D1461961

Marriages and Families

Relationships in Social Context

Karen Seccombe
Portland State University

Rebecca L. Warner
Oregon State University

THOMSON
WADSWORTH

Australia • Canada • Mexico • Singapore • Spain
United Kingdom • United States

To our children, Natalie, Olivia, and Ryan,
who keep us connected to what's really important.

Sociology Editor: Robert Jucha
Development Editor: Natalie Cornelison
Assistant Editor: Stephanie Monzon
Editorial Assistant: Melissa Walter
Technology Project Manager: Dee Dee Zobian
Marketing Manager: Matthew Wright
Advertising Project Manager: Linda Yip
Project Manager, Editorial Production: Trudy Brown
Print/Media Buyer: Rebecca Cross
Permissions Editor: Beth Zuber
Production Service: Robin Lockwood Productions

Text and Cover Designer: Lisa Buckley
Photo Researcher: Linda Rill
Copy Editor: Donald Pharr
Illustrator: Hans Neuhart
Cover Image: Circle of Love, 1996, © 2003
Michael Escoffery/Artists Rights Society
(ARS), New York
Compositor: G&S Typesetters, Inc.
Text and Cover Printer: Transcontinental
Printing/Interglobe

For more information about our products,
contact us at:
Thomson Learning Academic Resource Center
1-800-423-0563

For permission to use material from this text,
contact us by: **Phone:** 1-800-730-2214
Fax: 1-800-730-2215
Web: http://www.thomsonrights.com

Library of Congress Control Number: 2002115337
Student Edition: ISBN 0-534-55881-X
Instructor's Edition: ISBN 0-534-55882-8

Wadsworth/Thomson Learning
10 Davis Drive
Belmont, CA 94002-3098
USA

Asia
Thomson Learning
5 Shenton Way #01–01
UIC Building
Singapore 068808

Australia/New Zealand
Thomson Learning
102 Dodds Street
Southbank, Victoria 3006
Australia

Canada
Nelson
1120 Birchmount Road
Toronto, Ontario M1K 5G4
Canada

Europe/Middle East/Africa
Thomson Learning
High Holborn House
50/51 Bedford Row
London WC1R 4LR
United Kingdom

Latin America
Thomson Learning
Seneca, 53
Colonia Polanco
11560 Mexico D.F.
Mexico

Spain/Portugal
Paraninfo
Calle/Magallanes, 25
28015 Madrid, Spain

Brief Contents

Contents

Preface

Marriage and Family courses are popular on college campuses. Students of all ages crave information about love, sex, dating, relationships, marriage, and children. However, students tend to see these issues in individualized and personalized terms. Many textbooks do little to change this viewpoint. Marriage, family, and intimate relationships are discussed as though they exist in a vacuum—personal choice is emphasized without focusing on the structural conditions that shape these choices in the first place. Our goal is to offer students an introductory-level book that brings together a macrolevel, social structural analysis of marriage, families, and close relationships with the more microlevel, individualistic view that tends to dominate other textbooks. Throughout the text we weave together these two different perspectives as we explore the variety of intimate relationships that are part of family life.

The Importance of Social Structure

We illustrate the ways in which *social structure* affects even intimate relationships—how personal experiences, beliefs, privileges, and constraints are influenced by *social positions* and by *social institutions* such as the government, the economy, religious institutions, and the health care system.

Social positions, such as gender, race, and social class, affect personal relationships individually and jointly. Divisions of inequality based on gender, race and ethnicity, and social class pattern the structure of American families and the interaction that takes place within them. Our selection of a mate; our chances of marrying, bearing children, or divorcing; the amount of education we receive; the type of job we are likely to get; our health and our well-being are all affected by these critical dimensions of social position. For example, certain categories of people are less likely to marry than are others. Can you guess which groups are less likely to marry, and why?

Our social institutions also shape family life. Political and economic institutions have defined who and what a family is, thereby decreeing who is eligible or ineligible for something as basic as spousal health insurance benefits. Likewise, paid maternity leave is virtually unheard of in the United States, as are subsidized day-care centers and family allowances. How do these social institutions and their policies affect families? Not surprisingly, the United States has the highest rates of child poverty among industrialized nations.

A structural approach does not mean that we ascribe to a rigid determinism in which individuals have no choice in personal matters. Quite the contrary. To meet their needs, people choose, cope with, adapt to, and change social structures, including marriage, families, and intimate relationships. The goal of the book is to empower you to make appropriate choices and changes in marriage, families, and close relationships by introducing you to a *sociological imagination:* what you may have originally perceived as private, personal, and individual issues are in large part shaped by much broader social, historical, and cultural forces.

A Critical Perspective Shows the Diversity of Family Forms

Our book will also introduce you to a critical perspective which asks that you do not assume that families are monolithic or static, but rather acknowledge that they are ever changing. Humans construct their families to meet their needs; therefore, change is not necessarily something to be feared. Our goal is to recognize historical, cultural, and subcultural variations in the meanings and practices of family life. Because people live in different social locations and have different needs and desires, not everyone lives in the same type of family. We suggest that there is not one "right" type of family, and we respect the diversity in family styles adopted across social groups and locations. Throughout the text we encourage you to think critically about how your personal understandings of family are similar to or different from the perceptions of others.

A critical perspective also asks that we examine the assumptions, values, and ideologies that are used to define and characterize families and create social policy. Who gets to decide what a family is? When specific definitions of family shape social policies, what are the consequences for those who fall outside such definitions?

The Role of Social Science Research

One of the difficulties faced in a marriage and family course is the students' perceptions that the material is based on "common sense." Many marriage and family texts provide only a brief discussion of research methods to squelch this misperception. This book is different. We suggest that our knowledge of marriage, families, and close relationships is best grounded in both quantitative and qualitative social science research. The book offers a chapter devoted to the importance of research, the research process, how research and theory are interconnected, data-collection methods, and the political implications and ethics of research. In addition, throughout the text we explore the research methods used in particular studies rather than simply reporting their conclusions. Our goal is to inform and remind you that the conclusions drawn in the text are based on empirical evidence, not simply personal impressions or common sense. However, we also want you to recognize that empirical evidence is not necessarily value free; it exists within a historical, social, and political context. Researchers using particular theories will be led to ask particular kinds of questions. Those who advocate a particular type of family structure or process will look for empirical evidence to support their position. We want you to always ask where data come from and what the backgrounds are of those who collect and report family-related information.

The Integration of Macrolevel and Microlevel Perspectives

Another theme of this text is that microlevel and macrolevel factors work together to shape our opportunities, personal choices, privileges, and constraints. A microlevel perspective focuses on individuals' interactions in specific settings, such as communication skills, decision making, time management, and self-control. For example, a microlevel perspective may suggest that the best way to reduce the rate of domestic violence is to teach couples better communication skills. However, many relationship and family issues are social problems, not merely personal ones. Domestic violence, divorce, teen pregnancy, work–family stress, and inadequate child care cannot really be resolved unless we examine societal-level factors, including the way our social structure is organized to perpetuate these problems. For example, how do patterns of male domination or economic trends among women contribute to domestic violence? It is imperative that you use both macrolevel and microlevel perspectives to understand intimate relationships.

Marriage and Families draws upon multidisciplinary research in such fields as sociology, women's studies, family science, psychology, history, and anthropology. We focus on the latest and most influential quantitative and qualitative research published in the leading journals and books.

Chapter Overviews

Chapter 1 defines the concept of family and intimate relationships, and introduces the themes of the text. First, we suggest that social structures, including social institutions and statuses, profoundly shape our daily experiences, privileges, and constraints. Although it is easy to believe in "free choice" in personal matters, it is important that we recognize that choices are influenced by the social structure in which we live. A second theme is the value of a critical perspective illustrating that successful families can come in many types. Cross-cultural and historical variations show us that families are constructed by humans to meet our needs. Change is not necessarily something to be feared. A third theme is that empirical research is crucial to our understanding of families and close relationships. Many people have personal opinions about families that are based on nonobjective criteria. However, a scientific perspective, which draws on qualitative and quantitative data, can provide a clear window on the world. The fourth theme is that the microlevel and macrolevel influences in our lives are interrelated. Personal choice and interpersonal dynamics cannot be separated from broader social structures.

Chapter 2 addresses the diversity among social scientists in the theories and methods they use to understand families. We try to make clear that no one theory or method is better than others. The topics being explored and the questions being asked about families will draw on particular perspectives and strategies. All of the theories and methods discussed in this chapter will be referred to in subsequent chapters of the book. Our goal in this chapter is to provide you with the basic concepts necessary to understand and evaluate the research of family scholars.

Chapter 3 explores the significance of social structure and social status to understanding families, particularly the importance of gender, race, and social class. Each of these concepts is clearly defined, and numerous examples of their influence on families and relationships are offered. Gender, race and ethnicity, and social class help to shape a constellation of privileges and constraints that affect our personal relationships. These can result in having different life goals, opportunities, values, and choices. It is also critical that we recognize how these statuses interact with one another and shape our opportunities and constraints. One is not simply "rich." Rather, the privilege experienced by wealthy white men is likely to contrast vividly with the experience of wealthy Mexican American women, who must also deal with unique challenges associated with being a minority and female in the United States.

Chapter 4 concerns the concept of love. We begin by looking back over time to see how meanings associated with love (specifically, romantic love) have been shaped by the structure of society—its norms, values, and customs. Similarly, the organization of societies has shaped the ways we practice romantic love. Love is more than romance, however; it includes intense feelings we have for others that are not necessarily sexual. The love of a parent for a child, and the love between friends, are very important parts of our lives. We review the theories used to understand these attachments and explore contemporary research on loving relationships. This research reveals the considerable diversity in the meanings and practices of love, but also

indicates the important role that love plays in creating and maintaining family ties.

Chapter 5 explores the social side of human sexuality. This chapter shows the variety of ways in which our sexual norms, attitudes, and behaviors are related to our culture and to historical circumstances. These are dynamic and ever changing. Sexuality is only partly rooted in biology; it is also socially constructed. "Who am I?" and "What should I do?" are age-old questions that cannot be answered outside of the influences of the rest of society. Once again, what appear at first glance to be very personal choices—after all, what could be more personal than self-concepts, attitudes, and sexual behaviors?—are often shaped by larger social forces. The macrolevel and microlevel influences are intertwined.

Chapter 6 is on the subject of marriage in U.S. society. Although marriage has always been a central component of American life, fewer people are currently married today than has been the case for many years. Social scientists explain this "decline in marriage" by looking at both cultural features (changing values, cultures, and beliefs) as well as structural features (shifting economic and political conditions) of our society. This chapter also reviews literature on the quality and stability of marriages. What makes a happy marriage? What are the challenges that men and women face in trying to make their relationships work? We explore several explicit strategies that couples are using to construct high-quality marriages.

Chapter 7 continues some of our discussion from the previous chapter. While the number of people who are married at any given time has declined, the number of people who are single and the number who are cohabiting have increased. We find that, similar to our discussion of marriage, both structural and cultural factors play a role in these changing patterns of family life. Because of state laws regarding marriage, gay and lesbian couples must cohabit. In this chapter, we discuss the recent literature on gay/lesbian relationships and find that in many ways, "relationships are relationships." The quality and stability of cohabiting couples (gay/lesbian or straight) vary in response to the varieties of backgrounds and experiences that people bring to their relationships.

Chapter 8 turns our attention to another important dimension of family life—that of having children. Parents receive psychological benefits for having children, and children can offer social capital to their families. At the same time, the costs associated with having and raising children have been rising steeply, resulting in a reduction in family size. Another reason for fertility declines is the delay in childbearing. We review some of the consequences of these delays, including the increased prevalence of infertility treatments and an increasing interest in adoption. In this chapter, we also take a historical look at how the process of giving birth has changed. From midwives to doctors and back again, the options that women have for giving birth have become more responsive to an increasingly educated public regarding childbirth.

Chapter 9 explores the relationship between parents and children over time and across social locations. Research on parent–child relations shows that these relationships are sensitive to social structure. Families living in poorer communities have different socialization concerns than those living in more privileged communities. Families of color, and gay and lesbian families, also face different challenges that make parent–child relationships complicated. In this chapter, we also address the fact that the socialization of children is not always in the hands of parents. How families manage the care of children depends on who is involved and how the family is socially situated. We provide data to show that across all groups, the costs associated with child care have been rising sharply.

Chapter 10 sees all families as working families. However, how families have organized their work has changed over time. Today, the most common arrangement for families is that all adult members are employed. Both the income of the jobs held as well as the rhythms of work shape the ways in which families work to meet their needs. In addition to employment, families also require a significant amount of unpaid work at home. Who does the housework, child care, and other kin work is dependent on the other demands of family members and the norms about the appropriateness of certain divisions of labor. Finally in this chapter, we explore the effect that families have on the structuring of employment. More employers are now responding to family demands by offering a variety of benefits such as flexible work arrangements, family leaves, and employee assistance programs.

Chapter 11 focuses on family problems, particularly highlighting the ways in which some of the stressors and crises that families face have their basis in our social structure. The chapter emphasizes that many seemingly personal problems are really social problems and must be examined in their social context to really be eradicated or reduced. The chapter provides three vivid examples of the structural nature of problems experienced in families and personal relationships: poverty, domestic violence, and substance abuse. Our goal is to reveal that even though these problems are experienced on a deeply personal level, we must look beyond this level to obtain a greater understanding of the nature of these problems and their solutions.

Chapter 12 examines the demographics, correlates, process, and consequences of divorce. Although we may tend to think of divorce as a personal mechanism for ending an unhappy marriage, divorce is far more complex than that. Divorce is not simply a personal issue; there is an intricate weaving of macrolevel structural and microlevel personal factors that operate to explain rising and falling divorce rates and the repercussions associated with divorce. Despite its prevalence, divorce is usually a difficult and lengthy process for all involved. Divorce touches many aspects of our lives. Children are particularly vulnerable to the hardships associated with divorce, including a greater likelihood of poverty and other behavioral and social problems.

Chapter 13 explores the demographic and social implications of family relationships, remarriage, and stepparenthood after divorce. Broad social forces influence divorce, and they affect the type and quality of stressors that can occur in relationships that begin afterward. For example, given the low pay structure for many women, divorced women often struggle financially to support their families and raise them alone, although they often become closer to their children in the process. Moreover, although a common process, divorce and repartnering do not have clear norms in the United States. This is particularly apparent in stepfamily relationships, which have many unique characteristics and face many challenges when compared to two-parent biological families.

Chapter 14 reveals that our population is aging rapidly. These demographic changes will have profound implications for family life. No longer can the concerns of the elderly and of aging families be separated from those of younger age groups. Their needs influence and are influenced by other social institutions in society. Promoting good health and social and economic well-being, supporting intimate relationships, fostering positive bonds with adult children and grandchildren, and issues pertaining to retirement, widowhood, and formal and informal caregiving are some of the important subjects on the forefront of the national agenda. As our population continues to age, we will likely see these concerns become increasingly popular and discussed with even greater frequency. Issues that are currently viewed as individual problems (e.g., health, loneliness, caregiving) will increasingly become seen as social problems that require structural solutions.

Chapter 15 reviews the themes presented throughout the text and then asks what kind of family life we want for the twenty-first century. Families are not socially isolated entities that can survive solely on their own accord. Families can flourish only when we provide the support they need. While individual and community strengths are invaluable, this support must also come in the form of broad social and economic policies designed to help us care for one another. The United States has much to learn about family policy from other countries. It is likely that no one country has a model that could, or even should, be superimposed on the United States. However, our understanding of the power of social structure, using a critical perspective, having a respect for empirical data, and being able to link microlevel and macrolevel perspectives show us that other possibilities may indeed provide us with stronger, safer, and more resilient families.

Pedagogical Features

This first edition includes a number of pedagogical features specifically designed to make learning easier and more rewarding. They are designed to further elaborate on the themes outlined above.

Current Research and Statistics Every effort has been made to provide students with the most up-to-date research and statistics available for each topic. We draw liberally upon the 2000 Census and other cutting-edge government data to provide students with a current snapshot of demographic and social trends. Qualitative research is then used to bring these statistics to life. Students usually find personal narratives a compelling way to illustrate core concepts.

Boxed Inserts Students need opportunities to apply the material presented in the chapters. Our boxed inserts provide further enrichment and reinforce the primary themes of the book. These boxed inserts contain the following themes:

* *Focus on Family Research.* These boxes summarize the methods and results of recently published research on key topics from each chapter. For example, in Chapter 2 we present the results of a paper on marital satisfaction that recently received from the National Council on Family Relations the Reuben Hill Award for the Best Research Article Published in 2001. In Chapter 14 we profile a critical piece of research on the racial and ethnic variation in extended families in the United States.

* *Family Diversity.* These boxes illustrate the racial, ethnic, class, cultural, or historical diversity in relationships. For example, the issue of polygamy in Utah is explored in depth in Chapter 1. Chapter 8 includes a story of interracial adoption through the eyes of an African American girl raised in a European American family. And in Chapter 10, we look at how unemployment has a profound effect on marital and family relationships.

* *Family Narratives.* These boxes offer personal case studies relevant to material from the chapter. In Chapter 7 we hear from a woman who is living single in a world she sees as designed for married couples. A story of the trafficking of a girl for the sex industry is featured in Chapter 11.

* *Constructing Strong Families.* These boxes provide practical information or critically examine a program or social policy designed to strengthen families and intimate relationships. For example, Chapter 6 pro-

vides a helpful list of strategies to consider for interfaith relationships. Chapter 15 discusses the Head Start Program and the ways it provides educational enrichment to disadvantaged children.

Fact or Fiction Questions Students often find it useful to have ways of checking their comprehension of the material. We provide a number of these checkpoints in each chapter. Toward the beginning of a section of text, we pose a query, such as this one: *Fact or fiction: The United States government requires that all companies provide parental (maternal or paternal) leave.* As the student reads the next section of the text, the answer to this query should become obvious. Toward the end of the section we provide the correct response: *Fiction: The Family Medical Leave Act requires this only of companies with more than fifty employees. Most Americans work at companies with fewer employees.* By "testing" themselves, students can make sure they are retaining the pertinent information throughout the chapter.

Chapter Summaries In addition to a short conclusion at the end of each chapter, we offer students a series of questions that summarize the key topics in each chapter. Students can read the question and see what they remember from the reading. Then they can read our short summaries and return to any sections that might need to be reread.

Key Terms and Glossary To help students better retain critical information, important terms and concepts are boldfaced in each chapter and defined in a section called Key Terms at the end of each chapter. In addition, all key terms and their definitions are included in the glossary, at the end of the book.

Supplements

0-534-61044-7 *Instructor's Resource Manual with Test Bank*
This manual offers instructors a detailed lecture outline, learning objectives, classroom discussion and teaching suggestions, student activities, Internet activities, InfoTrac exercises, and more for each chapter of the text.

The test items include 50–60 multiple-choice questions and 10–15 true/false questions, all with page references to the text, as well as 5–10 short-answer questions and 3–5 essay questions for each chapter. Also included is a table of contents for the *CNN Today: Marriage and Family* video series and concise user guides for both InfoTrac College Edition and WebTutor.

0-534-61043-9 *ExamView® for Macintosh/ Windows*
Create, deliver, and customize tests and study guides (both print and online) in minutes with this easy-to-use assessment and tutorial system. ExamView offers both a Quick Test Wizard and an Online Test Wizard that guide you step by step through the process of creating tests. The test appears on screen exactly as it will print or display online. Using ExamView's complete word-processing capabilities, you can enter an unlimited number of new questions or edit existing questions.

0-534-56780-0 *Multimedia Presentation Manager for Sociology*
The easy way to great multimedia lectures! This one-stop digital library and presentation tool helps you assemble, edit, and present custom lectures. The CD-ROM brings together art (figures, tables, charts, and maps) from the text itself, pre-assembled PowerPoint® lecture slides, and CNN video. You can use the materials as they are or add your own materials for a truly customized lecture presentation.

0-534-58983-9 *Transparency Acetates for Marriage and Family 2004*
A set of four-color acetates consisting of tables and figures from Wadsworth's marriage and family texts is available to help prepare lecture presentations. Free to qualified adopters.

CNN Today Videos: Marriage and Family
Vol. I: 0-534-55257-9; Vol. II: 0-534-55258-7; Vol. III: 0-534-55268-4; Vol. IV: 0-534-55270-6; Vol. V: 0-534-55271-4; Vol. VI: 0-534-61897-9.
CNN's marriage and family videos allow you to integrate the news-gathering and programming power of CNN into the classroom to show your students the relevance of sociology to their everyday lives. Each video includes an annotated table of contents, descriptions of

the segments, and suggestions for their possible use within the course.

0-534-61891-X *Marriage & Family Case Studies CD-ROM*

This unique student CD-ROM includes important information about the text, direct links to book-specific study resources, and a series of 10 interactive case studies. The 10 case study videos are intended to provide a dramatic enactment illustrating key topics and concepts from the text. Students watch each video and answer critical-thinking questions, applying marriage and family theories. Students then compare their analysis with that of a marriage and family expert.

0-534-55885-2 *Study Guide*

This student study tool contains a chapter summary, detailed chapter outline, learning objectives, key terms with page references, Internet activities, and InfoTrac exercises for each chapter of the text. The guide also contains practice tests consisting of 20–25 multiple-choice and 10–15 true/false questions, all with answers and page references to the text, as well as 3–5 short-answer and 2–3 essay questions for each chapter.

InfoTrac® College Edition Four months of *free* anywhere, anytime access to InfoTrac College Edition, the online library, is automatically packaged with this book. The new and improved InfoTrac College Edition puts cutting-edge research and the latest headlines at students' fingertips, giving them access to an entire online library for the cost of one book! This fully searchable database offers more than twenty years' worth of full-text articles (more than ten million) from almost 4,000 diverse sources, such as academic journals, newsletters, and up-to-the-minute periodicals, including *Time, Newsweek, Science, Forbes,* and *USA Today.*

0-534-27359-9 *The Marriages and Families Activities Workbook*

What are your risks of divorce? Do you have healthy dating practices? What is your cultural and ancestral heritage, and how does it affect your family relationships? The answers to these and many more questions are found in this workbook of nearly a hundred interactive self-assessment quizzes designed for students studying marriage and family. These self-awareness instruments, all based on known social science research studies, can be used as in-class activities or homework assignments to help students learn more about themselves and their family experience.

The Seccombe/Warner Companion Web Site at Wadsworth's Virtual Society
http://www.wadsworth.com/sociology
Virtual Society features a wealth of online book-specific study materials created especially for this text, plus online chapters (on topics such as school violence), a student guide to Census 2000, "Sociology in the News," study resources, a career center, and much more. Specifically for instructors, there are password-protected instructor's manuals and e-mail access to Wadsworth editors. Click on the Student Companion Web site to find useful learning resources for each chapter of the book. Here are some of the Web site resources:

* Tutorial Practice Quizzes that can be scored and e-mailed to the instructor
* Internet Links and Exercises
  * CNN Video Exercises
  * InfoTrac College Edition Exercises
  * Flashcards of the text's glossary
  * Crossword Puzzles
  * Essay Questions
  * Learning Objectives
  * Interactive Activities based on the GSS survey in the Appendix
* Plus, new to Wadsworth's Virtual Society: a Marriage and Family Resource Center!

WebTutor™ Advantage on WebCT and Blackboard
WebCT: 0-534-55884-4
Blackboard: 0-534-55883-6
WebTutor—Web-based software for students and instructors—takes a course beyond the classroom to an anywhere, anytime environment. Students gain access to a full array of study tools, including chapter outlines, chapter-specific quizzing material, interactive activities, and videos. With WebTutor Advantage, instructors can provide virtual office hours, post syllabi, track student progress with the quizzing material, and even customize the content to suit their needs. Instructors can also

use the communication tools to do such things as set up threaded discussions and conduct "real-time" chats. "Out of the box" or customized, WebTutor Advantage provides powerful tools for instructors and students alike.

MyCourse 2.1

Ask us about our new *free* online course builder! Whether you want only the easy-to-use tools to build it or the content to furnish it, we offer you a simple solution for a custom course Web site that allows you to assign, track, and report on student progress; load your syllabus; and more. Contact your representative for details.

Acknowledgments

We are fortunate to be surrounded by many colleagues, friends, and family members who have helped to shape this book in important ways, from clarifying our thinking to providing technical support. Collectively, they have inspired and motivated us to summarize, critique, and reflect upon marriages, families, and intimate relationships to the best of our ability. This book is the result of their support, and we want to acknowledge them.

The story really begins with Dan Edwards, a former Wadsworth book representative who listened to our ideas for the textbook and provided the initial encouragement and connections to get the ball rolling. Without Dan, there simply would be no book.

Many colleagues have helped as reviewers of various versions of our text. Sally Gallagher and Mark Edwards of Oregon State University read early drafts and made excellent suggestions. Thanks also go out to those who provided original material and/or data that appear throughout the book. David Morgan (Portland State University), Shelley Nelson (Indiana University), Valerie Bredermeier (Portland State University), and Suzanne Smith (Washington State University Vancouver) wrote boxed inserts. Mark Edwards (Oregon State University) and Philip Cohen (University of California–Irvine) provided data that appear in several of our figures. We want to say a special thank you to Mark Edwards for his help in accessing the General Social Survey data that appear in the online Appendix.

Wadsworth has continued to provide us with excellent assistance, particularly the expert help of our editor, Bob Jucha. We also ap-

preciate the outstanding work of our development editor, Natalie Cornelison, Matthew Wright, Senior Marketing Manager, Stephanie Monzon, Assistant Editor (working on the supplements) and Dee Dee Zobian, Technology Product Manager (working on our Web site resources). Suzanne Smith, Washington State University Vancouver; Wanda M. Clark, South Plains College; and Rebecca Ford, Florida Community College at Jacksonville, wrote outstanding supplements for our text that will surely make using our book easier for both students and professors. The hard work at Robin Lockwood Productions made the final phases of this process nearly a breeze. Thanks to Robin, her copyeditor, Donald Pharr, and Linda Rill (photo researcher). We also appreciate the insights from reviewers all over the country, in a variety of different disciplines: Sampson Lee Blair, Arizona State University; Richard Bulcroft, Western Washington University; Carole Carrol, Middle Tennessee State University; Janice Chebra, University of Akron; Wanda Clark, South Plains College; Janet Cosbey, Eastern Illinois University; Tim Crone, Northern New Mexico Community College; Lillian Daughaday, Murray State University; Shannon Davis, North Carolina State University; Mark Eckel, McHenry County College; Rebecca Ford, Florida Community College at Jacksonville; Sandra French, Indiana University; Katherine Gilbert-Espada, Springfield Technical Community College; Michael Goslin, Tallahassee Community College; Richard Halpin, Jefferson Community College; Gerard Hoefling, Pennsylvania State University; Susan Mann, University of New Orleans; Clark McKinney, Southwest Tennessee Community College; Christine Monnier, College of DuPage; Carol Poll, Fashion Institute of Technology; Phyllis Raabe, University of New Orleans, Anisa Rhea, North Carolina State University; Cheryl Robinson, University of Tennessee at Chattanooga; Stacy Ruth, Jones County Junior College; William Smith, Georgia Southern University; George Stine, Millersville University; Jenny Stuber, Normandale Community College; Kinly Sturkie, Clemson University; and Deidre Tyler, Salt Lake Community College. To all of you, thank you.

Karen Seccombe I would like to extend my appreciation to my friends and colleagues who provided regular encouragement, support, and suggestions for topics, and who graciously helped me while I crammed a lifetime of transitions into just a few short years. In particular, I would like to thank J. Elizabeth Miller, Gary Lee, Karen Pyke, Kathy Kaiser, Heather Hartley, and Masako Ishii-Kuntz for all the support and mentoring that they have offered.

The Center for Public Health Studies and the School of Community Health at Portland State University have provided critical resources, including dedicated staff and graduate students who made valuable direct and indirect contributions to this project. Surely without them I would still be trying to figure out numerous technical tasks. Sincere thanks go to Christina Albo, Beth Bull, Renato Carletti, Gwen Kelly, Rick Lockwood, and Karen McNeil for their assistance in these tasks, among many others. Kim Hoffman has kept our health and welfare reform research project humming. Her expertise has allowed me the freedom to turn my attention to book writing as necessary.

And if it is ever appropriate to thank a co-author, this is the time. My twenty-year-long friendship with Becky Warner has withstood the test of co-authorship remarkably well, and I appreciate her talents and work ethic now more than ever. This truly was a collaborative effort, and I am most grateful for the opportunity to work with Becky on this project. We actually had fun writing this book together!

Finally, I would like to thank my family for surrounding me with all of the rich diversions that anyone could hope for. In particular, I'd like to pay tribute to the late Morgan and Jazz, who were always there for me, ready to romp, until the end of their days. I also offer my gratitude and love to my husband, Richard, and our daughter, Natalie Rose. Although generally I wouldn't recommend getting divorced, remarrying, having a baby, and planning an adoption while writing a book, I have to admit that somehow it has all worked out beautifully.

Rebecca Warner When we began this text, I was entering my second term as department chair. I thank William C. Krueger, chair of the Department of Rangeland Resources at Oregon State University, for providing me an office in his department that year so I could have space away from the constant demands of departmental business to begin the daunting task of getting caught up with the literature. A very heartfelt thanks goes to Kay F. Schaffer, dean of the College of Liberal Arts, for supporting me when I decided that this text, and my other research projects, needed my full attention and for allowing me out of my second term after only one year. And of course I thank everyone in my department (especially Gary Tiedeman) for their support in these efforts. Thanks to our office assistant, Tara Gerig, for the hard work of checking hundreds of references.

Thanks also to the many students at Oregon State University, including Kelsy Kretschmer and those enrolled in my family course in the University Honors College, for reading several of our chapters and giving us a critical student perspective on the material. Brandy Ota (graduate research assistant) provided considerable help in library research. My colleagues across campus came through numerous times to help me work through the ideas in this book. I owe a coffee to Sally Bowman, Flaxen Conway, Joe Hendricks, Bob Nye, Sam Stern, Alexis Walker, and Anisa Zvonkovic.

I am very fortunate to be living within eighty miles of my family of origin. My mother, Carolyn Warner, brother, Steve, and sisters, Pam and Patti, have always been a major source of strength and support. My husband, Brent, and son, Ryan, are my best friends and made sure that I was able to devote as much time as I needed to this project. They also took me away from it when I needed a break. Thanks to my extended family of friends who gave me perspective: Janet Lee, Sarah Ehlers, Sally Gallagher, and the women of Friday afternoon at Michaels.

Finally, thank you to Karen for inviting me on to this project. The ebbs and flows of writing this text were very much helped by our friendship. My favorite times were those we spent laughing.

© Tom Stewart/Corbis

Why Study Families and Other Close Relationships?

1

Family Portraits

Robert and Christina are a married couple in their early thirties. They are both employed full time in jobs that they enjoy. They have no children, by choice. Both feel that their careers are too time-consuming and require too much travel to allow them to spend much time raising children. They prefer a childfree lifestyle—devoting themselves to each other, their two dogs, and their cat feels like enough responsibility. Do you think Robert and Christina are a family? *Yes*

Julia and Mark are not married. They have lived together for seven years in a mostly monogamous union. They have a child together, a boy who is three years old. Julia, who is twenty-eight, stays home to care for their child. Mark, aged thirty-five, works full time to support Julia and their son. They are happy together and assume that they will stay together, but they acknowledge that they may not be sexually exclusive with each other. Julia and Mark have deliberately chosen to remain unmarried because they question the formal institution of marriage. They do not anticipate having any more children. Do they constitute a family? *Yes*

Lisa and Kathy have been romantically involved and have lived together for the past seventeen years. They are lesbians. Law forbids them to marry because they are both women, although they wish that the law would change. Despite not being allowed to marry, they think of themselves as life partners and see their future together. They both are in their mid-fifties and are currently saving money to buy a retirement home together on the coast. Do you think they are a family? *No*

Jessica, aged forty, has never married. Nonetheless, she desperately wanted a family and decided that she would adopt a child on her own. When she contacted several agencies and attorneys who specialize in adoption, she was told that there was a three- to four-year waiting list for a physically healthy infant or toddler. Jessica then decided to turn to foster care as a way to share herself with a needy child until she was able to adopt one of her own. After Jessica was screened and after she attended a thorough training, a nine-year-old girl named Nina was placed with her. Nina's mother cannot care for her because of a serious drug addiction, and the whereabouts of her father is unknown. Nina has lived with Jessica for over a year now, and it looks as though she will remain with her for a significant amount of time in the future. They have a warm and loving—although not always easy—relationship. Jessica provides the love and stability that were sorely lacking in Nina's previous home. Are Jessica and Nina a family? *Yes*

Bob and Rita were divorced nine years ago in a bitter court scene that was the final battle in their conflict-ridden marriage. They had two young sons at the time of the divorce who are now in their early teens. Bob moved out of state because of his job and has seen his sons only four times since the divorce. Bob usually sends them a birthday card and Christmas gift, but other than these, he contributes little to their support. He paid child support regularly for the first year after the divorce, but quit because he felt that Rita was spending the money foolishly, usually on herself. Visits with the children normally ended in another conflict between Bob and Rita, and he soon quit making an effort to see them. He has not seen them in five years. Are Bob and his sons a family? NO

These five scenarios point to the complexity of defining the common word *family*. We use the term in our everyday language. However, not everyone is in complete agreement about what constitutes a family. Some people believe that a couple must be legally married to be considered a family. Others think that children must be present, and still others believe that gay and lesbian partners do not really qualify as a family regardless of their level of commitment to each other. Today we are surrounded by childfree married couples, multigenerational families, unmarried adults who cohabit and sometimes have children, stepparents whose stepchildren reside with them only every other weekend, and gay and lesbian partnerships. These types of living arrangements are increasing, while the more traditional form—husband, wife, and children all living together—is on the decline. The Focus on Family Research box on page 4 draws upon the most recent U.S. Census Bureau data and other government information to illustrate some key demographic facts about families today, at least as families are defined by the government.

How Do We Define Family? AS A SOCIETY

With such a variety of relationships, how does one define *family*? This is not a trivial issue.

The celebration of family comes in many forms, as witnessed by these two couples who have exchanged vows revealing their love and commitment to one another.

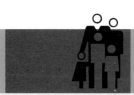

What do families look like today? How have they changed over time? This book is designed to address these issues. Just to give you a brief preview, let's examine some of the key statistics from the 2000 census and other governmental sources that will be discussed in more detail throughout the text.

A caveat must first be mentioned about government statistics because they have a number of limitations. For example, the racial and ethnic categories used have been highly criticized. "Hispanic" is used as a catchall category, but Hispanic groups are not homogeneous. What do Cubans, Mexicans, and Guatemalans really have in common? The "Hispanic experience" is not uniform. Hispanic groups comprise heterogeneous cultures that share a common language and colonial history. Likewise, until 2000, there was no mechanism for reporting biracial categories that reflect the growing diversity and complexity of racial and ethnic identification. Moreover, some argue that the definition of *family* that is used is limited; therefore, so is the information recorded. For example, the census does not record gay or lesbian families.

Nonetheless, government statistics, while imperfect, are an important source of information about our population. We rely on the census, vital statistics, and other records to update us on a number of social and economic trends. Our knowledge of many family issues is greatly informed by this information:

1. *Both men and women are postponing marriage.* Because of expanding opportunities and changing norms, people are marrying at later ages than in the past. Women now marry at an average age of 25, compared to 21 in 1970. Men now marry at an average age of 27, compared to 23 in 1970.

2. *The percentage of persons who have never married has declined.* In 2000, 3.6 percent of elderly women had never married, down from 5.9 in 1980. Among men, the decline in lifelong singlehood is less dramatic, but exists nonetheless: 4.2 percent of elderly men aged 65 and older had never married, down from 4.9 in 1980. In other words, people are now more likely to marry, not less likely.

3. *Family size is shrinking.* Fewer people are having three or more children today. Family size is particularly shrinking among black and Hispanic families. In 2000, 12 percent of black families contained three or more children, compared to 18 percent in 1980. Likewise, 18 percent of Hispanic families contained three or more children in 2000, compared to 23 percent in 1980. White families with three or more children declined to 9 percent from 11 percent in 1980.

4. *The divorce rate has declined in recent decades.* In the 1960s, the divorce rate began to rise rapidly, peaking at approximately 23 divorces per 1,000 married women around 1980. However, since this time, the rate of divorce has declined to approximately 19.5 per 1,000 married women.

5. *Single custodial fathers are less likely to be awarded child support than custodial single mothers (40 percent versus 61 percent, respectively).* Moreover, among those dads who are due court-ordered child support, they are also *less likely* to receive at least a portion of payments owed than are custodial mothers (57 percent versus 70 percent). In other words, it appears that mothers default on their child support obligations more frequently than do fathers.

6. *Mothers are increasingly likely to be employed for pay outside the home.* Although single mothers have usually had work outside the home, more married women with children are in the workplace than ever before. Today, nearly 40 percent of married couples with children have both parents working outside the home full time, and another 28 percent contain a full-time worker and a part-time worker. Only 28 percent of married couples today have only one wage earner, as compared to 55 percent in 1965.

7. *Single-parent households are on the rise, particularly among men.* Since 1970, there has been a 300-percent increase in single-parent households headed by mothers and a 500-percent increase in those headed by fathers. Today, approximately 26 percent of white families are headed by one par-

ent, as are 61 percent of black families and 34 percent of Hispanic families.

8. *Hispanic groups are now the largest minority in the United States at 12.5 percent of the population, or nearly 35 million people.* Hispanics make up 42 percent of the population in New Mexico, 32 percent in California, 32 percent in Texas, 25 percent in Arizona, and 20 percent in Nevada. Blacks constitute 12.3 percent of the U.S. population. But because birthrates and immigration are higher among Hispanics, it is estimated that their presence in the United States will continue to grow much larger than other groups. Mexican Americans, with a population of over 23 million, constitute 67 percent of all Hispanics. The second-largest Hispanic group is the catchall "other Hispanic" category (about 7 million), while persons of Puerto Rican descent are the third-largest group (about 3.2 million). Cubans make up less than 10 percent of all Hispanics, with a population of 1.2 million.

9. *The teenage birthrate is declining.* The birthrate among teenagers has declined by approximately 17 percent since 1990. This decline is occurring among all race and ethnic groups, and is particularly pronounced among African Americans.

10. *Unmarried couples living together is becoming increasingly common.* The number of unmarried couples has tripled since 1980, from roughly 1.5 million to 4.5 million. A large increase is also seen among the cohabiting elderly population, virtually doubling from 119,000 to 220,000 couples between 1980 and 1999.

11. *The percentage of people living in poverty has decreased.* Poverty rates among families, single adults, and children are down. Every racial and ethnic group has experienced a drop in both the number of poor and the percentage in poverty. There was more than a 15-percent decline in poverty rates between 1990 and 2000. In 2000, 9.6 percent of families and 16.2 percent of children lived below the poverty line.

12. *The rich have gotten richer, while middle- and low-income groups have lost ground.* The richest fifth of the population earns approximately 47 percent of the total national income, while the poorest fifth earns only 4 percent. The share of earnings received since 1980 has decreased for all groups, except among the highest-earning group. Moreover, the highest 5 percent of earners have made the most tremendous gains. Their share of income increased from 15 percent to 20 percent between 1980 and 1999.

13. *The elderly population has been increasing almost four times as fast as the population as a whole, and seniors now constitute 1 of every 8 people (35 million)* (Hetzel & Smith, 2001). In 1900 only a small portion of people—1 in 25—were aged 65 or older. It is likely that many younger people spent long portions of their lives rarely even seeing an elderly person.

14. *Persons aged 85 and over—referred to as the "oldest old"—constitute the most rapidly growing elderly cohort in the United States.* They now number over 4 million, or 10 percent of all elders, and 1.2 percent of the entire population in the United States (Hetzel & Smith, 2001). Because of the greater longevity of baby boomers, it is expected that the numbers of the oldest old will jump to 19 million in 2050. That would make them 24 percent of all elders and 5 percent of all Americans in just 50 years.

15. *Children are increasingly likely to live with a grandparent as their caretaker.* Approximately 4 million children now reside with a grandparent, and of these, 1.8 million do not have either parent living with them. These families are more likely to be poor, African American, and living in the South.

Critical Thinking

1. What other changes do you see occurring in families?

2. Do you think these changes are for the better or for the worse?

3. Why do you hold the opinions that you do? Where did your opinions come from?

Why Definitions Are Important

The definition has important consequences with respect to informal and formal rights. For example, neighbors, schools, and other community groups are likely to interact with family members differently than with other nonrelated groups who live together. Families even get special membership discounts to a wide variety of organizations that roommates or friends do not get. Even more important, the definition has important formal consequences that are legally recognized, such as access to a spouse's retirement benefits and health insurance. Under most employer insurance plans, only a worker's spouse and legal children can be covered by a health insurance policy. Lifelong but unmarried partners are excluded from coverage. If an unmarried couple has children, those children may receive health insurance coverage from their employed parent, but the partner may be excluded. These decisions involve billions of dollars in employer and government benefits, and affect millions of adults and children each year, as shown in the Constructing Strong Families box on page 7.

Legal Versus Social Science Definitions

The U.S. Census Bureau defines a *family* as two or more people living together who are related by birth, marriage, or adoption. Heterosexual or homosexual unmarried partners are excluded. This traditional definition continues to be the basis for the implementation of many social programs and policies. However, it has come under debate because it excludes diverse groups who consider themselves to be families.

Many social scientists believe that this definition should be expanded because it does not adequately reflect the reality of the rich diversity of family life in society today (Allen, 2000; Demo, Allen, & Fine, 2000;

Smith, 1993; Stacey, 1996). They suggest that if people feel that they are a family, these feelings should not be ignored because of rigid definitions. The focus should be on honoring diversity and being more inclusive of family relationships. However, not everyone agrees with this point of view.

FICTION

Affection is not included in the definition of family *used by the U.S. Census Bureau. If the term was included, then it is likely that unmarried heterosexual and homosexual partners would be counted as family. As it stands now, they are not.*

Is there only one family form, or should we recognize a plurality of family styles? Recently, the leading family scholarly journal published by the National Council on Family Relations changed its name from *The Journal of Marriage and the Family* to *The Journal of Marriage and Family* (deleting the word *the*), reflecting the growing recognition of multiple family forms. This change corresponds to the public's changing attitudes toward families. A 2001 study based on five large national data sources found increasing tolerance of family diversity since the 1960s. Americans are more likely to accept divorce, **cohabitation** (unmarried couples who are sexual partners sharing a household), remaining single, and being childfree as legitimate lifestyles, while at the same time also espousing that marriage, children, and a strong family life are important goals toward which they are striving (Thornton & Young-DeMarcho, 2001).

In this book we select the broader and more inclusive definition. We propose that a **family** is a relationship by blood, marriage, or affection, in which members may cooperate economically, may care for any children, and may consider their identity to be intimately connected to the larger group.

In most places around the country, unmarried adults who are in a long-term committed relationship and are responsible for each other's financial and emotional well-being are routinely denied benefits such as spousal health insurance or dental care, bereavement leave, and relocation benefits. "Domestic partners," as these relationships have been termed, have faced a number of obstacles simply because they lack the legal basis of marriage. Some domestic partners are heterosexuals who believe that the institution of marriage is irrelevant or unnecessary. Others are homosexuals who are not legally permitted to marry. However, employers are beginning to recognize that denying benefits to partners in committed relationships may not only be unjust but may also be bad for business.

Since 1982, when the New York City weekly *The Village Voice* became the first employer to offer domestic partner benefits to its lesbian and gay employees, a small but growing number of employers have followed suit. They voluntarily choose to offer benefits to an employee's unmarried partner, whether heterosexual or homosexual. These employers include at least 145 Fortune 500 companies, along with city, county, and state agencies. According to the Human Rights Coalition, the number of employers providing domestic partner benefits increased by 50 percent in the two-year period between August 1999 and August 2001, up to 4,285 employers.

Why do a growing number of employers offer benefits to domestic partners? One reason is simple fairness. Many employers believe that offering benefits to their employees' legally married partners but not to nonlegally married partners discriminates on the basis of sexual orientation and/or marital status. Because gays and lesbians cannot legally marry, their partners have traditionally been excluded from receiving benefits on the grounds that they are not legal family members of the employee. However, some employers have a formal policy against discrimination on the basis of sexual orientation and see the decision to offer domestic partner benefits as acting on behalf of this policy.

A second reason that more employers are offering domestic partner benefits has to do with the competition in today's labor market. In order to attract and retain a high-quality, diverse work force, employers are recognizing the importance of offering comprehensive benefit packages. Offering benefits has been found to be a sound business practice.

Sources: Employee Benefit Research Institute (June 2000). "Domestic Partner Benefits: Facts and Background." Available online at http://www.ebri.org/facts/0600fact2.htm; Human Rights Campaign Foundation (2002). "Frequently Asked Questions on Domestic Partner Benefits." Available online at http://www.hrc.org/worknet/dp/dp_facts.asp.

Critical Thinking

1. What are the arguments against offering benefits to same-sex partners? Are the arguments primarily financial or moral?

2. Should domestic partner benefits cover both homosexual and heterosexual relationships?

FACT OR FICTION?

Most health insurance policies in the United States will not cover "fictive kin," such as close friends and domestic partners, and allow them as beneficiaries on health plans.

We include **fictive kin** under the definition of family as well. Fictive kin are nonrelatives whose bonds are strong and intimate, such as the relationships shared among unmarried homosexual partners, heterosexual partners, or very close friends. In fact, these bonds may even be stronger than those between biological relatives. Fictive kin can provide important services and care for individuals, including assistance around the holiday season or through life transitions such as the birth of a child or a divorce (Dilworth-Anderson et al., 2001). As used throughout this book, *families* encompasses both fictive kin and more traditional definitions of family. We strive to embrace the abundance of intimate relationships on which humans thrive.

| FACT

Fictive kin are rarely allowed on health insurance, although domestic partners are occasionally included.

Themes of This Book

Our study of families will take the reader on a journey of self-discovery and greater societal awareness. This book has several key themes that are introduced in this chapter and then elaborated upon throughout.

First, we suggest that *elements of social structures profoundly shape our daily experiences, privileges, and constraints.* The social structure of a society provides the stable framework of social relationships in that society. It provides the framework for how we are to interact with others (Kendall, 1999). Seemingly personal choices that we make,

Will this woman continue to work after the birth of her baby? It is increasingly likely that she will do so, as the United States is the only industrialized nation that does not provide paid maternity leave.

such as marrying, bearing children, divorcing, the type of job we are likely to get, the type of child care we may use, our health and well-being, and the likelihood of living to see our grandchildren, are affected by our social structure.

A second theme introduces students to a critical perspective. *A critical perspective asks that we do not assume that families are monolithic or static, but rather acknowledge that they are ever-changing.* Families are constructed by humans to meet our needs; therefore, change is not necessarily something to be feared. Because families are ever-changing, it is a myth to assume that there is only one type of "true" family. Marriage and family patterns vary dramatically around the world, have varied historically, and vary today among different racial and ethnic groups. Intimate relationships reflect the social, political, and economic institutions in a particular culture in a particular time. A critical perspective also asks that we examine the assumptions, values, and ideologies that are used to define and characterize families and create social policy. For example, why is the United States the only industrialized country that fails to provide paid maternity leave for its citizens? Who benefits from such an arrangement?

A third theme of this book is *an appreciation for the role that social science research can play in understanding families and close relationships.* Many people have common-sense opinions about the family, which are often based on their personal experience or information filtered through peers or parents. However, we suggest here that a scientific perspective, which draws on empirical data, can provide a far more objective window on the world. It can inform us and offer a basis for our opinions and values.

Finally, a fourth theme is to *link the microlevel and macrolevel influences.* Personal interactions are shaped in large part by elements of social structure. For example, husbands and wives are not random actors.

© Amy Etra/PhotoEdit

Their interactions are reflections of broader societal expectations about gender. Yet we are not passive recipients of social structure. The task for each of us is to create a viable life even when constrained or limited by structural conditions.

The next sections of this chapter explore each of these themes in greater depth.

Theme 1: The Influence of Social Structure on Families

We live in a society with hundreds of millions of other people, most of whom also have families. Remarkably, each of these individuals and each of these families behaves in a relatively predictable fashion. That is because they all operate within a larger **social structure,** which is a stable framework of social relationships that guides our interactions with others. Social structure has several components: social institutions, statuses, groups, roles, and norms. Our first theme suggests that *elements of social structures profoundly shape our daily experiences, privileges, and constraints.*

The Family as a Social Institution

Because families and close relationships fulfill many of our personal needs, it is easy to forget that the family is also a **social institution.** A social institution is a major sphere of social life with a set of beliefs and rules that is organized to meet basic human needs. In addition to talking about *your* specific family, we talk about *the* family. Families are a social institution, in much the same way that our political, economic, religious, health care, and educational systems are social institutions. In early human civilizations, the family was the center of most activities. We

learned and practiced religion in families, educated the young, and took care of the sick. Over time, other institutions took on many of these functions. Today, we worship in churches, children are educated in schools, and we go to hospitals when we are sick.

Yet families continue to represent a major sphere of social life for most people. Families have an organized set of beliefs and rules, and they are arranged to meet certain fundamental needs. For example, despite a high divorce rate in the United States, people continue to want to marry, and most individuals agree on some fundamental rules between husbands and wives—for example, marital fidelity. While some people violate this rule and have extramarital affairs, such violations are generally looked down upon and discouraged.

Just as other social institutions cannot be understood in isolation, neither can families be understood without examining how they interact with and are influenced by the many forces within society. Families cannot merely be separated out as "havens" from the rest of society. Religious customs, the type of jobs that family members hold, residential location, and the political system, to name just a few, all shape family patterns, attitudes, behaviors, and opportunities. For example, these arrangements may influence which family members work outside the home, who has the primary responsibility for housework and other domestic labor, how children are raised and disciplined, and how power and decision making among family members will be allocated. For example, until recently in Afghanistan, the political system did not allow women to go to school or to work outside the home. Women had virtually no power either inside or outside the family.

Social Status and Families

Other important dimensions of social structure are the social positions that people occupy and the privileges and constraints that are attached to these positions. These are called **statuses.** We all occupy many statuses: you may be a daughter or son, student, employee, friend, roommate, and/or parent, to name just a few. A **master status** (or **statuses**) is the status that a person occupies that likely dominates over all the others.

Gender, race and ethnicity, and social class represent the major organizing constructs in our society. As we shall see in Chapter 3, these three statuses shape one's life in very dramatic ways; therefore, they are generally viewed as master statuses. For example, a recent Gallup poll surveyed families about their "ideal" arrangement combining work and parenthood. Only 13 percent of respondents said that the ideal situation for families is to have both parents working full time outside the home. Forty-one percent said that one parent staying home with the children is ideal, while the remainder claimed that the ideal situation is to have one parent work part time or work from the home. In both of these latter situations, when asked who it is that should work part time or stay at home, respondents either said the mother or that it doesn't matter. Very few persons suggested that the father curtail his full-time work activities (Gallup, 2001). As family scholar Katherine Allen writes, "If our goal is to study social structures and the processes related to families, we need ways to include more realistic understandings of the diversity of people's lives in our investigations" (2000: 8).

Theme 2: Using a Critical Perspective— The Myth of the Monolithic Family

Just as families in the United States are diverse, there is no single type of marriage or family pattern that is found exclusively throughout the world. There is widespread variation in what is accepted, tolerated, or even expected. First, we will examine variations around the world in marriage structures, patterns of authority, rules of descent, and patterns of residence. Second, we will compare family expectations in two industrialized nations, Sweden and Japan. Third, we will examine historical marriage and family patterns in the United States. These will illustrate the second theme: *a critical perspective shows us that a singular, monolithic family structure is largely a myth.*

Marriage Patterns

To most people in industrialized nations, the proper form of marriage is between one man and one woman (if not for a lifetime, at least for a period of time). We call this marriage pattern **monogamy,** and it is widely, although not exclusively, practiced throughout the world. However, because divorce rates are relatively high in many countries, including the United States, our marriage patterns have sometimes been described as **serial monogamy** because of our tendency to marry, divorce, and remarry.

Other societies practice **polygamy,** which allows for more than one spouse at a time. There are two types of polygamy. The most common of these is **polygyny,** which is the practice that allows husbands to have more than one wife. Although this practice is not legal in the United States, researchers estimate that approximately 30,000 American families currently practice polygyny. It is primarily found in Utah and other western states. In a study of these polygynous families, Altman and Ginat (1996) found that, on average, they contained four wives and twenty-seven children. Many of these families think of themselves as fundamentalist members of the Church of Jesus Christ of Latter-Day Saints (Mormon), but the Mormon church has not tolerated polygynous marriage since it was outlawed in 1890 and will

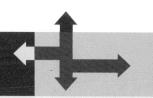

Utah Governor Mike Leavitt is facing a challenge: How strong of a stance should he take against polygamy, the practice of multiple spouses? When he took office in 1992, he swore to uphold the Utah Constitution, which forbids the practice. However, some people say that he refuses to flatly condemn the practice of polygamy and suggests that polygamy should be protected as a religious freedom. He has been thrown into the limelight by a high-profile child abuse case in 1998, in which Utah resident and practicing polygamist John Daniel Kingston allegedly whipped his sixteen-year-old daughter with a belt after she rebelled against an arranged marriage to Kingston's brother. She was ordered to become her uncle's fifteenth wife, but she refused, stating that all she really wanted to do was finish high school.

Some are quick to point out that Governor Leavitt is a member of the Mormon church. Mormons practiced polygamy in the middle 1800s during their move west; however, the church renounced the practice in 1890. Congress also passed tough laws against polygamy, and many persons who continued having multiple wives were imprisoned. Although the Mormon church had already outlawed polygamy, a wary Congress back in 1896 insisted that an anti-polygamy clause be included in the Utah Constitution when Utah was granted statehood.

The Mormon church has remained steadfast in its opposition to polygamy. Polygamists are summarily excommunicated from the church if discovered. Yet it is estimated that there are 30,000 polygamists in the western United States, with the highest number living in Utah. Many of these individuals are part of splinter groups from the Mormon church that have not been prosecuted. They claim they are practicing God's will.

Leavitt, in their defense, comments that polygamists are generally very hardworking, "good" people. He reportedly knew many polygamists while growing up in southern Utah. He feels that state resources are limited and that there may not be enough money to prosecute polygamists. "If you pump resources into polygamy and cohabitation, murderers and rapists walk," he said in defense of the lack of prosecution under his administration. Others also offer some support, or at least a blind eye, including the Utah Chapter of the National Organization for Women (NOW), a feminist group which says that polygamy could be a solution for the day-care problems faced by working mothers. Likewise, the Utah chapter of the American Civil Liberties Union said it would debate whether to back a possible lawsuit challenging the state's ban on polygamy.

But others suggest that the practice of polygamy is highly abusive of women and children—physically, sexually, emotionally, and spiritually. They suggest that polygamy must be stopped. "Leavitt's attitude is an insult to all of the women and children trapped in these relationships," said Roweena Erickson, a former polygamist wife and board member of the self-help group Tapestry of Polygamy. She believes that polygamy degrades women.

Meanwhile, John Daniel Kingston, the noted polygamist accused of trying to force his sixteen-year-old daughter to marry his brother, is a businessman and prominent member of the Kingston polygamist clan. It may have as many as 1,000 members and business holdings of up to 150 million dollars.

Sources: Adapted from Mike Carter (1998, Aug. 2). "Polygamy Bedevils Utah Governor." *Sunday Oregonian*, Sec. A, p. 9. Reprinted with permission of The Associated Press. Joyce Price (2002). "Polygamy Could Help Moms Who Work, Says Utah NOW." Available online: http://www.polygamy.com.

Critical Thinking

1. Who benefits from polygamy, and why do they benefit? Is anyone hurt by it?

2. Why has polygamy persisted despite such opposition to it?

This family photo shows Utah polygamist, Tom Green (top, red tie) with his five wives and some of his twenty-nine children in 2000. He was sentenced to prison for practicing polygamy and failing to support his family.

excommunicate members who are found to be practicing polygyny, as discussed in the Family Diversity box on page 11.

FACT OR FICTION?

Although there are a few societies in which men have more than one wife, there are no societies in which women have multiple husbands.

In contrast to the laws prohibiting polygyny in the United States, polygyny is tolerated in some nonindustrial societies in the world today, although we do not know its exact prevalence. It is more likely to be found in developing countries, including parts of Africa and South America. Where practiced, it is often supported by religious custom. Researchers Charles Welch and Paul Glick examined fifteen selected African countries and found that, depending on the country, between one out of five and one out of three married men had more than one wife. Obviously, not all men can have more than one wife, given existing sex ratios. They found that those who practiced polygyny tended to have two, or occasionally three, wives, but only rarely more than that (Welch III & Glick, 1981). Polygyny is primarily practiced by the wealthy. Having numerous wives is a sign of family wealth, education, and other dimensions of high status. It is used as a way to increase fertility within a family, since multiple wives increase the number of children born within the family. While Westerners may be tempted to assume that multiple wives would be jealous of or competitive with one another, a study based in polygynous Nigeria indicated that the wives tend to get along. When asked how they would feel if their husbands took another wife, approximately 60 percent said they would be pleased to share the housework, care of their husband, and child rearing, and to have someone to share things with (Ware, 1979).

The other type of polygamy is **polyandry,** which allows wives to have more than one husband. This type of marriage pattern is rare and tends to have several specific features associated with it (Cassidy & Lee, 1989; Stephens, 1963; Stockard, 2002). First, polyandry may occur in societies with hard environmental conditions, where poverty is widespread. Second, the multiple husbands are often brothers or otherwise related. For example, they may belong to the same clan and be of the same generation. Third, the marriage often takes place because it is seen to provide economic advantages to the men involved. For example, one husband may recruit his brothers or clan to come work on his land with him. Fourth, women's status is often low, with a limited role in the productive economy. Girls may be seen as burdensome to families; thus, female infanticide may be practiced as a way to eliminate having to care for girls. There is a shortage of women and girls for marriage. Janice Stockard describes a polyandrous marriage among Tibetans, where brothers collectively marry one wife (2002: 89):

> Married and living with two or more husbands in a household based on loyalty and cooperation among brothers requires management. Eventually the common wife is responsible for being sexually available to all of her husbands. The usual dynamic characterizing conjugal relations within polyandrous marriage is that the eldest brother enjoys an early and fairly exclusive honeymoon period. Given the age disparity among a set of brothers, it is not uncommon for the youngest brother(s)

to be too young to assume sexual relations. But each brother who is mature is welcomed into the marriage, as are the younger brothers as they become of age.

> All brothers are expected to be full partners in the marriage, and it is the wife's responsibility to see that each brother shares time with her in a rotational fashion. She must be careful to include each brother equally, sharing her affections and seeking to minimize signs of any favoritism on her part.

FICTION

There are some societies in which women are allowed to have multiple husbands. These societies are very rare.

Patterns of Authority

Women and men often receive drastically different treatment in many parts of the world. The term **patriarchy,** which means "rule of the father," refers to a form of social organization in which the norm or the expectation is that men have a natural right to be in positions of authority over women. Patriarchy is manifested and upheld in a wide variety of social institutions, including legal, educational, religious, and economic institutions. For example, the legal system may rule that women cannot vote, the educational system may enforce unequal or no formal education for girls, and religious institutions may attribute male dominance to "God's will." Patriarchy is the most dominant form of authority pattern. It is found to some degree in virtually every society.

A theoretical opposite to patriarchy is **matriarchy,** which is a form of social organization in which the norm or the expectation is that the power and authority in society should be vested in women. We refer to this as a "theoretical alternative" because no known cases of true matriarchies have ever been recorded.

In between these two extremes are authority patterns that could be best described as **egalitarian.** In these societies, the expectation is that power and authority are equally vested in both men and women. The United States and many other countries are headed in this direction, but it would be wrong to assume that all vestiges of patriarchy have been eliminated, as we will explore in Chapter 3.

Patterns of Descent

Where did you get your last name? How is property passed down? Who are considered to be your legal relatives? There are different ways in which a family's descent, or heritage, can be traced. Industrialized nations most commonly use a **bilateral** pattern of descent, in which descent can be traced through both male and female sides of the family. For example, the United States recognizes that both your mother's parents *and* your father's parents are related to you—you have, biologically, two sets of grandparents. Yet commonly found throughout the world is a **patrilineal** pattern, in which lineage is traced exclusively (or at least primarily) through the man's family line. A patrilineal society would recognize your father's relatives as your kin, but minimal connections would be established with your mother's side of the family. Vestiges of patrilineal descent can be noted in the United States, which practices primarily a bilateral model. These vestiges include (1) last names almost always reflect the fathers' lineage rather than the mother's, and (2) sons are sometimes given their father's

first names as well, and are then referred to as "Junior." There is no semantic equivalent for girls; they are not referred to as "Mary Anderson, Jr.," or as "Catherine Smith III."

Finally, a few societies can be characterized as having **matrilineal** descent patterns, characterized as having the lineage more closely aligned with women's families than with men's families. This is not the mirror opposite of a patrilineal pattern, however. In a matrilineal descent pattern, it is not women who are in positions of power to pass on their lineage; rather, women pass it on through their family side via their brothers or other male members of the family. Even in a matrilineal society a man retains the control over his own lineage. A child raised in a matrilineal society could have little to do with his or her biological father, at least where lineage is concerned. The biological father may retain ties of affection, but it is the child's maternal uncle who is the key figure in the child's life.

Patterns of Residence

Another dimension of the diversity of family patterns found worldwide is the residential patterns of a newly married couple. In industrial societies such as the United States, the expectation is for the couple to live separately from either set of parents. This is referred to as **neolocal;** the newly married couple establishes its own residence and lives there independently. Sometimes families will contain several generations, but the general expectation is for couples to establish their own homes. However, in some parts of the world **patrilocal** residence is practiced, defined as the expectation that the couple will live with the husband's family. Less common is a **matrilocal** pattern, the expectation that the newly married couple will live with the family of the wife. Where any of these three patterns operate, certainly not all couples adhere to the pattern, at least not for all of their lives. For example, in the United States, the expectation is for neolocal residence, with married couples living separately from their parents. However, some young couples move in with their parents because of financial considerations or the desire to share other kinds of assistance (Goldscheider & Goldscheider, 1994; Savage & Fronczek, 1993).

These different marriage and family patterns have real consequences for the way we experience family life. They reflect the expectations about whom and how we marry, where we should live, who should have power, and how we inherit and trace our lineage.

A Modern Contrast: Sweden and Japan

Families in modern industrial societies vary in style as well. Dating rituals may differ from one society to another, relationships between husbands and wives may vary, expectations of the ways in which parents should interact with their children may differ, and beliefs about whether the elderly should reside with their adult children vary sharply. The next section contrasts two industrialized nations, Sweden and Japan, to illustrate the variation found in industrialized nations today.

Sweden As one of the most affluent countries in the world with one of the highest average life expectancies found anywhere, Sweden is an interesting country in which to examine marriage and family patterns. Like many of its European counterparts, family support policies have always been considerably more generous than in the United States (Bergmann, 1997; Rainwater & Smeeding, 1995). For example, new parents in Sweden have generous maternity and paternity leaves in which they continue to receive pay and benefits (Haas, 1992; Haas & Hwang, 1995). These are available to both mothers and fathers, although fathers are less apt to take advantage of such benefits than are mothers. Right of citizenship guarantees health benefits, so access to prenatal and postnatal care is widespread. Compared to the United States, fewer babies are born prematurely, so their health is more secure. The **infant mortality rate,** defined as the number of deaths within the first year of life per 1,000 births in the population, is considerably lower in Sweden, at 5 per 1,000 versus 10 per 1,000 in the United States (Children's Defense Fund, 1997).

It was during the 1960s that Sweden's marriage and family patterns began to change rapidly. Sociologists David Popenoe and Jan Trost, two scholars examining demographic changes in Sweden's families, noted that the marriage rate decreased by approximately 40 percent in less than a decade. Many Swedes were (and are) choosing to marry later, as well as to not marry at all. Sweden has one of the highest average ages at first marriage and one of the lowest marriage rates found anywhere in the world. By 1980, the marriage rate was 78 marriages per 1,000 women within the 25–29 age group, compared to 109 in Japan, 117 in France, 127 in the United States, and 168 in England and Wales (Popenoe, 1987; Trost, 1985).

One reason for lower marriage rates is that in Sweden, marriage and cohabitation are virtually equally acceptable lifestyles. Children born within cohabiting relationships are not stigmatized. The parents have simply not chosen to marry, and there is no stigma attached to their single status.

The vast majority of mothers in Sweden are employed outside the home. Few women are full-time homemakers. Parents share domestic and parenting tasks to a greater degree than do parents in the United States, although the primary responsibility continues to fall to women (Calasanti & Bailey, 1991; Haas, 1992).

Yet Sweden has made a public effort to equalize domestic relationships. Generous family support policies are available by law to both fathers and mothers. For example, parents have several paid days off each year to care for sick children or to attend day-care or school functions. They can reduce their workday to six hours per day in order to have more time to spend with their children (Haas, 1992). There are generous paid maternal and paternal leaves at childbirth, and families are provided a stipend by the government to help defray the costs of raising children (Office of Research, Evaluation, and Statistics, Social Security Administration, 1999; United Nations Statistical Division, 2000). These policies were enacted to (1) encourage more couples to have children, as the birthrate in Sweden was dropping dramatically; (2) encourage more women to work outside the home, as Sweden needs additional workers; and (3) keep pace with Sweden's changing conceptions of gender and movement toward greater egalitarianism.

Japan In comparison to Sweden, Japan has a tradition steeped in segregated and traditional gender expectations. Women's and men's roles in work, family, and other social institutions are still highly differentiated, although some convergence has been noted in recent decades. For example, fewer mothers are employed full time outside the home in Japan than in any other industrialized nation, although the numbers are increasing somewhat. When mothers are employed, it is still expected that taking care of children is "women's work" while earning the family income is "men's work." Marital and family roles are more divided in Japan than in many other industrialized nations, including in the United States (Ishii-Kuntz, 1994; Kamo, 1990). Husbands often have a workday that extends well into the evening, and requires them to socialize with co-workers or clients. With husbands' extended absences from home, the bulk of child rearing and other domestic tasks falls onto the shoulders of women. But it is not simply that these jobs require long absences from home. Instead, an interplay of gender and the economy is operating—when women hold these jobs, they are still expected to take care of domestic responsibilities.

Marriage and family life are exceedingly important in the lives of the Japanese, arguably even more so than in other industrialized nations. For example, elderly Japanese often reside with their adult children and grandchildren even if they are in good health and financially stable. One study found that the proportion of the elderly aged sixty and over living in three-generational households was 32 percent in Japan, but only 1 percent in England, 1 percent in the United States, and 3 percent in Germany (Management and Coordination Agency, 1991). Although the proportion of Japanese who prefer to live autonomously is increasing, recent studies reveal that approximately one-half of married women still report that it is either a "good custom" or a "natural duty" to care for elderly parents (Ogawa & Retherford, 1993).

FACT OR FICTION?

Japan's traditional gender expectations have shown no real signs of change.

Another indicator of the primacy of marriage and family life to the Japanese is the comparatively very low rate of divorce. Di-

Men in Japan often work very long hours, and well into the night. These "hotels" provide a place to nap so that they can continue to work rather than go home to their families.

vorce is only one-fifth as common in Japan as in the United States, which has the highest rate in the world. This lower rate is likely due to several features of Japanese culture and family life: (1) Japanese culture stresses conformity and subordination of individual needs to those of the larger group; (2) the loss of income could be devastating to wives, who, if employed, likely earn considerably less than husbands; and (3) closeness and co-residence with other family members may buffer the effects of problematic marriages, as Japanese marriages are rarely couple-centered (Stack, 1992).

Yet, despite the apparent centrality of marriage and family in the heart of Japanese culture, recent trends show that some tre-mendous changes are taking place. Fewer women are marrying, and those who do are marrying much later than ever before (Raymo, 1998). Moreover, fewer women are bearing children, and those who do often have them relatively late in life. In 1970, fewer than 9 percent of women between the ages of 30 and 34 in Japan had remained unmarried, but this had increased to 20 percent by 1995 (Raymo, 1998).

FICTION

Japan is a society steeped in tradition, including traditional gendered expectations. However, this situation is beginning to change.

Most of this change is a result of delaying rather than forgoing marriage. However, it is also likely that some women who initially only anticipated delaying a marriage will ultimately remain unmarried for life (out of choice or by default). Why are women beginning to delay getting married? Reasons include (1) a growing gap in attitudes regarding women's roles in society, (2) increases in women's education and labor force participation, (3) an imbalance in the number of men to women, and (4) an increase in the attractiveness of single life while at the same time a decrease in the attractiveness of traditional marriages (Atoh, 1995; Raymo, 1998; Tsuya & Mason, 1995). In the book *Japan: The Childless Society,* written by a professor of French and sociology at a university in Tokyo, Muriel Jolivet (1997) outlines the pressures on women that make bearing and raising children unattractive. She suggests that the Japanese government, concerned about a birthrate that is far below replacement level at 1.46, criticizes women who choose not to have children as being "selfish." Yet, despite the stigma, many women in Japan are now resisting these social pressures and are limiting their family size. She reports that of women aged 40–49, more than 70 percent have had abortions.

Japan is experiencing tremendous economic and social transitions. These changes have enormous implications for marriage and family life. Next, we will illustrate that families have also varied rather dramatically from one historical period to another, and among different groups within historical periods.

The History of Family Life in the United States

Despite our perceptions to the contrary, families have always come in a wide variety of colors, shapes, and sizes, with divergent values and functions. Sociologist Stephanie Coontz, in her books *The Way We Never Were: American Families and the Nostalgia Trap* (2000) and *The Way We Really Are: Coming to Terms with America's Changing Families* (1997), reminds us that the images we have of families in the "good old days" of the past—of Dad at work as sole breadwinner, Mom as a full-time housewife and mother tending to the home all day, and a house in the suburbs—is largely a myth. This ideal type was popular for only a brief period primarily in the 1950s. But even then, not all families subscribed to this model. Lower-income families and many minority families did not share in the affluence of the 1950s or the suburban family lifestyle. Not all fathers were paid wages that could support a family; therefore, mothers were also employed. It is important to recognize that the 1950s style of family, which is held up and revered as an ideal model of family life today, is not only an aberration historically but never really existed for millions of Americans even during that period.

How to Study Families from the Past Piecing together the history of family life has become an active topic of research. Drawing on a variety of sources, historians and family scholars are attempting to weave together our "social history" to offer important insights about day-to-day life, customs, and lifestyles of ordinary citizens. This is a radical departure from the work of most historians, who focus on events such as wars, economic downturns, and other large-scale social events. Instead, social historians are interested in uncovering aspects of everyday family life (Degler, 1980; Schvaneveldt, Pickett, & Young, 1993). Because this field is still relatively new, our knowledge about the details of family life outside of the white middle classes is more limited. However, there are attempts to include those groups whose life stories have been previously ignored or are more challenging to piece together, including

African Americans, Latinos, Native Americans, Asian Americans, women, European immigrants, and the elderly.

Historians and family scholars look at diaries, letters, or other lengthy correspondence between people to understand the common, everyday experiences of families. They analyze historical records to get an aggregate picture about, for example, immigration trends, age at first marriage, or the average length of time between marriage and first birth. Census records; birth, marriage, and death registers; immigration records; slave auctions and other transactions; church records; newspapers and magazine articles; employment ledgers; and tax records can also provide insightful clues into the family lives of large numbers of ordinary people. Finally, scholars may rely upon **family reconstitution,** in which attempts are made to compile all available information about significant family events and everyday life within a particular family. Members of each generation who are still alive are interviewed, and they are asked to reconstruct their family history. A significant responsibility falls on the eldest members to reconstruct the generation that preceded them. Other documents will be combed as well; the goal is to reconstruct the family life and household patterns in the most precise manner possible.

Recreating the past is not easy. Historical researchers work as "detectives" and try to obtain the widest number of sources possible as they reconstruct the past. Numerous sources are sometimes available, but, unfortunately, clues can be scarce.

Family Life in Colonial America: European Colonists Several family historians, such as Peter Laslett, author of *The World We Have Lost* (1971), John Demos, author of *A Little Commonwealth* (1970), Steven Mintz and Susan Kellogg, authors of *Domestic Revolution: A Social History of American Family*

Families in colonial America were large by today's standards, and were the cornerstone of society.

Life (1989), and Carl Degler, author of *At Odds: Women and the Family in America from the Revolution to the Present* (1980), have given us some surprising glimpses into colonial family life. They show us that the family was the cornerstone of colonial society. It was the primary social institution, helping early immigrants adapt to life in the New World. The family was, first and foremost, a *business* because it was the central focus of economic production. Each household was nearly self-sufficient, and all family members—men, women, and children—worked together at productive tasks to meet their material needs, raising the food and making most of the clothing, furniture, and household goods that the family used.

FACT OR FICTION?

Most people in colonial America lived in large extended families, consisting of grandparents, parents, and children.

The family also served as a *school.* Formal schooling conducted away from home was extremely rare, particularly in early colonial times. Instead, it fell to parents to educate their children, to teach them how to read and write, and impart to them the vocational and technical skills that they would need in their adult life. Formal schools began to appear toward the end of the colonial period, but they were not mandatory; therefore, many children, especially girls, non-Europeans, and poor children, did not attend them.

The family also served as a *church*. Although churches flourished, families sometimes lived a great distance from them. Even in communities where churches were readily available, families worshiped and prayed together frequently in their home. Parents and children read the Bible together, one of the few readily available books and sources of moral instruction.

The family served as a form of *correctional institution*. Jails were rare. Instead, courts sentenced criminals and so-called "idle" people to live with more respected families in the community. Families were viewed as a natural setting in which to impose discipline and also to encourage reform.

Moreover, families were *health and social welfare institutions*. There were no hospitals, and there were few doctors during this period (Starr, 1984). Families, women in particular, took over the role of caring for the sick and infirm. Families also took care of the aging, the homeless, and orphans. These services were not pro-vided by outside social institutions, but by families—one's own or someone else's (Demos, 1970).

FICTION

Most people in colonial America lived in large nuclear families rather than extended families. The age at first marriage was relatively high, and life expectancy was short. This means that many grandparents died before their grandchildren were born.

Most people in colonial America lived in nuclear families. Newly married couples usually established their own households unless the parents were ill and needed care. Extended families, composed of grandparents or other family members, were the exception rather than the rule. Because the age at first marriage was relatively high and people didn't live very long, older adults may have died before their grandchildren were born.

Yet families in colonial America were large by today's standards, often containing six or more children. The age differences between children were large, and death rates were high. Siblings might have been twenty-five years apart in age. Therefore, some children were married and out of the house while other children were only babies.

It was common for husbands or wives to marry for second or third times because of high death rates. Therefore, children within a household commonly had stepsiblings or half-siblings. Some households also contained servants or slaves, and these were sometimes counted as household family members in statistical records. Peter Laslett, in his book *The World We Have Lost* (1971: 113), describes the results of a demographic count of a particular parish:

> The most remarkable effect of high mortality which can be recovered by Sampson's careful recordings in 1688 has to do with the number of times his parishioners found themselves remarrying after the loss of a spouse. He set out the rank order of every marital union in the village. There were seventy-two husbands in Clayworth in 1688, and no less than twenty-one of them were marked as having been married before: thirteen of them had been married twice, one a number of times unspecified, three

three times, three four times, and one five times. Of the seventy-two wives, nine had been previously married; one of the seven widowers and one of the twenty-one widows are known to have been married more than once. This may owe a lot to chance, but it is spectacular confirmation of the propensity of those who did get married in the English traditional world to go on marrying, at least until later life.

For both women and men, marriage and family were central events in life. Although marriages were often undertaken because of business or financial interests, love and affection between husbands and wives were anticipated. But how did men and women meet prospective marriage partners?

Dating   Dating took a very different form in colonial America from what it does today, and casual dating was frowned upon. Young women were usually not left alone to meet men. Young men had to ask the young woman's family for permission to see her, and the couple was usually chaperoned by friends or relatives. Parents, fathers in particular, exerted considerable influence over whom a son or daughter could date or marry.

Despite heavy parent involvement and a general lack of privacy, premarital sex and premarital pregnancy occurred with surprising frequency. According to some historians, nearly a third of women were pregnant at the time of their marriage (Demos, 1970). Sexual activity was generally confined to couples that were engaged or otherwise committed to be married. **Bundling** was a dating practice among some puritan New England groups and may have contributed to the rate of premarital pregnancy. Because a young man might have traveled a great distance to see his date or fiancée, and people

generally went to sleep early, he may have been allowed to stay the night at her house. Space was at a premium, so the young man and woman could continue their date by spending the night in a bed together, separated by a wooden board. Usually, bundling was reserved for young people who were engaged or otherwise seriously dating each other. The couple was supposedly under the watchful eye of the other family members, who likely shared the bedroom. It is unknown how many pregnancies resulted from "innocent" bundling, although we do know that premarital pregnancies occurred with relative frequency in colonial America.

Other women, including slaves or indentured servants, were particularly vulnerable to rape and coercion, and often bore children out of wedlock. Indentured servants were frequently young, poor, and alone in the United States. A family already living in the United States paid their fare on the condition that the indentured servant would work for the family for a period of seven years. Some indentured servants were treated like family members, while others were abused and exploited.

Relationships Between Husbands and Wives   Husbands and wives worked as a team to ensure that their family survived and thrived. A wife was considered her husband's helpmate but not his equal. Marriage was expected to be a partnership; however, the husband was considered to be the head of the family, and it was his wife's duty to obey him. New England clergymen often referred to male authority as "laws" that women must accept, and in the South, husbands denounced assertive wives as "impertinent." Females were thought to be morally weaker, a belief rationalized from the story of Adam and Eve, thus needing the authority of men.

At the same time, there was a shortage of women in colonial America, and this gender imbalance tended to enhance women's status and position. Compared to their counterparts in England, women in colonial America had more rights on average, including some measure of property rights and the right to make contracts. Some wills indicate that women could retain limited ownership of certain property after marriage. These rights varied from one colony to another, and sometimes from one community to another.

Women had crucial economic roles inside and outside the family. The division of labor was sharply divided. For the most part, wives did the cooking, sewing, cleaning, gardening, and certain farm chores, and produced many products for the family. Husbands did the planting and harvesting. Families needed the labor of women, and their duties were highly valued by society. Most women worked solely in the home, but their lives were anything but leisurely. As historian Carl Degler tells us,

> Over the long term of a lifetime [their tasks] were probably more arduous and demanding than those performed by the men. One traveler in 18th century Carolina reported that "the ordinary women take care of Cows, Hogs, and other small Cattle, make butter and cheese, spin cotton, and flax, help to sow and reap corn, wind silk from the worms, gather Fruit and look after the House." Looking after the house was itself a heavy task since that included not only cleaning the physical interior but the washing and mending of the family's clothes, preparing meals under the handicaps of an open fireplace and no running water, preserving various kinds of foods, making all the soap, candles, and most of the medicines used by the family, as well as all the clothes for the family. And

> then, as the quotation suggests, the women had to be ready at planting or harvest time to help in the fields. On top of this, of course, was the bearing and rearing of children. . . . Unlike the work of the husband-farmer, a woman's work went on after dark and at undiminished pace throughout the year. (Degler, 1980: 363–364)

Relationships with Children Families in colonial America had a different view of their children and a different conception of childhood from what we have today. Parents tended to be very strict; obedience to parental authority and to the teachings of the Bible was paramount. It was commonly believed that children were born with "original sin" and that they needed firm discipline and severe religious training to prevent them from going to hell. Discipline was strict in order to break their innate rebellion and selfishness. Firm guidance was seen as necessary to ensure that children would grow up to be productive members of society. Excessive tenderness could spoil the child.

Children were treated as miniature adults in many ways. There was no concept of adolescence as there is today. As soon as children were old enough to labor on the family farm or in the household, they were put to work. "Once the child had begun to assume an adult role and style, around the age of six or seven, the way ahead was fairly straightforward," writes historian Demos (1970: 150). Parents commonly sent their pre-teenage children away, "putting them out" or "farming them out" as it was called, so that they could learn a trade, develop a skill, and be better disciplined.

There were social class variations in child-rearing patterns then as there are today. Wealthy families tended to be more indulgent with their children than were poorer families. Yet child labor was nearly universal

Slave family ties were strong, when they were permitted to exist at all.

because their labor was needed for family survival.

Thomas Jefferson, former president of the United States, fathered children with one of his slaves.

Colonial America: African Americans and Slavery The first Africans forcefully brought to the United States were indentured servants, and after they served a specified amount of time, they were considered "free" and were able to marry and to purchase their own land. But by the late seventeenth century, the slave trade was well under way,

with a million Africans captured and brought to the United States against their will. Courts in the southern colonies abolished many of the legal rights of Africans.

Some prominent Americans, including Thomas Jefferson, publicly denounced slavery but privately supported it. In addition to his owning slaves, it is now generally agreed that he fathered children with one who has been identified as Sally Hemings, as discussed in the Focus on Family Research box on page 24.

It is generally agreed upon that Thomas Jefferson fathered children with one of his slaves named Sally Hemings.

Did Thomas Jefferson have a sexual relationship with one of his young slaves, Sally Hemings, and father a child with her? Her descendants have long claimed Jefferson as an ancestor. But for many years scholars, along with Jefferson's more obvious descendants, have denied it. Dumas Malone suggests in his book *Jefferson the President, First Term, 1801–1805,* that the charges of a sexual relationship with Sally Hemings "are distinctly out of character, being virtually unthinkable in a man of Jefferson's moral standards and habitual conduct."

Yet recent DNA tests performed on the descendants of Thomas Jefferson's family and of the family of Jefferson's slave, Sally Hemings, offer compelling evidence that the president of the United States fathered at least one of her children—her youngest son, Eston Hemings. It is likely that he also fathered at least one other son named Madison. The Y-chromosome is handed down directly from father to son, and all paternally related males will share it. There is less than a 1-percent chance that a person chosen at random would share the same set of Y-chromosome mutations that exist in the Jefferson lineage. It is possible that Jefferson's other relatives fathered the children with Sally, but it is unlikely. As Robert Gillespie, a lawyer who heads the Monticello Association, commented, "We've always agreed with mainstream historians that Jefferson wouldn't have fathered Sally Hemings' children." But he added that the DNA results are changing his mind.

There are no known images of Sally Hemings and only a few brief descriptions of her. Born in 1772 or 1773, she was the illegitimate half-sister of Jefferson's wife Martha, born to John Wayles and Elizabeth Hemings, a slave. Sally became Jefferson's property when he inherited the Wayles estate in 1774, and she arrived at Monticello as a very young girl in 1776. In her early childhood, Hemings probably served as a "nurse" to Jefferson's daughter. Later, while a widower and ambassador to France, Jefferson moved his family to France for a brief period and brought Hemings with them. In 1789, when she was 16 or 17, Hemings returned with the Jefferson family to Virginia and was pregnant. Her child was described as resembling Jefferson.

Thomas Jefferson did not free Sally Hemings, but he did release all her children before he died or in his will upon his death. His other slave families did not receive their freedom.

The evidence that Jefferson did indeed father a child with one of his slaves has caused some historians to critically reevaluate Jefferson. Others express more tolerance. "Within the larger world, the dominant response will be Jefferson is more human, to regard this as evidence of his frailties, frailties that seem more like us," said Joseph Ellis, whose 1997 book, *American Sphinx: The Character of Thomas Jefferson,* won the National Book Award. Indeed, the liaison between Jefferson and Hemings has been referred to by many as "a relationship," as though to minimize the exploitative nature of master–slave interactions. And writers often comment on Hemings's beauty and her near-whiteness. She has been described as "mighty near white . . . very handsome, long straight hair down her back." Jefferson's grandson described her as "light colored and decidedly good looking." Nonetheless, it should be remembered that Sally Hemings was not a free woman making a personal choice. It is unlikely that the inherent exploitation involved between a master and a slave could ever constitute "a relationship" in the traditional sense of the term. The true nature of their interaction, unlike the genetic DNA material, will probably forever remain a mystery.

Sources Adapted from "The Content of Jefferson's Character Is Revealed at Last, or Is It?" *New York Times Week in Review* (Nov. 8, 1998). *The New York Times* [Online]. Available at http://search.nytimes.com/search/daily/ ...te+site+60427+3+wAAA+Thomas%7E Jefferson; Dinitia Smith and Nicholas Wade. "DNA Tests Offer Evidence That Jefferson Fathered a Child with His Slave" (Nov. 1, 1998). *The New York Times* [Online]. Available at http://searach.nytimes.com/search/daily/... te+site+23051+5+wAAA+Thomas%7E Jefferson; The Plantation. 2002. "Thomas Jefferson and Sally Hemings: A Brief Account." Available at http://www.monticello.org/ plantation/hemings-jefferson_contro.html.

Critical Thinking

1. Why has it taken so long for this information to come to light?

2. Do you think that two people with such different levels of power could truly be in love or have a love affair? If not, then what was the nature of their sexual relationship? Was it rape?

For years, slavery has been used to explain current African American family patterns. African American families have been criticized for being matriarchal, assumed to be a carry-over from norms established during slavery. However, historians have begun to revise our conceptions of families under slavery. Instead of seeing slave families as inadequate, incomplete, or emasculated, historians are noting the resiliency of slave families (Sudarkasa, 1999; Wilkenson, 1997). The popularity of televised programs such as *Roots,* which vividly portrays the strength of family bonds under some of the most adverse conditions possible, and books such as *The Black Family in Slavery and Freedom,* by historian Herbert Gutman (1976), indicates that African family ties were strong when they were permitted to exist. Historians note the strength of the extended family and note that the relationships created by "blood" were considered more important than those created by marriage (Sudarkasa, 1999: 69).

In colonial America, it was not easy for a slave to find a spouse. In the North, most slaves were not allowed to associate with other slaves. They lived alone or in very small groups with their masters. In the South, most slaves lived on small plantations with ten or fewer other slaves. "Breeding," as it was termed, was not necessarily encouraged in the eighteenth century because many slave owners felt it was more expensive to raise a slave from childhood than it was to buy a mature slave.

However, by the early 1800s, the United States prohibited the importation of new slaves, and owners began to recognize the value of family relationships and childbearing among the slaves whom they owned. Some of these relationships were forged primarily for "breeding" purposes. At other times, real love developed between slaves. Yet slave marriages were fragile; one study conducted in several southern states reveals that over one-third of marriages were termi-

nated by selling off either the husband or the wife to another party elsewhere (Gutman, 1976). Another study reports that only 14 percent of slave couples said they lived together without some sort of disruption. Almost one-third of these were broken up by the master, but an even higher proportion of breakups were due to the death of one of the spouses (Blassingame, 1972). Yet, even when slavery tore apart families, kinship bonds persisted. Children were often named after lost relatives as a way to preserve family ties.

Prior to the Civil War, approximately 150,000 free African Americans were living in the South and another 100,000 were living in the North (Mintz & Kellogg, 1989). Yet even "free" African Americans were not necessarily allowed to vote or attend white schools and churches. Whites treated them as grossly inferior. Jobs were difficult to come by. Consequently, many free African Americans were poor, had high levels of unemployment, and were barely literate. Women had an easier time than did men in finding employment because whites sought them out as domestic servants. Moreover, the number of free women outnumbered free men in urban areas. Together, the high rates of poverty and the sex imbalance of free African Americans challenged African Americans' ability to marry and raise children. Therefore, it is not surprising that many children were reared in female-headed households. One study indicated that when property holdings, a key measure of income, are held constant, the higher incidence of one-parent families among African Americans largely disappeared (Mintz & Kellogg, 1989). Poverty shapes family life.

Industrialization and Immigration Family life changed considerably in the nineteenth century and the early twentieth century because of two primary factors. First, **industrialization** transformed an economy from a system based on small-family-based

© Bettman/Corbis

A family living in a dilapidated, but not uncommon, New York tenement building sits together in their bedroom.

life. By the late nineteenth century and early twentieth century, millions more came, primarily from Southern and Eastern Europe, including Greeks, Poles, Italians, Russians, and other Slavic groups. Other groups from Asia, such as the Chinese, later immigrated to work primarily in certain industries. Between 1830 and 1930, over thirty million immigrants came to the United States.

Immigrants were an important component of the changing economy and were employed in a number of key industries. A survey of twenty major mining and manufacturing industries found that over half of the workers were foreign-born. In clothing factories, the figure was over three-quarters. In packinghouses, steel mills, textile mills, coal mines, and a host of other industries, nearly half of the workers were immigrants to the United States.

The Poor and Working Classes Most immigrants were members of the poor or working class. Women were preferred over men in certain industries because they could be paid significantly less and were considered to be more docile and obedient. Many jobs became categorized and separated by sex. Men did the heavy manual labor. Women toiled in tedious and repetitive jobs that corresponded with their domestic skills, such as seamstress, laundress, or domestic servant to the rich. Men's and women's wages were low; consequently, children also often worked full time.

Weatherford, in her book *Foreign and Female: Immigrant Women in America, 1840–1930* (1986), describes the appalling conditions in which many immigrant families lived. Housing was crowded, was substandard, and often lacked appropriate sanitation facilities. Raw sewage was strewn about, causing rampant epidemics and disease in the neighborhoods in which immigrants congregated. Upton Sinclair describes the harrowing plight of immigrants in his best-sell-

agriculture to one of large industrial capital. Small family farms increasingly could not support themselves and folded, or else were bought out by large commercial farming companies. There was considerable movement to urban areas in search of jobs. "Work" became something that was increasingly being done away from the home. More and more goods and services were produced for profit outside the home, and families purchased these with money earned from the wages they earned at outside jobs.

Second, the large waves of **immigration,** as people moved to the United States, provided the labor fueling the industrialization. Millions of Irish, German, English, Scandinavian, and other Northern European immigrants came to the United States in the mid-1800s encouraged by the prospect of a better

ing novel *The Jungle,* originally published in 1906 as a story about an immigrant family from Lithuania. In describing some of the dreadful conditions in their neighborhood, he wrote of raw sewage and cesspools drawing flies and rodents where children played. Working conditions were also often dangerous, unsanitary, and inhumane. His book was influential in creating many new laws during the "progressive era" of the early 1900s to protect workers' health and safety. Sinclair describes the dangers of working in the meat-packing plants in Chicago:

> Of the butchers and floorsmen, the beef-boners and trimmers, and all those who used knives, you could scarcely find a person who had the use of his thumb; time and time again the base of it had been slashed, till it was a mere lump of flesh. . . . The hands of these men would be criss-crossed with cuts, until you could no longer pretend to count them or to trace them. They would have no nails—they had worn them off pulling hides; their knuckles were swollen so that their fingers spread out like a fan. There were men who worked in the cooking rooms, in the midst of steam and sickening odors, by artificial light; in these rooms the germs of tuberculosis might live for two years, but the supply was renewed every hour. There were the beef-luggers, who carried two-hundred pound quarters into the refrigerator cars; a fearful kind of work, that began at four o'clock in the morning, and that wore out the most powerful men in a few years. There were those who worked in the chilling rooms, and whose special disease was rheumatism; the time limit that a man could work in the chilling rooms was said to be five years.

> There were the wool-pluckers, whose hands went to pieces even sooner than the hands of the pickle men; for the pelts of the sheep had to be painted with acid to loosen the wool, and then the pluckers had to pull out this wool with their bare hands, till the acid had eaten their fingers off. (1981/1906: 98)

The strain on family life under these abysmal working and living conditions was severe and took its toll. Alcoholism, violence, crime, and other social problems stemming from demoralization plagued many families. Yet immigrants continued to crowd the cities in search of work because they hoped that it would lead eventually to a better life. Many immigrants hoped that if they simply worked hard enough, they would soon join the ranks of the middle and upper classes.

The Middle and Upper Classes In the middle and upper classes, the ideal family life involved separate spheres of activity. The husband was, ideally at least, the breadwinner, while the wife stayed home to rear the children and take care of the home. She no longer produced goods and services, but rather she consumed them in the process of caring for her family. The ideology of separate spheres has been called the **Cult of True Womanhood** and involved four virtues on the part of women: piety, purity, submissiveness, and domesticity (Welter, 1966). Women were supposed to be the guardian of the home and the moral values associated with it. A woman's task was to create a safe haven for her husband and family, removed from the harried world of work that her husband was becoming increasingly immersed in. Ideally, middle- and upper-class women were cut off from the outside world; they were considered too delicate to handle its harshness. They were "ladies." Other women in more challenging financial circumstances who had to work to support the family were looked down upon as being less than true and virtuous women.

During this period, ideas about children and the developmental stages associated with childhood began to change. Childhood and adolescence were increasingly viewed as distinct stages in the life cycle. Children were no longer considered simply miniature adults, perhaps because middle- and upper-class families no longer had to rely upon their labor. They were seen as individuals in their own right, not simply as extensions of their parents. Children were innocent, and they could be molded into good or bad citizens. There was a marked decline in the use of spanking and other firm disciplinary techniques (Degler, 1980).

Women had a critical role within the family: teaching children strong moral values. Child-rearing books played up the importance of mothers, while making the assumption that fathers would not be around very much. Women's child-rearing responsibilities were elevated in importance, and outside work was frowned upon because it would presumably take a mother away from her primary, natural, and most important work of all.

The Rise of the "Modern" Family— The Early Twentieth Century The early 1900s contained many social events that had a tremendous impact on the structure and dynamics of family life. There were two world wars, a depression, and the post-World War II affluence of the 1950s. Technological innovations were designed to reduce the amount of time spent on domestic labor. The automobile changed the ways families traveled and increased the number of readily available destinations. New residential patterns—migration to the cities in search of work, and the subsequent creation of suburbs and flight from the cities—increased travel and commuting time. Altogether, this decreased the time that fathers spent with their families.

These changes led to new lifestyles, family structures, and views about the family. Families moved away from being largely economic units to what has been called a **companionate family,** based on mutual affection, sexual attraction, compatibility, and personal happiness. Young adults freely dated without chaperons and placed a greater emphasis on romantic love and attraction in their search for mates than did their parents and grandparents. Families were smaller because children were increasingly viewed as economic liabilities rather than assets as they had been on the family farm.

This emphasis on a companionate family had an unexpected consequence. Alongside the growing dominant assumption that marriage should make couples happy, the United States witnessed rising divorce rates. Those who fell short of the ideal family increasingly ended their marriage.

National events and crises such as World War I, the Great Depression, and World War II caused dramatic shifts in family life. For example, during the Great Depression of the 1930s, millions of individuals and families became unemployed and impoverished. An estimated one out of four workers was unemployed and searching for work, although even this figure likely discounts seasonal workers (Gordon, 1994). Many families were dislocated, or members abandoned their families in search of paid work. Millions of families became transients going from town to town looking for work. Between one and two million were estimated to be homeless, sleeping in rat-infested shelters when they could afford or find them, on park benches, or under bridges. Finding enough food to feed their families and locating clothing, shelter, and heat were major hurdles for millions of people during this period (Watkins, 1993). Meanwhile, persons who were fortunate enough to continue to keep their jobs often faced large declines in their wages.

The stresses associated with impoverishment of this magnitude affected families in a multitude of ways. Some men who could not provide for their families became depressed and acted out their depression in destructive ways, such as excessive drinking, abusive behavior, or desertion of the family. Children were forced to become more independent and try to supplement family wages when they could. Dramatic male unemployment rates put pressure on women to resign from their jobs. Women workers were seen as taking jobs away from men, who had a greater right to employment. Even the government discriminated against women: approximately half of school districts fired married female teachers, three-quarters would not hire a married woman, and in 1932 a federal order stated that only one spouse could work for the federal government (Milkman, 1976; McElvaine, 1993).

World War II also contributed to a number of significant changes, including the dramatic influx of women in the labor market to help ease the shortage of workers caused by drafting men into the armed forces. Initially, it was not easy to encourage millions of women, often married and with children, to fill the available jobs. The government, in conjunction with media efforts, developed a large propaganda effort promoting employment as women's patriotic duty.

Surrounded by images of strong women employed in defense and manufacturing industries, women flocked to volunteer or work in paid positions. Efforts were made by employers to provide child care for children. Many women worked in jobs or held positions that they never dreamed that they would: they dug ditches, they operated forklifts, they worked in factories doing heavy labor, and they worked on the loading docks. Racial prejudice and discrimination were less apparent: all women's labor was sorely needed, and "color bars" that had previously limited the kinds of jobs minorities could hold were lifted, at least temporarily. For example, African American nurses, who were barred from serving in the military, were finally allowed in to ease the nursing shortage crisis.

Post-World War II   As World War II ended in 1945, and veterans returned from the war, families faced new challenges. Women, encouraged into paid work only a few years before, were now encouraged to give up their positions for the sake of men. Some women gladly did so, while others resisted because they enjoyed their newfound freedom, pay, and job experience. Some of the women who refused to quit were simply fired; few protective laws existed on the books to prohibit the arbitrary firing of women.

Divorce rates rose dramatically in the years after World War II, more than doubling the rate prior to the war. Several factors may have contributed to this dramatic increase. Some wives found that they could support themselves in their husband's absence and therefore decided to end an unhappy marriage. Others experienced tremendous strains when a husband returned from the war. The trauma of war contributed to depression and a wide variety of unhealthy coping mechanisms such as alcohol and violence. Meanwhile, some people had married prematurely, knowing each other for a very short period of time, but hastily marrying before the man left for war. Couples may have matured and grown in different ways during the husband's absence. When they were reunited, they recognized that they had little in common anymore.

During the period after World War II when women were no longer sorely needed in the workplace because of the veterans' return, family life was once again altered in dramatic ways. In the 1950s, women were

During the 1950s, the media portrayed sharply divided roles for men and women. Men were the kings of the castle, while women's lives revolved around domestic tasks.

encouraged to find fulfillment primarily as wives and mothers. In her influential book *The Feminine Mystique* (1963), Betty Friedan documents the push toward domesticity. Interviews with female college students revealed that their primary reason for attending college was to find a suitable male. Few women dreamed of jobs or careers. College women who were unattached by their senior year felt like they had failed in their ultimate mission—to get their "MRS. degree." Friedan's content analyses of women's magazines show a similar trend. Magazine articles, short stories, and advertisements glorified domesticity. Few women had jobs or careers; in fact, those who did were often portrayed as cold, aloof, and unfeminine. The "normal" or "natural" role for women was portrayed as a wife and helpmate to her husband, and as a mother to a large number of children.

During the 1950s the average age at first marriage dropped to an all-time low since records had been kept. The average age at marriage for women was barely nineteen. **Fertility rates,** or the number of births to women, climbed. The federal government underwrote the construction of homes in the suburbs, undertook massive highway construction projects that enabled long commutes from home to work, and subsidized low-interest mortgage loans with minimal down payments for veterans. Families, growing in size, craved the spaciousness and privacy of the new suburbs, where they could have their own yards rather than relying on community parks and play spaces for their children. In the suburbs, women cared for their children in isolation, volunteered in their children's schools and within the community, and chauffeured their children to various lessons and events. Television programs, women's magazines, and other media sources glorified women's domesticity. This representation can be seen in classic television shows from the 1950s and early 1960s such as *Ozzie and Harriet* and *Leave It to Beaver.*

In reality, this cultural image, strong though it was, was not attainable for many families. Working-class women and poor women, including many minority women, often worked full time or part time because their husbands did not earn enough to support the family. Even with their combined wages they could not afford expansive homes in the suburbs. Moreover, with the rising divorce rate after World War II and the rising rate of out-of-wedlock births, some women worked because they did not have a husband to support them. Nonetheless, the cultural image was powerful, and many women and men ascribed to this as an ideal, even if it was unlikely to be a part of their day-to-day reality.

Recent Developments: The Family Since 1970   As we have seen from our look at history, families are never isolated from outside events. The transformation of employment in the 1970s and the reduction in real income have contributed to a number of changes within the family. Declining wages among the middle classes, referred to as the "middle class slide," contributed to greater debt and the influx of married women with children into the labor force. Furthermore, despite a robust economy during the 1990s and at the beginning of the twenty-first century, the distribution of income has become increasingly skewed. Data from the U.S. Census Bureau show that the rich have made tremendous gains during the past few decades, while the middle and lower classes have experienced stagnation or a decline in real earnings, adjusted for inflation (Auerbach & Belous, 1998; Shapiro, Greenstein, & Primus, 2001).

The Middle Class Slide Beginning in the 1970s, our economy shifted from the relatively high-paying manufacturing jobs that predominated since the industrial era to lower-paying jobs in the service sector. Approximately three-quarters of workers are now employed in service jobs such as retailing, custodial work, banking, health care, education, or transportation. Moreover, union membership has declined along with job security and the fringe benefits that unions notoriously provide for their members.

Increasingly, workers are finding that temporary jobs with nonstandardized schedules are the best that they can find (Castro, 1993; Presser, 2000). Presser, a social demographer, notes that only 54.5 percent of workers have a standard full-time, 35-40-hour, Monday-through-Friday, daytime schedule. The remainder, nearly one-half, works nonstandard schedules, which include evenings, weekends, or rotating schedules (Presser, 2000). She found that, among couples with children, the risk of divorce increases up to six times when one of the spouses works between midnight and 8 A.M., as compared to daytime hours. These results were evident when controlling for such factors as the number of hours worked, the education level of spouses, previous marital experience, age differences, number of children, and the gender-role attitudes of both spouses.

Many families who consider themselves middle class have also noticed that their purchasing power has steadily declined because their incomes have failed to keep up with inflation. This is especially true for younger and lower-income workers. Almost two-thirds of workers making the minimum wage are adults aged twenty and over, and 40 percent of them provide the sole income for their families (U.S. News Online, Apr. 29, 1996). Adjusted for inflation, the value of the federal minimum wage had dropped by more than a dollar since the 1960s and 1970s, eroding in earnest in the 1980s. Some onlookers suggest that the minimum wage should be raised by $2 to $3 per hour so that full-time workers would be above the poverty line for a family of three, which was $13,738 in 2000.

In addition to lower real incomes, housing costs have become unaffordable for many people hoping to buy their first home. Likewise, the cost of a new car has risen faster than incomes over the past several decades. In the mid-1970s, the average family spent one-third of its income to purchase an average-priced car, but car prices have risen so dramatically that a family now spends approximately half of its income for the same purchase (Bennet, 1995).

Because of this "middle class slide," many families today not only work longer hours, but also an increasing number have both spouses employed full time outside the home yet still find themselves in alarming debt. One response to lower wages is to borrow money, which then must be repaid with interest. Credit cards such as Visa, MasterCard, and American Express are tempting to people with economic difficulties. Opportunities for receiving these cards are widespread. Total credit card debt has tripled over a recent ten-year period (Hull, 1995).

The middle class slide is also partly responsible for one of the most dramatic changes in family life during the past several decades—the increasing numbers of married women, often with children, who are employed outside the home. During the 1940s, women were encouraged to work as a part of their patriotic duty; in the 1950s, women were discouraged from employment; but by the late 1960s and 1970s, women began reentering the labor market. The number of married women who are now employed outside the home, including those with preschool-age children, has had remarkable influences on our culture. Families now rely on day care, after-school care, convenience foods, take-out fast-food restaurants, and a cadre of services catering to the need to juggle multiple demands.

In reviewing historical and cross-cultural variations in family life, we are reminded of the second theme of this book, that marriage, families, and close relationships are constructed by humans, so their structures are not monolithic. Families are ever-changing and adapt to a wide variety of historical and cultural traditions.

Theme 3: The Importance of Social Science Research—Is the Family Declining?

There is widespread concern today that the family is in trouble (Popenoe & Whitehead, 2002; Whitehead & Popenoe, 2002). Family researchers David Popenoe and Barbara Dafoe Whitehead, from the National Marriage Project at Rutgers University, express concern about "the neglect of marriage," "lack of commitment by men," "loss of child centeredness," "the rise in cohabitation," and "fatherless families." As David Popenoe writes,

> Like the majority of Americans, I see the family as an institution in decline and I believe that this should be a cause for alarm—especially as regards the consequences for children. In some sense, of course, the family has been declining since the beginning of recorded history—yet we've survived. But often overlooked in the current debate is the fact that recent family decline is unlike historical family change. It is something unique, and much more serious. (Popenoe, 1993: 527)

Television programs, newspapers, and magazines bombard us with stories about the demise of the family. We hear that in the "good old days," there were fewer problems: life was easier, family bonds were stronger, families had more authority to fulfill their functions, and people were happier. Abortion, divorce, teenage sex and parenthood, homosexuality, juvenile delinquency, and poverty are only some of the consequences attributed to the decline of the family and of "family values."

In contrast to this perspective, other family scholars remind us that these golden years of the past never really existed as we have fantasized them. They argue that families have always faced a myriad of challenges, including desertion, poverty, children born out of wedlock, alcoholism, unemployment, violence, and child abuse (Abramovitz, 1996; Coontz, 1997; Coontz, 2000; Demos, 1970, 1986; Gordon, 1994). They note that despite these problems, attempts to strengthen families through improved social services and financial assistance have been met with resistance. The United States has often demonstrated a reluctance to help strengthen families. Providing families with adequate child care, educational opportunities, jobs, health care, and housing is sometimes at odds with the U.S. emphasis on "rugged individualism." Instead, we are a nation that encourages our members to "pull ourselves up by our bootstraps."

For example, as Baca Zinn and Eitzen tell us (1996), these images of the "good old days" contain several critical myths about families:

* That families in the past were always stable and harmonious, free of conflict and social problems.

* That family units were independent and insulated from outside pressures.

* That families existed only in one traditional form, ignoring families that diverged from the middle class, two-parent, mother-stay-home model.

* That gender, race and ethnicity, and social class do not significantly shape family experiences.

* That family members always agreed with one another, ignoring the power relationships that accompany intimacy and that can lead to rivalries, conflicts, and abuse.

* That family changes are the cause of other social problems in society, such as poverty or juvenile delinquency. They remind us that parochial and nostalgic images of the past distort the reality of family life.

Yet how do we evaluate which of these views are correct? Answering this question requires us to return to the third goal of this book. *Rather than relying on common sense or personal experience to inform us about families, we should examine the information produced by social science research.* For example, we cannot just assume that divorce is fine for children, that women on welfare neglect their children, that only-children grow up to be spoiled, that teenage pregnancy is increasing, or that lesbians or gay men make bad parents. Instead, we must look to see what the research tells us about these issues.

The next fourteen chapters of this book will present and analyze the results of many empirical studies. Here we will touch on just a few examples of empirical research that shed some light on the controversy over whether American families are really deteriorating.

"Families Are Deteriorating"

People who feel that families are being threatened suggest that (1) Americans are rejecting traditional marriage and family life, (2) family members are not adhering to their roles within families, and (3) numerous social and moral problems result from the changes in families. They point to the recent data on the relatively high divorce rate in the United States, highest among industrial nations; the increasing percentage of single mothers who have children; the large number of people who choose not to marry or choose not to have children; the increased number of children in households with both parents employed full time; and the increased number of people who choose to cohabit instead of marrying. They may see these as indications that adults are becoming more selfish, putting their personal whims above their parental duties. They may also suggest that other social institutions, such as the education or social welfare system, undermine authority in families (Murray, 1984).

Are We Rejecting Marriage and Family Relationships?

We hear startling figures about family demise, and we worry that our society is now rejecting marriage and family relationships. Yet as these issues are explored throughout this text, you will see that many of these concerns reflect value-laden personal opinions that are not necessarily supported by empirical data. Therefore, we stand reminded of the third theme of this book: that empirical research can play a critical role in informing us about families and close relationships. Popular folklore or personal opinions about the family are often inadequate because they perpetuate biases and do not offer an objective lens through which to examine family life. We suggest here that a scientific perspective, which draws on empirical data, can provide a far more objective window on the world.

How has family life changed?

| FACT OR FICTION?

There has been a decrease in the commitment to marriage, children, and family since the 1960s.

Attitudes Research by Thornton and Young-DeMarco (2001), which used five national data sources, found less change in attitudes toward family life since the 1960s than many people think. They examined changing attitudes toward (a) gender equality; (b) freedom, autonomy, and tolerance for different family forms; and (c) the degree of commitment Americans have toward marriage and family life. Are Americans becoming detached from these institutions?

Examining data from the 1960s through the 1990s, the researchers found a long-term trend toward endorsing gender equality. All five studies found a greater expression of egalitarian attitudes, yet at the same time, Americans continue to endorse a gendered division of labor. Many people, especially men, believe that men should have primary responsibility outside the home while women's primary focus should be inside the home.

Second, Thornton and Young-DeMarco found a continued emphasis on and commitment to marriage, children, and family life. Both young and older Americans devote or plan to devote much of their lives to children and spouses. They see marriage as a lifetime commitment that should not be terminated except under extreme conditions, and view marriage and children as highly fulfilling. There is no evidence that this commitment has eroded over the past several decades. In fact, they note that some dimensions of family life are deemed even more important: young Americans in the 1990s were more committed than those in the 1970s to the importance of a good marriage.

| FICTION

Researchers found that the commitment to marriage, children, and family life has been relatively stable.

Third, the researchers found that this current commitment to marriage and children coexists alongside strong commitments to equality, tolerance, and freedom. A growing number of Americans believe that marriage and parenthood should be viewed as optional and voluntary choices. Americans have become increasingly tolerant of diversity. Although the vast majority plan to marry and have children, they are less likely to make blanket statements that this is what all people should do.

Another study, by the University of Michigan, examined how high school seniors feel about a number of marriage and family issues. Researchers have been collecting data from high school seniors since the mid-1970s, and the results indicate very little, if any, real decline in the way young people value marriage and family. Table 1.1 reports the percentage of seniors who said that having a good marriage and family life is "extremely important," and compares the answers of those who graduated in three different time periods. It appears that boys and

TABLE 1.1	Percentage of High School Seniors Who Said Having a Good Marriage and Family Life Is "Extremely Important," by Period		
	YEARS	BOYS (%)	GIRLS (%)
	1976–1980	69.4	80.2
	1986–1990	69.7	81.9
	1996–2000	72.9	82.1

Source: Monitoring the Future surveys conducted by the Survey Research Center at the University of Michigan. Adapted from B. D. Whitehead and D. Popenoe (2002). "Why Men Won't Commit: Exploring Young Men's Attitudes About Sex, Dating and Marriage." *The State of Our Unions* (The National Marriage Project).

girls who graduated from high school between 1996 and 2000 were *more* likely than those who graduated between 1976 and 1980 to rate having a good family life as extremely important.

The majority of high school students also agreed that it is "very likely" that they will stay married to the same person for life. There was a slight decline in the percentage of girls and boys who agreed with this statement in the late 1980s. However, as shown in Table 1.2, the latest round of data shows an upward trend, indicating that more girls and boys now see it very likely that they will find a life-time mate.

Despite the fact that young people value marriage and family life for themselves and hope to stay married forever, they are also becoming more tolerant of other lifestyle options. Girls, especially, increasingly recognize that cohabitation and singlehood could indeed be viable options for people, even if they themselves would prefer to marry. Table 1.3 reports the percentage of high school seniors who said they agreed, or mostly agreed, that "most people will have fuller or happier lives if they choose legal marriage rather than staying single or just living with someone." Again, the researchers compared the answers across different cohorts of high school seniors.

FACT OR FICTION?

The divorce rate has been declining since the 1980s.

TABLE 1.2	Percentage of High School Seniors Who Expect to Marry or Were Married, Who Said It Is "Very Likely" They Will Stay Married to the Same Person for Life, by Period		
	YEARS	BOYS (%)	GIRLS (%)
	1976–1981	57.3	68.0
	1986–1990	53.7	62.5
	1996–2000	58.1	64.6

Source: Monitoring the Future surveys conducted by the Survey Research Center at the University of Michigan. Adapted from B. D. Whitehead and D. Popenoe (2002). "Why Men Won't Commit: Exploring Young Men's Attitudes About Sex, Dating and Marriage." *The State of Our Unions* (The National Marriage Project).

TABLE 1.3	Percentage of High School Seniors Who Said They Agreed or Mostly Agreed That Most People Will Have Fuller and Happier Lives If They Choose Legal Marriage Rather Than Staying Single or Just Living with Someone, by Period

YEARS	BOYS (%)	GIRLS (%)
1976–1982	37.9	38.9
1986–1990	36.5	30.9
1996–2000	38.1	28.5

Source: Monitoring the Future surveys conducted by the Survey Research Center at the University of Michigan. Adapted from B. D. Whitehead and D. Popenoe (2002). "Why Men Won't Commit: Exploring Young Men's Attitudes About Sex, Dating and Marriage." *The State of Our Unions* (The National Marriage Project).

Behaviors Recent data from the U.S. Census Bureau (Fields & Casper, 2001) also suggest that Americans do not necessarily appear to be rejecting marriage, children, and family life. Figure 1.1 shows the marital status of the population aged 15 and over, by sex, for the years 1970 and 2000. These data represent snapshots in time—i.e., what the marital status of the population was in March 1970 and March 2000. First, we can see that the percentage of people who had "never married" has changed very little in 30

FIGURE 1.1 Marital Status of the Population 15 Years and Over by Sex: 1970 and 2000 (by percentage)

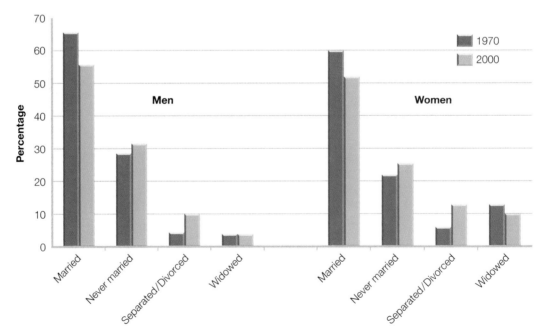

Source: J. Fields and L. M. Kasper (2001). U.S. Census Bureau, *Current Population Reports,* P20–537, "America's Families and Living Arrangements."

years, rising only 3 percentage points for both men and women. While this may initially look like rejection of marriage, this small increase is due to the *delayed age at marriage,* not an increased likelihood of remaining single over the life course. Women now marry at an average age of 25, compared to 21 in 1970. Men now marry at an average age of 27, compared to 23 in 1970. In fact, the percentage of people aged 65 and over who report to have never married was less than one-half of the rate it was in 1970, 3.6 percent versus 7.7 percent. In other words, people are more likely to get married now, not less!

The figure also reveals that between March of 1970 and March of 2000, the number of people who claimed to be currently divorced or separated increased almost three-fold for men and more than doubled for women. While again this may look like a rejection of marriage, a further look reveals that this is not the case. Divorce was on the rise in the 1970s for a multitude of reasons. However, the divorce rate began to level off in the 1980s and then decline in the 1990s. In other words, *divorce rates are going down, not up!* But more people claimed to have been divorced or separated in 2000 because they had not yet gotten around to remarrying. However, the majority of divorced persons eventually do remarry. In fact, nearly half of all marriages that occur are between couples in which one or both have been married before.

| FACT

The divorce rate in the United States has declined over the past several decades.

Figure 1.2 illustrates the size of households, again comparing 1970 with 2000. A cursory reading of this figure suggests that more people are living alone. Does this mean that we are rejecting marriage? Not neces-

FIGURE 1.2   Households by Size: 1970 and 2000 (by percentage)

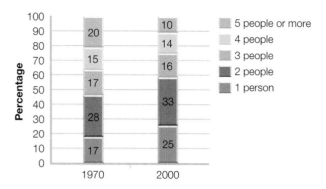

Source: J. Fields and L. M. Kasper (2001). U.S. Census Bureau, *Current Population Reports,* P20–537, "America's Families and Living Arrangements."

sarily. Remember, given that people are delaying the age at which they marry, it is not surprising that we see more one-person households. But if you look at the percentage of people who live in two- or three-person households (in other words, likely living with a spouse or partner and one child), you see that the figures have changed very little over time. In 1970, 46 percent of households consisted of two or three people, and thirty years later, the figure increased to 49 percent. In other words, these data suggest that *people still value marriage and intimate partnerships, and still value children.* What they tend to value less is *large* families, witnessed by the large decline in households containing five or more people.

Finally, the rise in the number of single-parent households is considered by many to be a cause for concern. Single-parent households, usually headed by women, have been blamed for a variety of family problems, including poverty, delinquency, teen pregnancy, and school dropouts. Eight percent of white households and 28 percent of African American households were female-headed with children in 2000. While this figure increased slightly since 1990 among whites (less than 1 percent), it actually decreased among African Americans. In other words, African Americans appear to be successfully reversing the trend that has caused such concern!

However, let us pause for a minute to ask why single-parent households are of such concern. As we will see in following chapters, single-parent families are indeed vulnerable to a wide variety of social problems. But researchers are careful to point out that most studies do not indicate that it is single parenthood, per se, that accounts for these problems. Rather, there are other issues that may be associated with single parenthood, such as an increased likelihood of poverty, that cause these various social problems. In other words, single parenthood may make poverty more likely to occur, but if we could do something to help fight poverty, then many of these social problems would be reduced significantly. One possibility is to expand family policies designed to strengthen all families.

FACT OR FICTION?

International research shows that changes in the traditional family structure have negative results for children.

An international comparison may shed some light on what could be done to eliminate poverty and improve child outcomes among single-parent households. Houseknecht and Sastry (1996) examined the relationship between the decline of traditional families and the well-being of children in Sweden, the United States, the former West Germany, and Italy. "Family decline" was measured by such factors as the divorce rate, the rate of nonmarital births, and the percentage of mothers with young children in the labor force. "Child well-being" was measured by the percentage of children in poverty, deaths of infants from abuse, and juvenile delinquency rates. The researchers found

that children seemed to fare best in both Italy and in Sweden. Interestingly, however, Italy had low levels of "family decline," while Sweden had significantly high levels. Thus, it appears that changes in the family structure do not necessarily have negative effects on children. Why did Italy with low levels of "family decline" and Sweden with high levels both have strong children? Because both countries have a wide variety of social policies and programs designed to help children and their families and keep them out of poverty, such as universal health insurance, subsidized day care, a dependent child grant from the government, expanded paid maternity leaves, and many other programs that help families stay strong. The authors conclude that poor child outcomes are the result of weak social policies that do not provide the support that our naturally evolving changing family structure requires. Poor child outcomes are not simply due to change, per se.

FICTION

Cross-cultural research shows that changes in traditional family structure do not result in negative child outcomes if a wide variety of social policies and programs are in place, such as health insurance and quality day care.

Theme 4: Integration of Micro and Macro Perspectives— Why Are Families Changing?

Why are families today in a state of change? The fourth theme of this text is that *microlevel and macrolevel factors work together to shape our opportunities, choices, privileges, and constraints.*

© Mark Richards/PhotoEdit

Increasing numbers of young people are delaying marriage, such as these college students.

Microlevel Perspectives on Family Change

Some analysts focus primarily upon a **microlevel** perspective, focusing on individuals' interactions in specific settings. They stress the importance of personal choices and internal relationships among family members. For example, a microlevel analysis may conclude that divorce would be reduced by teaching better communication skills, that a man who resorts to violence against his partner may need to learn to manage his anger, that a woman who feels the tension of balancing work and family demands should find a way to improve her time management skills, or that the teenage pregnancy rate would decline if families stressed the virtues of abstinence. A microlevel perspective fo-

cuses on personal decision making and the interaction between small groups of people in specific settings. This perspective concludes that families are changing because of the new choices that people are making, which reflect a new set of values.

Macrolevel Perspectives on Family Change

Although microlevel analysis is useful in many contexts, one of the themes of this textbook is to draw upon a **macrolevel** perspective as well. A macrolevel analysis examines the interconnectedness of marriage, families, and intimate relationships with the rest of society and with other social institutions. Families are not isolated entities. As one family scientist noted, "society makes families, and families make society" (Glazer, cited in Billingsley, 1992: 78). Seeing how families are influenced by larger social forces helps us to understand why we make the supposedly "personal choices" that we do. Divorce, domestic violence, work–family stress, and teen pregnancy are social problems, not simply individual ones. Meaningful solutions require that we examine the way that our social structure is organized to perpetuate these problems. For example, as you will see in Chapter 3, gender, race and ethnicity, and social class are critical dimensions of our social structure that have important implications for many of our personal relationships.

We shall provide one detailed example here.

An Example: Unemployment and Marriage Rates

William Julius Wilson has written extensively on the issue of inner-city unemployment, suggesting that the high unemployment rate of urban blacks contributes to their low marriage rate. In his well-known books *The Truly Disadvantaged* (1987) and *When Work Disappears* (1996), Wilson points out that marriage to inner-city African American men is seen as risky by many women because the men cannot support families on their meager wages. Furthermore, as factories and businesses move out to the suburbs or overseas, unemployment rates escalate. There is a shortage of employed African American men who are seen as good marriage prospects. Drawing upon a macrolevel perspective, Wilson shows us that our changing economy has a significant effect on individual microlevel choices relating to marriage and family patterns. Other research, using national data from the National Survey of Families and Households, indicates that African American women weigh economic

considerations heavily when deciding when to marry, even more heavily than white women do (Bulcroft & Bulcroft, 1993). In addition to high unemployment, or perhaps interrelated with it, are a multitude of other reasons that African American women may have a challenge finding a suitable mate. Homicide, violence, drug addiction, and prison have taken a tremendous toll on young African American men.

Therefore, it appears that families are changing because of the choices people make in conjunction with other larger developments in society. These may include changes in our economy, rising crime rates, immigration policies, technological advances, changes in women's opportunities, new conceptions of fatherhood, and a wide variety of social and political movements. Families are changing, but as we have learned, families have never been stagnant. They have always responded to other developments in society.

Human Agency Macrolevel forces that are seemingly outside of one's immediate control often shape our personal microlevel interactions. At the same time, being mindful to these social forces does not imply that we are passive recipients of them. Quite the opposite. **Human agency** is the ability of human beings to create viable lives even when they are constrained or limited by social forces (Baca Zinn & Dill, 1994; Baca Zinn & Eitzen, 1996). Rich, poor, male, female, young, old— we are all actively producing our lives, even in light of the social forces that help shape our opportunities. We do have free choice, but it is important to be mindful of the ways that we are influenced by the structure of the society in which we live.

Conclusion

This chapter highlights the four themes that will be elaborated on in the forthcoming chapters. First, we suggest that social structures, including social institutions and statuses such as gender, race and ethnicity, and class, profoundly shape our daily experiences, privileges, and constraints. Although it is easy to believe in "free choice" in personal matters, it is important that we recognize that we are influenced by the social structure in which we live.

A second theme is the value of a critical perspective. A critical perspective suggests that successful families can come in many types. Cross-cultural and historical variations show us that families are constructed by humans to meet our needs. Change is not necessarily something to be feared. A critical perspective also asks that we examine the assumptions, values, and ideologies that are used to define and characterize families and create social policy.

A third theme is that empirical research is crucial to our understanding of families and close relationships. Many people have personal opinions about families that are based on nonobjective criteria. However, a scientific perspective, which draws on empirical data, can provide a far more objective window on the world.

Finally, a fourth theme is that the microlevel and macrolevel influences in our lives are interrelated. Microlevel factors include issues of personal choice, inclination, and interpersonal dynamics. Macrolevel influences include broader social structures. Together, these shape our formation of families and close relationships.

Chapter Review

* *How does this chapter define* family, *and how does that definition differ from the one provided by the federal government for statistical purposes?*

We define families more broadly than the federal government does. We define family as a relationship by blood, marriage, or affection that may cooperate economically, may care for any children, and may consider the core identity of participants to be intimately connected to the group. Thus, this definition may include unmarried homosexual or heterosexual partners.

* *What are the themes of the book?*

This book has four main themes, which encourage students to see (1) how social structures shape our experiences, (2) the utility of a critical perspective in showing us that families are ever-changing, (3) the relevance of empirical research and the scientific perspective to studying families, and (4) how microlevel and macrolevel social forces are interrelated.

* *What is a social institution?*

A social institution is a major sphere of social life with a set of organized beliefs and rules that is organized to meet basic human needs. The family is a social institution.

* *But isn't the family in a state of decline since the "good old days" of families in the past?*

We tend to glorify the past. We assume that the 1950s model—i.e., Dad as breadwinner and Mom as homemaker—was the most common throughout history. This is incorrect. Many women and children worked long hours on the family farm or in factories. Many African Americans worked as slaves. Immigrants, the poor, and Native American families were often exploited. For many people, family life was harsh.

* *What is a "companionate family"?*

It is the current model, beginning in the early twentieth century. Families moved away from being largely economic units to being based on mutual affection, sexual attraction, compatibility, and personal happiness.

* *What types of economic changes have occurred since 1960?*

A number of significant economic changes have occurred, including the "middle class slide," increasing debt, and the influx of married women with children into the labor force.

* *What type of marriage and kinship patterns exist around the world?*

Marriage patterns include monogamy (including serial monogamy) and the two types of polygamy (polygyny and polyandry). Patterns of authority include patriarchy, egalitarian, and, theoretically at least, matriarchy. Patterns of descent include bilateral, patrilineal, and matrilineal, and residential patterns include neolocal, patrilocal, and matrilocal.

* *How would we characterize the differences between Sweden and Japan in the way they experience family life?*

Sweden and Japan are both affluent, industrialized nations. But the differences in family life and gendered expectations are significant. In the 1960s, Sweden's values and norms became increasingly permissive. Cohabitation is common, and Sweden's policy has made an effort to equalize domestic relationships. Japan is far more traditional, with segregated and traditional gender expectations. Marriage and family life are the foundation of Japanese culture. However, despite this, recent trends show that tremendous changes are beginning to take place in Japanese culture.

* *Is the U.S. family today in trouble?*

It depends on who you ask. Many people, including family social scientists, do suggest that the family is in a state of decline. However, others feel that this is a vast overstatement. Statistical data from the U.S. Census Bureau seem to indicate that people still value family life. Yes, the structure of the family is changing (for example, delayed age at marriage, lower rates of divorce, smaller families, more single-parent households), but many of these changes are the result of larger social forces outside of the family. Most of these changes do not particularly harm the family, and some of them might even be good for family members.

* *Why are families changing?*

There are two important forces operating. A microlevel view points to individual interactions in specific settings—for example, personal choices and internal relationships among specific family members. A second view focuses on macrolevel concerns, examining the interconnectedness of marriage, families, and intimate relationships with the rest of society and with other social institutions—for example, the economic system.

Key Terms

bilateral: descent traced through both male and female sides of the family

bundling: an arrangement in colonial America in which an unmarried couple would spend the night in a bed together, separated by a wooden board

cohabitation: the practice of unmarried couples who are sexual partners sharing a household

companionate family: a marriage based on mutual affection, sexual attraction, compatibility, and personal happiness

Cult of True Womanhood: the ideology of separate spheres for men and women

egalitarian: power and authority equally vested in both men and women

family: a relationship by blood, marriage, or affection in which members may cooperate economically, may care for any chil-

dren, and may consider their identity to be intimately connected to the larger group

family reconstitution: compiling all available information about significant family events and everyday life within a particular family

fertility rate: the number of births to women

fictive kin: nonrelatives whose bonds are strong and intimate

human agency: the ability of human beings to create viable lives even when they are constrained or limited by social forces

immigration: moving to a country from another country

industrialization: the transformation of an economy from a system based on small-family-based agriculture to one of large industrial capital

infant mortality rate: the number of deaths within the first year of life per 1,000 births in the population

macrolevel: a focus on the interconnectedness of marriage, families, and intimate relationships with the rest of society and with other social institutions

master status: the major defining status or statuses that a person occupies

matriarchy: a form of social organization in which the norm or the expectation is that power and authority in society are vested in women

matrilineal: lineage traced exclusively or primarily through women's families

matrilocal residence: the expectation that the newly married couple will live with the family of the wife

microlevel: a focus on individuals' interactions in specific settings

monogamy: marriage between one man and one woman

neolocal residence: the expectation that the newly married couple establishes its own residence and lives there independently

patriarchy: form of social organization in which the norm or the expectation is that men have a natural right to be in positions of authority over women

patrilineal: lineage traced exclusively (or at least primarily) through the man's family line

patrilocal residence: the expectation that the couple will live with the husband's family

polyandry: wives allowed to have more than one husband

polygamy: allows for more than one spouse at a time

polygyny: husbands allowed to have more than one wife

serial monogamy: marriage to one person at a time, but may include many marriages over the lifetime because of divorce, widowhood, and remarriage

social institution: major sphere of social life, with a set of beliefs and rules that is organized to meet basic human needs

social structure: a stable framework of social relationships that guides our interactions with others

status: the social positions that people occupy and the privileges and constraints that are attached to these positions

Resources on the Internet

These web sites have been selected for their relevance to the topics in this chapter. These sites are among the more stable, but please be aware that web site addresses change frequently.

American Association of Marriage and Family Therapists

http://www.aamft.org

The American Association of Marriage and Family Therapists (AAMFT) is a membership organization devoted to the advancement of marriage and family therapists. The web site contains information and resources for both family therapists and the public, such as information about a number of common problems that bring people to therapy, including alcohol problems, sexual difficulties, problems with children, infidelity, chronic illness, infertility, and divorce.

American Psychological Association

http://www.apa.org

The American Psychological Association (APA) is a scientific and professional membership organization that represents psychology in the United States. With 155,000 members, APA is the largest association of psychologists worldwide. The organization offers scholarly journals, an annual conference, and many other programs for students and professionals.

American Sociological Association

http://www.asanet.org

The American Sociological Association (ASA) is a membership association dedicated to advancing sociology as a scientific discipline and profession serving the public good. ASA encompasses sociologists who are faculty members at colleges and universities, researchers, practitioners, and students. Working at the national and international levels, the association aims to articulate policy and implement programs likely to have the broadest possible effect for sociology now and in the future.

National Council on Family Relations

http://www.ncfr.com

The National Council on Family Relations (NCFR) is a membership organization that provides a forum for family researchers, students, educators, and practitioners to share in the development and dissemination of knowledge about families and family relationships. It also establishes professional standards and works to promote family well-being. NCFR publishes two scholarly journals, sponsors an annual conference, promotes family life education, and fosters dialogue among family professionals.

U.S. Census Bureau

http://www.census.gov

This is the official government resource for social, demographic, and economic statistics. The site includes news releases, a subscription service, and a search facility.

Companion Web Site for This Book

Virtual Society: The Wadsworth Sociology Resource Center

http://sociology.wadsworth.com

Begin by clicking the Student Resources section. Next, click Marriage and Family, and then click the cover image for this book. Select from the pull-down menu the chapter you are presently studying. You will have easy access to chapter resources such as MicroCase Online exercises, additional Web links, flashcards, InfoTrac exercises, and practice tests (that can be scored). In addition, to enhance and help with your study of marriages and families, be sure to investigate the rest of the rich sociology resources at Virtual Society.

Visit InfoTrac College Edition

 Another unique option available to you at the Student Resources section of the Virtual Society web site described above is InfoTrac College Edition, an online library of hundreds of scholarly and popular periodicals. Here are three suggested key search terms for this chapter:

* Search keywords: *polygamy + United States*
* Search keywords: *family policy*
* Search keywords: *family + slavery*

Search recent years to get the latest information on these issues.

© John Henley/Corbis

Social Science Research and Family Studies

2

How Do We Know What We Know About Families?

We all have commonsense perceptions about families: what they are and what they should be. But how do we know what we know?

Personal Inquiry

If you check out your local newsstand, you will notice that a considerable number of magazines deal with issues about families and interpersonal relationships. There are entire magazines such as *Working Mother* and *Parenting* that address some of the major social changes that have occurred in family life, and the leading news magazines, such as *Newsweek* and *Time,* examine these issues routinely. For example, the cover story in the May 12, 1997, issue of *Newsweek* was called "The Myth of Quality Time: How We're Cheating Our Kids, What You Can Do." The article included research by leading sociologists, demographers, and psychologists that addresses the effects that two working parents have on children.

The article begins with an anecdote to set up the problem. A family living in New York City consists of a mother who is a lawyer, a father who is a journalist, and their two children. Because both parents are working long hours, the children spend a lot of time with a babysitter, and this babysitter also does some chores for the family, such as grocery shopping. One evening, the mother takes one of her children (a six-year-old boy) to the grocery store. While at the store, the son starts behaving in a way that distresses the mother (running up and down aisles, sliding on the floor). Not only was the behavior unnerving, but the mother was undoubtedly embarrassed when she heard a store clerk say, "So *you're* the mother."

How does this family respond to this "problem" of unruly children? They move to the suburbs, and the mother reduces her work schedule to part time. The parents feel that if they (especially the mother) were to spend more time with their children, the problems could be addressed. The authors of the article suggest that in the end it is the *quantity* of time more than the *quality* of time that makes the difference for children. In addition to this example, *Newsweek* cites a study by John Robinson and Geoffrey Godbey at Pennsylvania State University showing that over the course of a week, unemployed women spend almost twice the amount of time with children (12.9 hours) than do employed women (6.6 hours). Men, on the other hand, spend about 2.5 hours with their children each week regardless of their employment status (see Table 2.1). This certainly

TABLE 2.1	Average Time in Hours Parents Spend with Children Each Week by Employment Status*	
	HOURS PER WEEK	
	WOMEN	MEN
Employed	6.6	2.5
Unemployed	12.9	2.6

*Activities include bathing, feeding, reading, and playing.
Source: Adapted from Robinson and Godbey, *Time for Life* (Penn State Press), cited in *Newsweek,* May 12, 1997, p. 65.

Family-related topics are often the subject of news reports.

seems to justify the decision made by the family in the article. If the problem needs to be addressed by spending more time with children, then it is the unemployed mother who can produce the greatest return. Unemployed women are spending twice as much time with children as employed women are, and about five times as much as men who are not employed.

When thinking about the issues that *Newsweek* has defined as social problems (misbehaving children, inadequate time for parents to spend with children, the increase in the number of two-earner families), you may be left with a number of questions. What do we learn from this example? What do the numbers in the table really tell us? What is causing this social problem? Is it really a social problem? Why? Is the solution adopted by the family in the article the best way of addressing the social problem? Is this solution the most common one? Why? Is there anything else we can do about it?

You probably already "know" the answer to some, or all, of these questions. And the source of your "knowledge" is twofold.

First, your personal experience gives you information about the answers to these questions. You may have grown up in a household or family where there were two working parents, or you have been friends with someone who grew up in such a household. If so, this experience gives you a response to the questions posed. Your experience may lead you to agree with the article and its conclusions or to reject them. Understanding the world around us by using our own histories has been referred to as **experiential reality** (Babbie, 2001). Second, although you may not have experienced this arrangement firsthand, someone you know and respect has given you information about these issues. Parents, friends, and teachers all share their knowledge, ideas, and opinions with us, and we take for granted their understandings of the social world. We also know a lot of things because they are part of our culture. In fact, we may not even remember how we learned these things. For example, you know that when you go to someone else's house for dinner, you shouldn't sit at the "head" of the table. You probably learned this from watching your own family eat meals together for years. But who made that rule, and why does it exist? Knowing our world through information gathered from trusted others or through our culture is called **agreement reality.** Most of what we "know" about our world comes from these two sources. However, while there is nothing wrong with these modes of reality, social scientists are skeptical about relying on these sources alone to address social problems or to understand our social world. There is a risk involved here that your experiences, and the experiences and knowledge of those around you, will not be representative of the broader society. Your knowledge may be biased. Therefore, most family researchers use a *scientific* mode of investigation. Science is a set of systematic methods for investigating nature. **Social science,** then, is a set of systematic methods for investigating social relation-

ships and social structure. Table 2.2 summarizes attitudes adopted by social scientists. Not all family scholars agree with these attitudes; in particular, many family scholars challenge the idea there is one reality that can be objectively perceived by researchers (Allen, 2000). These scholars suggest that reality is in the eye of the beholder and therefore results in multiple realities.

Many students reading this text will not pursue a degree in the social sciences or a career in research. However, it is still important to understand the ways in which social science knowledge on family life is generated. The findings from social science research are important, for they often serve as the basis of social policies. Government and other social service agencies rely on the work of social scientists to inform and guide their work. Social science research is also used as the source for media coverage of family issues, as we saw in the opening discussion of this chapter. This relationship between social science research and both policy formation and media coverage is *not* perfect. Particular groups that may be interested only in a specific result sometimes fund research. And even if the research is not expected to have a certain outcome, the agency funding the research can make decisions about what to release from the findings or which results to emphasize (see the Constructing Strong Families box on page 52). What you should keep in mind as you are exposed to this media coverage of family issues is the question about the source of knowledge in the reports.

FACT OR FICTION?

Using data collected from students in college classes can result in biased knowledge about families.

Because the primary distinguishing characteristic of a social science approach is the methods used to generate knowledge,

TABLE 2.2	Twenty "Science Attitudes"

1. *Empiricism:* Scientists rely on observations—what we can see.
2. *Determinism:* Scientists believe that there are cause-and-effect relationships.
3. *A belief that problems have solutions:* If we can determine the cause of something, then we can craft a solution.
4. *Parsimony:* Scientists prefer explanations that are concise rather than complicated.
5. *Scientific manipulation:* Research designs must include adequate controls for alternative explanations.
6. *Skepticism:* Researchers are cautious and often check out the assumptions that underlie most theoretical statements.
7. *Precision:* The wording of hypotheses and research statements must be accurate.
8. *Respect for paradigms:* Paradigms are ways of looking at the world. Researchers always check to ensure that concepts and hypotheses are consistent with their paradigm.
9. *A respect for the power of theoretical structure:* If theories are useful, it is because their predictions can be proven empirically.
10. *Willingness to change an opinion:* When the data collected do not fit with a theory's prediction, the scientist must be open to challenging the theory.
11. *Loyalty to reality:* Scientists believe that they are able to observe reality. When observations don't match theories, scientists look for ways to explain observed reality.
12. *Aversion to superstition and an automatic preference for scientific explanation:* Even when observed relationships can't be explained, scientists do not look to superstition (for example, magic or chance) but to further scientific investigation.
13. *A thirst for knowledge, an "intellectual drive":* Scientists are always looking to expand on knowledge and to solve puzzles about the human condition.
14. *Suspended judgment:* Researchers will try hard to hold back making any conclusions until after all the data are in.
15. *Awareness of assumptions:* As mentioned in item 6, scientists are aware of assumptions behind more theories. It is expected that these will not be made explicit in research.
16. *Ability to separate fundamental concepts from the irrelevant or unimportant:* As scientists mature, they begin to recognize that not all data are relevant for what they wish to study.
17. *Respect for quantification and appreciation of mathematics as a language of science:* A good deal of social science research is quantitative—that is, based on mathematical summary. It is assumed that this type of analysis can reveal important patterns in human relationships.
18. *An appreciation of probabilities and statistics:* Probability and statistics allow scientists to make sense of the data they collect. They also help in understanding how to generalize their results (to what group[s] of people).
19. *An understanding that all knowledge has tolerance limits:* There is no absolute certainty in human behavior. Observations will cluster around a certain point, but there will always be variations.
20. *Empathy for the human condition:* Humans differ from nonhuman animals in significant ways. Humans can imagine and can make decisions based on their imaginations. Social science research must take human nature into account.

Source: Adapted from J. R. Schrock (1989). "Pseudoscience of Animals and Plants: A Teacher's Guide to Non-scientific Beliefs." *The Kansas School Naturalist, 35,* 3–15. Used with permission.

researchers do not rely only on personal experiences, but rather pay attention to the personal experiences of a wide range of people. Questions are asked about what experiences groups of people share and what kinds of things vary across groups. The same is true about the information we learn from listening to others. We always question the source of the information and how it differs from what others tell us. Social scientists are also more systematic in the way they approach the answers to questions. You will see in this chapter that although researchers vary widely in the approaches they use, there are some common elements of all research projects. The issues of *sampling, measurement,* and *data analysis* are key elements of scientific research and are part of every project, from inception to conclusion. Each of these will be discussed later in this chapter. But before we do that, let's step back and examine some of the ways in which our traditional methods of understanding the social world can be problematic.

Common Errors in Personal Inquiry Although it may be more comfortable to accept the words of our trusted friends and family, we can make a number of errors when relying only on the information we receive from others or our own experiences. One common error is that of **overgeneralization,** or using what we know about a subset of a group to incorrectly conclude something about the entire group. For example, let's say that a poll is taken in a college class; students are asked how many children are in their family of orientation (the family they were born into). The teacher calculates the average of the responses and finds that it is 1.2. What can be made of this number? Would you feel comfortable saying that the average number of children in American families is 1.2? In order to address this issue, we would want to know how representative this class is of the larger population. College students differ from others in ways that may be related to fertility. For example, college students are more likely to be middle class than the general population, and we know that fertility rates are lower among the middle and upper classes. Using college students, then, produces a **selection bias,** whereby the characteristics of the sample produce a non-generalizable result. Basing our conclusions on samples of convenience can lead to overgeneralization.

Students attending college are different from the general population (in age and social class) and therefore provide a limited view of family life.

Another common error is that of **selective observation,** or seeing only those things that are in line with our preferences or beliefs. It is very common for us to notice the characteristics of people around us. Social scientists will tell us that we live in relatively homogenous groups. That is, we look and think a lot like our neighbors and friends. Because this is true, we may only pay attention to those things that line up with what we—and our friends and family—believe are important. We may fail to see the diversity in experiences. For example, some students grew up in families where their fathers did the majority of household labor. When asked to do a research project on division of household labor, these students will come across research that suggests that their situation was not the norm. Responding to the research, some students might recognize that their family did not follow the norm, while others might discount the research, believing that it is biased or no longer valid. Discounting information that does not fit with your own views or experience is selective observation.

As a science, family studies research is free from bias.

When relying on personal experience as the primary source of knowledge, we must also be aware of the human ability to see, hear, or recall accurately. There is a tendency to notice some things and not others. People may remember parts of conversations, but not all. We typically don't take

The relationship among social science research, public policy, and the media is an important one. Because the work that social scientists do is relevant for designing policies that can help overcome critical social problems, results of such research are often cited by public policy agencies. In addition, social scientists are very often contracted to do research specifically for one agency that targets a particular issue. Because the government or privately funded "think tanks" want to get the word out about social problems, the media become a tool for disseminating information.

However, the transition of social science research from the academy to the public is not as smooth as some would like. Instead, information can be misrepresented or even dismissed depending on who is releasing the data or writing the reports. For example, in a recent symposium at the American Sociological Association meetings, several sociologists were asked to discuss how policy makers and the media use their work. What they had to say may not surprise you. One issue raised was that although the results of research were released to the media, what the media chose to highlight was incomplete and probably created a false impression of the work. For example, Peter Rossi, a sociologist at the University of Massachusetts, was contracted to study the effectiveness of the Food Stamp Program (FSP) and the Women, Infants and Children (WIC) program. The FSP is a program that provides to the poor coupons for food. The WIC program is designed to provide women, infants, and children who are at nutritional risk access to supplemental food. Rossi was charged with assessing these as "nutritional" programs. What he found was that the FSP was not effective as a nutrition program (people using food stamps did not have any better nutrition than those eligible who did not have food stamps) but that it was a useful program for other reasons and that its benefits warranted maintaining it. The WIC program, Rossi found, was a very effective nutrition program, and he argued that it too should be maintained. So what results were published in the media? "Federal Nutrition Programs Ineffective." This is certainly not what he concluded, but it did attract attention.

Rossi argues that controversy is often what makes news. The immediate effect on actual policy may be low, but it is the effect on public opinion that may have longer-term consequences. As politicians use the opinions of their constituents to decide how to vote, the swayed opinions resulting from biased headlines can result in the gutting of important social programs.

notes on our interactions. Not being able to observe everything, we may make the error of **inaccurate observations,** or observations based on faulty perception. This is different from the previous error of selective observation—the observer is not discounting information read or heard, but just does not read or hear all information.

Because the information we receive is not always without error, the conclusions made from them may be illogical or faulty. We need to remember that we are human beings and that we are social beings. *To err is human.* This does not mean that we are incapable of being good observers of social life. However, it does mean that we often come to closure on our inquiries too soon. We accept what we are told and/or what we experience as "truth." We don't go further. However, social scientists are skeptics. They aren't satisfied with what they know from personal experience. The world around us is too complex to rely solely on personal experience, and personal observations are tied to values, perceptions, and interests. If we want answers to questions that represent the plethora of experiences of people across time and space, we cannot be satisfied with only our personal experience or the opinions of those close to us.

Still another way that research is related to policy is that the media or policy makers may never pick up some research. Peter Rossi provides an example. He was asked to participate on a Bill Moyers television show as an expert on family preservation programs. These programs were designed to help families whose children were at risk for abuse and neglect. If the families received needed help and guidance, then children might not be taken from the home and put into foster care. When asked what he would say, Rossi said he would argue that the programs were ineffective (based on his research). He was thanked but told his views would not be included in the program.

Another example comes from the work of Kristin Luker. In her book *Dubious Conceptions: The Politics of Teenage Pregnancy* (1996), she presents the findings of her research on teen pregnancy. Her research, along with the research of others that she cites, suggests that contrary to popular opinion, "poverty has a more powerful effect on teen pregnancy than teen pregnancy has on poverty, and that teens make up a declining portion of unwed mothers." But the message of her research was ignored and has been disregarded in public policy debate. Luker suggests that social scientists are the "equivalents of nineteenth-century carriage makers" and are competing with well-funded think tanks that have full-time public relations staffs to get their message out quicker than social scientists can ever hope to do.

So what gets used, and how it is used, is not a scientific process. Although social researchers attempt to use "scientific" methods in their process of generating knowledge, others, who may in fact be more powerful in changing public views, do not.

Sources: P. H. Rossi (1999). "Three Encounters." *Contemporary Sociology: A Journal of Reviews, 28,* 1–4; K. Luker (1999). "Is Academic Sociology Politically Obsolete?" *Contemporary Sociology: A Journal of Reviews, 28,* 5–9.

Critical Thinking

1. What family issue have you seen recently covered by the media (television or newspaper)? What perspective do you think was used in analyzing the issue?

2. How were the data for the topic collected? Was the source of the data even provided?

3. What variables or other issues were left out of the news? Could there be another side to the issue?

| FICTION

Family researchers are human and therefore prone to bias. We select some things to study over others and choose to publish some findings over others.

Types of Social Science Research

There are many ways that social scientists go about studying family relations. These can be categorized in ways that address the types of questions asked in the beginning of this chapter about the *Newsweek* article on "The Myth of Quality Time." One type of research is **descriptive research,** which is designed to address quantitative questions such as these: How common is the situation of children growing up with two parents who are employed full time? Have the number of households fitting this description increased over time? A second type is referred to as **exploratory research,** which is interested in addressing questions about what it is like to experience these phenomena: How do people manage child care when they are employed? How do parents feel about their employment? How do children feel about their parents working? Exploratory research is particularly important when the topic under consideration is not well understood (lacking in prior theory and research). **Explanatory research** is a third type of research, which is meant to answer the question *why?* Why do the descriptive and exploratory findings occur? Why is it that the number of families with two earners has increased over time? Why do the rates vary by gender or ethnicity or social class? Why are the experiences uncovered in exploratory research occurring for some families more than others? And finally, a fourth type is **evaluation research,** which focuses on issues of what can be done to make a difference. Are there employer-sponsored programs that can help parents manage their family responsibilities better? What types of programs are more effective in helping families with delinquent children?

All of these types of research are commonly used in, and are very important for, studying families. And all of them are carried out in ways to avoid the problems of using everyday reasoning. By asking about how common some experience is, how this experience is related to other factors, and why such relationships occur, we can work to overcome the biases of our own opinions and ideas. Which type of research design is chosen will depend on the motivation for doing the research to begin with. Some motivations are academic—that is, researchers are interested in understanding the meaning of families in our lives. Other reasons are related to interest in social change. Policy makers working for the government and other social service agencies want to know why people make the choices they do and how we can change things so that everyone has the ability to make good choices. Researchers are also guided in their research by the theory or theories that they believe to be important. Theories can also suggest what to

study and how to study it. A variety of perspectives are employed to study families, and we will discuss the most frequently used theories here.

Theoretical Perspectives

Theories are made up of a set of statements that explains *why* certain relationships occur. The types of relationships we are interested in concern families and intimate relationships. For example, we may want to know why certain people stay married for a lifetime while others end a marriage through divorce. But the answer to this question doesn't come from just one theory. There are several theories that can help us get to the answer. The theories used in family studies vary in a number of ways. Some theories are designed to address more immediate or personal issues. For example, we may focus on the personality traits of the individuals in the relationship. Or the focus could be on individuals' expectations or desires, or the ways in which people interact with one another. These types of factors are the concern of microlevel theories. On the other hand, some researchers might be interested in whether or not relationships are less stable now than they were at a previous time in history. We could look at unemployment rates over time, or we might look at the laws that allow married people to obtain a divorce. Theories intended to explain these broader relationships in society are referred to as macrolevel theories. As we will see, there are also perspectives that attempt to include both types of variables. These types of theories will include characteristics of the individuals involved as well as characteristics of their environment. A brief overview of these theories and the types of questions asked can be found in Table 2.3.

TABLE 2.3	Family Theories	
THEORY	SOME BASIC QUESTIONS	SOME CRITICISMS
Ecological	• What are the factors involved in all four environmental systems (micro, meso, exo, and macro) that come together to shape family experiences? • How do families engage in practices that address the demands of these environments?	The categories are somewhat broad, and the relationships between systems are not always clear. In addition, the theory has not been applied for understanding more nontraditional family systems.
Structural Functionalism	• What are the needs that must be met by families? • What structures/relationships emerge in families to meet these needs?	This theory is conservative and tends to rationalize inequalities in families based on gender. It was developed on a white, middle-class model and is not as applicable for other groups.
Conflict	• Who benefits from structural relationships in families? • How do people's resources (education and income) affect relationships in families?	There is a tendency for this theory to focus on conflict and inequality and to minimize the extent of cohesion and stability in families.
Symbolic Interaction	• How do interactions within families help to construct meaning for those involved? • How does the status of the individual help shape family interactions and the meanings attached to them?	The focus on the way meanings get constructed through interaction can underestimate the influence of material resources on the structuring of such interactions.
Social Exchange	• What are the costs and benefits to certain family interactions for those involved? • What factors/resources are most influential in helping people obtain what they want in relationships?	This approach does not pay much attention to the way that resources get distributed in society in general.
Family Systems Theory	• How are the lines of communication in families problematic? • How do relationships between some family members influence other relationships in families?	This theory is vague and abstract, and it cannot be used to predict precise family outcomes.
Developmental Perspective	• What are the stages that families go through over time? • How do relationships change over the course of a family's life cycle?	Because stages are often based on ideal types, they can be limited in terms of describing the diversity of family experiences.
Feminist Perspectives	• How are families experienced in ways that are related to gender? • What are the consequences of gender for well-being in families?	There may not be sufficient recognition that not all women, or all men, are alike. Other factors, such as social class, race, and ethnicity, shape the way that gender is situated in families and other social settings.

Ellen Swallow Richards was the first woman admitted to MIT, and was the founder of the field of Home Economics.

The Ecological Perspective

The **ecological perspective** has its roots in the late nineteenth century, a time of rapid urbanization and industrialization and a concern about the health and welfare of families. Although the term *ecology* has been attributed to a German biologist, Ellen Swallow Richards introduced it for use in studying families in the United States. Richards was the first woman admitted to MIT, where she studied chemistry. She was very interested in improving people's lives and suggested that to do so would necessitate understanding the close connection between the behavior and health of people on the one hand, and the health of their environment on the other. Along with her colleagues at the Lake Placid Club, she proposed a new discipline that would integrate the sciences of the environment with the study of families and households. This interdisciplinary field was termed "home oekology (ecology)." Due to the organization of disciplinary boundaries (physical sciences and social sciences were seen as separate), this term was not adopted; rather, the new field was termed "home economics." But the influence of Richards and her colleagues was that this new field would use the methods and concepts of biology and natural ecology to show that human life and the environment are inseparable parts of a greater whole.

Contemporary use of the ecological perspective in the field of family studies is traced to Urie Bronfenbrenner (Bronfenbrenner, 1979). Bronfenbrenner further articulated this perspective by arguing that we can study human development by identifying the way in which immediate environments relate to more remote ones. He suggested organizing relationships into four systems. The most immediate is the *microsystem,* which defines the daily context (behaviors, roles, and relationships) in which human development takes place. For many of us, this is the family. However, the family frequently comes into contact with other settings for human development, and these are referred to as the *mesosystem.* For example, the mesosystem includes the relationship between families and day-care providers, schools, or play groups. *Exosystems* are those environments that are external to the family (structurally); however, because we participate in them, they affect human development. The most studied example of an exosystem, and how it is related to family functioning, is parents' employment. Finally, Bronfenbrenner argues that all of this is embedded in a *macrosystem.* This broader system is made up of the institutional patterns of culture: norms, values, and ideology. For example, we saw in Chapter 1 that the availability of parental leave varies widely across industrialized countries. Part of the variation is due to the differences in values and norms in these societies. The question of who is responsible for child care is answered differently in the United States than in Sweden. The United States is an individualistic society with a political system that emphasizes the rights and responsibilities of the person. As a result, we hold individuals accountable for their behavior. If you have a family and you have a job, it is up to you to figure out how to manage both. In a country such as Sweden, based on principles of democratic socialism, the society is seen as responsible for ensuring the rights of its members. Since most adults are employed, and most adults have families, the government assumes some of the responsibility in ensuring that the work in both arenas can get done. In sum, research intended to test the ecological theory of human development would be designed to include measures of the various systems that families interact with or are affected by.

Structural Functionalism

One way to think about families is to consider the function they serve in and for society and the function that roles within families serve in order for families to thrive. This perspective is called **structural functionalism.** Functionalists start with the assumption that society is a stable and orderly system. Societies are characterized by a consensus among their members, who share common values, beliefs, and norms. Functionalists also assume that certain requirements must be satisfied in order for a society to survive and that structures will emerge within the system to serve these functions. For example, functionalists would argue that we need economic, educational, religious, and familial structures because they serve critical survival functions for the society as a whole. What functions does the institution of the family serve? First, families produce new members for the system; second, they serve to socialize or train those new members to

work in that system. Without some structure to produce and socialize new members, societies could not survive.

The family itself is also a system made up of roles and relationships that are organized in ways to ensure its stability. Talcott Parsons and Robert Bales (Parsons & Bales, 1955), colleagues at Harvard in the 1950s, developed a functionalist analysis of family relationships. They argued that like larger systems, there are certain structures (role arrangements) that are optimal for system survival. For functionalists, these are **instrumental roles** and **expressive roles.** The instrumental leader of the family is responsible for taking care of the financial needs of the family while the expressive leader manages the emotions and nurturing tasks. It is assumed that these roles would align themselves with men (instrumental) and women (expressive) somewhat naturally. Primarily due to procreation, women would specialize in meeting the nurturing needs, while men, free from childbearing responsibilities, would devote their attention to wage earning. This assumed natural division of labor has been the subject of critique. While the number of marriages that followed this specialization in labor was at its peak during the time that Parsons and Bales were writing, it has never described a majority of marriages since (Coontz, 1992). Today, the majority of marriages are dual-earner relationships, with both women and men taking on instrumental and expressive roles in their families.

Robert Merton, another sociologist writing within the theoretical tradition of functionalism, expanded our understanding of the concept of functions. Merton suggested that some functions are intended and recognized (referred to as **manifest functions**) while others are not intended or well understood (called **latent functions**). For functionalists, the bearing and rearing of children is a manifest function of the family. In other words, it is understood to be part of family life. However, our traditional family struc-

Today the majority of marriages are dual-earner, and both partners engage in expressive and instrumental family activities.

ture has served some unintended functions as well. The expectation for women to be primarily responsible for domestic work and child care has resulted in maintaining their disadvantage relative to men in the labor market. Research indicates that time spent in domestic work has a direct negative effect on earnings for both women and men (Coverman, 1983; England, 2000). Traditional family structures have worked to reinforce male dominance.

Structural functionalism has been widely criticized by social scientists, especially those studying family relations. The assumption that all systems have a tendency toward equilibrium keeps us from recognizing that families experience considerable social change and conflict. And the emphasis on the optimal division of labor to maintain stability obscures the inequality that arises for women as a result of this division of labor. Parsons wrote in the 1950s, a time when the

heterosexual, single-breadwinner, middle-class family was not only more prevalent than it is today, but was also the basis for most samples in social science research. Recall from our earlier discussion that generalizing from nonrepresentative samples can lead us to a premature closure of inquiry. Certainly, families today do not look like families from the 1950s. Many alternative perspectives developed during the 1960s, partly as a reaction to the problems of functionalism. One of those perspectives is conflict theory.

The Conflict Perspective

The area of family studies, like most other social science disciplines, was heavily influenced by functionalism. Very little attention was paid to conflict, and when it was mentioned, it was more at the intra-individual level (e.g., how the individual manages multiple roles) and not focused on the relationships between individuals, or between the family and other social systems (Farrington & Chertok, 1993). However, as we've mentioned, the 1960s were times of rapid social change, and social conflict came to be seen as a basic element of human social life. **Conflict theory,** with its origins in the work of Karl Marx, Georg Hegel, and Frederick Engels, rejected the notion that societies were naturally in a state of equilibrium and argued that change is inevitable. There are several reasons why change is seen as certain. First, unlike functionalists, conflict theorists do not assume that people necessarily share the same values and interests. For example, within marriages, wives and husbands may have very different ideas about how to discipline children or how domestic labor should be divided. Whose interests and desires will be adopted? Conflict theorists would predict that people who hold positions of power in society are more likely to successfully pursue their own interests. Men,

© Laima Druskis/Stock Boston

who have access to important resources in our society, are hypothesized to have more control in relationships (Collins, 1986). However, this theory would predict that when women gain access to those important resources, they will hold more power in marriage, and relationships will be more equitable.

Another reason that conflict is inevitable is that even when groups do share values and desires in our society, the abilities to reach their desired states are not always equal. For example, all families may desire to own their own homes, but only those who have good-paying jobs, a savings account, and/or access to family wealth are able to do so (Edwards, 2001). Also, parents want/need access to medical care for themselves and their children. As we will see in more detail in Chapter 3, access to such benefits is associated with the types of employment that parents have, which in turn is related to race and ethnicity. Conflict theory points out that there will always be tension between those who have access to resources to achieve their goals and those who do not. The "have-nots" in our society include people of color, children, women, and the poor.

| FACT OR FICTION?

Social science theories focus on broad societal trends and cannot help us understand individual-level differences in family experiences.

Although functionalism and conflict theory derive from very different assumptions about human behavior, no research definitively supports one and rejects the other. Much of the research that you will read about in this text recognizes that there are situations in which we find considerable consensus in our society, and there are areas of systematic conflict as well. However, criticism has been leveled at both of these perspectives because they are very broad (they are macrolevel theories) and are not always useful in exploring the day-to-day behavior of individuals and families. We will need to look at microlevel perspectives such as *symbolic interaction* and *social exchange theory* to give us some insights on the face-to-face interactions in families and intimate relationships.

Symbolic Interaction

The term **symbolic interaction** was coined by Herbert Blumer in 1937. As the name of this perspective suggests, the primary focus is on how relationships are formed through the use and exchange of symbols. Symbols are understood to be things that have shared meaning. For example, a smile usually implies someone is feeling positive affect, while the sound of an infant crying suggests that the child is uncomfortable. Sounds, scents, visuals, and language are all symbols for which we have a common understanding (that is, within our culture). Day-to-day behavior is made up of the interaction of humans using such symbols. In fact, what is real to us is the product of our ongoing interactions with the physical and social world. And although some of our interactions are physical and seem instinctual (swerving the car to avoid hitting a child crossing the street, or grabbing the handrail when we slip on the stairs), our social interactions are always based on the meanings that we attach to the outside world. Because of the emphasis on the ways in which day-to-day interaction builds our reality, this perspective is often referred to as a *social constructionist* perspective.

Symbolic interaction is a very attractive theory to students of social science because it is grounded in the **empirical** world. That is, we can relate to its central ideas because they are based on things that are observable. For example, a symbolic interactionist who is

Symbolic interactionists suggest that men and women both show emotion in their relationships—but in different ways.

interested in exploring relationship satisfaction might look at the ways that couples express or communicate intimacy. It may be the case that couples exhibiting more outward signs of intimacy (hugging, holding hands) are happier on average than those who do not. Or researchers may find that the expression of intimacy is variable across cultures or groups and that physical shows of intimacy are stronger conduits for happiness among some groups than they are among others. Within relationships, expressions of intimacy may vary for women and men. For example, in a study of college students, Scott Swain (1989) found that young women and men exhibited some distinctive styles of intimacy. He found that while both young women and men use verbal cues to express their feelings, young men used more-active expressions of intimacy. The men in his sample said they expressed their positive feelings toward others by asking them to "do stuff" such as engage in sporting activities. The key for the symbolic interactionist is the salience that such symbols (like hugging or slapping someone on the back) has for those who are engaging in the interaction. If the symbols of intimacy are seen as important for a relationship, then individuals in a relationship will be happy when intimacy is expressed and unhappy when it is absent.

| FICTION

Social science theories cover both macrolevel as well as microlevel issues. Some theories even attempt to combine the different approaches to understand individual differences within broader social contexts.

Another key element of the symbolic interaction perspective is that the process of interaction, which is how we come to understand ourselves and our world, is ongoing and ever changing. Through continual interaction, we learn how to fulfill social roles, and we work to renegotiate them when times change. Symbolic interactionists recognize that interaction takes place within a structural context and that this structure influences the shape of interaction. Returning to the research on intimacy, Swain (1989) suggests that men choose to express their feelings in ways that are shaped by the contexts within which they take place. He says that men's intimacy

> is influenced by their awareness of the restrictive sanctions that are often imposed on men who express certain emotions, such as sadness or fear. Men's intimate verbal style is partially shaped by the fear of sanctions that may be imposed on emotional behaviors deemed culturally unacceptable. Homophobia and the difficulty men have disclosing weaknesses testify to the limitations they experience when attempting to explore certain aspects of their selves. These limitations of male intimacy may distance men from all but their closest men friends, and may also create a premium on privacy and trust in close friendships. Such limitations may be more detrimental later in life where structural settings are less conducive and supportive to maintaining active friendships. A college environment fosters casual access to friendships, and friendships may also be integral and functional for the successful completion of a degree. Thus, the sample in the present study may be experiencing an intimacy that is more difficult for men to maintain in job and career settings. (Swain, 1989: 84)

The recognition that individuals do not have complete control over their lives drives one of the criticisms of symbolic interaction. Although we do have the power to recreate and redefine, the social system into which we were born was not made by us. And this broader social system can constrain our actions and interactions.

Social Exchange Theory

Another perspective that has been important in the field of family studies is **social exchange theory.** Like symbolic interaction, it is a microlevel theory because the focus is on the interaction between individuals. Social exchange theory's early proponents included George Homans, who drew from the work of developmental psychology (and operant conditioning), and Peter Blau, who borrowed concepts from economics. Exchange theorists start with several assumptions about human behavior:

1. Humans are primarily motivated by self-interest.
2. Humans seek to maximize the rewards or profits in relationships while minimizing the costs or possible punishments.
3. Humans are rational beings and will therefore calculate the potential benefits and costs of all relationships.
4. The rules and/or importance of any exchange are variable across people and cultures.

There are also assumptions about the nature of relationships themselves:

1. Exchange is characterized by interdependence.
2. Exchanges are regulated by norms of reciprocity. (Sabatelli & Shehan, 1993)

An analogy is often made of social exchange to "market relations." People desire something from others. If they hold a resource that is valued by the other person, an exchange can take place. The norm of reciprocity says that both partners should perceive some gain or reward from the exchange or interaction. In other words, there should be a sense of balance. If the exchange results in a net loss for one partner, then the relationship may be in trouble. You might think about your relationship with a close friend. What does that friend bring to the relationship? What do you bring? Does it appear to you that the relationship is balanced? Have you ever ended a friendship because of an imbalance?

Social exchange theory has been used to explore issues such as dating, marital satisfaction, divorce, and other relationship patterns. An interesting articulation of social exchange theory is known as "resource theory." It follows the basic tenets of social exchange but recognizes that the balance of resources is not always equal. Classic studies by Blood and Wolfe (1960) suggest that men hold more power in marriage because they have greater access to valued resources (money, employment, status).

Critics of social exchange theory are quick to point out that this perspective leaves unanswered the question of how people come to hold varying amounts of resources in the first place. Why do men earn more than women? Why are there inequalities in education and occupation across ethnic groups? Access to resources is seen to be as important an issue as that of what we do with our resources.

Family Systems Theory

An interesting hybrid of macrolevel and microlevel theories is **family systems theory.** It incorporates basic assumptions of structural functionalism while having as its primary **unit of analysis** (the object of study) the interaction between members of families. This is distinct from other theories that target individuals or groups as the unit of analysis. The primary use of this theoretical perspec-

tive has been in the study of communication, particularly in clinical settings. There are several concepts that are central to systems theory (Ingoldbsy, Smith, & Miller, in press):

* A *system* is a collection of elements (here, family members and the roles they play) that interacts in ways to make it (the collection) a distinctly new entity. The family is a system, but it also includes subsystems, such as the parental system (husband/wife or couple) and the parent–child system.

* All families create *boundaries* around themselves and around the subsystems, helping to establish roles and responsibilities for family functioning. The ideal is to maintain sharp distinctions between systems. If not, families can become dysfunctional (e.g., a parent acting like a child).

* *Family rules* are created to ensure that families function well. They are the repetitive behavioral patterns that members engage in. Although some rules are created explicitly (a list of chores and who is to do them), many rules are created in ways that are not always obvious or even discussed.

* Systems theory assumes that all systems tend toward *equilibrium,* meaning that families will always work toward a balancing point in their relationships. A related concept is *homeostasis,* which implies that the inclination is for families to maintain the status quo. This can be a problem in families seeking therapy, for the natural tendency is *not* to change.

As these concepts suggest, systems theory has much in common with functionalism (Winton, 1995). However, it is different in terms of its unit of analysis. Ingoldsby and his colleagues suggest that we draw an image of the family as a set of circles, with each circle representing a member of the family. Then we should draw lines between these circles, representing the communication that takes place between the members. A systems theorist is primarily interested in the *lines* instead of the circles. If there is a problem within families, blame is not placed on individuals but on the patterns of interactions that occur between individuals. This approach is similar to that of symbolic interaction as it recognizes that individuals' actions do not take place in isolation. They are always part of *interaction,* or relationships. For example, if children won't do as their parents ask, the question is not "What is wrong with the child?" but "What is wrong with the relationship between parent and child?"

If we think about the lines as strings connecting objects in three-dimensional space (maybe like a mobile), we can see that pulling on one string can have a ripple effect on all of the objects (see Figure 2.1). An argument between parents influences children, and relationships between two siblings can spill over to interactions with parents, grandparents, and other family members.

Family systems theory is not without its critics. Klein and White (1996) suggest that although this approach has shown its usefulness in clinical settings, it is not as useful as a theory. If we look back at our definition of the term, a theory is expected to explain why relationships occur. Systems theory does not lend itself to very precise explanations for family interactions and cannot be used to make precise predictions about the outcomes of such interactions. Part of the issue is that the terms used by systems theorists are abstract or vague. For example, why do some rules get constructed, and why do some members of families have more power in defining rules than others? Another critique that has been noted about systems theory is that it has been used primarily to deal with

FIGURE 2.1   The Ripple Effect of Family Dynamics as Seen by Family Systems Theory

Systems theory recognizes that changes in any one member of the family will influence all other members of the family as well.

dysfunctional families. How well this approach works with families that are not in treatment has not been as thoroughly researched.

The Developmental Perspective

Another perspective that has had some influence on family studies is the **developmental perspective.** This approach, like the ecological perspective, incorporates factors from both the microlevel and the macrolevel to explain family behaviors and relationships (Rodgers & White, 1993). It starts with the recognition that families change over time and that they seem to go through a number of stages. Early versions of this approach articulated family stages as, first, married couples, followed by couples having and rearing children, then couples seeing their children leave home, and finally retirement and the death of a spouse. Families change shape over time, and the configuration of the family at any given moment (i.e., stage) will influence the experiences of its members. For example, marital satisfaction has been shown to decline from the early marriage through early child-rearing years, then increase again with children getting older and then leaving home (Rollins & Feldmen, 1970—although see a recent critique of this research in the Focus on Family Research box on pages 74–75.

A line of research often considered to be similar to this developmental one is referred to as the study of "life course." Within this tradition, social scientists, such as demographers, explore how individuals' lives change as people move through events in their lives. These events include marriage, childbearing, divorce, and movement through careers.

FACT OR FICTION?

Feminist theoretical perspectives have as their primary goal the belief in gender equality.

One of the major critiques of the developmental perspective is that it seems to assume that stages occur in the same order for everyone. Remember the childhood chant: "Sally and Ed, sitting in a tree, k-i-s-s-i-n-g; first comes love, then comes marriage, then comes Andy in a baby carriage." How often does this pattern occur? Given our discussion in Chapter 1, you have probably already thought about this criticism. As we move from looking at "the family" to "personal and close relationships," and recognizing that how people experience these relationships varies due to such issues as gender, age, ethnicity, and social class, we should be cautious about taking the developmental perspective too far (Scanzoni, 1988). Some have tried to move the focus away from the individual to a more structural and dynamic approach (Rodgers & White, 1993), but contemporary researchers have found that other perspectives, such as ecological theory or other mi-

crolevel theories, are better able to get at issues of family experience over time.

We've seen so far that there is considerable variation in theoretical perspectives that have been applied to studying family life. They vary in their assumptions about human behavior and orientations, and they differ in their level of analysis. Macrolevel theories are interested in patterns of behaviors that have become institutionalized, as well as the structure of, and interaction between, social institutions. Microlevel theories are more focused on the immediate relationships in day-to-day life. Feminist perspectives provide us with additional insights that are at both the macro and micro levels. Although they cannot be put strictly within one of the frameworks mentioned above, feminist perspectives emerged on the scene at about the same time as the critique of functionalism (the 1960s) and were primarily focused on inequality.

Feminist Perspectives

Feminist theoretical perspectives have emerged over the years alongside social movements designed to address gender inequality. There is not one unified feminist theory, but a number of perspectives and methods used to address both microlevel and macrolevel phenomena that work to create inequitable relationships between women and men. Osmond and Thorne (1993) lay out five basic themes that appear in feminist approaches. First, feminist perspectives place women's and girls' experiences at the center. The subject matter addressed is social life, but this social life is seen through the gaze of those who have been historically ignored. Second, gender becomes an organizing concept of social theory. Gender is seen not as a set of roles (as we saw in the functionalist viewpoint, where gender is associated with instrumental and expressive role arrangements), but as a set of relations. These relations are imbued with power and inequality, and are found in all parts of social life, not just in the family. Third, gender and family relations cannot be discussed outside of the sociocultural and historical situations in which they reside. How relationships are structured varies depending on social class, ethnicity, and geographic location. Recognizing the variation in the construction of family relations leads to the fourth theme of feminist perspectives: that there can be no single unitary definition for "the family." This concept was laid out for us in Chapter 1. Finally, what makes a feminist perspective quite different from other mainstream theories is that instead of taking a "value-neutral" stance, feminists understand that inequity exists and that it should be eliminated. Feminist theories are designed to uncover the mechanisms by which inequality is maintained so that new mechanisms can be constructed to dismantle it.

As you might guess, feminist theorists have been very critical of many of the theories we have discussed. For most microlevel, or interactionist, theories, the charge is that the constraining character of larger social structures is ignored. These broader structures influence the rules for interaction. Earlier we saw how age, situation (being in college), and gender shaped the expressions of intimacy given by young women and men (Swain, 1989). Another example comes from the use of social exchange theory. This theory assumes that all interaction is voluntary, with individuals rationally pursuing personal gain. Feminists would argue that relationships appear to be voluntary primarily for those with more resources. When people are without power or resources, they may often feel compelled to engage in an exchange.

Feminists are more drawn to the theory of symbolic interaction because it suggests that reality is socially constructed and can therefore be reconstructed. However, we still need to consider that within some relationships, the definition of the situation may not be the same for both partners. Jessie Bernard's classic study of marriage showed us that husbands and wives experience their marriages in different ways, with husbands appearing more positive than wives (Bernard, 1972). She argued that husbands' more favorable impressions are based on the fact that wives are expected to (and do) take on the major responsibility for domestic work and child care. This makes the time that husbands spend at home more relaxing; hence, they are happier. Current research finds that although men and women both benefit from marriage (when comparing married to single, divorced, and widowed individuals), it is still true that men benefit more from marriage than women do (England, 2000).

FACT

While most social theories include the notion of neutrality, feminist theories are explicit: gender inequality exists and should be eliminated.

So are there any problems with feminist perspectives? It is not surprising that much of the criticism comes from feminists themselves. Recall that looking at the world through the eyes of women is supposed to give us a view from the standpoint of the disadvantaged. But are all women equally disadvantaged? The current challenge is to recognize that race, ethnicity, social class, sexual orientation, and age are all very important cross-cutting ties with gender. In addition, around the world, women in developing nations face very different challenges than do women in advanced industrial societies. Poverty, environmental degradation, and starvation are critical concerns. Families, even when structured in a patriarchal fashion, may be the primary source of support and comfort for women in the developing world.

In the following chapters, we will bring up these various theoretical perspectives as they are used to understand the dynamics of families and intimate relationships. We do not advocate one particular theoretical perspective over another, but rather see various perspectives to be more relevant in some areas than others. It will depend on what questions we are interested in asking and what the substantive issue at hand is about.

The Role of Social Theory in Research

Theories are very useful for social researchers. They help point us to what types of questions we should ask and to whom we should ask them. Some researchers start with a theory and develop hypotheses about what they expect to observe. A **hypothesis** is a statement about the relationship between two or more variables that can be tested empirically. For example, social exchange theory tells us that those with more resources in a relationship hold the balance of power. Applying this argument to couples in dual-career situations, we would then hypothesize that partners who earn higher salaries will do less housework on average. The **variables** (characteristics that can take on different values) in this hypothesized relationship are the amount of "earnings" of spouses and the "time spent in housework." We would then collect data from dual-career couples by asking how much money each partner earns and how many hours each spends doing housework. If we find that the partner with the higher-paying job spends less time in domestic work, we have supported our hypothesis and therefore our theory. The process of starting with a theory, developing hypotheses, and then collecting data to test these hypotheses is called **deduction.** It is considered to be the traditional method in science, and it is used by those employing exchange theory

and conflict theory, for example. However, we don't always have theories that are explicit enough to explain or predict the types of relationships we are interested in studying. Therefore, other social scientists start with systematic observations of the world and move toward more abstract concepts or ideas. These ideas can form the basis of a theory. Others suggest that starting with theories and working with rigid hypotheses can keep researchers from seeing what's really going on. That is, we should start with observations and watch to see how relationships are constructed. By doing so, we might gain a clearer understanding of what's going on. This approach to social science research is called **induction.** Social scientists coming from the symbolic interactionist perspective and many using feminist approaches follow an inductive approach.

In reality, these approaches are part of an ongoing process of scientific inquiry, as shown in Figure 2.4. Research may begin with a theory or with data, but science depends on the continual movement between theory and observation. Theories must continually be tested in different environments and under different conditions. As new data become available, researchers use them to inform, modify, or refute theories. Because science is an ongoing process, it guards against the premature closure of inquiry. Our ultimate goal is to construct an understanding of how and why relationships occur—that is, what causes us to behave the way we do. This knowledge can be useful for communities. If we "know" what causes domestic abuse to occur, for example, we can work toward a solution to end it.

When Is a Relationship Causal?

Theories purport to tell us why variables are related to one another. As such, they tell us what causes us to engage in the behaviors we do. We want to know what causes some grandparents to be more involved with their grandchildren, or what causes children to use drugs, or what factors lead to teen pregnancy. These variables that we are interested in explaining are called **dependent variables.** The factors that we find to cause the dependent variable to occur are called **independent variables.** Establishing causal relationships between them includes meeting three criteria. The first criterion is that the *variables must be correlated.* That means that as one variable changes, so does the other. For example, as the education level of women has gone up, the age at marriage has also gone up. This is referred to as a **positive relationship,** for both variables change together in the same direction. A **negative relationship** is one where we find that as one variable increases, the other decreases. An example of this might be that as the education of women increases, the average number of children born to women decreases.

However, social scientists are not satisfied with correlation to establish a causal relationship. A second issue of primary concern is to establish *which of the variables comes first.* For an observed correlation to be causal, we should know which one causes the other to occur. The variable that changes first is the independent variable. The variable that changes as a consequence of the change in the former is the dependent variable. These appear to be tricky terms for many students. An example might help: there is a negative correlation between age at marriage and the likelihood to divorce. That means that people who marry later in life are less likely to divorce. As our knowledge of marriage and divorce makes clear, marriage precedes divorce; thus, age at marriage is the independent variable.

The third condition to establish a causal relationship is in many ways the most difficult to establish. This condition is the *lack of spuriousness.* A **spurious relationship** is a

FIGURE 2.4 The Wheel of Science

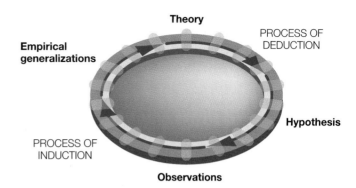

The process of scientific inquiry is represented by a wheel because it is an ongoing process that does not always begin at the same place. Some researchers begin with a theory and develop hypotheses to test the theory. Data are collected, and the hypothesis (the statement about what the researchers expect will occur) is assessed. Either the theory is supported or disproven (for the data). This is called *deduction.* However, theories are not always available to make predictions about what we want to study. In that case, researchers will collect data. Then, based on those observations, the researchers construct general statements about the relationships observed. These are called empirical generalizations because they are based on what is seen or heard. When researchers observe systematic patterns of relationships, they then instruct theories. This process is called *induction.*

correlation that exists between two variables only because another variable causes them both. For example, there is a correlation between divorce and children's problematic behavior. The correlation establishes the first criterion for causality. Since the divorce occurs prior to the problematic behavior in children, we have our second condition, and we call divorce the independent variable and behavior in children the dependent variable. However, it has been suggested that there are factors occurring in the relationship (marriage/family) prior to divorce that may be causing the divorce to occur as well as causing the problematic behavior in children (Furstenberg & Cherlin, 1991). These prior factors could include poor relationships between the parents, or between parents and children. This is yet another reason that science is seen as an ongoing process. We must keep an open mind when doing research and be thinking about reasons to question our findings.

Techniques of Social Research

As we suggested earlier, social scientists go about their research in many different ways. But no matter what the technique used, researchers need to address who will be studied (sampling), what information to collect from those studied (measurement), and how to make sense of the information once collected (data analysis).

Sampling Recall our initial discussion about how relying on information only from those with whom we have come in direct contact can be problematic for social scientists. To help overcome these problems, researchers try to draw samples that reflect the diversity in the population they are trying to study. The best way to do this would be to draw a **random sample,** one that gives every person in your target group an *equal* chance of being selected. It is the equivalent of a lottery. For example, let's say we want a random sample of students at a college or university. If we were to put all students' identification numbers in a hat, and draw out 100 of them, these 100 would be a random sample of our population. This type of sample is very difficult to do. First, it assumes that we have an exhaustive list of our population that we can draw from. Do such lists exist? If you wanted to study dual-career couples, where would you get such a list? How about if you wanted to study pre-school-age children?

Because random samples are difficult to obtain, researchers have devised strategies to get samples that are *representative* of

(that is, they look like) their desired populations in other ways. If you assume that the majority of people in the United States have telephones, you could draw a sample through random digit dialing. In fact, this is the way that the major polling firms come up with their predictions about who will win elections or about how people feel about some public issue. Another approach often used in large-scale research is *cluster sampling,* where people are initially divided up into collectivities (such as states, counties, regions), and then a sample is drawn of these collectivities. Among these groups, people are again put in clusters, and the clusters are sampled. Clustering and sampling are done until you reach the level of the individual (if that's what you are studying) and your final sample can be drawn. When samples are drawn in such a way that we can estimate the extent to which they represent the target population, they are called **probability samples.**

Many other techniques have been used to draw representative samples. However, it is not always possible, and maybe not even desirable, to do representative sampling. Here is just one example. Let's say we are interested in studying families that contain children who live with their fathers (and not mothers). Is there a list of such families anywhere? Not that we know of. So we could start by randomly calling people from the telephone directory and asking (1) if they are part of such a family and (2) if they would be willing to help us in our study. How long would this take? If we follow recently published research, we know that such families make up 5 percent of the population of households with children (see Chapter 1). That means that we would have to call many households, which would be very time consuming and very costly. The cost is also affected by geographic dispersion. What population do you want to study? The entire United States? Large metropolitan areas?

Rural areas? The Northeast? It would be quite easy to just give up. However, there are some *nonprobability* techniques that have been used to access small populations (Warner, 1986). One example is **quota sampling,** or selecting participants for your study in proportion to how many you need of various groups. If you know that certain characteristics are part of your target population, you try to control for them by including people with those characteristics. Our population is roughly 50-percent female, so you want to make sure your sample is gender balanced by making sure that about half of your sample is female. In studying dual-career couples, you might want to ensure a distribution that represents the categories of jobs that people hold (professional, technical, service, farm). Although there is no guarantee that you will get a representative sample, you are addressing the issue of representativeness. Another technique is **snowball sampling,** in which you start with one person (couple or family), then ask the person to identify someone like them. Think about trying to study alcoholic families who are trying to deal with the alcoholism. Imagine doing a random phone survey. However, you could attend an Alcoholics Anonymous meeting and recruit participants. These families may be able to get you in touch with others "like them."

| FICTION

Although results from nonrandom samples cannot be generalized to a broader population, they can provide useful information about families. Some research methods do not lend themselves to random sampling techniques but are superior methods for revealing more in-depth information about family relationships.

Because there is no way to estimate the extent to which these samples represent their target population, they are referred to as **nonprobability samples.** There are many other nonprobability types of sampling, but the issues in sampling that you should take forward with you throughout this book are as follows. First, what is the population that the researcher is trying to study? Second, how does the researcher identify participants for the study? Is it a representative sample? Third, what characteristics of the target population are covered, and which are not? If there are characteristics not covered in the sampling design, what are the consequences? Fourth, what should you conclude about who the results can be generalized to, and what needs to be done in future studies? Again, social scientists are skeptics. We continuously question what we hear and read.

Measurement The issue of measurement is a complex one. In general, we are interested in using measures that are **reliable** and **valid.** To be reliable, our measure should be consistent. That is, if we use the measure today, then use it on the same population next week, we should get similar results. Think about intelligence tests. If they are reliable, then your intelligence quotient should be the same if you were to take the test today, then take it again at another time. To be valid, a measure is actually getting at our variable of interest. Asking mothers "How many children do you have?" is probably a valid estimate of the fertility rate of your sample. But think of another example, regarding marital infidelity. You ask someone, "Have you ever had an extramarital affair?" The person responds "No." A week later you ask the same person the same question. The person again responds "No." This is a reliable measure of marital infidelity, for the response is consistent. Still, the person may be lying both times. How would you know? Obviously, a direct question about marital infidelity may not be the most *valid* way of learning about the behavior.

Surveys are the most frequently used method in family research.

Survey questions are likely to face challenges to validity when the research is on a sensitive topic. Respondents may be reluctant to tell a stranger about their sexual behavior or their views on homosexuality if they believe that their answers would be judged as nonnormative or socially unacceptable. In research, this is referred to as a **social desirability bias**.

How we decide what questions to ask, or what observations to make, depends in part on what theoretical perspectives we employ and what topic we are studying. The following section of the chapter explains the various techniques that are used when studying family relationships, but we'll see that no technique is the best overall; rather, each does a better job at addressing particular issues or research questions. The discussion is not exhaustive but is meant to cover the most widely used approaches: survey research, secondary analysis, field research, and experimental research.

Survey Research

Surveys are data-collection techniques that elicit information through the responses that individuals give to questions. This approach is arguably the most frequently used technique in the social sciences. Most people are probably very familiar with surveys, having filled out many in their lives. Surveys are popular because they can be efficient (easy, cost-effective), are quite flexible (can ask just about anything), and if done with a good sample, can produce results generalizable to a broader population.

There are generally three types of surveys. **Mail surveys** are self-administered questionnaires sent to respondents. A variety of issues regarding family life can easily be studied via a mailed questionnaire. However, an assumption needs to be made that the person intended to fill out the survey does so and that this person is able to provide answers to the questions. It is relatively easy for a respondent to answer a question about how much time has been spent cooking in the past week or how the respondent feels about an employer's responsibility to provide subsidized child care for working parents. Other questions are not particularly good for mailed questionnaires. Giving a detailed history of expenditures on children's school-related activities might be just the kind of question that causes a respondent to throw the questionnaire away. Or the respondent might just skip that question or make a wild guess. As you can surmise, getting valid and reliable answers to certain questions is related to the technique used to elicit them. Getting very complex data from respondents can depend on someone having direct contact with the respondent and spending time talking about family life.

Face-to-face surveys, or interviews done with respondents and the interviewer in conversation in the same place, are considered to allow researchers to get the highest-quality data. The interviewer can ask follow-up questions, probe for more detail after any answer, and make notations about the nonverbal cues given in an interview regarding certain questions. However, face-to-face interviews are very expensive because of the labor costs involved. Paying an interviewer the time to travel, do the interview, and transcribe interview notes can cost thousands of dollars, even for a relatively small sample. It will depend on the type of information you require for your study. It can also be related to the theoretical perspective you bring to the research. Following a symbolic interaction approach might suggest that you need observational data in addition to verbal responses, or at least it requires the opportunity for respondents to provide more-detailed responses. If you are interested in asking a smaller number of questions that require little energy on the part of the respondent, another type of survey might work better.

Telephone surveys require an interviewer to call up respondents and ask them a series of questions. Relative to other methods, including other kinds of surveys, telephone surveys are inexpensive. And results can also be obtained quickly. Telephone interviews can be done and analyzed within hours. If someone is interested in doing a descriptive study to see what people think about a public policy that is on an upcoming election ballot, a telephone survey would be the best approach. However, telephone surveys have faced some challenges in recent years as people are wary of phone calls from telemarketers and have started using new blocking techniques to screen calls.

Recall the important measurement issues of reliability and validity. We want to make sure that the responses we get from people really reflect what they think or how they act. How do we know that people tell the truth on surveys? And how reliable will the responses be? A sociologist at Washington State University has devoted a considerable amount of his career to studying survey research methodology. Don Dillman (1978, 2001) uses exchange theory to explore the quality and quantity issues in survey research. He argues that people will respond to surveys if they receive something in return for their time and effort. Some researchers compensate respondents with material rewards. Have you ever filled out a survey for the Nielsen ratings? Odds are if you did, you received a crisp dollar bill in your envelope. Social science researchers don't often have access to the type of resources needed to provide material rewards. Instead, researchers take advantage of an assumption about people's motivation to participate. If you make it clear that respondents' views are important, and establish trust with them, they are more likely to participate. Most of us like to think that how we live our lives and how

we think about things is "right," or at least "important." And as social beings, we like to share our views. Dillman would say that you will get the best data if you (1) maximize rewards (material or nonmaterial), (2) minimize the costs (the time it takes to answer and the energy involved in remembering), and (3) establish a relationship based on trust.

Secondary Research

Because surveys are relatively inexpensive to perform and can cover a large geographic area in a small amount of time, many large data sets have been accumulated that include information on a plethora of issues. Data sets such as the National Survey of Families and Households, National Longitudinal Surveys, and the Panel Study of Income Dynamics are available to most researchers for a minimal cost. These are often funded by the government or private foundations and include detailed information of residents throughout the United States. Using data collected by others for independent research projects is called **secondary research.** If you were to look at the major journals in the field of family studies, you would find that a large percentage of the research published uses data not collected by the authors of the paper.

> **FACT**
>
> *Most of the published research on families is based on some type of survey (mail, telephone, face to face). However, many researchers do not collect their own surveys, instead relying on publicly available data sets constructed by research institutes or centers.*

One of the benefits of these data sets is that they are **longitudinal** in scope; that is, data are collected from people at more than one point in time. As we noted earlier, establishing causality depends on establishing the time order in relationships, and longitudinal data can help do this. **Cross-sectional data,** or data collected at one point in time, can give us correlations between variables but may give misleading results. For example, in the Focus on Family Research box on pages 74–75, we see how a long-held belief in family scholarship about marital satisfaction has been challenged as we now have longitudinal data to really test our hypothesis.

Another major benefit of survey research is the access to large samples to obtain reliable data that can be generalized to larger populations. Yet there are a number of reasons that researchers may find surveys inadequate for addressing their research questions. You may be interested in nonverbal behavior or the relationship between what people say and what they do. Accounting for behavior is not always possible with surveys. People are not always cognizant of how they act, or they may not remember specific instances. Surveys can also produce an unnatural sense of things. That is, as people fill out surveys or answer questions that have a set number of responses, they may not be giving a true sense of how they think.

Field Research

In order to get a fuller picture of relationships, social scientists engage in a variety of methods that are referred to as **field research.** These techniques are a way to study naturally occurring social phenomena as they take place. Three of the most common field methods are participant observation, intensive interviewing, and focus groups. These techniques usually produce data we refer to as qualitative—that is, not likely to produce a large set of numbers to include in statistical analyses. Instead, the data are more detailed and give us a stronger sense of the meanings of actions in people's lives.

Participant Observation Just as it sounds, **participant observation** allows researchers to make observations about social life while participating in the activities being observed. Those being studied do not have to stop the normal course of their day to provide information. Researchers can interact with groups of individuals and take note (figuratively or literally) of how people think, feel, and act. Of course, researchers can also ask direct questions and allow respondents to talk while simultaneously carrying on other activities.

The term *participant observer* refers to a range of possible roles. In fact, some field researchers take the position of complete observer and do not participate in the activity being observed. This could occur in settings where the researcher would be a very awkward member, such as observing children's games or interactions between husbands and wives. As we will discuss later, there are serious ethical considerations when doing research, and in this case, it is important that the people being observed are doing so willingly. There are some examples of observation that take place without the consent of those being studied, called *covert observation,* but these are primarily examples of public behavior (for example, at sporting events or town meetings). At the other extreme we would find the *complete participant.* This may occur, for example, when a researcher is also a member of the group being studied, such as a group counseling session like AA. Issues may arise in this type of research about the ability of the researcher to remain objective in his or her research findings and analysis. The majority of field researchers adopt a stance in between. They participate in interactions, but as a researcher. The goal is to establish rapport with those being studied, making them feel comfortable. Once a sense of comfort is established, interactions become normalized.

© Natalie Fobes/Corbis

Social scientists use a variety of methods to collect data on families. Some researchers gather information via surveys, while others observe family interactions in more naturalistic settings. These settings might include private family celebrations such as birthdays, or public rituals such as those recognizing the passing of a family member.

Intensive Interviewing Although survey research in a face-to-face setting can elicit rich data, there is a distinction made between that technique and **intensive interviewing.** Intensive interviews rely on open-ended questions and have a very unstructured pattern of questions. One specific type of intensive interview is the *life history approach.* In this type of interview, respondents are given free rein to talk about their lives. The interviewer may have a few orienting questions, but the respondent covers information in whatever way deemed appropriate. In R. W. Connell's study *Masculinities,* for example, he argues that life histories provide a "rich documentation of personal experience" concerning the "making of social life through time" (Connell, 1995: 89).

The relationship between the interviewer and the research subject takes on increased salience as the subject matter discussed gets more detailed and personal. A basic ethical concern about not harming the participant (see pages 78–83) includes a different definition of the situation than that of the traditional survey. For example, many researchers now use the term *client* to refer to the subjects of the research, suggesting that the relationship is more than observer/observed. Other researchers also suggest that the text of the interview be returned to participants to ensure that their views are expressed in the way that they intended.

Focus Groups **Focus group research** is organized to elicit information from people brought together in small groups for open discussion on a topic of research. This approach has been used quite successfully by market researchers and political pollsters to

For many years, family scholars have argued that how people rate their marriages takes a U-shape over time. That is, in the beginning of marriages, couples rate their marriages relatively high; then, as time progresses, ratings decline. However, marriages recover later in life, and marital satisfaction again increases to levels not too dissimilar to those at the beginning of marriages (thus making a U-shape).

The primary reasons given for this curvilinear relationship reflect changes in family roles and structures over time. One significant change has to do with the presence of children. In the early stages of marriage, the couple devote all their energy to each other. Then, with the introduction of children into the relationship, there are increasing demands on the couple that shift their focus away from each other. Couples have less time to engage in adult-oriented leisure-time activities; instead, their time is consumed with child care. These shifts in responsibilities result in a decline in the satisfaction with the marriage itself.

As children age and reach the most challenging period of adolescence, the argument is that marital satisfaction will be at its lowest level. However, as children leave the nest, married couples can return to their one-on-one relationship and again do things that they enjoyed

prior to having children. Or they can move on to new activities, sharing them with each other. Some family researchers have also found that retirement can enhance marital quality as people (particularly husbands) leave high-stress jobs.

Most of the research supporting this hypothesis of U-shaped marital satisfaction was done in the 1960s and 1970s using cross-sectional data. Recently, however, Jody Van-Laningham and her colleagues (Van-Laningham, Johnson, & Amato, 2001) used data from a national seventeen-year longitudinal study (1980–1997) of married couples and found that over time, marital satisfaction did not follow a U-shape but followed either a continuous decline

or a decline before a flattening out of rates of satisfaction. Figures 2.2 and 2.3 represent the two views of marital satisfaction over time.

Why would cross-sectional data and longitudinal data produce such different results? The authors of this study suggest that the cross-sectional data reflected a **cohort effect:**

> The U-shaped association between marital duration and marital happiness is due to older marriage cohorts experiencing higher levels of marital happiness than younger marriage cohorts. These older cohorts—married at a time when people held more prag-

FIGURE 2.2 View of Marital Happiness Over Time Using Cross-Sectional Data

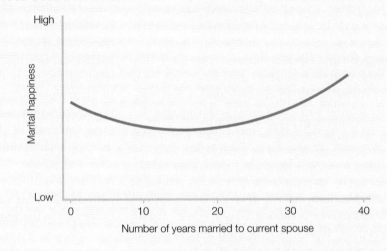

FIGURE 2.3 View of Marital Happiness Over Time Using Longitudinal Data

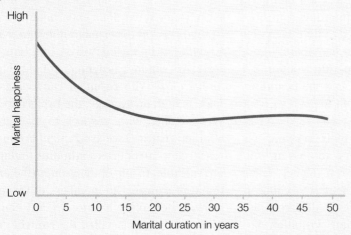

matic views about marriage, support for marriage was stronger, and couples were more committed to the norm of lifelong marriage—may have strengths that allow them to maintain high levels of marital happiness over the long haul. (2001: 1335)

Imagine doing a study in 1970. Couples who had been married for twenty years were married in 1950. As we will see throughout this text, marriage and family life were quite different in the 1950s than in subsequent years. These were the years of the baby boom and strong economic times, resulting in more stable jobs and income for men to support their families. Fast-forward to 1997 (the last year of this study), when those who have been married for twenty years were married in 1977. The 1970s saw significant social movements advocating gender equality in marriage. Along with significant downturns in the economy, this was the start of a major transformation from the "traditional marriage" of employed husbands/fathers and at-home wives/mothers to the dual-earner families that are more common today. These dramatic changes have produced greater challenges to couples in meeting their marital expectations. These challenges, in turn, may result in a lower rating of marital quality.

The significance of this study is to sensitize us to the implications that can be drawn from cross-sectional versus longitudinal data. We need to be careful when trying to use cross-sectional data to infer something about individual changes over time. For this type of inference, longitudinal data are necessary.

The rather "pessimistic" results of this study may also be discouraging. Is this what we can expect from marriage—a continual decline in happiness? The authors conclude by reminding us that, like all quantitative research, these results reflect patterns in the average change over time. Not all couples will experience a continuous decline in marital satisfaction. As we progress through this text, we will discover some of the factors that contribute to the enhancement or decline in marital quality.

Source: J. VanLaningham, D. R. Johnson, & P. Amato (2001). "Marital Happiness, Marital Duration, and the U-Shaped Curve: Evidence from a Five-Wave Panel Study." *Social Forces, 78,* 1313–1341.

Critical Thinking

1. What factors do you think lead to the general decline in marital satisfaction over time? Why?

2. The research cited here suggests that different cohorts of people approach marriage with different expectations. How are your views of marriage different from those of your parents? Why are they different?

see how people are responding to ads for products (market or political products) and has only recently been used widely by other social scientists (Morgan, 1997). This is also a useful technique for studying the public perception and use of public policies. Focus groups are group interviews. Their hallmark is the reliance on group interaction to produce information and insights that would be less accessible without the members' interactions. Focus groups generally contain six to ten people on average, and the facilitator may ask only a few questions to get the group talking about a particular topic. Topics could include widows sharing their grieving experiences, single mothers discussing the stresses of raising children alone, teens sharing their anxieties about sex, children whose parents have recently divorced discussing how they negotiate visitation between two households, and a multitude of other topics.

The benefit of focus groups is that the researcher can gather information quickly and relatively inexpensively. Focus groups are particularly good for gathering information unanticipated by the researcher. Respondents may develop a synergy not available in individual interviews, providing valuable insights into complex behaviors and motivation (Morgan & Kruger, 1993). However, focus groups also have some limitations. Because they are directed by the researcher/moderator, they are less naturalistic than participant observation. The setting is contrived, and the participants might wish to conform to the most outspoken opinions within the group. At the same time, other participants may express more extreme views in a group than they would in private. Focus groups work well on lively topics in exploratory research. For an example of how focus groups have been used in family research, see the Family Narratives box on pages 78–79.

Experiments

Experiments are a highly controlled method for examining cause and effect. They have been the hallmark of research in medical and biological research. In the social sciences, it is in psychology that we find the most frequent use of an experimental design. In the classical experimental design, control is achieved in various ways. One important feature is random assignment of participants into groups. The result of random assignment is that, on average, the two groups look very similar with respect to background characteristics. Once assignment is done, the researcher introduces a **stimulus** (independent variable) to one of the groups (the **experimental group**). The members of this group are watched to see if there are any changes. The other group is called the **control group.** Members of this group do not receive the stimulus and are used for comparison. The change over time for each group is measured and compared. If there are differences in the two groups, the change is then attributed to the stimulus. The random assignment of participants lets the researcher rule out other factors as the cause for change.

Let's take a simple example. Say we want to see if communication training will help make relationships happier. We recruit a sample of twenty couples and randomly put them in two groups. Dividing them randomly helps make sure that we don't have a bias in the groups. We would not want only those couples experiencing problems to be in the group that goes through a skills class. One group (experimental) takes a class that teaches communication skills. The other group (control group) does not. If the relationships of the couples in the experimental group improve while the couples in the control group remain the same, then we can conclude that the communication training works.

It is clear that having this type of control over the situation has real benefits. In a survey, we would not be able to have control over the background characteristics of those who sought out communication training and those who didn't. It would be very likely that those who sought out training were interested in improving their relationships anyway, and so would improve compared to others. In addition, a survey would not tell us how couples interacted prior to the training. Maybe these couples were happier to begin with or are the type of couples who enjoy taking classes that help them work on their relationship. Experiments allow the researcher more control over the design of the project and can help filter out these alternative explanations for change.

The other side of this issue of control is that the environment is contrived, or artificial. Being recruited for a study on communication in relationships keys participants into the issue on which they will be observed. Maybe people will change just because they know they are being observed. On one hand, this problem is addressed through the random assignment process. Both the couples in the experimental and control groups know they are being observed, so the likelihood that behavior will change because of observation is similar across both groups. Therefore, any additional change can be attributed to the communication class. On the other hand, there is still the possibility that taking the class works only when there is knowledge that couples are being monitored in some way. In our everyday lives we don't experience our relationships, or take communication classes, in a research situation. It may be the case that how training affects couples who seek it independently may be different from how it affects those who are assigned it in the laboratory. If experimental researchers suspect such an interaction effect, additional control groups can be added

to the experiment to sort out the various influences (Campbell & Stanley, 1963). The point to note here is that in experiments, considerable effort is made to anticipate the factors that will influence the research, and it is the researcher who controls this, not the participant.

Ethics in Social Research

In our discussion of the variety of techniques available to social researchers to answer their questions about families, we encountered a number of challenges. How do people feel about being observed? If they know they are being watched, will they change their behavior? Would it be right to observe people's behavior without telling them they are part of a research project? Can we deny people treatment because they are randomly put in a control group? What happens if participation in a study results in a participant's spouse finding out something previously kept secret? Most of us are cautious about filling out forms that come in the mail. How and why were we selected? These are very important questions, and answers to them must be anticipated before research is undertaken.

Concerns over the use of human subjects in research are relatively recent. Not until the middle of the twentieth century did the U.S. government get involved in the regulation of research using humans. Following World War II and the trial of twenty-three Nazi doctors and scientists who used humans in research that resulted in serious injury and deaths, the Nuremberg Code of 1948 was developed. It provided guidance for researchers using human subjects, which included gaining human subjects' consent to be included in research, anticipating and justifying the risks of the research, and guarding against serious mental or physical harm (Mitscherlich &

Focus groups are a form of qualitative interviewing that relies on open-ended discussions in small groups, typically with six to ten people. A "moderator," who is usually a member of the research team, leads the discussion. It helps to think of the term "focus group" as capturing the fact that the moderator provides the *focus* for the interview, while the data comes from conversations among the *group* members themselves.

In research on the family, focus groups sometimes bring together members from the same families. For example, consider a study that our research team did on "the sandwiched generation": adults who were caring for both their children and their older parents. The participants in these focus groups were couples where both partners worked, and our interview questions asked how they dealt with the multiple demands from their work, child care, and parent care responsibili-

ties. We usually had six people participating in these discussions, and some of the groups were made up of three couples. This format allowed each partner to compare his or her experiences to their partner's experiences. For example, the person in the couple who had the most flexible work schedule might take on more caregiving. In addition, having couples talking together allowed them to compare the differences in their families. For example, one family might have brothers and sisters who helped to care for an older parent, while another family might have all the elder-care responsibilities.

Often, however, it is neither practical nor wise to bring members of the same family together for a group discussion. For instance, in the study described above, it was frequently difficult for both members of a couple to attend the same group (even though the research team provided caregiving assistance). When it was not possible to

create groups that consisted of intact couples, we would often bring together separate groups of men and women. The difference between these groups and the "couple groups" was not just their homogeneity with regard to gender, but also the fact that none of the participants had their partner present in the same group. This allowed them to say things about their own point of view, and their feelings about their partner—things we might not have heard if we conducted all of the groups using couples.

As a general rule, focus groups avoid bringing together participants who are likely to be in conflict with each other. Instead, it is better to set up separate groups and then compare what they say. For example, if you are doing research on family issues for at-risk youth and their parents, it would probably make more sense to conduct separate groups for the teenagers and

---

Mielke, 1992). However, the effect of this code on U.S. researchers was weak, for it did not carry the weight of law and was not applicable to all types of human research.

| **FACT OR FICTION?**

To meet professional ethical standards, researchers must obtain informed consent from the participants in their research.

The most significant study for shaping the way research is regulated was a study

carried out between 1932 and 1971 by the Public Health Service to record the "natural history" of syphilis on African American men (Levine, 1988). As part of this research, hundreds of men were recruited to participate (both with and without syphilis). The men were not accurately informed about the purpose and extent of the research. Those with syphilis were denied treatment, even when it was discovered in the 1940s that penicillin was a safe and effective treatment. In 1972 the national press reported on this study, which produced 28 deaths, 19 cases of

the adults, rather than mixing them together. This approach has two advantages. First, each group feels more comfortable because they are talking to their peers—others who share a similar situation. Second, the researchers can compare the separate points of view that are expressed by each type of participant. For example, it would be interesting to know if the youths and parents agree on *what* the key problems are, even if they each blame the other for causing these problems. What is most important in a focus group is to bring together participants who are interested in talking to each other about the topic of the research. This is not likely to occur when the participants are so heterogeneous that it is difficult for them to relate to each other's experiences, or when there is conflict among different types of participants.

Fortunately, there are a great many situations where active group discussions occur simply by bringing together people who all share some of the same experiences or concerns. Here are some of the other topics that our research team has investigated using focus groups:

* We interviewed members of the Baby Boom generation, who were in their forties and fifties, asking them how their future retirement would differ from what their parents' generation is experiencing now. The Baby Boomers felt that they would have less financial security than their parents, and many of them felt that they would have to continue working longer, at least on a part-time basis.

* We talked to older women whose husbands had died in the past two years, and we asked them only one very broad question: What were the things that made their lives either easier or harder since they were widowed? They felt that the negative things other people did were at least as important as the positive or "supportive" things, and their most difficult problems involved negative aspects of relationships with their adult children.

* We asked family members who were caring for someone with Alzheimer's disease how they made the decision to seek a diagnosis. As these caregivers told their stories, it became clear that many of their decisions to seek a diagnosis had little to do with the symptoms of the disease itself. Instead, these caregivers often wanted a medical authority to validate the need for caregiving and help the family decide who would be the caregiver.

Author: David Morgan, professor of community health, Institute on Aging, Portland State University.

congenital syphilis, and 100 cases of disability. Shortly after, Congress formed the National Commission for the Protection of Human Subjects in Biomedical and Behavior Research, and this group produced the Belmont Report (1979), still used as the guide for ethical research. It includes the following principles:

1. *Respect for persons.* Research participants must be treated as autonomous human beings, able to choose for themselves whether they want to be part of a research study. Those persons with diminished autonomy (children and institutionalized persons) must also be protected.

2. *Beneficence.* Researchers have the obligation to ensure the well-being of those participating in their research. This includes maximizing the possible benefits of the research as well as minimizing the possible harms.

3. *Justice.* Participants must be treated fairly, with all benefits and risks shared evenly by those involved.

Institutional Review Boards

In 1991 the U.S. Department of Health and Human Services revised the regulations for protecting the rights and welfare of human research participants. Part of these new guidelines is the rule that for a research institution to be eligible for funding through any government agency, it must establish an **institutional review board** (IRB). These boards are made up of at least four members of the university community (with a variety of professional backgrounds) and one member not affiliated with the institution. The purpose of these boards is to review research proposals to ensure that they meet the ethical standards outlined above. Some institutions refer to this process as a human subjects review. Research proposals that include minimal risk to their participants may not need a full board review (these are referred to as "expedited reviews"), but all research including human subjects must be reviewed by an institutional authority.

When designing a research project that includes humans, researchers are required to submit an application to their IRB. The minimal federal requirements for these applications are that they address the following in their applications:

* Risk/anticipated benefit analysis. Risks must be minimized and must be reasonable in relation to benefits.
* Informed consent. The process used to inform participants must be described and the document used to gain their consent included in the application. The latter is often a typed page laying out the purpose of the research, the participants' rights, and a space for a signature implying their consent.
* Selection of subjects/participants. Selection of participants must be equitable, and the benefits and risks distributed equitably. Vulnerable populations must be protected.
* Safeguards for privacy and confidentiality of participants.
* A research plan for the collection, storage, and analysis of data.
* An appropriate research design/method that is scientifically valid.

FACT

Informed consent is based on the philosophical principle of respect for human subjects.

Ethical Concerns in Human Research

Social science researchers today are careful in thinking about their populations prior to doing research. As a scientific community, they believe that those who are part of research should be part of it willingly and should not be harmed physically, socially, or psychologically; as well, only the researcher should know the identity of participants. However, there are examples of research that have been questioned in terms of ethics. For example, a study conducted in San Antonio, Texas, in the early 1970s recruited Mexican American women to explore the effects of an oral contraceptive. The women were recruited as they arrived at a clinic seeking contraceptives. Although they did not know it, half of the women who received oral contraceptives were switched to a placebo after a period of time. The remaining women in the study initially received a placebo and then were switched to taking the contraceptive. Of the seventy-six women who participated in this study, ten became pregnant while taking the placebo. What are the ethical problems with this study? First, there was no informed consent. If the women had been told that for half of the time of the study they would be taking a pill that did nothing to prevent pregnancy, most, if not all, would not have consented. Second, the risks to the participants outweighed the benefits to science. Ten women who participated in a study to guard against pregnancy became pregnant. It is also reasonable to assume that some of these women participated in the study to get access to contraceptives without cost. They may have not been able to obtain contraception otherwise. This was a vulnerable population that should have been given additional protection (Levine, 1988).

If the San Antonio project were to undergo an IRB review today, it might not be approved without requiring further disclosure to the women before obtaining their consent. Even in projects that receive IRB approval, however, things may go wrong. If at any time during a research study it is discovered that the costs/harm outweigh the benefits of the gained knowledge, the study must be stopped until participants can be notified and harm can be reduced. For example, a major study by the National Institutes of Health on the effects of particular type of hormone replacement therapy (HRT) has recently been halted in order to notify participants of the potential risks of HRT. More than 16,600 women in the United States have been participating in a study in which roughly half received a form of HRT while the other half received placebos. While there have been some benefits shown for HRT (fewer hip and bone fractures and lower rates of colon cancer), there is an increased risk of heart disease. Because heart disease is serious (the number-one killer of women), it was determined that the potential harm outweighs the anticipated benefits (Writing Group for the Women's Health Initiative Investigators, 2002). All the women in the study have been notified to contact their doctors, find out if they were in the experimental or control group, and discuss whether to continue or discontinue their treatment.

When collecting information for research, it is important to get informed consent.

The potential harm that can occur to subjects in research is not just physical but can also be psychological, emotional, and/or social. One study that is discussed in many courses on research methods is that done by Laud Humphreys (1975). The goal of the study was to understand something about a population that had not been scientifically researched yet was the subject of public disdain and hostile acts. In order to collect data on male homosexuality, Humphreys engaged in participant observation in places known as "tearooms." He volunteered to be a lookout (called a "watchqueen") for men using public restrooms to engage in sex. His goal was not to expose these men, and once when Humphreys was arrested he went to jail instead of revealing his research and possibly being required to hand over information. Although he did interview a dozen men about their public participation in these tearooms, Humphreys was interested in collecting demographic information about the men in general. Who were they? What were their backgrounds? In order to learn this, he followed men out of the establishment and recorded their license plate numbers. About a year later, he posed as a "market researcher" and obtained name and address information from state officials. Humphreys then contacted these men and asked them to participate in a general health survey that he had designed earlier.

What are the ethical problems with this study? First, Humphreys deceived these men about the intention of his "health survey" and how they were selected. That is, they were not adequately informed. If they had been, his response rate most certainly would have gone down; they would not have voluntarily consented to participate. Second, the potential harm may have been great. The acts these men engaged in were illegal, and Humphreys could have been subpoenaed to turn over their names to police. Anticipating this, Humphreys was careful not to publish any information that might violate these men's confidentiality, and he burned all of his tapes and shredded incriminating material. Still, the men reading his work (which received considerable press coverage) must have been very concerned about what their "outing" would have done to them and their families.

In all types of research involving human subjects there is the potential for harm. Disclosing information about ourselves, and others, opens us up to critical evaluation. It might stir up bad memories and remind us of stressful events. There are also benefits. Those who participate can feel as though they are providing useful information that can help others. All researchers must weigh the risks and benefits of their research before proceeding. Most of the research included in this book poses minimal risks for participants. The examples above are not offered to suggest that social scientists are unethical but to emphasize that ethics are at the core of social science research.

Data Analysis

The types of data collected by family researchers are as variable as the techniques used. Surveys and experiments may produce numbers amenable to statistical analysis while field techniques produce data in the form of "narratives" or "text." In this section, we will briefly discuss a few of the ways data are presented in family research. The discussion is not meant to be a lesson in statistics but a guide to reading tables, charts, and graphs.

FACT OR FICTION?

Research indicates that mothers are more likely to have discussions that touch on birth control with daughters, while fathers are more likely to have discussions on such topics with sons.

Relationships Between Variables

Most of the time, we are concerned with how two variables are related—for example, whether parents are more likely to engage in discussions about sexual topics with sons than with daughters. In a recent study of parents and their eighth- through twelfth-grade children, family researchers were interested in exploring parent-teen communication regarding sexual topics (Raffaelli, Bogenschneider, & Flood, 1998). As part of their study, they reported the findings presented in Table 2.4. What we learn from this table is that discussions that take place between parents and sons are less likely to include talk of birth control (13.5 percent) than are discussions between parents and daughters (25.7 percent). In fact, the parent–daughter discussions are *twice as likely* to include mention of birth control. Compare the two numbers: 13.5 percent and 25.7 per-

TABLE 2.4	Birth Control as Part of Parent–Child Discussions	
	PARENT–SON DISCUSSIONS (%) (N=584)	PARENT–DAUGHTER DISCUSSIONS (%) (N=592)
Birth control part of discussion	13.5	25.7

Source: Adapted from Raffaelli, Bogenschneider, & Flood (1998). "Parent–Teen Communication About Sexual Topics." *Journal of Family Issues, 19,* 315–333.

TABLE 2.5	Birth Control as Part of Parent–Child Discussions, Controlling for the Gender of Parent and Child	
	PARENT–SON DISCUSSIONS (%)	PARENT–DAUGHTER DISCUSSIONS (%)
Mothers discussed birth control***	14.2	38.3
Fathers discussed birth control	12.7	8.4

***Relationship between discussions with sons and daughters statistically significant at the .0001 level.
Source: Adapted from Raffaelli, Bogenschneider, & Flood (1998). "Parent–Teen Communication About Sexual Topics." *Journal of Family Issues, 19,* 315–333.

cent. The second is almost twice the first. If these numbers were whole numbers (say, 13 families compared to 26 families), you could *not* say that one group was twice as likely as the other one is to discuss birth control. Why? Because you don't know the total numbers of each type of family. Therefore, researchers are more likely to present data in percentages, and doing so will allow for this type of comparison.

Let's try another table. Raffaelli and her colleagues also explored the communication between parents and teens and separated the results for fathers and mothers. These results are presented in Table 2.5. Recall that researchers strive to be very precise, so before generalizing these results to "parents," they decided to see if mothers and fathers had similar kinds of conversations with their daughters and sons.

There are many things to learn from this table. But this study is interested in whether or not parents talk about birth control more with sons or daughters. Recall that overall, it looks like parents talk about birth control more with daughters. So what do you find? Look at the first row for mothers. We see a similar trend. Mother–daughter discussions include more talk of birth control than do mother–son talks. The "***" that appears in the first row, and is footnoted at the bottom of the table, tells us that the difference is a statistically significant one. This means that in a sample of this size, this relationship is not likely to occur by "chance."

Now take a look at the second row, which summarizes the results for fathers. Here we see a difference in the *opposite* direction. That is, father–son conversations are slightly more likely to include a discussion of birth control than are father–daughter conversations. Because there are no asterisks, the authors are indicating that the observed relationship is not statistically significant. Father–son discussions are not that different from father–daughter talks with respect to the issue of birth control.

FICTION

Although the trend occurs generally, it is only statistically significant for mothers. Fathers are about as likely to converse with daughters about birth control as they are with sons (and it is less often than by mothers).

Tables are not the only way to present findings. Very often, especially in media presentations, charts are used. Notice how Table 2.5 would appear as a chart (see Figure 2.5). Sometimes when you look at a graph, you see things that you might not automatically see in a table. For example, it is obvious from the figure that the predominant form of communication that includes birth control is the mother–daughter conversa-

tion. What might explain this observed relationship? Traditional explanations might include the issue of pregnancy. Females get pregnant and therefore have "more at stake" when having sex. Still, with the risk of HIV infection, and our understanding that the use of a condom may work against the spread of HIV, it is somewhat surprising that so many fewer conversations occurred with sons.

Misleading Statistics   A discussion of statistics would not be complete without at least some mention of how statistics can be manipulated to tell a story. Social scientists operate on the assumption that *all* relevant data should be presented when discussing results. This certainly is not a universal assumption, as we saw in the box on pages 52–53. Regarding the work of Peter Rossi and that of Kristin Luker. Both of these social scientists had their research findings ignored in media presentations. However, what may be more prevalent in the social sciences is the incomplete coverage of a story, or "partial coverage." In the Focus on Family Research box on page 85, we see that the same data can be used to put forward more than one argument. Students of the family will want to make sure to not only read the text of papers or reports, but to actually look at the data presented and ask what is being learned. You may be surprised that your interpretations differ from those of the authors—and for the same table or chart. This brings us back to an issue we raised at the very start of this chapter. We all come to this class with "knowledge." This knowledge includes our experiences and information from others. But much of this knowledge is framed by the ideology that we use to make sense of our world. The preceding example of research suggests that birth control discussions taking place between parents and children depend on the gender of the parent and the gender of the child. But what can we make of these differences in conversations?

FIGURE 2.5   Percentage of Parent–Child Conversations That Include a Discussion of Birth Control

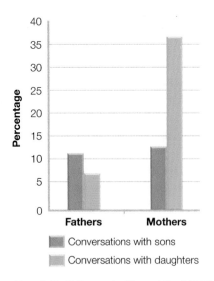

Source: Adapted from Raffaelli, Bogenschneider, and Flood (1998). "Parent–Teen Communication About Sexual Topics." *Journal of Family Issues 19,* 315–333.

The most prevalent family form is a two-wage-earner family. As women have increased their labor market activity, how has the division of labor at home changed? Are men picking up the slack? The data in Figure 2.6 represent the picture for what's happening at home for men and women. The first thing you might notice is that women have decreased their time in housework from 33.9 hours in 1965 to 19.4 hours per week in 1995. This is a 42-percent decrease. Men, on the other hand, have increased their time from 4.7 hours in 1965 to 10.4 hours per week in 1995. They have more than doubled their time in housework. Imagine having access to only the percentage change for men and women. It appears that men are changing more than women. A media headline might read "Men Are Doing a Lot More, Women Doing Much Less."

But let's look at the data another way. For each year, we can figure out the ratio of housework that is done by women. For example, in 1965 women did 33.9 hours, or 88 percent, of the housework. In 1975, women did 80 percent; in 1985, 68 percent; and in 1995, 65 percent. We see the same thing as before, that women's time is decreasing and men's is increasing; therefore, the percentage that women do is less. However, if we use these percentages, we notice that women are still doing the majority of the housework. You could not tell this from the change in men and women separately over time. We might see another headline: "Although Women and Men Are Both Employed, Women Still Do Almost Two-Thirds of the Housework."

Finally, notice that while women have continued to decrease the time they spend in housework, men have not continued to increase theirs. Consider the headlines: "The Stalled Revolution in Marriage" or "Men Have Maxed Out on Their Participation in Domestic Work."

The data used for these headlines are the same. *How* the data are used depends on the point that is being made.

Source: Data adapted from S. M. Bianchi, M. A. Milkie, L. C. Sayer, & J. P. Robinson (2000). "Is Anyone Doing the Housework? Trends in the Gender Division of Household Labor." *Social Forces, 79*(1), 191–228. Table 1, p. 208.

Critical Thinking

1. Which of the interpretations makes the most sense to you? Why?

2. What type of data would you need to convince you that housework was distributed equitably?

FIGURE 2.6 Who's Doing the Housework?

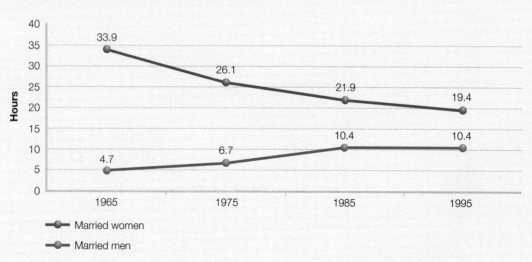

Are they a good thing or a bad thing? What we make of social science research findings is at least partly related to how we view the world.

Conclusion

There is considerable diversity among social scientists in the theories and methods they use to try to understand families. Recognizing this diversity is critical for addressing the themes of this book. Whether macro (functionalism), micro (symbolic interaction), or a merging of the two (systems theory), social science theories point to the structural arrangements that help to shape family relationships. A multiplicity of research designs provides us with data to help dispel myths (such as the myth of the monolithic family form) and reveal the complexities of family life. It is important to recognize that no one theory or method is better than the others. Over the course of this book, it will become clear that the topic covered and the questions asked will require different perspectives and methods. The underlying assumption of all these inquiries is the belief that social science research, carried out with respect for its participants, is beneficial for gaining knowledge and working to support and strengthen family ties.

Chapter Review

* How do we come to know about families?

Most of what we know about families comes from two sources. The first is personal experience. The source can be affected by bias because our particular lives are different from those of others. The other primary source of knowledge is from trusted others, including teachers, family members, texts, media, and other outlets. Social scientists, being skeptics at heart, are always cognizant of potential biases associated with the source of knowledge and engage in a scientific mode of inquiry using systematic methods to collect and analyze data.

* Does all social science research have the same goal?

Social scientists go about their work in many ways, and these have different purposes. Some researchers are interested in collecting data to get descriptions of general trends, while others are trying to uncover previously unexplored phenomena. Most social science research is interested in finding out why trends and patterns exist, and those trying to initiate social change can use this type of research to achieve their goals.

* What are the theories used by social scientists to explain family life?

Family scholars use a variety of perspectives. Some theories focus on macrolevel issues while others are more interested in microlevel phenomena. Macrolevel theories are interested in the ways in which the family, as an institution, is related to other social institutions. Questions refer to the relationship of family structure and functioning to other environments, such as neighborhoods, educational systems, and economic and political situations. Theories at the microlevel focus more on members of families and the relationships among those members. Theories also differ in terms of the assumptions they make about families. Some theories see families as smoothly functioning systems working toward a common goal, while other theories believe families are inherently in flux and always changing.

* What role does theory play in social science research?

Theories are very important for research on families because they help to guide the research process. The questions that are asked (hypotheses that are tested) by researchers often come directly from theoretical propositions. Theories also influence the type of research methodology that is employed. For example, theories that focus on interaction suggest an observational study, while theories that explore general trends in behavior suggest the use of large-scale surveys (such as the census).

* How do social scientists go about researching families?

Social scientists use a wide variety of research methods to study families. Depending on the type of information sought, studies can be large or small, can include face-to-face interaction, can take place with individuals or groups, or can be done in local, regional, or even broader social settings. The most commonly used technique in the social sciences is the survey. Surveys can be done via the mail, by telephone, or through interviews. Several large-scale research organizations engage in annual surveys that cover family-related behavior, and these surveys are used by researchers around the world.

* What are the common elements among research methods?

All researchers face three issues when engaging in social research. First is the sample. The best samples for generalizing to the population are those that are representative (covering the diversity in the population). However, smaller, nonrepresentative samples also provide key insight into areas not previously researched. The second issue is that of measurement. Researchers are particularly attentive to the subjects of reliability (collecting data in ways that are consistent) and validity (collecting data that actually measure what you intend to study). Finally, the issue of analysis is important. For quantitative researchers, the way in which data is presented can give certain impressions about family behavior. Statistical tests can reveal what variables are empirically correlated, but the question of what this means requires the researcher to make a theoretical evaluation.

* *Are ethical issues important for family research?*

Reputable researchers put the ethical treatment of participants in their studies at the forefront. Most universities and research centers funded by government agencies are required to get approval from a review board to ensure that participants in the research are involved voluntarily and will not be subject to undue harm as part of the research. Researchers are bound by requirements of confidentiality, meaning that they cannot make known any information about participants that allows others to detect who they are.

Key Terms

agreement reality: a way of knowing about our world through information gathered from trusted others or through our culture

cohort effect: people born in a particular time period exhibiting similar behavior patterns compared to people born in a different time period

conflict theory: a theoretical perspective that views social systems as always in flux. There is an uneven distribution of resources in society, and those with the most resources hold more power, or the ability to achieve their goals. Conflict the-

orists predict that those groups who have greater access to resources (education and income) will be more likely to have stable marriages.

control group: during experiments, the group members who do not receive the stimulus and are used for comparison

cross-sectional data: data collected at one point in time

deduction: the process beginning with a theory, developing a hypothesis, and then collecting data to test that hypothesis

dependent variable: the variable that we are interested in explaining. This variable changes as a result of changes in another (independent) variable.

descriptive research: the type of research designed to address basic quantitative questions such as "How many?" "How long?" "How much has changed?"

developmental perspective: a "stage" approach to analyzing family behavior. As relationships develop, they tend to go through somewhat predictable stages, just as the individual goes through developmental stages when growing up.

ecological perspective: a theoretical perspective identified with Urie Bronfenbrenner that studies human development and families by placing them in their environments. Environments range from the immediate day-to-day context (microsystem) to the broader cultural contexts (macrosystem).

empirical: that which is experienced through the senses. Empirical research is done by watching or listening to others to collect data.

evaluation research: the type of research designed to evaluate the effectiveness of structures or programs

experiential reality: understanding the world around us by using our own histories

experimental group: during experiments, the group members who receive the stimulus and are watched to note changes

experiments: a highly controlled research method for determining cause and effect. Used primarily by psychologists, it typically includes two groups of participants (experimental and control). One group receives a treatment; comparing the two groups over time can detect the effects of the given treatment.

explanatory research: the type of research designed to address questions of "why?"

exploratory research: the type of research designed to address questions about what it is like to experience a variety of situations

expressive roles: behaviors intended to manage the emotions and nurturing needs in families

face-to-face surveys: a way of eliciting information in which the researcher and participant engage in conversation in the same place

family systems theory: a perspective incorporating the basic assumption of functionalism but having "interaction" (as opposed to the individual) as its primary focus. When there is a problem within the family, this perspective looks at how people interact or communicate, instead of looking at the characteristics of the people involved.

feminist theoretical perspectives: theories that place women's and girls' experiences at the center instead of just applying knowledge based on samples of men to explain situations for women. Gender is always considered relevant because systems of power and inequality are found in all parts of social life, including the family.

field research: a method to study naturally occurring social phenomena as they occur

focus group research: a method of eliciting information from people who are brought together in small groups for open discussion on a topic of research

hypothesis: a statement about the relationship between two or more variables

(characteristics that can take on different values) that can be tested empirically (with observation)

inaccurate observations: observations based on faulty perceptions

independent variable: the causal variable. When this variable changes, it causes another variable (the dependent variable) to change.

induction: the process of beginning with observations, noting patterns, and developing theoretical understandings from these patterns

institutional review board: a committee that reviews research proposals at institutions, such as universities and institutes, to ensure the protection of human subjects in research. IRBs are required by law for those institutions that receive federal funding for research.

instrumental roles: behaviors intended to meet the tasks of financial support and leadership within families

intensive interviewing: collecting data through unstructured interviews in which questions are generally open-ended

latent functions: the unintended, or unanticipated, reasons for the existence of some structure. While traditional family structures are assumed to be efficient, they also serve to reinforce gender inequality.

longitudinal data: data collected at more than one point in time

mail surveys: respondents being asked to respond to questions by filling out a questionnaire. Mail surveys allow more privacy and time to answer, but may not produce detailed responses.

manifest functions: the intended reasons for the existence of some structure. Bearing and rearing children is a manifest function of the family in society.

negative relationship: one variable increasing (such as education), resulting in another variable decreasing (such as the likelihood to divorce)

nonprobability sample: the type of sample in which there is no way of estimating the likelihood that the people selected represent the population from which they were drawn

overgeneralization: using what we know from a subset of a group to incorrectly conclude something for the entire group

participant observation: a type of field method in which the researcher makes observations of a particular population by joining in on their activities

positive relationship: one variable increasing (such as age), resulting in another variable also increasing (such as income)

probability sample: a sample that is drawn in such a way that the researcher can estimate the extent to which it represents the target population. Random sampling is just one type of probability sample.

quota sampling: a nonprobability technique used to get a desired number of people (quota) in each category of people desired

random sample: a sample in which every person in the population has an equal chance of being selected for a study

reliability: a measure producing consistent results over time

secondary research: research based on data collected by someone else

selection bias: the results from a study being produced only because of the characteristics of the sample used. The results are nongeneralizable.

selective observation: seeing only those things that are in line with our preferences or beliefs

snowball sampling: a nonprobability technique that starts with a few people with the desired characteristics, then branches to people they know who also hold those desired characteristics

social desirability bias: responses given by a participant in a study because of an an-

ticipated judgment by others. Respondents say what they thing they should, or what is socially acceptable.

social exchange theory: a microlevel perspective that assumes that all interactions are based on rational self-interest. People will engage in an interaction if the benefits outweigh the costs.

social science: a set of systematic methods for investigating social relationship and social structure

spurious relationship: a relationship that exists only because of a third variable. Spurious relationships are correlational, not causal.

stimulus: during experiments, the independent variable that is tested

structural functionalism: a theoretical perspective aligned with Talcott Parsons and Robert Bales that sees the family as a structure meeting fundamental needs in society. Families produce and socialize new members to society.

surveys: the type of research that includes asking people to give information about themselves

symbolic interaction: a theoretical perspective aligned with the work of Herbert Blumer. The primary focus is on how relationships are formed through the use and exchange of symbols.

telephone surveys: the type of survey in which interviewers call people and ask them a series of questions

theory: a set of statements that explains why certain relationships occur

unit of analysis: the individual, group, or subject of study

validity: a measure producing an accurate picture of the concept or variable of interest

variable: a characteristic that can take on different values

Resources on the Internet

These web sites have been selected for their relevance to the topics in this chapter. These sites are among the more stable, but please note that web site addresses change frequently.

The Gallup Organization

http://www.gallup.com

The Gallup Organization takes periodic polls of people in the United States on their views on a variety of issues. Several of the tables and charts produced for this text came from Gallup polls. (Recently, this organization has begun to charge a subscription fee, so some information may not be available for free.) A recent search on the site for the subject of "family" produced survey results on the following topics: parents' views on mandatory school testing, parents' views on school shootings, adults' views on violence against children, and adults' attitudes regarding parental employment behavior.

The Urban Institute

http://www.urban.org

The Urban Institute is a nonpartisan economic and social policy research organization. The organization carries out research on national and local issues that are important to people in the United States. A variety of research methodologies are used, and a wide audience is the target for the results of this research. Included in that targeted audience are university students. Those interested in how families are responding to welfare reform, or the rise and fall of American youth violence, will find valuable research information on this site.

New York Times

http://www.nytimes.com

For students interested in exploring how social science research on families is presented in the media, try exploring a newspaper such as the *New York Times*. This web site's search engine will help you find information on a variety of family topics. To find out how local papers cover family issues, try locating your favorite paper on the Web.

Companion Web Site for This Book

Virtual Society: The Wadsworth Sociology Resources Center

http://sociology.wadsworth.com

Begin by clicking the Student Resources section. Next, click Marriage and Family, and then click the cover image for this book. Select from the pull-down menu the chapter you are presently studying. You will have easy access to chapter resources such as MicroCase Online exercises, additional Web links, flashcards, InfoTrac exercises, and practice tests (that can be scored). In addition, to enhance and help with your study of marriages and families, be sure to investigate the rest of the rich sociology resources at Virtual Society.

Visit InfoTrac College Edition

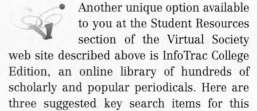

Another unique option available to you at the Student Resources section of the Virtual Society web site described above is InfoTrac College Edition, an online library of hundreds of scholarly and popular periodicals. Here are three suggested key search items for this chapter:

* Search keywords: *family + theories*
* Search keywords: *ethics + research*
* Search keywords: *media + family*

Search recent years to get the latest information on these issues.

© Gina Minielli / Corbis

3

The Importance of Gender, Race and Ethnicity, and Social Class

The Significance of Gender, Race and Ethnicity, and Class

Family experiences are shaped by the variety of privileges and constraints that we encounter, although many go largely unnoticed and we are unaware of the ways in which they affect us. As introduced in Chapter 1, however, our lives are influenced by a variety of structural, historical, and cultural forces. This chapter examines the impact of three critical dimensions of social structure: (1) gender, (2) race or ethnic background, and (3) social class.

To briefly illustrate how these master statuses influence us, consider the case of an unmarried, twenty-two-year-old, white, Christian, female college student who was raised in a middle-class family. Perhaps her father is a businessman, her mother a nurse. She would someday like to marry and have children. In her search to find her partner, what are the odds that she has ever dated a black man? What is the likelihood that she has ever dated someone who is Jewish or Buddhist? Would she date someone who is three or more years younger than herself? What are the odds that she has ever dated another woman? Moreover, how likely is it that she has dated one of the custodial workers at her university?

Why would she, in all likelihood, not consider these people as possible dating partners and lifelong mates? Certainly, there are individuals in all of these categories with whom she may have a tremendous amount in common. Yet she may avoid dating them al-together because doing so would violate **social norms,** or expectations that our society holds. Whether we are cognizant of them or not, dating and mate selection norms exist, and they are heavily influenced by social class, race and ethnicity, and gender. The young woman in our example veers away from certain groups of people that are somehow deemed unsuitable for her.

The Stratification System in the United States

As the example illustrates, many things, including our gender, race and ethnicity, and social class, affect opportunities, privileges, constraints, and the choices we exercise. These master statuses have a strong influence upon us throughout our lives. They are dimensions of **social stratification,** or the hierarchical ranking of categories of people within society. Some people have more, fewer, or at least different opportunities because of their gender, race, social class position, or combination of these.

"But Why Can't We All Just Be Equal?" There is a hesitancy to acknowledge the stratification found in society. Most people are self-conscious about noting differences, afraid that by noticing them they are guilty of endorsing unequal treatment. "Why can't we all just be equal?" students have asked. For example, whites worry that by "noticing" that the person sitting next to them in class is African American they may be exhibiting **racism,** the belief that certain racial or ethnic categories are innately superior or inferior to others. Shouldn't we just pretend race and ethnicity, and the differentiation we experience because of them, do not exist?

"Why can't we all just be equal?" ignores the fact that low-income families, for example, have significant difficulties even finding something as fundamental as housing. Using Census 2000 figures, the average wage needed to pay for a two-bedroom rental unit is $13.87 an hour, which at more than double the minimum wage is far more than many people and many families earn. Three states—Hawaii, New Jersey, and New York—have a "housing wage" greater than three times the minimum wage (National Low Income Housing Coalition, 2001). The lack of affordable housing causes many families to be homeless, to live in dilapidated dwellings without appropriate ventilation or heat, and to live in dangerous neighborhoods that are unsafe for children.

Acknowledging the ways in which race and ethnicity, gender, and social class shape our lives enlightens us in many ways. First, it allows us to concede that our private lives are indeed affected by what is happening in society around us. Many seemingly personal troubles, such as a divorce, unemployment, or sexual harassment, are experienced by others. Yet these events do not occur randomly throughout the population.

Certain categories of people are more likely to experience particular specific troubles. For example, persons with lower levels of education and income are more likely to divorce than are those with higher education and income, racial or ethnic minority members have significantly higher unemployment rates than do whites, and women are more likely to experience sexual harassment on the job than are men.

The Linkage Between Private Experience and Social Forces

The **sociological imagination** refers to the recognition that our personal experiences are, in large part, shaped by social forces within the larger society (Mills, 1959). The sociological imagination helps us place seemingly personal issues, such as mate selection, unemployment, power, sexual harassment, sexuality, poverty, wealth, cohabitation, division of household labor, and rape, into their broader social context. These events are not simply personal problems experienced by a random group of individuals. Instead, they result from structural and cultural forces in our society. For example, when a small number of people are unemployed, we might be tempted to dismiss their misfortune as their own fault: they are lazy and do not want to work; they quit school prematurely and have few skills of interest to employers; they are inexperienced and do not know how to look for a job. However, when as many as 15 percent of African American males aged twenty to twenty-four cannot find work, which is nearly three times the rate for whites of the same age, it is difficult to blame this problem solely on the personal characteristics of the unemployed (U.S. Census Bureau, *Statistical Abstract of the United States,* 2001). Instead, we need to examine the employment and economic structure in the United States and look for patterns of social inequality. Widespread unemployment within certain segments of the population is a social problem, not simply a personal one, despite the fact that the hardships are experienced on a personal level.

Understanding the ways in which race and ethnicity, gender, and social class shape our lives empowers us to make rational choices in our lives. We can go through life blindly unaware of societal influences upon us. But that would make for a largely dull and passive existence. Instead, race and ethnicity, gender, and class differences should not be ignored: differences can be reason for celebration, while the negative repercussions associated with these differences can be ameliorated.

Acknowledging racial differences does not have to translate into a relationship based on superiority or inferiority. Rather, it can improve our understanding of ourselves and the ways in which our society both empowers and constrains us. These privileges and constraints follow us as we mature and develop intimate relationships.

Likewise, many students are hesitant to acknowledge gender as an organizing construct in our society. They may recognize gender differences in sexuality and reproduction, but they are considerably less likely to believe that their personal relationships, goals, aspirations, expectations for marriage, job prospects and pay, and current and future roles are shaped considerably by their gender. It is easy to dismiss that "things have changed" when, for example, students are confronted with the results from studies that indicate that women earn considerably less than men do when both work full time (U.S. Census Bureau, *Statistical Abstract of the United States,* 2001). Instead, female students insist that they will have challenging and well-paying jobs. They are adamant that they will be an exception to the general trends. In other words, they prefer to ignore the ways in which gender influences lives. While they hope to be the "exception to the general trend," the trend remains nonetheless.

FACT OR FICTION?

Gender, race, and ethnicity are likely to affect your family experiences, but the effect of social class is minimal.

Finally, the ways in which class shapes our lives are perhaps even less clear-cut. People tend to spend time with other people who are most like themselves—people who live in the same neighborhoods, go to the same churches, go to the same schools, and share the same interests. Generally, these individuals also share the same social class, and they likely share the same values and set of social norms. However, lack of contact with individuals outside your social class can result in misconceptions about them. For example, the poor are often denigrated by the middle class and blamed for their own economic circumstances. They are ridiculed for living in a "culture of poverty" (Lewis, 1966). Public opinion surveys have found that a sizable portion of the population believes that the poor are lazy and unmotivated (Feagin, 1975; Hunt, 1996). Welfare recipients in particular are criticized for living off the "public dole" despite the fact that most welfare recipients are children (U.S. House of Representatives, Committee on Ways and Means, 1996). Yet many other people could also be accused of receiving substantial federal or state subsidies. College students also, arguably, live off the "public dole"; public state universities charge tuition rates only one-quarter to one-third of the real costs of college. Taxpayers—rich, poor, and in between, including people who have no college-age children at all—make up the difference. Yet the middle class is held up as the standard to which everyone else must strive. Those whose lives are structured differently are viewed as deviant.

Gender, race and ethnicity, and social class represent critical dimensions of diversity in our society. They have important implications for the ways that we organize our lives, including our lives within our families and close relationships (Demo, Allen, & Fine, 2000; Murry, Smith, & Hill, 2001). In this

Patriarchy can manifest itself in many ways and is imbedded in political, economic, and religious institutions. Despite modernization on many levels, these Islamic women must remain completely covered.

chapter we will introduce some of the keys to understanding these dimensions of diversity.

FICTION

Gender, race, ethnicity, and social class are all master statuses and are key determinants of many family experiences.

Gender and Patriarchy

Most U.S. citizens would be shocked if it was suggested that women should no longer vote or be allowed to drive a car, should eat a meal only after the men in their families have finished, and should otherwise be under the authority of men at all times. But these are the beliefs in many countries around the world.

Although biological sex differences are important, most differences in the way that men and women are treated have more to do with gender than sex. While **sex** refers to biological differences between men and women, and their role in reproduction, **gender** is the culturally and socially constructed differences between males and females found in the meanings, beliefs, and practices associated with "femininity" and "masculinity" (Kendall, 1999).

Cross-cultural research reveals that women and men often receive drastically different treatment in many parts of the world and that masculinity and femininity are defined and evaluated quite differently. The term *patriarchy*, which was introduced in Chapter 1, means "rule of the father." It refers to a form of social organization in which the norm or expectation is that men have a natural right to be in control of women. This dominance is beyond that found at the individual level, with one man asserting that he is the "boss" of his particular family. Rather, patriarchy is manifested and upheld in a wide variety of social institutions, including legal, educational, religious, and economic ones. For example, patriarchy is apparent in our religions. The Koran, a critical religious document for millions of people throughout the world, pronounces that God made men superior to women and that submissiveness is a natural part of femininity:

> Men are in charge of women. . . .
> Hence good women are obedient. . . .
> As for those whose rebelliousness
> you fear, admonish them, banish
> them from your bed, and scourge
> them.

Judaism has also traditionally taught patriarchy, as witnessed in this prayer said daily by male orthodox Jews:

> Blessed are thou, O Lord our God, King of the Universe, that I was not born a gentile. Blessed are thou, O Lord our God, King of the Universe, that I was not born a slave. Blessed are thou, O Lord our God, King of the Universe, that I was not born a woman.

Christianity, the dominant religion in the United States, also teaches patriarchy, as witnessed in the following passages in the New Testament (1 Tm. 2:11–15):

> Let a woman learn in silence with all submissiveness. I permit no woman to teach or to have authority over men; she is to keep silent. For Adam was formed first, then Eve; and Adam was not deceived, but the woman was deceived and became a transgressor. Yet woman will be saved through bearing children, if she continues in faith and love and holiness, with modesty.

| FACT OR FICTION?

The United States and most of Western Europe have virtually eliminated patriarchy.

Patriarchy, to some degree, is widespread and is found in every society. However, it exists on a continuum, and is more pronounced in some societies than in others. As women increase their economic status, relationships tend to become more egalitarian. However, it would be wrong to assume that patriarchy has been eliminated in countries like the United States. As we will see shortly, clear patterns of male dominance continue to exist.

But before those patterns are examined, we will first consider examples of patriarchy found in other parts of the world. It may be easier to identify patriarchy and social inequality elsewhere than it is within our own borders.

| FICTION

Patriarchy is found in all societies, including the United States and Western Europe, although its form and intensity may vary.

The Disappearance of Girls in China and India

A young woman living in a small village in China had just delivered a baby girl. There was no joy in the family, no celebrations of any sort. Instead, everyone was somber. The men filed out quietly so that the women could do what they knew they must do. They set about the grueling task of mashing poisonous seeds with oil to make a paste, which they hurriedly forced down the baby's throat. By the end of the day, the child had died, and the mother buried her in a nearby field. She felt remote sadness, but her primary emotion was anger at herself for not bearing a son.

In a town in another part of China, an American who worked as a volunteer in an orphanage witnessed the disposal of many bodies of young girls who had been abandoned by their families and left to die in the orphanage. She claimed that they were carted out in wheelbarrows, tossed into a dumpster, and ultimately taken away by municipal garbage collectors.

As illustrated above, perhaps the most extreme form of patriarchy is the deliberate killing of females, both before and after birth. No one knows exactly how many females have been killed in China, India, and other Asian countries, but thousands are

China's one-child policy, coupled with a preference for boys, has led to a widespread disappearance of girls. In some rural regions, boys outnumber girls by ten to one.

dying at the hands of their parents from gross neglect, abandonment, infanticide, and the selective abortion of female fetuses (Croll, 2001). Many researchers and policy makers around the world, including those in China itself, are alarmed. In 2000, 900,000 fewer female births were recorded than should have been, based on the number of male births, compared to a shortfall of 500,000 in 1990 (Beech, 2002). In some rural regions, boys outnumber girls by ten to one. If current trends continue, by 2020 the surplus of Chinese males will exceed the entire female population of Taiwan (*The Economist*, 1998). Who will these young men marry, when they become of marriageable age? This is a question China is currently facing, and some men are turning to first cousins so that they are not left without mates (Beech, 2002).

Reasons for Infanticide Why have all the girls disappeared? Countries like China and India are poor, and people struggle to keep their families fed and clothed. Coupled with widespread poverty are the patriarchal norms prevalent in these societies, norms in which boys are strongly favored over girls. Girls are viewed as an economic liability, whereas parents see boys as a better investment of their meager resources. Long-standing patriarchal customs have limited women's participation in the economic and political sphere; consequently, women have historically had few opportunities to support themselves and have had few avenues of political power. In many countries a woman's primary role is to become someone's wife. She leaves her own family behind and joins that of her husband. We see manifestations of this patriarchy in age-old customs such as the parents of a girl being required to offer an expensive dowry to the family of her prospective husband. Customs like these reinforce the preference for sons—daughters are seen as expensive, as wasting precious resources. Although the government in China has expanded women's opportunities in recent decades, and their work–family roles have expanded, long-standing patriarchal attitudes are slow to diminish.

Moreover, because of China's tremendous population explosion in the twentieth century, the Chinese government implemented a dramatic family planning policy beginning in 1979 that emphasized one-child families, with only few exceptions. Families who violate this policy face severe social and economic sanctions by the government. With pressures to have small families, coupled with the continued preference of sons over daughters, perhaps it is not surprising that female infanticide occurs, alarming though it may be.

Some governments are beginning to acknowledge the crisis and are taking some initial steps to stop it. For example, Chinese government officials have attempted to restrict the use of ultrasound scanners to determine the sex of the fetus. Ultrasound and amniocentesis, modern technologies that distinguish the sex of the fetus with a high degree of accuracy, allow female infanticide to be replaced by the selective abortion of female fetuses. In addition, a report by the State Family Planning Commission is promoting the idea that the birth of a girl is "just as good" as the birth of a boy, and it is calling for efforts to "eliminate the phenomenon of abandoning or drowning baby girls" (Herbert, October 31, 1997). Patriarchy is deeply entrenched, and its consequences continue to thrive.

Female Genital Mutilation

A second example of patriarchy is the painful and dangerous practice of "female circumcision," or what is more accurately referred to

© 2002 AP/Wide World Photos

Over 100 million girls and women alive today have had their genitals mutilated, a dangerous and excruciatingly painful procedure.

as "female genital mutilation" (Mackie, 1996). This medically unnecessary procedure is commonly practiced in more than two dozen countries in Africa and the Middle East, usually upon young girls between the ages of eight and twelve. In one form, **clitoridectomy,** the clitoris is literally cut out of the body. In the more extreme form, **infibulation,** the vaginal lips are also cut or scraped away, and the outer portion of the vagina is stitched together. A girl's entire external genital area is removed, leaving only a minuscule opening for menstrual blood and urine to escape the body. The procedure is done crudely; a layperson rather than a physician usually conducts it, while the victim is tied or held down. It is often done in a home or hut rather than a hospital, without an anesthetic, and the instrument used may be a knife, razor blade, or broken glass. Often, the girl's body is stitched together with thorn or catgut, and her knees are bound together for several weeks for the incision to heal itself and not tear open again when she walks. The procedure is excruciatingly painful and has many serious side effects.

Approximately 100 million women and girls alive today have had their genitals mutilated by cutting out their clitoris and/or vaginal lips.

Frequency and Support More than 100 million women alive today have had these procedures inflicted upon them. Rather than diminishing with modernization and increasingly public outcry globally, the practice appears to be spreading. In those countries where female genital mutilation is practiced, it is nearly universal, and it is sanctioned by strong patriarchal traditions. Even those who privately oppose it allow the procedure and intend to continue the practice. Failure to do so will make their daughters "different" or "promiscuous" and perhaps unmarriageable as a result.

FACT

This practice affects approximately 100 million women and girls today.

As shown in Table 3.1, data obtained from a large national sample of residents of Sudan show that women from diverse backgrounds favor the continuation of female genital mutilation, and the majority plan to have their daughters circumcised or infibulated (Williams & Sobieszczyk, 1997). Close to 90 percent of all women surveyed either had the procedure performed on their daughters or planned to do so. Support varied somewhat by age: 84 percent of women aged 23–24 have had or plan to have all their daughters circumcised or infibulated, compared to 92 percent of women aged 45–59. Nearly one-half of women who support some type of procedure favor continuation of the most severe form of infibulation. Those who favor the continuation of complete infibulation include women who (1) were also infibu-

lated themselves (52 percent), (2) have husbands who support it (48 percent), (3) have only an elementary education or less (42 percent), (4) reside in a rural area (43 percent), and (5) do not have electricity in the home (41 percent). These categories represent sizable portions of Sudanese society.

Few Sudanese women oppose circumcision outright. Women who are most likely to oppose the practice are those who have not been circumcised or infibulated themselves, are college educated, or have husbands who believe the custom should stop. But these groups are small in number in Sudanese society.

The health consequences of genital mutilation are swift, long lasting, severe, and include much more than a loss of sexual pleasure. Immediate consequences include possible shock, hemorrhaging, or bleeding to death. Soon afterwards, women face possible pelvic infection, dangerous scarring, and internal pain from urination and menstrual fluids that cannot properly escape the body. As the women mature, they may experience infertility, a greater likelihood of miscarriage, recurrent urinary tract infections, anal incontinence, and fissures. Intercourse will be painful, childbirth will be prolonged and obstructed, it is likely that the perineal area will be lacerated, and there is a greater chance of stillborn births.

The Roots of Female Genital Mutilation Why is this practice so popular, and why has it continued for so many years? It is deeply rooted in the patriarchal traditions in these societies. Women are expected to be subject to the control of men at all times, including sexually. Although no religion formally endorses female genital mutilation, it is widespread because of customs demanding that women be virgins at the time of marriage and insisting that they remain sexually faithful thereafter. Removing the clitoris, the source of women's sexual pleasure, ensures

| Respondent's Age in Years | ALL DAUGHTERS ARE OR WILL BE CIRCUMCISED (%) | FAVOR CONTINUATION | | | NUMBER OF CASES |
		NOT AT ALL (%)	MILD FORM ONLY (%)	SEVERE FORM (%)	
15–19	89*	13	47	40	98
20–24	84	20	42	38	444
25–29	86	19	45	36	861
30–34	88	17	45	38	714
35–39	90	17	43	40	809
40–44	89	17	39	44	476
45–49	92	17	38	45	403
Respondent Circumcised					
Not Circumcised	18	84	14	2	432
Less Severe	96	7	91	2	517
More Severe	97	10	38	52	2856
Husband's View					
Should Continue	100	2	50	48	2134
Should Stop	41	78	16	7	536
No Opinion	96	12	43	45	627
Opinion Unknown	79	27	42	31	508
Respondent's Education					
No Formal	86	17	41	42	2410
Primary	97	12	45	42	989
Secondary	83	33	52	15	368
Highest	34	74	24	3	38
Husband's Education					
No Formal	84	18	40	42	2002
Primary	96	11	43	46	1006
Secondary	92	20	50	30	648
Highest	65	50	44	7	149
Respondent's Current Residence					
Urban	88	22	45	33	1343
Rural	88	15	42	43	2462
Current Home Has Electricity					
Yes	90	23	42	35	1156
No	87	16	43	41	2649

TABLE 3.1 Percentage of Women Who Have or Plan to Have their Daughters Circumcised, by Selected Socioeconomic and Demographic Characteristics (Sudan Demographic and Health Survey, 1989–1990; N = 5,868)

*Data have been rounded to the next whole number.
Source: Adapted from Williams and Sobieszcyk, 1997.

Female genital mutilation has touched the lives of millions of women worldwide. Some of them live in the United States and Canada. Fatima, aged thirty-nine, was born and raised in Somalia before migrating to Canada, where she now lives. Canada, like other Western nations, has outlawed genital mutilation practices within its borders, but women often move there from other countries where they underwent the procedure as children. They were forced to undergo the practice because of patriarchal customs "rooted in superstitious contempt of women so deep that its victims, their mothers and daughters pay homage to the knife that mutilates them" (Rosenthal, 1993). Precise estimates are unknown, but it is likely that hundreds of thousands of infibulated and "circumcised" women now live in Western nations. Fatima describes the infibulation that took place when she was six years of age, and the ordeals that she has suffered since:

My sister, who is a year older, had it done on the same day I did. Four women held me down, spread my legs apart, and used a razor blade to amputate my clitoris and all of my vaginal lips. A thorn was used to sew the raw flesh together. . . . After the procedure was done, my legs were bound together from my heels to my thighs to stop me from moving. When my sister urinated, blood came out with the urine. It

scared me to death. I was unable to urinate at all. After three days, the thorns were removed. The next two weeks were an ordeal for both of us: I could only walk in small steps so that the wound wouldn't unseal while it was healing. But the real pain started at the age of 13 with the onset of my periods. I experienced terrible cramps and my periods were interminable. The blood could barely escape out of my vagina because I was stitched up so tightly. I met my husband in Somalia. . . . I was very frightened about our wedding night—that's when a man makes sure his bride is closed up and still a virgin. The following day, my vaginal area was frozen and I was literally cut open. If a man insists on having sex that same day, it's agonizing, but my husband was understanding and waited a few days for the area to heal. Even so, it was very painful. As a woman, I always expected sex to be painful. In Somalia, only a man has the right to enjoy sex. Although I have a loving husband, I still remember how scared I was on my wedding night, and I think about the pain. It's always been this way, so I don't know what I'm missing. . . . I've had problems giving birth too. Infibulation creates tough, hard scar tissue that can't dilate, so there's not enough room for the baby's head to come

out. I was in labor for three days with my first child and given an extended episiotomy. Some men insist on their wives being reinfibulated or sewn back up after they give birth to make their vagina tight again. Thank goodness that didn't happen to me. My mother didn't mutilate me to hurt me. She did it to secure me a marriage. Now I have three daughters, all under the age of ten. When they are older, they will thank me for having spared them from what I was forced to endure. (Ziv, 1997: 244–245)

Despite the illegality of female genital mutilation in the United States, evidence exists to suggest that it is happening here as well (Crossette, 1998). The U.S. Centers for Disease Control and Prevention estimated that more than 150,000 women and girls of African origin or ancestry in the United States may be at risk of having their genitals mutilated (Dugger, 1996). These procedures take place not in hospitals or surgical units but in the back alleys of our cities, or back in their homelands, and are conducted by men and women who often have no formal medical training.

Ahmed Guled is a recent immigrant to the United States from Somalia. His daughters are among the many girls who are at risk. The move from Somalia to Houston was not far enough to erase the cultural pressure that their father feels to radically alter the design of their bodies. He holds dear the all-American dream that his children, who now go to public elementary schools and are engrossed in American culture, will go to college and prosper in the United States. But he also clings to the belief that his daughters must have their clitorises cut off and their genital lips stitched together to preserve their virginity. He sees it as his parental responsibility. His wife concurs.

Many of the immigrant parents who are making these decisions about their daughters know little or nothing about female anatomy. They are told that if the clitoris is left alone, it will grow and drag on the ground; that if their daughters are left uncircumcised, they will be wild and will crave men; that no man from their home country will marry them uncircumcised; that circumcision aids in menstruation and childbirth (although the opposite is true in both cases); and that it is a religious—usually Islamic—requirement (although none of the major Islamic texts call directly for female genital mutilation). And so these women and their husbands come to the United States filled with misinformation and remain blindly dedicated to continuing this torturous tradition (Burstyn, 1995).

Changing this behavior will involve more than enacting a law. While laws prohibiting mutilation are an important first step, parents often circumvent the law by taking their daughters back to their country of origin to have the procedure done. Frequently, families will bring someone from the homeland to the United States to perform the circumcision or infibulation because it's cheaper to import someone to do it than it is to send several girls abroad. A taxi driver in Washington, D.C., who adamantly defends the practice says that he recently had his daughters altered this way. "I stood over her to make sure that she cut enough," he says. "I wasn't going to let my daughters have those things!" (Burstyn, 1995: 2–3).

Eliminating genital mutilation means finding a way to change the minds of parents like Guled. "What these women need is people who will educate them, not only about circumcision, but how to survive and assimilate in American society and still keep their culture and religion," said Miriam Diria, who assists refugees to the United States, and who is herself an ethnic Somali from Ethiopia.

Mimi Ramsey, another recent immigrant from Ethiopia, is devoting her life to educating immigrants in the United States about the horrors of female genital mutilation. She bows her head and prays aloud, "Please, God, save girls from being tortured." She is taking her message to the streets, meeting with parents in back alleys, in restaurants, and in their homes. At the Raleigh Studio, in Los Angeles, Ramsey gives a presentation and shows a film to an audience of thirty-two people. The viewers cannot help but cringe as they watch a young girl who is held down while the circumciser reaches for a razor blade. Mimi hangs her head and weeps. After the film, she can barely speak. Finally, she reveals her own story: "I was struggling and calling my mother. Little did I know that my mother had set me up. She paid for it to be done to me. My best friend was cut. She was my friend, my buddy. They did her the same day they did me, only she bled to death. What I'm doing now, I'm doing for her" (quoted in Burstyn, 1995: 9).

Sources: Adapted from Laura Ziv (1997, May). "The Horror of Female Genital Mutilation." *Cosmopolitan,* pp. 245–246; Linda Burstyn (1995). "Female Circumcision Comes to America." *Atlantic Unbound* [Online]. Available: http:/www.theatlantic.com/unbound/flasbks/fgm.htm; Barbara Crossette (1998, Mar. 23). "Mutilation Seen as Risk for the Girls of Immigrants." *New York Times,* sec. A, p. 3; Celia W. Dugger (1996, Dec. 28). "Tug of Taboos: African Genital Rite vs. American Law." *New York Times,* sec. A, p. 1; Abe M. Rosenthal (1993, July 27). "The Torture Continues." *New York Times,* sec. A, p. 13.

Critical Thinking

1. Is it ethnocentric of Americans and Europeans to denounce this practice? Why or why not?

2. Why is such a painful procedure practiced in many parts of the world?

3. How is female genital mutilation an example of patriarchy?

that they will not experience orgasm; thus, the likelihood of engaging in or enjoying sexual relationships outside of marriage is lessened. Among women whose entire external genital area has been removed, the opening that remains is so small as to forbid penetration. Husbands are virtually guaranteed that their wives are virgins. Intercourse is exceedingly difficult to accomplish and generally must be preceded by further cutting, tearing, or ripping to enlarge the opening.

Female genital mutilation persists because women's status is low and their options are few. Marriage and motherhood are the primary ways in which women receive recognition. Without marriage, they bring shame to themselves and to their families. Virginity is highly valued, and this procedure helps ensure that women's sexuality will be muted. If they are not circumcised or infibulated as customs decree, then their chances of finding a husband will be considerably reduced.

A small but growing number of women who have undergone mutilation are becoming more outspoken against the horrors of this practice. Local self-help groups are trying to educate others about its dangers, health consequences, and consequences for the status of women. The number of women speaking out and seeking change is also growing in Western nations, where many African women have migrated as adults. In the Family Narratives box on pages 102–103, a woman from Somalia who currently lives in Canada speaks out about her ordeal with genital mutilation as a child and the problems she has faced throughout her life because of it.

Many Western nations have now banned the practice within their own borders and in some cases are actively trying to put an end to it in those countries where it is performed by assisting local organizations to educate residents of its dangers (Dugger, 1996; Mann, 1994). Although some local residents have become outspoken critics of female genital mutilation, others are outraged that the United States and other Western nations are taking such a public stance in opposition of the practice. "We were taught that this was a way of ensuring a girl's good behavior," says one Somalian mother (Dugger, 1996), and she sees Western opposition as an attempt to obliterate a unique aspect of her cultural heritage.

Does Patriarchy Exist in the United States?

The United States is not without its own set of patriarchal norms and customs. A close look reveals a variety of ways in which male dominance pervades our social institutions. For example, most women routinely take their husband's last name when they marry (Scheuble & Johnson, 1993). Rarely do women keep their own name or hyphenate their name with their husband's. When Melissa Smith marries John Brown, she usually goes by the new name of Melissa Brown, or she may be called Mrs. John Brown, taking on both his first and last name. A study conducted in the Midwest with 258 college students found that 82 percent of college women planned to change their name to that of their spouse if they married, while another 7 percent reported that they would hyphenate their name with that of their husband's (Scheuble & Johnson, 1993).

Why does this custom persist? Some people may answer, "It's easier this way." "It helps make us a family to have the same name." "Why burden children with parents who have different last names from one another, or a long hyphenated name?" "It works out better this way for children's school and medical records." There are many reasons why it may be easier to have only one last name in a family. However, opposing arguments could also be made: changing one's name on all pertinent legal documents is time-consuming and confusing, and name changes can interfere with one's career trajectory or family history. Regardless of where one stands on the issue, it is important to note that the persons likely to change their last names at marriage are not randomly selected. It is virtually always *wives* who change their last name; husbands rarely do. The changing of wives' names is a carryover from older patriarchal customs where, upon marriage, a woman became the legal property of her husband.

The Construction of Gender

According to a famous Mother Goose nursery rhyme,

> What are little boys made of, made of?
> What are little boys made of?
> Frogs and snails
> And puppy-dog tails,
> That's what little boys are made of.
> What are little girls made of, made of?
> What are little girls made of?
> Sugar and spice
> And all things nice
> That's what little girls are made of.

Some people suggest that men and women have very different personality traits. Men are often considered to be naturally more aggressive, strong, and independent, whereas women may be considered more emotional, nurturing, and sensitive. Traditionally, people view masculinity and femininity as a set of distinct or even polar opposite traits. This philosophy suggests that men and women are complementary in nature, but the implications of this idea are that men and women are distinctly different and have little in common with each other.

Modern social science and biological research casts doubt on many of these assumptions, noting that men and women are far more alike than different (Lips, 1997). Yet researchers do note that men and women

are not identical—their differences extend beyond the biological ones necessary for reproduction.

FACT OR FICTION?

All differences between men and women are rooted in biology.

Some differences may be attributed to biology, including hormonal differences, such as women's higher levels of estrogen and progesterone, and men's higher levels of testosterone. This results in some of the biological differences well established in research (Deaux, 1984; Hyde & Linn, 1988; Maccoby & Jacklin, 1974). For example, infant mortality rates are higher among males, and their life expectancy is shorter (U.S. Bureau of the Census, *Statistical Abstract of the United States,* 2001). Males are affected by more genetic disorders and suffer from accidents at a higher rate than do females. However, despite being more vulnerable, males are, on average, physically stronger and more aggressive than females.

Given differences such as these, are other differences between men and women then due to "nature" or to "nurture"? That is, are they innate and biological, or are they learned in the social environment? Are they fixed, or are they flexible?

While there is no definitive answer yet, most social scientists suggest that differences are probably a result of both nature and nurture. That is, there is an interplay of biological and environmental factors operating. However, social scientists maintain that social and cultural factors are very powerful and that they shape biological factors. This can be clearly seen as we examine the wide variety of gendered expectations cross-culturally. What one culture defines as distinctly feminine behavior, another may see as quite masculine, as in the case of the well-known research by the famous anthropologist Margaret Mead (1935). She studied three tribes who lived within a short distance of one another in New Guinea. She found varying gendered expectations among the tribes. Among the Mundugumors, both men and women were aggressive and warlike. Both mothers and fathers displayed little warmth or tenderness toward their children. Among the Arapesh, the behavior of men and women was nearly the opposite. Both were nurturing and sensitive with their children and rarely engaged in aggressive competitive behavior with other tribes. Finally, in the Tchumbuli tribe, Dr. Mead found the reverse of what we would consider traditional gendered behavior. The women were the economic providers, while the men tended to care for the children. Cross-cultural research such as this, along with historical research that demonstrates a tremendous shift in gendered expectations over time, makes it difficult to deny the importance of social and cultural influences. Clearly, gender is, at least to some degree, socially constructed.

FICTION

Although biological differences are real, other differences between men and women are produced through the process of socialization.

The Constructing Strong Families box on pages 108–109 contains a "gender test" borrowed from a web site that claims it can identify whether you are male or female with virtually 100-percent accuracy, based on your answers to fifty simple questions. Take the test, and see if the web site can correctly identify you.

Gender Learning   Where do we learn expected gender behavior? We learn it through a process called **socialization,** which is a process of interaction whereby individuals acquire the knowledge, skills, norms, and values of their society. Socialization begins at a very early age. These norms are then reinforced in interactions with others, and through social institutions. **Gender socialization** is the teaching of cultural norms associated with being male or female. It may be a conscious effort, as in the case of a parent scolding a young son for displaying his emotions ("big boys don't cry"), or less consciously, as in the case of parents providing different toys for their children—dolls for their daughters and trucks for their sons. The various **agents of socialization,** or the primary groups responsible for this socialization, are discussed in following sections.

Parents   Family members, particularly parents, play a pivotal role in socializing children, including socializing them to gendered norms and expectations. Parents provide the first exposure to a particular culture: "These experiences include where they live, what they eat, whom they see, what they wear, how they talk, what type of medical care they get, what type of work they do, and a host of other small and large things" (Coltrane, 1998: 112). These experiences vary by social class and by race or ethnicity. They also vary rather dramatically from one culture to another (Heath, 1995).

These experiences vary by gender as well, as sociologists, psychologists, and family scholars have repeatedly shown (Bem, 1993; Lips, 1997; Maccoby, 1998). Because many parents believe that girls and boys are supposed to be different, they treat them differently. Research shows that this differential treatment begins early: baby girls are held more gently and cuddled more than boys are, and are kept in a more confined area. Parents of infant girls will describe their children as more dainty and delicate than will parents of infant boys, and the choice of dress usually reflects this idea (Rubin, Provenzano, & Luria, 1974; Stern & Karraker, 1989). This process of differential treatment continues throughout childhood, repeating itself over and over so that a self-

Children learn their expected gender norms from parents and other family members, schools, toys, peers, and the mass media. Here a child practices vacuuming, just like her mother.

fulfilling prophecy occurs that manifests itself far beyond any true existing biological differences. Solely on the basis of sex, parents may assign rules, toys, expected behavior, chores, hobbies, and a multitude of other cultural values or artifacts differently. When girls and boys are treated differently, not surprisingly they become more different. This distinction is seen by many parents as only natural and therefore becomes reinforced.

Schools Schools are another arena in which gender socialization occurs (American Association of University Women, 1992; Orenstein, 1994; Thorne & Luria, 1986). The **hidden curriculum,** which is the gender socialization that is taught informally in school, teaches girls to value silence, to value compliance, and to believe that academic achievement will mean forfeiting social desirability (Orenstein, 1994). For example, textbooks and readers predominantly tell stories of boys or men as main characters, relegating girls and women to the sidelines or showing them in a limited number of roles or occupations (Crabb & Bielawski, 1994). Although there has been considerable improvement in recent decades, one 1989 study found that two-thirds of the photographs in elementary school reading books still featured male characters (Purcell & Stewart, 1990). Compared to males, females are still overrepresented in domestic activities in children's books: cooking, cleaning, or taking care of children. Many of these books continue to have a wide circulation.

Sadker and Sadker (1994) report that teachers also contribute to socializing boys and girls differently. Boys are called on to answer questions more often than girls and are given more public praise by teachers. Teachers appear to have lower expectations for girls than boys—they solve the problem for the girls or give girls answers more quickly,

"Guys and girls are different in ways only *we* realize. In fact, without asking about your clothes, grooming, or chest, our Gender Test WILL predict, with 100 percent accuracy, whether you're a guy or a girl. How do we know? Well, deep down, your gender affects everything about you, from your favorite number to your views on Canada. If you're really wondering how the Gender Test works so well, realize that 4,750,463 people have taken the test (57 percent females; 43 percent males). And it's gotten smarter each time."

1. It's very important that you're honest during this test. Otherwise it wouldn't be as astounding when we guess your gender. So please think carefully about each question. Now, which shape do you prefer?

▢ ◯

2. Which color makes a better tee-shirt?

__green   __orange

3. Please pick a number.

__1   __6

4. Would you rather print or use cursive?

__print   __cursive

5. Would you rather be rich or famous?

__rich   __famous

6. On a camping adventure, you get separated from your friends. You haven't seen them in hours and you're completely alone in the woods. Would you . . .

__look for them   __stay put

7. Which is better, a happy ending or a total surprise?

__happy ending __total surprise

8. Would you rather fall to your death or drown?

__fall   __drown

9. When you get a headache, do you usually take painkillers?

__ yes   __no

10. And would you rather be deaf or blind? Seriously.

__deaf   __blind

11. Do you ever think about the beginning of time and wish you could've been there to witness it?

__yes   __no

12. If given the choice, would you rather . . .

__live forever   __die happy

13. Scientifically speaking, which do you think came first?

__chicken   __egg

14. Are clams alive?

__yes   __no

15. Which animal is smarter?

__a horse   __a pig

16. Do you think that one day there will be world peace?

__yes   __no

17. Please choose one:

__French fries __onion rings

18. Do you like having your picture taken?

__yes   __no

19. Would you rather be hungry or cold?

__hungry   __cold

20. Are you afraid of death?

__yes   __no

21. Our claim that we can guess everyone's gender is "impressive" and yet "retarded," writes one Spark fan. Which is it?

__impressive   __retarded

22. Back to gender questions. So, would you rather live in a blue bedroom or a white bedroom? Picture this in your head.

__blue   __white

23. Does Canada suck or what?

__yes   __no

24. Which would you rather be?

__completely and forever lonely
__bleed to death

25. Do you sleep on your stomach or on your back?

__stomach __back

26. Which word is grosser?

__moist   __used

27. For years philosophers have debated over what determines the future. Some say that fate exists, and that choice is an illusion. Others believe that we make choices of our own free will. What do *you* believe in?

__fate __the ability to choose

28. More important, do you prefer to drink with a straw?

___yes ___no

29. Consider the following sequences.

□ ○ □ ○ □ ?

Please choose whichever object you think fills in the blank better

◇ ○

30. And which is a better way to ship things:

___in a truck ___ on a boat

31. If you had two jobs to do, which would you do first?

___the easier one, to leave time for the harder one

___the harder one, to get it out of the way

32. Scenario: If you don't have the money by Tuesday, the kid dies. You can't get the money. Do you . . .

___call the cops
___call the kid's parents

33. Which number do you think fits better in the blank: 2, 4 ___?

___6 ___8

34. College is worth both the time and the money.

___true ___false

35. Technology always prevails.

___true ___false

36. Who will win?

___a ___b

37. Myths are often based on fact.

___true ___false

38. What is the greater value of the Internet?

___information ___communication

39. Best friends can be worst enemies.

___true ___false

40. In a certain light, nuclear war would be exciting.

___true ___false

41. Which is more correct?

___blue (colored light)
___blue (dark)

42. Which would you really prefer?

___a fair fight ___brass knuckles

43. Is consciousness an illusion?

___yes ___no

44. Do you associate better with people of your own gender?

___yes ___no

45. Do you like to go to the movies by yourself?

___yes ___no

46. Which is a better nickname for a male porn star?

___Black Jack
___The Slot Machine

47. Stop and think about your middle name for a second. Does it end with a vowel?

___yes ___no

48. Do you usually carry stuff in your pockets?

___yes ___no

49. Which place is worse?

___the hospital
___a courtroom

50. And finally, were you born in an even or odd year?

___even ___odd

Source: "The Gender Test" (1999). Available online: www.thespark.com/gendertest. Accessed July 18, 2002. Reprinted with permission of The Spark.com. See web site for scoring.

Critical Thinking

1. Which questions and their answers can you identify as decidedly masculine or decidedly feminine? Why?

2. Why do you think that men and women score differently on this test?

3. Why have nearly five million persons taken this test (at the time of this writing)?

whereas they expect boys to solve the problem themselves. They found that while girls generally excel over boys in all areas during grade school, this begins to change in middle school, and by high school the reverse is true. In coed schools, intelligent girls are often devalued. Another survey of over three thousand boys and girls between the ages of nine and fifteen conducted by the American Association of University Women (AAUW) found that, during adolescence, girls' self-esteem and self-confidence, including academic self-confidence, drop at an alarming rate, while boys' do not. This is particularly troublesome for Latinas, where the number who respond that they are "happy with the way I am" plunges 38 percent between the ages of nine and fifteen, as compared to 33 percent for white girls and 7 percent for African American girls (AAUW, 1992):

> The AAUW discovered that the most dramatic gender gap in self-esteem is centered in the area of competence. Boys are more likely than girls to say they are "pretty good at a lot of things" and are twice as likely to name their talents as the thing they like most about themselves. Girls, meanwhile, cite aspects of their physical appearance. Unsurprisingly, then, teenage girls are much more likely than boys to say they are "not smart enough" or "not good enough" to achieve their dreams. (cited in Orenstein, 1994: xvi)

Teachers use a number of methods to segregate young boys and girls, including giving them different chores, separating boys and girls into different lines, and forming competitive teams with one sex against the other. This gender segregation is central to daily life in schools and has been found to account for more segregation than race (Shofield, 1982). Thorne and Luria (1986) conducted an observation study of fourth- and fifth-grade children in four different elementary school playgrounds, classrooms, hallways, and lunchrooms. They noted that the amount of segregation varied not only by situation but also by individual school. They found that in an upper-middle-class private school in Massachusetts, 65 percent of the playground clusters were same-gender, compared with 80 percent in a matched, middle-class public school. They report that these separate groups and ritualized, asymmetric relations between girls and boys lay the groundwork for more overt sexual scripts of adolescence.

Toys, Games, and Peers Children's toys, games, and their peers also reflect our gendered culture and teach children important messages about what it means to be a boy, girl, man, or woman in our culture. Play tends to be sex-typed, with toys, games, and peer-group play styles differentiated on the basis of sex. A quick trip to any children's toy store will reveal that certain pink aisles specialize in "girl toys" (dolls and their accessories, arts and crafts, domestic toys) whereas others are reserved for "boy toys" (war games, sport accessories, action figures). Even very young children learn that the "wrong" aisles are to be avoided. A toy as seemingly gender neutral as a bicycle takes on great gender significance by its color. Bicycles for boys are *not* painted pink with white wheels! Moreover, while both boys and girls play with dolls, the type of dolls they play with varies dramatically. Dolls often reinforce traditional stereotypes. "My Baby Bundle," manufactured by Mattel, is an infant doll in a padded pouch that can be worn around a child's stomach. By simply pressing a button, the child can feel the baby inside kick and can hear its heartbeat, simulating an experience with pregnancy (Lawson, 1992). As another example, approximately 99 percent of girls between the ages of three and ten in the United States own at least one Barbie doll (Greenwald, 1996), and their clothing and furniture accessories constitute a near billion-dollar business for Mattel. Barbie's unrealistic body shape has been criticized for encouraging girls to be overly concerned with their body and thinness. At a minimum, the focus of the Barbie culture is on clothing and glamour. In contrast, dolls for boys are referred to as "action figures," and the focus is usually on anything but glamour or parenthood. Action figures such as GI Joe are rugged and warlike.

Psychologist Eleanor Maccoby has conducted research on young children's play groups. She found that children between the ages of two and three tend to sort themselves into same-sex peer play groups when provided with the opportunity to do so (1998). She found that children were more social with children of the same sex than they were with children of the other sex. She also noted that when girls were playing with other girls, they were as active as were boys playing with other boys. However, when girls were playing with boys, they frequently stood back and let the boys dominate the toys or games. Maccoby speculated that boys' rougher play and greater focus on competition were unattractive to girls, and girls responded by pulling back rather than by trying to exert their own play style. She also asserts that these young peer groups reinforce different interaction styles that carry over into adulthood: boys' groups reinforce a more competitive, dominance-oriented style of interaction, which carries over into adult male communication patterns that include greater interrupting, contradicting, or boasting. Girls' cooperative groups reinforce a style that contributes to adult female communication patterns that include expressing agreement and acknowledging the comments of others, and asking questions rather than making bold pronouncements.

The Mass Media The mass media, especially television, are an increasingly important mechanism for socializing children. Pre-

Boys don't play with "dolls." Instead, they play with "action figures." Why don't we call these toys dolls?

school-age children watch an average of 28 hours of television a week, increasing among school-age children to 4–5 hours during each weekday and 10 hours on Saturday or Sunday. By a child's eighteenth birthday, he or she is likely to have watched 25,000 hours of television—far more time than was spent in school (Clinton, 1996). As is the case with books, boys, especially middle-class white boys, are usually at the center of most television programming, with the most roles and showing the most activity (Barcas, 1983; Seiter, 1993; Spicher & Hudak, 1997). There are four times as many male characters as female ones in the Saturday morning cartoon lineup, according to one recent study of 118 cartoon characters in the Saturday morning programs (Spicher & Hudak, 1997).

A study conducted in three communities in Canada reveals the role that television plays in shaping attitudes toward gender (Kimball, 1986). One community had no television programming, another had only one station, and the third community had four stations. Kimball found that children living in communities without television had significantly less stereotyped views about gender than did the children who lived in communities with television. Additionally, Kimball found that when television was introduced to the community previously without it, children's attitudes became more stereotyped.

Other forms of media also present explicit gender expectations. A recent review of the cover of a magazine targeted toward young teenage girls, *YM,* revealed the following articles or features in one issue: "Get Asked Out More Often!—Guys Tell You How," "The Love and Sex Report—15,000 Girls on Pressure, Bad Reps & How Long to Wait," "Romance Secrets of Your Fave Stars," "Look Irresistible!—95 New Hair & Makeup Tips," and "30 Ways to Have More Fun on Dates" (*YM,* February, 2000). The message that is being sent to girls is that looks, attractiveness, romance, and pleasing boys are of the utmost importance.

Variation by Class, Race, and Ethnicity

There are significant class, race, and ethnic variations in the gender socialization process. For example, Hale-Benson (1986) has studied the socialization process of African American families and suggests that African American girls are more likely than their white counterparts to be encouraged by their parents to be independent and self-reliant. Consequently, African American children appear to hold fewer gender stereotypes than do white children (Bardwell, Cochran, & Walker, 1986). Likewise, gender socialization also appears to vary by parental education, one dimension of social class. Parents who have higher levels of education appear to be less sex-typed in the raising of their children than do those parents who have less education (Bardwell, Cochran, & Walker, 1986).

Gender's Influence Upon Our Family and Close Relationships

While gender is forged into all aspects of social life, it is particularly evident within families and close relationships. Jesse Bernard, the late sociologist who continued to be a prolific writer into her nineties, first introduced the idea of "his and her" marriage (Bernard, 1973). She suggests that husbands and wives often have very different perceptions of their marriage and that they experience marriage and intimacy differently. Researchers have found that when they ask husbands and wives identical questions about their marriage, they receive substantially different replies, even to straightforward factual questions. Moreover, husbands report being more satisfied with marriage than do their wives, on average.

Family scholars have come to acknowledge that the family is a **gendered institution,** meaning that gender organizes the way that families are organized, the way in which members interact, their practices, and their distributions of power. Most facets of daily family living—taking care of the children, the division of household labor, decisions about where the family will reside, and employment practices—are not the same for women and for men. Feminists point out that families are structured toward **male privilege,** referring to the advantages, prerogatives, and benefits that systematically accrue to men and are denied to women.

Example: Division of Household Labor

A striking example of gender's influence on our family and close relationships is the division of household labor. Studies of housework and child care show that, on average, women spend considerably more time on these responsibilities than do men at all ages of the life cycle (Coltrane & Ishii-Kuntz, 1992; Greenstein, 1996; Risman & Johnson-Sumerford, 1998; Robinson & Godbey, 1997). One study reported that women spent an average of 38 hours per week on domestic labor, compared to 18 for men (Greenstein, 1996). A similar although less dramatic pattern occurs with child care. Moreover, significant differences continue when the wife is employed, and when both partners are retired, and these differences persist at all income levels.

One of the best explanations for why women do a disproportionate share of the household labor is that we have defined such work as simply part of being a woman. Gender is often viewed as a reasonable and legitimate basis for distributing rights and responsibilities. West and Zimmerman, in their famous article "Doing Gender," write the following: "It is not simply that household labor is designated as 'women's work,' but that for a woman to engage in it and a man not to engage in it is to draw on and exhibit the 'essential nature' of each" (1987: 144).

Research findings suggest that husbands do very little domestic labor unless both they and their wives actively support gender equality and equality in their marital roles (Greenstein, 1996). In fact, gender is so central to the division of household labor that wives and husbands often compare their household workloads to other wives and husbands, rather than to each other, because gender, rather than their spouse, is considered to be the appropriate point of reference (Thompson, 1991).

Race and Ethnicity

The United States is a richly diverse nation (Parrillo, 1996). Many people immigrated to the United States from Europe, Africa, and Asia. Some came willingly, and others were coerced. Together, they joined the Native Americans and Mexicans who were already here and flourishing with many different cultures and languages.

The tensions that often resulted from this diversity cannot be ignored. People have killed, maimed, and raped for the right to label their ethnicity, their culture, and their "way of life" as supreme. Some groups have been nearly **annihilated,** or exterminated in the struggle, as was the case with Native Americans. There were frequent bloody battles and conflicts with white Europeans. Europeans used tactics such as the deliberate spread of smallpox and other diseases to Native Americans, who had developed no resistance to such diseases. Eventually, Native Americans were forced from their lands and "resettled" with small plots of land on which to make their homes to minimize conflict.

The United States has not always respected the rich diversity found within our borders. From the forcing of Japanese Americans and Alaskan Natives out of their homes and businesses and into internment camps during World War II to the continued prejudice and discrimination that many African Americans, Asians, Latinos, and Native Americans endure, members of ethnic groups have faced real barriers to full participation in American life. Not surprisingly, minority groups have had to adapt to these constraints.

The U.S. Population Is Becoming More Diverse

Data from the U.S. Census Bureau indicate that the racial and ethnic background of the U.S. population is quickly becoming more diverse. For example, there has been a significant change in the country of origin among immigrants. While in 1900, the majority of persons immigrating to the United States came from Europe, by the 1980s this situation had changed considerably. During

© Tony Freeman/PhotoEdit

Hispanics currently comprise 13 percent of the U.S. population, but are expected to increase to 24 percent by 2050. Hispanic families are characterized as large and close-knit.

Alaska Natives will remain at less than 1 percent of our population. The largest increases will be found among Asian Americans and Hispanics. The proportion of Asian Americans is expected to almost double between 2000 and 2050, from 5 percent to 9 percent, while Hispanics are expected to increase from 13 percent to 24 percent (U.S. Bureau of the Census, *Statistical Abstract of the United States,* 2001). The Family Diversity box on page 116 describes some of the changes facing first- and second-generation Hispanics. As these figures demonstrate, race and ethnicity will continue to matter a great deal.

The next section explores the ways in which race and ethnicity influence family life and close relationships. It begins by introducing some major concepts in the study of ethnic and race relations.

Defining Race, Ethnicity, and Minority Group

Race, ethnicity, and *minority group* are common terms. But what do they really mean?

Race Theoretically, **race** is a category composed of people who share real or alleged physical traits that members of a society deem to be socially significant. In the United States, this usually includes physical features such as skin color or hair texture. Nineteenth-century biologists created a three-part classification of races: **Caucasian,** comprising those individuals with relatively light skin; **Negroid,** comprising people with darker skin and other characteristics, such as coarse, curly hair; and **Mongoloid,** comprising those individuals who have characteristics such as yellow or brown skin and folds on their eyelids (Simpson & Yinger, 1985). However, people throughout the world

the 1980s, four times as many Asians and four times as many Hispanics migrated to the United States as did Europeans. These groups fled persecution in their war-torn countries or sought better economic and educational opportunities. By the late 1990s, immigration from Asia and Latin America slowed somewhat, but it still exceeded immigration from Europe by approximately 100 percent (U.S. Census Bureau, *Statistical Abstract of the United States,* 2001).

Figure 3.1 illustrates future population projections. By 2005, 69 percent of the U.S. population is expected to be white non-Hispanic. By the year 2050, whites will likely constitute only 53 percent of the U.S. population. Meanwhile, the percentage of African Americans is expected to increase only slightly between 2005 and 2050, from 12 percent to 13 percent. Native Americans and

display a tremendous array of racial traits. For example, many African Americans have a significant portion of Caucasian genes because many female African slaves were raped and impregnated by their white owners. Some African Americans may, in fact, have lighter skin than many people who call themselves Caucasian.

Most social scientists today suggest that narrow conceptions of race are not particularly accurate. Nor are these conceptions a useful way to understand the diversity of experience in American society and throughout the world. Narrow classi-fications force us to lump together all Hispanic groups under the classification "Caucasian," including Mexican Americans, Cuban Americans, and Puerto Ricans, despite their significant differences.

Ethnicity Instead of race, looking at **ethnicity**—which is defined as shared cultural characteristics, such as language, place of origin, dress, food, religion, and other values—may be a more useful concept. Ethnicity represents culture, whereas race attempts to represent biological heritage. People who share specific cultural features are referred to as members of an **ethnic group.** There are many different ethnic groups in the United States, and hundreds throughout the world. Even Caucasians may identify themselves as members of ethnic groups, such as Polish, German, or Italian, if they share interrelated cultural characteristics with others.

| FACT

Social scientists find ethnicity to be more useful because it deals with culture whereas race is biological.

Minority Groups Not all ethnic groups are considered **minority groups.** Usually when we talk about minority groups, we are not talking about the size of the group per se, but

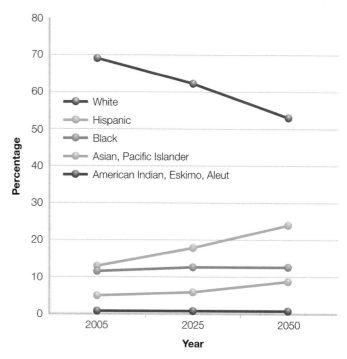

FIGURE 3.1 U.S. Population Projections, 2005–2050

Source: U.S. Bureau of the Census, *Statistical Abstract of the United States,* 2001.

rather a category of people who have less power than the dominant group and who are subject to unequal treatment. A minority group may categorically earn less money, have less representation in politics, and in other ways be socially disadvantaged. Most people would agree that all women and all people of color are members of minority groups; however, other ethnic groups such as Irish Americans are not. Minority groups experience negative treatment by other members of society. They may be denied opportunities or excluded from full participation in society. In some cases, minority groups may actually represent the statistical majority, as is the case with blacks in South Africa and with women in most societies around the world. Members of minority groups are often devalued and are treated with suspicion and contempt by other members of society.

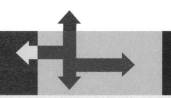

Hispanics are now the largest minority group in the United States, at nearly 13 percent, and they are at the cusp of a major change. In the past, their growth in numbers was due primarily to immigration. Large numbers of Hispanics migrated to the United States from Mexico, Central America, Cuba, and other regions. Now, however, the growth is fueled more by a high fertility rate. The population is expanding not so much because of immigration but because of children born to those immigrants.

This change poses many new and intriguing questions. How will the lives of the second generation be different from the first? Will the second generation do better economically? How much advantage comes from being raised and educated in the United States? Will the second generation speak English fluently? Will they retain their Spanish language and Hispanic culture? As their numbers grow, and as more are born in the United States, will prejudice or discrimination against Hispanics persist, will it change in format, or will it be largely eliminated?

A recent study for the Pew Hispanic Center attempts to answer some of these questions. Using data from the 1991 Current Population Survey from the U.S. Census Bureau, the authors found reason for optimism (Fry & Lowell, 2002). They report that there are strong indications that the majority of native-born children of Hispanic immigrants will move beyond the working-class jobs that are typical of their parents. Although the second generation is still largely young (four in ten are between sixteen and twenty-four years old), the early analyses indicate substantial economic gains from the first generation to the second. In looking to the future, they will likely receive more education, take jobs that demand greater skills, and be paid higher wages than the generation before them.

However, the news is not all good. The researchers predict that although the overall economic status of Hispanics is likely to improve, the movement forward is not nearly enough to bring the second generation to equality with non-Hispanic whites: "This large and

growing second generation, even though it is native born and a project of U.S. schools, seems likely to fall short of enjoying the kind of employment and the standard of living that most white Americans take for granted" (2002: 4). Why is this so? What role do you think prejudice or discrimination will continue to play? What other factors could account for the difference?

Source: Adapted from Richard Fry and B. Lindsay Lowell (2002). "Work or Study: Different Fortunes of U.S. Latino Generations." Pew Hispanic Center Report. Available online: www.pewhispanic.org.

Critical Thinking

1. How do prejudice and discrimination cease? Does a group need to become a statistical majority? Does the group need to completely assimilate (adopt the norms and values of the dominant group)?

2. What kinds of conflicts could emerge between first- and second-generation Hispanics? How are their lives different? Similar?

3. How do prejudice and discrimination affect families?

The next section discusses these forms of treatment.

Prejudice and Discrimination: Pervasive Problems

The late tennis star Arthur Ashe, an African American, was interviewed a few months prior to his death from AIDS. A sensitive reporter mentioned that the battle with AIDS, which Ashe contracted through a blood transfusion, must have been the heaviest burden he had ever had to bear. "No," Ashe responded. "It's a burden all right. . . . But being black is the greatest burden I've had to bear. Having to live as a minority in America. Even now it continues to feel like an extra weight tied around me. . . . Race is for me a more onerous burden than AIDS"

(Ashe & Rampersad, 1994: 126–127). He continued:

> My disease is a result of biological factors over which we, thus far, have had no control. Racism, however, is entirely made by people, and therefore it hurts and inconveniences infinitely more. . . . I am an optimist, not a pessimist. Still, a pall of sadness hangs over my life and the lives of most African Americans because of what we as a people have experienced historically in America, and what we as individuals experience each and every day. Whether one is a welfare recipient trapped in some blighted "housing project," or a former Wimbledon champion who is easily recognized on the streets and whose home is a luxurious apartment in one of the wealthiest districts in Manhattan, the sadness is still there. (Ashe & Rampersad, 1994: 127)

Ashe was speaking of the prejudice and discrimination experienced by minority group members. These are important but understudied phenomena that can profoundly affect stress, psychological functioning, and family relationships (Murry, Brown, Brody, Cutrona, & Simons, 2001).

| FACT OR FICTION?

Prejudice is an attitude, and discrimination is a behavior.

Prejudice   **Prejudice** is a negative attitude about members of selected racial and ethnic groups (Feagin & Feagin, 1994). It is a prejudgment that is usually negative, although not always so. Prejudice often comes from **stereotypes,** or an oversimplified set of beliefs about a group of people. For example, the stereotypes that African American girls have babies as teenagers, that Mexican Americans have many children, and that

A young boy lights a candle on the Kinara on December 26th, the first night of Kwanzaa. An increasing number of African Americans are joining in the celebration as a way to reclaim their family heritage.

Jews are stingy represent widespread prejudices that are prevalent in the United States. One recent study that was based on a large, nationally representative sample found that about half of white people stereotype African Americans as lacking motivation to improve their own lives (National Opinion Research Center, 1994).

Individual and Institutional Discrimination   While prejudice is an attitude, **discrimination** is a behavior. It involves actions or practices that have harmful impacts (Feagin & Feagin, 1994), and it can include the spoken or written word. Refusing to hire someone because of his or her race or ethnicity, refusing to sell your home to someone of a different ethnic background than your own, and demanding that your child switch teachers because of the teacher's race or ethnicity are examples of discrimination.

| FACT

Prejudice is an attitude, often resulting from stereotypes about certain groups.

Most of the time when we think about discrimination, we think of one person exhibiting a negative behavior toward another individual. This form of discrimination, appropriately called **individual discrimination,** is widespread and problematic. Although there are many laws that prohibit individual discrimination, it continues to occur and is often difficult to prove. However, we should also recognize that another form of discrimination exists that is at least as serious—**institutional discrimination.** This occurs when social institutions, such as the government, religion, and education, create policies and practices that are systematically disadvantageous to certain groups. Often, the resulting discrimination is unintentional and difficult to detect, thereby difficult to eradicate because the policies and practices are woven into the fabric of our culture and no one individual or group can be held accountable. Many people may not even question them because they are long-standing practices—"the way we always do things." For example, in 1994 the Denny's restaurant chain agreed to pay $45 million in damages to hundreds of African Americans in Maryland and California who filed a class-action suit alleging that they had been victims of discrimination by Denny's policies. They reported that the restaurant chain's policy included refusing service to them or requiring them to pay in advance for their meal. Similar allegations continue to occur. In May 1998, five customers of a Florida Denny's restaurant filed a lawsuit that claimed racial discrimination took place during their visit in August 1997. Two weeks prior to that lawsuit, a group of black sixth-grade boys from Baltimore also complained of discrimination related to poor service at yet another Denny's restaurant in Florida. Denny's asserts that the claims are frivolous and that the company has "become a lightning rod for this type of thing."

Another example: students in schools throughout the United States are routinely taught that Christopher Columbus "discovered" America, and we celebrate a holiday every year in his honor, Columbus Day. He is heralded as taming the savages who occupied the land and opening up the new world for the spread of European civilization. Yet this "truth" is really a social construction. Another version of the truth is that many people had been living rich and meaningful lives in this region long before Columbus and his associates sailed the seas. What might be the effect of this indoctrination on a Native American child who, all the while learning the virtues of Columbus's voyage, also knows that Columbus and his associates brought death and destruction to his or her people? More generally, how do prejudice and discrimination "feel" to their victim?

> Prejudice is something that you can't say, "It hurts my finger," or "It hurts here. Put the bandage here." You know it hurts. You don't know why. Maybe you say, "well, maybe I shouldn't think that. I should be above this." But you know it hurts. And it has an effect on you. . . . It stifles you. . . . It's little things that intimidate you that keep you from being your best. (Feagin, Vera, & Imani, 1996: 67–68)

How Do Race and Ethnicity Influence Our Family and Close Relationships?

This brief introduction to several key elements in the study of race and ethnicity leads us to wonder how they may influence family and close relationships. Do different racial and ethnic groups have different family patterns? The answer to that question is the proverbial "It depends," but many research studies do document key differences in family processes across racial and ethnic groups (Murry, 2000; Staples, 1994). For example, African Americans are more likely than whites to live in extended families; Native

Most ethnic groups, including African Americans, are far more likely to live in extended families than are whites.

Americans are more likely to be impoverished than other ethnic groups; Mexican Americans are less likely to have health insurance to cover their families' medical bills, which results in a variety of negative health outcomes for their families; and Vietnamese American teenagers are more likely to respect and defer to the wishes of their elders as compared to white, African American, and Latino teens (Kibria, 1997). Certainly, these are not absolutes: we are not suggesting that all African Americans live in extended families, that all Native Americans live in poverty, that all Mexican Americans are without health insurance, or that all Vietnamese teenagers comply with their parents' wishes. Instead of absolutes, we are describing tendencies, or the likelihood of these events occurring, in comparison with other groups. Two of these examples are elaborated below.

African Americans are more than twice as likely to live in an extended family than are whites.

Example: African Americans and Extended Families **Extended families** are those families that include not only parents and children but also other family members, such as grandparents, uncles, aunts, and cousins. Although extended families have never been the "typical" family structure in the United States, they were more prevalent in the past than they are today. The past century witnessed a long-term downward trend in the percentage of extended-family households and a movement toward **nuclear families,** consisting of only parents and their children. However, that downward trend in the prevalence of extended families was halted in the 1980s. The prevalence of extended families has begun to rise again, increasing from 10 percent of all households in 1980 to 12 percent in the 1990s. Extended families are more common among certain racial and ethnic groups, including recent immigrants and African Americans (Glick & Van Hook, 2002; Glick, Bean, & Van Hook, 1997).

Today, African Americans are more than twice as likely to live in extended families than are whites. Extended families may provide critical resources for the poor, and since African Americans are more likely than whites to be poor, part of the difference can be attributed to the need to pool income in order to survive. Families that pool their resources are more able to provide the necessities of food, shelter, and clothing.

FACT

African Americans at all income levels are more likely to live in an extended family.

However, economics does not explain the entire picture. Extended families are not simply a survival strategy among the poor; African Americans are more likely than whites to live in extended families regardless of income level. Even upper-middle-class or wealthy African Americans are more likely to co-reside with other family members. Rather than seeing extended families as a response to a problem such as poverty, and therefore considered deviant, they should be understood as a family strength.

African American families have a rich cultural heritage of drawing upon and sharing aid with other family members. One recent study of 487 African American parents aged 18 to 34, drawn from the National Survey of Black Americans, found that parents most often nominated their parents as the person they could count on for child-care assistance and parental guidance (Hunter, 1997).

This rich family and cultural heritage of African Americans is grounded in rural folkways (Wilkinson, 1997). In the varied African countries from which they came, important family rites, rituals, and ceremonies maintained the strong intergenerational ties within families. Ancestor worship and a belief in "a spirit world" were common (*African Americans: Voices,* 1993). In 1518, the first ship of African slaves came to the West Indies, and in 1619, slaves were first brought to the United States. This period of harsh and brutal bondage molded the form, structure, and patterns of interaction that existed among African American families then and that persist today. Despite the break-up of families, the rampant rape of female slaves by their white owners, and forced mate selection, "the institution of slavery only acted to reinforce the close bond that had already existed between mother and child" (Ladner, 1971: 279). Historians have shown us that extended families were highly valued during times of slavery. A review of 2,200 ex-slave narratives collected in the 1930s highlights the important role that grandparents played in the African American community, including raising children. Although many families were cruelly broken up by the slave trade, with family members being sold off to other white owners, African Americans nonetheless keenly appreciated older relatives, real and fictive, and co-resided whenever possible (Covey & Lockman, 1996). Herbert Gutman's *The Black Family in Slavery and Freedom* (1976) examines plantation records and census data for a number of cities between 1880 and 1925, and documents that two-parent households prevailed during slavery and after emancipation. The primary reason that families were broken up was the selling off of slaves by their white owners. Even when slavery destroyed biological families, kinship networks were rewoven so that unrelated slaves could join in and be a part of a family. Children were often named after uncles, aunts, and grandparents in order to keep the family name and symbolic sense of lineage alive.

Hatchett and Jackson (1993) note several features of African American families today:

* a high degree of geographical closeness

* a strong sense of family and familial obligation
  * fluidity of household boundaries, with a greater willingness to take in relatives, both children and adults, if the need arises
  * frequent interaction with relatives
  * frequent extended family get-togethers for special occasions and holidays

* a system of mutual aid, with extended families providing closeness, intimacy, and help with the day-to-day routines of raising children

Yet, despite the many benefits that an extended family can offer, the dominant ideology in the United States suggests that extended families are dysfunctional in some way (Smith, 1993). Too much interdependence is seen as weak. The desire to share assistance, or co-reside with other family members, is sometimes seen as a reflection that something is wrong rather than as a family strength.

Our culture idealizes and glorifies the traditional nuclear family, which consists of a husband who is the primary breadwinner, a wife who is primarily devoted to the care of her biological children whether or not she is employed, and their children (Smith, 1993). As Baca Zinn and Eitzen suggest,

> Rather than trying to explain why family patterns deviate from the alleged "normal" family, researchers have found a more fruitful approach lies in investigating how families are connected with larger social and economic forces. By looking at the social situations and contexts that affect families, we have gained a better understanding of why the family lives of people of color have never fit the mainstream model. (1996: 74)

Example: Mexican Americans and Health Insurance Health insurance is an important mechanism by which individuals and families in the United States access the health care system when they are sick or injured. Without insurance, many people are turned away at hospitals, doctors' offices, and clinics all over the country. The uninsured forgo visits to the doctor for all but the most urgent of conditions, they endure more suffering and disability, and they are more likely to die than those who have insurance (U.S. Congress, Office of Technology Assessment, 1992; Seccombe, 1995). They receive little preventive or primary care and must delay treatment until their conditions are serious and disabling (O'Brien & Feder, 1998; Wiegers, Weinick, & Cohen, 1998).

Unlike the health care systems in almost all industrialized nations (for example, Canada, Japan, England, France, and Australia) and many nonindustrialized nations, access to health care is not guaranteed to all Americans. In the United States, health care is not financed out of general tax revenues. Instead, when people become sick or injured, they must pay their own health care bills or rely on their health insurance policy to do so.

Most people who have health insurance receive it through their employer as a fringe benefit attached to their jobs. Usually, basic insurance covers only the individual worker, but for an extra charge the worker can include other members of his or her family on the policy. Unfortunately, not all employers offer health insurance to their workers or to their families. Employers are not required to do so, and many choose not to in order to save costs.

Consequently, 39 million persons, or approximately 14 percent of the population, lack health insurance in the United States (U.S. Census Bureau, Public Information Office, September 28, 2001). Some of these individuals are unemployed (or are dependents of the unemployed) and therefore do not have an employer to provide this benefit. Most, however, are employed but work at small businesses or in certain industries that do not provide this benefit to their employees. They do not qualify for Medicaid, Medicare, or any other public insurance programs and have no insurance program to help them pay for their medical bills. An additional 25–48 million people have insurance that is so inadequate that they would have great difficulty paying their medical bills if a health problem emerged (Weissman, 1996).

Not all of those who lack health insurance are adults. Fourteen percent of children under age fifteen have no health insurance at all from any source. These children are less likely to receive necessary immunizations and may be forced to forgo important periodic check-ups. Not surprisingly, they are sick more often than children with insurance and miss more school days as a result. They may fall behind in their education because of their illnesses or numerous sick days. Thus, being without insurance constitutes a serious social risk. Uninsured children are less likely to have a primary family physician and are more likely to use emergency rooms for their care. The doctors they see may lack the familiarity to assess and treat them properly, and may lack the rapport needed to advise a child's parents on a wide range of preventive measures as a private physician would do.

According to national data, Hispanic groups are particularly disadvantaged with respect to having health insurance. Approximately one-third of Hispanics are uninsured, compared to about 14 percent of Americans overall. Researchers have found that, of all Hispanic groups, Mexican Americans are the least likely to have health insurance (Amey, Seccombe, & Duncan, 1995). Only 52 percent of Mexican American families had insurance coverage for their entire family, as compared to 76 percent of Puerto Rican and Cuban families. Some of this is due to the unusually high unemployment rate among Mexican Americans. In October of 2001, the unemployment rate among first-generation Mexican Americans was 6.0, compared to 4.1 for non-Hispanic whites and 8.7 percent for second-generation Mexican Americans (Gonzales, 2002). Moreover, when employed, Mexican Americans are overrepresented in jobs where health insurance is not provided by an employer, such as agricultural work.

What does this mean for Mexican American families? Economic security is tenuous for any family when even one member is uninsured. One medical event can exhaust financial resources and pull a family into poverty. Mexican American families are particularly vulnerable to these conditions, and their family members suffer as a result. Children and adults are likely to go without needed health care and immunizations. Pregnant women are likely to forgo prenatal care, possibly resulting in a variety of negative health outcomes for themselves and their baby alike. To get the medical care they require may exhaust or seriously tax their financial resources. It is not a coincidence that Mexican American families, the group least likely to have insurance, are also more likely to live below the poverty line than are other Hispanic groups. Income and health insurance status are interrelated, and poverty can be both a cause and a consequence of the vulnerability of living without health insurance.

Social Class

It comes as no surprise to hear that income and wealth are unequally distributed in the United States. What may be more surprising is that disparities have grown in the past several decades. The rich are getting richer, and the poor are getting poorer. The magnitude in the inequality and the size of its growth are startling, given the strong economy during the 1990s.

Income, Wealth, and Inequality

Income refers to wages or earnings from employment or investments, while **wealth** is the total value of money and other assets, minus any outstanding debts. Wealth includes such items as stocks, bonds, and real estate. Figure 3.2 indicates the distribution of income in the United States. Commonly, the population is broken down into **quintiles,** or fifths of equal size. Twenty percent of the population resides in each quintile. Using this breakdown, we can see the distribution of resources among quintiles.

In an egalitarian society, all quintiles would have the same amount of income and wealth. We see that this is definitely not the case in the United States. Instead, the richest quintile earns approximately 47 percent of the income, while the poorest quintile earns only 4 percent (U.S. Census Bureau, *Statistical Abstract of the United States,* 2001). Moreover, the share of earnings received since 1980 has decreased for all quintiles, except among the highest-earning group. The rich have gotten richer, while middle- and low-income groups have lost ground. Moreover, the highest 5 percent of earners have made the most tremendous gains. Their share of income increased from 15 percent to 20 percent between 1980 and 1999.

Wealth is even more unequally distributed than is income in the United States. As illustrated in Table 3.2, families earning at least $100,000 per year have a median net worth of $511,000 and a mean net worth of $1,728,000. In comparison, families earning less than $10,000 have a median net worth of only $3,600 and a mean of $40,000. (The mean is skewed upward because of the

significant wealth of a few.) This disparity obviously translates into very different spending and consumption patterns.

Approaches to Measuring Social Class

Social class is an obscure concept, when compared to gender or ethnicity, because social class groups in the United States are not

FIGURE 3.2   Share of Aggregate Income Received by Each Fifth and Top 5 Percent of Families (1980–1999)

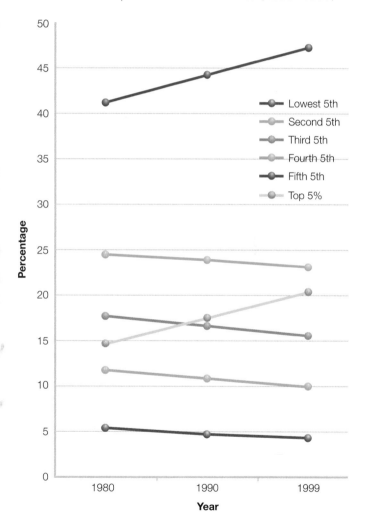

Source: U.S. Bureau of the Census, *Statistical Abstract of the United States,* 2001.

TABLE 3.2	Mean Family Net Worth in Constant (1998) Dollars, by Family Income		
FAMILY INCOME IN CONSTANT 1998 DOLLARS	PERCENTAGE OF FAMILIES	MEDIAN NET WORTH	MEAN NET WORTH
Less than $10,000	13	$3,600	$40,000
$10,000–$24,999	25	$24,800	$85,600
$25,000–$49,999	29	$60,300	$135,400
$50,000–$99,999	25	$152,000	$275,500
$100,000 and more	9	$510,800	$1,727,800

Source: U.S. Bureau of the Census, *Statistical Abstract of the United States,* 2001.

easily defined. Nor can we readily identify which people belong to which class. Social class boundaries are theoretically open so that people who gain schooling, skills, or income may experience a change in their social class position. However, we do know that social classes exist in a hierarchy and that they are based on income and wealth most apparently, but also on other resources, such as occupational prestige and educational level.

For Karl Marx, the nineteenth-century German economist and philosopher, one's social class results from one's relationship to the means of production. The capitalist class, or the **bourgeoisie,** owns the means of production. They own the land and money needed to operate factories and businesses, for example. Meanwhile, the **proletariat** are those individuals who must sell their labor to the owners in order to earn enough money to survive.

Max Weber, in contrast, developed a multidimensional approach, emphasizing (1) **wealth,** which, as we mentioned, is the value of all of a person's or a family's economic assets, including income, real estate, stocks, bonds, and other items of economic worth, minus debt; (2) **prestige,** defined as the esteem or respect a person is afforded; and (3) **power,** defined as the ability to achieve goals, wishes, and desires even in the face of opposition from others.

These differing views show us the complexity in defining social class with keen precision. It is also not clear how many social classes exist in the United States. While it might be safest to think of class as a continuum, for practical purposes most people tend to think of classes as categories. Today, people often define class as some combination of education, occupation, and income, and we sometimes call this **socioeconomic status (SES).** Sociologists have developed models of social class based on SES. One model includes six categories: (1) the upper class, (2) the upper middle class, (3) the middle class, (4) the working class, (5) the working poor, and (6) the underclass.

The Upper Class The upper class is the wealthiest and most powerful social class in the United States and consists of only about 5 percent of the population. Although this class is small in number, it has a tremendous influence upon the economy and the rest of society. Its members may have very high incomes, but more importantly, they own substantial wealth. They may be entrepreneurs, sit on the boards of major corporations, or get involved in politics by either running for

The upper class, who may live in mansions such as this, has tremendous influence and power in society.

office or by serving in key policy positions. Macionis (2001) suggests that the yearly income of the upper class is at least $145,200, although for many it exceeds that amount many times over.

Some families have been wealthy for generations. Names like Rockefeller, Kennedy, and Du Pont come to mind. These individuals and their families have been nicknamed "old money" or "bluebloods." They may belong to the exclusive *Social Register,* an annual listing of elites that has been published since the late 1800s, and prefer to socialize only with their peers. They belong to exclusive clubs, and their children attend private prep schools and Ivy League colleges, where applicants are carefully screened. There is very little mixing with other social classes; the Debutante Ball, which brings together unmarried young men and women to meet and socialize, carefully controls even dating. Researcher Susan Ostrander interviewed members of the upper class and asked them how they perceived their class position. As one respondent told her, "I hate to use the word 'class.' We are responsible, fortunate people, old families, the people who have something." Another respondent revealed that "I hate 'upper class.' It's so non-upper class to use it. I just call it 'all of us,' those who are wellborn" (Ostrander, 1980: 78–79).

Other members of the upper class, sometimes nicknamed "new money," have acquired their great wealth within one generation. They earned their money in business, entertainment, or sports. Despite their vast material possessions, which may be ostentatiously displayed, they lack the prestige of "bluebloods." Wealthy businessman Ross Perot, entertainer Oprah Winfrey, and real estate developer Donald Trump are examples of persons who have amassed great wealth within one generation.

The Upper Middle Class Approximately 20 percent of the U.S. population is categorized as "upper middle class." Persons in this group are often highly educated professionals who have built careers as physicians, dentists, lawyers, college professors, or business executives. Household income may be in the range of $75,000 to $150,000, perhaps even more if both husband and wife are employed. These families generally have accumulated some wealth, have nice homes in well-respected neighborhoods within the community, and play important roles in local political affairs. Education is strongly valued for their children: two-thirds of upper-middle-class children go on to college, and many continue into postgraduate education as their parents did.

The majority of Americans fall into the middle class.

The Middle Class With incomes of approximately $35,000 to $75,000 per year, 35 percent of the U.S. population can be thought of as "middle class." They are truly in the "middle," as the median household income in the United States is approximately $50,000 a year, so they fall squarely in this category. Members of the middle class work in occupations that may or may not require a college education and tend to be less prestigious on average than their upper-middle-class counterparts. Some occupations are classified as "white-collar" jobs, such as nurses, lower-level managers, and other semiprofessionals. Other occupations include highly skilled blue-collar jobs, such as in electronics or building construction. Traditionally, middle-class jobs have been secure and have provided a variety of opportunities for advancement; however, with corporate downsizing, escalating housing costs, and a generally rising cost of living, many middle-class families find their lives considerably more tenuous than in the past. Young middle-class families may find it difficult to purchase their first home in many cities around the country, and older middle-class families find that saving for both retirement and their children's college bills stretches their budget beyond its means. Consequently, it is increasingly common for both husband and wife to be employed outside the home.

Only one-third of Americans can be classified as middle class, with incomes between $35,000 and $75,000 per year.

The Working Class Members of the working class earn less than do middle-class families, and their lives are more vulnerable as a result. Approximately 25 percent of the U.S. population falls into this group. Some of these occupations may include those that require a short period of on-the-job training. Others require little more than basic literacy skills. Specific jobs may include salesclerks, factory workers, custodians, or semiskilled or unskilled laborers. Members of the working class report less satisfaction in their jobs than do those in higher social classes, and they experience less social mobility. The average income of working-class families is $15,000 to $35,000 per year, which is below the national average. Their income figures may be somewhat higher if both husband and wife are employed or if they work year-round. But these families generally live in modest neighborhoods and have difficulty sending their children to college, although many would like to. Family members must budget carefully to pay their monthly bills, as unexpected doctor or car-repair bills can wreak havoc on the family budget.

The Working Poor The working poor account for approximately 10 percent of the U.S. population. They are employed in minimum-wage or near-minimum-wage jobs, such as lower-paid factory jobs, seasonal migrant labor, or service workers in the fast-food or retail industry. Their wages are low, hovering near or only slightly above the poverty line, up to about $15,000 a year. Many workers receive no fringe benefits such as health insurance or sick pay. The working poor are very vulnerable. They live month to month and are unable to save money for the unforeseen but inevitable emergency. Unemployment is not uncommon. A sizable component of the working poor is represented by single mothers and their children. Some of these women intersperse work with bouts of welfare (Berrick, 1995; Edin & Lein, 1997; Seccombe, 1999). It is a vicious cycle: they work in a variety of low-wage jobs but then quit because the low wages and lack of benefits leave their families exceedingly vulnerable. They then seek the safety of welfare, where at least they can get their families' basic needs taken care of, such as food, shelter, and medical care. Then, faced with the stigma and hardship of day-to-day living on welfare, as revealed in the Family Diversity box on pages 128–130, they once again seek work. They begin their jobs with hopes for a better life, but once again they soon find that their health benefits have been reduced or eliminated, and their families are vulnerable once more. Then, again, they may turn to welfare for help.

Approximately 25 percent of the U.S. population falls into the category of "working class."

The Underclass The underclass, perhaps 3 percent to 5 percent of the population, comprises people who are extremely poor and often unemployed. Some cannot work because of disability or age. Others face difficult employment prospects because they lack education and job skills. Many reside in the inner cities, where job prospects are few because factories and businesses have moved out of town or overseas. Some, but not all, members of the underclass receive assistance from governmental welfare programs, perhaps drawing upon them for extended periods of time in order to live and survive. Their circumstances are bleak and may be exacerbated by racial or ethnic discrimination. Sociologist William Julius Wilson (1987) refers to these individuals as a "truly disadvantaged" underclass in America.

How Does Social Class Affect Our Family and Close Relationships?

Just as we saw with gender, race, and ethnicity, social class influences many aspects of family life. Consider the following two profiles.

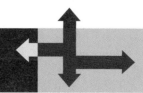

"Officials May Gain Welfare Insight" declares a recent headline in a Florida newspaper (*Gainesville Sun,* Sept. 2, 1997). A group of Florida legislators and state policy makers have signed up to be paired with a welfare recipient for one month "to walk a mile in the shoes of a welfare recipient." For thirty days, policy makers will talk on the telephone with their welfare "match" at least once a week, and they will do something with her related to her life, such as shopping with food stamps, visiting the welfare office, participating in training programs, or visiting a food bank. Perhaps most importantly during this month, they pledge to feed themselves and their families on a food stamp budget, although they will use cash rather than food stamps to purchase their food.

While this is an important step toward understanding the day-to-day experience of welfare recipients, it should not be confused with the actual realities of welfare existence. How is it different? The legislators' "welfare experience" is of short duration, takes place weekly at largely their convenience, and has a fixed beginning and ending point. They do not have to use "stigma symbols" such as food stamps during this period. Furthermore, they know that, at the end of thirty days, they may resume their upper-middle-class lifestyle, replete with expensive clothes, late-model cars, and dinners in lavish restaurants. Finally, because the experiment is

only temporary, there are no real decisions that need to be made to cope with the monotony, struggles, or stresses associated with poverty.

For welfare recipients in Florida, living with a child on $241 in cash and $208 in food stamps is not an experiment. In addition, many recipients would argue that it is not truly voluntary, that they are on welfare because they are "between a rock and a hard place, doing what I've got to do." Moreover, their stay on welfare is considerably longer than thirty days, and they do not have the security of returning to an upper-middle-class lifestyle afterwards. Women on welfare do not simply "rough it." Instead, they actually must learn how to live and survive on meager amounts, knowing full well that their financial circumstances may never improve considerably. Their clothes come from the thrift shops and garage sales, their cars are old and in disrepair, and dinners out are likely to be monthly excursions to a fast-food restaurant. Their stays on welfare are not an experiment. Unlike state legislators, women on welfare are not considered noble for enduring poverty of this magnitude.

What is life like on a day-to-day basis for someone who is poor? What kinds of decisions and struggles ensue, and how are these different from those faced by persons who are more affluent? Do the poor simply live a less-affluent version of the middle class dream and family ideal? Or have their lives

been significantly reconfigured in order to survive on a day-to-day basis?

Jana's life is a far cry from that of any state legislator's. She is a twenty-eight-year-old African American woman with four children. Her oldest child, a ten-year-old son, resides in a center for emotionally disturbed children located more than 120 miles away. Since Jana has no car, she relies on the Department of Health and Rehabilitation Services to take her to see him, but unfortunately, these visits are restricted to once a week. In between visits, she calls him on the telephone. "I miss him terribly," she told me.

Jana's other children are seven, four, and an eighteen-month-old toddler, all of whom live at home with her. She has, voluntarily, been sterilized so that she will have no more children. Their home is a dilapidated house in one of the poorest sections of town. The small two-bedroom structure sits on a small dirt lot without grass or other shrubbery. Walking up to the front door requires one to hop a series of makeshift steppingstones in order to prevent falling into large and deep holes in her yard. Several of these deep holes are adjacent to her front porch, a potentially dangerous situation for herself, her children, and visitors. From the front of the house, a broken living-room window was visible. No apparent attempt had been made to fix it. Thus, her house would be an easy target to burglarize, if only she had something to steal.

The brightly painted but chipping lime-green exterior of the house sharply contrasted with the brown, dark interior. The living room where we sat was very small and crowded. It was hot and stuffy, despite having the door wide open to a sunny 70-degree day in the middle of Florida's winter. The dirty dark carpet and the faded and well-worn furniture added to the dankness of the living room. A soiled blanket tacked up in the doorway partitioned off other rooms. Jana's home costs her $160 a month to rent, a sizable component of the $364 she receives in welfare aid and the $50 she receives some months in child support. Utilities average another $70 a month. The rent for her house is not subsidized, and she has no roommate. Thus, she pays approximately $230, or over half of her welfare grant and sporadic child support, for living quarters that, by most standards, would be deemed unfit and unsafe. However, her alternative, she tells me, is the housing projects, which she believes are even more stifling and dangerous for her children. Instead, they live month after month in their decaying house. Jana and her children will be there long after the Florida legislators have completed their noble month-long experiment and have gone back to their comfortable homes.

Jana has no telephone and no car. She cannot afford them, she tells me. Unlike most welfare recipients I met, she does not have an extended family network to help her out. She moved to Florida ten years ago to distance herself from an unhappy home life, "trying to make a change for myself." She chose Florida because an aunt lived there, but her aunt has since died. Jana is on her own, raising her children with only minimal help from the children's fathers. She has cultivated a strong friendship network to help out when needed, not surprising given her outgoing and gregarious personality. However, for the most part, if she cannot provide something for her children, they do without.

Her day-to-day living reflects both the tedium and struggle of being poor. It is tedious because it is predictable, month after month. There is little money for frivolous expenditures that add sparkle and interest to our lives. Jana takes no vacations, has no shopping trips to the mall, and rarely goes to a movie or out to dinner. She stays home day after day and takes care of her three children who live at home. She is up at 5:00 A.M. daily, awakened by her toddler, who shares her bed. "He gets up at 5 o'clock every morning. I mean every morning. And when he gets up, he gets out of bed and walks all the way around the house," she tells me sourly. There are no breaks. She has no husband or partner whom she can turn to and say "It's your turn." Instead, her day is spent getting her seven-year-old daughter off to school, taking care of her four-year-old and her toddler, cleaning the house, helping her daughter with homework when she returns from school, fixing dinner, and getting her family ready for bed. There is no money to vary the routine. She cannot hire a babysitter so that she can spend an evening out without her children. The tedium is stressful. "Sometimes I just go in my room and close the door and lay down on the bed. That's about all I can do. I just try to relax myself the best way I can because I get so stressed out sometimes that my head hurts. My head really hurts," she recounts.

Jana's life is also a constant struggle. It is not easy to pay the bills on time, to put food on the table, to pay for child care, to nurse sick children, to find a job, and to locate donations and charities to help benefits stretch throughout the month. A task as simple and common as grocery shopping poses its set of challenges. Without a car, and without a direct public transportation line, how does she get to the grocery store? With only $367 in food stamps, how can she buy enough food to feed her family for a month? Since food stamps cannot be used for nonfood items, how does she afford necessities like toilet paper, diapers for her baby, laundry detergent, cleaning supplies, and other toiletries and feminine hygiene products? "I use rags for just about everything, if you know what I mean," she winked.

For the more affluent, grocery shopping is a minor errand, conducted without a tremendous degree of thought. For Jana, like other

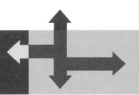

women on welfare, grocery shopping is a major ordeal and one that has to be dealt with every month. She does not like to rely on others and "owe" something to them, so she often walks to the grocery store, over a mile each way, taking her four-year-old and her baby with her. She "borrows" a shopping cart to tote them and haul her groceries in. Unfortunately, there are no sidewalks in her neighborhood, so she must take her montage out on the open roadway. Because of the logistical hassles, and to prevent herself from spending beyond her budget, Jana shops for groceries only once a month. Meals at the end of the month are "creative," she tells me, usually involving a dab of whatever she has left in the house. Peanut butter sandwiches made on day-old bread for several days in a row are not uncommon. "I try to make them with different kinds of jelly," she told me. Jana tries to avoid spending her welfare grant on food but usually finds that she runs short of food stamps and thus must spend thirty or forty dollars of her cash grant at the end of the month on food. When this is coupled with the additional fifty dollars she spends on nonfood necessities such as cleaning supplies, diapers, and toiletries, her meager welfare grant is virtually depleted for the month. She tries to squeeze out a family meal at a nearby fast-food restaurant, which they can walk to as a special monthly treat. Afterwards, there is little if anything left for a telephone, a car, or many other conveniences of modern living.

As we all know, unexpected costs or emergencies often impose upon even the best-made budgets. Buying a simple pair of children's shoes can wreak havoc in Jana's budget for the remainder of the month. What does Jana do when these unanticipated needs arise? Like other women on welfare, she lives month to month in a precarious

Example: "Tommy Johnson" and "Randall Simmons"

Profile 1

Name: Tommy Johnson

Age: twenty-nine

Father's occupation: janitor

Mother's occupation: nurse's aide

Community when growing up: Miami, Florida

Principal caretakers when a child: grandmother, neighbor, older sister

Education: Large public elementary and secondary schools in inner-city Miami. Emphasis on rote learning of basic skills. Security guards patrolled school. Occasional church camp during the summer. Classmates included sons and daughters of domestics, sales clerks, factory workers, service workers.

Family activities when a child: church, television, visiting with family members

First job: age sixteen, short-order cook at a fast-food restaurant in Miami

Hobbies: working on cars

College: Attended nearby community college. Quit after two semesters to take a full-time job.

First full-time job: age nineteen, sales clerk at auto parts store in Miami

Current position: Muffler installer at a national chain shop that is devoted to installing mufflers and brakes. Has been with the company for three years. Works Tuesday through Saturday, with occasional overtime. Annual earnings approximate $23,000 per year.

Marital status: Married at age twenty. Wife is employed part time, twenty hours per week as a sales clerk in a discount department store. Annual earnings approximate $8,000

juggling of bills. Paying her rent is her first priority, but on a couple of occasions the utility bill has gone unpaid and her electricity has been turned off. She vows to never let this happen again, as the turn-on charge is more than she can muster. She sometimes turns to the children's fathers, and they, on occasion, will buy the children food or clothing. She is also well versed in the location of charities, particularly those that will donate food. "See, I can get food. Food is no problem because they have the Catholic Charities and they will give you food when you need it. In addition, there is the Salvation Army and the Community Ministries. There are different places that you can go to and get help for food," she informs me. So she doesn't really feel that she or her children have ever gone to bed hungry. But without a telephone, and without transportation, even getting free help poses a difficulty. Therefore, instead, she usually ends up spending a portion of her cash benefit on food. Jana's day-to-day living, as is the case for the other women interviewed, is a nearly constant struggle in order to obtain a standard of living that falls well below what most people in the United States simply take for granted.

Source: Adapted from Karen Seccombe (1999). *"So You Think I Drive a Cadillac?" Welfare Recipients' Perspectives on the System and Its Reform.* Needham Heights, MA: Allyn & Bacon. Copyright © 1999 by Pearson Education. Adapted by permission of the publisher.

Critical Thinking

1. Why do you think that Jana is poor? Why can't she get out of poverty?

2. Do you think that the policy makers will gain a good understanding of what it is like to be poor? Why or why not?

3. How similar do you think Jana is to other welfare recipients?

---

a year. Together they have three children, aged seven, five, and two.

Family activities: bowling, church, watching television, city league baseball, visiting with other relatives.

Current residence: Owns a small, three-bedroom mobile home located in a trailer park in a lower-income Miami suburb. Comfortably furnished with older and well-worn furniture and appliances. Has two cars, a Ford Escort and a minivan, both of which are over seven years old.

Goals: To someday manage his own auto parts store, to send children to vocational college to learn a "good trade," and to be a good father and provider to his family.

Profile 2

Name: Randall Simmons

Age: twenty-nine

Father's occupation: real estate attorney

Mother's occupation: housewife and community volunteer

Principal caretakers when a child: mother and governess

Community when growing up: Beverly Hills, California

Education: Private elementary and secondary schools devoted to liberal and creative arts. Small student/teacher ratio. Supplemental tutoring in French, piano, clarinet. Fellow students were the sons and daughters of business leaders, physicians, and ambassadors. Spent summers in camps devoted to educational enrichment, including athletics and riding lessons.

Family activities as a child: Riding horses, theater, summer vacations in Europe, winter vacations at a condo in the Caribbean. His parents made generous donations to the performing arts community and were therefore granted season tickets for the family to music and dance events at the community theater.

First job: age twenty-six, attorney in large and prestigious law firm in West Los Angeles

Hobbies: riding horses (owns two horses, which are boarded approximately thirty five miles from home), golf, gourmet cooking

College attended: Bachelor of Arts degree from small, elite private college. Active in a campus fraternity and the college debate team. Attended law school at Stanford University, where father and uncle are alumni.

First full-time job: age twenty-six, attorney in large and prestigious law firm in West Los Angeles

Current job and earnings: Attorney in the same law firm. Works approximately fifty hours per week. Salaried, and annual salary approximates $200,000 a year. Also receives dividends of $150,000 a year from stocks and trust funds established by his wife's parents.

Marital status: Married at age twenty-seven. Wife is a community volunteer. She has a Bachelor of Arts degree in music from the same college as her husband. No children, but would like to have a baby within two or three years. Ideal family size is three children.

Family activities: international travel, theater, riding horses, golf at the country club

Current residence: 3,000-square-foot home in Pacific Palisades area of Los Angeles, located five blocks from a private beach on the Pacific Ocean. Parents helped with the down payment. Interior was professionally designed and furnished. Has two cars, a late-model BMW and a new Mercedes-Benz.

Goals: To make partner in law firm where he is currently employed within the next five to seven years.

Tommy Johnson and Randall Simmons, two young men who live in large metropolitan areas, could not have more different lives. The lifestyle of one is very economically privileged, the other considerably less so. Tommy and his wife could be described as being members of the working class. Both are employed, but their combined incomes afford a lifestyle significantly different from the lifestyle of Randall Simmons and his wife. Although both men work long hours and are highly motivated, the social class in which each was born has substantially shaped their opportunities, goals, and achievements. Tommy's parents were members of the working class; therefore, not surprisingly, he is also. Unlike Tommy, Randall grew up in a family that was able to lavish him with expensive trips and top-notch educational opportunities. He lived in a posh neighborhood. He received a wide variety of opportunities that were unavailable to Tommy, such as travel, music lessons, and riding lessons. Randall did not have to quit college in order to support himself; instead, he received extensive parental financial support that allowed him to attend an elite private university, to participate in extracurricular activities, and to graduate and further his education by attending law school. As expected, these opportunities have shaped his personal and family life and continue to influence him as an adult. They influenced his hobbies, his choice of mate, his choice of an occupation, and his type of residence. Theoretically, Americans can be anything they want to be, but in reality there is little substantial upward **social mobility,** or upward movement from one social class to another. People usually live out their lives in the same social class from which they come because of the norms that they learn and the constraints and privileges that they experience.

From Cradle to Grave From cradle to grave, social class standing has a significant impact on our lives in many ways. Briefly, class standing influences

1. our likelihood of being born in the first place, as birthrates are higher in lower classes

2. our health, including our chances of surviving the first year of life, and our overall life expectancy, which is dramatically less among lower-income groups

3. our gender expectations for boys and girls, men and women within the family, with egalitarian roles more likely to be found in the middle- and upper-middle-class groups, while upper and lower classes are more polarized

4. the values that parents socialize in their children, with working-class parents more likely to value conformity and obedience to authority, whereas middle- and upper-middle-class parents tend to value creativity and self-direction in their children

5. our likelihood of attending and graduating from college, with only part of the difference being due to finances per se, with much of the remainder related to the different value afforded to college education and the different structural constraints associated with being able to devote oneself full time to such pursuits

6. our dating and premarital sexual expectations and behavior, with girls from poorer households more likely to anticipate a nonmarital teen pregnancy, as well as more likely to have a child outside of marriage

7. our likelihood of marriage and age at first marriage, with upper-middle-class women less likely to marry than other groups and, when they do marry, marrying at later ages

8. our income and how money is spent in our family, with consumption patterns varying by social class

9. hobbies and pastimes within our families, with income shaping the way in which we view leisure and the opportunities we have to participate in leisure activities

10. the types of stresses we experience and coping mechanisms we employ, with wealthier individuals having a wider range of coping strategies available to them, such as travel, shopping, or working off stress physically in athletic clubs, whereas lower-income individuals may resort to coping mechanisms that provide a more immediate gratification, such as smoking or overeating

These are just a few of the many ways we are influenced throughout our lives by our social class membership.

FACT OR FICTION?

Gender, race and ethnicity, and social class interact and influence our opportunities, privileges, and constraints.

The Interaction of Gender, Race and Ethnicity, and Class

All people are affected by their social statuses: their gender, race or ethnicity, and social class. Moreover, these statuses interact with one another in many ways (Murry, Smith, & Hill, 2001). One is not simply male or female, rich or poor. For example, a person may be a white working-class male, a Chinese American upper-class male, an African American middle-class female, a white female in the upper class, or any multitude of combinations of statuses. Individually and collectively, these configurations influence our opportunities, privileges, and constraints. A study by family scholar Charlotte Olsen (1996) analyzed the opinions of African American adolescent women regarding their gender, race, and class as it related to their lives. She found that these young women felt that they had experienced male domination and male privilege, and saw these as major issues and potential obstacles for the achievement of their own life goals. Many instances of prejudice and discrimination were reported because of their race and gender. Most often they reported challenges and pitfalls with respect to getting a job and finding a husband of African American descent.

It is likely that Randall, the white affluent male featured above, would have different experiences had he been born of a different race, given the high degree of racism that persists in the United States. If he had been born poor, particularly a poor member of a minority group, his chances of making it to law school would be reduced, given the increased chances of going to poorly funded and inferior elementary and secondary schools. Moreover, had Randall been born female, her family may have steered her to other, more "feminine" pursuits instead of law. Perhaps "she" would be the nonemployed wife of a lawyer rather than a lawyer herself. And as a working-class minority female, the likelihood of her attending law school would be diminished even further.

Why is this? With financial aid seemingly available to all students, we must look beyond mere financial considerations. Women, ethnic and racial minority groups, and those persons within the lower social classes may have experienced different opportunities than affluent white males: they may be discouraged from attaining these goals by family, peers, and school counselors. For example, women may actively or more subtly be discouraged from graduate or professional school because of fears that a career will interfere with their ability to raise a family. When social class barriers or racial discrimination are added (e.g., having fewer role models or inadequate preparation because of attending poor secondary schools), it is not surprising that the entering classes in professional schools tend to reflect the background of Randall Simmons rather than of Tommy Johnson.

FACT

Gender, race and ethnicity, and social class interact with one another in important ways.

Conclusion

As this chapter has shown, gender, race and ethnicity, and social class are important to the study of marriages and families because they are important components of C. Wright Mills's position that many of our personal experiences are in large part shaped by broad social and cultural forces. Gender, race and ethnicity, and social class help to shape a constellation of privileges and constraints that follow into our personal relationships. These can result in having different life goals, opportunities, values, and choices. It is also critical that we recognize how these statuses interact with one another and shape our opportunities and constraints. One is not simply "rich." Rather, the privilege experienced by wealthy white men is likely to contrast vividly with the experience of wealthy Mexican American women, who must also deal with unique challenges associated with being a minority and female in the United States.

Chapter Review

＊ Why are gender, race and ethnicity, and social class important?

These three *social positions,* referred to as statuses, have a strong influence throughout our lives. Gender, race and ethnicity, and social class represent significant categories that shape our opportunities, constraints, and privileges.

＊ What is the sociological imagination?

The sociological imagination refers to the recognition that our personal experiences are, in large part, shaped by social forces within the larger society.

＊ What is the difference between sex and gender?

Sex refers to biological differences between men and women, and the role of these differences in reproduction; gender is the culturally and socially constructed differences between males and females found in the meanings, beliefs, and practices associated with "femininity" and "masculinity."

＊ What is patriarchy, and why is it important to the study of gender?

Patriarchy is a form of social organization in which the norm or expectation is that men have a natural right to be in control of women. Patriarchy is manifested and upheld in a wide variety of social institutions, including the legal, educational, religious, and economic institutions of society. Vestiges of patriarchy are found in virtually every society.

＊ What are two explicit examples of cross-cultural patriarchy?

Perhaps the two most vivid examples are female infanticide and female genital mutilation, both of which are practiced in many countries.

＊ How do we learn our gendered expectations?

Through a process of socialization. Agents of socialization include our parents, our teachers, and many other persons and entities. Conceptions of gender vary by race, ethnicity, and social class.

＊ Is the family a gendered institution?

Yes, gender contributes to the way that families are organized, how members interact, their practices, and the distributions of power.

＊ Is the United States becoming more diverse?

Yes. By the year 2050, projections are that whites will constitute approximately only 53 percent of the U.S. population. The largest increase will be among Asian and Hispanic groups.

＊ What is the difference between race and ethnicity, and which term is generally more useful?

Race is a biological concept. Ethnicity is generally far more useful because it focuses on shared cultural characteristics, such as language, place of origin, dress, food, religion, and other values. Ethnicity represents culture, whereas race attempts to represent biological heritage.

＊ What is the difference between individual and institutional discrimination?

Individual discrimination occurs when one person exhibits a negative behavior toward another individual. Institutional discrimination occurs when social institutions, such as the government, religion, and education, create policies and practices that are systematically disadvantageous to certain groups. The policies and practices are woven into the fabric of our culture.

＊ How many social classes are there?

There is no exact way to measure social class. A common typology compares and contrasts six categories: upper, upper middle, middle, working class, working poor, and the under-class.

* *How does social class affect our lives?*

Social class affects our lives in many ways, including the likelihood of being born, health status, gender expectations, the values that parents hold for their children, the likelihood of attending and graduating from college, dating and nonmarital sexual behavior, likelihood and age of marriage, income and consumption patterns, hobbies, and stress and coping mechanisms.

Key Terms

agents of socialization: the primary groups responsible for gender socialization

annihilated: exterminated

bourgeoisie: the capitalist class, which owns the means of production

Caucasian: part of a nineteenth-century biological definition of race comprising those individuals with relatively light skin

clitoridectomy: an operation in which the clitoris is cut out of the body

discrimination: behaviors, action, or practices that have harmful effects

ethnic group: people who share specific cultural features

ethnicity: shared cultural characteristics, such as language, place of origin, dress, food, and religion

extended families: families that include not only parents and children but also other family members, such as grandparents, uncles, aunts, and cousins

gender: culturally and socially constructed differences between males and females found in the meanings, beliefs, and practices associated with "femininity" and "masculinity"

gender socialization: teaching the cultural norms associated with being male or female

gendered institution: gender organizing the way that people are organized, the way that they interact, their practices, and the distributions of power

hidden curriculum: gender socialization that is taught informally in school

income: wages or earnings from employment or investments

individual discrimination: one person exhibiting a negative behavior toward another individual

infibulation: an operation in which the vaginal lips (and the clitoris) are cut or scraped away, and the outer portion of the vagina is stitched together

institutional discrimination: social institutions, such as the government, religion, and education, creating policies and practices that are systematically disadvantageous to certain groups

male privilege: the advantages, prerogatives, and benefits that feminists believe systematically accrue to men and are denied to women

minority group: a category of people who have less power than the dominant group and who are subject to unequal treatment

Mongoloid: part of a nineteenth-century biological definition of race, comprising individuals who have characteristics such as yellow or brown skin and folds on their eyelids

Negroid: part of a nineteenth-century biological definition of race, comprising people with darker skin and features such as coarse, curly hair

nuclear families: families consisting of only parents and their children

power: the ability to achieve goals, wishes, and desires even in the face of opposition from others

prejudice: a negative attitude about members of selected racial and ethnic groups

prestige: the esteem or respect a person is afforded

proletariat: those individuals who sell their labor to the owners

quintiles: the population as broken down into fifths of equal size

race: a category composed of people who share real or alleged physical traits that members of a society deem as socially significant

racism: the belief that certain racial or ethnic categories are innately superior or inferior to others

sex: the biological differences between men and women, and the role of these differences in reproduction

socialization: the process of interaction whereby individuals acquire the knowledge, skills, norms, and values of their society

social class: a hierarchy, based on income and wealth most apparently, but also on other resources, such as occupational prestige and educational level

social mobility: upward movement from one social class to another

social norms: expectations that our society holds

social stratification: the hierarchical ranking of categories of people within society

socioeconomic status (SES): a combination of education, occupation, and income

sociological imagination: the recognition that our personal experiences are, in large part, shaped by social forces within the larger society

stereotype: an oversimplified set of beliefs about a group of people

wealth: the total value of money and other assets, minus any outstanding debts

Resources on the Internet

These web sites have been selected for their relevance to the topics in this chapter. These sites are among the more stable, but please be aware that web site addresses change frequently.

Institute for Women's Policy Research
http://www.iwpr.org

The Institute for Women's Policy Research (IWPR) is a public policy research organization dedicated to informing and stimulating the debate on public policy issues of critical importance to women and their families. IWPR focuses on issues of poverty and welfare, employment and earnings, work and family issues, the economic and social aspects of health care and domestic violence, and women's civic and political participation.

National Organization for Women (NOW)
http://www.now.org

NOW is dedicated to making legal, political, social, and economic change in our society in order to achieve the goal of eliminating sexism and ending all oppression. NOW achieves its goals through direct mass actions (including marches, rallies, pickets, counter-demonstrations, and nonviolent civil disobedience), intensive lobbying, grassroots political organizing, and litigation (including class-action lawsuits).

Urban Institute
http://www.urban.org

The Urban Institute is a nonprofit nonpartisan policy research and educational organization established to examine the social, economic, and governance problems facing the nation. It provides information and analysis to public and private decision makers to help them address these challenges and strives to raise citizen understanding of these issues and trade-offs in policy making. Its work involves analysis of topics such as the working poor, welfare reform, and urban poverty.

National Association for the Advancement of Colored People (NAACP)
http://www.naacp.org

The primary focus of the NAACP continues to be the protection and enhancement of the civil rights of African Americans and other minorities. The NAACP works at the national, regional, and local levels to secure civil rights through advocacy for supportive legislation and by the implementation of its strategic initiatives. The NAACP also stands poised to defend civil rights wherever and whenever they are threatened.

Pew Hispanic Center

http://www.pewhispanic.org

The Pew Hispanic Center's mission is to improve understanding of the diverse Hispanic population in the United States and to chronicle Latinos' growing impact on the nation. The center strives to inform debate on critical issues through dissemination of its research to policy makers, business leaders, academic institutions, and the media.

Companion Web Site for This Book

Virtual Society: The Wadsworth Sociology Resource Center

http://sociology.wadsworth.com

Begin by clicking the Student Resources section. Next, click Marriage and Family, and then click the cover image for this book. Select from the pull-down menu the chapter you are presently studying. You will have easy access to chapter resources such as MicroCase Online exercises, additional Web links, flashcards, InfoTrac exercises, and practice tests (that can be scored). In addition, to enhance and help with your study of marriages and families, be sure to investigate the rest of the rich sociology resources at Virtual Society.

Visit InfoTrac College Edition

Another unique option available to you at the Student Resources section of the Virtual Society web site described above is InfoTrac College Edition, an online library of hundreds of scholarly and popular periodicals. Here are three suggested key search terms for this chapter:

* Search keywords: *poverty + female-headed household*
* Search keywords: *homelessness + mental illness*
* Search keywords: *health insurance + employment*

Search recent years to get the latest information on these family issues and to see articles that suggest solutions.

© Helen Norman /Corbis

The Meanings and Practices of Love

4

On a beautiful spring day, a man and woman met while wandering along a forest path. It was love at first sight. The young woman, thinking about what her guardians had told her about strangers, became nervous and returned home. The young man was distressed by her departure but was determined to find her again. After a long search, he arrived at her residence, but instead of seeing his true love, he was greeted by an evil woman. The man was captured and put into a prison cell. He was told that his true love had also been captured and put under a spell. The only way to break the spell was for the woman to be kissed by her true love. With the young woman in a trance and the young man in prison, it all seemed hopeless. Undaunted by his capture, however, feelings of love helped the young man struggle to free himself from prison. He hurried to find his true love, and on the way faced many struggles, including a direct confrontation with the evil woman. Victorious in his battle over evil, the young man found his true love and kissed her. She awakened, and they lived happily ever after. True love conquers all.

FACT OR FICTION?

"True love" defines a relationship that includes challenges and struggle.

This tale of love, as presented in the story of Sleeping Beauty, is a myth. It never happened. However, the elements of this story that make it the quintessential tale of love still resonate with us today (in Western culture). For example, the young couple falls in love at first sight. Many people believe in love at first sight, not only between romantic couples, but also between parents and children or between siblings and other family members. We often assume that love bonds us together in ways that are, in some ways, out of our control. It all seems so natural. Another important theme of this story is in its ending: "True love conquers all." If a couple that we know breaks up, we might believe that they were not really in love. If parents give up custody of their children, they must not have truly loved them. If best friends part and never communicate with each other again, the love they had for each other wasn't real. This belief in "true love" gives love a magical feature. It is something that just happens. It is love, or it is not.

However, maybe the most intriguing theme in our story of love is that at the very heart of this relationship is a struggle. The man in the story must fight against powerful, evil forces to get to his one true love. He never gives up. In other words, love isn't easy but is something that must be fought for. At first glance, this seems a bit contradictory. How can love be both about natural attraction and about struggle—at the same time? The reason is related to the notion that love is simultaneously an *ideal* and an *experience* (Swidler, 1980: 120). Ideals are part of our culture and help us set standards of what love should be. But they are often myths. Love in "real" life is not like love in "reel" life. The way that we experience love is shaped by the context in which it occurs. This means that love is related to historical periods and geographic space. Within those boundaries it is related to the social positions held by those in love (gender, age, social class, etc.). It is also related to the structural relationship of the people who love (parents and children, friends, romantic partners). All of these complexities make the attempt to achieve an ideal of love a challenge. Because we are all in different positions or situations in life, we all experience love in different ways. Still, within our culture we hold on to the ideals of love.

Although the "idea" of love is one that appears natural and unchanging, the "experience" of love takes place in a social context. As such, it is constantly challenged by situations specific to historical moments and social situations.

This chapter will address some of the complexities of the meanings and practices of love. In the first half of the chapter, we will begin by posing the question of "what is love?" Whether talking about love between parents and children, or between adults as lovers or friends, philosophers and social scientists have been intrigued by the varying ways that love has meaning for us. Next, we will cover the broad range of theories about how people experience love. This includes our understandings of how people are attached and/or attracted to one another and how they work to maintain love over time. Exploring the particular ways in which we practice love—again, focusing on romantic

love—will follow this discussion. We will pay more attention to other practices of love later in the book as we deal with issues such as marriage, parent–child relations, and aging families. The main topic of concern for us here is the practices that have been referred to as courtship, dating, and mate selection. In the last section of this chapter we will discuss the importance of friendships when thinking about love. Friendships can be very powerful in our lives. They can form the basis of other types of love (including romance). They can also serve to help us through transitions in love, such as breakups, divorce, or the death of a loved one. It should become clear that the ideals for love have real consequences for how we practice love. As mentioned above, our ideals and myths about love provide a frame of reference for us, helping us to have a language for interpreting our experience and providing meaning for our relationships with others.

What Is Love?

The topic of love has been written about perhaps more than any other topic in this book. Yet coming up with a definition of love is complicated, perhaps because most of us think about our love for another person in very individual terms. It is hard to imagine that the way we feel about our lovers, mothers, and best friends can be generalized to a one-size-fits-all statement. However, we suggest that some similarities across the types of loving relationships we enter will help us use the term *love* in a meaningful way. First, **love** is an *enduring bond* between two or more people. Although we would not argue that love is "forever," it is true that loving relationships are ones that we intend to be long lasting. Second, love is based on *affection* and *emotion*. When we love, or are in love

Love is an enduring bond between two or more people based on affection and emotion, and includes a sense of obligation. One way family members express their love for each other is through celebrations of important family events.

with, another person, we feel something different for that person. We also feel differently about ourselves when we are with him or her. Third, love includes a sense of *obligation* toward one another. When you love someone, you desire to help that person in times of need. This might include physical as well as emotional care. Focusing on these characteristics, we can see that love is central to family life. Love is a commitment to one another that is based on affection. If you were to make a list of the people you love, you would find that family members (related by blood, law, or commitment) make up the bulk of the list.

Family scholars have approached the study of love in a variety of ways. Some have focused on the first characteristic we listed for love—a bond. How do we come to attach ourselves to others, and what are the different types of attachments? Psychologists have long argued that there is a biological component to bonding that can be observed in early infancy. Infants become attached to their primary caregivers as a result of dependency. This initial bonding, or attachment, is believed to shape the way all other attachments are constructed throughout our lives, including the way in which adults become attached in romantic relationships. Other writers on love have focused on the diversity of styles or types of love. A look at the historical discussions of love suggests that love has always been appreciated as a multidimensional concept, but one that is strongly rooted in a particular historical moment. We will take a broad sweep of history to highlight some of the more powerful images of love that still have influence on us (in Western societies) today.

As It Was in the Beginning: Love as Attachment

One thing that seems innate about humans is that we are social. Without interaction with others, we could not survive. This notion forms the basis of **attachment theory** (Bowlby, 1969). In the beginning, infants and children stay close to parents/adults because they have to—for survival. But as people grow up, they continue to seek out relationships with others because the initial *need* for others develops into a *desire* to be attached to others. Those who use attachment theory suggest that the early attachments that infants make with their primary caregiver (usually the mother) will have implications for how they make attachments to others throughout life.

| **FACT OR FICTION?**

The quality of attachment between infants and their parents determines the quality of all subsequent adult attachments, including romantic attachments.

Early Attachments

Psychologist Mary Ainsworth and her colleagues (Ainsworth, Blehar, Waters, & Wall, 1978) have studied the early interactions between infants and their mothers. Experiments assessed infants' reactions when their mothers were temporarily removed from their sight. Ainsworth's findings suggested three basic patterns of reactions, reflecting the quality of the infants' attachments with

their mothers. Most infants (about two-thirds) were found to have **secure attachments,** in which infants feel safe when their mothers are out of sight. These attachments reflected children's confidence that mothers would be available when needed. The development of this confidence comes from mothers' having been warm, responsive, and consistently available to infants over time. In other relationships, mothers were found to be less predictable in their interactions with their infants, both in terms of their physical proximity and the levels of warmth exhibited. These types of relationships resulted in stress among infants, and they, in turn, developed insecure attachments. Some of these infants were characterized as **anxious/ambivalent:** insecure infants who became nervous when their mothers left and then showed rejection of their mothers when they returned. About an equal number of infants were characterized as **avoidant,** showing little attachment to their mothers. Ainsworth and her colleagues suggested that avoidant infants may have been neglected by their mothers in terms of their physical and emotional needs, and therefore have no expectation that the mothers would be there for comfort.

Over repeated interactions, infants/children develop a "working model" of attachment (Cassidy, 2000). Working models of attachment will continue to channel and shape close-relationship behaviors beyond infancy and childhood, and beyond the relationship to the primary caregiver. As individuals create new relationships, they rely in part on previous relationships to give them clues about what to expect from others. How will these new people feel about me, and how will they respond to me? Because initial attachments are expected to guide subsequent relationships, psychologists argue that we should expect infant attachment styles to be related to adult romantic relationships as well.

Adult Romantic Attachments

In several studies, adults have been asked to think back over their history of romantic relationships and to describe them by selecting from a list of statements. Hazan and Shaver (1987, 1990) found that adult romantic relationships also have three distinct types of bonds, corresponding to what we saw earlier describing infant attachments. The types, with some representative characterizing statements, are the following:

1. Secure attachments:
   - I find it relatively easy to get close to others and am comfortable depending on them and having them depend on me.
   - I don't worry about being abandoned or about someone getting too close to me.
2. Anxious-ambivalent attachments:
   - I find that others are reluctant to get as close as I would like.
   - I often worry that my partner doesn't really love me or won't want to stay with me.
   - I want to get very close to my partner, and this sometimes scares people away.
3. Avoidant attachments:
   - I am somewhat uncomfortable being close to others.
   - I find it difficult to trust them completely, difficult to allow myself to depend on them.
   - I am nervous when anyone gets too close, and often, others want me to be more intimate than I feel comfortable being.

However, there are two important differences between the bonds of love in early infant–parent attachments and those in adult romantic attachments. First, adult romantic relationships also include *caregiving.* For infants, attachment is dependent on receiving protection and comfort from another. But in adult romantic relationships, both partners must be involved in the role of caregiver. At some moments one partner can be stressed and in need of comfort, while at other times the other partner is the one in need. From a functionalist perspective, it is this mutual dependency that provides the stabilizing bond in marriage (Nock, 1998). Second, adult romantic relationships also involve *sex.* Those additional dimensions to adult love are believed to serve different functions and to develop in different ways over time, but they are empirically related to one another within attachment relationships. These distinctions have not yet received very much attention in social science research on attachment (Fraley & Shaver, 2000).

In addition to finding that romantic attachments were similar to infant attachments in orientation structure, Hazan and Shaver (1987) also found that characterizations of romantic attachments were correlated with respondents' memories of their early attachments with primary caregivers. Adults who were secure in their adult romantic relationships were most likely to be the ones to recall affectionate, caring, and accepting relationships with their parents (Levy, Blatt, & Shaver, 1998). However, notice from the wording of these relationships that the data used for this research are retrospective. That is, the correlations are based on memories of early attachments. Only one study has had the luxury of longitudinal data tracing individuals over time. Steele, Waters, Crowell, and Treboux (1998) correlated a measure of security at age one to security in adult romantic relationships and found it to be .17. Correlations from retrospective studies have been closer to .3. Certainly, more research needs to be conducted, but based on existing research, psychologists suggest that we consider the relationship between early and later attachments to be "moderate at best" (Fraley & Shaver, 2000).

Although the types of attachments formed early in life can influence subsequent attachments, research suggests that the long-term correlation is low. Many other social factors are important in shaping the quality of adult romantic relationships.

Many other concerns have been raised about using attachment theory, derived from research on infant attachments, to explain the complexities of romantic love. Some have argued that a three-category scheme of attachment styles is too limiting for adult relationships (Bartholomew, 1990), while some suggest that more attention be paid to other behavioral systems that are part of the loving experience (for example, caregiving and sex). For instance, research shows that the various dimensions of romantic love have independent (that is, differing) effects on things such as marital satisfaction. A recent review of a decade of theory and research on attachment concludes by suggesting that this approach cannot begin to explain the dynamic nature of love in relationships over time (Fraley & Shaver, 2000).

The Many Types and Styles of Love

Writings on love have always suggested that it is a complex and multifaceted phenomenon. Some of our earliest stories of love are from ancient Greek and Roman mythology. Roman stories of Venus, the goddess of love, and her son Cupid, along with the Greek tales of Aphrodite and her son Eros, are familiar to us. The writings of the Greek philosopher Plato were consumed with notions of love. Most of these treatises on love were about passion and adoration, but this passion was not channeled through marriage. For example, Plato wrote of love as something that existed between men. Women were not considered to be suitable partners for love, as they were considered intellectually inferior. Early Christianity included a type of love that was spiritual, religious, and ascetic. The ideal was to forgo all physical desires to obtain holiness. Therefore, marriage was considered to be something acceptable for those who could not control their carnal desires (Hendrick & Hendrick, 1992).

Tales of romantic love from the Middle Ages included the idea that true love was about something that was unattainable.

Romance Through the Ages

Ideals of love, as distinct from marital love, were prevalent up through the Middle Ages. By about the twelfth century, however, a rhetoric about sexual love between women and men emerged. Referred to as **courtly love,** it concerned the meanings and practices of love among the most privileged—those of the royal court. However, it is somewhat surprising that twentieth-century writers have used the term *courtship* to describe the process of mate selection, since the key to courtly love was that it was not obtainable (de Rougemont, 1956; Menocal, 1987).

Love in the Middle Ages In early-twelfth-century France, a new lyrical form took shape that has come to be labeled

Contemporary films often present love and romance in ways similar to stories from the Middle Ages.

and victorious in battle. Unlike their lords, who held their positions by birth, knights held more tenuous positions and were constantly aware of the need to be in their lord's favor. One way in which knights tried to display their devotion and maintain their good favor was through the offering of gifts. This gift service extended to the wife of the noble lord as well, and sometimes included gestures of sexual flirtation by the knights. It has been reported that knights would wear something that belonged to the lord's wife, such as a scarf, into battle. Because these interactions or relationships between a knight and a noble woman took place "at court," we can see the historical connection to the term "courtship."

The key to the story of the knight's love, as to the troubadour's, is that the love is unrequited. The knight who falls in love with the lady runs the risk of being caught in this forbidden love, hence proving disloyal to his lord. This struggle is shown clearly in the tale of Lancelot, who loves both his lord (King Arthur) and his lord's wife (Guinevere). Ann Swidler (1980) argues that it is just this struggle (she calls it the "duality of courtly love") that transforms and exalts the lover/knight: "Through an elaborate code of sexual flirtation combined with sexual restraint, courtly love heightened self-control, so that passion could inspire virtue, putting the power of sexual feeling behind the demands of self-perfection" (Swidler, 1980: 122). Swidler argues that this struggle takes a different shape over time and across social classes, but is a defining struggle in the quest for adulthood throughout time.

FACT

Much of the historical record from the Middle Ages came from the elite. Among the written record were poems and lyrics about men falling in love with royal women (whom they could never marry).

"courtly love" or "troubadour poetry." Poets, known as troubadours, wrote of passionate love felt for another person. However, this other, for whom the poet felt love, was unattainable because she was married (probably to the nobleman he served). It is believed that these intense feelings, potentially desperate since they were not returned, served as the power behind this lyrical form, providing the struggle that gave meaning to love (Menocal, 1987). Troubadours were brought to England from France because of the marriage between Eleanor of Aquitaine and Henry II, king of England (de Rougemont, 1956).

During the twelfth and thirteenth centuries, societies in Europe were made up primarily of two social classes: nobility and peasants. The nobility consisted of lords and their families, who had armies of men headed by knights, who, in turn, protected the land owned by the nobility. During the earlier part of the Middle Ages, knights were men who had distinguished themselves by being fierce

Another very important part of this early idea of romantic love is that it placed women in a position of adoration. As one historian notes (Owen, 1975: 25), "No longer is she the passive prey to his desires, but an ideal to which he must aspire from below, the focus of his every thought and energy." Rhetorically speaking, then, women were given power in the relationship between lovers. An example of such poetry can be found in the Family Narratives box on page 148.

It is important to remember that these narratives were written by, and for, members of the upper classes. The majority of people in Western Europe were peasants and not engaged in creating lyrics of love. However, these writings form the basis of our own love mythology and appear to continue as a theme over time. In particular, we focus on the part of the love myth that includes a struggle, sometimes against all odds, to obtain your object of love. Think about movies such as *Shakespeare in Love* and *Titanic*. Both have been box-office successes that look at love between people who just can't or shouldn't be together. But it is through the struggle that we come to know their relationships as true love.

Industrialization and the Feminization of Love Since the twelfth century, significant social changes have occurred. Populations have grown geometrically, and with the Industrial Revolution came a new economy with a growing middle class. It is argued that love has continued to be about the struggle to create one's own identity or to find one's place in the world, but that this quest now takes on a different meaning. Prior to the Industrial Revolution (prior to the eighteenth century), the household was the center of social life for most Europeans and Americans. People lived in smaller rural communities, and households were relatively self-sufficient, meaning that both the production and consumption of goods and services took place at home. The home was the place of employment, education, health care, and other social services. As pointed out by many scholars, there was not a clear distinction between the "public" and "private" spheres of life prior to the Industrial Revolution (Shorter, 1975; Ryan, 1979).

With population increases and industrialization, this type of household began to disintegrate. Land became scarce, and people moved from the country to new urban areas to work in shops and factories. This process led to the situation in which labor was exchanged for cash; then cash was used to buy goods and services. The home no longer was the place of employment, at least for men. Women continued to work at home, but because their labor was not remunerated (no earnings accumulated), their work was not defined as employment. However, because men were spending less time in the home, women became the de facto head of household. But what were they the "head" of? An increasing amount of women's time became devoted to caring for the needs of men and children (Ryan, 1979; Degler, 1980).

Along with the change in behavior came a new view about men and women, referred to by historians as the "ideology of separate spheres." This view exaggerated the differences between the world of women and that of men, and concluded that these two different life experiences were related to their personalities. Men were better suited for the harsh, difficult world of the new economy, while women were best suited for the work of caregiving (Welter, 1966). Rhetoric to this effect was evident in magazines, political speeches, and sermons across the United States. It served to perpetuate the view that love was "defined as what women did in the home; it had nothing to do with how men related to each other at work. Love became a private feeling, disassociated from public life, economic production, and practical action to help others" (Cancian, 1989: 18–19).

Bernard de Ventadour, a troubadour received at the court of Eleanor of Aquitaine (queen of England beginning in 1154), wrote the following poem. It provides an example of how the rhetoric of love included both the notions of "love as unrequited" and "love as the adoration of women."

When I see the lark fluttering its wings for joy in the sun's beam then falling back, entranced by the sweetness that enters its heart, ah, I am so sorely envious of all I see rejoicing that I wonder my heart does not straightway melt with desire.

Alas, so much I thought I knew of love, yet know so little! For I cannot help loving her from whom no benefit will ever come to me. She has plucked from me my heart and my being, herself and the whole world; and taking herself from me, she left me nothing but deep longing and desire.

Control and possession of myself I lost the instant she let me look into her eyes, a mirror full of delight for me. Mirror, since I reflected myself in you, sighs rising from the depths have slain me, and I have lost

myself like fair Narcissus in the fountain.

Source: D. D. R. Owen (1975). *Noble Lovers.* New York: New York University Press, p. 25.

Critical Thinking

1. Can you think of a more contemporary poem about love? What are the qualities that are assumed to be part of love?

2. Song lyrics are also poetry. What is your favorite love song? What do the words in this song tell you about what love is?

This process is what Cancian refers to as the **"feminization of love"** in the nineteenth century (Cancian, 1987).

There are two sides to this feminization of love. First, by separating home life from the world of remunerated labor, marriage can be based on a different set of qualities. Instead of dwelling on practical economic considerations, people were freer to base relationships on emotion. With this separation came more intimacy in family relationships. The outside world of work was seen as a dirty, cruel environment, and the family became a "haven in a heartless world" (Lasch, 1977). At the same time, because the day-to-day experiences of men and women became separate, it is also argued that the relationships between men and women became more unequal, therefore compromising the potential for real intimacy (Cott, 1977). A division of labor that results in men and women engaging in very different tasks results in little shared experience to discuss. As Cancian (1989) points out, a considerable amount of evidence about the lack of intimacy can be seen in the marriage manuals, popular magazines, and other writing of the time. To be a good wife and to be a good husband were two very different things. Although these two sets of traits were considered to "complement" each other, they may well have led to estrangement.

The lives of women and men today are becoming more similar. The majority of women are in the paid work force, and average levels of education are roughly equivalent for men and women. Cancian (1987) suggests this situation may lead to a more **androgynous** form of love, one in which both masculine and feminine qualities are both valued as important. Although these changes certainly describe a trend, we still hold on to notions of love that are related to gender (as we will see in a later section).

Love in the Consumer Age Since industrialization, many countries have undergone more dramatic changes in the organization of social life. The twentieth century is really a story of the movement from a family-wage economy to a family-consumer economy (see Chapter 10). Today, we find that very little production goes on in the home. Rather, most adult members of households work for an income, which is then used to buy what is needed to survive. This change in the social organization of production has shaped our ideals about love. Contemporary writers who have paid attention to the shifting meanings and practices of love point out that the struggle of love today is about the tension between the profit orientation of our capitalist economy and the idealism of families as places of free, nonmonetary expressions of emotions (Coontz, 1992).

Eva Illouz (1999), in her work *Consuming the Romantic Utopia,* argues that the power of romantic love and the mythology that goes along with it is critical today. The reason that it is so important is that it provides an opportunity to experience (or envision) utopia in an otherwise unromantic society. First, we start with identifying the primary values of Western society. Williams (1970) suggests that among our most important American values are achievement and success, hard work, and efficiency and practicality. These values fit well with a capitalistic economic system that emphasizes self-interest and the creation of profit. Next, think about what our contemporary ideals of love include. Romantic love, Illouz argues, would appear to be the antithesis of capitalism. When in love, we believe we are not profit-oriented; rather, we give of ourselves freely. Holding on to romantic love, then, is a way for us to rebel against the system in which we live. Recall that in courtly love the knight struggled to win the love of the nobleman's wife against the laws/prohibitions of the land. Love appears to always include a physiological/emotional attraction that becomes embedded in a struggle (Swidler, 1980).

What this brief history of the conceptions of love has shown us is that love is complex and that it changes over time. Yet some of the notions of love from these historical periods are still with us. We still believe that love includes a struggle. But what we are struggling against depends on the organization of society and our place within it. We turn now to recent research on how people experience loving relationships. We'll see that traces of the past emerge again in identifying how love is defined today.

John Lee's Styles of Love

Canadian sociologist John Lee (1973, 1988) reviewed thousands of sources on the treatment of love across the centuries, including most of the ideas cited above. He sifted through the writings and came up with thirty statements reflecting what he saw as the diversity of notions about love. After giving the statements to a sample of young (under thirty-five), white, heterosexual men and women in Canada and Britain, he published what is now the most-cited contemporary work on the styles of love. These are meant to suggest "ideal types" of love. The six styles of love are seen as distinct from one another, yet relationships can be characterized by more than one style of love.

* **Eros.** This style of love derives from the Greek god Eros, son of Aphrodite. The stories of Eros were about passion. *Eros* forms the root of the word *erotic.* It is the type of love that is overpowering and seems to sweep us off our feet. This is the type of love that is most often presented in movies, television, and other types of popular culture. Sex is often central to relationships within this style of love. Eros describes love that wants to be all consuming.

* **Ludus.** This type of love is more carefree and nonpossessive. It is considered to be more about fun than commitment. As with eros, sex is often part of the relationship, but it is different from eros in that a committed sexual partnership is not central to the relationship. In fact, these couples may be involved in a number of sexual relationships. Although some might view this type of love as problematic (from a moral standpoint), it is not intended to be a love that harms the individuals involved.

* **Storge.** This type of love (pronounced STOR gay) characterizes couples whose love develops slowly over a period of time. It describes the relationship among couples starting out as friends with similar interests, who then move the relationship forward into a more committed one. Sexual intimacy comes much later in these relationships, with much more emphasis being paid to shared activities and interests. Lee suggests that storgic couples who break up are the couples most likely to remain friends.

* **Pragma.** As it sounds, this is a down-to-earth (pragmatic) style of love. You can imagine an individual making a list of all the things important in a relationship and then comparing that with a partner. Being compatible on key issues is important for the maintenance of these relationships. As a relationship develops, such couples take the time to reflect on where they are and where they are going. Mid-course corrections can be made, or couples can break up.

* **Agape.** This type of love (pronounced ah GAH pay) is also referred to as altruistic, meaning that partners are completely selfless, always giving without any thought of getting something in return. Lee refers to this as a classic example of Christian love that is *always* patient and giving. Lee's study did not produce any examples of an agapic lover.

* **Mania.** Manic relationships are the most problematic. This type of love is characterized as possessive and obsessive. Partners are very demanding of each other, wanting to know their whereabouts at all times. Spending time apart is painful and can produce considerable anxiety. The manic lover may try to force his/her partner to a commitment without waiting for love to develop. These are volatile—and the least satisfying—relationships.

From a developmental perspective, some have argued that types of love develop over time (Walster & Walster, 1978). In adolescence, the most typical type of love would be mania, developing toward eros in early adulthood. Storge and pragma would develop later on in life. However, recent research on love attitudes across family life stages does not support this strictly generational correlation with styles of love. Montgomery and Sorell (1997) gave the Love Attitude Scale to 122 males and 128 females ranging in age from 17 to 70. Their findings suggest that age is less important than marital status. Singles were more likely to hold manic and ludic love attitudes than were married adults, and these young singles were much less likely to hold the attitude of agape:

> These differences likely exist because the commitment endemic to marriage generally precludes low-commitment "playing around" Ludic attitudes and the obsessive, uncertain Manic attitudes that are characteristic of courtship. Marriage, on the other hand, may encourage self-giving love and the subordination of individual needs and preferences to those of the mate or the relationship to an extent that is not appropriate in courtship. (Montgomery & Sorell, 1997: 59–60)

There are a variety of styles of love, and relationships can be
characterized by more than one style.

Clyde Hendrick and Susan Hendrick have developed a Love Attitude Scale to assess styles of love. Below are some questions from that scale. In thinking about a current relationship, we can respond to the following items in terms of level of agreement. Adding up scores for each subset will suggest which styles of love are more characteristic of the relationship.

For each of the following characteristics, assign points as follows:

1	=	strongly disagree
2	=	moderately disagree
3	=	neutral
4	=	moderately disagree
5	=	strongly agree

POINTS	TYPE OF LOVE
	EROS
_____	My partner and I were attracted to each other immediately after we first met.
_____	My partner and I have the right "physical chemistry" between us.
_____	Our lovemaking is very intense and satisfying.
_____	I feel that my partner and I were meant for each other.
_____	*TOTAL FOR EROS*
	LUDUS
_____	I try to keep my partner a little uncertain about my commitment to her/him.
_____	I believe that what my partner doesn't know about me won't hurt her/him.
_____	I have sometimes had to keep my partner from finding out about other partners.
_____	I could get over my affair with my partner pretty easily and quickly.
_____	*TOTAL FOR LUDUS*
	STORGE
_____	It is hard for me to say exactly when our friendship turned into love.
_____	To be genuine, our love first required caring for a while.
_____	I expect to always be friends with my partner.
_____	Our love is the best kind because it grew out of a long friendship.
_____	*TOTAL FOR STORGE*

Recall that this is a typology, or a set of ideals. Few, if any, couples can be characterized in terms of only one type of love described here. This typology might be useful in helping us understand how couples come together and which couples may be most, and least, likely to have long-term relationships. It has been argued that the styles may correlate with the categories of attachment discussed previously. Eros, agape, and storge appear to

PRAGMA

_____ I considered what my partner was going to become in life before I committed myself to her/him.

_____ I tried to plan my life carefully before choosing my partner.

_____ In choosing my partner, I believed it was best to love someone with a similar background.

_____ A main consideration in choosing my partner was how she/he would reflect on my family.

_____ *TOTAL FOR PRAGMA*

MANIA

_____ When things aren't right with my partner and me, my stomach gets upset.

_____ If my partner and I broke up, I would get so depressed that I would even think of suicide.

_____ Sometimes I get so excited about being in love with my partner that I can't sleep.

_____ When my partner doesn't pay attention to me, I feel sick all over.

_____ *TOTAL FOR MANIA*

AGAPE

_____ I try to always help my partner through difficult times.

_____ I would rather suffer myself than let my partner suffer.

_____ I cannot be happy unless I place my partner's happiness before my own.

_____ I am usually willing to sacrifice my own wishes to let my partner achieve hers/his.

_____ *TOTAL FOR AGAPE*

Source: C. Hendrick and S. Hendrick (1996). "Gender and the Experience of Heterosexual Love." In J. T. Wood (Ed.), *Gendered Relationships* (pp. 144–146). Mountain View, CA: Mayfield Publishing Company. Used by permission.

be more secure types of love, while mania is more anxious/ambivalent, and ludus is closest to avoidant (Hendrick & Hendrick, 1992). To see how you approach love, see the Constructing Strong Families box on pages 152–153.

Sternberg's Triangular Approach to Love

Another approach to exploring the multidimensional character of love comes from the work of Robert Sternberg (1986, 1988).

Sternberg's **triangular theory of love** can help us explore the different types of relationships that are characterized as love, and how they can vary in terms of intensity. He argues that love has three elements: intimacy, passion, and commitment. *Intimacy* is the emotional component of a relationship, capturing the ways in which partners connect with each other. *Passion* is the motivational piece of the relationship, tapping into the components that produce arousal and physical attraction. Finally, the element of *commitment* represents the cognitive dimension. Each partner makes decisions about wanting to maintain the relationship. Individuals will differ in the emphasis they place on these three elements, and the relative emphases can change over time. When couples are matched on their desires in these dimensions, relationships are stable ("perfectly matched"), although the more likely situation is that compatible couples will be "closely matched." The further individuals are from each other on these dimensions, the more unstable the couple becomes.

Sternberg also suggests a number of kinds of love based on various combinations of the elements of intimacy, passion, and commitment. As in the work of Lee, these combinations describe more ideal notions rather than descriptions of actual relationships. (These types of love are summarized in Table 4.1.) For example, when someone is high in terms of all three components, Sternberg calls this "consummate love"—it is all that love can be. Infatuation describes the situation where there are passion and intimacy, but no commitment. And commitment alone, without passion or intimacy, is seen as not really being love at all.

Empirical research using Sternberg's typology suggests that the way intimacy, passion, and commitment are experienced can change over time. A recent study shows that among heterosexual couples, traditional ways of expressing intimacy, passion, and commitment decline over time (Reeder, 1996). This decline wasn't related directly to the length of time that couples in this study were together; rather, it was more closely associated with the age of the individuals involved. As we'll see in the next chapter, research indicates that individuals engage in sex less often as they get older (Michael, Gagnon, Lauman, & Kolata, 1994). While there are some biological reasons for a decline in the frequency of sex, it is also the case that American culture does not tolerate public displays of intimacy between older individuals as much as it does among younger people. A look at popular television programs and movies will give you an idea of who is "allowed" to publicly express their feelings of romantic love. Few media productions show physical expressions of love among the elderly or the infirm.

The work of John Lee and the work of Robert Sternberg are good examples of just how complex love can be. We began by defining love as being about an enduring bond that is based on affection and includes a sense of obligation. Now we understand that what goes into creating such bonds varies by individual, varies over time, and varies in the relative emphasis that individuals place on the dimensions of their loving relationships. Although in theory these discussions could be applied to all types of loving relationships, in reality they have been developed and applied primarily to romantic relationships, especially heterosexual relationships. We will return to a discussion of the love in other types of relationships shortly. First, we turn to the theories about romantic attraction. Here the questions turn from those about how love is defined to questions about how people fall in love and how love develops. These are theories about "attraction" and the developmental character of love. A summary of them can be found in Table 4.2.

TABLE 4.1	Sternberg's Types of Love			
TYPE		COMMITMENT	PASSION	INTIMACY
Liking	A close relationship without passion or commitment	–	–	+
Infatuation	Love at first sight	–	+	+
Empty love	Not really love	+	–	–
Romantic love	Not necessarily long term, but a close relationship with passion	–	+	+
Companionate love	May have started with passion, but moves on to a commitment based on shared interests	+	–	+
Fatuous love	Sometimes called deceptive love because the commitment is based on the unstable component of passion	+	+	–
Consummate love	The love of our dreams— very difficult to maintain	+	+	+

TABLE 4.2	Contemporary Theories About Love and Mate Selection
THEORY	BASIC ASSUMPTIONS OR ARGUMENTS
Sociobiology	All humans have the instinct to pass on their genes (inclusive fitness). People fall in love with those whom they sense will maximize their inclusive fitness. Men prefer younger and more physically attractive women. Women prefer men who are more financially secure.
Attachment theory	The primary human motivation in life is to be attached to other people. Connections are established through physical contact and expression of emotion. The style of attachment that is developed between an infant and adult will affect the infant's long-term potential for success in love. Attachment can be secure, anxious/ambivalent, or avoidant.
Reiss's wheel theory of love	Relationships develop in stages. Stages are rapport, self-revelation, mutual dependence, and need fulfillment. Couples can move both forward and backward through the stages.
The filter theory of love	Factors that initially attract are not necessarily the same as those that maintain a relationship. In the beginning, people of similar characteristics are attracted to each other. After time, need complementarity develops.
Sternberg's triangular theory of love	Love has several dimensions: intimacy, passion, and commitment. The relative weight of each dimension depends on the needs of the individuals and on the stage of the relationship.
Equity theory	Relationships work best when those involved sense there is a fair exchange. When inequity is sensed, relationships tend to dissolve.
Feminist theories	Love, like other experiences in our lives, is closely related to the structure of gender relationships. Love is corrupted by an unequal balance of power.

Theories About Attraction and the Development of Love

Scientists and social scientists approach the question of attraction from different angles. Two of the main approaches are biological/chemical and social/psychological.

Biological and Chemical Theories About Love

Sociobiology, as an evolutionary theory, argues that all humans have an instinctive impulse to pass on their genetic material. According to sociobiologists, men and women have very different strategies for doing so. To understand why, we start with the following statement: motherhood is a fact; fatherhood is a hypothesis. When a child is born, we *know* that the woman delivering the child contributed to its genetic material and is the biological mother. Without testing, however, we can't immediately prove who the father is. Sociobiologists suggest that over time, this difference has led men and women to approach love (or desire) in different ways (Buss, 1994). Men, trying to ensure they pass on their genes, may look to establish more than one romantic attachment. Having multiple partners increases the probability of success in becoming a parent. Women, on the other hand, knowing that their children are theirs, can be more selective about entering into a relationship with a man. Sociobiologists point to this as an evolutionary process that over the centuries has produced the behavioral patterns (dating and sexual relations) we observe today. For example, research indicates that men report having more sex partners over time than do women (Michael et al., 1994). Over half of men have five or more partners in a lifetime, while only 29 percent of women do. However, it is important to remember that sex is only one component of romantic love.

Men and women report wanting basically the same thing when it comes to love.

In addition to the number of people that men and women look to mate with, sociobiology also gives us clues as to the *type* of people men and women are attracted to. Women, who are physically restricted through pregnancy, childbirth, and the child-rearing years, tend to seek out older men. Older men are more likely to be of higher status and therefore more capable of taking care of the woman and her children financially. Men's attraction, on the other hand, tends toward women who are the most fertile—that is, younger women. This can be seen in the age differences in dating and marriage. Age is not the only thing that biologists note to be important in selecting a partner, or falling in love. Men prefer waists to be 60–80 percent the size of hips (an indicator of fertility potential) while women prefer men with softer facial features, as these features suggest feelings of warmth and trustworthiness (Singh, 1993). And it is argued that all humans are attracted to symmetrical facial features, because these features are expected to decrease the likelihood of reproductive abnormalities. In sum, attraction is rooted in our biology and may be something we don't consciously think about. Falling in love just happens.

In a major study by David Buss (1989), data were collected from more than 10,000 individuals from 33 countries. The interest was in testing the predictions from evolutionary theory about human attraction. Buss found that men across cultures were more likely to value physical attractiveness and relative youth in their potential mates, while women were more likely to value financial capacity (see Figure 4.1a, b, c). Although Buss argues that these findings provide support for evolutionary theory, he cautions that the data have some limitations. The sample is not

FIGURE 4.1a Traits Desired in "Choosing a Mate"

FIGURE 4.1b

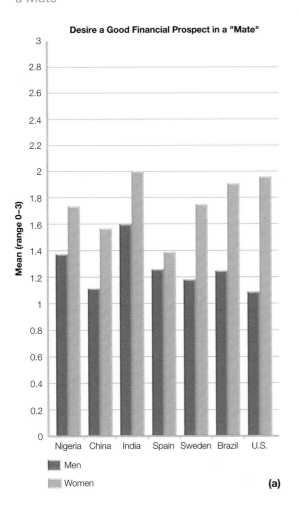

(a)

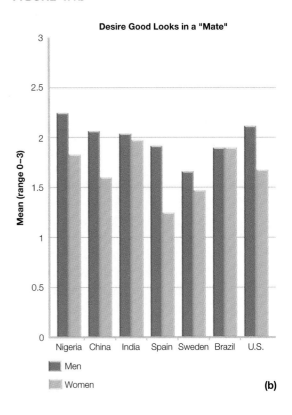

(b)

FIGURE 4.1c

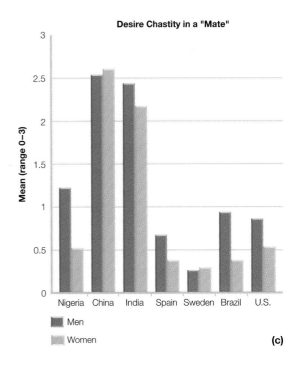

(c)

Source: D. M. Buss, (1989). "Sex Differences in Human Mate Preferences: Evolutionary Hypotheses Tested in 37 Cultures." *Behavioral and Brain Sciences, 12,* 1–49.

representative and is biased toward more-educated individuals. People with more education may have access to knowledge about other cultures (either through literature, popular culture, or travel). This means that cultural diffusion may have taken place. With the rapid distribution of Western culture, it would not be surprising to see similarities in attitudes and ideas. In addition, Buss argues that there is considerable overlap in the distributions of preferences among men and women showing that not all men, or all women, think alike. And finally, he found that traits such as "kind/understanding" and "intelligent" were even more important than looks, age, or income for everyone (regardless of gender). This suggests that the strongest part of attraction may not be sex-linked.

| FACT

Cross-cultural research shows that women and men place kindness, understanding, and intelligence at the top of their list of what they want from a potential life partner.

A related approach that looks toward biological factors affecting love includes **biochemical theories.** These theories start with the assumption that we are naturally drawn to certain features over others. When we establish eye contact with the person who holds those features, our brain releases a chemical (dopamine) that gives us a rush. And this rush is experienced as "sexual attraction." As a couple gets acquainted, other natural chemicals such as norepinephrine and phenylethylamine are also produced. These result in dilated pupils, sweating, skin flushes, and stomach "butterflies." These physiological experiences are cues to us about whom our potential partners in love might be.

Before concluding that love is merely a product of biochemical forces, we should take into account that these feelings we label "sexual attraction" are similar to the physiological sensations we label "fear" and "anger." That is, when faced with situations that make you afraid, a very similar set of natural chemicals is released and you experience comparable physiological symptoms (butterflies, sweating, etc.). An often-cited piece of research about the physiological determinants of emotion is that by Stanley Schacter (1964). Schacter injected subjects with a drug that produced a physiological reaction of arousal. The participants in his research project were asked to identify their feelings when put in different situations. He found that subjects would identify their experience of the *same* drug as one of "elation" or "anger" depending on the situation he put them in. What this suggests is that the chemicals produced are not *automatically* connected to falling in love. It is the *interpretation* of the physical feelings that is also important.

We certainly cannot deny that there are physiological factors involved in attraction, emotion, and caring. But this research suggests to us that we should also look beyond initial physiological responses to factors in our environments in order to explain the meaning and process of falling in and out of love. Expanding to more social perspectives also allows us to be more inclusive. Much of the previous discussion assumes heterosexual attraction. Most of the theoretical perspectives that follow were developed for, and applied to, heterosexual relationships. However, there is no reason to limit them to male–female romances. Researchers including gay and lesbian couples in their research find that, in most ways, "relationships are relationships" (Mackey, O'Brien, & Mackey, 1997). At the same time, we will see later in this chapter that how people behave with romantic others does vary because cultural norms define what is acceptable public behavior.

Social Psychological Theories About Love

Social psychological approaches to studying love include the issue of initial attraction but also focus on how that initial attraction develops into what we label as love. As couples get to know each other better, their relationship takes on different qualities. These theories are often referred to as "stage theories" because they identify a set of steps that couples go through in their relationship. Like much of what we've discussed so far, these approaches are not meant to characterize all couples as moving in identical ways. Rather, these approaches suggest to us patterns of relationship development among romantically involved couples.

Reiss's Wheel Theory of Love Reiss's theory was initially developed and used in the 1960s and 1970s, and argues that love develops in stages (Reiss, 1960; Reiss & Lee, 1988). In the beginning, people meet and establish *rapport.* It is most likely that people meet based on shared interests. That is, we are most likely to meet people who are near us in physical proximity and are doing things that we like to do. As a result, the people we meet also are likely to share cultural norms and values. After establishing rapport, couples move to a second stage of *self-revelation,* in which they begin to share more about themselves. The things we share become more personal with time, and we begin to let the other know about our innermost thoughts, desires, fears, and weaknesses. After sharing these very personal aspects of themselves, couples may move on to a third stage of *mutual dependence.* In this stage, partners will really begin to open up and start to depend on the other (who knows a lot about you) to respond in a caring manner. And finally, couples that have become dependent on each other can move on to a stage of intimacy called *need fulfillment.* Recall in our discussion of attachment theory the assumption that people need others to survive. We also need others to help us develop our sense of self and to validate who we are.

Reiss argued that these stages form an ever-moving wheel as couples meet, share parts of themselves, and become dependent on each other. But the movement is very much affected by the environment around the people involved. As we learn more about our partners, we may discover an incompatibility in lifestyles or values. This may lead to the severing of relationships (Martin & Luke, 1991) or to stepping back a stage in the development of the relationship. The development of the relationship can move fast or slow, and it can move forward or backward.

| FACT OR FICTION?

The popular saying "opposites attract" is the best predictor of who falls in love.

The Filter Theory of Love Kerchoff and Davis (1962) were two of the first researchers to explore the development of love using longitudinal data. That is, instead of comparing couples just beginning a relationship to couples that have been together for a long time, they followed the same couples over time. What they found was that the factors that initially attract people to each other are different from the factors that sustain them. In the beginning, similarity in social characteristics is important and serves as the first *filter.* One's level of education, social class background, and religion provide exposure to different people, and these people become the initial pool of eligibles. The term **homogamy** is used in theories of mate selection (discussed in Chapter 6) to refer to this process of being attracted to people with similar social characteristics. Within this aggregate of individuals, you then look for those who hold similar attitudes and values.

This second set of factors will *filter out* some of the initial potential candidates. It is usually among this set of people (people with both similar social characteristics and similar attitudes and values) that you find enduring partners. But in deciding with which of these partners to establish an enduring relationship, there are additional considerations. According to filter theory, the final step (or filter) is one of identifying *need complementarity*. Here the issue may be to find someone to provide balance to what you have to offer. A shy person may want to be with a more outgoing person. A person who would like to be the at-home parent may look for someone who wants to be the primary economic provider. In other words, this theory says that the two adages—"birds of a feather flock together" and "opposites attract"—are both accurate descriptions of love relationships. They just describe different stages of relationships. The filter theory is similar to the wheel theory, for it shows that the basis of a relationship changes over time and that as you discover more about your partner, you can become more or less attached.

| FICTION

Or at least it is not totally true. Initially, people are attracted to others who are very much like themselves in terms of social characteristics. As a relationship develops, however, some couples may decide to stay together because they have traits that provide a balance.

Equity Theory The **equity theory** developed by Walster and Walster (1978) suggests that **relationships** work *best* when both people involved feel as though there is a "fair exchange." This should not be confused with the idea that what is exchanged must be the same. Someone who is very shy might be attracted to someone who is more outgoing so

that together they have balance. But what this theory does assume is that through a process of negotiation, people will work out relationships that seem fair to them. When a person perceives personal disadvantage in a relationship, that individual is more likely to consider ending the relationship than when a situation of equity is perceived (Blair, 1993). This theory complements those mentioned earlier by suggesting that people want and/or need many different things from relationships. Those things are determined by the way individuals have been socialized by the culture they live in. It is different from the other theories in that its fundamental assumption is that people are attracted to partners who value balance or fairness.

Feminist Perspectives on Love As we discussed in Chapter 2, there is no single feminist theory on society and culture. However, feminists across different disciplines recognize that gender is an important factor in understanding our lives. And the experience of "love" is not unlike the experience of other family or intimate relationships. Because the organization of social relationships in our society reinforces the power of men (patriarchy), love becomes another way in which men have the opportunity to control women. Our popular culture provides us with stories of love that include women and men "becoming one," and the one is the man. The majority of women are born with the name of their father and die with the name of their husband. Some feminists argue that because patriarchal love is such a powerful part of our society and our psychology, it is "the pivot of women's oppression" (Firestone, 1970). Feminists agree with conflict theorists in arguing that love is corrupted in a society to the extent that there is an unequal balance of power. However, feminist theorists recognize that love, even patriarchal love, varies across time and across societies. It is important to remember that love is a social construction and, as such, has the potential to be a liberating experience if only society were structured to support relationships among and between equals. Recall that Francesca Cancian predicts the development of a more androgynous type of love in a society where women and men take on similar activities in education and employment.

In Chapter 3 we discuss the importance of looking at how social forces shape our personal experiences (the sociological imagination). In this chapter, we've seen that what love means, and how it is achieved, vary considerably over time. Still, we hold on to a definition of love that appears to be a bit static. That is, we don't often recognize that love is also variable within moments of history. Although biological theories might suggest that class and race make no difference to love (men and women are suspected to be drawn to people of the opposite sex who maximize the ability to pass on their genes), other social theories suggest that opportunities for attraction depend on being in the proximity of others. Our society is very much segregated by race, ethnicity, and social class. This segregation works as a filter for physical proximity and will therefore provide different opportunities for love. Within heterosexual couples, there also appear to be some important differences in the meanings of love—those between women and men.

Gender and Love

| FACT OR FICTION?

Men are the first to fall in love in heterosexual relationships.

If we are to believe popular culture, women are in charge of love. There is a popular term for films about love: "chick flicks." Maybe part of this idea is related to the feminization

of love that we discussed earlier (Cancian, 1987). Because women became the ones in charge of the household and its members, they were seen as the experts on love. Surveys show that, in fact, men report falling in love sooner in heterosexual relationships than do women (Kephart, 1967; Montgomery & Sorell, 1998). Research also shows that men are more likely than women to fall in love for reasons related to physical attractiveness (Allgeier & Wiederman, 1991). Women, on the other hand, appear to be a bit more cautious about love, taking a bit longer and using a wider variety of factors in deciding if they are in love. These characteristics include physical attractiveness but also traits of ambitiousness, industriousness, and financial prospects.

Are these tendencies natural? As we saw earlier in this chapter, sociobiologists suggest that they are natural and related to maximizing our genetic fitness (Buss, 1994). Women's reproductive potential is such that they can have only a certain number of children in their lifetime. In order to ensure that they produce children who are successful, they need to make sure that the father of their children has just the right traits. Men, on the other hand, who can be a bit looser, are freer to fall in love without consideration of a lot of different traits.

If this were the case, we might not see much variation over time in how women and men fall in love and decide with whom to live their lives. However, research clearly shows that the reasons for falling in love do change over time and appear to be more closely associated with the structure of gender in our society. Historically, women have been more economically dependent on men in marriage. If the survival of your children is related to the economic standing of your husband, it makes good sense to select a partner who, in addition to being attractive, is also well situated. This is initially consistent with the sociobiology argument, but it differs in that it places its emphasis on the context in which we live. And it suggests that as the context changes, so too will the reasons for falling in love.

In survey research, men do report falling in love sooner than women do.

Over the course of the last forty years, surveys indicate that women and men give some similar responses to questions about the role of love in selecting a partner. About 85 percent of men and women now say that they would not marry without love. In the 1960s, women were more open to marrying without love, as long as their other desires in a partner were met. What was the reason for this change? Since the 1960s, women's economic dependence on men in marriage has declined. With the majority of women, wives, and mothers in the paid labor force, the pressure to have a husband/partner who will take sole responsibility for economic support has declined. With less *need* for a husband as a provider, women can focus on other qualities for their enduring relationships. Or, as Dana Vannoy (1991) argues, when gender roles become more balanced, so too will the capacities for love.

But we should caution that employment situations are still not equal for women and men. We'll see in Chapter 10, on working families, that occupational and income disparities based on gender are still a reality of our labor market. As a result, men still have more financial independence than women, so we can expect to continue to see some differences in the ways men and women approach relationships.

Another way in which gendered notions of love are revealed is through popular culture. Magazines and advice columns still emphasize the man in the role of provider (Coltrane, 1998). Popular movies, such as the hit film *You've Got Mail,* starring Meg Ryan and Tom Hanks, continue to present traditional gender roles. In this very nineties film about love, the two main characters fall in love over the Internet, suggesting that love can be based on qualities totally independent of physical characteristics. However, the story doesn't end with falling in love online. As it turns out, Ryan's character owns a small children's bookstore started by her mother, and the business is struggling due to a new, larger bookstore in the neighborhood, which is owned by Hanks's character. Online, Hanks tries to help Ryan find ways to fight against the corporate giant and respond to its aggressive owner (not knowing, of course, that he is the corporate giant). She is not successful in her fight and has to sell her mother's business. Meanwhile, she continues her relationship with Hanks and ultimately meets him face to face. What happens when they discover their other (business) relationship? Do they discuss the contradiction in the Hanks character—he had wanted her to fight the corporation while he was working to run a small owner out of business? No. In fact, nothing is really ever discussed. It is OK, because they are *in love.*

The Practices of Romantic Love

Just as the meanings of love have varied over time, across cultures, and across social groups within cultures, so too have the ways in which we practice love. Later in the chapter we explore friendships, and later in the book we cover the ways love is expressed in marriage and in families with children. For now, we continue with our discussion of romantic love. Over the last several hundred years, U.S. society has changed dramatically. Along with those changes have come new ways of meeting, getting to know each other, and falling in love. Whether it's called courtship, calling, dating, or hanging out, these practices are all focused on love.

Historical Views on Courtship and Dating

Courtship in Early America During colonial times, interactions between unmarried individuals were highly supervised, not surprising when we consider the organization of social life prior to 1800 in the United States. Social life centered on family and community, and the primary economic activity was agriculture. Opportunities for interaction, then, occurred either at public social gatherings or in the homes of families. At social gatherings, parents could influence whom their daughters and sons met, and who might be invited to their homes for a visit. Because distances between farms were great and transportation was not very fast, it was not uncommon for the visitor (most likely a young man) to spend the night. It was during this period that a practice developed known as *bundling* (also called *tarrying*), which we first mentioned in Chapter 1.

A dating practice that emerged during the eighteenth and nineteenth centuries was **calling.** This practice, like the earlier "visits," primarily entailed men coming to visit women in their homes. In the upper social classes, this has been written about in women's diaries and portrayed in films. An interesting argument about this practice is that because women and their families had the opportunity to control the visit (who was *allowed* to call), women held more power in the development of romantic relationships than men. Carol Smith-Rosenberg (1975) suggests that even in the eighteenth century, when women were expected to be passive and not express hostility or criticism, they found ways to do so when an unwanted suitor came to call:

> When one such unfortunate came to court Sophie DuPont she hid in her room, first sending her sister Eluethera to entertain him and then dispatching a number of urgent notes to her neighboring sister-in-law, cousins, and a visiting friend who all came to Sophie's support. A wild female romp ensured, ending only when Sophie banged into a door, lacerated her nose, and retired, with her female cohorts, to bed. Her brother and the presumably disconcerted suitor were left alone. These were not the antics of teenagers but of women in their early and mid-twenties. (Smith-Rosenberg, 1975: 20)

However, this control still took place in a social system in which women held very limited power. Cott (1978) argues that in the 1800s, marriage was the primary means for women to support themselves financially; therefore, they could not be in complete control of their relationships with men. Economics still played an important role in their lives, and both their parents, who had an incentive to encourage contacts with certain men, as well as the men themselves, who were the ones to initiate contact, influenced women. Cott quotes a very articulate eighteen-year-old who understood women's precarious position in that they had the "liberty of refusing those we don't like, but not of selecting those we do" (1978: 229).

Industrialization, Consumerism, and the Emergence of Dating Significant shifts in unmarried individuals' dating behaviors occurred after 1900. Rapid industrialization resulted in rural to urban migration and the shifting of the place of work from farm to factory. The changing economy brought with it a higher standard of living and the opportunity in a cash economy to save some discretionary money. Uses for this discretionary money could be found in the growing commercial recreation sector of the economy.

A growing commercial recreation center in the early twentieth century, such as the dance hall, provided opportunities for dating couples to spend time together without parental supervision.

Movie theaters, amusement parks, and night-clubs were all part of the urban scene. Technological innovations in transportation (especially the automobile) provided the chance for couples to get away from home and parental supervision, and public social settings gave couples a place to go. It was a time when dating entered the arena of consumption (Bailey, 1988; Illouz, 1999).

In the early part of the past century, other social changes influenced interactions between those who were unmarried. Child labor laws limited the time that children could work, and mandatory education required that they spend time in school. These two changes resulted in a longer period of childhood, which was termed **adolescence** by G. Stanley Hall in 1904. Schools were also co-educational, which created an environment for girls and boys to interact socially. As relationships developed, couples could spend time alone together, away from parental supervision, at the movies or a dance club. These couple interactions were called **dating**.

Beth Bailey (1988) argues in her book *From Front Porch to Back Seat: Courtship in Twentieth Century America* that this movement of interaction away from home and parents brought with it a change in power dynamics. Like others, Bailey saw the *calling* system as one that favored women (and their families). Now that *dating* took couples away, it was the peer group and the economics of these individuals that took control. This economic system favored men, whose money was used to pay for the date. Men were expected to initiate, plan, and pay. Women's responsibility was to control men's behavior (sexual advances) within the relationship.

The first major college study on dating was done by Willard Waller (1937) at Penn State University. There, Waller studied the behavior of fraternity men on a campus in which men outnumbered women about six to one. In this system, dating became a very organized system in which men and women were rated in terms of their dating value (his article was called "The Rating and Dating Complex"). Men received higher scores or were put in the top "class" when they had access to automobiles, could dance well, and had more money. Women were held in higher regard if they dressed well, had good conversation skills, and were considered popular. Waller argued that in this system the goal was to be in a higher class, which would bring an enhanced reputation and the ability to get the best dates.

Some have criticized this early research, suggesting it may have reflected a situation unique to the particular institution or Greek life on college campuses (Gordon, 1981). Later attempts to replicate Waller's work found a bit more complexity to dating that included more than just an attempt at status enhancement. For example, Vreeland (1972) explored dating at Harvard in the 1960s and discovered that although some followed the more *instrumental* pattern that Waller found at Penn State, others were interested in dating for different reasons. Some wanted to pursue possible marriage partners (*traditional* dating), others wanted to find friendship (*companion* dating), and some saw dating as a process of intellectual stimulation (*intellectual* dating).

Like the "stage models" proposed for studying the development of love in the 1960s and 1970s, approaches were put forward for categorizing dating. Bernard Farber (1964) suggested that dating goes through the following stages: (1) dating, (2) keeping company, (3) going steady, (4) private agree-

ment to marry, (5) announcement of engagement, and (6) marriage. LeMasters (1957) also proposed stages: (1) group dating in middle or junior high school, (2) dating, (3) steady dating in high school, (4) pinning in college, (5) engagement, and (6) marriage. Like our discussion of such theories on love, stage theories on dating are "ideal forms" and do not cover the diversity in the development of relationships.

Contemporary Patterns of Interaction: Going Out or Hanging Out

The 1970s saw many political movements, including a resurgence of the women's movement, and dating became less structured. Title IX legislation, which mandated that girls be allowed access to sports programs in ways comparable to boys, has resulted in increased coeducational experiences. Boys and girls play together on basketball, soccer, baseball, and other sport teams, at least up to middle school. Sex segregation in the curriculum has declined, and girls and boys now take similar classes and take them together. Colleges have coed dormitories. And in the work force, the opportunities for women and men to engage in similar types of occupations or jobs, and to do them together, have increased.

FACT OR FICTION?

In general, attitudes about gender in relationships have become less conservative over time.

These structural changes in the lives of children and adults have been followed by a shift in attitudes among men and women regarding gender relationships. A recent study by Brewster and Padavic (2000) using data from the General Social Survey finds that attitudes about gender relationships have become more liberal over time. In 1977 the ma-

Just How Much Have Attitudes About Gender Relationships Changed?

From 1977 to the present, the General Social Survey has included four items that reflect adult attitudes about gender relationships. Responses to these statements range from strongly agree, agree, disagree, to strongly disagree. A recent analysis of people's responses to these items show the following trends:

STATEMENT	PERCENTAGE GIVING THE CONSERVATIVE RESPONSE	
	1977	1996
It is more important for a wife to help her husband's career than to have one herself.	57	21
It is much better for everyone if the man is the achiever and the woman takes care of home and family.	66	38
A preschool child is likely to suffer if his or her mother works.	67	46
A working mother can establish just as warm and secure a relationship with her children as a mother who does not work.	51	33.5

In 1977, the majority of Americans gave conservative responses to these statements. As of 1996, the majority did not. However, keep in mind that the data in this table reflect two points in time. Recent research by Brewster and Padavic (2000) explores the change in attitudes for all the years between 1977 and 1996, and also suggests reasons for the shifts in attitudes over time. Their findings reveal a number of important trends (and maybe some surprising ones).

The first thing they point out is that the support for conservative attitudes is not declining in a linear fashion over time. The dramatic shifts in women's labor market participation in the 1970s and 1980s were accompanied by similarly dramatic shifts in attitudes. However, now that the majority of women (and mothers) are employed, attitudes appear to be changing more slowly. This is an example of a curvilinear relationship (see Chapter 2).

jority of Americans held the view that the preferred situation is one in which women emphasize domestic pursuits while men focus on financial matters. As of 1996, the majority of Americans no longer supported this ideal (see the Focus on Family Research box above).

| FACT

More than twenty years of research on attitudes about gender in families show that people are less likely to support a relationship between men and women that restricts women to taking care of home and family while expecting men to be the sole breadwinner.

These changes in gender relationships have changed the way that men and women interact in the dating process. Women are now more likely to initiate relationships, and dating can no longer be put into strict categories or stages. No longer is dating seen as the linear process moving straight toward marriage, but as the way to meet some basic social needs. "Going out" on dates allows the opportunity for people to develop friendships and intimacy. It gives people a chance to

Another finding was that differences in attitudes remain for women and men (specifically, men show more conservative attitudes than women each year of the survey), *and* the changes in attitudes over time are greater for women than for men. Despite the age of the respondents, men are more conservative than women with respect to their views on the division of labor, and men appear to be more resistant to changing their views.

Finally, the results of this study suggest that while those with higher education are more liberal than those who hold less education, the effect of education on attitudes is declining over time. Several decades ago, the percentage of people getting a college education was smaller and allowed this group to experience events very different from others. Now, a much higher percentage obtains higher education, *and* the experiences of all

people (regardless of education) have changed with respect to issues of employment for women. Therefore, the effects of education and employment experiences on attitudes are more widely felt.

In general, attitudes are less conservative today than they were twenty years ago. However, the rate of attitudinal change has declined due to the fluctuations in people's views in recent years. The authors suggest that these fluctuations be explored in relation to a number of period effects. For example, the spotlight on child care has brought considerable media attention to problems associated with children being cared for outside the home. In addition, the rise in conservative political movements may be getting people to question the roles of men and women in the family and in the labor market. At the same time, projections are that increasing numbers of women will enter the la-

bor market in the coming years and that this trend may keep views about the gendered division of labor relatively liberal.

Source: K. Brewster and I. Padavic (2000). "Change in Gender-Ideology, 1977–1996: The Contributions of Intracohort Change and Population Turnover." *Journal of Marriage and Family, 62,* 477–487.

Critical Thinking

1. How would you respond to the statements used in the survey? How might your answers compare to those of your parents and your friends?

2. Can you think of some of the social forces we've discussed in this book that relate to the diversity in opinions on these statements?

3. Do you think attitudes will continue to change in the same way that they have over the last twenty years? Why or why not?

---

learn about their social selves as well. What does it mean to be an adult woman or man? As opposed to earlier practices that seemed to pair people up, new practices of "group dating" or just "hanging out" emerged wherein groups of people were less restricted by rules about who they are (or should be) attached to.

In a series of studies conducted in the 1980s and 1990s on college campuses, researchers found that young adults continue to maintain traditional notions about dating and, in fact, still behave in relatively traditional ways. In the first of this series, Rose and Frieze (1989) asked about 100 students to identify at least 20 things that *would occur* on a "first date." From these lists they pulled the items mentioned by more than one-quarter of the respondents and constructed a "dating script." Although there were many items listed as expected behaviors for both men and women, there were several items listed by only one gender or the other. For women, the activities suggested more passive behavior, while for men they were more active. Rose and Frieze (1993) followed up this study by asking students to identify activities/behaviors that *actually occurred* on first dates. They found remarkable similarity between what students had suggested would occur and what actually did. Men were more proactive (in planning and doing) while women were more reactive (waiting for the date, being polite). Laner and Ventrone (1998, 2000) have replicated these findings at another university. They found the following activities to be associated with *both* women and men on first dates:

* Deciding what to wear
* Grooming and getting dressed
* Going to dinner or a movie
* Some sort of conversation
* Thanking a date

However, women had a unique script that included waiting to be asked out on a date, buying a new outfit, waiting for the date, eating light, going to the bathroom to primp, and calling a friend to discuss the date. For men, the script included some other activities. They needed to ask someone for a date, prepare the car, get money, plan the date, buy flowers, pick up the date, open doors for date, pay the bill, and walk the date to the door when returning home. Both men and women agreed on these gendered scripts, suggesting that although attitudes about relationships have become more egalitarian, this shift has not been translated into the dating behavior of all college students. When it comes to dating, many young people still hold on to traditional practices.

FACT OR FICTION?

Dating on college campuses today continues to show gender differences in the ways women and men approach "courtship."

It is not so surprising that these scripts are still with us when we look at how the popular press presents ideas about dating. From advice columns in the 1930s to best-selling books about relationships in the 1960s, messages about gender-specific approaches to interacting with the opposite sex were common (Coltrane, 1998). For example, in a widely published advice column, Dorothy Dix helped women establish courtship rituals that included physical preparation (enhancing your beauty to attract a man) and more emotional displays (showing him that you depend on him). In the 1960s, an exceptionally popular book called *Fascinating Womanhood* encouraged women to be obedient and supportive (even if you don't agree with your man). Rose and Frieze (1989) found that these gender-specific pieces of advice continued to appear in dating guides published in the 1950s through the 1980s. Even current guides perpetuate such advice. For example, Laner and Ventrone (2000) take a brief look at *The Complete Idiot's Guide to Dating* (Kuriansky, 1996) and *Dating for Dummies* (1997). In *The Idiot's Guide* we learn that men and women still approach dating in different ways. Men are told to "be romantic, listen attentively, agree to do things with her family/friends, build her trust, spend time cuddling, do not expect or demand sex, learn about her body." Women, on the other hand, should learn the following: "do not expect him to profess love for you soon, do not push him into commitment, do not snoop, do not nag him into talking about his feelings, take the initiative sometimes, do not take everything personally, loosen up your inhibitions, do not compare him to other lovers," and "accept him without judgment" (Kuriansky, 1996: 491). This is interesting advice when research suggests that men will claim to fall in love first. You don't need to buy an *Idiot's Guide* to get ideas about how men and women should relate to one another. Television shows, books, popular music, and movies all provide clues.

It is not only traditional notions about dating or "scripts" for dating that maintain a traditional flavor; other rituals also reveal the importance of gender. For example, how can we tell when a couple is "going steady" or in some way dating exclusively? Beth Bailey (1988) traced dating patterns in the second half of the twentieth century and found examples such as getting pinned, exchanging ID bracelets, and wearing corduroy "steady" jackets. Other examples include wearing a boyfriend's class ring or wearing a "promise ring." Most of these rituals focus on women's display of the relationship.

| FACT

While both men and women report that they engage in grooming behaviors prior to a date, men are more likely to be cognizant of the need for money, whereas women are more focused on their appearance.

Public displays of gender are also reinforced by the multi-million-dollar business devoted to engagement and wedding rings (Ingraham, 1999). Advertising by jewelry companies suggests that "diamonds are forever" and a good investment for a young couple. DeBeers, the largest diamond manufacturer, spends about $75 million per year in advertising. Part of the advertising provides us with the helpful suggestion that the engagement ring should cost at least two months' salary for the groom.

The buying of a ring by a man for a woman to wear prior to their marriage helps to perpetuate the patriarchal idea of male ownership of women. Although the majority of men and women exchange rings at their wedding ceremonies, it has been the wearing of rings by women that has the longest history. Called a "betrothal ring," it signified the transfer of property (a woman) from father to groom. The intended would wear the ring on her right hand until the wedding ceremony, and then her husband would switch the ring from the right to the left. Contemporary practice is for the woman to wear two rings, an engagement ring worn prior to the wedding and then another added at the time of the ceremony. It is estimated that about 75 percent of all first-time brides wear engagement rings (Ingraham, 1999).

Variations in Dating Practices: Social Class, Ethnicity, and Sexual Identity

As the previous discussion suggests, dating can be related to resources. Whether a date takes place at the local cinema or the opera house may depend on the ability to purchase the tickets to the event and the resources to obtain the appropriate thing to wear. Although people with the means to spend a lot may choose not to, the point is that the option to go to expensive restaurants and theaters and buy expensive gifts *without going into significant debt* makes the possibilities for dating very different across social classes.

Those who study the upper socioeconomic classes have long suggested that dating is socially controlled in order to maintain their distinctive place in society. People in the upper class are said to have **class consciousness.** That is, they understand their position in society and establish practices that help to maintain this system and their place in it. Private schools, private clubs, and gated communities are examples of how people segregate themselves by social class. But it is also important for upper-class families to make sure that their children fall in love with the "right" kind of people. Debutante balls and private social clubs serve as mechanisms to introduce young people to "appropriate" dating partners. The first debutante ball in the United States was in Philadelphia in 1748, but these gatherings continue to be held today throughout the winter and spring seasons. The cost of the balls can range from $25,000 to $250,000 (which is the amount Henry Ford II spent) but may also be sponsored by local charities as fund raisers (and are then tax deductible) (Domhoff, 1998).

Members of the upper classes in our society are not the only ones who engage in

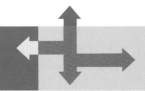

In 1998, online romances became the subject of the movie *You've Got Mail,* starring Tom Hanks and Meg Ryan. The two meet online and exchange e-mails, even though they are both in relationships with other people at the time. In the end, they fall in love, meet each other in person, and "hit it off." And, believe it or not, that is exactly what is happening for many "real-life" couples.

With millions of people surfing the World Wide Web, it's no wonder online romances are blooming. Although many believe that the Internet promotes isolation, online dating is connecting people across the country and around the globe. Match.com, for instance, a popular online dating service, currently serves more than 100,000 people. As the popularity of these services and chat rooms continues to increase, meeting someone online becomes less and less farfetched.

As far as who is dating whom, online romances tend to follow general off-line standards. In general, Internet personal ads follow the same format as those found in the newspaper. People tend to seek people of the same race, similar age, and similar education levels. Because of the makeup of online populations, this gives an advantage to those of certain races and income levels. As Alecia Wolf (1998: 17) points out, the typical Internet user is "overwhelmingly white, male, and well educated, with a higher than average income in a white-collar professional career." In fact, statistics show that though African Americans make up 12 percent of the general population, they represent only 5 percent of Internet users. Eighty-seven percent of Internet users are white, while only 74 percent of the general population is white. And, with a median income of $60,000,

the average Internet user is making far more than average in the general population. With the exception of romances between people from different countries, then, online romances involving Internet users from the United States are much more likely to involve white, college-educated individuals. Though the Internet is often touted as the "great equalizer," providing access and opportunities across the lines of race, class, and gender, the fact remains that certain groups are overrepresented in online communication.

Despite this current lack of diversity, online romances continue to bloom, often bringing together individuals who most likely never would have met otherwise. Take the story in the Friday, April 21, 2000, edition of the *San Francisco Chronicle*.

David Martin posted his profile with an online dating service and soon found himself in an e-mail rela-

practices to mark their distinctiveness. Others who are also interested in celebrating their distinctive cultures create situations for their children to introduce them to adult life and interacting with others. One example of this is the *quinceañera,* a kind of coming-out party for Latinas. This type of party is held at the time of the young woman's fifteenth birthday and usually includes a mass followed by a party. The woman's family buys the daughter a special dress, and it is expected that she will/can begin dating after this celebration.

FACT OR FICTION?

The Internet is the "great equalizer." Dating online produces higher proportions of intergroup (ethnic, race, social class) relationships than dating in an off-line setting.

Although the upper classes and some religious or ethnic groups plan ways to introduce their children to potential dating partners, most young people meet each other in public places: the workplace, at school, and through friends. The new public space known

tionship with a woman named Dorthia. The two are now living together in California and see nothing peculiar about meeting some-one online. Similarly, in honor of Valentine's Day 2000, *48 Hours* ran a segment on a Greensboro, North Carolina, man who met his girlfriend online. The couple met through Match.com and then met face to face.

Online romance doesn't always work out, and breakups, just as in "real-life" relationships, can be devastating. According to an article in the *Washington Post,* online dating has its drawbacks. The levels of self-disclosure increase in online relationships, often making the relationship particularly fragile. And there is an even greater risk of deception when dating someone via the Internet. Because of this deception and the element of fantasy that the Internet allows, many online romances don't carry over into "real-

life" relationships. Chat rooms such as "Married and Flirting" allow users to be in two marriages at once: one online and one in "real life." Complications arise because some see these online marriages as extramarital affairs.

Certainly, online romance is not for everyone, but it is becoming more and more common despite its drawbacks. In fact, right-wing radio talk show host Rush Limbaugh met his wife online. Still, experts urge people to be careful in cyberspace, especially when it comes to dating. What you "see" online is not always what you get. Just as with relationships that start face to face, sometimes they work and sometimes they don't. With the increasing number of people looking for love online, this may be more than just a passing fad. Who knows? Maybe you'll find your next love online.

Shelley L. Nelson, Indiana University

Reference cited: A. Wolf (1998). "Exposing the Great Equalizer: Demythologizing Internet Equity." In B. Ebo (Ed.), *Cyberghetto or Cybertopia? Race, Class, and Gender on the Internet* (pp. 15–32). Westport, CT: Praeger.

Critical Thinking

1. Have you ever met anyone online? If not, would you ever consider doing this? Why or why not?

2. What do you think are the odds of an online relationship succeeding compared to one in which the people met off line? If you think the odds might be different, why do you think so?

3. Do you think there should be some kind of rules for people using chat rooms and online dating services?

as the Internet also provides an avenue to find friends and potential partners (see the Family Diversity box on pages 170–171). However, some groups have a difficult time meeting others in our society because of social stigma. Those are gays, lesbians, bisexuals, and transgendered (GLBT) individuals (these identities will be discussed at greater length in the next chapter). It is still illegal for people to marry someone of the same sex. According to the General Social Survey, 24 percent of Americans think homosexuality is "always wrong" for adults, and the vast ma-

jority think it is always wrong for teens (see http://csa.berkeley.edu:7502). Because the general sentiment is not strongly supportive of gay/lesbian relationships, the public spaces that are created for GLBTs are limited, and in many areas they are just nonexistent. They tend to be found in "gay ghettos" and are often under the watchful eye of police. Huston and Schwartz (1996) also note that even when gays or lesbians meet, they then have a difficult time maintaining a relationship. The options for public places to spend time are limited, so many date by

New technologies provide new ways for people to meet others for friendship or romance.

going to personal residences. In addition, because of discrimination at work, many gays and lesbians choose to stay "closeted" about their sexual identity and dating relationships to save their job.

| FICTION

First, Internet users are not as diverse a group as the general population. In addition, when meeting people online through dating services or chat rooms, people ask questions about the social characteristics of others. This produces as much homogamy as in the general population.

Research on GLBT relationships is very limited. Much of the discussion is about sexual practices and not about dating practices. But the little research that has been done suggests that GLBT dating practices have many similarities with heterosexual dating relationships. Those relationships that last the longest are those in which the partners have a greater sense of equity. Research also suggests gender differences that are similar to the relationships of straight women and

men. Gay men tend to have shorter relationships with more partners, while lesbians tend more toward "serial monogamy." They have several relationships over a lifetime, but one at a time. Straight men are also more likely to have more partners and to have more than one at a time, as compared to straight women.

Intergroup Dating

We've mentioned that romantic relationships in our culture are quite homogamous. That is, we tend to spend most of our time with people who look like us, act like us, and think like us. As we can see in Table 4.3, the majority of people in both long-term and short-term relationships are similar with respect to ethnicity, education, age, and religion. But this is not always the case. No national figures exist on the prevalence of interethnic dating, but as we'll see later in this book, the percentage of interethnic marriages has increased; therefore, we can assume that the number of people dating interethnically has also increased. The same is probably true with respect to other kinds of intergroup dating, such as interfaith dating.

There are several possible explanations for the fact that some people date others from different ethnic groups or religions, but there is very little research to test these ideas. One explanation refers us back to the notion of a "pool of eligibles." For most groups, the numbers of available (unmarried) men and women is roughly equal across age groups. For others, the pool of eligibles is more limited than for others. For example, the work of Robert Staples, William Julius Wilson, and others suggests that the historical conditions faced by African Americans have resulted in a skewed sex ratio. Specifically, the number of eligible black men is far fewer than the number of eligible black women, from adolescence throughout adulthood (Wilson, 1997). Reasons for the skewed

TABLE 4.3	Percentage of People in Sexual Relationships Who Hold Similar Characteristics		
CHARACTERISTICS	PEOPLE WHO ARE COHABITING (%)	PEOPLE IN LONG-TERM RELATIONSHIPS (%)	PEOPLE IN SHORT-TERM RELATIONSHIPS (%)
Race/ethnicity	88	89	91
Education	87	83	87
Age	75	76	83
Religion	53	56	60

Source: Adapted from Michael et al. (1994), Table 3, p. 46. Observations are of sexually active partnerships in the past year. Short-term relationships are those partnerships lasting less than one month.

sex ratio include higher rates of crime and incarceration, crime victimization, and health-related deaths among African American men than among African American women. These factors result in fewer opportunities for African American women to date or marry African American men (Staples, 1994).

The opportunity to meet people from varying social, ethnic, or religious backgrounds is also related to migration patterns that bring people in contact with others along with the residential or schooling choices of adults for themselves and their children. Research suggests that when a group is in the minority in their environment, they are more likely to perceive intergroup dating as a viable option. An example of this can be found in the literature on interfaith dating. Marshall and Markstrom-Adams (1995) studied high school students who attended one of two types of schools. One school was a Jewish high school in a neighborhood that was predominantly Jewish (called the majority context). The other schools attended were either public or private, but not oriented to Judaism (called the minority context). Students going to school in the majority context were less open to interfaith dating than were students in the minority context. The authors of this study argue that the larger pool of same-faith dating partners existed in the majority con-

text; therefore, students did not have to face alternatives. Similar arguments have been proposed regarding the dating practices of other religious groups (Francoeur, Koch, & Weis, 1998) as well as those of a variety of ethnic groups (Fujino, 1997; Shibazaki & Brennan, 1998; Tucker & Mitchell-Kernan, 1995; Ross, 1997).

A recent study by Marisol Clark-Ibáñez (2000) explored a number of potential explanations for interethnic dating using a sample of college students. These included students who were African American (4 percent), Latino/a (28 percent), Asian American (12 percent), Filipino/Pacific Islander (3 percent), Middle Eastern (3 percent), Indian (1 percent), non-Hispanic white (40 percent), and of mixed ethnicity (9 percent). One of the strengths of her research is that she distinguished between those who have dated interethnically only once from those who have done so more frequently. She found that social network theory was very useful in explaining the extent of interethnic dating. This theoretical perspective looks at the "availability" of various dating patterns but recognizes that there are different levels of interaction with those people with whom one can potentially interact. Some people may casually interact with ethnic others, while others may interact more closely (in living groups, at social gatherings, or in small classes).

As our society becomes more diverse, the number of interethnic couples is increasing.

Among those in Clark-Ibáñez's sample, the respondents who had more ethnically diverse social circles were more likely to date interethnically at least once. But the distinguishing factor among those who have interethnically dated more than once or twice was the diversity of the respondents' parents' friends. This factor is likely to indicate longer-term interaction with people of different ethnic groups, but more importantly it shows a climate of acceptance of ethnic others as friends.

Another intriguing finding in the research on interethnic dating is that men are more likely to date among people of different ethnic groups than are women (Clark-Ibáñez, 2000; Sprecher & Felmlee, 1992). The argument here is that women may be more influenced by pressure from friends and family than men are. Social networks work as a kind of social control, and in a society where marrying within one's own group(s) is still the norm, women may feel more pressure to conform.

Overall, the extent of intergroup dating has increased over time in the United States, and this trend probably reflects the same kinds of forces that have resulted in more freedom of choice in dating partners and less parental control over the dating process.

The Downside to Love

Falling in love is a powerful emotion, filled with positive affect. When we are *in love,* we think it will last forever. However, nothing about love is guaranteed. Although research on breaking up is not abundant, it suggests that the majority of dating relationships break up after a few years. For example, one study found that about a third of dating couples break up after three months and about 40 percent after nine months (Berscheid, Snyder, & Omoto, 1989), while another study finds that 58 percent break up after four years (Sprecher, 1994). Recall from our earlier discussion that relationships develop over time and that after initial stages of attraction, couples learn more about each other. During this process, individuals may discover differing interests or values. Differing communication styles also appear to be a common reason for breaking up. Reasons for ending a romantic relationship are similar in heterosexual and same-sex relationships (Kurdek, 1991).

One of the fascinating findings in contemporary research on romantic relationships is that the reasons that some couples break off relationships are the same as the reasons for being attracted to each other in the first place (Felmlee, 1995; Pines, 1997). These relationships are referred to as "fatal attractions," where *fatal* refers not to being "deadly" but to being "prophetic" or "foretelling" (Felmlee, 2001: 263). In her most recent study, Diane Felmlee (2001) found a number of fatal attractions among a sample of 125 undergraduates in a general education course. For example, some individuals are attracted to others who are "nice" or "considerate." Later, the same people get described as too nice because they are not willing to open up and be honest for fear of hurting their partner. Others claimed to be initially attracted to people with "strong" personalities, only to argue later that these same personalities were "stubborn." Other fatal attractions included those that went from being seen as funny to flaky, outgoing to over the top, caring to clinging, quiet to close, exciting to scary, physically attractive to high maintenance, laid-back to lazy, and successful to workaholic. Not all couples recognizing these differences break off their relationships. Becoming disenchanted with one characteristic of a partner does not necessarily translate into disenchantment with the relationship.

Another theme in the research on romance focuses on the potential benefits of romantic relationships. Later in this book we will see that there is considerable evidence suggesting that adult romance (via marriage and cohabitation) brings some benefits to individuals in terms of greater happiness and better health. However, research on romantic attachments during adolescence suggests just the opposite (Joyner & Udry, 2000). Following almost 8,000 seventh through twelfth graders over the course of one year, Joyner and Udry found that those who entered into romantic relationships were more likely to experience increases in depression compared to those without romantic attachments. Adolescent females were significantly more affected by romance than were adolescent males. Females were also more likely to become less happy over time when they were involved romantically. Increases in alcohol problems and delinquency were associated with those involved in romantic relationships, and there were no differences between males and females.

Why would romance bring adolescents down? One of the findings from the study just mentioned is that romantic attachments were negatively correlated with school performance and relationships with parents.

That is, over time those who enter romantic relationships tend to do more poorly in their schoolwork and experience more problems with their parents. Romance includes a lot of emotion work, both positive and negative (Larson, Clore, & Wood, 1999), which can affect the time and energy one has for involvement in other types of relationships. It is also possible that adolescents who have problems in school or at home seek out romantic relationships and hence are more likely to be depressed and unhappy. The romance may not help.

Other, more serious problems can also occur in romantic relationships. Recall earlier in the chapter that one of the "styles of love" identified by John Lee is "mania," an obsessive type of love. This is the most problematic type of love, for feelings of possessiveness and jealousy can hinder the development of positive self-esteem and self-worth. In other romantic relationships, aggression and violence may also result. We will return to this subject in the next chapter.

The point to recognize here is that love is idealized in our culture and that we expect more from our romantic relationships than is humanly possible. We want someone who is strong yet gentle, outgoing yet reserved, assertive yet caring, etc. In expecting too much, we can set ourselves (and our relationships) up for failure.

Love and Friendships

If we stop and think back on our experiences of loving others, we may find that some of our most endearing and enduring loving relationships have been with friends. The study of friendships is relatively new to social scientists because of the historical emphasis in Western societies on heterosexual romantic love. The idea of falling in love is taught to us as a story of a woman and a man. And friendship, if it is part of this process, is seen as good for the relationship. But friendships independent of romance are, or can be, suspect. First is the idea that men and women can never be "just friends." It is assumed that spending too much time together is bound to result in sexual relations. Second, same-sex friendships have not been considered to be very important because they are seen as secondary to heterosexual relationships. Lillian Rubin's study of 300 men and women between the ages of 25 and 55 shows that the intensity of friendships is dependent on whether or not there is a "love interest" around (1985: 114). If there is, friendships with others will wane or disappear. She argues that we all understand this, so whether it's our friend who pulls back or we who pull back, it is seen as normal. Friendships will always take a back seat to romance. Finally, same-sex friendships can be perceived as problematic in our culture because of **homophobia,** an unrealistic fear of homosexuality that is particularly acute among men (Lehne, 1998). Traditional notions of masculinity include independence and control. In relationships with women, men are expected to be the ones in control, and their ability to be in such a position is supported by our cultural norms and social institutions (patriarchy). Norms regarding relationships between men are not so clear. Does one partner lose out in terms of control, hence compromising masculinity? Fears about the compromise to masculinity create confusion about close friendships among men.

| FACT OR FICTION?

Women are more intimate in their same-sex friendships than are men.

Fears and confusion aside, research is clear that friendships are beneficial for our health and well-being. Friendships have been shown to lower blood pressure, heart rates, and cholesterol. One study covering a nine-year span found that those who had the highest number of friends reduced their risk of death by over 60 percent. Particularly beneficial are friendships among women. A recent review of the literature finds that women are more likely than men to seek out same-sex friends, especially in times of stress, and that these friendships are beneficial in women's responses to that stress (Taylor et al., 2000). Although this particular review suggested that the tendency for women to seek out other women may be rooted in our evolutionary past, social historians also point to the ways in which societies are organized as explanations for why women's friendships are both more accepted and encouraged.

Historical Research on Same-Sex Friendships

Carol Smith-Rosenberg (1975) studied friendships between women by exploring letters written between 1760 and 1880 in the United States. Because these letters do not represent the diversity in the population at the time, she presents her work as a study of literate middle-class American women. What we learn from her work is that friendships, like romantic love relationships, are best understood by placing them within their historical period. During the eighteenth and nineteenth centuries, the majority of people lived in very gender-segregated worlds. Labor at home was divided along gender lines, and most of one's day was spent with others of the same gender. Historians of this period show that women in urban areas spent time visiting other women, often for tea or to share in domestic pursuits, while rural women spent time with their children or extended periods of time visiting other families, sharing work with other women. Although women and men did spend time together, their interactions were subject to more strict codes of conduct. Smith-Rosenberg argues that women developed very strong intimate bonds with other women. The letters that women wrote to each other show an affinity that included a longing for physical contact and verbal expressions of love. Take, for example, the correspondence between Jeannie and Sarah. They met while on vacations with their families and subsequently went to boarding school together. As Jeannie wrote,

> I want you to tell me in your next letter, to assure me, that I am your dearest. . . . I do not doubt you, and I am not jealous but I long to hear you say it once more and it seems already a long time since your voice fell on my ear. So just fill a quarter page with caresses and expressions of endearment. (1975: 314)

Whether or not these two women engaged in sexual relations is not the issue to focus on here. Instead, we should see how certain environments allow for the freedom to create relationships with a broad range of feelings and emotions. The United States in the nineteenth century was such an environment for middle-class women. Living in single-sex or "homosocial" networks allowed for the development of these intimate—and seemingly sensual—relations among women.

We are beginning to see similar arguments being constructed around men's friendships with other men through history. Recall that the writings of Plato suggested that men's love for one another was the superior love. More recently, Karen Hanson (1992) studied men's friendships in antebellum New England and also found what appeared to be romantic friendships among men. She argues that these friendships may have been as common as those among women during that time. Her study focused on a time period that we referred to earlier as that of "separate spheres" for women and men. So it was not only women who were living in homosocial worlds (as Smith-Rosenberg calls them), but men were as well. Following from the title of Smith-Rosenberg's

earlier work, Hanson asks if there was also a "*male* world of love and ritual" in early-nineteenth-century New England (1992: 37).

In the United States in the nineteenth century, it was not uncommon for men to spend a considerable amount of time together and on occasion to share a bed. In rural America, families would get together for exchanging services, whether it was to raise a barn or to help in times of harvest. Men and women were both frequent visitors or hosts and spent time with others of the same sex. There did not appear to be a fear of same-sex friendships, for such relationships did not present a threat to masculinity or femininity. The terms *heterosexuality* and *homosexuality* are more recent creations, therefore not part of the vocabulary of this time (Spenser, 1995). As a result, men were also allowed the freedom to establish intimate bonds with other men. Letters exchanged between men reveal the quality of men's friendships. In one example, Hanson tells us about the friendship between two men who had worked together in New Hampshire in the 1830s. Although the letters exchanged between these men varied in content and style, they were not without a hint of the romantic tradition that Smith-Rosenberg found. In one letter, a Mr. Beal wrote that he

> can not forget those happy hours [th]at we spent at G. Newcombs and the evening walks; but we are deprived of that privilege now we are separated for a time we cannot tell how long perhaps before our eyes behold each other in this world. (Beal to Nims, March 21, 1832) (Hanson, 1992: 48)

This research presents us with a view of friendships among men and among women that were varying in intensity and the potential for romantic attachment. The key here is that romantic or physically intimate same-sex relationships could exist in earlier parts of our history because nineteenth-century

What we've seen from the historical study of both women and men's same-sex friendships suggests a pattern. In environments where there is considerable segregation along gender lines, the opportunity for intimate friendships among women and among men is greater. Alternatively, the ways in which friendship sentiments are expressed make them appear to be more intimate. Using data on nonindustrialized societies randomly drawn from the Human Relations Area Files, Daphne Spain (1992) found that there is a statistically significant relationship between the existence of "men's huts" and the extent of male solidarity. These data are based on ethnographies of cultures that relied primarily on hunting and gathering, horticulture, or agriculture for subsistence. Of the 81 societies used for her study, 22 (or 27 percent) had "men's huts." These huts are referred to by a number of names, including ceremonial huts, bachelor's huts, or clubhouses, but they all serve a similar purpose.

They are places where men spend time together away from women. While in these huts men practice politics (decisions regarding their village), discuss religion and culture (initiation rites), and plan activities (hunting, warfare). Spain suggests that the huts provide men the opportunity to develop strong ties with other men and create a sense of solidarity. Her statistical analyses showed that in societies with men's huts, men are more likely to have a higher degree of solidarity than will men in societies without men's huts.

Another very important finding from her research is that the power that men hold relative to women is greater in those societies with men's huts than in others. This may be one of the major differences in the relationship between gender segregation and same-sex friendships for men and women. While both women and men in gender-segregated environments have been shown to develop more intimate friendships with same-sex friends, this situation doesn't nec-

essarily translate into greater power for women. More recent research on the existence of separate men's clubs suggests that groups such as the Masons, Odd Fellows (Clawson, 1980), and Boys Scouts (Hantover, 1978) have had the consequence of creating solidarity among men and reinforcing their greater power/status relative to women.

Critical Thinking

1. Do you belong to any organizations or groups that have only people of your gender? If so, do you think that this setting provides an opportunity for you to develop closer relationships with these individuals?

2. Have you ever been in a situation where you've been "outnumbered" by the other gender? Do you think that the gender composition of friendship groups can influence the types of behaviors and activities of the groups?

culture allowed it. Friendships also vary by cultural context, as can be seen in the Family Diversity box above.

Contemporary Research on Friendships

Most of the research in the 1970s and 1980s on same-sex friendships concerned comparisons between the quality and quantity of men's versus women's attachments. Men and

women were found to have about the same number of friends, but men's friendships appeared less personal or intimate compared to friendships among women (Pleck, 1975; Rubin, 1985). Women were found to be more self-disclosing (verbal) while men spent time with other men engaging in activities. In other words, women *talked* about things while men *did* things. In Chapter 2 we presented the work of Scott Swain (1989) on intimacy in men's friendships. His study found that the college-aged men he interviewed expressed a considerable desire for intimacy. But because of cultural prescriptions about appropriate behavior for men, along with the homophobia that exists in our culture, men created close connections to other men through side-by-side physical activity. Instead of hugging or holding hands, men played sports and showed signs of intimacy through slaps on the back or high-fives.

What this research tells us is that both men and women consider their friendships to be important but are constrained by the context within which they can interact with friends. In a recent study of same-sex friendships, Karen Walker (1994, 2001) suggests that if we look a bit closer at same-sex friendships, we may find that men are more intimate with other men than previously thought. First, Walker finds that when she asks the men and women in her sample general questions about their friendships, they reinforce the gendered experiences just mentioned. That is, men talk more instrumentally about their friendships, saying that they like to share activities. Women focus more on their friends as people to share feelings with. Walker suggests that these discussions may just reflect the respondents' acceptance of cultural norms about appropriate forms of masculinity and femininity in same-sex relationships. (This is a kind of social desirability bias—see Chapter 2— whereby survey respondents say what they perceive to be culturally accepted.) She argues that this type of bias exists because when she asked about specific friends, she found that men were as likely to report sharing feelings with their male friends as women were to report sharing feelings with other women.

| FICTION

Historical evidence shows that both women and men have had very intimate same-sex relationships. Contemporary research sug-

gests that although women may admit to having more-emotional relationships in general, men also admit to more closeness if asked about specific friends.

Variations in Friendships: Social Class and Race/Ethnicity Another very interesting finding in Walker's research is that there appears to be a difference in styles of friendships across social class. She finds that friends who were characterized as working class had been friends much longer than those in the middle class. They were more likely to have grown up in the same neighborhood and to continue living there as adults. The longevity of the friendships allowed friends more opportunity to become intimate and share much about themselves. They knew each other better. Friendships among people in the middle class appeared to be of shorter duration. Occupations in the middle and upper-middle classes often require geographic mobility. Although friendships can be maintained over time, they are less likely to be maintained face to face and are more likely to be done over the phone or through the mail. Another structural difference between working and middle-class individuals is that those in her sample who were working class experienced more crises in their lives. Unemployment, substance abuse, and family health problems were more frequent. Although there were crises among those in the middle class, they were less severe, on average, and of shorter duration. To the extent that intimacy is built in a relationship by sharing problems, Walker found that working-class friendships had more opportunities for intimacy.

Clyde Franklin's (1992) work on friendship among black men suggests that racial/ethnic differences, as well as social class, shape relationships among men: "Because working-class black males experience greater isolation from mainstream society than upwardly mobile black men, they may not internalize the same taboos against male

Although cross-sex friendships are possible, others often make assumptions about men and women who spend time together.

to succeed in life, they have a more competitive relationship with others, including their friends.

Friendships Between Women and Men

Up to now, our discussion has been about same-sex friendships. It is clear that the meaning and experience of friendships vary across time and space. Intimacy is apparent in relationships among women and among men, but how that intimacy is practiced or acted out depends on the structure of gender, class, and racial/ethnic relations in our society. What about friendships between women and men? Can there be true friendships, or are they possible only either prior to a romantic commitment or as part of a romantic relationship?

Friendships between women and men have not received much attention in the literature, but this is partly due to the fact that they are less likely to occur, and when they do, they are not as likely to endure as either same-sex friendships or romantic heterosexual ones. As we suggested earlier, this is because they are believed to be part of the developmental process of romantic engagement (friends become lovers or lovers later become friends) or because cross-sex friendships are threatening to our heterosexual social order. Swain's (1992) study of college students shows that male–female friendships are difficult to maintain. There are continual questions about the sexual boundaries in the relationship. He found that it was not uncommon for the friends to have to explain to others that they were "just friends."

The struggle to maintain friendships also comes from inside the relationship. We've already discussed some of the differences between men and women in how they practice intimacy. Men are socialized to be less verbal, while women learn to desire self-disclosure. To the extent that these differences exist in the friendship, conflict may arise over perceptions of the other's commit-

same-sex friendships, which result in non-self-disclosure, competitiveness, and non-vulnerability" (1992: 203). Franklin found working-class black men expressing strong sentiments about their friends because they trusted them. They shared experiences, including the experience of being black in a society with a long history of racism. Among middle-class black men, however, he found more "cool" relationships. Like Walker, Franklin suggests that upwardly mobile people are not as likely to be linked to a specific geographic area, and in their striving

ment to the relationship. Another challenge to people in cross-sex friendships results from a power imbalance between men and women in our society. Booth and Hess (1974) found cross-sex friendships to be less homogeneous than same-sex friendships. That is, there are more likely to be differences in the age, education, and occupational experiences of the men and women. And these differences usually put men in a position of power. This situation may have changed. Women's level of education has risen, relative to men's, and women are more likely to be working side by side with men in occupations that were previously male dominated. Future research may find that cross-sex relationships have reflected these changes. At the same time, Swain (1992) argues that whether or not structural imbalance exists, cross-sex friendships exist in a culture that continues to support notions of gender inequality. For example, when a couple is out to dinner, the check may be automatically given to the man because of the assumption that he is in financial control.

Whether the relationships we form are with those of the same sex/gender or not, the important thing to realize is that these relationships are important. They help us to explore ourselves in environments that are accepting and affirming. They also help us to be healthier and to live longer lives. Friendships can be enduring bonds that include caring and commitment. Using the definition offered at the start of this chapter, friendships are loving relationships.

Conclusion

Much of the literature on the meaning of love has focused on romantic heterosexual love. We can trace our contemporary definitions to stories (many of them myths) from medieval Europe, where love was sung by the troubadours as something a man felt for a woman he could not have. This struggle to attain the impossible (referred to as unrequited love) is sometimes associated with the struggles that people face as they move toward adulthood. The goal of this struggle is to find someone with whom you share a bond of affection and emotion, a bond that will last a lifetime.

How people experience love is very much shaped by the structure of society—its norms, values, and customs. The way in which our societies are organized around social class, race/ethnicity, gender, and age sets up opportunities for people to meet and fall in love. Changes in the economy and major technological innovations have also shifted patterns and behaviors of courtship. However, love is more than romance; it includes intense feelings we have for others, feelings that are not necessarily sexual. The love of a parent for a child, and the love between friends, are very important parts of our lives that are also shaped by the social and cultural environment. Family research on loving relationships reveals the considerable diversity in the meanings and practices of love, but also indicates the important role that love plays in creating and maintaining family ties.

Chapter Review

* *What do we mean by the term* love*?*

Although love is experienced in a variety of ways, there are a number of common features. Our definition of love is of an enduring bond between two or more people that is based on affection and emotion, and includes a sense of obligation toward one another. Using this definition is useful when looking at a variety of types of love, including the love of parents for children, the love of romantic partners, and the love of friends for one another.

* *How do we learn to love?*

One thing is certain about human beings: we are social by nature. We cannot live without having relationships with other people. Psychologists suggest that our first relationships in life, those with our primary guardian, shape the way that we approach relationships with others. If we have secure relationships with our primary caregiver, we are likely to have similar types of romantic attachments as adults. However, even though early attachments are important, they cannot explain the dynamic and complicated ways in which we learn to love others later in life.

* *How have meanings of love changed over time?*

Love is a social construct. As such, the way it is defined and experienced will vary depending on who is involved and where and when it occurs. This is why we read about love as something that occurs only between men during ancient Greece (Plato), as a sexual flirtation between men and women who cannot be together in the Middle Ages (courtly love), or as a feminine quality concerning the care of family members during the mid-nineteenth century (feminization of love). In contemporary society, we recognize that love can be experienced in a variety of ways and that the quality of love between two people can change over the duration of their relationship. Love is not static.

* *What is it that attracts people to each other for romantic love?*

There are a number of theories that attempt to explain the processes of attraction. Biological theories suggest that attraction is rooted in our evolutionary past. In order to pass on our biological heritage, we are attracted to others who have the highest probability of procreative success. Social scientists focus more on the ways in which we are socialized and the exposure we have to others. We tend to develop relationships with others who are like us socially (norms, values, social class) and are physically near to us. After initial attraction, relationships are maintained by individuals getting to know each other better and working out a balance in terms of what is given to each other. Couples stay together when relationships are more balanced.

* *Do men and women want the same thing from love?*

The short answer to this question is yes. Research suggests that most people, regardless of gender, look for romantic partners who are kind, understanding, and intelligent. After that, however, gender does show a difference. Men are more likely to value physical attractiveness and youth in their potential partners, while women place a higher value on financial capacity in men. Sociobiologists suggest this syndrome is related to the differences between men's and women's procreative strategies, but again social scientists suggest we look at the way in which societies are organized. Women are still at a disadvantage in terms of occupational opportunities and income, and will therefore put more emphasis on financial capacity in a partner. If this explanation is better than the biological one, then we should expect women to emphasize economics less as they become more equal to men in the labor market.

How have the ways that people "date" changed over time?

Dating is a concept that emerged in the twentieth century. However, women and men were engaging in romantic interactions much earlier than that. The interactions were shaped by the social organization of society at the time. In our agrarian past, young couples might get together as part of community events. With industrialization and the emergence of larger cities, middle-class couples would gather in the parlor of a young woman's parents' home. With the advent of public transportation and the automobile, romantic relationships developed away from homes and more in public spaces (movie theaters, dance halls). Similar types of activities occur today, but couples are more likely to do things in larger groups when they are young (high school). Physical proximity is also less a factor in meeting due to the creation of the Internet and dating services.

What leads people to date people who differ from them in terms of social characteristics?

The majority of people date others who are like them socially. However, social forces have provided more space for interaction among diverse groups; therefore, interethnic/racial friendships (and dating) are more common. This is also true of dating among people of different religions and social class. When opportunities to meet different people increase, the odds of befriending others with different social characteristics also increase. Children whose parents are part of a diverse social network are also more likely to date people from different social groups.

Is friendship a type of loving relationship?

Friendships are very important to people. They help us to live longer and healthier lives. Throughout our history are stories of friendships that are enduring and affectionate, and ones in which people are committed to help-ing out without expecting things in return. Both men and women seek and maintain same-sex friendships. Historical and cross-cultural research suggests that when societies structure situations for men to have close friendships with other men, it gives them an advantage in society. For women, psychological research suggests that friendships are also critical, especially in the reduction of stress. Maintaining cross-sex friendships is difficult in our society.

Key Terms

adolescence: the period of life that occurs between childhood and adulthood. The term was not used until the twentieth century.

androgynous love: a type of love that includes both traditional feminine traits and masculine traits

anxious/ambivalent attachments: seen in infants who become nervous when their mother leaves the room and can show rejection when she returns

attachment theory: the theory that the way in which infants form attachments early in life will affect their relationships in later life

avoidant attachments: seen in infants who show little attachment to their mother

biochemical theories of love: biological theories that suggest humans are attracted to certain types of people. When the attraction occurs, the brain releases natural chemicals.

calling: a dating practice of the eighteenth and nineteenth centuries in which a man would make a call on a woman in her home. It may have been more prevalent among the middle class.

class consciousness: people understanding their socioeconomic position in society and engaging in practices that help to maintain the system and their place in it

courtly love: a term derived from the Middle Ages, when poets or troubadours would write songs of love and present them at the court of their aristocratic/royal masters. This type of love was initially considered to be unrequited.

dating: used to describe the interactions that take place between romantically attached people away from the oversight of parents

equity theory: suggests that relationships work best when both people involved feel as though there is a fair exchange, or balance, in the relationship

feminist theories of love: theories that see the organization of romantic relationships as mirroring the power of men over women in society

feminization of love: the process beginning in the nineteenth century whereby love became associated with the private work of women in the home—namely, nurturance and caring

filter theory of love: sees relationships as developing over time and the traits that attract individuals to each other changing with that development

homogamy: refers to the practice of dating or marrying someone who holds similar social characteristics

homophobia: an unrealistic fear of homosexuality

intergroup dating: the type of dating in which individuals hold different social characteristics (such as different religious beliefs or levels of education)

John Lee's styles of love: includes six types of love that describe the way in which couples are attracted to each other. For example, ludus is the love of passion while pragma is a down-to-earth type of love.

love: an enduring bond between two or more people who show affection and a sense of obligation toward one another

Reiss's wheel theory of love: a developmental theory that shows relationships moving from the establishment of rapport, to self-revelation, to mutual dependence, and finally to need fulfillment

secure attachments: seen in infants who feel safe when their mothers are out of sight

sociobiology: an evolutionary theory that argues that all humans have an instinctive impulse to pass on their genetic material

triangular theory of love: sees love as having three elements: intimacy, passion, and commitment. Each relationship will vary depending on the type and level of these elements.

Resources on the Internet

These web sites have been selected for their relevance to the topics in this chapter. These sites are among the more stable, but please be aware that web site addresses change frequently.

American Film Institute's Best Love Stories
http://www.filmsite.org/afiloves.html
The American Film Institute (AFI) distributed a ballot to 400 nominated film artists (directors, screenwriters, actors, editors, cinematographers), film critics, and film historians. They were asked to select the best love stories in feature-length films. The films had to be in English and, regardless of genre, had to show a romantic bond between two or more characters, whose actions and/or intentions provide the heart of the film's narrative. Check them out against your favorites.

American Psychological Association
http://www.apa.org
The web site for the American Psychological Association includes at least five years' worth of press releases from its premier journal. Just click on the word "Releases," or type in the address—http://www.apa.org/releases—and you will find the results of studies on

many of the topics in this chapter, including attachment theory, dating, and sexuality.

Gallup Organization

http://www.gallup.org

The Gallup Organization takes periodic polls of people in the United States on their views on a variety of issues. Several of the tables and charts produced for this text came from Gallup polls. You can track changes in people's views on sexuality outside of marriage, views about gays/lesbians, and views about gender roles.

Loggia

http://www.loggia.com/myth/index.html

Loggia is a web site that explores the arts and humanities. Within the site are the stories from mythology that often frame our contemporary ideas about love. Click on the link for "lovers & legends" to read the Greek tales about Eros and Psyche, Echo and Narcissus, or the many affairs of Zeus. Stories of love from the Romans are also available on this site.

Companion Web Site for This Book

Virtual Society: The Wadsworth Sociology Resource Center

http://sociology.wadsworth.com

Begin by clicking the Student Resources section. Next, click Marriage and Family, and then click the cover image for this book. Select from the pull-down menu the chapter you are presently studying. You will have easy access to chapter resources such as MicroCase Online exercises, additional Web links, flashcards, InfoTrac exercises, and practice tests (that can be scored). In addition, to enhance and help with your study of marriages and families, be sure to investigate the rest of the rich sociology resources at Virtual Society.

Visit InfoTrac College Edition

 Another unique option available to you at the Student Resources section of the Virtual Society web site described above is InfoTrac College Edition, an online library of hundreds of scholarly and popular periodicals. Here are three suggested key search items for this chapter:

* Search keywords: *love + families*
* Search keywords: *mate selection*
* Search keywords: *love + friendships*

© Yang Liu/Corbis

Sexual Identity, Behavior, and Relationships

5

"The Sex Skill Men Adore"

"You've Cheated, Should You Tell?"

"Faking Orgasms: Will He Really Know?"

"Love Your Breasts, Even If They Are Small"

"10 Sex Tips That Will Drive Him Wild"

"New Places to Make It"

Sexual behavior was once largely hidden from public view. No more. Media depictions of sexuality are as close by as the magazines in the grocery store checkout line. No longer do headlines such as the ones above blare from only "pornographic" magazines. Mainstream women's and girls' magazines such as *Redbook* and *Seventeen* also use sex to sell more copies. The *Sports Illustrated* annual swimsuit edition, featuring bikini-clad women in provocative poses, sells twice as many copies as any other issue of the magazine. Television, radio, film, and the World Wide Web also use sex to entertain and to increase their profits. These media bombard us with clear images of what it means to be sexual. Yet what do they really tell us about being a woman? About being a man? About condom use? About sexually transmitted diseases? Are these media trying to inform us or exploit us? While two-thirds of prime-time television programs contain sexual content, less than 10 percent refer to any possible risks or responsibilities associated with sex ("T.V. Sex Misses Opportunities," 1999).

| FACT OR FICTION?

Sexual behavior may be a universal and natural physiological experience, but atti-

tudes and sexual behaviors can vary from one culture to another.

Historical and Cultural Influences

Compare the attitudes toward sexuality in these two cultures: among the Mangaia people of Polynesia, both girls and boys are expected to have a high level of sexual desire in early adolescence. At the age of thirteen or fourteen, boys are given explicit instructions about how to please a girl through kissing, fondling, and cunnilingus, along with specific techniques for giving her multiple orgasms. Boys are taught these techniques through personal experience with an older female teacher. It is critical that a boy learn these techniques quickly. Soon he will begin sexual relationships with a girl his own age, and if he fails to satisfy her, she will likely publicly denounce him and his lack of sexual skill.

In contrast to the Mangaia, the Dani of New Guinea show little interest in sex beyond what is needed for reproduction. Sexual intercourse is performed quickly, and female orgasm is virtually unheard of. After childbirth, mothers and fathers abstain from sex for five years. Sexual affairs are rare or nonexistent (Strong, DeVault, Sayad, & Yarber, 2002).

Sexual behavior may be a universal and natural physiological experience, but our attitudes and our behaviors are highly variable. This variation is far more than random personal likes or dislikes. Different cultures have significant variations in what are considered acceptable sexual behaviors.

This variation reflects far more than random personal likes or dislikes. Across different cultures, there are significant differences in what are considered acceptable sexual behaviors.

We can also see this variation in the United States. Differences in sexual attitudes and behaviors occur across historical periods, between racial and ethnic groups, across social classes, and between women and men. For example, in Chapter 4 we mentioned that sexual relationships prior to marriage have always been quite common; in fact, many couples were expecting their first child at the time of marriage even in the seventeenth century. However, the *context* for sexual behavior prior to marriage is very different today from what it was in colonial America. Americans now have more sexual partners, begin sexual activity at an earlier age, are less likely to view sexual activity solely as an act of procreation, and if pregnancy occurs, often view marriage as only one of several options available.

Our culture also addresses sexuality much more openly and publicly now. At the turn of the twentieth century it was illegal to provide people with information about birth control (what little there was), yet today many unmarried teenagers already know about and have used various methods of birth control. Sex is commercialized and a part of teen (and adult) culture via magazines, movies, and television. A quick look at programming on regular television or cable channels suggests that sex sells, and sells quite well. We have seen the emergence of an entire profession to study sex, **sexology**—a field comprising a multidisciplinary group of clinicians, researchers, and educators concerned with sexuality—and the result of this research is widely spread through televi-

sion, magazines, and high school and college courses.

In addition to these changes in cultural climate, we also spend more time as unmarried adults, thereby increasing the likelihood of having nonmarital sex. In 1890 the average age at **menarche,** or women's first menstrual period, was 14.8 years, and the average age of marriage for women was 22 years. By 1990, the average age at menarche had declined to 12.5 years, and the average age at marriage had risen to 24 years, resulting in 4 more years as an unmarried yet physically mature woman. This provides a bigger "window of opportunity" for young people to explore their sexuality.

This chapter will illustrate a number of ways that our sexuality is rooted in social and cultural norms (Andersen & Taylor, 2002):

1. Sexual attitudes and behaviors vary dramatically in different cultures.
2. Sexual attitudes and behaviors change over time.
3. Sexual identity is learned.
4. Social institutions channel and direct human sexuality.

But before looking more closely at how sexual norms, attitudes, and behaviors are related to our culture, how these vary across place and time, how we learn these norms, and how our institutions channel sexuality, we must begin with a discussion of what we mean by the term *sexuality*.

Defining Sexuality

Defining sexuality is much more difficult than we might imagine. In his recent anthology of historical narratives about sexuality, Robert Nye (1999) suggests that two fundamental questions about sexuality have been addressed over time. One question is "Who am I?" It emerged alongside the development of individualism in the West. First used in the

1800s, sexuality referred to one's sexual feelings. Here, *sexual* is a limited word meaning either the feelings associated with being male or female, or the feelings associated with the act of procreation.

The second question is "What should I do?" Responses to this question have included long-standing ethical debates about sexual conduct. Nye traces these discussions from Plato, through the Middle Ages and the Enlightenment, to contemporary Western discourse. He shows us very clearly that "the past is like a foreign country" when we try to understand contemporary sexual practices. However, his work shows us that the concern for regulating sexual behavior has been with us as long as we have had historical records.

More contemporary usage of the term *sexuality* encompasses a broader view. We now recognize that sexuality is both *physical* (sexual response is related to our anatomies) and *social* (sexual response is influenced by cultural and social practices) (Lorber, 1994).

"Who Am I?"

Regarding sexuality, the answer to the question "Who am I?" is not as straightforward as common sense would dictate. Sex, gender, and sexual orientation are three related yet distinct components of the answer for any human being.

Sex

The answer to the question "Who am I?" begins with our **sex.** Recall that our definition of sex referred to biological differences and one's role in reproduction. Typically, people think of two sexes, based on genitalia: male and female. But categories are not always this clear-cut. There are **hermaphrodites,** or those born with genitalia that do not clearly identify them as unambiguously male or female. The rate of hermaphroditism is approximately .012 per 1,000 live births

(Blackless, Charuvastra, Derryck, Fausto-Sterling, Lauzanne, & Lee, 2000). Hormonal errors during prenatal development produce a variety of congenital defects, such as having a gonad of each gender (a testicle and an ovary) or gonads that combine testicular and ovarian tissue (Rathus, Nevid, & Fichner-Rathus, 1993). The genitals are usually surgically reconstructed to adhere to the child's genetic chromosomes, either XX for a female or XY for a male.

Gender

A second layer of response to the question "Who am I?" concerns one's **gender,** which, as you recall from Chapter 3, refers to the culturally and socially constructed differences between males and females found in the meanings, beliefs, and practices associated with femininity and masculinity. These are learned attitudes and behaviors, not biological or physical qualities. We are born male or female, but we learn the cultural and socially prescribed traits associated with masculine or feminine patterns of behavior.

Historically and in most societies throughout the world, men and women have been viewed as far more different than alike. We even refer to one another as the "opposite sex." Yet the idea that men and women are opposite from each other is seriously flawed. We all possess both masculine and feminine traits; however, most of us primarily display the gendered traits that are associated with our sex. Females are more "feminine" and tend to behave in culturally prescribed feminine ways, and males are more "masculine."

FACT OR FICTION?

Most cross-dressers or transgendered individuals are heterosexual.

Of course, not everyone fits so neatly into his or her prescribed category. Some

Girls' play often emphasizes nurturing behavior whereas boys' often emphasizes violence or aggression.

people have an identity that does not conform to their biological anatomy. **Transgendered** individuals are those who feel as comfortable, if not more so, in expressing gendered traits that are associated with the other sex. A man may feel as relaxed, comfortable, and "normal" engaging in feminine traits, such as wearing certain clothing (e.g., dresses), engaging in particular grooming practices (e.g., painting nails), or in having feminine hobbies as he does in engaging in masculine ones—or even more so. Likewise, some women are also transgendered, although transgendered women are not usually as obvious to us because we allow women more leeway to behave in traditionally masculine ways (e.g., wearing men's clothing, acting aggressively). Individuals who wear the clothing associated with the other sex are also referred to as

cross-dressers. They may don the attire only occasionally (e.g., when going out of town on business trips), at regular intervals (e.g., after work in the privacy of their own home), or routinely in public, where they may try to "pass." There is a diversity of experience (Dixon & Dixon, 1991).

FICTION

Most are heterosexual, and many are married and have children.

It is estimated that at least 1 in 50,000 individuals over the age of 15 in the United States has discordant sex and gendered identities (Cloud, 1998). A small number of transgendered individuals harbor a deep sense of discomfort about their sex and wish to live fully as members of the other sex. Usually referred to as **transsexuals,** these individuals undergo sex reassignment surgery and hormone treatments, either male to female or female to male. Although surgery cannot alter the internal reproductive organs of the other sex, it can generate the likeness of external genitals. Surgery is expensive, and the preparation for it is time-consuming and emotionally taxing. Yet it is estimated that perhaps 25,000 Americans have undergone sex reassignment surgery (Cloud, 1998).

Perhaps not widely known is that most cross-dressers or transgendered individuals consider themselves to be heterosexual, and in fact many are married and have children. More information about this phenomenon can be found in the Family Diversity box on pages 192–193, "Questions Asked by Wives and Mates of Cross-Dressers."

Sexual Orientation

In addressing the first question, "Who am I?," we have discussed sex and gender. The next layer of response to this question concerns **sexual orientation,** or the sexual and romantic partner of choice. It is distinguished from other components of sexuality, including biological sex and gender (American Psychological Association, 1998). A **heterosexual** orientation refers to an attraction and preference for developing romantic and sexual relationships with the other sex (a man and a woman). A **homosexual** orientation refers to attraction and preference for relationships with members of one's own sex (two men or two women). Homosexual men may be referred to as "gay males," or just "gay." Homosexual women are often referred to as "lesbians." The term **bisexual** indicates an orientation in which a person is attracted to both males and females (engaging in both heterosexual and homosexual partner choice).

| FACT OR FICTION?

Researchers suggest that sexual orientation is clearly either heterosexual or homosexual, except for the rare person who is bisexual.

Sexual orientation refers to an identity—i.e., how someone sees himself or herself. Persons usually express a sexual orientation consistent with their behaviors, but this is not always the case. For example, it is possible that someone who engages in homosexual activities now and then may still see himself or herself as a heterosexual. The person may even be happily married and have children. In other words, people may engage in homosexual behaviors but still think of themselves and refer to themselves as heterosexuals. Coming to identify oneself as a gay man, lesbian, or bisexual is usually a lengthy and complex process and involves more than simply engaging in sex.

Determining the percentage of persons who are gay, lesbian, bisexual, or heterosexual is difficult because of identity issues and because of the way the terms are measured in research. In Western society, sexuality is typically constructed in a binary fashion: one is either homosexual or heterosexual. But these strict dichotomies are not found in all cultures, and imposing them keeps us from understanding the diversity that exists in our society with respect to sexuality.

Classifications and Frequency Before the work of Alfred Kinsey and his colleagues in the 1940s and 1950s, scientists generally viewed homosexuality and heterosexuality as separate and distinct categories. However, in his pioneering work on human sexuality, Kinsey reported that he found sexuality more appropriately placed on a seven-point continuum (1953). Persons in category 0 were considered exclusively homosexual, whereas those in category 6 were considered

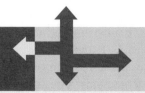

Question 1: Is my husband (boyfriend, friend) gay because he likes to cross-dress?

Renee: Most cross-dressers are not gay.

Merissa: Most male cross-dressers are attracted to females. The desire is to emulate one's love object, not be a love object to another man. The "turn-on" is femininity, not masculinity; therefore, relatively few cross-dressers are gay.

Question 2: Why does he wear the clothes of the opposite sex?

Renee: Most cross-dressers find comfort in wearing the clothes of the opposite gender. Another reason is the release of tension.

Merissa: Most cross-dress because they enjoy it. It is rewarding. The nature of that reward is entirely up to the individual. It may be nothing more than a "turn-on," or an escape, or it feels good, or narcissism, or a way to express an otherwise repressed part of one's personality. Whatever the reason, be it emotional, sensual, or sexual, or all three, it is one thing—rewarding.

Question 3: Will the cross-dresser ever stop dressing, or will this behavior continue throughout his lifetime?

Renee: Some cross-dressers stop from time to time (purge) but usually continue after a period of time. Sometimes when a cross-dresser reaches a very mature age he stops, but that is extremely rare.

Merissa: A cross-dresser will possibly if not probably stop, mostly because of "boredom" and not because of any "cure." However, if he does stop, he will most likely start again. I've never known anyone to be "cured" of the desire. I've never known a case where repressing or denying the desire worked. I've also known people to "purge" but all that did was stop the cross-dressing, not the desire. I've seen many people "purge" and "deny," and I've seen the tragic consequences— guilt, fear, hatred, even suicide.

Question 4: Will he ever become a transsexual and have the operation to change his sex?

Renee: Most trans-gendered people are just that . . . trans-gendered, not transsexual, and when they learn of themselves they realize they are both, not just one or the other. Transsexualism is a very rare thing to have happen to any individual. Usually the "either black or white" person has the most problems with transsexualism because they must be "either/or" and not "both."

Merissa: I don't know of anyone who has ever become a transsexual. Most transsexuals have known or suspected what they were from early childhood. In fact, the reverse is usually true. Most people who suspect themselves of being transsexual will learn to live without having surgery. . . . Very few will eventually come to the conclusion that re-assignment surgery is, in fact, correct for them.

Question 5: Will my spouse want to appear in public cross-dressed, or will cross-dressing at home satisfy him?

Renee: Some cross-dressers are very good at being able to go into the public eye and be what they appear to be. This does not mean that all people who cross-dress will try to appear in public with their adopted role.

Merissa: Some will be quite content to have the freedom to dress at home. For most, though, being "all dressed up with no place to go" is extremely frustrating. Fortunately there are a growing number of good support groups with activities programs that provide places to go and things to do without danger.

Question 6: Should our children be told that my spouse or mate cross-dresses, or should we keep it away from them?

Renee: Some cross-dressers have told their children at a very young age. Others have never told their children. Still others wait until "their children are old enough to understand." There are many ideas, but I think the best way to put it is on a "need-to-know" basis. If both decide there is a need to know, then the children should be told.

Merissa: "To tell or not to tell" is strictly up to the individual. From my observation it seems to work better if the children know and are taught to treat it for what it is—no big deal! I'm just uncomfortable with people making themselves vulnerable to being caught in a lie by people as important as their children. However, I'm even more uncomfortable with people telling their children, and treating it as mommy or daddy's "condition." As for children being harassed at school, children are harassed at school anyway, and at what age do you teach your children how to cope and put up with other people's problems? As for creating gender-conflicted children—I haven't seen it happen. People have to decide what is right for their own families.

Question 7: Should we tell our close friends and relatives that he is a cross-dresser?

Renee: This can be handled on the "need-to-know" basis. Do relatives have to know? Do friends have to know? Is there a reason for people to know?

Merissa: The consequences of not telling them can be severe—fear, blackmail, ulcers, stress, etc. The consequences of them knowing, or at least being able to cope with the possibility of them finding out, are less severe. My suggestion is don't bother telling them if they don't need to know, but be prepared to tell them if necessary; and above all, treat it for what it is—no big deal!

Question 8: What is the average age most cross-dressers started?

Renee: It seems as though the ages range from 6 to 12 years old. Many do start later and earlier.

Merissa: Many start as young children when playing "dress up" is fun, and perhaps emotionally rewarding. Others start as older children when "vanity" sets in, and they enjoy looking at themselves all dressed up and pretty, and feeling good. Others start with puberty, and dressing up is a "turn-on." Others start when they first discover that cross-dressing is rewarding (somewhere between the ages of 2 and 104). In short, there is no average age.

Question 9: Is it true that the cross-dresser actually has two personalities?

Renee: Some cross-dressers say that there are two completely different personalities, one male, one female. Others claim that there is only one.

Merissa: No, unless the person is completely schizoid. . . . Expressing oneself as a different person is little more than giving one's personality a broader range of expression.

Question 10: Does the cross-dresser have more respect for his mate because of cross-dressing?

Renee: Yes! The cross-dresser is able to more easily identify with the needs of the mate.

Merissa: I would like to think so, and many do, but that's not always the way it is. Many cross-dressers focus so much on their own needs that they are oblivious to their spouse's feelings. . . . I would love to see couples give each other the sensitivity, love, and respect each deserves. We are developing wives/couples support groups across the country to deal specifically with that.

Source: Excerpts from "Questions Asked by Wives and Mates of Cross-Dressers," by Renee Chevalier and Merissa Sherrill Lynn (1991). *Wives, Partners, and Others: Living with Cross-Dressing*, edited by Jan and Diane Dixon. Wayland, MA: Educational Resources Publications.

Critical Thinking

1. What type of stigma do you think cross-dressers face?

2. Why do you think that male cross-dressers are more stigmatized than female cross-dressers?

TABLE 5.1	Percentage of Respondents Aged 20–35 at Each Level of the Kinsey Heterosexual–Homosexual Continuum		
RATING	CATEGORY	FEMALES (%)	MALES (%)
0	Entirely heterosexual experience		
	Single	61–72	53–78
	Married	89–90	90–92
	Previously married	75–80	—
1–6	At least some homosexual experience	11–20	18–42
2–6	More than incidental homosexual experience	6–14	13–38
3–6	Homosexual as much or more than heterosexual	4–11	9–32
4–6	Mostly homosexual	3–8	7–26
5–6	Almost exclusively homosexual	2–6	5–22
6	Exclusively homosexual	1–3	3–16

Source: Based on data from A. Kinsey, et al. (1953). *Sexual Behavior in the Human Female.* Philadelphia: W. B. Saunders, p. 488.

exclusively heterosexual. He found that many persons' sexuality could best be described as falling somewhere in between these two points, as shown in Table 5.1, with various degrees of homosexual interests and experience. Overall, nearly 50 percent of men and 28 percent of women Kinsey surveyed had experienced homosexual erotic interests. Thirty-seven percent of men and 13 percent of women reported to interviewers that they had at least reached an orgasm through homosexual activity. However, this did not mean that these persons identified themselves as homosexual. Most of them thought of themselves as heterosexual. He found that only about 1–3 percent of women and 4 percent of men were exclusively homosexual. In other words, more people are having same-sex experiences than report homosexual or bisexual orientations.

FICTION

Kinsey's work revealed that sexual orientation should best be thought of as a continuum, with many people falling somewhere between the two extremes.

Many have criticized this research because of its sample (nonrandom and relying heavily on certain segments of the population). Another, more recent study (see Figure 5.1) suggests that the percentage of men who have had homosexual experiences since turning age eighteen is closer to 5 percent and is 4 percent for women (Michael, Gagnon, Laumann, & Kolata, 1994). A nearly equal number (6 percent of men and 4 percent of women) reported that they had felt sexually attracted to individuals of the same sex. This study, conducted by researchers at the University of Chicago, was based on a random sample of 3,432 people between the ages of eighteen and fifty-nine.

Keep in mind that having had a homosexual sexual experience is different than holding the *self-concept* of being gay or lesbian. Michael and associates (1994) asked their respondents "Do you think of yourself as heterosexual, homosexual, bisexual, or something else?" They found that 2.8 percent of men and 1.4 percent of women claimed *either* a homosexual or bisexual self-concept. Note that the percentage of persons who see themselves as homosexual or bisexual is substantially smaller than the percentage of persons who have had a same-sex sexual experience or who would find it appealing. Like Kinsey's earlier work, this suggests that sexual behavior is not simply binary.

Researchers suggest that people usually choose their sexual orientation.

What Causes Sexual Orientation? There are many theories about the origins of a person's sexual orientation. Today, most scientists agree that sexual orientation is likely the result of a complex interaction of biological (genetic or hormonal), environmental, and cognitive factors (American Psychological Association, 1998). In 1975 the American Psychological Association removed homosexuality from the official manual (DSM) that lists mental and emotional disorders, claiming that previous research was biased. Psychologists, psychiatrists, and other mental health professionals generally agree that homosexuality is not an illness, mental disorder, or emotional problem. They believe that human beings cannot choose their sexual orientation.

| FICTION

Most researchers believe that human beings cannot choose their sexual orientation.

A recent study of college students indicates that many gays and lesbians had inklings of their sexual orientation when they were quite young. In the survey, 17 percent of gay and bisexual men and 11 percent of lesbian and bisexual women reported that they knew that they were gay or bisexual as early as grade school (Elliott, Brantley, & Johnson, 1997). Uncertainty about sexual orientation declines with age, from 30 percent of twelve-year-old students to 5 percent of seventeen-year-old students (Ramafedi, Resnick, Blum, & Harris, 1992).

The origin of sexual orientation is a hotly debated issue. Some of the people who oppose civil rights for gays and lesbians argue that homosexuality is a lifestyle choice (unlike race or gender)—a choice that they disagree with; therefore, gays and lesbians should not be subject to the same civil rights protections as are other groups. But evidence is emerging to suggest that the biolog-

FIGURE 5.1 Percentage of Men and Women Aged 18–59 Who Reported Dimensions of Homosexual Orientation

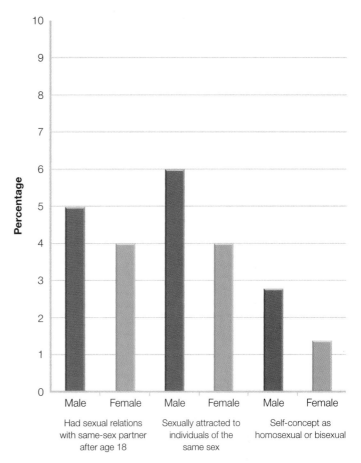

Source: *Sex in America: A Definitive Study.* 1994, Michael, Robert, Gagnon, John H., Laumann, Edward O., and Kolata, Gina. Boston, MA: Little, Brown, and Company.

Most scientists believe that sexual orientation is a result of a complex interaction of biological, environmental, and cognitive factors. Recent surveys suggest that 2–3 percent of men and 1–2 percent of women claim to be homosexual or bisexual.

ical component of sexual orientation may be larger than was once thought. Although the research is preliminary and far from definitive, it brings the debate into a new light.

One study focused on sibling pairs, one of which was known to be gay or lesbian (Bailey & Pillard, 1991; Bailey, Pillard, Neal, & Agyei, 1993). The sibling pairs were made up of identical twins, who share genetic material; fraternal twins, who share half their genetic material; and adopted siblings, who share no genetic material. The researchers found that 52 percent of the male identical twins and 48 percent of the identical female twins were both homosexual. This percentage is significantly higher than was the case among fraternal twins, who share only half of their genetic material (22 percent and 16 percent for fraternal male and female twins, respectively). Finally, adopted siblings, who share no genetic material, were the least

likely to both be homosexual (11 percent and 6 percent for adopted male and female siblings, respectively). This finding suggests that homosexuality may contain an important biological component.

Another study examined the relationship between the sexual orientation of fifty-five gay or bisexual fathers and their eighty-two adult sons at least seventeen years of age (Bailey, Bobrow, Wolfe, & Mikach, 1995). The study found that over 90 percent of the sons were heterosexual, unlike their fathers. Furthermore, gay and heterosexual sons did not differ on potentially relevant variables, such as the length of time they had lived with their fathers. Thus, the researchers question environmental influences and suggest that they do not appear to be as significant as was previously assumed.

Some researchers suggest that homosexuality is more common on the maternal side, fueling a discussion that homosexuality may be passed through women (Hamer & Coupland, 1994). Another researcher, a neuroscientist, performed autopsies on the brains of recently deceased men and women whose sexual orientation was established (LeVay, 1991). He found that a small region in the center of the brain involved with sexual response was smaller among gays than among heterosexual men. However, there were only forty-one subjects in the sample, and just six were women.

Scientists interpret these results with caution—the studies are often based on small and nonrandom samples. Even if specific genes were eventually isolated that could be directly linked to sexual orientation, our behavior is also shaped and molded by our environment. It is unlikely that something as complex as intimacy and attraction can be taken completely out of its cultural and historical context. Genes may encourage a person to act in a particular way, but fantasy, courtship, sexual arousal, and sexual behavior are all shaped by particular cultural and historical norms.

Attitudes Toward Gay and Lesbian Relationships The stigma against homosexuality in our society continues. Although attitudes about gay and lesbian relationships have become more tolerant over the last several decades, as shown in Figure 5.2, the majority of the population continues to see homosexual behavior as wrong to some degree. According to a national poll conducted each year by the National Opinion Research Center (NORC), just over 10 percent of Americans accepted homosexuality as "not at all wrong" in 1973. That figure fluctuated during the next three decades, and by the late 1990s the percentage of acceptance almost tripled (28.2 percent). When asked if they believe that homosexuality is something one chooses, 56 percent of Americans state that it is something you have no choice over.

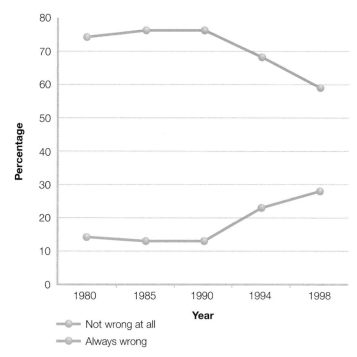

FIGURE 5.2 Attitudes Toward Homosexuality

Source: General Social Surveys. Available online: http://www.icpsr.umich.edu/GSS//rnd1998/merged/cdbk-trn/homosex.htm

Women are more likely to feel this way than are men.

Adolescents, who are struggling with a multitude of issues, are a group that may be particularly intolerant of diversity. In a fourteen-city survey, nearly half of lesbian and gay adolescents reported that they lost a friend after coming out to him or her (Ryan & Futterman, 1997).

Some people have very strong negative feelings toward homosexuality. This is referred to as **homophobia,** derived from the root words meaning "fear of homosexuals." Because prejudice may not necessarily be a clinical "phobia," the term **anti-gay prejudice** is often used instead. Homophobia, or anti-gay prejudice, can take many forms, including use of derogatory names (e.g., *queer, faggot, fairy, dyke*); telling disparaging jokes; barring or discriminating against gays and

The brutal murder of Matthew Shepard brought to national attention the violence that is directed toward gays and lesbians.

lesbians in employment, housing, or other contexts; and violence. The U.S. Justice Department claims that gays and lesbians are subjected to physical violence more than any other minority group, and there are indications that anti-gay violence has been increasing (Wertheimer, 1988). The news media paid a great deal of attention to the case of Matthew Shephard, the gay man in Wyoming who was tied to a fence, pistol whipped, and left to die. This horrendous crime outraged the public and led some state legislatures to add violence against gays and lesbians to their hate-crime statutes.

Anti-gay prejudice may be derived from several factors, including (1) a deep insecurity concerning one's own sexual orientation or gender identity, (2) a strong or fundamentalist religious belief, and (3) ignorance con-

cerning gays and lesbians (Marmor, 1980). Interestingly, most people recognize that there is a likely genetic basis for sexual orientation (i.e., no choice involved), yet many still believe it is wrong. Anti-gay prejudice adversely affects both homosexuals and heterosexuals. It creates fear, anxiety, misunderstanding, and hatred. For example, heterosexuals may restrict same-sex friendships, or heterosexual males may act hyper-masculine out of fear that they may be misinterpreted as being gay. Likewise, the delay in our country's response to HIV/AIDS has been attributed to anti-gay prejudice (Shilts, 2000). In his best-selling book, *And the Band Played On: Politics, People, and the AIDS Epidemic,* Randy Shilts illustrates the ways in which the labeling of HIV/AIDS as the "gay" disease kept us from acting as quickly or as thoroughly as would have been the case if another group had initially contracted the disease.

"Who Am I?" Revisited

The answer to the first question "Who am I?" invariably involves a close examination of our sex, our gender, and our sexual orientation. For many persons, these three components operate in predictable ways: if you are a woman, you behave in ways our culture considers feminine, and you are romantically and sexually attracted to men. Likewise, if you are a man, you act in ways deemed masculine, and you are attracted to women. However, these three components do not operate in this fashion for all people. As we have seen in the above discussion, there is tremendous diversity. Sex, gender, and sexual orientation are interrelated, but they are separate and distinct components of who you are.

"What Should I Do?"

Robert Nye suggests that, in addition to "Who am I?" the second fundamental question about sexuality asks "What should I do?" Answers to this question regarding what is or is not appropriate sexual conduct have been debated throughout time. Norms regarding appropriate sexual activity have varied dramatically historically, and they vary cross-culturally today. What has been defined as deviant, aberrant, or perverse in one time or place may be seen as normal sexual behavior elsewhere. There are few universal sexual trends. Although we tend to think of our sexual interests and behaviors as solely reflecting our individual personality and personal choices, this view is misguided.

Sexual Behavior Prior to the Twentieth Century

Images of early American sexuality in folklore are those of prim and proper Puritanism, and sexually repressed Victorianism. These views are somewhat exaggerated and a bit misleading (Weiss, 1998). Yes, it is true that sexuality was generally not a topic of conversation in polite society and that sexuality was valued primarily within the context of marriage. Religious and medical authorities in the United States and England widely believed that women did not experience sexual desires or obtain much pleasure from a sexual relationship. Women who did were considered dangerous or evil (Ehrenreich & English, 1989).

Myths and stereotypes surrounded males as well. Sexual intercourse was seen as draining a man of his natural vitality; therefore, engaging in it too frequently (e.g., more than once a month) was not recommended. The Reverend Sylvester Graham (1794–1851) preached that even a loss of an ounce of semen was equal to the loss of several ounces of blood (Bullough, 1976). Masturbation was considered perverse or dangerous for men, and virtually unheard of for women, as shown in the excerpts from an early medical book in the Family Diversity box on pages 200–202. Each time a man ejaculated, he was thought to be risking his physical health. Graham encouraged men to control their sexual feelings by adopting a diet based on whole-grain flours. His name is still identified with a cracker he developed in the 1830s to help men control their sexual urges—the graham cracker!

Despite these views, the actual sexual behavior of early Americans was not quite as repressed and prudish as it would seem at first glance. Sexuality was valued in the confines of marriage. Puritans and Victorians accepted erotic pleasure in marriage as long as it was based on mutual affection, respect, and comfort. An early study conducted in 1892 by a woman physician, Clelia Duel Mosher, discovered that many women experienced sexual pleasure and orgasm. Her sample was small and nonrandom, containing only forty-four women, but she found that thirty-five of the forty-four women reported that they desired sexual intercourse, and thirty-four women reported experiencing orgasm (Gay, 1984). However, pleasure alone could not justify a sexual relationship. The expected goal was, ultimately, the need and desire for children.

Nonmarital sex was discouraged, but it was a frequent occurrence nonetheless. A study that compared marriage dates and baptisms in one community in Massachusetts between 1761 and 1775 reported that one-third of the women were pregnant at the time of their wedding (cited in Reiss, 1980). Another study conducted in various communities throughout New England showed the percentage of nonmarital pregnancies to be somewhat lower, about 11 percent (D'Emilio & Freedman, 1988). Although precise numbers are hard to obtain, it is likely that these figures underestimate the true frequency of nonmarital intercourse for three reasons. First, many women who engaged in intercourse did not become pregnant and therefore would not be included in these statistics. Second, some women who did become pregnant may have aborted their fetuses, had spontaneous miscarriages, or had their baby

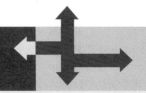

The following is an excerpt on masturbation that was published in a book titled *Sexology*. It was edited by Professor Wm. H. Walling, A.M., M.D., and was published in 1904. Our purpose for reprinting this excerpt is to show the attitudes and misconceptions surrounding male and female masturbation at the turn of the century.

Masturbation, Male.

Viewing the world over, this shameful and criminal act is the most frequent, as well as the most fatal, of all vices. In our country, however, it is second in frequency—though not, surely, in importance—only to the crime of libertinism. It is encountered in all ages, from the infant in the cradle to the old man groaning upon his pallet. But it is from the age of fourteen to twenty that its ravages are most frequent and most deplorable. Nothing but a sense of inexorable duty, in the hope of effecting a radical reform by awakening the alarm of parents and teachers to the enormous frequency and horrible consequences of this revolting crime, could induce the author to enter upon the sickening revelation.

Granted that, as already stated, it must, if persevered in, reveal itself, it is only the most aggravated cases that are brought to notice, and these usually are hopeless and incurable. The vast majority escape detection, and the practice in such, though indulged to a comparatively moderate extent, does not the less seriously, but only the less completely, impair the intellect and lay the foundation of physical, mental and moral maladies, the causes of which are usually as unsuspected as they are consequently persistent in their operation.

Perhaps the most constant and invariable, as well as earliest signs of the masturbator are the downcast, averted glance, and the disposition to solitude.

Prominent characteristics are, loss of memory and intelligence, morose and unequal disposition, aversion, or indifference to legitimate pleasures and sports, mental abstractions, stupid stolidity, etc. A distinguished German physician, Gottlieb Wogel, gives the following truthful picture:

"The masturbator gradually loses his moral faculties, he acquires a dull, silly, listless, embarrassed, sad, effeminate exterior. He becomes indolent; averse to and incapable of all intellectual exertion; all presence of mind deserts him; he is discountenanced; troubled, inquiet whenever he finds himself in company; he is taken by surprise and even alarmed if required simply to reply to a child's question; his feeble soul succumbs to the lightest task; his memory daily losing more and more, he is unable to comprehend the most common things, or to connect the simplest ideas. The last crisis of melancholy and the most frightful suggestions of despair commonly end in hastening the death of these unfortunates, or else they fall into complete apathy, and, sunken below those brutes which have the least instinct, they retain only the figure of their race."

According to Dr. Franck, "Masturbators are not only a charge upon society, but are even dangerous," and this celebrated physician exhorts to exercise over them the most active supervision.

As we have said of the physical, so also can we say of the moral punishment of the masturbator. Perhaps, even a small proportion of the whole number die in this manner; yet, in this comparatively small minority, *those who persist in the practice will sooner or later surely be included.* Let no one delude himself with the false assumption that he can be exempt from this universal law. *There will be no exemption!* Those who persist will surely die the death most horrible of all deaths; and those who practice the most limited and most occasional acts of onanism will surely be punished in proportion to their crimes; while the very individuals who seem to escape, are those who most surely carry the punishment for the remainder of their lives, never live to attain old age, and most frequently fall victims to some grave chronic disease, the germs of which they owe to this detestable vice. Or an acute malady, which they resist far less readily than others, cuts the thread of their existence in the prime of their manhood.

Let those who read these pages reflect upon the numberless instances, which must have come within the observation of all medical or lay observers, of youths who stood high in their classes, and ranked quite as intellectual prodigies up to a little beyond the age of puberty, say from fourteen upward—who suddenly, without obvious cause, became stupid as dunces, or losing their vivacity, seemed to fail rapidly in intelligence, and to disappoint the high hopes which had been entertained of them. Ninety-nine per cent of these examples are cases in point.

Masturbation, Female.

Alas, that such a term is possible! O, that it were as infrequent as it is monstrous, and that no stern necessity compelled us to make the startling disclosures which this chapter must contain! We beseech, in advance, that every young creature into whose hands this book may chance to fall, if she be yet pure and innocent, will at least pass over this chapter, that she may still believe in the general chastity of her sex; that she may not know the depths of degradation into which it is possible to fall. We concede that only a widespread existence of the crime could justify this public description of its consequences. We believe that a smaller proportion of girls than of boys are addicted to it, but the number is nevertheless enormous, and the dangers are all the greater, that their very existence is so generally ignored.

Beyond all dispute the crime exists. We translate the following from an acknowledged high medical authority, the "*Dictionnaire des Sciences Medicales.*"

"Naturally more timid and more secret than boys, the effects of their reunion, although very fatal, are less than in the latter. At the same time a culpable negligence in the boarding-schools of 'young ladies,' too frequently allows to be introduced there the disorders of masturbation. This practice is dissembled from the impenetrative or careless eyes of the teacher under the guise of friendship, which is carried, in a great number of cases, to a scandalous extent. The most intimate *liaisons* are formed under this specious pretext; the same bed often receives the two friends. . . ."

With them, as with boys, the genital organs may be constitutionally endowed with excessive predominance of action, which masters all the affections, all the movements of the economy, and causes them to titillate incessantly that part of those organs which is the seat of the keenest sensibility. Very little girls are often thus borne along, by a kind of instinct, to commit masturbation. The famous Dr. Deslandes makes the astounding statement, which can only be true of the French nation, that "a great number of little girls, and the majority of adolescents, commit this crime! There is no young girl who should not be considered as already addicted to or liable to become addicted to this habit." All physicians admit that it is very difficult—almost impossible, in fact—to ascertain the origin of many of the diseases of unmarried women which they are called upon to treat, and, if the cause be perpetually in operation, they will prescribe with fruitless results. The broken health, the prostration, the great debility, the remarkable derangements of the gastric and uterine functions, too often have this origin, and when the cause is investigated the subject alleges great exertions, intense trouble, unhappiness, etc., but is silent as to the real cause, which, perhaps, after all, she does not herself associate with her maladies. The utmost penetration can only cause one to suspect the truth, but a question skillfully put will generally reveal all.

The symptoms which enable you to recognize or suspect this crime are the following: A general condition of languor, weakness, and loss of flesh; the absence of freshness and beauty, of color from the complexion, of the vermilion from the lips, and whiteness from the teeth, which are replaced by a pale, lean, puffy, flabby, livid physiognomy; a

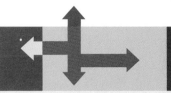

bluish circle around the eyes; which are sunken, dull, and spiritless; a sad expression, dry cough, oppression and panting on the least exertion, the appearance of incipient consumption. It is not uncommon to see the shape impaired.

The moral symptoms are similar to those of the opposite sex. They are sadness or melancholy, solitude, or indifference, an aversion to legitimate pleasures, and a host of other characteristics common to the two sexes.

We could give facts almost without number in reported cases, to show the prevalence and destructive nature of this vice among girls in our own country, but we forbear; the subject is painful and revolting even to contemplate. We believe that we have said enough to terrify parents into the needed precautions against it. If so much has been accomplished our object is fully realized. We remark, however, in conclusion, that it is not sufficient to use merely ordinary precautions of a judicious watchfulness; direct and skillful interrogation must be from time to time employed, at least in every suspected case. The subject should never be avoided through false delicacy, and such lessons should be imparted on the dreadful consequences of the habit, as shall effectually deter the perpetrators from persisting in it. It were far better to acquaint even pureminded and perfectly innocent girls with the existence of such a vice, while teaching them its horrible consequences, than, through a false modesty or mistaken motives of delicacy, to fail in imparting the requisite information in a single case.

Source: *Sexology, the Family Medical Edition* (1904). Prof. Wm. H. Walling, editor. Philadelphia: Puritan Publishing.

Critical Thinking

1. How have views toward masturbation changed since this essay was written?

2. How do the attitudes toward male masturbation and female masturbation differ?

3. How do attitudes toward women in society more generally influence attitudes toward women's sexuality?

without marrying. They too would not be reflected in the statistics. Third, African slaves were not legally allowed to marry. Therefore, they would not be represented in the statistics at all.

Social Changes in the Twentieth Century

The twentieth century witnessed a number of new social trends that began to shape sexual behavior and marriage and family life (Weiss, 1998). These include the following key factors with widespread implications:

* industrialization, along with urbanization and the eventual emergence of suburbs surrounding metropolitan areas

* a shift in the family from an economic-producing unit to that of a consumer

* the entry of men, and later increasing numbers of women, into the paid labor force

* the development and expansion of formal education in public schools, especially among women and minorities

* technological innovations, especially the automobile

How did these changes affect sexual behavior and relationships? These developments led to a great deal of questioning about sexuality and gender expectations. Traditional values, often based on religious principles, began to give way to more hedonistic views.

Both men and women began to see sexual gratification as a right, at least within the confines of marriage. Marriage was increasingly connected to romance—husbands and wives were viewed as companions attending to each other's physical, emotional, and sexual needs. Specifically, some of the changes during this period included the following:

* the development of effective contraceptives
* greater privacy and autonomy
* increased leisure and affluence
* the development of an adolescent subculture
* new forms of private transportation such as the automobile, allowing greater freedom
* a shift to a more companionate marriage based on love and mutual attraction
* increased independence and employment, social, and legal opportunities for women
* an increasing divorce rate
* health care breakthroughs, such as antibiotics to cure some sexually transmitted diseases
* the development of research, education, and therapy, which helped trigger a greater understanding of sexual behavior
* the women's movement, along with increased college attendance and increased freedoms

Famous Research in Human Sexuality

The twentieth century ushered in important new research that changed the way we conceptualized and understood sexuality, as well as the way we documented changing sexual attitudes and behaviors. Sigmund Freud (1856–1939) focused much of his work on

The Granger Collection, New York

Despite our thinking to the contrary, the birth records available in early America reveal that unmarried couples were often sexually active.

the study of the psychosexual development of children and how it affected adult life and mental condition. He believed that we are all born with biologically based sex drives. These drives must be channeled through socially approved outlets; otherwise, the individual will experience conflict within himself or herself, the family, or society at large. In 1905 Freud wrote *Three Essays on the Theory of Sexuality,* in which he developed his theory of infantile sexuality and tried to demonstrate the link between adult sexual "perversions" and distorted childhood sexual expressions. Although his work is controversial today, particularly his understanding of female sexuality (e.g., the phenomenon of penis envy), it has had a large influence on the field of psychology.

One of the first large surveys on human sexuality, and mentioned earlier, was the pioneering work of Alfred Kinsey (1894–1956) and his associates. Kinsey was a highly respected zoologist and biology professor at Indiana University who was asked in the 1930s to teach a new course in sexuality and marriage. In preparing his lectures, he found that there was very little reliable research about sexuality. He set out to change this. His work, which brought great notoriety, includes *Sexual Behavior in the Human Male* and *Sexual Behavior in the Human Female* (otherwise known as *The Kinsey Reports*), which were published in the 1940s and 1950s. These reports are based on interviews with approximately 11,000 men and women, and they provide a complete sexual history of each respondent. Although from a nonrandom and biased sample, these data served for decades as a major source of statistics on sexual behavior. The Kinsey Institute, located at Indiana University, remains today a major center for research on sexuality.

Kinsey's findings can be touched upon only briefly here. In general, he found that Americans—both men and women—were far more sexually active, and enjoyed sexual activity more, than previously imagined. For example, he found that among women born after 1900, more than one-half reported to their interviewer that they had sex before marriage, a percentage that greatly exceeded common beliefs. Because of the nonrepresentativeness and biases of the sample, however, it is always a bit dangerous to extrapolate Kinsey's findings to the total U.S. adult population. Nonetheless, his work provided the first real description of the sexual behavior of at least a certain segment of the population.

William Masters's and Virginia Johnson's ground-breaking research addressed two important features of sexuality: (1) the physiology of human sexual response and (2) the treatment of sexual dysfunction. Rather than relying on the survey methods used by Kinsey, they adopted observational designs within a laboratory setting. They used so-phisticated instrumentation to measure the physiological responses during masturbation and sexual intercourse of nearly 700 individuals, including 276 married couples, 106 single women, and 36 single men. The married couples engaged in intercourse and other forms of mutual stimulation. The unmarried subjects participated in studies that did not require intercourse, such as masturbation. The participants experienced more than 10,000 orgasms in these controlled laboratory conditions! The findings of this research were published in the book *Human Sexual Response* (1966) and have served as the springboard for many further studies. Masters and Johnson found it useful to divide sexual response into four states, now well-known as "the sexual response cycle"— (1) desire, (2) excitement, (3) orgasm, and (4) resolution—claiming that they are experienced by both men and women in a similar fashion. Other researchers since this pioneering inquiry have questioned the sexual response cycle, acknowledging that we still know very little about women's sexual response, as shown in the Focus on Family Research box on pages 206–207. John Gagnon, a sociologist and noted sex researcher, suggests that scientists (who are largely male) have failed to study women's sexuality adequately because of stereotypes and fears about women's bodies and sexual desires. He explained that men worry that "if she enjoys it too much, will she do it with someone beside me?"

Another book written by Masters and Johnson, *Homosexuality in Perspective* (1979), was based on similar laboratory observations of the sexual response of homosexual subjects. Their research provided new insights on the workings of sexual response, in particular the similarities rather than the differences between men and women, and between heterosexuals and homosexuals. Finally, Masters and Johnson developed clinical techniques for the treatment of sexual dysfunctions. Their book *Human Sexual Inadequacy* (1970) continues to be an important resource in the growing field of sex therapy.

Since these early studies, there have been many additional research projects, most of which attempted to replicate Kinsey's work on sexual behaviors by using survey methods. One study, funded by the Playboy Foundation, and later nicknamed the Hunt Report, profiled sexual behavior in the 1970s. It was based on a random sample of 982 men and 1,044 women from 24 American cities. Journalist Morton Hunt wrote up the results in the book *Sexual Behavior in the 1970s* (1974). The survey asked more than 1,000 questions about the respondents' sexual histories and attitudes. In addition to the written questionnaire, researchers conducted small-group discussions among participants about national trends in sexual behavior. These data provided a much-needed update to the Kinsey studies and allowed for interesting comparisons and contrasts of behavior changes over a generation. However, this study was also based on a sample of urban dwellers; therefore, the results cannot really be generalized to the target population, like Kinsey's work before it. Not all Americans live in cities, and it is possible that the sexual behavior of urban dwellers differs significantly from those who live in the small towns and rural regions of our nation.

FACT OR FICTION?

It is impossible to do a survey on human sexuality with a random sample of people.

Contemporary Research in Human Sexuality Perhaps one of the best surveys to date was conducted in 1992 by the National Opinion Research Center (NORC) and the University of Chicago. This study was based on face-to-face interviews with a random sample of 3,432 American adults aged 18–

59. The results are reported in the books *The Social Organization of Sexuality: Sexual Practices in the United States* (Laumann, Gagnon, Michael, & Michaels, 1994) and *Sex in America: A Definitive Survey* (Michael, Gagnon, Laumann, & Kolata, 1994). The respondents were selected using the same sophisticated sampling techniques that are used in other social and political research, and 80 percent of those contacted agreed to participate, ensuring that the findings are far more representative and generalizable than previous research. This large-scale study, like Kinsey's work, focuses on a wide variety of attitudes and behaviors—marital, nonmarital, heterosexual, and homosexual—and examines differences by age, racial, ethnic, gender, and class subgroups. Although the sample omits people aged 60 and over, so we are not able to learn about the sexual activities of the elderly, it nonetheless gives us the first truly scientific study of sex among younger adults in the United States. Many of these findings will be reported in the next sections.

Another excellent source of data is the Youth Risk Behavior Survey (YRBS) conducted biannually for the Centers for Disease Control and Prevention (CDC). It measures the prevalence of several health-risk behaviors, including sexual behavior, contraceptive use, sexually transmitted diseases, and unintended pregnancy. The 1999 YRBS was based on a representative sample of 15,349 students in grades 9–12 in 41 states and the District of Columbia. This study provides important information regarding the sexual behavior of youth in the United States.

The National Survey of Family Growth (NSFG) is another contemporary survey that gives us important information about human sexuality. It has been conducted six times by the National Center for Health Statistics (NCHS): in 1973, 1976, 1982, 1988, 1995, and 2002. In each case, the survey was based on personal interviews conducted in the

In this era of blatant sexuality, it is surprising that very little is known about the physiology of women's sexual response. In the early 1970s, Julia Heiman, a psychologist at the University of Washington and the director of the reproductive and sexual medicine clinic, was one of the first to study the sexual response of women. She used a device that detects blood flow into the vagina and determined that women, like men, get sexually excited by erotic talk, not just by romance. Even though the majority of the fields of science have progressed, Dr. Heiman's work, now thirty years old, represents about as far as we have come.

Why do we remain ignorant? According to John Gagnon, a sociologist at the State University of New York at Stony Brook, "For most medical professionals, a woman's genitals are still 'down there.'" Dr. Gagnon believes that scientists do not really want to find out what gives a woman pleasure and how to enhance that pleasure. As he explains, men worry that "if she enjoys it too much, will she do it with someone besides me?"

James H. Greer, a professor of psychology at Louisiana State University and an inventor of the tampon-like device that was used in Dr. Heiman's ground-breaking study, believes there is tremendous resistance to understanding women's physiological sexual response. Consequently, many of the questions involving women's sexual response have gone unanswered.

Part of the problem with this type of research stems from the lack of an appropriate method to measure women's physiological sexual response. Many have stated that Dr. Heiman's earlier study involving blood flow into the vagina did not measure the correct organ. She should have measured the clitoris instead, her critics argue. But it is extremely difficult to study the sexual response of the clitoris. According to Dr. Heiman, "The clitoris is so sensitive that simply touching it could trigger a response." Until better measuring devices are developed, these questions will not be answered.

In the meantime, many women are unsatisfied with their sex lives, and increased knowledge could serve both them and their partners well. Dr. Leiblum, a psychologist at the Robert Wood Johnson Medical Center in New Brunswick, New Jersey, notes that surveys invariably find that more women than men

homes of a national sample of women aged 15–44 in the civilian, noninstitutionalized population of the United States. The main purpose of the surveys was to provide reliable national data on marriage, divorce, contraception, infertility, and the health of women and infants.

| FICTION

There are a number of excellent surveys of sexuality that have used large, random samples of the population.

Research studies such as these, which are based on representative samples of the population, helped to both change and document sexual attitudes and behaviors. They helped to redefine the answer to the question "What should I do?" by changing what was seen as normative behavior—for example, "If everyone else seems to enjoy sex, or is engaging in a certain type of sexual behavior, then, hey, why shouldn't I?"

Sexual Expression

We have been discussing the ways in which our sexual behavior is socially constructed by the norms of our culture in a particular historical time. We now focus on specific sexual behaviors commonly practiced in the United States, using data from collected by the NORC and the University of Chicago, from the

complain of sexual difficulties. She believes that most women can have orgasms while masturbating: "when they don't feel pressured to perform, and when they don't feel concerns about how they look or how they are formed or how they smell." However, it is much easier and more socially acceptable for scientists to talk about the psychological problems associated with women's sexual response than it is to discuss the physiological reasons.

Pfizer, the drug company that developed Viagra, has taken an interest in determining if Viagra can help improve women's sex lives. The research originally conducted on this new drug focused solely on its physical effects on erections. Soon the company began to redirect its efforts. Dr. Quirk, a physician at Pfizer, developed a questionnaire in order to determine women's perceptions about sex. She asked women questions relating to how often they have sex, how quickly they respond to sexual stimulation, and how confident they are as sexual partners. The results seem to show a relationship "between women's symptoms of sexual dysfunction and worries about the future of their sex lives." For example, 34 percent of the women in her study who reported having difficulty becoming aroused also reported that they worry about the future of their sex lives. But can Viagra help improve women's sex drive? It helps men achieve erections; however, it does not increase men's desire for sex.

In order for society to support research on women's sexuality, "People would have to view women's sexual desire as an important issue," Dr. Heiman states. If there is a problem to treat and, perhaps even more importantly, a market for a new drug, drug companies may be the first ones to further study women's sex lives. Ironically, it may be the quest for profit that finally encourages us to learn more about women's sexual response.

Source: Adapted from Gina Kolata (June 21, 1998). "Women and Sex: On This Topic, Science Blushes." *New York Times*, "Women's Health," p. 3.

Critical Thinking

1. What aren't women clamoring for more scientific information about their bodies and their sexual response?

2. What political or social factors impede our knowledge about women's sexual response?

Youth Risk Behavior Survey, and from other smaller-scale surveys.

Masturbation **Masturbation** refers to sexually stimulating one's own body. It involves rubbing, fondling, and stimulating the genitals, but it can also include other body parts such as the breasts. People report that they masturbate for relief of tension, for relaxation, for physical pleasure, to aid falling asleep, or because a partner is unavailable.

Among Americans aged 18–59, nearly 60 percent of men and 40 percent of women report that they have masturbated in the past year (Michael et al., 1994). Men are also likely to masturbate more frequently than are women: more than 25 percent of men,

but less than 10 percent of women, report masturbating at least once a week. (See Figure 5.3.)

| FACT OR FICTION?

There are many differences in the sexual behaviors of whites and African Americans.

Attitudes toward masturbation vary among different ethnic groups. African Americans and Hispanics are more likely to say that they had never masturbated during the past year than were whites: 68 percent, 65 percent, and 56 percent, respectively (Laumann et al., 1994). Among those who masturbate, whites also report masturbating

FIGURE 5.3 Percentage of Men and Women Aged 18–59 Who Reportedly Engaged in Masturbation During the Past Year

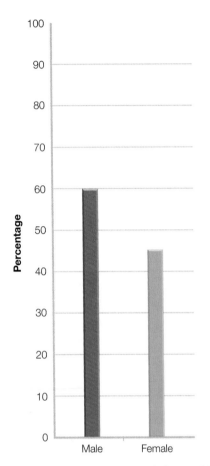

Source: Robert T. Michael, John G. Gagnon, Edward P. Laumann, & Gina Kolata (1994). *Sex in America: A Definitive Survey.* Boston: Little, Brown.

more frequently than do African Americans or Latinos. These differences have cultural influences. Whites begin sexual activity later, on average, than do other groups, particularly African Americans. Therefore, whites may regard masturbation as an acceptable and normative alternative to sexual intercourse, whereas African Americans may see it as a sign of sexual inadequacy and deviance. In contrast, Hispanics are more likely to regard masturbation as sinful, given the influence of the Catholic church, and

are therefore less likely to engage in this behavior.

As we saw in the Family Diversity box on pages 200–202, masturbation was considered morally repugnant in the Victorian era and was blamed for a wide variety of medical ills. Today, we know that masturbation is not harmful. Although some religious leaders may still see masturbation as wrong, most health care providers, sex researchers, and therapists see masturbation as normal sexual behavior. A former U.S. Surgeon General, Jocelyn Elders, even proposed that information about masturbation be included in sex-education programs in the schools. Her view, misconstrued as advocating that schools teach children *how* to masturbate, was publicly criticized, and former President Clinton eventually fired her because of it.

Kissing   **Kissing** is one of our earliest sensual experiences. From sucking as infants to the kiss between lovers, our mouths and lips are very sensitive to touch. Kisses are the stuff of fairy tales: a kiss has the inordinate power to bring a prince or princess back to consciousness.

Kissing is probably the most common and most acceptable form of sexual expression in the United States. Both men and women regard kissing as a romantic act (Tucker, Marvin, & Vivian, 1991). Lesbian couples tend to engage in the most kissing, heterosexual couples next, and gay couples the least (Blumstein & Schwartz, 1983), but even among gay men, 85 percent claim that hugging, kissing, and snuggling are favorite activities (Lever, 1994).

Oral Sex   **Oral sex** is oral stimulation of the genitals. **Cunnilingus** is oral stimulation of the woman's genitals by her partner; **fellatio** is oral stimulation of the man's genitals. According to the recent large-scale study of sexuality of persons aged 18–59, 79 percent of men reported having received oral sex, as did 73 percent of women (Michael et al., 1994). It is becoming a normative part of the sexual scripts of many people. (See Figure 5.4.)

Whites are considerably more likely to engage in and receive oral sex, both cunnilingus and fellatio, than are African Americans and Hispanics (Staples, 1973; Sterk-Elifson, 1994; Wilson, 1986). For example, 81 percent of white men reported that they have given oral sex to their partners, as did 51 percent of African American men and 66 percent of Hispanic men. Likewise, 75 percent of white women reported giving oral sex to their partner, as did 34 percent of African American women and 56 percent of Hispanic women. In another study, which focused on undergraduate college students, Belcastro also found that African Americans were less likely to engage in oral sex (1985). He reports that 48 percent of the African American college women surveyed reported performing fellatio, compared to 82 percent of the whites. One study, based on in-depth interviews with 33 African American woman under age 20 to over age 59, found that two-thirds of the respondents generally agreed with the following statement provided by one of the respondents:

> Those kinds of sex are wrong. Human beings are not created to do those kinds of things. It is evil and disgusting. . . . Anal sex got men in trouble. . . . Oral sex should make people vomit. It is sex invented by whites. . . . Prostitutes are willing to do that and that causes major relational problems. . . . Masturbation is also wrong. You are not supposed to touch your body. . . . I would accept it from a boy, but there is no need for girls to touch themselves at those places. (Sterk-Elifson, 1994: 112)

Sexual Intercourse Most people think that the term **sexual intercourse** refers to

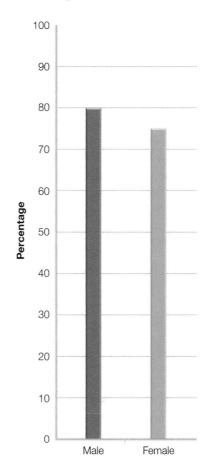

FIGURE 5.4 Percentage of Men and Women Aged 18–59 Who Reportedly Have Received Oral Sex (Fellatio or Cunnilingus)

Source: Robert T. Michael, John G. Gagnon, Edward P. Laumann, & Gina Kolata (1994). *Sex in America: A Definitive Survey.* Boston: Little, Brown.

vagina–penis penetration, but actually the term refers to any sort of penetration, including anal penetration. This could be by same-sex partners or not. While oral sex may be appealing to large numbers of adults, anal intercourse is viewed far less favorably. Researchers found that only 1 percent of women and 5 percent of men reported that anal sex was very appealing (Michael et al., 1994). Probably not coincidentally, anal intercourse has the highest risk of HIV infec-

FIGURE 5.5 Mean Age at First Intercourse by Birth Cohort, Race, and Sex

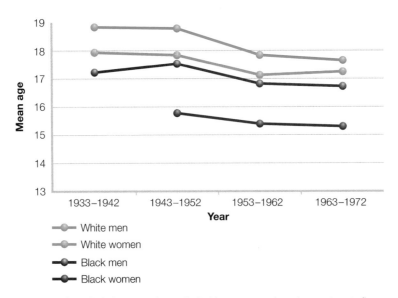

Note: This figure includes respondents who had intercourse no later than age twenty-five and who have reached their twenty-fifth birthday by the date of the interview. Missing segments indicate insufficient number of cases for a particular category (> 30). Whites were computed from the cross-section sample; blacks were computed from the cross-section and the over sample.

Source: Robert T. Michael, John G. Gagnon, Edward P. Laumann, & Gina Kolata (1994). *Sex in America: A Definitive Survey.* Boston: Little, Brown.

tion among all sexual behaviors because of the possible blood contact caused by tears in the rectum wall.

Generally speaking, most people use the term *sexual intercourse* synonymously with *vaginal intercourse,* or *coitus.* Consequently, we will do the same in the following discussion.

Figure 5.5 shows the average age at first intercourse for men and women, African Americans and whites, and different birth cohorts. We can see that the average age of first intercourse has declined somewhat for all groups over time, although the decline in age may not be as large as imagined. Individuals born between 1963 and 1967 began to have intercourse a year (or less) earlier than individuals born between 1933 and 1942.

Figure 5.5 shows us that African American men in all age cohorts generally begin to have intercourse before age 16. They are followed by African American women, who,

on average, begin to have sexual intercourse around the age of 17. White men, on average, begin to have sexual intercourse around age 17.5 or 18, depending on the age cohort. The largest drop in age at first intercourse, more than a year, has occurred among white women, who also are the oldest at the time of first intercourse. White women born between 1933 and 1945, prior to or during World War II, were nearly 19 at the time of first intercourse. However, among white women born between 1963 and 1967, the average age declined to approximately 17.5 years.

Table 5.2 reveals the number of reported sexual partners since age 18 by survey respondents. Nearly half of men aged 18–59 reported having no more than 4 partners (44 percent), as did nearly three-quarters of women (70 percent). In contrast, at the other end of the continuum, 17 percent of men reported having 21 or more partners, as did 3 percent of women. Clearly, men are

	0	1	2 to 4	5 to 10	10 to 20	21+
SEX						
Men	3%	20%	21%	23%	16%	17%
Women	3%	31%	36%	20%	6%	3%
RACE/ETHNICITY						
White	3%	26%	29%	22%	11%	9%
Black	2%	18%	34%	24%	11%	11%
Hispanic	4%	35%	27%	17%	8%	9%
Asian American	6%	46%	25%	14%	6%	3%
Native American	5%	28%	35%	23%	5%	5%
EDUCATION						
Less than high school diploma	4%	27%	36%	19%	9%	6%
High school graduate or equivalent	3%	30%	29%	20%	10%	7%
Some college, vocational	2%	24%	29%	23%	12%	9%
Finished college	2%	24%	26%	24%	11%	13%
Master's/advanced degree	4%	25%	26%	23%	10%	13%

TABLE 5.2 Number of Sexual Partners Since Age 18 Reported by Adults Aged 18–59

Source: Robert T. Michael, John G. Gagnon, Edward P. Laumann, & Ginal Kolata (1994). *Sex in America: A Definitive Survey*. Boston: Little, Brown.

more likely to report having a greater number of sexual partners than are women.

Racial and ethnic differences are noted as well. Asian Americans report sexual intercourse with fewer partners since age 18 than do other groups. For example, the table reveals that 77 percent of Asian Americans report 4 or fewer partners, compared with 58 percent of whites, 54 percent of African Americans, 66 percent of Hispanics, and 68 percent of Native Americans. And only 3 percent of Asian Americans report having 21 or more sexual partners.

| FACT

For example, African Americans, on average, are less likely to masturbate, they begin to engage in sexual behavior at an earlier age, and they are less likely to engage in oral sex.

Finally, Table 5.2 reveals that persons with more formal education are more likely to have had sexual intercourse with more partners since age 18 than are those with less education. Sixty-seven percent of persons with less than a high school diploma have had no more than 4 partners, compared with 55 percent of those with at least a master's degree. Likewise, only 6 percent of those with the least education have had 21 or more partners, as compared with 13 percent of persons with the highest levels of education reported here. These differences could be a function of age or marital status. That is, perhaps those with less education are younger than those with higher levels of education. Moreover, persons with less education tend to marry at younger ages, thus likely restricting their number of partners over the course of their adult lives.

Confusion Over the Source of Women's Pleasure Sexual intercourse is often viewed as the "ultimate" sexual act; indeed, it is sometimes referred to as "having sex," as though other sexual activities are simply preliminaries for sexual intercourse. For example, oral or manual stimulation may be seen as "foreplay." While this makes sense from a procreative standpoint—since sexual intercourse is needed to make babies—it does not make complete sense to the many women who are more likely to have orgasms from manual or oral stimulation than from sexual intercourse itself. Many women prefer or need additional clitoral stimulation beyond that which is provided in sexual intercourse in order to reach orgasm. For example, one study based on in-depth interviews with 33 African American women who ranged in age from under 20 to over 59 revealed that none of the woman experienced an orgasm during their first sexual intercourse (Sterk-Elifson, 1994). One-third of the women, mainly middle class and under age 30, explained to the interviewer that they began reaching orgasm with their partner later, often by telling him that they preferred some clitoral stimulation. Three-quarters of respondents, particularly the younger ones, reported that they had faked an orgasm to please their partner. As one woman suggested, "A guy would not feel a real man if he can't get his lady to come. A woman doesn't lose anything if she fakes it" (Sterk-Elifson, 1994: 114). Shere Hite, who conducted surveys with more than 3,000 women in the mid-1970s, found similar results: the pressure from their partners to have an orgasm during intercourse was so strong that the majority of women reported faking orgasms (Hite, 1977).

Sexologists have often been confused over woman's sexuality and where the source of her pleasure really lies. They debated between vaginal versus clitoral orgasms, claiming that the former were more "mature" than the latter, although we now know that this opinion is incorrect. Women who did not have orgasms in intercourse were thought to have female sexual dysfunction (FSD) and to need treatment. Sex therapists and educators taught women who failed to have or-gasms in intercourse to first masturbate and, when achieving success there, to then switch to sexual intercourse with their partner, since orgasm in intercourse was considered "normal" and the ultimate goal.

Even today it has been promoted that four in ten women experience some form of sexual dysfunction (Laumann, Paik, & Rosen, 1999). Textbooks on marriage and the family and human sexuality still occasionally promulgate such ideas, referring to the need for stimulation beyond intercourse for orgasm as "secondary orgasm dysfunction," as though it suggests the need for treatment (Rice, 1999).

Research now shows us that the clitoris is, in many ways, the female counterpart of the penis. Both organs receive and transmit sexual sensations. However, while the penis is directly involved in reproduction, the clitoris is unique in that it serves no known purpose other than providing sexual pleasure. It is ironic that many cultures, both past and present, have viewed women as unresponsive to sexual stimulation when it is they, not men, who possess a sexual organ that is apparently devoted solely to providing pleasurable sensations.

Sexual Scripts

We may like to think that our sexual behavior is spontaneous and represents our unique individual likes and dislikes, but in reality even this personal aspect of our lives is highly shaped by social and cultural forces. Our sexual attitudes and behaviors are organized and directed by **sexual scripts,** which are the norms or rules regarding sexual behavior, including number and type of sexual partners, activities, attitudes, and even purposes for engaging in sexual relationships. For example, our culture prohibits sex with animals, with children, or with someone to whom you have paid money. It does not prohibit sex among unmarried people, those who share a different religious faith, or those who are of a different race or ethnic background. However, such is not the case in all societies. Sexual scripts act as a blueprint, informing us what is expected and appropriate, and what is inappropriate and taboo. Gendered expectations are a critical component of sexual scripts because the sexual norms for males and females are socially constructed and remain highly differentiated in any culture (Fracher & Kimmel, 1992).

Where Do We Learn Our Sexual Scripts?

We learn our sexual scripts from at least three different sources (Laumann et al., 1994). First, we learn from the culture in which we live, including our parents, our friends, and the mass media. Second, scripts are learned from the interpersonal communication between two individuals as they begin, and attend to, their personal relationship. Third, sexual scripts also reflect personal views of sex, based on people's unique personal feelings, desires, and fantasies. We must look beyond biology, because the sexual scripts that people learn appear to be far more influential than biological factors: "That we are sexual is determined by a biological imperative toward reproduction, but *how* we are sexual—where, when, how often, with whom, and why—has to do with cultural learning and meanings transmitted in a cultural setting. . . . Sexual beings are made, not born . . . sexuality is learned in roughly the same way as anything else is learned in our culture" (Fracher & Kimmel, 1992: 440–441).

Gender and Sexual Scripts: The Double Standard

Do gender differences exist in attitudes toward sex, expectations for sexual behavior, and reported sexual behaviors? Yes. Sexual scripts are distinctly different for women and

Magazines such as this reveal the double standard in our sexual scripts.

men. Traditionally, men have been allowed far more permissiveness in sexual behavior whereas women are more likely to be socially punished for their sexual experiences, particularly their nonmarital experiences. This disparity has been referred to as the **double standard.** Men are expected to be assertive in seeking sexual behavior, to be always ready for sex, with orgasm as the goal rather than intimacy. In contrast, women are to walk a fine line by being "sexy" yet not "too sexy." They must make themselves desirable and attractive to the attentions of men, but by becoming too desirable or attractive they risk being labeled "easy" or "cheap." They must be careful not to appear to be too interested in sex. Men may be complimented as "studs" for their participation in nonmarital sex with a large number of partners, but the words *slut* and *whore* are derogatory terms commonly used to describe sexually active women.

The sexual double standard has declined substantially today compared to in the past.

Has the Double Standard Declined?

Some scholars suggest that the double standard has declined in recent generations—that both men and women are allowed to engage, in nonmarital sex with few social repercussions. Although the double standard may have declined to some degree, people are still more tolerant of nonmarital sexual activity among men than among women, particularly on the first date (Hatfield & Rapson, 1996), in uncommitted relationships (Hynie, Lydon, & Taradash, 1997), or with a large number of partners over time (Rubin, 1990). Hynie, Lydon, and Taradash (1997) found that the double standard is held by both men and women: even women perceive other women more negatively if they have had sex in an uncommitted relationship than if they have had sex in a committed one. Using harsh sexual terms to refer to sexually active girls is common among people of all ages, including preadolescent boys, middle and high schoolers, college students, and other adults (Fine, 1987; Hatfield & Rapson, 1996; Rubin, 1990).

In her book *School Girls,* Peggy Orenstein found that the fear of being labeled a slut in middle school profoundly affects how girls see themselves and directly influences how they relate to both other girls and to boys. She describes one interview with Evie, a typical middle school girl who is keenly obsessed with pointing out the girls at school who are "sluts." Evie is learning the rules, or scripts, about sexuality. She explains to Orenstein, in her middle school language, that sex "ruins" girls but enhances boys, that boys have far fewer constraints than do girls, that sexual behavior for girls is containable,

but for boys it is inevitable and excusable: "Boys only think with their dicks" (1994: 57). Girls who fail to follow the scripts are shunned. If they dare to complain about the scripts, or confront a boy who is pressuring them for sex, it is *their* reputations that are on the line. "The thing is, we don't have control," Evie explains. "He could just say that we were asking for it or that we wanted it. Then everyone will think we're sluts" (1994: 65). As Orenstein comments,

> There is only one label worse than "schoolgirl" and that's her inverse, the fallen girl, or in student parlance, the slut. A "slut" is not merely a girl who "does it," but any girl who—through her clothes, her make-up, her hairstyle, or her speech—seems as if she *might*. Girls may protest the prudish connotations of "schoolgirl," but they fear the prurience of "slut": in order to find the middle ground between the two, a place from which they can function safely and with approval, girls have to monitor both their expressions of intelligence and their budding sexual desire. They must keep vigilant watch, over each other and over themselves.

The Double Standard in Current Sexual Behavior

Given the strongly gendered sexual scripts in our society, it is not surprising that the most recent large-scale study of human sexuality by NORC and the University of Chicago found significant differences between men and women in their sexual behavior. In the national survey, with a representative sample of 3,432 adults, men reported thinking about sex more often than did women (54 percent versus 19 percent reported thinking about sex several times a day) and having more sexual partners (33 percent versus 9 percent having 10 or more sex partners since age 18) (Michael et al., 1994). Men and women also report different motivations for sexual behavior. With respect to sexual intercourse, men report the desire for sexual pleasure, conquest, and the relief of sexual tension more often than do women, who are more likely than men to emphasize emotional closeness and affection (Michael et al., 1994).

| FICTION

Although it has declined somewhat, it still prominently exists. Both men and women are more critical of women's sexual activity outside of marriage or a monogamous relationship.

An analysis of the double standard is critical because it adversely affects both women and men. It contributes to a lack of knowledge about women's sexual needs, it fosters the mistaken idea that women have less important sexual needs, and it perpetuates the notion that male sexuality should be the normative baseline for eroticism and sexual activity. It objectifies women by keeping them as the "objects of desire" rather than recognizing their own human sexual needs. Furthermore, it inhibits communication between partners, it can increase the likelihood of relationship violence, and it prevents individuals from seeking help when a sexual problem does occur.

The double standard is commonly found throughout the world, in both industrialized and nonindustrialized nations. Sometimes it even lays the foundation for government social policy. The Family Diversity box on page 216 illustrates how the double sexual standard has affected government policy in Japan. While Viagra, the drug developed to treat male impotence, was approved by the Japanese government in less than six months, the birth control pill, heralded around the world as a relatively safe way to control fertility, has only recently been approved. Could this disparity reflect that men's sexual pleasure is seen as more important than women's?

Sexually Transmitted Diseases

In the United States today, more than 65 million people have an incurable sexually transmitted disease (STD). An additional 15 million people become infected with STDs each year, and half of these cases are incurable (Cates, 1999). STDs, along with other diseases and epidemics, are the focus of **epidemiologists.** They work as health detectives to piece together a picture of the disease.

Despite the fact that STDs are widespread and can strike people of any age, sex, or sexual orientation, most people remain unaware of the risks and consequences of all but the most publicized STDs—human immunodeficiency virus (HIV) and AIDS. Yet, as shown in Table 5.3, epidemiologists at the Centers for Disease Control (CDC) show us that the **prevalence** of STDs, which is the estimated number of people currently infected,

TABLE 5.3	Magnitude of the STD Epidemic	
STD	PREVALENCE	INCIDENCE
Chlamydia	2,000,000	3,000,000
Gonorrhea	N/A	650,000
Syphilis	N/A	70,000
Herpes	45,000,000	1,000,000
Human papillomavirus (hpv)	20,000,000	5,500,000
Hepatitis B	417,000	120,000
Trichomoniasis	N/A	5,000,000

Source: Cates (1999).

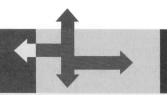

Japan took only six months to approve the impotence-treatment drug Viagra, which left many people asking why the birth control pill has sluggishly been in review by the Japanese government for nearly a decade. Many women in Japan were upset about their government's refusal to approve the birth control pill, while the quick passage of Viagra has stirred new concerns.

Women's groups and the media accused the government of sexism. Midori Ashida, who heads a Tokyo-based group that is pushing for the pill's acceptance, states, "When old guys want something, they get it. But when women want something, nothing happens. . . . Japan is still a male-dominated society."

The Health Ministry in Japan estimates that anywhere from 8,000 to 7,000,000 Japanese men suffer from impotence. However, advocates of the birth control pill claim that approval of the birth control pill will serve far more people and be of better benefit than Viagra. In Japan, unwanted pregnancies are a common occurrence, and statistics show that one in five of these ends in abortion, for a total of roughly 340,000 abortions per year. Japan's abortion rate is somewhat lower than that of the United States but far higher than that of the Euro-pean nations. The risks of pregnancy and abortion far outweigh any possible side effects of the pill, supporters claim.

The Health Ministry claims that the number-one reason that the pill spent so long in review is the government's concerns about the possible side effects. However, more than 300 million women around the world use birth control pills, and recent studies show few if any long-term ill effects.

Moreover, the Health Ministry is concerned that acceptance of the pill will cut into the use of condoms, which may contribute to the spread of AIDS. Others cite fears about the destruction of moral values. However, the government does not seem at all concerned with the possible side effects of Viagra. Of the Americans who have taken Viagra since it was first made available, 130 have died, mostly from heart attacks. One Japanese man who used Viagra has died.

Advocates of the birth control pill finally met with success. In June 1999, within a few months after the outcry over the approval of Viagra, the Japanese government decided to allow limited sale of the pill. It will require a doctor's prescription and will not be covered by public health insurance.

Why the delay in the pill when Viagra was approved quickly?

Takaichi Hirota, a spokesman for Pfizer, believes that Viagra won quick approval because the company provided hard data on the drug. However, others believe that the quick passage of Viagra and the foot dragging on the pill were more likely related to the Japanese government's goal of raising the rapidly declining birthrate of the nation. The birthrate in Japan is at an all-time low of 1.39 births per woman, and government officials are worried that this trend will increase the elderly population. The increasing elderly population may create a serious financial problem for Japan.

Source: Adapted from Yuri Kageyama (Feb. 11, 1999). "A Tale of Two Drugs Irks Japan's Women." *The Oregonian*, A-6, reprinted with permission of The Associated Press; Ginny Parker (June 2, 1999). "Japan Approves Birth Control Pill." Associated Press. Available online: http://www.yourkweekly.com/1999news/6_2_w2.htm.

Critical Thinking

1. What is the logic used by Japanese officials for quickly approving the drug Viagra while stalling on the approval of birth control pills?

2. What are the social and cultural factors that may also account for these decisions? In the official debate about Viagra and birth control pills, are these factors explicit or implicit?

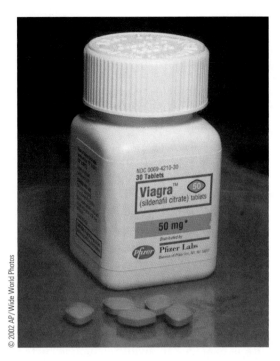

Viagra was approved by the Japanese government quickly, yet it took decades for birth control pills to be approved. Does this reflect a double standard?

and the **incidence** of STDs, which is the estimated number of new cases every year, are staggering (CDC, 2001c). The direct and indirect costs of the major STDs are nearly $17 billion each year (Eng & Butler, 1997).

Although STDs such as chlamydia and herpes are widespread across all racial and ethnic groups, average STD rates tend to be higher among African Americans than whites. Some of this disparity can be attributed to differences in risk behaviors (i.e., beginning sexual intercourse at an early age, multiple partners, unprotected intercourse, level of drug use) and social conditions such as poverty and access to health care. However, part of the disparity is also due to the fact that African Americans are more likely to seek health care in public clinics that report STDs more thoroughly than do private providers (CDC, 2001c). Consequently, the statistics may actually be underreporting the rates among whites.

| FACT OR FICTION?

HIV is the most common STD in the United States today.

Genital Herpes

Genital herpes (also known as HSV-2) is the most common STD in the United States, with 45 million people currently infected, and 1 million new cases every year. In other words, approximately one in five Americans is infected with genital herpes (Fleming et al., 1997; McQuillan, 2000). Genital herpes, in addition to the pain and inconvenience caused by the virus itself, can put people at greater risk for HIV because the lesions can facilitate HIV transmission.

The first outbreak, which is often the most painful, lasts an average of twelve days and may occur anywhere from a few days to a few weeks after exposure. Small bumps, called vesicles or papules, appear on the genitals. They may first itch, then blister, and finally rupture, forming painful ulcers.

The recurrent painful lesions of genital herpes can be treated, but the infection itself cannot be cured. Drugs can be used to reduce the symptoms. Some people with herpes have no noticeable symptoms and pass the disease on to others unaware.

Women are more likely to have herpes than are men because male-to-female transmission is more efficient than transmission from females to males. It is most common among African American females, with rates of over 50 percent, compared to 19 percent of white women. The percentage of people infected increases with age because once a person is infected, it is incurable; however, the prevalence of infection has increased most rapidly among white teens and young adults. Herpes prevalence among white teens aged twelve to nineteen is five times greater than the prevalence in the 1970s (CDC, 2001c; Fleming et al., 1997).

Genital herpes is far more common than HIV and is the most common STD.

HIV and AIDS

HIV or AIDS receives more media attention than any other STD because it is so deadly and because of the political implications surrounding its discovery and treatment (i.e., the fact that it was initially labeled a "gay disease"). AIDS is caused by infection with a virus called *human immunodeficiency virus,* passed from one person to another through blood-to-blood transmission, sexual contact, and pregnancy, delivery, or breastfeeding. Most people with HIV will develop full-blown AIDS. The CDC reports that scientists have different theories about the origin of HIV, but none have been proven.

History and Development In the early 1980s, physicians in a number of U.S. cities began to notice that numerous cases of rare diseases were occurring among otherwise strong and healthy men. Kaposi's sarcoma, a

type of cancer of the blood vessels, and pneumocystis carinii pneumonia, a usually mild lung infection, had become deadly diseases because of a breakdown in the immune system. The term **acquired immunodeficiency syndrome,** or AIDS, was given even before the virus responsible (HIV) was discovered.

At first, AIDS seemed to be confined to few groups: gay men, people with hemophilia, and Haitians. Some have argued that because the disease did not seem to run through the entire population, but among groups who had faced stigma and discrimination, the government was slow to act (Shilts, 2000). It was labeled a "gay disease" and stigmatized. As Pat Buchanan, a conservative leader and former U.S. presidential hopeful said, "The poor homosexuals—they have declared war upon nature and now nature is exacting an awful retribution" (cited in Strong et al., 2002: 538).

Current Status The cumulative number of AIDS cases in the United States reported to the CDC through December of 2000 is 774,467. There have been even more HIV cases—nearly 900,000. Again, it is likely that all of these individuals will someday develop AIDS. Minority groups have been particularly hard hit. Epidemiologists estimate that although African Americans make up only 12 percent of the U.S. population, they have 37 percent of reported AIDS cases. Approximately 1 in 50 African American men and 1 in 160 African American women are infected with HIV. Likewise, Hispanics represented 13 percent of the population in 1999 but accounted for 19 percent of the new AIDS cases reported that year (CDC, Division of HIV/AIDS Prevention, 2001). For prevention programs to be particularly effective in minority communities, the CDC recommends that they be culturally sensitive. While race and ethnicity alone are not risk factors for HIV and AIDS, underlying social and economic conditions (e.g., higher rates of poverty, substance abuse, limited access to

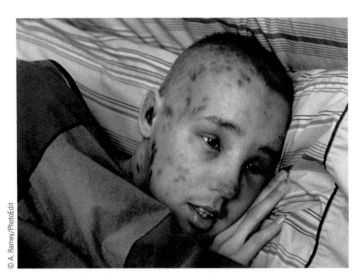

© A. Ramey/PhotoEdit

By the end of 2000, 448,060 people in the U.S. had died from AIDS. Although the number of deaths has declined in the past few years, there is still no cure for AIDS.

FIGURE 5.6 Annual New HIV Infections (N ≈ 40,000)

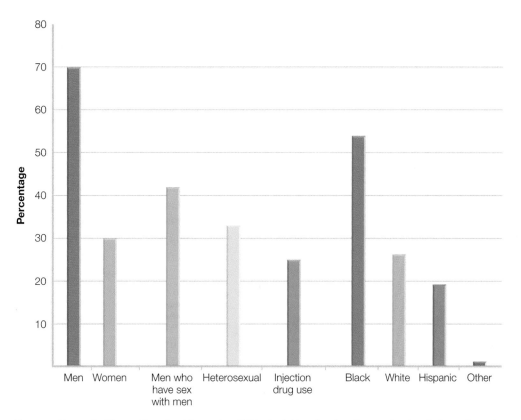

Source: Centers for Disease Control and Prevention, 2001a. Available online: http://www.cdc.nchstp/od/news/At_a_glance.pdf.

health care, cultural diversity, and language barriers) may increase the risk of infection.

By the end of 2000, 448,060 people had died of AIDS, although the number of deaths is decreasing somewhat because of new HIV treatments. The number of deaths declined 17 percent from 1997 to 1998 and 8 percent from 1998 to 1999, down to 16,765 in 1999. More people are living with AIDS than ever before.

These same HIV treatments have also slowed the progression from HIV to AIDS. The number of new AIDS cases declined 13 percent between 1997 and 1998, and 3 percent between 1998 and 1999, down to 41,849. Nonetheless, despite this optimistic news, there are still approximately 40,000 new cases of HIV each year in the United States alone, and it is likely that they will all eventually turn into AIDS. Today, there remains no known cure. Figure 5.6 illustrates the distribution of the new HIV infections each year according to race, risk factor, and gender.

Adolescent Sexual Behavior, Pregnancy, and Births

An important theme in this chapter is that our sexual norms, attitudes, and behaviors are influenced by the culture in which we live. We will provide an in-depth example. An examination of adolescent pregnancy can show us how even such personal issues as sexuality are socially produced and are related to our culture.

The Framing of a Social Problem

Adolescent pregnancy, and thus adolescent sexual behavior more generally, are considered to be major family policy concerns and public health challenges in the United States. Approximately 900,000 U.S. women under age 20 become pregnant each year (Alan Guttmacher Institute, 2000). Approximately 40 percent of U.S. women become pregnant before the age of 20 (Baldwin-Grossman, Walker, Kotloff, & Pepper, 2001), and more than three-quarters of these pregnancies are unintended (Alan Guttmacher Institute, 1998). Moreover, the United States has one of the highest teenage birthrates in the developed world: twice as high as England's, three times as high as Australia's, four times as high as Germany's, six times as high as France's, eight times as high as the Netherlands', and fifteen times as high as Japan's (Berne & Huberman, 1999; Singh & Darroch, 2000). Why are rates so much lower in other countries? This situation is, arguably, due to policies in those countries that include mandatory, medically accurate sex education programs that provide comprehensive information and encourage teens to make responsible choices; easy access to contraceptives and other forms of reproductive health care; the social acceptance of adolescent sexual expression as normal and healthy; and governmental and social programs that allow needed services such as medical care, education, and other social services (Berne & Huberman, 1999).

The negative consequences of early parenting in the United States have been well documented (Adams & Kocik, 1997; Brooks-Gunn & Chase-Landale, 1991; Annie E. Casey Foundation, 1998; Coley & Chase-Lansdale, 1998; Fergusson & Woodward, 2000; Maynard, 1997; Hoffman, 1998; Ventura, Matthews, & Curtin, 1999). Teen mothers are 2.5 times as likely to die in childbirth as are older mothers, their infants are twice as likely to have low birth weight, and their infants are nearly 3 times more likely to die within the first month of life. Furthermore, teen mothers are more likely to drop out of school than are other teens, are considerably poorer, and are more likely to receive welfare. Adolescent mothers are also less knowledgeable about child development than are other mothers, are less prepared for child rearing, and are more likely to be depressed. Therefore, it is not surprising that social workers, health professionals, educators, researchers, and parents and teens themselves are alarmed at the relatively large number of teens—both young women and men—who are involved in adolescent pregnancies.

Contemporary Trends

For some good news, the 1990s witnessed substantial declines in teenage birthrates. Teenage pregnancy and abortion are at their lowest points since they were first measured in the early 1970s. Likewise, birthrates are similar to those that prevailed between the mid-1970s and the mid-1980s (Henshaw, 1999). As shown in Figure 5.7, in 1986 ap-

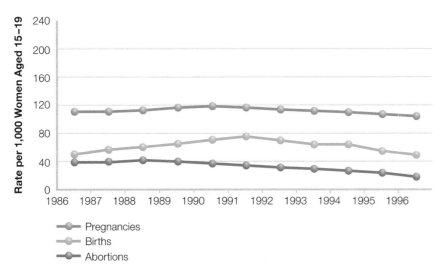

Source: Alan Guttmacher Institute (1999). *Teenage Pregnancy: Overall Trends and State by State Information.*

proximately 107 pregnancies occurred per 1,000 women aged 15–19. By 1990, that rate had climbed to 117 per 1,000. By 1996, the rate declined by an impressive 17 percent, to 97 pregnancies per 1,000 teenage women. Figure 5.7 illustrates the decline in birthrates and abortions since 1986 as well.

The declines are widespread, occurring with both younger and older teens. Even among teenagers 14 and younger, a group that has always had relatively low rates of pregnancy compared to older teens, the declines are substantial. Approximately 17 pregnancies occurred per 1,000 teen girls in this age group between the mid-1980s and 1993. By 1996, the number was reduced to 13 per 1,000.

Declines have also occurred across racial and ethnic groups. Figures 5.7, 5.8, and 5.9 illustrate the pregnancy, abortion, and birthrates for white, African American, and Hispanic teenage women. Historically, white teenagers have had lower rates than African Americans or Hispanics. Through most of the 1990s, African American teens had the highest rate. However, the birthrates

of African American teens have dropped even more dramatically than those of whites; therefore, the gap between these two groups has narrowed. Moreover, the birthrates among Hispanic teens have declined only slightly, so they now have the highest birthrate.

What accounts for these trends? Obviously, declines in birthrates reflect changes in (a) the level of teenage pregnancies and (b) how these pregnancies are resolved. Since

Teenage birthrates have declined substantially over the past decade, due to more effective contraceptives, and an increase in abstinence.

FIGURE 5.8 Among Non-Hispanic White Teenagers, Birthrates Have Fallen Less Steeply Than Pregnancy Rates Because of Large Drops in Abortion Rates

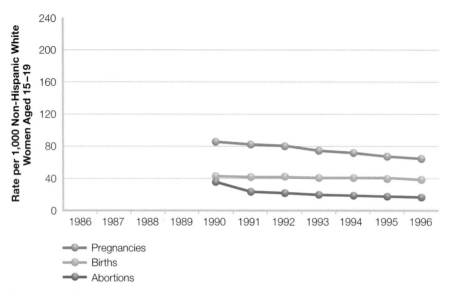

Source: Alan Guttmacher Institute (1999). *Teenage Pregnancy: Overall Trends and State by State Information.*

FIGURE 5.9 Pregnancy Rates, Birthrates, and Abortion Rates Among Black Teenagers Have All Dropped by About 20 Percent

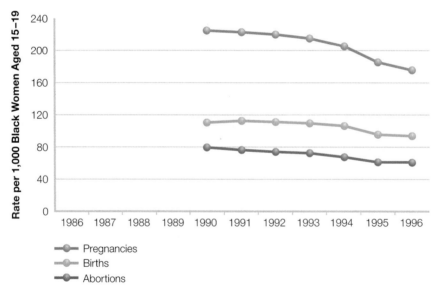

Source: Alan Guttmacher Institute (1999). *Teenage Pregnancy: Overall Trends and State by State Information.*

FIGURE 5.10 Hispanic Teenagers' Pregnancy Rates and Birthrates Have Only Recently Begun to Decline

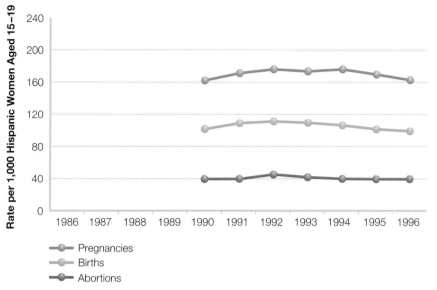

Source: Alan Guttmacher Institute (1999). *Teenage Pregnancy: Overall Trends and State by State Information.*

we know that the abortion rate among teens also declined during this period, it appears that the decline in teenage birthrates is attributable to the reductions in the pregnancy rate. The important question then remains: Why did the pregnancy rate decline?

Reasons for the Declining Rate of Adolescent Pregnancy

Many social trends have contributed to the reduction in adolescent pregnancy. The data below are primarily from the 1988 and 1995 National Survey of Family Growth (NSFG), which contains large, nationally representative samples of more than 1,500 teenage women. The NSFG is one of the best and most recent statistical sources available to address these issues. (These data are found in the report by the Alan Guttmacher Institute, *Why Is Teenage Pregnancy Declining?*

The Roles of Abstinence, Sexual Activity, and Contraceptive Use [2000].)

1. *An increase in abstinence has occurred.* According to the NSFG, the proportion of all teenagers who had ever had sexual intercourse decreased by 2 percent between 1988 and 1995, to 51 percent. Calculations indicate that approximately one-fourth of the drop in teenage pregnancy during this seven-year period resulted from increased abstinence (i.e., a decrease in the proportion of adolescent women who had sexual intercourse), the other three-quarters of the change being due to changes in behavior among those having sex, as outlined below.

2. *The average frequency of sexual intercourse has changed.* Among teens who acknowledge being sexually active, nearly twice as many reported not having sexual intercourse at all during the past year in

1995 as did teens in 1988 (9 percent versus 5 percent). However, this decline is somewhat offset by the fact that a larger proportion of teens in 1995 said that they had intercourse in every month of the year (43 percent versus 35 percent). Consequently, the average exposure to sexual intercourse among sexually active teenage women has changed little.

3. *Teens are using more-effective contraceptive methods.* The NSFG examines teens' use of contraception at three points in time: (a) the first time they had intercourse, (b) during the month preceding the survey, and (c) the last time they had intercourse. The most dramatic increase between 1988 and 1995 is in the number of teens who report using contraception during their first sexual intercourse (75 percent in 1995 versus 65 percent in 1988). Moreover, teenagers are increasingly adopting hormonal methods, such as implants or injections, which are long-acting and have the lowest failure rates of all reversible methods. Generally unavailable in 1988, they accounted for 13 percent of the use among teens in 1995. Condom use increased only slightly, while reliance on oral contraceptives declined substantially. Because of this shift in methods between 1988 and 1995, teens (at least those who use contraceptives) are now less likely to become pregnant.

What has contributed to these changes among teenagers? Research is inconclusive, but some results point to the following:

* The rise in balanced sex education programs that teach young people to take responsibility for their sexual health and include information about delaying intercourse and about conception (Franklin, Grant, Corcoran, Miller, & Bultman, 1997; Kirby, 1997).

* Open and honest parent–teen communication, which has been shown to lead to less risky sexual behaviors among teens (Holtzman & Rubinson, 1995; Hutchinson & Cooney, 1998; Rodgers, 1999). African Americans report higher levels of parent–teen communication than do whites, which may explain their larger decline in recent birthrates (Hutchinson & Cooney, 1998).

* Concern and fear over contacting HIV/AIDS, which has contributed to greater condom use and other safe sex practices (Holtzman & Rubinson, 1995).

* The recent availability of long-acting hormonal birth control methods, which have the lowest failure rates of all reversible methods.

Conclusion

This chapter has shown us a variety of ways in which our sexual norms, attitudes, and behaviors are related to our culture and to historical circumstances. These relationships are dynamic and ever changing. Sexuality is only partly rooted in biology; it is also socially constructed. "Who am I?" and "What should I do?" are age-old questions that cannot be answered outside of the influences of the rest of society. "Who am I?" addresses issues related to sex, gender, and sexual orientation. These are interrelated, although not always in a predictable manner. With respect to sexual expression, our cultural attitudes and behaviors have changed over time. A number of important studies give us some key insights into our sexual selves. Yet, despite what we may think of as personal choices, sexual scripts—norms—largely explain our attitudes and behaviors. These sexual scripts continue to be different for men and women, a situation called the double standard. Even our social policies must be examined in their social and historical context. Once again, what appear at first glance to be very personal choices—after all, what could be more personal than self-concepts, attitudes, and sexual behaviors?—are often shaped by larger social forces. The macrolevel and microlevel influences are intertwined.

Chapter Review

* *What do we mean by "sexuality"?*

Sexuality is not necessarily easy to define, even though the word is in popular usage. Here we address two critical components, identity and behavior.

* *What is the difference between "sex" and "gender"?*

Sex refers to the biological differences and one's role in reproduction, whereas gender refers to culturally and socially constructed differences associated with masculinity or femininity.

* *Don't sex and gender go together? Aren't women feminine and men masculine?*

It's not that simple. First, what is defined as feminine and masculine can vary dramatically from one culture to the next, or from one historical period to the next. Second, some people are transgendered: their physical sex and their gendered feelings don't match in the predicted fashion.

* *How do we learn our gendered behavior?*

We learn it from a process called socialization, which involves parents, schools, toys, games, peers, and the mass media. We learn gender through our daily interactions with others and through our dealings with social institutions.

* *What do we mean by "sexual orientation"?*

We are referring to the sexual and romantic partner of choice. Kinsey's early work showed that sexual orientation exists on a continuum from completely heterosexual to completely homosexual. While the number of people who are exclusively homosexual is small, many people lie somewhere in between these two polar points. Bisexuals are attracted to both males and females.

* *Were people in the Victorian era really as sexually repressed as we have been led to believe?*

Our views are somewhat exaggerated and a bit misleading. Yes, they certainly held some different views and inhibitions as compared to today, but sexuality was alive and well. In fact, it's estimated that somewhere between 10 percent and 30 percent of Victorian-era brides were pregnant on their wedding day.

* *How can researchers possibly do a survey on sexual behavior? Isn't that too personal to study? Won't people lie?*

On the contrary, a number of excellent studies of human sexuality have given us keen insights into values and sexual behaviors. The most useful studies involve large and representative samples.

* *What are some popular forms of sexual expression?*

There are many forms of sexual expression, including masturbation, kissing, oral sex, and sexual intercourse. Gender, class, race and ethnicity, and age all influence these experiences.

* *What are sexual scripts, and where do we learn them?*

Sexual scripts are the norms regarding sexual behavior, and we learn these through the various agents of socialization. We also learn them from interpersonal communication and from our own unique personal desires.

* *Are sexual scripts different for men and women?*

Yes. This disparity is referred to as the "double standard." Men are allowed far more permissiveness in sexual behavior than are women.

* *How do we measure the frequency of sexually transmitted diseases?*

The prevalence of STDs, which is the estimated number of people currently infected, and the incidence of STDs, which is the estimated number of new cases every year, show that the numbers are staggering.

* *What is the most common STD?*

Genital herpes is the most common STD, with 45 million currently affected (prevalence) and approximately 1 million new cases a year (incidence).

* *What is AIDS?*

AIDS is a deadly disease that has killed hundreds of thousands of people in the United States alone. It is passed through blood-to-blood transmission, sexual contact, and pregnancy, delivery, or breastfeeding. The disease has been highly publicized, primarily because its first known victims were gay men.

* *How large of a social problem is teenage pregnancy?*

Approximately 900,000 women under age 20 become pregnant each year in the United States, and most of these pregnancies are unintended. However, the teen pregnancy rate, abortion rate, and birthrate are at their lowest points since they were first measured in the early 1970s. Declines are seen among younger and older teens, and across all racial and ethnic groups.

* *Why has teen pregnancy declined?*

Abstinence is more common, the average frequency of sexual intercourse has declined, and teens are using more-effective contraceptive methods.

Key Terms

acquired immunodeficiency syndrome (AIDS): a deadly disease passed from one person to another through blood-to-blood transmission, sexual contact, and pregnancy, delivery, or breastfeeding

anti-gay prejudice: very strong negative feelings toward homosexuality. (This term is preferred over *homophobia.*)

bisexual: an orientation in which a person is attracted to both males and females

cross-dressing: wearing the clothing associated with the other sex

cunnilingus: oral stimulation of a woman's genitals by her partner

double standard: men being allowed far more permissiveness in sexual behavior

epidemiologist: a "health detective" who works to piece together a picture of disease

fellatio: oral stimulation of a man's genitals by his partner

gender: culturally and socially constructed differences between males and females found in the meanings, beliefs, and practices associated with femininity and masculinity

hermaphrodites: those born with genitalia that do not clearly identify them as unambiguously male or female

heterosexual: attraction and preference for developing romantic and sexual relationships with persons of the other sex

homophobia: an unrealistic fear of homosexuality. See *anti-gay prejudice.*

homosexual: attraction and preference for relationships with members of one's own sex

incidence: estimated number of new cases of a disease every year

kissing: one of our earliest sensual experiences

masturbation: sexually stimulating one's own body

menarche: a woman's first menstrual period

oral sex: oral stimulation of the genitals

prevalence: estimated number of people currently infected with a disease

sex: biological differences and one's role in reproduction

sexology: a field made up of a multidisciplinary group of clinicians, researchers, and educators concerned with sexuality

sexual intercourse: penetration, including vaginal and anal

sexual orientation: the sexual and romantic partner of choice

sexual scripts: the norms or rules regarding sexual behavior

transgendered: a condition in which a person feels as comfortable, if not more so, in expressing gendered traits that are associated with the other sex

transsexuals: individuals who undergo sex reassignment surgery and hormone treatments

Resources on the Internet

These web sites have been selected for their relevance to the topics in this chapter. These sites are among the more stable, but please be aware that web site addresses change frequently.

Kinsey Institute

http://www.indiana.edu/~kinsey

The mission of the Kinsey Institute is to promote interdisciplinary research and scholarship into the fields of sexuality, gender, and reproduction. The site features a library and a catalog, research projects, training info, clinics, and links.

Alan Guttmacher Institute

http://www.agi-usa.org

The Alan Guttmacher Institute is a nonprofit organization focused on sexual and reproductive health research, policy analysis, and public education. The institute's mission is to protect the reproductive choices of all women and men in the United States and throughout the world. The institute supports people's ability to obtain the information and services needed to achieve their full human rights, safeguard their health, and exercise their individual responsibilities regarding sexual behavior and relationships, reproduction, and family formation.

Tri-Ess

http://www.brendat.com/tri-ess1.htm

Tri-Ess is an educational, social, and support group for heterosexual cross-dressers, their spouses or partners, and their families.

PFLAG

http://www.pflag.org

Parents, Families & Friends of Lesbians & Gays (PFLAG) is a national nonprofit organization with more than 80,000 members and supporters and more than 460 affiliates in the United States. PFLAG promotes the health and well-being of gay, lesbian, bisexual, and transgendered persons, their families, and their friends through support aimed to help cope with an adverse society, education to enlighten an ill-informed public, and advocacy to end discrimination and to secure equal civil rights.

Henry J. Kaiser Family Foundation

http://www.kff.org

The Henry J. Kaiser Family Foundation is an independent philanthropy focusing on the major health care issues facing the nation, including reproductive and sexual health.

Companion Web Site for This Book

Virtual Society: The Wadsworth Sociology Resource Center

http://sociology.wadsworth.com

Begin by clicking the Student Resources section. Next, click Marriage and Family, and then click the cover image for this book. Select from the pull-down menu the chapter you are presently studying. You will have easy access to chapter resources such as MicroCase Online exercises, additional Web links, flashcards, InfoTrac exercises, and practice tests (that can be scored). In addition, to enhance and help with your study of marriages and families, be sure to investigate the rest of the rich sociology resources at Virtual Society.

Visit InfoTrac College Edition

 Another unique option available to you at the Student Resources section of the Virtual Society web site described above is InfoTrac College Edition, an online library of hundreds of scholarly and popular periodicals. Here are three suggested key search terms for this chapter:

* Search keywords: *pregnancy + teenage*
* Search keywords: *sexuality + elderly*
* Search keywords: *AIDS + Africa*

Search recent years to get the latest information on these issues.

© Claudia Kunin /Corbis

Making Commitments: Marriage

6

... to have and to hold from this day forward, for better for worse, for richer for poorer, in sickness and in health, to love and to cherish, till death do us part.

More than two million women and men say these words each year as they move their relationships toward what they hope will be a lifetime commitment. The odds of making such a lifetime commitment are declining. Marriages are occurring less frequently than ever before, and among recent marriages, it is estimated that close to half will end in divorce. This can be a pretty depressing statistic to learn, especially for those who are anticipating marriage for the first time. The majority of Americans (regardless of class, gender, or ethnicity) place marriage at the top of their priority lists (Cherlin, 1992; Tucker & Mitchell-Kernan, 1995). "Having a happy marriage" is seen as either "one of the most important objectives" or "a very important objective" for over 90 percent of Americans (Glenn, 1996). A majority placed it higher than "good health" or a "good family life." So why are we unable to sustain something we value so highly?

FACT OR FICTION?

Marriages are legal relationships among consenting adults.

There is not an easy or simple answer to this question, and it has been puzzling scholars for years. Some suggest that our culture of individualism and the increasing secularization of religion have resulted in a lessen-

ing of our commitment to lifelong marriage. These cultural shifts, along with the greater acceptance of cohabitation, sex and childbearing outside of marriage, and divorce, work together to lessen the social sanctions associated with nonmarital lifestyles. Others argue that who gets married and stays married is related to one's social and economic position. Finding a "good match" is more difficult for some than others. Lower rates of marriage among African Americans and higher rates of divorce among people with less education and lower-paying jobs can be seen as indicators of the unequal access to resources for building successful partnerships. Americans want to marry but believe that marriage brings with it the responsibility to be economically self-sufficient. For those who have fewer resources, or do not have access to potential partners with resources, marriage (especially an enduring one) is less likely. This perspective sees structural shifts in the economy, and growing economic inequality, as the culprits behind the declining rates of marriage.

In this chapter, we will explore these structural and cultural explanations for the statistical decline in the rates of marriage. In doing so, we will use the following definition of **marriage:** a legally and socially recognized relationship between a woman and a man that includes sexual, economic, and social rights and responsibilities for partners. This definition calls attention to the fact that marriage, although it is a legal contract between two individuals, is also a matter of public concern. State laws establish the rules for marriage and its dissolution. At the same time, members of society maintain norms and sanctions for appropriate behaviors related to marriage.

| FICTION

Marriages are legal relationships, but just the consent of the adults is not sufficient. Each state has its own laws about who can and cannot marry. In no state can two people of the same sex marry.

We begin the discussion of marriage by exploring its importance throughout American history. Marriage was often used as a metaphor for good government during the creation of our new nation. Political leaders in the colonies did not believe their relationship with England was one that allowed them freedom of choice. They argued for a government that functioned like marriage: men and women are believed to enter into marriage freely. Once married, the couple becomes united into one unit. The husband, as head of the household, works to protect and defend his wife. He represents her in all legal matters. Governments should be the same. Men should elect their representatives, who would then protect and defend their rights and represent them in governmental affairs (Hartog, 2000).

However, laws regarding marriage have changed since the establishment of the United States, and the "union of man and wife" means something very different today. We no longer view a husband and wife as one person in law but as equal partners in domestic exchange. This view is evident in marriage and family law, with the introduction of concepts such as "community property" and "shared custody" of children in the case of divorce. However, while laws have become much more egalitarian, contemporary research on wedding rituals and the negotiation of marital relations suggests that vestiges of more-traditional notions are still part of marriage.

Census data reveal that fewer people are married today than ever before, and those who do marry are delaying it longer than their parents and grandparents did. Both structural and cultural features of U.S. society are related to the likelihood that people marry and the age when they marry. The data comparing long-term marriage to its alternatives suggest that marriage brings a premium in terms of health and economic well-being, but we will also take a look at whether marriage brings the same premium to all who enter. Finally, we take up the issue of what makes a marriage successful. Marriages are hard work. For some, the difficulty comes from trying to maintain a traditional division of labor in an economy that puts pressure on wives and mothers to work. For others, it means trying to create an egalitarian marriage in a patriarchal society—one that still evaluates men on their ability to provide and women on their ability to nurture. But whatever the challenge, it appears that the majority will take it on.

The Importance of Marriage in U.S. History

Marriage has existed in some form in most countries around the world. It is recognized as an important factor in ensuring the success of societies. For example, it can serve a political function by joining together two families. Because the institution of marriage has been closely connected with the socialization of children, marriage can also serve as a way of ensuring intergenerational continuity (Farrell, 1999). As well, marriage is important to the individuals within societies. The overwhelming majority of Americans desire to get married and eventually do so. In his recent book, *Marriage in Men's Lives,*

Steven Nock (1998) argues that most Americans hold the following views about marriage today:

1. Marriage is a free personal choice, based on love.
2. Maturity is a presumed requirement for marriage.
3. Marriage is a heterosexual relationship.
4. The husband is the head, and principal earner, in a marriage.
5. Sexual fidelity and monogamy are expectations for marriage.
6. Marriage typically involves children.

Although these are individuals' beliefs about what a marriage should be today, historians tell us that these ideas have come to be important through the course of U.S. history. (For a view of marriage in another culture, see the Family Diversity box on page 234.) In this section we will briefly review the meaning of marriage from colonial times through the twentieth century. Our review will suggest how marriage has gone from a community-centered institution to one that is considered to be primarily a private matter. At the same time, marriage has always been regulated by the state; therefore, marriages are simultaneously private and public concerns.

Marriage and the Formation of a Nation

During the early part of the eighteenth century, marriage was typically seen as contracted in a community context. It was not meant as a rite of passage into adulthood but rather as a commitment between already mature adults to participate in community life. Marriage was also recognized as an instrumental arrangement, necessary for the survival of the individual and the community. Because such alignments were critical, communities played an important role in ensuring their success, from the wedding (Gillis, 1996) throughout the course of the marriage (Farrell, 1999). A shift began later in the eighteenth century from a view of marriage as being an instrumental one grounded in the community to a more emotional or affective one that takes place in private. The shift was very much connected to the development of a new nation separate from Great Britain.

Borrowing from the writings of French Enlightenment thinker Baron de Montesquieu, the founders of the U.S. government argued that marriage, like government, was a "union based on consent" (Cott, 2000). This *heterosexual* union established a system of authority in which husbands were put in the position of *heads of household*. As the heads of households, husbands were expected not only to support their wives and children but also to represent them legally. The marriage "union" literally meant that the husband and wife were "one," and that one was the husband. Wives did not have the right to vote, own property, or enter into any legal agreements without the consent of their husbands. Because they did not hold independent legal status, wives also could not be tried for a crime. But their husbands, their freely chosen representatives, would represent them and ensure their protection. Marriage paralleled the new form of government. Drawing on late-eighteenth-century writings, Nancy Cott says that women were called on to

> "chearfully [sic] submit to the government of their own chusing [sic]," arguing that "women by entering upon the marriage state, renounce some of their natural rights (as men do, when they enter into civil society) to secure the remainder." A wife gained "a right to be protected by the man of her own choice," just as "men, living under a free constitution of their own framing, are entitled to the protection of the laws." (2000: 17)

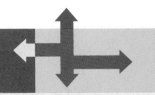

Family scholars have argued that there is an international convergence toward a nuclear family system in which companionate marriages predominate. In companionate marriages, the conjugal relationship is of primary importance; hence, researchers have been concerned with the factors that lead to more-satisfying marriages. In this chapter we have focused a considerable amount of attention on the quality of marital relationships, with the primary target being U.S. relationships. How appropriate would it be for us to apply the assumptions and perspectives of this work to other societies? Ellen Efron Pimentel (2000) addresses this question in a study of marital relations in China. She finds that although there has been some movement in China to a more Western notion of marriage, long-standing cultural practices make studying marital quality in China distinctly different from studying marriages in Western culture.

Over the course of the past century, China has experienced dramatic social change. Marital relationships have been part of these changes. The Marriage Laws of 1950 and 1980 resulted in less family control over marital relationships, and the expectation for women to be employed outside the home brought women and men together in contexts independent of parents and extended families. At the same time, a long

history, which includes arranged marriages, patrilineal/patrilocal kinship customs, and a belief in making intergenerational ties more important than the marital relationship, still influences family relationships today. Based on interviews with close to 1,800 wives and husbands in Beijing, Pimentel finds that both social forces can be seen in the study of marital quality. Her measures of marital quality include indicators of how close the couple feels and the extent to which there is disharmony in the relationship.

Similarities to Western findings about marital quality include the following:

- A curvilinear relationship between age of children and marital quality among couples who married with "free choice." That is, like U.S. couples, satisfaction in marriage is lower with the presence of children than it is without them (prior to having children and when children have grown).

- Couples are happiest when they both hold egalitarian views and share in decision making. Also similar to research in the United States is that only wives appear to be happier when the housework is shared. Husbands are not as concerned with this aspect of sharing.

However, several findings point to the distinctiveness of Chinese culture. These findings include the following:

- Chinese spouses' views on what makes a "good" or "bad" marriage are not dependent on the extent to which the couple spends time together independent of other family members.

- Parents continue to have influence over their children's choices of a marriage partner. Both husband's and wife's parents' approval results in significantly higher scores on measures of marital quality.

The results from this research suggest that there may be a movement toward convergence in marital/family structures, with greater emphasis being put on marriage (and hence the quality of marriage). However, "If Chinese marriages and families are converging toward a Western pattern, it is with some distinctive characteristics in hand" (2000: 46).

Source: Based on E. E. Pimentel (2000). "Just How Do I Love Thee? Marital Relations in Urban China." *Journal of Marriage and Family, 62,* 32–47.

Critical Thinking

1. Why do you think that parents' approval is important for marital quality in Chinese marriages? Why do you think this is not such an important factor in the United States?

2. Do you think there are groups in the United States for which parental approval and acceptance are more important for marital quality?

Monogamy has not been the only accepted form of marriage in American history. For example, Mormons allowed for the marriage of one man to more than one woman until 1890.

Cott argues that these analogies between marriage and government worked well because they coincided with the prevailing Christian model of marriage. In this model, husband and wife "shall be one flesh" and man shall be "head" of his wife, as Christ was the head of the church. A scripture reading sometimes used in wedding ceremonies suggests how the analogy works:

> Wives, submit yourselves unto your husbands, as unto the Lord.
>
> For the husband is head of the wife, even as Christ is the head of the church: and he is the savior of the body.
>
> Therefore as the church is subject unto Christ, so let the wives be to their own husbands in every thing. (Ephesians 5:21)

FACT OR FICTION?

Monogamy has been the only practiced form of marriage in American history.

Another important part of Christian marriage is *monogamy*. Although early European settlers did not believe polygamy was ever an option, they did understand that monogamy was not a universal feature of marriage. International travelers' writings on life in other cultures indicated that belief systems supporting only monogamous unions were in the minority. Even in this new land, there were groups, such as the Iroquois, that allowed polygamy. Some of these original inhabitants were also known for kinship practices that challenged notions of male headship. Iroquois groups followed matrilineal descent and patterns of matrilocal residence. As a horticultural society in which women were the primary horticulturalists, while men were migratory hunters, it made sense that families would organize themselves around the more geographically settled wives (Brown, 1975). Some Native American groups were also known to permit premarital sex and divorce with remarriage. This posed a challenge to early European settlers, for it was seen as immoral, promiscuous behavior. As Native Americans were forced into treaties and resettlement, government officials would try to impose Christian forms of marriage on Native Americans by offering them land in exchange for the relinquishment of their tribal affiliations and practices (Cott, 2000).

Returning to Nock's (1998) summary of contemporary beliefs about what marriage should be (free choice among mature adults, heterosexual monogamy, male headship), we can see they are ideas basic to the establishment of the first government of the United States. Freely formed unions, with authority established on the consent of the partners, made for a consistent approach to relationships between free people. But because the new country did not establish a national church, instead establishing a basic separation of church and state (along with the tolerance of a diversity of religious practices), marriage and family relationships were left to states to regulate. In a vast and growing nation, state laws about marriage varied. An interesting finding from historical records is that cohabitation without the solemnization of matrimony (what we might call "common law marriage") was not at all uncommon in parts of this country. "Living in tally" was most likely to occur in the southern and western regions, where people did not have ready access to officials to conduct ceremonies, or among poorer people who did not have the resources to pay for a marriage license or the cost of a wedding. These informal yet pragmatic partnerships were accepted in

local communities and considered legitimate in courts. Southern states sought to legitimate informal unions when there were children.

Redefining Marriage in the Nineteenth Century

The institution of marriage faced many challenges throughout the next century, especially during the time of emancipation. The passage of the Thirteenth Amendment, intended to eliminate slavery, had the potential to do much more. Early language used in introducing the amendment included the phrase that "All persons are equal before the law, so that no person can hold another as a slave." Senators worried that such language had the potential to threaten the power of men as heads of households—some might argue that wives were not unlike slaves. Wives' domestic work was for the benefit of their husbands, and wives held no independent rights to vote or own property. Making the point that wives entered this relationship voluntarily (which made them distinct from slaves), the phrase was pulled, and in its place was "Neither slavery nor involuntary servitude . . . shall exist within the United States" (cited in Cott, 2000: 80). Being a wife included "voluntary servitude."

American marriage was also challenged by those resisting monogamy as the only acceptable form of marriage. Mormons in the Utah Territory advocated a type of "plural marriage" whereby men are allowed more than one wife. They argued that monogamous marriage had the potential to isolate couples from the broader community, thereby threatening to tear at the seams of society. Other alternative communities established types of "complex marriage" (e.g., the Oneida community led by John Humphrey Noyes) as a more stable way of bonding members of communities. Throughout the second half of the nineteenth century, dozens of these communal, and separate, societies

Prior to the twentieth century marriage included more rigid roles for wives and husbands.

sprung up in the Midwest and the Northeast, presenting a challenge to the institution of monogamous marriage. Social movements supporting a belief in individualism threatened to weaken the community "glue" that was believed to unite people.

FICTION

Some Native American groups, as well as early settlers (Mormons), practiced polygamy. Also, some alternative communities in the mid-nineteenth century practiced a type of group or "complex" marriage.

The response was to make monogamous marriage itself the glue or the type of social bond that could unite a country. As we saw in previous chapters, husband and wife in the nineteenth century were part of a complementary relationship. Husbands, perceived as the more innately individualistic partners, were expected to take on the challenge of the new economy to support their families. Wives became the moral guardians of the home because they were assumed to have more pious, pure natures. Spouses, with their separate roles, needed each other to create a whole. This separation of spheres also meant the community became associated more with the world of men, while women's world (family) was less a public concern.

However, it didn't take long for this system to change yet again, and with it the meaning of marriage. The first wave of the women's movement began with women working for the emancipation of slaves, but did not end after the passing of the Thirteenth Amendment. The first Women's Rights Convention was held in 1848 in Seneca Falls, New York, where women formed their own constitution demanding equal civil rights for all citizens, regardless of sex. Many women, committed to their domestic obligations, were at the forefront of the Reform Movement at the turn of the century. At the same time, women were increasingly seeking advanced

The vast majority of those who marry do so in some type of ceremony or ritual. Friends and family are invited to these ceremonies to share in a merging of public and private commitments. On the private side, men and women fall in love and want to announce this to others. But because marriage is also a state-controlled relationship, the announcement includes a couple's acceptance of social conventions (Oswald, 2000). Weddings, like other rituals, can also be seen as important symbolic representations of a **rite of passage,** or one of the mechanisms used by society to denote movement from one phase of life to another. The term derives from anthropologist van Gennep's (1960) *rites de passage* and can be used to show how wedding ceremonies signify the transition between being single and being married. The three stages of a rite of passage are separation, transition, and incorporation. *Separation* occurs at the beginning of the ceremony. In the traditional Christian wedding,

held in a church, the bride is walked down the aisle by her father and given to the groom. The minister asks "Who gives this woman to be married?" Sometimes the question is answered "I do," by the father, but in more recent ceremonies the response is "Her mother and I do." The ceremony then follows a pattern that helps with *transition.* The wedding official tells the couple of the significance of their vows and their obligations to each other in marriage. After an exchange of vows and rings, the presiding authority pronounces the couple (sometimes "man and wife" or, more recently, "husband and wife") married. They have now become one (*incorporation* has occurred), and they walk back down the aisle they had used to enter the ceremony as single individuals.

Symbolically embedded in this rite of passage is the notion of male authority or headship in marriage. Wedding announcements hint at the transition of a woman from one home to another (not the transition

of a man). The walk down the aisle suggests that fathers (or parents) give their daughters to husbands. Brides may say vows that include the word *obey,* and the vast majority of women change their surnames from their father's to their husband's. At the end of the reception the new wife tosses her bouquet to single women while her husband tosses her garter to single men. Husbands do not lose their flowers or undergarments, and they do not change their names. Studies exploring the meanings that weddings have for those involved find that brides don't often think about the symbolic representation of male authority and headship, but see their marriage rituals as just a matter of "personal preference" (Currie, 1993).

Marriage rituals include not only the wedding ceremony but often pre-wedding showers as well. Most showers are organized by women, for the bride, and are held at someone's house (Cheal, 1989). Gifts that are given to the bride-to-be include

degrees and looking for ways to put their educations to work. Together these women worked in the public arena, arguing for a marriage between equal partners.

Marriage in the Twentieth Century

The Industrial Revolution resulted not only in the separation of the spheres of work expected for men and women but also the sep-

aration of marital relations from community control. This situation led to what sociologist Ernest Burgess characterized as the transition from *marriage as an institution* to *marriage as a companionship* (Burgess & Locke, 1945). In Chapter 1, we defined an *institution* as a major sphere of life with a set of beliefs and rules that is organized to meet basic human needs. Prior to the twentieth century, marriage held rather strict rules and beliefs about the appropriate roles for husbands and wives, parents and children. Marriage,

items that are considered to be useful for keeping house. The most common gifts are things for the kitchen. Brides now register for their showers, and guests can log on to web sites to purchase items that the bride has decided she wants for her house. Rituals of gift giving at wedding showers help to reinforce traditional notions of gender. First, "gift giving" reflects a more general notion of giving and nurturing, which are part of traditional femininity. Second, the gifts given suggest the types of activities that women can expect to be involved in throughout their marriage. Third, by having showers as all-female activities, women can establish a network with other women, creating a "female consciousness": "Women acquire a heightened consciousness of their obligations to preserve and nurture life through their domestic labor" (Cheal, 1989: 91).

Although the majority of magazines designed to help prospective brides plan their weddings still maintain a quite traditional approach, there are some that challenge tradition. Lori Leibovich has started a new web site called Indiebride.com (see the Resources on the Internet section at the end of this chapter). As she puts it,

All bridal magazines . . . contain the same articles: registering for china, planning a honeymoon, selecting a florist and, most importantly, finding the elusive perfect dress. . . . Every magazine I opened was filled with checklists and planners to guide me from the engagement through to the honeymoon, reminding me of the thousands of tasks I had to complete. Some of the chores were obvious, such as booking a caterer. Others, like choosing a "going away outfit" for the honeymoon, were simply perplexing. I'm not even sure my mother, who was married in 1964, had a "going away outfit." About six months into the wedding-planning process, when my office was strewn with wedding "To Do" lists, and our guest list had inexplicably ballooned to 204 people, my bridal magazine feeding frenzy came to a screeching halt. It was the day I saw the April/May 2001 issue of *Modern Bride* with a huge headline instructing brides to "Jump for Joy!" I realized then that if I was the editor of a bridal magazine, the cover line would have been "Jump Off a Bridge!"

And thus, Indiebride was born.

Critical Thinking

1. If you plan to get married, what ceremonies and rituals do you plan to include? Why? What meaning do they have for you and your family?

2. If you have been married, what ceremonies and rituals did you have? Is there anything you would change if you could do it again?

---

as the center of family life, served a number of important societal needs, from economic to social.

As the new century got under way, a number of other social changes occurred that encouraged this movement of marriage away from its community control to a focus that was more personal, based on companionship between wives and husbands. These social changes included (1) the changing experiences of youth, (2) a sexual revolution, and (3) changing life-course patterns.

Changing Experiences of Youth As we saw in Chapter 4, the relationships between men and women prior to marriage went through some significant changes around the turn of the twentieth century. Middle-class dating in the nineteenth century was characterized as "calling" and took place within family homes. With urbanization and the development of a variety of entertainment options away from home (dance halls, theaters, etc.), couples began "dating" or interacting away from families. Another factor reinforcing this separation from family was the increase in education among youth.

Because youth spent more time together, away from parents, there was a tendency to focus more on their personal growth and the development of their relationships with romantic others (Coontz, 1992). This focus carried forward into marriage. Couples were relatively free to make decisions about marrying based on love, and less on the more instrumental considerations of earlier generations of youth. This relative freedom has continued, and today we have a view of marriage, as outlined above, that has "personal choice" as a primary component.

A Sexual Revolution Most of the studies on dating in the early 1900s recognized that heterosexual interactions in public places increasingly included sexual activity (Illouz, 1999; Bailey, 1988). As couples get to know each other better, they would increase their levels of intimacy, and there is some evidence that more individuals did not wait until marriage to have sex. Once married, couples were able to get information about birth control, resulting in a separation of sexuality from procreation. This heightened attention to sexuality, both before and during marriage, hastened the shift of the meaning of marriage toward a more companionate model.

Later in the century, another phase of the sexual revolution occurred. Following the somewhat conservative (and unique, according to Coontz [1992]) decade of the 1950s, we experienced a significant liberalization of attitudes regarding sex (reviewed later in this chapter). Part of the impetus for these attitudinal shifts was the technological innovations in birth control. Without the fear of pregnancy, sex could become even more associated with intimacy.

Changing Life-Course Patterns Partly as cause, partly as consequence, the changes just noted were associated with an increasing diversity in the structuring of the life course. Prior to the turn of the twentieth century, individuals would move somewhat more quickly from being a child to being an adult, from being single to being married and having children. Today, the length of time from leaving parental homes to getting married has increased, and the ordering of life events is also more variable. Some continue to follow the traditional sequence of events, while others are having children before (or outside of) marriage, and others are refraining from both marriage and children. More-tolerant attitudes are also associated with assigning fewer stigmas to cohabitation and divorce, and a growing acceptance of gay and lesbian relationships.

What all of these shifts have done is to help make marriage something that includes greater demands for affection, intimacy, and friendship, known as the companionate marriage. However, for the first sixty years of the twentieth century, this companionship did not have as a primary emphasis the notions of equity in marital roles. Assumptions about gender in marriage included women's primary responsibilities being toward domestic work and child care, while men's first priority was toward economic support of wife and children. This will be referred to shortly as the *specialization* model of marriage. The last third of the twentieth century saw a movement away from the companionate, yet specialized, marriage to one that is more *independent* and *symmetrical*. Like the movement toward "androgynous love" that we discussed in Chapter 4 (Cancian, 1987), marriages have also become relationships in which both partners are expected to engage in behaviors once associated with only one gender or the other. One way we can see the changes in how couples approach marriage is through the rituals and ceremonies surrounding marriage. However, note that vestiges of our past are still present among these

Marriages are becoming more independent and symmetrical in terms of marital relations.

rituals (see the Constructing Strong Families box on pages 238–239).

Over the course of the last two hundred years, the meaning of marriage has taken a number of turns. It began as an instrumental relationship grounded firmly in the community. Slowly, the community took on many of the obligations that were part of marriages (education of children, health care, etc.), and marriage and family relations became more private. Marriages at one point were between companions (male and female, of course) with complementary skills and natures that together would make a strong foundation for family life. Now marriages are more likely to be seen as something between partners in which obligations are negotiated based on personal interests and desires. Therefore, it may be surprising that despite the greater emphasis on marriage being a satisfying relationship, the rates of being married are declining, along with the likelihood of having one "until death do you part." What is happening to American marriages?

FACT OR FICTION?

The age at which people first marry has been rising steadily over the past 100 years.

The Decline in Marriage Rates: Are Americans Giving Up?

Some social scientists are concerned about the state of marriage in American society. They suggest that rising divorce rates and increases in cohabitation and childbearing outside of marriage indicate a collapse in the perceived value of marriage (Whitehead & Popenoe, 1999). Data collected as part of the 2000 census show that 58 percent of men and 55 percent of women are currently mar-

ried. This is down from 67 percent of men and 62 percent of women thirty years ago (see Figure 6.1). As the number of years spent between reaching adulthood and marrying increases, so does the opportunity for premarital sex and cohabitation. Rising rates of singlehood, cohabitation, premarital sex, and nonmarital childbearing are all seen as challenges to the institution of marriage. However, a majority of Americans continue to want to be married, and most do get married (Coontz, 1992; Goldstein & Kenney, 2001). The primary reason for the decline in marriage rates is that people are **delaying marriage** until later in life. Nevertheless,

FIGURE 6.1 Percentage Married, 15 Years Old and Over, by Sex and Race: 1950 to Present

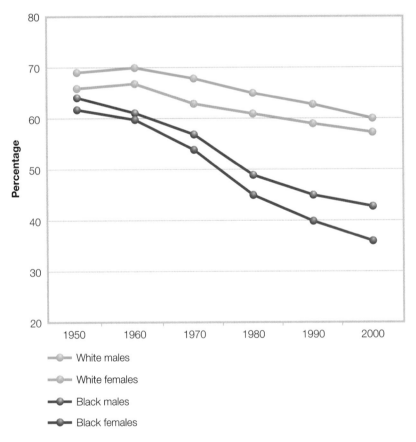

*1950 and 1960 data are for the population 14 years old and over.
Source: Fields and Casper (2001).

rates of marriage are changing, and it is important to explore some of the reasons why.

Delayed Marriage

Data show that since about 1960, the age at first marriage has been increasing (Fitch & Ruggles, 2000). However, if we take a look at data covering a longer period of time, we see that these upward trends are a somewhat recent phenomenon. In Figure 6.2, median age at first marriage is shown for native-born whites from 1850 to 1999, and figures for native-born blacks from 1850 to 1990 are displayed in Figure 6.3. We can see that for all groups, age at first marriage has not been on

FIGURE 6.2   Median Age at First Marriage for Native-Born Whites, 1850–1999

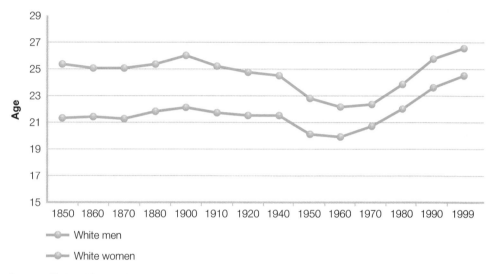

Source: Fitch and Ruggles (2000), Table 4.1, p. 83. Data for 1930 unavailable.

FIGURE 6.3   Median Age at First Marriage for Native-Born Blacks, 1850–1990

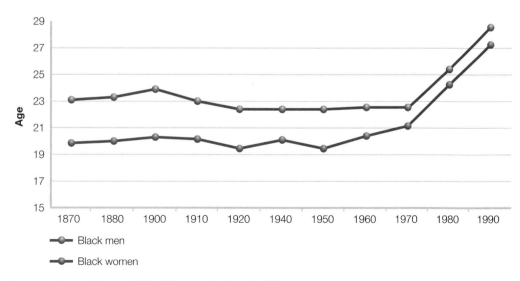

Source: Fitch and Ruggles (2000), Table 4.2, p. 84. Data for 1930 unavailable.

a steady increase, but rather has gone up and down over the last century and a half. A similar trend exists for those who have never married (see Figures 7.3 and 7.4 in the next chapter). Both of these figures show that marriage rates vary in nonlinear ways, and they appear to be different for blacks and whites. The reasons for these trends include structural changes in the economy and occupational opportunities, but also reflect broader cultural shifts in the norms, attitudes, and values of Americans regarding marital and sexual relationships.

FICTION

Although age at marriage today is higher than it has been in the last 100 years, it has not been a linear increase. Rates were high in 1900, dropped to their lowest point in the 1950s, then rose again.

Economics and Marriage Rates

In Chapter 2 we introduced a perspective known as *exchange theory*. Related to the economic theory of rational choice, this model is often used to explain why people decide to marry (Becker, 1981). Most Americans say they marry for love, but love is not the only reason. Other considerations include whether you believe you and your partner can make a successful go of it. This entails at least one partner being economically well situated. Traditionally, this partner is the husband. Becker (1981) starts with the assumption that marriage works because of the mutual dependence that derives from **specialization**. Husbands focus on labor market activity while wives devote their efforts to domestic production. This view is similar to the model of marriage that emerged with industrialization and the separation of spheres of work for women and men. Both spouses are able to maximize

their individual skills by focusing their energies on specific tasks. Then, by sharing the fruits of their labor with their spouses, they can provide for each other in a complementary relationship.

This theory was popular among functionalist sociologists such as Talcott Parsons and Robert Bales (1955), who wrote about marriage during a time when married couples were more likely to practice specialization in their division of domestic labor. But there is some question about whether or not this theoretical perspective continues to explain marital behavior when the majority of married couples are both employed. Current research suggests that the effect of economic activity on the age at marriage and the likelihood of marriage varies by both gender and race/ethnicity.

FACT OR FICTION?

Employment is now an important criterion for marriage for both men and women.

Men's Employment and the Delay in Marriage Men are more likely to marry when they are employed, and many will wait until they are more settled financially before tying the knot. The ability to obtain secure employment is related to the structure of the economy and the availability of jobs. For example, at the end of the nineteenth century, the United States was a primarily agricultural society. However, during this time there was a decline in the availability of land, which resulted in fewer opportunities for young adults to make their own way. The result was a delay in marriage for men (see the 1880–1900 section of Figures 6.2 and 6.3). However, industrialization brought increased opportunities (particularly for native-born white males) for higher-paying jobs, perhaps explaining the drop in age at first marriage following 1910.

During the years of 1870 to about 1940, median age at first marriage for native-born whites and blacks followed similar patterns. After 1940, the patterns of age at first marriage differed for native-born blacks and whites in two ways. First, the declines in age at first marriage did not occur for native-born blacks as they did for native-born whites following World War II. The other major difference between the two groups is that the increase in age at first marriage was much more dramatic for black men and women following 1960. By 1990, black women were marrying for the first time at the age of 27.3 (the rate was 23.6 for white women), while black men married at the age of 28.6 (25.8 for white men). A considerable amount of research shows that marriage rates are sensitive to economic conditions (Bennett, Bloom, & Craig, 1989; Oppenheimer, Kalmijn, & Lim, 1997). When economic conditions are favorable for establishing an independent household that can support more than one person, marriage rates go up. When jobs are scarce, people delay marriage, and the number of people who never marry increases as well. These correlations between jobs and marriage are particularly important for men.

Fitch and Ruggles (2000) analyzed the occupational distribution for men from the mid-nineteenth century to the present. They showed that the age at first marriage for men is closely associated with employment rates as well as the type of occupations held by those employed. A comparison of the occupational distribution for native-born black and white men since 1940 explains the divergence in marriage trends for these two groups. For black men, the biggest change in occupational distribution from 1940 onward is a significant decline in participation in agricultural work and a concomitant rise in the number of these men who were out of the labor force entirely. In 1940, agriculture employed over 30 percent of black men in the

United States, but by 1960, the level had dropped to 6.5 percent. During this same time period, the percentage of black men who were not employed rose from 9.5 to 22.3 percent. On the other hand, data show that native-born white men did not experience as dramatic a decline in agricultural employment, and they did not show major increases in unemployment. Also, their unemployment was more likely to be associated with educational activities. Instead, the biggest shift for native-born white men was toward higher-income, nonfarm occupations. With employment that allowed for relative economic security, native-born white men had higher odds of getting married than did black men, and they did so at younger ages.

Women's Employment and the Delay in Marriage Economic opportunities for women are also related to the age at first marriage and the likelihood that women will eventually marry. However, the data indicate that women's employment opportunities do not keep them from marriage; instead, employment only encourages a delay. In one way, this relationship for women works in a similar way as it does for men. That is, occupational success is increasingly dependent on higher levels of education. Time spent pursuing education results in the deferral of marriage. In addition, women's earning potential also appears to make them better marriage prospects. This is the part of the argument that appears to contradict the old paradigm about what makes marriage work. Becker (1981) suggested that marriages reach their peak of efficiency when one spouse (the husband) specializes in employment while the other spouse (the wife) devotes primary energy to domestic work and child care. So why would men be looking for a wage earner when what they require is a good homemaker?

A more recent conceptualization about marriage shifts the focus to a **new home**

One of the popular explanations for the "decline in marriage" is women's increased labor market activity. This argument is based on notions of specialization in marriage. If wives are expected to be the primary caregivers at home, and to be flexible with their labor market activity when children are present, then it can be most efficient for couples to specialize in their division of labor. Husbands can devote their undivided attention to employment, increasing their odds of being economically successful. From this model, then, we can predict that men who have the best earnings potential will be the most likely to be married. When women are employed, however, the opposite occurs. Bringing in an income implies that women are no longer dependent on men for economic security. This suggests that women don't have to get married and would be especially unlikely to marry if they expect that marriage will bring additional work without pay (housework).

This popular explanation has come under scrutiny in the recent past, especially with changes in labor market activity. Economic shifts in the United States have produced a situation in which families are now dependent on more than one wage to survive. With this structural change, one suggestion is that women with strong employment prospects will actually be more attractive (in an economic sense) and therefore more likely to get married. What has shifted here is the "bargain" that needs to be reached for marriage formation. No longer is there an exchange between two people who engage in different types of activities, but between two people who have a more symmetrical relationship.

A recent study by Megan Sweeney of UCLA has attempted to test the adequacy of these ideas for explaining marriage formation in contemporary society. She uses data from two cohorts of individuals—(1) those born between 1950 and 1954 (early baby boomers) and

(2) those born between 1961 and 1965 (late baby boomers)—to test the theories of Becker and Oppenheimer. If Becker is correct, then for both cohorts, men's employment prospects will have a significant effect on the likelihood to be married, while women's employment prospects should decrease their marriage odds. If Oppenheimer is correct, then we should find that the effect of women's employment on the likelihood to marry should become more positive over time. In addition, the relative effect of men's employment should decline (as both men's and women's employment are important for a good marriage bargain).

Based on her analysis, Sweeney finds more support for Oppenheimer's theory. Among her findings are these:

1. Women's employment among the early cohort has an insignificant (*not* negative as Becker predicts) effect on marriage formation, but among the new baby boomers, women's

socioeconomics. Andrew Cherlin (2000) argues that we are in an economic climate that is not conducive to single-earner families. In this environment, women with economic potential are more attractive to men. A considerable amount of empirical research supports this argument (Oppenheimer et al., 1997). Cherlin, as well as others (Goldscheider & Waite, 1991), suggests that a more realistic model for examining the relationship between economics and marriage is one that assumes "symmetry" in marital relations instead of "specialization" (see the Focus on Family Research box above for the most recent research in this area). Both wives and husbands are expected to participate in wage earning, and they are less likely to consider marrying someone who is unlikely to hold a job (South, 1991). Recent research also suggests that symmetrical marital relations can provide insurance in case of death, divorce, or the loss of earning capacity by a spouse employment prospects are more important and actually increase the odds of getting married. Findings were generally similar for white and black women.

2. Men's employment shows a positive effect on the likelihood of marriage for both cohorts. Although the effect of employment status diminishes slightly for the later cohort, it remains a very important consideration for men's likelihood to marry.

It is important to note that this study focuses on individuals, not couples. Becker's theory is really about the trade-offs that occur between husbands and wives in structuring their family work. Future studies need to include relative earnings potential within relationships to help test these ideas more clearly.

Sweeney summarizes her study as follows:

Despite these limitations, the results presented here clearly suggest that the economic context of contemporary marriage is dominated more by concerns about the affordability of marriage than by efforts to maximize the benefits of specialization. This is not surprising, given that the majority of young women in recent cohorts continue to work in the labor market after marriage. For Becker's (1981) model of specialization and trade to produce optimal benefits within marriage, the partner specializing in the labor market must be able to earn enough to support his family at a desirable standard of living. Women must view marriage as a secure long-term contract, such that their specialization in domestic labor does not leave them economically vulnerable should their marriages end before old age. In light of declining male earning power, growing perceptions of economic "need," and high rates of marital disruption, these old rules simply do not apply to the current regime of marriage. (2001: 144)

Source: Based on M. M. Sweeney (2002). "Two Decades of Family Change: The Shifting Economic Foundations of Marriage." *American Sociological Review, 67,* 132–147.

Critical Thinking

1. How important is it for you to marry someone with strong employment prospects? Why?

2. How important is it for you to have strong employment prospects before you get married? Why?

3. Which model of marriage ("specialization" or "symmetrical") do you see as the dominant model of the near future? What factors influence the prevalence of one model over the other?

(Oppenheimer, 2000). As we will see later, negotiating symmetrical marriages can pose a significant challenge (Schwartz, 1995).

FACT

Prior to the 1960s, a man was perceived as needing to have a job prior to marriage. Today, with the increasing importance of women's earnings for families, women's employability is critical for marriage as well.

Shifting Norms, Values, and Attitudes and Their Effects on Marriage

Shifts in the way people think about marriage and intimate relationships are also influencing the shape of family life. Arguments about changing values and beliefs, and the effects they have on marriage, take place at two levels. At the structural level, some have argued that there is increasing secularization in religion and that this leads to a weakening of moral values. Without a strong link to a core set of values, there are fewer social sanctions for behavior. At the individual level, the argument is that people are becoming more tolerant of nonmarital lifestyles and that this tolerance can encourage, or at least reinforce, nonmarital practices such as cohabitation and premarital sex. Although the link between values and behaviors is a controversial and contested one, the research is clear that some attitudes about marital and sexual relationships have changed.

FACT OR FICTION?

Americans are less supportive of a traditional division of labor in marriage today than they were twenty to thirty years ago.

At the beginning of this chapter we presented a set of beliefs about what a marriage should be, according to sociologist Steven Nock (1998). These beliefs included ideas about marriage as a monogamous union of a woman and man. This relationship usually includes the desire for children and exhibits a conventional division of labor in which men are the primary wage earners. Contemporary attitudes about the requirement of marriage to follow these patterns are changing, and the change in these attitudes is seen as challenging the institution of marriage itself (Waite & Gallagher, 2000). Views about premarital sex, cohabitation, the gendered division of labor within marriage, and childbearing outside of marriage have become more liberal, and these liberal views make nonmarital lifestyles (such as cohabitation and single parenting) more acceptable.

Attitudes About Premarital Sex   In a review of data on family-related attitudes over the last three decades of the twentieth century, Axinn and Thornton (2000) found strong evidence that there has been a shift in Americans' attitudes. For example, in the mid-1970s, 56 percent of women and 46 percent of men agreed that premarital sex is always, or almost always, wrong. By the mid-1990s, the figures had dropped to 46 percent of women and 32 percent of men. However, this liberalization has not been shown to extend to views about extramarital sex. Americans have remained consistently negative about such behavior throughout the last few decades. Most of these findings also indicate gender differences in views about sex before and outside of marriage. In both cases, women are less accepting of nonmarital sex than are men.

Attitudes About Cohabitation   Views about cohabitation, while also becoming more accepting, show a slightly different gender pattern. Today, people of all ages are more likely to agree that living together is a good idea than they were in the past (Axinn & Thornton, 2000). And the number of men who are open to this pattern of living is greater, on average, than for women. However, the increase in levels of acceptance over the recent past has been greater for women than for men. Some have suggested that women may be more likely to view cohabitation as an opportunity to test out a relationship with a man and to assess his willingness to construct a symmetrical marriage (Clarkberg, Stolzenberg, & Waite, 1995).

Attitudes About the Gendered Division of Labor   The desire for more-symmetrical marital relations appears to be on the rise. More than ever, Americans are less accepting of the traditional views about specialization in marriage. In the 1970s, the majority of Americans agreed that "it is more important for a wife to help her husband's career than to have one herself" and that "it is much better for everyone if the man is the achiever and the woman takes care of home and family." By 1996, a minority of adults held this view. Similar shifts in attitudes have been found among teens (Axinn & Thornton, 2000).

A minority of Americans agree with the statement "it is much better for everyone if the man is the achiever and the woman takes care of home and family."

Attitudes About Nonmarital Childbearing Finally, the relative weight put on being married prior to having and raising children has shifted so that today people believe that marriage is no longer a prerequisite for having children. According to a recent Gallup poll, Americans are split in their views about the morality of nonmarital childbearing. In 1997, 47 percent said it was morally wrong to have a baby if a woman was not married, 50 percent said it was not wrong, and 3 percent had no opinion. There was not much difference between men and women, but age did influence adults' views. Younger adults are much more likely to accept nonmarital childbearing than are older adults. In Figure 6.4 we see that views in the United States

FIGURE 6.4 International Views on Nonmarital Childbearing. Percent saying it is morally wrong for an unmarried woman to have a baby.

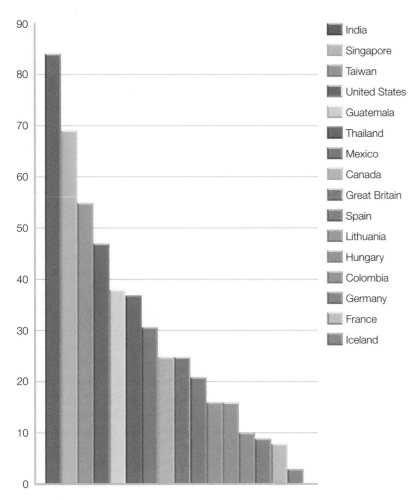

Source: Global Study of Family Values, © 1997 The Gallup Organization. All rights reserved, used with permission.

are quite different from views in other countries. The most accepting views come from Western European countries (Germany and France) while East and South Asian countries (India, Singapore, and Taiwan) were at the other end of the cultural spectrum. According to the Gallup poll, these differences are consistent with the variation in views on other family-related issues, such as the desired number of children, the value placed on children, and the desired gender of children. Where you find people who think childbearing belongs only in marriage you are more likely to find a desire for more children, a higher value placed on having children, and a greater likelihood of desiring male children.

Another way to see that attitudes are changing is to look at the views of those who are young and have not yet been married or started a family. Based on longitudinal data from high school students, Axinn and Thornton (2000) found that fewer teens today believe "childbearing outside of marriage is destructive to society." The shift toward more-liberal attitudes has been greater for young women than for young men. In a recent longitudinal study, college students were asked to rank their expectations about marriage. Some expectations for marriage remained stable. For example, from 1967 to 1994, students still ranked "love and affection" as their primary expectation for marriage (from a list of eleven expectations). However, the expectation for "healthy and happy children" in marriage dropped from second to fourth, being replaced by "companionship" and "economic security." At the same time, the expectation for marriage to be about "satisfactory sexual relations" dropped in its ranking. The authors of this study argue that with changes in our society, love and companionship are relatively more important for marriage, while sex and children (although important) may no longer be the primary considerations for marriage (Barich & Bielby, 1996: 149).

In sum, attitudes about marriage and sexual relations have changed considerably over the last several decades. Americans are now more accepting of premarital sex, cohabitation, less-traditional domestic practices, and childbearing and child rearing outside of marriage. But the interesting finding from this body of research is that despite views that challenge traditional notions of marriage, the majority of Americans continue to endorse marriage, want to marry, and eventually do (Ahlburg & De Vita, 1992; Axinn & Thornton, 2000). Marriage still holds a special place in people's lives. Their expectations about marriage have changed, but they still believe that it is a good thing. But why is this the case? What benefits occur from marriage?

The Marriage Premium: Happiness, Health, and Economic Security

Arguments in favor of marriage include that married people are happier, healthier, and financially better off than those who are not married (Waite & Gallagher, 2000). By pooling resources, married couples can provide a variety of support mechanisms that enhance their well-being. These include financial resources through combined incomes, greater access to health care, and help from parents. In terms of social support, husbands and wives are expected to stick it out "for better or worse, in sickness and health." So if spouses become sick or unable to work, a built-in support person can help them. Of course, the flip side to this is that the healthy spouse who takes on the caregiving may face significant costs.

Young people believe that married people are happier than those who are not, and this belief has not changed over the last

© John Henley/Corbis

Marriage is correlated with better physical health and well-being.

three decades (Axinn & Thornton, 2000). Data from the General Social Survey throughout the 1990s confirm what high school students expect from marriage. Married people are more likely to say they are very happy with their life in general (40 percent) than those who are single or cohabiting (just under a quarter). Those who are separated (15 percent) or divorced (18 percent) are the least likely to report being very happy (Waite & Gallagher, 2000: 67). At the other end of the spectrum, married people are the least likely, compared to the other groups, to say they are unhappy with their lives. Married people also benefit in terms of other dimensions of psychological well-being, including lower rates of depression, higher levels of self-esteem, having closer personal relations with others, a stronger sense of personal growth, and feelings of being more in control of one's life (Marks & Lambert, 1998). Using data from seventeen countries, Stack and Eshleman (1998) argue that the correlation between marital status and well-being can be found outside the United States as well.

Physical health and well-being have also been shown to be enhanced by marriage. A review of the research shows that those who are married live longer and are less likely to die from all the leading causes of death (coronary heart disease, stroke, pneumonia, many kinds of cancer, cirrhosis of the liver, automobile accident, murder, and suicide). Lillard and Waite (1995) followed individuals throughout life transitions from the mid-1960s on and found that staying married increased the odds of living until the age of sixty-five. Nine out of ten men who remained married lived to see age sixty-five, while those who did not stay married had lower odds (two out of three lived to age sixty-five). For women, the odds of living to age sixty-five were 90 percent if they remained married, 80 percent if they did not.

Finally, many have commented on what is referred to as a **marriage premium,** or the higher average earnings of people who are married compared to those who are not. The concept of the marriage premium has been applied primarily to white men. Cornwell and Rupert (1997) developed a hypothesis that married men are more productive than single men for several reasons. First, married men are thought to work harder because they know they are supporting others. A second reason behind the marriage premium for men is that employers may discriminate in favor of them (Reskin & Padavic, 1999). A third—and maybe the most important—reason for men's marriage premium is that wives still shoulder most of the responsibility for housework and child care. Using 1999 data, Chun and Lee (2001) find that after controlling for age, work experience, education, and other background factors, married men earn an average of 12.4 percent more per hour than never-married men. However, this wage premium declines when wives are employed. Married men with "at-home" wives earn 31 percent more than unmarried men, while married men with wives employed full time have a smaller advantage, earning 3.4 percent more. With the increases in women's employment, then, we should anticipate that the marriage premium will be on the decline.

Waite and Gallagher (2000) suggest that women experience an economic advantage from marriage as well, although it is not necessarily in terms of their individual earning potential. Rather, the argument is based on the assumption that married couples stay together "over the long haul" and pool their resources. These resources include the husband's salary and help from in-laws. In short, the economic advantage for women in marriage is indirect. It comes from staying with a man who does experience a marriage premium.

There are many explanations for why married people may fare better than those who are not married. Married people can be better off financially by pooling their income and other economic resources. They are more likely to have access to health care through employer insurance. However, we can't forget that being married is a positive attribute in U.S. culture. Because marriage is a matter of public concern, the treatment of married people may be better than the treatment of single, divorced, or cohabiting people. Research comparing financial help received by families with children finds that 29 percent of married couples received some kind of financial help while fewer cohabiting couples (24 percent), formerly married mothers (19 percent), or never-married mothers (14 percent) received economic assistance from family members (Hao, 1996). Those who are married also have two sets of parents, so the total amount of financial support given to them is likely to be much greater as well.

FACT OR FICTION?

Men benefit more from marriage than women do.

While marriage provides some important benefits to those involved, research also shows that part of the reason married people are healthier is that healthier people are more likely to get married in the first place (Lillard & Panis, 1996). This is referred to as a **selection effect.** We saw earlier in this chapter that when people (especially men) have access to stable employment, they are more likely to get married. Stable employment brings income, better health and other employment benefits, and a positive sense of self. Therefore, the factors that lead people to marry in the first place (and to stay married over the long haul) are also factors that help explain the better health and income among the married. Because of this correlation, the marriage premium for men has also been referred to as the "prospective marriage" premium (Cornwell & Rupert, 1997).

Does Marriage Benefit Everyone Equally?

Most scholars do not challenge the findings regarding better health and greater wealth among married people as compared to the unmarried (on average), although the reasons for this finding are under debate. However, many have also warned that we are not getting the entire picture about marriage if the only comparison is between people who are married and those who are not.

"His" and "Her" Marriage

In her classic study of marriage, Jessie Bernard (1972) argued that there are two marriages in American society: "his" and "hers." Based on data collected in the 1960s, she argued that marriage was an institution that benefited men but did not do much for women. Many have challenged her data and arguments regarding the **his and her marriage** (Waite & Gallagher, 2000), but the debate often includes arguments based on different sets of comparisons (England, 2000). What about the data that compare married women to married men? Do women and men gain equally from the institution of marriage?

The data presented above regarding marital happiness over time found that, on average, married people are happier than those who are not. Waite (2000) documents the trend in happiness for both married men and women over time (1972–1976) using the General Social Survey. First, she finds that a majority of women and men report being "very happy" with their marriage. However, she also finds that the percentage of men who report being "very happy" is greater than the percentage of women who do. The differences are small but statistically significant. In addition, the percentage of married people reporting to be "very happy" has declined over the twenty years of data, with the decreases being larger for women than for men.

In some ways, men seem to benefit from marriage more than women. Women are more likely to exhibit signs of psychological distress (anxiety, demoralization, depression, and worry) than are men. But the greatest differences in distress are found between married women and men (Mirowsky & Ross, 1989, 1995). Similarly, the health benefits that accrue from marriage are greater for men than they are for women. Although the mortality rates are higher for single people than married people, they are 50 percent higher among women while they are 250 percent higher among men (Ross, Mirowsky, & Goldsteen, 1990).

One of the reasons that marriage provides more benefits to men than women is that marriage changes men's behavior more dramatically. Of particular relevance are destructive behaviors such as drinking, taking drugs, and taking other behavioral risks. Research shows that single men are more likely to smoke, drink, drink and drive, and get into fights than are married men (Ross et al., 1990). At the same time, married men are more likely to say that someone monitors their health (Umberson, 1992) than are nonmarried men or married or nonmarried women. And the person who is most likely to monitor a husband's behavior is his wife. Married men are also more likely than married women to depend exclusively on their spouses for emotional intimacy. Research indicates that having the social support that comes through emotionally intimate relationships can improve physical health and survival (Ross et al., 1990). In sum, men get more from marriage than women because they reduce their risky behavior, and they get the support they need to maintain a healthy, productive lifestyle.

The advantages that women derive from marriage come through different sources. Women's behavior does not show as much change from being single to being married.

In this way, women aren't being saved from themselves through marriage as men are. However, being married increases women's chance to have a better standard of living. Marriage typically includes companionship and someone to share a life with. But the differences in marital experiences of men and women must be addressed; they can be the key to understanding why marriage benefits men more than women.

| FACT

Men's behavior changes more with marriage than does women's. Married men are healthier, happier, live longer, and earn more than their nonmarried counterparts. The comparison for women is not so clear.

The Division of Domestic Labor

The evidence regarding the **division of domestic labor** between husbands and wives is clear on two points. First, regardless of age, race, or ethnicity, wives are more likely to devote more time to housework (and child care) than are husbands (Walker, 1999). Second, although there has been some change in the division of labor in the recent past, wives still do a disproportionate share (Brines, 1993; Gupta, 1999; Bianchi et al., 2000).

Although this inequity in the division of household labor exists across a variety of families, there are some significant variations. For example, husbands are more likely to do housework if their wives are employed (Blair & Johnson, 1992; Ishii-Kuntz & Coltrane, 1992), but they do not do *more* housework than their wives when wives are employed (Marini & Shelton, 1993). Higher levels of education are associated with more time spent in domestic work among men, while younger men are more active at home than older men. Other research finds more balance in the division of labor among men and women of color. Both African American men and Hispanic men have been shown to be more involved in domestic work than are white men (Coltrane & Valdez, 1993; Shelton & John, 1993). Again, the divisions are not equitable, but the research indicates that the inequity in division of labor is variable across marriages.

This unequal division of labor has a number of consequences. First, when husbands spend less time in domestic work, wives can sense more disadvantage in the relationship. A sense of disadvantage is related to lower levels of marital satisfaction (Suitor, 1991) and a greater likelihood for wives to anticipate divorce (Katzev, Warner, & Acock, 1994). Doing housework is also related to reports of health problems (Bird & Fremont, 1991) and depression (Kurdek, 1993a). In a recent national study, Bird (1999) looked at how the performance of housework affected mental health. She found that it was not the amount of time that people spend doing housework but the relative proportion of housework that people do that affects mental health status. For those who were married and employed, the best mental health was associated with roughly a 50-percent split in household labor. This finding was true for both men and women. Anything less than an equitable split resulted in more psychological distress, and the highest levels of distress were associated with people who do 90 percent or more of the housework. With wives spending more time in domestic activity (Bird found married women do more than twice the amount of labor than husbands), this suggests an important explanation for how men benefit more from marriage than women do.

The primary way in which the unequal division of labor in marriage negatively affects wives is that it puts them in a position of lower bargaining power in marriage, a precarious situation if a marriage comes to an

Although marriages are becoming more symmetrical in some respects, women still do more of the routine housework.

end. As discussed previously in this chapter, the traditional model of marriage is one of *specialization* (Becker, 1981). Husbands invest in employment while wives invest in family care. This division of responsibility and work increases men's income, allowing for a higher standard of living for the household, wives included. Women's domestic work benefits husbands by making them more productive. However, by taking time out of the labor market, wives put themselves in an awkward position (England, 2000). If something happens to end a woman's marriage, she will be at a significant disadvantage when returning to paid employment. She will have lost her earnings edge through a depreciation of skills. Husbands' investments in the traditional marriage, on the other hand, are "portable." They have continuous labor market experience and up-to-

date skills so that their earnings potential is higher. England (2000) argues that even while in a traditional marriage, the portability of men's investments gives men bargaining power in the decision-making process. Wives are dependent on husbands' earnings and therefore will be at a disadvantage in the family negotiation process.

Race, Ethnicity, and the Benefits of Marriage

As has been the case for much of family-related research, samples have been heavily weighted toward European Americans. Recent research suggests that not only are there differences among racial/ethnic groups with respect to their attitudes about marriage and their rates of marriage (as noted above); there are also some differences in the likelihood of various groups experiencing a marriage premium.

In a number of studies including variation in racial and ethnic identification, the findings suggest that many people of color believe more strongly in marriage than do whites. For example, Oropesa and Gorman (2000) found that Latinos and Asians were more likely to agree that "it is better to marry than stay single" than were non-Latino whites or blacks. The differences between the views of blacks and non-Latino whites were small, with blacks being slightly less likely to see a benefit to marriage. One of the reasons for the differences found in the study was the nativity of the respondents. Latinos and Asians were more likely to include those born in other countries, and the countries of origin for these groups are known to hold more pro-marriage views. In fact, the foreign-born in each group, including non-Latino whites and blacks, were more supportive of marriage over singlehood than were their native-born counterparts.

These differences in attitudes about marriage might predict that people of color would have higher marriage rates overall. However, rates of marriage do not automatically follow people's desires (Tucker, 2000). According to the 2000 census, the highest rate of marriage for women is among Asian and Pacific Islanders while the highest rate for men is among whites. The lowest rates of marriage for both men and women are among blacks. Many structural factors are at play here. First, high rates of unemployment among black men place them in positions that may not be conducive to marriage. Both black women and men are more likely to believe that economic security prior to marriage is important than are white men and women (Bulcroft & Bulcroft, 1993). Second, a skewed sex ratio among some black communities makes it difficult for all women to find marital partners (although there is some indication that the sex ratio is changing in

some areas). Third, it has been suggested that the relationship between employment and marriage varies among men and women. Even when controlling for economic opportunities, black women are still less likely to marry than are white women in similar situations (Lichter et al., 1992). Oropesa and associates (1994) have found that the correlation between economic opportunities and marriage rates is not as strong among Mexican Americans, who have relatively high marriage rates in spite of considerable economic problems.

Finally, recent research suggests that the marriage premium is variable not only across gender but across racial/ethnic groups as well (Cohen, 1999). As shown in Figure 6.5, among all racial/ethnic groups, men experience a clear marriage premium. For each group, men's hourly wages are higher when married compared to those who have never married, were married previously, or are cohabiting. For women, the relationship is not as clear. Among non-Hispanic black women, marriage is associated with higher wages. For non-Hispanic white women, it is the never-married group that commands higher wages, and among Hispanic women, those who are cohabiting earn higher wages.

More research on racial/ethnic variation in marriage rates and experiences is needed. The evidence presented here suggests that how marriage works in our society is variable across groups. When reading or listening to arguments about the costs and benefits of marriage, it is important to know just who is being compared to whom.

We started this section by asking whether marriage has equivalent benefits for everyone. Not all people appear to have equal access to marriage, and among those that do, it seems that men are the primary beneficiaries. The main reason for this is the unequal distribution of labor within marriages. Although women are increasingly

FIGURE 6.5   Median Hourly Wages in 1999 by Marital Status

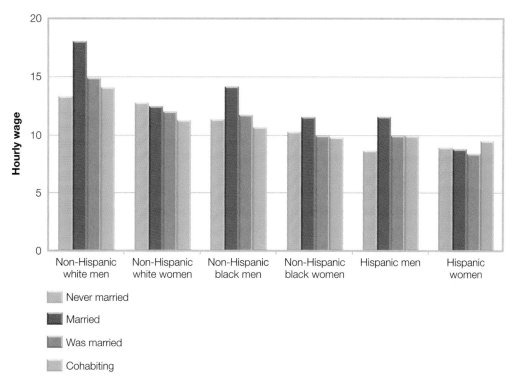

Source: 1998–2000 March Current Population Surveys. Data calculated by Phillip N. Cohen, Department of Sociology, University of California, Irvine.

likely to be employed, husbands have not made up for this by taking on a fair share of the domestic work. Still, if couples stay together over the long haul, the data tell us that, on average, married people will be happier, healthier, and better situated financially than those who are single (particularly those who are divorced). We turn now to a discussion of what it takes for a marriage to be successful. How can people hang in there so that everyone receives a marriage premium?

Marital Satisfaction and Success

There are a variety of ways to conceptualize a "successful marriage." One dimension is stability, or the likelihood that a couple re-

mains married. Staying together, as we have seen, benefits couples in terms of health and wealth, and therefore can be viewed as a success. However, another important dimension includes the notion of the quality of the relationship. Are both partners happy or satisfied with their relationship? Do they see it as a fair one? Although these two dimensions (stability and quality) are empirically related, researchers find that they are not identical. Stable or enduring marriages may not be equally satisfying to both partners. In one of the early studies of "enduring marriages," Cuber and Harroff (1966) found that marriages work well in a variety of forms. The majority of marriages function in a "utilitarian" form, including (1) the **conflict-habituated marriage** (filled with tension and conflict), (2) the **devitalized marriage** (exists without much passion), and (3) the **passive–congenial marriage** (little conflict but little excitement). Much less common were the **vital** or **total marriages,** in which married partners invested a considerable amount of their energy in each other and gave their marriage priority over other aspects of their lives. The study shows us that marriage can be successful (enduring) without necessarily being "very happy" or "very satisfying."

Another consideration in studying marital quality is the multiple dimensions of "satisfaction" in marriage. In a recent review of the literature on how satisfaction is conceptualized and measured, Bradbury and colleagues (2000) suggest several important points regarding how we think about marital quality. First, there are multiple ways of measuring **marital satisfaction.** These include evaluative judgments about the relationship as well as specific behaviors and interaction patterns. Second, marital satisfaction cannot be seen as just the *absence* of dissatisfaction. Research suggests that the things that can lead to a distressing marriage are not the same things that in their absence lead to a satisfying marriage. Third, it may not be useful to have just one indicator of marital happiness (such as "I am satisfied with my marriage"), for spouses may hold both positive and negative evaluations of a marriage. Finally, most research is cross-sectional, assessing views at one point in time, and does not capture the dynamic nature of marriage. Satisfaction can increase and decrease, and at variable rates, over the course of a marriage.

What Makes a Successful Marriage?

With the wide variability in the conceptualization and measurement of marital satisfaction, it makes sense that research has produced mixed results on just what makes a marriage satisfying and enduring. However,

several categories of factors have continued to show some relationship to marital quality. These are the backgrounds and characteristics that people bring to marriage, the life events and transitions that are experienced in a marriage, and the way that spouses spend time together.

Backgrounds and Personal Characteristics Spouses bring to their marriage a history that affects their views, interaction skills, and behaviors. One of the background characteristics that shapes marriage is the nature of the parents' marriages. For example, a considerable amount of research indicates an intergenerational transmission of divorce (Amato, 1996; McLanahan & Bumpass, 1988). In addition, whether or not parents were divorced, current marriages are also likely to be affected by the level of satisfaction that parents had while married. In other words, both the stability and the quality of the parents' relationship help shape children's approach to their own marital relationships.

The relationship that children have with their parents also influences the relationship they develop with their spouses. Recall in Chapter 4 Bowlby's (1969) theory about attachments, which suggests that the type of attachment formed between parents and children will carry forward into the children's relationships with others. Marital quality has been shown to be enhanced when spouses recall having "secure" attachment styles, versus avoidant or anxious, with their parents (Feeney, Noller, & Callan, 1994).

| FACT OR FICTION?

Satisfaction in marriage increases as the marriage matures.

Another personal characteristic associated with marital quality is the extent to which spouses believe that they are in charge of their married lives. Myers and Booth (1999) looked at how one's **marital locus of control** is related to the satisfaction with a marriage and the response to marital strain. When marriages experience tensions, those who feel less control over their lives become more dissatisfied. At the other end of the locus of control spectrum, those who have a strong sense of being in command are better able to weather the stresses and strains to their marriage. Marriages can experience strain in many ways. Some of them can be expected (such as having children); however, spouses normally do not anticipate other types of strain (such as unemployment).

Life Events and Transitions Strains, or challenges, to marriage can occur throughout the duration of a marriage; therefore, we should expect that levels of marital quality will vary over time. Early research on the changes in marital quality over the life cycle suggested a U-shaped relationship between the length of marriage and satisfaction with it (Rollins & Feldman, 1970). Marriages begin with high levels of satisfaction and then show a decline, hypothesized to be the result of having children (Waite & Lillard, 1991). Young children require a considerable amount of time and energy, detracting from the time and energy that spouses have for each other. These early models of marital quality over the life cycle propose that satisfaction levels begin to rise again as the family enters a stage where children are in school. Satisfaction continues to rise, returning eventually to the levels experienced early in the relationship. Recent research has begun to complicate this model. First, declines in satisfaction begin even prior to the birth of a child (White & Booth, 1985). Second, Glenn (1998) finds that levels of satisfaction do not recover their original highs at any subsequent point in the marriage, for a couple of reasons. First, routinization occurs with the settling in of a relationship, and as with other

relationships, this can be accompanied by a lowering satisfaction. Second, having children is not the only change that occurs in a marriage. People change jobs and change their interests and attitudes, and changes are often associated with adjustments in the relationship. These adjustments probably explain why satisfaction with marriage continues to be challenged over the course of a marriage (VanLaningham et al., 2001).

Recent research also suggests considerable variability among couples in terms of the effect children have on the quality of the marriage. Cox and associates (1999) found that the transition to parenthood is less likely to be associated with a decrease in marital satisfaction if a pregnancy was planned. It also helps when parents show stronger mental health (fewer depressive symptoms) and stronger problem-solving skills. An interesting finding in this study was that the gender of a child also makes a difference. Marital satisfaction is more negatively affected by the birth of a daughter, especially when the daughter is the result of an unplanned pregnancy. In related research, having only daughters has been shown to increase the

© Jose Luis Pelaez, Inc./Corbis

Marital satisfaction is challenged by the introduction of children into the family as children demand more of their parents' time.

odds of divorce (Katzev et al., 1994; Morgan, Lye, & Condran, 1988). Attitudes regarding a preference for sons (Pederson, 1982) are still prevalent in the United States and abroad, and may influence parents' sense of marital satisfaction with the births of their children.

Levels of marital satisfaction are the highest in the beginning, then decline with the birth and raising of children, the routination of family life, and the introduction of life events.

Other transitions or life events are not planned for in marriage, and these, too, can influence the way spouses feel about their marriages. The declining health of a parent, a spouse, or a child can bring stress to a relationship. So too can an unanticipated layoff from employment, particularly challenging when one spouse is the primary breadwinner for the family. Lillian Rubin's (1994) study of working-class families suggests that employment is at the core of a husband's sense of self. Unemployment places a strain on the marital relationship because it challenges a man's concept of being a good husband. Other dimensions of employment also affect marital relationships. When spouses want to be employed, and are employed in satisfying jobs, marriages experience less stress from employment demands.

Relationship Dynamics Married couples spend their time together in a variety of ways. Early in a marriage, before children arrive, couples may spend a considerable amount of time together in shared activities. The more time couples spend doing things together that they enjoy, the happier they are. One of the ways that spouses spend time together in marriage is in sexual activity, and this obviously influences the quality of the relationship.

Recent studies find that both the frequency of sex (Call, Sprecher, & Schwartz, 1995) and the satisfaction with sex (Edwards & Booth, 1994) are positively related to spouses' general satisfaction with marriage. Christopher and Sprecher (2000) caution us about assuming the causal ordering here. Does a satisfying sexual relationship make a marriage satisfying, or is it a satisfying marriage that makes sex good? Their review of research over the last decade suggests that the combination is most likely reciprocal but that longitudinal research is needed to get a clearer answer.

We've already mentioned that there is a relatively inequitable division of labor in marriage, with wives doing more household labor regardless of their employment status. This interaction dynamic can have an effect on the satisfaction in marriage (Dillaway & Broman, 2001). Those spouses who are dissatisfied with the division of household labor report being less satisfied with their marriages. This relationship has been found to be stronger than that between marital satisfaction and age, educational attainment, or wife's employment status (Suitor, 1991). The key to this relationship is what spouses want, or expect, in terms of the division of domestic responsibilities. When the work is done according to expectations, then spouses are happy, regardless of what the split is (Lavee & Katz, 2002). But when spouses want something different from what they have (and this occurs more frequently for wives), then there is a negative effect on feelings about the marriage. Being clear about what spouses want or expect in marriage is vital, and this suggests that communication in marriage is important for developing satisfying relationships (see pages 264–266).

Marital quality has declined as a result of the changing gender relations in society.

Changes in Gender Relations and the Effect on Marital Quality Throughout this book we have seen that the ways in which men and women structure their relationships have changed over time. At one time, men and women engaged in specialization in the division of domestic labor, but today we find that marriages are more symmetrical. Wives are more likely to be employed today, compared to earlier decades, while husbands have shown some increase in the amount of domestic labor they provide (Robinson & Godbey, 1997). How do these changes affect the quality of marital relationship?

Using data from two national samples reflecting different marriage cohorts, Rogers and Amato (2000) set out to explore the changes in gender relations between age cohorts, the changes in levels of marital discord (an indicator of marital quality), and the relationship between the two. They found that compared to the older cohort, younger wives provided a greater share of family income, husbands contributed a greater proportion of housework, both held less traditional attitudes about gender, and younger wives experienced more work–family demands. In terms of marital quality, the authors found that rates of happiness did not vary by cohort but that younger husbands and wives did experience greater marital discord. Marital discord included indicators of conflict, measures of marital problems, and the proneness to divorce. The findings with respect to the relationships between gender relations and marital discord were interesting. Within cohorts, nontraditional gender roles and attitudes were correlated with more marital discord. However, most of the changes in gender relations and attitudes over time did not explain the changes in marital discord. Only the increase in women's "work–family demands" was a significant predictor of the decline in marital quality. This study suggests that becoming more egalitarian in relationships is not necessarily the problem in

marriage. It's when the changes place conflicting demands on spouses that relationships become strained.

FICTION

Although levels of marital quality are lower today than in previous times, the changing gender relations in marriage are not the primary cause of the decline. The conflicting demands of work and family explain more of the stress on marriage.

Covenant Marriage

Increasing concerns over the challenges of creating and maintaining a successful marriage have created a growing marriage movement. Although much of the marriage movement is rooted in religious communities, it has also produced political change. In three states—Arizona, Arkansas, and Louisiana—a "covenant marriage" is now legal. This type of marriage is somewhat different from standard marriages in that it specifies a unique set of legal standards in addition to those already in place in state law. These standards are designed to increase the level of commitment that couples make to each other at the time of marriage. Those who are already married can convert their marriages to this type. The specific components of covenant marriage are as follows:

1. Some type of marriage preparation.
2. A full disclosure of all information that could reasonably affect the decision to marry.
3. An oath of lifelong commitment to marriage.
4. Acceptance of limited grounds for divorce, such as abuse, adultery, addiction, felony imprisonment, or separation for two years.
5. Marital counseling if problems threaten the marriage. (Hawkins, Nock, Wilson, Sanchez, & Wright, 2002: 166)

Covenant marriages are not required in any state, and few couples in covenant marriage states have selected it (less than 5 percent in Louisiana, for example). A recent study of attitudes about the concept of covenant marriage finds that it has a higher chance of being adopted in some places than in others (Hawkins et al., 2002). States with people who hold more conservative views on politics and gender roles, and those in which people are more religiously active, are the ones most likely to pass legislation supporting covenant marriage. Within such states, there will also be variations among residents in their likelihood of contracting such a marriage, with these differences based on their political and religious beliefs. Also, some parts of covenant marriage will receive more support than others. A majority of the adults in this survey agreed that it is a good idea for couples to get counseling before marriage and to be willing to seek it if trouble arises during a marriage. Less popular were the ideas of restricting mechanisms for divorce, such as a required waiting period: "In this respect, there is more support for attempts to build better marriages and support troubled ones than to restrict divorces" (Hawkins et al., 2002: 174).

Communication in Marriage

Communication is central to the development of a relationship. Through communication, couples create their marriage. Individuals also create their own identities as husbands and wives. Good communication, which includes being open and honest, helps couples come to a shared understanding of their marriage and can make their relationship more resilient to all the potential stressors that we've just reviewed (Fitzpatrick, 1988). Communication is particularly important for marital problem solving. All marriages will, at some time, include challenges that need to be worked out. A recent review of longitudinal studies found that marital problem-solving behavior was the best predictor of marital satisfaction and stability of all the demographic, intrapersonal, and interpersonal factors assessed (Karney & Bradbury, 1995).

One of the primary ways that communication can help create satisfying marriages is through **self-disclosure,** or telling your spouse something about yourself (thoughts or feelings). However, for self-disclosure to benefit a relationship, there must be reciprocity and support. That is, both spouses should feel free to be honest with each other and also be supportive of the feelings being shared by each other. Disclosing feelings can involve risk, for not all feelings are positive. But if spouses support each other in sharing both the good and the bad, a trust can develop. Lack of support, or a negative response to self-disclosure, on the other hand, can be detrimental to the quality of a relationship (Derlega, Metts, Petronio, & Margulis, 1993). From a social exchange perspective, self-disclosure will enhance a relationship when both partners are open and supportive.

Gender and Communication

There has been a considerable amount of discussion about the extent to which self-disclosure is a gendered matter in communication (Tannen, 1990). Although the research does not clearly identify differences between men and women in the amount of disclosure, the way in which people disclose has been shown to vary between women and men (Rubin, 1983; Swain, 1989). While women tend to be more verbal in disclosure of their feelings about the relationship, men tend toward more physical displays. For example, Lillian Rubin's study found that husbands were frustrated by wives' complaints about their lack of affection. Husbands believed they were giving it their best shot. Wives seemed to want more than just the presence of men in their lives; they wanted more regular verbal displays of affection. "Tell me you love me," she says. "I'm here, aren't I?" he responds.

This disparity leads to a kind of misunderstanding between husbands and wives. Both are self-disclosing, but they are not always given credit for it. It may be the perception of disclosure that makes the difference in the quality of marriages (Davidson, Balswick, & Halverson, 1983). Women not seeing as much disclosure from their husbands as they want may help to explain why women show lower overall rates of satisfaction in marriage than do men.

Most of the research on communication is based on interviews in which spouses are asked to say how they communicate and what they think of their partner's communication. An alternative approach, of actually observing interactions between wives and husbands, has been shown to be a better predictor of marital quality. Spouses are less happy, in both the short term and the long term, when they are observed communicating negative content and emotions. Another twist in methodology is to actually monitor physiological changes in spouses as they communicate. Measures such as temperature and heart rate can be even better predictors of marital satisfaction and stability than observational data (Levenson & Gottman, 1983; Gottman, 1996). Findings from research using this type of methodology suggest that, as in the interview studies, men and women show different styles of communication. Husbands are more likely to either withdraw emotionally, or physically leave, during an argument than wives are. The results here suggest that both verbal communication and nonverbal communication are closely linked to the way in which married couples evaluate their relationships. As well, early gender socialization that encourages different styles of expression can carry forward into marriage and affect the way in which couples relate to each other.

As we have seen throughout this book, gender differences also vary across racial and

Verbal and nonverbal communication are important components of marital interaction.

ethnic groups. In a study of couples that had been together at least twenty years, Mackey and O'Brien (1998) found that African American husbands were less likely to withdraw during marital conflicts than were Mexican American or non-Hispanic white husbands. This finding seems in line with other family research that suggests that African American men are more likely to share in other dimensions of family life (domestic work and child care) (McLloyd et al., 2000; Shelton & John, 1993). Mackey and O'Brien also suggest that African American men may feel more safe at home than in their relationships in other contexts, so they can be more open in interpersonal conflict with their wives.

Communication and Problem Solving

The research on marital communication has focused primarily on its benefits for problem solving because effective problem solving is an excellent predictor of marital satisfaction and marital stability (Gottman, 1994, 1996). Especially important work in this area has been conducted by social psychologist John Gottman and his colleagues. As mentioned above, much of this work on marital communication has taken place in a laboratory setting, where researchers can make direct observations of the verbal and nonverbal communication behaviors of spouses during problem-solving events. Over the past several decades, Gottman has been able to show that conflict and anger are common in marital relationships. When problems occur, spouses can become upset and exhibit negative affect toward their partner. However, neither conflict nor anger, by itself, produced unhappy marriages headed for divorce. Instead, Gottman found five behaviors that were more important in predicting divorce:

1. *Contempt.* This is an attitude of superiority to one's spouse. One way in which spouses exhibit contempt is by rolling their eyes while their partner is talking.

2. *Defensiveness.* When feeling as though you are being attacked, the response is to try and defend yourself and your position in an argument.

3. *Criticism.* This includes negative evaluations of the other's behavior or feelings.

4. *Stonewalling.* A type of listener-withdrawal technique through which some partners show they are refusing to listen to their spouse.

5. *Belligerence.* This is a challenging behavior meant to establish power in the relationship.

In one of Gottman's most recent studies, he and his colleagues extended their work by observing 130 couples at the beginning of their marriage, then following them for 6 years (Gottman, Coan, Carrere, & Swanson, 1998). At the end of the 6 years, there had been 17 divorces. Gottman and associates discovered that the pattern of communication among the divorced couples was significantly different from that of the other married couples. Among divorced couples, there was a negative start-up of conflict by the wife, followed by a husband's refusal to accept influence from his wife. The wife then reciprocated with negativity in kind, and no effort was made by the husband to deescalate the negativity. For the couples that ended the study in happy, stable marriages, there was more positive affect in the exchange, including humor, affection, and interest.

Gottman is not the only researcher to find that wives are more likely to initiate conflict discussions in marriage (Ball, Cowan, & Cowan, 1995). As we saw above, women are more likely to self-disclose than are men, whether the feelings are positive or negative. This finding certainly should not be confused with the idea that wives start all the arguments in marriage. Rather, women are more likely to verbalize their feelings. The cause of the negative feelings can emerge from a variety of locations and situations.

The recommendation from this particular study is that both husbands and wives can work on communication styles to reduce the amount of negative affect (such as belligerence, contempt, or defensiveness) and hence reduce the likelihood of unhappiness and divorce. For example, wives should work to "soften the start-up" of conflict. Husbands, on the other hand, should learn to accept influence from their wives and reduce their own negative affect. Another way of putting this is that husbands should learn to share power in their marital relationships. As we'll see in this next section, power in marriage affects more than just communication.

FACT OR FICTION?

The spouse who earns the most in a marital relationships is the one who has more power.

Conflict and Power in Marriage

Couples do not always agree when they communicate, a fact that is plausible for a number of reasons. Although most marriages are relatively homogamous, partners are not identical in all regards. They enter marriage with relatively different attitudes, interests, and resources. Marriage is an ongoing relationship, one that requires negotiation. Couples will enter the negotiation process with different styles, and as relationships progress, couples will alter or modify their behaviors even more.

Outcomes of negotiations depend on the issue currently at hand and the relative power that spouses have to bargain over the issue. Questions about who does what in the household, what types of jobs spouses take, or how families spend their leisure time all must be negotiated. **Power** is defined as the ability to carry out goals, wishes, and desires, even in the face of opposition. Most marriages should not be seen as relationships filled with opposition, where one tries to dominate the other. But there are situations where spouses may not be "of the same mind." When looking at power in marriages, the question is this: Are outcomes of negotiations random? Or do some spouses have an edge in getting an outcome that is to their advantage?

Sociologists have been studying marital power for years. One of the first major studies, by Blood and Wolfe (1960), found that the socioeconomic status of spouses is influential in making family decisions. Occupations can set rather strict demands on the household. Some jobs require geographic mobility, while others require odd hours of work. Blood and Wolfe found that the spouse with the most prestigious job can use that in the marital bargaining process. The income associated with the job is also positively associated with the ability to influence decision making, as is spouses' relative level of education.

Based on this early work, researchers have hypothesized that in marriages where the occupational prestige, education, and income of spouses are more equal, so too will be the relative power in the relationship. However, evidence suggests that things don't follow this pattern directly. No matter the relative occupational status (job and income), husbands still continue to have more power in marriage than wives. This can be seen in decision making and in the division of household labor. In a recent study of "status-reversal couples," where wives had jobs that brought in higher incomes than their husbands, Tichenor (1999) found that husbands continue to be advantaged.

This continued asymmetry in power, even in marriages where husbands do not earn more than their wives, is related to Americans placing a higher value on men's employment while valuing women's domestic work more. In intensive interviews, Tichenor (1999) found that husbands and wives would even try to hide any behaviors that suggested that men were doing more of the domestic labor. It seems that wives and mothers judge themselves as *wives and mothers,* using their domestic performance as the measure of success. The self-judgment of men as *husbands and fathers* is more closely associated with their occupational achievements (Pyke, 1994; Rubin, 1994).

FICTION

Research suggests that husbands continue to be advantaged in marital relationships, even when their wives earn more.

So in what type of marriage do we find that power is more shared? As you might expect from this discussion, it takes not only a sharing of the responsibilities of family life (paid work as well as work for home maintenance), but just as important is a belief in the value of women's employment. When wives' employment is supported, negotiations are more balanced (Blaisure & Allen, 1995; Risman & Johnson-Sumerford, 1998). We will see that this is a struggle in our discussion of peer marriage below.

Sources of conflict and power are part of most marriages because partners are not the same people. They have different ideas and interests, but also are different genders, have different levels of education, and are usually of different ages (husbands are usually older than their wives). With variation in marriages, potential for conflict always exists. These differences usually do not classify marriages as *heterogamous*. Factors more likely to be included in a study of heterogamous marriages are couples' being of different racial/ethnic groups or different religions.

Peer Marriage

A growing number of couples understand the challenges they face in marriage. Aware of the stress that comes from trying to "have it all," couples are making efforts to construct fair and equitable marriages. Some refer to these as "feminist" marriages because they focus on the awareness that society is structured in ways that put women at a disadvantage in marriage (Blaisure & Allen, 1995). Married mothers are expected to take on a "second shift" of housework and child care when they are employed (Hochschild, 1989). This means that dual-worker marriages can easily benefit husbands without a conscious effort on their part to resist doing domestic work. Pepper Schwartz (1995) studied couples she refers to as being in **peer marriages**: relationships in which couples consider themselves to have "equal status or standing in the relationship." She interviewed fifty-seven couples that tried to maintain no worse than a 60–40 split on housework, child care, and financial decision making. She found that such relationships were a lot of work. Both wives and husbands were likely to have been raised with more-traditional notions of gender, ones in which husbands were expected to be the primary breadwinners and wives the domestic caretakers. In addition, friends, family, and employers continued to reinforce this socializa-

tion during the marriage. Schwartz found that couples needed to continually monitor their behavior and regularly check in with each other to maintain balance.

Blaisure and Allen's (1995) study of twenty "feminist" married couples further articulated the work involved with challenging conventional expectations for heterosexual couples. They showed that all of the husbands and wives they interviewed practiced "vigilance, defined as an attending to and a monitoring of equality, within and outside of their relationship" (1995: 10). This process included the following:

1. *Critiquing gender injustices.* Couples engaged in regular dialogue about the ways in which their egalitarian views were challenged. Such challenges included messages given by commercials and comments made to them by friends and co-workers that reinforced traditional views and put down men and women who acted outside traditional boundaries.

2. *Public acts of equality.* Couples continued to use their own last names, put the wife's name first on documents, and challenged others who questioned a partner's role.

3. *Husbands' support of wives' activities.* Husbands offered help in wives' career pursuits and supported them in their efforts to be politically active in feminist causes.

4. *Reflective assessment.* Couples engaged in active monitoring of the relationship and talking about each other's commitments to the family.

5. *Emotional involvement.* Couples found that open communication regarding their emotions was important in mediating potentially conflicting situations.

In looking at these explicit commitments to creating an egalitarian relationship, we could be talking about all marriages, not just those in which the spouses claim to be feminists. The key to satisfying marriages is to know what you want from a marriage *and* communicating that expectation to your partner. Some couples might consider making up their own marriage contract, explicitly stipulating their goals and expectations. Others may want to be more informal but maintain open channels for ongoing evaluation.

| FACT OR FICTION?

The overwhelming majority of married couples are of the same racial classification.

Heterogamous Marriages

Heterogamous marriages are those in which spouses do not share certain social characteristics, such as race, ethnicity, religion, education, age, and social class. We saw in Chapter 4 that the structure of dating relationships is such that the vast majority of dating couples are similar in race, religion, and social class. When couples get married, they are even more alike. The overwhelming majority of marriages are between people of the same racial classification (see Table 6.1). In terms of religion, one study estimates that about 90 percent of all Protestants, Catholics, and Jews are married to people of the same religious group (Glenn, 1982). But, as with many other attitudes about marriage and family life, attitudes about marrying outside of one's race or religion have become more liberal over the last several decades. And this change in attitude is associated with shifts in behavior. In this section we will discuss three of the ways in which marriages are heterogamous in our society: interracial/interethnic marriages, marriages between people of different social classes, and interfaith relationships. Research suggests that even with some shifts in attitudes, heterogamous marriages can be a challenge to maintain.

Interracial and Interethnic Marriages

Marrying someone of a different racial designation has not always been legal in this country. During the nineteenth century, with the concerns over impending emancipation, states created **miscegenation laws,** or laws forbidding interracial marriage. Even the Fourteenth Amendment, which guaranteed civil rights to all citizens regardless of race, could not override states rights to regulate marriage (Cott, 2000). It was not until 1967 and the U.S. Supreme Court ruling in *Loving v. Virginia* that people of different racial groups were free to marry in any state in the United States. Since that time, attitudes about interracial and interethnic dating and marriage have become more liberal. The number of marriages taking place between people of different racial/ethnic groups is also on the rise. A recent review of literature on intermarriage shows that rates of endogamy (marrying within groups) are as follows: African Americans (95 percent), Asian subgroups (75 percent), Hispanic subgroups (65 percent), American Indians (45 percent), and European Americans (45 percent) (Kalmijn, 1998). However, these rates are a bit deceptive. For example, when members of Hispanic subgroups marry outside their own subgroup, they are likely to marry another Hispanic from a different subgroup. The same pattern is found for European Americans: marriages are more likely to take place between members of different European American subgroups than between European Americans and other racial/ethnic groups. Asians, on the other hand, are more likely to marry European Americans when

TABLE 6.1	Characteristics of Married Couples: March 2000	
CHARACTERISTIC		PERCENTAGE
Age Difference		
Male 6 or more years older than female		19.6
Male 2 to 5 years older than female		36.3
Within 1 year of each other		31.8
Female 2 to 5 years older than male		9.0
Female 6 or more years older than male		3.3
Race Difference[a]		
Same-race couples		97.4
Both white		86.6
Both black		7.1
Both Asian and Pacific Islander		3.4
Interracial couples		1.9
Black/white		0.6
Black/Asian and Pacific Islander		—
White/Asian and Pacific Islander		1.2
Hispanic Origin Difference[b]		
Both Hispanic		8.4
Neither Hispanic		88.5
One Hispanic and one non-Hispanic		3.1
Education		
Male more education than female		24.5
Male and female same education		54.1
Female more education than male		21.4
Employment Status		
Male only employed		22.4
Female only employed		6.8
Neither employed		17.3
Both employed		53.5
Earnings Difference[c]		
Male $30,000 or more higher than female		29.5
Male $5,000 to $29,999 higher than female		29.3
Within $4,999 of each other		26.3
Female $5,000 to $29,999 higher than male		11.1
Female $30,000 or more higher than male		3.8

— Represents zero or rounds to zero.

[a]This race comparison is regardless of Hispanic origin.

[b]This difference does not consider race. People of Hispanic origin may be of any race.

[c]Includes people with no earnings or loss.

Note: Data are not shown separately for the American Indian and Alaska Native population because of the small sample size in the Current Population Survey in March 2000.

Source: Fields and Casper (2001), Table 8.

marrying out than they are to marry people of other Asian subgroups.

While publicly expressed attitudes suggest tolerance, not all interracial couples have an easy time of it. First, acceptance is not randomly distributed across racial/ethnic groups. Acceptance of the idea of interracial marriage is least likely among whites. Second, not all interracial/interethnic marriages are equally likely to occur (Rosenfeld, 2002). A recent study of 540 couples found the most common interethnic relationships were those between non-Hispanic whites and Latinos/as (close to half of such couples in the study) (*Washington Post*/Kaiser Family Foundation/Harvard University, 2001). Next in frequency were "Asian-non-Hispanic white" marriages (20 percent), followed by "African American-non-Hispanic white" and "non-Hispanic white-Native American" couples (each at 10 percent). The differences found in this study (which included both married and cohabiting couples) are similar to those for married couples only (see Table 6.1). Among interracial married couples, "white-Asian/Pacific Islander" couples (1.2 percent of all marriages) are twice as likely to occur as "black-white" couples (.6 percent of all marriages).

FACT

Even though the number of interracial marriages is increasing, the majority of people marry within their own racial groups.

Lower levels of acceptance for African American-white and white-Native American marriages are most likely related to the long history of struggle between such groups. Although most miscegenation laws were passed in states to keep blacks and whites from marrying, Arizona once prohibited the marriage of whites and Native Americans, and California once denied marriage between whites and "Mongolians." Social–political histories in the regions of the United States have shaped views about race and ethnicity (Omi and Winant, 1986), in turn influencing laws and practices regarding marriage between members of varying groups.

Recent studies of interracial/interethnic marriage show how the pressures from "outside" (broader norms in society) as well as "within" families can make these marriages challenging. In a study of Chinese and Korean communities, Kibria (1997) found that a sense of identity as Chinese or Korean was very important. It provided an affiliation with others who share values and customs along with a history. As a result, endogamous marriages are valued. At the same time, second-generation Chinese and Korean young adults find themselves in more-diverse communities, and the opportunity to date and marry those outside their ethnic group increases. Kibria found that among Asian American subgroups, people were more accepting of relationships between people of different ethnic groups. Both Chinese and Koreans face similar histories in the United States with respect to prejudice and discrimination. Therefore, intermarriage between these two groups allows for the creation of a pan-Asian American history and culture, and helps in maintaining a distinct identity.

Marriage Across Social Class Boundaries

The extent to which there are opportunities to meet and marry others outside one's social position influences the rate of endogamous marriages. In the United States, an ideology of equality suggests that people are free to marry anyone they choose, rich or poor, and that social class does not matter. As we mentioned in Chapter 4, the idea of marrying across class lines is a common theme among American movies. Still, the majority of people

When couples are dating, interfaith conflicts may not be particularly serious. Even in the initial years of marriage, difficulties may not be significant. Many couples defer resolution of their interfaith status until later in marriage, perhaps when their first child arrives. Working out differences in religious beliefs can be a challenge. Below are a variety of ways that couples can work on resolving these differences.

Withdrawal

Both spouses withdraw from organized religious activity. They might stop attending church and avoid religious discussions within their marriage. This has the advantage of minimizing friction over differences in religious tradition. But this may not be sustainable. Often, one or both spouses will want to become religiously more active later in life—perhaps after the birth of a child. Membership and activity within a faith group may be such an integral part of one or both spouses' spirituality that they cannot suppress it for long.

Conversion

One spouse converts to the religion of the other. This has the advantage of avoiding friction due to religious differences, but only if the conversion is sincere and accepted without pressure. The partner who has given up their religious faith for their spouse's may

- Feel unfairly treated, either at the time or in the future.
- Feel resentment for being pressured into converting.
- Find that their family of origin is angry and disappointed.
- Find it difficult to worship God in their new faith tradition.
- Have intellectual problems with new doctrines that they must accept.
- Miss the cultural traditions associated with their old faith tradition.
- Have feelings of renunciation or even betrayal of their faith tradition.

Compromise

Both spouses convert to a compromise religion. Here, both spouses leave their religious tradition and settle on a new faith group. This could be a denomination "halfway" between their original religions. As examples,

- A Methodist and a Roman Catholic might decide to join an Episcopal/Anglican church. The Methodist might be relatively comfortable with the choice, since he or she would still be in a Protestant denomination; the Catholic would still enjoy the majestic church rituals, which would be similar to those to which he or she was accustomed.
- A Christian and a Buddhist might join a congregation affiliated with the Unitarian Universalism Association. The UUA is a church that has members from many different traditions: Aboriginal, Buddhism, Christianity, Hinduism, Judaism, Neopaganism, etc. The purpose of a UU congregation is to support one another in the development of a personal spiritual path.

Some of the disadvantages associated with the conversion option (#2 above) may also apply here. In particular, both of the families of origin may be angered at the decision.

in the United States marry within their social class levels.

Research shows a couple of themes with respect to the pattern of marriages that do cross boundaries. First, there appears to be more endogamy at the extremes of the economic spectrum. The very rich and the very poor live somewhat more segregated lives (geographically and culturally) than do those in the middle. Second, a couple of lines in the socioeconomic hierarchy are harder to cross than others. In terms of occupations, marriages are the least likely to cross the blue-collar/white-collar line. With respect to education, intermarriage is least likely between those with and those without college educa-

Multifaith

Both spouses affiliate with both denominations. They might go to one church each Sunday morning and the other each Sunday evening. Or they might go to a Sunday service at alternate churches on successive weeks. Each would support the other in his or her religious activity. If church regulations permit, they might even join each other's church. Each can grow to understand and appreciate the other's religious heritage.

Ecumenical

The two spouses merge their religious traditions and become an ecumenical family. They examine each other's religious traditions and, in essence, combine the two faith groups within their family. They work to establish common ground in their beliefs. The couple engages in the same path towards unity as many Christian denominations are attempting today. Since there are only two adults involved, the merger can be accomplished in weeks rather than the decades or centuries that formal denominations often take. They might satisfy their needs

for fellowship by joining with other similar couples to form a house church.

Diversity

If the spouses have a high level of commitment to their faith, any form of compromise may be intolerable. Each spouse may choose to follow separately his or her own past religious heritage. They would continue to go to their own religious services and celebrate different holy days. This is considered the least desirable approach by many couples because it reduces the amount of time that they spend together and diminishes the level of companionship in their marriage. This may be compensated for by a substitute joint activity.

Do Nothing

In many cases, organized religion plays a minimal role in the lives of one or both spouses. They might feel that their commitment to religion is so low that they would not want to spend the time and energy needed to resolve their religious differences. Irritants due to religious and cultural differences might not

justify the effort to resolve them. They might decide to let things slide for the moment and resolve conflicts in the future as they develop.
B. A. Robinson, Coordinator, Ontario Consultants on Religious Tolerance

Source: B. A. Robinson (2002). *How Interfaith and Intra-faith Couples Handle Religious Differences.* Retrieved 27 July 2002 from http://www.religioustolerance.org/ifm_diff .htm. Reprinted with permission.

Critical Thinking

1. Is religion important to you? Would you consider a person's religion before dating or getting married? Why?

2. Which of the methods above seems the most appropriate in the case where two people with different religious beliefs have married?

3. Are there any pairs of religions that you think would be more or less compatible than others?

---

tions. The hypothesis for why these hard lines occur is that occupation and education serve as both indicators of preferences/tastes and predictors of economic success. Rates of class endogamy are declining in industrial societies because educational and occupational opportunities are more available (Kalmijn, 1991, 1998).

Interfaith Marriages

Intermarriage based on religion is not looked upon as suspiciously in the United States as is interracial/interethnic marriage. Interfaith marriages can still be challenging, however (see the Constructing Strong Families box on pages 270–271). Religion provides beliefs about what is right and true, and dif-

Cokie Roberts (ABC News) and her husband Steve wrote about the challenges of their interfaith marriage (she's Catholic, he's Jewish) in their book, *From This Day Forward* (William and Morrow Company, 2000).

ferences in beliefs can test a marriage. Which church you get married in, what holidays you celebrate, and how children will be raised are all issues that require more negotiation than is normally found in religiously endogamous marriages.

Variations in fundamental beliefs and religious practices suggest that people from some faiths are more likely to intermarry than others. Some research suggests that Catholics and some Protestants (e.g., Baptists) are less likely to intermarry than are other types of Protestants or Jews (Glenn, 1982). Over time, rates of intermarriage based on religion have increased but, again, more for some groups than for others. Both Catholic–Protestant and Jew–Gentile marriages have shown significant increases over the last few decades. The exception to these trends of interfaith marriage is found among conservative Christian groups, whose rates of endogamy have been more stable.

Overall, rates of intermarriage based on race, ethnicity, class, and religion have increased, both in the United States and in other industrialized nations. Our country is built on the notion that we are free to choose whom we marry. The decision to marry should be based on love. At the same time, marriages do not exist in a vacuum. Although couples are in love, they live in communities that have various opinions and beliefs. Prejudice still exists in American society, and there are consequences for those who marry someone in a different social location than their own.

Conclusion

Having a happy marriage is a high priority for most Americans, yet data reveal that the number of married people in the United States has been declining for the last forty years. One of the themes that we highlight in this book is the importance of using social science research to explore such perplexing findings. Research indicates that one of the primary reasons for the decline in the number of married people in our society is that people are delaying marriage. Surveys find that we are as likely to desire marriage as the generations that preceded us did but that we are more likely to put marriage off until later in our lives. The reasons for the "delay" in marriage versus the "decline" in marriage are both structural (changes in the economy) and cultural (changes in people's attitudes).

Another important theme of this book is the role of social structure. Within the structure of American society, people hold different social statuses; these statuses will frame the way people experience family relationships. For example, marriage is an institution for people who are heterosexual. Although there has been some movement toward legalizing same-sex marriage, this chapter has excluded the study of same-sex relationships (we will remedy this exclusion in the next chapter). Second, considerable research has shown that the opportunities to form a marriage vary also by race, ethnicity, and social class. For both men and women, successful employment appears to be a prerequisite for marriage. This condition puts some in our society at a considerable disadvantage. Finally, we've seen that the experience of marriage is also related to gender, with men receiving relatively more advantages from marriage than women do. Despite these challenges, the struggle to establish and maintain strong family ties (of which marriage is one) is a central concern of our society.

Chapter Review

＊ How have marriages changed over time?

Marriage has always been an important part of U.S. society. During the time of the American Revolution, political speakers often argued that our government ought to be patterned after marriage: a union entered into freely. Marriages were also important to individuals within society. Marriage was the transition to adulthood and necessary for individuals to survive. As time went on, the wider community took on the responsibilities that were once a central part of marriage. This left marriage to develop into a relationship based more on companionship than instrumental needs. In the more recent past, marriages were still based on affection, but the change was in the way marital relations were structured. Marital relations are now more symmetrical than those of previous generations, with wives providing a greater share of the family income and husbands providing a higher percentage of domestic labor.

＊ What does the decline in marriage rates mean?

For the past forty years, the number of people who are married at any given time has declined. Although some argue that this means that people care less about marriage, it is still true that the majority of Americans want to marry and will do so—eventually. What appears to be the biggest shift is that people are delaying marriage.

＊ What are the reasons behind the delay in marriage?

Both structural and cultural changes affect the age at which people marry. Employment opportunities have been shown to affect the age at which men marry over the last century. Because of the emphasis on men as the primary breadwinner, men will delay marriage until they are in a position to be able to help support a family. In the last few decades, women have stepped up their labor market activity and now provide a significant proportion of family income. With this change, research indicates that women's employment opportunities are also important predictors of the age at marriage. In addition to economic factors, cultural shifts in attitudes have also been linked to the delay in marriage. More-liberal views on premarital sex, greater tolerance of cohabitation and childbearing outside of marriage, and an expectation for more egalitarian gender relations in marriage have all influenced people's choices to delay marriage until they find the right person.

＊ What is the marriage premium?

The marriage premium is a term initially developed to explain the higher earnings of married versus single men. It has been expanded to cover the notion of family earnings by including the evidence that women who stay married will have higher lifetime family income (via both themselves plus their husbands) compared to women who are not married. Broadening the concept even further is the idea that married people are happier, are healthier, and live longer.

＊ Does marriage benefit everyone equally?

In general, men benefit more from marriage than women, partly because men are more likely to significantly change their behavior when married, taking fewer risks. However, more important is that in marriage, wives are more likely to provide support services for husbands that benefit their earning capacity as well as their ability to remain healthy.

＊ What are the factors associated with marital satisfaction and success?

There are a variety of ways to assess marital satisfaction and success, from evaluative statements, to the lack of conflict, to whether a couple divorces or not. Research in this area is extensive but often focuses on a number of key issues. One is family history. We often use our parents as role models as we learn how to relate to our partners. The level of satisfaction with marriage is not static and can change over the course of the marriage. Satisfaction with marriage is the highest in the beginning. As time goes on, and relationships become more routine, levels drop off. We also get preoccupied with other activities as marriages grow, including the raising of children and the developing of careers. As couples have less time and energy to devote strictly to the marriage, satisfaction can decline. Recent research finds that couples report more marital conflict when there are conflicting demands on their time. Communication in marriage can be critical for overcoming these challenging life events.

* *Are married couples more alike or more different?*

In general, marital couples are quite similar in terms of social class backgrounds, race/ethnicity, and religion. However, we are free to marry people different from ourselves, and rates of interethnic and interfaith marriages have increased. These couples face challenges both from the broader society as well as from their families. Interracial marriages can experience discrimination from a society in which interracial marriages have not always been legal. In interfaith marriages, couples can have strained relationships with families and with each other during significant holidays. To the extent that the religions practiced differ in beliefs, couples may find negotiating relationships to be problematic.

Key Terms

conflict-habituated marriages: marriages that include frequent conflict. These may be enduring marriages, however.

delayed marriage: a trend for women and men to marry at a later age

devitalized marriages: enduring marriages that exist without much passion

division of domestic labor: the way in which domestic responsibilities are divided in a family

heterogamous marriage: a marriage in which spouses do not share certain social characteristics, such as race, ethnicity, religion, education, age, and social class

his and her marriage: a term developed by Jessie Bernard to describe the different ways in which wives and husbands experience marriage

marital locus of control: the extent to which spouses believe they are in charge of their married lives

marital satisfaction: typically measured by asking spouses how happy they are with their marriage

marriage: a legally and socially recognized relationship between a woman and a man that includes sexual, economic, and social rights and responsibilities

marriage premium: people receiving more benefits (higher incomes, better health) when married as compared to being single

miscegenation laws: laws forbidding interracial marriage. These laws existed at the state level until 1967.

new home socioeconomics: a perspective on marriage that views roles as taking on a more symmetrical pattern

passive–congenial marriages: enduring marriages that include little conflict but also little excitement

peer marriages: marriages in which couples consider themselves to have equal status or standing in the relationship

power: the ability to carry out goals, wishes, and desires, even in the face of opposition

rite of passage: one of the mechanisms used by society to denote movement from one phase of life to another *self-disclosure:* telling your spouse something about yourself (thoughts or feelings) in an honest fashion

selection effect: occurs when the factors that give rise to one family process are the same as those that give rise to another. For example, married people are generally healthier than single people, in part because healthier people are more likely to marry in the first place.

specialization model of marriage: a type of marriage in which each spouse focuses his or her primary energy on a certain set of activities. For example, one spouse may be the breadwinner while the other spouse takes care of domestic responsibilities.

vital (total) marriages: marriages in which couples give primacy to the marriage over other aspects of their lives

Resources on the Internet

These web sites have been selected for their relevance to the topics in this chapter. These sites are among the more stable, but please note that web site addresses change frequently.

National Marriage Project

http://marriage.rutgers.edu

The National Marriage Project is a nonpartisan, nonsectarian, interdisciplinary initiative located at Rutgers University. Its mission is to strengthen the institution of marriage through research that can educate the public and inform social policy. According to the web site, "the problem is this: marriage is declining as an institution and childbearing and child rearing, with devastating consequences for millions of children."

Council of Contemporary Families (CCF)

http://www.contemporaryfamilies.org

Established in 1996, CCF is a nonprofit organization designed to bring contemporary research about families into the national conversations about what families need and to provide insights on how to meet those needs. The site provides summaries of recent research as they relate to hot media topics.

Indiebride.com

http://indiebride.com

This web site was established as a counter to the more traditional wedding/bridal magazines. It encourages prospective brides to take control of the process by planning a wedding that more accurately matches their interests and lifestyle.

Companion Web Site for This Book

Virtual Society: The Wadsworth Sociology Resource Center

http://sociology.wadsworth.com

Begin by clicking the Student Resources section. Next, click Marriage and Family, and then click the cover image for this book. Select from the pull-down menu the chapter you are presently studying. You will have easy access to chapter resources such as MicroCase Online exercises, additional Web links, flashcards, InfoTrac exercises, and practice tests (that can be scored). In addition, to enhance and help with your study of marriages and families, be sure to investigate the rest of the rich sociology resources at Virtual Society.

Visit InfoTrac College Edition

 Another unique option available to you at the Student Resources section of the Virtual Society web site described above is InfoTrac College Edition, an online library of hundreds of scholarly and popular periodicals. Here are three suggested key search terms for this chapter:

* Search keywords: *marriages + families*
* Search keywords: *marital satisfaction*
* Search keywords: *marriage + communication*

Search recent years to get the latest information on these issues.

© Larry Williams/Corbis

Making Commitments: Singlehood and Cohabitation

7

* They are hostile toward members of the opposite sex or are homosexual.
* They are immature and unwilling to assume responsibility.
* They are unattractive or unhealthy.
* They are socially inadequate.
* They are over-focused on economics.
* They are just unluckily isolated by geography, education, or occupation.

These are a few examples of things said about people who are not married (Cargan & Melko, 1982; Waehler, 1996). In a society where most people want and expect to be married, it is sometimes difficult to understand why someone would choose any other type of adult living arrangement. Often when people are confused about the behavior of others, particularly those who are considered to be outside the norm, they create a *stereotype,* or an oversimplified set of beliefs about that group of people (see also Chapter 3). However, the reality is that there has been a significant shift in the United States and Europe such that fewer people are married at any given time. As more people are choosing to construct meaningful relationships that are not legally bound, like marriage, it is important to look beyond stereotypes and ask what is going on.

Demographers have documented notable increases in rates of singlehood, cohabitation, and delayed marriage. Moreover, although fertility rates have declined overall, the likelihood of procreation outside marriage has increased (mostly within consensual unions). In addition, marriages are much less stable today than in the past.

These shifts have been particularly dramatic since the end of World War II and, taken together, have been referred to as "the second demographic transition" (Lesthaeghe, 1995, 1998).

In the previous chapter, we saw that both structural and cultural patterns help us to understand the reasons for the delay, or decline, in marriage. These same sets of factors are important for looking at the rise in other types of living situations. In this chapter, we will explore the relationship between broad social forces and the rates of singlehood and cohabitation over time. Whether we conceive of singlehood as "not currently married" or "never married," data suggest significant increases in singlehood over the last thirty years. We ask why people might choose a single lifestyle in such a pro-marriage environment. Is it really a choice? And what are the consequences of living single for personal well-being?

We will also take a look at cohabitation, or unmarried couples who are sexual partners and sharing a household. Rates of cohabitation are up 70 percent from ten years ago. What is behind this trend? What are some of the advantages and disadvantages of cohabitation versus marriage? Some couples don't have the option to marry. Gay and lesbian couples are restricted from marriage by law, so cohabitation becomes their only option for union formation. Others who do have the option to marry may choose to cohabit to test the waters before making a legal contract. Those who have been through the dissolution of a marriage may see cohabitation as a good alternative to repeating past failures. And some may choose to cohabit for financial reasons.

If we assume that people are entering cohabiting relationships out of choice, should we expect them to have qualitatively different relationships than those who marry? That is, if people choose not to marry, is it because they want to create alternative types of relationships? We will take a look at the research on cohabiting couples (heterosexual as well as gay and lesbian) in this chapter to see how they compare to married couples.

In a rapidly changing society, the options for constructing families and intimate relationships are becoming more diverse. Although other texts refer to these living arrangements as "alternative" lifestyles (that is, as alternatives to marriage), we prefer to consider singlehood and cohabitation as two increasingly common options for people as they strive to build meaningful connections in their lives. Our goal is to understand why these options are relatively more common today, and what the implications are for people who choose them.

Singlehood

Family scholars writing within the developmental or systems models (see Chapter 2) often use a kind of typology to organize their approach to understanding families over time. The centerpieces of these typologies are typically marriage and child rearing, and the tasks and responsibilities that emanate from them. For example, early work by Duvall (1977) proposed a sequence that begins with a "couple without children," progresses through stages with children of different ages, a stage of "launching" when children leave home, and ends with "empty nest" and "retirement" stages. This type of family scheme leaves out households in which the adult(s) are single and/or without children.

More recently, McGoldrick, Heiman, and Carter (1993) have introduced an important stage of "young adult" prior to the couple formation (i.e., singles), but the stage is only a temporary one. These typologies are useful in exploring the way in which people negotiate relationships and how they create their adult identities. However, with the growing number of Americans living outside of marriage, it also makes sense for us to think about what it means to be single in a society that has marriage at the center of families.

Living Arrangements of Singles

In the broadest sense, we can define *singlehood* as synonymous with "not married." This would include those who have never married, those who are cohabiting, and those who are divorced or widowed. Although the census tells us that the number of those "not married" is increasing, it is important for us to recognize and explore the varieties of single lifestyles. In this first section, we will deal with **singlehood** as those unmarried and noncohabiting individuals who do not have children. Most of those who are in this category of being single live independently. Figure 7.1 indicates that from 1970 to 2000, the percentage of both men and women living alone has risen. For men, the rate has gone from 5.6 percent in 1970 to 10.7 percent in 2000. For women, the rate has gone from 11.5 to 14.8 percent. Overall, women are more likely to be living alone, but the increase over time has been greater for men.

Other singles are not living single. These are people who live with other family members (such as parents), in dorms, or in group homes. Living arrangements vary by gender and age. Figure 7.2 shows that a sizable proportion of the unmarried who are 18–24 years old are living at home, but men are more likely to do so than women. By the time

FIGURE 7.1   Household Type, 1970 to 2000

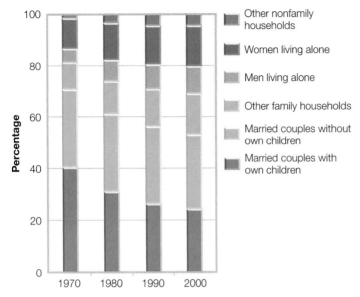

Source: Fields and Casper (2001).

Rates of singlehood are higher today than at any other point in history.

What these data point out is that being single does not necessarily mean that a person will be living alone but that the living arrangements of singles are related to age and gender. Among younger adults, singles (especially single men) are very likely still living with their parents. And this age group is more likely to be doing so today than in previous generations. Among older adults (over age 65), singles are more likely to be women who are living alone.

A very difficult thing to measure is the rate of singlehood for those who never marry. There is some evidence that the percentage of people who remain single for a lifetime is increasing. Figures 7.3 and 7.4 show the rates of those who have not been married by the age of 45. Being unmarried at 45 is not a guarantee of singlehood for life, for we don't know if those currently 45 and older will marry in the future. One estimate for men is that by the age of 45, only 5 percent of those who are single will end up marrying (Chudacoff, 1999). Therefore, using the age range of 45–54 gives us a baseline on which to compare data over time. The results are interesting. For native-born whites (Figure 7.3), the percentage of those who have never married has a nonlinear trend. Comparing this pattern to the data we presented in the previous chapter on age at first marriage, the pattern looks similar, except for about a 20-year lag. The peak of the curve for age at first marriage is around 1900 while the peak of the never-married chart is around 1920. This suggests a *cohort effect.* Twenty years after the peak in age at first marriage, we find a high percentage still not married.

they are 25–34 years old, most women and men are living with a spouse (women more than men), but more are also living on their own by this time. Fewer are living with their parents, but 25–34-year-old men are more likely to be living with parents than are women in this age group (12.1 percent and 5.4 percent, respectively).

Older adults also show some gender differences in living patterns. Among those who are 65 to 74 years old, women are much more likely to be living on their own while men are more likely to be married and living with their spouses. Among the 75 and older population, about half of the women are living alone while a majority of men are still living with a spouse. Since women still have a life expectancy that exceeds men, and women are likely to marry men who are older, a greater proportion of the elderly women who are both single and living single can be predicted.

FIGURE 7.2 Living Arrangements of Younger and Older Adults: March 2000

18 to 25-Year-Olds

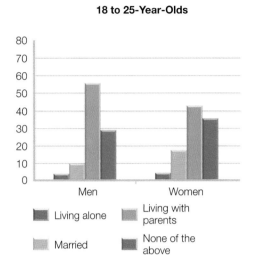

25 to 34-Year-Olds

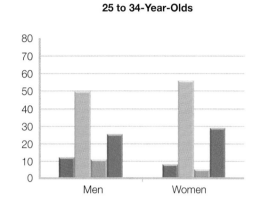

65 to 74-Year-Olds

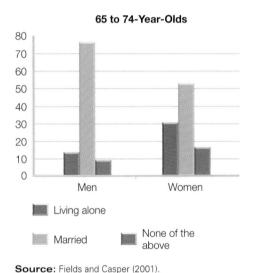

75 Years Old and Over

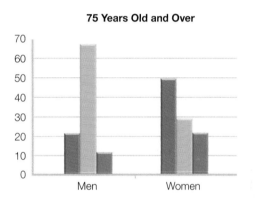

Source: Fields and Casper (2001).

The findings for native-born blacks (Figure 7.4) are different. Rates for the never-married have been relatively constant for women (until recently) but quite variable for men. And there doesn't seem to be a consistent correlation between age at first marriage and the percentage of never-married as there was for whites. One exception appears in the most recent years. That is, among blacks, age at first marriage and the percentage of never-married are both increasing during the same time period. This is referred to as a **period effect,** or correlated behavioral patterns during one time period.

FIGURE 7.3 Percentage of Native-Born Whites Never Married, Ages 45–54, by Gender, 1850–1999

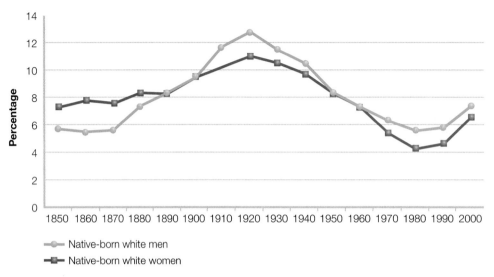

Native-born white men

Native-born white women

Source: Fitch and Ruggles (2000), Table 4.3, p. 85.

FIGURE 7.4 Percentage of Native-Born Blacks Never Married, Ages 45–54, by Gender, 1870–1990

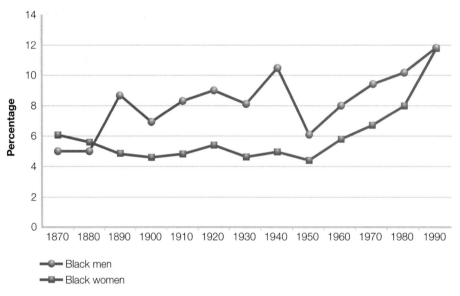

Black men

Black women

Source: Fitch and Ruggles (2000), Table 4.3, p. 85.

Although rates of singlehood have increased over the last century, rates are comparable to those in 1900.

The data here are interesting as they suggest that age at marriage, which we know is increasing, is positively correlated with the likelihood that people will never marry during their lifetime. If these trends continue, significant numbers of the current population will be living single for a lifetime (England, 2000). What do we know about singles? Why have the rates of singlehood varied over time? How are the lives of those who remain single different from those living in married or other family arrangements? Although there is not an abundance of research of singlehood, what work has been done suggests that social forces (structural and cultural) play a significant role in both rates and experiences.

Explanations for Changing Rates of Singlehood

Figures 7.3 and 7.4 indicate that rates of singlehood among those aged 45–54 had a local peak just after the turn of the twentieth century. Although the trends were not linear, rates declined somewhat over the century (at least for whites) until more recently, when rates have again increased. Might there be factors in the two time periods that are similar and therefore help to explain why more people were single at such an age? Social scientists have proposed a number of structural (demographic and economic) as well as cultural (norms and values) features of American society to help understand variations in the rates of singlehood.

Structural Factors One commonly used explanation for rates of singlehood is demography. Specifically, during some periods of time, and in some locations, there is an excess or shortage of one sex or the other, making marriage for all impossible. At the start of the twentieth century, imbalanced sex ratios existed in much of the western United States due to migration (from the East Coast) and immigration patterns. In a recent study of bachelors from 1890 to 1930 in major urban centers, sex ratios were found to be very skewed (Chudacoff, 1999). In San Francisco, for example, the ratio of males to females between the ages of 25 and 34 was 4 to 1 in 1890 and 2 to 1 in 1920. Over half of the men in San Francisco were single in 1890, and 75 percent of men with one foreign-born parent were single that year. However, this same study found that sex ratios in other cities were skewed in the opposite direction. Baltimore and Boston had surpluses of women and still had higher than average rates of singlehood for both men and women. The author of this study suggests the need to look beyond demographic factors.

Today, demographic factors may be playing a role, at least for women's rate of singlehood. First, women outnumber men in all age groups above the age of 20, and by the time women reach the age of 65, they represent approximately 57 percent of the population. Second, this imbalance is exacerbated by **hypergamy,** the practice of women marrying older men.

Another important structural feature of our society is the economy. We saw in the previous chapter that in times of economic crisis, people will delay marriage. The economy was undergoing significant change from an agricultural to an industrial society at the start of the last century. This led to an increase in unemployment among men, which in turn produced higher ages at first marriage and the increase in rates of singlehood. Today, we are experiencing another crisis in our economy as we shift away from industry toward a service economy (discussed in more detail in Chapter 10). Unemployment rates are high, and wages have stagnated. Age at first marriage is similar to that of a century past, and the rates of singlehood are similar. Economic uncertainty has been particularly problematic for people of color and can help to explain the high rates of singlehood among African Americans (Tucker & Mitchell-Kern, 1995).

Cultural Factors   Although structural factors set the context within which relationships take place, it is also important to look at the "desirability" of singlehood versus marriage. Marriage has always been valued in our culture, but for varying reasons. If the value of marriage is that it brings economic and social security, then when the opportunity exists for attaining such goals exists outside of marriage, we might expect rates of singlehood (via a delay in marriage at least) to increase. At the turn of the last century, financial independence could be found outside of marriage for men (Chudacoff, 1999), and today evidence suggests that both men and women are capable of supporting themselves outside of marriage (England, 2000). When the structural conditions are right, cultural responses (shifts in attitudes) often follow.

During agrarian times in our history, parents, church, and communities had a strong influence on the lives of young people. After 1900, the influence of such groups began to erode, and greater opportunities for public diversions emerged. For example, the first decade or so of the century saw the emergence of dance halls, amusement parks, sporting events, saloons, theaters, social clubs, and pool halls, to name a few (Peiss, 1986). The availability of transportation, via streetcars and automobiles, made getting out to these social activities much easier. Young men and women were able to spend more time with each other without parental supervision, and it may be this freedom that encouraged a delay in marriage (and therefore higher rates of singlehood).

For men during this period, additional cultural support helped those who lived a single lifestyle (Chudacoff, 1999). For example, the Young Men's Christian Association (YMCA) and its counterpart in the Jewish community (Young Men's Hebrew Association) were intended to be a place for unmarried, middle-class men who otherwise might be tempted by the corrupting influences of the time. Male-only social clubs also served the more privileged classes, with many offering junior divisions for single men under 30. Public acceptability for "bachelorhood" was promoted via magazines such as the *National Police Gazette,* which has been characterized as the *Playboy, National Enquirer,* and *Sports Illustrated* of its time. These emerging organizations, associations, and publications helped to support a kind of "bachelor subculture" in the early 1900s.

The situation for single women was different from that of men. Whereas it was understood that in a changing economy it was necessary for men to seek out new opportunities for work before getting married, women were still defined by a domestic role. Clubs supporting the public activities of single women were not prevalent. However, the rising number of single women at the turn of the twentieth century did result in a variety of experiences that challenged traditional notions of femininity (Chambers-Schiller, 1984). Middle- and upper-class white women were central to philanthropic movements to aid the poor and were at the forefront of the feminist movement, which fought for women's independence and freedom of choice. Poor, working-class single women and single women of color entered the paid work force, starting a trend in women's employment that has never waned.

Today, cultural forces also help make singlehood a more acceptable lifestyle for both women and men. Social movements in

Kautz Family YMCA Archives, University of Minnesota, Minnesota Collection

The YMCA was designed to meet the needs of the growing numbers of single men during the first decades of the twentieth century.

the 1960s and 1970s, including the women's movement, gay/lesbian movements, and civil rights movements, served to challenge the status quo, including traditional marriage. Higher rates of education for men and women mean that marriage is delayed and people spend more time single. Higher rates of divorce have produced a larger contingent of singles later in life, including singles with children. Support groups, popular magazines, and popular culture (movies and television) all serve as cultural mechanisms to help de-stigmatize singlehood. However, this does not mean that singles no longer face any challenges to their legitimacy. As we'll see, there is considerable diversity among singles, and experiences with singlehood are varied.

Variations Among Singles

Stein (1976, 1981) developed a typology of singles based on two characteristics: (1) whether or not the person is single voluntarily or not and (2) whether being single is a temporary or stable condition. There are four possible combinations, and Stein argued that these groups of singles would differ in terms of the effect on their lives of being single:

* *Voluntary temporary singles.* A significant proportion of this group is made up of those who have never been married, but are delaying it. Many are pursuing education or establishing a career. However, this group stays open to marriage and probably will eventually marry.

* *Voluntary stable singles.* People in this group want to be single and want to be so for a long time (maybe for life). This group might include priests and nuns, who take a vow of chastity. But it can also include those who are eligible to marry but choose not to. These could be cohabiters or people living single.

* *Involuntary temporary singles.* We might think about these singles as

those who are actively searching for a mate but are unable to find a suitable one. The desire among this group is to be married, but for a variety of reasons marriage is delayed (against their wishes).

* *Involuntary stable singles.* A number of people who would like to be married are more than "delayed." Some can expect to be single for life even though they may not want to be. The elderly, especially women, may get to a point where searching is fruitless. In some regions where male unemployment is high, women may be closed off from eligible mates. And gays and lesbians who want to marry are denied a legal avenue to do so.

FACT OR FICTION?

Women are more likely to have "never married" than are men.

This typology is useful in pointing out the variability in singles in terms of intentions and the duration of this status. But it's important to recognize that people may move across categories over time. Both individual choices as well as social forces are involved in determining what category a single falls into.

These differences also play out in terms of the ways in which people are single. For example, women are more likely than men to be single because they are divorced, widowed, or separated (22 percent of women and 5.1 percent of men). Men, on the other hand, are more likely to have never been married than are women (31.3 percent of men to 25.1 percent of women). This is true of men in all age groups. Of course, there are differences by race, as we saw in Figure 7.4. Black men and women are equally likely to be never-married today.

FICTION

Whereas women are more likely to be single because they are divorced, widowed, or separated, men are more likely to have never been married.

A Typology of Bachelors A recent study of the psychology of heterosexual, long-term bachelors over the age of 40 suggests that bachelors share some important traits but are also different in terms of how they manage their single identity (Waehler, 1996). Similarities among these never-married men include (1) staunch independence and self-determination, (2) emotional detachment in relationships with women, (3) interpersonal passivity, and (4) idiosyncratic thinking. At least the first three traits are in line with traditional notions of masculinity. Men are expected to be independent, emotionally aloof, and less involved in sustaining emotional relationships (Chudacoff, 1999).

However, the author of this study finds some differences between bachelors that are related to their individual experiences and life histories. He suggests that there are three types of bachelors:

* *Flexible bachelors.* These men are quite comfortable with their status of being long-term singles. They are somewhat indifferent toward marriage. It is expected to happen, maybe someday, but they are not in any rush. Most of these men have good memories of relationships with their parents and other family members, and feel at ease in settings that include married people, children, or other singles.

* *Entrenched bachelors.* These men hold fast to their independence from others. They are quite satisfied with their single lives and are not intimidated by social pressures to marry. However, this indif-

ference can be problematic for them by interfering with their ability to have long-term relationships with others. These men are more self-absorbed and inflexible. It might be men among this group who evoke stereotypical responses.

* *Conflicted bachelors.* This is the largest group of long-term single men. They are the most ambivalent about being single. Aware of the costs and benefits associated with marriage and single-hood, these men seem to be "psycholog-ically invested in both" types of life-styles. They worry about the decisions they have made and are concerned about what to do next. This is the group most likely to marry, but their ambiva-lence results in an approach that is akin to waiting for the right one, then finding the grounds to keep her at arm's length. (Waehler, 1996)

Although there has not been a typology created for single women, research reveals considerable diversity among them as well. Single women, like single men, are often conflicted or ambivalent as they work to cre-ate a satisfying and productive life. Women, in particular, struggle to construct an inde-pendent identity in a social world that has viewed them as "relational," or dependent on men. In a study of single women aged 35 and over, Tuula Gordon (1994) found that women spoke of the importance of being in control: in control of their emotions, their finances, and their space. A 40-year-old "voluntary single" woman put her struggle this way:

In my generation of women—what I've seen and what I've heard is that women were taught that they're nothing—they're not fulfilled in life unless they have a man. And that's a dependency problem for them, that they must outgrow to become inde-

The majority of long-term single men are ambivalent about their marital status. While they desire marriage, they also enjoy a single lifestyle.

pendent. It would be like learning a typing system and then having to unlearn that. . . . I'm having to make . . . my way in life in a different way without relying on another per-son. . . . I'm creating my own life. . . . I wasn't brought up that way. (Gor-don, 1994: 166)

This study revealed that in spite of obstacles, single women who were successful in their pursuits for independence were happy. Many have relocated to communities that have a higher proportion of single people and more social support networks.

Experiencing the Single Life

Stages in the Life Cycle for Singles To explore some of the issues involved in negoti-ating and living a single life for both women and men, Schwartzberg and associates (1995) have proposed a developmental model not unlike those mentioned at the beginning of this section. Their model does not assume a common blueprint for singles but does suggest that the issues that are addressed do

TABLE 7.1	Stages of the Single Adult Life Cycle	
LIFE CYCLE STAGE	**EMOTIONAL PROCESS**	
Not yet married	Shifting the relationship with the family. Restructuring interaction with the family from dependence to independence. Taking a more autonomous role with regard to the world outside the family: work and friendship.	
The thirties: entering the "twilight zone" of singlehood	Facing single status for the first time. Expanding life goals to include other possibilities in addition to marriage.	
Midlife (forties to mid-fifties)	Addressing the fantasy of the ideal American family: accepting the possibility of never marrying and accepting the possibility of not having own biological children. Defining the meaning of work, both current and future. Defining an authentic life for oneself that can be accomplished within single status. Establishing adult role for oneself within family of origin.	
Later life (fifties to when physical health fails)	Consolidating decisions about work life. Enjoying fruits of one's labors and the benefits of singlehood. Acknowledging the future diminishment of physical health. Facing increasing disability and death of loved ones.	
Elderly (between failing health and death)	Confronting mortality. Accepting one's life as it has been lived.	

Source: Schwartzberg, Berliner, and Jacob (1995), p. 56, Table 4.1.

follow an age-related chronology. At each stage of the model, individuals will have certain tasks and relationships to address. Each will bring different sets of emotions, and all will help to shape one's definition of self. This model is summarized in Table 7.1.

In their twenties, singles are among the "not married yet" population. Many of their peers are getting married, reminding them of normative expectations regarding marriage. With the increased age at first marriage, however, they are not yet out of sync with the majority of their friends. By the time that singles reach their thirties, they have entered the "twilight zone of singlehood." This is the time when singles tend to reevaluate their decisions about living arrangements, work, and friendships. Because singles in their thirties are most likely to be both sup-

porting themselves economically as well as domestically, it is also a time for the blurring of gender distinctions. Both men and women need to engage in paid labor as well as unpaid labor. Singles in this stage begin to feel more out of sync with their peers. In coming to terms with their singlehood, they may begin to settle in—buying a home, for example—or think about having children without marriage.

By the time that singles reach the age of forty to their mid-fifties, they are learning to "develop alternative scripts." Those "fantasies" held about the perfect life need to be reevaluated, and some decisions come to a head (see the Family Narratives box on page 289). For women, this includes a real assessment about the likelihood of having biological children. Some singles in this stage face

After interviewing and writing about thirty single women negotiating their way through a world defined by marriage, Lee Reilly gave the following thoughts about her own status as a single woman:

Twenty-five years ago, it was at a bonfire on this beach that I watched Tommy Piage, the boy I adored, take Barbara Pott's hand and walk off into the darkness. It's here that my best friend, Nicki, and I watched the moon landing and toasted—with orange soda—to our honeymoons on the moon. We planned our waterfront weddings that day; the minister would be perched on the lifeguard stand.

The place has changed, of course. The beach has widened since I huddled around illegal bonfires watching boys and girls pair off. Today is gray and windy, a wet, off-season day exhaling the last gasps of a storm that blew through two days ago. It's the kind of day when locals dressed in rubber suits fish the breakers for blues, and people walk the shoreline wearing jeans and leather jackets. It's cold.

Then, suddenly, on the 17th Street beach I spot four men in tuxedos and four women in long, fancy dresses that trail in the sand. They're standing near the dunes, encircled by pots of purple, yellow, and orange mums; a Jeep stands by, ready to sweep them away if the weather gets any worse or the ocean gets any closer.

She is wearing white satin and a half-veil that attaches to her blond hair, which is swept up off her neck and twisted in a sophisticated knot. The groomsmen, the groom, and a bridesmaid—dressed in bright jewel blue, a fluffy dress she'll never wear again—are shuffling around while the photographer, a woman in pants, sets up the last shot. How the bride must have worried about the weather! I think watching her consult with her maid of honor; she must have known that the northeaster would linger. Did she consider renting the Firemen's Hall? Did she worry about her dress, her hair, her mascara? Did she pack a few umbrellas in the Jeep, just in case? And when the vows came, did the wind whip away her words, and the guests lean in to hear better?

They're packing up the mums now, all those young, dark-haired men in formal suits, and the bride is climbing the dune to join her waiting bridesmaids. But she can't do it; her high heels disappear into the slipping sand, the wind fills her veil like a spinnaker, and she falters. Finally she takes off her white shoes, digs her stockinged toes deep into the damp sand, bunches up the satin skirts in her hands, and climbs. And as she climbs, the garter on her thigh peeks through a nearly full-length slit in her skirt.

It is a silly picture, this barefoot bride on the beach, and I wish I had a camera—to have the picture and to hold it, to keep it in mind as I walk to the lighthouse and later as I write. It is a moment, a confirmation, a challenge. It's a mirror, clean and fresh and accurate. Maybe it's a conclusion.

The conclusion is this: that a young girl dreamt of being a bride on a beach and she was; and another young girl dreamt of being a bride on a beach and she wasn't. But both have so many more dreams to create and fulfill, to dream and lose, to love and recover, that this one dream cannot be the only determinant of quality in their lives.

For if it is, then we each failed ourselves.

Source: Reilly (1996), pp. 202–203.

challenges in terms of their perceived role in their families of origin. Grappling with these issues can be less problematic for those who have more "embracing" definitions of what families are. At about the age of fifty, singles begin to "pull it all together." This is a stage that is not too dissimilar to the one faced by married people in middle age. The considerations that must be addressed include planning for retirement, preparing for old age, firming up a will, and enjoying the fruits of one's own labor (a career at its peak).

As singles reach the "elderly stage," they face another challenge similar to married elderly people: moving from being self-sufficient to being cared for by others. This is the stage that concerns some people because of the assumption that singles don't have anywhere to go or anyone to go there with. We will return to a discussion of this topic, but research does not support the notion that those who are single and/or without children fare any worse in old age.

Gay and Lesbian Singles In some ways, the developmental process works similarly for gay and lesbian singles. Careers develop over time, and decisions about having biological children happen for all women at similar times. Yet gay singles face not only the stigma of singlehood but also potential discrimination from a society characterized by homophobia and heterosexism. Whereas heterosexual singles can eliminate any stigma of singlehood by getting married, gay and lesbian singles cannot.

In order to apply the developmental model proposed above, it is important to consider a number of modifications. First, an important component to be included is the development of a gay/lesbian identity. For some, this may occur earlier in their lives; for others, it may be later. The timing of this development will affect how these singles relate to co-workers while developing careers, and how they relate to other family members. Some develop a gay or lesbian identity after spending time in a heterosexual relationship, and they may have children. This situation makes family relationships more complicated, for society does not have ready-made normative guidelines for these family relationships. As we'll see a bit later, the "coming out" process for gays and lesbians can be smooth or challenging depending on their social locations. Some environments, and families, are more embracing than others.

Another difference comes at the time that singles consider having children (biolog-ical or adoptive). Many states do not allow gays and lesbians to adopt children, and those who are considering having children biologically are faced with the costs of in-vitro fertilization, artificial insemination, or obtaining a surrogate.

Finally, considerations made in planning for old age may also be different for lesbian and gay singles. A long history of discrimination may result in fewer resources available for later life. If relations with families became strained in the coming out process, the ability to have close family ties in old age is reduced. Some evidence suggests that gay and lesbian older people are less likely to participate in senior citizen activities than are others (Hammersmith, 1987). However, as views about gays and lesbians become more liberal in our society, we may find that in the future these differences are not as great.

The Consequences of Singlehood

By now, we've seen a considerable amount of research suggesting that singlehood is an increasingly common status in U.S. society. Less well understood are the consequences of being single. Some of the research summarized in the previous chapter indicates that singlehood disadvantages both women and men in terms of general life satisfaction and health. Men, and some women, also receive a marriage premium via higher earnings. However, this research has not as yet articulated differences by comparing those who are single by choice to those who are married by choice.

FACT OR FICTION?

Single adults are less likely to be happy with their lives compared to married adults.

Psychological and Physical Well-Being
Marriage can bring a number of significant assets to adults. It provides a sense of mean-

ing to their lives, a meaning that is above and beyond the individual (Waite & Gallagher, 2000). Marriage also encourages sharing and watching out for each other. The desire among Americans to be married suggests that marriage is important to them and can enhance people's lives and make them happier. Using data from the General Social Survey from 1972 to 1996, Waite (2000) finds that marriage is indeed associated with higher levels of general happiness. This is true when comparing married individuals to either the never-married or the previously married. The marriage benefit is relatively consistent over the 24 years of data collected, although Waite finds that it is stronger when the comparison is married to previously married than for married to never-married. In other words, the divorced and widowed are particularly disadvantaged, suggesting that "intention" may be important when making these comparisons. The never-married may include more intentional singles; therefore, the differences in happiness between them and married individuals are smaller.

Those who are voluntarily single and have never married are more likely to be happy with their lives.

| FACT

However, the differences in rates of happiness are larger when comparing married to previously married than when comparing married to never-married.

Another benefit often attributed to marriage is better health. The mechanisms associated with this difference vary by gender. For men, the advantage comes from having women take care of them more often, while women's advantage comes from living in a higher-income household with better health benefits (from husbands' employment). Over the last three decades, women's ability to be economically independent has increased, so the beneficial effect of marriage may have declined. Again drawing on the General Social Survey, Waite (2000) finds no significant differences in self-reported health among married and nonmarried individuals, regardless of whether the nonmarried are never married or previously married. However, the direction of the relationship for never-married men and women was different. Never-married men reported lower levels of health than did married men (and the relationship approaches statistical significance), while never-married women reported slightly higher levels of health than did married women. It's important to recognize that these are not direct comparisons of health and that there is a limited amount of research on this topic.

What these comparisons have neglected to identify is whether or not the never-married were living that lifestyle voluntarily. The majority of Americans want to get married, and if they are single because they haven't been able to find a mate, we would expect them to be less satisfied with their lives than those who have been successful in finding a marriage partner. But what about the consequences for men and women who are choosing to be single? As more people are remaining single consciously and voluntarily, should we expect that the consequences associated with being single would be more positive, or at least less negative? (Forsyth & Johnson, 1995).

Although not a direct test of this idea, a recent study shows that perceptions about marriage and marriage opportunities do influence women's psychological well-being (Tucker & Mitchell-Kernan, 1998). The authors were interested in three dimensions of well-being: depression, anxiety, and life satisfaction. They asked the women in their sample about their views on the "value of marriage" and whether or not they perceived a "good marriage market for women like themselves" in general and the "availability of dates" for themselves personally. After controlling for age, education, and neighborhood income, both single Latinas and single white women showed higher rates of depression when they found themselves without available dates. Single Latinas also exhibited higher rates of depression and anxiety when they saw a poor marriage market for women like themselves. Single white women were less satisfied with their life in general when they felt dates were not available for them. What these findings indicate is that when single Latinas and white women aren't seeing their situations relating to marriage in a positive light, they will be disadvantaged psychologically.

The findings were not significant for black women, even though they are in a more precarious marriage market than are other women. It is also interesting because in this survey black women placed a higher value on marriage than did Latinas and white women. The authors propose two explanations for this finding. First, among both black women and men there is a pervasive view of a "male shortage." Believing that marriage opportunities are dim, black women are more prepared for the situation of not being married and are less affected by a poor marriage market. Second, remaining single has become more normative and visi-

ble, which means that there is less stigma associated with being single.

Economic Well-Being Many have argued that marriage is beneficial because it brings a more secure financial position for households. For women and children, the benefit can come from having access to a man's salary and benefits, while for men, marriage is associated with the possibility of higher earnings. For couples to benefit from the *marriage premium,* wives/mothers put more effort into domestic care so that husbands/fathers can be free to devote their energy to employment. Single people are at a disadvantage because they do not have the support at home that married people (men, at least) do.

In the previous chapter, Figure 6.5 showed that the marriage premium exists for many people. The only group for which marriage was associated with lower earnings than those who were never married was white women. For all men, and for black and Hispanic women, being married had higher economic returns than did being never married, cohabiting, or being previously married. Why are white women unique? There are a couple of things to be considered. First, white married couples are more likely to have a traditional division of labor at home than are other racial/ethnic groups (Coltrane & Valdez, 1993; Shelton & John, 1993). As a result, marriage is more likely to interrupt white women's labor market activity, which in turn reduces their earning power. Second, black women who have never married are more likely to have children living with them, depressing black women's earning potential compared to that of white women.

Another interesting trend observed in Figure 6.5 was that for men and black women, cohabiting also brought a wage premium over being never married. For men, this makes sense because of the traditional division of labor that exists in most coupled households. For black women, living with a man (married or not) provides some kind of support that benefits her labor market activity.

Most research on the economic consequences of singlehood, like that on psychological consequences, does not distinguish between those who are single by choice or not, or between different types of singlehood. An interesting issue emerging among singles is whether or not they are actually being discriminated against relative to married people in the labor market. The American Association for Single People has become quite active in pursuing legislation that will counter what it sees as unfair treatment by employers. It is working to address disparities in employment benefits, insurance, credit, housing, survivor rights, consumer discounts, and much more. One study indicates that the vast majority of single employees (about 80 percent) believe that their employers are more concerned with the needs of married employees with children than they are with the needs of single employees.

In sum, the consequences of being single are not automatically positive or negative. They depend on what type of singlehood is being explored. They are also related to the broader social conditions that single people face. Age, gender, social class, and race and ethnicity are important factors to consider when looking at all types of family and household situations—including singlehood. Generally speaking, singles fare better when they *want* to be single, and have the resources to survive in today's economy. Many years ago, Margaret Adams (1976) argued this as well by suggesting that there are three essential criteria for developing a successful and satisfying single life:

1. The capacity and opportunity to be economically self-sufficient.

2. The capacity and opportunity to be psychologically autonomous.

3. A clearly thought out intent to be single by choice.

More research in this area is needed. Approximately 46 percent of Americans are not married. The numbers within this group who have never married are increasing, especially in the last twenty years. We don't have a clear picture of whether or not these lifestyles are voluntary or how temporary they are. But with the increased attention to the "decline in marriage," it would make sense to take a look at the variety of singles in order to learn the advantages and disadvantages of not being married in a society that is "marriage prone."

Heterosexual Cohabitation

Living together without being married is not a recent creation. Although direct measures of **cohabitation** were not available until very recently, we saw in the previous chapter that cohabitation was not all that uncommon in the eighteenth century. Officials qualified to marry couples were not always available in a geographically dispersed country, and the cost of a marriage license kept some couples from applying. However, this did not mean that early European settlers supported cohabitation without marriage. Rather, couples were supported in their relationships *until* they could get married. In other cases, courts made decisions about property and child care for cohabiting couples as if they were married (Cott, 2000). Marriage has always been the desired adult relationship, and communities worked to support its centrality in their lives.

The situation is drastically different today. An increasing number of Americans support cohabitation. The National Opinion Research Center data for 1994 show that 42 percent of adults believe "it is all right for a

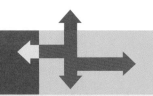

Cohabitation is not just a pattern associated with the United States, nor is the United States alone in experiencing an increase in the rate of cohabitation. Similar increases have been reported for other industrialized nations, such as Canada, France, Australia, Norway, and Sweden (Blanc, 1987; Carmichael, 1990; Leridon, 1990; Wu & Pollard, 2000). In fact, cohabitation is actually more prevalent in Scandinavian countries than it is in the United States (Duvander, 1999). Part of the reason for the higher rates of cohabitation in Sweden is that the government ensures similar rights and benefits for households headed by a married couple as those headed by cohabiters (i.e., domestic partnerships). It might be predicted that when the government provides no incentives to marry (tax benefits or greater access to health care), marriage would become a thing of the past. However, as in the United States, the majority of people in Sweden do eventually marry. Only 15 percent of women and 23 percent of men have not married by the age of 46. Marriage, it appears, is here to stay.

© 2001 AP/Wide World Photos

Cohabitation is viewed more positively in Scandinavia, even for the Crown Prince of Norway who cohabited with his fiancée prior to marriage.

Many Scandinavian countries have created registered partnerships for any cohabiting couple regardless of sexual orientation. Denmark was first in 1989, followed by Norway in 1993 and Sweden in 1994. However, this legislation does not allow for adoption, and other countries do not recognize these unions. Just to the north of the

United States, the Federal Liberals (the political party in power in Canada) proposed a bill in early 2000 that would extend legal rights, obligations, and benefits that are currently associated with married couples to cohabiting couples. This would apply to all cohabiters, regardless of sexual orientation. If the sentiment of the populace makes a

couple to live together without intending to get married," while a third also believe that "it's a good idea for a couple who intend to get married to live together first." The actual practice of cohabitation is so common that the majority of marriages (first marriages and remarriages) begin with cohabitation (Bumpass & Lu, 2000). In this section, we will look at current trends and patterns in cohabitation, reasons why cohabitation has in-

creased, and cohabitation's effects on marital stability and children.

Rates and Patterns of Heterosexual Cohabitation

Data estimating the rates of cohabitation suggest that there has been a significant increase, most notably in the last two decades (Casper & Cohen, 2000). Census 2000 data

difference, this bill stands a relatively good chance at becoming law. A recent Gallup poll in March of 2000 found that 43 percent of Canadians are supportive of same-gender marriage (up from 36 percent a year ago) and that 61 percent believe homosexuals living as married people should receive the same tax and employment benefits.

Another reason behind the varying rates in cohabitation around the world is the relative trend toward individualism and autonomy that can be seen in the many worldwide social/emancipation movements (Lesthaeghe, 1995). Rates of cohabitation are going up in places such as rural Siberia (Mikheyeva, 2000) and Nicaragua (Baker, 2000). In July 1979, the Sandinista National Liberation Front came in to power in Nicaragua after a lengthy political struggle. The goal of the Sandinistas was to work toward the empowerment of all people by redistributing the resources within the society. Part of this transformation included the movement of gender ideology from one of *machismo* to one of *equality*. *Machismo* is a belief about

gender relations "predicated on a series of oppositions between men and women. It emphasizes male virility and all things considered 'masculine'" (Baker, 2000: 310, note 2). However, in transforming society, the new government worked to change *women,* not men. Women were encouraged to participate in new income-generating projects and become economically independent while men were not expected to alter their behavior. Even after the revolution, men maintained their sexual freedom in marriage, for men are seen as *needing* more than one sexual partner. Women did not have such freedoms either before or after the revolution.

Suzanne Baker argues that this change in Nicaragua has resulted in a situation where women and men have different preferences regarding living arrangements. Women reported a preference for informal relationships while men preferred formal (marriage) ones. If the church marries a couple, divorce is next to impossible. So if women feel neglected or abused, it is difficult to leave the relationship. By living in in-

formal unions, Baker argues that women can maintain a sense of freedom and keep options open for themselves and their children. During the time of her study, she found that 60 percent of unions in Nicaragua were "informal"—that is, not validated by a civil or religious ceremony.

What this brief look at the variation in cohabitation around the world tells us is that cohabitation varies by social context. Politics, religion, and values all help to structure the situation whereby cohabitation becomes more prevalent and what the consequences of increased cohabitation will be for other unions and family relationships (Seltzer, 2000).

Critical Thinking

1. How are politics, religion, and values shaping family structure (particularly cohabitation rates) in this country?

2. As cohabitation rates continue to rise, do you think they will have an effect on politics, religion, and values?

show a 72-percent increase in cohabitation in just ten years, from 1990 to 2000. Data from the National Survey of Families and Households show that 33 percent of women report having *ever* cohabited by 1987. Eight years later (using data from the National Survey of Family Growth, 1995), the percentage had increased to 45 percent (Bumpass & Lu, 2000). The percentages are even higher when looking only at those who cohabit prior

to their first marriage. Among those women who married for the first time between 1980 and 1984, 46 percent report to have cohabited. But among those women marrying for the first time a decade later (1990–1994) 59 percent lived together before their marriage. Although the majority of the cohabiting experiences for these women were with their "husband-to-be," the percentage of women cohabiting with someone other than the first man they married rose from 5 to 16 percent. (For a comparison to cohabitation in other countries, see the Family Diversity box on pages 294–295.)

(see the Family Diversity box on pages 294–295.)

College students are the most likely group to cohabit.

Variations Across Race, Ethnicity, and Social Class   Using data from the National Center for Health Statistics, Figure 7.5 shows slightly lower rates of cohabitation than those reported by Bumpass and Lu (2000) but also shows the variations by race/ethnicity and type of cohabitation. Several points can be observed. First, note very little difference in the overall rates of cohabitation across racial/ethnic lines. There is a slightly higher percentage of non-Hispanic whites having reported cohabiting than other groups, and their rates are increasing the fastest. Second, in terms of the type of cohabitation, among all racial/ethnic groups the most frequent pattern is to cohabit before the first marriage (the data are for 15–44-year-old women). The only difference between groups appears to be that non-Hispanic blacks are more likely to have co-

FIGURE 7.5   Cohabitation Experience of Women Aged 15–44, 1995

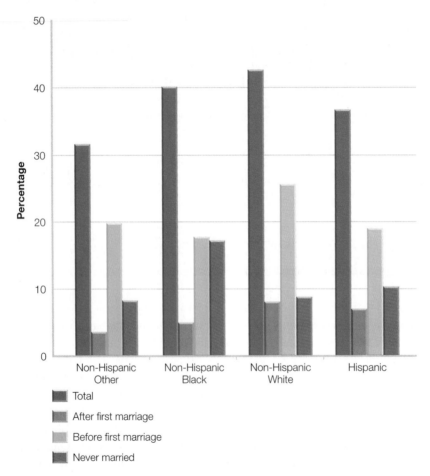

Source: U.S. National Center for Health Statistics (1997).

habited without ever marrying than are others. This finding may be partially explained by economic and demographic considerations, and it will be discussed below when we look at the reasons for the rise in heterosexual cohabitation.

One of the ways in which cohabitation looks different from marriage is that it is more likely to occur for those at the lower end of the socioeconomic scale (Thornton, Axinn, & Teachman, 1995). For example, Bumpass and Lu (2000) found that 59 percent of women with less than a high school education had cohabited, while 46 percent of those who had a high school degree, 39 percent with some college, and 37 percent of those who completed college had cohabited. Although these differences are statistically significant, we should note that cohabitation is still quite common among people of all levels of education, even among those who have graduated from college (almost two-fifths). So when we look at the data across subgroups by age, race/ethnicity, and education, cohabitation appears to be a common experience and on the increase for all groups.

Rates of cohabitation go down as the level of education goes up.

Cohabitation and the Presence of Children One final characteristic of cohabitation is that it is increasingly likely to involve children. Since the rise in cohabitation has occurred among those previously married (divorced or widowed) as well as among the never married, we would expect children to be present. Close to half of those who cohabit following divorce have children living with them. However, perhaps the biggest change has been in the relative proportion of children born to unmarried women. Table 7.2 contains information about the family structure in which children were born in two time periods (1980–1984 and 1990–1994) and re-

veals several interesting findings. First, looking at the first row of data for the total picture, we see that the majority of children born in both time periods were born to married parents (79 percent and 71 percent). The rate of births to married parents did decrease, but notice that the decrease was countered *more* by the situation of children being born to cohabiting parents than to mothers who were not in a cohabiting relationship with a man. The rate of children born to unmarried and uncoupled mothers rose only slightly, from 15 percent in the early 1980s to 17 percent in the 1990s. However, the total rate of children who were born to cohabiting mothers doubled over this time period (from 6 percent in the 1980s to 12 percent in the 1990s). Another way of looking at this change is to look at the data in bold print. In the earlier cohort, 29 percent of children who were born to unmarried mothers were born to mothers who were cohabiting. By 1990–1994, that rate went up to 39 percent. In other words, close to half of all children born to unmarried mothers were coming home to two parents.

Children are more likely born to married parents than to cohabiting parents.

When controlling for other factors, we see that the likelihood of children born to cohabiting mothers (versus unmarried mothers without male partners) is greater among those with lower levels of education. In terms of race/ethnicity, over half of the children born to unmarried Hispanic and non-Hispanic white mothers are born to cohabiting mothers. The rate is half that for black children (22 percent).

Cohabitation has been shown to be a very short-lived experience. Almost half of cohabitations last less than a year, one in six lasts three years, and only one in ten endures for five years. Many of those who end their

TABLE 7.2 | Percentage of Births to Mothers, 1980–1984 and 1990–1994, by Marital Status/Union

| | 1980–1984 | | | PERCENTAGE OF BIRTHS TO ALL UNMARRIED WOMEN | 1990–1994 | | | PERCENTAGE OF BIRTHS TO ALL UNMARRIED WOMEN |
	MARRIED (%)	UNMARRIED/ COHABITING (%)	UNMARRIED/ NO UNION (%)	THAT WERE TO COHABITING WOMEN	MARRIED (%)	UNMARRIED/ COHABITING (%)	UNMARRIED/ NO UNION (%)	THAT WERE TO COHABITING WOMEN
Total	79	6	15	**29**	71	12	17	**39**
Education								
<12 years	57	16	27	**37**	48	29	23	**41**
12 years	76	6	18	**25**	68	13	19	**39**
College 1–3 years	87	3	10	**23**	79	8	13	**35**
College 4+ years	95	1	9	**20**	94	2	4	**20**
Race/Ethnicity								
Non-Hispanic	88	4	8	**33**	81	10	9	**50**
Black	38	13	49	**21**	27	17	56	**22**
Hispanic	79	10	11	**48**	67	18	15	**53**

Bumpass and Lu (1998, 2000). Data for 1980–1984 from the National Survey of Families and Households. Data for 1990–1994 from the National Survey of Family Growth.

cohabiting relationship do so by getting married (around half); however, this percentage has been decreasing. It appears that cohabitation, like marriage, is becoming less stable over time.

Over 70 percent of children are born to married parents.

In sum, cohabitation is becoming quite common among all groups of Americans. It is a short-lived experience, with about half of cohabiting couples marrying within a few years and the other half splitting up. As well, a major shift is occurring in the presence of children in cohabiting relationships due to both the rising rates of cohabitation among divorced people and the increased likelihood of cohabiting couples to have children themselves. These are some significant changes in family structure, and as with the discussion on the decline in marriage rates, scholars are not clear on just why they are taking place.

What Explains the Rise in Cohabitation?

Explanations for the rise in cohabitation parallel our discussion in the previous chapter, on marriage. Both cultural and structural forces are proposed to explain why these shifts in family structuring are occurring, although most family scholars recognize that the two sets of factors are mutually reinforcing (Axinn & Thornton, 2000; Lesthaeghe, 1998).

Cultural Factors Recall that in terms of cultural issues, the focus is on norms, attitudes, and values. One value that ranks quite highly in American society is "individualism." Americans believe that they have rights as individuals to choose where they work, where they live, and with whom they live. And the key to this deeply held value is that

© Digital Vision/Getty Images

Establishing a career has resulted in a delay in marriage and a rise in cohabitation.

individuals shouldn't have to be accountable to someone (including the state) for their own desires and interests (as long as these are legal). Research that correlates attitudes with the likelihood of cohabitation supports the argument that individualism is a relevant value for union formation. One study that followed 12,000 high school seniors into their thirties found that (1) women (but not men) who placed a high value on their career success, and (2) men (but not women) who placed a high value on the "leisure to enjoy my own interests," were significantly more likely to enter cohabitation as a first union (versus marriage) (Clarkberg, Stolzenberg, & Waite, 1995). This is an interesting finding, for it suggests that people are anticipating a loss of independence with marriage and may be opting for an alternative. However, *what* people fear losing depends on gender. Women may understand marriage as sacrificing their careers, while men see marriage as a restriction of their leisure time.

Structural Factors   The other factors that are emphasized in explaining the increase in cohabitation are structural ones. Over the last century, the demand for women's labor has been on the rise. As women spend more time on education and employment activities, they are likely to delay marriage. The longer the time spent as an adult before marriage, concomitant with the more liberal attitudes about premarital sex, the greater the odds of cohabitation.

In the previous chapter, we reviewed research about structural inequalities in the labor market that make the "pool of eligibles" smaller for some groups than for others. African American women and women in geographic areas with high levels of male unemployment are less likely to find economically independent men to marry (Oppenheimer, 2000). The decision for women to marry is often based on knowing that their partner is economically self-sufficient (Manning & Smock, 2002). This attitude is most prevalent among African American women (Tucker & Mitchell-Kernan, 1995). The combination of attitudes, along with limits in structural opportunity, decreases the odds of marriage and increases the odds of cohabitation.

The relationship between attitudes and behavior, between culture and structure, is a close one. Good arguments can be made about which is the causal factor, but many family scholars are now proposing that family formation be seen as a product of "feedback loops" (Axinn & Thornton, 2000). Structural situations, such as labor market demand, can set up particular behavior patterns (delayed marriage). These behavioral patterns, in turn, can reinforce certain attitudes (acceptance of premarital sex and/or cohabitation). Subsequently, these attitudes may provide support for other behaviors (actual cohabitation). One argument states that

attitudes and values have strong intergenerational ties to behavior as well. Delayed marriage, reduced childbearing, and divorce in one generation are associated with similar behaviors in the next generation. Likewise, children who grow up in households with cohabitation may be more likely to cohabit as adults. Mothers' attitudes and values regarding marriage are particularly important in the intergenerational transmission process. Children's behavior has been found to be closely associated with the attitudes of their mothers, even when controlling for children's own attitudes and values. These researchers suggest that current patterns of family behavior will have long-term consequences for family formation in subsequent generations.

FACT OR FICTION?

Married couples who cohabit prior to marriage are more likely to divorce than are married couples who did not cohabit.

The Effects of Cohabitation on Marriage and Children

There are some concerns about the rise in cohabitation. Some worry about it as a moral issue due to their belief that it is wrong for people to engage in sexual activity prior to marriage. Others are worried because of research that links cohabitation with a higher likelihood to divorce. The impact of union disruptions on children makes up another set of concerns and leads to the question in general of what impact cohabitation has on relationships and the children involved. In this section, we will look at the research that focuses on this question.

Cohabitation and Subsequent Marital Stability   Cohabiting relationships are not very stable. Very few couples cohabit more than a couple of years, and estimates are that only about half of couples who cohabit will marry (for a more detailed look at the transition from cohabitation to marriage, see the Focus on Family Research box on pages 302–303). Marital relationships are also less stable if the couple had been in a cohabiting relationship prior to marriage than if they had not (Axinn & Thornton, 1992). However, some suggest that the problem of marital instability is only likely to occur when couples have been in more than one cohabiting relationship prior to their marriage (DeMaris & MacDonald, 1993).

There are two primary explanations for the correlation between cohabitation and subsequent marital instability. First are the differences between those who cohabit and those who do not, specifically in terms of education and attitudes. Those with less education and those who value independence are more likely to cohabit prior to marriage. It is also the case that marital instability is greater for these same groups; therefore, those couples would have divorced regardless of their premarital cohabitation. This is referred to as a *selection effect,* and there is empirical research to support it. The factors that give rise to cohabitation are the same as those that give rise to marital instability (Lillard, Brien, & Waite, 1995). The second explanation of cohabitation and marital disruption focuses on the experience of cohabitation itself and how it changes the individuals involved. Waite and Gallagher argue that "the great theme of marriage is union," while that "of cohabitation is individualism" (2000: 44–45). Those choosing cohabitation are somewhat more "individualistic" to begin with, but this tendency can be reinforced during the cohabitation. And those who enter without such individualistic tendencies may develop them because of the cohabitation. For example, couples who cohabit are less likely to pool their incomes than those who are married. As a result, individuals maintain their independence from each other financially. In addition, being in a rela-

tionship that does not carry with it the legal obligation to stay together may encourage cohabiting couples to accept their relationship as "temporary." These attitudes and behaviors are then thought to carry forward into marriage and make married couples more accepting of the idea that relationships need not be permanent. One study that followed people from age eighteen to twenty-three found that cohabitation was associated with greater tolerance for divorce (Axinn & Barber, 1997). Those who did not cohabit, but rather lived in other "nonfamily" arrangements (with roommates or on their own), did not experience a change toward more tolerance. The data also indicated that the longer people cohabited, the less enthusiastic they became about marriage and childbearing. And the largest effect on attitudes about divorce was found among those whose cohabitation ended by dissolving the relationship (versus getting married). The authors of this research suggest that dissolving cohabitation is similar to the dissolving of a marriage in that it makes people more tolerant of divorce.

| FACT

Cohabitation is positively correlated with the likelihood to divorce.

Popenoe and Whitehead, who have led a major charge to discourage cohabitation, sum up this argument this way:

> Although cohabiting relationships are like marriages in many ways— shared dwelling, economic union (at least in part), sexual intimacy, often even children—they typically differ in the levels of commitment and autonomy involved. According to recent studies cohabitants tend not to be as committed as married couples in their dedication to the continuation of the relationship and reluctance to

In July 2002, the Centers for Disease Control and Prevention (CDC) released a report on cohabitation, marriage, divorce, and remarriage, based on the most recent wave of the National Survey of Family Growth (NSFG). In 1995 the NSFG interviewed more than 10,000 adult women aged 15–44. The report provides clear evidence that successful cohabitations, like successful marriages, are related to the communities in which people live as well as individuals' race, family background, and education. Two cohabitation experiences that are featured in this study help to show the variations in cohabitation:

1. The probability that a first premarital cohabitation makes the transition to marriage within five years.
2. The probability that the first cohabitation breaks up within ten years.

By exploring these two "endings" to cohabitation, we can see that prior experiences and current social locations are important in shaping cohabitations.

Transition to Marriage

Overall, 58 percent of those who have cohabited for at least three years have made the transition to marriage, and 70 percent of those cohabiting for at least five years have married. There are considerable variations among women, with white women and women with higher levels of education making

the transition to marriage at higher rates than women of color and those with less education. Also positively correlated with the transition to marriage are having lived in a two-parent family throughout childhood, having no children at cohabitation, or, if there were children, that

the children were born after the onset of cohabitation.

Community-level factors are also important for the transition to marriage from cohabitation. As we can see in Figure 7.6, making the transition to marriage is more likely to occur in communities with higher

FIGURE 7.6 Probability That an Intact Cohabitation Makes the Transition to First Marriage Within 5 Years, by Community Male Unemployment Rate, Median Family Income, Percentage Below Poverty Level, and Percentage Receiving Public Assistance: United States, 1995

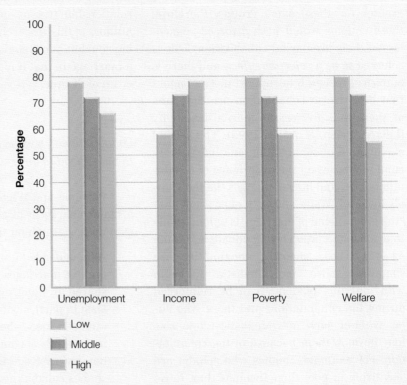

Source: Bramlett and Mosher (2002), Figure 10.

median family income levels, lower rates of male unemployment, fewer people below the poverty level, and fewer people receiving public assistance (welfare). Although not shown here, the report indicates that these community-level factors play a more significant role for black women than for non-Hispanic white women.

Probability of First Cohabitation Disruption

Turning to the likelihood of a first cohabitation to be disrupted (break up), the variations among groups are a mirror opposite of those for the transition of cohabitation to marriage. Disruptions are more likely to occur for black women than for Hispanic or non-Hispanic white women, are more common for those raised in single-parent households, and are more common for those with lower levels of education. In terms of community-level factors, Figure 7.7 again reveals a mirrored trend. Cohabiting couples who live in areas with lower median family incomes, higher male unemployment, higher rates of poverty, and more households reliant on public services are at greater risk of cohabitation disruption.

The general finding of this report is that the likelihood for both marital and cohabiting relationships to succeed is related to a similar set of factors. Being situated in a better position (economically and educationally) provides resources for couples to draw on to develop lasting relationships. When people are in challenging environments, it appears that relationships are challenged as well.

Source: Bramlett and Mosher (2002).

FIGURE 7.7 Probability That the First Cohabitation Breaks up Within 10 Years, by Community Male Unemployment Rate, Median Family Income, Percentage Below Poverty Level, and Percentage Receiving Public Assistance: United States, 1995

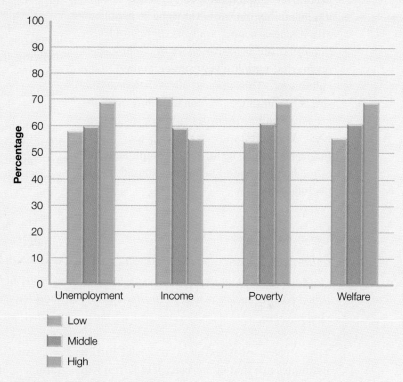

Source: Bramlett and Mosher (2002), Figure 16.

Critical Thinking

1. After reviewing these findings, how likely do you think you would be to have a successful cohabitation and/or marriage?

2. Can you imagine other people you know being either more or less successful at cohabitation or marriage than you? What makes them different?

terminate it, and they are more oriented toward their own personal autonomy. It is reasonable to speculate, based on these studies, that once this low-commitment, high-autonomy pattern of relating is learned, it becomes hard to unlearn. (1999: 5)

There is some evidence that the effects of premarital cohabitation on subsequent marital instability may not always be so problematic. Using a cohort analysis, Schoen (1992) finds that the negative effect of cohabitation on marital stability is stronger among older cohabiters. This makes sense because the social acceptance of cohabitation has increased, and so has the number of cohabiters. As cohabitation becomes a more "normalized" family form, its consequences for other family-related behaviors should be expected to change.

The Effects of Cohabitation on Children

Estimates are that 40 percent of children will spend some time growing up in a cohabiting household (Bumpass & Lu, 2000). Although there has not been much research on how this finding affects children (primarily due to the fact that longitudinal data are not available), here are a couple areas of concern about the effects of cohabitation on the well-being of children. One issue concerns the financial situation of such households while the other focuses on the way in which cohabitation increases the number of transitions that children must face while growing up.

Financial stress is more likely to occur in cohabiting than married households for two reasons. Selection into cohabitation is related to income and education. Cohabitation is more frequent among those with lower levels of education and income. Therefore, children born to cohabiting parents are more likely to be at a disadvantage economically (Manning & Lichter, 1996). Also, after divorce, single parents (primarily mothers) are more likely to begin a cohabiting relationship if they are experiencing economic difficulties. Finally, cohabiting couples are less likely to pool their incomes, making it less likely that children will gain the benefit of living in a cohabiting two-earner household (Bauman, 1999). The basic argument here is that cohabitation does not take care of the financial problems of single-parent households. Longitudinal research suggests that cohabitation and economic uncertainty are "mutually reinforcing in the lives of children" (Graefe & Lichter, 1999: 216).

Another area of concern is how cohabitation is more likely to result in frequent family transitions (Graefe & Lichter, 1999), which can have negative consequences for children's well-being (Wu, 1996). These children are twice as likely to experience relationship disruption than children born to married parents because cohabitation is a relatively short-term experience (Bumpass & Lu, 2000). Children born to cohabiting parents may encounter two types of changes. One transition is from living in a household headed by a cohabiting couple to one headed by a married couple. Another is the movement from a two-parent cohabiting household to a single-parent (usually mother) headed household. This second type of tran-

TABLE 7.3	Characteristics of Unmarried Male–Female Couples: March 2000

CHARACTERISTIC	PERCENTAGE
Age Difference	
Male 6 or more years older than female	24.7
Male 2 to 5 years older than female	28.6
Within 1 year of each other	25.5
Female 2 to 5 years older than male	12.0
Female 6 or more years older than male	9.1
Race Difference[a]	
Same-race couples	94.6
Both white	79.5
Both black	12.6
Both Asian and Pacific Islander	1.2
Interracial couples	4.3
Black/white	2.3
Black/Asian and Pacific Islander	—
White/Asian and Pacific Islander	1.8
Hispanic Origin Difference[b]	
Both Hispanic	8.7
Neither Hispanic	85.5
One Hispanic and one non-Hispanic	5.8
Education	
Male more education than female	23.2
Male and female same education	49.0
Female more education than male	27.9
Employment Status	
Male only employed	18.2
Female only employed	10.7
Neither employed	6.0
Both employed	65.0
Earnings Difference[c]	
Male $30,000 or more higher than female	14.3
Male $5,000 to $29,999 higher than female	40.6
Within $4,999 of each other	23.6
Female $5,000 to $29,999 higher than male	17.5
Female $30,000 or more higher than male	4.0

— represents zero or rounds to zero.

[a]This race comparison is regardless of Hispanic origin.

[b]This difference does not consider race. People of Hispanic origin may be of any race.

[c]Includes people with no earnings or loss.

Note: Data are not shown separately for the American Indian and Alaska Native population because of the small sample size in the Current Population Survey in March 2000.

Source: Fields and Casper (2001).

women (2 percent marry and 4 percent cohabit) (Raley, 2001). When a pregnancy occurs during cohabitation, non-Hispanic white women are again more likely to marry prior to the birth of the child than are black women or Puerto Rican women. If cohabitation were seen as an acceptable alternative to marriage in terms of childbearing, then we should not see a difference in the rate of marriage before childbirth among racial/ethnic groups. Because of the connection among cohabitation, childbearing, and marriage, the argument is that cohabitation is a precursor to marriage for non-Hispanic whites while it is more of an alternative to marriage for black and Puerto Rican women (Manning, 1993; Oropesa, 1996).

Finally, most of the writing on heterosexual cohabitation suggests considerable variation among cohabiters. The ability to construct meaningful relationships while preparing for marriage, or in lieu of marriage, depends in part on the broader social context within which it takes place. People's views about cohabitation have changed, and as attitudes become more liberal, we may find that cohabitations last longer and do not have such a negative effect on subsequent marriages. Or we may find that the meaning of marriage itself will change (Seltzer, 2000). It may be too early to tell just what role cohabitation plays in the scheme of family relationships, but it appears to be here to stay and deserves the continued attention of social scientists.

We turn now to another type of cohabiting relationship—that of lesbians and gay men. This type of cohabitation faces even more obstacles than heterosexual cohabitation, and the struggle for acceptance has an effect on the couples themselves.

| FACT OR FICTION?

The majority of Americans support marriage for gay and lesbian couples.

Gay and Lesbian Cohabitation

Americans are divided on their views about same-sex relations. Gallup polls show that in 1999, 50 percent of Americans believed that "homosexual relations between consenting adults should be legal," while 43 percent said they should not (http://www.gallup.com/poll/indicators/indhomosexual.asp). But saying that these consenting relationships should be legal is not the same as saying they should receive the same types of support as marriage. Figure 7.8 shows that about one-third of Americans support legal marriage for lesbians and gay men. Slightly more (40 percent) support the right for gays and lesbians to make a "legal commitment" to each other in which they can receive the same rights and benefits as couples in traditional marriage. The difference here is probably due to religious convictions about the meaning of marriage as a relationship between a man and a woman.

| FICTION

Although the majority of Americans support the legality of gay/lesbian relationships, fewer support marriage for such couples.

The Desire for Enduring Relationships

Research indicates that sexual orientation does not differentiate Americans from one another in terms of their desire for long-term romantic relationships. And, despite the fact that state laws have not supported the right of everyone to choose whom to marry, many lesbian and gay men have been successful in forming satisfying, enduring relationships (Mackey, O'Brien, & Mackey, 1997). A review of the studies of same-sex couples shows that, like married couples, the majority report they are satisfied with their relation-

FIGURE 7.8 Views About Same-Sex Marriage.
Do you think marriages between homosexuals should
or should not be recognized by the laws as valid, with
the same rights as traditional marriages?

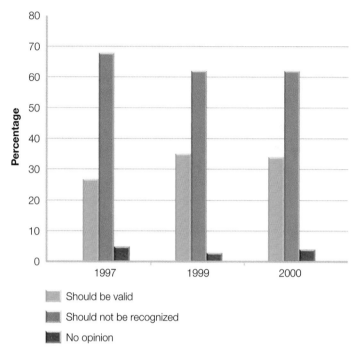

Should be valid

Should not be recognized

No opinion

ships and are happy (Patterson, 2000). In a finding that is somewhat different from the reports of married couples, where a specialization in the division of labor appears to be the preferred pattern (Brines & Joyner, 1999), same-sex cohabiting couples are the most satisfied and have the most enduring relationships when they sense equity in the relationship and a sharing of domestic activity (Blumstein & Schwartz, 1983; Peplau & Cochran, 1990).

In heterosexual (straight) couples (either cohabiting or married), we saw that the division of labor is very closely aligned with gender. For couples that include two people of the same gender, the model for their relationship is based on other factors. Early work on same-sex couples referred to the alternative model as a "friendship" model. This is because gender is a source of power in heterosexual couples, setting up hierarchical relationships. In same-sex couples, this hierarchy is less evident (at least one that is based on gender), giving the couple a more equal playing field. However, even with a more "equal start" to negotiating relationships, lesbian and gay couples are not without conflict or struggle. In some ways, relationships fall prey to similar forces as those experienced by straight couples. And gender is not irrelevant, for there are some differences between lesbians and gay men in how they approach and construct cohabiting relationships.

Research finds that like married couples, the majority of gay/lesbian couples report they are satisfied with their relationships.

Relationship Dynamics Among Gay and Lesbian Cohabiters

In many ways, the relationship dynamics of gay and lesbian gay cohabiters are similar to those of heterosexual cohabiters. However, gays and lesbians face additional conflicts in the work force and in reactions from their family members.

Challenges Faced by Gay and Lesbian Couples Marriage is still the preferred state, and cohabitation does not receive either the same legal or social support as marriage (Waite & Gallagher, 2000). Lack of social acceptance makes cohabitation stressful. However, attitudes are more supportive of heterosexual cohabitation than they are of gay and lesbian relationships, and this adds a layer of stress. One of the ways in which lack of support for gays and lesbians is evident is in employment. Studies show that same-sex households lag behind heterosexual households in income (Lukenbill, 1995), and we've seen that economics are influential in setting the context for family life. In his recent book *No Place Like Home,* Christopher Carrington argues that gay/lesbian/bisexual

families that are financially secure are able to build "stable identities, families, and communities" (1999: 211). The combination of the social and economic discrimination experienced by lesbians and gays, like that of other disempowered groups in our society, inhibits their attempts to have enduring relationships.

Another area in which cohabiting couples encounter problems is relatives. Again, like straight cohabiters (Aquilino, 1997; Nock, 1998), gay and lesbian couples get resistance from family members about their cohabitation. Of course, lesbian and gay couples have an added pressure that has implications for their relationship. Do they tell their families about their sexual relationship (referred to as "coming out")? First, couples may disagree on whether to disclose their sexual orientation, and to whom, and this disagreement introduces conflict into the relationship. Second, if and when they do come out, the reaction of family members adds additional strain. Research shows that the reaction of family members (in particular, the parents) varies by a number of factors. Religion, race, and ethnicity influence opinions. Many religious orientations support only heterosexual unions, and some racial/ethnic groups are also less supportive in their attitudes (for example, some Hispanic groups) (Morales, 1990). Negative reactions are also more likely to come from older parents, those with less education, and those who had strained relationships with their children prior to learning of their gay or lesbian identity. The quality of the relationship between parents and children is the best predictor of how parents will respond to news of their children's homosexual orientation (Cohen & Savin-Williams, 1996; Savin-Williams, 2001).

Power and Conflict in Relationships Within the relationship itself, gay and lesbian couples enter alike in terms of gender, but on other characteristics they might be quite different. Age, education, religion, income, race/ethnicity, and values can vary as much as those among straight couples. These characteristics are conceptualized as resources for relationships by exchange theorists, and they have a bearing on how couples negotiate their interactions. We saw in previous sections that among heterosexual couples (married and cohabiting), differentials in resources had implications for power in the relationship. Those with more resources did less domestic labor and had more decision-making authority. This same theoretical perspective has been applied to same-sex couples, but the interesting finding is that it works for gay men but does not work well for lesbians. That is, gay men are advantaged in their relationships when they have higher incomes, education, and other resources relative to their partners. Although the findings across a variety of research efforts are not completely in agreement, it seems that resources do not affect the balance of power in lesbian relationships as much as they do in gay or heterosexual relationships (Blumstein & Schwartz, 1983; Peplau, Veniegas, & Campbell, 1996). One of the reasons for this difference relates to the construction of masculinity and femininity. Masculinity is more closely aligned with occupational and economic performance, while femininity is seen as also including success in relationships. As a result, the outcome of employment activities may be more central to gay and straight men in developing their own identities as well as their relationships with others.

In a major study of lesbian, gay, and heterosexual cohabitation, Kurdek (1994) found that when cohabiting couples disagreed, they all seemed to disagree about very similar types of things. All types of couples said they had experienced conflict around (1) power issues (finances and equality issues), (2) intimacy (affection and sex), (3) personal flaws (personal habits), and (4) personal distance (time spent away at work). And power and intimacy were ranked first and second in terms of frequency among couples of all types. Kurdek did observe a few differences, however. First, heterosexual cohabiters were more likely to argue over differences in values and views on political and social issues. Lesbian and gay men share experiences in discrimination, so they come together as couples with some similarities in attitudes about social issues. A considerable amount of research shows that men and women differ, on average, in their opinions about social issues (political, family, and gender issues), so coming together in a relationships sets up the opportunity for disagreements. The second difference occurred between lesbian and gay couples, with gay men reporting more arguments over previous lovers. Gay and lesbian communities (groups who identify as a circle of friends and supporters) are small, and it is more likely that ex-lovers will remain in contact. This physical presence provides a reminder of past relationships and can cause or reinforce feelings of jealousy.

FACT OR FICTION?

Trends in relationship quality (conflict, sexual relations, intimacy) are similar among heterosexual and gay/lesbian couples.

Friends are an important source of support for gay and lesbian couples. A recent qualitative study of couples that had been together a minimum of fifteen years found that success was closely connected to having a network of support (Mackey, O'Brien, & Mackey, 1997). When asked to comment on family, religion, therapy, and friends as sources of support for their relationships, married couples mentioned family first, while gay and lesbian couples mentioned friends. Family members, including parents and siblings, maintained connections with their lesbian or gay family member, but relationships were more ambivalent. Ambivalence is common when learning to interact with a new family member (daughter- or son-in-law), but it can be more uncertain when that new member is gay.

Relationships Are Relationships The study by Mackey and colleagues (1997) also allows for a comparison between gay/lesbian and straight couples over time. All couples had been together for at least fifteen years. Mackey and associates compared these couples on the level of conflict, sexual relations, and psychological intimacy at three points in time over the course of their years together. In general, they argue, "relationships are relationships." Changes on these dimensions of relationships (conflict, sexual relations, psychological intimacy) showed very similar patterns over time. For example, reported conflicts increased initially in all types of relationships, but then they decreased later. Satisfaction with sexual relations showed a decline for all types of couples, and psychological intimacy, like conflicts, shifted in similar ways over time. As conflicts increased, intimacy suffered. However, with subsiding conflict over time, higher levels of intimacy returned.

| FACT

Research suggests that "relationships are relationships," and shifts over time are similar among gay/lesbian couples and heterosexual couples.

These trends held for all types of couples, although the levels of conflicts, satisfaction, and intimacy varied by group. In general, heterosexual couples showed lower levels of conflict, higher rates of sexual satisfaction, and higher levels of intimacy on average than did gay and lesbian couples. We should keep in mind that maintaining relationships is more difficult for gays/lesbians because these relationships are negotiated in a relatively nonsupportive social context.

Comparing gay to lesbian couples, lesbian couples showed the highest levels of reported conflict, lower levels of sexual satisfaction, and lower rates of intimacy. The authors of this study argue that lesbians, more than any other group, spent a considerable amount of time negotiating their relationships. Doing housework, earning incomes, and financial planning were all talked about extensively due to concerns over ensuring an equitable relationship. Because of more conversation and negotiation, there was more opportunity to learn about their differences in opinions. Lesbians were also more likely to push the negotiations until they felt they both understood and agreed on a situation. Gay men, Mackey and associates found, took the approach of "a buck is a buck" to figure out how to handle household finances. The argument here is that women are more likely to articulate their feelings; therefore, we may not be getting a complete picture from gay men. These differences aside, the research suggests that the types of issues that need to be negotiated are quite similar across couples. And how relationships change over time also appears to follow comparable paths.

| FACT OR FICTION?

Gay and lesbian marriages are legal in some states.

Should Same-Sex Couples Be Allowed to Marry?

The debate over whether same-sex couples should be allowed to marry is ongoing. There has been some movement in the United States to gain more rights for same-sex couples, but to date, no state allows for same-sex marriage, and thirty-six states have specific anti-same-sex-marriage laws. In addition, in 1996 the United States passed the Federal Defense of Marriage Act (H.R. 3396), which made marriage, in the eyes of federal law, something between men and women. And in case any state tried to make same-sex marriage legal, this act also made it clear that no other state was obligated to honor the marriage if the couple moved to that state.

Issues that are at the center of the debate include (1) the benefits that accrue to married couples that are denied to cohabiters and (2) the protection offered by the law to equitably settle cases of union dissolution. Marriage is legislated at the state level; therefore, the benefits/rights of marriage vary. But in general, some of the benefits of married couples include transfer of property without taxation, access to the health care and other employment benefits of one's partner, family visitation rights in hospitals, family leave benefits, cheaper auto insurance rates, and reductions in the legal costs of adopting children. In terms of legal protection, when a couple divorces, the court can attempt to compensate for the unpaid domestic labor of a spouse who works at home by calculating the prevailing wage for such work and including it in the divorce settlement. These benefits and protections are being sought for gay and lesbian families as "equal protection under the law."

| FICTION

At press time, no states permit gay/lesbian marriage. Some states allow for domestic partner benefits, but this is not the same as marriage.

Some counters to this argument issue from two camps. Some observers follow their religious beliefs and see marriage as the union of a man and a woman. Marriage is the foundation of family through the bearing and rearing of children. Another argument against marriage comes from those who believe that marriage itself is a discriminatory institution that benefits only the economically well off. By legalizing marriage for gays and lesbians, marriage would introduce this inequality into the gay and lesbian communities (Carrington, 1999). From this perspective, the argument is that we should be ensuring the rights of individuals to choose whom they want to share their property with, whom they want as their guardians, and who can visit them when they are sick. In terms of the protections that marriage brings to couples in the case of divorce, some courts and legislatures have not shown much recognition of the value of unpaid labor in divorce settlements (Singer, 1997). This means that allowing lesbian and gay couples to marry would not protect them from situations where one partner invested more time in unpaid domestic work and desired some compensation for that work when the relationship ended.

Because marriage is valued in our society, many lesbian and gay couples desire the social recognition that might come with it. Married couples are more active in kin networks, holidays, and gift exchanges, and these types of family experiences can be very satisfying. They can help keep the couple together through their connections to each other's families.

Forming Legal Partnerships

Because of the concerted effort by the federal government to refuse to legalize same-sex marriage, some individuals, employers, and states have tried to find ways to provide benefits and protections for cohabiters, regardless of sexual orientation. Two ways in

Social movements supporting lesbian and gay unions have occurred in the U.S. and around the world. Although same-sex marriage is not allowed in any state, some states have established the existence of domestic partnerships.

which unions may be formalized are (1) rights and responsibilities within the union and (2) rights and responsibilities with respect to the state and other third parties (Seltzer, 2000). The former can be done through couples drawing up marriage-like contracts, usually with a lawyer (see the Constructing Strong Families box on page 315). In this contract, the couple can lay out their expectations with respect to property and financial matters. The contract may not be binding in all states, but it can serve as a mechanism for couples to communicate their intentions and desires. Many issues cannot be contractually decided in this matter, and these fall into the second category, of rights

and responsibilities. States have the right to decide on taxation laws, while employers have the right (within limits) to decide how benefits are distributed to their employees.

Several states and cities, and some employers, have made modifications to allow for domestic partner benefits (Wisensale & Heckart, 1998). As we saw in Chapter 1, the creation of domestic partner benefits by employers is one way to achieve more equitable treatment of both straight and gay/lesbian cohabiting couples. A recent study finds that 18 percent of the workers in the United States work for firms that offer coverage for domestic partners. Eleven percent of workers are in firms offering such coverage to

For people who cohabit, gay or straight, contracts can be a way to help negotiate the relationship. Because open communication can benefit a marriage, drawing up a contract is one way of explicitly sharing interests, desires, and expectations. Young people in their twenties are less likely to want to draw up a contract. They are also less vulnerable if they break up because they probably have not accumulated much property or wealth. However, as people get older and do begin to collect assets (home, car, savings account), contracts can help if a cohabiting couple breaks up. Below are tips that can help in drawing up a living-together agreement:

1. Decide how you want to handle your financial and property ownership. It may be unpleasant to make plans for dividing property in case you split, but you'll be happy you did if your relationship does end.

2. Don't try to write the contract in one sitting or in one contract. Relationships are complicated. Take time to discuss the situation.

3. Cover the basics of property and money. Do all your possessions now belong to both of you? Or do you both keep what you had coming in? What will you do about gifts given to you as a couple? And things you buy together?

4. Don't get personal. Anything you detail about kitchen chores or garbage duty probably won't be enforceable in court. The court may also decide to throw out the entire agreement.

5. Don't mention sex. If the court sees a connection between sex and money or services, it may toss the agreement.

6. Be free of other entanglements. Don't write a living-together agreement until both of you are free from past relationships.

7. Fabulously wealthy? Get legal advice before signing an agreement.

8. Erase the perception of a power imbalance. Get legal advice if you're an experienced, older lawyer dating an inexperienced, wealthy nineteen-year-old. A court may not believe your agreement otherwise.

9. Agree in advance to mediate disputes so you can avoid costly court time.

10. If you move to a new state, revisit your agreement to make sure it reflects state law.

Source: Reprinted from *Living Together: A Legal Guide for Unmarried Couples* by Toni Ihara, Frederick, Hertz, and Ralph Warner, Nolo, Copyright 2001, htt://www.nolo.com

Critical Thinking

1. Can you think of things that you might want to include in a contract with your life partner?

2. Can you think of things that you would *not* want to put in such a contract? Why would you leave these things out?

same-sex partners (Kaiser Foundation & Health Research Educational Trust, 1999). It is up to the employer to determine the guidelines for establishing a domestic partnership. An employee is usually required to submit documentation, which can take the form of a written statement or evidence of some financial arrangement such as a joint lease or mortgage.

Domestic partner legislation is a relatively recent phenomenon, but it is attracting attention around the United States as well as in other countries. It is important to recognize the broader social context within which such relationships take place to understand the relative likelihood of their support, whether it be for heterosexual or same-sex unions.

Conclusion

In the previous chapter, we saw that the proportion of the population that is married has declined over the last several decades. If not married, what are the living arrangements for adults? This chapter explored some of the living arrangements that have become more common, including living independently and cohabiting. We presented these not as alternatives to marriage; rather, we looked at them as options for people as they strive to build meaningful connections in their lives.

Because marriage is a central part of our society, many myths/stereotypes exist about those who don't marry. Attitudes include viewing singles as selfish and as unable to attract a partner. Social science research reveals a variety of singles with many reasons for not marrying. In addition, the consequences of being single are related to this variation. Although in general those who are single are less happy than those who are married, the differences between the groups are greatest for married versus previously married, and least for married versus never married.

Many of those who are single are not living single, but are cohabiting. A considerable amount of research has been conducted on both gay/lesbian and heterosexual cohabitation and suggests that relationship dynamics are similar to married couples. That is, relationship quality varies in response to the varieties of backgrounds and experiences that people bring to relationships. Differences between heterosexual cohabitation and marriage are that cohabitations are less stable in general than marriages, and such couples are more likely to be economically challenged. Gay and lesbian cohabitations are also different from marriages in that they cannot transition to marriage and still represent stigmatized relationships in our society.

Chapter Review

⁕ How and why have rates of singlehood changed over time?

The rates of singlehood (unmarried and non-cohabiting individuals without children) show a curvilinear trend over time. That is, rates declined for much of the twentieth century but began to rise in the last few decades. The reasons behind these changes are both cultural and structural. Structural factors include demographic shifts that result in skewed sex ratios and shifts in the economy that create financial uncertainty. The availability of partners and opportunities to support families are important considerations in the likelihood of remaining single. Economic opportunities for women have also produced a situation where women are less dependent on men for economic survival. This change might create a more supportive cultural climate for women to remain single. Social movements in the 1960s and 1970s challenged the status quo, including traditional marriage.

⁕ What is it like to be single in our society?

Experiences of being single can depend on whether people are single voluntarily or not, and whether it is a stable or temporary state. Of course, singles can change in these characterizations over time. Data suggest that men are more likely to be single for a lifetime than are women. The consequences of being single are not automatically positive or negative but depend on what type of singlehood is being explored. In general, singles fare better when they want to be single and have the resources to survive in today's economy.

⁕ Who is more likely to cohabit?

Rates of cohabitation are rising for all groups, but in contemporary society rates are higher for those at the lower end of the socioeconomic scale. Cohabiting couples are less likely to have children than are married couples, but the number of children born to, or live with, cohabiting parents has increased significantly over the last few decades.

⁕ What explains the rise in cohabitation?

As with singlehood, social scientists look toward both cultural and structural factors to explain rising rates of cohabitation. Americans value their independence and are increasingly likely to support lifestyles to maintain it. At the same time, our economy has encouraged women's employment and required higher levels of education. The result is a delay in marriage, but not a delay in developing close relationships. Those who face economic uncertainty due to fewer employment opportunities also delay marriage and are more likely to cohabit.

⁕ What effect does cohabitation have on marriages and children?

There is a positive correlation between cohabitation and divorce. Some argue that cohabitation encourages attitude change so that people become more accepting of relationships as temporary and then carry forward this attitude into marriage. Others suggest that those who cohabit are more likely to come from groups in our society that have a higher risk for divorce anyway. However, cohabitation's negative effect on marriage may be declining as cohabitation becomes more normative in our society. Because those who cohabit have lower incomes on average, children living with cohabiting parents are also more likely to be economically disadvantaged compared to children with married parents. One of the biggest challenges faced by children in cohabiting households is the exposure to a greater number of transitions. Since cohabiting couples are less stable than married couples, children may experience more structural changes in family membership.

⁕ How do gay and lesbian cohabiters compare to heterosexual cohabiters?

In one way, cohabiters are the same; they desire committed romantic relationships. They are also equally susceptible to social forces such as shifts in the economy. Some research on long-term couples (straight and gay/lesbian) finds similarities in terms of the types of issues that need to be managed in the relationships. However, gay and lesbian couples are different from heterosexual couples in some ways. Gay and lesbian couples are more likely to have a friendship model compared to a model of specialization as found in marriage. Gay and lesbian couples also face the stigma of their sexual orientation in a society that is based on heterosexual marriage. Challenges also exist in the way that gay and lesbian couple negotiate their relationships with their families.

Key Terms

cohabitation: the practice of unmarried couples who are sexual partners sharing a household

conflicted bachelors: men who are ambivalent about their single status and the most likely to marry among long-term bachelors

entrenched bachelors: single men who hold fast to their single status

flexible bachelors: single men who are comfortable with their being long-term singles but are not opposed to marriage

hypergamy: the practice of women marrying older men

period effect: patterns of behavior correlated because they occur during the same time period

singlehood: the state of being unmarried and noncohabiting

stable versus temporary singles: singlehood that is long-standing as opposed to short term or transitory

voluntary versus involuntary singles: those who want to be single as opposed to those who would rather be married but have not been successful in finding a partner

Resources on the Internet

These web sites have been selected for their relevance to the topics in this chapter. These sites are among the more stable, but please note that web site addresses change frequently.

American Association for Single People
www.singlesrights.com
The American Association for Single People was created to work toward maintaining equal protection under the law, regardless of marital status. The organization is nonprofit and nonpartisan. The web site includes a variety of essays on the rights of singles as well as links to data sources and summaries of current legal and corporate policies that affect the lives of single people.

Alternatives to Marriage Project
www.unmarried.org
The Alternatives to Marriage Project (AtMP) is a national nonprofit organization advocating equality and fairness for unmarried people, including people who choose not to marry, cannot marry, or live together before marriage. Included on this site are discussions of legal and social issues related to lifestyle choices. Statements are both proactive and reactive. For example, there is a response to the CDC report highlighted in the Focus on Family Research box on pages 302–303.

National Gay and Lesbian Task Force
www.ngltf.org
Founded in 1973, the National Gay and Lesbian Task Force works to eliminate prejudice, violence, and injustice against gay, lesbian, bisexual, and transgendered people at the local, state, and national level. On this web site are summaries of contemporary research and many charts and graphs showing how

different states legislate issues regarding gay/lesbian relationships. The issues covered include laws on domestic partnership, same-sex marriage, and adoption.

Companion Web Site for This Book

Virtual Society: The Wadsworth Sociology Resource Center

http://sociology.wadsworth.com

Begin by clicking the Student Resources section. Next, click Marriage and Family, and then click the cover image for this book. Select from the pull-down menu the chapter you are presently studying. You will have easy access to chapter resources such as MicroCase Online exercises, additional Web links, flashcards, InfoTrac exercises, and practice tests (that can be scored). In addition, to enhance and help with your study of marriages and families, be sure to investigate the rest of the rich sociology resources at Virtual Society.

Visit InfoTrac College Edition

 Another unique option available to you at the Student Resources section of the Virtual Society web site described above is InfoTrac College Edition, an online library of hundreds of scholarly and popular periodicals. Here are three suggested key search terms for this chapter:

* Search keyword: *singles* or *singlehood*
* Search keywords: *cohabitation + heterosexual* (or *same-sex*)
* Search keywords: *cohabitation + children*
* Search recent years to get the latest information on these issues.

© Ariell Skelley/Corbis

The Transition to Parenthood

8

One way to get an idea of what is on the minds of Americans regarding family life is to take a look at popular magazine covers. Here are four cover stories appearing in the last couple of years:

* "The New Single Mom: Why the Traditional Family Is Fading Fast, What It Means for Our Kids." *Newsweek,* May 28, 2001.
* "The Name of the Father and the Making of a New American Family." *Rolling Stone,* February 3, 2000.
* "The Truth About Fertility: Why More Doctors Are Warning That Science Can't Beat the Biological Clock." *Newsweek,* August 13, 2001.
* "Babies Vs. Careers." *Time,* April 15, 2002.

What are these stories about? In "The New Single Mom," *Newsweek* writers address a number of trends, including the increasing number of cohabiting couples who are raising children, the rising numbers of gay and lesbian parents, and the growing popularity of women choosing parenthood outside of marriage. The *Rolling Stone* piece follows up one of these themes by telling the story of a lesbian couple (Melissa Etheridge and Julie Cypher) who became parents by finding a sperm donor (David Crosby). The issues here reflect the demographic trends we've been discussing in this book. The heterosexually married couple with biological children is statistically on the decline. Replacing this family are increasing numbers of single-parent households, cohabiting parents, and households without children at all.

The last two magazine cover stories are about fertility and women's biological clocks, and they bring up the most recent concern of the medical community—the postponement of parenting. Although advances in medical technology have allowed women and men to delay parenting into their forties (and sometimes fifties), doctors are concerned about the impact of this delay on women in particular and society in general. **Fecundity** (women's biological capacity to produce) declines significantly later in life, and bearing a child after the age of forty can be a very expensive proposition. Because fertility treatments are not successful much of the time, many women and men invest considerable time and energy with nothing but disappointment in the end. The American Society for Reproductive Medicine sees this to be a serious enough problem that it has started a new ad campaign. A sign on the side of buses in New York, Chicago, and Seattle features an hourglass in the shape of an inverted baby bottle accompanied by a warning: Advancing Age Decreases Your Ability to Have Children.

This warning plays on a very common idea in our society, which is that women and men *desire* children. If not careful, people could jeopardize their chances of reaching their goals. However, the desire to have children is embedded in a complicated social world. The understanding of the negative effects of having children on women's employment (referred to as *opportunity costs*) is resulting in women postponing having children while they finish their education and get their careers established. As we have seen, the average age at first marriage is increasing, and the majority of children (70 percent) are born to married parents. Therefore, children are increasingly born to older parents.

Issues surrounding fertility, including *when* to have children, *how* to achieve parenthood, and with *whom* people parent, are the subjects of this chapter. We review historical rates of fertility and address the relative costs and benefits of children for parents and families. Children are an expensive project, but they can bring significant joys for parents and can improve connections between them and extended family and community members. At the same time, those who do not have children may experience other benefits in their lifestyles and relationships. For example, childless couples have a lifetime earnings advantage over those who do not have children. Next, we explore the varieties of ways in which people are going about becoming parents. Heterosexual married couples have children in a relatively well-defined culture of parenthood. There are well-established norms regarding the

way men and women interact during pregnancy, childbirth, and the rearing of children. Those who parent without partners, or those who parent with partners of the same sex, find a more challenging environment in which to become parents. Finally, we turn our attention to the ways in which pregnancy and childbirth are socially organized in our society. We live in a time when changes in family life seem fast but inevitable. How we respond to these changes will depend on the meanings we attach to parenting in our lives.

Fertility Among Women in the United States

The majority of Americans say that they want to have at least one child. However, in the last thirty years, there has been a dramatic drop in the average number of children that people report as ideal. The Gallup Organization first asked a sample of Americans about family size in 1936. That year, two-thirds of Americans said they thought having 3 or more children was ideal. The average number reported was 3.6. Keep in mind that the number of children born to women to maintain the current population, or the population **replacement rate,** is 2.1. Views on desired family size then remained relatively constant for close to 40 years. By 1973, the average "ideal" number of children had dropped to 2.8, with only half of the respondents saying that 3 children constitute the model number. Rates continued to drop during the 1970s, and by 1980, Americans' views reached their lowest statistical point (average of 2.5 children, with only 40 percent saying 3 or more are ideal), and similar views are held today. Controlling for gender, Gallup found that there was no difference between men's and women's views about ideal family size. A comparison of Americans' views with those of people in other countries can be found in Table 8.1.

TABLE 8.1	Global Study on Family Values, 1997
WHAT IS THE IDEAL NUMBER OF CHILDREN FOR A FAMILY?	
NATION	PERCENTAGE REPORTING 3 OR MORE
Iceland	69
Guatemala	61
Taiwan	52
United States	41
France	49
Singapore	47
Mexico	42
Canada	33
Lithuania	33
Thailand	30
Great Britain	24
Hungary	24
Colombia	23
Germany	17
Spain	18
India	12

Source: *Global Study of Family Values.* © 1997 The Gallup Organization. All rights reserved. Available online: http://www.gallup.com/poll/specialreports/pollsummaries/family.asp

FIGURE 8.1 Fertility Rates for Women Aged 15–44 by Age and Race/Ethnic Origin, 2000

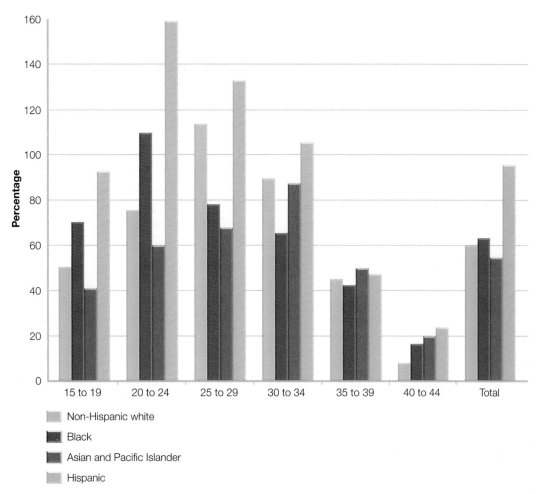

Non-Hispanic white

Black

Asian and Pacific Islander

Hispanic

Note: Hispanics can be of any race.
Source: Bachu and O'Connell (2001).

Variations in Fertility Rates Over Time

Fertility rates are measured in a number of ways. One measure is the **annual fertility rate,** the number of births per 1,000 women in a given year. In 2000 there was an annual fertility rate of 64.5, or about 65 births per

1,000 women aged 15–44. In Figure 8.1, however, we see that the rate was variable across age and racial/ethnic groups. Hispanic women had the highest fertility rate (95.1) while Asian/Pacific Islander women had the lowest (54.6). Looking at the shape of the graph, we see a curvilinear trend in fertility rates by age. That is, rates increase from the teens through the twenties, then decline. However, notice that the peaks of these curves vary by race/ethnicity. For black and Hispanic women, fertility rates peak in the 20–24-year-old group, while for non-Hispanic white

A growing number of women are choosing to have children later in life. Below are comments from women who had their first baby between the ages of 40 and 45, revealing some of the specific joys and challenges of having children at a nontraditional age.

You all had your first baby when you were at least 40 years of age. Could you tell me a little bit about your situation?

Joan I didn't plan to have my first baby at 42. It just sort of happened this way. I married my first husband when I was in my late twenties. We thought we would have at least two children, maybe even three, well before my fortieth birthday. But, well, it wasn't a very good marriage. After a few years, I felt that the marriage was a mistake. But it took me a number of years to get out of it. During this time I knew that I should never have a child with him. Boy, am I glad. We'd be fighting over child custody, visitation, and support—I just know it! I was 35 years old when we divorced. I hoped to remarry and even joined a few singles-type clubs to speed the process along, but it took me almost five years to find the right man. When I met Nick, we both just knew we belonged together. We married nearly one year after our first date. That's pretty quick, I guess, but I knew it was the right thing to do. Less than two years later, Olivia was born. She's beautiful! She's wonderful! I couldn't be happier.

Renee I've been married for a long time, but during my twenties I was completely focused on getting my education. I have a Ph.D. in chemistry. Some people had babies in grad school, but that seemed like so much work! It was hard enough just being in grad school, let alone trying to juggle that with taking care of a little one. No way! And then in my thirties I was pretty focused on my career. Academic jobs aren't easy to find in my field. I did a post-doc and then landed a tenure-track job. I really love my work and hoped to establish myself as a well-respected chemist. I don't mean to sound judgmental, but I never wanted to be in a situation where I had to put my child in day care for 50 hours a week. I know lots of people who do that. But I just felt that I didn't want to have a child until I could be home with it more. You know, people think that academics have these great flexible schedules. Yeah, maybe it's flexible, but we also work 50 hours a week or more. By the time I had tenure and had made full professor, and felt like I could finally let my hair down a little bit, I was 43 years old. Luckily, when we decided to have a baby, it didn't take very long to get pregnant. I know a number of people who struggled with infertility. Evan was born when I was 44.

Carole The stories of your quick pregnancies make me so envious! It took me fifteen years and virtually all the technology in the world that we could afford to bring Faith into the world. That's why I named her Faith—we just wouldn't give up. My husband and I have been wanting children since we were first married. We waited a few years just like a lot of married couples do, and when we were in our late twenties we decided to start a family. But nothing happened. Years and years were going by. Do you have any idea how stressful infertility is? Stressful, demoralizing, sad, lonely, painful, you name it. It's also expensive. Our health insurance does not pay all of the costs of the treatments that I've received. We owe a lot of money. My husband, Stan, got a small inheritance when his grandmother died, and we've used all that money and a lot of our own. But hey, look what we got for our money! It's all worth it. We don't have the money or the stamina to go through this again, so Faith is it. Plus, I'm 45. I'm not even in the fertility statistics, am I? Don't they stop calculating at 44? Ha!

Amy My husband and I didn't really want children. We've been very happy just being on our own. We both have pretty demanding jobs, but we also like to hike and travel around on weekends. We were just pretty comfortable in our own lives and didn't see a reason to change it. In fact, I used to feel sorry for people with young kids sometimes. You know, like when you see parents struggling in a restaurant trying to have a conversation over little Johnny's temper tantrum. But then, when I was 40, I found out I was pregnant. What a shocker. It still is a mystery to me. Rick and I talked about nothing else for two entire weeks. It seemed like eternity. Should I have an abortion? Should I have the baby? We decided to have the baby. I'm pro-choice and all, but it seemed selfish to have an abortion. I mean, I can see it if I was a teenager, or unmarried, or in a bad financial situation, or whatever. But I'm none of those things. Rick and I are just fine financially. So we made the decision to have the baby. It's definitely been an adjustment for both of us, but overall, we are very, very happy that we made this decision. I like being a mom more than I would have imagined.

What have been some of the good things about having a baby at this age?

Joan The good thing for me is that I'm finally in a committed relationship that is healthy. We truly are one happy family. Maybe not a "big" happy family, but happy nonetheless. It's nice to have a child in relationship that is rock-solid. Some people have that when they are young. I didn't.

Renee For me, the best thing about waiting is that I don't have to struggle so much between my career and my family. I'm not trying to build them both simultaneously. My friends who had children in grad school or early in their career had to work so hard, but they ended up shortchanging both work and their children, in my estimation. Several were denied tenure, which is a very stressful and demoralizing experience. And some spoke of not get-

ting home from work until after the baby was in bed. Personally, having a baby later in life has worked out great for me. I can cut back at work and coast for a few years, and I'm not in jeopardy. I'm only working part time. Plus, financially, it is much easier. We don't struggle so much over the costs. And kids can be very expensive. I can't believe all the gear they need. I don't know how two twenty-something-year-old kids can do it.

Carole Well, I don't see that many benefits in having children later, because, as I said, I wanted them a long time ago. My waiting wasn't by choice. But Renee is right; most people are much better off financially in their forties than in their twenties. We're not, but that's because we had to pay for much of our fertility treatments out of pocket.

Amy I also feel a bit more settled down. I've sowed my "wild oats," so to speak. I mean, I've already done a lot of hiking, biking, and other things I like to do. I've been to Europe twice, Hawaii three times, and even to New Zealand and Australia. Even though my pregnancy was a bit of a surprise—that's an understatement; it was a major surprise. But even though it was a surprise, I think I have an easier time staying home and being a mom right now because I've already done so many things. Actually, it feels kind of good to not be on the go for a while! I never thought I'd be a stay-at-home mom, but I kind of like it.

What have been some of the challenges about having a baby at this age?

Joan There are a lot of rude people in the world. They know nothing about your situation but make judgments. I actually had someone at work tell me, to my face when I was visibly pregnant, that I was too old to have a baby. Can you believe it? They were very aggressive and rude. I am a healthy and active woman. I went home and cried. I guess another downside is that if you start your family later, you can run out of time to have another one. We'd like another child, but I can't exactly wait three years to do so. They will have to be close in age. But I kind of like that idea too. Hopefully they will be close in spirit if they are close in age.

Renee The biggest challenge for me was my fear about birth defects. I was plagued with fears during my entire pregnancy. I even had trouble sleeping and had many really scary dreams. I breathed a sigh of relief when my ultrasound showed no defects, but some defects don't show up. Definitely, the biggest drawback is the higher rate of birth defects. I mean, we all would prefer a healthy baby, right? Having a child when you are over 40, even over 35, really decreases those odds. At 44, I had about a 1 out of 50 chance of having a baby with Down syndrome, not to mention all the other difficulties out there.

(continued)

Carole Yes, the fear about birth defects, no doubt about it. Oh, also, since most of my friends and relatives had their babies 15 years ago, no one had any gear that we could borrow. Babies need a lot of things—car seats are just the start. Luckily, we were given several baby showers by colleagues at work, and my husband's colleagues too. People knew about our infertility, so they were really kind to us.

Amy I keep hearing from people that I'm not supposedly as energetic as I was when I was 20. But I haven't really noticed a decline. Yeah, it's hard to get up with Sean three times a night. But I'm not sure I would have found that any easier when I was 20. Biologists say we decline as we age, so I guess it's true, but I think it's a bit over emphasized. It's probably true for most Americans who lead a sedentary lifestyle. But I haven't really found it to be true for me. I still try to run at least four days a week. It's more of a challenge to find the time to run. I just get up earlier and run before Rick leaves for work. Pretty soon, when Sean is old enough, I'll buy one of those jogging strollers.

Source: Stories compiled by Karen Seccombe.

Critical Thinking

1. At what age do you plan to have your first child? Why? For those of you who have a child, did you plan the age at which you would become pregnant?

2. Do you know any "older than average" parents? What challenges/joys have they experienced?

women the peak occurs in the 25–29-year-old group, and for Asian/Pacific Islander women the peak occurs in the 30–34-year-old group. These differences suggest that the latter two groups of women are more likely to be delaying childbearing. In fact, data from the Current Population Survey indicate that the rates of first births for women in 2000 show similar trends to those displayed here for the overall annual rates (Bachu & O'Connell, 2001).

Although these rates are interesting, they do not give us an indication of the **total fertility rate,** the total number of children ever born to women. The Census Bureau estimates these rates by looking at women in the 40–44 age group because the overwhelming majority of women in the United States have stopped having children by the age of 45. Only 2 percent of all children born in 2000 were born to women over the age of 40. Still, the figures are not precise because an increasing number of women are giving birth later in life (see the Family Narratives box on pages 324–326). Using these estimates, the rate of total fertility in 2000, or the average number of children born to women, was 1.9. Looking back in time, the average number of births per woman was at around 4.0 in 1900. Rates fell during the Great Depression to about 2.2 births per woman, then increased to a high of 3.7 births per woman in 1957 (the height of the **baby boom**). Like annual rates, total fertility rates vary by race and ethnicity. On average, non-Hispanic white and Asian/Pacific Islander women have 1.8 children. Black women have 2 children. And only Hispanic women have an average number of children (2.5) that is above the population replacement level.

These figures can also be disaggregated to look at the diversity in family configurations. Not all women have the same number of children. Among women between the ages of 40 and 44, the most common scenario is to have two children (about 36 percent). The next most likely scenario is to have *no* children (19 percent), followed by one child (17

FIGURE 8.2   Fertility of Women Aged 40 – 44

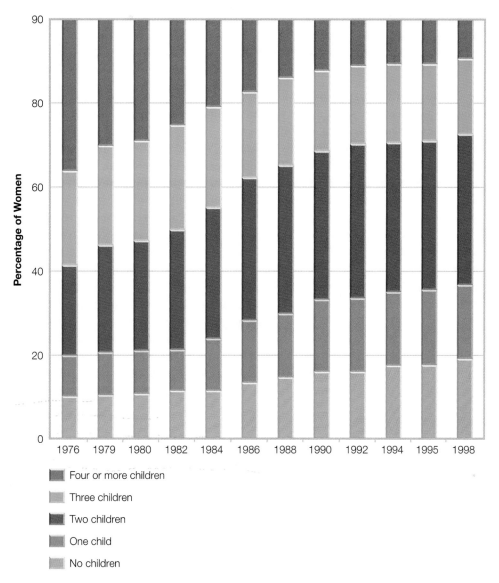

Four or more children
Three children
Two children
One child
No children

Source: U.S. Census Bureau http://www.census.gov/population/socdemo/fertility/table#2.pdf

percent), or three children (18 percent). However, notice the shift that has taken place in just the last 25 years (Figure 8.2). In 1976, the most common situation was for women to have had *four or more* children, followed by three children. The number of women who had not had any children by the age of 44 in 1976 was half of what it was twenty years later.

| FICTION

Although the fertility rate is lower today, the change has not been linear. Fertility dropped during the first thirty years or so of the last century, then rose to the century's highest rate in 1957. It has been declining ever since.

| FACT OR FICTION?

Among those women who have completed childbearing, the most likely scenario is to have had only one child.

There are two things to keep in mind when looking at these data. First, as already noted, the number of women who are having children past the age of 44 is increasing. This fact would alter both the average number of children ever born to women, as well as the percentage who never have a child. Second, because these findings are for women currently between 40 and 44, we can't generalize their behavior to other groups of women. Maybe women who are now in their twenties will exhibit different fertility patterns from women currently in their forties.

| FICTION

It is still more common for women to have two children than one. The second-most-likely scenario is to have had no children.

Why the Decline in Fertility in the United States?

In agrarian societies, such as the United States prior to the twentieth century, children were a valuable source of labor for families. From an early age, children were taught skills that would directly benefit a family's ability to survive. The transition to an industrial economy brought about a significant change in the expectations for children to participate in the family economy. Both fathers and children spent more time away from home as fathers took on paid employment and children were required to attend school. This shift (which will be addressed more fully in the next chapter) re-

sulted in children becoming an economic burden to families rather than an economic asset (Zelizer, 1985).

The Economic Costs of Having and Raising Children

An economic approach to understanding fertility views children as "resources" for families (Caldwell, 1982). In contemporary American society, children provide fewer economic resources for parents and families. They are less likely to be directly involved in economic production (income generation) for their families; instead, parents have to expend significant resources to raise their children. These **direct costs** of raising children include housing, food, child care, and education. There are also **opportunity costs** in raising children. Parents, most often mothers, will limit or modify their labor force participation to care for children, decreasing the earning power of both women and families (Bianchi & Spain, 1986). The direct and opportunity costs associated with having children are believed to be the primary reasons for the fertility decline in the United States and in other industrial economies.

| FACT OR FICTION?

Adjusting for inflation, raising a child to the age of eighteen today can cost around a quarter of a million dollars.

What Does It Cost to Raise a Child? On average, for a middle-income family of two, the cost of raising one child to the age of eighteen is $165,630 (in 2000 dollars). This is an increase of about 13 percent over the costs incurred in 1960 (Lino, 2001). However, this estimate glosses over some important issues, so it's worthwhile to see how the estimate gets constructed. The U.S. Department of Agriculture (USDA) collects household expenditure data that allow for estimates of the

Middle income families will spend over $150,000 (on average) to raise a child to age eighteen.

costs of raising children. The categories of expenditures include the following:

1. Housing expenses (shelter, utilities, furnishings, and equipment)

2. Food expenses (food and nonalcoholic beverages purchased at a store, at a restaurant, or at school)

3. Transportation expenses (purchase of a vehicle, finance charges, gasoline and oil, maintenance and repairs, insurance, and public transportation)

4. Clothing expenses (children's apparel, footwear, cleaning expenses, repair, and storage)

5. Health care expenses (medical and dental services not covered by insurance, prescription drugs, and health insurance premiums not paid for by employers)

6. Child care and education (day-care tuition and supplies, babysitting, elementary and high school tuition, and books and supplies)

7. Miscellaneous expenses (personal care items, entertainment, and reading materials)

The largest portion of these expenses for the raising of children is housing (33 percent of the total cost) followed by food (18 percent). The proportion spent on other items, as well as the actual dollar estimates for these expenses, varies considerably. One way in which costs vary is that they depend on how many children parents have. More children can produce "economies of scale." When sharing a house with another, you can split the cost, which is considerably less than the cost of two independent houses. The same can be said for purchasing food, utilities, and other household equipment necessary for family care. So while the total cost of raising children goes up with more children, the per-child cost goes down. Costs of raising children also vary by how old they are. Generally, the costs go up as children age. The cost of living also varies by region of the country, whether people live in an urban or rural area, and by the neighborhood that people live in within their city or town. All of these considerations factor into estimates for the price of raising a child. To get a general idea, the USDA presents the scenario of a two-parent household with two children. The costs reported are for the youngest child. Here is what the USDA finds for the year 2000:

* Families earning below $36,000 a year will expend between $6,280 and $7,380 per year for one child.

* Families earning between $36,000 and $64,000 will expend between $8,470 and $9,860 per year for one child.

* Families earning above $64,000 a year will expend between $13,000 and $14,260 per year for one child.

These estimates are probably conservative because they do *not* include two important expenses. First, the estimates do not include the cost of a college education. Although tuition and costs of college vary, the average cost of a good in-state university can be around $10,000 a year. Second, these costs do not include the "opportunity costs" mentioned above. These are the lost wages of the parent who takes time out of the labor market to care for a child. These lost opportunities become increasingly important as the numbers of married and single mothers in the work force continue to rise. It is hard to predict what these lost wages might be, but they include the actual lost wage and the job experience that is lost during the time off. Time out of the labor market has a negative effect on earnings when people return to work, for they are competing with others who have continuous labor market experience. Including college and opportunity costs, the total expense of raising a child would be considerably more than the estimates provided by the USDA.

Another very important consideration is inflation. Saying that parents will spend $8,000 in one year assumes we are thinking in 2000 dollars. But how will those dollars translate to future dollars? And since we know that costs increase as children age, how will this affect the estimate? The USDA figures that for a child born in 2000, and adjusting for inflation, the total direct cost of raising that child to the age of eighteen ranges from $171,460 for the lower-income group to $340,130 for the highest-income group. The middle-income family will pay $233,530 by the year 2018 (Lino, 2001). One recent attempt at including the additional costs of college and the lost wages of a middle-class parent calculates the total cost of raising one child born in 1997 to be about $1.5 million by the time the child reaches the age of twenty-two in the year 2019 (Longman, 1998).

| FACT

Depending on family income levels, parents can expect to pay between $171,000 and $340,000 for a child born in 2000.

Why Do People Have Children?

With the rapidly rising economic costs involved in having and raising children, we might ask why people are having children at all. The economic theories that have been used to predict the decline in fertility over time are not quite adequate for addressing this question. They predict that the decline in the marginal utility of children (their economic value) leads to a decline in fertility, but they do not explain why people continue to have children even when they present a "net cost." This approach doesn't take into account the value that children have to people *other* than their material resource value.

We live in a society where people think that families (and especially women) are not complete without having children.

The Value of Children

The most basic value of children to society is that children sustain it. Without children, we would be extinct in a relatively short period of time. However, our question here is more about the reasons that people would want to have children independent of propagating the species. With the availability of safe and effective birth control, we have choices about whether to have children, how many children to have, and when to have them. Demographic theories suggest that when we have the choice, we make rational decisions based on maximizing our economic position. As indicated in the last section, children don't appear to be economically advantageous. So why would a rational economic actor choose to have them? There are several categories of reasons that family scholars propose to explain people's fertility decisions. At the cultural level, we live in a society that ideologically supports childbearing. Women are raised with ideals about finding true love that translate into marriage and children. Because we are raised to believe in the value of having children, there are psychological benefits to achieving these societal goals. Still, in a society founded on notions of individualism, the critical role that children play

may be that they provide a mechanism for linking us to one another. We'll discuss each of these ideas in turn, then move on to address the question of what happens for those who do not have children.

Pronatalism **Pronatalism** can be seen generally as an attitude embedded in culture and social policy that supports and encourages childbearing. We can see a positive view of childbearing in our culture situated in the rituals surrounding pregnancy and childbirth. Women have baby showers to celebrate this change of status in their lives. The importance of having children can also be seen in the great lengths that people will go to have a child on their own, find a surrogate to bear a child for them, or adopt (see the Constructing Strong Families box on page 332 for an example of how controversial this quest can become). Some suggest that having children is like a "cultural imperative." Families are "complete" when they include children (Caldwell, 1982).

We adopt a variety of rituals and events to celebrate having children, and women can be stigmatized if they are unable to have children. This emphasis on childbearing is called pronatalism.

A considerable amount of research suggests that stereotypes about women and childbearing stigmatize those who do not have children. For example, cultural constructions of femininity align it with sexuality and reproduction (Hird & Abshoff, 2000; Gillespie, 2000), and the ultimate fulfillment in life for women is believed to be having a child (Ulrich & Weatherall, 2000). These conceptions of femininity and womanhood result in women who do not have children feeling either incomplete or deficient (Morell, 2000) or being viewed by others as selfish or abnormal (Letherby & Williams, 1999).

In 1996, John and Luanne Buzzanca finally had a child. They named her JayCee. After spending five years trying to have a child on their own, the Buzzancas hired a surrogate mother, Pamela Snell, to have a baby for them. Pamela was convinced that John and Luanne would be dedicated, loving parents. So she signed a contract with the Buzzancas to have a donated fertilized egg implanted in her uterus. She carried the child, gave birth to JayCee, and then gave her to the Buzzancas to raise.

Things didn't go as planned. Not long before Pamela gave birth to JayCee, John filed for divorce. He refused to provide child support in the divorce agreement, arguing that the child wasn't his (it was donated sperm) and that he signed the agreement with Pamela Snell only because his wife had begged him to.

Pamela (the surrogate) became upset about giving birth to a child that she assumed would go to two loving parents. Her concern led her to pursue steps to become JayCee's legal mother. Because she carried and gave birth to JayCee, she argued that she was the legal mother.

However, things became a little bit more complicated. The fertilized egg that was implanted in Pamela's uterus was not her own. In the course of legal proceedings, the woman who had donated the egg was found. Erin Davidson, the donor, had no idea that her egg had been given to Pamela. She had signed an agreement with a different couple to provide eggs to be fertilized with sperm from the husband of that couple. These eggs were to be implanted in the wife's uterus. Not all the fertilized eggs were used, and the couple believed they signed a form to have the remaining eggs destroyed. Unknowingly, they checked the box to donate the eggs to science. One of these eggs was given to Pamela to carry.

So who is JayCee's parent?

- Erin Davidson, who donated the egg?
- The unidentified man who provided the sperm?
- Pamela Snell, since she gave birth to her?
- Or the Buzzancas?

In 1999 a state appeals court decided that the Buzzancas are JayCee's legal parents and that John would be required to pay $400 per month in child support for an additional thirteen years.

Source: Adapted from television and print news. Summarized on http://cbsnews.com/now/story/0,1597,9352-412,00.shtml, accessed August 17, 2001.

Critical Thinking

1. Who do you think should be the legal parent of JayCee? Why?

2. What do you think about the obligation of Mr. Buzzanca to pay child support for JayCee until she is eighteen years old?

3. Should there be any laws regarding the use of donated sperm and eggs?

Pronatalism is also an attitude supported by social institutions. A number of examples from religious teachings suggest the positive value of children (Monach, 1993). In the book of Genesis, Adam and Eve are commanded to be fruitful and multiply, while in other passages we learn that childlessness is an indication that God has withdrawn his favor. The Roman Catholic church supports procreation through its opposition to birth control. Orthodox Jews are expected to forgo contraception and to bear at least one daughter and one son.

Pronatalist views are also argued as central to the politics surrounding birth control and fertility (Morell, 2000). Many insurance companies do not pay for birth control prescriptions for women, but they do pay for men's prescriptions for Viagra. As mentioned at the outset of this chapter, the medical community has also taken an interest in warning women about delaying childbearing for fear of becoming infertile. One of the consequences of this campaign might be to influence women to have children earlier than they had anticipated because of the fear of infertility.

These attitudes and policies all encourage women to think seriously about having children. Having children is a way to make their lives complete. For those with certain religious beliefs, having children is doing the right thing in the eyes of God. For others, being a mother is believed to be a natural part of womanhood. Therefore, we should expect some psychological benefit for those who become parents.

Participating in their children's activities can broaden parents' social networks.

Psychological Benefits Some of the earliest work on articulating the value of children suggested that having children provides many psychological benefits (Hoffman & Manis, 1979). It is quite satisfying for parents to see parts of themselves in their children. They can be proud of their children's accomplishments and take some credit for their children's successes. Parents even have the option of experiencing things vicariously that they may not have experienced themselves as children. Having children is also an opportunity for novelty, stimulation, and fun—doing those things that you might not otherwise do with adults. For those who respond to society's pronatalist stance, or the cultural imperative to have a child, having children can provide pleasure. Parenthood is also seen as one clear indication of reaching adulthood (Hogan & Astone, 1986).

Parents feel responsible for ensuring the safety of their children and helping them become competent social beings. As parents do their jobs of parenting, children will present a number of challenges as well as opportunities. Children can expand friendship networks for parents through their school and extracurricular activities, and they can

get parents to become interested in new and different types of activities. These friendships and activities can be very satisfying for parents.

We should point out that the literature on voluntary childlessness (discussed below) does not refute these arguments, but suggests that in contemporary society not all adults want children. For those who do not want to have children, the psychological payoff comes from being childfree. The key to feeling good about your fertility behavior is that it be in line with your fertility desires.

Children Provide Social Capital Drawing on the work of anthropologists, Schoen, Kim, Nathanson, and Fields (1997) argue that the value of children is in their capacity to facilitate ties or networks. In many cultures, children can help to form alliances between families and communities. These alliances occur through the marriage of children from different families. In the upper classes of the United States, we can also see how children can grow up and marry into families that will ensure the maintenance of wealth (see Chapter 4). The marriage of children from two families can solidify social placement.

For most people, however, the benefit of family and social networks is that they provide various types of support. People with access to a broader network of family and friends are able to draw on people with a diverse set of skills. This idea of the benefit of social integration (here facilitated through having children) is what Coleman (1990) refers to as **social capital.**

One of the ways that children can facilitate social capital is through solidifying ties among their parents, grandparents, and other kin. We saw in our chapter on marriage that parents are more likely to provide economic support (such as the down payment on a house) for their adult children when they are married and when they have children. Grandparents and other relatives are also more likely to help in other ways. They are more likely to provide physical help (housekeeping and child care) as well as emotional support (through more frequent contact) (Hogan, Eggebeen, & Clogg, 1993; Rempel, 1985).

In addition to generating social capital, having children is also suggested to reduce the uncertainty in people's lives (Friedman, Hechter, & Kanazawa, 1994). Some young people face challenges in terms of access to education and employment, making their futures seem unclear or uncertain. Having children, as mentioned before, is seen as a way to reach the status of adult. And children are expected to provide connections and networks that might not be obtained otherwise. Reducing uncertainty, then, may help to explain the inverse relationship between fertility and social class. Those who hold the highest-status occupations and earn the highest salaries are the ones with the lowest fertility and the ones who are most likely to be voluntarily childless (Ramu & Tavuchis, 1986). These are also the people whose lives hold less uncertainty.

Some family theorists argue that children are more valuable today than ever before. In a society characterized as individual-istic, connections to others have taken on greater salience. We have reached a stage, according to Beck and Beck-Gernsheim, where

> Traditional bonds play only a minor role and the love between men and women has likewise proved vulnerable and prone to failure. What remains is the child. It promises a tie which is more elemental, profound and durable than any other in this society. The more other relationships become interchangeable and revocable, the child can become the focus of new hope—it is the ultimate guarantee of permanence, providing an anchor for one's life. (1995: 73)

Delayed Childbearing

Whatever the value of children, one thing is perfectly clear: women are postponing having them. In a recent study comparing fertility data from 1970 through the mid-1990s, Martin (2002) found that the average age at first birth has risen almost 2.5 years. In the years from 1970 to 1974, women were, on average, 22.6 years old when they gave birth for the first time. By the period of 1990–1994, the average age had risen to 25.1. This study also points out that age at first birth is strongly correlated with women's levels of education. In the most recent time period studied, the average age at first birth for women with a high school degree was 23.7, 29 for women with a bachelor's degree, and 31.9 for women holding a master's degree. This delay in family formation affects women and families in a number of ways.

FACT OR FICTION?

The majority of women having children later in life are doing so as single women.

Although older people face difficulties having a child, they can bring additional resources to childrearing. This is because older parents are more likely to be educated and working in jobs that bring higher salaries.

Consequences of Postponing Childbearing

For women who are postponing having children well into their thirties or forties, there is a chance that they will not be successful. Despite the visibility of celebrities such as Jane Seymour, Mimi Rogers, Madonna, and Susan Sarandon, who have had children in their forties, many women are not able to conceive without the help of reproductive technologies such as in vitro fertilization (IVF). A report using data from the Centers for Disease Control and Prevention indicates that the costs of fertility treatments are in the thousands of dollars (some insurance companies cover partial costs) and that a relatively low percentage of these treatments (around 19 percent) result in a successful birth (Longman,

1998). Because of the increased difficulties associated with later pregnancy and births, older first-time parents may not be able to achieve their ultimate desired family size.

Although most of the attention on **delayed childbearing** has been focused on women, a recent study by researchers at New York University and Israel's Ministry of Defense suggests that we pay attention to men's reproductive decline as well. Findings from this study were that men who fathered children between the ages of 45 and 49 were twice as likely as those under 25 to have children who developed schizophrenia. Men over 50 were three times as likely. Although this research has yet to be replicated, it does raise the issue of how fertility is more than just an issue about women's bodies.

Alongside these potential costs, however, are some benefits for the parents and children. Older parents are more likely to be married, highly educated, and working in professional careers with higher incomes (Bachu, 1993). This tendency may result in more secure parenting styles, and it certainly provides the opportunity for children to have better access to material resources (Martin, 2002). Some parents may find it a challenge interacting with the parents of their children's friends because of the age difference. And one study done by an economist who had his third child at the age of 52 found that children of older parents show heightened concerns about the health of their parents (Carnoy, 1990). Because the number of older parents continues to rise, this challenge may be lessening. In addition, parenting support groups are forming in many communities as a way to connect older parents.

Delayed childbearing is also associated with another trend, the increasing number of people who do not parent. Fecundity declines with age, and some women and men who delay childbearing long enough may become infertile. Others who delay may discover that they enjoy the freedom that a life without children can have. Still others never intend to have children. The experiences of going through life without children are related to the reasons that adult do not have children.

| FICTION

Most older parents are married.

Remaining Childless or Childfree

The recent trends of delayed childbearing, having fewer children, and remaining childfree are receiving considerable attention by scholars and from the popular press. In the United States, we are having children at a rate below replacement value, and about 20 percent of women between the ages of 40 and 44 have not had children and are not expected to (see Figure 8.3). Is there reason for alarm? If we look at census data from the past one hundred years, we find that the current trends are not unique (Morgan, 1991). For women born in the middle of the nineteenth century, close to 15 percent remained childless. The percentage of women who did not have children increased somewhat steadily over the next several decades, reaching a peak for those women born in the 1901–1910 cohort. These are women who were in their childbearing years during the Great Depression, and about 25 percent of these women remained childless. Following this period, rates of childlessness began to fall sharply, and by the time we reach the birth cohort of 1925–1935 we find that closer to 10 percent remained childless. The childbearing years for these women were the 1950s, which have been characterized as the baby boom, or the years of the highest fertility rates for women in the twentieth century. Since that time, childlessness is again on the rise. Demographers are predicting that we will soon match the peak observed earlier in the last century (Rindfuss, Morgan, & Swicegood, 1988).

One of the reasons for the fluctuations in rates of childlessness is that these rates correspond to the rates of marriage. The periods in which significant numbers of people remained single throughout adulthood also had higher rates of childlessness. This finding fits with more contemporary research indicating that marriage is still one of the best predictors of whether or not a woman will have a child (Heaton, Jacobson, & Holland, 1999). However, Morgan's (1991) analysis of census data at the state level shows that rates of childlessness even among those who marry have followed the patterns shown above and that the actual rates of childlessness are not much lower once the "never-married" are taken into account.

Reasons for Being Childless/Childfree

It is pretty clear that remaining childless, like becoming a parent, is the outcome of a process, and one that is quite variable (Matthews & Martin Matthews, 1986; Rindfuss, Morgan, & Swicegood, 1988). Some women may have early desires to remain childless but then either change their minds and/or become pregnant by chance. Others may desire children but postpone having them initially. During this postponement period, women may develop interests (career or otherwise) that are not conducive to raising children. Still others may delay long enough that when they do try to get pregnant, they cannot. As a result, asking women *why* they are childless will depend on where they are in the process. A recent study of women who have not had children summarizes the differences in reasons for being without children as choice, chance, or happenstance (Cain, 2001). And, depending on whether women are happy with their decision/circumstance, the term used to describe women without children can be either **childfree** or **childless**.

Research among women who are post-childbearing age (55 years old+) indicates a variety of reasons for not having children. The majority of women (72 percent) in a recent Canadian study (Connidis & McMullin, 1999) reported that they were childless by circumstances other than "choice." Married women's circumstances leading to childlessness were primarily physical problems, age, and fate. Among the women who said they were childless by choice (28 percent), the reasons varied by whether or not the women were married. Married women gave reasons such as their spouses' preferences, practical concerns, and altruism (concern over their role in overpopulation). Single women who

FIGURE 8.3   Percentage Childless, Women Aged 40–44

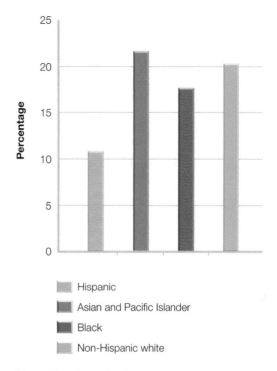

Note: Hispanics can be of any race.
Source: Bachu and O'Connell (2001). Adapted from Table 1.

remained childless by choice focused on reasons of altruism as well, but also mentioned fate and the desire for self-actualization (wanting to be free to do things for themselves).

FACT OR FICTION?

People who do not have children are socially disadvantaged compared to those who have children.

Consequences of Childlessness

One of the reasons for people having children is that they provide social capital, the means for social integration that can provide benefits for parents. Does this mean that childless

Couples who choose not to have children often develop other interests more fully.

adults are less well integrated in their families and communities? There is some evidence that childless married couples do have fewer visits with family members and receive less help from them (Rempel, 1985). However, this doesn't mean that the childless are without support. Ishii-Kuntz and Seccombe (1989) find that married couples without children develop strong marital ties and rely on each other rather than on family and friends. Among older adults, childless persons are no less likely than those with children to have someone to confide in or to provide financial or emotional support (Connidis & McMullin, 1994). However, who they confide in is more likely to come from networks of friends and other relatives.

An intriguing finding regarding childlessness among the older population is that perceived advantages and disadvantages do not always coincide with actual experiences. For example, Connidis and McMullin (1999) find that older adults perceive the primary advantages for being without children in later life to include financial wealth, fewer worries, and greater freedom. In fact, those who were childless in this study did have a lifetime earnings advantage over those who had children. However, perceptions did not always corre-

late with actual experiences. The most commonly reported ideas about the costs of childlessness are loneliness and lack of companionship. However, those who perceive these disadvantages are not more likely to be lonely or report less help from others than are those who do not expect these consequences. The researchers suggest that older people may be more likely to claim these as disadvantages because of the general views in our culture regarding childbearing (pronatalist views), not because of a real difference in well-being among the childless. Recent research on younger women who are currently mothering finds support for these common views in society about what having children means for adults. When asked how they would feel if they never had children, the most common responses given by both middle- and working-class mothers were empty/incomplete, sad/lonely, and less self-worth/sense of failure (McMahon, 1995).

As mentioned above, the key to the consequences of being without children is whether or not it is a desired situation. Those who have a strong interest in having children but are unable to do so are viewed as child*less,* and the consequences may include feeling incomplete or dissatisfied. However, this does not mean that involuntarily childless adults are doomed to lives of misery. New identities, formed around relationships with other family members and friends, can be constructed. Others, who do not have the intention or desire to have and raise children, are the child*free.* Although still facing a stigma in a relatively pronatalist society, they negotiate networks of friends and families that can be as supportive as those created by adults with children.

FICTION

Research findings suggest that people without children establish networks of family and friends that provide support.

Having Children Outside of Marriage

In earlier chapters, we described a number of social trends about family formation. For example, we saw that the age at marriage has increased over time, and this reflects the longer period of time that women and men are spending in educational and occupational pursuits. We also noted a significant increase in the incidence of cohabitation, as a precursor to marriage or as an alternative to marriage. One of the consequences of these trends is the increase in the "risk" or "opportunity" of having children outside of marriage. Data reported in the National Vital Statistic Reports (Ventura & Bachrach, 2000) indicate that the number of births to unmarried women increased from 1.17 to 1.3 million over the decade of the 1990s. However, this increase, which averaged about 1 percent per year, represents a slowdown from the 1980s, when the average annual increase was nearly 6 percent. Another way of looking at the trend in births to unmarried women is presented in Figure 8.4. Here we see the percentage of all births in a single year that were to unmarried women. The trend line shows a steady increase over most of the period until 1994. At that time, the percentage actually dropped, and since that time there has been little change. One-third of all births are to unmarried women.

Variations in Nonmarital Childbearing

Who are these women who are having children outside of marriage? In Table 8.2, we see that the percentage of never-married women who have at least one child has increased. In 1990, 18.1 percent of never-married women had had a child, and by 2000 that percentage had gone up to 23.3 percent (or just over one in five never-married women). Education shows an inverse relationship to nonmarital fertility (Bumpass & Lu, 2000). With higher levels of education, women are more aware of, and have better access to, contraception, which allows them to plan their childbearing. Higher educations are also related to occupational pursuits, which in turn are related to delayed childbearing (Martin, 2000). On the other hand,

FIGURE 8.4 Percentage of Births to Unmarried Women, 1940–1999

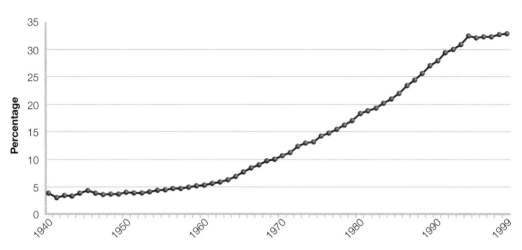

Source: Ventura and Bachrach (2000). Adapted from Table 1, page 17.

TABLE 8.2	Characteristics of Never-Married Mothers, 1990–2000: Percentage of Women in Each Group Who Have Had a Child		
	1990 (%)	1995 (%)	2000 (%)
Total	18.1	20.9	23.3
EDUCATIONAL ATTAINMENT			
Less than high school	18.3	18.7	19.1
High school, 4 years	26.5	37.1	40.5
Some college	14.0	16.9	21.7
Bachelor's degree+	7.0	6.8	8.2
LABOR FORCE STATUS			
In labor force	14.9	18.3	24.2
Not in labor force	25.5	26.6	21.2
OCCUPATION			
Managerial and professional	8.9	10.2	14.1
Other	14.8	18.9	26.7
RACE/ETHNICITY[a]			
White non-Hispanic			14.8
Black			44.8
Asian/Pacific Islander			10.6
Hispanic (any race)			32.9

[a]Race and ethnicity were measured differently in 1990 and 1995, making comparisons unreliable.
Source: U.S. Census Bureau (http://www.census.gov/population/socdemo/fertility/tabH4.pdf). Internet release date: Oct. 18, 2001; accessed Jan. 24, 2002.

women with lower expectations regarding education and occupation are more likely to consider having a child outside of marriage as an acceptable option (Abrahamse, Morrison, & Waite, 1988).

Race and ethnicity are also associated with the likelihood of **nonmarital childbearing.** Part of this relationship has to do with socioeconomic status (Bumpass & McLanahan, 1989; Trent & Crowder, 1997). Access to financially secure marriage partners is more limited for some, especially for black women. There is also evidence of greater acceptance of nonmarital childbearing among blacks and Hispanics (Oropesa, 1996; Trent & South, 1992).

Other factors related to nonmarital childbearing are cohabitation and childhood family structure. Close to 40 percent of non-marital births are to cohabiting couples (Bumpass & Lu, 2000), and cohabitation is offered as a primary cause of the increases in nonmarital childbearing over the last twenty years (Raley, 2001). In terms of family structure, women who spent some time in a single-parent family while growing up are more likely to have a child without being married (McLanahan & Sandefur, 1994). Possible explanations include the intergenerational transmission of values (greater acceptance of single parenting) as well as being at greater risk for teen pregnancy (due to less supervision of adolescents' behavior).

Given the possible consequences of single parenting for both parents and children, why would women have children outside of marriage? Evidence suggests that the majority of women desire marriage (see

Chapter 6) and believe that the best situation for having children is as part of a good marriage. At the same time, the availability of "eligible" marriage partners is variable across different groups. Moreover, lesbians who want children are legally restricted from being married. Therefore, many women with strong desires to be mothers face a difficult challenge: How can I have children when marriage doesn't appear to be an option for me? In this section, we'll take a look at a variety of situations in which single women are having children.

Single Mothers by Choice

In 1992, Vice President Dan Quayle made a speech arguing that single women having children outside of marriage was a major social problem threatening families in the United States. He used the case of a fictional character on television, Murphy Brown, to build his argument. He condemned "Murphy" for choosing to parent alone and even made an analogy between her behavior and the "lawless social anarchy" that led to the riots in Los Angeles in 1992 (Sidel, 1996). Although Mr. Quayle has changed his rhetoric a bit (he now focuses on the rights of fathers instead of the behavior of women), he still sees "extraordinary turmoil and dysfunction in families today" (Quayle, 2001). There has been considerable debate about the issue of single parenting, especially regarding those who begin their lives as parents without a partner. The concern is usually centered on the effects of single parenting on children (McLanahan & Sandefur, 1994). Others have picked up on Quayle's argument about the importance of fathers, arguing that single-mother families challenge the true meaning of the family (Blankenhorn, 1995; Whitehead, 1993). Despite the public concern, the reality is that increasing numbers of women are making a conscious decision to have children without being married.

Middle-Class Single Mothers Middle-class women who desire children but do not see a "good man" on the horizon have joined forces in a group called "**Single Mothers by Choice** (SMC)." Jane Bock (2000), of the University of Wisconsin–Green Bay, interviewed women in SMC to explore the ways in which they approached becoming mothers in a society that stigmatizes single mothers. She finds that these middle-class women believe they have a right to become mothers on their own. They justify their position by comparing themselves to "other" single mothers such as teen mothers or mothers on welfare, arguing they are prepared for motherhood because of the following factors:

* *Age.* Unlike teenagers, these women, who are in their thirties and forties, believe they are old enough to know what they are doing. At the same time, they are reaching a critical point in their lives where their ability to have a child is declining.

* *Fiscal capability.* Most of these women spent their twenties and thirties focused on careers and had managed to situate themselves quite well financially.

* *Responsibility.* As middle-class women, they understand basic issues of survival and how to maintain a safe, secure environment for themselves and a child. They believe that marrying "just to be married" would not be a responsible act for either themselves or their children.

* *Emotional maturity.* Being a mother requires self-confidence and a strong sense of morality. Their age, education, and social class position bring relative emotional maturity to these women.

Constructing their identities as "good mothers" depends on their own characteristics as well as a relative comparison to other single mothers. By establishing their place in a "hierarchy of mothers," they pass on the stigma of nonmarital childbearing to others while justifying their own decisions.

Working-Class and Poor Single Mothers
Studies of women who are working class or poor show that they also give serious consideration to marriage. Most of these women desire a good relationship, but they want to make sure they make smart decisions about who they partner with. Poor women of all racial and ethnic groups find fewer acceptable partners in their neighborhoods; therefore, marriage is seen as risky. While waiting for Mr. Right, women face biological issues in their fertility. Kathryn Edin's (2000a, 2000b) research in poor communities in nine Philadelphia metropolitan neighborhoods suggests that the justifications for single motherhood focus on (1) affordability, (2) respectability, (3) trust, and (4) control.

Poor women live in neighborhoods where male unemployment may be three to four times the national average, making the pool of "eligible" marriage partners somewhat less attractive. Among the women in Edin's study, marriage included a prerequisite of economic stability. Being married to someone who is economically stable can bring status in poorer communities. However, the instability of the financial situation of men can make single parenting relatively more *affordable*. Edin found that lack of *respectability* for men kept poor women from marrying them (or at least they deferred marriage). Many of the black, Puerto Rican, and white poor women in her study suggested that they had a lack of *trust* for the men in their community. They worried about these men in terms of their sexual fidelity, their ability to handle money, and their ability to parent. In precarious environments, where jobs are insecure, women worried that men would not stick around and commit to their families. Finally, the women in Philadelphia suggested that being a single parent brought a sense of *control* to their lives. They enjoyed feeling as though there was some-

thing in their lives that was not subject to be taken away (by men or by their employers). The women in this study desired marriage, but marriage to them was about a partnership, where both partners were equally committed to providing economic and emotional support. In the challenging neighborhoods of many poor communities across the country, this combination is difficult to find.

Although the percentage of women having children outside of marriage is increasing among all age, class, and racial/ethnic groups, it is still more likely to occur for those who grew up in single-parent households, particularly households that were poor. Thus, the women studied in Edin's project are likely to see their children also become single parents. Wu and Martinson (1993) explored three possible reasons for this intergenerational transmission of family formation. One explanation is that girls who grew up in single-parent households are socialized to see these family structures as acceptable or desirable. Another idea is that households with only one parent are less likely to exercise control over their children's behavior than are households with two parents, increasing the odds of a pregnancy for their daughters. However, these researchers find that neither of these explanations adequately explains the relationship among family structure, poverty, and nonmarital childbearing. Instead, they argue that for black and Hispanic women, experiencing disruptions early in life (parental divorce, geographic mobility) was more closely associated with childbearing outside of marriage. At the same time, when childbearing occurs outside of marriage, a network of support embedded in African American neighborhoods and families can help support unmarried mothers (Hill, 1999).

Racial/Ethnic Single Mothers The data we've presented show that single black and Hispanic women are more likely to have children than are white or Asian/Pacific Islander single women. There have been several explanations given for these differences. One concerns the social characteristics of different racial/ethnic groups. Because black and Hispanic women tend to have lower levels of education and be economically disadvantaged relative to other groups, they are more likely to make different decisions regarding fertility behavior. Like the research on poor women just mentioned, these women make decisions based on the availability of men and their economic stability. A study in inner-city Chicago found that when fathers are employed, they are twice as likely to marry the mother of their first child (Testa, Astone, Krogh, & Neckerman, 1989).

Another explanation, somewhat more controversial, is that patterns of childbearing outside of marriage have led to a decline in the value placed on marriage among some racial/ethnic groups. In one study of black, white, Mexican, and Puerto Rican women and men, Renata Forste and Marta Tienda (1996: 124) found that "black respondents were more likely to emphasize the declining value of marriage and their tolerance for out-of-wedlock childbearing, while Hispanic and white parents underscored the role of economic distress in male abandonment of families." What is not clear from research to date is whether this difference reflects a "racial subculture or a temporary adaptation to chronic and extreme deprivation."

The evidence does suggest that in terms of racial/ethnic variations in fertility, a variety of explanations are possible and that singles having children is not a "black–white" issue. Rather, it reflects a combination of factors. First, we live in a pronatalist society. Most Americans want children and state that they think the best situation involves marriage. A study comparing 51 single mothers to 51 demographically similar married mothers found no differences in the motivation to mother (Seigel, 1995). Second, we live in a society where women expect more-egalitarian relationships from marriage. In the study

just mentioned, the researcher found that the difference between married and single mothers was in how they viewed relationships with men. Single mothers were more "ambivalent" and also less willing to accept compromises in their relationships. Third, we've also seen in the last two chapters that economic stability, as a prerequisite for marriage, is an important goal. As long as the ability to achieve all of these things simultaneously varies across the population, we can expect to see variations in family formation patterns, including the existence of single-parent households.

| **FACT OR FICTION?**

There has been a decline in the number of teens giving birth over the last several decades.

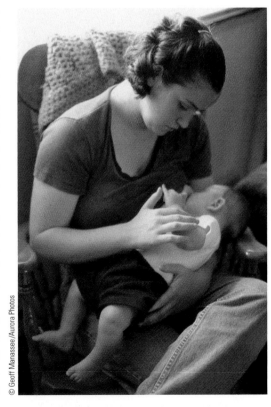

Having children outside of marriage captures public attention, especially when the mothers are teens.

FIGURE 8.5 Percentage of Never-Married Teens (Aged 15–19) Who Have Had a Child, 1998

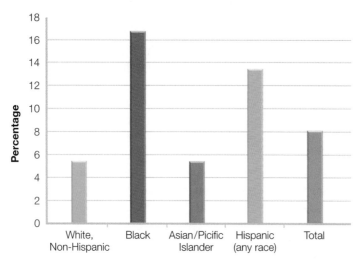

Source: U.S. Census Bureau, Table 1. "Distribution of Women by Number of Children Ever Born, by Race, Age, and Marital Status." Internet release date: October 24, 2000. http://www.census.gov/population/socdemo/fertility

Teen Mothers

About 10 percent of 15–19-year-old women become pregnant each year in the United States (Alan Guttmacher Institute, 1999). Of these pregnancies, close to two-thirds end in a birth (about one-third end in abortion). (For variations in rates by race/ethnicity, see Figure 8.5.) However, many observers are surprised to find that teen birthrates are declining. Between 1991 and 2001, birthrates for 18–19-year-old women were down 20 percent, and the birthrates for 15–17-year-old women were down 35 percent (Martin, Park, & Sutton, 2002). These birthrates are the lowest they've been in over 50 years (U.S. National Center for Health Statistics, 2000). So what is behind the concern? An increasing percentage of first births to teens (age 15 to 19) are to those who are not married (Bachu, 1999). In the early 1930s, 14.5 percent of the teens having their first child were not married. This figure increased slightly to about 16 percent by the early 1950s. After 1960, the numbers went up dramatically so that by 1975 one-third of the first births

among teens were to unmarried women, and by 1995 the rate was almost three-quarters. An additional 14 percent of teens conceived their first child and subsequently married. The result is that close to 90 percent of women who have a first birth in their teen years are conceiving outside of marriage.

| FACT

According to the Alan Guttmacher Institute, the number of teens giving birth is lower today than it has been in the last fifty years.

The heightened concern also reflects the fact that two people may be negatively affected. Some of the teen mothers themselves are children, whose lives are dramatically altered by the experience of having and rearing children. Reports are that teen mothers are less likely to complete their schooling, will be employed in jobs that bring lower incomes, and are less likely to be in enduring marriages (those that do not end in divorce).

These experiences, in turn, can negatively affect the well-being of their child.

Recent research challenges the argument that teen pregnancy itself is the primary cause of women's subsequent economic position. Kristin Luker (1996) argues that those women who are the most likely to be teen parents are also those who would have done poorly in school and in the labor market even if they had delayed parenting. An intriguing study that attempted to test this idea compared teen mothers to their sisters who had not become teen parents (Hoffman, Foster, & Furstenberg, Jr., 1993). The assumption is that both of these young women would have experienced similar situations in terms of structural opportunities as well as similar socialization experiences. These researchers find that when controlling for the background characteristics of these women, the effects of teenage childbearing on the mothers themselves are not as severe as others have suggested, but they still remain. Teenage mothers are less likely to complete high school, are at risk of having more children than are other women, and are disadvantaged economically.

Likelihood of Marrying After Conceiving Premaritally Premarital or out-of-marriage childbirth is of concern primarily because it affects the life experiences of children. Children growing up in single-parent households, particularly households headed by women, are at a disadvantage in terms of access to economic resources. How likely is it that women who conceived prior to being married ever get married? About 10 percent of women who conceived their first birth in 1990–1994 married prior to the birth of that child (Bachu, 1999). Census data that follow women several years out suggest that about 23 percent of these women will marry within five years. This is a significant decrease from earlier decades. Between 1930 and 1970, at least half of all women who conceived prior to marriage subsequently married (within

five years). The likelihood of eventually marrying is also related to characteristics of the mother. Those who are more likely to marry prior to the birth of their child are women in their thirties, high school graduates, and non-Hispanic white women. Another factor in this scenario is cohabitation. Using national longitudinal data, Manning and Landale (1996) found that at least for white women, cohabitation hastened marriage. It may be for these couples that marriage was planned and the pregnancy just moved the date up. Or, if marriage wasn't necessarily planned, a pregnancy might have encouraged it. These researchers also found that the relationship between cohabitation and premarital pregnancy and birth was not a factor for non-Hispanic black women or Puerto Rican women. There may be differing explanations for these nonfindings. For black women, we have already mentioned that they are less likely to cohabit and that the availability of suitable marriage partners among black men is restricted. The argument for Puerto Rican women refers more to cultural beliefs and practices that do not stigmatize women for childbearing outside of marriage (Oropesa, 1996).

FACT OR FICTION?

There has been a greater increase in the rates of single-father households than of single-mother households.

Single Fathers

The majority of single parents are women, and the number of single mothers is on the rise. However, the number of single parents who are men has also been increasing. In 1970, there were 393,000 single-father families. In the 2000 census, the number had risen to 2,000,000, a 500-percent increase (compared to the 300-percent increase for

TABLE 8.3	Single-Parent Households as a Percentage of All Families, 1970–2000					
	WHITE		BLACK		HISPANIC	
	MAINTAINED BY		MAINTAINED BY		MAINTAINED BY	
	MOTHER (%)	FATHER (%)	MOTHER (%)	FATHER (%)	MOTHER (%)	FATHER (%)
2000	20.7	5	55	6	28.4	5.7
1990	18.8	3.8	56	4.3	29	4
1980	15	2	49	3.2	24	1.9
1970	8.9	1.2	33	2.6	N/A	N/A

Note: Hispanics can be of any race.
Source: http://www.census/gov/population/socdemo/hh-fam/tabFM-2.txt

single-mother families). As we can see in Table 8.3, increases have occurred for single parents across racial and ethnic groups.

The majority of men become single fathers as a result of ending a relationship with the child/children's mother (66 percent), with most becoming divorced (see Figure 8.6).

Still, one-third of men become primary parents without ever having been married. Garasky and Meyer (1996) find that the situation of single fathers is related to race. Compared to white fathers, African American fathers are less likely to have been married to the mother of their child/children. Recent

FIGURE 8.6 Percentage of Single Parents in Each of the Marital Status Categories

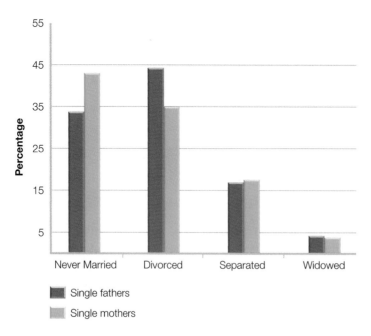

Source: http://www.census.gov/populationsocdemo/hh-fam/p20-537/2000/tabFG5.pdf

Although still a minority of single parents, fathers are increasingly likely to take sole responsibility for their children.

studies suggest a variety of reasons for men gaining custody of their children (Grief, 1995; Hamer & Marchioro, 2002; Roy, 1999). These include (1) mothers who are unable to financially support the child/children, (2) mothers who are found to be physically and/or psychologically unfit to have custody, (3) mothers who do not want the full-time responsibility of caring for the child/children, (4) fathers who want to remain actively involved in their children's lives, and (5) children requesting that they live with their fathers after the divorce or separation of their parents.

FACT

Rates have risen more for single-father households, but recall from Chapter 2 that rates can be deceiving. Single-mother households still represent the overwhelming majority of single-parent families.

Making the transition from shared to single parenting presents challenges to fathers. In a culture where it is widely accepted that mothers are primarily responsible for the nurturing, physical care, and emotional development of children, men find it difficult to be viewed by others as legitimate parents (Hamer & Marchioro, 2002). However, a comparison of single fathers and single mothers suggests that both do equally well in terms of the primary parenting behaviors of housekeeping, child rearing, and nurturing. Single mothers and single fathers are also similar in terms of their own perceptions of their abilities to manage family and work responsibilities (Heath and Orthner, 1999).

Diversity Among Single Fathers Because men earn more than women, on average, we might expect that they are better able to care for their children financially than single mothers are. However, there is considerable diversity among single fathers, and many experience financial as well as social challenges. African American single fathers are particularly at risk. While 10 percent of white single fathers are below the poverty line, 24 percent of African American single fathers fall into this category. African American fathers are also more likely to hold jobs with lower incomes on average, and jobs that are less likely to come with insurance and other benefits (Chadwick & Heaton, 1999).

The reasons that low-income fathers become custodial parents are similar to those of other fathers. However, the way in which low-income fathers negotiate their parenting responsibilities is necessarily different. In contrast to middle-income custodial fathers, who are more likely to use day cares and sitters for their children, lower-income fathers are more likely to use relatives to help with child care (Hamer & Marchioro, 2002). Although part of the reason for using kin is the economic situation of lower-income fathers, Hamer and Marchioro suggest that income is not the only reason. The African American custodial fathers who made up their sample relied on kin who were not in any better economic shape than the fathers. Still, the kin networks helped fathers to manage their parenting and work responsibilities and more generally to come to grips with the transition to this new role of primary parent. Other studies have shown that African American custodial mothers also rely on kin groups to get by (Seccombe, 1999), making low-income African American single fathers more like African American single mothers than like middle-class white single fathers.

Lower-income single fathers recognize that money is not the most important factor in having and raising their children. One unmarried father in Chicago, who wanted to have an active role in raising his kids, put it this way:

> To me, that's the easy way out: give [the kids] some money and then run off. The money doesn't comfort them at night. They can't say "Hey, Dollar Bill, I had a nightmare last night" and expect the Dollar Bill to rock them and hold them. Money is there because it is a necessity. But if you give a child love and attention, money is the last thing they are going to look for (quoted in Roy, 1999: 432).

Gay and Lesbian Parenting

Family law in the United States typically recognizes three types of legal parents: (1) those who have a child biologically, (2) those who adopt the legal or biological child of their married partner, or (3) men who are living with their wife who has a biological child (Dalton & Bielby, 2000). Lesbian and gay couples are at a disadvantage when it comes to parenting. While lesbians are able to biologically reproduce through donor insemination (and therefore are recognized by law as a parent), their partners cannot be legally related to the child without adoption. Second-parent adoptions for gay and lesbian couples are not possible in some states, and are certainly a challenge in all states. (Maps showing state restrictions/opportunities for adoption or second-parent adoption by gay and lesbian adults can be found on the National Gay and Lesbian Task Force web site [http://www.ngltf.org].)

These legal challenges are also accompanied by other challenges that gays and les-

Michael Galluccio and his partner Jon Holden hold their jointly adopted children. The couple set a state precedent when they jointly adopted in 1997 in New Jersey.

bians face in their communities. Societal norms about parenting are similar to the legal definitions. Parenting is seen as something done by a woman and her husband. We know how to treat married couples that are expecting a child, and we have elaborate rituals to celebrate it. And for those who need some guidance, a long history of expert advice gives expecting mothers help on how to be a "good mother" (Grant, 1998). These self-help books construct a rather polarized version of parenting, with mothers and fathers taking on very different roles, although both are seen as necessary for having and raising a child. Even without the help of expert advice, heterosexual couples take on rather polarized roles in childbearing and child rearing. Susan Walzer's (1998) recent study of heterosexual couples' transition to new parenthood found that even among those who claimed they wanted to balance child-care responsibilities, there was a "channeling" toward gender-specific parenting roles by cultural imagery, family members, and friends.

Because there are no taken-for-granted assumptions about gay and lesbian parenting, the definitions and boundaries of parenthood must be consciously thought through and continually negotiated (Dunne, 2000; Weston, 1991). Many family researchers suggest this may not be a bad thing. By having to work through each step of the process, couples can articulate their feelings and come to more shared understandings. Couples must also negotiate their relationships as parents with their family, friends, co-workers, and other community members. We will return in the next chapter to the issue of gay and lesbian parents and actual parenting practices. Now we will turn to a process that is increasing among a variety of people, not just gays and lesbians: adoption.

Adoption

Traditional ideology about families includes the assumption that a "real" family is one based on blood ties. The result of such ideology is a stigma for families with adopted children as being "second best" and adoption as "second choice" (Wegar, 2000). Both parents and children feel the effects of this negative labeling. Parents face automatic assumptions by others that they must be infertile. Children may have to face feelings about having been rejected by their biological parents. In fact, trying to counteract such stigma has been stated as an important motivator for adopted children seeking out their biological parents (March, 1995). On a more positive note, it appears that there has been a reduction in the social stigma attached to adoption. The greater acceptance of adoptive families as "normative" comes with a greater acceptance of diversity in family forms in general. There has also been greater public attention given to adoption because women who delay childbearing are running into issues of infertility. Costs associated with infertility treatments along with the time and

stress involved have led many people to seek alternatives. As more people seek out adoption, and more attention is given to it, adoption becomes another viable option for family formation.

While the demand for children to adopt has been increasing, the number of children (particularly infants) available for adoption is declining. One reason for the drop in available infants is effective birth control, which reduces the number of unplanned pregnancies. In addition, single women, who might previously have opted for adoption after an unplanned pregnancy, are now more likely to keep their children. This situation has resulted in increased diversity in adoption, which now commonly involves transracial/transethnic and international adoptions.

Types of Adoption

Like the regulation of many family matters (e.g., marriage and divorce), legal adoptions are handled at the state level, meaning that they vary across the country. In general, there are two types of adoption. **Public adoptions** are those in which children who are in the public child welfare system are placed in permanent homes by either a government-operated agency or by a private agency that is contracted by a public agency to place these children. **Private adoptions** include the placement of children in nonrelative homes through the services of a nonprofit or for-profit agency that is licensed by the state. In what is also called an *independent adoption,* children are placed in homes by their birth parents through a certified facilitator (who may be a doctor, clergy member, or attorney). Private adoptions represent the majority of all adoptions, with one of the reasons being that prospective parents often want young children, particularly infants. Children available through the public child welfare system tend to be older. In Table 8.4 we see that only 2 percent of the available children in 2000 were under the age of one year. Sixty-five

TABLE 8.4 | Adoption Statistics

GENERAL ADOPTION STATISTICS

Number of children in the United States waiting to be adopted (3/31/2000)	134,000
Number of children adopted from the public foster care system in 1999	46,000

AGES OF:	WAITING CHILDREN	ADOPTED CHILDREN
Under 1 year	3,084 (2%)	835 (2%)
1–5 years	44,648 (33%)	20,758 (45%)
6–10 years	47,785 (36%)	16,467 (36%)
11–15 years	33,654 (25%)	6,999 (15%)
16–18 years	4,829 (4%)	896 (2%)

GENDER OF:	WAITING CHILDREN	CHILDREN ADOPTED
Male	61,734 (52%)	22,961 (50%)
Female	22,961 (50%)	23,039 (50%)

RACE/ETHNICITY OF:	WAITING CHILDREN	CHILDREN ADOPTED
Black	53,240 (45%)	19,979 (43%)
White (Non-Hispanic)	37,306 (32%)	18,152 (39%)
Hispanic	14,438 (12%)	6,734 (15%)
American Indian/Alaskan Native	1,337 (1%)	496 (1%)
Asian/Pacific Islander	917 (1%)	639 (1%)
Unknown	10,763 (9%)	

Source: Adoption and Foster Care Analysis and Reporting System (AFCARS). Data submitted for the reporting period 10/1/99 through 3/31/00. Available online: http://acf.dhhs.gov/programs/cb/publications/afcars/apr20

percent were at least six years old. Also noted in the table is the racial/ethnic composition of this group of children. Whereas African Americans make up about 12 percent of the U.S. population, they make up 45 percent of children available for adoption. This has proven to be a topic of considerable debate among welfare providers in recent years.

Transracial Adoption

The disproportionate number of African American children in the public welfare system has prompted some movement to increase **transracial adoption,** or the placement of children in families of a different race/ethnicity. The Multiethnic Placement Act, passed in 1994, makes it illegal for agencies to deny transracial adoption. Behind the passage of this act was the concern that without such placements, ethnic minority children would be left permanently in the foster care system (something that is meant to be temporary). Research also indicates that children's development in transracial families, on the whole, is not hindered by such adoptions (Simon & Alstein, 2000). However, there is also unease regarding transracial adoption. For example, the National Association of Black Social Workers opposes interracial adoption because it alienates children from their own culture or ethnic community. When children are immersed in an ethnic culture different from their own, they may find they are expected to suppress their ethnic identities. An example of the anxiety caused by transracial adoption for children can be seen in the Family Diversity box on page 352.

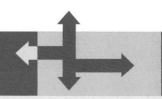

It was just last summer that I really came to understand how many things my extended family members and I experience differently from one another. My childhood expectations were the same as any kid's. I wanted my extended family to love me, to be happy to see me at family occasions, and to let me have the cookies when mom and dad wouldn't. As I have grown up, I have developed, as we all do, more realistic expectations of myself and my family.

My mom's side of the family lives in Chicago, my dad's side in New York. I live in California. We see each other one to three times a year. Before I go any further, let me tell you that I was adopted at birth, transracially. All of my extended family is white and I am black. Last summer, my aunt and I got into a discussion about a particular celebrity's double-murder court trial (you know . . . what's his name?). So, we were discussing the trial and I brought up the racial issue. Immediately, my aunt asked, "Why would you think race is part of this?" I tried to explain my point of view. I was shocked when I suddenly understood what I had never understood in my entire life: my aunt, who loves me with all of her heart, found it impossible to see that my experience and views of the world differed from hers because we are different races. She seemed to be shocked that I viewed the world as a person of color. She seemed surprised at what I was saying. She seemed

not to understand why I was getting so distressed. Most of all, she seemed not to understand why the trial mattered so much to me.

Why did this conversation matter so much to me? It was about two things. The first was about her inability to understand that if an African American person and a Caucasian person are involved, race is a component that matters. The other was her inability to realize that my opinion was shaped by my experiences as an African American woman.

Since that conversation last summer, I have spent a lot of time thinking about my frustration about it. In my opinion, people of color are always conscious of race. White people may not be. People of color see things from a perspective shaped by their experiences; white people do as well. The important thing to understand here is that the two are always different. In this society, it is not possible for them not to be. This difference is not a bad thing, when all points of view have equal value. A variety of viewpoints enriches our lives by creating diversity. But this difference *is* a bad thing when we don't understand that "our" point of view is not the only one. When we're in the majority, it is easier to fool ourselves into believing that our thoughts are universal. When we are in the minority, we are more aware of being different and are bound to be more sensitive about being heard and having our views valued. The gulf between

white and black consciousness was being played out in my own white family. I felt my views were not granted equal value. I know that this inequality was not my aunt's intention, but it is what happened. My aunt thought that we would see things the same because we are family and share a family history. What she couldn't get was the part that was different: my race. She couldn't see me as a member of both my race and my family. It had to be either/or.

As a result, I've learned that if I expect my family to be able to include my racial experiences as part of who I am, I need to help them understand how important this is to me. When they don't recognize the place race holds, it feels like they are excluding the most basic part of me. I need them to be conscious of the ways race affects my life and to understand that if it affects my life, then it affects their lives also, because we are family.

By Liza Steinberg

Source: "Up Close and Personal: Personal Profiles." *Pact: An Adoption Alliance.* http://www.pactadopt.org/profiles/race-family.html. Accessed September 3, 2002. Reprinted with permission.

Critical Thinking

1. Imagine growing up in a family that was of a different race than yours. Do you think you would have been treated differently? How so? Why?

2. Imagine adopting a child of a different race. How would you approach the issue of race with that child?

One way a transracial adoptive family can demonstrate their aware-ness of, and sensitivity to, their children's cultural heritage is to participate in activities honoring that heritage. These five parents walk with their adopted Asian children in an Asian-American festi-val parade.

Many agencies and organizations are working to balance these concerns. The Child Welfare League of America has estab-lished standards of Excellence for Adoption Services that include the following:

* When consistent with the child's best interest, the agency providing adoption services should honor the birth par-ents' request that a family of the same race or ethnic background adopts the child. The child's adoption, however, should not be denied or delayed if the agency is unable to recruit adoptive parents of the child's race or culture and adoptive parents of other cultural or racial groups are available.

* All children deserve to be raised in a family that respects their cultural heri-tage. In any adoption plan the best in-terests of the child should be para-mount. . . . Assessment and prepara-tion of a child for a transracial/transcultural adoption should recognize the importance of cul-ture and race to the child and his or her experiences and identifications. The adoptive family selected should demonstrate an awareness of and sen-sitivity to the cultural resources that may be needed after placement. (Child Welfare League of America, 2000)

International Adoption

Another increasingly popular type of adop-tion is **international adoption**. Children who are citizens of a foreign nation are adopted by U.S. individuals or families and brought to live in the United States. The number of international adoptions has doubled in the last decade. The U.S. State Department reported a total of 16,396 children adopted from other countries in 1999. The most frequent sites of adoption were China (25 percent), Russia (26.5 percent), South Korea (12 percent), and Guatemala (6 percent). International adoptions can be expensive (averaging about $20,000) (Varnis, 2001), and the struggles to maintain children's cultural heritage are as problematic as those for domestic transracial adoptions. Social forces behind the growth in international adoptions are similar to those shaping domestic adoption (increasing infertility) but also include the perception by prospective parents that they are more likely to find a younger child, and to find that child sooner than they would in the United States.

Single-Mother Adoption

We have noted in previous chapters a growing number of single parents (particularly mothers). Most of the rise is due to divorced parents living with their biological children. However, another rising trend is for single women to look to adopt children. Data from the Adoption and Foster Care Analysis Reporting System indicate that this group of adopting parents is different from adopting couples in some important ways. Single women adopted almost a third of the children available through the public child welfare system in 1998. About two-thirds of these women were African American, and 70 percent of the children adopted by single women were African American (Maza, 2002). Similar to married couples, most of these women adopt children of the same racial/ethnic group. As single parents, they are less likely than married couples to adopt siblings or children with mental, physical, or emotional disabilities. However, they are more likely than married couples to adopt older children. Single women play a critical role in the welfare system by offering permanent homes to children who are the most difficult to place (racial/ethnic minority and older children).

Having a Baby: More Than Biology

Whether choosing to become a parent as a married or single person, in a cohabiting or married relationship, or earlier or later in life, the process of having children is a profound interweaving of biology and culture. The biological aspects of pregnancy, birth, and lactation are universal. However, these events are far more than merely biological phenomena. How we conceive children, and how we birth, feed, and raise them, are shaped by important historical, cultural, and structural norms. Let us provide a detailed example—childbirth—that will illustrate that "having a baby" is much more than a natural biological process.

The Social Construction of Childbirth in the United States

Something as seemingly natural as childbirth can take place in wildly different environments with varying norms and expectations, and be a microcosm of the political power structures and authority patterns in society. What may be considered normal, healthy, and appropriate childbirth practices in one culture or historical period may be viewed as dangerous or barbaric in another. Childbirth can serve as an explicit reminder of the ways that our lives are socially constructed. The medical establishment, the economic system, the political culture, and the degree of technological sophistication all play a part in defining the birthing process.

Childbirth Prior to the Nineteenth Century

Until the nineteenth century, doctors were virtually absent during childbirth. Instead, childbirth was considered "women's business" and was attended only by other women: midwives, mothers, sisters, and friends (Wertz & Wertz, 1989). Doctors, virtually all of whom were men, were considered suspect—why would they want to be so intimately involved in birth, and what could they possibly have to offer? Even husbands and partners were excluded. They awaited the news of the birth elsewhere, away from the commotion.

Midwives are women who are trained to help women give birth (Litoff, 1978). Prior to the nineteenth century, this training was informal rather than administered in a formal school setting. Women learned to be midwives by working as apprentices to other midwives, assisting with births until they were skilled enough to go out on their own. They held the philosophy that, generally speaking, childbirth is neither an illness nor a medical event. They believed that almost all women have within them the ability to deliver children. A midwife, along with a mother, sister, and friend, was there to help the woman do what she already knew how to do.

The Medicalization of Childbirth

The nineteenth century began an erosion of confidence in midwives and a growing dependence on male physicians in childbirth. This trend was due to a complex set of forces, many of which had little to do with the safety of birth itself.

As the field of professional medicine began to grow, there were a number of clashes between midwives (and other lay healers) and physicians. A large and diverse group of practitioners engaged in substantial competition over clients. Physicians reasoned that if they could expand into new fields such as delivering babies, they could secure their future (Starr, 1982). They believed that families who came to a doctor for childbirth would likely continue to use that person as their source of medical care.

In order to achieve their professional dominance, physicians began a full-fledged attack against midwives (Sullivan & Weitz, 1988). They claimed that childbirth was inherently dangerous, that it required medical assistance, and that midwives were inadequately trained to deal with the complex nature of delivering babies. As criticism mounted, fewer middle-class or upper middle-class women were attracted to midwifery as an occupation. Doctors then played up the social class and racial differences between themselves and the midwives. Gradually, one's choice of birth attendant was seen as an element of social prestige—having a white, upper-class, male attendant was considered far more prestigious than being attended to by a minority or working-class female attendant. Thus, the **medicalization of childbirth** began.

Meanwhile, America's interest with science and the medical model grew during this period. In her book *In Labor: Women and Power in the Birthplace,* Barbara Katz Rothman (1991) suggests that with the rise of the medical model, physicians gained tremendous status, all but eliminating other health care providers, including midwives. In 1915 the *Boston Medical and Surgical Journal* reported that midwives were "inconsistent with the methods and ideals of civilization and of medical science in this country" (1915: 785).

A change in the status of the patient occurred as well. Instead of being in control of their own care, women surrendered to the power and authority of doctors—the doctor knows best. Wealthy women were the first to flock to male doctors for childbirth, lured in large part by the promise of new technology and painkillers. In the early 1900s the German method of "twilight sleep" was introduced in the United States—a combination of morphine for pain relief and scopolamine to cause women to have no memories of giving birth (Rooks, 1997). Since it was difficult to apply technology to childbirth in the home, births were moved to a hospital setting. A hospital birth became a status symbol for women. Not only would they be offered pain relief and the utmost in technological intervention, whether needed or not, but they would also have the prestige of being attended to by an upper-class white man.

FICTION

Midwifery is a very old profession. Prior to the development of professional medicine, most women had their children at home accompanied by female relatives, friends, and midwives.

By 1900, physicians in hospital settings were attending approximately one-half of births in the United States, largely along social class lines, although only 5 percent of births were in the hospital (Germano & Bernstein, 1997; Rooks, 1997). By 1970, virtually all births (99.4 percent) occurred in hospitals, usually attended by physicians. Women routinely had their pubic areas shaved, were strapped down to cold metal labor and delivery tables (the most painful and unnatural position), were given drugs that fogged the mind of mother and baby, were given enemas to empty the bowels (which often empty on their own in the early stages of labor), were hooked up to I.V.s and external fetal heart monitors that limit a laboring

woman's mobility (which can increase her pain), and were given episiotomies (the controversial cutting through the perineum toward the anus to enlarge the vaginal opening). Husbands and partners were often barred from the birth or required to wear full hospital regalia. Babies were born into bright spotlights and were taken away by hospital staff immediately after birth. The Family Narratives box on page 357 provides a typical description of medicalized birth in the 1970s, as told by a woman who is both a registered nurse and a certified midwife today. As she reveals, "I cried when I saw my first birth in nursing school . . . not because it was such a miracle, but because it was so violent."

Today, hospital births remain at approximately 99 percent (Rooks, 1997), with only 1 percent of births occurring in free-standing birth centers or at home. Medical interventions remain routine, although many of the above interventions have been altered dramatically, depending on hospital policy. Yet in the United States, approximately one out of four babies is born via cesarean section, a shockingly high number according to the World Health Organization (WHO). Nearly two-thirds of women have an episiotomy, and most women receive invasive fetal monitoring, are hooked up to cumbersome I.V.s, and receive drugs that numb the body as well as relieve some element of pain, practices that research findings deem to be usually unnecessary or even dangerous.

FACT OR FICTION?

For most women, having babies at home is as safe as having them in a hospital.

The Movement to Reclaim Birthing

The medicalization of childbirth has come into question over the past several decades. As recognized in a number of European na-

I cried when I saw my first birth in nursing school (1973). I had created a mental picture of women as strong and primal in labor, and viewed the process as sacred, natural, and at the same time, ordinary. I cried, though, not because it was such a miracle, but because it was so violent.

The mother was alone (because her husband was told to wait in the waiting room); she lay medicated and exhausted in a narrow bed, constrained by a fetal monitor. Just as she was ready to push, her doctor insisted on spinal anesthesia, which completely immobilized her from the waist down. Two nurses dragged her in a sheet from her bed to a cart. She was wheeled from her labor cubicle back to the surgical stainless steel delivery room, where she was pulled from the cart to the delivery table. Nurses lifted her floppy, numb legs into stirrups, fully exposing her genitals. One nurse shaved the mother's pubic area and washed her denuded perineum with cold betadine solution, while another aimed the glaring surgical light hanging from the ceiling. The doctor, fully gowned, gloved and masked, entered and perfunctorily cut her episiotomies, applied forceps to her baby's head, and pulled him out.

When she spontaneously reached for her newborn, the nurses frantically yelled, "Don't touch him!" The worried mother's arms recoiled as she asked, "Why not? What's wrong?" only to learn, "The drapes are sterile. Keep your hands under the drapes." And the doctor handed her baby to the nurse.

The child she had dreamed about for months was taken to the far end of the delivery room, out of reach, even out of sight. The distraught mother could hear him screaming as his feet were needlessly and repeatedly slapped—until the nurses and doctor were satisfied that his lungs were "healthy."

As a student-nurse, I often found myself standing out in the hall by the labor and delivery rooms, bewildered and disturbed. Even though I wasn't aware of homebirths and midwives at the time, I knew women did not have to give birth *this* way.

Shortly after, I learned about midwifery. Once I began my midwifery training at the Frontier Nursing Service in Hyden, Kentucky (1977), I knew I had come home. Everything I learned and did made sense to me. During the next five years, I practiced midwifery in the hospital and a birth center, and also attended women at home.

By Pam England

Source: England and Horowitz (1998). *Birthing from Within.* Albuquerque, NM: Partera (pp. xvi–xvii). Used with permission from Pam England and Rob Horowitz.

Critical Thinking

1. If you were going to have a child (or your partner was), how do you picture the birth?
2. What do you think has influenced your preferences?

tions, it has also become apparent in the United States that hospitalization and technological intervention are not always needed to deliver healthy babies and in fact can sometimes make things worse. Although medical technology can indeed save lives, it is not without emotional, physical, and financial costs. Millions of Americans die needlessly through all types of unnecessary surgeries and medical procedures. Medical decisions are not infallible. In a *New England Journal of Medicine* study of fifteen cases in which physicians sought court orders to force cesarean deliveries on mothers who disagreed with their diagnosis, researchers found six of the mothers delivering healthy babies vaginally. The remaining nine women were forced to have cesareans, so we cannot tell whether these operations were unnecessary as well (Kolder, Gallagher, & Parsons, 1987).

Mounting evidence suggests that births outside hospital settings are at least as safe and perhaps even safer than births in a hospital for average, low-risk women (e.g.,

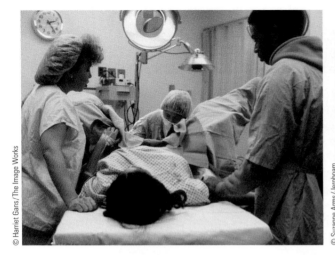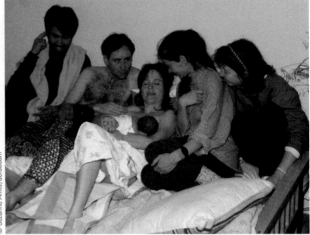

Dissatisfaction with the structure of hospital births has resulted in some women choosing alternatives for childbirth. Home births provide the opportunity to include more family and close friends in the experience.

women who are not diabetic, are not having twins, or do not have other identified fetal or maternal health problems). Nonhospital births that involve limited medical intervention actually have better outcomes with respect to low birth weight, fetal distress, cesarean section, and infant mortality (Cawthon, 1996; Janssen, Holt, & Myers, 1994; Sullivan & Beeman, 1983). One study, which matched 1,046 hospital births with 1,046 home births, found that women giving birth in a hospital were five times more likely to have high blood pressure in labor, nine times more likely to have a severe perineal tear, three times more likely to have a postpartum hemorrhage, and three times more likely to have a cesarean. Serious repercussions occurred for the babies as well. Babies born in a hospital were six times more likely to have had fetal distress before birth, four times more likely to have needed assistance to start breathing, and four times more likely to have developed an infection. There were no birth injuries at home, but thirty infants in the hospital suffered injuries from their birth (Mehl, Peterson, Witt, & Hawes, 1977).

FACT

Research has found that having a child at home is safe for most women and can even provide a healthier experience for mother and child.

Armed with this information, many people are seeking a more natural approach. Options include (1) prepared childbirth, (2) attempts at restructuring the hospital environment, (3) free-standing birth centers, and (4) home births.

Prepared Childbirth—Reclaiming Control

In the 1960s and 1970s, many women and their partners complained of feeling disconnected from birth. Women were looking for a more natural way to deal with the pain and anxiety of birth, one that would involve their husbands or partners. Prepared, or natural, childbirth was popularized by Fernand Lamaze (1970) and Grantly Dick-Read (1972). The goals include helping women and their partners to become more knowledgeable and confident, and thus more active in the birth process. Lamaze focuses on the use of breathing and other exercises throughout labor and delivery in order to separate the physical uterine contractions from the conditioned response of pain. Dick-Read focuses on physical relaxation exercises to ease muscle tension and thus ease pain and stress in childbirth. These methods can be used instead of, or in addition to, pain medication.

Restructuring the Hospital Environment

Not so long ago in a typical U.S. hospital, a mother giving birth usually lay flat on a table, working against the force of gravity. This position is largely for the convenience of the physician; it is not the most comfortable or efficient position for childbirth. In other cultures, women give birth in a squatting, kneeling, or standing position, or they use a birthing chair. In recent years, women began to demand that hospital policies and their physical environments change so that a mother's needs be given greater priority. For example, women have demanded that hospital birthing rooms be changed so that they are more personal and homelike, and less sterile and cold. Many hospitals have responded to these requests and attempt to offer a cozier and more comfortable environment for the laboring woman and her partner. She may be allowed to write her own birth plan, she may no longer be transferred to a different room between labor and delivery, and she may be able to have more free use of alternative positions for delivery. Hospital policies vary widely with respect to such accommodations; therefore, it would be wise for prospective parents to investigate each hospital carefully.

Birth Centers

Birth centers are a popular option in Europe (Odent, 1984) and are beginning to gain some popularity in the United States. Birth centers are free-standing facilities not associated with a hospital. They view childbirth as a normal, healthy process that can be attended to by skilled practitioners, including midwives, physicians, and naturopathic doctors. Birth centers usually present a homelike setting and offer clients the personal autonomy to decide the conditions surrounding the birth, while at the same time offering a degree of medical security that many couples find appealing. For example, many birth centers offer the woman the opportunity to give birth in a large tub of warm water, with her spouse or partner in the tub with her. Laboring and giving birth in water is a desirable option for some women because of the natural pain relief that warm water provides. However, insurance companies are less likely to cover births within a birthing center.

Home Births

Less than 1 percent of births occur at home in the United States, yet those women who give birth in their own homes are nearly unanimous in their praise of doing so. With skilled attendants (such as midwives) present, women with low-risk pregnancies have outcomes at least as safe at home as in hospitals (England & Horowitz, 1998; Sullivan & Beeman, 1983). Also, some women prefer to give birth in the loving confines of their home. At home, they can set the mood of their choosing (e.g., lights, music, water), they can avoid being pressured to use technological intervention or drugs, they can invite whomever they want to come into the room to witness the birth, and they can give birth in whatever position (or room of the house) that pleases them. One study found that 91 percent of the women who had their last baby at home said that they would prefer to have their next baby at home. Among those who had experienced both a home birth and a hospital birth, 76 percent preferred the home birth: "Being in our own bedroom, in our house, people could come and go as they wished. It was very relaxing and peaceful. Afterwards we all sat around and talked, we had champagne and a party.

It was a celebration! We did it! It was not a 'Whew, I'm glad that's over' kind of experience" (England & Horowitz, 1998: 113).

Not all pregnant women are good candidates for a home birth. Those who are the best candidates are healthy, are nonsmokers, are willing to cope with the pain and hard work of labor without drugs, live where midwives are available, live within thirty minutes of a hospital, and, most important, are able to cope with additional expenses not covered by insurance plans. Hospital births are most appropriate when women have chronic medical problems, are experiencing prenatal problems, and want to have access to hospital services and the use of drugs (England & Horowitz, 1998).

Men's Participation in Childbirth

Historically, men have not played very active roles in the childbirth process (except as doctors). This is changing, and men are now frequently present for births at home and in hospitals, even in the case of cesarean births. Although much of men's participation comes from their partners' desires to have them involved, men have increasingly taken initiative to bring attention to their participation.

Prospective fathers are not only involved in births, but also in the preparation for birth. However, the messages that men receive in our culture about how to get involved in the process are sometimes confusing. An example comes from Forrest Seymour (http://www.fathersjournal.com/Essays/Pregnant.html), who has been writing his thoughts on fathering for an online journal. Here is what he had to say about being a "pregnant father":

> Rather than a delineated pregnant father role, or even a clear set of options, we get instead mixed messages. On the one hand, expectant fathers are supposed to get involved, go to all these appointments and classes, read the books, know the lingo, be able to hold his own in a conversation about perineal massage, placentas or Braxton–Hicks contractions. And yet, when people are doling out sympathy about what a pain pregnancy is, it's the mom who gets the attention. I've lost count of the number of times I've stood in a group and felt basically invisible as everyone twitters on about Nancy's pregnancy. Men and women alike exclude the father from pregnancy conversation. I've even caught myself doing it. The mother of course is the one who is, in fact, pregnant, but, if we want fathers to include themselves in the pregnancy, then we must include them in our attentions.

Some of the confusion that men face when approaching the subject of pregnancy and childbirth is related to traditional notions of masculinity (Connell, 1995; Kimmel, 2000). From the time that males are little boys, they are told to "be tough" and "don't cry." Yet, when interacting with partners who are pregnant, they are expected to "be nurturing" and "be supportive." How to negotiate these simultaneous demands is a challenge for those involved. Research on men and pregnancy is advancing, along with guidance for those who are interested in getting more involved in the process (e.g., Shapiro et al., 1995).

Conclusion

Normative definitions about families traditionally include children. Children are necessary for the survival of the species, but they also play an important role in family life. Parents receive psychological benefits from having children, and children can offer social capital to their families. At the same time, the costs associated with having and raising children have been rising steeply. Economists argue that the cost of having children has been the primary cause of the significant decline in fertility rates in the United States and other Western nations. The other primary reason for fertility declines is the delay in childbearing. People are waiting longer to get married and have children, thus reducing the total number of children born to each woman.

Those who delay childbearing long enough face increased risks of infertility. The costs associated with infertility treatments are high, and the success rates of these treatments are low. As a result, there is greater interest now in adoption. Gay and lesbian couples, who also face challenges in having children, are also pursuing adoptions. However, the reduced fertility rate in the United States has meant that there are fewer children to adopt. Consequently, many people are pursuing international adoptions.

Diversity in the process of having children has helped to reduce the stigma associated with family forms not rooted in blood. However, stigma can still affect those who do not have children at all (whether by choice or not). Assumptions about people without children are similar to those we saw about single people in Chapter 7. However, research indicates that people who do not have children can develop family and friend networks that are satisfying and that integrate them into their communities.

Chapter Review

* How have fertility rates varied over time, and how do they vary by ethnicity?

Fertility rates have declined over the last hundred years, but not in a linear fashion. The average number of births declined from 1900 through the Great Depression, then rose to a peak in 1957 (the height of the baby boom). Since then, rates have declined. Current fertility rates vary by race and ethnicity. Hispanic women have the highest overall total fertility rate (2.5) while non-Hispanic white and Asian/Pacific Islander women have the lowest (1.8). The population replacement rate is 2.1.

* Why have fertility rates declined in the United States?

There are two main reasons for the decline in fertility. First is the direct cost of having and raising children. The USDA estimates that in 2000 dollars, the cost for a middle-income family to raise a child to age eighteen is $165,630, up 13 percent from forty years ago. The second reason is the opportunity costs, experienced primarily by women, of having children. When mothers take time out of the labor market to raise a child, they are losing wages. They also forgo job experiences and training so that when they reenter the labor market they are at a disadvantage relative to when they left.

* With the high costs of children, why do people have any?

We live in a society that is characterized as pronatalist. This means that we culturally support the notion of having children and believe that families are not complete without them. At the individual level, children are expected to bring many psychological benefits to adults. Parents often see bits of themselves in their children and are proud of their accomplishments. At the social level, children bring social capital. They provide opportunities for parents to create and maintain networks within families and communities.

* Are there consequences of delaying childbearing until later in life?

Both costs and benefits are associated with delaying childbearing. In terms of costs, the likelihood of conceiving goes down with age, and increasing numbers of prospective parents must invest a considerable amount of time and money in technologies to enhance conception (such as IVF). However, older parents tend to be more financially secure, and their children may benefit from having more economic resources.

* Why make a distinction between being childless and childfree?

Even in a pronatalist society, women and men may choose to go through their lives without having children. For those who choose to be childfree, friends provide the social capital to maintain networks. Some women and men have a great desire to have children but cannot, for a variety of reasons. When involuntary childlessness occurs, people are more likely to experience sadness and loneliness.

* Why is there an increase in the rate of childbearing outside of marriage?

Childbearing outside of marriage is increasing among most groups of women. One important explanation for nonmarital births is the rise in cohabitation, which accounts for close to 40 percent of such births. Among the women who are single (not cohabiting) and who have children, there are a variety of reasons for having a child. Some middle-class women believe that they have earned the right to have a child because they are more physically, emotionally, and financially responsible. Waiting for "Mr. Right" may keep them from ever having children. Women in working-class and poorer communities also face the problem of finding an appropriate match. Because these women desire economic stability, it may be better for them to be cautious about marriage. However, having children is a valued part of their lives, and waiting for a good marriage compromises their options.

* What challenges do gays and lesbians face when deciding to have children?

Because marriage is legal only between a man and a woman, state governments do not recognize both parents without the process of adoption. Some states do not allow gays and lesbians to adopt. Societal norms are similar, recognizing heterosexual parents more readily. Since there are no taken-for-granted assumptions about gay/lesbian parents, these parents must work hard to negotiate relationships with friends, family, and members of their communities.

* How is adoption organized in our society?

Adoptions are regulated at the state level. There are two basic types: public and private. Private adoptions are more common because of the limited availability of children through the public child welfare system. Available children are disproportionately older and are from racial/ethnic minorities, producing an increase in the number of transracial adoptions and the seeking of children for adoption from other countries.

* How have pregnancy and childbirth changed over time?

Until the nineteenth century, childbirth was "women's business," and doctors were not involved. As the field of professional medicine developed, however, childbirth was taken over as a medical procedure. Women began to have their children in hospitals, instead of at home, and their experiences were determined by the latest technology. Today, many women are trying to reclaim the process of childbirth. Restructuring hospitals, the creation of birth centers, home births, and the

use of midwives are changes that promise to give women and their families a more positive, healthy experience. Recently, fathers have also become more active in the process, from pregnancy through childbirth.

Key Terms

annual fertility rate: the number of births per 1,000 women in a given year

baby boom: a cohort in which the average number of children born to women reaches a peak compared to cohorts prior to and subsequent to it—in the United States, the most significant baby boom took place between 1946 and 1964

childless versus childfree: terms referring to those who do not have children, either because they want to but cannot get pregnant or because they choose not to have children, respectively

delayed childbearing: putting off having children until someone is older, often related to the increased time spent in education and career development

direct costs of raising children: expenditures for children, including housing, food, child care, and education

fecundity: women's biological capacity to reproduce

international adoption: children who are citizens of a foreign nation being adopted by U.S. individuals or families and brought to live in the United States

medicalization of childbirth: a transition in the nineteenth century away from the use of midwives in childbirth, instead relying on physicians

midwives: women who are trained to help women give birth

nonmarital childbearing: having children outside of marriage

opportunity costs of raising children: negative effect of childbearing and child rearing on women's employment in terms of experience and income

private adoption: the placement of a child in a nonrelative home through the services of a nonprofit or for-profit agency that is licensed by the state. Also called an *independent adoption.*

pronatalism: an attitude embedded in culture and social policy that supports and encourages childbearing

public adoption: an adoption in which a child who is in the public child welfare system is placed in a permanent home by either a government-operated agency or by a private agency that is contracted by a public agency to place such children

replacement rate: the number of children who need to be born to each woman to maintain the current population

single mothers by choice: women who choose to have children without being married

social capital: regarding children, this term refers to the value of children for integrating families into the broader community

total fertility rate: the total number of children ever born to women

transracial adoption: the placement of a child in a home with a family of a different race

Resources on the Internet

These web sites have been selected for their relevance to the topics in this chapter. These sites are among the more stable, but please be aware that web site addresses change frequently.

Center for Nutrition Policy and Promotion
http://www.cnpp.usda.gov
This site is associated with the U.S. Department of Agriculture. We obtained the data on the costs of raising children from this site.

You can go further and check out how costs vary across areas of the country.

National Association of Childbearing Centers
http://www.birthcenter.org
Here you can find answers to frequently asked questions about birth centers or childbearing in general. You can locate birth centers in your own area where you can visit and get more information.

Parents Without Partners
http://www.parentswithoutpartners.org
Parents Without Partners is an international organization that addresses the concerns of single parents. Never-married, divorced, separated, and widowed parents can connect with other single parents to discuss their concerns and ideas. A student interested in the topic can find links to research and publications concentrating on single parenting.

National Adoption Information Clearinghouse
http://www.calib.com/naic
The National Adoption Information Clearinghouse is a national resource that offers comprehensive information on all aspects of adoption. The general public can access a library collection, databases with adoption resources, publications, and information about federal and state legislation. Links to dozens of other Internet sites on adoption are also available.

Companion Web Site for This Book

Virtual Society: The Wadsworth Sociology Resource Center
http://sociology.wadsworth.com
Begin by clicking the Student Resources section. Next, click Marriage and Family, and then click the cover image for this book. Select from the pull-down menu the chapter you are presently studying. You will have easy access to chapter resources such as MicroCase Online exercises, additional Web links, flashcards, InfoTrac exercises, and practice tests (that can be scored). In addition, to enhance

and help with your study of marriages and families, be sure to investigate the rest of the rich sociology resources at Virtual Society.

Visit InfoTrac College Edition

Another unique option available to you at the Student Resources section of the Virtual Society web site described above is InfoTrac College Edition, an online library of hundreds of scholarly and popular periodicals. Here are three suggested key search terms for this chapter:

* Search keywords: *fertility + ethnicity*
* Search keywords: *child + care*
* Search keywords: *single + parents*
* Search recent years to get the latest information on these issues.

© Walter Hodges/Corbis

Relationships Between Parents and Children

9

Thank you. What a thrill. Members of the Academy, thank you. . . . Dad, who's here tonight, thank you for teaching me how to soldier through tough situations and Mom, for teaching me how to do it gracefully. (Marcia Gay Harden, Best Actress in a Supporting Role, *Pollock*)

I'd like to thank . . . my father for showing me the power of caring; my mother for teaching me never to give up; my brother for looking out for me and my godmother for giving me a million and one reasons to believe. (Benicio Del Toro, Best Actor in a Supporting Role, *Traffic*)

Each year at the Academy Awards we listen to long, rambling acceptance speeches from actors, directors, and other winners. In many of these speeches, we hear mention of family, particularly parents. As these two excerpts from the seventy-third Annual Academy Awards in 2001 (http://www.oscar.com/oscarnight/winners/winners.html) show, adults are aware of the important role that parents play in their lives. Some winners also thank their children. Children are reported to open, or re-open, adults' eyes to the fantasy, fun, and creativity in life. In other words, the interaction between parents and children in families is important. It helps to shape who we are, and we continue to grow and learn as human beings as a result of this interaction.

In this chapter, our goal is to explore the relationship between parents and children. We begin, as before, by recognizing that relationships are socially constructed. How parents and children relate to one another varies across social locations over time. A brief overview of parenthood and childhood in the United States can reveal some of these variations. The rest of the chapter addresses the contemporary scene of parent–child relationships. We cover the normative expectations for parenting as well as the varieties of styles and practices of parenting. Of particular interest will be the ways in which social class, race/ethnicity, gender, and family structure help shape the environments in which parents and children are socialized. Finally, because of the changing family/work relationship (in particular, the increase in dual-earner families), we look at the current state of child care. Now that a majority of parents are employed, who is taking care of children and what implications this issue will have for children's development and well-being are important considerations.

Many other topics could also be explored here, but because of space and organization, we will discuss them later. For example, parent–child relations do not end when children leave home. We discuss the lifelong character of parent–child relations in a chapter on families in later life. Moreover, not all relationships between parents and children are positive, and child abuse is a serious problem that needs attention. This subject is addressed in the chapter on family crises.

| FACT OR FICTION?

Children have always been thought of as innocent beings.

A Brief Historical View of Parenthood and Childhood

A large literature focuses on the social construction of motherhood and fatherhood. One of the main arguments made in this literature is that the process of constructing the meaning of parenthood is a dialectical one (Lupton & Barclay, 1997). Understanding what it means to "mother" can't be achieved without exploring what it means to "father." As well, understanding the meaning of parenthood necessitates an understanding of the meaning of childhood. To be a "good" parent includes meeting the needs of children.

Contemporary views see children as precious and innocent beings, ones in need of intensive physical, psychological, and emotional care (Hays, 1996; Zelizer, 1985; Farrell, 1999). We hear this from parents when they say something like "I want them to be happy, healthy, and successful in whatever it is that they choose to do." A quick look at the historical record suggests that these desires for children have been socially constructed, although certainly not evenly across class or racial/ethnic lines. First, people in most (if not all) societies over time have been concerned with the health of children. Children are physically dependent on adults for the first several years of their lives. But the challenges to being healthy have varied considerably in different historical periods, and the responsibility of parents for ensuring the health of their children has also varied. Second, historical research suggests that an emphasis on children's ability to be successful, or independent, did not emerge as an area of concern for parents until the nineteenth century, when the occupations of children did not necessarily follow the path of their parents. Third, the emphasis on happiness for children is a much more recent phenomenon, one that has occurred only as the issues of ensuring children's health and preparing them to be successful have been addressed by institutions beyond the family.

Being a good parent includes meeting the needs of children. Although parents have always been concerned about the physical health of their children, today the concern focuses more on intellectual and mental health.

Parents and Children Before Industrialization

Child rearing in most, if not all, cultures includes protecting children from physical harm until they reach an age at which they can take care of themselves. The issues of *what* physical harm children face, *how long* they must be protected from it, and *who* is responsible for providing the protection have changed dramatically. Historians suggest that during the Middle Ages, the harm children faced was due to their own sinful nature (Badinter, 1981). Care of young children was the province of others, not parents, who were also concerned about the effect of children's less than pure nature on the broader community. Phillip Aries's (1962) classic study of childhood suggested that the concept of childhood itself didn't even exist in the Middle Ages. Using portraits, literary references, diaries, and archaeological records, Aries showed that there is little evidence of the recognition of children per se. No public rituals were held for grieving the death of an infant, no headstones existed to mark their graves, and no special clothing, toys, or games existed to demarcate this period in people's lives.

FICTION

In the Middle Ages, infants were thought to be born with a sinful nature and to need strict discipline in order to develop.

Colonial New England provides evidence of a time in this country when adults believed that children were born with sinful natures. Salvation, it was believed, was possible only through a very long and difficult process of strict disciplining of children, including physical punishment. However, parents were not necessarily the ones responsible for providing all of this strict discipline (Gillis, 1996). The **putting-out system** was common, in which children were sent to work for another family to learn a skill or a trade. This other family was also seen as responsible for the care of the children. It would not be until the next century that mothers were given the primary responsibility for their children's development.

Alongside these religious beliefs were structural conditions that made parenting a more emotionally detached practice. Birthrates were very high in the colonial period, birth intervals were short, and high infant mortality was a fact of life. Houses were also quite small, and because the labor of all adults was necessary for survival, older siblings may have looked after younger children as often as parents did. It has been suggested that these demographic and social arrangements created more distant connections between parents and their children. If children were not expected to live to the age of "independence," parents may have tried to maintain more instrumental (versus expressive) relationships with their children.

Parents and Children in the Era of Industrialization

During the nineteenth century, dramatic transformations occurred in the organization of society and changed the ways we think about parenthood and childhood. Processes of industrialization, urbanization, and immigration resulted in a more complicated class system. With the ideological and physical separation of places of employment from the domestic sphere, and the lengthening of the time that children were under the care of parents, mothers became responsible for their children's nurturance and safety. Children were no longer seen in terms of their sinful natures, and their protection focused on proper moral development and sheltering them from the corrupting external world. It was during this period that mothers became the main target for parent training. Movements focusing on social reform became popular, and magazines about mothers and infants were widely circulated. An interesting contradiction existed during this time of social reform in that the proponents of this new arrangement, whereby women would be exclusively committed to the moral development of their children, were not likely to practice what they preached. Women of the privileged classes, who were at the heart of the Reform Movement, had women as domestics to care for their homes and children. However, the important point is that this middle-class rhetoric became quite popular and set the stage for the even more intensive parenting expected of women in the twentieth century.

FACT OR FICTION?

The number of years spent in "childhood" is greater today than in earlier generations.

The turn of the twentieth century began yet another phase in the reconstruction of childhood (Jones, 1999). The Child Study Movement was under way, and the government got involved in regulating childhood. For example, the U.S. Children's Bureau was established in 1912 to help guard against the exploitation of children as workers. However, not all concern about children's working was about their physical safety. Labor unions, trying to protect the jobs of their members, also lobbied for the passing of child labor laws. As cheap labor, children posed a threat to adult men seeking employment.

The public concern about the child was evidenced by the kindergarten movement, the playground associations, and the enforcement of compensatory schooling. Along with these concerns about children came concerns

Photo by Lewis Wickes Hine © Corbis

The period in a child's life we know as adolescence did not always exist. Prior to the twentieth century children moved into adult roles earlier in their lives.

about mothers' abilities. Their "instincts" and "virtues" were no longer sufficient. Scientific understandings of child development also transformed motherhood (and fatherhood) and demanded serious attention to children's moral, cognitive, and emotional development. The period of time spent in childhood was expanded, and this new stage of development was formally labeled and recognized as *adolescence*. The number of magazines and journals about parenting and child development grew, and "expert" advice was pursued more frequently by a geographically mobile society in which people depended less on community. Instinctual motherhood was replaced by scientific motherhood (Apple, 1997).

| **FACT**

Historians have traced the existence of a period of adolescence only to the early part of the last century.

As mentioned at the outset of this brief historical overview, the changes in childhood and parenthood were uneven over time. During the twentieth century, the Great Depression and World War II kept children from being completely innocent creatures. Children living in working-class urban areas, children living in immigrant and racial/ethnic communities, and children living in the Southwest or the frontier states continued to have an early entrance into adult activity. However, the ideological construction of childhood did continue to be one of a period of innocence, and certainly the period following World War II saw the revitalization of the home, along with women's and children's place in it. Scientific theories emerged about the innate attachments between mothers and infants having long-term implications for development, and we see the institutionalization of what sociologist Sharon Hays (1996) calls **intensive mothering**. However, not all societies organize parenting responsibilities in just these ways. For a comparison with a matrilineal society, see the Family Diversity box on pages 372–373.

Contemporary Parenthood and Childhood

In contemporary Western societies, many social forces have come together to create a situation in which parent–child relationships are seen as central to the identity of most people. We live in a global market economy that requires mobility, and we face the reality of several occupations/careers in our lifetimes. Although rates have fluctuated over the century, family sizes are now smaller, and life expectancy is greater. Therefore, while the amount of time that adults spend parenting has decreased, they spend that time focusing on fewer children. And child rearing has increasingly become a single-parent or multi-household phenomenon. Some have argued that the contemporary scene is one characterized more by an individualistic orientation rather than a community orientation (Beck & Beck-Gernsheim, 1995). What this means for families is that parents may become the primary source of both the successes and the failures of their children.

| **FACT OR FICTION?**

Socialization in families refers to the ways that parents teach their children.

Parent–Child Relationships

When we think about the relationships between parents and children in families, we often think first about how parents socialize children. Because parents are older and the ones responsible for minor children, we assume that part of this responsibility is to teach children and provide for them so that they can grow up and become adult members of society. While parents do have a lot to

In the northeastern corner of India, in the state of Meghalaya, lives a matrilineal group known as the Khasi. As a matrilineal society, Khasi recognize kinship through the female line. Any two people are related if they share a mother or a common female ancestor. In this type of society, the socialization of children is the responsibility of more than just the biological parents. It also includes maternal uncles and members of the broader kin group and society.

At the broadest level of family organization is the clan, or *kur.* The basis of the kur is the belief that people of this group all descended from a common female ancestress. It is an exogamous unit, meaning that marriage is not allowed to another member of one's kur. Several kur will live together in one village, called the Shnong.

At the more local level of family organization is the "ïing." The ïing can be viewed as a domestic group, generally consisting of those who live together and are related by blood. As an example, a ïing could include a mother, her husband, and her unmarried children. However, the ïing could also include the mother's brother(s). As a matter of practice among the Khasi, the elder daughters will move out of their mother's ïing when they marry, each forming a residence with her husband. Out of obligation, the youngest daughter will remain in her mother's home, bringing her husband to live with them (matrilocal residence). In this way, the original ïing is perpetuated by the youngest daughters of each generation.

The ïing is the primary unit of socialization of children. In Khasi they say that the ïing is "Ka thymmei jong ka longbriew man birew," or "the epicenter of upbringing of the human person." It is within this group that significant events (marriage and other family rituals) and processes (inheritance) take place. At the same time, because multiple ïing will belong to the same kur, and all live within the same village (Shnong), it is important that family affairs be coordinated. Therefore, the responsibility to socialize children lies not only with the adults in their immediate household but also with related adults living in other households. The individuals/groups that perform vital roles in socializing children are the following:

Ka Kmie (Mother)

- The mother in Khasi society is referred to as "Ka nongri—ïing" (it means she is the keeper of the domestic group). It is her duty and responsibility to care, feed, clothe, and spend more of her time with the children. It is unthinkable of Khasi mothers to break these primary duties.

- Every child, both male and female, looks up to her for support, and more so in time of crisis.

- The children of the ïing learn the basic values, norms, and patterns of behaviours from the mother. She teaches them about the clan relations and the rules of clan exogamy, forms of address to elders, and the rules of respect to abide by in the society.

- The children are specifically oriented to respect the father's mother, father's siblings, and other members.

- Another important role of the mother is that she listens and keeps watch over the children at all times. It is interesting that even married children, both male and female, will confide in her. On many occasions they will even seek her advice.

teach children and are held legally responsible for their care, this view keeps us from seeing that the relationship is not a one-way street. Children can also have a profound influence on their parents. Children's interests, personalities, and experiences outside the family can shape the way parents interact with them (Holloway & Valentine, 2000). They can also shape a parent's identity *as a* parent. Being a good parent includes taking care of children's needs. But what those needs are will depend on the child.

Interactions between parents and children also take place within a broader social

It is expected that the mother care for the unmarried and married children at all times. It is through her that the unity and solidarity of the ïing are maintained.

U Kpa (Father)

- The father is known as "U ba lah ba iai" (a provider for the family and the well-being of the children). As a provider of the family, he has to generate income to meet the basic needs of the children.
- He is also the protector of the children. He keeps watch over the children (both young and old).
- As the children grow into adulthood, the father takes the role of regulator of the lifestyles of his children. He instills in his children the path of righteousness.

U Kni (Mother's Brother)

- He meets and discusses regularly with his nephews and nieces to know about and provide advice on their well-being.
- He inculcates the basic values of righteousness and the values of healthy lifestyles.
- He controls and reprimands any inappropriate actions committed by children.

- He protects the interests of the group at all times, especially those that affect the nephews and nieces. He is the manager and authority in the rites of passage.
- He supports them in their needs and assists them in their times of crisis.

Ki Kur (Clan Members)

- It is the duty and responsibility of every clan member to support and to protect each other.
- The clan members inculcate each other on the rules of mutual respect and maintenance of social order.
- Each member has the right to control and reprimand other clan members should their actions go against the social norms and values.

Ka Shnong (Village)

- The village council's primary responsibility is to promote the welfare of the younger generations. It facilitates their growth and well-being.
- The village council, the elders, and the adult population teach the younger members the values of

respect and social order and to follow the rules and regulations of the village.
- Younger members are protected by the village and receive support in times of crisis.
- The village and its elders control and reprimand the younger generations in case they deviate from social norms and practices.

Source: A. Kyrham Nongkynrih, Senior Lecturer, Department of Sociology, North Eastern Hill University, Meghalaya, India.

Critical Thinking

1. Recall from Chapter 1 that the United States practices bilateral descent and neolocal postmarital residence. How do these differences in kinship organization shape the responsibilities for childhood socialization?

2. In what ways have your aunts, uncles, and other family members been involved in teaching you about your culture?

and cultural environment. Financial situation, region of the country (including urban or rural residence), and cultural traditions are just a few of the variations of context that set the stage for family interaction. In this section, we will review the research on parent–child relations, beginning with work that focuses on how parents can influence children's development and well-being. Then we will turn things around and ask how children can influence parents' development and the quality of interactions between parents and children. Finally, we will broaden the discussion by placing these relationships in social context, looking in particular at issues of social class, race/ethnicity, gender, and sexual orientation.

| FICTION

Socialization in families is not a one-way street. Parents are also socialized via interaction with their children, a process called reciprocal socialization.

Parent Effects in Families

We've seen how being a parent is historically and socially situated, but within all these situations, parents have goals for themselves and their children (Okagaki & Divecha, 1993). Three broad parenting goals include (1) ensuring the physical health and survival of children, (2) preparing children for becoming self-sustaining adults, and (3) encouraging the development of positive personal and social behaviors in children. Most family researchers recognize that these goals are all part of what are considered to be "socialization concerns" (Peterson & Hann, 1999). If we define *socialization* as the process of interaction whereby individuals acquire the knowledge, skills, norms, and values of their society, then parents are responsible for teaching their children to become socially *competent*. Parents have a variety of ways to go about socializing their children. These are referred to as *styles* of parenting.

| FACT OR FICTION?

The most effective style of parenting is one is which parents give their children complete discretion to do what they want.

Parenting Styles

One approach to studying the styles that parents use in interactions with their children is to develop a typology of the variety of ways that information gets communicated to children. The most widely known typology is one by Baumrind (1978, 1991). She identified three styles of parenting correlated with children's development of social competence:

- **Authoritarian.** These parents often use arbitrary or punitive means of controlling children. Parents exhibit lower levels of nurturance, communication, and support in their interaction with children.
- **Permissive.** Parents are very nurturing and supportive, and do not exert very much control over their children's behavior.
- **Authoritative.** This parenting style includes communication that involves reasoning with children. Parents' influence is seen as rational, not coercive. Parents provide guidance and set limits for children.

Baumrind (1991) argues that the authoritative style of parenting is the most successful in promoting social competence in children. Competence is measured as social responsibility, independence, achievement, friendliness, and cooperativeness with others. Other researchers have found that authoritative parenting approaches are associated with better school performance, higher self-esteem among children, less deviance, and better peer relationships (Steinberg, Lamborn, Dornbusch, & Darling, 1992; Durbin, Darling, Steinberg, & Brown, 1993; Baumrind, 1991). Authoritarian (versus authoritative) child-rearing practices, on the other hand, have been shown to have negative consequences for children's school performance (Dornbusch, Ritter, Leiderman, Roberts, & Fraleigh, 1987).

Using typologies to describe the ways in which parents care for their children can be problematic. These typologies often do not include the entire scope of parenting styles (i.e., they are not exhaustive). Baumrind (1978) provides examples of two other possible styles ("quasi-authoritarian" and "harmonious") that may be effective in some families. Typologies also do not allow parents to fall into more than one style for all interactions with children (i.e., the styles are not mutually exclusive) (Peterson & Rollins, 1987). It may be that the style of parenting employed will depend on the situation, so parents could employ different styles over the course of raising their children. However, this particular typology has come into question in terms of its generalizability. Most of the research supporting the relationship of these parenting styles to child outcomes has studied European American middle-class families. Other research suggests that parenting techniques that are appropriate for middle-class white families may not be as effective for families that must cope with economic deprivation and racial/ethnic discrimination (Julian, McKenry, & McKelvey, 1994; Baumrind, 1978). We'll also see below that the interpretation of parenting styles is affected by the values of the observers of family interaction.

FICTION

The more effective style of parenting is referred to as "authoritative," wherein parents set ground rules and explain them to children in rational conversations.

Parenting Practices

In addition to the styles of parenting, family scholars are also interested in the particular behaviors parents engage in that influence their children, referred to as "child-rearing practices." Two of the broad categories of practices that have received considerable attention are *support* and *control.* Supportive behaviors include showing physical affection, being verbally affectionate, and showing acceptance. Very little research has been done to suggest how supportive behaviors can help create socially competent children (Peterson & Hann, 1999), but it is well ac-

Authoritative parenting includes communication that involves reasoning with their children. It is considered to be the most successful strategy for developing independence and responsibility.

cepted that supportive parenting promotes positive social development. When children feel supported by parents, they learn to trust them. Children are then more likely to take their parents' advice on how to behave. (See the Constructing Strong Families box on page 376 for a useful list of family problem-solving strategies.)

Parental Support Supportive parenting practices encourage children to get involved in activities that enable independent decision making and enhance social competence. Supporting behaviors vary depending on the age of the child. When children are very young, parents will be more physical in their support. Smiles for children getting dressed on their own and hugs when children pick up their toys are examples of supportive behavior. For older children, supportive parents are more likely to use verbal encouragement, praising children for their accomplishments. Other examples of **parental support** include talking to children about their involvement in activities outside the family that can enhance intellectual and/or spiritual development.

In a review of literature on how parents interact with children, David Demo (1992) argues that things are a bit different today than

All families face challenges and must find constructive ways to respond to them. Family researchers have found a variety of ways that families can approach problem solving and have also noted that these approaches take considerable work. But problem solving is worth the effort. It resolves family conflicts that would otherwise detract from the quality of family life. Effective problem solving enhances the quality of communication among family members and can increase feelings of caring and warmth. It also helps parents and children develop skills they can apply to other situations in their lives. Below is a summary of the basic steps that are used in problem solving. They are from a publication about foster families, but the general rules can be applied to all families.

1. Define the problem.
   - Describe your own perception of the problem.
   - Ask for other ideas about the problem.
   - Listen carefully and help each child "hear" what the others are saying.
   - Agree on a definition.
2. List possible solutions.
   - Take turns contributing many ideas.
   - List all ideas and don't evaluate them until later.
   - Be creative and include crazy ideas.
   - Listen carefully without judging or lecturing.
3. Decide on the best solution.
   - Take turns evaluating each idea.
   - Talk about what might happen if the family followed the idea.
   - Give each idea a "plus" or "minus" accordingly.
   - Select one idea that everyone rated a "plus." If no idea is rated "plus" by everyone, combine several ideas or return to Step 2.
4. Make a plan.
   - Write down exactly how the solution should work. Decide who will do what, where, and how.
   - Ask whether everyone agrees to the plan.
   - Decide how long to give the plan a try.
   - Put the plan into action.
5. Evaluate the plan.
   - Meet again and ask each person how well the plan is working.
   - Decide whether the plan needs revision or will be continued.

Source: Ozretich, Vuchinich, Pratt, and Bowman (2001). *Enriching Foster Family Relationships Through Problem Solving: Guidelines for Foster Parents* (Oregon State University Extension Service No. EC 1517). Corvallis, OR: Oregon State University. Used with permission.

Critical Thinking

1. Imagine a problem that your family has faced. Could these guidelines have helped you address that problem?

2. How would one's position in the family (parent, child, grandparent, aunt/uncle) influence this approach to problem solving?

---

in the past. With the increase in dual-earner families and single-parent families, parents are less likely to be able to have consistent face-to-face opportunities to support their children. Does this mean that parents are less supportive of, or less attached to, their children today? Demo's answer is no. What has changed is the shape of parent–child interactions and the way in which support is conveyed. Contemporary interactions are more likely described as "supportive detach-ment," whereby parents let their children know how they feel and provide structural arrangements that are conducive to their children's development.

Parental Control   In contrast to the limited literature on how supportive behaviors translate into social competence among children, considerably more is known about another parenting behavior: control. **Parental control** is defined in terms of the behaviors exhibited by parents in their attempts to influence their children's lives (their behavior and well-being) (Peterson & Rollins, 1987). There are two types of control that have been shown to be influential in children's social development. One is called **parental induction,** a type of control in which parents actively communicate with their children using reason. Parents try to help children see why they have established rules or limits for their behavior, why violating these rules is not acceptable, what effect their behavior will have on other people, and how children can work to make their behavior more acceptable to others (Peterson & Hann, 1999). Induction is really more of a psychological method of control; it focuses on children being able to mentally work through what they are taught and see how it applies to them. By developing a rationale for certain types of behaviors, children can develop a sense of right and wrong, and learn how to take into account the concerns of others. This parenting practice is also expected to help strike a balance between children's conforming to parents' wishes and making autonomous decisions. Induction can be effective in socializing both internalized states (it can enhance children's self-esteem) and externalized behaviors (it encourages the selection of prosocial behavior) (Stafford & Bayer, 1993).

The other type of control exhibited by parents is through **monitoring** or supervising their children's behavior, which can be accomplished through the observation and/or management of children's schedules, activities, and friends. It is most effective when parents follow a consistent set of rules and check their children's observance of them. The process of monitoring children is much simpler when children are very young, for they are more likely to be in their parents' presence. As children age, however, supervision becomes more complicated. Children spend an increasing amount of time away from parents when they are older due to school activities and friends.

Research on the effects of parental monitoring suggests that a lack of supervision can lead to problems. Parents are not the only agents of socialization for children. Children learn through their interactions with teachers, with friends, and with forms of popular culture (movies, television, magazines). If parents are monitoring their children's behavior, they can have some control over their children's exposure to these other sources of information. When parents have less control, children can be exposed to a broader variety of stimuli, not all in line with their parents' interests or desires. As a result, insufficient monitoring has been shown to be associated with higher rates of antisocial behavior, delinquency, deviant peer association, sexual risk taking, and drug use (Barber, Olsen, & Shagle, 1994).

A concept related to monitoring is **parental involvement.** Involved parents spend more time with their children in a variety of interactions, from play and conversation to helping out with homework and attending children's events (Gerard & Buehler, 1999). When parents are more involved in their children's lives, they are more capable of supervision or monitoring. Therefore, it is not surprising that children with involved parents are less likely to become involved in delinquency (Amato & Rivera, 1999; Gerard & Buehler, 1999).

Excessive Control Up to this point, we have been referring to the control of children's behavior as having a positive, linear relationship to children's social development. That is, the more control shown, the better off a child is. However, parents can be excessive in their controlling behaviors, compromising children's development of social competence. Often, parents over-control through manipulation of their children's emotions. Because of psychologically controlling behavior such as instilling anxiety or guilt, or withdrawing love, parents become less effective agents of socialization. The consequences for

When parents withdraw from their children they become less effective agents of socialization.

children include lower levels of self-esteem and higher rates of depression, suicide, eating disorders, and other internalized problems (Barber, 1992; Peterson & Hann, 1999).

A recent study of high school students shows how the various types of control (including excessive control) can influence children's involvement in problem behavior. Rodgers (1999) found that for both male and female students, higher degrees of parental monitoring were associated with fewer sexual risk-taking behaviors. In this study, monitoring was measured by asking students to respond to items such as "I talk to my parents about the plans I have with my friends" and "If I'm going to be home late, I'm expected to call my parents and let them know." Sexual risk-taking behavior was assessed by asking students about the number of sexual partners they had in the past year, the type of birth control used (effectiveness), and the consistency of contraceptive use. Low-risk students were those who were

monogamous and who used consistent, effective birth control. These low-risk students were also the ones who had a relationship established with their parents for reporting on their whereabouts.

Another type of parental control was also important for predicting sexual risk taking, but it was important only for girls. When girls saw their parents as psychologically controlling, they were *more* likely to take risks sexually. Rodgers measured psychological control in terms of whether students perceived their parents as using "guilt mechanisms." When Rodgers compared the behavioral (external) and psychological (internal) mechanisms of control, it was psychological control that had a larger effect on girls (for boys, it was the behavioral dimension of monitoring). Why would internalized control have a larger effect for girls? Rodgers suggests that for girls, sexuality itself is a more internalized event. Girls/women are more likely to engage in sexual activity when they are in an ongoing, developing relationship. Sex is a form of emotional intimacy that helps to create stronger feelings about each other: "Females may be more affected by psychological control by their parents because sexual relations represent an emotional connection with others" (Rodgers, 1999: 107).

Parents can also be excessive in terms of their behavioral control. Excessive behavioral control, referred to in the literature as **punitiveness,** includes verbal or physical attempts at controlling children's behavior without a rational explanation. This type of excessive control has also shown to have negative (and long-term) effects on children (Aquilino & Supple, 2001). A relatively common response of children to punitiveness on the part of their parents is hostility and resistance. Children become less attached to their parents and are less likely to develop the social skills that parents desire in them (Stafford & Bayer, 1993). And because children turn away from coercive parents, they turn to others (peers) and through these interactions can develop a higher risk for delinquency (Straus, 1994).

In sum, the literature on parenting suggests that to achieve socialization, parents should be supportive, use rational forms of control, and be responsive to their children's capabilities (Day, Peterson, & McCracken, 1998). When parents use excessive forms of control (psychological, verbal, and/or physical), children become less attached to their parents and are less likely to internalize the types of traits that parents would desire for them. Instead, they may be more influenced by other agents of socialization, such as peer groups. These arguments regarding the influence of parenting practices on children make sense, but they do not take into account the fact that children are not just recipients in the socialization process. Socialization results from interaction, and interaction requires at least two social actors. Therefore, it is important to take into account the role that children play in this process and look at the ways in which children can socialize their parents.

Child Effects in Parent–Child Relationships

People frequently say that having children changed their lives. But what does that mean? In what ways do children change the lives of parents? First, just the sheer presence of children changes the way parents go about family life. We saw in Chapters 6 and 7 that marriage and cohabitation are likely to encourage the specialization of labor between men and women. The transition to parenthood also reinforces, and often increases, gender specialization (Hays, 1996; Walzer, 1998). Having children can also affect marital relations, with marital satisfaction declining after the birth of a child (VanLaningham et al., 2001; Waite & Lillard, 1991). But in this section we ask something more specific: How do the characteristics of children influence parent–child relations? Although this is not a question that has been well-researched (Ambert, 1992), there is some evidence that the temperaments of children, their perceived capabilities, and their gender all influence parents and family interaction processes.

The photo albums for most families contain many pictures of smiling people. Babies are laughing, and children are playing. But most of us who have spent time with young children know that babies are not always smiling and children's behavior is not always playful. As children's moods, emotions, and behavior change, so too will parents'. Research focusing on the parents of infants suggests that they respond differently to their children when the children are smiling, irritable, or crying (Maccoby & Martin, 1983; Peterson & Rollins, 1987). Irritable infants may have interrupted sleeping patterns, which can cause parents to feel tired and stressed. Toddlers who have difficult temperaments also seem to negatively affect parents' moods and reactions. In part because such children are more active, parents have been shown to use more reactive forms of control when their toddlers misbehave (Bates, 1989). Overall, however, the literature on temperament effects on parents is mixed (Peterson & Hann, 1999). Children with challenging temperaments may influence parents, but the effects are very likely to be shaped by the context within which parent–child relations take place. Some parents may have more resources to face difficult challenges. Whether the support comes from another parent, a family member, or a child-care provider, having access to support helps parents get the rest they need to be supportive. In addition, the way in which parents interpret their children's moods and behaviors can also affect how they respond to their children (McBride, Schoppe, & Rane, 2002). When parents perceive their children to be more emotionally intense, they experience more stress. Other research (Dix, Ruble, & Zambarano, 1989) finds that when parents are relaxed and supported, they can give more balanced responses to their children's potentially challenging behavior or temperament.

Parents' Expectations and Children's Capabilities In addition to socializing children to be socially competent, being a "good parent" also includes keeping children healthy and safe (Ruddick, 1989). What is entailed in keeping children safe is historically specific, as we saw in the beginning of this chapter. In contemporary society, we take much for granted. Advances in medical knowledge and technology mean that pregnancy and childbirth are relatively safe for mother and child. Immunizations and medical treatment also mean that infant mortality has declined and parents can be less concerned about the odds of their children not reaching adulthood due to disease.

But even with advanced technology, not all parents have healthy children. Anne-Marie Ambert's (1992) review of the literature on parenting children with severe chronic illnesses and disabilities suggests that every part of the parent–child relationship is affected when a child's health is compromised. Parents of children with fragile bones or bodies cannot hug, cuddle, or roughhouse with their children for fear of inflicting pain. Children with severe physical health problems are also more likely to have emotional problems, presenting additional challenges to parents. And because disabled children are often stigmatized in our society, their parents are required to put in additional time trying to negotiate friendships and safe environments for them. Ambert's own research also shows that mothers of severely ill children are very sensitive to how they are viewed by others. Mothers she spoke with reported that the looks they received from others led them to think that others believed that they (the mothers) were to blame for their children's problems. Because good parents are those who protect their children, these women had failed as mothers (in their own eyes).

In the previous section, we noted that parents respond to children, in part, based on their interpretations of their children's temperament. Parents also make assessments regarding their children's capabilities and competencies and will engage in parenting styles and practices accordingly (Dix et al., 1989). For example, if parents believe that their children do not have the potential to reach a certain goal, they may be less likely to engage in punitive parenting practices with their children when they don't make that goal. On the other hand, when children are seen as having potential, but do not behave in a certain way, parents may employ more disciplinary practices.

Parents also base their judgments of children's behavior on a comparison with

STONE SOUP   **BY JAN ELIOT**

Raising sons or daughters can bring different opportunities for interaction.

their own values and norms. When children either meet parents' expectations or exceed them, parents experience positive affect, and this influences their feedback to children. Negative affect for parents, and negative behavioral feedback to their children, are the consequences of children not meeting their parents' norms. Parents' expectations are related to their experiences with their own parents, as well as their social position. Social class, religion, race/ethnicity, and gender are all influential in the establishment of normative behaviors for both parents and children. We will discuss all of these factors in more detail below, but in terms of specific characteristics of children that influence parents, we turn now to how children's gender shapes parent–child interaction.

FACT OR FICTION?

Parents' involvement with children is affected by the gender of their children.

Children's Gender A considerable amount of research by social psychologists tells us

that parents treat their infants differently depending on the gender of the child (Leaper, 2002). Parents have been shown to be more physical with male infants, while they interact with daughters by using more visual and auditory stimuli (Maccoby & Martin, 1983; Rubin, Provenzano, & Luria, 1974). The big question is whether or not this interaction is based on actual sex differences in infants that call for different responses from parents or if it results from parents' perceptions of sex differences and their differential expectations for their sons and daughters to develop certain levels of physical and verbal competency. One of the ways we can see the influence of parents' expectations (and the norms of the broader society) is through the types of toys that are bought for very young children. Before children are old enough to state a preference, adults are more likely to buy sports-related toys for boys and dolls for girls. If we take a trip to our local toy store, it becomes clear that these "choices" are well understood. There are primary-color aisles for boys and pastel aisles for girls. Whatever biological propensities exist in young children, our culture is set up to re-inforce those qualities that lead girls and boys in different directions in terms of interests and temperament.

When children are older, parents are also more likely to expect different domestic activity from their daughters than from their sons. Although parents may perceive sex-related competencies (boys are better at outdoor tasks requiring physical strength) and "sex"-related interests (boys are not very interested in cooking), it is safe to say that the chores assigned to children are likely to be ones that both boys and girls can perform. The point is that we don't really know if it is biological sex that is the key here or the more socially constructed gender of children that makes the difference in how parents interact with their children. But what seems pretty clear is that whatever the biological propensities of children, parents and other adults interact with girls and boys differently. These differences in treatment reinforce what we know to be traditional stereotypes for masculinity and femininity.

Another intriguing finding from social science research is that fathers' behavior is particularly responsive to the gender of their children. For examples, fathers are more engaged with their sons, and with their children overall when there are sons (Harris & Morgan, 1991; Barnett & Baruch, 1987). When fathers are more involved with child rearing, mothers are happier; hence, marriages are more stable (Katzev, Warner, & Acock, 1994; Kalmijn, 1999; Morgan, Lye, & Condran, 1988).

FACT

However, the relationship is stronger for fathers.

Fathers' employment behavior is also responsive to the gender of their children. Economists have documented that having children changes the way that parents approach their labor market activity. With the birth of a child, parents begin to "specialize" their division of labor, with mothers taking on more domestic activity and limiting their labor market participation while fathers increase their labor market time. Although these patterns occur for parents of daughters as well as sons, the increase in fathers' labor market time after having sons is 2.5 times that of the increase after having daughters (Lundberg & Rose, 1999). In addition, men's wages are higher when they have sons than when they have daughters. These results suggest that "men work more and/or harder" when they have sons (Lundberg & Rose, 1999: 11). Similar analyses conducted for mothers show insignificant effects of child gender on their labor market activity.

FACT OR FICTION?

The majority of parents in the United States claim that they do not care if they have a girl or a boy (if they have only one child).

But what is it about children's gender that elicits different behavior from parents? One explanation is that parents are expected to play a more significant role in the lives of same-sex children to provide gender-specific role modeling. One of the concerns about "absent fathers" in our society is the resulting lack of appropriate role modeling. However, we've seen that mothers' behavior is not so responsive to the gender of their children. The time that mothers spend interacting with children and the time spent in employment are not correlated to children's gender the way fathers' are. Another explanation may be related to the preferences of parents (especially men) for sons. Opinion poll data show that 42 percent of adults in the United States say they have no preference for having a son or a daughter (if they could only have one child). But among the 58 percent who did have a preference, the scales tipped in favor of sons. Thirty-five percent of adults said they would like a son (60 percent of those

FIGURE 9.1 Gender Preferences for Children

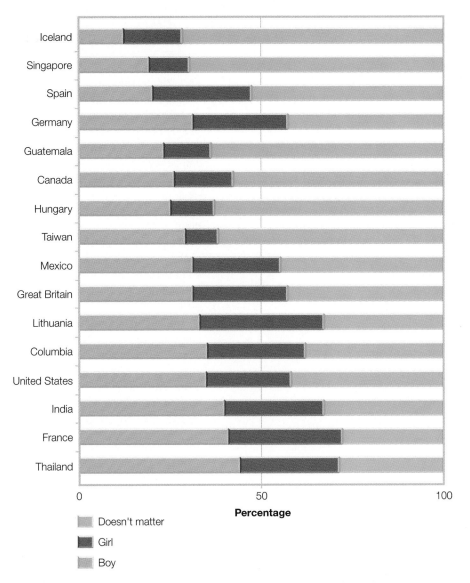

Percentage

Doesn't matter

Girl

Boy

with a preference), while 23 percent preferred a daughter (see Figure 9.1). The report also noted that men in the United States are slightly more likely to have a gender preference than are women. Of the countries included in the survey, U.S. men ranked fifth out of the sixteen countries in terms of having a son preference. In Chapter 8, we learned that marriages sometimes experi-

ence a decline in satisfaction with the birth of a child but that the effects are mediated by whether or not the child was "planned" (Cox, Paley, Burchinal, & Payne, 1999). A related argument might be that fathers are more involved with children when their desires for sons are met. Although research has not addressed these relationships directly, they point to broader conceptions of gender in our

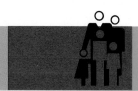

In a recent conference at Pennsylvania State University, family researchers came together to explore "Children's Influence on Family Dynamics: The Neglected Side of Family Relationships." Although these researchers are not dismissing the powerful role that parents play in families, they presented work that strongly encourages us to consider children as active, causal agents themselves (referred to as child effects). Doing so helps to elaborate on how reciprocity in family relationships more fully explains the dynamics involved in a variety of family outcomes.

One paper at this conference focused on an issue that has been the subject of considerable research—the relationship between parental monitoring and child outcomes. Researchers Margaret Kerr and Håkan

Stattin, from Örebro University in Sweden, argue that there may be reason to doubt the literature positing a causal relationship between the two, with parental monitoring being the independent variable. One reason for concern is the way "parental monitoring" has been measured. In much of the highly respected and widely cited research, parental monitoring is measured by responses to four items on a scale. These items ask if parents

1. know exactly where child is most afternoons after school
2. really know a lot about where child goes at night
3. really know a lot about what child does with free time
4. really know a lot about where child is most afternoons after school

In an earlier study, Stattin and Kerr (2000) tested the idea that knowing these things about children was directly a consequence of actual behaviors by parents (such as solicitation of information or controlling behaviors). They found that knowledge was not correlated with parents' initiatives; rather, parents' knowledge was based on their children's willing disclosure of their own behavior. In other words, researchers have been attributing something to parents that should be attributed to adolescents (a child effect).

These findings led the researchers to go one step further. Maybe the direction of the relationship, one in which parents' behavior is seen as the variable that produces change in the behavior of their adolescent children, should be ques-

culture that give rise to the expectations and desires of parents.

| FICTION

Fifty-eight percent of Americans prefer a child of a specific gender. Of those, 60 percent prefer a boy.

Reciprocal Socialization

What the previous discussion suggests is that socialization is a **reciprocal** process in families. Both parents and children are influenced by the behavior, attitudes, and orientations of the other. Reciprocity does not mean that the effects are identical from parents to children and children to parents, or that the strength of the relationships is equal. What it implies is that socialization is a process, one in which parents and children learn and develop through ongoing interaction. The dynamics of this process help create and sustain long-term relationships between parents and children as well. An interesting recent study questioning the direction of effects between parents and children is summarized in the Focus on Family Research box above.

An example of reciprocal socialization can be seen from the literature just reviewed. The styles and practices of parenting

tioned. They collected data from both youths and their parents at two points in time (N=1,283, youths in eighth and then tenth grade). They included youth self-reports on delinquency, youth disclosure of information to parents, parents' solicitation of information, and parental controlling behavior (e.g., setting curfews). What they found might be surprising. They found that parenting behavior at time 1 did not predict delinquency at time 2. Instead, it is the youths' delinquency at time 1 that produced a change in parenting behaviors. And the specific outcome was that the delinquency at time 1 led parents to be *less* involved in monitoring activities. In more detailed analyses, the authors find that parents may be reducing their monitoring effects in order to avoid conflicts with their children.

Because this research represents a small slice of family lives, when children are adolescents, it does not explain how they got to this point. It may well be that earlier behavior by parents set up the situation that existed by the time children in this study reached eighth grade. In this case, then, we can argue that over the long term it is the reciprocal relationships (the interactions) between parents and children that need to be studied.

This study raises important issues about what we study and how we study it: "What we know is limited to what we have tried to know, and, for the most part, that has been how parents *influence* adolescent adjustment—a unidirectional question. A challenge for future research, then, is to inquire about how to pose research questions that can

give us the largest set of possible answers" (2001: 33).

Source: Kerr and Stattin (2001).

Critical Thinking

1. Thinking back on when you were younger and living with your parent(s), do you agree that what parents know is a reflection of what children tell them?

2. Why do children keep information from their parents? Is there anything that could encourage children to be more forthcoming?

shape the way that children learn, but they also can influence the way that children respond to their parents. Parents using coercive models of parenting may find that their children do not respond to them or others in positive ways. These interactions can escalate, and minor problems can develop into more serious acts of antisocial or delinquent behaviors later on. On the other hand, early parenting styles that are more likely to elicit a trust in and respect for parents can work toward closer relationships between parents and children later in life.

It is also very important to look beyond the parent–child interaction to the broader context within which families live. We've argued above that parenting is a process that involves parents' providing for their children, giving them the skills and tools necessary to be effective members of society. To raise socially competent children includes passing on relevant values and norms, and these may be different among people of different religions, social classes, and ethnicities. In addition, being able to protect children is related to the social positions of families. Some parents face challenges to protecting or caring for their children related to economic conditions, while other parents face struggles stemming from discrimination based on race and ethnicity. Because parents' beliefs about their ability to care for their children affect their parenting behaviors, it is critical to remember the ways that social context shapes how parents and children interact.

Social Class and Parent–Child Relations

One of the important ways in which social context plays a role in parent–child relations can be seen by looking at families across the spectrum of social class. As we saw at the beginning of this chapter, people have struggled to provide a safe and secure environment for their families throughout history. But even within historical periods, not all families face the same sets of challenges to raising healthy or competent children. We live in a society where the majority of people consider themselves "middle class." However, the considerable variation in the occupations and incomes of Americans can affect the ways in which parents spend time with their children (see Chapter 3 for a review of the definition of social class and its implications for families).

The structure of parents' employment can place constraints on family interactions. First, the amount of time spent in employment activities will directly affect the time available for families to be together. The more time parents spend away from home, the less time they have to interact with or monitor their children (Voydanoff, 1987). Second, jobs can also set parameters for when the time is spent. Parents working the swing shift or the graveyard shift will have different hours available than parents who are working days. Finally, some jobs can induce stress. Parents working in low-wage, dead-end jobs without the opportunity to get ahead can bring job stress home, in turn decreasing the quality of interactions with other family members, including children. Reasoning with children about their behavior and providing support for the development of new skills are harder to do when a parent is depressed or distressed because of work.

Another critical implication of employment for families is income. The ability to have shelter, food, and clothing varies in our society. Close to a million children experience a spell of homelessness each year (Burt & Aron, 2000). Many poor families live in run-down neighborhoods and send their children to schools where their health and safety are also at risk (Seccombe, 2000). (We will discuss the problems of poverty more generally in Chapter 11.) The economic standing of parents affects their ability to protect their children (physically) and to provide the type of socialization experiences we've been talking about in this chapter. At particular risk for poverty are single parents (especially women) and families in which parents have experienced unemployment.

Social class also affects parent–child relationships through the transfer of class-related values. In his *Class and Conformity*, Melvin Kohn (1977) argues that the structure of employment shapes workers' orientations. For example, parents employed in working-class occupations (assembly-line work, jobs requiring physical labor) are in working environments that are more supervised or controlled. To be successful in their jobs, working-class employees must conform to company rules and policies, and they would face discipline if they did not. Therefore, working-class parents come to value conformity and obedience. Parents employed in middle-class occupations (teachers, managers, those in professional positions) have very different employment demands. They are given more autonomy in their work schedules and engage in fewer routine activities. For them, being successful might involve coming up with new ideas or finding solutions to problems. Kohn argues that these job-related values are generalized to other areas of people's lives, including child-rearing values. He found that working-class parents are relatively more likely to value obedience, conformity, and good manners in their children. Middle-class parents place more emphasis on independence, self-direction, and curiosity.

Research since Kohn's early work has generally supported his ideas. Parents employed in occupations that require more complexity place a higher value on self-direction and autonomy in their child-rearing strategies. Work that requires less complexity is associated with child-rearing values that include obedience (Kohn & Schooler, 1983; Crouter & McHale, 1993). A recent study of children aged eight to ten and their families reveals how these values get transferred from parents to children through day-to-day interactions and language (Lareau, 2002). For example, white and black middle-class parents engage in what Lareau calls "concerted cultivation." They enroll their children in a number of organized activities that they believe transmit important life skills. Talking with their children is the preferred form of discipline. Compared to middle-class children, working-class and poor children are involved in significantly fewer organized activities and spend their free time developing ties with extended family and neighborhood friends. Their parents are more likely to issue directives and to place more emphasis on physical punishment.

The long-term effect of differential socialization may be the reinforcement of social class itself. As children are encouraged to value different approaches to work, they may find that certain types of jobs or training are more or less appealing to them. At the same time, having been socialized with different orientations may make individuals more or less successful in obtaining different types of employment. As Lareau concludes from her study, "Differences in family life lie not only in the advantages parents obtain for their children, but also in the skills they transmit to children for negotiating their own life paths" (2002: 749).

Although social class variation continues to exist, among all parents there has been a shift toward valuing autonomy in children over obedience (Alwin, 1996). Valuing autonomy in children is consistent with U.S. values and culture. The increasing emphasis on such values in child rearing is in line with other socio-demographic changes in our society, including a decline in fertility; an increase in independent living; changing patterns of marriage, cohabitation, and divorce; and changes in the gendered division of labor.

Race/Ethnicity and Parent–Child Relations

Early work on race, ethnicity, and parent–child relations started with an understanding of socialization based primarily on white (European American) families. This understanding included a model of parenting whereby children were seen as benefiting most from an authoritative (versus authoritarian) style of parenting. African American and Latino families were found to be more likely to use an authoritarian model of parenting, which included being more strict with their children. Because prior research found that this style of parenting was associated with higher rates of behavioral problems and decreased school performance, the impression was that these families were "deficient." However, there is evidence "that the 'stricter' parenting styles of African Americans may be more in the eye of the (European American) beholder than in African American parenting" (McLoyd, Cauce, Takeuchi, & Wilson, 2000: 1082). One study recruited both African American and non-African American adults to observe mother–daughter interactions. The participants were asked to characterize the interactions in terms of how restrictive the mothers seemed and how much conflict they observed. The non-African American observers perceived both more restrictive parenting behaviors and more conflict than did the African American observers. Differences in the interpretations of behaviors of Chinese American parenting styles have also been observed (Chao, 1994). These studies point to the difficulty in learning about different families when we compare them to a norm established by a single group.

Over the past ten years, however, research has shifted in focus from this deficit approach to one that puts families of color at the center of analysis, asking how they approach the socialization of their children. Probably one of the most notable features of family life for people of color is that in addition to the challenges European American families have faced historically, parents of color have also had to face prejudice and discrimination based on their race and/or ethnicity (see Chapter 3). Discrimination can affect family life in many ways. First, it has an effect on the ability of parents to gain access to jobs that can provide economic security (Wilson, 1987). According to the 2000 U.S. Census (www.census.gov/hhes/income/histinc/f05.html), family income across racial/ethnic groups was reported as follows:

- Non-Hispanic white families earned $56,442.
- Asian and Pacific Islander families earned $61,504.
- African American families earned $34,204.
- Families of Hispanic origin earned $35,050.

Poverty is unevenly distributed across racial/ethnic lines. In 2001, 7.4 percent of families with children under the age of 18 were living in poverty. The percentage of blacks and Hispanics in such families living in poverty was over three times as high (25.6 percent and 23.2 percent, respectively) (U.S. Census Bureau, 2002). Recall that the average annual expenditure for a child in families in the lower third of the income distribution is about $6,500 (see Chapter 8), a factor that puts some families at greater risk when trying to satisfy basic economic needs.

Prejudice and discrimination based on race/ethnicity can also affect children's development of a positive identity or sense of self (Peters, 1985; Collins, 1996). Parents must act as a buffer between their children and the negative images of them in the larger society. Racial/ethnic families can help their children in a number of ways. One feature of many racial/ethnic families is that they tend to have developed broader kinship networks (Zinn, 1993). In their struggles to overcome a variety of social forces throughout history, ethnic groups have created diverse family forms. African Americans (Sudkarasa, 1997; Collins, 1996), Hispanics (Griswold del Castillo, 1998; Leyendecker & Lamb, 1999), and Asian Americans (Glen, 1993) have constructed extended-family systems with informal social support networks that include several households. Children may have access to many adults who can care for them physically and emotionally. Another way that families adapt to racial/ethnic discrimination is parents' engaging in practices that encourage their children to learn about their cultural heritage and to develop a sense of pride in who they are.

FACT OR FICTION?

Parents in racial/ethnic families face additional concerns when raising their children.

Research on African American families finds that goals for children are quite similar to those of white families—the desire is for children to be happy, secure, and successful ("socially competent") (S. A. Hill, 1999). However, in addition to socializing the values leading to social competence, racial/ethnic

Racial/ethnic minority families often celebrate events to recognize their cultural heritage. Here a Latino family celebrates a daughter's fifteenth birthday (quinceañera).

parents must also help their children develop and apply these skills in a world that is not race/ethnic neutral. They do this by incorporating racial/ethnic socialization as an explicit part of their parent–child relations. Racial socialization has been defined as an "attempt to prepare their children for the realities of being Black in America" (Taylor, Chatters, Tucker, & Lewis, 1990: 994). Racial socialization is not only an issue for black parents, nor is it only an issue for people of color. European American parents are also involved in teaching their children about race and ethnicity. However, the point of such teaching is usually about tolerance, acceptance, and inequality. For parents of color, an added dimension is the preparation for being a potential victim of intolerance, nonacceptance, and inequality (McLoyd et al., 2000).

Boykin and Toms (1985) addressed this additional burden on African American families. They refer to it as the **triple quandary of socialization,** and it is applicable to par-

ents of all families of color. It includes the following parenting approaches:

1. *Mainstream socialization.* Parents prepare children for success in American society, emphasizing the development of self-confidence, ambition, hard work, and respect. These values transcend race and are intended to focus on human values.

2. *Minority experience socialization.* Parents prepare their children to respond to race-related problems in American life: prejudice and discrimination. Parents share their own experiences with prejudice and help their children respond to new incidents as they occur.

3. *Cultural expressions.* These parent–child interactions revolve around learning the history of one's ethnic group(s). Parents might identify prominent historical figures from their ethnic group who can serve as role

models, and they can encourage their children's participation in cultural events celebrating their ethnic heritage. The difference between this and minority experience socialization is that it is intended to bring people of certain ethnic groups together (across social class lines) to recognize the legitimacy of their heritage.

| FACT

In addition to general concerns about raising competent children, racial/ethnic parents must also help to prepare their children for the potential of prejudice and discrimination. They must also supplement school learning to help their children create a positive sense of racial/ethnic identity.

A recent study comparing racial/ethnic groups finds that racial socialization occurs to varying degrees across racial and ethnic families (Phinney & Chavira, 1995). For example, African American parents are more likely to interact with their children regarding problems and solutions for prejudice than are Mexican American parents. Less likely than either African Americans or Mexican Americans to engage in such interaction are Japanese American parents. The extent to which parents engage in racial socialization is related to factors such as whether or not they were socialized in regard to race issues when they were children, whether or not they perceive racial prejudice in their place of employment, and the extent to which their identity and self-concept are centered in their communities. In a recent study of African American families with elementary school children, Hughs and Johnson (2001) found that parents are particularly attentive to issues of racial socialization when their children report unfair treatment by adults. It is hard to imagine *not* socializing children about race, given that parents are expected

to protect and prepare a child for adulthood. However, parents of color are not completely consumed with the issue of race. Shirley Hill (1999) suggests that African American parents do not have precise plans about what to say and what to do regarding racial socialization. Instead, the response emerges from the particular experiences of black parents (or other parents of color). The most important part of racial socialization concerns the development of positive self-esteem and a positive sense of self as a person of a particular racial/ethnic group (Thornton, 1997).

Gender and Parent–Child Relations

We have already addressed many ways in which gender is important for shaping the relationships between parents and children. Historically, the roles, expectations, and meanings of parenthood have been aligned with whether or not we are talking about mothers or fathers. And even though these meanings have shifted over time, with greater expectations for fathers to be involved in child rearing, most researchers find that mothers still do the lion's share of child care. The division of family labor also affects children and what are acceptable behaviors and activities for them (Cunningham, 2001). The gender of children shapes relationships among family members as well. We've seen that parents respond to sons and daughters in different ways and that parents expect different things from their children according to gender. The result of these interactions is the construction of the children's concept of their selves as gendered (West & Zimmerman, 1987). Children learn about what it means to be a daughter or son, boy or girl, by watching their parents and engaging in family rituals and activities. Although the family is just one of the many socializing agents in a child's life, the family is a child's first exposure to gender and probably the most important one (Crouter, McHale, & Bartko, 1993). We'll see that gender gets constructed in families in a variety of ways related to the structure of the household (number and gender of parents, age and gender of children) and the race/ethnicity of families.

The majority of children under the age of eighteen are living with two parents (see Figure 9.2). There is some variation across racial/ethnic groups, with non-Hispanic white (79 percent) and Asian and Pacific Islander children (84 percent) being more likely than Hispanic (68 percent) or American Indian and Alaska Native children (62 percent) to be living with two parents. The only group for which a majority of children do *not* live with two parents is black children (38 percent). The majority of black children are living with their mothers only. The ways in which parents are involved with their children are related to race, ethnicity, and household composition. When children live with only one parent, they get exposure to a single role model who is involved in the full range of parenting activities: economic, physical, and emotional care. With two parents, it is possible to see both parents involved in all types of care, but it is more likely for children to experience the gender specialization in domestic behavior that we've seen emerge in marriages and families. From these different situations, children are given clues about what is appropriate behavior for them to develop. In other words, children learn what it means to become a socially competent man or woman.

In families with two parents, mothers are generally more involved in child care than are fathers (Aldous, Mulligan, & Bjarnason, 1998; Barnett & Shen, 1997; Walker, 1999). Part of the reason is that mothers are still less likely to be employed than are fathers, making the amount of time available to provide child care greater for mothers. But

Children learn what it means to be a boy or girl by watching their parents.

when both parents are employed, fathers usually still have an earnings advantage over mothers, giving fathers a bargaining resource to *not* engage in household labor, including child care (Coltrane & Ishii-Kuntz, 1992). (We discuss this bargaining approach to explaining the division of labor in Chapter 2.) Following this approach, we would expect fathers to be more involved in child care if their wives are employed. This idea has been supported by research showing fathers' time being directly responsive to the hours that

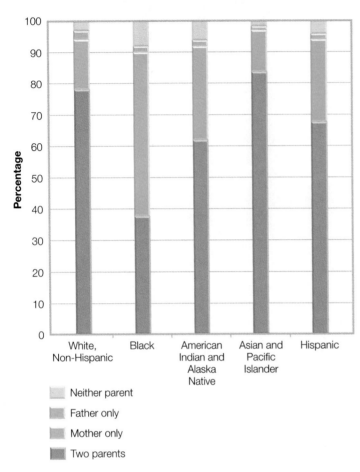

Neither parent

Father only

Mother only

Two parents

Source: Fields (2001).

when mothers were employed, this study revealed that even when both are employed full time, mothers still provide more child care than fathers do.

Another feature of household composition that appears to be related to parent–child interactions is sibling structure. Crouter and associates (1995) found that children's interaction with parents became more gender specific when they had a younger sibling of the opposite gender. Daughters became more involved with their mothers when they had younger brothers, while sons interacted more with fathers when they had younger sisters. The findings here are like those mentioned above. When there are family members of both genders (father and mother, daughter and son), there tends to be a greater specialization in domestic activity.

As we learned above, fathers' involvement is also related to the gender of their children. Fathers spend more time with their sons in particular, but with all their children if they have sons (Aldous et al., 1998; Barnett & Baruch, 1987; Harris & Morgan, 1991; Harris, Furstenberg, & Marmer, 1998). Mothers' time with their children has not been found to be related to the children's gender. Reasons for this differential may be due to expectations by parents, and by society in general, for fathers to be gender-specific role models for their sons. Mothers are expected to be child-care providers in general and therefore are expected to care for all children. Also, some activities that children are involved in encourage fathers' greater involvement with sons. Most team sports are still gender segregated, and fathers might find it easier to interact with their sons in activities that they participated in as children (such as football, baseball, or Boy Scouts). This is not to say that parents won't, shouldn't, or don't get involved with both daughters and sons. But our society is still organized in ways that reinforce differential involvement with children depending on gen-

their wives work (Blair & Johnson, 1992), especially when young children are in the family (Deutsch et al., 1993). Using data from the National Survey of Families and Households, Aldous and her colleagues (1998) found that when children were young (preschool age), fathers did about one-third the amount of child care that mothers did. With older children, fathers' time increased so that they provided almost two-thirds the time mothers did. And although the time differences between mothers and fathers were smaller

Statistics show that fathers in Japan spend an average of 17 minutes a day with their young children. This finding has been printed on posters in hopes that men will be encouraged to do more at home. Women are demanding that men learn how to care for their young children's basic needs such as changing diapers, and irritated men are demanding that the government stay out of domestic situations (especially this one).

It seems that even Parliament members are shocked by the government's campaign suggesting that in "the model family" men and women should split child care. In defense of dads across the country, Parliament member Yasuo Ichikawa said, "Many fathers start working early and work late, and mothers take care of the family and respect the father." Another voice against change is banker Noboru Yamada, who said, "We just don't have time." Yamada has two grown children, and he said that when his children were young, though he changed a diaper only about every six months, he spent more than a few minutes a day with his kids. He then went on to add that this occur-

rence happened only every "ten days or two weeks."

The Health Ministry has sponsored a campaign of television ads and posters featuring one of the most famous fathers in the country: a hip, young dancer. The dancer is holding his infant son, and the caption reads "A man who does not help in child rearing cannot be called a father." This ad has provoked a hostile reaction from angry fathers, who call the Health Ministry, telling the government to mind its own business.

The media uproar is once again focused on the relationship between the sexes. In 1996 a United Nations survey concluded that Japanese men significantly trailed men in other advanced industrialized countries in the time spent helping out around home. With Japan's birthrate dropping to an all-time low (1.39 births per woman), reasons for this trend are linked to women delaying marriage and children. A factor believed to contribute to this situation is fathers' general reluctance to help out at home. Economic upheaval in Japan is forcing social changes, and with increasing demands for dual-income families,

men are pitching in more at home since they need their wife's salary. However, many men are not helping out, and the change is not happening evenly since fathers are resisting the pressure to take over nontraditional fatherhood roles. Many men feel the discussions are very one-sided right now. Takeshi Mito, an electronics salesman, feels that men are being ignored and says, "Guys are hurting too."

Source: Written by Valerie Bredemeier. Adapted from Mary Jordan and Kevin Sulivan (LA Times–Washington Post Service). "Japan Pushes Dads to Spend More Than 17 Minutes a Day with Kids." Appeared in the International section of the *Sunday Oregonian*, May 9, 1999, page A16.

Critical Thinking

1. Do you think the situation in Japan is that different from the situation in the United States? Why or why not?

2. Families in Japan are feeling the crunch of "economic upheaval." How might economic challenges affect other aspects of families (in addition to gender relations)?

der, a fact that may also be true in many other countries as well. See the Family Narratives box above for how fathers' participation (or lack of it) in children's lives is causing a bit of a national uproar in Japan.

Another way in which parental involvement has been shown to influence children's gender is through the nature or quality of the relationship that adults had with their parents when they were younger. Using data from the National Survey of Children, one study found that gender orientations held by young adults (aged 18–22) were not correlated with whether fathers had resided with their families when they were younger (aged 7–11). However, sons were likely to hold more-egalitarian views about gender (regarding work/family roles) when they had had nurturing relations with their fathers (Hardesty, Wenk, & Morgan, 1995).

Racial/Ethnic Variations in Gender Socialization

There is some evidence of racial/ethnic variation in the division of labor among parents. Research shows that the division of labor is relatively more equitable among African Americans than among European Americans (although women still do a larger proportion) (McLoyd, 1993). Some have suggested that African American men have more time available for domestic work due to higher rates of unemployment, but research finds that the greater involvement holds regardless of the employment status of men (Shelton & John, 1993; Coltrane, 2000). To the extent that children model after their parents, this research suggests that children in African American families may learn less traditional notions about gender in families (McLoyd et al., 2000).

Direct parental involvement with children shows less variation across racial and ethnic groups. A review of the literature on families of color finds that African American, Hispanic, and European American fathers spend comparable amounts of time in primary activities and in monitoring children (McLoyd et al., 2000). When differences do occur, fathers of color show slightly higher levels of involvement, and they are less likely than European American fathers to be differentially involved with sons compared to daughters.

Variations in family practices across racial and ethnic groups are related to the different historical, social, and cultural experiences of families. Historically, families of color have not had the same opportunities to construct a traditional division of labor that keeps women out of the labor force. Because of the centrality of employment for both women and men, for example, African American parents are more likely to emphasize similar traits for daughters and sons (S. A. Hill, 1999).

Parents of all racial and ethnic groups vary to the extent that they practice gender-specific family practices or emphasize gender differentiation for their children. Religion, education, and employment patterns all contribute to ideas about what parents think are appropriate activities and experiences for girls and boys. When parents hold religious beliefs that women and men are intended to engage in different behaviors that complement one another, they are more likely to model this behavior and/or teach it to their children (Gallagher, 2003). Parents with higher levels of education are more likely to hold egalitarian views and practice more sharing in their domestic behavior. And when both parents in a two-parent family are employed full time, their children are more likely to experience variations in gender displays. These differences have been shown to exist across racial and ethnic groups.

Two recent longitudinal studies show that parents' division of labor has a long-term effect on their children's division of labor and their ideas about gender when they are adults. For example, data from a study following children from age one to thirty-one indicate that sons who grew up in households where their mothers were at home full time while their fathers were employed later held more-traditional views than those sons who lived in families with two employed parents (Cunningham, 2001). This same study found that when fathers were involved in stereotypically female tasks early in a son's life, the son was more likely to engage in such tasks as an adult. A daughter's adult household behavior was more likely to be shaped by her mother's employment behavior than by her mother's domestic behavior.

In another study, Crouter and associates (1995) found that when parents have a traditional division of labor, adolescent children are more likely to specialize in the tasks that they perform in the household. Along with the longitudinal study just mentioned, this work suggests that "family characteristics during childhood shape individuals' understanding of the symbolic meaning of particular behaviors for identifying and enacting gender" (Cunningham, 2001: 199).

In sum, gender gets socialized in families through the ways in which family members spend time with one another. When parents have a more specialized division of labor within the family and assign tasks to children aligned with gender, children are more likely to grow up and emulate these behaviors themselves. On the other hand, when children grow up observing different parenting practices (shared parenting or single parenting), their exposure to a variety of presentations of gender encourages less stereotypical views. But although the ways in which children construct their family lives as adults are shaped by their early family experiences, many other factors also influence their decisions. In some ways, traditional gender ideals get reinforced outside family life. Schools, the media, and peer culture all encourage differentiated views about gender. In other ways, experiences outside of families of orientation can challenge the influence of traditional socialization. Education, employment experiences, and interactions with friends can all play important roles in socializing gender.

FACT OR FICTION?

Children who grow up with gay and lesbian parents are more likely to become gay themselves.

Gay and Lesbian Families

The family lives of gays and lesbians have been under scrutiny during the past several decades. Normative definitions of family are closely aligned with heterosexuality, making the notion that lesbian or gay parents can raise children a questionable one in our society (Weston, 1991). What we know about gay and lesbian parents and families is somewhat limited. The research available is not extensive and has been the subject of political debate. A considerable amount of this research has been undertaken as a response to judicial cases regarding child custody. In order to show that lesbian and gay parents either should or should not get custody of children following a divorce, researchers have collected data and presented these data in ways that can be used to support their arguments. For those in support of lesbian and gay parental rights, the approach has been to show "no differences" between gay and straight parenting styles and practices, while those who oppose same-gender parenting relationships look for as many differences as possible.

In a research paper published in the *American Sociological Review,* Judith Stacey and Timothy Biblarz (2001) attempt to review some of these studies in order to get past the politics and understand the dynamics of parent–child relationships in light of parents' sexual orientation. Their review is consistent with other reviews (Patterson, 1998, 2000) in that there are no differences in the psychological well-being of children raised in families with either heterosexual parents or gay/lesbian parents. To date, all measures of the quality of parent–child relationships show no measurable differences between families. Also consistent with other reviews, lesbian mothers do not differ from heterosexual mothers in terms of their psychological "fitness" to parent. In fact, when differences occur, lesbian mothers had somewhat more positive outcomes on measures of mental health than did heterosexual mothers.

However, the "no differences" argument is not supported in other areas, but the findings are not clearly in one direction or the

© Najah Feanny/Stock, Boston

Research suggests that children growing up with lesbian parents are less likely to follow gender stereotypes because their parents also don't follow traditional divisions of labor.

other. These differences are in (1) parenting practices, (2) children's gender preferences and behavior, and (3) children's sexual preferences and behaviors. In terms of parenting practices, researchers have looked for indications of parenting skills thought to aid in the development of children's social competence (Baumrind, 1978). On this issue there is pretty consistent evidence that lesbian and gay parents are as "skilled" as heterosexual parents, and in some studies, lesbian and gay parents have higher rates of these desired skills. In another area of parenting practices, research indicates that lesbian partners in two-parent households are more likely to share responsibilities for family work and child care than are heterosexual parents. Together, these findings provide evidence for the argument that children are not disadvantaged in gay/lesbians families with respect to developing social skills.

Another area where differences emerge is in children's gender preferences and behavior. In one study comparing 56 children living with divorced lesbian mothers to 48 children with divorced heterosexual mothers, it was found that sons across the two household types did not differ with respect to their preference in television programs, games, or toys. However, daughters of lesbian mothers were more likely to play in ways that are considered stereotypically masculine (Green, Mandel, Hotvedt, Gray, & Smith, 1986). Daughters of lesbian mothers were also more likely than daughters of heterosexual mothers to have occupational aspirations considered to be more masculine, such as doctor, lawyer, engineer, or astronaut. The findings for sons are more mixed; some studies indicate no difference, and a few suggest that sons are less aggressive and hold less traditional views on gender. Stacey

396 ● Families at Work I PART THREE

and Biblarz (2001: 177) suggest that this is a very logical finding from a variety of theoretical perspectives: "Children who derive their principal source of love, discipline, protection, and identification from women living independent of male domestic authority or influence should develop less stereotypical symbolic, emotional, practical, and behavioral gender repertoires."

Probably the area that has received the most public concern is whether or not gay and lesbian parents socialize their children to be gay or lesbian. Most of the research in this area has been problematic because it does not follow children into adulthood, when sexual identity takes clearer form (Patterson, 2000). However, one study has included longitudinal data from children: *Growing Up in a Lesbian Family* (Tasker & Golombok, 1997). This study included 39 children growing up in a lesbian family and 39 children growing up in a heterosexual single-mother family. The results included the finding that children raised by lesbian mothers were more likely to have had a homoerotic experience or to anticipate that they might. However, the researchers found no significant differences between children across the two types of families in terms of their likelihood to claim a gay, lesbian, or bisexual identity when they reached adulthood.

| FICTION

Although children in gay and lesbian families are more nontraditional in some respects (toy preference, career preference), they are no more likely to have a gay/lesbian identity when they grow up.

Several cautions are necessary when reviewing this research. First, large-scale, longitudinal research on lesbian, gay, and bisexual families is quite recent, meaning that the samples of most prior research are small and sometimes noncomparable. Second, there is considerably less research on gay families,

so generalizing from the research on lesbian mothers mentioned above is difficult. Finally, we need to be careful not to conclude that the differences between children in gay/lesbian families and heterosexual families are caused by the sexual orientation of parents. Lesbian and gay families are much more likely to live in cosmopolitan areas (San Francisco, New York) and socially progressive communities (university towns). These communities are much more tolerant of diversity in sexual orientation and lifestyles (Stacey & Biblarz, 2001) and may be influential in socializing children toward more-liberal views on sexual orientation independent of their parents. Also, gay and lesbian families confront a stigma in a society where heterosexuality is the norm. Like families of color, gay/lesbian families face the challenges of discrimination, which may lead these parents to develop a broader array of parenting skills that help prepare their children to face challenging social interactions (Oswald, 2002).

Who Is Taking Care of the Children?

Up to this point, we have emphasized how social context is important for shaping the interaction between parents and children. One very important component of our social world that has had tremendous implications for raising children is the participation of parents in employment. Specifically, there have been dramatic shifts in the employment patterns of women, wives, and mothers in the last century. In 1948, about one-quarter of women with children of school age (6–18) were employed, while fewer mothers with preschool-age children were employed (10 percent). Today, 77 percent of mothers with school-age children are employed. A majority of mothers of preschool-age children (64 percent) are also employed (Cohen & Bianchi, 1999). One of the consequences of

The majority of children under age five receive some kind of care other than from parents. For those spending time in child care centers, experiences vary widely. One major source of variation is the teacher/child ratio.

this change is that women are having fewer children. Even with fewer children, however, employed women and their families face the challenge of negotiating care for their children. Parents employ a variety of child-care arrangements for their children, depending on the age of the child and the structure of their other obligations. Two-earner families might attempt to find employment during different sets of hours so that one parent can always be available for the children. Single parents, on the other hand, are more likely to depend on relatives or more formal arrangements. But across all family types, the demand for child care is increasing, and to meet the demand, most parents use more than one arrangement to care for their children when they cannot.

FACT OR FICTION?

Parents provide all the child care for the majority of children under the age of five.

Caring for Preschool-Age Children

The majority of children in this country under the age of five receive some kind of care other than that of their primary parent (usually considered to be the mother). In 1995, 14.4 million children (or about 75 percent) were in some kind of regularly scheduled child care. On average, this group of children spent about 28 hours per week in child care (Smith, 2000). Although preschoolers were more likely to be taken care of by someone other than their designated parent when that parent was working or in school (98 percent of children), it was also quite common for children of nonworking primary parents (44 percent) to have others care for them at least some time during the week.

The types of arrangements used by parents include both the use of relatives (particularly grandparents, which we discuss in

FIGURE 9.3 Child-Care Arrangements for Children from Birth Through Third Grade, 1999: Percentage of Children by Age and Type of Care

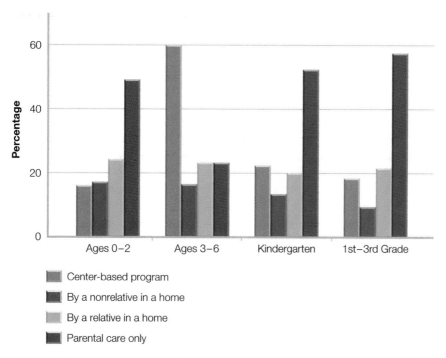

- ■ Center-based program
- ■ By a nonrelative in a home
- ■ By a relative in a home
- ■ Parental care only

Source: U.S. Department of Education, National Center for Education Statistics, National Household Education Survey. Accessed at www.childstat.gov/ac2001/pop7.htm on Sept. 26, 2001.

Chapter 14) as well as nonrelatives in either home-based care or in organized facilities. Young preschoolers (aged 0–2) are most likely to be cared for by parents only. Parents are much more likely to use center-based programs for their children when they are between the ages of 3 and 6 (see Figure 9.3). A greater variety of programs are available for parents of children in this older age group. In addition to day care centers, which are primarily facilities to watch children, pre-kindergartens and other educational programs are designed to give children a head start on preparing for elementary school.

| FICTION

About 75 percent of children under the age of five receive some kind of regularly scheduled child care.

Negotiating care for children can be challenging for employed parents. Like the term implies, "day care" facilities are often not open in the evenings (or on weekends). Parents working the afternoon or night shift face a significant barrier to using organized facilities. Other types of nonrelative care— for example, taking children to another person's home to be watched with a small group of other children—are also restrictive in terms of the hours that they are available. Parents find themselves in need of care at variable times as they work overtime or need to put in additional days of work. Because of the demands of employment, and the relatively limited supply of most day care facilities, most parents report using more than one type of child-care arrangement (average of 2.2 types of care). The most common combination of care was to use both an organized facility and another nonrelative (28 percent of parents of children under age five). The second most common was to use a nonrelative and the "other parent" (23 percent) (Smith, 2000).

This use of the "other parent" is an interesting finding. The data for this report (Smith, 2000) come from the Survey of Income and Program Participation. The survey identifies a "designated parent" to provide information. In married-couple families, mothers were the designated parent (if at all possible). So, when their fathers were caring for children, it was characterized as "child care." This rhetorical style reinforces the notion that when fathers are involved with children, it is considered to be "helping out the mother." In single-parent families, the other parent (nonresident) also played a role, although it was more minor. The other parent was more likely to be involved in child care in a single-parent family when that other parent was the mother: nonresident mothers were three times more likely to be involved in caring for their preschoolers than were nonresident fathers.

Caring for School-Age Children

As children reach the age of kindergarten and first grade, parents are relieved of some of the challenges of finding child care. The majority of children in the United States are in school, averaging about 35 hours a week. But with many parents working more than 35 hours, other arrangements still need to be made. Like parents of preschoolers, parents of children between the ages of five and fourteen use multiple arrangements (an average of 2.8 arrangements). The types of care available for older children are different. Outside of school, these children are involved in a variety of enrichment activities, such as sports, les-

sons, and club activities. But, like younger children, school-age children also spend time with other relatives (other parent, grandparents, or siblings).

Children Engaging in Self-Care As children get older, parents begin to give them increasing amounts of responsibility, part of which is to care for themselves (Kurz, 2002; Polatnick, 2002). The public image of children caring for themselves is not always positive. A term sometimes used to describe children who are responsible for their own care is "latchkey" children. During the 1970s and 1980s, when the employment of mothers began to rise dramatically, quite a bit of media attention was given to latchkey children and the issue of their safety. Like the concern about children in the care of "strangers," people's understanding of children as innocents who need adult supervision and care led many to worry about this trend.

Data from 1990–1995 suggest that the numbers of children who are engaging in **self-care** are not on the rise. In 1990, 12 percent of 5–13-year-olds spent some time in self-care, and this figure had not changed five years later. The stabilization of these rates is probably the result of a stabilization of employment patterns for mothers. In 1990, 75 percent of mothers whose youngest child was between six and seventeen (when they are most likely to be allowed to care for themselves) were employed. By 1995, the rate had gone up only one point, to 76 percent.

As we can see in Figure 9.4, the likelihood of grade-school-age children being in self-care is correlated with age. The biggest change comes between the ages of ten (when 14 percent of children use self-care) and eleven (24 percent in self-care). This is the time when many children are transitioning between elementary and middle school. They are taking on more responsibility in many aspects of their lives.

FIGURE 9.4 Percentage of Children Aged 5–14 in Self-Care, 1995

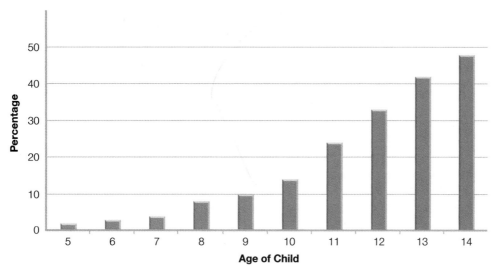

Source: Smith (2000).

The cost of one year of care for a four-year-old is more than the cost of one year of college tuition.

The Costs of Child Care

When parents are faced with selecting a child-care arrangement, they must consider a number of things, including the quality of care and the cost of care. Both of these issues have implications for the availability of care. The cost of child care has risen dramatically. One report suggests that from 1985 to 1995, costs went up 45 percent (Smith, 2000). Currently, estimates are that parents spend between $4,000 and $6,000 per year, but it is not uncommon for annual costs to rise to $10,000 (Schulman, 2000).

The amount depends on whether families live in rural or urban areas, the type of care selected, and the age of the child. Costs are higher in urban areas, for center-based care, and for infants. Based on a survey of all 50 states, researchers at the Children's Defense Fund find that child-care costs are one of the biggest expenses faced by families. In 49 of 50 states, the annual cost of care for a four-year-old exceeds the average cost of a year of college tuition. Infant care, which runs over $1,000 more per year than care for a four-year-old, costs more than the average annual college tuition in *every* state. Table 9.1 shows comparisons across the country.

FACT

This is true for 49 of the 50 states.

The amount that parents spend on child care varies depending on income level. Those with higher incomes can afford to pay for child care that is considered higher quality (low teacher/student ratio, high levels of training for providers). Estimates are that nonpoor families spend around 7 percent of their income on child care (Schulman, 2000), while the poor spend over 30 percent of their

TABLE 9.1	Comparison of Average Child Care Costs in Urban Areas to Average Annual Public College Tuition Costs		
	AVERAGE ANNUAL COST IN A CHILD-CARE CENTER		
STATE	FOR A 12-MONTH-OLD	FOR A 4-YEAR-OLD	AVERAGE ANNUAL COST OF PUBLIC COLLEGE TUITION
Alabama	$4,242	$3,672	$2,621
Alaska	7,176	6,019	2,769
Arizona	4,965	4,352	2,158
Arkansas	3,900	3,640	2,590
California	6,995	4,858	2,609
Colorado	6,760	5,096	2,685
Connecticut	8,086	6,405	4,345
Delaware	6,297	5,510	4,462
Florida	5,708	4,255	2,022
Georgia	6,032	4,992	2,442
Hawaii	7,815	5,505	2,880
Idaho	5,881	4,814	2,380
Illinois	8,840	5,304	3,845
Indiana	6,552	4,732	3,490
Iowa	6,750	6,198	2,869
Kansas	5,824	4,889	2,392
Kentucky	4,992	4,368	2,516
Louisiana	4,680	4,160	2,379
Maine	7,670	5,790	4,058
Maryland	8,461	4,774	4,359
Massachusetts	12,978	8,121	4,012
Michigan	6,268	4,830	4,277
Minnesota	10,414	7,436	3,866
Mississippi	3,692	3,380	2,859
Missouri	6,604	4,784	3,550
Montana	5,720	4,680	2,795
Nebraska	5,720	4,680	2,627

income to pay for child care (Smith, 2000). And even though low-income families are paying a significant proportion of their earnings on child care, it is a relatively small amount of money. The amount of money available for child care means that low-income families are often left with fewer options to choose from and that most of the options are lower-cost—hence lower-quality—care programs for their children.

Some families at the lower end of the income scale are eligible for publicly available child care, such as Head Start. About 3 percent of children receiving care in 1995 were involved in Head Start. It is certainly true that the supply of child care is not adequate to meet the demand. We'll see in Chapter 15 that other countries have done a much better job in taking care of children's care needs than we have. Early child care is important for children's cognitive and social development.

The Quality of Child Care

When considering child care, parents are understandably concerned about the quality of care provided. A number of issues are in-

| | AVERAGE ANNUAL COST IN A CHILD-CARE CENTER | | |
STATE	FOR A 12-MONTH-OLD	FOR A 4-YEAR-OLD	AVERAGE ANNUAL COST OF PUBLIC COLLEGE TUITION
Nevada	5,850	4,862	1,956
New Hampshire	9,046	6,520	5,753
New Jersey	6,610	5,252	4,951
New Mexico	5,607	4,801	2,180
New York	9,048	8,060	3,905
North Carolina	6,968	5,876	1,958
North Dakota	4,961	4,627	2,868
Ohio	7,240	5,672	4,258
Oklahoma	4,967	4,108	2,068
Oregon	7,680	5,580	3,561
Pennsylvania	7,384	6,188	5,327
Rhode Island	7,752	6,365	4,158
South Carolina	4,004	3,900	3,520
South Dakota	4,846	4,243	3,038
Tennessee	5,200	4,420	2,495
Texas	5,356	4,160	2,432
Utah	5,928	4,550	2,174
Vermont	6,864	5,980	6,751
Virginia	6,136	4,857	4,160
Washington	7,696	6,604	3,151
West Virginia	5,538	4,238	2,337
Wisconsin	7,526	6,104	3,113
Wyoming	4,160	4,056	2,330

Notes: Data for Indiana, Mississippi, and Rhode Island are statewide (not only urban areas). Suburban data are provided for New York. North Carolina and Oregon data are medians; the rest are means.
Source: Schulman (2000).

volved in determining quality, from health and safety concerns to questions about the type of activities and interactions that take place while children are in care. As we'll see in the section that follows, the issue of quality is of critical importance for children's physical and cognitive development. Parents who are searching for quality care can find an abundance of help in guidebooks and on the Internet. Most of these resources suggest considering the following factors before selecting a care facility (whether a child-care center or an in-home facility):

- *Teacher/child ratio.* States set standards for day care centers and for in-home care. Ratios will be smaller for younger children (that is, fewer children per adult). Teacher/child ratios are important not only for the physical safety of children, but also for the facility's ability to provide stimulating and enriching activities for cognitive development.
- *Total number of children in care.* Beyond the ratio of teachers to children, centers that have larger numbers overall can be loud. Parents also report that

children have more opportunities to catch colds and therefore get sick more often.

- *Physical environment.* Is the facility clean? Is it safe? When was it last tested by the state or licensing board? How often are facilities tested in this state?

- *Philosophy regarding curriculum and play.* What types of educational opportunities are provided for children? What types of toys and playground equipment are available?

- *Training of child-care providers.* The Children's Defense Fund finds that as of 1999, 39 states did not have any requirement for training at child-care centers. For those that do, training may include prior experience, courses in health and safety (first aid, CPR, and food handling), or high school, community college, or university courses dealing with issues of child development.

Finding quality child-care facilities may not be easy. One recent study found that seven in ten facilities provide "mediocre" care, and one in eight provides such low-quality care that children are physically at risk while in attendance (Helburn, 1995). One of the primary reasons for low-quality care is economics. Hiring and maintaining qualified child-care providers is expensive. The average annual salary for child-care workers is $15,430 (Children's Defense Fund, 2001), and very few of these workers receive benefits (health insurance, retirement) as part of their employment. The result is an occupation with a very high turnover rate. About one-quarter of early-childhood teachers leave their jobs each year; closer to 40 percent of child-care assistants do so. And without significant subsidies from government or business, parents must pay for the entire cost of child care.

The Effects of Child Care on Children

Surveys of Americans about the best way in which to take care of children suggest that people understand the demands on parents' lives. The majority of those surveyed over the last ten years or so say that they do not think children are harmed by having two working parents. At the same time, most people think the best arrangement is for at least one parent to work only part time in order to take care of children.

Many people have concerns about putting children in the care of nonrelatives. On television, we regularly see stories about child-care workers who physically harm children. In the spring of 2001, a report was released based on data from a comprehensive longitudinal study of children and families sponsored by the National Institute of Child Health and Human Development (Belsky, Weinraub, Owen, & Kelly, 2001). This study included 1,364 children and their families at ten different locations across the United States. Among the findings of this study was one that caught the attention of many: children who were in child care (any regularly scheduled care by anyone other than the mother) for more than 30 hours per week during the first 4.5 years of their life were more likely to be rated by observers as aggressive than were those who had been in regular child care for fewer than 10 hours per week. This report found its way to most national news broadcasts and made most of the major newspapers. However, it also caught the attention of social scientists, who found the report somewhat problematic. One response appearing through the National Council on Families (Schaefer, 2001) included some concerns regarding the meaning of the data and the decision of media to focus on only one part of the broader study:

1. A finding of equal importance in this study (that did not receive attention) is that both groups of children exhibited levels of aggression within a normal range. The levels did not indicate clinical-level psychological or behavior problems for either group.

2. The actual percentage of children rated as aggressive was low for both groups. The percentage of children in the 30+ hours of child care category who were rated as aggressive was 17 percent, while 6 percent of the 10 hours of child-care group were rated aggressive. Alternatively stated, a majority of both groups were non-aggressive.

3. Additional findings from the larger NICHD study included the result that the quality of child care was the most consistent predictor of child functioning (with higher quality being associated with greater social competence, greater cooperation, and fewer problem behaviors). (NICHD Early Child Care Research Network, 1997, 1998)

Although this study suggests differences in the outcomes of children's experiences in different types of care, it needs to be put in context. The reality is that child care is needed by a significant proportion of families. If additional research reinforces these findings regarding aggressive behavior, then the question is what we do with this information. Does it mean that children should be kept out of child care? What should parents do about employment? We should also remember the positive components of child care in terms of cognitive capabilities for children and the finding that the quality of care is important in its effects on children's subsequent social behavior. If quality child care were available, and affordable, for all children, working families would certainly be helped.

Conclusion

In this chapter, we have explored the relationships between parents and children over time and across social locations. The majority of the literature in this field typically conceptualizes this topic as the process of socializing children into competent adults. What we found is that this perspective makes some assumptions about parent–child relations that are problematic. One assumption is that socialization is a process going from parent to child. Research suggests that interactions between parents and children also influence parents as well. Children are active agents in constructing their social worlds, and they can help shape family activities as well. Future research must pay attention to the reciprocity in the relationships between parents and children.

We also discovered that how parents and children interact is related to social structure. Families living in poorer communities have different socialization concerns than those living in more privileged communities. The resources of local environments structure family members' health and safety. Families of color, and gay and lesbian families, also face different challenges that make parent–child relationships complicated. Facing discrimination in the broader community can challenge parents' and children's attempts at constructing positive identities.

Finally, we discovered that the work of socializing children is not always in the hands of parents. With increasing labor market participation by both mothers and fathers, children are spending more time in the care of others. These others vary by the location of families. Again, the resources available to families, depending on social class and community organization, make the care of children a very complex matter. Regardless of place, however, the costs associated with caring for children are increasing and reinforce the dual-worker family form.

● *How have parent–child relations changed over time?*

Parents have always taken responsibility for the care of children. However, *what* they need to protect their children from, *how long* they must be protected, and *who* is the most responsible for it have changed. During the Middle Ages, children were believed to have a sinful nature. Entire communities (not just parents) took the responsibility for socializing children into productive members of society. Childhood was relatively short. Later, children came to be viewed as having been born innocent. Today, they remain children for longer periods of time (through adolescence), and individual families (especially the mother) take responsibility for children's proper socialization.

● *In the relationship between parents and children, what difference can parenting styles and practices make?*

Parents organize their responsibility to their children in a variety of ways. One aspect of child rearing is the *style* that parents take. The style that has been shown to be the most effective is authoritative parenting, where parents communicate in a reasoned way with their children. Authoritarian parenting is not as beneficial to children. In terms of parenting practices, parents provide both support and control. Supportive parents encourage and praise their children for their accomplishments. Control refers to the way in which parents monitor their children's activities and how they get involved in their children's lives. Higher levels of supervision and involvement benefit children; excessive supervision or control does not.

● *In what way do children influence parent–child relations?*

Children are born with, and develop, certain capabilities. These capabilities affect the way in which they interact with their parents.

Children who show potential in some area may elicit parental support and encouragement. Gender plays a role here because boys and girls are differentially involved in some activities, and these activities require different amounts and types of parental involvement. Children who have special needs engage their parents in other ways. Basically, children provide opportunities for parents to provide behavioral feedback independent of parents' desires and interests.

● *What is meant by reciprocal socialization?*

Socialization in families is not a one-way street from parent to child. Parents and children are both actors in an ongoing relationship. This means that we do not view children as the only recipients in the socialization process and that they too can shape the quality and quantity of interaction within families.

● *How does social class shape parent–child relations?*

One of the basic ways in which social class influences family life is through the financial resources that are available. But another important factor is the type of jobs that parents hold. Whether parents are working standard or nonstandard hours affects how much time they have to spend with children, as well as when that time falls during the day. Parents' occupations have also been related to the transfer of certain value orientations. When parents work in supervised or controlled environments, they tend to value conformity, while parents in occupations with more autonomy place a higher value on self-direction and curiosity. Over time, however, all parents have experienced a shift in valuing autonomy because the desire for autonomy is more consistent with U.S. culture.

● *How do race and ethnicity shape parent–child relations?*

In most ways, parent–child relations are similar across racial/ethnic groups. Parents want to have happy, healthy, and successful children. However, how this is accomplished varies by race and ethnicity. In a society where discrimination still exists, parents and children of color face additional challenges. Along with schools, parents need to socialize children into mainstream culture, but they are left alone to try to help their children prepare for prejudice and discrimination. They also address the issue of helping their children develop strong racial/ethnic identities. This three-pronged approach is known as the "triple quandary of socialization" for families of color.

● *In what ways is gender socialized in families?*

Parents set an example of gender in terms of how they organize family work. When mothers take primary responsibility for domestic work, children learn that this is a woman's responsibility. Men appear more responsible for earning family income. Fathers who are differentially involved with their children based on the gender of children can pass on notions of appropriate behavior for boys and girls.

● *Are gay and lesbian families different in the way that children are socialized?*

A review of the research including lesbian families suggests that on all measures of the quality of parent–child relationships, there are no differences between lesbian families and families with heterosexual parents. However, lesbian and gay parents do show a tendency to be more egalitarian in their role-modeling behavior. Their children also exhibit more nontraditional behaviors, but they are no more likely to grow up to be gay than are children raised by heterosexual parents.

● *Who is taking care of our children?*

The majority of children under the age of five receive some kind of care other than that of their primary parent. When children are under the age of two, the most likely scenario other than care provided by a parent is for them to be cared for by a relative in a home. Once children reach the ages of three to five, a center-based program is the usual form of alternative care. Once children start school, they tend to use after-school programs, school-related activities, and self-care.

● *How much does child care cost, and what effect does it have on children?*

The costs of child care can be staggering. In all but one state, the annual cost of care for a four-year-old exceeds the average cost of a year of college tuition. The effect of child care on children's well-being is debatable. A large national study found that children in alternate care for extended periods of time showed higher rates of aggression, but the study also showed that the quality of care can be a deciding factor. Families without the resources to access high-quality child care are the families that may need it the most.

Key Terms

authoritarian parenting: parents using arbitrary or punitive means of controlling their children

authoritative parenting: includes communication that involves reasoning with children

intensive mothering: the view that a mother is the most appropriate parent and the one who should take on the primary responsibility for caring for children

monitoring: observation and/or management of children's schedules, activities, and friends

parental control: behaviors exhibited by parents in their attempts to influence their children's lives

parental induction: a type of control in which parents actively communicate with their children using rational thought

parental involvement: parents spending more time with their children in a variety of interactions, from play and conversation to helping out with homework or attending children's events

parental support: supportive behaviors exhibited by parents to encourage social competence

permissive parenting: a style of parenting whereby parents are very nurturing and supportive, and do not exert very much control over their children

punitiveness: verbal or physical attempts at controlling children's behavior that do not have a rational explanation

putting-out system: in pre-industrial society, a practice in which parents would send their children to live with another family in order to learn a skill or trade

reciprocal socialization: a recognition that parents influence child development but that children also influence the development of parenting

self-care: children in charge of taking care of themselves

triple quandary of socialization: the additional socialization responsibilities of parents of color

Resources on the Internet

These web sites have been selected for their relevance to the topics in this chapter. These sites are among the more stable, but please note that web site addresses change frequently.

ChildStats.gov

http://www.childstats.gov

This is the official web site of the Interagency Forum on Child and Family Statistics. It provides access to research and reports on a variety of topics related to children and their families. One comprehensive report worth looking at is "America's Children: Key National Indicators of Well-Being," the annual monitoring report on the status of U.S. children. Another recent publication is on nurturing fathers.

American Psychological Association

http://www.apa.org

The web site for the American Psychological Association includes at least five years' worth of press releases from its premier journal. Just click on "Releases," and you will find the results of studies on many of the topics in this chapter, including socialization, parenting, and children's well-being.

Administration for Children and Families (ACF)

http://www.acf.dhhs.gov/index.htm

This federal agency funds state, local, and tribal organizations to provide a variety of family assistance programs to their communities. Through this site you can see what's been funded in your area and the results of funded programs.

Companion Web Site for This Book

Virtual Society: The Wadsworth Sociology Resource Center

http://sociology.wadsworth.com

Begin by clicking the Student Resources section. Next, click Marriage and Family, and then click the cover image for this book. Select from the pull-down menu the chapter you are presently studying. You will have easy access to chapter resources such as MicroCase Online exercises, additional Web links, flashcards, InfoTrac exercises, and practice tests (that can be scored). In addition, to enhance and help with your study of marriages and families, be sure to investigate the rest of the rich sociology resources at Virtual Society.

Visit InfoTrac College Edition

 Another unique option available to you at the Student Resources section of the Virtual Society web site described above is InfoTrac College Edition, an online library of hundreds of scholarly and popular periodicals. Here are three suggested key search terms for this chapter:

* Search keywords: *childhood + socialization*
* Search keywords: *child + care*

* Search keywords: *parents + children*
* Search recent years to get the latest information on these issues.

© Jim Craigmyle/Corbis

10

Working Families: The Intersections of Paid and Unpaid Work

W hen people talk about "work," they typically mean that which is done for an income. However, social scientists conceive of work more broadly. **Work** can be defined as activity that creates something of value, either goods or services. One way of determining value is to look at how much people get paid for doing different types of it. For example, those involved in occupations that require more mental labor (physicians, lawyers, business executives) usually receive higher incomes than those who do manual labor (janitors, machine operators, cooks). This suggests to us that Americans place a higher value on mental work over physical labor. But not all work of value is paid directly. Housework and care for family members are types of work that have value to us, but they do not produce wages when done for our own families. The work of family members to sustain their livelihoods has been the subject of much of this book. Some domestic work is mental (organizing schedules, planning budgets) while other domestic work is physical (child-care activities, meal preparation, housecleaning).

The distinction between paid and unpaid work emerged as a consequence of industrialization. Whereas once all family members worked in relative close proximity to produce their livelihoods (mostly on farms), today family members work in a variety of settings and rely on both paid and unpaid work to survive. Still, this distinction between types of work has had implications for how we study families. We often see the phrase *work and families*. The two terms imply that they are separate spheres. As a result, much research has focused on one or the other. When looking at an introductory sociology text, we notice that the chapter on "the family" is separate from the one on "the economy." Following this conceptual separation, family scholars have asked questions about how one affects the other.

More recently, family scholars are abandoning this approach to studying families for two reasons. First, both paid work and unpaid work are necessary for families. People cannot be productive at work without the support of family members: physical preparation (being clothed and fed) as well as mental preparation (socialization). All families are working families. Second, changes in the **labor force participation** of women and men have produced the situation where the most common form of couple families (with and without children) is the dual-earner family. A majority of mothers, including mothers of preschool-aged children, are employed, meaning that the majority of adult family members are involved in both paid and unpaid work. Recognizing that couples are less likely to engage in "specialization" (see Chapter 6), a new vocabulary is emerging to apply to working families. Now we hear about work/family linkages, intersecting work and family roles, and the synergy of paid and unpaid work (Galinsky, 2001; Voydanoff, 2002).

This chapter begins with a historical view of the relationship between families and economic life since the seventeenth century. The movement from agricultural to industrial production had important implications for the ways in which families organized their work. In the most recent past (the twentieth century), two key processes shaped family dynamics: women's employment and economic restructuring. After reviewing these trends, we address how employment and family work affect each other. Although we review these two issues in separate sections, it is important to keep in mind that the relationship between family and employment is a reciprocal one; the effects go both ways simultaneously. We will end this chapter by commenting on the ways in which families and places of employment are struggling to meet the needs of working families for tomorrow.

Historical Perspectives on Families and Work

The last three hundred years have seen a remarkable transformation in the social organization of work. In general, we have gone from organizing work around the seasons and the land to organizing work around the clock. During the seventeenth century, most families in what we now call the United States were connected to the land. The eighteenth and nineteenth centuries saw a move-

ment from an economy based primarily on agriculture to one dominated by industrial production. The twentieth century saw further transformation away from industrial production to a more diverse economic system with a rapidly growing service sector. In this section, we will review these broad transitions and discuss their implications for how families survive. We will follow a method of organization proposed by historians that looks at three historical periods of families and work: (1) the family-based economy, (2) the family-wage economy, and (3) the family-consumer economy (Tilly & Scott, 1978). It is a model that has been developed primarily through research on white family history. Therefore, we will pay attention to the ways in which these periods of history do not exist with hard boundaries. The extent and rate of change in the social organization of work are variable across racial and ethnic groups, as well as across social classes and geographic regions. Recognizing that these categories for organizing history are not rigid, we have decided to use them because they do capture major social and economic transformations that have changed the way all families work.

The Family-Based Economy

The **family-based economy,** one in which households are the basic unit of economic production, characterized much of the seventeenth and early eighteenth centuries. It included small farms, artisans' shops, large plantations, and haciendas, and it required the work of all members of a household for survival. Most households were relatively self-sufficient and were not involved in generating a surplus to sell on the market. Labor in this period was divided along the lines of age and gender. On small farms, men were primarily responsible for agricultural work, and women were involved in a variety of domestic production activities. Along with children, women would do the cooking and

In early America the family was the primary economic unit in society, with family members working in close proximity with one another.

cleaning, but also tended gardens and orchards and kept animals for producing eggs, butter, and milk. Women also engaged in spinning and weaving to produce family clothing and made other household items such as soap and candles.

One of the defining characteristics of this economic period was that the rhythm of work was determined by the season, and seasons varied by region of the country. Weather and soil conditions dictated what crop was planted, when it was planted, and when intensive labor was needed for planting and harvesting crops. During these peak labor times, the division or line between men's work and women's work became less rigid. Harvest often required the labor of all household members. Men and boys were involved in activities traditionally thought of as women's work, such as the production of linen. In a family-based economy, all members of the household were active in producing the goods they needed to survive.

Although this pattern characterized a sizable number of European American families during the colonial period, there was considerable variation across race, ethnicity, social class, and region of the country. Even among whites in colonial America, historians have documented variation in the work of women, primarily along the lines of social class. For example, upper-class women were less involved in the actual production of household goods. Their work would more accurately be described as management. They gave instructions to servants (some had slaves) and supervised the work of others.

In the seventeenth and early eighteenth centuries, there is also evidence of women working in jobs typically thought of as men's work. Women worked as innkeepers, shopkeepers, crafts persons, and keepers of taverns. Some women worked as servants in other people's households. Some servants were "indentured," having come to America to work for a specified period of time with a family, after which they could be released from their service. Many of these working women were widows, or poor women, who needed to receive economic compensation to maintain their children's and their own livelihoods (Kessler-Harris, 1981).

The experiences of men and women of color were also quite different from those of white settlers in colonial society. The most dramatic difference occurred for African men and women brought to the colonies as slaves. Estimates are that more than 9.5 million Africans were captured and forced into slavery in the United States and parts of the Caribbean (Genovese, 1972). Although some black men and women worked as indentured servants or in various trades (primarily in the North), the majority of Africans arriving in this country (men, women, and children) were used as field labor in support of cash crops, primarily in the South.

In addition to doing the same types of field jobs as men, black women were required to provide domestic help for white women (mistresses of the plantation) (Jones, 1985). African families had some division of labor along gender lines. Women were primarily responsible for the care of their children. When they could get the materials, it was men who would build furniture for their families while women produced household goods such as soap and candles. In order to survive, however, slave families had to be much more flexible in their distribution of labor. While black men and women worked in the fields and homes of their white masters, it was often the responsibility of grandparents, and other slaves unable to do physical labor, to care for children.

The family work life among Native Americans also differed by region of the country and by tribal affiliation. It is estimated that Native Americans spoke more than 200 languages and made up more than 600 distinct societies (Coontz, 1988; Snipp, 1989). As with other groups during this historical period, the

The family work life of Native Americans differed by region of the country and tribal affiliation. Most took advantage of the natural resources surrounding their communities.

and community affairs (Hesse-Biber & Carter, 2000).

White colonists found Native American family structure to be somewhat suspect. Particularly concerning was the role that women played not only in agricultural production, but in community decision making as well. Some groups, such as the Iroquois, were matrilineal and matrilocal societies (see Chapter 1). Starting in the East and moving westward, European settlers pushed Native Americans off their land, with dramatic effects on their culture and traditions. As Native American land came under the control of the U.S. government, there was less opportunity for men to hunt. In these societies, men turned to agriculture, depriving many women of their traditional working roles. Missionaries and officers of the U.S. government also worked to help reorganize families away from extended kin groups (especially matrilineal ones) in order to follow their own pattern of nuclear family structures, in which men were the heads of households (Amott & Matthaei, 1996).

The Family-Wage Economy

The transition from an agricultural to an industrial society brought with it a major transformation in family work. The decline in available land for farming meant that considerable numbers of families were no longer able to be completely self-sufficient. Men increasingly left the home to work for wages. The production of household goods by women in the home also declined, and as the center of labor moved from the household to the factory, the **family-wage economy** was created. This transition to an industrial economy in which wages were necessary for survival took place over the later part of the nineteenth century and the early part of the twentieth century.

During the early years of industrialization, the majority of men were still involved

work of all members of society was necessary for communities to survive. In general, there was a gendered division of work whereby men were responsible for hunting, fishing, and/or warfare, while women were primarily involved in agricultural activity and other domestic production. Most Native American groups were quite resourceful in their use of natural resources. Women would gather plants to be used as food and medicine, and bark and grasses to be used for the production of cloth. In societies that depended more heavily on hunting, men had more authority within the community and kinship systems were patrilineal. In those societies that relied more heavily on agriculture, the labor of women was more central, resulting in women having considerably more control over family

in agriculture. New industries, in need of a steady supply of cheap labor, therefore turned elsewhere to recruit their workers. One group targeted early in the growth of textile manufacturing was young women. For example, Francis Cabot Lowell recruited young single women from New England farm families to work in his textile mills in Massachusetts. He advertised this work as a respectable route for young women to help out their families financially, save for a trousseau, or to help send a brother to college (Kessler-Harris, 1981). But the conditions in most factories were hazardous, and by 1845 the workers in the Lowell mills had organized themselves into the Female Labor Reform Association. They argued that their long hours were not appropriate for the minds and bodies of young women. In response, the mills stopped hiring young single women and turned to a recently arrived group of immigrants from Ireland. Seven years later, the majority of mill workers in New England were foreign-born women and men who worked for very low wages.

The organization of work in other parts of the country during this period had different effects on families and the organization of family work. As in the Northeast, industrialization in other areas pushed people into the wage-labor market in order to acquire the cash necessary for family survival. In the Southwest, Chicanos/as were primarily employed on large industrialized farms, requiring a seasonal migration of families. Many men found jobs in the growing areas of mining and railroads. Women were more likely to find jobs in canning, in textile factories, or as domestics (Baca Zinn & Eitzen, 1999). Chinese immigrant men were also recruited to come to America to work in the mines and railroads of the West, but the Chinese Exclusion Act of 1882 kept these male laborers from bringing family members over with them. The act was renewed through 1902, meaning that Chinese immigrants estab-lished what is referred to as a "split-household family" in which men worked in the United States and sent money home to their families (Glenn, 1983). In the early part of the twentieth century, Chinese women began immigrating to the United States and were most likely, along with Japanese immigrant women, to find employment in domestic work. Domestic employment continues to be an important avenue of work for immigrants today, particularly among Latinas (Romero, 1992).

At the same time that industrialization was altering the work patterns of men and many women so that they were required to exchange their labor for wages, an urban middle class (primarily white) emerged in which men became wage laborers while women restricted their work to unpaid labor in the home. Life for these relatively privileged women was dramatically different from the lives of the women who were involved in paid labor. However, it was the lifestyle of these middle-class white women that became the model for what true womanhood was meant to be.

When such major differences exist among the working patterns or lifestyles of different groups of people (along the lines of gender, social class, or race/ethnicity), it is common for people to develop ideas that help explain such stratification. An **ideology** is a belief system that seeks to explain and justify certain conditions. An ideology that emerged during this time period to help justify a system of gender difference is known as the **domestic code** (Kraditor, 1968). This code defined women's proper role as the nurturer of men and children. Arguments put forward in sermons and popular magazines of the time suggested that the world of work had become a dangerous place. It was rough, competitive, and required individuals (men) to be selfish in order to be successful. Instead of working to restructure the corrupting environment of paid work, it was argued that

Although industrialization helped to create a separation of spheres of work for men and women, not all women had the option to stay out of the paid labor force.

children and regenerating moral character in their husbands. This transition meant that what was once men's responsibility in the family, being the guiding force for children's moral and educational development (Vinovskis, 2001), now became the primary responsibility of mothers.

The domestic code was intended to apply to all women, but it certainly was not relevant for poor women, immigrant women, and women of color. As we mentioned above, many women did not have a choice about whether to engage in paid labor. Following emancipation, both African American men and women sought out employment although their occupational opportunities were more limited than those for whites. The majority of men who found employment did so in southern tobacco and textile industries. Large numbers of African Americans migrated north for jobs in manufacturing. African American women, like men, found jobs in agriculture and manufacturing, but they were also employed as domestics or laundresses. This legacy of slavery has meant that African American women are more likely than white women to be in the labor force. Even as early as 1870, almost 40 percent of African American married were employed for wages, while 98 percent of married white women reported they were "keeping house" (Jones, 1985).

families should become a place of comfort for men. Middle-class wives, who were spared the involvement in paid labor, would serve the role of constructing a retreat for men that would be compensation for their efforts in employment.

Historian Barbara Welter (1966) argues that this ideology about women's proper roles included assumptions about the fundamentally different natures of women and men. Women were seen as holding some virtues not necessarily part of men's nature. These virtues were piety, purity, submissiveness, and domesticity. Such innate qualities made women perfectly situated to be the caretakers of innocent children and hardworking husbands. Mothers could help to stabilize society by generating moral character in their

The Family-Consumer Economy

During the twentieth century, American families continue to rely on wage earners for survival. As we just noted, by the turn of the century there began a dramatic shift as most men, and many women, entered paid employment. This trend has continued, and today the majority of men and women combine paid employment and unpaid domestic work. The two-earner family is now the predomi-

416 • Families at Work | PART THREE

nant family structure for families with children. Several major trends have contributed to this new organization of families and work. First, after the turn of the twentieth century, household goods and services were increasingly being produced outside the home, and with new methods of mass production they became much cheaper than making them at home. Industrial technology was also applied to the materials needed to perform housework, changing the way domestic work was performed. Second, institutions of education and welfare began to remove other family functions from the home. Young, sick, or aging family members could now be cared for elsewhere. And third, growth in the service sector, including the fast-food industry and entertainment industries, moved other activities (meals and leisure) to places outside the home. These shifts meant that what went on inside the home focused less on production and more on the organization of consumption and reproduction. Tilly and Scott (1978) called this period of economic organization the **family-consumer economy.**

In her book *The Way We Never Were,* social historian Stephanie Coontz (1992) argues that mass production also had the result of turning the majority of women into income earners. Early in the century, increasing numbers of single women, women of color, and poorer women were drawn into employment in the growing service sector of the economy. But large-scale producers recognized that to be successful in business, they also needed mass consumers. Married women were increasingly drawn into employment with the promise that the income would allow them to purchase new material goods that in turn would provide their family a better standard of living. Advertising agencies were created, and they targeted homemakers, who were assumed to be the ones purchasing most household goods. What was created was a "rhetoric of need" whereby families saw what could be had by increasing the income in their household. Middle-class women's employment could help "keep up with the Joneses."

The Changing Dynamics of Working Families Today

Many social forces have come together to influence the employment structure of families. They include both push and pull factors. A changing economy away from industrial production to service sector employment means a decrease in real wages for men. This has challenged a family's ability to survive on one income and has pushed women into paid employment. At the same time, women's education has increased so that today the majority of college students are women. With higher levels of education, women are becoming more likely to want to work.

Table 10.1 contains data from the Census Bureau collected each month. In 1965 the majority of married couples (with and without children) were one-earner couples (almost exclusively it was husbands who were the earners). By 1997, these types of couples represented slightly more than one-quarter of all married couples. The modal form is now the two-earner family among married couples (with or without children). In fact, the most likely scenario today is for married couples to have two full-time earners (43.5 percent of all married couples, 38.7 percent of married couples with children). As expected, the majority of single parents are employed full time (59.1 percent).

In this section we will take a closer look at the employment changes for women, but also for men. We will see that as women's

TABLE 10.1 Percentage of Married Couples and Children's Parents with One, One and a Half, and Two Earners, 1965–1997

| | ALL MARRIED COUPLES (%) | | | CHILDREN'S PARENTS | | | | |
| | | | | MARRIED COUPLES (%) | | | SINGLE PARENTS (%) | |
Year	1 Earner	1.5 Earners	2 Earners	1 Earner	1.5 Earners	2 Earners	Part-Time	Full-Time
1965	50.8	16.9	25.5	55.4	17.7	19.1	17.3	50.2
1970	47.6	19.7	27.4	50.0	22.0	22.6	21.3	50.8
1975	42.9	21.4	29.2	45.0	23.4	25.0	18.4	48.4
1980	35.8	22.8	34.0	37.5	25.1	29.8	18.9	54.3
1985	31.8	23.9	37.6	34.0	27.3	31.7	17.9	51.1
1990	27.2	25.3	43.0	29.6	29.1	36.9	17.3	56.8
1995	25.8	25.9	42.2	28.0	29.2	36.8	19.8	52.7
1997	26.0	24.6	43.5	28.0	28.0	38.7	19.1	59.1

Source: Current Population Survey. Adapted from Waite and Nielson (2001), p. 31, Table 1.4.

employment has increased, men's has actually slightly decreased. A multitude of factors are involved, but a very important variable to consider is the changing structure of the U.S. (indeed the global) economy.

Changes in Women's Employment

The last hundred years have seen a relatively steady growth in women's employment, although there were three periods of marked fluctuations (Kessler-Harris, 1982; Edwards, 2001). The first deviation from a general linear increase came around the time of the Great Depression, when the percentages of women engaged in paid worked declined. Men were given priority in hiring, and businesses established practices of firing married women first in time of layoffs. In fact, 26 states passed laws forbidding married women to be employed. This did not remove all women from the labor force, but it did stall their progress. A second shift in the steady increase in women's employment came during the time of World War II, but the shift was in the opposite direction. This was a significant period for women's employment, not so much because it allowed more women to work but because it gave women the opportunity to work in well-paid industrial jobs. The demand for women's labor also meant that the government provided on-site child care so that mothers could work. Women who had already been in the labor market also experienced some upward mobility as new women entered the labor force. After the end of the war, many women were required to give up their jobs for men. But unlike popular portrayals of the postwar era, not all women returned home to become homemakers. Kessler-Harris (1982) finds that the upward trend in women's employment rates persisted after the war in a pattern that was really just a continuation of the earlier positive trend. Looking ahead to Figure 10.4, we can see this broader trend. In this figure we have charted data points once per decade. Without the data points for each individual year, women's employment appears to show a continuously increasing trend.

FACT OR FICTION?

The majority of mothers refrain from paid employment until their children are in kindergarten.

The third shift in employment rates occurred in the 1970s and is represented by acceleration in women's employment, particularly among women with children (see Figure 10.1). Using data from the Bureau of Labor Statistics, Edwards (2001) notes that the employment rate for mothers of preschoolers went up about .9 percentage points per year from 1950 to 1969. Starting in 1970, the rate increased to about 1.6 percentage points per year. Changes in the rate of employment have been attributed to a number of causes. One approach considers women's desires to work. With advanced education, women are more likely to develop a commitment to careers and be less likely to interrupt their career trajectories when they have children. Other reasons relate to the need for mothers of young children to be employed. In the 1970s, for the first time in memory, men's earnings could not guarantee a standard of living comparable to that obtained by their fathers (Oppenheimer, 1982). In addition, Americans have shown an increasing commitment to consumption (Schor, 1998), establishing a rhetoric of need. The result is that in order to keep up with their expectations for a lifestyle comparable to that of their parents, as well as to keep up with the Joneses, American mothers felt pressure to stay in the labor force when they had young children.

FIGURE 10.1 Annual Employment of Mothers (United States, 1948–2000)

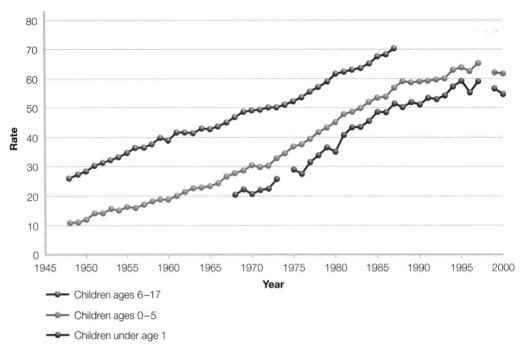

Source: U.S. Bureau of Labor Statistics. Chart produced by Mark E. Edwards, Department of Sociology, Oregon State University.

| FICTION

As of 2000, the majority of mothers of preschool-age children are engaged in paid labor.

It is also important to note that this trend of increasing employment of young mothers, although applying to all women, applies specifically to white, middle-class mothers. Working-class mothers, single mothers, and women of color have always had relatively high rates of employment; hence, the extent of change for these women was not as dramatic in the 1970s. The issue here is that the experiences that have been part of many women's lives for years are now becoming normative for most women.

The combination of the demand for women workers along with the increased

availability of women with higher levels of education has resulted in an increase in real wages for women. In Figure 10.2 we can see that using constant 2001 dollars, women working full time and year round have gone from an annual median income of just over $15,000 in 1955 to $30,420 by 2001. However, men's median incomes have not shown a consistently positive trend. Starting in 1955, men earned about $23,716. Incomes rose until around 1985, at which point they declined, not rising again until the late 1990s.

The increases in income for women mask some important differences among them. It is only for college-educated women that earnings have seen such an increase (Bianchi & Spain, 1996). Earnings of less-educated women, who are more likely to be in the service sector, did not see a rise. Other important distinctions among workers and

FIGURE 10.2 Full-Time, Year-Round Workers by Median Income and Sex: 1955–2001 (Using 2001 Dollars)

Source: U.S. Census Bureau. Current Population Survey, Annual Demographics Supplements (2002). Online: http://www.census.gov/hhes/income/histinc/p36.html. Accessed February 1, 2003.

families become invisible when using these data. We include data only for full-time, year-round workers in order to make the figures comparable. Yet it is important to note that many women and men are working part time *not* by choice. These are more likely to be people working in economic sectors with less stable employment. If we were to include those who are part time involuntarily, the figures would be lower.

FACT OR FICTION?

The reason that the number of men employed has gone down over the last thirty years is that women are taking men's jobs.

Earnings differences between women and men also show variation across racial and ethnic groups. In Figure 10.3 we see that when comparing full-time, year-round workers, men in each racial/ethnic group have higher incomes than women in that group. The differences between men and women are greatest for whites and Asian American/Pacific Islanders. Black and Hispanics, earning much less than Asian Americans/Pacific Islanders or whites, show the least amount of gender differences in earnings.

Compared to women's employment, men's rates of employment have been declining somewhat since 1970 (see Figure 10.4). The reasons for this decline are related to changes that have occurred in the economy. These changes include loss of jobs that have been traditionally held by men, while the numbers of jobs more often held by women (in the service sector) have increased. It is important to note this because women are not taking men's jobs—men's jobs are disappearing. Some of these jobs have disappeared due to the movement of jobs overseas, while other jobs have been eliminated by technological innovations. Jobs in manufac-

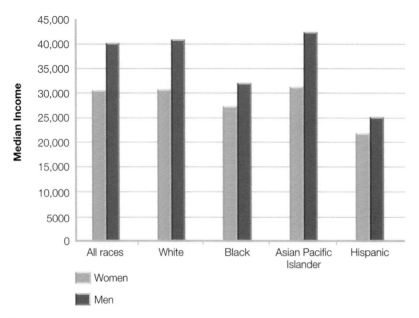

FIGURE 10.3 Median Annual Income for Full-Time, Year-Round Workers by Race/Ethnicity and Sex, 2001

Note: Hispanics can be of any race.
Source: U.S. Census Bureau. Current Population Survey, Annual Demographics Supplements (2002). Online: http://www.census/gov/hhes/income/histinc/ (tables 36 and 36a through 36d). Accessed February 1, 2003.

turing have been the hardest hit. It was just these types of jobs that helped to ensure a "family wage." That is, these jobs had income and benefits that allowed families to survive on one income. A quick look at the restructuring of the economy will help us to see how employment opportunities are related to the ways in which families organize their work.

| FICTION

The reason that the rate of men employed has declined over the last thirty years is that the types of jobs traditionally held by men (in manufacturing) have disappeared.

Changes in the Economy: Economic Restructuring

Sociologists refer to the transformations in the structure of employment as **economic restructuring.** The result of these changes has been to create a much more diverse work force. On the one hand, job growth has occurred in professional and administrative occupations. These jobs require significant investments in education and training, and also bring higher incomes and better benefits. On the other hand, there has also been substantial growth in occupations in the service sector. These jobs require little training but also provide limited compensation (wages and benefits) (see Table 10.2). Several key processes summarize the transformations over the last century: (1) **deindustrialization,** (2) technological advances, and (3) **globalization.** These trends are interrelated and have implications for workers in terms of the availability of jobs, the opportunity to obtain a livable wage, and the certainty with which they will have jobs for an extended period of time. These, in turn, are important for understanding how families organize work.

FIGURE 10.4 Labor Force Participation of the Civil Population, 1870–2000: Percentage of Women and Men in the Labor Force

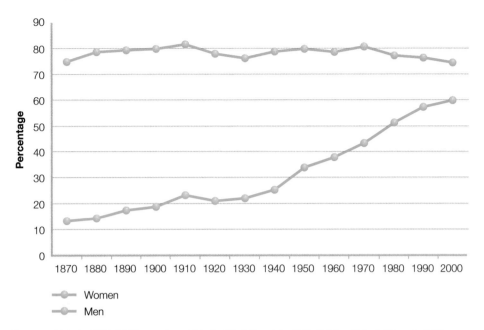

Source: Data for 1870–1960 come from *Historical Statistics of the United States, Colonial Times to 1970,* Part 1, Series D 11-25. U.S. Census Bureau (1975). Data from 1970–2000 come from *Statistical Abstract of the United States* (2002).

The U.S. economy is no longer one based primarily on the industrial production of goods. We continue to engage in the production of goods, but fewer people in the United States are involved in such work. Enhancements in production equipment mean fewer people are needed for production jobs. In many areas of production (e.g., cars, computers), much of the work is now done overseas. Recall that at the beginning of the last century, most workers were employed in agriculture. By the end of World War II, the majority of those employed were in manufacturing. By the end of the century, the vast majority of those employed were in what is called the **service sector.** Service sector employment includes the provision of services (cleaning, child care, and food preparation) as well as information processing (banking, computer operations, and clerical work). The loss of jobs in manufacturing has been devastating for some families. These jobs have a history of being controlled by unions, and they offer higher pay and benefits. Displaced workers have had to find jobs in new sectors of the economy where income and benefits are not sufficient to meet family needs. Again, this shift is probably responsible for a portion of the increase in women's employment, especially since World War II.

FACT OR FICTION?

The growth in new jobs in the economy is in high-paying as well as lower-paying jobs.

As mentioned above, there has also been growth in professional and technical jobs that provide higher levels of compensation (income and benefits). The consequence of this change is that for new workers, or people looking for work, the opportunities are at the extremes of the occupational ladder. Those with higher levels of education

TABLE 10.2	Employment Projections for Job Growth: Top Ten Occupations for Job Growth Between 1998 and 2008, Along with Required Education and Training			
OCCUPATION	NUMBER OF NEW JOBS (IN THOUSANDS)	PERCENTAGE CHANGE FROM 1998 TO 2008	HOURLY EARNINGS (BY QUARTILE RANK)*	EDUCATION AND TRAINING REQUIRED
Systems analysts	577	94	1	Bachelor's degree
Retail salespersons	563	14	4	Short-term on-the-job training
Cashiers	556	17	4	Short-term on-the-job training
General managers and top executives	5,551	16	1	Work experience plus bachelor's degree
Truck drivers, light and heavy	493	17	2	Short-term on-the-job training
Office clerks, general	463	15	3	Short-term on-the-job training
Registered nurses	451	22	1	Associate's or bachelor's degree
Computer support specialists	439	102	1	Associate's degree
Personal care and home health aides	433	58	4	Short-term on-the-job training
Teacher assistants	375	31	4	Short-term on-the-job training

*Quartile ranks based on the Occupational Employment Statistics hourly earnings. Ranks: 1 = $16.25 and over; 2 = $10.89 to $16.14; 3 = $7.78 to $10.88; 4 = below $7.77.
Source: U.S. Census Bureau, *Statistical Abstract of the United States* (2000). Table 670, p. 419.

and training will fare much better than those with less education. As we saw in Chapter 3, the income distribution in the United States is widening. Part of this can be explained by the changing structure of employment.

Two related features of economic restructuring that have influenced employment are technological innovation and globalization. Probably the most significant innovation in our time is the computer chip. It's hard to imagine a time when computers were not involved in our daily lives. We buy e-tickets to fly, we order just about anything over the Web, and we use e-mail (and e-cards) to stay in contact with family and friends. Computers have revolutionized not only our own per-

sonal lifestyles but also the organization of work. Work can be done at any time of the day and from anywhere around the world, so some workers may be able to work from home. (This option is used by only a fraction of U.S. workers.) It is also true that people are more likely to be working what are considered "nonstandard" hours (or shift work). Although married people are less likely than those who are single to be involved in shift work, it is estimated that close to one in three parents in two-earner couples works nonstandard hours (Presser, 1995). For some families, shift work allows them to juggle the demands of child-care responsibilities. However, research suggests that shift work relates more to the demands of employers than to the needs of employees and their families. Another significant effect of technological enhancements in the work process is that many jobs (especially computer-related jobs) can be transferred overseas, where labor costs are much lower than they are in the United States. Also leaving the country are many jobs that use assembly-line production processes. Many companies are exporting the work of putting together apparel or computers. Although as consumers we may benefit from the lower costs of such products, a concurrent effect is job elimination in this country.

| FACT

The largest growth in jobs can be found at both ends of the pay scale. At the upper end are jobs such as systems analyst or general managers, which require significant education. At the other end are jobs such as cashiers and retail salesworkers, which require short-term on-the-job training.

Along with these features of economic restructuring comes an increased dependence on contingent workers. These are people who do not hold regular or permanent jobs. They work in seasonal employment or in short-term jobs available with temporary peaks in certain sectors of the economy. Part-time or seasonal employees are used in all types of jobs, from agricultural work, which has high demand seasons, to colleges and universities, which need a supply of temporary instructors to meet temporary increases in enrollment. Although such work occurs in all occupational categories (with high and low wages), contingent workers are more likely to be in the lower-paying jobs within each sector. Most contingent workers do not receive health care and other benefits. Recent estimates put contingent workers as making up close to 30 percent of the labor force (Kalleberg et al.,

© Spencer Grant/PhotoEdit

An increasing number of parents in dual-earner families are working nonstandard hours. This results from both the need for child care as well as the changing structure of the economy.

2000). Women and people of color are much more likely to be in the lower-paying contingent pool of workers, meaning that they are more likely to be in a situation of uncertainty in providing for their families.

In sum, economic restructuring has produced a work force that is much more diverse. Jobs are less stable, and earnings have stagnated (especially for men's jobs). The result is that the majority of adult family members combine employment with their unpaid

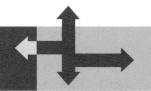

Economic restructuring, combined with a recession in the early 1990s, resulted in the elimination of a number of jobs. Particularly hard hit were people in the working class. When unemployment occurs, it can place stress on marital and family relations. Lillian B. Rubin interviewed families that experienced unemployment in the 1990s and found that unemployment posed a number of challenges, particularly if men in families had lost their jobs. She argues that this is true for two reasons. First, men have been the ones with higher earnings, meaning that the loss of their job will have more serious financial consequences for the family than women's (in a two-parent family). Second, she argues, employment is more closely linked to men's identity than to women's: "Going to work isn't just what he does, it's deeply linked to who he is. . . . Ask a man for a statement of his identity, and

he'll almost always respond by telling you first what he does for a living. The same question asked of a woman brings forth a less predictable, more varied response, one that's embedded in the web of relationships that are central to her life" (Rubin, 1994: 104).

Through her interviews with working-class men, Rubin found a variety of responses to unemployment, which varied over the length of time that men were without employment. At first, men appeared to be in state of shock and denial ("How could this happen?"). But, feeling relatively positive at first, men would stay busy at home with repairs and other household work. One woman Rubin interviewed mentioned that her husband was so busy at home that he didn't even stop to watch football as he did before. The husband responded, "If I don't keep busy, I feel like I'll go nuts. . . . I don't know, maybe I'm

kind of scared if I sit down there in front of the TV, I won't want to get up again . . . besides, when I was working, I figured I had a right" (1994: 106). Many fathers also increased the time that they spent with their children, which was seen as a positive thing from the viewpoint of the children.

For most of these families, men's unemployment shifted the division of family work. Women had to increase their hours at work to compensate for the loss of men's wages. Although many of the couples agreed this was acceptable, the traditional notions about what a family ought to be were in the backs of their minds. One woman said, "I'm not sure what I think anymore. I mean, I don't think it's fair that men always have to be the support for the family; it's too hard for them sometimes. And I don't mind working; I really don't. In fact, I like it a lot better than being at home with the

work at home. Therefore, social scientists have moved from asking questions about *why* there is an increase in women's (especially mothers') employment to asking *how* "contemporary families juggle the spheres of work and family and how this juggling influences children, parents, employers, and the state" (Edwards, 2001: 184). We are also moving away from thinking about "work" and "family" as two distinct spheres. As we make clear by the title of this chapter, families are at work—both inside and outside the home. The topics that family researchers are more concerned with are about how work gets organized and performed.

Unemployment and Families

Economic restructuring has not only affected the way in which jobs are organized but has also affected the sheer availability of jobs. Recent economic downturns have also altered the availability, producing higher rates of unemployment. For example, in just one year (from 2000 to 2001), the proportion of families with at least one unemployed member rose from 5.7 to 6.6 percent (Bureau of Labor Statistics, 2002). Especially hard hit were families of color. While 5.5 percent of white families contained an unemployed

house and the kids all the time. But I guess deep down I still have that old-fashioned idea that it's a man's job to support his family . . . like maybe I won't respect him so much if he can't do that. I mean, it's okay for now" (1994: 109). Men responded in similar ways: "Don't get me wrong; I'm glad she has her job. I don't know what we'd do if she wasn't working. It's just that . . . I know this is going to sound pretty male, but it's my job to take care of this family. I mean, it's great that she can help out, but the responsibility is mine, not hers" (1994: 109).

When periods of unemployment continue for longer periods, additional stress sets in. The loss of health care benefits and insurance can threaten a family's health. Not being able to pay bills, such as the car or mortgage, introduces fears of having to live on the street. Men's sense of self becomes increasingly tested, and the "financial and emo-

tional turmoil that engulf families when a man loses his job all too frequently pushes marriages that were already fragile over the brink" (1994: 120). Some families had problems with alcohol, and others saw incidents of domestic violence. For some, the outcome was divorce. As one woman stated, "We had problems before, but we were managing. Then he got laid off, and he couldn't find another job, and, I don't know, it was like he went crazy . . . there was no talking to him" (1994: 120).

The point of Rubin's research is that unemployment is more than about economic loss. It also challenges notions of who we are and our abilities to maintain strong families. Rubin argues that the psychological consequences can be as difficult as the economic ones. One man who lost his job as a long-distance hauler is now working as an orderly in a nursing home. In a very

emotional exchange, he said, "This is not the kind of job for a guy like me. It's not just the money, it's . . . it's like I got chopped off at the knees, like . . . aw, hell, I don't know how to say it. . . . What the hell's happening to this country when there's no decent jobs for men who want to work?" (1994: 124).

Source: Based on Rubin (1994).

Critical Thinking

1. How might unemployment be experienced differently among families in the middle class?

2. With the significant increases in the number of dual-earner families, do you think that women will begin to have an identity that is grounded more centrally in their employment, as Rubin argues it is for men?

member, 9.9 percent of Hispanic families and 11.4 percent of black families had an unemployed member in 2001. However, all family groups experienced an unemployment increase over this one-year period.

Unemployment and its effects on families have been the topic of much research, particularly following times of economic crisis (see the Family Diversity box on pages 426–427). A considerable body of research was generated following the Great Depression suggesting that unemployment can have deleterious effects on those unemployed, as well as on the relationships of the unemployed with their partners and children (Ko-

marovsky, 1940; Elder, Liker, & Cross, 1984). This early work focused primarily on men's unemployment because men were considered the primary breadwinners in American families. The general finding of this research is that when men lost their jobs, they became irritable and tense. This psychological distress was passed on to wives and children through punishing behaviors. Research conducted in the 1970s and 1980s after major plant closings in the Midwest supports these findings by showing correlations of unemployment to declines in physical and mental health of those experiencing layoffs (Perrucci et al., 1988). Similar findings regarding declines in family relationships have also been found for midwestern families experiencing the loss of jobs due to economic declines in the agricultural sector of the economy (Elder, Conger, Foster, & Ardelt, 1992).

Research exploring the most recent economic downturn has not yet been published. However, recent data from others countries suggest that similar findings should be expected. Based on a longitudinal study in Denmark, Christoffersen (2000) finds that for those who experience long-term unemployment (around three years or more), the greater is the likelihood of divorce or separation, hospitalization of parents for psychiatric and drug abuse problems, exposure to domestic violence between parents, crime among parents (especially fathers), lower rates of high school graduation for children, and higher rates of children's hospitalization due to abuse.

Is unemployment always catastrophic? Hamilton, Hoffman, Broman, and Rauma (1993) find that many of the negative effects of unemployment can be largely reversed by re-employment, although this certainly is conditioned on the length of time between jobs. For those who experience longer periods of unemployment, the depression initially caused by the first layoff can result in a reduced likelihood of getting another job. However, other factors can help to mediate the negative effects of unemployment. According to Nancy Vosler (1994, 1996), who has done work on dislocated manufacturing workers and their families, the effects of unemployment on couples' relationships and on children can be buffered by the state of the families prior to, and during the time of, unemployment. These factors include the following:

* Resources more external to the family (re-employment opportunities and opportunities for education and retraining)

* Resources more internal to the family (savings and extended-family and friend support)
* How the family defines the situation, as challenge or failure (family coping skills)
* Intra-family relationships (marital/ couple relationship and parent–child relationships)
* Family structuring of roles and willingness to restructure them (physical and mental health of family members)

Women's Unemployment and Families
Very little systematic research has been done on women's unemployment and how it affects their relationships with families. Part of the reason is the common assumption that employment is more central to men's identity than to women's and that, historically, married women have had more flexible employment histories. However, with the dramatic increase in women's employment (especially among married women and mothers), along with the rise in single-parent families headed by women, such research should be forthcoming. One recent study, done in Israel, finds that gender makes very little difference in the effects of unemployment on perceived stress and financial strain (Kulik, 2000). Only in terms of physical health were women more likely to have more negative effects than men. This study found that "family status," for both women and men, was the crucial factor. Those experiencing the most difficulty following compulsory unemployment were those who were widowed or divorced, for they had less access to support through another adult's employment.

Research conducted specifically on African American single mothers finds that unemployment can have serious implications for relationships between mothers and children (McLoyd, Jayaratne, Ceballo, & Borques, 1994). This study suggests that unemployment is related to maternal depression, which in turn is correlated with increased punishment of adolescent children. In earlier work, Elder and colleagues (1984) found that fathers experiencing unemployment during the Great Depression became irritable and angry, and consequently became more punishing in their relationships with wives and children.

One significant difference emerged in this study when compared to earlier work on men's unemployment. Earlier studies found that unemployment produced financial strain, which in turn led to greater psychological distress among parents (Conger et al., 1992). In the study by McLoyd and colleagues, African American single mothers did experience greater financial strain when unemployed, but women's perception of financial strain did not produce higher rates of depression. One explanation for this nonfinding is that the women in this study were among those who were living in more extreme economic conditions, conditions that may be more permanent than those of other families:

> In most of the families [in this study], severe financial pressures and efforts to cope with these pressures were probably chronic, rather than episodic, with unemployment and work interruption serving to worsen an already bleak financial situation. Over time, mothers may have habituated to these pressures. (McLoyd et al., 1994: 583)

Single Fathers and Unemployment As mentioned in Chapter 8, the number of men who have physical custody of children has increased in the recent past. According to the Bureau of Labor Statistics (2002), these families appear to be among the hardest hit in the most recent economic downturn. While the number of married-couple families with an unemployed member rose 17 percent from the previous year and the increase for families maintained by women was 10 per-

cent, the increase for families maintained by men was 31 percent. It should be noted that even with such changes, female-headed families with an unemployed member (1.3 million) are three times more common than male-headed families with an unemployed member (433,000).

A recent ethnographic study of single African American men who are trying to maintain (or build) strong relationships with their children suggests that unemployment, in light of current welfare reform legislation, can be a major impediment for parent–child relations (Roy, 1999). The author of this study spent three years working in a fatherhood program based in a Chicago community college. The men who participated in this program had been proven to be the fathers of children born to women receiving public assistance, and they were required to engage in training programs and/or jobs in order to pay state-mandated child support. However, this support was filtered through the state, and part of the amount was siphoned off to pay for the service of matching up fathers to children and monitoring support. The result, Roy suggests, is that these fathers felt reduced to "dollar bills" and resented that the state would not allow them to give money directly to their children (and their children's mothers) and would not accept in-kind support such as spending time with their children and other types of social support.

Employment of Children

Although most of the research focusing on employment by family members addresses the work of mothers and fathers, many children are also likely to be earning a wage. The most recent data on children's employment come from the 1997 National Longitudinal Survey of Youth. These data indicate that 57 percent of fourteen-year-olds and 64 percent of fifteen-year-olds report holding some type of job. The type of job held varied by gender,

TABLE 10.3	Percentage of Youths Employed at Ages 14 and 15			
	ANY JOB (%)	EMPLOYEE JOB ONLY (%)	FREELANCE JOB ONLY (%)	BOTH EMPLOYEE AND FREELANCE JOBS (%)
TOTAL WORKING AT AGE 14	57.2	14.4	33.3	9.4
Sex				
Male	55.2	18.5	27.1	9.7
Female	59.2	10.1	39.9	9.2
Race or Ethnicity				
White	64.3	16.1	36.8	11.4
Black	43.3	10.2	27.3	5.8
Hispanic origin	41.3	11.3	24.6	5.4
Household Annual Income				
Less than $25,000	48.6	13.9	28.1	6.6
$25,000–$44,999	62.7	16.3	37.3	9.1
$45,000–$69,999	63.0	13.6	36.5	12.9
$70,000 or more	63.5	13.9	38.5	11.0
Family Structure				
Two-parent family	61.0	15.0	35.4	10.6
Female-parent family	53.9	13.6	32.6	7.8
Not living with parents	39.4	8.0	28.5	2.9
TOTAL WORKING AT AGE 15	63.7	23.9	26.1	13.7
Sex				
Male	63.4	29.3	21.9	12.2
Female	64.1	18.2	30.6	15.3
Race or Ethnicity				
White	71.8	27.0	27.9	17.0
Black	43.6	14.9	21.4	7.3
Hispanic origin	47.9	19.8	21.4	6.7
Household Annual Income				
Less than $25,000	52.3	21.4	20.0	10.9
$25,000–$44,999	70.9	26.1	30.1	14.7
$45,000–$69,999	69.4	22.5	29.6	17.3
$70,000 or more	75.6	26.2	33.4	16.0
Family Structure				
Two-parent family	67.3	24.2	28.7	14.3
Female-parent family	63.6	23.4	25.4	14.8
Not living with parents	43.3	20.8	17.3	5.1

Source: The National Longitudinal Survey of Youth, 1997. Table adapted from U.S. Department of Labor (2000).

race and ethnicity, household income and family structure (see Table 10.3).

At fourteen, females were slightly more likely to hold a job than were males, but the numbers were similar among fifteen-year-olds. However, the types of job held in both age groups were different. Males were more likely to hold employee jobs (such as working at a restaurant or supermarket), while females were more likely to be in "freelance" jobs (such as babysitting). In terms of race and ethnicity, whites were more likely to hold any type of job than were black or Hispanic youths. Why these differences occur has been a matter of speculation. Researchers point out that labor market opportunities may be variable, with fewer opportunities in the neighborhoods and communities where children of color live. This suggestion is consistent with other findings that black and Hispanic youths are more likely to be unemployed (but looking for work) than are white youths.

Family structure and household income are also related to youth employment. Those most likely to hold jobs are living in two-parent families or in households with higher incomes. Again, there has not been enough research to answer the question about why these differences occur. However, youths in single-parent households and those living in lower-income households may have greater work responsibilities at home and have less time for outside jobs. For fourteen- and fifteen-year-olds to get to jobs, they need access to parents or reliable public transportation for rides. Transportation may be less available to youths in lower-income homes or those living with one parent. Finally, youths living in poorer neighborhoods face the situation of higher area unemployment rates. Taken together, the suggestion is that the social location of youths will shape their employment opportunities and experiences.

One of the important factors to consider regarding youth employment is that employment earlier in life will affect subsequent employment (Gardecki, 2001). Therefore, the lower levels of employment that we see for black, Hispanic, and lower-income youth may result in less opportunity for upward social mobility as adults. Another issue regarding children's employment is the ways in which children use the money they earn. We can expect in this consumer-oriented society that some of the income will be used for clothes and entertainment. However, some youths are also likely employed either to help support their families or to save for college.

A recent book suggests that youths in economically disadvantaged families are more likely to engage in work at home (housework, child care) without receiving any financial compensation (Winton, 2003). This situation may produce their lower rates of "freelance" jobs in the data above. It is probably also the case that youths in lower-income families are using their earnings to provide material support for their families. Further analyses of this relatively new data set will help address some of these questions that emerge from the patterns observed.

The remainder of this chapter will focus on families at work. We begin by looking at unpaid work in the home. Some significant changes have occurred in what gets done and how, but less change has occurred in terms of who does what type of work. Following this section, we will look at the intersections of work in the labor market and work at home, and how these situations relate to dimensions of family well-being.

Family Work at Home: Housework, Child Care, and Kin Work

As we saw at the beginning of this chapter, the organization of work in the household has changed. Whereas all family members once worked relatively near to one another

New technologies for housework were not labor-saving devices as they helped produce a raised standard of housekeeping and cleanliness.

to jointly produce the necessary goods and services to survive, we now have a situation where work is conceptually separated into paid and unpaid work. Each type of work has important implications for the other. We just described some of the ways that employment has changed; here we turn our attention to how unpaid domestic work has changed. Unpaid work at home has typically been studied as consisting of three sets of interrelated activities: housework, child care, and kin work.

Housework: What's to Be Done, and Who Does It?

We typically think of industrialization as having two major effects: (1) it separated the spheres of work of men and women, and (2) it created a very different type of work schedule for those who entered paid employment (i.e., from farm to factory). Industrialization has also had an effect on the organization of work that takes place in the domestic sphere. Industrial technology brought about mechanized modes of production that permeated both the factory and the home. For example, the first vacuum cleaner was sold in 1859; the dishwasher was available in 1865. The

introduction of such new technology resulted in the restructuring of housework. It provided the potential for lessening the physical demands of cleaning, but it also resulted in a rise in the standards for work at home. However, these effects did not take place overnight.

No distinction may be more important than that between the invention and diffusion of technology. To exploit the new cleaning technologies, households needed to be equipped with both indoor plumbing and electricity. Yet half of the households in New York City still used an outdoor "privy" in 1893 (Strasser, 1982), and less than one-quarter of homes had electricity in 1917 (Cowan, 1983). It wasn't until the third decade of the twentieth century that a majority of households were set up to take advantage of these labor-saving devices.

However, the result was not a reduction in the workload for women. Joann Vanek (1974), in tracing housework over much of the twentieth century, argues that new technology for domestic work has had the result of raising the standards of housekeeping for women. Early in the century, women spent a considerable amount of time doing housework because it was all done by hand. For example, laundry could take an entire day and therefore was done maybe once a week. With the introduction of washing machines and dryers, women were able to do laundry in much less time. Did this mean that they spent less time overall in laundry? No, says Vanek; they just did it more often.

New technology also resulted in the creation of new tasks for homemakers such as cleaning toilets and bathtubs. Labor-saving devices may have made the work less arduous, but it did not free up much time. Between 1926 and 1968, the total amount of time that full-time housewives spent in housework went up from 52 to 55 hours a week.

In the early part of the twentieth century, Frederick Taylor began doing time and motion studies. His goal was to make workplaces more efficient. The work of Taylor in restructuring the workplace was also brought into the home (Strasser, 1982). For example, Christine Frederick wrote in the *Ladies' Home Journal* in 1912 about how "household engineers" could apply Taylor's principles of work efficiency. Taylor's main argument related to separating mental work from physical work. Managers would plan, and workers would do the physical labor. In the household, however, women had to be both manager and physical laborer. So Frederick suggested that women do their planning all at once, and in advance of an event such as preparing a meal. Then women were to take a rest. Kitchens were designed to minimize movement while preparing a meal, leading to women getting the most out of their day. When it came time to prepare a meal, women didn't even have to think about it. Many of these ideas are still used in designing kitchens today. Although kitchens are much larger, they are working centers where you can do baking, cooking, and cleaning separately.

FACT OR FICTION?

As women spend more time in the labor market, the time they spend in housework declines.

Time Spent in Housework Today One clear finding from social science research is that within households, less time is spent on housework today than in past decades (Bianchi et al., 2000). People are spending less time at home (more time in employment), families are smaller (fewer numbers of children), technology has improved, we eat out more, and some people now pay someone else to do their housework. While people spend less time doing housework, in families headed by a married or cohabiting couple it is still women who are doing more of it (Shelton & John, 1996). Using data from time diaries (see Figure 2.5 on page 433), Bianchi

and associates (2000) found that from 1965 to 1995, married women decreased the total time spent in housework from about 34 hours a week to 19.4 hours (a decrease of 43 percent). Married men, on the other hand, increased their hours from 4.7 to 10.4 hours a week (an increase of 120 percent). A couple of ideas should be noticed here. First, recall from Chapter 2 that numbers can give different pictures. Using the percentage changes makes a case for significant change among men and women, with men picking up their level of involvement. However, although married men have doubled their time, they still do only about half as much housework as married women do. Second, notice that men did not show any change in behavior, on average, between 1985 and 1995. And women's decrease in housework time also declined less steeply (from 21.9 to 19.4 hours) over this decade. Arlie Hochschild (1989) noticed this trend in her study and referred to it as a **stalled revolution.** While married women continue to increase the amount of time they devote to paid employment, men's involvement at home appears to be stabilizing.

FACT

While women's time in domestic work has declined and men's has risen (less rapidly), women still do almost twice as much as men.

Another interesting dynamic in household labor is the considerable gender segregation in the types of work done. While women do close to twice the amount overall, they invest about four times the effort in meal preparation and cleanup, five times the effort in housecleaning, and 9.5 times as much effort in laundry. Married men are more likely than married women to devote their efforts to outdoor chores, repairs, and bills (between one-third and two-thirds more time). The total amount of time devoted to the tasks in which men do more is between four and seven hours a week, while the tasks women perform more frequently (meals, cleaning, laundry) take between ten and twenty hours per week. The point to be noted here is that married women are more likely to be involved in the more time-consuming housework. These tasks are less optional than the tasks that men perform, and they are more likely to be considered boring and repetitive.

Explanations for the Division of Household Labor

Research on the division of household labor is extensive. Early studies on household labor tended to look at a predefined set of tasks (for example, cooking, laundry, lawn care) and had respondents answer questions about who did more of each task. For each task, the respondent would typically say one of the following: (1) wife does all, (2) wife does more, (3) wife and husband share, (4) husband does more, or (5) husband does all. It was not uncommon for researchers to ask these questions of only one spouse. Critiques of this research focused on the potential bias of selecting a predefined set of tasks, the limited response categories provided for the questions, and the fact that most studies used a reconstruction method asking people to remember work done in a past time (Warner, 1986). An alternative methodology employed more recently is that of time diaries. It is a more time-intensive methodology, but this method allows respondents to record whatever work they perform (not just from a list), to provide more precise estimates of time spent in various activities, and to record work as it is done instead of from memory. It is really the preferred technique among social scientists to study household division of labor, and scores of studies have been completed using this approach.

Several major reviews of the division of household labor research have been done over the past decade (Walker, 1999; Shelton & John, 1996; Coltrane, 2000). The focus of these reviews has been both on the actual amount of time that women and men spend in domestic labor and, more interestingly, on the explanations for the gender inequity in the division of labor. In general, three sets of factors have been presented as important in understanding why couples divide housework in the ways that they do: (1) relative resources, (2) time availability, and (3) gender ideology.

FACT OR FICTION?

The most important predictor of who does the housework in families is the time that is available to do housework.

Relative Resources The relative resources hypothesis originated with the studies of marriage by Blood and Wolfe (1960) and is grounded in exchange theory. The assumption is that household labor is something to be negotiated and that the work is not necessarily desirable. Therefore, the people who will end up being assigned these undesirable tasks are most likely those spouses who hold less power in the relationship. Using social exchange theory (see Chapter 2), power or authority in families is related to the amount of resources (valuable commodities in an exchange) held by an individual. The types of things that are considered valuable include income, age, and education.

Tests of the relative resource hypothesis find that when wives earn a higher proportion of the couple's income, they do less housework, their husbands do more housework, and the gap between the number of hours each puts into housework is smaller. Similar findings occur regarding age. When wives are the same age as their husbands, they do less housework than if they are younger. Younger wives put in relatively more time than their husbands. In terms of education, the couples with higher levels of education have more equitable divisions of labor (Shelton & John, 1996). Wives are particularly advantaged in relationships where they have a college degree and their husbands do not (Bianchi et al., 2000).

Time Availability The time-availability explanation is related to the structure of family life and the other commitments held by family members (Shelton, 1992). The amount and type of housework that needs to be performed depend on how many people are living in a household. When there are children in the home, especially young children, more work needs to be done. Although children increase the housework time of both fathers and mothers, children increase mothers' housework three times more than fathers'.

Time is also restricted by the number of hours that someone is employed. When wives work longer hours, they do less housework and husbands do more, making the gap between them shrink. Husbands' work hours have a different effect: not altering their own housework time, but increasing their wives', making the gap in time greater (Bianchi et al., 2000). These gender differences suggest that time alone is insufficient to explain the distribution of housework.

| **FICTION**

The best predictor of who does the housework is gender. Women do the majority of housework regardless of their other time demands, such as employment.

Gender Ideology The **gender ideology** perspective for explaining the division of labor proposes that attitudes regarding appropriate roles for men and women influence people's family behaviors. When individuals hold more-egalitarian views about what men and women should do, they are more likely to act in more egalitarian ways. That is, they are more likely to negotiate a balanced division of labor. Empirical support is not always consistent for this hypothesis, with some arguing that women's egalitarian views are

consistent predictors of housework sharing (Coltrane, 2000), while others argue that men's attitudes are better predictors of housework than are women's (Shelton & John, 1996). Part of the inconsistency is related to the great variability in the measurement of household labor (time diaries versus retrospective studies). Measures of gender ideology are also not used consistently across research studies. But recent findings regarding ideology make two important points. First, when both partners in a relationship are similar in their attitudes, they are more likely to act on them. Couples who are egalitarian in their thinking are more likely to be egalitarian in the division of household labor. Second, research that has included measures of relative resources and time availability along with measures of gender attitudes finds that the former play a more important role in determining the actual division of labor (Bianchi et al., 2000).

| **FACT OR FICTION?**

Daughters are more likely than sons to increase their time in housework when their mothers are employed.

Children's Participation in Housework

As children age, parents tend to increase their responsibility for household tasks. We've already seen research suggesting that the types of tasks are often assigned based on gender. Boys are more likely to be expected to engage in outside tasks (including carrying out garbage) while girls are more likely to be assigned cleaning and meal-related tasks, especially when households have both sons and daughters (Crouter et al., 1995).

Another relevant question for us in this chapter is whether or not children's household responsibilities respond to the employment status of their parents. Should we expect children with two wage-earning parents

Daughters do more housework on average than sons, especially when they have two full-time employed parents.

daughters appear to do more housework than sons in all types of households, the largest discrepancy is found in households with two full-time employed parents. The time that girls increased their household labor the most was on weekends (similar to their full-time employed mothers) while boys showed little variation in their involvement between the weekdays and weekends.

Why does the gender disparity exist? Like the gendered division of labor between men and women, parents may believe that their daughters are more suited to some types of domestic work. Gender socialization often includes preparation for adult family roles. To the extent that we continue to believe that women's identity is more closely aligned with their relationship to kin, while men's identity is more closely aligned with their relationship to employment, we can expect that women and girls will assume greater responsibility for all types of family/kin work (Ferree, 1991; Hochschild, 1989).

| FACT

Most of this increased time for daughters is accumulated on the weekend, as is true for employed mothers.

to be more active in housework than those in two-parent, single-earner households? Research is mixed, with some studies finding that children do spend more time in housework when they have an employed mother (Winton, 2003) or two employed parents (Benin & Edwards, 1990), while others have found little difference in the time spent in housework by children when controlling for the mother's employment (Bianchi & Robinson, 1997). However, one finding that is relatively consistent across studies is that daughters are more responsive to parents' employment status than are sons (Manke, Seery, Crouter, & McHale, 1994). Although

Child Care

Most of the studies that have explored domestic labor have focused on housework. As we saw in chapters 8 and 9, a considerable amount of work gets done in families to care for children. In family literature, a distinction is made between a number of categories of care. These include three main areas: (1) activities devoted to meeting children's basic physical needs; (2) activities that are focused on children's emotional, educational, and recreational needs; and (3) the responsibility of organizing for children's general well-being. As we saw in earlier chapters, mothers and fathers are both involved with all types of child care, but fathers are still less engaged with and accessible to their children (Pleck, 1997), and fathers are more likely to spend their time interacting with children in recreational activities. However, there is some evidence that African American fathers are less likely to limit their interactions with children to specific areas (Hill, 1999).

The time parents spend with children has increased over time, regardless of the parents employment situation.

FACT OR FICTION?

Parents are spending fewer hours engaged with children today than they were twenty years ago.

In this chapter, our attention is focused on the ways in which domestic work (here, child care) is related to the changes in family work over time. An important question is whether or not the increase in dual-earner families has altered the ways in which parents care for their children. Media attention often plays on the issue of time. Now that the majority of mothers are employed, the suggestion is that parents have less time to spend with their children. (The fear among some is that less time with children will result in a lower quality of child care. We address the question of the effect of employment on children's well-being in a subsequent section.) The issue of just how much time parents are spending with children is itself an interesting one. Figure 10.5 shows the amount of time that fathers and mothers are engaged with their children per week. Several interesting findings emerge. First, the data show that the average time that both parents spend with their children increased between 1981 and 1997, regardless of family employment situation. Second, in the most recent year of data, fathers spent slightly more time with their children when their wives were employed than when they were not. Notice this was not true in 1981. Finally, the data do indicate that nonemployed mothers spent more time per week with their children than did employed

mothers. However, it is also important to see that employed mothers in 1997 spent slightly more time with their children per week (about half an hour more) than did nonemployed mothers in 1981.

Not shown in this figure but reported in its source (Sandberg & Hofferth, 2001) are the changes in time spent by married mothers compared to single mothers. Over the period between 1981 and 1997, mothers in two-parent families increased the time they spent with children (regardless of whether they were employed). The time that single mothers spent did not change. Based on these findings, the authors suggest that concerns about the increasing numbers of employed mothers and single mothers regarding the time they have available for their children are largely unfounded.

FICTION

Whether looking at mothers, fathers, employed or at-home mothers, or married or single-mother families, parents spend more time with their children today compared to twenty years ago.

FIGURE 10.5 Children's Time with Parents, 1981 and 1997, by Employment Status of Mothers

Time Spent with Mothers Per Week: Hours Engaged or Accessible

■ 1981
▧ 1997

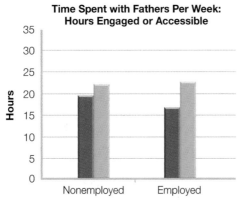

Time Spent with Fathers Per Week: Hours Engaged or Accessible

Note: Data for mothers include mothers in single and two-parent households.
Source: Sandberg and Hofferth (2001).

Kin Work

Most empirical research on family work focuses on those things that are observable, in particular the amount of time spent doing something. A category of family work that remains relatively invisible to observers, but is critical to family life, is **kin work,** defined as "the conception, maintenance, and ritual celebration of cross-household kin ties" (di Leonardo, 1987). Included in this work are tasks such as sending birthday cards to relatives (and remembering when those birthdays are), organizing holiday and family gatherings, calling sick relatives to offer help, and keeping track of relatives' preferences for gifts, food, and communication. Kin work is like housework and child care in that it is most likely to be the work of women. It is different in that it cannot be easily replaced with hired labor. It also differs from much of other family work in that it crosses family and household boundaries. But it may be just this type of work that "fulfills our cultural expectation of satisfying social life."

In addition to housework, child care, and kin work, family scholars also point to other dimensions of family labor that are critical for some families (Haas, 1999). For example, a growing number of families are taking on the responsibility of elder care. Although spouses are usually the ones involved in the care of a frail elderly person, adult children are the next in line. Another example of kin work can be found in those marriages in which one partner is the main provider. Here, family work can also entail "spousal career support," including entertaining, networking, volunteering, or providing organizational support. In both of these types of family work, women are more likely the ones doing the work (Dwyer & Seccombe, 1991; Haas, 1999).

In sum, while the picture of employment has changed significantly over the last hundred years, the picture of domestic life has changed less so. While women are spending less time in housework to adjust for the increase in time spent at work, men are doing somewhat more (although still only half as much as women). Employment has affected families in many other ways, and we now address the broader questions of how work outside the home can have an effect on marriage and children.

The Effect of Employment on Families

For many years, researchers have adopted a strategy for studying families and work while maintaining an assumption of separate spheres: employment and family. As such, considerable attention was given to how the one activity affected the other. For example, how will women's employment affect the relationships between spouses, or between parents and children? Conversely, how will the responsibility for domestic work (housework, child care, kin work) affect employment opportunities and outcomes?

Out of this research came two important concepts that help us begin to understand the reciprocal and dynamic interaction of employment and family life. One concept is that of **role overload**: people taking on too many roles that have conflicting demands. This has been particularly relevant for understanding varying rates of psychological well-being among married mothers compared to married fathers (Menaghan, 1989). The mothers who are the most depressed are those who are employed and get little to no help from their husbands in negotiating child care. The least-depressed employed mothers are those who have husbands who are involved fathers (Ross & Mirowsky, 1988).

Another important concept is that of **spillover,** the notion that the demands involved in one sphere of work can carry over into work in another sphere. Work demands can spill over in a couple of ways. One is related to the structural demands of work. Some employers demand that workers be on site for specific hours of the day or days of the week. Those who are involved in certain occupations may be required to travel for their work. With these demands, parents may find it necessary to use a variety of types of child care, which can result in their missing out on some of their children's activities (for an example of one such occupation, see the Focus on Family Research box on pages 440–441). On the other hand, family work demands can spill over into employment. Taking care of sick children or aging parents may mean that people have to shift employment so they can manage family responsibilities. It should not be surprising that the spillover between work and family is not symmetrical for women and men (Pleck, 1977; Bielby & Bielby, 1989; Marks, Huston, Johnson, & MacDermid, 2001). Because men continue to earn more than women, and their jobs are considered to be more important for families, the boundaries around family are more permeable. That is, fathers are more likely to miss out on children's activities because of work than to miss work for family responsibilities. Women, on the other hand, have more permeable employment boundaries.

The second way in which spillover appears is in terms of the stressors involved in the two spheres of work. When they face stress on the job, parents can come home and react more negatively to their spouses' or children's demands (Crouter et al., 1999; MacDermid & Williams, 1997; Doumas, Margolin, & John, 2002). Parents who are pressured to work overtime, to work nonstandard hours, or to take on a second job are tired when they come home, and the tension becomes part of family interaction. One particularly stressful situation affecting family relationships is when a parent loses a job (we address family stress in more detail in Chapter 11). Stress at home can also affect employment performance. Even if child care can be arranged, it is difficult for parents to focus on their work knowing that a child is sick.

Using these concepts, we will now take a closer look at some areas that have concerned researchers and policy makers about

In this chapter, we explore how the structure of the U.S. economy, and the types of jobs that family members hold within it, set up opportunities and constraints for family life. Depending on the number of hours worked and the patterning of the hours worked, families must structure and restructure their lives. Research on families employed in one industry, coastal fishing, finds that these families have a unique pattern to their lives. Their family rhythm is dictated by the demands of the fishing season, the weather, the type of fish sought, and the changing regulations of the fishing industry. Zvonkovic, Manoogian, and Mc-Graw (2001) conducted focus groups and qualitative telephone interviews with husbands and wives in fishing families (the majority with children) on the Oregon coast. Husbands, as the fishermen, were gone sometimes five days per week or up to four months at one time. Wives, who were involved in unpaid fishing-related work (such as bookkeeping) and other paid employment, would remain home and be the primary parent. From the conversations with fishing families, the researchers discovered four distinct phases experi-

enced by families in fishing communities. Each phase was experienced somewhat differently by husbands and wives, and presented considerable challenges to family members.

Phase I: Departure. As family members prepared the boats for their trips to sea, they also prepared themselves for the time spent apart. It was an emotional time for everyone, with some anger on the part of wives (being left behind to do everything) and some guilt on the part of husbands (not being there to help out with children). In general, however, husbands were a bit more practical in their views and tried to distance themselves emotionally:

> We pretty much accept it, I mean, I discussed with my wife before we ever got married that I was a fisherman and that I'll probably be a fisherman for the rest of my life. So, you know, that's something that had to be accepted. (2001: 144)

Phase II: Separation. Fishing is a dangerous occupation requiring husbands to be focused on their specific tasks and surrounding environment, resulting in husbands talk-

ing about this phase as being exclusively about their own work: "I have to keep my mind on the business of catching fish and staying alive. I can't afford to daydream about my kids at the 'wrong time' or I might not get home . . . ever" (Conway, Gilden, & Zvonkovic, 2002). Wives, on the other hand, had much to do while their husbands were away. In their day-to-day lives, they became single parents. Although this is a challenge that produces considerable stress, most of the wives enjoyed their independence and ability to take care of themselves and their children. As one wife said, "It gets real long and hard, but I'm proud" (Zvonkovic et al., 2001: 146). Many of the wives also connected with one another and via these friendships established a sense of normalcy in their lives.

Phase III: Homecoming. Homecoming was a second stage of preparation. It typically began during the second half of the fishing trip and continued to the beginning of the time back together as a family. Fishermen referred to the midway point of their trip as "hump day" and admitted that they began thinking more about their families and an-

the changes in family work dynamics. We will begin by looking at how employment affects families. Specifically, we will explore the effect of employment on marriages and on children's well-being. Then we will see how family work shapes the structure and rewards of employment.

The Effect of Employment on Marital Relationships

Earlier in this book we discussed the notion of specialization in marriage. This perspective on marriage argues that marriages can benefit from a situation in which husbands

ticipating time together. However, an important factor that shaped the homecoming was the success of the fishing trip. If things went well, then husbands arrived home much happier. It was a time of excitement for both husbands and wives, but wives tended to think more about transitioning everyone to being back together.

Phase IV: Reunion. While the homecoming held some excitement and romance, the reunion was a bit more challenging. Families had to shift again, this time from a one-parent to a two-parent system. Husbands reported being a little nervous about reentering, noting that "when I get back it takes me awhile to kind of fit in again" (Zvonkovic et al., 2001: 150). From the wives' perspectives, it looked like this:

> Your husband's gone five months and he comes home and all of a sudden, you've got this stranger in your house, who wants to take over everything, you know, and you've been in control and the kids resent it. . . . Because the rules are so different. (2001: 151)

Fishing families are not all the same. Families vary in terms of the schedules of the fishing industry and the particular patterns of fishing for different types of fish. Families will also vary by the way in which wives organize their work, both paid and unpaid. However, even with all of this complexity, common themes do emerge (Manoogian-O'Dell, McGraw, & Zvonkovic, 1998). All the fishing families in this research depend on the sea for their livelihoods; therefore, husbands must be away from their families for a period of time. To respond to this structural condition, fishing families must be flexible and learn to create and manage space that includes husbands/fathers and space that does not include them. Fishing families must also find alternatives to face-to-face communication patterns familiar to other families as ways to keep up on the activities of one another. Interviews with fishing families revealed that they used audiotapes, videotapes, journals, photo stories, and scrapbooks so that fathers could get a sense of what went on while they were at sea. With the increasing use of cell phones, fathers can also communicate with their families when the weather permits, and they can use e-mail when at port in other locations. It was the conclusion of these researchers that fishing families face no more stress than other families per se. Rather, it takes some work to adjust to the ebb and flow of the coastal fishing industry.

Sources: Based on Manoogian-O'Dell, McGraw, and Zvonkovic (1998); Zvonkovic, Manoogian, and McGraw (2001); and Conway, Gilden, and Zvonkovic (2002).

Critical Thinking

1. What other types of occupations require extended absences for family members? Do you think they also follow this four-phase model?

2. This research was based on information from the adult members of families. What do you think children in these families might have to say about the prolonged absence of a parent? How might it affect parent–child relations from their perspective?

devote their primary energies to employment activities while wives devote their energies to domestic work (Waite & Gallagher, 2000). This system is suggested to have long-term benefits in terms of economic well-being for families. The emphasis on men's employment over women's is related to the fact that men's wages exceed those of women's, even in similar occupations. The emphasis on domestic work by women, then, is partially related to their lower earning capacity but also to assumptions about women's nature and preferences. With these more traditional notions about marriage and family, we might expect

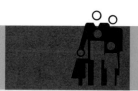

Votive candles and patriotic placards line the streets as they report for work and leave work. Millions of television viewers cheer with them at small victories or cry with them as they bury one of their own. Since September 11, 2001, Americans have taken a renewed interest in and shown amazing support for the police as they go about their job of protecting and serving the public. And we may have a better understanding about the nature of police work. But what happens in the homes of police officers when the shift is over and they return to their families? Although our interest may be new, the transition from society's guardian to family member is as old as the profession.

In "The Remains of the Workday," published in the November *Journal of Marriage and Family,* Nicole Roberts and Dr. Robert W. Levenson (2001) examine the effect of job stress and physical exhaustion on the marriages of nineteen male police officers and their spouses. The authors conclude that job stress in these marriages is toxic for marital interaction and certainly contributes to the high rate of divorce in police marriages.

Levenson and Roberts, psychologists at the University of California–Berkeley, studied the emotional cost of work as indicated by measures of job stress and exhaustion. They asked if job stress and exhaustion contribute to ways of interacting that could lead to declines in marital satisfaction and ultimately to marital dissolution. Nineteen male police officers and their spouses provided information about themselves and their marriages. These couples completed a thirty-day diary and visited the laboratory four times to report on stress and exhaustion and to participate in videotaped in-teractions. During these visits, physiological responses such as cardiac rate and electrodermal response were recorded. Both observed and measured physiological responses showed that greater stress related to greater physiological arousal. Husbands who experienced high levels of physical exhaustion, as measured in the pre-conversation period, showed even higher responses during the conversation period. These responses to exhaustion dampened the positive quality of the marital interaction. The findings also suggest that wives who sense the stress may assume a defensive and vigilant posture either in anticipation of difficult interactions or as a way of minimizing the husbands' stress.

The researchers found it especially interesting that husbands' physical exhaustion was reflected only in husbands' physiology, and not that of the wives: "Wives do

that the increase in women's employment would pose a couple of challenges to the marital relationship. First, when women are away from home, they have less time to spend with their partners. If husbands are used to more time devoted to them, women's employment can lead to a decline in marital satisfaction. Second, women's employment might provide them with independent income, meaning that they are not dependent on husbands for survival. Lower dependency could lessen employed wives' commitment to marriage.

Research about the effects of women's employment suggests there can be positive effects for some and negative effects for others. In terms of financial issues, it appears that women's employment has a generally stabilizing effect on marriages (Greenstein, 1990). Two-income marriages have an earnings advantage over one-income marriages, and for those who are working at lower-wage jobs, a woman's earnings can keep the family out of poverty. However, an important contextualizing factor in this relationship is whether the couples desire a two-earner relationship. When couples prefer husbands to be the primary breadwinner, but their situation doesn't allow it, marriages experience more stress (Pyke, 1994).

not have to 'mobilize' for dangerous and difficult marital interactions when dealing with an exhausted husband in the same way that they would when dealing with a stressed husband."

Dr. Ann Crouter, of the Department of Human Development and Family Studies at Penn State, calls the research "A fascinating glimpse into the emotional processes linking policemen's work and family lives. I particularly liked the focus on both stress and exhaustion. The findings clearly suggest that stress is problematic in the ways it spills over into marital interaction."

Dr. Crouter also points out that the results are consistent with other research on the transmission of emotion between work and family. She concludes that we need a better understanding of specific occupations and their work-related stresses to know how marriage might be affected negatively by paid work.

Dr. Cedric Alexander, of the Department of Psychiatry, University of Rochester Medical Center, provides short- and long-term therapy for police officers and their families. Dr. Alexander believes the Levenson and Roberts research demonstrates the challenge that confronts police officers and their spouses. He notes that patients report general job-related stress, and this stress may precipitate depressed moods, anxiety, or post-traumatic stress. That job stress shows up in marital interaction, states Dr. Alexander, "certainly aligns with much of the work I do on a daily basis."

The results of this study might predict an unhappy outcome for many police families, and for any family where one partner is engaged in a high-stress occupation. However, researchers Levenson and Roberts, and reviewers Crouter and Alexander, agree that we should screen individuals as they enter a high-stress profession and build counseling and family support into those professions before stress has a detrimental effect on individuals, marriages, or families.

Source: Adapted from National Council on Family Relations, *Journal of Marriage and Family* press release, November 16, 2001 (http://www.ncfr.org/about_us/j_press_release.asp). Accessed November 29, 2001.

Critical Thinking

1. What other jobs do you think would be particularly stressful for families?

2. What job do you hope to have after college? In what ways might that job introduce stress into your family life?

Because of the assumption that men will be employed (it's part of our definition of masculinity), less research has been conducted on the implications of men's employment on marital relationships. A recent longitudinal study of dual-earner families with adolescent children explored the effect of husbands' work hours and work overload on the quality of their marriages (Crouter et al., 2001). Data were collected from both husbands and wives. The authors found that when husbands worked sixty hours per week or more, on average, they spent less time with their wives in shared activities. However, this did not result in a less positive evaluation of the marriage by either wives or husbands. What did appear to affect the quality of the marriage was when husbands felt "overloaded" with employment demands. Feeling like "I can't ever seem to get caught up" resulted in both partners' feeling less marital love (lower levels of closeness) and reporting higher levels of marital conflict. The conclusion of this study is that the time one spends at work is less important than the pressures that employment brings.

Another important component of work structure is whether employment follows standard hours (daytime, weekdays) or nonstandard hours, also referred to as **shift**

Stress can spill over from parents' employment to family interaction. Parent-child relations are challenged, in particular when parents feel overloaded by their employment.

work (evenings, nights, weekends). As we mentioned earlier, one in three dual-earner families with children includes a spouse doing shift work (Presser, 1995). Consistent with the research just summarized, shift work can negatively influence marital relationships. First, it limits the time available for couple interaction, interaction that can aid commitment. Second, working nonstandard hours can be physically stressful, spilling over to marital relations. Using data from the National Survey of Families and Households, Presser (2000) finds one type of shift work (night shifts) that has negative effects on marital quality but finds that these effects occur only when there are children. Without children present, couples are better able to negotiate the demands of their working relationship. With children, however, couples experience more stress with shift work, especially when that shift is at night. When working at night, parents must sleep during the day, which is particularly difficult to manage when children are at home. Without sufficient sleep, marital relations are compromised. These research findings applied to both mothers and fathers who worked night shifts. For an interesting example of how

stress can spill over from one particular occupation (police work), see the Focus on Family Research box on pages 442–443.

The Effect of Employment on Children's Well-Being

The vast majority of the interest in the effect of employment on children has focused on the impact of *women's* employment. The changes in women's employment have been more marked than men's in the last thirty years. With women's continued responsibility for domestic work, the concern is that when women take on an additional role, something may suffer: the children. More recently, researchers have also been asking what effect men's employment has on children. Along with concerns over changes in men's employment (longer hours, involvement in shift work) and the reality that dual-earner households are now the modal form for families with children, we need to ask how the health and well-being of children are related to the overall structure of employment in families.

Women's Employment and Children's Well-Being The literature on child outcomes associated with maternal employment is diverse in terms of the issues that it addresses. One well-researched topic is the effect of mothers' employment on mother–child attachments. Recall from Chapter 4 that attachment theory hypothesizes that when the mother is not present for extended periods in an infant's life, that infant is less likely to develop secure attachments with his or her mother (Ainsworth, 1964). Early attachments have consequences for children in their ability to form secure attachments later in life. Older studies did suggest a negative relationship, finding that insecure attachments were more common among children with employed mothers. Subsequent research based on larger, more diverse samples has not been able to replicate these negative results (NICHD Early Child Care Research Network, 1997). Some have suggested that the earlier studies that found negative effects were done in a time when employment among mothers of infants was less normative than it is today (Han, Waldfogel, & Brooks-Dunn, 2001).

Another area of concern is how mothers' employment affects the cognitive development of children. A major study using the National Longitudinal Survey of Youth found that early maternal employment was not consistently related to a wide variety of child outcomes (Harvey, 1999). A couple of specific findings that did emerge were that when mothers worked a higher number of hours in the first three years of a child's life, it was associated with slightly lower vocabulary scores (only up to age nine) and that early employment was correlated with more positive outcomes for children in lower-income families. Using the same data, but employing a longitudinal design and controlling for race, Han and associates (2001) found that early maternal employment had different effects on non-Hispanic white children than on African American children. Specifically, the authors found that when white mothers were employed early in a child's life, the child showed lower vocabulary and math scores at ages three and four and again at ages seven and eight. The effect of early maternal employment on African American children was insignificant. As with the variation in results over time on mother–child attachment, these findings may be related to the fact that among African American families, maternal employment is more normative.

Men's Employment and Children's Well-Being Men's employment can influence their children's lives in several ways. Certainly, the income that men provide for families is critical. Fathers' earnings, independent of mothers', are associated both with enhanced educational attainment and the psychological well-being of children as they become young adults (Amato, 1998). In families where fathers are not resident (in the case of separation, divorce, or parents never marrying), the important issue is about how much of the father's income gets passed on to children through support payments. In this situation, the outcomes are similar. When fathers (resident or not) financially support their children, this results in better educational outcomes and fewer behavior problems for children (Amato & Gilbreth, 1999).

One of the concerns mentioned in the research about women's employment is that the more time they spend at work, the less time they have for their children. However, there has been little concern over men's employment hours, probably because for years the norm has been for fathers to be employed as close to full time as possible. We saw earlier that the number of hours men work, along with when those hours take place, has become more variable. In her study of *The Overworked American,* Juliet Schor (1991) provided data suggesting that adults increased their working hours by 163 hours a year (one additional month) between 1969 and 1987. The stress of this "overwork" was proposed as having negative implications for families, especially children. Recent studies that address how the number of hours that fathers work influences their relationships with children find that the sheer number of hours does not appear to make a consistent difference in children's well-being (Harvey, 1999; Crouter et al., 2001). However, when fathers work longer hours *and* feel overloaded by this work, their relationship with their children is compromised (Crouter et al., 2001).

| FACT OR FICTION?

Research indicates that maternal employment has very few negative effects on children's well-being.

The Moderating Effect of Child Care Quality on the Relationship Between Parental Employment and Children's Well-Being A growing body of evidence suggests that the type of alternative care provided for children while their parents are at work can make a difference in terms of their development. The largest study to date is the ten-site study by the National Institute of Child Health and Development's Early Child Care Research Network. Findings from this research indicate that alternate child care in the first year of life does not have detrimental effects on children's development (NICHD, 1997). However, the quality of the care does make a difference (Han et al., 2001), particularly so for low-income families compared to high-income families (Brooks-Gunn, Klebanov, Liaw, & Spiker, 1993). The cost of high-quality child care is prohibitive for some families, as was shown in the previous chapter. It is among just these families that the need for child care may be the greatest.

Other studies that have paid attention to nonparental care and its effect on older children suggest that the key issue is supervision (monitoring). When children are unsupervised after school, they have a higher likelihood of engaging in externalizing behavior (deviant behaviors). Marshall and colleagues (1997) found that for lower-income children, spending time in an after-school program had a positive effect on adolescents' behaviors. When children are supervised after school, they also do better in some areas of academics, such as math (Muller, 1995).

This review of the effects of employment on family life indicates that it is not employment per se that affects family life. Rather, it is the structure of employment and the ability of parents to work out alternative care for their children that are important in understanding how work matters. Also, parents' desires regarding their work are important. When parents are working too little or too much, this can produce strain on family relationships. The organization of work (family and employment) can also be looked at from the opposite perspective. Instead of asking how families are influenced by employment, an equally important question is this: How do families affect employment behaviors?

| FACT

Research has shown that what is most important when considering the impact of maternal employment on children's well-being is to control for whether or not mothers have access to quality child care.

The Effect of Families on Employment

The concept of spillover includes the idea that family concerns and responsibilities affect the way in which family members approach their employment behaviors. The traditional assumption is that this spillover is more relevant for women. Taking care of partners, children, and sometimes aging parents consumes a considerable amount of time and energy. Therefore, because women are responsible for domestic care, there will be consequences for their employment. These consequences are thought to include (1) women being less interested in their employment and being less satisfied with their jobs than men, (2) women being less committed to their jobs, and (3) women's lower commitment resulting in fewer rewards from their employment (Haas, 1999). Research focusing on these relationships for both women and men has begun to challenge these hypotheses.

Attitudes Toward Employment

If we assume that women not only are responsible for domestic work but also that it is their preferred activity, then we might expect that women will view their jobs in different ways than men do (Lorence, 1987). In particular, women should be expected to find less satisfaction in their paid employment than men, who are socialized to see employment as key to their identity *as* men (Rubin, 1994). However, no empirical evidence supports this assertion. First, women and men are about equally likely to find their paid work satisfying. Second, for women and men alike, marital status, number of children, and the job characteristics of one's partner do not influence job attitudes (such as commitment or satisfaction with work). What does seem to make a difference to employees is the characteristics of the jobs themselves. People are more satisfied with their work when it has more value (they are paid more), when they are given more autonomy, when more skill is involved, and when the work is interesting.

Commitment to Employment

The majority of adult men and women in U.S. families are employed. So, in one sense, we can see that family responsibilities are not keeping people completely from work. However, some aspects of employment are affected by family responsibilities. These include the number of hours that people work, whether employment is full time or part time, the number of hours/days taken off work to care for family, and productivity on the job. In all of these categories of work-related behavior, family responsibilities continue to influence women more than men.

When men and women become parents, their work hours shift, but in opposite directions. Fathers tend to increase their hours of employment while women are more likely to decrease theirs (Lundberg & Rose, 1999). We saw in Figure 10.1 that a majority of mothers, even mothers with infants, are employed. However, many of these women are employed only part time. Some of these mothers are employed part time by choice,

with others working part time involuntarily. These latter women are the underemployed, and they are disproportionately women in lower-wage jobs and also single mothers. On the other end of the employment spectrum, mothers who are the least likely to experience any disruption in their employment behavior are those who hold high-status jobs, those with longer work histories, and those who have access to good maternity benefits. There are no racial differences in these employment patterns for women (Yoon & Waite, 1994).

Family demands also spill over into paid work when parents must care for sick children, spouses need to care for ailing partners, or adults need to care for aging parents (Ferber & O'Farrell, 1991). In most of these situations, women are the ones who are most likely to miss work because of family duties. Mothers are more often the parent called by school officials when a child is sick, and this can result in taking more time off work or in a lowering of their productivity at work. However, when fathers are more involved as parents, they are just as likely to miss work to care for sick children.

The Availability of Child Care and Commitment to Employment Research on the effect of family responsibilities on women's employment patterns suggests that it is not a lack of interest in or a lack of commitment to work that explains why women miss work or have lower productivity when children are sick or need assistance. Rather, it is the availability of quality, reliable child care that makes a significant difference. The availability of alternative care for children is variable across families. Depending on the situation of the parents, there are different types of challenges in locating care. For example, single parents are more likely to be without access to care from the other parent. Parents who are working certain types of shift work (especially night work) may find that child care is not available at all. Those working overtime or on-call must seek flexible child care, which can be scarce. And most parents find it a challenge to access (physically or financially) a high-quality care environment for their children. All of these factors are important when parents establish their working schedules.

As with other areas of family research, little is known about how fathers negotiate their employment to accommodate the needs of children, but there is pretty clear evidence that mothers do. We know that the majority of women are employed. At the time of the birth of a child, a mother needs to make a decision about whether to leave her employment or alter her time at work. Overall, women with children, especially young children, are more likely to exit a job in any given month than are women without children or are men. Some of the mothers leave because of their desire to be at home with their child. However, researchers at the University of Michigan find that the accessibility of formal nonparental child-care arrangements (including center care) also significantly affects women's employment (Hofferth & Collins, 2000). When mothers have to travel more than ten minutes to the nearest care facility (center- or home-based care), they are more likely to leave their jobs.

In addition to the general issue of availability of care, specific characteristics of child care, such as cost, stability, and flexibility, play relatively more or less important roles in women's employment activity depending on the wage level of the mother employed. For example, mothers with jobs bringing in lower wages are more influenced by the flexibility of care, which may be related to the types of occupations they hold (or the tenuousness of their employment). Women with moderate incomes make decisions about leaving their jobs based on the cost and stability of care. Women earning higher wages are more often influenced by the stability of child care (Hofferth & Collins, 2000). The point of this research is to show

that women make decisions about their employment patterns based on their family's child-care needs. This type of information can, and should, be useful to employers as they try to attract women workers into their places of business.

The Effect of Domestic Work on Wages

The third way in which women's domestic work is thought to affect their employment is by depressing the rewards they receive for their jobs. About twenty years ago, Shelley Coverman (1983) explored the relationship between housework and wages. She found that the more time people spend in housework, the lower their wages. Although the relationship was negative for both men and women, it was greater for women. Why would time spent in housework have a stronger impact on women's wages than on men's? A recent study finds that the answer to this question can be found in the type of housework done by women versus men (Noonan, 2001). The author of this study grouped household tasks into three groups: "female" tasks (preparing meals, washing dishes, cleaning house, and washing clothes), "male" tasks (outdoor and other household maintenance and automobile maintenance), and "neutral" tasks (shopping, paying bills, and driving other household members from place to place). She discovered that only the "female" tasks had a significant effect on wages. To explain this relationship, we should think about how these groups of tasks vary. "Female" tasks are those activities that must be performed daily and are the least flexible. These types of activities may be the ones that tax a person's energies the most, resulting in a negative effect on work performance (availability and productivity). Noonan also found that the negative effect of "female" tasks on wages held for both women and men. The results here are interesting. We've mentioned that the overall distribution of domestic work has become more equitable over time. However, it appears that the total time spent is less important than the time spent in certain types of family work.

Juggling Family Work

In the final chapter of this book, we will address the issue of how the federal government has responded to the changes in family dynamics. However, other steps can be taken at the level of the organization or business that could help families coordinate their work efforts. The phrase "family friendly" is now used to describe those businesses that are providing benefits or opportunities to families to make their organization of work easier. At the same time, individual families themselves can construct meaningful combinations of work at home and at their places of employment. (For individual coping mechanisms employed by families, see the Constructing Strong Families box on page 450.)

| FACT OR FICTION?

The number of families in which husbands stay at home while wives take primary responsibility for breadwinning is on the rise.

Diversity in Family Styles

The result of the dynamic changes in families' working lives has been the construction of a very diverse set of families. Although it is quite common for families with children to include parents who are employed (and employed full time), the structuring and type of employment vary quite a bit. There are at least three broad categories of family styles, with each including a number of subtypes. Each style of family represents a way of organizing family work. We have already discussed the variety of types of employment opportunities for family members and the consequences of employment for marriages and families. Here we address the economic consequences of varying family types.

The Two-Person Career This type of family has two adults, but only one of them is formally employed (the vast majority of the employed are men). However, the partner who is not formally employed is very actively involved in supporting the career of the partner by doing the domestic work, plus a type of kin work termed "spousal career support" (Haas, 1999). The support role can include the following (Haas, 1999; Pavalko & Elder, 1993):

1. Being an unpaid partner by doing some of the same work that the partner is involved in. These partners might go out on the stump for their politician spouse, or they may provide emotional support to others, as in the work of a pastor.

2. Being an auxiliary worker by providing work that would otherwise have to be hired out by their spouse's business, such as bookkeeping, scheduling, or maintaining an office.

3. Being an enabler. This work might include entertaining clients or community volunteer work that brings prestige to the employed partner.

4. Doing emotion work. The supporting partner can encourage a partner to continue or can help smooth things over if times get rough.

The term **career** is a specific one, referring to an occupation with the opportunity for upward mobility and one that requires higher levels of education and training. Although most data sources do not make a distinction regarding single-earner families in which the employed person is in a career versus a job, the important point is that this type of couple is on the decline. In 1997,

All families must coordinate activities to get family work accomplished. Things are a bit more complicated when more than one family member works. Below are several of the more common approaches that families use to respond to this challenge.

Cutting Back on Paid Work

Specialization in family roles	This strategy is most common among families with young children. Typically, mothers will stay at home while fathers take full responsibility for family financial support. Those families in which parents work in lower-paying jobs, and single parents, are not as likely to find this option viable.
Going part time	Like specializing in family roles, going part time is an option available only to those families in which one wage earner can earn enough to compensate for the lower wages of the other partner. Research on the effects of cutting back on work suggests that it has a negative effect not only on family finances but also on women's self-esteem.

Cutting Back on Housework

Delegating household chores to others	Parents typically expect children to do chores around the house. The research is mixed on whether children of employed parents are more likely to do household chores than are children with only one working parent, but among those who do, it is daughters who appear to pick up more of the slack. Children are more likely to watch younger siblings than they are to do either housework or elder care. Husbands are likely to do more when their wives work, but this strategy of delegating chores appears not to make the division of household labor completely equitable.
Paying for someone else to do the housework	Employment statistics show that many people (primarily women) work as domestics. Some are part of a business (such as The Maids) while others organize their own work.

Psychological Approaches

Prioritizing one role over another	Some dual-earner couples may be employed, but specialize in terms of who is seen as primarily responsible for one area. By prioritizing one area, lack of success in the other may not have as severe consequences in terms of psychological well-being.
Becoming a supermom	Some women attempt to maintain high standards for housework, child care, and employment, but typically at the expense of their own needs.
Developing organizational skills	This approach is also referred to as cognitive restructuring. To decrease role strain, parents focus on the positive outcomes of holding multiple roles and downplay the problems associated with doing so.

Source: Based on Haas (1999).

28 percent of couples with children under the age of 18 included an employed husband and a stay-at-home wife, compared to 55.4 percent of such couples in 1965 (see Table 10.1).

One particular type of single-earner couple that is small in number, but increasing, is the household in which wives are employed and husbands are not. These men are referred to as **househusbands,** and they are found in about 4.4 percent of married couples. These families are not as prevalent because men still have an earnings advantage over women; therefore, families can maximize earning potential through men's employment. However, another deterrent is the social pressure for men to be the primary breadwinner in families. The househusband style of family is more likely to be a temporary style, employed during periods of men's unemployment or work stoppage.

Dual-Earner Families Although we refer to the dual-earner family as the modal type of families with children, there is considerable diversity among dual-earner families. One difference is between those with two full-time employed parents and those with at least one partner employed part time. In 1997, 56.6 percent of women were employed full time, and another 23.4 percent were employed part time. One in five women was not employed at all. Having children made a slight difference, with married women with children being more likely to be employed part time (28.3 percent) than full time (28.3 percent). Only slightly more were not employed at all (23.1 percent). For single mothers, the trend is reversed. They are more likely to be employed full time (58.2 percent) than are other women (Waite & Nielson, 2001).

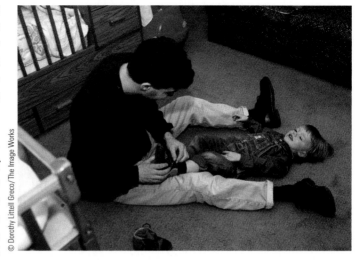

Because men continue to have an earnings advantage over women, the percentage of men who are househusbands is small, although this number is on the rise.

| FACT

It is estimated that there are now over one million families in which men take on the role of homemaker.

Families with two employed adults have an earnings advantage. For example, in 1998 the median family income for two-income couples was $60,669 while the median income for one-income couples (wife not in the labor force) was $36,027. These figures do not account for the presence of children. However, recent figures suggest that even controlling for household composition, dual-earner families with children have at least a $10,000-per-year income advantage over those families with one earner (Waite & Nielson, 2001).

We've already addressed the diversity in employment that has occurred with economic restructuring. There are significant differences in the types of employment that men and women hold, and these differences have consequences for family life. When people are involved in shift work, a trading-off pattern of working at home often occurs. Some dual-earner couples adopt a "commuter marriage" whereby partners live and are employed in different locations. This type of family is most likely to occur with professional couples and couples without children. The situation is particularly stressful, both financially and emotionally (Winfield, 1985).

Single-Earner/Single-Parent Families The number of children who will experience living in a single-parent family is rising, due to a higher divorce rate along with an increase in the number of children who are born to women outside of marriage, including a growing number of cohabiting couples that have children. Most of these families are female, single-headed households. What that means is that household incomes will be, on average, lower. Recalling the figures above for family income by number of income earners, female-headed households earned a median of $21,023, which is about 60 percent of what one-income couples made. When men are the single heads of households, they do somewhat better, although single men do earn less than married men (Waite & Gallagher, 2000). The median income for families headed by a single male was $32,960 (91 percent of that of one-earner couples and almost 50 percent more than that of female single heads of household). Single parents face all the same child-care issues that couples do, with the additional problem of having less access to the other parent to help out.

Employers' Responses to Working Families

Family researchers are not the only ones to pay attention to changing family dynamics. Employers are now very much involved in designing "family-friendly policies" that will allow for employees (single, cohabiting, married, or parents) to be available for work. Like family scholars, businesses are also changing their thinking from a view of employment as separate from family life to one that sees a "synergy" between work inside and outside the home (Galinsky, 2001). This new thinking suggests that the most productive workers on the job are those who are also the most productive at home. Having the time and energy to attend to all family work is the goal. To this end, a number of strategies have been tried by business:

* *Flexible work arrangements.* Employees are able to move from full time to part time and back again without penalty. Other types of flexibility include working from home, job sharing, and daily flextime (working seven hours one day and nine the next to be full time).
* *Leaves.* The Family Medical Leave Act (see Chapter 15) applies only to businesses of a certain size; therefore, it excludes most employees in this country. However, some businesses are following suit and providing maternity/paternity leaves that guarantee an employee a comparable job after a leave of absence.
* *Child-care assistance.* This can include an on-site care center or a child-care subsidy (such as being able to pay with pre-tax dollars).
* *Elder-care assistance.* This may include either long-term-care insurance for family members or financial support for local elder-care programs.
* *Employee assistance programs.* These are designed to help employees resolve family problems. They also include retraining programs for employees who are reassigned to new positions that require a different skill set.
* *Supportive workplace cultures.* Businesses might offer training programs for supervisors to help them understand the multiple demands on employees or to become more sensitive to issues of diversity that hinder strong communication.

Who is more likely to offer such benefits? According to a 1998 survey done by the Families and Work Institute (Galinsky & Bond, 1998), the most frequent predictor is the type of industry. Finance, insurance, and real estate businesses are the most likely to provide a variety of programs and supportive policies. The least likely are the wholesale and retail trades. Another important factor is company size. Larger companies are better positioned to offer a variety of benefits.

Something that is as important as company size is the proportion of top executive positions in the company that are held by women or by minorities. As we might expect, women and people of color are more familiar with the stresses and strains involved in negotiating family work. They are more likely to be in lower-earning positions and are more likely to be in single-parent situations. It is not surprising, then, that the next most important predictor of benefit provision is the percentage of the work force that is women. When women make up a majority of workers, employers' hands are forced. They must take into consideration the concerns of many who are responsible for the care of others.

The actual number of businesses that offer these types of benefits is small but growing. Employers realize that productive workers are good for business, but coming to an understanding of the ways that employees' family lives influence that productivity may take some time. We should expect that if women and people of color continue to find their way into the upper levels of management (which is slowly occurring), companies may be pushed even more quickly toward creating a family-friendly atmosphere. Sociologist Kathleen Gerson (1993) points out another potentially revolutionary effect of these policies. If they are adopted, we may well begin to see a more balanced distribution of work at home. Both mothers and fathers could become involved parents without jeopardizing their opportunities for job or career advancement. With this dramatic change, it will make sense for us to think about family work in a much more synergistic way.

Larger companies are better positioned to provide employees with benefits such as on-site child care facilities.

Conclusion

All families are working families. That is, everyone in families is involved in creating something of value, whether it is a good or a service. How families have organized their work has changed over time. Prior to industrialization, families were likely to be all working domestically to produce their livelihood. After industrialization, family members began leaving home to exchange their labor for wages. Today, the most common situation is for all adult members to be employed. The type of occupations held by people in the United States is changing because of the processes of economic restructuring, technological innovations, and globalization. These have produced a much more diverse labor force, with people working a variety of hours organized in many different ways.

A great deal of social science research has looked at the effects of these diverse employment patterns on families. This research suggests that how employment affects families depends on a number of factors. First, when the rhythm of employment clashes with the rhythm of families, stress can result. Another important factor is whether one's employment results in compensation adequate to meet family needs. Finally, when the particular employment pattern of family members is desired (they want to be employed), families adjust better to the demands of jobs. One of the themes of this text is to show how structural arrangements (availability of jobs and the structuring of jobs) influence the flow of family life. At the same time, the beliefs and values attached to family mediate the way these structural conditions shape family experiences.

While it is expected that most adult family members will be employed outside the home for pay, the unpaid work at home still needs to get done. Housework, child care, and other kin work are still necessary components of family work. Like paid work, unpaid domestic work is divided among family members in a way that reflects the positioning of each member. Those who are working more hours and earning more income (more likely husbands and fathers) tend to do less of this work. People also hold varying ideas about the appropriateness of certain divisions of household work. For all types of unpaid domestic work, women are still believed to be the ones responsible.

Finally, we've seen in this chapter that families have had an effect on the structuring of employment. More employers are now responding to family demands by offering a variety of benefits such as flexible work arrangements, family leaves, and employee assistance programs. The actual number of businesses offering these benefits is small, however, meaning that families must continue to juggle their schedules and obligations in order to keep up with family work.

Chapter Review

* How has the relationship of the family to the economy changed over time?

Prior to industrialization, families were places of work. All members of families were involved in producing the goods and services needed to survive. After the mechanization of production, there was a decline in reliance on home production, and many family members (primarily men but also less-privileged women and women of color) had to exchange their labor for wages so that the families could survive. This process has continued. The production of most goods now takes place outside of the home, and most goods must be purchased, resulting in the changing functions of families from production to consumption.

* How has economic restructuring affected family dynamics?

Transformations in the structure of employment, including deindustrialization, technological advances, and globalization, have produced a much more diverse work force. Growth is most likely in the service sector, although there is also growth in the top tier of occupational categories. This situation has resulted in more diversity in family styles. The declines in traditionally male occupations that brought higher wages, along with the increases in women's employment, have produced the dual-earner family as the most popular form.

* What are the different categories of work that continue to be done by families at home?

Domestic work is typically divided into three categories: housework, child care, and kin work. Kin work includes the work necessary to maintain connections across households within families. For all categories of domestic work, women do more of it. Variations in the distribution of family work at home are related to the time each member has available to do the work, the amount of resources held by each family member (income, age, and education), and the attitudes that family members hold regarding the appropriateness of certain types of work for women and men.

* What are the implications of employment for marital relationships?

The effect of employment on marriage depends on a number of issues. Marriages can be enhanced when both husbands and wives are involved in work that they enjoy. If partners are employed more or less than desired, or in jobs that require nonstandard hours of work, marriages experience stress and instability. Income from having two earners can have a stabilizing effect, especially for those in lower-wage jobs.

* How does parents' employment affect children's well-being?

Most research on this question has focused on the influence of mothers' employment. Recent large-scale studies find that mothers' employment per se does not affect children's well-being. Fathers' employment can have an effect, especially relating to their economic provision for the family. Probably the most important finding is that the availability of reliable, quality child care can make a difference for children's well-being in families with employed parents.

* In what ways do families influence employment?

Because of traditional notions about women's preference for domestic work, it was assumed that women's employment would be negatively affected by demands from family. However, research is pretty clear that commitment to work and the satisfaction with work are more closely associated with the type of occupation that people hold. Having children does increase the likelihood for women to take time off work (using sick pay or family leave). Involved fathers are also more likely to miss work when they have children. Again, a key issue here is whether parents have access to child care. Women are much more likely to leave a job to care for children when quality child care is inaccessible.

* *What types of strategies do families employ as they juggle work responsibilities?*

The ways in which families juggle work are quite diverse. A pattern that has seen a significant decline is the single-earner couple. More prevalent today are dual-earner couples with children and single-parent families. The way in which families organize work is related to the types of jobs that people hold and the types of demands for work at home.

* *How have employers responded to the needs of families?*

Employers have been slow to catch up with the demands of working families. The types of benefits employers are experimenting with are flextime, family leaves, family care assistance, employee assistance programs, and supportive workplace cultures. The businesses that are more likely to have these benefits are larger companies that have higher percentages of women and people of color in decision-making positions.

Key Terms

career: an occupation with the opportunity for upward mobility and one that requires higher levels of education and training

deindustrialization: the process by which economies switch from being based on industry to ones based more on service sector production

domestic code: an ideology that emerged during the nineteenth century to help justify a system of gender difference

economic restructuring: transformations in the structure of employment

family-based economy: a society in which households are the basic unit of economic production

family-consumer economy: a system in which family work focuses less on production and more on the organization of consumption and reproduction

family-wage economy: a society in which the center of labor moves from the household to the factory

gender ideology: belief systems about the similarities and differences between women and men

globalization: the process by which our economy is no longer bounded by national borders

househusbands: husbands who focus their energies on unpaid domestic work

ideology: a belief system that seeks to explain and justify certain conditions

kin work: the conception, maintenance, and ritual celebration of cross-household kin ties

labor force participation: the rate of involvement in paid labor

role overload: a situation that occurs when people take on too many roles that have conflicting demands

service sector: part of the economy that includes the provision of services (cleaning, child care, food preparation) as well as information processing (banking, computer operations, and clerical work)

shift work: a type of employment that runs by the clock and can occur at intervals around the clock

spillover: a situation in which the demands involved in one sphere of work can carry over into work in another sphere

stalled revolution: the dramatic changes made by women in taking on both paid and unpaid work for the family while men made fewer changes in their level of domestic work

work: activity that creates something of value, either goods or services

Resources on the Internet

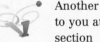 These web sites have been selected for their relevance to the topics in this chapter. These sites are among the more stable, but please be aware that web site addresses change frequently.

Alfred P. Sloan Centers

(1) Center for Working Families, University of California–Berkeley
http://workingfamilies.berkeley.edu

(2) Cornell Employment and Family Careers Institute
http://www.blcc.cornell.edu/cci/cci.html

Both of these university-based organizations are composed of an interdisciplinary group of faculty, graduate students, and researchers who study working families over the life course. The sites can provide copies of publications and working papers representing the most recent research on a variety of topics related to families at work.

Council of Contemporary Families (CCF)
http://www.contemporaryfamilies.org

Established in 1996, CCF is a nonprofit organization designed to bring contemporary research about families into the national conversations about what families need and to provide insights on how to meet those needs. The site provides summaries of recent research projects as they relate to hot media topics.

9 to 5: National Association of Working Women
http://www.9to5.org

9 to 5 is a national, grassroots organization dedicated to strengthening women's ability to work for economic justice. It was founded in 1973. This site provides data on issues of sexual harassment, discrimination, and work/family issues. The site provides opportunities for women to share ideas and experiences and get involved in political activities around the country.

Companion Web Site for This Book

Virtual Society: The Wadsworth Sociology Resource Center
http://sociology.wadsworth.com

Begin by clicking the Student Resources section. Next, click Marriage and Family, and then click the cover image for this book. Select from the pull-down menu the chapter you are presently studying. You will have easy access to chapter resources such as MicroCase Online exercises, additional Web links, flashcards, InfoTrac exercises, and practice tests (that can be scored). In addition, to enhance and help with your study of marriages and families, be sure to investigate the rest of the rich sociology resources at Virtual Society.

Visit InfoTrac College Edition

Another unique option available to you at the Student Resources section of the Virtual Society web site described above is InfoTrac College Edition, an online library of hundreds of scholarly and popular periodicals. Here are three suggested key search terms for this chapter:

* Search keywords: *families + employment* (or *unemployment*)
* Search keywords: *working + families*
* Search keywords: *families + stress*

Search recent years to get the latest information on these issues.

© DiMaggio/Kalish/Corbis

11

Family Crises and Stress: Poverty, Domestic Violence, and Substance Abuse

For years, "Brenda" endured severe abuse and her husband's controlling behavior. She was not allowed to finish high school, get a job, handle money, or associate with friends. Her four sons witnessed her beatings and were subject to extreme punishment by their father. They were made to stand in the cold without shoes or coats, threatened with having their pets killed, and not allowed to spend time with friends or participate in extra-curricular activities after school.

After her husband was arrested for battery, Brenda and her children fled to a domestic violence shelter in a Midwestern state. There, she attended weekly meetings for survivors of domestic violence, as well as weekly parenting meetings and life skills classes. Her 12-and 14-year-old sons participated in a teen support group to help them deal with deep feelings of guilt over their anger toward their mother and fear and rage toward their father. Each child was assigned a male mentor, to whom they responded very well. The 4- and 6-year-old, who both had severe speech delays, got full assessments and follow-up treatment. All boys were enrolled in the Boys' and Girls' Club, which they loved. The program's legal clinic helped Brenda get a divorce and file for custody. She got a job as a cafeteria worker and was promoted several times.

Five years later, Brenda and the children are doing remarkably well. She is still working and maintains an apartment. The older boys, who worked during high school to contribute to the family's earnings, now have high school diplomas, are working, and in good relationships. Brenda still writes often to the program staff and includes pictures of her children, which serve as a record of the family's success.*

FACT OR FICTION?

A crisis can be either positive or negative.

Family Crises and Stressors

It is inevitable: all families will face a crisis at some point. A **crisis** is a critical change of events that disrupts the functioning of a person's life. We tend to think of crises as negative events that serve as turning points—for example, the death of a child, the loss of a job, or a divorce. Surely these are crises, but not all crises are negative. The adoption or birth of a baby and sending a child off to college are usually thought of as positive events, yet they may also bring a critical change that disrupts family relationships and family functions.

When people live together in families, they develop certain patterns of interacting with one another. They may fall into predictable and comfortable routines. For example, family members may divide up house-

*Children's Defense Fund *The State of America's Children Yearbook 2000*. Reprinted with permission.

TABLE 11.1	The Ten Most Common Family Stressors

1. Finances and budgeting
2. Children's behavior
3. Insufficient time as a "couple"
4. Lack of shared responsibility in family
5. Communication with children
6. Insufficient time for "me"
7. Guilt for not accomplishing more
8. Relationship with spouse
9. Insufficient family "play time"
10. Overscheduled family calendar

Source: Curran (1987).

hold chores in a mutually agreeable way, they may take certain types of family vacations at a particular time of the year, and they may have certain spending or saving patterns. A family crisis, either positive or negative, can upset all of these routines. An unexpected job loss could require that spending and saving patterns be altered and could put vacation plans on hold indefinitely. The birth of a baby may drastically alter the division of household labor that a couple has developed over the years.

FACT

Although we often think that crises are only negative, many positive and happy events are also crises.

Sometimes, a crisis is completely unexpected. A child playing kickball in the street is hit and critically injured by a drunk driver. A woman finds a note from her husband telling her that he is in love with someone else and that their marriage is over. A teenage girl unexpectedly finds out that she is pregnant. Other crises evolve more slowly from **family stress,** which is defined as tensions that test a family's emotional resources. Stressors can vary in their type and in degree. They can occur outside the family (e.g., coping with a

hurricane or other natural disaster) or within it (e.g., alcoholism). Family stress may differ from other types of personal stress because of the interpersonal dynamics involved. What do you think are the most common family stressors? Take a guess, and then check your answers in Table 11.1.

A family crisis often follows a reasonably predictable pattern. There are three distinct phases: (1) the event that causes the crisis, (2) the period of disorganization that follows, and (3) the reorganizing that takes place afterward. Family members may find, afterward, that they function at a level similar to just before the crisis. On the other hand, they may find that they have been strengthened and are more effective as a family, or they may be weakened by the crisis. Burr and Klein (1994) interviewed fifty-one families that had experienced a family crisis. Adults in these families were asked to draw a graph that illustrated how the crisis affected their overall family functioning over time, including such things as marital satisfaction, communication, and family togetherness. The results are shown in Figure 11.1. Approximately one-half of the families fell into a "roller-coaster" pattern, where family functioning came back to the previous level after a drop attributable to the crisis. The other half of the respondents experienced different reorganization patterns.

The remainder of this chapter will examine three crises that are, unfortunately, common: (1) poverty and economic problems, (2) domestic violence, and (3) substance abuse. Certainly, many other significant issues are problematic for families, but these three examples will illustrate that family crises occur in a social context. Although they are experienced on a personal level, they are *social problems* as well as personal ones. Crises are influenced and affected by our cultural values, norms, and gendered expectations. To better understand the complex web of causes, consequences, and solutions, we need to look beyond individual personal experiences. We should not lose sight of this.

Poverty and Economic Problems

In 2001 the U.S. Census Bureau reported seemingly good news—median income in the United States was up, and poverty rates among families, single adults, and children were down. "Every racial and ethnic group experienced a drop in both the number of poor and the percentage in poverty, as did children, the elderly and people ages 25 to 44. . . . And on the income side, this was the fifth consecutive year that households experienced a real annual increase in income," reports Daniel Weinberg, Chief of the Census Bureau's Housing and Household Economic Statistics Division (U.S. Census Bureau, Public Information Office, 2001).

FACT OR FICTION?

Ten percent of children live below the poverty line.

This "good news" from the Census Bureau is based on cross-sectional data that allow for comparisons of the poverty rate over time. Table 11.2 reports the poverty rate for 1980, 1990, and 2000. By 2000, the figures had dropped to 11.3 percent, 9.6 percent, and 16.2 percent, for the general population, children, and families, respectively (Dalaker, 2001). Poverty rates declined over 15 percent between 1990 and 2000. Table 11.3 reveals that much of this decline occurred in only one year—between 1999 and 2000. The poverty rates for 2000 matched or exceeded the all-time low for all ethnic groups. Researchers and policy makers will be watching attentively to see whether the decline in poverty continues or reverses itself during

FIGURE 11.1 Five Patterns of the Effects of Stress on Family Functioning

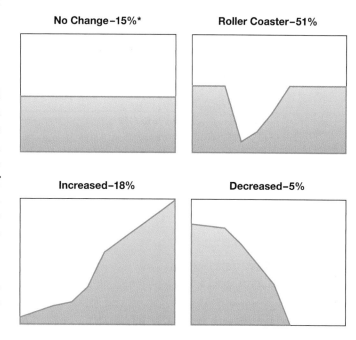

*Percentage of families in the Burr and Klein (1994) study.
Source: Burr, Klein, et al. (1994), pp. 70–78, 159.

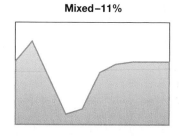

TABLE 11.2	Percentage of Individuals, Families, and Children in Poverty: 1980, 1990, 2000		
	1980 (%)	1990 (%)	2000 (%)
Individuals	13.00	13.50	11.30
Families	11.50	12.00	9.60
Children	17.90	19.90	16.20

Source: Dalaker (2001).

TABLE 11.3	Groups Matching or Surpassing in 2000 Their All-Time Low Poverty Rates			
CHARACTERISTIC	2000 POVERTY RATE (%)		STATUS	SIGNIFICANT DECREASE, 1999–2000
Blacks	22.1		New all-time low	Yes
White Non-Hispanics	7.5		Matches all-time low	No
Asians and Pacific Islanders	10.8		Matches all-time low	No
Hispanics	21.2		Matches all-time low	Yes
All people	11.3		Matches all-time low	Yes

Source: U.S. Census Bureau Public Information Office (2001b).

the economic downturn that has characterized the early part of this decade.

| FICTION

Over 16 percent of children (nearly one out of six) live in poverty.

Amid the good news about declining poverty is a second, contrasting story. The U.S. economy has undergone tremendous restructuring. Despite a seemingly robust economy during the 1990s, other indicators of economic well-being offer somewhat less reason for optimism:

* Inequality in income and **wealth** (a total economic package including stocks, real estate, and other assets in addition to income) has steadily increased, and the gap between rich and poor is the largest in recent history.
* Many employed individuals remain financially vulnerable.
* The purchasing power represented by the poverty line has been steadily eroded.
* Families leaving welfare for work earn wages averaging only $6.50 per hour—far below what is needed to lift them out of poverty.
* The percentage of individuals living in "extreme poverty" (i.e., less than 50 percent of the poverty line) has remained stable during the past few decades at nearly 40 percent of the poor, 5 percent of the general population, 7 percent of children, and 17 percent of children in female-headed households.
* Unemployment rates are rising and are at their highest levels in decades. Minority-group members and teens are particularly hard hit.

© Tony Freeman/PhotoEdit

Many families were left behind in the economic boom of the 1990s. Inequality grew during the boom and continues to grow today.

* The percentage of poor children who are "food insecure" (i.e., have difficulty obtaining enough food, have reduced quality of diets, report anxiety about their food supply, or experience moderate to severe hunger) has increased between 1995 and 1999 (the latest data available).

* Approximately 39 million Americans have no health insurance whatsoever. Millions more have insurance that is woefully inadequate to meet their needs.

* Finally, given the terrorist attack on September 11, 2001, the U.S. economy has weakened on many fronts. It is likely that more people will fall victim to poverty and economic insecurity as the jobless rate rises.

TABLE 11.4	Average Poverty Lines by Family Size in 2002
One person	$8,860
Two people	$11,940
Three people	$15,020
Four people	$18,100
Five people	$21,180
Six people	$24,260
Seven people	$27,340
Eight people	$30,420
Nine people	$33,500

Source: Federal Register (2002).

How Is the Poverty Line Calculated?

The **official poverty line** was established by the Social Security Administration in 1964 (Orshansky, 1965) as a way to measure the number of people living in poverty. Survey data in the early 1960s indicated that families spent approximately one-third of their income on food. Therefore, the poverty line was calculated from the estimated annual costs of a minimal food budget designed by the U.S. Department of Agriculture and then multiplied by three, a method that continues today (U.S. House of Representatives, Committee on Ways and Means, 1996). This food budget parallels the current "Thrifty Food Plan," which forms the basis of food stamp benefits and is the least expensive food plan developed by the U.S.D.A. (Family Economics and Nutrition Review, 1997). It is far below the amount that most middle-class families spend on food. Individuals or families with annual incomes below this established threshold are counted as "poor."

As shown in Table 11.4, the poverty line varies by family size. It also varies by whether the individuals are over or under age sixty-five, and whether a person lives in the forty-eight contiguous states or in Alaska and Hawaii, as food costs are expected to differ. It is revised yearly based on inflationary changes in the Consumer Price Index. The 2002 poverty line guidelines reported by the Department of Health and Human Services averaged $15,020 for a family of three and $18,100 for a family of four (Federal Register, 2002).

A quick budgeting exercise, as shown in the Constructing Strong Families box on page 464, will illustrate that the poverty line is inadequate to meet the needs of families. Even when families create a bare-bones budget, the poverty line is still too low to meet basic needs. However, only families living on less than this amount are represented in the poverty statistics. Meanwhile, other families that are living on incomes only slightly above the poverty level are still teetering on the margins, but they are not counted in official statistics. They are living

The 2002 poverty line for a family of three is $15,020 a year, which comes to about $1,200 a month. This means that a family with three people in it (e.g., a single mother and two children, or two parents and one child) are counted as poor only if they live on less than $1,200 a month. If they live on more than this amount, they are not counted as poor. Is this poverty line reasonable? Could your family of three live on this amount?

Let's find out by examining a sample budget. The cost of living varies somewhat from one community to another, so you may quibble over the cost of specific items in this budget. For example, maybe rents are higher (or lower) where you live than the estimate provided below. These are just sample estimates. Plug in figures that better represent costs in your community if you feel that these are inadequate. The question is this: Is it reasonable to assume that a family of three in the United States can live on $1,200 a month? Keep in mind that someone who works full time, year round, at approximately $6.75 an hour would earn this amount. Many full-time workers earn considerably less.

SAMPLE EXPENSES

Rent (two-bedroom apartment):	$600
Utilities (heat, electric, phone):	$100
Food:	$400
Toiletries:	$50
Travel (insurance, gas, upkeep, bus passes):	$100
Total	$1,250

Already we have gone over budget. What can we cut back on?

- A cheaper apartment, or one in a less desirable part of town? Don't forget that two children live here.

- Lower the utility bill by keeping the house colder? This is one reason that poor children are sick more often.

- Eliminate the telephone? Doing so could be dangerous in case of an emergency.

- Cut back on toiletries? Toilet paper, shampoo, and tampons are basic needs.

- Eliminate bus passes or car maintenance? How will the family get to work, to school, or to grocery stores?

We are over budget, and we haven't yet included other basic needs for this family:

Clothing:	$100
School supplies:	$25
Health insurance:	$300
Entertainment:	$100
New total:	$1,775

Assumption: Even this revised budget assumes that the family already has a household set up. There is no money included to buy furniture, a car, or household items such as towels or dishes. In other words, even $1,775 a month is unrealistically low.

As you can see, the poverty line is an inadequate measure of poverty. For all practical purposes, a family of three living on $1,250, $1,500, $1,775, or even $2,000 is still extremely vulnerable.

Critical Thinking

1. If the poverty line is as inadequate as it appears, why doesn't the federal government increase it to a more realistic level?

2. How does a family make ends meet if a parent earns poverty-level wages?

month to month in tenuous circumstances, hoping to keep the worst at bay.

Inequality in Wealth and Income

Another way to assess the social cost of poverty is to explore it in **relative** rather than absolute terms—how are the poorest U.S. households doing relative to others? Have the lowest groups made gains or experienced losses over time compared to the middle class and the wealthy? In other words, have income disparities increased or decreased over time? A comparative assessment shows us how the poorest in our nation are doing relative to everyone else, another mechanism to measure the economic well-being of our most vulnerable. Some suggest that looking at the degree of inequality is a better predictor of many dimensions of health and well-being than simply looking at poverty rates.

As discussed in Chapter 3, data released by the U.S. Census Bureau and the Congressional Budget Office (CBO) show dramatic increases in disparities in both income and wealth over time in the 1980s and 1990s. The poor groups have experienced significant declines over time, while the wealthiest groups have made tremendous gains. Inequality is increasing.

Consequences of Poverty

Impoverished families and those experiencing **economic hardship** (e.g., low income, income loss, and unstable work) face a higher degree of stress, disorganization, and other problems. The Children's Defense Fund presents a model (Figure 11.2) summarizing the deleterious multidimensional and complex effects of poverty on children. Poverty is not simply about money. Its effects can be far-reaching and devastating. Poverty con-

tributes to (a) lack of food, (b) family stress, (c) neighborhood problems, (d) fewer resources for learning, and (e) housing problems. These effects, in turn, lead to further negative consequences.

Consequences for Adults

The potentially harmful health effects of poverty on adults are numerous. For example, poor adults have significantly higher morbidity (sickness) and have a lower life expectancy than other adults. They are more likely to work in dangerous occupations and live in unsafe neighborhoods, and their homes are more likely to be located near toxic sites. A review of virtually any medical sociology textbook will reveal that income is highly correlated with health and disease, using both objective and subjective measures (Cockerham, 2001; Weitz, 2001).

Poverty affects adults in other ways as well. One issue with far-reaching consequences for families is that poor men and women are less likely to marry (White &

The poor often work in dangerous occupations or live in contaminated areas. How likely is it that farm workers breathe in dangerous chemicals?

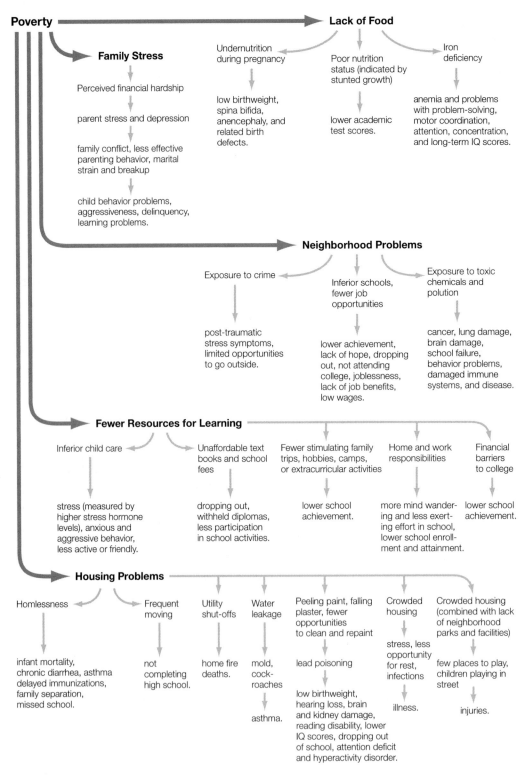

Source: Children's Defense Fund, *Wasting America's Future,* (1994), p. 12. Reprinted with permission.

Rogers, 2000). Poverty undermines economic security and makes men less attractive marriage partners. For example, Wilson suggests that key factors in explaining the falling marriage rate among inner-city African Americans are their declining employment opportunities as jobs move to the suburbs or overseas (1987, 1996). Unemployed or underemployed men are not deemed to be good marriage prospects. Indeed, in another study based on in-depth interviews with young unmarried mothers, it was found that neither young mothers nor their parents supported marriage to a man who was not employed (Farber, 1990).

Poverty and other forms of economic hardship also undermine marital stability (Conger, Rueter, & Elder, 1999; Vinokur, Price, & Caplan, 1996). They are associated with lower levels of marital happiness and greater marital conflict because of the higher degree of stress involved in such a situation. Conger, Ge, and Lorenz (1994) suggest that poverty and economic hardship can lead to greater levels of depression, which can then lead to hostile marital interactions such as anger, resentment, and hostility among partners, lowering marital quality. As one wife, in a study of distressed rural families, put it,

> I . . . highly resent my husband's debt and selfishness. I would like a better home and to be able to be rewarded for my hard work instead of being limited by his failures and debts. I'm tired of his bills always being a pressure. (Conger et al. 1994: 188)

FACT OR FICTION?

Poor children have more health problems than do wealthier children.

Consequences for Children

Perhaps even more alarming are the negative effects of poverty on children. These neg-

ative consequences have also been well-documented and appear to intensify the longer a child is impoverished. Perhaps foremost, compared to other children, those reared in poverty have poorer physical health and more chronic health problems.

Physical Health   Research is unequivocal on the relationship between poverty and health. Only 68 percent of children in families below the poverty line were reported to be in very good or excellent health in the National Health Interview Survey (NHIS), compared with 86 percent of families at or above the poverty line (Federal Interagency Forum on Child and Family Statistics, 2000). Poverty puts the health of children at risk by increasing the frequency of low-birth-weight babies and inadequate nutrition, which in turn increases their likelihood of serious chronic and acute illness (Children's Defense Fund, 1998, 1994; Weigers, Weinick, & Cohen, 1998). Children living in poverty have a higher risk of infant mortality because of biological factors such as low birth weight, birth defects, and environmental hazards during the fragile first year of life. Mothers also often receive inadequate prenatal care.

Poor children continue to suffer from a variety of ailments at higher rates than do more affluent children. For example, they are more than 3 times likely to be iron deficient, 1.5 times more likely to have frequent diarrhea or colitis, twice as likely to suffer from severe asthma, and 1.5 times more likely to suffer partial or complete blindness or deafness (Children's Defense Fund, 1994). Moreover, poor preschoolers are 3 times more likely than their more affluent counterparts to have lead levels in their bloodstream of at least 10 micrograms of lead per deciliter of blood, a level at which harmful effects to the brain and nervous system have been noted. An estimated three million poor children may be at risk of impaired physical and mental development related to ingesting

© Skjold/Jeroboam, Inc.

Nutritious food is important for the physical, mental, and emotional growth of children, yet many children do not get enough good food to eat. Food stamps help but families often run out of food by the end of the month and turn to food charities or do without.

lead-based paint flaking off the walls of older homes (Needleman, Schell, Bellinger, Leviton, & Allred, 1990).

FACT

Poor children have more chronic and acute health problems.

Finally, as many as twelve million children a year go without food at some point every month (Jackson, 1993), suffering the immediate pain of hunger and the more longterm consequences of malnutrition. Without proper nutrition, children are in a weakened state. They run the risk of more frequent colds, ear infections, and other infectious diseases; impaired brain function; and stunted growth. They are also more vulnerable to lead and other environmental toxins. Data from the Continuing Survey of Food Intake by Individuals (CSFII) indicate that the percentage of households claiming that they sometimes or often did not have enough to eat increased from less than 8 percent to approximately 11 percent among low-income families between 1989 and 1991. The age group most likely to be affected were youths aged twelve to nineteen (reported in Lewit & Kerrebrock, 1997).

Children (and adults) living in poor families are not only at a higher risk for serious medical problems, but often these problems go untreated. Some poor children have **Medicaid,** the government-sponsored insurance program for low-income persons. However, children (and adults) on Medicaid are less likely to have a regular physician providing them with continuous care, and they are more likely to use emergency rooms than doctors' clinics (U.S. Congress, Office of Technology, 1992). Furthermore, many poor children do not receive Medicaid. In fact, 14 percent of children under the age of eleven had no health insurance from any source in 1998, including Medicaid, and a third of these children were living below the poverty line (Office of Health Policy, 1998).

Children's Mental Health, Adjustment, and Well-Being Children living in poverty have more socioemotional and behavioral problems than do more affluent children. They are more likely to suffer from depression and social withdrawal; to have peer relationship difficulties; low self-esteem, and behavioral and conduct disorders; and to do poorly in school (Conger, Conger, & Elder, 1997; Dumka, Roosa, & Jackson, 1997; Downey, 1994; Duncan, Brooks-Gunn, & Klebanov, 1994). Gerard and Buehler explain how poverty influences pre-adolescent and early-adolescent problem behaviors:

> The association between poverty and youth problem behaviors may be explained by possible links among educational quality of home environments, academic difficulties, and increased problem behaviors. Poor families have fewer resources to commit to educationally relevant tools such as computers, books, and calculators. This type of impoverishment is associated with academic failure (Downey, 1994), which, in turn, may prompt or sustain misbehavior or emotional distress in school. (1999: 356)

Economic conditions in early childhood have a large impact on student achievement. Why is this?

Weinger (1998) conducted a qualitative study in order to hear directly from children how they are affected emotionally by poverty. She found that poor children have a very difficult time holding on to positive self-images. They view poverty as a deprivation and perceive messages in society that are highly critical of the poor. She found that they internalize many of these negative messages.

Academic and School Achievement Children living below the poverty line are more likely to suffer academically than are children who are not poor (Federal Interagency Forum on Child and Family Statistics, 2000). Overall, poor children receive lower grades, receive lower scores on standardized tests, are less likely to finish high school, and are less likely to attend or graduate from college than are nonpoor youth (Downey, 1994; Duncan, Brooks-Gunn, Yeung, & Smith, 1998; McLanahan & Sandefur, 1994; Pong, 1997; Teachman, Paasch, Day, & Carver, 1997).

Specifically, Smith, Brooks-Gunn, and Klebanov (1997) found that children in fami-

lies with incomes less than one-half of the poverty line scored between 6 and 13 points lower on various standardized tests than did children in families with incomes between 1.5 and 2.0 times the poverty line. In all cases, the differences were statistically significant. Children living in families whose incomes were higher, but still below the poverty line, also did significantly worse on a majority of tests than did the higher reference group. Economic conditions in early childhood have the biggest effect on levels of achievement.

Smith and colleagues also examined the consequences of poverty upon young children's cognitive ability, verbal ability, and early school achievement. They used three different types of assessment: IQ, verbal ability, and achievement tests. They found that the duration of poverty had a significantly negative effect on all three assessment tests. Moreover, they noted that the degree of poverty also affected children's scores: children's cognitive abilities dramatically increased as family income increased from very poor to near poor.

Poor African American and Hispanic children experience more frequent and more severe poverty than do whites, with fewer prospects for improvement in their economic circumstances. This increases their risk of dropping out of school or being involved in a teen pregnancy.

Mediating Effects Within the Family: Stresses, Parenting Styles, Discipline, and Abuse

Poverty affects how parents interact with their children. The **Home Observation of the Measurement of the Environment (HOME)** is a widely used interview and observation measure of parent–child interaction. Its measures include maternal warmth and learning experiences provided to the child, and it is associated with a variety of child outcomes. Poverty has a significant effect on the quality and stimulation of the home environment, even after controlling for the effects of other variables. Improvements in family income have the strongest effects on improving the quality of the home environment for children who were born to a poor family.

| FACT OR FICTION?

Child abuse is more likely to occur among the poor.

Researchers have also found that parents are less nurturing, are more authoritarian, and use more inconsistent and harsh physical discipline as a family's economic situation worsens (McLoyd, 1990). Moreover, while child abuse occurs in many different type of households, poor children have a higher probability of being abused, neglected, and injured more severely by the abuse than do their more affluent peers (Children's Defense Fund, 1994; Gelles, 1992). As Gelles reports (1992: 271),

Abusive violence is more likely to occur in poor homes. Specific social and demographic characteristics increase the likelihood that poverty will lead to abuse. Poor young parents who are raising young children have an elevated risk of using the most abusive forms of violence toward their children, as do poor single mothers.

What is it about an impoverished family environment that increases the likelihood of negative outcomes for children? One likely culprit is that parents who are living in poor conditions have a high level of stresses related to their situation. Parents with low and unstable incomes experience more emotional distress and see themselves as less effective parents than do parents with higher incomes.

Increased social support from family and friends reduces the amount of stress that poor families experience, reduces the degree of violence or harsh discipline that children may experience, and fosters improved self-esteem and the ability of children to overcome adversity (Bowen & Chapman, 1996; Hashima & Amato, 1994). However, some of the most vulnerable poor families, such as those that are homeless, tend to have very little social support.

Other possible causes of child maltreatment include the lack of social capital and possible antisocial qualities of the parent(s). For example, high levels of male unemployment are significantly associated with child abuse and deprivation. McLanahan and Sandefur (1994), drawing upon a variety of national data sources, found that children growing up in a single-mother household are more likely to have poorer academic performance, to be teen parents, to engage in delinquent acts, and to experience a variety of other negative outcomes that undermine their chances of future success. These researchers also exercise caution in interpreting these findings (1994: 2):

Domestic Violence and Abuse

Researchers note that child abuse occurs more often in poor homes, likely because of the added stress of poverty.

But are single mother and father absence therefore the root cause of child poverty, school failure, and juvenile delinquency? Our findings lead us to say no. While living with just one parent increases the risk of each of these negative outcomes, it is not the only, or even the major cause of them. Growing up with a single parent is just one among many factors that put children at risk of failure, just as lack of exercise is only one among many factors that put people at risk for heart disease.

Extrafamilial Mediating Effects: The Neighborhood

Poor children are increasingly isolated from the nonpoor in their neighborhoods and communities, and live in inner cities where violence, crime, truancy, loitering, and a sense of despair predominate (Massey & Denton, 1993; O'Hare, 1995). Some findings suggest that those neighborhoods characterized by "poverty, excessive numbers of children per adult resident, population turnover, and the concentration of female-headed families are at highest risk for maltreatment" (Coulton, Korbin, Su, & Chow, 1995: 1262). Drake and Pandey (1995) found a positive relationship between neighborhood poverty and three types of maltreatment: neglect, physical abuse, and sexual abuse, with the strongest relationship appearing between neglect and neighborhood poverty. Of course, this does not mean that these types of acts occur only in lower-income communities; rather, it means that they are *more likely* to occur there than in higher-income communities.

What do Oprah Winfrey, Tina Turner, and Pamela Anderson have in common? In addition to being celebrities, they all have had the frightening experience of being abused within their families. Tina Turner and Pamela Anderson reportedly were victims of violence by their partners. Oprah Winfrey revealed that several members of her extended family sexually abused her as a child. We find domestic violence to be particularly abhorrent because we like to idealize families as safe havens. Yet for many people, especially women and girls, this is not the case.

This section will explore the issue of domestic violence, indicating how this too occurs in a social context. Although domestic violence is experienced on a personal level, it is a social problem affected by our cultural values, norms, and gendered expectations. We will begin with a discussion of how we define and measure domestic violence. We will then look at violence in dating relationships, since the abuse often begins there. We will next cover spouse/partner abuse, a topic that has received a great deal of attention by researchers over the past three decades. This section will then focus on child abuse, including sexual abuse and the international trafficking of girls and women for sexual purposes. We conclude with a look at elder abuse.

How We Define and Measure Domestic Violence

Domestic violence can encompass physical, economic, sexual, and psychological abuse. Many abusive situations involve more than one type (Hamby & Sugarman, 1999).

In 1975 and 1985, Murray Straus and his colleagues conducted some of the earliest nationwide studies of spouse/partner abuse in the United States. They conducted interviews with more than 2,000 married or cohabiting adults with children between the ages of 3 and 17. They developed an important conflict assessment tool known as the **Conflict Tactics Scale (CTS)** that is still commonly used today (Straus, Gelles, & Steinmetz, 1980). In the CTS, people are asked about how they deal with disagreements in relationships. The following list is used in part or in its entirety in a variety of studies:

Non-aggressive responses:

   Discussed an issue calmly

   Got information to back up your side of things

   Brought in or tried to bring in someone to help settle things

   Cried

Psychologically aggressive responses:

   Insulted him/her or swore at him/her

   Sulked or refused to talk about the issue

   Stomped out of the room or house

   Did or said something to spite him/her

Physically aggressive responses:

   Threatened to hit him/her or throw something at him/her

   Threw or smashed or hit or kicked something

   Threw something at him/her

   Pushed, grabbed, or shoved him/her

   Slapped him/her

   Kicked, bit, or hit him/her with a fist

   Hit or tried to hit him/her with something

   Beat him/her up

   Choked him/her

   Threatened him/her with a knife

   Used a knife

A review of research studies using the CTS has found that women tend to show *higher* rates of physical aggression than men (Sugarman & Hotaling, 1989). For example, a recent study of college students reports that women were more likely than men to be physically aggressive (43 percent versus 23 percent), and women were less likely to report being a victim of physical aggression (34 percent versus 40 percent). This may seem surprising. Indeed, these findings have been criticized because the CTS does not take into account the meaning of violence/aggression in our culture and the context in which it takes place.

One potential problem with using the CTS to conclude that women are more physically aggressive than men is that physical violence perpetrated by men may be underreported (Browning & Dutton, 1986; Edleson & Brygger, 1986). Men are less likely than women to remember their own acts of violence, and they may not perceive their acts as abusive. It is also true that for most acts of physical violence, the consequences are more serious for women than for men (Miller & Simpson, 1991). Another problem is that the CTS is framed as a scale of "conflict resolution"; respondents are asked to tell the researcher how they have responded to a situation of conflict or disagreement. Some have argued that violence and abuse can take place without a preceding disagreement; therefore, the CTS may underreport some violence. Finally, the CTS does not include acts of sexual violence or aggression, which are far more likely to be perpetrated by men.

Michael Johnson and Kathleen Ferraro (2000) present a different typology of violence and abuse. In their seminal review of domestic violence research, they note that it is important to make distinctions among types of violence, the motives of perpetrators, the social locations of both partners, and the cultural context in which violence occurs. They identify four patterns of violence (Johnson & Ferraro, 2000; Johnson, 2000). "Common couple violence" (CCV) arises out of a specific argument in which at least one partner lashes out physically. It is less frequent than other types of abuse, and it is less likely to escalate or involve severe injury. Yet this type of violence is usually captured in research studies. "Intimate terrorism" (IT) is motivated by a desire to control the other partner. It is more likely than CCV to escalate over time and to cause serious injury, although some cases of IT involve relatively little injury. The primary feature of this type of abuse is the general desire for control. "Violent resistance" (VR) is the nonlegal term associated with self-defense. Research on VR is scarce, but it is conducted almost entirely by women. VR may be an indicator that a woman will leave her abusive partner soon. "Mutual violent control" (MVC) refers to a pattern of behavior in which both partners are controlling and violent. They are battling for control. Again, this is an understudied phenomenon.

Dating Violence

About one-third of dating relationships include some type of aggressive behavior. We presume that dating is about having fun, exploring your own identity, and getting to know someone else. It seems like the last place for violence to occur.

One feature of this type of violence that is also alarming is that it is not likely to be reported to authority figures. One reason may be that dating is perceived as a short-term relationship; therefore, when violence occurs, the victim will end the relationship. Young people may also fear their parents' reaction to their poor choice of dating partners. Particularly problematic with respect to underreporting is the incidence of sexual violence. Data collected from college students in the 1980s found that less than 5 percent of victims of sexual assault reported the assault to authorities, and half of the victims told no one about the assault (Koss, Gidycz, & Wisniewski, 1987).

Sexual Aggression and Rape in Dating Relationships The frequently used measure of sexual aggression comes from the

© Inc. Yuri Dojc/The Image Bank-Getty Images

Several national studies show an alarming rate of domestic violence. One study found that 8 percent of women had been raped and 22 percent physically assaulted by someone close to them.

work of Mary Koss and her colleagues (Koss, Gidycz, & Wisniewski, 1987). The Sexual Experiences Survey (SES) asks about a variety of behaviors related to sex, including items about the use of threats, force, or alcohol to obtain sex from another. They found that over half of college women across the United States had experienced some form of sexual aggression. Fifteen percent had been raped, another 12 percent had experienced attempted rape, 12 percent had experienced sexual coercion, and 14 percent had experienced unwanted sexual contact. Men were less likely to have reported perpetrating sexual violence against women. Only 4 percent admitted to initiating a rape, and 3 percent said they attempted it. The vast majority of men who admitted to forcing sexual relations said that it was definitely not rape. What is rape then, if not forced sexual relations?

A very chilling finding from research on relationship violence is that the victim often believes that the perpetrator of the violence loves her/him (Lloyd, 1991). Michael and colleagues (1994) found that of the 22 percent of women in their national sample who had reported to have been forced to do something sexual by a man, all but 4 percent knew the man, and 46 percent said they were in love with him.

Spouse/Partner Abuse

Spouse abuse and partner abuse were not widely discussed among family scientists until the 1970s. Few researchers studied the topic, and few marriage and family textbooks included information about this important "dark side" of families. What we knew about abuse was based on small, nonrepresentative samples from the isolated case files of social workers, psychologists, and police. These data have the potential to be very biased since only certain types of abuse, and certain types of abusers, come to the attention of professionals.

However, since the 1970s, with the help of the women's liberation movement and a spotlight on women's issues, family and social scientists have been trying to piece together a more accurate depiction of this phenomenon (Gelles & Straus, 1988; Straus, 1979; Straus, Gelles, & Steinmetz, 1980). They have been trying, with some success, to amass large and representative samples to understand how often spouse/partner violence occurs, who is likely to be a victim, and its causes and consequences.

Frequency of Violence and Abuse The results from the early surveys by Straus and colleagues (1980) show an alarming rate of abuse in the United States. These results have been confirmed in more recent studies such as the National Violence Against Women Survey (NVAW), conducted by the National Institute of Justice (NIJ) and the Centers for Disease Control (CDC). This 1997 study contains information on violence and abuse among 16,000 adult men and women randomly selected from across the United States. It found that among all women who reported being victims of rape or physical assault, the perpetrator in 76 percent of the cases was an intimate partner (defined as current and former spouses, opposite and same-sex cohabiting partners, dates, boyfriends, and girlfriends). For men, most rapes or assaults were perpetrated by strangers (60 percent), with only 18 percent of perpetrators being an intimate partner (NIJ, 1998). The details of how this landmark study was conducted can be found in the Focus on Family Research box on page 475.

| FACT OR FICTION?

Nearly 5 percent of women (one out of twenty women) report being the victims of domestic violence.

Table 11.5 reports the percentage of women who have been raped or physically assaulted by an intimate partner over the course of the respondents' lifetime. The table compares the victimization rates between men and women. We see that especially for women, violence by an intimate partner is a relatively common occurrence. Nearly 8 percent of women have been raped, and 22 percent have been physically assaulted by someone close to them. The corresponding figures for men are 0.3 percent and 7.4 percent, respectively. The most common types of violence experienced by women are being pushed, grabbed, or shoved (18 percent) and

In order to better understand the prevalence, incidence, and consequences of domestic violence, the National Institute of Justice (NIJ) and the Centers for Disease Control and Prevention (CDC) jointly sponsored a national telephone survey in 1995–1996 on this critical topic. This landmark survey is known as the National Violence Against Women (NVAW) survey. It focused on rape, physical assault, and stalking both over the previous year and throughout one's life. The sample included both men and women so that comparisons could be made on violent victimization. The nationally representative sample was drawn from random-digit dialing of all households containing a telephone in the fifty states and the District of Columbia. A total of 8,000 women and 8,000 men aged eighteen and older were interviewed. Only female interviewers surveyed female respondents, and both male and female interviewers surveyed the male respondents. The telephone interview was conducted in Spanish when needed.

Several features of the NVAW survey set it apart from other victimization surveys:

- It was based on a large, representative sample of men and women; therefore, we can be highly confident that the percentages reported are accurate within a few percentage points.

- State-of-the-art techniques protected confidentiality and minimized the potential for retraumatizing victims.

- Information about both the prevalence (lifetime and annual) and incidence of violence was gathered. Therefore, estimates can be compared with other surveys.

- Specific questions focused on rape, physical assault, and stalking victimization.

- Detailed information about the characteristics and consequences of victimization was gathered, including injuries sustained and use of medical services.

- Information was gathered in a way that allowed tracking of victimizations by the same perpetrator (e.g., the victim's ex-husband).

- Comparisons can be made between men and women, and among different ethnic groups.

National data such as these provide important insight into domestic violence for criminal justice and public health researchers and practitioners, legislators, policy makers, and intervention planners at all levels of public and private practice. The NVAW survey reveals that violence against women is much more common than previously thought. The knowledge gained from surveys such as the NVAW has the power to call the nation's attention to how pervasive the problem is, and how many women face danger in our communities. The knowledge gained from empirical data is the first step in ameliorating such violence.

Critical Thinking

1. Why is research conducted in this fashion more accurate than earlier research from therapists' case files?

2. The researchers compared rates of violence between men and women, and between racial/ethnic groups. What other comparisons do you think are important?

TABLE 11.5	Percentage of Persons Raped and Physically Assaulted by an Intimate Partner in Lifetime by Type of Assault and Sex of Victim*	
TYPE OF ASSAULT	WOMEN (%) (n=8,000)	MEN (%) (n=8,000)
Rape	7.7	0.3
Total physical assaults by intimate partner	22.1	7.4
Threw something	8.1	4.4
Pushed, grabbed, shoved	18.1	5.4
Pulled hair	9.1	2.3
Slapped, hit	16	5.5
Kicked, bit	5.5	2.6
Choked, tried to drown	6.1	0.5
Hit with object	5	3.2
Beat up	8.5	0.6
Threatened with gun	3.5	0.4
Threatened with knife	2.8	1.6
Used gun	0.7	0.1
Used knife	0.9	0.8

*Intimate partner includes current or former spouses, opposite-sex cohabiting partners, same-sex cohabiting partners, dates, and boyfriends/girlfriends.
Source: National Institute of Justice and Centers for Disease Control and Prevention (1998).

being slapped or hit (16 percent). Almost 1 percent of women have had a gun or knife used on them.

| FICTION

The statistics are much higher than this: Twenty-two percent report being assaulted by a spouse or partner, and 8 percent have been raped.

Differences between women's and men's rates of physical assault by an intimate partner become greater as the seriousness of the assault increases. For example, women were two to three times more likely than men to report that an intimate partner threw something at them or pushed, grabbed, or shoved them. However, in looking at the more dangerous assaults, women were seven to four-

teen times more likely to report that they had been beaten up, choked, tied down, threatened with a gun, or had a gun used on them.

Table 11.6 reports the percentage of women who had been raped or physically assaulted in their lifetime by race and ethnic background (by all persons, not just intimate partners). Overall, nearly one in five report having been raped at least once in their lifetime. Over half of all women have been assaulted. Because some women have experienced both, respondents were asked if they had ever been raped and/or assaulted, and over half claimed that they had. American Indian/Alaska Native women are most likely to have been raped and physically assaulted. Over one-third had been raped, and 61 percent had been assaulted. In contrast, Asian/Pacific Islanders were the least likely to have experienced this abuse.

Factors Associated with Abuse The National Violence Against Women (NVAW) survey reveals that most women are raped and assaulted by intimate partners. Yet most men do not abuse their partners. What specific factors are associated with spouse/partner abuse? Several characteristics increase the odds of abuse (although they do not make abuse inevitable):

* *Youth.* In most violent relationships, the partners are under the age of thirty.
* *Low levels of education.* Often, the husband/male partner has a high school diploma or less.
* *Aggressive behavior.* The husband/male partner may have shown aggressive tendencies such as fighting with others or injuring or killing a pet.
* *Low income or employment problems.* The family income may be below or near the poverty line, or the man may be unemployed.
* *Drug or alcohol use.* Often, one or both partners use drugs or alcohol fre-

	TOTAL (%) (n=7,850)	WHITE (%) (n=6,452)	HISPANIC* (%) (n=628)	AFRICAN AMERICAN (%) (n=780)	ASIAN/ PACIFIC ISLANDER (%) (n=133)	AMERICAN INDIAN/ ALASKA NATIVE (%) (n=88)	MIXED RACE (%) (n=397)
Rape	18.2	17.7	14.6	18.8	6.8	34.1	24.4
Physical assault	51.8	51.3	53.2	52.1	49.6	61.4	57.7
Rape and/or physical assault	55	54.5	54.9	55.1	51.9	64.8	61.2

*Persons of Hispanic origin may be of any race.
Source: National Institute of Justice and Centers for Disease Control and Prevention (1998).

quently and may try to excuse conflict and violence because of this habit.

* *Abuse in family of orientation.* One or both partners may have witnessed or experienced abuse as children.

* *Cohabitation.* The couple may be cohabiting rather than married.

Coping with Violence and Abuse: Leaving and Staying   A common question that is asked is "Why do women stay in an abusive situation?" However, the truth is that most do not stay. A recent longitudinal study revealed that by 2.5 years, three-quarters of battered women had either left the relationship or the abuse had ended (Campbell, Rose, Kub, & Nedd, 1998).

Leaving is often a *process* rather than a single event. It may be difficult for some women to garner the courage or logistics to leave immediately. This is where the typology discussed by Johnson (2000) and Johnson and Ferraro (2000) comes into play. The diverse types of spouse/partner abuse have repercussions for one's ability to leave the situation. For example, men engaged in intimate terrorism (IT) foist on their victims a wide range of control tactics that can cripple a victim's sense of command over her own

life. This generally is less the case with couples engaging in common couple violence (CCV). What are some of these control tactics that may make it difficult for victims to leave an abusive and violence relationship?

* *Blaming the victim.* The perpetrator may blame the victim for the abuse: "If you weren't so stupid, I wouldn't have to hit you." After hearing blaming comments often enough, some women believe them. Their self-esteem is eroded,

© Mary Kate Denny/PhotoEdit

Some communities offer abused women and their children a short-term place to live to escape their abuse. Unfortunately, these shelters are often filled to capacity.

and they begin to believe that they must deserve the abuse and be unworthy of a positive, loving relationship.

* *Shame.* Feelings of embarrassment and shame are common among abused women because they know that many other women are not abused. They worry that other people will look down on them for either provoking the abuse or for tolerating it. Likewise, they may be embarrassed at how their spouse/partner will be perceived by others. Therefore, abused women may try to hide their bruises when they go out in public by applying make-up or wearing certain types of clothing (e.g., scarves, hats).

* *Financial dependency.* Some women are particularly vulnerable because they are financially dependent on men. Perhaps they have children to support and do not have specific job skills or recent employment experience. Some perpetrators foster this economic dependence by not letting their wives/partners establish credit in their own name and refusing to put their names on checking, savings, or other accounts.

* *Isolation.* Abused women are often isolated. The isolation may be initiated by the abuser as a control tactic, or it may be initiated by the woman out of shame. In either case, abused women are often cut off from family and friends. They may cease going to church, to work, or to school. They have little social support and no one to turn to for a "reality check."

* *Fear of retaliation.* Fear is an important reason that some women linger in abusive relationships. The perpetrator may have threatened the woman, her children, or even her pets. Because he has been abusive before, the threats are real, so many victims live in fear.

* *Love and hope.* Many abused women harbor fantasies that their abuser will somehow miraculously change. They do not want the relationship to end; they just want the abuse to stop. They love their spouse/partner and believe that if they just work harder in the relationship, or if external forces change, the abuse will somehow stop. Sometimes it does; more often it does not.

* *Commitment to the relationship.* When we marry, we agree to take our partner "for better or worse, until death do us part." Although we take these vows seriously, most people would probably leave an out for particularly harsh circumstances that would include domestic violence. But not everyone feels this way. Some people, perhaps based on religious grounds, believe that they must endure their marriage regardless of the costs.

* *Fear of being alone.* Many people are afraid of being without a spouse or partner. They have low self-esteem and are unsure whether they can live alone and take care of themselves. Women have been socialized to derive a great deal of their social status through their affiliations with men. When this is coupled with possible financial dependence, we can see why some women may be hesitant to leave an abusive situation.

Child Abuse

A mother hits her child. Is this child abuse? Does it matter if the mother uses an open hand or a *fist*? How about if she uses an *object* to hit her child? Does it matter if her hitting leaves a *welt*? Does the *reason* for hitting the child make a difference? How about the *age* of the child? Does it matter *where* the child was hit? Does it matter how *often* the child is hit?

Few people spank children today.

Not all forms of child abuse are clearcut and obvious. For example, most adults believe that it is appropriate to use corporal punishment on children. In the second National Family Violence Survey, conducted in 1985, 56 percent of parents reported having slapped or spanked a child; 31 percent pushed, shoved, or grabbed a child; 10 percent hit a child with an object; and 3 percent threw something at a child during the preceding twelve months. Parents used corporal punishment an average of nine times during that period (Straus, 1994). Using data from the National Survey of Families and Households relating to parents with a child between the ages of one and eleven, another study reports mothers are more likely to spank their children than are fathers (44 percent versus 31 percent, respectively). Boys are more likely to be spanked than girls are (Day, Peterson, & McCracken, 1998).

FICTION

The majority support spanking and use it as a form of discipline.

Murray Straus, a leading researcher in domestic violence, argues that corporal punishment is detrimental to children and teaches them violent and abusive behavior (Straus, 1994). He suggests that it serves to legitimize other forms of violence. For example, adults who were hit as adolescents are more likely to hit their spouses and physically assault someone outside the family, states in which teachers are allowed to hit children have a higher rate of student violence and a higher murder rate, and nations where teachers favor corporal punishment have a higher infant murder rate. Yet many parents continue to believe that the context of the spanking, slapping, shoving, and so on

may, in some cases, justify it. But exactly what is that context? There is a wide range of opinion about when, how, and under what conditions it is appropriate to use corporal punishment.

Nonetheless, some acts against children are unambiguously abusive. Physical abuse is "an attack on a child that results in an injury" and violates our social norms (Straus, 1994: 8). According to the National Center on Child Abuse and Neglect, about five million children in the United States are reported as abused or neglected. Nearly one million of these cases are confirmed (U.S. Department of Health and Human Services, National Clearinghouse on Child Abuse and Neglect Information, 2002), but the true rate is probably higher than this. An estimated 1,100– 2,000 children die as a result of abuse and neglect each year. Annually, more children under the age of four die from abuse and neglect than from falls, choking, drowning, fires, or motor vehicle accidents.

Abuse occurs in all income, racial, religious, and ethnic groups and in all types of communities. Female victims slightly outnumber male victims, especially in cases of sexual abuse. African American children have the highest rates of abuse, followed by American Indians/Alaska Natives, Hispanics, whites, and Asian/Pacific Islanders. Sixty percent of perpetrators are female.

Types of Child Abuse There are several different types of child abuse. **Physical abuse** involves inflicting physical injury and harm upon a child. This may include hitting, shaking, burning, kicking, or in other ways physically harming a child. Among substantiated child abuse cases, approximately one quarter involve physical abuse. The most extreme cases may result in the death of a child. One study based on abused children admitted to a pediatric intensive care unit found that the most common causes of death were skull fracture and internal bleeding (Irazuzta,

By day the young girls watch television soap operas, giggle and pore over the pages of fashion magazines. But as dusk descends on Cambodia's brothels the young girls begin to touch up their make-up and adjust their stylish blouses and short skirts. They are preparing to entertain men, both local and foreign, who pay for an hour or a night of sex with them.

While research on child sex workers is only beginning in Cambodia, experts and international organizations agree on one thing: the problem is growing rapidly.

More than one third of all sex workers in Cambodia are estimated to be children, mostly girls aged 12 to 17, or nearly 20,000 children. The demand for younger girls, especially virgins, is accelerating in response to growing customer demand for AIDS-free sex, coupled with the illusion that younger girls are unlikely to be HIV-positive.

Of the 236 women released during a police raid of brothels last year in the north-eastern town of Battambang near the Thai border, more than a quarter were under the age of 18. The burgeoning industry in Cambodia entraps not only local children but also those from Vietnam and, according to some reports,

from China's southern provinces. Although the most highly publicized cases of sexual violation of children spotlight tourists and businessmen from other countries in Asia or the West, the majority of clients are still local men.

Child sex workers are pushed or lured into the trade by a number of complex factors. While poverty is often the main factor cited, well-organised crime rings, inadequate law enforcement and the breakdown in family and community support systems, compounded by the low status of girls, all converge to foster the trade.

More often than not, young children are trafficked from rural to urban areas, taking advantage of the vulnerability of the rural poor. Many others are imported from neighbouring countries, victims of vast and sophisticated criminal networks established by local and foreign business interests.

Like many young girls in Tuol Kok or Svay Pak, two of the largest red light districts that ring Phnom Penh, Ari is guarded about revealing her age. Relief workers place her at no more than 15, although she insists she is 18. She is less reluctant to describe the circumstances that brought her to the dingy brothel

where she is kept a virtual prisoner.

"My family is poor and so my mother pledged me for $500 to help feed my eight brothers and sisters. I am the most beautiful," Ari says with pride. Most of the money she makes goes directly into the pocket of a brothel owner, leaving little to pay off the debt she now shoulders.

How Ari came into prostitution is a familiar story to the local organizations researching child sexual exploitation. According to NGOS (Non Governmental Organizations Associated with the United Nations), the majority of child sex workers are abducted by middlemen (or women), sold or pledged by parents, relatives, neighbours or boyfriends, or deceived with the promise of jobs or marriages. Often children are hired out or sold by their families to agents who may or may not reveal the true nature of the work.

The agent may promise a job as a domestic servant, factory worker or waitress at a wage many times higher than is customary in rural areas. In a smaller percentage of cases, say experts, children knowingly enter prostitution to help support their families.

One recent study found that 50 percent to 65 percent of commercial sex workers reported being forced

McJunkin, Danadian, Arnold, & Zhang, 1997).

Neglect is the most common form of abuse, and it involves the failure to provide for the child's basic needs. Approximately one half of substantiated cases of abuse are based on neglect. Neglect can be physical, such as failing to provide adequate food, clothing, shelter, a safe environment, or medical care to a dependent child. Emotional or psychological neglect occurs when a parent (or caretaker) fails to meet a child's most

into the sex business. Of these, an alarming 86 percent were deceived or sold into the trade by people familiar to them.

Upon arriving at a brothel, a young girl is typically kept locked in a back room to protect her virginity, which will fetch a large sum. The going price for a week with a virgin in Phnom Penh is estimated at $300 to $500, with the price dropping dramatically after that. Many of these girls are then resold to other brothels for $30 to $100.

Trafficking of very young girls, experts say, is bolstered by the widespread beliefs that sex with a virgin rejuvenates an adult or that engaging in sex with a younger child offers protection from HIV/AIDS. Children, though, are more susceptible to infection since the immature lining of their vaginas and anuses is more easily torn, creating sores and bleeding that speed the spread of the virus.

Ari says she plans to leave the brothel in one month, once the debt is paid off. Even if this turns out to be the case, which is highly unlikely, the question remains: what will become of her?

"Many prostituted children face overwhelming difficulties reintegrating into their families and communities, where they are ostracized and labeled for life as prostitutes," says Bjorn Ljungqvist, UNICEF representative in Cambodia. More often than not, once in the trade they find it hard to break the cycle. And for those young girls who are HIV-positive, the future is particularly grim.

According to the World Health Organization, HIV/AIDs is rapidly coming to be recognized as one of the biggest health crises in Cambodia. A recent survey conducted in three provinces by the Cambodian Centre for the Protection of Children's Rights found that 38 percent to 40 percent of commercial sex workers had tested HIV-positive.

In most brothels, the young girls are kept as long as they are disease-free. When they are found to be seropositive, they are put on the streets to fend for themselves.

Few studies have assessed what happens psychologically to a child forced to endure months or even years of sexual and emotional abuse. The loss of self-esteem and the personal trauma to a prostituted child brought about by constant degradation is difficult to imagine.

As difficult to contemplate is how children can be reintegrated into their families and communities, when it was precisely those they trusted most who sold them into the sex trade.

"To be effective, any programme to reintegrate the child back into society must combine psychological support for the child and the family, training in other useful skills and improvement in the family's economic situation," Ljungqvist says.

Source: Adapted from Madeline Eisner (1996). "Ari's Story." United States Embassy, Stockholm, Sweden. Available online:http://www.usemb.se/children/csec/press_contact.html. Reprinted with permission.

Critical Thinking

1. How is this a social problem rather than Ari's individual issue?

2. What would it take to eliminate the trafficking of children such as Ari?

3. What will become of Ari as she ages? When she's thirty, forty, or fifty years old?

basic need: love and affection. This could involve chronically cold and distant behavior towards a child or allowing a child to witness spousal abuse or some other dysfunctional behavior in the family. An extreme form of neglect is outright abandonment.

Emotional abuse, accounting for about 6 percent of substantiated cases, can be verbal, mental, or psychological maltreatment that destroys a child's self-esteem. Abuse of this nature often includes threatening, degrading, or humiliating the child and can

The sexual trafficking of teenage girls is big business in many parts of the world. Many girls are sold into sexual slavery by their parents, often tricked by the promise of a "better life" for their daughters.

involve extreme or bizarre forms of punishment, such as confinement to a dark room or being tied to a chair for long periods of time. Emotional abuse probably occurs far more frequently than what can be substantiated. The scars are not as visible as with other types of abuse.

Sexual abuse involves inappropriate sexual behavior with a child for sexual gratification. It occurs in about 13 percent of substantiated child abuse cases. It could include fondling a child's genitals, making the child fondle the perpetrator's genitals, and progressing to more intrusive sexual acts, such as oral sex and vaginal or anal penetration. Sexual abuse also includes acts such as exhibition, or in other ways exploiting the child for sexual purposes.

Sexual Trafficking Sexual abuse is rapidly increasing in developing nations. An estimated one million children, mostly girls, enter the multi-billion-dollar sex business each year (World Congress Against the Commercial Sexual Exploitation of Children, 2001). In **sexual trafficking,** many are coerced, kidnapped, sold, deceived, or otherwise trafficked into sexual encounters, as shown in the Family Narratives box on pages 480–481. Increasingly around the world, girls are sought out in the mistaken belief that they are less likely to be HIV-positive. In reality, they are most vulnerable to HIV infections because their bodies are physically unready for sex and may tear more easily.

The trafficking of children results from a broad range of factors. Increasing poverty, inequality, and economic crises have occurred in the last few decades in many countries. Coupled with patriarchal norms in which women and girls are disvalued, some families sell their daughters to traffickers or put them in vulnerable positions as domestic workers in far-off urban locations. Moreover, globalization has triggered an influx of money and goods, further aggravating disparities between rich and poor, and promoting new levels of consumerism.

Children who are trafficked into prostitution face a multitude of dangers. In addition to injuries and disease associated with multiple sexual encounters, they may become dangerously attached to pimps and brothel operators and become financially indebted to them. Moreover, they may become addicted to drugs that have been used to subdue them. If the children do manage to escape and return to their families, they may be rejected because of the stigma associated with prostitution.

Factors Contributing to Child Abuse It is easy to attribute child abuse to mental disorder, but fewer than 10 percent of abusers suffer from mental illness. Instead, we must look to a complex combination of social, cultural, and personal factors to explain child abuse. No single explanation fits all cases. The following are potential risk factors.

Stress Families that experience a great deal of stress are more likely to abuse their children (Gelles, 1979). The stress could be brought on by a number of different factors, including illness, unemployment, marital conflict, and financial problems. Sometimes, specific traits of the child are associated with stress. For example, premature infants who require special care, and who may cry harder and more frequently, have an increased risk of abuse. Likewise, children with physical or developmental difficulties are more likely to be abused. Alcohol and drug use are key risk factors for abuse. They can aggravate stress, decrease coping skills, and impair judgment.

Social Isolation Parents (and other caretakers) who abuse children tend to be socially isolated. They may have little contact with other family members, have few friends, and belong to few community organizations. Sometimes, this isolation predates the abuse (i.e., they abuse because they are so isolated), and in other families the abuse may predate the isolation (i.e., they isolate themselves to hide the abuse from others). Regardless, these families lack social support to help them with their stress, their anger, and the challenges of raising children.

Learned Behavior A parent is more likely to abuse his or her child if the parent was abused as a child. This has been dubbed the *intergenerational transmission of violence*. It has been estimated that approximately 30 percent of abused children become abusive parents themselves, ten times the rate of all parents (Kaufman & Zigler, 1987). Parents who are able to break the cycle of abuse realize, perhaps through therapy or a supportive partner, that the abuse was wrong, and

they have learned other ways to deal with their frustrations.

Unrealistic Parental Expectations It is fairly easy to have unrealistic expectations about parenthood and about children. Very little in life prepares us for the stress and challenges associated with being a parent. While we require a test to verify fitness to drive an automobile, virtually anyone can become a parent. No required course or formal certificate verifies that we have mastered a certain level of knowledge and skills. Therefore, some people become parents with little information regarding child development and little sense of the self-sacrifice required to be a parent. This ignorance can translate into lashing out in undesirable and destructive ways.

Family Structure Several demographic characteristics of parents have been identified as risk factors, including age, marital status, and socioeconomic status. Young parents, especially teens, are more likely to engage in abusive behaviors because they have little knowledge about child development, have unrealistic expectations about parenthood, and are unprepared for its demands. Single parents are more likely to abuse their children than are married parents. Low socioeconomic status is another risk factor. Parents who earn less than $15,000 per year are 12–16 times more likely to physically abuse their children, 18 times more likely to sexually abuse them, and 44 times more likely to neglect them (Sedlak & Broadhurst, 1998). It had been argued that this social class difference is due to the fact that abuse in low-income households is simply more likely to be detected by social workers. But researchers now believe that child abuse is indeed more common among low-income households. The most common explanation for this difference is that low-income parents are under a great deal of

TABLE 11.7 Total Annual Cost of Child Abuse and Neglect in the United States

DIRECT COSTS	ESTIMATED ANNUAL COST
Hospitalization Rationale: 565,000 children were reported as suffering serious harm from abuse in 1993. One of the less severe injuries is a broken or fractured bone. Cost of treating a fracture or dislocation of the radius or ulna per incident is $10,983. Calculations: 565,000 × $10,983	$6,205,395,000
Chronic Health Problems Rationale: 30% of maltreated children suffer chronic medical problems. The cost of treating a child with asthma per incident in the hospital is $6,410. Calculations: .30 × 1,553,800 = 446,140; 446,140 × $6,410	$2,987,957,400
Mental Health Care System Rationale: 743,200 children were abused in 1993. For purposes of obtaining a conservative estimate, neglected children are not included. One of the costs to the mental health care system is counseling. Estimated cost per family for counseling is $2,860. One in five abused children is estimated to receive the services. Calculations: 743,200/5 = 148,640; 148,640 × $2,860	$425,110,400
Child Welfare System Rationale: The Urban Institute published a paper in 1999 reporting on the results of a study it conducted estimating child welfare costs associated with child abuse and neglect to be $14.4 billion.	$14,400,000,000
Law Enforcement Rationale: The National Institute of Justice estimates the following costs of police services for each of the following interventions: child sexual abuse ($56), physical abuse ($20), emotional abuse ($20), and child educational neglect ($2) (cross-referenced against DHHS statistics on number of each incidents occurring annually). Calculations: sexual abuse—217,700 × $56 = $12,191,200; physical abuse—381,700 × $20 = $7,634,000; emotional abuse—204,500 × $20 = $4,090,000; and educational neglect—397,300 × $2 = $794,600	$24,709,800
Judicial System Rationale: The Dallas Commission on Children and Youth determined the cost per initiated court action for each case of child maltreatment was $1,372.34. Approximately 16% of child abuse victims have court action taken on their behalf. Calculations: 1,553,800 cases nationwide × .16 = 248,608 victims with court action; 248,608 × $1,372.34	$341,174,702
Total Direct Costs	**$24,384,347,302**

stress, have lower levels of education, have inadequate support systems, and have higher rates of substance abuse. However, they are also more likely to be young and unmarried—two other factors associated with child abuse.

Consequences of Child Abuse Child abuse has numerous physical and emotional consequences for children (Kemp, 1998). Abuse leaves approximately 18,000 children permanently disabled each year. Negative

TABLE 11.7	Total Annual Cost of Child Abuse and Neglect in the United States

INDIRECT COSTS	ESTIMATED ANNUAL COST
Special Education Rationale: Over 22% of abused children have a learning disorder requiring special education. Total annual cost per child for learning disorders is $655. Calculations: 1,553,800 × .22 = 341,386; 341,386 × $655	$223,607,830
Mental Health and Health Care The health care cost per woman related to child abuse and neglect is $8,175,816/163,844 = $50. If the costs were similar for men, we could estimate that $50 × 185,105,441 adults in the United States cost the nation $9,255,272,050. However, the costs for men are likely to be very different, and a more conservative estimate would be half of that amount.	$4,627,636,025
Juvenile Delinquency Rationale: 26% of abused or neglected children become delinquents, compared to 17% of children as a whole, for a difference of 9%. Annual cost per child for incarceration is $62,966. Average length of incarceration in Michigan is 15 months. Calculations: 0.09 × 1,553,800 = 139,842; 139,842 × $62,966 = $8,805,291,372	$8,805,291,372
Lost Productivity to Society Rationale: Abused and neglected children grow up to be disproportionately affected by unemployment and underemployment. Lost productivity has been estimated at $656 million to $1.3 billion. Conservative estimate is used.	$656,000,000
Adult Criminality Rationale: Violent crime in the United States costs $426 billion per year. According to the National Institute of Justice, 13% of all violence can be linked to earlier child maltreatment. Calculations: $426,000,000,000 × .13	$55,380,000,000
Total Indirect Costs	**$69,692,535,227**
Total Costs	**$94,076,882,529**

Source: Prevent Child Abuse America (2001).

health consequences continue into adulthood for many victims, including increased rates of gynecological problems, migraine headaches, digestive problems, asthma, and a host of other disorders (Cunningham, Pearce, & Pearce, 1988; Hyman, 2000).

Perhaps even more insidious are the emotional scars left behind. Child abuse often has devastating and long-term emotional consequences. For example, physically abused children tend to be more aggressive and more likely to get involved in delinquent

activities, are more likely to have difficulty in school, and are more likely to be involved in early sexual activity, including teen pregnancy (Prevent Child Abuse America, 2001). Even as adults, children who have been abused are more likely to suffer from nightmares, depression, panic disorders, and suicide ideation (Briere, 1992; Hyman, 2000).

As shown in Table 11.7, the annual *direct* costs of child abuse in the United States are estimated at $24.4 billion, taking into account increased rates of hospitalization, chronic health problems, use of the mental health care and child welfare systems, law enforcement costs, and use of the judicial system. *Indirect* costs total $69.7 billion, for a total *cost* of $94.1 billion (Prevent Child Abuse America, 2001). The physical, emotional, and financial costs of child abuse are far too great to ignore.

Elder Abuse

Difficult as it is to imagine, each year hundreds of thousands, perhaps even millions, of older persons are abused, neglected, and exploited by family members and others close to them (U.S. Department of Health and Human Services, Administration on Aging, 2001). Many of these elders are frail and vulnerable, and are dependent on others to meet their basic needs.

What constitutes **elder abuse**? Generally accepted definitions include (1) *physical abuse,* which is the willful infliction of physical pain or injury, such as slapping or bruising; (2) *sexual abuse,* which is the infliction of nonconsensual sexual contact of any kind; (3) *psychological abuse,* the infliction of mental or emotional anguish such as humiliating, intimidating, or threatening; (4) *financial or material exploitation,* which is improperly using the resources of an older person without his or her consent, for someone else's benefit; and (5) *neglect,* which is the failure of a caregiver to provide goods or services necessary to avoid harm or mental anguish, such as abandonment, denial of food or water, or delaying needed medical services.

A large national study conducted in 1996 by the National Center on Elder Abuse found the following (National Center on Elder Abuse, 1999; U.S. Department of Health and Human Services, Administration on Aging, 2001; Tatara & Kuzmeskus, 1997):

* There were 551,011 reported and substantiated cases of persons aged sixty and older experiencing abuse in a one-year period.

* Reports of elder abuse to adult protective services increased over 150 percent between 1986 and 1996. This increase dramatically exceeded the 10-percent increase in the elderly population during this time period.

* Because only one-quarter of abuse cases are reported and substantiated by adult protective service agencies, it is likely that the true extent of elders who are abused each year may approximate two million. Like other forms of domestic violence, elder abuse often goes unreported because the elderly are reluctant or unable to talk about it to others.

* Persons aged eighty and over are particularly vulnerable. They suffered abuse two to three times more than their proportion of the older population.

* Among known perpetrators of elder abuse, 90 percent were family members. Two-thirds of the perpetrators were adult children or spouses.

* Neglect is the most common source of abuse (55 percent), followed by physical abuse (15 percent), and financial/material exploitation (12 percent).

Who Are the Perpetrators and the Victims? Elder abuse is extremely complex. Generally, a combination of psychological, social, and economic factors, along with the mental and physical condition of the victim and the perpetrator, contribute to the occurrence of elder maltreatment. Two-thirds of elder abuse perpetrators are family members of the victims, typically serving in a caregiving role. Caring for frail older people is a very difficult and stress-provoking task, particularly true when older people are mentally or physically impaired, when the caregiver is ill-prepared for the task, or when the needed resources are lacking. Under these circumstances, the increased stress and frustration of a caregiver may lead to abuse or willful neglect. Some researchers have found that elders in poor health are more likely to be abused than those in good health. They have also found that abuse tends to occur when the stress level of the caregiver is heightened as a result of a worsening of the elder's impairment.

Researchers have found that abusers of the elderly (typically, adult children) tend to have more personal problems than do nonabusers. Frequently, adult children who abuse their parents suffer from such problems as mental and emotional disorders, alcoholism, drug addiction, and financial difficulty. Because of these problems, these adult children are often dependent on the elders for their support. Abuse in these cases may be an inappropriate response by the children to the sense of their own inadequacies (National Center for Elder Abuse, 2001).

Why Do Family Members, Dates, and Partners Abuse?

A quick survey of your classmates would probably indicate that everyone abhors domestic violence and abuse. Then why the high incidence? There tend to be two types of perspectives. One focuses on the societal and cultural causes of violence, while the other focuses more on the individual causes. Both factors come into play.

FACT OR FICTION?

Rape and sexual aggression are universal; they are practiced in every culture in the world.

Societal and Cultural Level Causes: Patriarchy This perspective focuses on male domination and the overall cultural climate that tolerates or even promotes violence, especially violence against women and children. It suggests that violence is more likely to occur in those households (and in those societies) in which men are dominant and try to control women and children. Men may hold the power and authority in their families (and in society at large), and see women and children as their "property." Women and children have been trained not to challenge men's authority over them.

Anthropologist Peggy Sanday (1981) has written about sexual aggression around the world. She finds that rape is not universal. It is absent in some cultures. Other cultures are more rape-prone, and these are cultures in which women hold relatively low political and economic status, cultures that hold rigid rules about the relationships between men and women, and cultures that encourage boys to be tough, aggressive, and competitive.

FICTION

Some cultures have no concept of this phenomenon.

Although patriarchy is more evident in countries where women cannot drive, vote, or be seen in public without extensive covering of their face and bodies, patriarchy is evidenced in American society as well. Men establish their dominance by eschewing any semblance of femininity. "You throw like a girl," "You're a sissy," and "Quit acting like a woman" all show contempt for the feminine. Men are taught that toughness, competitiveness, and controlling behavior are masculine attributes, and many adopt these attributes with a vengeance.

One consequence of patriarchy is to blame women for the violence. A review of high-circulation "women's magazines" between 1970 and 1997 (e.g., *Teen, Glamour, Good Housekeeping,* and *Essence*) found that articles on domestic violence were likely to frame the problem in terms of its being the victim's problem (Berns, 1999). Although the magazines may have been trying to give women clues about how to take charge of their lives, the message was that relationship violence is a private problem, to be addressed by the individuals involved.

Another recent study explored the role of the victim's style of dress in perceptions of rape. Workman and Freeburg (1999) studied 632 college students (75 percent non-Hispanic white, 14 percent non-Hispanic black, 2 percent Asian, 2 percent Hispanic, 7 percent other) by having them read a rape scenario, look at photographs of the victim, and attribute relative responsibility to the perpetrator and victim. Overall, men attributed more responsibility to the victim and less to the perpetrator than did women across all groups. But among both men and women, more responsibility was placed on the victim when she was pictured wearing a short skirt than when the photograph showed a victim in a moderate-length or long skirt.

What differences might these findings make? If young people hold beliefs about heterosexual relations that are tolerant of male sexual aggression (especially when women wear certain types of clothing), this might help explain why men underreport their violence (i.e., it is seen as "normal") and why women may not report being a victim to authorities.

Individual Level Causes: Social Learning Theory and the Intergenerational Transmission of Violence

This perspective suggests that we learn norms and behaviors by observing others and that this learning is transmitted from one generation to another. Our families of orientation are our primary source of early learning. Therefore, it makes sense that many adults who abuse their spouses, partners, or children learned this behavior in their own families. Perhaps they witnessed abusive or violent behavior between their own parents, or perhaps they were abused as young children. **Social learning theory** predicts that when we observe people engage in certain types of behavior, we learn scripts for our futures. In this case, the script includes an acceptance of aggressive behavior between people whom we believe to care for one another.

Research suggests a tendency towards an **intergenerational transmission of violence**—the theory that violence is a cycle potentially passed down to dependents (Egeland, 1993; Foshee, Bauman, & Linder, 1999; Ronfeldt, Kimnerling, & Arias, 1998; Straus, 1994). The transmission of violence can begin early. Male preteens and teenagers who were physically punished more frequently by their fathers are more likely than other boys to commit acts of animal cruelty (Flynn, 1999). Likewise, adults who witnessed abuse are significantly more likely to abuse their dates, spouses, partners, or children.

However, that being said, it is also true that most people who witnessed or experienced abuse as children do *not* abuse others. A study by Straus, Gelles, and Steinmetz (1980) reports a startling statistic from their research—sons of the most violent parents are 1,000 times more likely to abuse their spouses than are the sons of nonviolent parents, but this also translates into a rate of 20 percent. In other words, 80 percent of those sons witnessing the most extreme forms of violence do *not* abuse their own wives. Therefore, it is very important to note that the "intergenerational transmission of violence" is referring to a greater likelihood of engaging in violence—it is not referring to determinism. Many persons who witnessed or experienced abuse as children grow up to be loving, supportive partners and parents without a hint of domestic violence and abuse.

Substance Abuse

Substance abuse causes more deaths, illnesses, and disabilities than any other preventable health condition. Tobacco alone causes about 430,000 deaths each year, fol-

Nearly one-third of adults report that alcohol has been a cause of trouble in their family.

Despite the party image of alcohol, 30 percent of adults report that alcohol has caused trouble in their families.

lowed by 100,000 deaths from alcohol, and nearly 16,000 from illegal drugs (Schneider Institute for Health Policy, 2001). Many people focus on the social, financial, and emotional costs of illegal drugs—cocaine, marijuana, heroin—and pay less attention to legal ones—alcohol, tobacco, prescription medications. Yet inappropriate use and overuse of these legal drugs can be even more dangerous, disruptive, and deadly than the others. For example, more than 6,000 children die each year because of parental smoking, which can cause Sudden Infant Death Syndrome (SIDS), respiratory infections, or low birth weight (caused by smoking during pregnancy). Thirty percent of adults report that alcohol has been a cause of trouble in their family, and nearly 20 percent report that drug abuse has been problematic (Sinson, Yi, Grant, Chou, Dawson, & Pickering, 1998).

Approximately 30 percent of adults claim that alcohol has caused trouble in their families.

Some people turn to drugs to escape problems, but excessive use inevitably exacerbates problems rather than providing a meaningful escape. Drug and alcohol abuse can result in financial ruin, marital instability, serious health problems, job loss, legal problems, domestic violence and child abuse, and death. Granted, most people who occasionally drink, smoke, or take drugs will not have negative experiences or become dependent. However, individuals who consume greater and more frequent quantities, have addictive properties in their personality and environmental influences, and have addiction in their families of orientation are more likely to become dependent.

When someone is addicted, it is difficult to quit or to curtail use. The physiological and psychological addiction produces cravings, increased tolerance, and compulsive use of the drug. It may take multiple attempts or intervention by a third party or agency (e.g., treatment center) to get rid of the dependence.

All groups in society are affected by substance use and abuse. In 1998, nearly 14 million Americans were using illegal drugs, 52 million smoked cigarettes regularly, and 113 million reported that they had used alcohol in the past month. However, there are some significant differences in use patterns. For example, young adults under age thirty-five are more likely to use virtually all types of drugs than are older adults, and men are more likely than women. People with more education are more likely to drink, but those with less education are more likely to drink heavily, to smoke, and to use illegal drugs (especially among those under thirty-five). Whites are more apt than African Americans or Hispanics to drink alcohol; however, American Indians and Alaska Natives are most likely to be dependent on it (Schneider Institute for Health Policy, 2001). As was the case with poverty and domestic violence, substance abuse is influenced and affected by a complex web of cultural values and norms. To better understand the causes, consequences, and solutions to this crisis, we need to look beyond individual personal experiences and examine the social context in which substance abuse occurs.

Alcohol

Alcohol is the most widely used recreational drug in our society. It is consumed by adults and children, even though the drinking age in all states is now twenty-one years of age. Alcohol is the most commonly used drug among young people, with 50 percent of high school seniors reporting drinking in the past 30 days and 32 percent reporting being drunk at least once during this period (Schneider Institute for Health Policy, 2001). It is the most popular drug on college campuses; its use far exceeds marijuana and cocaine use. Twenty-five percent of college students get drunk at least ten times a month (Lowe Family Foundation, 2001).

Alcohol is also the most widely abused drug. A new analysis of data collected in 1992 on 42,800 Americans, the latest data available of this magnitude, reveals that approximately one in four U.S. children is exposed to family alcoholism while growing up (Grant, 2000). There are an estimated fourteen million alcoholics in the United States—one in every thirteen adults. Alcoholism is more common among whites than among minority groups, men than women, and is highest among young adults aged eighteen to twenty-nine and lowest among adults aged sixty-five and over.

Alcoholism has serious health consequences, the most extreme being death. Alcohol is a factor in 38 percent of automobile fatalities (U.S. Department of Transportation, 2000). Despite the fact that white males are most likely to drink, twice as many African Americans die from alcohol use as do white males (Stinson & Nephew, 1996).

What Is Alcoholism? **Alcoholism** is a chronic condition lasting a lifetime; therefore, it is often labeled a "disease." It includes the following four symptoms (National Institute on Alcohol Abuse and Alcoholism, 2001):

* *Craving.* A strong need or urge to drink.
* *Loss of control.* Not being able to stop drinking once drinking has begun.
* *Physical dependence.* Withdrawal symptoms, such as nausea, sweating, shakiness, and anxiety, after stopping drinking.
* *Tolerance.* The need to drink greater amounts of alcohol to get "high."

Alcoholism can develop insidiously. Often, the lines between recreational drinking, problem drinking, and outright alcoholism are unclear. Seemingly innocent recreational alcohol use can turn into a problem when it interferes with work, strains family relationships, or involves the law (e.g., drunk driving). Full-blown alcoholism is an addiction. People who suffer from alcoholism have little or no control over the frequency or amount they drink. They are usually preoccupied with drinking, have blackouts after drinking, and suffer frequent hangovers. They may drink alone and deny that they have a problem. Alcoholics usually have a variety of social and health problems that accompany their out-of-control drinking, such as violent and abusive relationships, frequent absenteeism from work, and a high rate of accidents and illnesses.

FACT OR FICTION?

Alcoholism is unrelated to genetics.

What Causes Alcoholism? How and why alcoholism develops is still a bit of a mystery. Obviously, people who drink heavily on a regular basis will be more likely to become alcoholics than those who rarely drink, but there is more to the story than this.

Alcoholism is caused by a mixture of genetics and the social environment. Children of alcoholics are at increased risk. One study found that children with one alcoholic parent have a 52-percent chance of becoming alcoholics themselves. With two alcoholic parents, the chances of becoming alcoholic jumped to 71 percent (Wells, 1982). But is this due to heredity or the environment in which children are raised? Answers are inconclusive, but studies on animals, fraternal and identical twins, and children who have been adopted lead researchers to believe it is a bit of both. For example, studies of women who had been adopted at birth have shown a significant association between alcoholism in adoptees and their biological parents. However, the relationship is far from absolute. Therefore, researchers suggest that the multiple genes a person inherits; environmental issues such as lifestyle, coping skills, depression, learned behaviors, peer pressure, and social support; and a myriad of other social factors can contribute to alcoholism (National Institute on Alcohol Abuse and Alcoholism, 1992, 2000). As the National Institute on Alcohol Abuse and Alcoholism reminds us, "risk is not destiny" (2001: 2).

| **FICTION**

Alcoholism is likely caused by a mixture of genetic and social environmental factors.

Just because alcoholism tends to run in families doesn't mean that a child of an alcoholic parent will automatically become an alcoholic. Some people develop alcoholism even though no one in their family has a drinking problem. By the same token, not all children of alcoholic families get into trouble with alcohol. Knowing that you are at risk is important, though, because then you can take steps to protect yourself from developing problems with alcohol.

Substance Abuse in the Family

It is not only drug abusers and alcoholics who suffer consequences of their actions, but also the entire family. The home can become a chaotic battlefield, affecting family members from infancy to old age.

Consequences for Children The youngest victims are those born of dependent mothers. For example, children born with **fetal alcohol syndrome** (FAS) suffer a series of mental and physical birth defects, including mental retardation, growth deficiencies, and abnormalities of the central nervous system and organs caused by alcohol use by a pregnant woman (National Organization on Fetal Alcohol Syndrome, 2001). It is not known precisely how much alcohol must be consumed during pregnancy for these results to occur, so pregnant women are usually advised to

Women who drink significant amounts of alcohol while pregnant place their babies at great risk for Fetal Alcohol Syndrome (FAS).

avoid alcohol entirely. Because the fetus is small, its blood-alcohol content will be much higher than that of the mother. A woman may hardly notice the effects of her drinking, but meanwhile her fetus is getting drunk. Not all women take this advice, however. More than 2,000 infants are born every year in the United States with FAS (Schneider Institute for Health Policy, 2001). It is the third most common birth defect and second leading cause of mental retardation in the United States (Donatelle, Davis, & Hoover, 1991). In addition, because alcohol can also be passed on to a child via breast milk, most doctors advise nursing mothers to limit their use of alcohol and to refrain from drinking for several hours before nursing.

Drug and alcohol abuse in a family can strain children's lives socially as well as medically. Children from alcoholic and drug-addicted families are more likely to have problems with depression, aggression, peer relationships, delinquency, school performance, and emotional issues than are their peers whose parents do not have problems with alcohol. Reports of child abuse have increased dramatically in recent years, and many of these are associated with alcoholism. These problems stem from the painful emotional climate and turmoil in the home. Families in which one or both parents are alcoholics usually contain many dysfunctions. Their environment is often unpredictable, chaotic, and filled with broken promises. Children may be asked to keep inappropriate secrets (e.g., "Don't tell Mommy that you saw Daddy smoking pot"), to live by arbitrary and rigid rules (e.g., going to bed unusually early so parents can drink), and to cope with chronic disappointment (e.g., parents making promises that they repeatedly do not keep). Many children of substance abusers receive inadequate nurturing. Unlike a spouse, however, who can choose to leave the situation, children in dysfunctional families are trapped. They cannot leave. In-

stead, they may be forced to play one of several roles (McGaha, Stokes, & Nielson, 2000):

* *Chief enabler.* Usually the spouse, but sometimes the oldest child, this person puts aside personal feelings and becomes increasingly more responsible for control of the alcoholic and the family.

* *Family hero.* This person tries to better the family situation by succeeding in the environment outside the home. Often, this is done for self-worth or positive recognition for the family. The hero often feels like a failure because the alcoholic's behavior does not change.

* *Scapegoat.* Not willing to work as hard as the hero for recognition, the scapegoat pulls away in a destructive manner, bringing negative attention to the family.

* *Lost child.* This individual takes care of his or her personal problems and avoids trouble. Often ignored by the family, this individual faces problems alone, which often brings loneliness and personal suffering.

* *Mascot.* To deal with the personal pain and loneliness, this member is charming and funny in times of stress. This behavior relieves the pain for some family members, but does not help the mascot deal with personal pain and loneliness.

The Constructing Strong Families box on page 493 reveals a number of important ways in which children can be helped by the caring assistance of other relatives and friends, even if their parents' drug use or drinking continues.

It is difficult to assess the magnitude of the pain of living with a parent who abuses drugs or alcohol, and the degree to which it carries over into adulthood. Only recently have we really acknowledged that the trauma

With one out of every four children living in a family touched by alcoholism, the United States is facing a rampant problem with potentially serious and long-term consequences. Children of alcoholics (COAs):

- Are at high risk for alcohol and other drug problems
- Often live with pervasive tension and stress
- Have higher levels of anxiety and depression
- Are more likely to do poorly in school
- Often experience problems with coping

The good news is that they can be helped to bounce back from the effects of their families' problems. The child in an alcoholic home may be helped whether the alcoholic stops drinking or not. It is not necessary to do anything to change the adult's drinking behavior. Single acts of kindness and compassion can make a big difference:

- Tell them that they did not cause alcoholism and cannot cure or control it. But they can learn to cope with it. Make clear that children are not responsible for solving grown-up problems.

- Understand that COAs often build up defenses against the pain, shame, guilt, or loneliness they may feel. They may show off, act tough, keep secrets, or hide. You may help them by accepting them for who they are. Encouraging them to share their thoughts and feelings will help them learn to trust others and accept and adjust to their lives.
- Get them involved in something about which they feel good. It can be something small like taking care of a pet; or a hobby such as collecting rocks, or stamps, or comic books; or a sport. Go slow, don't push, but keep trying.
- Do something with them on a regular basis, even if it's only twice a year, such as on the 4th of July or Martin Luther King's birthday. Providing some consistency and showing that adults can be counted on are important assurances for young people who may have experienced many broken promises and unpredictable parental behavior.
- Gently help them get positive attention from others. Let them know they are wonderful, special, and cared about just because they are who they are.

- Help them see life as really living even though there are many times and situations that may be very painful. Help them see beyond their present circumstances. Help them feel connected to nature, art, and history; to heritage, culture, religion; to their community. Help them build a larger picture of their lives and their worlds than their families' current problems.
- Help them understand that it is okay to ask for help. Assure them that getting help is a sign of strength. Offer some examples from your own life so they'll know how it's done and that it really is okay.

Source: The National Clearinghouse for Alcohol and Drug Information, 1995. *The Fact Is Alcoholism Runs in Families.* Reprinted with permission.

Critical Thinking

1. What may be the best way to approach a child of an alcoholic about the situation he or she is in?

2. In addition to family members, what other adults could get involved and make a difference in the life of a child of an alcoholic?

that children suffer could be long term. For example, adult **children of alcoholics (COAs)** still suffer the consequences of their parents' drinking. As a group, they often have little grasp of what is considered "normal" family behavior. Many suffer from low self-esteem, have trouble forming and maintaining close relationships, and have other emotional difficulties (McGaha, Stokes, & Nielson, 2000). COAs have been referred to as suffering from **post-traumatic stress disorder,** a condition first attributed to soldiers in combat. The

FIGURE 11.3 Heavy Alcohol Users Have Problems Working, 1997 (Full-Time Employees, Aged 18–49)

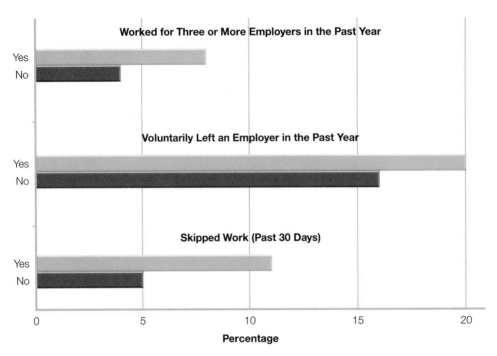

Source: Adapted from Zhang, Huang, & Brittingham (1999).

term is now used more widely to refer to people who have been subjected to levels of trauma beyond the range that could be considered "normal" and who experience the following symptoms: (1) re-experiencing the trauma, (2) psychic numbing, (3) hypervigilance, and (4) survivor guilt (Donatelle, Davis, & Hoover, 1991).

Consequences Among Adults Substance abuse can leave a marriage very shaky, or break it up altogether, because the relationship usually centers around the drinking or drug-using member: his or her moods, health, feelings, work situation, stresses, and coping. The needs of the other spouse, as well as the needs of the children, are ignored or subsumed under the needs of the alcoholic. Tensions and conflicts are commonplace.

Two interrelated sources of marital conflict are financial and work issues. Fre-

quent purchase of drugs and alcohol is expensive (e.g., a six-pack of beer a day can cost upward of $2,000 a year, and other drugs may cost considerably more). At the same time, many abusers find it difficult to keep working on a regular basis. Some are absent from work frequently, missing out on pay after their sick-leave benefits expire. As shown in Figure 11.3, 11 percent of heavy alcohol users reported that they skipped work during the past thirty days. Twenty percent of heavy alcohol users reported that they voluntarily left an employer in the past year. Eight percent of heavy alcohol users reported that they worked for three or more employers during the past year (Zhang, Huang, & Brittingham, 1999).

Perhaps one of the most disconcerting effects of drug and alcohol abuse is the increased likelihood of domestic violence (Caetano, Nelson, & Cunradi, 2001). As shown in

Figure 11.4, a U.S. Department of Justice study reports that over three-quarters of victims of domestic violence (nonfatal) claimed that their assailant had been drinking, doing drugs, or both (U.S. Department of Justice, Bureau of Justice Statistics, 1998). This finding includes both incidents that were and were not reported to police.

A recent large nationwide study of 1,635 African American, white, and Hispanic adults examined the relationship between spousal (and intimate-partner) violence and alcohol dependence. Violence was measured using the Conflict Tactics Scale and included violence that occurred in the past twelve months and involved one or more of the following: threw something; pushed, grabbed, or shoved; slapped; kicked, bit, or hit; hit or tried to hit with an object; beat up; choked; burned or scalded; forced sex; threatened with a knife or gun; used a knife or gun. Alcohol dependence was measured during those twelve months and included the salience of drinking, impaired control, withdrawal, relief drinking, tolerance, and binge drinking. As shown in Table 11.8, men who report alcohol dependence are at least two to three times more likely than other men to perpetuate male-to-female domestic violence. One-third of white men with alcohol dependency symptoms committed an act of domestic violence during the previous twelve months, compared to 10 percent of white men without symptoms. Sixty-one percent of alcohol-dependent African American men committed acts of domestic violence, compared to 17 percent of African American men without alcohol-dependent symptoms. And 29 percent of Hispanic men with dependent symptoms were violent, compared to 15 percent without dependent symptoms. Within each ethnic group, the difference in the rate of violence between those who are dependent on alcohol and those who are not is statistically significant (Caetano et al., 2001).

Spouses and partners deal with drug abuse and alcoholism in a number of differ-

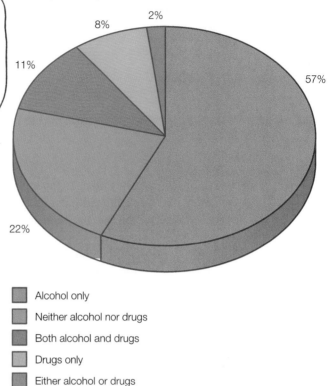

FIGURE 11.4 Percentage of Female Victims of Nonfatal Intimate Violence Reporting Alcohol or Drug Use by Assailant

- Alcohol only
- Neither alcohol nor drugs
- Both alcohol and drugs
- Drugs only
- Either alcohol or drugs

Notes: Assailant includes current or former spouse, boyfriend or girlfriend. Domestic violence between intimates in this survey includes nonfatal violence: rapes, robberies, or assaults. Because these data are based on victim's perceptions of violence, murder and manslaughter are not included, although they are part of domestic violence. These data include both incidents reported and those not reported to the police and exclude victims who were not able to distinguish alcohol or drug use by the offender.
Source: Data are from the National Crime Victimization Survey, as reported in U.S. Department of Justice, Bureau of Justice Statistics (1998).

ent ways. **Co-dependency** refers to a relationship pattern in which a person assumes responsibility for meeting others' needs to the exclusion of acknowledging his or her own needs. It is far more than simply caring for another person. Instead, co-dependent people lose their sense of their own identity and become "addicted to the addict" (Donatelle, Davis, & Hoover, 1991). They are often unaware of their own feelings, are extremely devoted and attached to their partner, and turn the other cheek despite

TABLE 11.8	Relationship Between Perpetration of Intimate-Partner Violence and Perpetrators' Problem Status: Male-to-Female Partner Violence (Male Perpetrator)		
PERPETRATOR PROBLEM	WHITE (%)	BLACK (%)	HISPANIC (%)
No alcohol dependence	10	17	15
Alcohol dependence	33	61	29
No drug dependence	11	21	17
Drug dependence	25	52	27

Source: Adapted from Caetano, Nelson, and Cunradi (2001).

personal humiliation. They take far too much responsibility for their addicted partner, and role boundaries are blurred between them (Kitchens, 1991).

Usually, a co-dependent spouse or partner engages in **enabling behaviors**. The partner will do things to cover for, support, or in many different ways enable the alcoholic to continue to drink. These could include things like calling an employer to claim that a spouse is sick when he or she is actually suffering from a hangover, lying to other family members or friends about the spouse's drug use, buying alcohol or drugs for the spouse, conducting additional household chores to compensate for the lack of domestic labor done by the abusing spouse, or in other ways sending messages that it is OK to continue drinking or doing drugs.

Substance Abuse Treatment

More than eighteen million people in the United States need treatment for alcohol abuse, and another five million people need treatment for their abuse of other drugs. Overall, fewer than one-quarter who need treatment actually receive it (Schneider Institute for Health Policy, 2001).

FACT OR FICTION?

There are several reliable cures for alcoholism.

There is no known absolute cure for alcoholism other than abstinence. Most alcoholics refer to themselves as "recovering" throughout their lifetime rather than as "cured." Most professionals believe that recovering alcoholics can never resume drinking again, even on a limited basis. Among those who do receive care, the most popular treatment strategies involve peer-group support such as that found in Alcoholics Anonymous (AA) or treatment at inpatient and outpatient facilities.

Self-help programs, such as Alcoholics Anonymous, have proved helpful to millions of alcoholics and their families.

There is no known complete cure for alcoholism other than abstinence.

Drug and alcohol treatment is considerably less expensive than the alternatives. A report by the Institute of Medicine reveals that the cost to treat cocaine addiction in an outpatient facility is less than $3,000. Treatment in a residential setting costs approximately $12,500, yet incarceration costs nearly $40,000, and untreated addiction could cost even more (Institute of Medicine, 1996). Timely treatment reduces crime, lowers health care costs, and enhances productivity.

The most successful programs involve the entire family. For example, AA has key programs for family members. Al-Anon's goals include helping families and friends of alcoholics recover from the effects of living with the problem drinking of a relative or friend. Similarly, Alateen is a recovery program for young people.

Conclusion

The focus of this chapter is family problems, particularly the ways in which some of the stressors and crises that families face have a basis in our social structure. Crises and stressors that we experience can be either negative or positive, but usually we focus on those that are more negative. Sometimes a crisis is completely unexpected, but other crises evolve more slowly from family stress. Stressors can vary in their type and in degree. They can occur outside the family or within it. Family stress may differ from other types of personal stress because of the interpersonal dynamics involved.

Here we have identified the findings of social science research surrounding three specific family problems to illustrate the types of crises and stressors that families can experience: (1) poverty and economic problems, (2) domestic violence, and (3) substance abuse. Our goal is to reveal that even though these problems are experienced on a deeply personal level, we must look beyond this level to obtain a greater understanding of the nature of these problems and their solutions. Many family problems are really *social problems*, not simply personal issues, and therefore require that we examine them in their social and cultural context.

Chapter Review

* What is a family crisis?

A crisis is a critical change of events that disrupts the functioning of an individual or a family. A crisis can be positive or negative, although we usually think of crises as negative. Examples of crises include divorce or death.

* What is family stress?

Family stress includes tensions that test a family's emotional resources. They vary in type and degree, but are often a process rather than one event. Living with an alcoholic spouse or parent or with an illness in the family are examples of stressors.

* Aren't these types of problems simply personal issues that people experience in their own way?

No, not completely. Many family crises and stressors are social problems, not merely personal ones. To understand issues like poverty, domestic violence, and substance abuse, we need to understand that some of the causes, consequences, and experiences are socially constructed.

* Why do we have growing inequality in the United States?

Changing tax laws give breaks to wealthier households, and wage distributions have become more unequal, with more highly skilled, trained, and educated workers at the top experiencing significant wage gains while those at the bottom experience losses because of global competition. Other factors are the decline in union membership, the decline in the real value of the minimum wage, and the increasing use of temporary workers. As well, female-headed households, which tend to have lower incomes, are increasingly common, and men with higher-than-average earnings are increasingly likely to marry women who also have higher-than-average earnings.

* Is the poverty rate decreasing?

Yes, data from the Census Bureau show a decline in poverty in 2000 from previous years. However, this is somewhat misleading. Social inequality is on the rise, and other indicators show that many low-income families in the United States are increasingly vulnerable.

* What are the consequences of poverty?

There are many social and health consequences for both adults and children, most of which are negative. For example, impoverished children suffer far more health risks from infancy on, including higher rates of infant mortality. They are also more likely to suffer from depression, have behavioral problems, and do poorly in school.

* How big of a problem is domestic violence?

Violence against intimates is more common than many people imagine. It can include violence and aggression between spouses and partners, in a dating relationship, child abuse, and other types of abuse (e.g., sibling, elder).

* What is the Conflict Tactics Scale?

The CTS is a commonly used assessment tool that asks respondents how they deal with disagreements in relationships. It focuses on violent behaviors.

* What explains domestic violence?

Researchers generally point to two lines of theoretical explanations. One looks at structural causes, such as patriarchy. Another explanation focuses on individual-level causes, including social learning theory and the intergenerational transmission of violence.

* How large of a problem is substance abuse?

It is a large problem. Thirty percent of adults report that alcohol has been a source of trouble in their family, and nearly 20 percent report that drug abuse has been problematic. Thousands die from drugs and alcohol every year. Problems affect the entire family.

* *What is alcoholism?*

It is a chronic condition that lasts a lifetime, with craving, loss of control, physical dependence, and increased physical tolerance. The causes are still not completely understood, but alcoholism is generally thought to result from a mixture of genetics and the social environment.

* *How can alcoholism be cured?*

There is no known absolute cure for alcoholism other than abstinence. Most alcoholics refer to themselves as "recovering" throughout their lifetime rather than "cured." Most professionals believe that recovering alcoholics can never resume drinking again, even on a limited basis. Among those who do receive care, the most popular treatment strategies involve peer-group support such as that found in Alcoholics Anonymous (AA) or treatment at inpatient and outpatient facilities.

Key Terms

alcoholism: alcohol addiction—a chronic condition lasting a lifetime; therefore, it is often labeled a "disease"

children of alcoholics (COAs): children who still suffer the consequences of their parents' drinking. They often have little grasp of what is considered "normal" family behavior, suffer from low self-esteem, have trouble forming and maintaining close relationships, and experience other emotional difficulties.

co-dependency: a relationship pattern in which people assume responsibility for meeting others' needs to the exclusion of acknowledging their own needs; they often lose their sense of their own identity

Conflict Tactics Scale (CTS): a commonly used scale based on how people deal with disagreements in relationships

crisis: a critical change of events that disrupts the functioning of a person's or a family's life

economic hardship: low income, income loss, and unstable work

elder abuse: abuse of an elderly person that can include physical abuse, sexual abuse, psychological abuse, financial or material exploitation, and neglect

emotional abuse: verbal, mental, or psychological maltreatment that destroys self-esteem

enabling behaviors: doing things to cover for, support, or in many different ways enable the alcoholic or drug addict to continue without change

family stress: tensions that test a family's emotional resources

fetal alcohol syndrome (FAS): a series of mental and physical birth defects, including mental retardation, growth deficiencies, and abnormalities of the central nervous system and organs, caused by alcohol use by a pregnant woman

Home Observation of the Measurement of the Environment (HOME): interview and observation measure of parent–child interaction that examines maternal warmth and learning experiences provided to the child. It is associated with a variety of child outcomes.

intergenerational transmission of violence: the theory that sees violence as a cycle that is passed down to dependents

Medicaid: government-sponsored insurance program for low-income persons

neglect: the failure to provide for basic needs

official poverty line: a measure established by the Social Security Administration in 1964 as a way to determine the number of people living in poverty

physical abuse: inflicting physical injury and harm

post-traumatic stress disorder: a condition in which previous trauma manifests itself as (1) re-experiencing the trauma, (2) psychic numbing, (3) hypervigilance, and (4) survivor guilt

relative poverty: the condition of the poorest U.S. households relative to others in society

sexual abuse: inappropriate sexual behavior with a child for sexual gratification

sexual trafficking: a multi-billion-dollar industry in which children are coerced, kidnapped, sold, deceived, or otherwise trafficked into sexual encounters

social learning theory: learning ways of living by observing people as they engage in certain types of behavior

wealth: a person's or family's total economic package, including stocks, real estate, and other assets in addition to income

Resources on the Internet

These web sites have been selected for their relevance to the topics in this chapter. These sites are among the more stable, but please be aware that web site addresses change frequently.

Joint Center for Poverty Research
http://www.jcpr.org

The Northwestern University/University of Chicago Joint Center for Poverty Research supports academic research that examines what it means to be poor and live in America. JCPR concentrates on the causes and consequences of poverty in America and the effectiveness of policies aimed at reducing poverty. The center's goal is to advance what is known about the economic, social, and behavioral factors that cause poverty and to establish the actual effects of interventions designed to alleviate poverty.

National Coalition Against Domestic Violence
http://www.ncadv.org

Information and referral center for the public, the media, battered women and their children, and agencies and organizations.

National Institute of Justice
http://www.ojp.usdoj.gov/nij

NIJ is the research and development agency of the U.S. Department of Justice and is the only federal agency dedicated to researching crime control and justice issues. NIJ provides objective, independent, nonpartisan, evidence-based knowledge and tools to meet the challenges of crime and justice, particularly at the state and local levels.

U.S. Department of Health and Human Services
http://www.os/dhhs.gov

The U.S. Department of Health and Human Services (HHS) is the U.S. government's principal agency for protecting the health of all U.S. citizens and providing essential human services, especially for those who are least able to help themselves.

Companion Web Site for This Book

Virtual Society: The Wadsworth Sociology Resource Center

http://sociology.wadsworth.com

Begin by clicking the Student Resources section. Next, click Marriage and Family, and then click the cover image for this book. Select from the pull-down menu the chapter you are presently studying. You will have easy access to chapter resources such as MicroCase Online exercises, additional Web links, flashcards, InfoTrac exercises, and practice tests (that can be scored). In addition, to enhance and help with your study of marriages and families, be sure to investigate the rest of the rich sociology resources at Virtual Society.

Visit InfoTrac College Edition

 Another unique option available to you at the Student Resources section of the Virtual Society web site described above is InfoTrac College Edition, an online library of hundreds of scholarly and popular periodicals. Here are three suggested key search terms for this chapter:

* Search keywords: *poverty + health*
* Search keywords: *domestic violence + child*
* Search keywords: *alcoholic + gender*

Search recent years to get the latest information on these social problems and to see articles that suggest solutions.

© Bob Mitchell /Corbis

The Process of Divorce

12

The following is a "letter of goodbye" written by a woman in a divorce recovery class. The letter is intended to help her let go of the grief caused by a relatively recent and painful divorce.

Goodbye*

Goodbye to the New House that I spent endless afternoons and weekends looking for—making sure that it met all the rigid requirements. I'll probably never find another house like that again. It was so much more than a house—it represented an end to looking, an achievement of a goal; a new beginning; a readiness for our family to begin. And now I'm back at the beginning of the beginning. So very far away from that place I'd worked so hard to get to. God, I was so tired of searching and so grateful to have found it, and now I've lost it all.

Goodbye to the home we were making for our future. Goodbye to the tulips we planted in the Fall, but that we never saw together in the Spring when it came time for them to bloom. Goodbye to the plans we made for the nursery and fixing up the old cradle for the baby we never had.

Goodbye to all that potential our new beginning was bringing up. Goodbye to the confidence and satisfaction I felt as "your mate"—the well-defined role; knowing what was expected of me.

Goodbye.

I've wanted so badly to say goodbye. To let go of you. To push you swiftly and completely from my life as you have done with me.

What is it that I'm holding on to? Promises?

The good old "as-soon-as-we" promises. . . .

Degrees . . . Travel . . . Jobs . . . Honeymoon . . . Money . . .

Funny how they changed to "as-soon-as-*I*" promises.

I loved you because you were the other half of a marriage that I needed very badly in order to feel whole. Because you were the future father of our family. Because I needed someone to care for, to nurture, to parent; you made me feel needed.

This woman crafts a "letter of goodbye" to her former spouse as a way to let go of the past.

© Larry Williams/Corbis

* From *Rebuilding: When Your Relationship Ends,* 3rd ed. © 2000 by Bruce Fisher and Robert E. Alberti. Reproduced for Karen Seccombe by permission of Impact Publishers® P.O. Box 6016, Atascadero, CA 93423. Further reproduction prohibited.

I guess I've already said goodbye in more ways than I would have thought possible. You've been gone for a year and a half. Somehow I'm still here; all here; and nowhere, not even on the final decree, does it say that I am now only half a person with only 50 percent of the purpose, of the value that I once had. I am not trying to say goodbye to my self-worth or dignity—I've not really lost that—but rather I am trying to say goodbye to my need for your credibility stamp on those feelings in order to make them valid.

The last goodbyes are the positive ones. For they are the goodbyes to the negatives.

Goodbye to the feelings of enslavement.

Goodbye to your picky little dislikes—onions, mushrooms, olives, and my flannel nightgown, and getting up early, and Joni Mitchell, and my friend Alice, and going to the zoo.

Goodbye to your lack of direction, and your lack of creativity, and your lack of appreciation, and your lack of sensitivity.

Goodbye to your indecisiveness and your stifled, dried-up emotions, and your humorless sense of humor.

Goodbye to feeling ashamed of getting angry and showing it, feeling embarrassed for being silly, and feeling guilty when I knew the answer and you did not.

Goodbye,
Trisch

This letter illustrates the pain, the grief, and the difficult process of letting go that is associated with divorce or ending an intimate relationship. Although "Trisch" had been divorced for a year and a half, she was still grieving, and hoped that writing this letter would provide her with the peace and serenity that had so far eluded her.

Divorce disrupts plans for the future. It shatters a daily routine. In a world of secondary relationships, there is hope that marriage might provide closeness and intimacy.

When that relationship is destroyed, feelings of rejection, anger, hurt, betrayal, defeat, and fear are common. You must face the seemingly impossible task of starting anew. Daily patterns and dreams for the future must be amended.

Given the difficulty that divorce causes for the divorcing couple, their children, and the larger community of family and friends, we might logically assume that divorce is a rare occurrence. But, as we all have learned from our experiences and from the mass media, divorce is very common, particularly in the United States. How common is it?

FACT OR FICTION?

Half of all marriages end in divorce.

Divorce in the United States

We often hear that "half of all marriages end in divorce." But what does this mean? Does it mean that half of all the marriages that occurred last year also ended in divorce? Of course not. Some people think that it refers to the **ratio of divorces to marriages in a given year.** Let's say that 100,000 couples married last year, and 50,000 divorces were granted. On the quick surface it looks like 50 percent of marriages ended in divorce. But this doesn't really make sense because the marriages took place in only one year, but the divorces are from marriages that may have taken place decades ago. Therefore, this is not a very useful comparison.

Others use the statement "half of all marriages end in divorce" to mean, quite simply, that if the current rate of divorce continued over the next several decades, approximately half of all marriages would ultimately end in divorce at some time during that period. While this makes more sense and may have some truth to it, it is not a very accurate way to present the frequency of divorce because, historically, divorce rates have fluctuated dramatically. We certainly cannot expect the divorce rate to remain at today's rate over the next thirty or forty years. It may go up, or it may go down. For most of history, as we shall see shortly, it has gone up. However, since about 1980, the divorce rate has actually been in a slight decline.

What then is a better way of understanding the frequency of divorce, and what do we mean by a "divorce rate"? One way is to examine the rate of divorce per 1,000 population. In the United States, this amounts to 4.0 per 1,000 population (U.S. Census Bureau, 2001). This is a common way of reporting divorce data, and it can allow for comparisons over time or across countries.

However, not all people have married, so it makes more sense to solely focus on how many married people get a divorce. Therefore, a more useful way to measure the frequency of divorce, one that also enables us to make comparisons, is to talk about the number of divorces that occur out of every 1,000 married women. This is called a **refined divorce rate.** It also allows us to make statewide comparisons, international comparisons, and comparisons over time. The refined divorce rate is approximately 19.5 per 1,000 married women (U.S. Department of Health and Human Services, 2001). This is the number of divorces divided by the number of all married women in the United States. So, in a recent year, approximately 20 out of 1,000 married women, or 2 percent, received a divorce. This number is much less sensational than "half of all marriages end in divorce," but it is a considerably more accurate and useful measure.

This refined divorce rate is **cross-sectional,** meaning that it is a rate at only one point in time. It provides a one-year snapshot of how many married women divorce. But certainly, the other 980 out of 1,000 women who didn't divorce that particular year *could* get a divorce the following year, or the year after that, or ten years later. Therefore, even though a married woman had a 2-percent chance of divorcing last year, she has a far higher chance of divorcing over the course of her married life. Just how high these chances are is unknown. If the current rate continues, which is unlikely according to family demographers, her chances are approximately 50 percent (Cherlin, 1999). This is where the frequently cited but erroneous "half of all marriages end in divorce" statistic comes from. We don't know whether half of all current marriages will end in divorce.

FICTION

This is a faulty way of calculating divorce rates. The more common and accurate method is the refined divorce rate, which is approximately 19.5 divorces for every 1,000 married women in a given year.

Another useful way to conceptualize the frequency of divorce is by examining how many people in the population have actually been divorced. In Table 12.1, based on data from the U.S. Census Bureau, we can see that approximately one-third of all women age

TABLE 12.1	Percentage of Formerly Married Women Who Have Divorced, by Age and Race: 1990			
AGE	ALL RACES (%)	WHITE (%)	BLACK (%)	HISPANIC (%)
20–24	12.5	12.8	9.6	6.8
25–29	19.2	19.8	17.8	13.5
30–34	28.1	28.6	26.6	19.9
35–39	34.1	34.6	35.8	29.7
40–44	35.8	35.2	45.1	26.6
45–49	35.2	35.5	39.8	24.6
50–54	29.5	28.5	39.2	22.9

Source: Adapted from U.S. Census Bureau (1997), p. 107.

thirty and over who had been married have also been divorced. Overall, the chance of divorce is higher for middle-aged African American women and slightly lower for Hispanic women of all age groups than it is for whites. Rank and Davis's research (1996) indicates that African American wives and husbands are considerably more likely than whites to perceive that they would be happy outside of marriage and that other aspects of their lives would not be as damaged by a divorce. However, the table also reveals that

Divorce is more strict in patriarchal societies where women have few legal rights. Women can only request a divorce under narrow circumstances, if at all.

among women under age thirty-five, it is white women, not African Americans, who are more likely to have divorced.

Cross-Cultural Trends in Divorce

If we look at countries other than the United States, we find that the rate of divorce is related to several factors. First, a country's level of socioeconomic development is positively related to divorce. Less-developed countries in Africa, Asia, and Central and South America have significantly lower divorce rates than do more developed industrialized countries in North America and Europe (Trent & South, 1989). For example, grounds for divorce among the Hindus in India include adultery, abandoning one's religion and adopting another one, and having a contagious sexually transmitted disease (Engel, 1982), but not simply irreconcilable differences, as is the case in many developed nations.

China, which has undergone rapid socioeconomic development, has also had a surge in its divorce rate. Between 1990 and 1994, the divorce rate in China virtually doubled, catching media attention (Faison, 1995). The rapid increase is due to many factors, including new social and economic freedom. Most divorces are initiated by women now, which indicates the increases in women's rights and opportunities in recent years.

A second factor that may influence how rarely or frequently divorce occurs is the dominant religion that is practiced, especially in less-developed countries. For example, much of Central and South America is dominated by Roman Catholicism, which strictly forbids divorce in all but the most extreme circumstances. In Italy, an industrialized but largely Catholic nation, divorce was illegal until the 1980s. Likewise in Ireland, the Catholic church was successful at forbidding divorce until 1997. Religious institutions play a strong role in defining cultural norms toward divorce and other moral issues.

Third, divorce tends to be more restrictive in patriarchal societies, where women have few legal rights (Amato, 1994; Chang, 1993; Neft & Levine, 1997). Paul Amato suggests the following: "the greater the inequality between men and women in a given society, the more detrimental the impact of divorce on women" (1994: 217). In many countries, men are allowed to divorce their wives for almost any reason, yet women are not allowed to initiate divorce except under the most extreme circumstances. In Muslim countries, for example, husbands can unilaterally divorce their wives by repeating this sentence three times in front of witnesses: "I divorce thee." In contrast, a wife seeking a divorce must go to a religious court and prove that her husband has failed to support his family or has otherwise had a harmful moral effect on the family (Neft & Levine, 1997).

Moreover, the laws regarding child custody and spousal support are designed to perpetuate male dominance and control. In Taiwan, custody of children goes automatically to the father, based on the tradition that children carry on the father's family name. In an exchange to obtain custody of children, some women pay their husbands large sums of money (Chang, 1993). In Iran, wives are entitled to spousal support for only three months, despite the very limited economic opportunities available to women in that country. Most divorced women must therefore return to their families, often in shame. In India, a woman rarely receives any of the marital assets, for these are assumed to belong to her husband and his family. Many Indian women do not even ask for child support out of fear that their husbands will also try to gain custody.

Until recently, women in Egypt could not file for divorce except under the most extreme circumstances. As shown in the Family Diversity box on page 508, with the support of the country's Muslim religious establishment, the law now allows women to initiate a divorce. Among the region's countries, only Tunisia has a similar law.

| FACT OR FICTION?

The United States has the highest rate of divorce in the world.

Although cross-cultural divorce rates are related to socioeconomic development, dominant religious institutions, and level of patriarchy, other cultural factors also come into play. The United States has the highest rate of divorce in the world. As shown in Figure 12.1, we have a divorce rate almost double that of Sweden, Canada, and France, and over ten times that of Mexico. Yet these countries, with the possible exception of Mexico, are highly developed and industrialized nations, have diverse religious institutions, and have relatively low levels of patriarchy. So why is the U.S. rate so much higher?

FIGURE 12.1 Divorce Rates per 1,000 Population for Selected Western Countries (1966)

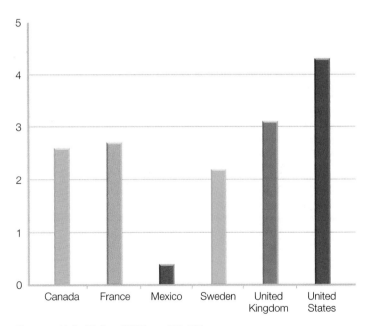

Source: United Nations (1998), pp. 383–385.

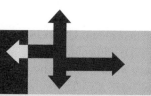

Nirmin says her husband used to lock her in his family's building and beat her, and the beatings did not end when she became pregnant one month into their marriage. Another woman, Wahad, said her husband, a colleague of her brother's, beat her at the slightest provocation and became increasingly violent after the birth of two children and increasing financial pressure. Until recently, these women's choices would be few without permission from their husbands. They could possibly get a divorce on grounds of abuse, but doing so would necessitate an inordinate amount of proof, and could take literally years to be granted.

On Wednesday, March 1, 2000, women like Nirmin and Wahad were among the first Egyptian women to file for divorce under a new law that allows wives to initiate a divorce with relative ease. The law was passed after a bitter debate. Some feared that changing the divorce law would cause a domestic upheaval.

Women's rights in Egypt and elsewhere in the Middle East are governed by ancient traditions that justify a wide range of restrictive rules and customs for women—all the way from what can be worn outside the family home to female genital mutilation. It is in this context that we see the restrictions on divorce.

Family law in Egypt and most other Muslim countries is based on a 1,400-year-old Islamic legal code known as Sharia. It allows for a Muslim man to be granted a no-fault divorce automatically. But a women is entitled to one only if she successfully and unequivocally proves to a court that her husband beats her, is a drug addict, is sterile, or does not support the family. But even under these grounds, many women still find that they are stymied for years by judges who discount their complaints. Moreover, even when granted a divorce, her husband can appeal the decree indefinitely. It was not unusual for a divorce request to stay in the courts for over a decade. "I always see women crying because they have no one to provide for them," said Fathi Shaheen, who has made his living for the past forty years helping illiterate women prepare their requests for divorce.

But in early 2000, Egypt enacted one of the Muslim world's most sweeping reforms related to families. For the first time, a woman can divorce her husband with or without his consent on grounds of incompatibility. But if the divorce is granted over the objections of her husband, she then must renounce all financial claims and return money given at the time of marriage. However, depending on circumstances, she will also be able to call on the government to garnish his wages if he refuses to provide for the children. If he refuses or cannot pay, she will be able to draw upon a special state bank to provide for her family. The new law allows a woman to simply declare before a judge that she wants a divorce. The judge will give the couple a three-month period to try to reconcile, six months if they have children. If the woman does not change her mind, a divorce is granted.

The law has faced strong criticism from some Islamic fundamentalists and from some lawmakers who say women cannot be entrusted with no-fault divorce. But an alliance of moderate Muslim clerics, women's rights advocates, judges, and divorce lawyers endorsed the changes. They began a public relations effort to convince people that the law is a modern rendering of the equal rights that Islam bestows on women. While no one predicts an avalanche of divorces because of long-standing Egyptian custom, at least the avenue is open to women who now seek it.

Source: Adapted from Sachs (2000) and Schneider (2000).

The United States has the highest rate of divorce in the world. Most other countries have considerably lower rates.

Historical Trends in Divorce in the United States

Some people suggest that the current high divorce rate in the United States indicates the recent decline of family values. But divorce and desertion have been historically common in the United States (Cherlin, 1999; Degler, 1980; Phillips, 1991; Wright, 1889). Although legal divorce was rare and difficult to obtain prior to the mid-nineteenth century, separation and desertion occurred in its place. Women in colonial America had few legal rights, and their ability to initiate divorce was limited. Colonies recognized adultery and desertion as grounds for divorce, and some allowed divorces on grounds of violence. But because of patriarchal norms, few divorces were granted to wives because of a husband's adultery. In fact, few divorces were granted to wives, period. Husbands were the head of the household. They needed, and therefore controlled, their wives' labor, sexuality, children, and ability to terminate the marriage. An early study of marriage and divorce conducted in the mid-1800s examined twenty-nine cases of divorce based on "cruelty" in which the wife was the defendant. In almost every case, the "cruelty" committed was that the wife was attempting to break out of the traditional subordinate role in one way or another (Wright, 1889). Half of these cases were based on her refusal to do domestic chores, such as keeping her husband's clothes in repair or cooking his meals.

Early feminists such as Susan B. Anthony, Elizabeth Cady Stanton, and Amelia Bloomer all spoke out in favor of making di-

© Corbis

Early feminists hoped to make divorce more available to women in order to help them out of dangerous or cruel marriages that they were trapped in.

vorce more available to women as a way to improve women's rights and position in marriage (Degler, 1980). By the mid-nineteenth century, the divorce rate began to rise. It became easier for women to initiate and obtain a divorce on grounds such as their husbands' mental cruelty, chronic drunkenness, or failure to support the family. Men had always had access to initiating a divorce. What changed was that divorce gradually became a remedy available to women as well.

The changes in divorce laws reflected the changing nature and contributions of men and women regarding the family. With industrialization, the dominant middle-class and upper-class norm was one of "separate spheres." A man was expected to work to

FIGURE 12.2 Divorce Rates per 1,000 Population and Married Women in the Years 1940–2001

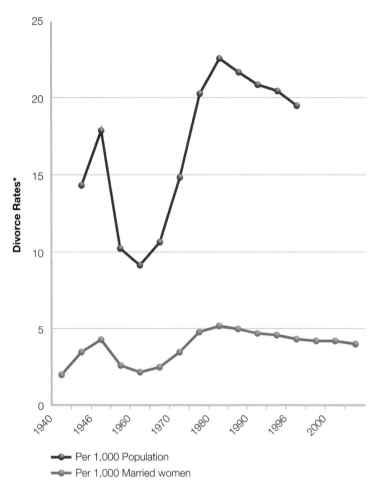

*Rates per 1,000 married women for 1940 and 1998–2001 not available.
Sources: U.S. Census Bureau (2001); U.S. Department of Health and Human Services, 2001.

tion, drunkenness, and failure to provide (Degler, 1980).

The divorce rate rose steadily between 1860 and 1940. Until 1880, fewer than 2 married couples out of 1,000 obtained a divorce each year. The rate doubled between 1880 and 1900, from 2 to 4 couples per 1,000. It nearly doubled again over the next 20-year period, to approximately 8 per 1,000 married couples in 1920. The rate of divorce dropped somewhat during the Great Depression. It is unlikely that the drop was because marriages were happier during this period. Instead, it is likely that many unhappily married couples simply couldn't afford to get divorced or needed to keep the family together for sheer survival. After the Depression, the divorce rate continued to rise. By the mid-1940s, it was triple the rate just ten years earlier. Why the dramatic increase? Perhaps many "shotgun" marriages occurred hastily as soldiers were going off to war. At the end of World War II, when couples got back together, some found that they had less in common than they originally thought, or couples faced difficulties that they had not imagined in their hurry to marry. Consequently, they divorced. Approximately 18 out of 1,000 marriages ended in divorce during this peak period.

The rate of divorce in the United States has been rising over the past two decades.

support and care for his wife and children in the home. He was to provide for them in a fair and loving manner. When he routinely abused his responsibilities toward his family, courts looked more favorably on a wife seeking a divorce. During the five years from 1872 through 1876, approximately 63 percent of all divorces granted to women were on grounds indicating that their husbands were neglecting to fulfill their duties toward them, including grounds of cruelty, deser-

Figure 12.2 illustrates the trends in the divorce rate in the United States between 1940 and 2001. After the rush of divorces following World War II, the divorce rate dropped considerably, down to around 10 per 1,000 married women. During the 1950s, the divorce rate remained relatively low. As discussed in previous chapters, this decade was unusual: women married younger and had more children than in prior decades. But by the 1960s the divorce rate began to rise again, peaking at approximately 20.3 divorces per 1,000 married women around 1980. However, since this time, the rate of divorce has declined to approximately 19.5 per 1,000 married women and 4.0 per 1,000 population.

The divorce rate has been declining since 1980.

Why did the divorce rate rise so rapidly during the 1960s and 1970s? Why has it declined since then? We will explore these two questions in the next sections, where we look at the factors that are associated with divorce.

Why Did the Rate of Divorce Increase During the 1960s and 1970s?

We could ask individuals why they divorced, and we would get many different answers: "We fell out of love," "We grew apart," "We are just too different," "She met someone new," "He doesn't listen to me," "We disagree about how to spend money." Instead of settling for a host of miscellaneous answers, family sociologists and other family scientists try to look at the *patterns* of why people divorce. The explanations that couples offer tend to focus on individual personal problems or concerns, such as those illustrated above. In fact, a common response is "We have irreconcilable differences." But family scholars want to look at macrolevel structural factors as well as microlevel personal explanations to find important patterns that help us understand why people divorce. This includes understanding why the rate of divorce climbed so rapidly during the 1960s and 1970s in virtually every industrialized nation (Goode, 1993). For example, were more people really experiencing marital difficulties and falling out of love during this period than ever before? Or is it that people were openly doing something about their marital difficulties? And what prompted this openness?

Macrolevel Societal Factors Associated with Divorce

The 1960s and 1970s were a period when many cultural changes were occurring in our society. Many of these changes influenced our personal lifestyles and choices. Some of these are outlined below.

"No-fault" divorce means that any married person can request a divorce without blaming his or her spouse.

Changes in Divorce Laws   Until recently, to be granted a divorce, one partner had to file suit against the other. One spouse had to blame the other for violating their marriage vows, or in other ways making the marriage intolerable. Common grounds for divorce included mental cruelty, adultery, and desertion. In other words, one person had to be found at fault, even if no one partner really was to blame. It is likely that many spouses concocted stories to impress upon a judge their desire to divorce. For example, a husband and wife who were unhappily married and wanted a divorce may have, together, made up a story about domestic violence or about one spouse having an extramarital affair. These stories may have been successful in getting a judge to grant a divorce, but they may have had unintended and long-term consequences. Being found "at fault" could affect custody arrangements, property settlements, and alimony awards.

Begun in the 1960s, "no fault" divorce legislation implies that a couple can request a divorce without having to blame one another.

Beginning in the 1960s, states slowly began to amend their laws to reflect **no-fault divorce.** This means that a couple could go before a judge without having to blame each other. Instead, they could simply say that they had irreconcilable differences and that they wished to divorce. Beginning in Oklahoma in 1953 and Alaska in 1962, no-fault divorce laws spread through the states during the 1970s. By 1987, the final holdout, Utah, had enacted no-fault divorce legislation (Nakonezny, Shull, & Rodgers, 1995).

FACT

A divorce is legally easy to obtain; no-fault divorce means no reason other than "irreconcilable differences" need be given—no party need be at fault.

It is not clear how the passage of no-fault divorce laws affected the divorce rate. Part of the confusion lies in the fact that the divorce rate was already rising rapidly prior to passage of this legislation (Glenn, 1997). So there was certainly more going on than just a change in the law. However, some evidence also suggests that a high number of divorces occurred immediately after the leg-

islation was passed (Nakonezny, Shull, & Rogers, 1995; Rodgers, Nakonezny, & Shull, 1997). This may indicate that there was a backlog of unhappy couples waiting until the legislation went into effect so that they could divorce more easily and simply, without blaming the other or concocting a sham to appease a judge.

Women's Employment Traditionally, couples were tightly bound together because they needed the labor of each other to survive and support their families. On the farm, women and men worked together, often side by side, to meet their basic needs. In early industrial society, members were also interdependent economically, but not necessarily in the same way as on the family farm. Instead, women were often economically dependent on men to support them. In exchange for financial support from their husbands, wives provided a variety of housekeeping and child-care functions. Poor and immigrant women were often employed outside the home, yet they earned wages that were significantly lower than their male counterparts. Their incomes were usually insufficient to support a family; consequently, these women still depended on men to support them and their children. During early industrialization, middle-class and upper-class women often didn't work outside the home at all; thus, they were virtually dependent on their husband's financial support.

This pattern of wives' economic dependence continued through most of the twentieth century. However, as we saw in Chapter 10, middle-class married women increasingly began securing paid employment. During World War II, assisting in the war effort was considered patriotic. After the war, most middle-class married women did not work outside the home for pay, especially if they had young children. However, the norms regarding married women and work during nonwar times gradually began to change.

These changing norms were particularly evident during the 1960s and 1970s, when a rapid explosion in employment occurred for married women with children. Today, the majority of married women are employed, include those with a child under age one.

This change in women's employment patterns has enabled women to more easily support themselves. Although their wages continue to lag significantly behind men's, and many women still earn near-poverty-level wages, the fact remains that women can now more easily end an unhappy relationship because they can come closer to supporting themselves than ever before (Heidemann, Suhomlinova, & O'Rand, 1998; Martin & Bumpass, 1989). Most research has found that women who are more self-sufficient, such as those who have higher incomes or who earn more than half the household income, are more likely to divorce than are those who are economically dependent (Heckert, Nowak, & Snyder, 1998; Hiedemann, Suhomlinova, & O'Rand, 1998; Ono, 1998). Moreover, women are more likely to divorce when working in an occupation that is relatively male-dominated, thereby increasing the likelihood of meeting new potential partners (South, Trent, & Shen, 2001).

Changing Attitudes Toward Divorce
Forty years ago, it would have been unlikely for any person known to have divorced to be elected to a major political office. Yet in 1980, Ronald Reagan's divorce did not prevent him from being elected President of the United States. And in the 1992 presidential election, candidate Bob Dole's divorce was barely mentioned. Attitudes toward divorce are changing as divorce becomes more common. In the past, people who divorced were deeply stigmatized. Women, in particular, bore the brunt of the stigmatization. For example, the term *divorcée*, which was applied to women only, had sexually suggestive connotations.

The changing attitude toward divorce is probably both a consequence of an increasing divorce rate and a cause of it. As divorce becomes less stigmatized, unhappy couples may consider it an appropriate way to end their relationship. Moreover, some couples contemplating getting married may see marriage as only semipermanent, noting that they can "opt out" if it doesn't work. Knox and Zusman report that only 8 percent of 620 never-married undergraduate college students agreed with the statement "I would not divorce my spouse for any reason" (1998). Defining marriage as only semipermanent resembles a self-fulfilling prophecy: if partners enter marriage with the idea that it could end, it is more likely to do so.

But the stigma toward divorce, although reduced, has not been eliminated. Although attitudes toward divorce are less disapproving than in the past, disapproval of divorced *individuals* continues (Gerstel, 1987). Family, friends, co-workers, and neighbors all want to know who is to blame, often in moralistic tones. Those who initiate divorce are viewed as the "bad guys," and they must deconstruct the relationship in a way that will define themselves to others as victims rather than the perpetrators of divorce.

Cultural Norms Immigrants to the United States often face new attitudes about gender roles, and these can stress relationships and increase rates of divorce. Often, gendered expectations are far more traditional and fixed in the country of origin. For example, immigrants from Latin America or the Middle East are more likely to believe that a man's primary responsibility is to earn a living and support the family, while a woman should tend to the home and children. Yet, after immigrating to the United States, they find less support for these traditional expectations. For example, it may take both spouses' working to make ends meet financially. One study of Iranian immigrants to the

United States found that men were more likely than women to retain traditional viewpoints. Women tended to adopt views more similar to those of mainstream America (Hojat, Shapurian, Foroughi, Nayerahmadi, Farzaneh, Shafieyan, & Parsi, 2000). This difference, coupled with women's increased job opportunities, paved the way to potential conflict. "Americanized" women are disdained, and becoming too Americanized can jeopardize both mate selection and marriage. While the divorce rate approximates 10 percent in Iran, it is estimated to be as high as 66 percent among Iranian immigrants (Tohidi, 1993).

Microlevel Individual Factors Associated with Divorce

In addition to the macrolevel societal forces that influence divorce rates, specific sociodemographic characteristics may also influence the risk of couples divorcing. Our personal histories do matter. Some of the most important characteristics include (1) having parents who have divorced; (2) marrying at a young age or marrying at an unusually late age; (3) the presence of children; (4) having a child conceived or born outside of marriage; (5) having all daughters rather than at least one son; (6) being a member of certain ethnic or racial minority groups; (7) having lower levels of education or, for women in particular, unusually high levels of education; (8) having a low income; (9) dissimilarity between husband and wife; and (10) the couple's ages.

Parental Divorce Persons whose parents have divorced are themselves also more likely to divorce. Several studies have found that divorce has negative long-term consequences for children's mental health that continue into their own adulthood, such as emotional problems, anxiety, and depression (Chase-Lansdale, Cherlin, & Kiernan, 1995; Cherlin, Chase-Lansdale, & McRae, 1998). Additionally, children of divorced parents marry younger, generally have lower incomes, are more likely to be involved in a nonmarital pregnancy, and are less likely to go to college, which puts them in several higher risk categories (McLanahan & Sandefur, 1994; Saluter & Lugaila, 1998). Moreover, perhaps adult children model their own parents' behavior or they learn destructive habits, such as poor communication skills or family violence.

Age at Marriage Marrying young tends to be one of the greatest factors that influence the chance of divorce (Kurdeck, 1993b; Martin & Bumpass, 1989; Waite & Lillard, 1991). Teen marriages are at a particularly high risk because teenagers tend to be poorly prepared for marriage and its responsibilities. Generally, teens do not have the maturity of people in their twenties or thirties—they do not yet know what kind of adult they will be or what type of spouse they are best suited for. As well, teen marriages are often precipitated by a premarital pregnancy, which increases the likelihood of the marriage failing. Practically speaking, they are also likely to have low incomes and to have had their education interrupted, also putting them in a higher risk category.

Presence of Children Couples who have children are less likely to divorce (Waite & Lillard, 1991). Specifically, families with preschool-aged children or families with many children are less likely to experience divorce. This, of course, says nothing about the quality of these marriages—people may stay in unfulfilling marriages because they feel that it is the appropriate thing to do for their children's sake. But regardless of marital quality, it remains that married couples who are childfree are more likely to divorce than those couples who have children.

Nonmarital Childbearing Couples who bear a child or conceive prior to marriage have higher divorce rates than do other couples. Part of this may be explained by the fact that a nonmarital pregnancy may encourage people to marry when they may not otherwise have chosen to do so. It may also encourage them to marry before they are financially or emotionally ready. Pregnancy, caring for a newborn, and raising a child put additional strains and stresses on a relationship. Two people who have not yet had the opportunity to truly get to know themselves and their partner may have a difficult time transitioning to their role as parents.

| FACT OR FICTION?

Mothers who have at least one son are less likely to perceive that their marriage could end in divorce than are mothers who have only daughters.

Sons Versus Daughters Researchers have found that mothers who have at least one son are less likely to perceive that their marriage will end in divorce than mothers who have only daughters (Katzev, Warner, & Acock, 1994). As discussed in the Focus on Family Research box on page 516, this is primarily because fathers in families with boys are more engaged with their children; therefore, mothers perceive the relationship as more equitable and stable.

| FACT

The gender of children is an important predictor of divorce. Presumably, men are more invested in their families if they have sons instead of daughters.

Race and Ethnicity The likelihood of divorce varies for different racial or ethnic groups, as shown in Figure 12.3. This figure reports the percentage of the white, black, and Hispanic population that was divorced in 1980 and in 2000. Among whites, 6 percent were divorced in 1980, increasing to 9.8 percent in 2000. This increase is larger than the

FIGURE 12.3 Percentage of Population Currently Divorced, by Race and Ethnicity (1980 and 2000)

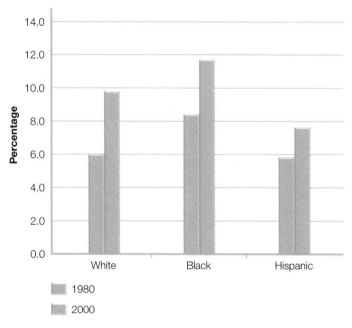

■ 1980
■ 2000

Source: U.S. Census Bureau (2001).

Divorce occurs less frequently in families with sons. Why do you think this is the case?

Research on marital quality and stability tells us that a key feature to sustaining a relationship is the perceived equity in the relationship. When both individuals involved believe there is an equitable and just division of responsibilities, they are happier than if they perceive the situation to be unjust. We also know that the perception of fairness or equity in a marital relationship is related to the actual involvement of the partners in their family life. That is, when the division of domestic labor (housework and child care) is skewed so that one spouse is doing disproportionately more than the other, dissatisfaction is likely to occur (especially for the person with the position of relative disadvantage).

But what are the factors that influence the relative involvement of parents in family life? Katzev,

Warner, and Acock (1994) find that the gender of children in the household is something to consider. Our culture expects fathers to be involved with their children, but especially so when there are sons. Using data from the National Survey on Families and Households, the researchers found that having at least one son in the family did increase the time that fathers spent with children. Although it did not affect the time spent in housework, this increase in involvement resulted in wives sensing more equity. In turn, these mothers were less likely to view their marriages as unstable. In addition, having at least one son also directly influenced wives' perception of the stability of their marriage. The reasons for this direct effect may be that boys continue to hold greater value in our society;

therefore, having sons enhances the relationship between husbands and wives.

The model estimated for this research appears in Figure 12.4. All relationships shown are statistically significant.

Source: Katzev, Warner, and Acock (1994).

Critical Thinking

1. Why do you think that fathers who have sons are more invested in their marriages?

2. Do you think we would find the same effects for mothers who have only daughters—are these mothers more invested in their marriages?

3. Do you agree with the authors that sons are valued in society more than daughters are? What evidence can you find for your opinion?

FIGURE 12.4   Relationship of Child Gender to Marital Instability

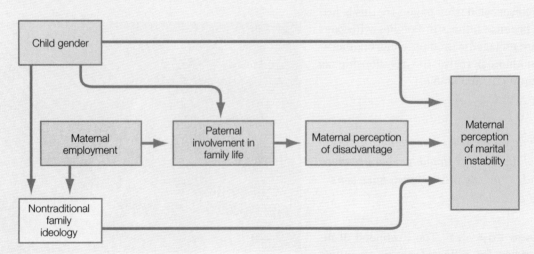

Source: Katzev, Warner, and Acock (1994.)

increase among blacks: 8.4 percent were divorced in 1980, increasing to 11.7 percent in 2000. Hispanic groups have relatively low rates of divorce, at 5.8 percent and 7.6 percent, respectively, in 1980 and 2000.

It is not altogether clear what explains the difference in divorce rates among racial and ethnic groups. Senator Daniel P. Moynihan (1965) has suggested that the effects of slavery continue to cause a relatively unstable family structure among African Americans, including husband absence and higher rates of nonmarital births. Other scholars suggest that the difference may have more to do with the lack of jobs for urban African American males and high rates of unemployment and poverty (Cherlin, 1981; Wilson, 1996). Likewise, what might explain the relatively lower rate of divorce among most Hispanic groups? The most common explanation is a cultural one, focusing on the primacy of the family in Hispanic culture; the importance of Catholicism, which does not recognize divorce; and the norms of male domination known collectively as *machismo*.

Education On average, persons with lower levels of education are more likely to divorce than are persons with higher levels of education (Kurdek, 1993b). A college degree reduces the risk of divorce (Lillard & Waite, 1993). But the relationship is less clear-cut for women than it is for men. Some studies suggest that women with very high levels of education are also more likely to divorce, especially later in the marriage, because doing so contributes to their ability to be economically independent (Heidemann, Suhomlinova, & O'Rand, 1998).

Income Divorce is more common among persons with lower incomes than among those with higher incomes. Financial and job-related stresses can contribute to the deterioration of a marriage. While certainly not all wealthy couples have happy marriages

and not all couples with lower incomes are doomed to unhappy or unstable unions, researchers have found that financial issues are a major contributor to marital problems (Conger, Elder, Lorenz, Conger, Simons, Whitbeck, Huck, & Melby, 1990; Kurdeck, 1993b). Unemployment, poverty, and financial strains increase the likelihood of family violence and disruption, and decrease displays of affection. In a study of separation and divorce conducted by Spanier and Thompson (1987), 56 percent of couples claimed that a major source of conflict was over the amount of money they had. Precisely *who* earns the money is also of importance. Nontraditional couples in which wives earn between 50 percent and 75 percent of the household income are more likely to separate or divorce than are other couples (Heckert, Nowak, & Snyder, 1998).

Degree of Similarity Between Spouses When spouses are similar to each other in socioeconomic characteristics such as age, religion, and race or ethnic group, they are less likely to divorce. Couples who are very different on one or more of these dimensions face increased stresses and complications in their marriages. They may have different values and norms about gender, how to spend religious holidays, how to socialize their children, or what to do about an unhappy marriage. For example, Jones (1996) compared the likelihood of divorce among a sample of Chinese, Japanese, Filipino, Hawaiian, and Caucasian couples. Jones reports that interracial or interethnic marriages are more likely to end in divorce than are marriages between persons of the same racial or ethnic group, and suggests that one reason may be the difference in views toward divorce that ethnic groups display.

The Couple's Ages The likelihood of a couple divorcing declines dramatically with age. This decline may be because unhappy

The likelihood of a couple divorcing declines with age. Unhappy marriages have either already ended or the couple may have resigned themselves to the relationship.

couples divorce long before ever reaching middle or old age. Or it may be because unhappy couples decide that it would be better for them to remain married than it would be to divorce at this stage in life. Dividing up many years worth of joint assets (e.g., home, retirement accounts, savings) could be problematic. For these reasons, three-quarters of divorces occur before age 40, and only 1.3 percent occur after age sixty-five (Johnson, 2001). Because divorce is so rare among the elderly, they have few peers with which to share their experience, exacerbating the sense of isolation and loneliness that usually accompanies divorce.

The Process of Divorce

Rarely is divorce a quick, easy, and painless event. Usually it is a long, difficult, and painful *process*. Although the divorce decree may be granted in a matter of minutes by a judge, most couples have gone through a long period in which they have had to analyze, redefine, and reorganize not only their relationship but also nearly all aspects of their lives (Ganong & Coleman, 1994). This

period often takes many years. It may include a separation to provide the emotional distance to work on resolving marital problems, and then sometimes a reconciliation, and then finally a divorce. In a study involving in-depth interviews with thirty divorced persons, Hopper (1993) found that all respondents said that they were well aware of their marital problems for a long time, sometimes for ten to twenty years.

Another study, involving a national sample of more than 1,000 people interviewed several times between the years 1980 and 1992, reports that marital problems identified in the first interview in 1980 predicted divorce up to twelve years later (Amato & Rogers, 1997). These studies reveal that couples who divorce tend to report problems in the marriage as early as nine to twelve years before the actual divorce occurs.

Drawing upon an exchange perspective, some researchers examine how couples think about their commitment to the marriage and how they weigh the barriers to divorce as well as the more positive alternatives to their marriage. Johnson, Coughlin, and Huston (1999) highlight three distinct components of marital commitment: (a) the personal desire to stay married, (b) feelings of moral obligation to stay married, and (c) feelings of constraint to stay married. They note that these three measures are not necessarily highly correlated with one another.

Knoester and Booth (2000), using a national sample of 1,184 individuals, illustrate the importance that people place on possible barriers to divorce. These are reported in Table 12.2. Adults place "children's suffering" and "not lose a child" as the two most important factors in keeping a marriage together.

FACT OR FICTION?

Husbands and wives tend to see marriage problems differently.

	The Perceived Importance of Barriers to Keeping		
TABLE 12.2	One's Marriage Together (N = 1,172)		

BARRIER TO DIVORCE	NOT VERY IMPORTANT (%)	SOMEWHAT IMPORTANT (%)	VERY IMPORTANT (%)
Child's suffering	32	18	50
Religious beliefs	35	24	41
Dependence on spouse	28	39	33
Not lose a child	43	11	46
Financial security	26	50	24
Spouse's independence	31	38	32
Not leave residence	58	23	19
Family and friends	66	22	12

Source: Adapted from Knoester and Booth (2000).

Gender Differences

The reasons for getting a divorce, and the process itself, are experienced differently by men and women. Although each person may experience negative feelings, including guilt, depression, embarrassment, failure, and/or low self-esteem, divorce is experienced differently by husbands and wives because of the gendered opportunities and constraints deeply embedded in our society.

These gender differences can be seen even in the first stage in the process of divorce—voicing marital problems. Amato and Rogers (1997), drawing on a national sample, found that husbands and wives differ in their reports of marital problems. Women report more marital problems than do their husbands although, interestingly, Amato and Rogers found that women tend to blame themselves for many of these marital problems. It is possible that this finding reflects women's subordinate position in many marriages and results in wives monitoring and interpreting their marriage more often than do husbands (Thompson & Walker, 1989). Table 12.3 illustrates gender differences in the reporting of various marital problems by husbands and wives. We can surmise from these data that husbands and wives see the problems in their marriage very differently.

The first two columns of Table 12.3 report the percentage of husbands and wives who attribute a particular problem to the *husband.* The second two columns of the table report the percentage of husbands and wives who attribute the same problem to the *wife.*

In the first two columns, we see that husbands were more likely than wives to say that their own hurt feelings, criticism, moodiness, and absence from home caused problems in the marriage. Wives claimed that it was their husbands' jealousy and irritating habits that contributed to marital problems.

We also see that spouses evaluate wives' contributions to marital problems differently, as reported in the second set of columns. Wives were more likely than husbands to report that their own anger, hurt feelings, criticism, moodiness, lack of communication, and drinking or use of drugs caused problems in the marriage. Husbands claimed that their wives' jealousy contributed to marital problems. It seems that husbands and wives see different problems affecting the relationship.

	Percentage of Husbands and Wives Reporting Specific Marital Problems Due to Their Spouse's or Their Own Behavior			
TABLE 12.3				

	HUSBAND'S BEHAVIOR REPORTED BY		WIFE'S BEHAVIOR REPORTED BY	
	HUSBANDS (%)	WIVES (%)	HUSBANDS (%)	WIVES (%)
Gets angry easily	20	20	13	23*
Feelings are easily hurt	14	11*	35	42*
Jealous	10	13*	13	11*
Domineering	13	13	7	9
Critical	18	14*	9	14*
Moody	23	17*	19	27*
Does not talk to the other	18	18	12	16*
Has had sex with someone else	4	4	2	2
Has irritating habits	12	18*	8	10
Not home enough	19	15*	4	4
Spends money foolishly	11	12	8	7
Drinks/uses drugs	6	7	1	1

*The difference in percentages between husbands and wives is statistically significant.
Source: Adapted from Amato and Rogers (1997).

FACT

Research indicates that men and women voice different types of marital problems and often have different reasons for initiating divorce.

Phases of a Separation

A marital separation is often a prolonged and painful process in and of itself. Ahron and Rodgers (1987) describe four phases. In the first phase, (1) *pre-separation,* one or both partners begin to think about the benefits of a separation. They may first fantasize about leaving and being free of the responsibilities associated with marriage. But when thinking about the logistics, it is common for people to experience anxiety, sadness, fear, anger, and loneliness concurrently. At the same time, couples may not fully reveal to friends and family their intention to separate. They may continue to attend family functions together, or they may concoct a story to explain a partner's absence from events.

During the (2) *early separation phase,* couples are faced with a series of issues to address as they separate. Who will be the one to move out? How shall we work out financial matters, such as the house payment, the car payment, and other bills? How do we explain this to our children? How should parental responsibilities be divided? Should family, friends, and teachers be told and, if so, how? In addition, couples may have conflicting feelings about both the separation and the possibility of divorce looming over the horizon.

In the (3) *mid-separation phase,* the realities of daily living set in. These may include the pressures of maintaining two households, the difficulties of arranging visitation for the children, and the harsh economic realities of living on a reduced income. Sometimes the pressures of daily living are difficult to handle, and the couple reconciles simply to avoid these pressures rather than because they have resolved the problems that are in the relationship. But the underlying problems may resurface again, causing another separation or leading directly to a divorce this time around.

Finally, during the (4) *late separation phase,* a couple must learn to live as singles. This includes tackling the challenging tasks mentioned above. They must also decide on the next step to take. Not all separated couples divorce. Many continue to work on the problems they faced as a married couple and then successfully reconcile (Wineberg, 1994). Others remain separated indefinitely (Morgan, 1988). They may live separately but not divorce because of financial reasons, such as not being able to afford legal fees, or opposition on religious grounds. Others may decide that their marital problems cannot be rectified, so they seek a divorce.

The Many Dimensions of Divorce

Divorce is usually a drawn-out process because there are so many emotions involved, decisions to be made, laws to adhere to, and so many people in different arenas affected. Divorce is not simply the ending of a relationship between two people; it is the altering or even severing of many personal and legal ties. A divorce may signal the death of relationships with other family members; with friends who find themselves taking sides; with neighbors whom you will rarely see now that you have moved away; with community groups of which you are no longer a member or can no longer afford to join; with even your children, whom you may see infrequently (Kitson, 1992; Miller, Smerglia, Gaudet, & Kitson, 1998). Bohannon (1971) refers to these different dimensions as the **stations of divorce**: the emotional, legal, economic, co-parental, community, and psychic dimensions of divorce. These dimensions are interrelated, and together they be-

gin to capture the complexity of the divorce experience. Several will be discussed below.

The Emotional and Psychic Divorce

This stage begins long before any legal steps are taken. One or both partners may feel angry, resentful, sad, or rejected. Generally, one spouse initiates the break-up of the marriage. Vaughan, who interviewed people about this process, refers to this person as the "initiator" (1990). This person has the advantage of preparing emotionally for the separation and using its threat as a way to demand change. But Hopper's research, which involved in-depth interviews, found that the labels of "initiator" versus "noninitiator" of the divorce were virtually accidental and random (1993). He found that both spouses were generally aware of multiple marital problems, experienced discontent and contemplated divorce or separation, and were ambivalent about the best way to resolve the marital problems. But he also noted that once their labels as either initiators or noninitiators emerged and took hold, these became the basis of distinct vocabularies used throughout the divorce. Despite mutual uncertainty, discontent, and ambivalence before the divorce, divorcing couples could easily identify who initiated the divorce—the initiator is the person who made the final decision. A woman who is a noninitiator, and in the middle of a divorce after twenty-five years of marriage, illustrates the randomness with which these labels are applied:

> Eleven years back I was ready to take steps. Yeah, I was ready to leave. And he was the one that convinced me, "No, I'm worth fighting for, and the relationship is worth fighting for, and let's work on it." I was ready to leave then, and he knew it, and I was real serious. (Hopper, 1993: 805)

Seven years ago in a light summer rain I got married in a meadow of wildflowers in the mountains of Colorado. The morning of the wedding, my soon-to-be husband and I went running with our friends, and called it the Dowry Dash. We talked about wearing our running shoes to the wedding, but our friends decided it wouldn't be a good idea, as it would be too easy to run away if one of us got the jitters.

People said rain at a wedding brings lasting happiness. They must be right, because I still feel happy. Today it's cool, gray and raining—just like our wedding day—with the tall grass and willows in the field behind our house generously soaked from the morning's shower.

Things change in seven years. Today I performed a ceremony to say goodbye to my soon-to-be ex husband, to symbolically put the marriage behind me so I can start my new life. I found a tape of the music played during the wedding and put it in my Walkman. I sat down on the floor and sorted through old photos from races and good times my husband and I had shared with our running friends.

Then I removed the photograph of my husband from the leather frame my sister gave me and replaced it with one of my dog,

Joanie, sitting alone, looking wind-blown and happy. I called Joanie over to show her the picture that will now sit on my desk, and through tears, explained why this was so.

Afterwards I took her for a run in the rain, down to the field on a narrow path, through thick weeds and tiny yellow wildflowers, both of us getting wet from the light drizzle. We stopped momentarily by a ditch, watching the muddy water flow downstream. I imagined the water carrying away my pain, flushing me clean.

Rounding the curve, my eyes caught sight of a beautiful white poppy in the field, several yards off the path. It was the only flower out there in acres of high, green vegetation, and its white color stood out like a single cloud in a clear blue sky.

I ran over to it through the dripping grass, jumping over tall weeds, then bent down to take a closer look. I separated the delicate wet petals with my fingers.

The poppy reminded me of the calla lilies I carried in my wedding; still, it was different. This flower had a genuine, thorny, wild look—the way I've heard people describe me. A bright yellow display of anthers surrounded a five-sided centerpiece of deep maroon. It had a rough, spiky stem and leaves. The livery hairs on the stem gave it a

mature, stalwart look.

Standing alone in the rain-soaked meadow, the poppy had been strong enough to weather the morning's downpour; its petal hadn't collapsed. As we ran further away, I could still see it, a brilliant white dot in the carpeted shades of green and yellow framed by cottonwood and willow trees. Standing out there in the drenched field, the poppy looked happy—soft yet tough, determined to live among the thick stalks and grasses.

Later, when Joanie and I arrived home, I was still thinking about the flower. I stood on the back doorstep, watching the sun begin to break through the clouds. In the meadow 400 yards away, I could see the poppy, distinct and proud. It was looking upward at the broken sky, its arms outstretched in the rain, smiling confidently, happy to be alive.

By Alene Nitzy

Critical Thinking

1. Why are ceremonies and rituals so important?

2. Which life changes tend to have rituals associated with them, and which ones do not? Why is that?

Vaughan reports that the initiator commonly expresses general discontent at first, but without attributing it to the marriage per se. The initiator may try to alter the relationship or the spouse's behavior by suggesting such things as a new job, having a baby, or in some other way changing the nature of the relationship substantially.

Research suggests that, generally speaking, women tend to show better emotional adjustment after a divorce (Arendell, 1995; Zeiss, Zeiss, & Johnson, 1980). Men often have a more difficult time after a divorce, and in some cases this stress is so extreme that it can lead to increased illness or an early death (Riessman & Gerstel, 1985). For a variety of reasons, men who are separated, widowed, or divorced have higher mortality rates than do comparable women. First, males are less likely to see themselves as the initiator of the divorce (Braver, Whitley, & Ng, 1993). Second, they have a weaker network of supportive relationships (Arendell, 1995). Third, men are more dependent on marriage (Hemstrom, 1996). The image of the carefree bachelor, free from the pressures of a wife and children, does not fit the reality of many men's lives. Many men, particularly those men who were in traditional marriages, have less experience in maintaining a household. Coupled with the loss of their spouse and children, many men initially find the tasks of cooking, cleaning, shopping, and other routine household tasks to be daunting.

As time moves on, most people adjust to the separation and divorce. The "psychic divorce" refers to the regaining of psychological autonomy and beginning to feel whole and complete again as a single person. In this aspect of the divorce experience, people must learn to distance themselves from the still-loved and hated aspects of the ex-spouse (Bohannan, 1971). Masheter's (1997) study of 791 divorced couples obtained from courthouse records from seven counties in one state reports that respondents have significantly better adjustment to divorce if they fit into one of two categories: (1) high degree of friendship and low levels of preoccupation with the ex-spouse, and (2) high hostility towards the ex-spouse and low levels of preoccupation with him or her.

The Family Narrative box on page 523 examines one woman's "letting go" ceremony. It gave her the finality needed to say good-bye to her ex-spouse.

The Legal and Co-Parental Divorce

The couple must end their relationship legally as well as emotionally. This involves dividing up their assets and property, including the home, cars, savings, and retirement accounts. It also means dividing up their debts, including credit cards and loans. Few couples can make these decisions easily. Hiring attorneys to iron out the division of assets can average over $10,000. However, most divorce settlements are reached through informal negotiation rather than through the courts (Jacob, 1992). **Divorce mediation** is a nonadversarial means of resolution whereby the divorcing couple, along with a third party

Divorce mediation has helped many couples negotiate the terms of their divorce decree.

such as a therapist or trained mediator, negotiate the terms of their financial, custody, and visitation settlement.

One survey of more than 400 divorced persons found that after one year, women tend to be more satisfied than men with a number of legal aspects of divorce, including custody of children, visitation, property, and financial settlements (e.g., medical insurance, school expenses, travel)—with the notable exception of child support (Sheets & Braver, 1996). Another study of 1,666 adults with household incomes of at least $100,000 found similar results: 37 percent of the men believed that the division of assets was equal, compared to 52 percent of the women (Hammonds, 1998). These findings are interesting, especially given the data presented in the next section indicating that women's standard of living declines more dramatically than men's following a divorce. Perhaps it takes women a few years to feel the brunt of their financial situation?

In the no-fault divorce laws found in the United States, both partners are treated as equals, theoretically. Each is supposed to receive half of the family assets, and the former wife is expected to support herself and contribute to the support of their children. Yet one study reports that fathers without custody of children received 47 percent of the assets, whereas mothers with custody received 28 percent (Quinn, 1993). Most fathers continue to have significant assets. According to the National Longitudinal Study of Youth, 70 percent of thirty-year-old nonresidential fathers have positive assets, such as car equity, stocks and savings, and housing and business equity. Among these men, assets average over $100,000 in 1993 dollars (Pirog-Good & Amerson, 1997).

But how does a couple, or the court, divide up an asset such as a college degree that one spouse earned while the other worked full time at a low-wage job to support him or her? In 1979 a Kentucky court had such a case before it, *Inman v. Inman*. The couple

met while undergraduates at a university, and both had intended to attend medical school. Mr. Inman attended medical school first while Ms. Inman supported him, with the understanding that after he received his medical degree it would be her turn to attend medical school. Instead, the couple separated a year after Mr. Inman finished his studies. In court, Ms. Inman asked that she be awarded compensation for her husband's medical degree, arguing that she had paid for it in the anticipation of joint benefits, but because of the divorce only Mr. Inman would reap the benefits. After hearing her arguments, the court ordered the husband to reimburse her for the costs of his medical school, plus inflation and interest (Weitzman, 1985).

When children are present, the legal issues surrounding divorce become more complex. The couple must try to design and agree upon co-parenting strategies. For example, there is the issue of custody. Where will the children live, and who will have the right to make important decisions about their lives?

Legal Custody **Legal custody** refers to who has the legal authority to make important decisions concerning the children, such as where they will go to school, where they will reside, and who will be notified in case of a health emergency or school problem. It may have nothing to do with the child's living arrangement.

In the past, legal custody was usually given solely to the parent with whom the child lived. But this is changing. Increasingly, noncustodial parents (usually fathers) retain their legal rights with respect to their children, referred to as **joint legal custody**. Joint custody of children is estimated at approximately 13 percent (Cancian & Meyer, 1998). Wilcox, Wolchik, and Braver (1998) report from their multi-year study of custody issues after divorce among 378 families that mothers' sociodemographic characteristics were relatively unimportant in predicting their opinions about sharing legal custody. Instead, mothers were more likely to prefer joint legal custody, as opposed to sole maternal custody, when they were (a) experiencing low levels of conflict with their ex-husband, (b) experiencing low levels of anger/hurt over the divorce, (c) experiencing fewer visitation problems, (d) perceiving the ex-husband to be more competent as a parent, (e) experiencing little psychological distress, and/or (f) receiving social support to maintain the father–child relationship. Mothers' income, age, and religious affiliation; their ex-husbands' income; and their children's gender and ages were not associated with a particular preference. Fathers with joint legal custody, compared to fathers without custody, pay more child support, spend more time with their children, and have more overnight visits with their children (Seltzer, 1998).

Physical custody refers to the place where the children actually reside. The court maintains that living arrangements should be based on the best interests of the child, which theoretically should not discriminate against men or women in any systematic way. In the vast majority of divorces, mothers have physical custody. However, men generally do not want physical custody (Cherlin, 1999). When men do sue for custody, they win either sole or joint custody more than 70 percent of the time (Mansnerus, 1995).

Noncustodial fathers report a poorer relationship with their children than do fathers who are either married or divorced and reside with their children (Shapiro & Lambert, 1999). Shapiro and Lambert speculate on why co-residence is so important to fathers' evaluations of their relationship with their children. First, we may be seeing a selection effect: single fathers with custody may value their relationship with their children more, which is why they sought custody in the first place. Second, the presence of children in the home allows the father a greater sense of control over their lives. Third, co-residence may also free the father from the aggravation

associated with negotiating future visits. Fourth, living together may encourage fathers to become more involved in their children's lives.

Shapiro and Lambert also note that there are psychological costs to living with children. Fathers who reside with their children after a divorce are less happy than both divorced nonresidential fathers and married fathers. The researchers suggest two possible explanations. First, children in the home demand time and energy and limit personal freedom. Second, single parenthood may be more emotionally taxing for males than females because of their socialization experiences and smaller close-confidant networks.

King and Heard (1999), using a national data set based on interviews with 1,565 single mothers, report that the percentage of mothers who are satisfied with fathers' visitation is highest in families in which fathers either visit most often (88 percent) or once a week (76 percent). As shown in Table 12.4, mothers are least satisfied (and report more conflict) when fathers have low to intermediate levels of contact.

In a growing number of cases, approximately 16 percent, families and courts are deciding on **joint physical custody,** meaning that children spend a substantial portion of time in the homes of both parents, perhaps alternating weeks or days within a week. Be-

TABLE 12.4	Percentage of Mothers Satisfied with Father's Visitation	
FREQUENCY OF VISITS	MOTHERS WHO ARE SATISFIED (%)	MOTHERS WHO REPORT CONFLICTS (%)
None	71	7
Once a year	58	26
Several times a year	59	33
One to three times a month	66	34
Once a week	76	30
Several times a week	88	22

Source: Adapted from King and Heard (1999).

In "joint physical custody" arrangements, children have two homes that they share nearly equally.

cause this arrangement requires a tremendous amount of cooperation, it tends to work best when both parents want it and are willing to work with each other to provide smooth transitions for the children (Buchanan, Maccoby, & Dornbusch, 1991). It generally does not work well when there is conflict or tensions among parents or when one parent feels like the arrangement was foisted upon him or her. Arditti and Madden-Derdich (1997) report that mothers in joint custody arrangements often report better relationships with their ex-spouses. However, this may be a cause, rather than a consequence, of joint custody.

Joint physical custody is controversial. Critics suggest that it is disruptive to children's routines and school schedules. They claim that it can exacerbate conflict between parents because no two parenting strategies are identical, and that situation creates loyalty conflicts for children. Supporters suggest that it lightens the economic and emotional responsibilities of single parenthood and that it provides men with the opportunity to routinely care for and nurture their chil-

dren—which, in turn, is in the child's best interest.

Child Support Noncustodial parents have a legal responsibility to support their children. For much of this country's history, this was done as a private arrangement by the former spouses; the noncustodial parent (usually the father) negotiated with the mother a **child support order,** a legal document delineating the amount and circumstances surrounding the financial support of noncustodial children (Garfinkel, Meyer, & McLanahan, 1998). Not surprisingly, the amount of awards varied widely, even among similar types of families. In the past, the administrative authority for child support was left to the local courts, and an individual judge had the power to decide whether the residential father should be required to pay and what the payment should be. Enforcement was minimal; usually, the burden of pursuing overdue payments was left to the mother.

Prior to 1979, the data on child support are sketchy. By 1979, the Census Bureau added questions pertaining to child support to its Current Population Survey (CPS), and these data began to provide a clearer picture: only 60 percent of mothers with children who were eligible for child support had a legal arrangement requiring the father to pay. And of the 60 percent of fathers with child support orders, one-half of them paid the full amount due, one-quarter paid only a portion of what was due, and one-quarter paid nothing (U.S. Census Bureau, 1983).

FACT OR FICTION?

Approximately one-quarter of parents ordered to pay child support fail to pay the full amount regularly.

Since the mid-1970s, the federal government has stepped up efforts to improve the collection of child support payments. A series of laws were passed aimed at increasing the proportion of eligible children with a child support order, increasing and standardizing child support orders, and increasing collection rates (Garfinkel, Meyer, & McLanahan, 1998). These include the Child Support Enforcement (CSE) amendment to Title IV of the Social Security Act and establishing the federal Office of Child Support Enforcement (OCSE), which requires all states to establish comparable state offices and which provides federal funding to augment states' funding of enforcement.

How successful are these stepped-up efforts? Overall trends in child support have not improved dramatically since the 1970s, as shown in Figure 12.5. Approximately one-half of noncustodial parents with a child support decree pay the full amount. Yet this graph reveals that court awards to never-married women—the group least likely to receive child support—have increased fourfold

between 1976 and 1997 (Urban Institute, 1999). How then is it possible that the trends in child support show virtually no improvement? The answer lies in sheer demographics. There is a tremendous increase in the number of never-married mothers. This large increase depresses any improvement we might see in overall rates of child support receipt. Thus, although there have been some successes, when looking at single mothers as a whole, the proportion who receive child support has remained virtually unchanged since the mid-1970s (Urban Institute, 1999).

FICTION

One-half fail to pay the full amount regularly.

Some spouses may request **alimony.** This is payment by one partner to the other, usually husband to wife, and is generally only temporary. It is designed to support the

FIGURE 12.5 Percentage of Single Mothers Receiving Child Support Between 1977 and 1997, by Marital Status

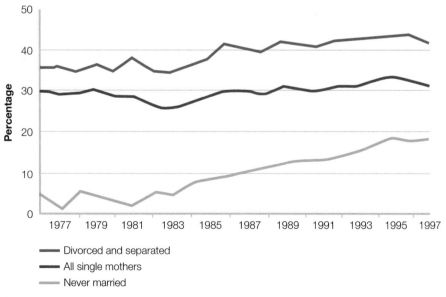

Source: The Urban Institute (1999).

more dependent spouse for a period of time. The legal system assumes that women can be self-supporting following a divorce but recognizes that a small segment of women may need some short-term financial assistance, especially if they have been out of the labor market for a period of time raising children. However, alimony is not commonly awarded.

The Economic Divorce

Policy makers and researchers are concerned with the economic consequences of divorce for men, women, and children. A recent study of 9,824 individuals approaching retirement found that those who had divorced had considerably less wealth than those who had remained married throughout their adult lives (Wilmoth & Koso, 2002). Marital history is particularly important to women's wealth outcomes. The researchers also found that remarriage offset much of the negative effects of divorce.

FACT OR FICTION?

Both men and women's standard of living declines after a divorce.

Weitzman (1985) concluded from a sample of Los Angeles residents that the economic consequences of divorce are devastating for women and children. She estimated that women's standard of living declined by 73 percent while men's actually increased by 42 percent. Peterson (1996), in a reanalysis of these data, found that the discrepancy was not quite as large as Weitzman had concluded; he found that women's standard of living was reduced by 27 percent while men's increased by 10 percent. The precise figure here is subject to debate, but both sides agree that the economic fallout of a divorce tends to favor men over women and children. African American women are especially vulnerable after a divorce (Pollock & Stroup, 1994).

FICTION

On average, a woman's standard of living declines while a man's improves.

As Weitzman reports, after a divorce, fathers become *single,* and mothers become *single parents,* meaning that child-rearing responsibilities have a significant effect upon a woman's lifestyle. For example, a woman's employment opportunities may be more restricted than those of her ex-husband because the demands of children may force her to alter her work schedule, reduce her ability to work overtime, and limit opportunities for travel, relocation, and further training needed for advancement. Nearly half (49 percent) of all female-headed households (combined group of divorced, never-married, and widowed women) have incomes in the bottom quintile of incomes in the United States (the poorest 20 percent of household incomes) compared to only 28 percent of male-headed households. One reason is the lower wages paid to women generally.

Some women have intermittent work histories. Some couples have a mutual agreement that, at least while the children were young, the husband will support the family while the mother stays in the home to take care of their children. Not surprisingly, after several years of unemployment, some women are not able to reenter the labor force easily. Their skills might be outdated, and they cannot command high salaries. Yet the legal system expects mothers to become self-supporting quickly.

Consequently, many single mothers and their children live in poverty. Over one-third of female-headed households are poor. Low wages coupled with sporadic and inadequate child support doom many children to live in impoverished homes. Things are quite different in many other industrialized nations, including most of Western Europe, where the government intervenes and assists families to a greater extent than in the United States.

For example, in France, where the unemployment rate is 50 percent higher than in the United States, the rate of child poverty is 6 percent, as compared to approximately 20 percent here. As economist Barbara Bergmann notes (1996), the difference is due to the extensive commitment made by the French government to improve the conditions for children, such as by providing free health care, free public nursery schools, low-cost child care, and family allowances to help parents better provide for their children.

The Community Divorce

Marriage joins families and friendship networks. Divorce, in contrast, breaks them apart, sometimes in a confusing and bitter fashion. Relationships between former in-laws or friends whom the couple shared together frequently deteriorate or vanish altogether. Divorced people may feel uncomfortable with their old friends because of their allegiances. Also, their married friends may become reluctant to remain friends with a divorced person because he or she may be seen as a threat to their own marriage by challenging the couple to examine the strengths and weaknesses of their marriage.

One group that has grabbed media attention and legal protection in their quest to maintain ties after a divorce is grandparents. Grandparents are recognized as important kin who provide unique benefits to children (Spitze, Logan, Deane, & Zerger, 1994). As Wallerstein and Blakeslee write, based on their ten-year study of the effects of divorce on children (1989: 111),

> Grandparents can play a particular role, especially if their marriages are intact: symbolic proof to children that relationships can be lasting, reliable, and dependable. Grandparents also convey a sense of tradition and special commitment to the young that extends beyond and over the parents' heads. Their encouragement, friendship, and affection has special meaning for children of divorce; it specifically counteracts the children's sense that all relationships are unhappy and transient.

Virtually all states now have statutes that grant grandparents visitation rights in some contexts, including the opportunity to

© Rob & Sas/Corbis

Virtually all states now have laws that give grandparents the opportunity to secure visitation rights with their grandchildren after divorce.

Most people assume that persons stuck in bad marriages will be happier when they divorce. But is this true? A team of family scholars conducted a research study designed to examine this question. The answer appears to be a resounding "No."

The research team, headed by Dr. Linda Waite of the University of Chicago, used data collected by the National Survey of Family and Households. Out of more than 5,000 married adults, 645 reported being unhappily married. Five years later, these same adults were interviewed again. Some unhappily married people continued to stay married, but many had divorced during these five years. The researchers then compared detailed and complex measures of psychological well-being between these two groups— those who remained married and those who chose to divorce.

First, the study found that, on average, unhappily married adults who divorced were no happier than those who remained married on any of the twelve separate measures of psychological well-being. For example, divorce did not generally reduce or eliminate feelings of depression, raise self-esteem, or increase a sense of mastery. This was the case regardless of income, race, gender, or age.

Second, the researchers also found that two-thirds of unhappily married spouses who stayed married over these five years reported that their marriages had improved. Interestingly, those who were in the least-happy marriages at the time of the first interview reported the most dramatic turnaround.

"Staying married is not just for the children's sake. Some divorce is necessary, but results like these suggest the benefits of divorce have been oversold," says Dr. Waite.

Why doesn't divorce make people happier? The authors of the study suggest that while divorce eliminates some stresses, it creates new ones as well, which can have deeply negative consequences. These can include the response of one's spouse to the divorce; the reactions of children; potential disappointments and aggravations in custody, child support, and visitation orders; new financial stresses; health problems; and new relationships.

To follow up on the findings that two-thirds of unhappy marriages had become happy five years later, the researchers also conducted focus group interviews with 55 formerly unhappy spouses who had turned their marriages around. The focus groups revealed that many of these currently happy couples had periods of serious family problems, including such things as alcoholism, infidelity, verbal abuse, neglect, depression, illness, and work problems.

However, why did these marriages survive while others did not? Spouses interviewed in the focus groups generally had a low opinion of the benefits of divorce and had friends and family members who encouraged them to stay married.

go to court to seek visitation rights against a custodial parent who has refused them the opportunity to see their grandchild. However, these statutes are beginning to be challenged on the premise that they violate parental rights.

Difficult as all these dimensions may be, people who divorce do so because they assume that they will be happier afterward. However, as shown in the Focus on Family Research box above, a large recent research study calls this "divorce assumption" into question.

Consequences of Divorce for Children

Approximately one-half of all divorce cases occur among families with children. While presumably at least one of the spouses

Because of their commitment to marriage, these couples invested great effort in overcoming or enduring problems in their relationships. The stories of how their marriages became happier fell into three broad headings:

- *The marital endurance ethic.* Most commonly, couples reported that their marriages got happier not just because partners resolved problems but because they stubbornly outlasted them. Over the course of time, many of the sources of conflict eased.

- *The marital work ethic.* Spouses actively worked to solve problems, change behavior, and improve communication. They consulted with counselors or clergy, they enlisted help or advice from relatives, and they rearranged schedules to spend more time together.

- *The personal happiness epic.* Marriage problems did not diminish appreciably; however, married couples found alternative ways to improve their own happiness and build a good and happy life despite a mediocre marriage.

These results raise an important question: Would unhappy spouses who divorced have been happier if they had remained in their marriages? The research team cannot say for sure. In most respects, the unhappy spouses who divorced and those who stayed married were similar in terms of demographics. Those who ended up divorcing tended to be a little younger, had lower incomes, and were more likely to be employed and to have children, but the differences were not large. However, there is one important difference between the two groups. Unhappy marriages that ended in divorce were more than twice as likely to contain violence, 21 percent to 9 percent, respectively. While no one should have to endure violence, the researchers suggest that if only these worst-case marriages ended up in divorce, we would expect divorce to be associated with improved psychological well-being. The fact that it is not suggests that benefits associated with divorce for many low-conflict marriages may be "oversold."

Source: Adapted from American Values (2002). *Does Divorce Make People Happy?* For further information or to order a copy, contact www.americanvalues.org. Reprinted with permission.

Critical Thinking

1. The results of this study challenge the conventional wisdom that unhappily married couples will be happier if they divorce. Do you have any personal experience (as a child or an adult) that relates to this issue? How does your experience confirm or conflict with their findings?

2. How would you design another study to further examine this issue?

---

chooses to divorce, it isn't necessarily the case that the children have any choice in the matter. They live with the decisions made by their parents. Very few children want their parents to separate and divorce. In one study involving twenty-eight children whose parents had separated, all the children wanted their parents to get back together (Holroyd & Sheppard, 1997).

What are the social and psychological effects of divorce on children? It may be helpful to distinguish between short-term effects and long-term effects.

Short-Term Effects of Divorce on Children

The first year or two after a divorce has been labeled a "crisis period" for both adults and children because of the grief and the numerous challenges that they experience (Chase-Lansdale & Hetherington, 1990). During this highly stressful time, parents may be distracted and preoccupied with their own grief and distress, thereby ignoring the needs of their children. While in the throes of this crisis period, parents may not be able to offer the support, nurturance, and discipline that their children need. Some, in fact, turn to their children for comfort and support, putting their children in adult roles that may be well beyond their years.

One team of researchers found that these issues do not only occur after the divorce, but beforehand as well (Sun & Li, 2002). Using a large and nationally representative sample, the researchers examined the extent to which children's academic performance and psychological well-being before and after their parents' divorce compared with their peers in families whose parents did not divorce. They looked at four different points in time, from approximately three years before the divorce to three years after the divorce, and found significant differences between the two groups.

Before, during, and immediately after a divorce, children often feel guilty and depressed. Young children in particular may feel that they are responsible for their parents' conflict and divorce—that if they had just behaved better, their parents would not have felt the need to separate. Their world as they have known it has come to an abrupt end. At the very least, it will be modified substantially.

In the crisis period, children generally face a number of situations that they must learn to cope with. These may include (a) handling parental conflict, (b) dealing with the loss of a parent, (c) living with a reduced standard of living, and (d) adjusting to many transitions.

Handling Parental Conflict Sometimes parents involve children inappropriately in their disputes. They may try to use the children as a weapon to hurt the ex-spouse, get them to take sides in a dispute, or use children as a way to pry out information. Parents may communicate their anger and hostility toward each other to their children, and demean and ridicule their ex-spouse. Children experience tremendous stress in these situations. During and after a break-up, children have fewer emotional and behavioral problems if their parents can cooperate or at least minimize overt conflict in front of them.

FACT OR FICTION?

Nearly half of divorced children see their fathers less than once a month.

Dealing with the Loss of a Parent During a separation and after the divorce, children most often live with their mothers, and many children see their fathers only sporadically, if at all. Bianchi (1990) found in her study that more than 60 percent of noncustodial fathers did not contact their children at all over a one-year period. Judith Seltzer's study, drawing upon a representative sample of adults who were married when their child was born, found that after a divorce, over 20 percent saw their fathers once a year or less, and nearly half of the fathers saw their children less than once a month. Only 12 percent of fathers reported seeing their child at least several times a week (Seltzer, 1991).

Why do so many noncustodial fathers fail to see their children regularly? The issue is more complex than we might first think. Certainly, many fathers *choose* to ignore their children. But residential parents (generally mothers) may also interfere with the relationship between father and children in one of the following ways:

1. Being unsupportive of access.
2. Not cooperating in arranging visits.
3. Being inflexible in altering visitation schedules.
4. Discouraging children from visiting. (Pearson and Thoennes, 1998)

Over 20 percent saw their fathers once a year or less, and nearly half of the fathers saw their children less than once a month. Only 12 percent of fathers reported seeing their child at least several times a week.

A Reduced Standard of Living As discussed above, the standard of living among mothers and their children often drops dramatically after a divorce, requiring an adjustment by everyone. Certain types of clothing, outings, vacations, or other aspects of a lifestyle that were the norm prior to the divorce may no longer be possible. Given the severely limited budgets of most divorced families, consumption patterns must change drastically. Teenagers may need to work at after-school jobs to provide basic necessities for the family.

Adjusting to Transitions A divorce requires that both children and adults go through many transitions, some of which can be confusing to children. The departure of one parent is likely only the first of many transitions to come. If the legal settlement requires that assets be divided, then it is possible that the family's home will be sold, necessitating a move to a new house or apartment. Two-thirds of divorced mothers move in the first year after a divorce (McLanahan, 1983). For children, this may involve new schools, new neighborhoods, new friends, and leaving behind all that was familiar. Children must also adapt to a visitation schedule with the noncustodial parent and adjust to seeing him or her in unfamiliar surroundings. Over time, both parents are likely to resume dating, and children will therefore meet new partners of their parents. Cohabitation is increasingly common, so many children must also adapt to other adults moving in (and out) of the household. Finally, since most single parents eventually remarry, chil-

dren will likely experience stepparent relationships. These issues are discussed more fully in the next chapter.

Longer-Term Effects of Divorce on Children

Many research studies suggest that the effects of divorce on children continue to be felt for years after the actual divorce occurs. While most children adjust adequately over time to the transitions in their lives, a sizable minority continue to be plagued by depression or other behavioral problems. In the 1970s and early 1980s, Wallerstein and Blakeslee conducted a longitudinal study of sixty families in the San Francisco area who had experienced a divorce, following them for ten years. This is a small and nonrepresentative sample; consequently, we should be careful about interpreting and generalizing the results. But the early findings are illuminating and have set the stage for later research. The researchers found that, ten years following a divorce, over a third of the children were still depressed and suffering from a number of behavioral problems related to the divorce (Wallerstein, 1983; Wallerstein & Blakeslee, 1989).

Divorce doesn't harm children over the long term.

Amato and Booth (1991), using a national sample of 2,033 married adults, compared the well-being of those adults who had experienced the divorce of their parents with those adults whose parents had not divorced. They found that the adults whose parents had divorced were more likely to report to be more depressed and to have lower social, family, and psychological well-being, although the differences were not large. However, they also found that adults who grew up in conflict-ridden homes with parents who remained married to each other *also* experienced greater emotional problems. Moreover, they noted that adults who grew up in low-stress but divorced homes were about as happy as adults who grew up in low-stress homes with parents who remained married. Thus, Amato and Booth conclude that divorce doesn't always have harmful effects, especially if the parents' divorce causes minimum disruption in children's lives.

Other researchers have compared the achievements of children, adolescents, and adults who grew up in divorced and nondivorced households (Amato & Keith, 1991; Bianchi, 1990; Biblarz & Gottainer, 2000; Cherlin, Chase-Lansdale, & McRae, 1998; McLanahan & Sandefur, 1994; Spruijt & Goede, 1997; Sun & Li, 2002). Often using large, nationally representative samples, they have noted that parental divorce is related to a variety of negative outcomes. Children whose parents divorce are more likely to become pregnant prior to marriage or impregnate someone, drop out of school and have lower academic achievement, experience more behavioral problems, use alcohol or drugs, have poorer health, suffer from depression, and be idle or unemployed. For example, Biblarz and Gottainer (2000) used the 1972–1996 General Social Surveys, which are representative samples from more than 35,000 people in the United States, to compare outcomes of children who grew up in single-mother families because of divorce or widowhood to those of children in two-biological-parent families. They found that, even when controlling for important background factors such as race, gender, mother's level of education, year, and age, children from single-mother homes produced by parental divorce are significantly less likely than those from two-biological-parent families to complete high school, attend college (given high school completion), or graduate from college (given college en-

try). As adults, they are also likely to hold occupations that are generally lower in status, and they have a lower level of general psychological well-being. In contrast, children from widowed single-mother homes did not differ significantly from two-biological-parent families on any of these variables except having slightly lower odds of completing high school.

Recent research suggests that many children suffer long-term effects from divorce.

These findings certainly do not mean that *all* children from divorced households experience these outcomes. Many children whose parents have divorced lead happy, well-adjusted, and successful lives. It simply means that they are more likely to have these problems than are children from families in which parents have not divorced. In fact, many of these negative outcomes are related to the higher rates of poverty among children growing up in divorced households and are less apt to occur if the family has adequate financial resources. The lack of economic resources can result in stress for parents and children alike.

Age and Gender of the Child The children's ages at the time of the divorce and their gender seem to be important factors in understanding their adjustment. Divorce tends to be most detrimental to younger children, and boys tend to suffer more than girls (McCabe, 1997; Pagani, Boulerice, Tremblay, & Vitaro, 1997). Boys are more likely than girls to do poorly in school and have behavioral problems such as increased aggression, anxiety, or easy distraction, particularly among those who have little contact with their fathers (Bianchi, 1990). But Wallerstein and Blakeslee (1989) suggest that we might be seeing a "sleeper effect," meaning that behavioral problems in girls are simply delayed somewhat until adolescence or adulthood. They noted from their interviews that many girls and young women whose parents had divorced seemed to have a lingering sadness about the divorce. They were also often hesitant and fearful of making a commitment themselves.

Which Is Worse, Divorce or Marital Conflict?

The amount of conflict experienced during a divorce has important consequences for how easy or difficult it is for children to adjust to the situation, and how long lasting their trauma may be. Are children better off when their parents remain married despite high levels of conflict or when their parents end their marriage?

Children do not fare well when they experience tremendous conflict, violence, and name-calling, and also when they are put in the middle of their parents' struggle. This is true regardless of whether parents divorce or remain married. In fact, many researchers suggest that it is the amount of conflict rather than a divorce per se that causes the most harm to children. For example, a study by Amato and Booth (1997), based on telephone and in-person interviews conducted in 1980 and 1992 with a nationally representative sample, found that children who were in families with high marital conflict in 1980 were actually doing *better* in 1992 if their parents had divorced than if they had stayed together. They also found that children from low-conflict families were *worse* off if their parents divorced than if their parents had remained together.

These findings suggest that the worst situations for children are to be in either a high-conflict marriage that does not end in divorce or a low-conflict marriage that does end in divorce. If a marriage contains severe conflict, a divorce may indeed be better for the children than to be subjected to a family in continued turmoil. Sociologist Susan Jekielek found similar results using a large sample of families from the National Longitudinal Surveys of Youth (1998). Looking at 1,640 children between the ages of six and fourteen, she found that children in high-conflict but intact families had lower levels of well-being than did children whose highly conflicting parents divorced.

However, most unhappy marriages do not display extreme forms of conflict. In the

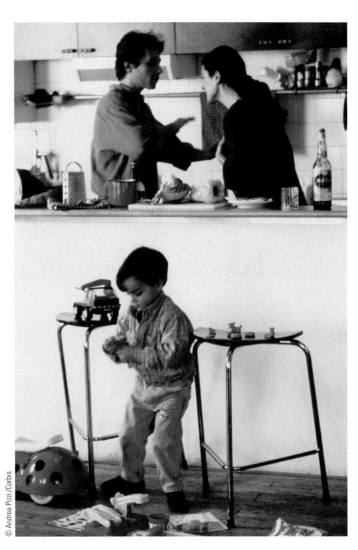

© Andrea Pizzi/Corbis

Are children in conflict-ridden homes better off if their parents divorce? It depends on the severity of the conflict, researchers say.

longitudinal study by Amato and Booth (1997), only one-quarter of parents who divorced between 1980 and 1992 reported any sort of domestic violence or reported that they disagreed "often" or "very often" with their spouse. Only 30 percent reported at least two serious quarrels during the previous month. Consequently, the authors conclude that the majority of children whose parents divorce probably experienced relatively low conflict and therefore would be better off if their parents had stayed together:

> If divorce were limited only to high conflict marriages, then divorce would generally be in children's best interest. Instead, with marital dissolution becoming increasingly socially acceptable, it is likely that people are leaving marriages at lower thresholds of unhappiness than in the past. Unfortunately these are the very divorces that are most likely to be stressful for children. Consequently, we conclude that the rise in marital disruption, although beneficial to some children, has, in balance, been detrimental to children. Furthermore, if the threshold of marital unhappiness required to trigger a divorce continues to decline, than outcomes for children of divorced parents may become more problematic in the future. (1997: 20)

Conclusion

Divorce is a common feature of U.S. society. Although we may tend to think of it as a personal mechanism for ending an unhappy marriage, divorce is far more complex than that. Divorce is not simply a personal issue; an intricate weaving of macrolevel structural and microlevel personal factors operates to explain rising and falling divorce rates. Despite its prevalence, divorce is usually a difficult and lengthy process for all involved. Divorce touches many aspects of our lives. Children are particularly vulnerable to the hardships associated with divorce, including a greater likelihood of poverty and other behavioral and social problems. But as we will see in the next chapter, sometimes divorce is not solely the ending of a relationship. With high rates of remarriage, divorce can also allow for the beginning of a new family unit.

Chapter Review

* What is the best way to calculate the divorce rate?

Many different methods are used to calculate the divorce rate. Some of them are misleading. The best method is the refined divorce rate, which is the number of divorces for every 1,000 married women.

* What factors are related to divorce, cross-culturally?

There are several important factors, including the country's level of socioeconomic development, the dominant religion that is practiced, and the degree of patriarchy.

* Is the rate of divorce in the United States currently increasing?

No. Although the rate of divorce in the United States has varied tremendously, it has been declining somewhat since 1980.

* Why did so many divorces occur in the 1960s and 1970s?

Many societal factors were involved, including changes in divorce laws, the rise in women's employment, and the changing attitudes toward divorce. Individual reasons for divorce include a parental divorce, age at marriage, the presence of children, nonmarital childbearing, the sex composition of children, race and ethnic background, education, income, and degree of similarity between spouses.

* Is divorce experienced differently by women and men?

In some ways yes, because of the gendered opportunities and constraints embedded in our culture. For example, women are more likely to report marital problems. They are also more likely to be impoverished after a divorce.

* What are the many dimensions of divorce?

Dimensions of divorce include the emotional and psychic divorce, the legal and co-parental divorce, the economic divorce, and the community divorce.

* Are child support and alimony common?

Virtually all divorcing couples with children have a child support order that outlines the amount of monthly support, its duration, and other specific features of the arrangement. However, despite this order, many noncustodial parents fail to make their full payment on a regular basis. Alimony is a payment to the spouse. It is awarded with far less frequency.

* What types of custody arrangements are available?

Legal custody refers to who has the legal authority to make decisions concerning the children. It may be either joint or sole. Physical custody refers to the place where the children actually reside. This can also be joint or sole.

* What are the consequences of divorce for children?

The consequences may vary depending on the age and gender of the child. However, a growing number of research studies suggest that divorce is often more harmful for children than we had previously thought. In very-high-conflict marriages, children may be better off if their parents divorce. In lower-conflict marriages, which constitute the majority of divorce scenarios, the children do more poorly than other children on a number of key indicators.

Key Terms

alimony: payment by one partner to the other, designed to support the more dependent spouse for a period of time

child support order: a legal document delineating the amount and circumstances of the financial support of noncustodial children

cross-sectional: a rate at only one point in time

divorce mediation: a nonadversarial means of resolution whereby the divorcing couple, along with a third party such as a therapist or trained mediator, negotiate the terms of their financial, custody, and visitation settlement

joint legal custody: a custody agreement allowing noncustodial parents (usually fathers) to retain their legal rights with respect to their children

joint physical custody: a custody agreement having children spend a substantial portion of time in the homes of both parents, perhaps alternating weeks or days within a week

legal custody: given to the parent who has the legal authority to make important decisions concerning the children after a divorce, such as where they will go to school, in what community or state they will reside, or who will be notified in case of a health emergency or school problem

no-fault divorce: a style of divorce in which a divorcing couple can go before a judge without having to blame each other

physical custody: the home where the children actually reside after a divorce

ratio of divorces to marriages in a given year: a misleading way to calculate the divorce rate suggesting that if 100,000 marriages took place last year, and 50,000 divorces occurred, then 50 percent of marriages end in divorce

refined divorce rate: the most appropriate way to measure divorce, based on the number of divorces per every 1,000 married women

stations of divorce: the interrelated emotional, legal, economic, co-parental, community, and psychic dimensions of divorce, which together begin to describe the complexity of the divorce experience

Resources on the Internet

These web sites have been selected for their relevance to the topics in this chapter. These sites are among the more stable, but please be aware that web site addresses change frequently.

Parents Without Partners

http://parentswithoutpartners.org

Parents Without Partners provides single parents and their children with an opportunity to enhance personal growth, self-confidence, and sensitivity toward others by offering an environment for support, friendship, and the exchange of parenting techniques. Provides free referrals to local PWP chapters, which offer social and educational opportunities for single parents.

National Fatherhood Initiative

http://www.fatherhood.org

The National Fatherhood Initiative (NFI) was founded in 1994 to stimulate a society-wide movement to confront the growing problem of father absence. NFI's mission is to improve the well-being of children by increasing the number of children growing up with involved, committed, and responsible fathers in their lives. NFI offers a quarterly newsletter and a catalog of books and videos focusing on fatherhood issues.

Divorce Source

http://www.divorcesource.com

Divorce Source offers an effective way to locate information and communicate with professionals and individuals sharing similar thoughts and experiences. Details alimony, child custody, and child support issues, and offers a state-by-state breakdown of resources.

Single Parent-Tips

http://www.singleparent-tips.com

Offers advice on custody, visitation, dealing with ex-spouses, legal matters, and effective parenting for single parents.

Companion Web Site for This Book

Virtual Society: The Wadsworth Sociology Resource Center

http://sociology.wadsworth.com

Begin by clicking the Student Resources section. Next, click Marriage and Family, and then click the cover image for this book. Select from the pull-down menu the chapter you are presently studying. You will have easy access to chapter resources such as MicroCase Online exercises, additional Web links, flashcards, InfoTrac exercises, and practice tests (that can be scored). In addition, to enhance and help with your study of marriages and families, be sure to investigate the rest of the rich sociology resources at Virtual Society.

Visit InfoTrac College Edition

 Another unique option available to you at the Student Resources section of the Virtual Society Web site described above is InfoTrac College Edition, an online library of hundreds of scholarly and popular periodicals. Here are three suggested key search terms for this chapter:

* Search keywords: *divorce + children*
* Search keywords: *single mother + poverty*
* Search keywords: *divorce + child custody*

Search recent years to get the latest information on these issues.

© Philip Lee Harvey/Stone-Getty Images

13 Family Life, Partnering, and Remarriage After Divorce

Now it's like we're sisters. That's how it changed when they got divorced. We started growing up together. It's like she had to start growing up all over again. Since then, it's just like we're sisters, and it makes it kind of tough when there is a conflict because I don't hesitate to talk back to her which you shouldn't do with your mother. It's so different. (female college student, age six at the time of her parents' divorce)

My relationship with my mother was just mediocre (before the divorce). After the divorce, things have changed in the sense that there's much more equality between the two of us. Before, it was always me crying on my mom's shoulder, and now it's me crying on my mom's shoulder and my mom cries on my shoulder. (female college student, age seventeen at the time of her parents' divorce)

Before my mom was like staying home completely for me and my brother, so I guess I was pretty close. She was pretty much the household mother. But when the divorce happened, she went back to work and we didn't see her as much. But we were still pretty close. Now we're very close. She's got to work and spends the majority of her time doing that, but now I understand it. (Female college student, age seven when her parents divorced)

| FACT OR FICTION?

Most people who are interviewed after a divorce claim that it was the wrong decision and that they have many regrets.

Being Single Again

After divorce, many relationships change. The above excerpts, from a study of 58 college students whose parents had divorced, reveal that divorce should not simply be viewed as an unhappy ending of a husband–wife relationship (Arditti, 1999). Severing a destructive relationship allows each partner to go his or her own way—to begin anew, whether it be to begin a new job, go back to school, cultivate a new friendship network, or find a more compatible partner.

Relationships Between Custodial Parents and Children

Although divorce can be a devastating experience, divorce can also be a positive new step in developing or strengthening other family relationships. For example, one study based on a representative sample in the United States found that children from single-parent families report that they talk to their mothers more often than do children in two-parent families (McLanahan & Sandefur, 1994). Although it is true that children whose parents divorced are more prone to experience negative outcomes (see Chapter 12), it is also true that most children do not experi-

Researchers have found that family relationships change after a divorce. Many mothers and daughters become more like friends.

with their custodial parent (mostly mothers) as generally close and satisfying. Most were very pleased that their mothers moved away from a more authoritarian parenting style. They perceived an increased closeness because of a more equal relationship.

Yet positive shifts in parental and children's roles after a divorce have rarely been studied. Instead, most scholars begin from a deficit model—that a home without two parents is somehow a "broken home." However, there is some evidence that after a divorce the relationship between mothers and their children is characterized by greater equality, intimacy, and companionship (Guttman, 1993). In the book *Separating Together: How Divorce Transforms Families,* the authors suggest that rigid authority structures and firm boundaries between parent and child often collapse after a divorce, and despite our thinking to the contrary, this may not necessarily be a bad thing (Stewart, Copeland, Chester, Malley, & Barenbaum, 1997). The authors report that rigid role boundaries are not associated with better outcomes for children and are associated with worse outcomes for mothers.

The Emotional Effects of Divorce

Most people who are interviewed after their divorce say that it was the right decision for them and that they have few regrets overall. One study found that over 90 percent of divorced men and women said that their lives were better after the divorce than before (Albrecht, Bahr, & Goodman, 1983). Another study that interviewed people ten years after their divorce reports that 80 percent of the women, but only 50 percent of the men, reported that they were happy to be out of their marriage (Wallerstein & Blakeslee, 1990). This does not mean that their lives are completely happy now or that these individuals initiated or even wanted the divorce at the

ence such outcomes, and instead lead happy and well-adjusted lives. Many children continue to have warm and loving relationships with one or both of their parents. Strong positive relationships are more likely to occur between children and the one parent with whom they continue to live, more so than with their noncustodial parent. In fact, it is these positive relationships that help to beat the odds against negative outcomes, such as dropping out of school or teen pregnancy. A primary factor in children's short-term and long-term adjustment to divorce is how effectively the custodial parent—usually the mother—functions as a parent (Furstenberg & Cherlin, 1991).

Arditti (1999) found that her college-age respondents described their relationships

time. Rather, they are reflecting, weighing the pros and cons, and have decided that divorce was the right decision.

Most claim that it was the right decision and that they have few regrets.

The divorce may not be completely behind them, however. Ten years after the divorce, about half the women and one-third of the men still felt anger towards their ex-spouse. Divorce tends to have a negative effect on adults' psychological well-being. Overall, people who are divorced tend to be less happy than people who are married (Waite & Gallagher, 2000).

Issues for Custodial Mothers: Downward Mobility

Often, the first few months or years after a divorce are a difficult time, with a multitude of conflicting emotions: elation, anger, depression, and sadness. This range of emotions sometimes makes it initially difficult to provide steady and secure parenting to children. It is not uncommon to witness for a period after a divorce more lax supervision, inconsistent discipline, and disorganization (Furstenberg & Cherlin, 1991). Quite often, this situation is exacerbated by the significant financial loss that many families face.

As discussed in the previous chapter, divorce can dramatically alter a family's standard of living. Divorce tends to reduce the money available to the woman, particularly if she has children to care for. Economist Rebecca London (1996), using data from a large, nationally representative sample, found that divorced mothers were twice as likely to receive welfare benefits (formerly called AFDC) as never-married mothers were. Ironically, divorce actually increases the standard of liv-

ing among noncustodial fathers, including those fathers who faithfully pay their child support.

Terry Arendell (1986) conducted in-depth interviews with approximately sixty women after a divorce to see how they fared financially. Most women initially assumed that after the divorce they would be able to maintain a middle-class lifestyle for themselves and their children. In particular, women in their twenties and thirties were confident that they could find or maintain employment that would provide sufficient income for their families. Older women were less confident about their earning capabilities but generally assumed that the difference in income would be made up by child support and alimony payments. Consequently, instead of focusing on financial matters, most recently divorced women claimed that they were more worried about the psychological effects of divorce on their children.

However, over time it became clear to virtually all women in the study that they had grossly underestimated the degree of financial hardship that they and their children would face. Ninety percent of them found that their incomes plummeted to the poverty line immediately after the divorce and remained very low for years. Most cut their expenses drastically or moved to cheaper housing so that they could pay their monthly bills. Few had any extra money left over after paying for the minimum necessities. Most felt trapped in their present situation and worried that their future would not improve. Women of all ages and at all income levels talked about the anxiety, depression, and despair that were associated with their financial difficulties—about trying to make ends meet after a divorce:

> I've been living hand to mouth all these years, ever since the divorce. I have no savings account. The notion of having one is foreign to me as in-

surance—there's no way I can afford insurance. I have an old pickup that I don't drive very often. In the summertime I don't wear nylons to work because I can cut costs there. Together the kids and I have had to struggle and struggle. Supposedly struggle builds character. Well, some things are not character building. There have been times when we've scoured the shag rug to see if we could find a coin to come up with enough to buy milk so we could have cold cereal for dinner. That's not character building (Arendell, 1986).

I owe $16,000 on this house. I could get about $135,000 for it, so I have a large equity. But it would have taken all of that to get that condominium I looked at, and my payments would still have been about $400 a month. I don't know how I'll be able to keep up the house, financially or physically. The house needs painting, and I can't keep up the yard work. I'd like to move. I'd like a fresh start. But the kids don't want to move, and I can't imagine how I'll handle all of this once they're gone. When the alimony stops, there'll be no way I can manage a move. I'm stuck here now (Arendell, 1986).

Essentially, I took an $80,000 drop in annual income. And I had to borrow again last year. This year I finally sold the house, and that was the only way I've made it. My change in lifestyle has been tremendous. Just my heating and electricity bill for our home was $350 a month. We just barely got by on $2,000 a month. I stopped buying clothes for myself. And I rented out a room in the house. It was a huge house, and that helped out. I let the cleaning woman and the gardener go. I didn't paint. I let the property taxes go until I sold the house and paid them then. I quit taking trips. This house I'm in now has much lower operating expenses. My son doesn't have the same things he'd had. His grandparents buy most of his shoes and clothes now. He used to have lots and lots, so it's been a change for him (Arendell, 1986).

I don't have a future. I can sit around and cry about that for a while, but then I have to move on and ask, what am I going to do about it? And there's not much I can do. What career can I start at my age? How do I retrieve all those years spent managing a family? (Arendell, 1986)

Custodial Fathers: A Rapidly Growing Group

After a divorce, most children reside with their mothers. However, the number of single fathers has grown rapidly in recent years, increasing 25 percent between 1995 and 1998 alone (U.S. Census Bureau, 2000c). This represents a jump from about 1.7 million to 2.1 million single dads, while the number of single mothers remained constant at around 9.8 million. Consequently, men now constitute one-sixth of the nearly twelve million single parents in 1998, up from one-seventh in 1995 and one-tenth in 1980. This means that approximately 3.1 million children live in a single-parent household headed by their father, a figure that has tripled since 1980.

Forty-four percent of these fathers are single because of a divorce. Of the remainder, 35 percent had never married, 12 percent were separated, 5 percent were widowed, and 5 percent were separated for reasons other than marital discord. The vast majority of single fathers are white (83 percent), and another 13 percent are African American or

Hispanic. Their average age is 38, with only one out of nine single fathers being under the age of 25.

In the past, fathers usually could not obtain custody of their children unless the mother was proven to be unfit or there were other extenuating circumstances. Today, fathers may seek and gain custody for a wide variety of reasons, often through mutual agreement with the mother. Fathers may step in because the mother is physically, emotionally, or financially unable to care for the children or because they simply want to maintain a sense of family. Moreover, fathers may seek and obtain custody at the request of their children, who for a variety of reasons may prefer to live with Dad rather than with Mom.

Table 13.1 indicates how children living in single-father households fare, as compared to children living with both biological parents. From the table we see that they have lower incomes, are twice as likely to be impoverished, have less-educated fathers, and are more likely to live in rental housing rather than in their own home. While these households are more vulnerable than two-parent families, they do have higher incomes than those headed by single mothers.

One study of African American custodial fathers found that they often gained custody by default rather than explicit choice, but the transition to full-time custody was made easier by the use of extended family support networks.

Parenting Among Low-Income and Working-Class African American Fathers Most studies of custodial fathers focus on the experience of white fathers who obtain custody following a divorce. A study by Hamer and Marchioro (2002) notes that, relative to white men, African American males

TABLE 13.1	Social and Economic Indicators for Children Living with Both Parents and Those Living with a Single Father	
CHILDREN LIVING WITH BOTH PARENTS	CHILDREN LIVING WITH A SINGLE FATHER
48.6 million children	3.1 million children
No significant increase between 1980 and 1998	Threefold increase between 1980 and 1998
1997 median family income: $52,553	1997 median family income: $29,313
Approximately 1 in 10 were poor in 1997.	Approximately 2 in 10 were poor in 1997.
86% had at least one parent with a high school diploma.	77% had a father with a high school diploma.
29% had at least one parent with a bachelor's degree or higher.	1% had a father with a bachelor's degree or higher.
One-quarter lived in rental housing.	One-half lived in rental housing.

Source: U.S. Census Bureau (2000).

are less likely to have ever married the mothers of their children. Therefore, what are the circumstances in which low-income and working-class African American men come to gain custody of their children, how do they transition to full-time parent, and what type of social-support networks do they use in parenting? The researchers interviewed twenty-four men from an impoverished midwestern urban area. They found that the fathers generally became full-time fathers by default, often without any explicit discussion with the mother. Some mothers gradually withdrew from parenting by leaving their children more and more with the father. Other mothers more abruptly disengaged themselves from their children. Most fathers were reluctant to accept their children but did so because of pressure or because they assumed the situation would be only temporary:

> I thought, "hey, she'll go in [into drug rehabilitation center], get cleaned up, and come and get these kids."
> But no! [laughing] It did not happen that way at all. These kids have been living with me; they are my pride and joy and have been since '94, that's when they came to live with Daddy. But in the beginning I tell you, I did not want any part of it and they [Child Service Workers] had to practically threaten me to do it—they made me realize there was no other place for my kids to go, and my kids had been through a lot of bad things with their mother. I didn't know the extent of it until they was living with me. (quoted in Hamer & Marchioro, 2002: 121)

The fathers' transition to full-time parenting was difficult for several reasons. First, they lacked confidence in their parenting abilities. Second, they had little money and found it difficult to provide for their children. Third, they had to make drastic changes in their lifestyle and give up a degree of freedom.

The transition to full-time parenting was made easier by the use of extended-kin support networks and shared living arrangements. Eight of the twenty-four fathers lived with other family members, usually parents or siblings. These, and those that lived independently, depended on family to help with babysitting, preparing children's meals, doing the laundry, and a multitude of other parenting tasks: "If it weren't for my family, times would be very, very rough" (2002: 124).

FACT OR FICTION?

Noncustodial fathers are more likely to pay their court-ordered child support for their children than are noncustodial mothers.

Single Fathers and Child Support An examination of child support among custodial parents reveals some interesting facts, according to the U.S. Census Bureau (2000c). For example, single fathers are less likely to be awarded child support than are custodial single mothers (40 percent versus 61 percent, respectively). Moreover, among those dads who are due court-ordered child support, they are also *less* likely to receive at least a portion of payments owed than are custodial mothers (57 percent versus 70 percent). In other words, it appears that mothers default on their child support obligations more frequently than do fathers.

Then why do we talk about "deadbeat dads" rather than "deadbeat moms" or "deadbeat parents"? One reason is the sheer number of noncustodial fathers who owe child support as compared to women. Since mothers constitute 85 percent of custodial parents, it stands to reason that the absolute number of fathers who owe support is far greater than the number of mothers who owe support. So, while mothers may be overrepresented among "deadbeats," their actual size in the population is comparatively small.

It is noncustodial mothers, not fathers, who are more likely to be "deadbeats."

The second reason that we seem to be more focused on "deadbeat dads" than "deadbeat moms" is that fathers who receive child support have higher average incomes than mothers who receive it. As we saw in Chapter 10, women tend to earn much lower incomes than men. Therefore, single-mother households are particularly vulnerable and in need of child support payments. Among fathers and mothers who received child support, their level of support was comparable, less than $4,000, on average. However, that amount represents a larger percentage of single mothers' overall budget, given their lower incomes.

Dating After Divorce

There are many paths after a divorce. Some adults, feeling angry or betrayed, swear that they will never marry again. Others desperately look for mates to ward off loneliness or financial difficulties (Ahrons, 1994).

Generally, finding a new partner is the most important factor in improving life satisfaction for both men and women, although research suggests that it is more critical to men than to women (Hetherington, Law, & O'Conner, 1993). Men tend to thrive in the security of marriage. Using data from a large, nationally representative sample, sociologist Adam Shapiro (1996) found that, compared to divorced persons, remarried individuals have significantly lower rates of both economic and psychological distress and depression. Economic issues significantly contributed to women's distress and depression, much more so than for men.

If the divorcing partners are young and were married only a short time, it may not be very difficult for them to begin dating again. In contrast, dating and courtship may be more difficult or awkward for people who have been married for a long time because they may be unaware of changing dating norms. Common questions may include these: Is it OK for a woman to initiate a date? Who does the paying? Should I meet him or her at the restaurant or be picked up at my house? Who pays for the babysitter? What sexual expectations will there be? Am I supposed to like her children right away? Are my children supposed to like him right away? Trying to guess the answer to these questions can make people uncomfortable.

One study asked remarried women to indicate the number of men whom they had dated prior to meeting their future spouse. The average number was between three and five dating partners. Ten percent had dated only their future spouse, and one-third of the women indicated that they had dated more than ten men prior to meeting their future spouse (Montgomery, Anderson, Herington, & Clingempeel, 1992).

© RF/Corbis

How does dating in middle age differ from dating among young adults?

Cohabitation and Repartnering As we learned in Chapter 7, cohabitation is becoming quite common, with the majority of the population living with a partner before marriage. Cohabitation is increasingly common among previously married and middle-aged adults (Chevan, 1996), and over half of these relationships have children present. As with those who have never married, cohabitation is often viewed as an extension of serious dating. It may lead to marriage, or it may not. However, in their research during the 1980s, Bumpass and Sweet (1989) found that 60 percent of remarried people had lived with a partner (not always their spouse) prior to remarrying. This figure is presumably higher today. Chevan, using a large national data source, reports that the increase in the percentage of unmarried people between the ages of 40 and 59 who are cohabiting is almost as large as among individuals under the age of 40, increasing from 0.2 percent of the population aged 40–59 in 1960 to 10.8 percent in 1990. In fact, Bulcroft and Bulcroft (1991) found that among single persons over age 55 who date, cohabitation is favored almost as much as marriage. Thus, for many divorced persons, cohabitation may not simply be a precursor to marriage; it may replace it altogether. This is why some researchers interested in relationships after divorce prefer to focus on **"repartnering"** rather than "remarriage" per se (Lampard & Peggs, 1999).

There is great diversity in the rate of repartnering and remarriage. In one longitudinal study of 57 women who had remarried, 17 percent of the women cohabited with their future husband within one year of separating from their former spouse. Another 19 percent waited more than seven years (Montgomery, Anderson, Herington, & Clingempeel, 1992).

When a couple decides to remarry or cohabit, the decision usually occurs quickly after the relationship begins, unlike first marriages, in which dating may last for years before a commitment to marry. In their study of remarriage, Montgomery, Anderson, Hetherington, and Clingempeel (1992) found that 80 percent of the women in their sample dated their future spouses for no more than a year before cohabiting with them. Of these women, 38 percent dated for three months or less prior to cohabitation. Things progress more quickly because divorced men and women may feel that they do not need as much time to get to know each other. They have learned from past mistakes, are more focused about what they are looking for in a partner, or are a better judge of character. Yet Ganong and Coleman (1989) found that among couples who were preparing for remarriage, many fail to address critical issues: fewer than 25 percent discussed financial matters with their partner, and 13 percent reported that they did not discuss any substantive issues at all.

FACT OR FICTION?

Remarriage is a recent feature of family life in the United States.

Remarriage

We often talk as though **remarriage,** and the new family structures that it creates, is a modern invention. However, remarriage has *always* been a common feature of family life in the United States (Phillips, 1997). In early U.S. history, life expectancy was considerably lower than it is today, and many adults died when they were relatively young (by today's standards). Since it was difficult to maintain a household as a single adult, a quick remarriage was often a fact of life. If children were present, the remarriage substituted a new parent for the old one.

Remarriage has always been a feature of our culture, but the reasons for it have changed from widowhood to divorce.

Despite the prevalence of remarriage, it took until the 1970s for researchers to begin to take a real interest in the subject. The reason for this recent interest is that *divorce* rather than death has now become the leading precursor to remarriage (Cherlin, 1992). Today, nine out of ten remarriages occur following a divorce, unlike in the past. A remarriage that occurs after a divorce has very different characteristics from a remarriage that occurs after death. Namely, the ex-spouse is still alive, perhaps living within the vicinity and exercising his or her parental rights. This provides many challenges that were not faced in the past. Consequently, it is not surprising that the research on remarriage and on blended families has skyrocketed, with three times more articles published in the 1990s than in the preceding ninety years combined (Coleman, Ganong, & Fine, 2000).

Remarriage in Other Societies

Just as divorce laws and norms vary cross-culturally, so do laws and norms regarding remarriage.

Nonindustrial Societies We tend to see the most restriction in nonindustrial societies, perhaps because of religious beliefs or because of strong patriarchal norms. For example, one study found that 22 percent of tribal societies restrict remarriage, and these restrictions are almost always more limiting or more punitive for women than for men (Hatfield & Rapson, 1996). Some Indian groups restrict remarriage for women. For

example, Rajput widows are treated harshly: their heads are sometimes shaved, they are required to stay indoors, they are forbidden to participate in religious ceremonies, and they are treated by their own family and the rest of society as unclean and polluting. These norms likely come from the old tradition known as "sati" or "suttee." In medieval India, this meant "a good and virtuous wife," and she was expected to be loyal, innocent, self-sacrificing, and self-effacing. She was to live through her husband; therefore, if he died, she was expected to throw herself on his funeral pyre or to be buried alongside him. If she resisted, her family forced her to commit suicide so that they, rather than the widow, could inherit the couple's property and would be spared the burden of supporting her. Those widows who lived were forbidden to remarry or to have sexual relations. Until the nineteenth century, the practice of sati was relatively common, although the British and some Indian groups opposed the custom. Finally in the 1980s, the Indian Parliament passed a law forbidding sati, in response to women's organizations protesting the custom; it was still occasionally practiced (Hatfield & Rapson, 1996).

Industrial Societies: The Example of Japan Variations in views toward divorce and norms regarding remarriage are also found in industrialized societies. For example, rigid gender discrepancies in remarriage rates are noted in Japan, discrepancies that are larger than found elsewhere. Japanese men are 1.28 times more likely to remarry than are Japanese women, while the comparable figure in the United States is somewhere between 1.05 to 1.10 times (Cornell, 1989). Meanwhile, the hardships resulting from divorce are significant for women in Japan. Divorced women and their children face stigma, and it is likely that they will experience significant economic problems. Since

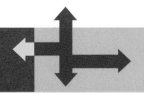

Arab Americans originate from several Arabic-speaking countries in the Middle East, including Syria, Iraq, Egypt, Palestine, Lebanon, Jordan, Yemen, Saudi Arabia, and Kuwait. Early immigrants to the United States were largely Christian, while today they are primarily Muslim. Religion plays a key role in Middle Eastern culture and is a critical social boundary. Religious institutions play a major role in society, and religious norms provide a strict code of behavior that all Arabs should follow. These norms are particularly clear in the realm of dating, marriage, divorce, and remarriage.

The family is the basic unit of social organization for Arab Americans, and it helps soften the economic and emotional challenges of adjusting to a new country and new culture. Arabs are encouraged to think of their family first, themselves as individuals second. Consequently, it is not surprising that families,

reflecting religious traditions, place a strict control and watchful eye over intimate relationships.

Dating, in the usual American sense, is rare among traditional Arab Americans, particularly females, although this is a source of tension between generations. One study found that 37 percent of males claimed to have never dated. In comparison, 80 percent of females claimed to have never dated, and another 10 percent reported that they "hardly ever" dated (Ba-Yunis, 1991). Instead, marriage in the Arab American community is closely controlled by regulating interaction between single men and women, and parents often arrange marriages. The behavior of females is more closely monitored than that of males because women are expected to be virgins when they marry; to lose their virginity is seen as dishonoring the entire family. While in the Middle East dating is necessarily re-

stricted for males because females are so highly guarded, this is not so in the United States. The Arabic culture tolerates Arab American males dating and having sexual relationships with non-Arab females. However, strong pressure is exerted on Arab American males to marry women of their cultural background.

The family is usually involved to some extent in the marriage. Arab Americans tend to marry younger than do many other Americans, although this depends on many factors, including their education level. The marriage is contracted and witnessed by men. Among Muslim families, a sum of money is paid by the groom's family to the bride's family, most of which goes to the bride herself. In some cases the entire sum is paid before the marriage, but in other cases only a portion is made at that time, and the remainder is set aside in a trust in case of divorce.

many mothers do not work outside the home in Japan, reentering the labor market after an absence is difficult. Work skills are likely to be very rusty.

Despite these problems, one study found that many women in Japan do not want to remarry, despite the social and economic benefits that marriage in their culture could give them. Forty-six percent of divorced women between the ages of 20 and 29 report that they do not want to marry again, as compared to only 19 percent of men the same age. Furthermore, the percentage of women who claim that they do not want to remarry

increases among older age groups so that 64 percent of women aged 30–39, 68 percent of women aged 40–49, and 82 percent of women aged 50–59 claim that they do not want to get married again (Cornell, 1989). This seems counterintuitive. Wouldn't women want to marry when they face poor economic prospects while solo? And wouldn't older women be more inclined to want to marry, given traditional socialization patterns and their lower levels of work experience?

Cornell (1989) suggests that the answer may be a combination of both deliberate choice and acknowledged resignation to one's

Among Arab Americans, divorce carries a heavy stigma, and it is strongly discouraged. It casts a shame on the entire family, not simply the divorcing couple. Extended families will usually try to intervene to prevent the couple from ending their marriage. One study conducted in Canada found that the divorce rate in the Muslim population was only 2.2 percent for males and 3.1 percent for females. The divorce rate is low because of the primacy of family relationships and the importance of upholding family honor. A divorce would likely disgrace the family.

A divorce leaves women at a disadvantage in many ways. Because many have limited education and work experience, they have difficulty supporting themselves. Some turn to welfare, while others turn to their families for aid. Women also usually do not get custody of the children; they belong to the fa-ther's family. Attitudes toward this are changing, however. One study in 1987 reported that nearly one-half of Arab Americans (45 percent) believed that women should be granted custody of children until the children turn eighteen (Haddad & Lummis, 1987). But single parenthood is considered abnormal by Arab Americans unless the parent is a widow or widower.

Following a divorce, it is usually easier for a man to remarry than it is for a woman. If a divorced Arab American woman remarries outside of the Arab community, she risks losing her support and the ties to the community. In contrast, men who remarry outside the Arab community are generally not ostracized to the same degree.

Some adolescents are challenging these long-standing religious and cultural norms within families. Many of these norms are obviously in conflict with the patterns in main-stream America to which children have become accustomed. They feel torn between two different cultures. Although they may appear to be assimilating, older Arab Americans try hard to maintain their roots and traditions. The customs of having a large and involved family and of expressing loyalty to the group rather than to the individual are a source of tremendous ethnic pride.

Source: Adapted from Aswad (1997).

Critical Thinking

1. As Arab Americans become assimilated, how difficult do you think it will be for them to maintain their traditions regarding divorce and remarriage?

2. Are traditional Arab American customs surrounding divorce and remarriage patriarchal or egalitarian? How do you think an Arab American would respond to this question?

fate. Because Japan is a society in which divorce is heavily stigmatized and thus relatively rare, women who seek divorce are likely to be those who have strong negative feelings about their partner and the institution of marriage. They are mavericks who may choose to remain single. On the other hand, because Japan is a society with strict gender roles, wives are considered primarily responsible for the quality of the marital relationship. Its failure is viewed as *their* failure. Divorced women are viewed with suspicion and distrust, and they may be referred to as *kizu mono* (damaged goods). These women may not be "chosen" for remarriage, so they are resigned to remaining unmarried.

Subcultural groups in the United States also have varying views about divorce and remarriage. For example, the small but growing Arab American community has strict religious traditions that regulate dating, marriage, divorce, and remarriage, as shown in the Family Diversity box on pages 550–551.

FACT OR FICTION?

Whites are more likely to remarry than are other racial or ethnic groups.

Women who remarry after a divorce are on average thirty-four years of age, while men are thirty-seven years. Given their ages, it is likely that they will begin their second marriage with children.

Demographic Trends: Who Remarries, and When?

Remarriages often take place rapidly. As shown in Table 13.2, 28 percent of women remarry within two years after a divorce (Bramlett & Mosher, 2001). Younger women are more likely to remarry than are older women. Among women who divorce when under the age of 25, 81 percent are remarried within ten years, as compared to 68 percent who were aged 25 or older when divorcing. Some people remarry quickly: nine percent of women remarry within six months after a divorce. It is likely that most of these individuals had met and begun the new relationship well before the divorce was final or were separated but waited to go through with the final divorce until they had met a new partner. The average (mean) length of time between a divorce and remarriage is approximately four years (Coleman, Ganong, & Fine, 2000), although men remarry more quickly than do women.

The average age of persons who remarry has increased among both men and women. Women who remarry after a divorce are on average 34 years of age, up from 31 years in 1980. Likewise, the average age of men who remarry is 37 years, up from 34 years in 1980. Men and women who remarry after their spouse dies are considerably older.

		AGE	
DIVORCED WOMEN WHO HAVE REMARRIED AFTER	TOTAL (%)	LESS THAN 25 YEARS (%)	25 YEARS AND OVER (%)
6 months	9	9	9
1 year	15	17	14
2 years	28	28	27
3 years	39	41	37
4 years	47	49	44
5 years	54	57	51
6 years	59	64	55
7 years	62	67	58
8 years	68	72	63
9 years	71	77	65
10 years	75	81	68

TABLE 13.2 Probability of Second Marriage by Time After First Divorce and Woman's Age at Divorce: United States, 1995

Note: This table includes all first divorces of women aged 15–44 in 1995.
Source: Bramlett and Mosher (2001).

Racial/Ethnic Differences in Remarriage
Whites are more likely to remarry than are other racial or ethnic groups, and they remarry more quickly. National data shown in Figure 13.1 indicate that by two years after a divorce, 30 percent of whites have remarried, compared to 14 percent of African Americans and 19 percent of Hispanics. By fourteen years after a divorce, the rates of remarriage for whites and Hispanics are comparable, 84 percent and 80 percent, respectively. Among African Americans at this stage, only 57 percent have remarried.

FACT

Whites are more likely to remarry.

Why are minority groups, particularly blacks, less likely to remarry than are whites? The answer to this question may be related to the same reason that minority groups are less likely to marry in the first place. There is often a shortage of available, marriageable men, particularly in inner-city urban areas (Wilson, 1987, 1993). With jobs moving out to the suburbs, urban minority males face high rates of unemployment. The newer suburban jobs are difficult to get to for urban dwellers because public transportation is limited to suburban areas. Along with racism and discrimination, many males living in the inner cities experience poverty, and some, in their despair, resort to coping mechanisms such as drug use or violence. Harvard sociologist William Julius Wilson suggests that these conditions significantly reduce the pool of men eligible for marriage.

FACT OR FICTION?

Women are more likely to remarry after a divorce than are men.

Gender Differences in Remarriage Men are more likely to remarry than are women, and they do so more quickly. Approximately

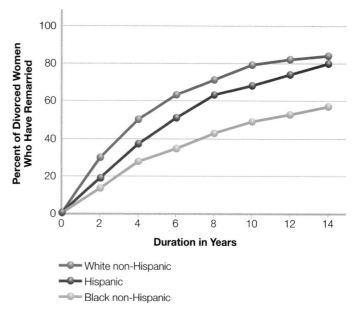

FIGURE 13.1 Probability of Remarriage by Duration of Divorce and Woman's Race/Ethnicity: United States, 1995

Source: Bramlett and Mosher (2001)

two-thirds of women remarry, whereas three-quarters of men do. Men remarry, on average, within three years, compared to five years for women. But gender alone does not predict when or if a person will remarry. For women, the likelihood of remarriage is lower when they are older, have more education, are employed, or have children (particularly children under age six). Table 13.3 indicates the gender differences in "repartnering" (either cohabitation or marriage) by age and duration. These data were drawn from the General Household Survey, a large representative sample of adults in the United States (Lampard & Peggs, 1999). As we can see, among persons under the age of thirty, gender differences in repartnering within three years are virtually nonexistent, although gender differences are accentuated when we examine the five-year trend. However, we see more dramatic differences among individuals

TABLE 13.3	Percentage Repartnering (Remarriage or Cohabitation) by Age at End of First Marriage and by Sex		
AGE AT END OF FIRST MARRIAGE		WOMEN (%)	MEN (%)
Had Repartnered by 3 Years:			
16–29 years		40	41
30–39 years		31	42
40–49 years		18	36
50–59 years		0	41
Had Repartnered by 5 Years:			
16–29 years		56	64
30–39 years		46	55
40–49 years		23	49
50–59 years		7	46

Source: General Household Survey. Reported in Lampard and Peggs (1999).

divorcing as they age. Among couples divorcing in their thirties, only 31 percent of women had repartnered within three years, as compared to 42 percent of men. Within five years, 46 percent of women in their thirties had repartnered, compared to 55 percent of men. These differences are accentuated among couples divorcing in their forties and fifties. For example, the table reveals that less than 1 percent of women who divorce during their fifties will repartner in three years, while 41 percent of their male counterparts will do so.

FICTION

Men are more likely to remarry than are women, and they do so more quickly.

The reasons for these gender differences are complex. Part of this difference is by choice: some women simply do not want to remarry. If they can support themselves and their families easily enough, they might not feel the need to remarry. But for many other individuals who would like to remarry, cultural norms make it more difficult for women to find available spouses.

Why Do Men and Women Not Remarry at the Same Rate? There are a number of reasons that help to explain why men are more likely to remarry and do so more quickly than women:

1. *Men are able to initiate contact more easily.* Men have a lifetime of socialization experiences that have encouraged them to be the initiator in personal relationships. Many women, particularly older women, have never asked a man out on a date. When they were younger, to do so would have been considered "improper." Even today, women are generally socialized to, and are therefore more comfortable in, the role of being chosen rather than actively doing the choosing themselves. The ritual of the high school "Sadie Hawkins" dance illustrates this concept. It is a one-time event that says it is OK for a girl to go ahead and ask a boy out on a date. Notice there is no special high school event needed to grant permission for a boy to ask a girl out on a date. Boys are expected to initiate contact in most contexts.

In addition, men often have a wider social network than do women. They have a larger circle of causal friends and acquaintances, and these can be drawn upon to meet potential partners. Men are more likely to have worked outside the home for a longer period of time and are more likely to be in managerial or professional positions that require skills at initiating and directing conversation. Moreover, because their incomes are considerably higher than those of women, men have more money to treat someone to a dinner, movie, or some other type of date.

2. *There is a double standard of aging.* As men age, they are considered to be more "distinguished." Their graying hair, increasing wrinkles, and weight

gain are offset by their increased occupational prestige or financial assets. However, when women age, they are usually considered less attractive and therefore less desirable.

3. *The pool of eligible partners is larger for men than it is for women because of cultural norms.* It is unusual for women to marry men who are much younger than themselves. Instead, women generally marry men who are older, or at least the same age. When a female is 22 and a male is 25, this is not particularly problematic because the size of the pool of eligible partners is relatively equivalent. But imagine this same couple 30 years later. The female is now 52, and the male is 55. Do they still have an equal chance at finding partners? No. Cultural norms can be particularly cruel to older women. A 55-year-old male could easily marry a 35-year-old woman without people giving it much thought. He would not be considered deviant. In fact, many people would think that they both made a good "catch" (he benefits from her youth and sex appeal; she benefits from his financial status). But older women are not granted the same latitude. Although theoretically a 55-year-old woman could also marry a 35 year-old man (i.e., it's certainly not illegal to do so), it is deviant enough that it would likely draw some negative attention. In fact, many people would wonder what he sees in such an "old woman" or why she is "robbing the cradle."

4. *Women are more likely to have children living with them.* Women who have custody of children are less likely to remarry than are women who do not have children or do not have custody, as shown in Table 13.4. Again using data from the General Household Survey, we see the likelihood of repartner-

© George DeSota/Newsmakers-Getty Images

Men are more likely to remarry and remarry more quickly compared to women. One reason for this is the double standard of aging. Aging makes men "distinguished." However, older women are considered less attractive and therefore less desirable.

ing by women (either marriage or cohabitation) according to the number of children that they have (Lampard & Peggs, 1999). This table shows that, within three years, 48 percent of women without children are likely to remarry, as compared to 33 percent of women with one child, 31 percent of women with two children, 21 percent of mothers with three children, and 23 percent of mothers with four or more children. Similar patterns exist among women if we examine repartnering over five years or even over ten years.

TABLE 13.4	Percentage Repartnering of Formerly Married Women, by Number of Children, Over Time		
NUMBER OF CHILDREN	3 YEARS (%)	5 YEARS (%)	10 YEARS (%)
0	48	63	80
1	33	48	63
2	31	45	62
3	21	34	53
4 or more	23	31	47

Source: General Household Survey. Reported in Lampard and Peggs (1999).

Why do children influence women's likelihood of repartnering? One reason is that women may not have the time or financial resources to date. Another reason is that some men are hesitant to take on the financial and emotional responsibility that comes with a ready-made family. Another reason is that stepfamilies have a unique set of issues that can strain a relationship, discussed below. Some women may be hesitant or very cautious about remarrying and thus bringing a new person into established family relationships. Finally, children may try to sabotage their mother's relationships out of fear or jealousy.

Remarried Relationships

How are relationships different the second (or third) time around? Are people happier in their subsequent marriages?

Power and Equity Between Spouses Remarried couples tend to perceive their relationships as more equitable than was the case in their first marriages (Crosbie-Burnett & Giles-Sims, 1991; Pyke, 1994; Pyke & Coltrane, 1996). Women often believe they have more power and autonomy regarding financial and other decisions. One study compared data from 111 remarried and first-married spouses and found that remarried spouses endorsed more autonomous stan-

dards in child rearing, friendships, and finances (Allen, Baucom, Burnett, Epstein, & Rankin-Esquer, 2001). Different reasons have been offered for this increased feeling of autonomy, power, and equity:

1. Women have greater levels of financial resources.
2. Women seek more power because of specific experiences in their prior marriages.
3. Men concede more during marital conflicts than they did in their first marriages.
4. Both remarried men and women have expanded their ideas about their roles in marriage. (Coleman, Ganong, & Fine, 2000)

Despite feelings of greater equality and autonomy, domestic labor is not shared equally among remarried couples (Ishii-Kuntz & Coltrane, 1992; Pyke & Coltrane, 1996; Demo & Acock, 1993). Household chores remain largely based on gender, with males and females doing different types of tasks and spending an unbalanced amount of time on those tasks. Pyke and Coltrane (1996) reported research with 215 men and women who were in second marriages following a divorce and residing in Southern California. They used both interview and survey data to examine the marital processes underlying the division of household labor—to examine how the *meanings* associated with housework, paid work, and earnings affect the allocation of domestic labor. They suggest that not everyone evaluates the equal sharing of tasks, or women's financial contributions to the family, in the same way. For example, in some families these may be perceived as threats rather than positive attributes. Pyke and Coltrane found that the early housework experiences in previous marriages were used as the point of reference for their current situation. Consequently, for many women this comparison tempered their feelings that housework should be shared and instead increased their feelings of gratitude that "he helps." Therefore, many women were grateful for even an unequal division of domestic labor because it was at least less unequal than in the previous marriage. One surprising finding, also related to using the previous marriage as a referent, was that husbands who had extramarital affairs were less likely to share housework. Extramarital affairs in the first marriage facilitated feelings of entitlement and gratitude by both the husband and his new wife. Men's fidelity was used to help excuse them from participation in what they might see as mundane tasks. One man in the study justified doing little housework in his remarriage this way: "I'm home and I'm not drinking or doing drugs. I should be considered a good guy."

| FACT OR FICTION?

Remarriages have a higher incidence of divorce than do first marriages.

Satisfaction and Stability of Remarriages Returning to our question of the happiness of remarriages, we find that they are not necessarily happier than first marriages. In fact, some research shows that second (and third) marriages are somewhat less happy than first ones and are more prone to divorce (Ceglian & Gardner, 1999; Hobart, 1991). This finding may reflect a selection bias—people who remarry obviously consider divorce as an option to end an unhappy relationship. But remarried couples also tend to more openly express criticisms and anger than do couples in first marriages (although this is not always a negative trait). Remarried couples are also generally more prone to disagreements, but these are largely related to issues surrounding stepchildren. Stepchildren generally make the remarried relationship more tense because of arguments between stepchildren and stepparents, or between stepparents on issues related to

child rearing or discipline (Brown & Booth, 1996; Kurdek, 1999).

Generally speaking, remarriages have a higher incidence of divorce than do first marriages. After ten years of remarriage, 47 percent of remarried women under the age of twenty-five have divorced again, compared with 34 percent of remarried women who are twenty-five or over. However, one recent study among couples who are both over age forty-five at the time of remarriage found that they had very low rates of divorce. Clarke and Wilson (1994) suggest that older couples may be more careful in selecting their spouses, or are more reluctant to divorce again.

Figure 13.2 reports the percentage of women who get divorced again after a remarriage, across racial and ethnic groups. The figure reveals that blacks have the highest rate of re-divorce, followed by whites. Hispanics have the lowest rate of re-divorce. After ten years of remarriage, 48 percent of

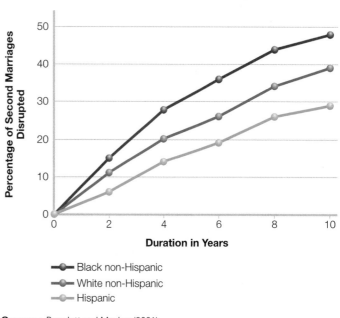

FIGURE 13.2 Probability of Second Marriage Disruption by Duration of Marriage and Wife's Race/Ethnicity: United States, 1995

Source: Bramlett and Mosher (2001).

African Americans, 39 percent of whites, and 29 percent of Hispanics have divorced again.

The likelihood of divorce is higher in subsequent marriages.

According to Ihinger-Tallman and Pasley (1987), the instability of a remarriage may reflect a problem in one or more of four main areas that are critical to marital success:

1. *Individuals may fail to make a real commitment to remarriage.* Having lived through at least one divorce, people may see that divorce is a remedy for an unhappy or unfulfilling marriage. Consequently, they may not make the necessary effort to resolve problems; instead, they use divorce as a way out. Compared to the larger pool of first marriages, remarriages contain a larger proportion of people who have certain personality characteristics that make them less likely to work towards successful solutions to marital problems and predispose them to end relationships more frequently, such as persons with emotional problems, alcoholics, drug abusers, or those who are physically violent.

2. *The couple may fail to become a cohesive unit.* Developing bonds between adults with separate and perhaps lengthy life histories, including other families, may be difficult. Couples must learn to think of themselves as a "we," not simply an "I." Given the complexity surrounding remarriages, there is bound to be conflict and confusion over new rules, new norms, and new ways of allocating assets. Children may wittingly or unwittingly pit one parent against the other: "But Mom said I could!" To avoid this type of dilemma, the new couple must make a concerted effort to work together to develop a new set of rules.

3. *Individuals may fail to communicate appropriately with each other.* This is a common problem, perhaps exacerbated in a previous marriage where communication patterns were problematic. Learning how to communicate more effectively is difficult and time consuming, but it is critical in order to break old, destructive habits that interfere with developing a strong family.

4. *Remarried couples must deal with more boundary maintenance issues than do couples in first marriages.* In addition to in-laws, there are also ex-spouses to contend with. This can be a source of tension if child custody, visitation, or child support disagreements drag on. Furthermore, remarried families with children in them have to establish new boundaries—what are the new expectations among family members?

Remarriage Among the Elderly The demographic structure among older persons makes it challenging for older women to remarry in the advent of divorce (or widowhood). There are only 82 men aged 65–74 for every 100 women of the same age group (Hetzel & Smith, 2001). When this demographic imbalance is coupled with norms regarding mate selection (i.e., husbands are expected to be older), we can see that it makes it all the more difficult for women to remarry—difficult, but not impossible.

A number of features can make remarriage between older adults quite successful. First, when elders remarry, they usually do not have to worry about stepparenting issues to the same degree as do younger persons who remarry. Although their adult children may disapprove of the remarriage, the children are generally living on their own and are not directly affected by the new union. This can ease a tremendous burden associated with remarriages. Second, older adults may be financially established and therefore experience less stress and conflict over money. Third, older adults may benefit from the wisdom that comes from a lifetime of experience and seek partners who offer comfort and companionship.

Stepfamilies

Since many couples who remarry or cohabit also have children, let us now turn to the topic of **stepfamilies**. Sometimes stepfamilies are called *blended families* or *reconstituted families,* although these have been criticized as "catchy media phrases" that set up unrealistic expectations since stepfamilies rarely really blend.

Stepfamilies are families in which one or both of the adult partners has at least one child, either residing with them or elsewhere. This definition does not necessarily require the adult partners to be married. Indeed, the majority of children first enter a stepfamily through their parent's cohabitation rather than through marriage, although often the parent later marries. This definition also does not require the adult parent to have been married when the child was born. It is relatively common among low-income and African American stepfamilies to have been preceded by a nonmarital birth rather than a divorce (Bumpass, Raley, & Sweet, 1995). Children in stepfamilies are referred to as *siblings* (biologically related from same parents), *stepsiblings* (not biologically related, but parents now married to each other), *half-siblings* (share one parent biologically), *mutual children* (children born to the remarried couple), *residential stepchildren* (live in the household with the remarried couple more than half of the time), and *nonresidential stepchildren* (live in the household less than half of the time).

Stepfamilies can have many positive attributes. For example, greater exposure to a wide variety of behavior patterns and life-styles can be beneficial to children in many ways. They can learn to see the diversity in lived experience. They also may benefit from living with an adult who is possibly more objective. Biological parents sometimes have a difficult time with this objectivity. For example, if a teacher sees problems with a young student, a biological parent may be defensive while a stepparent can more easily step back and objectively observe the situation. Children may also benefit from an increased standard of living made possible by two incomes and their parent's greater happiness at being involved in another relationship.

Stereotypes of Stepfamilies: The Wicked Stepmother

Despite the prevalence of stepfamilies and the possible benefits of living in one, societal views towards them are remarkably negative. Stepfamilies are often stigmatized as harmful environments for children and adolescents, a view that is shared in many different cultures (Ganong & Coleman, 1997). For examples, views of the "wicked stepmother" are rampant, found from Shakespeare to Cinderella, with connotations of cruelty, jealousy, and neglect. From where did these stereotypes emerge?

We guess that these stereotypes are rooted in the stepfamilies of preindustrial society. Families needed the labor of two parents to provide food, shelter, and clothing for the family. When one spouse died, which was most often the wife, given the dangers of childbearing, a husband had little choice but to remarry after a quick mourning. Most people thought it would be very foolish, not to mention unmanly, to attempt to raise and provide for his children alone. So economic necessity, along with patriarchal norms, led him to remarry as soon as possible. Yet his remarriage choices were often limited. Women who were his same age were likely to be already married. Consequently, a second (or subsequent) wife may have been considerably younger than her husband, perhaps by even twenty years. Indeed, she could be the same age as some of his older children! This large age difference between a husband and wife contributed to her being viewed and treated as though she were a child rather than a spouse. Coupled with patriarchal norms, she had little power in the relationship and little authority over children in the household despite having to cook for them, clean after them, and in other ways raise them. We can see how feelings of jealousy, cruelty, or neglect could surface. The way for the stepmother to gain some bit of power was to have children of her own. Not surprisingly, the issue of favoritism between her own and her stepchildren could emerge, exacerbating strained stepfamily relationships and contributing to the stereotype of the "evil stepmother" (Cherlin, 1999; Mitterauer & Sieder, 1982).

Negative views of stepfamilies as deficient or problematic continue to thrive. Family scholars have reviewed the coverage of stepfamilies in marriage-and-family college-level textbooks and found that such texts still focus largely on problems rather than on the positive outcomes of stepfamilies (Coleman, Ganong, & Goodwin, 1994).

Types of Stepfamilies

Although we often talk about *the* stepfamily, as though there is only one type, we know otherwise. Berger (1998) points out the diversity within stepfamilies. Types include the following:

* Stepfamilies in which a child lives with his or her married parent and stepparent.
* Stepfamilies in which children from a previous marriage visit with their remarried parent and stepparent.
* An unmarried couple living together in an arrangement in which at least one

of the partners has children from a previous relationship who live with or visit them.

* A remarried couple, with each of the spouses bringing children into the new marriage from the previous marriage.
* A couple who not only bring children from a previous marriage but also have a child or children of their own.
* A remarried couple, both of whom have children from a previous marriage. The children may live in another state and have very little contact with the remarried couple.

Stepfamilies: A Normless Norm

Stepfamilies differ from nuclear families in many ways. In a traditional two-parent family, a child is biologically related to both sets of parents, unlike in a stepfamily, where the biological tie is to only one parent.

Stepfamilies have been referred to as a **normless norm,** meaning that they are common enough to be considered normative, yet the expectations, obligations, and rules within these families are vague and confusing (Lamanna and Reidmann, 1997). Roles are ambiguous, and people do not know what is expected of them. Over a third of children born in the United States today will be in a stepfamily before reaching age eighteen (Bumpass, Raley, & Sweet, 1995; Ganong & Coleman, 1994). However, there is no socially prescribed script for how family members are expected to relate with one another. What names do children use for their stepparent? To what extent can stepparents discipline their stepchildren? How are stepparents and stepchildren supposed to feel about one another? What relationships are counted as "family"? Do stepparents and their stepchildren even include one another as part of their "family"? For example, your ex-husband's new wife is technically a stepparent to your children, but what if your children are grown and out of the house? Would they refer to her as "my dad's new wife" or as "my stepmother?" Sociologist Lynn White found in her research a tremendous variation in the way members of stepfamilies count who is a "family member," as shown in the Focus on Family Research box on pages 562–563.

Features of Stepfamilies When remarriages involve children from previous unions (marriage or otherwise), the family dynamics become increasingly complex. The characteristics of stepfamilies have been pointed out by Emily and John Visher (1979) and the Stepfamily Association of America (2000), among others:

1. *Stepfamilies come about because of a loss.* The loss may be because of death or because of divorce. Regardless of the reason, endings are difficult because they mean adjusting to loss and change, and separating from old ties. Both children and adults grieve over their losses. Children grieve over the loss of a parent, even if the nonresidential parent visits regularly; the loss of stability; the loss of their fantasy about the way they want life to be; and the loss associated with such things as their old home, school, neighborhood, or friends. Adults grieve over similar things: the loss of a partner, the loss of their dreams about the way they thought marriage would be, and the losses involved in change.

2. *The parent/child relationship has a longer history than the new couple's relationship.* This fact can make it challenging for the adults to consider their relationship the primary, long-term one. The incoming marriage partner can feel like an intruder or an outsider. The close relationships that develop between divorced parents and their children, as shown in the opening vignette

of this chapter, sometimes mean that the new spouse has a difficult time joining the family. This new person has not been a part of funny or tragic family memories, or a part of developing sentimental traditions. The environment can feel alienating and unwelcoming. "Why does he like those kinds of yucky foods?" children may wonder. "Why do her children expect to open their gifts on Christmas Eve instead of Christmas day?" the new stepfather may ask himself. "Don't his children know the value of saying grace before meals?" the stepmother may wonder about her stepchildren who visit every other weekend. The fact that remarried families come together from diverse backgrounds accentuates the need for tolerance of differences. In time, the family can develop meaningful shared experiences and rituals. This usually does not happen quickly or spontaneously, and it involves effort among all members. It takes time to develop a sense of shared family history.

3. *There is a biological parent outside the stepfamily unit and an adult of the same sex as the absent parent in the household.* Important relationships may end abruptly or fade over time. Some fathers have no contact with children after a divorce or after an ex-spouse remarries. About 26 percent of custodial remarried mothers report that their child's father is deceased or of unknown whereabouts (reported in Mason, 1998). Sometimes, siblings are split between different households and rarely see one another. Meanwhile, there is a new adult in the household of the same sex as the absent parent. "Is he supposed to be my 'new dad?'" a teenager wonders. "No way!" How can the transition be smooth? The two must develop understanding for each other. Some behaviors such as discipline are particu-

FOCUS ON
FAMILY
RESEARCH

Who's Counting? Quasi-Facts and Stepfamilies
in Reports of Number of Siblings

It would seem that most of us would be able to say immediately how many brothers and sisters we have. Yet for a large number of people, this apparently is not the case.

Using data on approximately 9,400 adults interviewed in 1987–1988 and again in 1992–1994 to analyze sibling relationships over the life course, an unexpected discrepancy in the number of siblings was discovered by family sociologist Lynn White. The number of siblings that adults reported tended to change dramatically between interviews. White anticipated that a significant portion of older respondents would lose siblings between interviews (because of death), so it seemed reasonable that 15 percent of the sample reported fewer siblings in the second interview. Unexpectedly, however, another 16 percent reported *more* siblings in 1994

than in 1988. How is it that these adults gained siblings?

Overall, the simple question "How many siblings do you have?" is apparently more complex than it appears. Even within a five-year span, adults appeared to change their count of siblings. Both underreporting and overreporting of siblings were more likely among respondents with complex family structures. Estranged full siblings, brothers- or sisters-in-law, one's father's new wife's children from her first marriage, half-siblings, and perhaps friends and fictive kin may be counted in some circumstances or in response to some questions and may not be counted in others.

It should not be surprising that counts of stepsiblings and half-siblings are sensitive to question wording or perhaps are just plain unreliable. We are often not sure if these

people are relatives, much less what we should call them. Should a stepfather's nonresident minor children be regarded as stepsiblings? How about the adult children of a mother's new husband? Because 38 percent of respondents whose parents remarried between waves of the survey reported additional siblings, it appears that some may have counted the latter connections as stepsiblings. Because one-third of those who acknowledged residential stepsiblings and half-siblings in childhood increased the number of reported siblings when the residence rule was relaxed, it appears that many are also willing to count stepsiblings or half-siblings with whom they had only visiting relationships during childhood. However, another one-fourth cease counting stepsiblings or half-siblings with whom they lived during child-

larly touchy. Under what conditions should a stepparent discipline his or her stepchild? Expectations surrounding discipline may vary drastically from one family member to another. Research suggests that stepchildren reject stepparents who use discipline too early in the relationship (Bray, 1992; Ganong, Coleman, Fine, & Martin, 1999).

4. *Most children in stepfamilies hold membership in two households, with two sets of rules.* Two households can be a very positive experience. Theoretically, they can provide twice the love, twice the number of positive experiences, twice the number of family va-

cations, and twice the parental involvement in the child's schooling or other activities. However, membership in two households can also create confusion and conflict, including playing one parent off against another (Beer, 1992). "But Dad lets me stay up until 9:00 at his house, so why do I have to go to bed at 8:30 here?" "Mom lets me watch that TV program, so why won't you?" Two households can also create loyalty conflicts (Beer, 1992). For example, suppose a son feels close and loving to his new stepmother but at the same time learns (verbally or nonverbally) that his biological mother, whom he

hood once the wording of the question no longer instructs them to count these relationships.

Family scholars acknowledge that "relations acquired by marriage are automatically eligible to be relatives" but that such a construction is far from automatic (Furstenberg, 1981: 134). In a report based on the National Children's Study, Furstenberg (1987) reports that when asked to list those they included in their family, 19 percent of the interviewed children omitted a natural sibling, but 41 percent of those living with stepsiblings failed to include at least one. Further, 31 percent of children failed to list their residential stepparent as a member of their family, compared with only 7 percent who omitted a biological parent. Similarly, 15 percent of the parents with residential stepchildren failed to list them, and 1 percent

failed to list residential biological children.

Left to their own devices, it appears that respondents will use widely different definitions of who is family and, probably, who is stepfamily. Moreover, these definitions may change from one week to the next. Unless we wish to abandon the notion of family structure completely and say that family is whatever you say it is, social scientists need to agree among themselves who should be considered stepkin. For example, what is a stepsibling? Is it anyone whose parent is married to your parent? What if you have never even met this person? Or is a stepsibling only someone who has actually co-resided with you as a child? Moreover, what if your parent wasn't married to his or her partner but cohabited instead? Because 60 percent of all Americans will be part

of a stepfamily at some point in their lives (Bumpass, Raley, & Sweet, 1994), a growing portion of Americans—and data analyses—will face these ambiguities.

Source: Adapted from White (1998).

Critical Thinking

1. If you have stepsiblings, how would you answer the researchers' questions?

2. What can researchers do to improve the validity and reliability of respondents' answers?

3. Are there other ambiguities like this that researchers may face when they do research on families?

---

also loves, does not like the stepmother. Perhaps the biological mother resents her ex-husband remarrying, period. Perhaps she resents her ex-husband's increased income, if in a dual-earner household, while she herself is still experiencing a tremendous economic struggle. Perhaps she does not care for the values the stepmother holds, or perhaps she resents having another woman get emotionally close to and care for her child. Regardless of the reason or its validity, the child may feel pulled in two directions. To allow himself to respond affectionately to the stepmother risks alienating the biologi-

cal mother. To please Mom requires rebuffing the stepmother, which would displease her and his father.

Living in two families can pose challenges, but it helps to have family boundaries that are flexible so that children can move from one family to another more easily. One study with ninety-five teenagers who lived in remarried family households found that this flexibility is the critical variable to explaining teens' happiness with their family relationships (Henry & Lovelace, 1995). Specifically, adolescents who perceived their remarried families to be more flexible reported greater satis-

Living in two different family households can be challenging, and it helps to be flexible so that children can move from one household to the other more easily.

faction with both the overall remarried family household and the parent–stepparent relationship.

African American families have adopted this model of flexibility more readily than whites; their families tend to have more fluid and permeable boundaries so that children can feel comfortable in more than one household (Crosbie-Burnett & Lewis, 1993; Hunter & Ensminger, 1992). African American children are more likely than other children to spend portions of their childhood in extended-family households or in other flexible arrangements. For example, one study, conducted in the largely African American community of Woodlawn, outside of Chicago, examined living arrangements of children between the first grade and adolescence. The study found that among African American children who lived in two-parent households when in first grade, 10 percent had lived in a two-parent extended family by the time of adolescence, 30 percent had lived with a single parent, 10 percent had lived in a one-parent extended family, and approximately 2 percent had lived with family members other than parents (Hunter & Ensminger, 1992).

5. *The stepparent may be thrust into the role of "instant parent" with no previous parenting experience.* He or she is expected to play a knowledgeable parent role in the household. Biological parents have the opportunity to grow into parenting roles as their children grow; however, stepparents are often expected to adjust instantly as though parenting is an inborn skill. For biological parents, the bonding process results in being more tolerant of their children's personalities and behaviors than someone who does not know them as well or does not have a sense of history with them. The reverse is also true. Children are bonded to (and thus often more tolerant of) their biological parents.

6. *The role models for stepparents are poorly defined.* Part of this problem stems from the fact that the legal status of stepparents and the rights of parents are remarkably different (Mason, 1998; Mahoney, 1994). For example, parents, just by virtue of a biological tie, have child support obligations, custody rights, and inheritance rights. These exist regardless of the social and emotional bonds between parent and child. In contrast, stepparents in most states have no obligation during the marriage to support their stepchildren. They also do not have any legal custody right. Consequently, if the marriage terminates through either divorce or death, stepparents generally do not have the automatic right to custody or even to visitation. Moreover, in the case of divorce, they have no obligation to pay child support, regardless

of whether their stepchildren have long depended on their income (Mason & Simon, 1995).

Given this legal backdrop, we can see that the social role of stepparenting also has few rights or privileges attached to it. Nonetheless, stepfamilies often compare themselves to biological families and have expectations regarding family life that are naive. For example, members may have unrealistic expectations of one big happy family paralleling the popular television show of the early 1970s, *The Brady Bunch*. But roles and emotional bonds take time to develop. There is little agreement about the stepparenting role, even among members within a particular family. Stepfathers seem to be more satisfied with their family life if they adopt a father-like role (Marsiglio, 1992), whereas stepmothers are less likely to assume a mother-like role and, instead, act as something more akin to a friend (Church, 1999).

The top show of the 1970s, *The Brady Bunch*, made living in a stepfamily look easy.

| FACT OR FICTION?

Adolescents tend to attribute more negative motives to stepparents' behavior than they do to their own parents in identical situations.

7. *Step-relationships are new and untested, and they are not a given as they are in other families.* Even when the new groups are in tune with one another, they do not have the comfort of really *knowing* that there is an unconditional bond of caring and love. Outward signals and signs are continuously needed in many stepfamilies to show that caring and loving really exist. Researchers note that affection and genuine "liking" are found more often between stepparents and stepchildren when stepparents intentionally tried to get their stepchildren to like them (Ganong, Coleman, Fine, & Martin, 1999), especially at the beginning of the relationship (Bray & Berger, 1993; Hetherington & Clingempeel, 1992). However, stepchildren also play active roles in developing positive emotional bonds with their stepparent. Hetherington and Clingempeel (1992) found that stepfathers eventually withdrew from stepchildren when they felt that their overtures early in the marriage were being ignored.

By Patti Posner

I was divorced in 1986, when my daughter was eight years old. When I started dating and realized that perhaps one day I would remarry, I remember thinking that I would like to marry a man who already had children. I never thought about what it would mean to be a part of a step or blended family, and just how that would impact my life.

In 1990 I married a man who had two children. My husband also has an ex-wife, ex-in-laws, plus his ex-wife's long-time live-in significant other. The coming together of my daughter and myself, my husband, his children, his ex-wife, her significant other, and her parents has been a very difficult task.

It is very difficult to form a blended and extended family. Part of the dilemma of blending families is that there are few, if any, cultural guidelines to follow. For example, we know how to behave and what is expected of us when we become in-laws. But we really do not know what our role is with our spouse's ex-spouse. There is no language for these new members of our extended family, nor do we think of them as friends. They may actually be seen as intruders, and a relationship built on this type of foundation can be very draining.

My own story is probably not all that different from the many other women who have married men who have previously been married. It took over eight years for the adults to come together. For years I felt in the midst of an angry tug of war. My husband's relationship with Jane (ex-spouse) was based on anger and fighting. I was hurt when my husband was unable to set boundaries for himself and for letting Jane manipulate him. I felt that Jane was trying to control her children in ways that were interfering with my life with my new husband. It seemed that no matter what my husband and Jane did, I had to enter into the picture, and would become angry and frustrated as well. The two main issues that I was confronted with were control and anger. And then I had to learn to deal with issues of jealousy. I had no role model, and I was very confused by all the emotions because of having Jane in my life. I think all three of us really had no idea of how to behave: for Jane and my husband, to be cordial ex-spouses who share and love their children; for Jane and myself, who had the awkward relationship of having been married to the same man; and even for myself and my husband, on how to deal with his ex-wife.

Adolescence is a particularly challenging time to forge new emotional bonds, and conflicts may arise or escalate during this stage (Hetherington, 1993). Using vignettes of various family situations, Russell and Searcy (1997) found that adolescents responded to their own biological parents in a friendlier and more supportive way than they did to stepparents in identical situations. They tended to attribute negative motives to stepparents' behavior but not to their parents' behavior.

8. *The children in stepfamilies have extra sets of relatives.* Living in a stepfamily offers the chance for many additional

FACT

Stepchildren are harder on their stepparents than they are on their parents.

relationships, including relationships with an extra set (or two) of grandparents, aunts and uncles, and cousins. The ties between these relatives can vary dramatically from no contact to close relationships. For example, some stepgrandchildren have little relationship with their stepgrandparents, while others have an especially warm one. The outcome of these relationships depends largely on the investment that

There were no road maps for any of us to follow. The difficulties between the three of us kept growing, and none of us were capable at the time to make the necessary adjustments. I could no longer take having Jane call our home, because most times an argument would ensue. I did not know how to pull myself out of the turmoil. I did something that may sound radical; I sent a note to Jane asking her not to call our home and explained that I could no longer deal with the arguing.

A year later I came to a halting revelation: I can choose to be married to my husband, and if I do, then his ex-wife must be a part of the picture. I sent another note, this time asking her to simply put the past aside and to begin again as friends. I give Jane much credit because she has been able to do this with dignity.

Our first meeting was for her son's college graduation. The whole family went, myself, my husband, all our children, Jane and her boyfriend, and her parents. Our first few minutes were a bit awkward, and then we eased into a relationship. Her boyfriend and I have an inside take on "our family," as we share the sense of being "the in-laws." In the past two years we have shared several family events. Having been able to succeed at this relationship has been and continues to be a very gratifying and healing experience.

Source: Adapted from Patti Posner (2002). "One Family's Journey to Healing." Stepfamily Network, Inc. Available online: http://www.stepfamily.net. Reprinted with permission of Stepfamily Network, Inc.

Critical Thinking

1. If remarriage is so common, why are the relationships so awkward? Why do we not have a common understanding of language, behavior, expectations, and responsibilities?

2. What kinds of issues would cause such tension between the current wife and the ex-wife? Are these issues similar to or different from the issues among current and ex-husbands?

3. What prompted the author to send a note to her husband's ex-wife? Do you think that this was an appropriate action? Why or why not?

---

the stepgrandparents make (Cherlin & Furstenberg, 1994). The possibilities are one of the exciting by-products of stepfamilies.

Multiple Relationships and Dynamics
Ahrons and Rodgers (1987) discuss the different relationships involved in a stepfamily, illustrating that remarriage may involve the addition of new family members in all three generations: parents, children, and grandparents. Let's take a look at their hypothetical case. Nancy and Jim recently divorced, after many years of marriage. They had two children together, Ellen and David, who were aged eight and ten, respectively, at the time

of the divorce. Both children have continued to live with their mother, Nancy. They spend every other weekend, six weeks in the summer, and some holidays with their father. Two years after the divorce, Jim married Elaine, who is the custodial parent of a six-year-old daughter named Jamie. The next year Nancy remarried a man named Craig, who had also been divorced, and has joint custody of two daughters, aged six and eleven. Within the next four years, Jim and his new wife, Elaine, had two children of their own, a son and a daughter.

When Ellen and David, the two children of Nancy and Jim, are fifteen and seventeen, their family looks like this: they have two biological parents, two stepparents, three stepsisters, a half-brother, and a half-sister. The extended family has also grown to include two sets of stepgrandparents, two sets of biological grandparents, and an expanded network of aunts, uncles, and cousins.

Former Spouse Subsystem Ahrons and Rodgers (1987) have dissected the components of these relationships and uncovered the features that make them so complex. First, there is a former spouse subsystem. This relationship becomes increasingly complex as former spouses remarry or become involved in significant relationships. The Family Narratives box on pages 566–567 gives one woman's story about coming to terms with her husband's ex-wife.

Tensions are more likely to arise if one of the former spouses marries quickly before other family relationships have been reorganized and stabilized. For the spouse who remains single, the marriage may bring to light jealousy, old feelings, or animosity. With respect to Jim's remarriage to Elaine, Nancy said this:

> When Jim told me he was getting married, I reacted with a cutting comment, saying that I hoped she was better prepared for long evenings alone than I was. But what I was really scared about was that he would be different with her than he was with me. What if he had *really* changed? I realized that I wanted his marriage to fail. Then I would know that I was right in divorcing him. (Ahrons & Rodgers, 1987)

Jim's remarriage initiates a complex set of changes for all participants. Even though Nancy and Jim have been divorced for two years, Jim's remarriage caused their relationship to change even further. Jim experienced many conflicts:

> When Elaine and I decided to get married I felt guilty and like I needed to tell Nancy immediately. I dreaded telling her. When I did tell her she didn't say much, but I knew she was feeling upset. I wanted the kids to be part of the wedding and I knew Nancy was going to feel jealous and left out. I'd feel much better if she had someone else in her life. Elaine's relationship with her ex-husband is nothing like my relationship with Nancy and she didn't understand my wanting to ease Nancy's pain by not flaunting my new life at her. (Ahrons & Rodgers, 1987)

Because of the children that they had together, Nancy's and Jim's lives are intertwined, yet Nancy is faced with abiding by a new set of loyalties—Jim's new life with Elaine. It is difficult for Nancy to see that Elaine's needs are important or that Elaine is a significant person to the children or to Jim. Six months after Jim's remarriage, Nancy summarized it this way:

> Things have changed a lot since Jim remarried. He's less willing to accommodate when I need to change plans around the kids. He always has to check with Elaine first. I really resent that—the kids should come first. I invited Jim to Ellen's birthday party but he couldn't come because of plans he had made with Elaine and her child. And I feel uncomfortable calling him at home about anything. Elaine usually answers the phone, and I feel like she's listening the whole time. Jim has asked to take the kids on a week's vacation to visit Elaine's parents over Easter. I know it's his time with the kids but I think he should give them some special time and not make them spend it

with Elaine's family. (Ahrons & Rodgers, 1987)

Researchers find a pattern of deteriorating co-parental relations after remarriage, particularly if the ex-husband remarries and the ex-wife does not. The number and frequency of shared child-rearing activities (e.g., birthday parties) are highest when both partners are single, and lowest when only the husband has remarried. Conversely, conflict is highest when only the husband has remarried, and is lowest when both are single.

Remarried Couple Subsystem Second, Ahrons and Rodgers (1987) discuss the remarried couple subsystem. Remarried couples overwhelmingly report that they are unprepared for the complexities in remarried life, including the exchange of children, money, and decision making. When Jim and Elaine married, they fantasized about their plans for blending their families, minimizing the problems and remaining optimistic that they could cope because of the love that they share. But many of the problems created more stress than they had imagined. As Elaine describes it,

> When Jim and I decided to get married, I was surprised by his feelings about Nancy. I didn't have any of those feelings about my ex, Tom. When Tom remarried last year it didn't make much difference in my life. He hadn't seen much of Jamie [their daughter] anyway and he just saw her less after he remarried. It was a relief not to have much to do with him. So, after living alone with Jamie for three years, I was really excited to have a family again and give Jamie more of a dad. But it's not working out that way. Jamie is angry a lot about not having time alone

> with me, which ends up with Jim and me fighting a lot. Jim feels badly about not spending enough time with his kids, and when the kids are together, it just seems to be everyone fighting over Jim. And I feel resentful at not having enough time alone with Jim. Between every other weekend with his kids and the long hours we both work we never seem to have time alone together. Last Friday we were finally spending an evening all alone and, just as I was putting dinner on the table, Nancy called. Jim and I spent the next two hours talking about Nancy. It ended up spoiling our whole evening. (Ahrons & Rodgers, 1987)

Elaine's concerns are not unusual. Remarriage when children are present requires reorganization and realignment, and these are usually neither simple nor quick.

Sibling Subsystem A third subsystem discussed by Ahrons and Rodgers is the sibling subsystem. The typically competitive struggles among siblings can become a heated battle in remarried families as children must learn to share parental time, household space, and parental affection. The authors suggest that the transition to remarriage may, in fact, be more stressful to children than the transition to divorce because the newly married parent is preoccupied with his or her new mate and may neglect the children in the transition.

Nonetheless, although some children reject a new sibling, others may welcome one. Some stepsibling relationships remain close even into adulthood. White and Reidmann (1992) analyzed national data and examined the degree to which biological siblings and stepsiblings remained in touch in adulthood. They found that adult biological siblings kept in contact significantly more often than did stepsiblings (one to three times a month versus only several times a year), but only .5 percent of stepsiblings were so estranged that they did not know the whereabouts of their stepsibling. Adults who are most likely to keep in contact with stepsiblings include women, African Americans, younger persons, and those who live physically close to their stepsiblings.

Most stepparents believe that their role in the family should be that of "parents" to the stepchild, while stepchildren are more likely to believe that stepparents should be "friends."

How Similar Are the Views of Stepparents, Parents, and Stepchildren?

To explore how stepfamily members see the role of the stepparent, and how consistent their views are with one another, family researchers Mark Fine, Larry Ganong, and Marilyn Coleman conducted a study of forty families in which each stepparent, parent, and one child between the ages of ten and nineteen were surveyed. One question asked respondents to describe the "ideal way" that the stepparent should relate to stepchildren. Possible responses include distant relative, teacher, friend, stepparent, acquaintance, advisor, boss, parent, uncle/aunt, enemy. The results showed that parents and stepparents were in general agreement—about half identified "parent" as the ideal way that stepparents *should* relate to stepchildren. Moreover, they felt that this was the role they were currently taking. They believe that a stepparent should act much like a parent does in a nuclear, first-marriage family. However, the stepchildren felt differently. They believed that the role of "friend" was the most

appropriate way to relate. These different views have the potential for conflict if clear expectations are not communicated (Fine, 1997).

Stepparents and stepchildren are likely to disagree on the stepparent's proper role.

How Do Children Fare in Stepfamilies?

In their decade review of the research published during the 1990s on remarriage, Coleman, Ganong, and Fine (2000) found that one-third of the studies dealt with the effects of remarriage (or repartnering) on children. The bulk of this research focused on the academic achievement of young and adolescent children living in stepfamilies, their psychological well-being, and their likelihood of exhibiting behavioral problems. A number of large national studies were conducted using data gathered from a representative sample of people in the United States (along with data from other countries as well). Children in stepfamilies were generally compared to children living in two-parent biological families and to children living in single-parent families (usually due to divorce).

On average, children growing up in stepfamilies have outcomes that are similar to children in biological two-parent families.

How do children from stepfamilies fare? The news is not particularly encouraging. Just as we reported in the previous chapter, that children from single-parent households face an increased chance of certain negative outcomes, so do many children who live in stepfamilies. In other words, the well-being of children in stepfamilies is no better on average than the well-being of children in divorced single-parent families.

FICTION

On average, children growing up in stepfamilies are more likely to have outcomes that parallel single-parent households than biological two-parent households.

Certainly, not all stepchildren experience problems. Many stepchildren grow up feeling secure in happy, loving homes made possible by their parent's remarriage. It is estimated that 100,000 stepchildren are adopted by their stepparents every year, likely indicating their mutual love. Among minority groups in particular, living in a stepfamily is reported to often have significantly positive effects on a child's well-being. Family researchers have found that high-quality relationships with stepfathers, and to a lesser extent with noncustodial fathers, may have a positive effect on internalized problems, such as depression or feelings of worth, and on externalizing problems, such as impulsivity and restlessness (White & Gilbreth, 2001). As one adopted son, now an adult, put it,

> Looking back, I think the "legal" adoption really isn't too important to me now, except for some consistency between my folks' and my last name. What was significant then was the act of the adoption and what it signified. It was a very validating experience, though I couldn't have articulated that as a child. My mom had picked a new person in her life, and that person had chosen me as his son, in whole. And I chose him to be my dad. The adoption was the stamp of approval on his choice and mine. (Sample, 1999)

Despite these important findings, research indicates that in terms of potential

How do children growing up in stepfamilies fare? This is a growing area of research for family scholars.

difficulties, children living in stepfamilies often have more in common with children from single-parent homes than they do with children residing in biological two-parent families (Hoffmann & Johnson, 1998; McLanahan & Sandefur, 1994; Pong, 1997). We can see that, in general, stepchildren (and children living in single-parent households) earn lower grades in school, complete fewer grades, and score lower on achievement tests (Bogenscheider, 1997; McLanahan & Sandefur, 1994; Pong, 1997; Teachman, Paasch, & Carver, 1996). They also have higher rates of depression and emotional problems, particularly when conflict between two households is present (Zill, Morrison, & Cioro, 1993; Hanson, McLanahan, & Thomson, 1996). They are also more likely to exhibit behavioral problems such as involvement with alcohol and drugs, nonmarital childbearing, idleness, or being arrested (Coughlin & Vuchinich, 1996; Hoffman & Johnson, 1998; McLanahan & Sandefur, 1994). For example, a study based on 194 males found that living in either a stepfamily or single-parent family more than doubled the risk of delinquency that began by age fourteen, including arrest. However, it did not increase the risk of delin-

Remarriage and partnering create many stresses for children, including possibly moving to a new home.

munity) related to the divorce. Remarriage does not repair these deficits completely, perhaps because stepparents are expending resources on their children from a prior union or because stepparents are not fully invested in their stepchildren (Bogenscheider, 1997; McLanahan & Sandefur, 1994). Children reared in stepfamilies created by marriage do seem to fare better than children living with parents in a cohabiting union, at least with respect to income and likelihood of poverty (Morrison & Ritualo, 2000).

A third explanation suggests that quality parenting may be compromised as parents get involved in new relationships because they are *investing time and energy into their new relationships rather than into child rearing.* For example, parents may not spend as much time talking with their children, helping them with their homework, or monitoring their friends and activities as they did prior to the remarriage because they are preoccupied with their new partner (Downey, 1995; Pong, 1997). This reduced involvement, in turn, can lead to problems in children.

A fourth explanation is related to the *lack of norms* for stepfamily behavior. This perspective suggests that stepchildren fare worse, on average, than children in two-parent biological families because stepfamily members are unsure how to relate to one another. They do not know how to express their feelings, and there is a lack of institutional support for helping them overcome difficulties (Visher & Visher, 1996).

These theories draw heavily upon psychology (stress and individual adaptation) and sociology (social roles and structural contexts). But there are other views as well. An evolutionary perspective, which draws upon sociobiology, points to the lack of biological ties between stepparents and stepchildren. It suggests that *stepparents who are also biological parents will discriminate in favor of their genetic children* (Flinn, 1992); their stepchildren may have academic, emotional, and behavioral problems as a result.

quency that began at a later age (Coughlin & Vuchinich, 1996). But again, let us also remember that the vast majority of stepchildren do well in school and do not have emotional, behavioral, or delinquency problems.

Explanations for Added Risk Why do children living in stepfamilies face an increased chance for these outcomes? Several theoretical explanations have been proposed. The most common center around the notion of *stress,* suggesting that remarriage and repartnering involve many stressful changes and potential conflicts for both adults and their children (Crosbie-Burnett, 1989). These stresses include possibly moving to a new residence and adapting to new family members and new routines, both of which could contribute to poorer school performance, depression, and behavioral problems (Menaghan, Kowalski-Jones, & Mott, 1997).

Another explanation focuses primarily on *economic and social capital deprivation.* This theory suggests children living in stepfamilies and in single-parent families are disadvantaged because of their lower incomes and reduced levels of social capital (connections to other adults or institutions in the com-

How Do Adults Fare in Stepfamilies?

Despite the excitement of being in a new loving relationship, both men and women usually have to make significant adjustments to living in a stepfamily. For example, if a woman's new husband has children, she will have to learn to at least accept them, if not develop affection for them. Most likely, they will visit on a part-time basis, but often the visit is for extended periods of time (e.g., six weeks in the summer).

She may also have to learn to accept the alimony and child support payments that go towards maintaining her husband's previous wife and children from that union. Average child support payments are about $300–$400 a month, but they can go significantly higher than that, depending on the husband's income and the number of children he is supporting. Feeling resentful over the payments (e.g., "we could buy a new car with that") will do little towards developing a smooth and harmonious relationship with her new husband or his children.

A wife may also need to deliberately work towards encouraging her children to accept her new spouse, and vice versa. Younger children are usually more accepting than adolescents, and make for a smoother transition. It is more difficult for adolescents to accept their mother's new relationship because they may not want to accept new authority figures into their lives or admit that their mother is having a sexual relationship with someone new. Likewise, adults do not always find teens immediately lovable!

Men in stepfamilies face a similar set of concerns. They must learn to get along with their wives' children, who likely reside with them on a full-time basis. Moreover, since child support, even when given regularly, is not intended to cover the full costs of caring for the children, the new husband may find that he must financially support his stepchildren while also paying for his own. Finally, if he has children who now reside elsewhere with their own mother, he must also find ways to encourage his new partner to accept these children, and minimize the problems that could arise from part-time residence or visitation.

FACT OR FICTION?

One key step that stepfamilies can do to be more successful is to nurture and enrich the couple relationship.

Strengthening Stepfamilies

The Stepfamily Association of America (SAA) knows that living in a stepfamily is not always easy for the parent, child, or stepparent. It has developed a list of recommendations that can enhance the stepfamily's success (2000). These include the following:

* Nurture and enrich the couple relationship. *Affirm each other frequently by demonstrating affection, being open and honest, spending time together without the children, and fighting fairly.*

* Reveal and understand emotions. *Deal with and resolve the loss, bitterness, or guilt that often exists after a divorce. Encourage the children to express and process their feelings as well.*

* Have realistic expectations. *All members of the stepfamily need time to get to know one another before remarriage takes place. Instant love is a myth.*

* Develop new roles. *Understand that a new family is being created and that all members will be developing some new roles and changing other roles.*

* Seek support and see the positive. *Learn about stepfamily dynamics and seek positive support from family, friends, or organizations. Emphasize the positive because stepfamilies have many strengths.*

On this Father's Day I believe not only biological fathers should take a bow but also stepfathers. As the biological dad in a stepfamily, I am acutely aware of the fact that my daughter spends part of her time with her stepdad and mom too. She is shared by two families who love her.

When Father's Day rolls around, I get all the gifts and recognition as her dad. That's great, and I eat it up and enjoy my breakfast in bed to the fullest. And while I am like the bright sunshine for my daughter, she also enjoys delightful moonlight. So on this Father's Day, I want to recognize the efforts of my daughter's stepdad.

His name is Richard, and I hardly know him. Although we share fatherly duties, we share very little else. I know his birthday and his last name. We hardly ever talk beyond the handful of sentences a year at school functions or when calling my daughter over the phone. What do you think about my daughter? Does she make you happy with her vivacious ways?

Can she make you laugh with her jokes? Do you hurt inside when she cries? Do you read her stories when she goes to bed? You are a mystery to me, but of the few things I do know about you I am grateful.

When my daughter comes home, she sometimes relates a story about how Richard did a nice thing for her. How you took her miniature golfing, let her steer the car in the parking lot, took her out for ice cream. She thinks your parents are great, and she loves the horseback riding lessons your job helps buy her. It's not hard to see that she has come to love you in a special way as a very important member of her extended family.

I know the difficulty you must have experienced with her in the beginning because, you see, my daughter has a stepmother too. It was hard for all of us to get used to the changes whirling around us, especially her at such a young age. Only time and patience has helped heal old wounds. I just want to encourage you not to take it hard

whenever my daughter gets upset about you. She does that to me and her stepmom, too! It's all part of growing up—no matter what one's age.

So while I'm going to enjoy this Father's Day to the fullest, please accept my gratitude. You are an important male influence for my daughter, and I appreciate your kindness and love towards her. I hope one day society will have the courage to face up to the reality of stepfamily situations. My dream is for stepfathers—and stepmothers—to each have their own special day of honor.

By Tom Wohlmut

Source: Tom Wohlmut (2001). "Thanks to a Stepfather on Father's Day." Stepfamily Network, Inc. Available online: http://www.stepfamily.net. Reprinted with permission of Stepfamily Network, Inc.

Critical Thinking

1. Do you think that this father is typical or atypical? Why?

2. In what ways might his positive attitude affect his daughter?

The Stepfamily Association of America lists this as the first step in creating strong, healthy stepfamilies.

The Family Narratives box on page 574 illustrates this positive thinking. It is a letter written from a father to a stepfather, letting him know how much he is appreciated.

Conclusion

This chapter examines family relationships after divorce. Most people who divorce are happy that they did so, although divorced persons tend to have lower psychological well-being than do married persons. But divorce, and the relationships that begin after divorce, are influenced by broader social forces. For example, given the low pay structure for many women, divorced women often struggle financially to support their families and raise them alone, although they often become closer to their children in the process. A small but growing number of single men are raising children. They too suffer financially compared to two-parent families but are considerably better off than single mothers, on average.

Most divorced persons remarry or repartner within three to five years after the divorce. A stepfamily consists of a remarried or repartnered couple in which at least one of the spouses has a child from a previous relationship. Stepfamilies have many unique characteristics compared to two-parent biological families and face a number of specific challenges. Social science research has proved invaluable in understanding the special concerns that stepfamilies face. For example, research has found that children living in stepfamilies may exhibit a range of personal, social, and behavioral problems that more closely resemble those of children living in single-parent households than those of children whose parents have not divorced. While not all children in stepfamilies exhibit these types of problems, social science research has made us aware that they are a potentially vulnerable group in need of special care and support.

Chapter Review

* *What types of relationships do custodial parents have with their children after a divorce?*

Many studies show that custodial parents are often closer to their children and have a more peer-like relationship after divorce.

* *Do people have many regrets after a divorce?*

Most studies reveal that people are generally pleased after they divorce and feel that, overall, they made the right decision.

* *What is the biggest issue for women after a divorce?*

The first few months or years after a divorce are a difficult time. One of the most pressing issues is the downward mobility that many women face. Most women underestimate the amount of financial hardship that they and their children may confront.

* *What are some issues facing fathers after a divorce?*

The number of custodial fathers is increasing rapidly. Nearly one-half of these fathers are single because of divorce. They are less likely to be awarded child support than single mothers; when awarded it, they are less likely to receive it.

* *How much dating and/or cohabiting do divorced people do?*

According to one study of women, the average number of men they had dated prior to meeting their future spouse was between three and five dating partners. Ten percent had dated only their future spouse, and one-third dated more than ten men. Cohabitation is quite common and, for some couples, replaces marriage altogether.

* *Is remarriage a new phenomenon in the United States?*

Remarriage has always been a common feature of family life in the United States. How-ever, it is now most likely to be a result of a divorce, whereas in the past it usually resulted from the death of a spouse.

* *Which groups in the United States are more likely to remarry?*

Nearly three-quarters of all people who divorce in the United States eventually remarry. The average length of time between a divorce and remarriage is approximately four years. However, whites are more likely than minority groups to remarry, and men are more likely than women.

* *Why do men and women not remarry at the same rate?*

There are several reasons, including that men are able to initiate contact more easily, the double standard of aging sees older women as not as attractive as older men, the pool of eligible partners is larger for men, and women are more likely to have children living with them.

* *How strong and stable are remarried relationships?*

Remarried relationships can be fragile. Women do feel that they have more power in their relationships regarding financial and other decisions. However, overall, subsequent marriages are not necessarily happier than first marriages. Their rate of divorce is higher.

* *What is a "stepfamily"?*

A stepfamily is one in which one or both of the adult partners have at least one child, either residing with them or elsewhere. There are many different types.

* *What do we mean when we call stepfamilies a "normless norm"?*

We mean that although they are becoming very common (a norm), the expectations, obligations, and rules within these families are vague and confusing.

* *What are some of the unique features of stepfamilies?*

Stepfamilies come about because of a loss; the parent–child relationship has a longer history than the new couple's relationship; there is a biological parent outside the stepfamily unit and an adult of the same sex as the absent parent in the household; most children in stepfamilies hold membership in two households with two sets of rules; the role models for stepparents are poorly defined; step-relationships are new and untested, and they are not a given as they are in other families; and the children in stepfamilies have extra sets of relatives.

* *How similar are the views of stepparents, parents, and stepchildren?*

Generally, stepparents and parents seem to agree that the role of the stepparent should be as close as possible to a parent. Stepchildren see it differently. They believe the stepparent should act more in the role of a friend.

* *How do children fare in stepfamilies?*

There are many studies that address this issue, focusing on the academic achievement, psychological well-being, and behavioral problems of children living in stepfamilies. The results of these studies usually indicate that children growing up in stepfamilies have an increased chance of negative outcomes compared to children growing up in biological two-parent households. It appears that the well-being of children in stepfamilies is no better, on average, than the well-being of children in divorced single-parent families, perhaps due to stress, economic and social capital deprivation, the parents' investing their time and energy into the new relationship rather than into their children, the lack of norms for stepfamily behavior, and/or stepparents' discriminating in favor of their own genetic children.

* *How do adults fare in stepfamilies?*

Adults also face a series of financial and emotional challenges in adjusting to a stepfamily.

* *How can stepfamilies be strengthened?*

The Stepfamily Association of America (SAA) has a number of recommendations, including nurturing and enriching the couple relationship, revealing and understanding emotions, having realistic expectations, developing new roles, seeking support, and seeing the positive in the situation.

Key Terms

remarriage: a subsequent marriage. This area is gaining new interest because divorce rather than death has now become the leading precursor to remarriage.

repartnering: establishing a new relationship after divorce but not remarrying

stepfamilies: families in which one or both of the adult partners has at least one child, either residing with them or elsewhere

stepfamilies as a normless norm: the idea that stepfamilies are common but that the expectations, obligations, and rules within these families are vague and confusing

Resources on the Internet

These web sites have been selected for their relevance to the topics in this chapter. These sites are among the more stable, but please be aware that web site addresses change frequently.

Stepfamily Association of America
http://www.stepfam.org
The Stepfamily Association of America is a national organization dedicated to providing support and guidance to families with children from previous relationships.

Stepfamily Network

http://www.stepfamily.net

The Stepfamily Network is a nonprofit organization dedicated to helping stepfamily members achieve harmony and mutual respect in their family lives through education and support.

Wedding Planner & Guide—Second Weddings

http://www.wedplan.com/secwed.htm

Offers advice to couples planning a second wedding on points of etiquette and general concerns.

Companion Web Site for This Book

Virtual Society: The Wadsworth Sociology Resource Center

http://sociology.wadsworth.com

Begin by clicking the Student Resources section. Next, click Marriage and Family, and then click the cover image for this book. Select from the pull-down menu the chapter you are presently studying. You will have easy access to chapter resources such as MicroCase Online exercises, additional Web links, flashcards, InfoTrac exercises, and practice tests (that can be scored). In addition, to enhance and help with your study of marriages and families, be sure to investigate the rest of the rich sociology resources at Virtual Society.

Visit InfoTrac College Edition

 Another unique option available to you at the Student Resources section of the Virtual Society web site described above is InfoTrac College Edition, an online library of hundreds of scholarly and popular periodicals. Here are three suggested key search terms for this chapter:

* Search keywords: *cohabitation + children*
* Search keywords: *remarriage + age*
* Search keywords: *stepfamilies + conflict*

Search recent years to get the latest information on these issues.

© Jim Erickson /Corbis

Families in Middle and Later Life

14

"Grow old along with me. The best is yet to be." —Robert Browning

"Will you still need me, will you still feed me, when I'm sixty-four?" —The Beatles

"It's not the years in your life, but the life in your years." —Cary Grant

"Age, I do abhor thee. Youth, I do adore thee." —William Shakespeare

"Old age is always 20 years away." —Jack LaLanne

"Women are not forgiven for aging. Robert Redford's lines of distinction are my old-age wrinkles." —Jane Fonda

Couples who marry in their mid-twenties can expect to live another fifty or sixty years. This chapter focuses on marital and family relationships when couples reach the middle and later years of life. We begin by looking historically at the role of the elderly in families. Then we examine the changing demographic structure—people are living longer than ever before, and this has many pronounced effects on our family relationships. We then explore the process of family transitions, such as when children leave home and when parents become grandparents. We next examine the marital and sexual issues that aging couples may experience. The chapter concludes with a look at the growing research on how families care for frail elders, including the dark side of elder care—elder abuse. It will become clear that aging is far more than a biological process. The aging *experience* is largely social in nature, and it is shaped by cultural and historical influences.

Aging in Historical Perspective

Many people relish the thought that elders were highly respected in the past. However, historians have largely debunked the myth of the "golden age," when all seniors supposedly commanded respect, power, and prestige. Instead, we now realize that many elderly persons in early America were quite marginalized. The elderly poor were despised and treated as outcasts. Elderly black slaves continued to be bought and sold at the mercy of their owners. Elderly women were largely dependent on their spouses for financial and social standing since they were not allowed to own property themselves, and when their spouses died, often so went their livelihood. Many elders never experienced "retirement"—they continued to work in dangerous or dirty jobs to put food on the table and have a roof over their head. Only a small segment of the elderly population—property-owning white males—experienced the status and prestige that we generally associate with old age (Farrell, 1999).

Before the Nineteenth Century

During the seventeenth and eighteenth centuries, with a strong Puritan influence in agrarian colonial America, older, white, property-owning males were seen as among God's "selected people" (Fischer, 1977). They had made it! They had fought off myriad diseases that plagued people during this period, avoided or recovered from life-threatening accidents, and otherwise escaped death. Property-owning older white males commanded the respect of their community members and dominated the power circles. Even seating arrangements in New England meeting houses were arranged according to age, with "graybeards" having the best seats in the house.

At home, elderly, white, property-owning males maintained patriarchal control over their land. Their family was a "business"—a critical agency of economic production and exchange. Each household was relatively self-sufficient, and family members were inextricably tied to one another. All members—young and old, male and female—had critical tasks.

Ideally, early American households were nuclear, with adult children located nearby, often even on the same land. This family style has been called a "modified extended family system" (Greven, 1970). Adult sons often continued to live at home until their fathers passed away or until they received land as a wedding gift (Demos, 1986). Only between 12 percent and 18 percent of households in the late nineteenth and early twentieth centuries contained extended family members outside the immediate nuclear family (Hareven, 1977).

Fischer (1977) illustrates the common and powerful grip fathers had over their sons in his description of the Holt family from Andover, Massachusetts. The senior patriarch, Nicholas Holt, established himself as a wealthy landowner with the help of his five sons. He retained strict control of his property and refused to relinquish any land to his sons until he was seventy-seven years old. Only at his death, when his sons were middle-aged and had been married for a number of years, did they finally achieve financial independence. This pattern continued in the next generation. Henry Holt, Nicholas's son, had eight sons of his own. None of them received land until Henry was seventy-three, at which time four of them had been married for between seven and seventeen years. Owning property was equated with economic and social power. Fathers were reluctant to relinquish this power, and sons had little choice but to bide their time and wait their turn. Old age had its advantages. But on occasion, landowning fathers would retire and turn over the family farm to a son with the provision that the son would take care of his aging parents. Aging parents made contracts with their sons specifying that, in exchange for their care in old age, they would provide their son with land. The fact that parents relied on formal contracts rather than just an informal agreement speaks volumes about the potential insecurities between the generations (Smith, 1973).

Early census takers found that people commonly exaggerated their age, reporting that they were older than they actually were. People exaggerated their age because being older was considered a privileged status, at least in the idealized culture of white property owners. Today it would be difficult to imagine most adults inflating their age. This illustrates that our ideas about aging are both socially constructed and continually changing.

The Nineteenth Century and Beyond: Cultural and Structural Changes

Historians begin to see some evidence of changing cultural ideals about aging in the nineteenth century. This is likely due to cultural and structural changes that occurred

FAMILY DIVERSITY — Aging and Social Policy in Canada

As in the United States, approximately 12–13 percent of Canada's residents are aged sixty-five or older, but by 2025 the proportion of the elderly will increase to nearly 19 percent. In comparison with the countries of Western Europe, Canada is considered to be a youthful country, but this will change by 2025, when the number and proportion of elderly will increase significantly. As with the United States, this change will be costly because public programs for the elderly are the largest single category of expenditures.

Canada's first critical program for the elderly was its Old Age Pensions Act of 1927. Although begun nearly a decade before our Social Security program, it was not universal. It provided a pension of just $20 a month to low-income persons over the age of seventy. By 1951, the pension had increased to only $40, and it continued to be offered only to the poor. A major change occurred in 1952: the Old Age Security Act was passed, which extended the $40 pension to everyone, regardless of income, at age seventy. Several changes have been made since then, including the following:

- A drop in age of eligibility from seventy to sixty-five
- Establishment of the Guaranteed Income Supplement
- Full annual cost-of-living adjustments
- Establishment of the Spouse's Allowance
- Extension of the Spouse's Allowance to all low-income widows and widowers aged sixty to sixty-four
- Extension of benefits and obligations to same-sex common-law partners

Moreover, the amount of the benefit has been raised significantly. Elderly Canadians receive a flat rate, depending on how long they have lived in Canada. A person who has lived in Canada after reaching age eighteen for periods that total at least forty years may qualify for a full Old Age Security pension. Those with less tenure receive less. Unlike in the United States, this pension is not based on earnings— everyone is entitled to it by right of citizenship.

This pension is not intended to be a person's sole means of support. Consequently, a second tier of pension benefits was adopted in 1967 for those who have little or no other income. Called the Guaran-

---

in the process of moving from an agrarian to an industrial economy. Patriarchal power began to wane as more and more sons moved away from their fathers' farms to the city in search of manufacturing work. Family members became more independent of one another because of the distance between the cities and farms.

Over time, as this new breed of workers grew older in their manufacturing jobs, they often found that they could not keep up with younger workers and were displaced by them. Old age ceased to be an asset and was considered an economic liability (Farrell, 1999). With geographic mobility, aging parents could not always rely on their children to take care of them when they became ill or frail.

By the second half of the nineteenth century, elderly persons living in poverty were becoming increasingly conspicuous. Almshouses, which housed or provided charity to needy people, were increasingly made up of elderly persons with no money and no family members to turn to for help (Haber, 1983). Americans began to shift from viewing aging as a natural process to seeing it as a period of life characterized by physical and mental decline, dependence, and weakness. During this period, geriatrics emerged as a branch of medicine that focused on medical symptoms of mental and physical decline

teed Income Supplement, this second tier is based on income, as is the case in the United States. The employer and the employee each contribute to the pension plan. In addition to these public pensions, employed persons in Canada, as is the case in the United States, have access to pension plans established by their employers and to personal savings plans.

Canada's program is significantly different from the Social Security program offered in the United States. First, Canada offers a safety net for all its citizens by providing all the aged, regardless of their earnings or participation in the labor force, a basic pension. Only the second tier is tied to labor force participation. In contrast, in the United States, Social Security is strictly tied to labor force participation and wages, and no general support is offered.

Second, in Canada, national health insurance, sickness benefits, and family allowances are provided to all citizens and are paid for by public taxes. Canadian physicians are generally private, self-employed, fee-for-service practitioners, but unlike their U.S. counterparts, they do not deal with numerous insurance companies. Physician fees in Canada are paid by government-sponsored national health insurance according to rates negotiated with government officials in each province. Private health insurance is generally prohibited except for some supplemental benefits.

With a rapidly rising elderly population, Canada is faced with increasing financial pressures to continue to provide for the health and well-being of its elderly. Canada's approach to dealing with its elderly is similar to how it deals with the needs of all its citizens regardless of age—people are provided a basic level of services regardless of their ability to pay. These services are guaranteed by right of citizenship.

Source: Adapted from Cockerham (1997); Human Resources Development Canada (2002).

Critical Thinking

1. Why do you think the Canadian system differs so much from the U.S. Social Security program?

2. Do you think the United States might expand its program to more closely resemble the Canadian model? Why or why not?

(Hareven, 2000). Social reformers, policy makers, and early researchers not only noted a positive correlation between old age and poverty, but many suspected a causal relationship operated as well. They felt that poverty was an outcome of industrialization because the elderly simply could not keep up with younger persons in the factories and industries (Epstein, 1922).

In the late nineteenth century and the early twentieth century, few companies had private pensions for seniors, and the government did not provide public pensions. Consequently, elderly persons who could still physically work usually did so. In 1900, two-thirds of men over the age of sixty-five were employed, as compared to only about 16 percent of men (and 10 percent of women) today (U.S. Census Bureau, 2000a). Many other industrialized nations had created publicly funded programs that provided pensions for the elderly. Germany implemented such a program in 1889, Great Britain in 1908, Sweden in 1913, Canada in 1927, and France in 1930 (Cockerham, 1997). The Family Diversity box on pages 582–583 illustrates the features of the Canadian model.

| FACT OR FICTION?

Today, the poverty rate of the elderly is below that of the rest of the population.

During industrialization, older workers had difficulty keeping up with younger workers in the fast paced, often dangerous working environments.

In the United States, bills for public pensions were introduced many times between 1900 and 1935 with no success. But during the Great Depression it became obvious that the elderly could not rely on jobs, private pensions, savings, or their families for finan-

cial support. While people of all ages were vulnerable during these hard times, the elderly were particularly hard hit. By 1935, unemployment rates among those sixty-five and older were well above 50 percent (Hardy & Shuey, 2000). Pension plans were still relatively rare. A federal commission determined that nearly half of all seniors in the United States could not realistically support themselves (Achenbaum, 1978). The Social Security Act was born in 1935 as a response to the poverty that enveloped many of our nation's elders. The act, referred to today as simply **Social Security,** is many programs under one umbrella, including Medicare, Medicaid, cash welfare assistance, and cash assistance for survivors and for seniors. But Social Security has become synonymous with a cash-assistance entitlement program for seniors. It is seen as an earned right for seniors, not as a form of welfare (Trattner, 1999).

Payments from Social Security have successfully reduced the percentage of seniors who are impoverished. Today, the poverty rate among the elderly is slightly below that of the rest of the population and is considerably lower than the poverty rate of children, as shown in Figure 14.1. In 2000, 10.2 percent of persons aged 65 and older were in poverty, compared to 11.3 percent nationally, 16.2 percent of children under age 18, and 9.4 percent of adults aged 18–64.

FIGURE 14.1   U.S. Poverty Rates, 2000

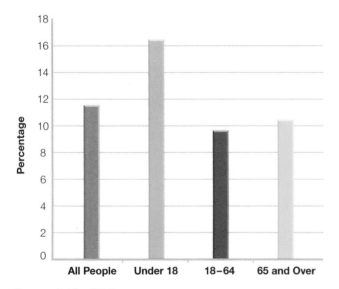

Source: Dalaker (2001).

FACT

The poverty rate among the elderly is slightly below the rate for the population as a whole, but subgroups of elders—e.g., the oldest-old, women, minorities—have high rates of poverty.

The decrease in poverty has brought increased security and leisure time to many elderly persons. Partly due to their significant increase in numbers, seniors today wield increasing political clout. The AARP (formerly known as the American Association of Retired Persons) is the second largest social organization in the United States, after the Roman Catholic church! (Farrell, 1999). Invitations to join are generously extended to all persons at age fifty. Since half of the membership is not retired, the organization recently changed its name to simply AARP.

The Demographic Revolution

The United States is in the midst of a powerful revolution, although you generally do not see people demonstrating in the streets. Yet this revolution is destined to reshape the nation and the world. It is a demographic revolution. Only a century ago, birthrates were high and life expectancy was short. Therefore, only a small portion of people—1 in 25—were aged 65 or older (3.1 million) in 1900. It is likely that many younger people spent long portions of their lives rarely even seeing an elderly person. But the elderly population has been increasing almost four times as fast as the population as a whole, and seniors now constitute 1 of every 8 people (35 million) (Hetzel & Smith, 2001). In fact, elderly persons now outnumber teenagers. The elderly population has grown substantially during the twentieth century.

. . . And will continue to rise well into the twenty-first century

According to projections made by the U.S. Census Bureau, the elderly population will more than double between now and the year 2030 to approximately 70 million, as shown in Figure 14.2. By then, as many as 1 in 5 Americans could be aged 65 or older. Much of this growth will occur between the years 2010 and 2030 as the **baby boom generation** (those born after World War II through the early 1960s) ages.

FIGURE 14.2 U.S. Census Bureau's Projections on Elderly Population Growth

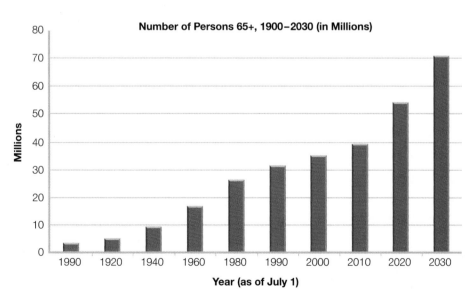

Source: U.S. Census Bureau

One of the 50,000 centenarians in the United States celebrates her 100th birthday with her great-granddaughter.

beyond his African American counterpart (U.S. Census Bureau, 2001).

As life expectancy increases, many persons will live far longer than our average statistics suggest. Persons aged 85 and over—referred to as the "oldest old"—constitute the most rapidly growing elderly cohort in the United States. They now number over 4 million, or 10 percent of all elders, and 1.2 percent of the entire population in the United States (Hetzel & Smith, 2001). Because of the greater longevity of baby boomers, it is expected that the number of oldest old will jump to 19 million in 2050. That would make them 24 percent of all elders and 5 percent of all Americans in just 50 years.

FACT OR FICTION?

Who lives to be 100? Research finds that most centenarians are white, wealthy males.

The number of persons living to be at least 100 years old is increasing dramatically as well. Twenty years ago, there were only 15,000 centenarians in the country. Today, there are over 50,000, and by 2050, the U.S. Census Bureau predicts that this figure could increase tenfold. Dr. Leonard Poon heads a centenarian study at the University of Georgia. "We want to see what influences longevity and adaptation in old age," he writes. (By the way, some centenarians turned down his request to participate in the study because they were "too busy.") One of these centenarians, Mary Sims Elliott, 104, was working on her autobiography, writing poetry, and trying to influence her church's position on social issues. Now she's 105, and her autobiography, *My First One Hundred Years,* was just published (Purdy, 2000).

Although there remains a large degree of variation, the study has drawn up a general portrait of a centenarian. "She":

* lives by herself or with her children
* has an income of $4,000–$7,000

...Especially for the "oldest old"

Life expectancy, or how long a person can expect to live from birth, is going up. Life expectancy is usually calculated from birth—for example, a girl born in 1998 can anticipate living 79.7 years and a boy 74.1 years. This is a significant increase from a century ago, as medical advances have eliminated or significantly reduced many infectious diseases, such as influenza, smallpox, and measles, that killed many people in the past. However, life expectancy can be calculated at any age. If we successfully pass through several dangerous periods—childhood, adolescence for males, childbearing years for females—then our life expectancy goes up. By age 65, females can expect to live another 17.8 years, compared to 15.9 years for males (National Center for Health Statistics, 2001). Life expectancy varies across racial and ethnic groups. For example, a white girl born in 1999 can anticipate living an average of 5 years longer than an African American girl born in the same year. Likewise, a white boy born in 1999 may live an average of 6 years

* has vision and hearing problems
* takes two medications a day
* wants to avoid institutionalization
* is feisty and wants to have her way
* is generally satisfied with life. (Purdy, 2000)

Most centenarians are poor females.

. . . Consequently, more people face dependency, and more people will need to care for the dependent

We have made vast improvements in medical technology, drugs, and procedures during the twentieth century, and people live considerably longer and in better health as a result. Most elderly who live outside of institutions, particularly in the younger cohorts, report being in excellent or good health. Nonetheless, as more people live to the oldest ages, we will see more chronic conditions such as arthritis, osteoporosis, and senile dementia. These types of conditions result in people needing assistance in various **activities of daily living (ADL)** such as cooking, cleaning, bathing, and home repair. Who will provide this care to an increasing number of seniors? Most do not really require the complete care provided in nursing homes. Instead, most will turn to their adult children, often in their fifties, sixties, or even seventies themselves, to provide care.

Elderly women outnumber elderly men . . .

Because men have higher death rates than women at every age, more women make it to old age than do men. The differences, especially in the older age cohorts, are substantial. As shown in Figure 14.3, there are 82 men for every 100 women for those aged

FIGURE 14.3 Sex Ratio of People 55 Years and Older, by Age, 1999

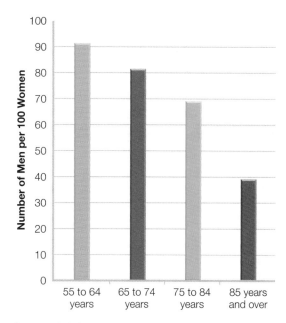

Source: U.S. Census Bureau (1999).

The sex ratio becomes very imbalanced among the older age cohorts; therefore women spend an increasing amount of time sharing the company of other women.

65–74. By ages 75 to 84, there are only 69 men alive for every 100 women. And among the oldest-old groups (85 and over), there are over twice as many women alive as men—49 men for every 100 women (Hetzel & Smith, 2001)

. . . Consequently, while most elderly men are married, most elderly women are not

Living arrangements and marital status among the older population differ considerably between men and women as they age (Hetzel & Smith, 2001). As shown in Figure 14.4, most elderly men are married, which is not the case for elderly women. Over three-quarters of men aged 65–74 are married, compared to only slightly more than half of women. Even among the oldest-old cohort, more than half of men are married, com-

pared to only 12 percent of women in this age group. In contrast, women are far more likely than men to be widowed. As the figure reveals, only 8 percent of men between 65 and 74 are widowed, compared to nearly one-third of women the same age. The vast majority of women age 85 and over are widowed, compared to only 38 percent of their male counterparts.

Many elderly women live alone . . .

A consequence of the different rates of widowhood is the fact that elderly women are far more likely than men to live alone. Forty-one percent of elderly women live alone, compared to only 17 percent of elderly men (Fields & Casper, 2001).

However, these averages mask the diversity in living arrangements found among persons of different racial and ethnic back-

FIGURE 14.4 Percentage of People 65 Years and Older Who Were Married with Spouse Present or Widowed, by Age and Sex, 2000

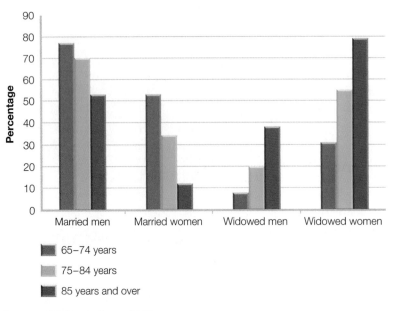

Source: U.S. Census Bureau (1999).

FIGURE 14.5 Percentage of People 65 Years and Older Below
Poverty Level, 2000

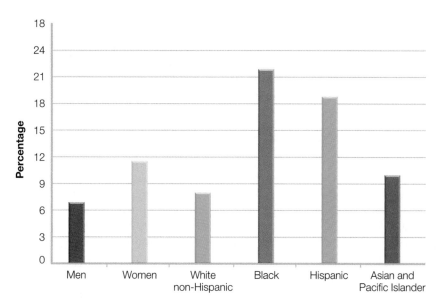

Source: Dalaker (2001).

grounds. Asian American elders, in particular, are less likely to live alone and are far more likely to live in an extended-family arrangement than are whites. The differences, and the cultural reasons behind them, are elaborated upon in the Focus on Family Research box on page 590.

. . . Consequently, older women are more likely to live in poverty than are men

Poverty is a serious problem faced by many older women, as shown in Figure 14.5. Nearly 12 percent of elderly women live in poverty, and the figure increases as women join the ranks of the oldest old. Figure 14.5 also reveals that the likelihood of being in poverty varies across racial and ethnic groups. Older African Americans are the most vulnerable, with nearly one-quarter living in poverty.

Family Transitions

Over time, families undergo a number of important transitions, such as the birth of children, the launching of those children, becoming grandparents, and retirement. These experiences and their timing are dictated in part by cultural norms. Despite considerable variation in when people experience certain transitions, as a culture we share a remarkable consensus regarding the appropriate ages at which these events *should* occur (Settersten & Hagestad, 1996). However, these norms are subject to change.

Midlife as Crisis

There is a lot of talk about the **midlife crisis** that people supposedly experience as they approach middle and old age. The assumption is that midlife is a time of trauma during which people focus on what they have failed

With Whom Do They Live? Living Arrangements of Elderly Chinese, Japanese, and Non-Hispanic Whites in the United States

Living arrangements of elderly persons are of interest to family scholars and gerontologists. Particularly at issue has been whether the elderly live in extended families, nuclear families, alone, or in an institutional setting. In many Asian countries, the three-generation extended family is an important and prevalent family type. It is estimated that more than half of rural persons at least sixty years old, and more than a third of their urban counterparts, live in three-generation households. The cultural patterns of these living arrangements are deeply rooted in the tradition of filial responsibility and respect towards elders. Adult children feel a moral obligation to take care of their parents. And despite rapid industrialization in Japan, the honorable status of the elderly there has remained stable. The elderly continue to be integrated into their children's families.

However, does this pattern continue after Asians migrate to the United States? In the United States, extended families have never been very common. Even during the preindustrial era, co-residence among the generations was temporary and not widespread. This pattern of nuclear family arrangements continues to predominate, overall, at least with respect within the white, non-Hispanic majority population. Cultural values stress individualism and personal freedom, and these often endure into later years.

Using data from the 1980 U.S. Census on 8,502 elderly persons, sociologists Yoshinori Kamo and Min Zhou examined the residence patterns of elderly Chinese, Japanese, and non-Hispanic whites. They compared the living arrangements between the unmarried and married elderly, and between males and females. Furthermore, they examined these patterns in California, Hawaii, and elsewhere in the United States.

As shown in the table, they found that elderly Chinese and Japanese men and women are far more likely to live with their children than are whites. This is particularly the case for older women, but significant differences are also seen among men. For example, in Califor-

nia, 43 percent of unmarried elderly Chinese women and 37 percent of unmarried elderly Japanese women live with their children (in their children's household), compared to only 9 percent of unmarried elderly white women. Differences are even more pronounced among married persons. Although norms in the United States promote privacy and independence among married couples, in California, 24 percent of married elderly Chinese women and 12 percent of married elderly Japanese women live with their children in the children's household, as compared to only 2 percent of married elderly white women. The trends in Hawaii and elsewhere in the United States parallel those found in California. Co-residence with adult children is far more common for elderly Chinese and Japanese men and women than it is for whites.

Source: Adapted from Kamo and Zhou (1994).

to achieve (e.g., in employment) or focus on the changes in their family (e.g., children leaving home). The media play up the notion of a midlife crisis by showing middle-aged men buying fancy new sports cars or divorcing their wives and taking up with women twenty years their junior. Despite the talk, most of the transitions during this period are not as traumatic as we are led to believe. Many of the changes are expected, even anticipated. Midlife is generally as happy as any other time of life.

Perspectives for Understanding Development and Change

Several perspectives explain how people develop and change over time. The three most common perspectives are known as the life-stage perspective, the life-span perspective, and the life-course perspective. Briefly, the **life-stage perspective** contends that development proceeds through a fairly set pattern of sequential stages that most people experi-

Percentage of Chinese, Japanese, and Non-Hispanic Whites, Aged 65 or Older, by State, Who Live with Their Children

	CALIFORNIA	HAWAII	ELSEWHERE IN UNITED STATES
Unmarried (%)			
Chinese			
Male	17	10	20
Female	43	36	58
Japanese			
Male	21	30	11
Female	37	45	33
White			
Male	11	10	3
Female	9	19	12
Married (%)			
Chinese			
Male	18	4	18
Female	24	4	30
Japanese			
Male	7	8	5
Female	12	9	14
White			
Male	1	1	1
Female	2	2	1

Source: Kamo and Zhou (1994).

ence. These are considered to be age-linked and relatively universal. Transition from one stage to another is largely dependent on how successful a person was in an earlier stage.

The **life-span perspective** proposes that development is a multidirectional, lifelong process. Development consists of both positive and negative changes, and always involves gains and losses. This perspective notes that there is a great deal of individual variability, for development is dependent on social and cultural conditions.

The **life-course perspective** focuses on age-related transitions that are socially produced, socially recognized, and shared. Aging is a lifelong process influenced by social structure, historical forces, and culture. Glen Elder identifies four principles of the life-course perspective (1998):

* the principle of historical time and place
* the principle of timing in lives
* the principle of linked lives
* the principle of human agency

Elder's work shows us how individuals change over time, how their transitions are connected to other family members, and how these changes reflect social and historical conditions.

One such transition occurs when children move out of their parents' home. They may leave home for college or simply to get their own apartment. Another transition is when children marry. Another occurs when children become parents and their parents become grandparents.

Increasingly, we see that parents must also deal with *unexpected* transitions in their adult children's lives (Allen, Blieszner, & Roberto, 2000), such as when adult children move back home to live with them (Goldscheider & Lawton, 1998; Lee & Dwyer, 1996). However, even during these transitions, parents and children continue to have close, enduring ties. As Zarit and Eggebeen comment,

Parent–child relationships are a life-span issue. Rather than ceasing when children are launched from the family, these relationships endure with often complex patterns of interaction, support and exchange that wax and wane around key transitions in the adult years. (1995: 119)

Children Leaving Home

Frances Goldscheider, a sociologist and demographer, has referred to the home in which one was raised as "the safety net young adults often need" as they embark on a complex set of transitions (1997). Children may leave home for school, work, travel, or marriage. For example, over two-thirds of first-year college students live away from their parents' home (American Council on Education & University of California, 1998). Adult children leave, but an increasing number now return to the parental home in times of need. Approximately 40 percent of all adult children return to their parents' home for a period of at least four months (Goldschieder & Goldschieder, 1994). Many return, move out, return, and move out once again. Why is this?

In the past, a woman's primary reason for leaving home was marriage (Goldscheider & Goldscheider, 1994). Among men, the most common reasons for leaving home were either marriage or to join the military. Given these reasons, few of these adults moved back into their parents' home. But today, the route out of the parental home is significantly less likely to involve marriage or the military. Young adults branching out on their own do so because of school or simply the desire to live on their own (Ward & Spitze, 1996). They are affected by a broader economic picture. Housing costs, job opportunities, and wages all influence people's ability to live independently. Most return to their parents' home because of graduation from college, employment prospects that soured, or the desire to save additional money rather

Approximately 40 percent of adult children move back in with their parents for at least four months.

than because of a marriage or military service ending. Few adult children move back with their parents specifically to give them assistance (Ward & Spitze, 1996).

Advantages and Disadvantages of Returning Home Children who return home face a myriad of advantages and disadvantages. On the plus side, both parents and their adult children have reported a number of benefits, and approximately 70 percent of parents have reported that they thought co-residence worked out "very well" (Aquilino & Supple, 1991). Young adults may experience greater emotional and economic security living with their parents. If they have children of their own, they may benefit by having a grandparent participate in child care. Likewise, older adults may benefit by having their children near them to provide assistance in various tasks of daily living, such as yard work, cooking, and cleaning. Older adults may also appreciate having their grandchildren live with them.

Co-residence also has some marked disadvantages, however (Ambert, 2001). It can alter the older parents' life course significantly. They may not be able to retire as early as they wish, they may have to postpone plans to travel, they may need to reorganize their own finances in order to offer assistance to their children, they may need to rearrange furniture and space within the house, and they may find themselves doing extra cooking and cleaning. Children often return home when they have special needs (i.e., little or no money), and parents may feel obligated to help them out regardless of their own personal and financial situation.

Older parents and adult children may return to the roles that they played when the children were teens. Parents may try to establish a curfew or establish rules governing their adult child's behavior or clothing. If the adult child has lived alone for a period of time, then he or she is likely to resent these rules and see them as intrusions.

Almost all adults in the United States do eventually live separately from their parents. As they do, their relationships change again.

Young Adult–Older Parent Relationships

Overall, relationships between older parents and their adult children improve as the children leave home, cohabit, marry, and are employed (Aquilino, 1997; White & Rogers, 1997). Both generations report strong feelings of connection to each other, although parents often have stronger feelings of attachment to their children than their children have to them (Lynott & Roberts, 1997). Generally, adult children and their parents want to get along, and therefore try to avoid those topics that cause tension in the relationship. Few adults report overt hostility or conflict with their aging parents. One study found that only 5 percent of adults reported frequent conflict with their aging mothers and 6 percent reported frequent conflict with their aging fathers (Cicirelli, 1983).

A survey conducted by AARP, Harvard University, and the University of Southern California with a sample of 1,500 randomly selected adults was designed to explore intergenerational solidarity (Silverstein & Bengston, 2001). Solidarity included a number of dimensions: *structure* (factors such as geographic distance that constrain or enhance interaction), *association* (frequency of social contact and shared activities among family members), *affect* (feelings of emotional closeness, affirmation, and intimacy among family members), *consensus* (actual or perceived agreement in opinions, values, and lifestyles among family members), *function* (exchange of instrumental and financial assistance and support among family members), and *norms* (strength of obligation felt toward other family members).

Researchers identified five types of intergenerational relationships based on these dimensions of solidarity, which are indicated

TABLE 14.1	Latent Classes of Intergenerational Relations
CLASS	DEFINITION
Tight-knit	Adult children are engaged with their parents based on all six indicators of solidarity.
Sociable	Adult children are engaged with their parents based on geographic proximity, frequency of contact, emotional closeness, and similarity of opinions but not based on providing assistance and receiving assistance.
Obligatory	Adult children are engaged with their parents based on geographic proximity and frequency of contact but not based on emotional closeness and similarity of opinions. While only about one-third of children in this class are engaged in providing and receiving assistance, this proportion is slightly higher than that for the sample as a whole.
Intimate but distant	Adult children are engaged with their parents on emotional closeness and similarity of opinions but not based on geographic proximity, frequency of contact, providing assistance, and receiving assistance.
Detached	Adult children are not engaged with their parents based on any of the six indicators of solidarity.

Source: Silverstein and Bengston (2001).

in Table 14.1. They include the following: tight-knit, sociable, obligatory, intimate but distant, and detached.

The *tight-knit* group, in which adult children are engaged with their parents on all six indicators of solidarity, is most characteristic of an extended family that owns a business together, while the *detached* represents the most pronounced isolation among extended families. Relationships in the other three groups are connected on some but not all dimensions of solidarity.

The researchers noted that nearly one-third (31 percent) of adult child–mother relations fell into the *tight-knit* category, the most common type. Only 7 percent of adult child–mother relations fell into the *detached* category, yet this was the most prevalent type of relationship among adult children and their fathers (27 percent). The *tight-knit* category was the third most common type among adult child–father relations, with 20 percent falling into this category (Silverstein & Bengston, 2001). Bonds with mothers, especially between daughters and mothers, appear to be strong and enduring (Walker & Allen, 1991).

The researchers also found racial, ethnic, and social class variations with respect to adult children's relationships with their mothers. For example, whites are more likely than African Americans to have *detached* maternal relations. Whites are also more likely to have *obligatory* relations than are African Americans and Hispanics. These findings support the claims that family relations among minority groups are more cohesive and are based more on altruism and less on obligatory feelings. No differences were detected in relationships with fathers.

Income level was found to be negatively associated with solidarity among adult children and their mothers. That is, adult children with lower incomes were more likely to have *tight-knit* maternal relationships than were those with higher incomes. This is consistent with findings from other research studies (Silverstein & Bengston, 2001).

Child Partnering and Marriage

An important transition experienced by most families is the child's marriage. When a child marries, he or she brings a new person into the family. A new daughter- or son-in-law can create new opportunities for family closeness as well as the possibility for new tensions.

Women are largely responsible for maintaining ties among family members. This is called **kin-keeping.** Therefore, daughters-in-law play a critical role in fostering and maintaining contact across the generations. Rossi and Rossi (1990) note that sons have greater contact with their parents after they marry than they did prior to marriage. The reverse is true for daughters, who actually have less contact with their parents after they marry. The explanation for this may be found in our expectations about what it takes to be a "good" daughter-in-law. She is expected to be the kin-keeper for her new family. Therefore, she may try to build good relations with her husband's family by initiating more frequent contact. She may, temporarily at least, decrease contact with her own relatives.

Most adult children receive substantial help from their aging parents, far more than they give.

Assistance from Aging Parents

Most adult children receive substantial help from their aging parents. Until parents are very old and frail, they give far more assistance to their children than they receive from them. They may lend money to their adult children for a down payment on a new house or a new car, they may provide child care to grandchildren, they may help pay for a grandchild's college tuition, or they may provide their adult children with extra cash in times of personal need such as a family illness or a divorce. Gallagher (1994) found that older and middle-aged adults spend almost twice as many hours helping relatives as do younger adults (forty-one and forty-two hours versus twenty-one hours per month) and more than three times as many hours helping their immediate family members (thirty-three and thirty-two hours versus eight hours per month).

Until parents are very old and frail, adult children generally receive far more assistance from their parents than the reverse.

Financial assistance received from aging parents is usually not an ongoing arrangement, but rather is given as a lump sum for a particular need. Consequently, if we look at cross-sectional data, which represent a snapshot in time, the data will suggest that most aging parents are not providing assistance to their children. For example, one national survey found that only 17 percent of adults reported getting $200 or more from their parents within the previous five years, and only 4 percent reported receiving more than $200 (Eggebeen & Hogan, 1990). However, cross-sectional data mask the true extent of the financial assistance that is shared over the course of time.

Co-residence

Some parents and their adult children live together in one household. Although co-residence is relatively uncommon, with only about 8 percent of families adopting this model, we see in Table 14.2 that co-residence is rare among some ethnic groups and relatively common among others (Glick & Van Hook, 2002). For example, less than 6 percent of white parents and children co-reside, but nearly one third of families from Southeast Asia do, as do nearly one quarter of families from Central and South America.

Why do families co-reside? Do they live together to better care for a frail and dependent parent, or to care for a dependent child? Or do they live together for other reasons? Table 14.2 also shows whether there is a dependent adult or child in the family. Again, we note interesting variations across racial and ethnic groups. For example, while Asian groups largely co-reside to care for a

TABLE 14.2	Percentage of Parent–Adult Household Co-residence, 1995–1998			
	TOTAL (%)	DEPENDENT PARENT (%)	NEITHER DEPENDENT (%)	DEPENDENT CHILD (%)
Total	8	3	3	3
Non-Hispanic White	6	2	2	2
Asian	24	14	6	4
East Asian	20	13	5	3
Southeast Asian	29	15	9	5
Other	21	12	4	5
Mexican	21	8	7	7
Other Hispanic	18	8	6	4
Cuban	14	7	5	3
Puerto Rican	14	4	6	4
Central/ South American	23	12	6	5
Black	15	4	5	5

Source: Glick and Van Hook (2002).

dependent parent, this is not the case among Mexicans.

Grandparents and Their Grandchildren

Almost all parents eventually become grandparents. On average, first grandchildren are born when grandparents are in their late forties, although the age is increasing as young couples wait longer to have children. Some people may not become grandparents until their eighth decade (Walker, Manoogian-

Grandparents today are more likely than those in the past to be emotionally involved in the lives of their grandchildren.

O'Dell, McGraw, & White, 2001), while for others, more than forty years may pass between the birth of a first and last grandchild. Compared with children in the past, children today are more likely to have all four grandparents alive when they are born, and most will continue to have at least two grandparents alive when they reach adulthood (Szinovacz, 1998; Uhlenberg & Kirby, 1998).

Grandparenting in the Past and Today
The role of grandparent has changed over the past century (Cherlin & Furstenberg, 1986). First, it has become a role distinct from parenting itself because grandparents are now unlikely to still have their own children living in the home. Second, it has changed because the elderly are healthier, are better educated, and have greater economic security than in the past. Third, grandparents, grandfathers in particular, are now more likely to recognize the importance of having direct emotional involvement with young children. Grandfathers have opportunities to participate in nurturing children that seemed unavailable to them as fathers, or to grandfathers in the past (Cunningham-Burley, 2001). Finally, families can more easily travel long distance and communicate by way of telephone or computer.

Families are now able to construct their own understandings of what it means to be a grandparent (Walker et al., 2001). Relationships between grandparents and their grandchildren vary tremendously, but most grandparents find their relationships meaningful and report that fun and pleasure are key components of the relationship. In their national study of grandparents, Cherlin and Furstenberg (1986) found that over half of grandparents reported a **companionate** relationship with their grandchildren: they enjoy recreational activities, occasional overnight stays, and even babysitting. The relationship is intimate, fun, and friendly. Grandparents reported that they enjoy spending time with their grandchildren but that they "are ready

FIGURE 14.6 Percentage of Grandparents Engaging in Activities with Grandchildren Over the Past 12 Months

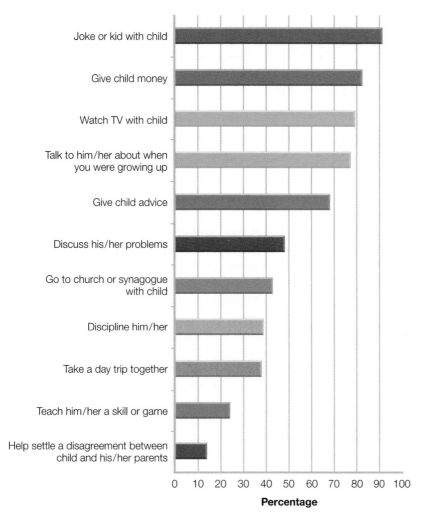

Source: Cherlin and Furstenberg (1986).

to leave the tough work of parenting to the parents" (Cherlin & Furstenberg, 1986: 56). As one grandmother said,

> Afterwards the grandchildren go back home where, of course, they find the routine, the direction of their parents. I get the good part, because I can play, enjoy myself; that is, I have no direct responsibility. . . . A grandparent is left with the more enjoyable part, and so I have a great time. I enjoy being a grandmother. . . . I chose to be a grandmother such that when she arrives it's great fun. (Gattai & Musatti, 1999: 38)

Nearly one-third of grandparents had **remote,** or emotionally distant, relationships with their grandchildren, usually because they lived far away. Another 15 percent were more **involved,** with more frequent interaction or possibly even living together. Figure 14.6 shows the percentage of grandparents engaging in various activities with their children during the previous twelve months.

Cherlin and Furstenberg (1986) also point to the changing relationship between grandparents and grandchildren. They found a marked shift in the balance between respect and affection. They asked all respondents in a national survey, "Are you and the [study child] more friendly, less friendly, or about the same as your grandparents were with you?" Forty-eight percent reported that they were "more friendly" while only 9 percent said "less friendly." Similarly, 55 percent claimed that their relationship with the child was "closer" than their own relationship with their grandparents, and only 10 percent said that it was "not as close." When respondents were asked about respect, most reported no difference. However, 22 percent said that they were more respectful of their grandparents whereas only 2 percent believed that their grandchildren showed them greater respect.

FACT OR FICTION?

Most grandchildren feel closer to their grandmother than to their grandfather.

Differences Between Grandmothers and Grandfathers Grandparenting styles are different for women and men. Grandmothers are more likely to be involved in planning and orchestrating family activities, nurturing their grandchildren, and assuming caregiving responsibilities (Walker et al., 2001), consistent with their role at all ages of being the family "kin-keeper." Women tend to have the responsibility for maintaining family contact. For example, it is usually the women in the family who are responsible for sending greeting cards on holidays and birthdays. Family scholars show us that kin-keeping carries over into the grandmother role as well. In contrast, grandfathers are more likely to focus on practical issues and spend more time exchanging help and services with their grandsons than with their granddaughters (Hagestad, 1985; Cherlin & Furstenberg, 1986). One consequence of this difference in

style is that family members generally feel more obligation and are closer to their grandmothers than to their grandfathers (Rossi & Rossi, 1990). Perhaps this is why grandmothers report greater satisfaction and overall meaning in grandparenthood than do grandfathers (Somary & Stricker, 1998).

FACT

Grandmothers and grandfathers have different styles of interaction, and grandchildren generally report feeling closer to their grandmothers.

Racial and Ethnic Differences in Grandparenting Styles A small number of studies have looked at the variation in the grandparent role across ethnic and racial groups. These studies reveal that in racial and ethnic minority families, grandmothers frequently have important and influential roles in child rearing, often mimicking parent-like behavior (Dilworth-Anderson, 2001; Hunter, 1997; Kivett, 1993; Morgan & Kunkel, 1998; Uttal, 1999).

A study by psychologist Andrea Hunter (1997) examined African American mothers' and fathers' reliance on grandmothers for parenting support. She used a sample of 487 parents aged 18 to 34 from the National Survey of Black Americans, examining their responses to the following questions: (a) "Do you have anyone who gives you advice about child rearing or helps you with problems having to do with children? If yes, what is this advisor's relationship to you?" and (b) "Do you have someone to count on to take care of the children? If yes, what is this person's relationship to you?" She found that 57 percent of the mothers and 56 percent of the fathers reported that they relied on grandmothers for parenting support, relying on them more frequently than anyone else. The majority of these persons said that they receive both advice and child care from the grandmothers.

Another study of Apache grandmothers shows how the roles of grandparents are socially constructed and can vary dramatically from one culture to another. The author notes four key differences between Apache and "Anglo American" grandparenting styles (Bahr, 1994):

* *Obligation and responsibility.* An Anglo American grandparent is a "spoiler" of grandchildren, one who may interact or give gifts but who can also have meaningful relationships with his or her grandchildren with only minimal obligation and responsibility. Among the Apache, particularly among grandmothers, grandparenting means heavy obligation and responsibility. The grandmother's role is that of a parent substitute within the family. There is virtually no such thing as minimal involvement and responsibility.

* *Gender differences in grandparental role behavior.* In Anglo American society, grandmothers are somewhat more important than grandfathers because they tend to have warmer and closer relationships with their own children as well as their grandchildren. Among the Apache, the importance of grandmothers far exceeds the importance of grandfathers. Although Apache and Anglo patterns are similar, it is the magnitude of the difference between grandmothers and grandfathers that is striking. This is a function of grandmothers' greater longevity but also the cultural norm of greater affinity and responsibility to children.

* *Grandparents as part of a viable, functioning family network.* In Anglo families, kinship ties among parents, adult children, and grandchildren are valued, but households tend to be independent. Economics and residence are rarely shared. The preference is for families to be independent of one another. In Apache families, not only are kinship ties valued, but households are also likely to be extended and often involve cross-generational members, including grandparents, aunts, uncles, and cousins. Family households have loose, permeable boundaries. Family members are highly interdependent, and this is seen as a real strength.

* *Economic security and economic responsibility.* Among Anglo Americans, grandparenthood and retirement are times of fairly secure economic status. Grandparents are likely to own their own homes and have accumulated savings. They are not responsible for rearing or educating their grandchildren or supporting their adult children. There are few if any economic demands made on them. In Apache families, being an elder and a grandparent is a time of heavy economic demand. Grandparents, including grandmothers, may be economically responsible for the support of their adult children and grandchildren. They may continue to work in the formal or informal sector of the economy so that they can provide some or all of the assistance to their often multi-generation family. They remain active and influential participants in community life.

Three theories are often used to explain why racial and ethnic minority families are more likely than white families to use grandparents (and other kin) to provide child care for their grandchildren (Uttal, 1999). The *cultural* explanation suggests that these practices are the product of different cultural experiences and adaptations. The *structural* explanation views these child-care arrangements as an adaptation to structural constraints, such as racism or poverty. The *integrative* explanation combines the first two perspectives, suggesting that these arrangements are due to the intersection of cultural values with structural constraints, operating alongside gendered expectations.

In her in-depth interviews with seven African American mothers, seven Mexican American mothers, and seventeen Anglo American mothers, Uttal (1999) found that the major difference among the groups was how the mothers *felt* about using kin for care. Anglos tended to feel that relying on grandparents and other kin was inappropriate or problematic, whereas African American and Mexican American mothers willingly accepted this help because they felt that it was appropriate and acceptable (even if not necessarily ideal, in their minds). Unlike the others, the white mothers in her study were particularly concerned about being a burden or imposing, as indicated by this statement:

> I don't think I'd want to be that owing to her. In debt to your mommy! I just don't like it when someone does a favor for you. There's an implied obligation that if someone does something for you, you should do something for them. I think it's better to pay for someone's services, and get it over with. I'd feel this big obligation.

Grandchildren and Grandparents Living Together A growing number of children live with their grandparents. We commonly think of these as families in which the grandparents move into the homes of their adult children and grandchildren because they are too frail to live independently. But there has been a new twist in co-residence patterns that has received attention. Instead of the common pattern of an older generation moving into a house maintained by their adult child (and grandchildren), grandchildren (and sometimes their parents) are moving into a house maintained by the grandparents.

Researchers first began to notice this trend in the early 1990s, when the U.S. Census Bureau reported that 4.9 percent of all children under age 18 were living in a home maintained by their grandparents (Bryson & Casper, 1999). As shown in Figure 14.7, by 1997 that figure had increased to 5.5 percent, or 3.9 million children.

Sometimes, one or both of the child's parents also live with the grandparent. But as shown in Figure 14.7, the greatest growth has occurred among grandchildren living with one or both grandparents with no parent present. Of the 3.9 million grandchildren living with grandparents, approximately 1.5 million live there without their parents. Mothers and fathers are absent for many reasons—death, desertion, incarceration, drug problems, physical or mental illness,

FIGURE 14.7 Percent of Grandchildren Under 18 Living in Grandparents' Home by Presence of Parents

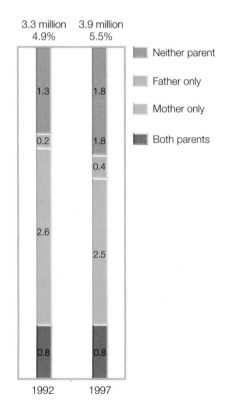

Source: 1992 and 1997 Current Population Surveys as reported in *Marital Status and Living Arrangements: March 1992*, Table 4, and March 1997, Table 4.

employment problems, HIV/AIDS, and child abuse, among others. One study of 129 grandparents raising their grandchildren examined the situations that precipitated this relationship (Sands & Goldberg-Glen, 2000). The study found multiple problems in the homes of the grandchildren's parents that led the grandparents to take over the care of their grandchildren. The most commonly reported problem was substance abuse, but the parents' inability to care for the child, neglect, and psychological and financial problems were also cited as factors. When the grandparents in this study first began to take care of their grandchildren, only one-third expected to be the caregiver until the children grew up. But at the time of the interview, over three-quarters of grandparents reported this expectation.

What are some of the characteristics of these intergenerational families that are maintained by the grandparents? (Bryson & Casper, 1999; U.S. Department of Health and Human Services, Administration on Aging, 2001). Several characteristics are discussed below:

Almost four million children live with their grandparents.

1. *Co-resident grandmothers outnumber co-resident grandfathers five to three.* There are a number of reasons that grandchildren are more likely to reside with a grandmother than a grandfather. One reason is that women live longer; therefore, they are more likely to reach an age where they have grandchildren. Another reason is that women are more likely than men to assume a caregiving role; therefore, grandmothers may feel more obliged to take in grandchildren. Grandmothers are also more likely to be widowed and have lower incomes, so they may want to live with their children or grandchildren for companionship or support.

2. *The majority of grandparents raising their grandchildren are younger than sixty-five.* One-third are younger than age fifty, and nearly half are between fifty and sixty-four. Only one out of five is aged sixty-five or older.

3. *Grandchildren in grandparent-maintained families are more likely to be African American, younger, and living in the South,* compared with grandchildren who live in intergenerational households maintained by their parents.

4. *Grandchildren in grandparent-maintained families are more likely to be poor than other children are.* While nearly 20 percent of all children live below the poverty line, that figure rises to 27 percent for children who live with their grandparents in their grandparents' home. They are also more likely to receive public assistance (56 percent versus 36 percent of all children) and are twice as likely to be without health insurance coverage (33 percent versus 15 percent).

5. *Grandparent caregivers face challenges.* Most grandparents are not particularly eager to take on their grandchildren's care but feel that it is a last resort and that they have little choice in the matter (Hayslip, Jr., Shore, Henderson, & Lambert, 1998; Jendrek, 1994). In addition to financial difficulties, grandparents are prone to feelings

of emotional strain as well as feelings of helplessness, isolation, and decreased life satisfaction (Bowers & Myers, 1999). Grandparents often neglect their own physical and emotional health because they give priority to the needs of their grandchildren. They sometimes encounter problems that can require them to seek legal authority to make decisions on behalf of their children regarding medical care, school enrollment, immunizations, and public assistance and other support services. Some of these issues can be seen in the Focus on Family Research box on page 603, which is based on an in-depth interview with a grandparent who is raising a grandchildren.

In a study of twenty-two African American grandmothers raising their grandchildren, one woman offered the following suggestion about how social service agencies could be more responsive to the financial and emotional challenges she faces:

> Agencies need to provide workers to come out to the home to see how things are going, counsel the family, and help them cope with the changes and difficulties. I always had my only daughter living with me, but now I must adjust to four grandchildren. (Rodgers-Farmer & Jones, 1999)

Relationships with Siblings

Most older people have siblings, although the likelihood of having a living sibling declines with age. The special nature of sibling relationships can make them particularly important as we age—they are the longest lasting of all family connections. Siblings can provide connections to the past, an anchor to the present, and assistance in the future.

Over the course of adult life, sibling relationships tend to become closer and more compatible, and rivalries and conflicts decline. Some have suggested that the relationship represents a U-shaped curve, with a high level of closeness in childhood and early adulthood, decreasing closeness in middle adulthood as siblings become absorbed in jobs and children, and then a return to closeness and intimacy as they approach middle age (Ross & Milgram, 1982; Bedford, 1995). However, closeness likely depends on geographic proximity, gender, racial/ethnic background, and whether siblings have children, as well as on personal interests and temperament (Bengston, Rosenthal, & Burton, 1990). Older adults tend to evaluate their relationships with sisters as closer than those with brothers. Moreover, African Americans are more likely than whites to report feeling closer to their siblings and are more likely to live within two miles of them.

FACT OR FICTION?

The age at which people retire has increased since 1950.

Retirement

Work provides us with income, but for many of us, work is also an important part of our identity. "I *am* a professor," "I *am* a firefighter," "I *am* a doctor" is how we describe our work: we *are* the occupation. Consequently, retirement is a notable transition not only because of the reduced income, but also because it alters a major identity. However, it appears that many people eagerly await this change and see retirement as a legitimate, earned privilege (O'Rand, 1990). The median age at retirement has fallen from sixty-eight years in 1950 to sixty-three today, during a time when life expectancy has increased (Macionis, 2001). This reduction of the retirement age reflects more than just personal whim. It also reflects a convergence of public and private employment policies. People now retire earlier because of publicly funded Social Security, because employer-sponsored

When asked to describe a typical day Cheryl stated: "My day starts at 6:30 or so, trying desperately to get the oldest ready for school and the baby fed and dressed. The kids go to school, I drop Agatha off at day care, and then I go to the office. I pick them all up at the end of school, go home and do some things around the house and try and get dinner ready as I help the kids. Donny, my husband, usually gets home and then helps the kids before and after we eat. We get them to bed, get ready ourselves, and try to get a little sleep before they start waking up in the night."

What makes Cheryl and Donny's story different from millions of other working couples raising young children is that they are not the biological parents of John (age 10), Becky (age 6), and Agatha (age 2), but are their grandparents. Larry, their son and the father of the children, abuses alcohol and other drugs along with the children's mothers. According to Cheryl, this resulted in "abuse, neglect, things like gating the children into a bedroom while they were gone or using, and not feeding the kids all day or changing a single diaper." Once Cheryl discovered this she "took them. . . . I mean it was very hard because I knew it would change our lives but it was also easy to do for the children because my main concern was for their safety and well-being."

Since this decision was made Cheryl and Danny's lives have changed dramatically. As she said, "There's no retirement now. Financially this is very difficult. It has also been stressful on our marriage since we only have one child and are now raising three and Donny travels a lot for his job. We don't have many friends anymore because they don't want us tagging along with children to do adult things. And now instead of traveling and enjoying simply being grandparents, we're parents again." However, when I asked Cheryl if it was worth all the changes to their lives she smiled at me and said, "I love these children. They didn't ask for this. They didn't deserve all this. So I try to give them the best normal world possible. And they don't call me grandma; they call me mom. We may be second generation, but this is my family and these are our kids."

As for John, Becky, and Agatha, despite a frightening beginning in this world they are now thriving in their current environment. While this is the story of only one family, it is a good depiction of many of the families like this in today's society. I interviewed Cheryl and Donny, along with forty other grandparents raising grandchildren in a large metropolitan area, to determine how this phenomenon affects the grandparent–grandchild relationship, and how everyone involved adjusts to this parenting arrangement. I found that grandparents today are removing children from harmful situations and families and providing them with safe and loving homes, often at the expense of their own long awaited "golden years." However, they see the shift from grandparents to parents of these children as a positive change for everyone in the end.

By Suzanne R. Smith, Ph.D.

Source: Suzanne R. Smith, Ph.D., associate professor of human development, Washington State University–Vancouver. Reprinted with permission.

Critical Thinking

1. What are some of the challenges and rewards for grandparents who raise their grandchildren?

2. What are some of the challenges and rewards that the grandchildren may experience?

3. Do you think these challenges and rewards for grandparents and grandchildren may be different across race, ethnicity, or social class? If so, how and why?

Throughout history most people have had to work to support themselves. There was no such thing as "retirement." Today workers retire at an average age of fifty-nine, despite living another twenty years or more.

pension or savings plans are more common, and because many employers are inducing older persons to exit the labor force due to a surplus of labor (Hardy & Shuey, 2000).

FICTION

The age has declined from 68 years in 1950 to 63 years today.

The Social Construction of Retirement A systematic retreat from work at a specific age—retirement—is a social construction. Most people throughout history, as well as across cultures today, have had to work to support themselves. They were not systematically exempt because of their age. Widespread retirement did not exist until relatively recently.

For significant numbers of the elderly to be able to withdraw from the labor force, four conditions must exist in a society (Morgan & Kunkel, 1998). First, a society must produce an economic surplus that is large enough to support its nonemployed members. Second, there must be a mechanism in place to divert some of that surplus to the nonemployed members such as through a pension or government transfer program.

Third, nonemployed members should be viewed positively by the rest of society, and their activities or leisure must be seen as legitimate. Finally, the nonemployed members must have accumulated an acceptable number of years of productivity to warrant support by the other members of society. These conditions materialized in the United States after the industrialization of the nineteenth and twentieth centuries.

Gender and Retirement Typically, retirement is seen as a transition that is important primarily to older men. But as more women enter the labor force, retirement is no longer a male-dominated event. It is also no longer a one-time irreversible event. Today, with almost half of the work force made up of women, and with the majority of workers married to other workers, couples are forging new retirement paths. Couples face not only two retirements, but they must also coordinate their retirements and address whether to take up other paid work after they retire.

Researchers at Cornell University conducted a five-year study of retirement with 762 men and women between the ages of fifty and seventy-two who were selected from six large employers in New York. Respondents were interviewed three times. The key questions addressed were how gender and career pathways influence the planning and timing of retirement and how the timing of retirement, stresses of the retirement transition, and re-employment decisions affect marital quality and retirement satisfaction for both women and men (Cornell Gerontology Research Institute, 2000).

FACT OR FICTION?

Women report being happier in retirement than men do.

The researchers found that workers today retire at the average age of fifty-nine, six years earlier than in previous generations. They noted tremendous variation in age at retirement, ranging from the forties to "never." The men in the sample began to plan for retirement earlier than did the women (ages forty-nine and fifty-four, respectively) although they retired at similar ages (Han & Moen, 1999). The researchers also found that the process of retiring was associated with a decrease in marital quality for both men and women (Moen, Kim, & Hofmeister, 2001). Newly retired men and women both report more conflict in their relationship, compared to couples who had not retired or those who had already retired. Conflicts arise in these families more often when one spouse, particularly the wife, is still employed while the other spouse begins to retire. This escalated conflict may be due to their difference in role status and power, with men in this cohort being happier when their wives conform to more traditional gender norms (Moen, Kim & Hofmeister, 2001; Szinovacz & Harpster, 1993). A study based on more than 1,000 men and 1,000 women aged fifty-five and over found that wives who continued to work after their husbands retired reported less satisfaction with their marriages than did other wives (Lee & Shehan, 1989). Lee and Shehan speculate that this may be due to their dissatisfaction with the division of household labor, as husbands increase their participation in housework only slightly after they retire. In another study, of more than 2,000 individuals, Myers and Booth report similar conclusions:

> Our findings suggest that the division of labor within and outside the household is one of the most troubling areas. . . . Husbands' persistent resistance to housework, coupled with feeling threatened by their wife's occupational success (Hochschild, 1989) suggest that men retiring now will have poorer quality marriages than those who retired when female

labor force participation was at much lower levels. (1996: 354–355)

Given the differences in men's and women's employment experiences over the life course in terms of continuity, occupations, pay, and expectations, it is possible that they would have different experiences associated with retirement as well. The researchers found that overall, men are more satisfied with retirement than are women. Seventy-one percent of men and 56 percent of women report that they are happier in their retirement than in the five years just before retirement (Quick & Moen, 1998). While good health and a comfortable post-retirement income are some of the most important predictors of happiness during retirement, there are some interesting differences among men and women as well. For example, part-time employment is linked to retirement satisfaction among men, but this is not the case among women. The researchers speculate that women are more likely to be busy with volunteer work or other family activities and feel less inclined to seek further employment for pay. Women who had more year-long employment gaps during their working years are more likely to be satisfied in retirement, perhaps because retirement is a less dramatic transition for them.

FICTION

Seventy-one percent of men and 56 percent of women report that their retirement years are better than the five years just before retirement.

The Aging Couple

Most married older couples have a relationship that has endured many years. They have faced life and its transitions with a partner: the birth of a child, the raising of children, employment opportunities, finding the balance between work and family, their children's departure from the home, and becoming a couple once again. Experiences such as traveling, expanded leisure, grandparenthood, and day-to-day living will be enhanced by sharing them with a spouse.

Marital Satisfaction

How does the degree to which couples are satisfied with their spouses and their relationship change over the life course? One early study of 400 couples married in the 1930s involved a longitudinal comparison of marital satisfaction over 20 years. Each member of the couple was evaluated soon after their marriage, and then again 20 years later. Using a number of different measures, the study found that marital satisfaction had diminished over time (Pineo, 1961).

More-recent studies have usually been cross-sectional, since it is very difficult to track couples for twenty, thirty, or forty years to conduct a longitudinal study. Cross-sectional studies generally report that the marital satisfaction of couples may instead be curvilinear, or U-shaped. This means that a marriage begins with a high level of satisfaction, but it begins to drop as couples have children, and then rises again when the children leave home (Morgan & Kunkel, 1998).

However, the definitive answer to how marriages fare over time is not yet available. Sociologist Norval Glenn (1998) examined several cohorts of families over a ten-year period (marriages in the 1930s through the 1980s), and his work casts doubt on whether marital satisfaction actually rises after the children leave home. He found no evidence of the upturn; he suggested instead that variation in marital quality may simply be due to cohort differences—i.e., people of different cohorts, or ages, have different expectations about marriage. A couple who married many years ago may be more likely to emphasize duty and responsibility in marriage, and focus less on how the relationship can be personally fulfilling. Therefore, it would not be surprising to see that their marriage is self-rated as happier than that of someone younger, who has expectations about marriage that primarily focus on what the relationship can do for him or her personally.

Alzheimer's Disease Perhaps the ultimate test of marital quality or cohesiveness is what happens to the couple when one person develops **Alzheimer's disease (AD).** Currently, about four million persons have AD, and the risk increases with age, with nearly half of persons aged eighty-five and over experiencing symptoms. Given the rapidly changing demographics outlined earlier in this chapter, AD is expected to increase substantially in the coming decades.

Kaplan (2001) conducted in-depth interviews with sixty-eight individuals who had spouses institutionalized for AD. Her goal was to learn to what degree they perceived themselves as still married. Five groups representing different degrees of couplehood emerged in her interviews. From the highest level of couplehood to the lowest level, she called these "Till Death Do Us Part," "We, But," "Husbandless Wives/Wifeless Husbands," "Becoming an I," and "Unmarried Married." These themes are summarized in Table 14.3. She found that one-third of the spouses reported that they felt fully enmeshed in the relationship ("Till Death Do Us Part"). Another third were in the middle, "Husbandless Wives/Wifeless Husbands." The other third fell into the other three categories. Eight reported that they felt far removed from being a couple: "Unmarried Married."

FACT OR FICTION?

Almost one-quarter of married elders report that they have had sexual intercourse at least once during the previous month.

	TILL DEATH DO US PART	WE, BUT…	HUSBANDLESS WIFE/WIFELESS HUSBAND	BECOMING AN "I"	UNMARRIED MARRIED
Description	Internalized being part of a "We"; know no other way to consider selves	Some sense of "We" but recognize no longer have mates able to participate in marital relationship	Ambivalence; see spouse as no longer who he/she was; therefore, marriage can't be the same	Recognize that married life no longer includes two people, but one	Legally married, but don't feel married
Couplehood Status	Very strong; past marital history is important to current couplehood; speak in terms of "We/Us"	Less of a "We" than in the past; offer clarifiers to describe state of couplehood ("I feel married, but … ")	"In limbo" regarding whether feel married or not; marriage is now "just being there" for spouse	Feel that "my life goes on" as an "I" because fewer perceptions of "We" and more of an "I"	No couplehood; perceive marriage as completely over
Coping	Optimistic; unwilling to "fall apart"	Uncertainty regarding balancing desire for "We" with reality that everyday life is more an "I"	No longer take spouse into account; experience isolation	Facing prospect of having lost spouse and of being alone	May experience anger and question remaining married
Future Outlook	Anticipate feeling like a "We" as long as spouse is alive	Adjusting to being less of a "We" than desired	Difficult time reconciling whether to get on with life as part of a "We" or an "I"	Adjusting to being an "I"; thoughts of dating again	Establishing identity as an individual and not as one of a pair

TABLE 14.3 Typology of Groups with Alzheimer's Disease

Source: Kaplan (2001).

Sexuality

A very common misconception about the elderly is that they are no longer sexually active. In a classroom, any discussion of elders' sexuality is largely met with snickers or looks of disbelief. But as the data below reveal, if an elderly person is married or partnered, it is quite likely that he or she is still sexually active. One national study asked married adults aged 60 and older "About how often did you and your husband/wife have sex during the last month?" Fifty-three percent indicated that they had sexual intercourse at least once during the previous month. In fact, among those who said that they were sexually active, one-half claimed to have intercourse once a week or more (Marsiglio & Donnelly, 1991).

Although frequency of sexual activity declines with age, many older persons are

Do elderly persons engage in sexual relationships? The answer is overwhelmingly, yes.

still sexually active. Marsiglio and Donnelly (1991) also found that, among those married respondents aged 66 and older, 44 percent reported having sex in the previous month. Among the oldest cohort of individuals, aged 76 and over, 24 percent were sexually active. Data such as these take many people by surprise.

FICTION

The correct answer is over one-half!

In *The Social Organization of Sexuality,* Laumann and colleagues (1994) report national data indicating that elderly men are more likely to be sexually active than women are. For example, among those aged 65 to 69, approximately 75 percent of men report they are sexually active, as do about 40 percent of women. By 85 to 89, approximately 45 percent of men report they are sexually active, compared to only 5 percent of women. The large gender differences are due to the fact that many more women are widowed and are thus less likely to have available sexual partners than are men. When a partner is available, many couples continue to engage in sexual relations. But the lack of a sexual partner should not be taken as proof

that interest in sexuality disappears in later life. Studies have noted that about one-third of women over age 70 and slightly less than one-half of men over age 70 report masturbating (Marsiglio, Scanzoni, & Broad, 2000). It appears to be time to debunk the myth that the elderly are asexual.

The Division of Household Labor

As children leave the home, and with changes brought on by retirement, the aging couple may alter certain dimensions of their lives. One area that has been studied is the division of household labor (Coltrane & Ishii-Kuntz, 1992; Szinovacz, 2000). Most studies show that the division of household labor changes little as a couple ages (Brubaker & Kinsel, 1985). For the most part, long-established patterns continue.

Using a large, nationally representative, longitudinal sample of seniors in which one spouse was employed at least ten hours a week at the first interview (Time 1), Szinovacz (2000) examined how retirement changed a couple's allocation of domestic labor. She found that retirees spend more time in housework than do their employed counterparts, including in tasks that were considered to be in their partner's domain. Retiring husbands whose wives continue to work outside the home take on more responsibility; however, when the wife retires, she appears to take charge again of her domain.

Childfree Older Families

One of the many benefits that we assume will accrue from having children is that we will be happier in old age. In fact, the potential for rewards and companionship in later life is noted as a primary reason for having children (Glenn & McLanahan, 1981). If this is the case, then how do older childfree couples fare? A substantial number of older couples do not have children, either voluntarily or involuntarily.

Most analyses suggest that couples without children are virtually as happy in later life as those with children (Glenn & McLanahan, 1981, Rempel, 1985). Couples without children rely on their spouses, friends, and other kin for their social support. Some research, but not all, indicates that they may be a bit more isolated than couples with children, but their finances are generally better, and they report being happy (or unhappy) as frequently as do those with children. The childfree are more likely than other older adults with children to go to a nursing home when their health deteriorates and they are unable to take care of themselves.

| FACT OR FICTION?

Research on widowhood tends to focus on younger persons (under age forty) since death is unexpected and presumably more difficult during this period.

Widowhood

The death of a spouse stands as one of life's most stressful events. It means the loss of a companion and friend, perhaps the loss of income, and the ending of a familiar way of life. Many widowed men and women experience extreme sadness, weight loss, loneliness, insomnia, and depression. Widowhood can occur at any point in the life cycle, but because it is most likely to occur among the elderly, research tends to focus on that population. Nonetheless, when people become widowed at a younger age, their difficulty may be exacerbated because death during young adulthood and middle age is so unexpected. Few of their friends are likely to be widowed, so they may stand alone from their peer group in an important way.

Approximately 13.5 million persons are currently classified as "widowed" in the United States, and 85 percent of them are women. However, the number of persons who have *experienced* widowhood is much larger than that, and is less gender lopsided, for

There are 13.5 million persons classified as "widowed" in the United States. The vast majority are women.

some have remarried (Berardo & Berardo, 2000). There are three primary reasons for the significantly higher rates of widowhood among women than men. First, mortality rates among females are lower than for males; therefore, they live to older ages. The life expectancy of females at age sixty-five exceeds that of males by nearly seven years. Second, wives are typically three to four years younger than their husbands and consequently have a greater chance of outliving them. Third, widowed women are less likely to remarry than are widowed men. Eligible men are scarce because our cultural norms encourage older men to date and marry younger women, but not the reverse (Berardo & Berardo, 2000).

| FICTION

Research on widowhood tends to focus on the elderly since widowhood is far more common within this age group.

One of the more popular perspectives on death and dying is based on the work of Elisabeth Kübler-Ross (1969). Her work with 200 primarily middle-aged cancer patients indicated that there are often five somewhat distinct stages that dying people and their loved ones experience. Although her work has been criticized on grounds that not everyone experiences these stages, nor do they experience them in this order, her work is useful nonetheless. Her five stages are the following:

* *Denial.* Many people first refuse to believe that they or a loved one is dying. They may ask for additional medical tests, desire a second or third opinion, or in other ways deny that death is near.
* *Anger.* When coming to grips with the truth, some people become angry. They may project this anger on other friends, family, people who are well, or medical personnel.
* *Bargaining.* The dying person or loved one may try to forestall death by striking a bargain with God.
* *Depression.* Depression may set in when the dying person or their loved ones realize that they cannot win the fight against the illness. They may be depressed over the symptoms of their condition (chronic pain) or their treatment (hair loss). As they see and plan for their future, the loss they face can feel overwhelming.
* *Acceptance.* Eventually, a patient or loved one may come to accept the approaching death. In doing so, they may reflect on their lives together.

It is not clear whether widowhood is more difficult for men or women, although the preponderance of research points to men's greater difficulty. Some studies report that men and women experience similar physical and emotional difficulties over time (see Brubaker, 1991, for a review). But most studies suggest that males who lose their spouse have a more difficult time because they are less likely to have same-sex widowed friends, are more likely to be older, may have poorer health themselves, have fewer family ties, and are not proficient in domestic tasks (Berardo, 1970; Burgess, 1988; Siegel & Kuykendall, 1990; Stroebe & Stroebe, 1983; Umberson, Wortman, & Kessler, 1992).

On the other hand, older women have largely been dependent on their husbands,

and when widowed, they may find two substantial difficulties. First, their incomes are profoundly reduced. Not all widows benefit from generous life insurance policies, investments such as stocks and bonds, or employer pension plans. Two-fifths of widows fall into poverty at some time during the five years after their husbands' death, a higher proportion than for divorced women (Berardo & Berardo, 2000). Second, widows may find that they face the daunting practical problems of maintaining a house alone (Johnson & Barer, 1997). A study of 201 widows drawn from public death records in a midwestern metropolitan area found that financial problems were not a primary cause of stress for widows (although they were a major cause of stress for women getting divorced). The researchers found that practical support such as help with home repairs significantly decreased widows' stress (Miller, Smerglia, Gaudet, & Kitson, 1998).

Social class, race, and ethnicity are related to different experiences in widowhood. Lopata (1973, 1979) found that working-class couples are more likely to live in sex-segregated worlds; consequently, they experience less disorganization in their lives immediately after the death of a spouse. However, finances may be more vulnerable than is the case among the middle class. Researchers have noted that whites have fewer children, are less likely to live in extended families, are more likely to live alone, and have fewer active support systems following widowhood than do minority elders. Therefore, in many ways they are more prone to loneliness and isolation.

Health and Caregiving

As we age, our health is likely to decline in a number of ways, and we are increasingly likely to need someone to help us with many of the things that we used to do for ourselves:

cooking, cleaning, home repairs, and perhaps even personal care. The health status of older adults is a result of a complex set of factors, including individual ones such as diet, exercise, and heredity, and structural factors such as socioeconomic status, racism, and access to health care.

According to the most recent National Long Term Care Survey, more than seven million persons are informal caregivers—providing unpaid help to older persons who live in the community and have at least one limitation on their activities of daily living (U.S. Department of Health and Human Services, 2001). **Gerontologists**—persons who study the elderly—have measured the degree of physical impairment by using a common set of activities of daily living (ADLs), such as bathing, dressing, eating, getting into and out of bed, walking indoors, and using the toilet. By using a common set of measures, gerontologists can track elders' degree of impairment and can make some comparisons across different samples. More than six million Americans are unable to perform at least one of these ADLs by themselves, and approximately five million are so severely disabled that they are unable to carry out three or more self-care tasks. Gerontologists estimate that the number of older persons needing significant and long-term care may increase dramatically over the next fifty years as the number in the oldest-old cohort increases: fourteen million elders may need significant care by 2020, and twenty-four million by 2060.

Formal Versus Informal Care

Some elderly persons rely on **formal care,** which is care provided by social service agencies on a paid or volunteer basis. This could include a variety of types of care: paid visiting nurses, meals or housecleaning programs, a paid personal attendant, or nursing home care. Few elderly persons live in nursing homes, although that number rises with age. Most people do not need that intense level of care, cannot afford such care, and would rather be cared for within their communities outside of institutions. However, 22 percent of persons eighty-five and older live in nursing homes, and 40 percent of elders are likely to spend some time in a nursing home at one point or another in their lifetime (AARP and the Administration on Aging, 1997; Soldo & Agree, 1988).

FACT OR FICTION?

Most caregiving to frail elders is provided by family members rather than by social service agencies.

In contrast to formal care, the majority of elders rely primarily on **informal care**—i.e., unpaid care by someone close to the care recipient. About 85 percent of informal care is provided by family members: usually a wife, daughter, husband, or son. About 23 percent of caregivers are the wives of the care recipient, while 13 percent are husbands, 29 percent are daughters, and 9 percent are sons. Other relatives (e.g., nieces, siblings, grandchildren) or even friends or neighbors also sometimes serve as informal caregivers. They provide a wide variety of hands-on care and continue to do so even after an elder is institutionalized (Keefe & Fancey, 2000).

FACT

Family members provide about 85 percent of needed caregiving to frail elders.

A spouse is generally the first person in line to provide care if she or he is able (Stone, Cafferata, & Sangle, 1987), and among spouses, wives tend to care for their husbands rather than the reverse. This may be a function of the fact that men have shorter life expectancies and may need care earlier than women do, as well as a function of gendered expectations: women have been the caregivers and kin-keepers in their families.

When a spouse is unavailable or is unable to provide this level of care, adult children, usually daughters, step in (Lee, Dwyer, & Coward, 1993). This is particularly true for African American and Latino families, for which adult children constitute about 75 percent of caregivers, compared to 40–60 percent in white families (Montgomery, 1996). Many of these adult daughters have children under eighteen to care for in addition to their disabled parent. These women are sometimes referred to as the **sandwich generation** because they are in the middle, providing care to members of cohorts on both sides of them. One study of 273 married respondents who provided care found that having children, particularly daughters, seems to increase rather than decrease the amount of time spent in caregiving to frail relatives. The researchers found that children are more likely to connect the generations rather than constrain the help that both mothers and fathers provide (Gallagher & Gerstel, 2001).

There are differences in caregiving across racial and ethnic lines. Using the National Survey of Families and Households, family scientist Nadine Marks found that Hispanic Americans were less likely to be caregivers than were non-Hispanic whites. This finding seems counterintuitive, given the close family ties emphasized in many His-

panic families. She speculates that this finding may be due to the fact that Hispanics are more likely than non-Hispanic whites to be recent immigrants whose elderly relatives reside elsewhere. This difference persists even when differences in income are held constant.

Caring for elderly parents or a spouse can be a labor of love, but it is also time intensive, potentially expensive, and often stressful. Most caregivers provide assistance seven days a week, with nearly half reporting twenty-one hours or more of care per week, with little help from formal services (American Association of Retired Persons and the Travelers Foundation, 1988). Adult daughters and sons are also likely to be employed outside the home, so they provide care to their relative on top of an already tight schedule. Furthermore, 40 percent of caregivers report spending their own money for care-related products, services, or activities. These sums can be substantial for people on a fixed income or for people who are caring for their children as well as for a parent.

Given these challenges, researchers have noted considerable strain among many caregivers, both spouses and adult children. Most caregivers report experiencing emotional strain, and nearly half are clinically depressed. Caregivers use prescription drugs for depression, anxiety, and insomnia two to three times as often as the rest of the population (Scharlach, 1991).

Organizations such as the National Family Caregivers Association (NFCA) support family caregivers and speak out publicly for caregivers' needs. NFCA espouses a philosophy of self-advocacy and self-care based on the belief that

Caregivers who choose to take charge of their lives, and see caregiving as but one of its facets, are in a position to be happier and healthier individuals. They are then able to have a higher quality of life and to make a more positive contribution to the well

The "sandwich generation" refers to the group of adults who are caring for their frail elderly parents as well as their own children.

© Barros & Barros/The Image Bank-Getty Images

1. Choose to *take charge* of your life, and don't let your loved one's illness or disability always take center stage.

2. Remember to *be good to yourself.* Love, honor, and value yourself. You have a very hard job and you deserve some quality time, just for you.

3. *Watch out* for signs of depression, and don't delay in getting professional help when you need it.

4. When people offer to help, *accept the offer* and suggest specific things that they can do.

5. *Educate yourself* about your loved one's condition. Information is empowering.

6. There's a difference between caring and doing. *Be open to technologies and ideas* that promote your loved one's independence.

7. *Trust your instincts.* Most of the time they'll lead you in the right direction.

8. *Grieve for your losses, and then allow yourself to* dream new dreams.

9. *Stand up for your rights* as a caregiver and a citizen.

10. *Seek support* from other caregivers. There is great strength in knowing you are not alone.

Source: National Family Caregivers Association (2002). *Ten Tips for Family Caregivers.* Available online: http://www.nfcacares.org. Reprinted with permission of the National Family Caregivers Association, Kensington, Maryland, the nation's only organization for all family caregivers.

Critical Thinking

1. Why is caregiving so stressful?

2. Is caring for an elder more or less difficult than caring for a child?

being of their care recipient, all of which has a positive impact on society and health care costs. (NFCA, 2002)

The Constructing Strong Families box above provides ten important tips to address the common needs and concerns of caregivers.

Conclusion

Our population is aging rapidly. The elderly population has been increasing almost four times as fast as the population as a whole, and elderly persons now outnumber teenagers. Persons eighty-five and over—referred to as the "oldest old"—represent the fastest growing cohort in the United States.

These demographic changes will have profound implications for family life. No longer will the concerns of the elderly and of aging families be separate from the rest of us. Their needs influence and are influenced by other social institutions in society. The AARP is the second largest social organization in the United States, after the Roman Catholic church, and has achieved great success in actively promoting the concerns of an aging population. Promoting good health and social and economic well-being, supporting intimate relationships, fostering positive bonds with adult children and grandchildren, and matters dealing with retirement, widowhood, and formal and informal caregiving are some of the important issues on the forefront of the national agenda. As our population continues to age, we will likely see these concerns become increasingly public and discussed with even greater frequency. Issues that are currently viewed as individual problems (e.g., health, loneliness, caregiving) will increasingly become seen as social problems that require more structural solutions.

* *In the past, were the elderly treated better than they are today?*

Attitudes toward the elderly have been mixed. Rich, white, property-owning elderly men were generally treated with respect. However, poor or minority elders were often despised and treated as outcasts.

* *Why was Social Security created?*

With industrialization increasing, and patriarchal power waning, poverty was becoming more conspicuous. Elders seemed particularly vulnerable because few were covered by employer pensions.

* *What do we mean by a "demographic revolution"?*

The aging population is rapidly increasing today and will continue to rise during the twenty-first century. By the year 2050, one in five Americans could be aged 65 and over. This has tremendous repercussions for many aspects of social life.

* *How has the process of adult children leaving home changed?*

Adult children are less likely to leave home for marriage or to join the military than they were in the past. Instead, now they leave home for college or to take a job. These types of transitions are less "final" than those of the past; therefore, children today are more likely to return to their parents' home for a period of time.

* *What type of relationship do parents have with their adult children after they finally do leave home for good?*

Approximately one-third of adult children–mother relations fall into the "tight-knit" category. Only 7 percent fall into the "detached" category. Most adult children receive substantial help from their older parents—until parents are very old and frail, most aging parents give far more assistance to their children than they receive from them.

* *What type of relationship do grandparents have with their grandchildren?*

Most report a companionate relationship, meaning that they enjoy recreational activities, enjoy occasional overnight stays, and have fun together. A growing number of grandparents are raising their grandchildren because of the parents' absence or unsuitability for parenthood.

* *How is retirement a "social construction"?*

Historically, and in many societies today, there is no such thing as retirement. People had to work to support themselves, and they were not exempt from that task because of their age. Retirement is a relatively recent concept. Moreover, it is seen and experienced differently by different groups in our society.

* *Are the elderly satisfied with their marriages?*

Most researchers have found that marriage begins with a high level of satisfaction, but the satisfaction begins to decline as couples have children, and then rises again when the children leave home. However, at least one researcher has found no evidence of the upturn; he suggested instead that variation in marital quality may simply be due to cohort differences—people of different cohorts, or ages, have different expectations about marriage.

* *Are the elderly sexually active?*

Yes, if an elderly person is married or partnered, it is quite likely that he or she is still sexually active. Sexual feelings and behavior continue throughout our lives.

* *Is widowhood experienced differently by men and women?*

Generally speaking, yes. Most widowers are females: they have longer life expectancies, they are generally several years younger than their husbands, and they are less likely to remarry. Consequently, because of their greater number, they may have more avenues for social support. However, they are also more likely than widowed men to live in poverty.

* *What do we mean by "caregiving"?*

It is often used to refer to caring for a frail elderly person, although technically speaking, caregiving can be done with any age group. In this chapter, caregiving refers to primarily "informal care," which is unpaid care by someone close to the care recipient, usually a wife, daughter, husband, or son.

* *Is caregiving stressful?*

Caring for elderly parents or a spouse can be a labor of love, but it is also time intensive, potentially expensive, and often stressful. Most caregivers provide assistance seven days a week, with nearly half reporting twenty-one hours or more of care per week, with little help from formal services.

Key Terms

activities of daily living (ADLs): general day-to-day activities such as cooking, cleaning, bathing, and home repair

Alzheimer's disease (AD): the most common form of dementia, or the loss of mental functions such as thinking, memory, and reasoning

baby boom generation: those persons born after World War II through the early 1960s

companionate grandparenting: enjoying recreational activities, occasional overnight stays, and even babysitting, with an emphasis on fun and enjoyment

formal care: care provided by social service agencies on a paid or volunteer basis

gerontologists: persons who study the elderly

informal care: unpaid care by someone close to the care recipient

involved grandparenting: grandparents and grandchildren engaging in frequent interaction or possibly even living together

kin-keeping: maintaining ties among family members

life-course perspective: a theory that sees age-related transitions as socially produced, socially recognized, and shared—a product of social structure, historical forces, and culture

life expectancy: how long a person can expect to live from birth

life-span perspective: a theory that sees development as a lifelong, multidirectional process that consists of both positive and negative changes involving gains and losses

life-stage perspective: a theory that sees development as proceeding through a fairly set pattern of sequential stages that most people experience

midlife crisis: a time of trauma during which people focus on what they have failed to achieve (e.g., in employment) or focus on the changes in their family (e.g., children leaving home)

remote grandparenting: emotionally or physically distant grandparent behaviors

sandwich generation: family members who are in the middle, providing care to members of cohorts on both sides of them—parents and children

Social Security: many programs under one umbrella, including Medicare, Medicaid, cash welfare assistance, and cash assistance for survivors and for seniors

Resources on the Internet

These web sites have been selected for their relevance to the topics in this chapter. These sites are among the more stable, but please be aware that web site addresses change frequently.

AARP (formerly known as the American Association of Retired Persons)
http://www.aarp.org

AARP represents more than 34 million members aged fifty and over. Over half of the members are working, while the remainder are retired. Its goal is to increase the quality of life of older Americans, and it does this through advocacy, volunteer opportunities, education, and social opportunities. It publishes a number of magazines and newsletters.

American Society on Aging

http://www.asaging.org

Professionals rely on the American Society on Aging to keep them on the cutting edge of knowledge about aging. ASA offers educational programs, publications, information, and training resources.

National Family Caregiving Association

http://www.nfcacares.org

The National Family Caregiving Organization (NFCA) is a grass-roots organization created to educate, support, empower, and speak up for the millions of Americans who care for chronically ill, aged, or disabled loved ones.

National Institute on Aging

http://www.nih.gov.nia

This U.S. government agency provides information on the latest research on aging. It also provides a number of links to additional relevant sites.

Companion Web Site for This Book

Virtual Society: The Wadsworth Sociology Resource Center

http://sociology.wadsworth.com

Begin by clicking the Student Resources section. Next, click Marriage and Family, and then click the cover image for this book. Se-

lect from the pull-down menu the chapter you are presently studying. You will have easy access to chapter resources such as MicroCase Online exercises, additional Web links, flashcards, InfoTrac exercises, and practice tests (that can be scored). In addition, to enhance and help with your study of marriages and families, be sure to investigate the rest of the rich sociology resources at Virtual Society.

Visit InfoTrac College Edition

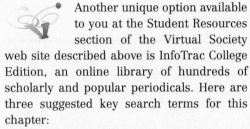 Another unique option available to you at the Student Resources section of the Virtual Society web site described above is InfoTrac College Edition, an online library of hundreds of scholarly and popular periodicals. Here are three suggested key search terms for this chapter:

* Search keywords: *caregiving + elderly*
* Search keywords: *retirement + gender*
* Search keywords: *grandparents + African American*

Search recent years to get the latest information on these issues.

© Macduff Everton /Corbis

15

Looking Ahead: Helping Families Flourish

W

hat are children's lives like today?

1 in 2 preschoolers has a mother in the labor force.

1 in 2 children will live in a single-parent family at some point in childhood.

1 in 2 never completes a single year of college.

1 in 3 is born to unmarried parents.

1 in 3 will be poor at some point in their childhood.

1 in 3 is behind a year or more in school.

1 in 4 lives with only one parent.

1 in 4 was born poor.

1 in 5 is poor now.

1 in 5 lives in a family receiving food stamps.

1 in 5 is born to a mother who did not graduate from high school.

1 in 5 has a foreign-born mother.

1 in 6 has no health insurance.

1 in 7 has a worker in their family but still is poor.

1 in 8 never graduates from high school.

1 in 8 is born to a teenage mother.

1 in 12 lives at less than half the poverty level.

1 in 12 has a disability.

1 in 13 was born with low birth weight.

1 in 24 lives with neither parent.

1 in 26 is born to a mother who received late or no prenatal care.

1 in 60 sees their parents divorce in any year.

1 in 138 will die before their first birthday.

1 in 910 will be killed by guns before age 20. (Children's Defense Fund, 2000)

Looking Forward

What kind of people do we hope to be in the twenty-first century? What kind of world do we want for our children? This chapter looks forward to future possibilities. It examines the individual, political, and policy choices that we must make to create a more compassionate environment for our families. What is it that families need to really flourish? We will take a creative look at numerous options and opportunities that could improve the health, security, and well-being of families, drawing from the experiences of other nations as well as our own.

This look forward requires that we take stock of and review the basic themes of our study of families and close relationships. First, we have learned that *social structures, including gender, race, and class, profoundly shape our daily experiences, choices, and constraints within families and intimate relationships*. They operate individually and collectively to shape our lives.

Second, we have learned that *a critical perspective shows us that changes in families are normal and nothing to inherently fear because current family structures are not sacred or inviolable, but are ever-changing.*

Third, we have gained a respect for social science research. Our knowledge of families and intimate relationships *should be based on scientific data rather than reliance on stereotypes, popular opinion, or common sense.*

Fourth, we recognize the ways that *microlevel and macrolevel influences are linked to one another.* Our personal choices often emerge from broader social forces in our lives.

Themes

In this section, we will review these four themes in more detail.

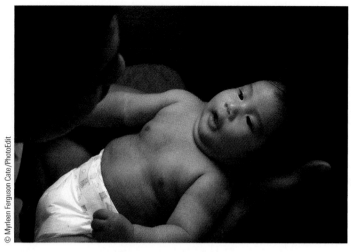

What kind of world do we want for our sons and daughters?

The Importance of Social Structure

This book has examined family and close relationships over the life course. One of our goals has been to introduce a view that synthesizes a structural analysis of marriage, families, and close relationships with the more individualistic psychological view that tends to dominate popular thinking. We have hoped to illustrate the ways in which social structure interacts with intimate relationships—how personal experiences, choices, and beliefs are influenced by historical and cultural forces, by social positions, and by social institutions. Often, these forces are far beyond the control of any one individual.

In particular, we have focused on the ways in which gender, race, and class, individually and in conjunction with one another, affect close relationships. The structure of families, and the interaction that takes place within them, are patterned by divisions of inequality based on gender, race, and class within the United States. Seemingly personal choices, such as our chances of marrying, of bearing children, of divorcing, the amount of education we receive, the type of job we are likely to get, the type of child-care program we use, our health, and our well-being, are affected by these critical dimensions of social stratification. We suggest that gender, race, and class are far more than attributes of individuals.

However, a structural approach does not mean that we subscribe to a rigid structural determinism in which people have no choice. Quite the contrary. People choose, cope with, adapt to, and change social structures, including marriage and families, to meet their needs. **Agency** is the ability to create viable lives even when constrained by structural forces (Baca Zinn & Eitzen, 1996). Our goal is to empower students to make the needed choices and changes in their marriage, families, and close relationships by introducing them to a sociological imagination: the recognition that our personal experiences are, in large part, shaped by social forces within the larger society.

A Critical Perspective Illustrates That Families Are Not Monolithic

Our second theme has been to introduce students to the fine art of critical thinking. A critical perspective asks that we do not blindly accept the commonsense explanation of why things are the way they are. Instead, we acknowledge that marriage, families, and close relationships are constructed by humans; therefore, their structures are not monolithic or sacred. There are, have been, and will continue to be a multitude of family types, and these are influenced by social, political, economic, historical, and cultural conditions. A critical perspective does not consider the present organization of families as inviolable, nor does it assume that some other particular organization would necessarily be a panacea for all our domestic problems. Something is not "truth" or "fact" just because it has been accepted as such in the past. A critical perspective examines families not as something static, but as something out of which change and growth can occur. Change is not necessarily something to be feared.

A critical perspective also examines the assumptions, values, and ideologies that are used to define and characterize families. We all have values, and all policies and programs reflect some set of core values. Some of these are designed to maintain the status quo. For example, we hear that welfare recipients are lazy, that mothers of young children should stay at home and not work outside the home, that gay and lesbian relationships are very different from heterosexual ones, and that divorce is bad for children. A critical perspective may ask "Who benefits from such opinions?" Critical theorists recognize that popular opinion and social institutions can support or reflect existing power relationships. For example, nuclear families, long dominant among white families, have been viewed as the norm, while extended families, more dominant among African Americans and other minority groups, have been viewed as deviant. Minority family structures have been seen as deficient and not measuring up to the ideal model.

An Appreciation of Social Science Research

A third theme is to provide an appreciation for the role that research can play in understanding families and close relationships. As opposed to "common sense," a scientific perspective, which draws on empirical social science data, can provide a far more objective window on the world. For example, you cannot assume that the poor routinely buy steak with food stamps just because you have always heard it is so, and you cannot assume that all partners have an equitable division of household labor just because that is the type of relationship your parents have. Instead of relying on "common sense" or "personal experience," which are often based on stereotypes or other fallacies, empirical data can help us understand the distribution of specific phenomena, under what conditions these phenomena occur, and the meanings that people assign to these phenomena. For example, popular stereotypes convey that women place a greater importance on love than do men. Pick up a copy of any "women's magazine," and you will find a number of stories devoted to finding, satisfying, and

Empirical data can provide important insight into social issues, but cannot tell us what is right or wrong morally. Some decisions remain personal.

keeping a mate. Yet, as you recall from Chapter 4, empirical data from a number of studies have found that men are more distraught after a relationship ends than are women.

Empirical data cannot tell us what is right or wrong. For example, data cannot tell us whether abortion should be legal or illegal. Nor can they tell us under what conditions abortion should be legal or illegal. However, empirical data can tell us other important information that may help us answer these vexing questions. Data can tell us how many abortions occurred last year, among what age groups, the percentage of unmarried women who had abortions, the level of support from their partner or parents, the percentage who would reportedly seek an illegal abortion if a legal abortion were unavailable, and the reported range of feelings from regret to relief that women feel after having an abortion. Data collected to address these types of questions can help discussions of abortion and help inform personal choices. As such, data can also offer a basis for values. Your values and opinions can be just as easily shaped by data as by popular folklore.

The Interconnectedness of Microlevel and Macrolevel Influences

A microlevel perspective focuses on individuals' interactions in specific settings, and it includes such things as personal choices and internal relationships among family members. For example, a person may choose to drop out of high school and thereby limit potential employment opportunities. But choices do not exist in a vacuum. A macrolevel analysis examines the interconnectedness of marriage, families, and intimate relationships with the rest of society and with other social institutions. Families are not isolated entities. They are influenced by a wide variety of social issues outside the family, including things such as the unemployment rate, racism, the quality of schools in the

neighborhood, and crime rates. To continue this example, the person who chooses to drop out of high school may be influenced by school overcrowding. He or she may feel lost in the crowd, with little individual support or mentoring from teachers, parents, or peers. It is important to draw the connections between microlevel and macrolevel perspectives.

However, being aware of macrolevel issues does not imply that we react passively to them. Human agency is the ability of human beings to create viable lives even when these lives are constrained or limited by social forces. We all actively produce our lives, even in light of the social forces that help shape or restrict our opportunities. Recognizing this delicate balance between microlevel and macrolevel influences in our lives is our fourth theme.

What Do Families Need to Flourish?

As we look back upon the preceding chapters, we have seen many changes that are based on a natural evolution of family demographics, needs, and functions. However, other changes represent a unique historical set of challenges. For example, as more women join the labor market, how do families cope with juggling work and family demands? Perhaps even more important, what is there to help them cope? As our economic structure becomes increasingly polarized, how do families deal with the outcomes of increasing economic inequality in the United States? What mechanisms could we employ to help struggling families? Finally, how do families manage the surge in the elderly population that will require an increasing number of adults to care for their aging and infirm parents, and what do families need to help them cope? These questions have two interrelated points. First, what is it that "healthy" families need in order to thrive?

Second, recognizing that many families face a particular set of challenges—poverty, abuse, and neglect, for example—what is it that challenged families need in order to become resilient? We may find that their needs are more similar than different.

FACT OR FICTION?

Family resiliency is the study of how some families and family members lead happy, productive, and well-adjusted lives in spite of major obstacles.

Family Resiliency

We know that many people, both adults and children, do not have picture-perfect family lives. As we have discovered in the preceding chapters, many people experience racism or sexism, grow up in impoverished environments, are deeply tormented by divorce, or are victims of child abuse or other types of domestic violence. Yet despite the toll that these events can take, some adults and children overcome this adversity and lead successful, well-adjusted, and competent lives. In the face of life's many obstacles, they have overcome most or all of them. These individuals are resilient. **Resilience** is a multifaceted phenomenon that produces the ability to thrive despite adversity. The term is derived from Latin roots meaning "to jump (or bounce) back" (Silliman, 1994). It can be defined as the capacity to rebound from adversity, misfortune, trauma, or other transitional crises and be strengthened and more resourceful (McCubbin, McCubbin, Thompson, Han, & Allen, 1997; Walsh, 1998, 2002):

> A family resilience perspective fundamentally alters that deficit-based lens from viewing troubled families as damaged and beyond repair to seeing them as challenged by life's adversities. Rather than rescuing so-called "survivors" from dysfunctional families, this approach engages dis-

tressed families with respect and compassion for their struggles, affirms their reparative potential, and seeks to bring out their best. (Walsh, 2002: 130)

Although most social scientists seem to focus on problems rather than resiliency per se, the Kauai Longitudinal Study is a notable exception (Werner, 1994, 1995; Werner & Smith, 1989, 1992). This study, based on 698 children born in 1955 on the Hawaiian island of Kauai, examined the long-term effects of growing up in high-risk environments, following the children for nearly forty years. Most of the children were born to unskilled sugar plantation workers of Japanese, Filipino, Hawaiian, Portuguese, Polynesian, and mixed racial descent. Fifty-four percent of the children lived in poverty. Approximately one-third (210) were considered "high risk" because of exposure to a combination of at least four individual, parental, or household risk factors such as having a serious health problem, familial alcoholism, violence, divorce, or mental illness in the family. The children were assessed from their perinatal period to ages one, two, ten, eighteen, and thirty-two years.

The research team found that two-thirds of high-risk two-year-olds who had experienced four or more risk factors developed learning or behavior problems by age eighteen. However, this also meant that one-third did not. These children developed into stable, competent, confident, and productive adults, as rated on a variety of measures. In a later follow-up, at age forty, all but two of these individuals were still successful. In fact, many of them had outperformed the children from low-risk families.

Perhaps a key finding was that resiliency can be developed at any point in the life course. Among the two-thirds of high-risk children who had learning or behavioral problems at age eighteen, one-half of them did not exhibit these problems at age thirty.

Instead, they had satisfying jobs, had stable marriages, and in other measures were deemed successful by the research team. The researchers noted that teenage delinquency is not automatically a precursor to a life of crime. Meanwhile, a few individuals identified as resilient at age eighteen had developed significant problems by age thirty.

FACT

Social scientists usually study family problems, *but there is a growing interest in how and why families thrive in spite of adverse conditions.*

The evidence shows us that many adults and children reared in poverty (and other disadvantaged statuses) do overcome their adversities. Why is this?

Individual, Family, and Community Factors Most research on resilience has focused on three types of factors to improve resiliency in the face of adverse conditions: (1) individual traits and disposition, (2) family protective and recovery factors, and (3) community strengths. **Individual-level protective factors** include such traits as a positive self-concept, sociability, intelligence and scholastic competence, autonomy, self-esteem, androgyny, good communication and problem-solving skills, humor, and good mental and physical health (Garmezy, 1991; Rouse, 1998; Walsh, 1998; Werner, 1994). Wolin and Wolin (1993), in their review of research and clinic experience, identified seven traits of adults who survived a troubled childhood: insight (awareness of dysfunction), independence (distancing self from troubles), supportive relationships, initiative, creativity, humor (reframing the situation in a less threatening way), and morality (justice and compassion rather than revenge). For example, the resilient high-risk adolescents in the longitudinal Kauai study had developed a sense that obstacles were not insur-

mountable, and they believed that they had control over their fate. They had a high degree of self-esteem and self-efficacy, and many developed a special skill or hobby that was a source of pride.

Family protective and recovery factors are central features of the resiliency literature. **Family protective factors (FPF)** are those characteristics or dynamics that shape the family's ability to endure in the face of risk factors. **Family recovery factors (FRF)** assist families in "bouncing back" from a crisis situation (McCubbin, McCubbin, Thompson, Han, & Allen, 1997). Key characteristics of resilient families are warmth, affection, cohesion, commitment, and emotional support for one another. However, if parents are not able to provide this environment, other kin (e.g., siblings, grandparents) may step in to provide it. Resilient families generally have reasonable and clear-cut expectations for their children. They participate in family celebrations, share spiritual connections, have specific traditions, and follow predictable routines. Moreover, resilient families generally share core values regarding financial management and the use of leisure time, even when money and time are in short supply (Abbott & Meredith, 1998; McCubbin & McCubbin, 1988; Silliman, 1998; Stinett & Defrain, 1985; Walsh, 1998).

There are also **community factors** (e.g., geographic space, social networks, religious and faith-based fellowships) that affect resilience (Silliman, 1998; Miller, 2000). Community institutions are important in the process of developing resilient youth and fostering resiliency among adults. Blyth and Roelkepartian (1993) indicate several key community strengths. First, a strong community has opportunities for participation in community life. For youth, extracurricular activities in school, religious youth groups, scouting, or other activities help to bond them to their school, churches, or communities. In these settings, they can learn important skills such as teamwork, group pride, or

Strong and caring community institutions, including churches, can help to foster resilient youth.

leadership. Adults also have a frequent need for opportunities to hone these skills. Second, Blyth and Roelkepartian suggest that a strong community should have avenues provided to contribute to the welfare of others. Volunteer activities can foster a sense of inner strength and self-esteem. Third, a strong community provides opportunities to connect with peers and other adults. Resiliency is more likely when people have access to a role model, a friend, or a confidant. For youth, teachers may play a critical role in providing this type of social support. Finally, Blyth and Roelkepartian propose that healthy communities have adequate access to community facilities and events for youth, indicating the importance of a funding priority for education and youth activities, with a functioning committee focusing on youth issues.

What Is Missing? Structural Conditions

A broader, systemic view of resiliency—the recognition that strengthening families requires the interaction of individual, familial, and community contingencies—is gaining proponents (Walsh, 1998, 2002). While this broader view pays homage to ecological and developmental nuances, it still places its focus on individual conditions. It virtually ignores the position that national and statewide policies must play in strengthening families. Can we really expect families to be resilient without this assistance? For example, how do we best help a wife who is battered by her husband? Should we focus on getting her in therapy so that she can develop a greater sense of her own self-worth that eventually allows her to end the relationship? This may be an important component of resiliency, but it is insufficient. Most battered wives do not seek therapy because they do not have time, money, or trust in therapists. Even when therapy is helpful, it occurs *after the fact,* when the psychological, physical, and emotional damage has already been done. As Walsh warns,

> We must be cautious that the concept of resilience is not used in public policy to withhold social supports or maintain inequities, based on the rationale that success or failure is determined by strengths or deficits within individuals and their families. It is not enough to bolster the resilience of at-risk children and families so that they can "beat the odds"; we must also strive to change the odds against them. (1998: 12)

In addition to strong individual attributes, an involved family, and a supportive community, developing sound economic and social policies designed to strengthen all families (healthy as well as vulnerable ones) can go a long way toward giving families and youth the necessary tools to master resiliency.

This leads us back to the first component of our question: What is it that "healthy" families need to thrive? They too will benefit. Policy decisions—particularly at the national level—have the potential to dramatically improve our lives.

Family Policy

The United States is conspicuously void of a national family policy. It seemingly has no comprehensive, collective vision for families, unlike that of other industrialized nations (Bergmann, 1996; Bogenschneider, 2000; Elrod, 1999; Kamerman & Kahn, 1978). The policies that are in place are "selective" in nature and are available only to a few, rather than "universal" policies available to all citizens.

Selective Versus Universal Policies

The United States has a long history of "rugged individualism" and a distrust of government and governmental programs. U.S. policies reflect and promote the concept of self-sufficiency. They expect people to be in charge of their own destinies, with little tolerance for those who seem to be unwilling or unable to pull themselves up by their "bootstraps" (Quadagno, 1982; Trattner, 1999). Borrowing from early English "poor laws," our policies evolved over the seventeenth and eighteenth centuries, and they make clear distinctions between "worthy" needy people (i.e., people who cannot support themselves through no fault of their own) and the "unworthy."

Not surprisingly then, the United States has wallowed in a laissez-faire approach in which families are largely left to fend for themselves. Many of the programs we do have tend to be selective, meaning that persons need to meet some eligibility requirement to qualify for benefits. Often, people must meet certain income thresholds—re-

ferred to as **means-tested.** For example, people have to be below a certain income to qualify for Medicaid. These income thresholds are kept relatively low to limit the number of users of the program and thus control their costs. Yet not all programs in the United States are means-tested. Police protection, fire protection, and public education are available to all persons, regardless of income. It is not always clear to the observer why some programs are available to everyone and others are not. Why is education a "right" but health insurance a "privilege" available only to those with generous employers or who are so poor as to qualify for a government program?

When we compare the philosophy of the United States to the philosophies of most of Europe, Canada, and other places, we see vast differences in approaches. Most industrialized nations have an interrelated, coordinated set of proactive and **universal** economic and social programs to help strengthen all families. Universal programs are not means-tested; rather, they are available to everyone. For example, as shown in Table 15.1, in a recent review of twenty-four industrialized nations, the United States is the only country that has no universal health insurance coverage, paid maternal/parental leave at childbirth, or a family allowance/child dependency grant (U.S. Social Security Administration, 1999). While the United States thinks of these issues in individualistic terms and expects parents to fend for themselves, other countries have specific policies to ensure that all people can receive these benefits. But many parents in the United States are not able to "fend for themselves." How do you go about getting health insurance when an employer does not offer it and the costs of purchasing it yourself far exceed your budget? How do you arrange for paid maternal leave after the birth of your child when an employer tells you that you will be fired if you don't quickly come back to work? How do you go

TABLE 15.1

	Child safety Net Policies in 23 Industrialized Countries Compared with the United States		
COUNTRY	UNIVERSAL HEALTH INSURANCE/ HEALTH CARE	PAID MATERNAL/ PARENTAL LEAVE AT CHILDBIRTH	FAMILY ALLOWANCE/ CHILD DEPENDENCY GRANT
Australia	Y	Y	Y
Austria	Y	Y	Y
Belgium	Y	Y	Y
Canada	Y	Y	Y
Czech Republic	Y	Y	Y
Denmark	Y	Y	Y
Finland	Y	Y	Y
France	Y	Y	Y
Germany	Y	Y	Y
Hungary	Y	Y	Y
Iceland	Y	Y	Y
Italy	Y	Y	Y
Japan	Y	Y	Y
Luxembourg	Y	Y	Y
Netherlands	Y	Y	Y
New Zealand	Y	Y	Y
Norway	Y	Y	Y
Poland	Y	Y	Y
Portugal	Y	Y	Y
Spain	Y	Y	Y
Sweden	Y	Y	Y
Switzerland	Y	Y	Y
United Kingdom	Y	Y	Y
United States	N	N	N

Source: Social Security Administration (1999).

about finding a family allowance, when most people in the United States have never even heard of such a program?

| FICTION

The United States has a weak national family policy.

In other countries, these programs are financed by **progressive** forms of taxation—those who earn more pay a higher percentage of their income in taxes. These countries have adopted these programs because their residents favor structural explanations for poverty and inequality, and therefore look for structural solutions. U.S. citizens are much more likely to equate poverty and its consequences with individual failure, immorality, lack of thrift, or laziness. For example, when asked "Why are there people in this country who live in need?" 39 percent of Americans blamed personal laziness, compared to only 16 percent of Swedes (World Values Survey, 1994).

Here we outline several specific policies (out of many possibilities) that, if enacted or expanded, could help all families thrive, as well as strengthen the circumstances of those families that are most vulnerable and offer them a genuine opportunity for resiliency. We compare our policies with those

Among industrialized countries, the United States ranks:

1st in military spending

1st in military exports

1st in Gross Domestic Product

1st in the number of millionaires and billionaires

1st in health technology

1st in defense expenditures

10th in eighth-grade science scores

14th in the proportion of children in poverty

16th in living standards among our poorest one-fifth of children

16th in efforts to lift children out of poverty

17th in low-birthweight rates

18th in the gap between rich and poor children

21st in eight-grade math scores

Last in protecting our children against gun violence

According to the Centers for Disease Control and Prevention, U.S. children under age fifteen are:

12 times more likely to die from gunfire,

16 times more likely to be murdered with a gun,

11 times more likely to commit suicide with a gun, and

9 times more likely to die in a firearm accident

than children in twenty-five other industrialized countries combined.

Source: Children's Defense Fund. *The State of America's Children Yearbook 2000.*

Critical Thinking

1. If the United States has the highest number of millionaires and billionaires, then why are we ranked so low on other indicators of health and social well-being?

2. How can private citizens promote a shift in the government's spending priorities?

---

of other nations, examining what they can teach us about strengthening families. As shown in the Constructing Strong Families box above, the United States can certainly learn something from other nations.

General Policies Needed to Support Families

National Health Insurance The lack of health insurance is a serious and disturbing social problem in the United States because health insurance is one of the primary mechanisms of accessing health care services. Thirty-nine million Americans, or 14 percent of the population, had no health insurance in 2000 (U.S. Census Bureau, Public Information Office, September 27, 2001). Millions more are "underinsured"—their high deductibles or co-payments render their insurance virtually useless except in the most catastrophic conditions.

FACT OR FICTION?

The United States is virtually the only industrialized nation that does not offer universal health insurance coverage to its citizens.

In the United States, approximately three-quarters of working adults receive their health insurance from an employer. It is considered a fringe benefit of their employment and a supplement to their wages. However, employers are not required to offer health insurance to their workers, and an increasing number are choosing not to do so. This mechanism of employer-sponsored insurance is virtually unheard of in other industrialized nations, as well as in many nonindustrialized ones. Instead, these countries have **national health insurance,** meaning that access to health care is considered a

The United States provides no paid maternity leave, unlike virtually all other countries, including poor nations such as Bangladesh, India, and Mozambique.

public right of all citizens. It is viewed as a public good, like education, police protection, and parks, and is therefore funded out of taxes and general revenues. Consequently, health care coverage is universal in these countries. Virtually no one is uninsured.

FACT

The United States leaves health insurance financing largely to employers or private citizens.

Having health insurance can make a tremendous difference in the amount and type of health care that people receive. Without insurance, both adults and children in the United States use the health care system less often, are less likely to have a regular source of health care, more often rely on emergency rooms for their treatment, and may experience unnecessary pain, suffering, and even death (Kaiser Commission on Medicaid and the Uninsured, 1998).

For example, as shown in Table 15.2, the United States has one of the highest maternal mortality rates of any developed nation, due to the large number of women who fail to get prenatal care because they are without insurance and no doctor will see them. Approximately 8 out of every 100,000 women die giving birth in the United States, a far cry from the rate of 1,100 per 100,000 women in Mozambique, but a rate higher than that of Italy, Ireland, Finland, the U.K., Sweden, Switzerland, or Spain (United Nations Statistics Division, 2000, Table 3b).

Low-income workers in the United States are particularly hard-hit with respect to being uninsured. The working poor are twice as likely to be uninsured as are poor persons without jobs (Berk & Wilensky, 1987). Over one-half of minimum-wage jobs fail to provide health insurance to their employees, compared to only 1 out of 10 jobs that pay over $15 an hour (Cooper & Shone, 1997). Moreover, the working poor generally do not qualify for public health insurance programs even when their employers fail to insure them. Although Medicaid and state Children's Health Insurance Programs (CHIP) were designed to fill in the gaps, the safety net appears to be woefully inadequate as millions remain uninsured.

Being without insurance is extremely stressful to families. They know that without insurance, they may not be able to get needed care. In in-depth interviews with mothers on welfare, Seccombe (1999) found that they commonly rated Medicaid as their most important benefit. It was evaluated as more important than food stamps, subsidized housing, or even the welfare check itself. For many women, the fear of losing their Medicaid was a primary reason that they "chose" not to work or terminated their employment.

Parental Leave   Another critically important way to invest in families is by providing paid **parental leave** after the birth of a child (or some other serious family event). As Canada's Prime Minister Jean Chretien has said,

> There is now overwhelming scientific evidence that success in a child's early years is the key to long term healthy development. Nothing is more important than for parents to be able to spend the maximum amount of time with newborn children in the critical early months of a child's life. Therefore, I am proud to announce today that the government will introduce legislation in this parliament to extend employment insurance maternity and parental benefits from the current maximum of six months to one full year. (October 13, 1999, cited in Center for Families, Work, and Well-Being, 2001)

What "scientific" information is the prime minister referring to? A growing body of research is informing us of the benefits that paternal leaves have for children, their parents, and their parents' employers (Center for Families, Work, and Well-Being, 2001; Galtry, 1997; Glass & Riley, 1998; Ruhm, 1998). Long leaves are associated with better maternal health, vitality, and role function, and lower rates of infant mortality. Moreover, women are likely to breast-feed for longer periods if they have extended leave benefits. The benefits of longer parental leaves also extend to employers. Women are more likely

TABLE 15.2	Maternal Mortality Rate (per 100,000 Live Births)
	RATE

Developing Nations	
Bangladesh	440
Bolivia	390
Cuba	27
Egypt	170
India	410
Kenya	59
Mozambique	1100
Republic of Korea	20

Developed Nations	
Canada	—
Denmark	9
Finland	6
Ireland	6
Italy	7
Japan	8
Netherlands	7
Spain	6
Sweden	5
Switzerland	5
United Kingdom	7
United States	8

Source: Adapted from United Nations Statistical Division (2000), Table 3b.

to return to work after childbirth in those countries that have more-lengthy leaves. It is more cost-effective to develop a well-planned parental leave policy than it is to rehire and retrain new employees.

FACT OR FICTION?

The United States is more likely to offer paid maternity leave than developing nations (e.g., Bangladesh or Bolivia) but less likely than developed nations (e.g., Canada or Sweden).

The United States has, by far, the least generous parental leave policy of any nation, including poor and developing nations, as

TABLE 15.3	Maternity Leave Benefits (1998)	
	LENGTH OF MATERNITY LEAVE	WAGES PAID IN COVERED PERIOD
Developing Nations		
Bangladesh	12 weeks	100%
Bolivia	60 days	100% of minimum wage + 70% of wages
Cuba	18 weeks	100%
Egypt	50 days	100%
India	12 weeks	100%
Kenya	2 months	100%
Mozambique	60 days	100%
Republic of Korea	60 days	100%
Developed Nations		
Canada	17–18 weeks	55% for 15 weeks
Denmark	18 weeks	100%
Finland	105 days	80%
Ireland	14 weeks	70% or fixed rate
Italy	5 months	80%
Japan	14 weeks	60%
Netherlands	16 weeks	100%
Spain	16 weeks	100%
Sweden	14 weeks	360 days @ 75%; 90 days @ flat rate
Switzerland	8 weeks	100%
United Kingdom	14–18 weeks	6 weeks @ 90%; flat rate afterward
United States	12 weeks[a]	0

[a]Applies only to workers in companies with 50 or more workers.
Source: Adapted from United Nations Statistical Division (2000), Table 5c.

shown in Table 15.3. The Family Medical Leave Act of 1993, signed by former President Clinton, requires employers with more than fifty employees to allow twelve weeks of *unpaid* leave. Employers in small firms are not required to offer leaves. This situation results in about 2 percent of employed women working in places where they are not offered even unpaid maternity leave (U.S. Census Bureau, 2001). Among those who work in larger employee settings, the reality is that few people can take unpaid leave anyway. Therefore, many come back to work shortly after their short-term disability, vacation, or sick pay has been exhausted. In a survey about the use and impact of family and medical leave, 34 percent of workers said they needed but did not take leave (Commission on Family and Medical Leave, 1996). Data from the Census Bureau indicate that the percentage who did not take maternity leave because they could not afford to was even higher. Lower-educated and minority women were least likely to take leave after giving birth (U.S. Census Bureau, 2001). By way of contrast,

FICTION

The United States is far less likely to offer paid maternity leave than any other nation.

- Denmark offers eighteen weeks of paid maternity leave at 100 percent of salary.

- In the Netherlands, women receive sixteen weeks of paid maternity leave at 100 percent of salary. They may also take unpaid leave for six months or reduce their working hours by half for up to six months while they receive 75 percent of their salary for those leave hours.

- Spain offers 16 weeks of leave at 100 percent of salary.

- Sweden allows for 450 days of leave per child until the child is 8 years old. The time can be configured as the parents choose. Of the 450 days of leave, at least 30 are reserved for the mother, and 30 are reserved for the father, with the remaining days being split as the parents wish. Parents receive 75 percent of their income for the first 360 days, while for the remainder it is a flat rate. Some employers offer a supplement that replaces a parent's full salary for up to four months.

- The United Kingdom allows maternity pay at 90 percent for six weeks, and 12 weeks at a flat rate. It also offers 40 weeks of unpaid leave.

- Canada provides up to 17–18 weeks of maternity benefits, and 10 weeks of parental leave benefits for fathers. (Center for Families, Work, and Well-Being, 2001; United Nations Statistical Division, 2000, Table 5C)

Parental leave is also far more generous in poor or developing nations than it is in the United States. Even in Bangladesh, one of the poorest nations on Earth, women receive twelve weeks of maternity leave, paid at 100 percent. Mozambique offers sixty days of maternity leave at 100 percent of pay.

Courtesy of Karen Seccombe

Why does U.S. policy offer no paid parental leave after the birth of a baby?

Flexible Time and Place of Employment

The adoption of more flexible work environments could do much to enhance families. Many parents report a high degree of tension in trying to balance work and family demands, including marital tension, shorter periods spent breast-feeding infants, less involvement with their older children, and depression (Beatty, 1996; Bumpas, Crouter, & McHale, 1999; Crouter, Perry-Jenkins, Huston, & Crawford, 1989; Lindberg, 1996). Flexibility in the timing of work, known as **flextime,** and in the location of work, **flexplace,** are high on the agenda of families and family scientists. One IBM study of more than 6,000 employees found that job flexibility improved the tenuous work–family balance that many face, even after taking into account other factors such as number of hours worked, hours spent in domestic labor, marital status, occupation, and gender (Hill, Hawkins, Ferris, & Weitzman, 2001).

Employers have generally been more willing to accommodate flexible hours than to give employees more leeway in where the work is done. Most large companies claim to offer some type of flextime. A recent study of more than 1,000 U.S. companies found that approximately two-thirds allowed periodic flextime but that only one-quarter allowed it on a daily basis (Galinsky & Bond, 1998). However, Hill and colleagues (2001) make the suggestion that employees may not feel that flextime is truly available without repercussion, for corporate norms seem to dictate longer hours than ever before (Shore, 1998).

"Flexplace," sometimes referred to as telecommuting or "virtual office," is less common. Among the more than 1,000 companies studied by Galinsky and Bond (1998), about one-half allowed employees to work at home occasionally, and one-third allowed employees to work at home on a regular (but usually part-time) basis.

Increasing the flexibility of work environments could be beneficial to working parents by decreasing commuting time and the stresses associated with fighting rush-hour traffic, and allowing them to synchronize their work schedules with their children's activities and other family responsibilities.

FACT OR FICTION?

A worker earning $5.15 an hour year-round earns under $11,000 a year, several thousand dollars below the poverty line for a family of three.

Living Wage   At $5.15 an hour in 2003, the minimum wage has been criticized as being far too low to support a family. Many families earning minimum wage are living below the poverty line, and they need programs such as food stamps to make ends meet. A worker earning $5.15 an hour earns $10,712 a year, several thousand dollars below the poverty line for a family of three. Likewise, the purchasing power of the minimum wage has

eroded over the past several decades. Adjusting for inflation, the actual value of the minimum wage in 2001 was $7.00 in 1978. The value has been steadily declining since then (U.S. Census Bureau, 2001). The minimum wage has eroded, and it is no longer sufficient to support even a small family.

In response to this concern, the living wage movement has gained significant foothold in at least sixty local governments, including New York City, Baltimore, Portland, Chicago, and Minneapolis. A typical **living wage** ordinance requires contractors and businesses receiving governmental financial assistance to pay a minimum wage that is deemed a "livable wage" in that community. Usually, wages range from 150 percent to 225 percent of the federal minimum wage. The argument made is that public money should not be used to create jobs that keep people poor. Pay should provide a wage on which a family can reasonably expect to live, ultimately decreasing the number of persons who will be dependent on social programs. Living wage movements have also expanded their goals to include health benefits, vacation days, and other benefits (Employment Policies Institute, 2001; Religious Action Center of Reform Judaism, 2000).

Critics of living wage legislation claim that these laws actually harm those people they are intended to help by reducing their work opportunities. Critics charge that as the price of labor increases, a loss of jobs will result, and people will be even worse off than before. They suggest that a better alternative is a targeted wage subsidy that "lifts the income of those most in need without raising labor costs to employers" (Employment Policies Institute, 2001). Wage subsidies are usually administered as federal tax credits. This strategy would, in essence, shift much of the financial burden from the local governments to the federal government, which is supposedly better able to absorb these costs. An example of a wage subsidy, or tax credit for low-income persons, is the Earned Income Tax Credit (EITC), described below.

The minimum wage is not a livable wage for a family.

Earned Income Tax Credit The **Earned Income Tax Credit (EITC)** is a refundable federal tax credit for low-income working families. The credit can reduce the amount of taxes owed and result in a tax refund to those who claim and qualify for the credit. To qualify for the credit, the adjusted gross income for 2000 must be less than $31,152 for a family with more than one child, $27,413 for a taxpayer with one child, and $10,380 for a family without children.

The EITC has been applauded for lifting millions of families out of poverty each year. In the United States, where family allowances, health insurance, and worker benefits are largely excluded from national policy, the EITC is considered one of the country's largest sources of assistance for poor and low-income families (Hotz, Mullin, & Scholz, 2001; Schiller, 2001). It is a cash subsidy that applies to low-income workers. The EITC was enacted in 1975 and expanded in the 1990s, and now more than 19 million taxpayers receive nearly $32 billion in EITC payments.

Not surprisingly, the EITC has had a positive effect on employment because it offers a real supplement to wages for those low-income workers who qualify. The EITC has been credited with making it easier for families to transition from welfare into work (Ellwood, 1999; Hotz, Mullin, & Scholz, 2001). Ellwood's research on single mothers' employment suggests that welfare reform accounts for only half of the changing employment of female-headed households. The

Some communities have adopted "livable wage" ordinances that require businesses receiving governmental financial assistance to pay a wage that is deemed "livable" in that community, usually 150–225 percent of the minimum wage.

EITC, and other work supports, account for roughly 30 percent of the change, and the relatively robust economy accounts for the remainder (Ellwood, 1999).

More than one-half of all payments go to families who live below the poverty line. The vast majority of benefits (80 percent) are

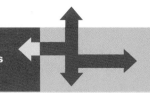

"I can only imagine what someone who makes $40,000 or $50,000 a year needs," wonders Dr. Cline, a surgeon living in Austin, Texas, who earns nearly $300,000 per year. Wonder indeed. The median household income in the United States is under $50,000 a year. Dr. Cline earns nearly six times the median income yet sees himself as struggling financially and in need of tax relief. Owning a home with a swimming pool in the fashionable part of town, having a car, and hiring a full-time nanny to help care for their children seem like the norm rather than luxuries to the Clines. As the following excerpt from the *New York Times* reveals, the rich are often far removed from the struggles of many lower-income families and do not understand why tax relief or programs such as the EITC are available for the poor.

Well-Off But Still Pressed, Doctor Could Use Tax Cut (*New York Times*, April 7, 2001)

Dr. Robert Cline lives in a graceful four-bedroom house with a pool in a tree-shrouded neighborhood considered one of the more desirable in town. His income approached $300,000 last year, ranking him among the wealthiest 2% of all Americans.

And yet Dr. Cline, 39, a surgeon, says he does not feel rich. "The perception is that someone like me doesn't have any concerns other than getting a new car," said Dr. Cline, who drives a 10-year old Acura.

In the hierarchy of wealth in America, a scale that ballooned drastically upward during the booming 1990s, Dr. Cline is at the low end of the high end. His annual income far surpasses what most Americans will ever earn, yet it is dwarfed by the fortunes of the super-rich who have built limestone mansions on the western hills of this city. When Dr. Cline and his wife, Tasha, offered a visitor a ride-around tour, they drove through a mansion-filled compound called Stratford Hills. The message was clear: They are rich, not us.

For Dr. Cline, a Republican who voted for Mr. Bush, the philosophical basis of a tax cut echoes the president's own points that everyone, regardless of income, should get a tax cut and that since the wealthy pay more, their tax savings should be larger. "You know, I think I pay too much in taxes," he said. "I'm sure everybody feels the same way, but I do, too." In fact, Dr. Cline stands to see a significant tax cut under the plans moving through Congress. If Mr. Bush ultimately succeeds in achieving the $1.6 trillion cut, the family could save nearly $12,000 a year.

When he began his practice, Dr. Cline took out a $100,000 loan to start his business and feed his family. Slowly his practice grew.

His family grew much faster. When they moved to Austin, they had just one child; by 1998 they had three children under the age of 4. When he and Tasha decided to have a fourth and final child, they instead had twin girls, Monroe and Eva, now both nearly 3. There were complications, and Eva has required extensive medical attention; her annual medical expenses—the amount paid out of pocket to meet the insurance deductible—exceed $10,000.

paid to workers with wages below $9.78 an hour. The maximum benefit for a family with two or more children is $3,888. For a family with an income of approximately $10,000 per year, the EITC reflects nearly a 40-percent increase, or approximately $2.00 an hour (Hotz, Mullin, & Scholz, 2001). This increase in income provides a critical element of security for poor families. It can contribute to basic necessities, it can enable families to make special needed purchases, or it can be used as a savings cushion to offset a future job loss, illness, or other situation that can leave families vulnerable.

The EITC, a key element of the U.S. safety net, has lifted millions of working families out of poverty. At the same time, the EITC has had less impact than it could. Its el-

In 1998, the family moved into their current four-bedroom house in the fashionable Tarrytown neighborhood. The house cost $667,000—a stretch for them—but it was only five minutes from Dr. Cline's office, and the overheated real estate market offered few bargains.

But when Mrs. Cline unexpectedly became pregnant with their sixth child and only son, Saylor, now 9 months old, they found they had already outgrown a house they could barely afford. Saylor sleeps in a walk-in closet converted to a nursery.

Mrs. Cline, 35, a former actress, said she does not want to be perceived "as the whining rich." Her days are spent chasing children and ferrying them to schools, doctors and soccer games. With six children under the age of 7, the family spends about $26,000 annually for a 40-hour-a-week nanny, though her hours will be cut in half when the three oldest girls enroll in school this fall.

Mrs. Cline said she shops at the cheaper grocery stores—her mother-in-law clips coupons for her—and that new clothes for the children are a rarity. She said that the family rake their own leaves, paint their own bedrooms, clean their own pool. "We don't have the luxuries that you would think in this tax bracket," she said. "Of course, I'm sure that having six kids doesn't help."

Dr. Cline added: "I can only imagine what someone who makes $40,000 or $50,000 a year needs with a family my size."

For Dr. Cline, money is not a consuming issue, not something he covets. Yet, he said, "with what I do, I guess my expectation was that I was not going to worry about money. And here I am worrying about money."

Once again, the family is house-hunting. The real estate boom has tacked another $200,000 in appraised value onto their house. But they are having a hard time finding a five-bedroom house in a neighborhood they like for less than $1 million. One option would be to move further out to the suburbs, where houses are cheaper but the commute is longer. Dr. Cline said he was a city guy and hated the thought of moving.

"I don't think I'm unique, especially in the medical community," he said. "We know other families that are moving into smaller houses for the same reasons."

From the tone of the debate in Washington, Dr. Cline said, it was obvious that a tax cut is coming, but not yet clear for whom and how much.

"My point to you is that I need one, too," he said.

Source: Adapted from Yardley (2001). © 2001 by The New York Times Co. Reprinted with permission.

Critical Thinking

1. What are the controversies surrounding offering tax cuts for wealthy individuals such as Dr. Cline?

2. Do you think Dr. Cline understands the lifestyle of the average American?

igibility is restricted to those with exceptionally low incomes. Few families with a breadwinner earning $10 an hour would be eligible for the EITC. However, for all practical purposes, these families are still on the economic margins. As shown in the Family Diversity box above, wealthy families do not always understand what it is like to live on the margins.

Welfare Reform: Temporary Assistance to Needy Families (TANF) Welfare has been one of the most vexing social policy concerns in the United States. Its principal cash program, **Temporary Assistance to Needy Families (TANF),** formerly called Aid to Families with Dependent Children (AFDC), has been accused of fostering long-term dependency, family breakups, and illegitimacy

(Murray, 1984, 1988). Welfare recipients are stigmatized. They are viewed as lazy and unmotivated, looking for a free ride at the expense of the taxpayer (Seccombe, 1999).

There has been a major push in the United States to get people off welfare and into work. Both Republicans and Democrats have tried to reconstruct welfare or end it altogether. Former President Clinton signed sweeping welfare reform legislation, which became federal law on July 1, 1997. Turning many of the details of welfare law over to states, it set lifetime welfare payments at a maximum of five years, with the majority of adult recipients being required to work after two years.

FACT OR FICTION?

Families leaving welfare for work are almost always better off financially after leaving welfare.

Since the passage of welfare reform, many people have left welfare, usually for low-wage work. These changes, coupled with the expanding economy and low unemployment rate of the 1990s, contributed to a dramatic initial drop in the number of families receiving TANF. From March 1994 to March 2001, national caseloads fell by over 50 percent, declining from 5 million to 2.1 million families (U.S. Department of Health and Human Services, 2001).

Families leaving welfare for work are not necessarily better off financially (Edin and Lein, 1997; Loprest, 1999; Center for the Study of Women in Society, University of Oregon, 2001). As shown in Figure 15.1, the results of a nationwide study reveal that families leaving welfare are more likely to be employed than are other low-income families, yet they are struggling with housing and food costs.

Statewide studies of families leaving welfare support the national reports. An Oregon study that followed 725 former welfare recipients until 18–21 months after leaving TANF revealed that the average monthly take-home pay of the employed was $1,016. Although this figure is significantly more than their previous welfare check, it renders them ineligible for a number of important services. Many families expressed significant economic hardship: 80 percent had paid bills late, 40 percent depended on money or gifts from family or friends to get by, 30 percent had eaten at a food kitchen or received a food box, and 20 percent had skipped meals because of lack of money (Center for the Study of Women in Society, University of Oregon, 2001). In Florida, 43 percent of families leaving TANF reported that at some point they had "no way to buy food" (Tweedie, Reichert, & O'Connor, 1999).

Other countries have a different approach to welfare. For example, in her book *Saving Our Children from Poverty* (1996), economist Barbara Bergmann states that only one-quarter of single mothers in France receive welfare-type benefits, compared to two-thirds of single mothers in the United States. The reason for this difference is not because France is stingy. In contrast, France has made a successful commitment to enhancing low-tier jobs, improving the conditions surrounding low-tier work so that these

Skyrocketing housing costs leave many families with few options other than to live in squalor.

FIGURE 15.1 Proportion of Low-Income Parents Experiencing Hardships in the Last Year, and Proportion Currently Employed, 1997

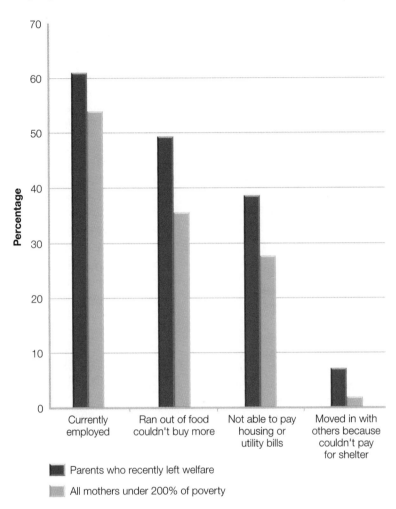

Source: Loprest (1999), Chart 4 and Table 4.

jobs pay a living wage. As well, the government does not automatically eliminate an array of benefits that are vital to a family's well-being. A single mother in France who moves from welfare to work retains approximately $6,000 in government cash and housing grants. She continues to receive health insurance and pays only a small amount for child care, as do all French citizens. Therefore, even though France has an unemployment rate that is 50 percent higher than that of the United States, its poverty rate is considerably less. In contrast, the Family Narratives box on pages 638–639 shows us how single mothers in the United States try to survive.

FICTION

Families are often poorer when they leave welfare because they may no longer receive certain benefits, such as health care or subsidized housing.

How do single mothers in the United States survive meager welfare benefits and low-wage work? In many other countries, they would qualify for an array of government benefits to help them make ends meet. But in the United States, they are largely left to their own devices. One study of 214 welfare and 165 wage-reliant mothers found a number of crafty and deceptive strategies. Some strategies were illegal because they were not reported to the welfare agency. But the mothers claimed that without this type of assistance, their families would be destitute. What are some of their survival strategies?

1. **Contributions from Family, Friends, Boyfriends**

   "The kids give me a headache about clothes. Usually my mom, brother, or sister-in-law gives me money to buy them clothes. I can't afford it. I get clothes at church and other charitable clothes giveaways, or at garage sales. My kids haven't had any store-bought clothes paid for by me for eight or nine years. Mama buys them shoes when we visit her. It's cheaper where my mother lives."

   "He sometimes gives me money. When I sent her up there to his mother's house, he buy her Pampers and baby food, but all he puts into my hand is a $20 bill. I mean, what does he expect me to buy with $20? I can't even buy but two boxes of Pampers with $20. He's coming over here tonight to bring her back, and I said I needed $40 'cause she need so many things right now. But I don't think he gonna bring it. He always says he's gonna bring money, but he never does because he's never working steady. If he doesn't bring money this time, I am not gonna let her go up there to his mother's house to visit anymore."

2. **Reported Work**

   "Working overtime if I have to, anything to get a few extra dollars. I try to get to work one-half hour early, and leave one-half hour late, that's an extra five hours worth of pay each week! It comes in handy."

3. **Unreported Side Jobs**

   "I wish I could report my job, I really do. But then I just couldn't make it right now, not until I get a raise or some overtime. I dream about the day when I can go in and tell my caseworker, 'I don't need your assistance, I got a job.' I dream about the day I can kiss welfare good-bye."

   "I'm pretty resourceful. Where I live we have a pretty big

Specific Policies for Children

Children are a particularly vulnerable group because they are dependent on others to meet their basic needs of food, shelter, clothing, and love. What can we do to improve their circumstances and therefore improve their resiliency and chance for a good life?

Early Childhood Intervention **Early childhood interventions** are attempts to maintain or improve the quality of life of young children. While most of the care that young children receive comes from families, other relatives, or friends, early childhood interventions are those formal supports designed to augment this care, including the following:

* Public health and social welfare programs that provide prenatal care, immunizations, or food and nutritional supplements, including the feeding program Women, Infants, and Children (WIC)
* Child-care programs designed to ensure high-quality providers or to pro-

garage, and I collect junk, trash pick—I'm the ultimate trash picker—and I go to garage sales. I have my friends picking up stuff in alleys and at garage sales for me too. They're all like, 'oh, let's grab this for her!' whenever they see some old crap. Then on weekends, I'll get this friend of mine to help me load his pickup and we get a table at the flea market for about $50. Some weekends I'll make $200 or $300 on old junk I might have paid $20 total for, but that's not all the time."

4. Underground Work

"Some of our friends will sell drugs. I know some of my friends who have turned tricks. Usually, some people do it for their family, and some people do it for drugs. At one point I did sell drugs in order to keep my family [together]. When my husband left, and I had to make sure I could pay my bills. That's what I did."

"My brother, he sells stuff out of the back of his car, you know, like stolen stuff for real cheap prices. I could work for him any time I wanted to, but I don't want my kids to think I'm a criminal."

5. Agency-Based Strategies

"I don't like to beg, but I will for the kids. I go to a church where they give you canned goods, tuna, spaghetti, tomato sauce, eggs . . . I've been twice in two months. They don't like you to show up too often, but if you really need it, they'll give it."

"This morning I went to Catholic Charities and got a $20 voucher for the Market Basket [grocery story]. You can only go once a year. They're cutting back a lot of programs: no more emergency assistance, no more back payments in rent, no more rent assistance. These cuts will affect me a lot. I will have to dig deep. I don't know what I am going to do."

Source: Edin and Lein (1997), pp. 143–191.

Critical Thinking

1. Do you think that women in other nations resort to these same survival strategies? Why or why not?

2. Do any of these survival strategies bother you, personally? If so, why?

3. How do our social policies promote the need for these types of survival strategies?

vide financial assistance to families needing child care

* Programs to promote early childhood development, such as parenting classes, Head Start, preschool, and kindergarten

* Income or other support "safety-net" programs. (Children's Defense Fund, 2000; Karoly et al., 1998)

Researchers from RAND, a prominent research institute in California, conducted a project to determine whether or not early childhood intervention programs are successful in helping children later in life (Karoly et al., 1998). They examined nine specific social programs in which evaluations had been performed that assessed a variety of measures of well-being: (1) educational achievement (e.g., high school graduation, grade repetition, achievement in the short term and long term); (2) cognitive and emotional development (e.g., IQ in the short and long term, behavioral measures); (3) health status (e.g., emergency room visits, teen pregnancy rates); and (4) economic well-being (e.g., employment, income, welfare participation, involvement with crime or delin-

Early childhood interventions can improve quality of life and strengthen families.

quency). Experimental designs were used to randomly assign children to either one of the programs or to a "control group" (i.e., no program). Children were then compared on the above measures.

The researchers found that each program favorably affected at least one measure, and most of them affected several measures. In other words, children enrolled in these programs had better outcomes than did those who were not enrolled. For example, they had lower rates of teen pregnancy, and they were less likely to repeat a grade or be on welfare. However, it is important to clarify that no program was successful on all measures:

> Nonetheless, our review supports the proposition that, in some situations, carefully targeting early childhood interventions *can* yield measurable benefits in the short run and that some of those benefits persist long after the program has ended. (Karoly et al., 1998: xiii)

The Constructing Strong Families box on pages 642–643 describes the Head Start program, which is designed to improve school readiness and basic cognitive skills for low-income preschool-aged children. This pro-

gram currently serves more than 900,000 children and has helped millions of others since it began in 1964.

FACT OR FICTION?

Less than half of custodial mothers receive the full amount of their court-ordered child support.

Child Support   In the United States, 23 million children under age 21 have parents who do not live together (Grall, 2000). Inadequate **child support** payments from the noncustodial parent to the custodial parent have hurt many families. In 1997, only 42 percent of custodial mothers received the full amount of their court-ordered child support payment, and 27 percent received only a partial or sporadic payment. Even fewer custodial fathers received their court-ordered award, with only 32 percent receiving their full payment and 26 percent receiving a partial payment. Of the $29.1 billion of child support due, only $17.1 billion (58.8 percent) was received (Grall, 2000). A national policy to bolster child support enforcement could help millions of families escape poverty and obtain economic security, and thus improve family outcomes.

Since 1988, the federal government has made greater efforts to secure child support from the absent parent with passage of the Family Support Act. The act included withholding child support from fathers' wages, requiring states to adopt uniform standards for setting child support awards, and implementing computerized systems for locating delinquent parents. Some states take additional steps, such as intercepting tax returns, withdrawing funds from bank accounts, suspending drivers' licenses, or even putting nonpayers in jail (Garfinkel, McLanahan, & Robins, 1994). Despite these efforts, compliance is still woefully inadequate. Overall, the proportion of women who receive court-ordered child support has changed little since the mid-1970s (The Urban Institute, 1999). Consequently, child support enforcement was an important component of the welfare reform changes of 1996, and states must now comply with more rigorous federal guidelines (Institute for Research on Poverty, 2000). The long-term effects of welfare reform are still unknown. The U.S. Census Bureau (2000c) reports no significant change in child support received between 1995 and 1997, but other early reports suggest that there has been a modest increase (Sorensen & Halpern, 1999).

FACT

Only 42 percent of custodial mothers receive the full amount owed to them, and even fewer custodial fathers receive child support.

Will further enforcing child support orders significantly reduce poverty? A study in Wisconsin found that child support payments from fathers of children on welfare would average between $200 and $460 a month if child support laws were perfectly enforced (in mid-1990s dollars), which could improve the lives of impoverished children considerably (Brien & Willis, 1997). Sorensen (1997) reported that if all noncustodial fathers paid the same percentage of their income in child support as payers did, they would pay, on average, between 12 percent and 15 percent of their income, averaging between $2,837 and $3,321. Although this would not bestow great wealth on these families, it would nonetheless make their lives more comfortable and secure (especially given that child support payments are not taxed).

Child-Care Policies As we saw in Chapter 10, child-care costs for employed parents are expensive. Costs for full-time day care can run up to $10,000 a year or more per child,

© Tom Rosenthal/SuperStock

In many countries, quality day care for children is available to all parents at a very low cost, or no cost at all. In the United States, quality day care can cost upward of $10,000 a year per child.

while in-home nanny services are in the range of $20,000–$25,000 per year. Given that most families have more than one child, and they are spaced only a few years apart, many families have day-care bills that are approaching $20,000 per year. These costs are comparable to, or even exceed, costs for college, and they are out of the reach of many families. Yet where is the "financial aid" to help these parents?

Head Start began in 1965 as part of the War on Poverty program launched by the administration of President Lyndon B. Johnson. Nearly half of the nation's poor people were children under age twelve, and Head Start was developed to respond to the needs of poor children as early as possible. A few privately funded pre-school programs for poor children in inner cities and rural areas had shown marked success in raising children's intellectual skills. Research showed that early intervention through high-quality programs enhances children's physical, social, emotional, and cognitive development; enables parents to be better caregivers and teachers to their children; and helps parents meet their own goals, including economic independence. Moreover, many low-income chil-dren also had unrecognized health problems and had not been immu-nized. Head Start was envisioned as a comprehensive program that would provide health and nutritional services to poor children while also developing their cognitive skills. The program aimed to involve parents as well. Many parents of children in the program were employed as teach-ers' aides so that they would under-stand what their children were learning and help carry on that learn-ing at home.

The program was political from its inception. Head Start was launched with much fanfare by Lady Bird Johnson, Lyndon Johnson's wife, and presidents from Lyndon Johnson to Bill Clinton have praised the program and taken credit for its successes. Measuring the pro-gram's actual success is not a simple matter, however. Head Start is said to save taxpayers money, be-cause children who attend Head Start are more likely to graduate high school and get a job than their peers who do not attend Head Start. However, the precise long-term benefits of Head Start are difficult to gauge, and researchers disagree even about the short-term benefits. Nevertheless, one government pub-lication states that in the long term, $6 is saved for every $1 invested in the Head Start program. Other stud-ies merely suggest that Head Start graduates are more likely than their peers to stay in the proper grade level for their age in elementary school.

Most programs are half-day, and include lunch. The curriculum is not the same in every program, but in most cases school readiness is

No federal loans, scholarships, or work-study programs pay for child care. Families themselves pay most of the costs. Looking at child-care expenditures, overall, approxi-mately 60 percent of the costs are borne by families, with the public and private sector paying the remaining share. In contrast, families pay an average of only one-quarter of the costs of their child's college expenses.

There are two ways the public sector can chip in for the costs of child care. One mechanism is a child-care tax credit on the family's income tax form. Under current law, the Child and Dependent Care tax credit can cover between 20 percent and 30 percent of expenses to care for children younger than age thirteen. There is a dollar limit on the ex-penses toward which families can apply the credit: $2,400 for the care of one, $4,800 for two or more. The lower the family's income, the higher the allowable percentage.

As a second option, available only if an employer offers this benefit, a family can set aside up to $5,000 pre-tax dollars for child care. They do not pay taxes on this amount, so if a family is in a 25-percent tax bracket, it is as though they are getting a 25-percent bonus on this money ($1,250). This is a real boon for many families. However, there are two problems with this program. First, given that most child-care costs far exceed $5,000, these savings, while helpful, are inadequate

stressed. Children may be taught the alphabet and numbers and to recognize colors and shapes. Health care is an important aspect of the program, and children in Head Start are monitored to keep them up to date on their immunizations; testing is also available for hearing and vision. Many programs are integrated to include children with special needs such as a physical or mental handicap. Class size is limited to between seventeen and twenty children, with two teachers. Parents are encouraged to volunteer their time in the classroom, or to work as teachers' aides.

Head Start began by primarily serving four-year-olds, who attend Head Start for one year before starting kindergarten. However, with the reauthorization of the Head Start program in 1994, Congress estab- lished a new program for low-in- come families with infants, toddlers, and/or pregnant women called Early Head Start. The Early Head Start program provides resources to com- munity programs to address the needs of younger children and their families. Its goals are similar to Head Start—to demonstrate the im- pact that can be gained when early, continuous, intensive, and compre- hensive services are provided to pregnant women and very young children and their families.

Head Start served approximately 900,000 children across the nation in the fiscal year 2001. Fifty-eight per- cent were age four or older, 35 per- cent were three, and 7 percent were under three. Four percent of children were Native American, 30 percent were Hispanic, 34 percent were Afri- can American, 30 percent were white, 2 percent were Asian, and 1 percent were Hawaiian/ Pacific Islander. Seventy-seven per- cent of Head Start families had an- nual incomes of less than $15,000 per year.

Source: Adapted from *Gale Encyclopedia of Childhood & Adolescence* (1998); Head Start (2002, 1999).

Critical Thinking

1. Why is it so difficult to measure the exact financial impact of Head Start?

2. Why did Head Start initially fo- cus on only four-year-olds, and why did it take another thirty years to include younger children?

to meet the needs of most families. For ex- ample, if the real cost of child care is $10,000, and by law the 25-percent tax benefit can be taken on only half of that amount—$5,000—it thereby reduces their real savings by half, to 12.5 percent. Second, wealthier families, which are in a higher tax bracket, save more money than do lower-in- come families, which are in a lower tax bracket. Therefore, a program like this is highly regressive: the wealthier end up get- ting a higher benefit than do those families that need it the most.

How do other countries deal with the is- sue of child care, and what can we learn from them? Table 15.4 illustrates the per- centage of children in publicly funded child care in fourteen countries. Of the countries listed, the United States ranks last in the per- centage of children in publicly funded pro- grams, with only 1 percent of children aged two and under, and 14 percent of children aged three to school age, in publicly funded programs (cited in Ontario Coalition for Bet- ter Child Care, 2000). Compare this with Denmark, where 48 percent of children up to age two and 85 percent of children aged three to school age are in publicly funded day care. Or compare the United States with France and Belgium, where 20 percent of children up to age two and 95 percent of chil- dren aged three and older are in publicly

TABLE 15.4	Publicly Funded Child Care	
	PERCENTAGE OF CHILDREN IN PUBLICLY FUNDED CHILD CARE	
	AGE 0 TO 2 (%)	AGE 3 TO SCHOOL AGE (%)
Australia	2	26
Belgium	20	95
Canada	5	35
Denmark	48	85
Finland	32	59
France	20	95
Germany	2	78
Italy	5	88
Luxembourg	2	58
Netherlands	2	53
Norway	12	40
Sweden	32	79
United Kingdom	2	38
United States	1	14

Source: Cited in Ontario Coalition for Better Child Care (2000).

funded day care. In the United States, the costs of child care are largely borne by the parents themselves. Quality care is seen as a private good rather than a public one, even though we all benefit from having well-cared-for and educated children.

France can provide us with an example of what is possible (Bergmann, 1996). French parents at all income levels receive a great deal of government assistance with child care. Day-care centers for young children or smaller, family day-care units are readily available, staffed by an educated and valued work force that is well paid and receives full benefits. Free public nursery schools are available for children aged 2½ to 6, and by the time they are 3, virtually all of French children attend. There is also a well-coordinated before- and after-school care program for a nominal fee. These programs are universal and are available to all citizens regardless of income. Because they are universal, there is no stigma attached to using them. They are considered to be programs that all families may need.

Specific Policies for the Elderly

As shown in Chapter 14, both the sheer number and the proportion of elderly persons within the population are increasing dramatically. Consequently, we are facing new challenges in trying to deal with our changing demographic structure and care for the most frail members of our society. Here we will look at several policies related to the economic well-being and health of the elderly, comparing the policies of the United States to those of other nations.

Social Security and Economic Well-Being As indicated in Chapter 14, nearly 10 percent of elders live in poverty. Yet to truly understand the economic well-being of the elderly as a whole, we must examine more than just the poverty line. Many elderly live only slightly above the poverty line. They are not represented in the statistics, but they are vulnerable nonetheless.

Moreover, subgroups of elderly vary wildly in income and assets. An eighty-year-old African American female who lives alone is significantly worse off than a sixty-six-year-old married white male. Gender, race, and age interact to significantly influence median income and the likelihood of living in poverty. Sociologists refer to the notions of **cumulative advantage** and **cumulative disadvantage** to describe how early life chances influence one's status in later life. Individuals who have greater opportunities for financial success (i.e., white males) can build upon their successes to perpetuate their advantages into older age, while those who have faced disadvantage carry these over, often resulting in poverty.

Ideally in the United States, elders' income comes from three primary sources: (1) retirement benefits from Social Security, (2) payments from private pensions, and (3) income from assets and personal savings.

The imagery used by the Social Security Administration is that of a "three-legged stool"—all three legs are needed in balance for the stool to provide support.

The United States is one of approximately 155 countries that have some sort of financial program for elders, known here as Social Security (discussed in Chapter 14). Each program operates somewhat differently but provides at least some minimal benefit to help the elderly survive. Some programs serve virtually everyone above a certain age threshold, such as in the United States and the United Kingdom, while others serve only a smaller fraction that meet some eligibility requirement. In China, less than one-quarter of elders are covered, while in Mexico the figure is about one-third.

The amount of money provided to participants in these programs also varies. Figure 15.2 compares the disposable incomes of elderly couples and females living alone to the median disposable income of citizens in seven countries, adjusted for size of household. It appears that all programs provide greater coverage for married couples than they do for females. This discrepancy is particularly acute in the United States. Elderly married couples are better off, on average, than are other married couples, while elderly females living alone earn only 62 percent of the amount of female-headed households nationally. In fact, elderly females who live alone in the United States are among the poorest of the seven countries. Only in Australia are females worse off. It appears that our "three-legged stool" may be adequate for married couples, but something is clearly amiss for widowed, divorced, or never-married women.

Health Policy Health care is a rapidly growing segment of the U.S. economy, and the elderly frequently use health care services.

FIGURE 15.2 Elderly Median Household Income as a Percentage of National Median Household Income, by Country

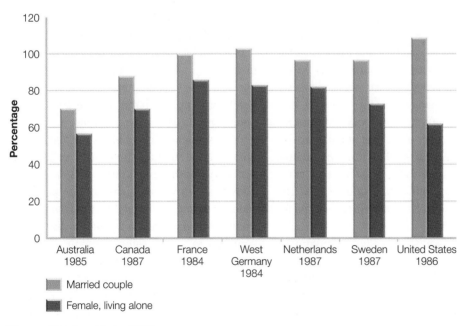

Source: Kinsella and Tauber (1993).

Medicare is a federal program designed to provide health care for the elderly. However, it does not cover all health care costs.

Since most elderly persons no longer work, how do they get their health insurance? **Medicare** is a federal health insurance program for people aged sixty-five and older (and some people with disabilities under sixty-five, including people with permanent kidney failure requiring dialysis or a transplant). Medicare was created in 1965, and today it is virtually universal among the elderly.

Medicare is actually made up of two distinct programs. Part A is sometimes called "hospital insurance." Most people receive Part A automatically when they turn 65, and they do not have to pay any monthly premiums for it. It covers overnight stays in hospitals, 100 days in a skilled nursing facility, hospice care, and some home health care. The yearly deductible (the amount that the recipient must pay before Medicare chips in) was $792 in 2001.

Part B is sometimes called "supplemental insurance." It is optional and requires a $50 monthly premium. Part B covers 80 percent of the costs of such things as doctors' fees, outpatient hospital treatment, and lab services. The other 20 percent, which is re-

ferred to as a **co-payment,** is the part that the elderly pay out of pocket. In addition to the monthly premium and co-payments, there is a yearly deductible of $100 (U.S. Department of Health and Human Services, 2001).

FACT OR FICTION?

Medicare, the health care program for the elderly, covers virtually all their costs.

Medicare has made health insurance far more affordable and available to elders. Because it is a universal program rather than means-tested, it has virtually no stigma attached to it.

Yet Medicare is not without its critics. Given high deductibles, co-payments, and payments for things not covered under Medicare, most elderly persons spend thousands of additional dollars each year on medical care, averaging 21 percent of their medical costs (Committee on Ways and Means, 1997). Their health care is far from free. In fact, even with Medicare, rising costs and gaps in coverage result in elders paying more out of their own pockets today than they did before Medicare existed (Morgan & Kunkel, 1998). Consequently, nearly 70 percent of elders have some form of additional insurance, known as a "medigap" policy. The poorest elderly may qualify for Medicaid, the health care program that is designed to serve poor persons, regardless of age.

In any case, our health care system is not designed to serve the elderly well. This is certainly not the sole fault of Medicare, but it does dampen the efficiency of the program. Elders commonly suffer from chronic conditions, such as arthritis or heart disease. In contrast to these needs, our health care system is geared towards acute care, such as surgical or "high-tech" treatments to fix short-term problems. Many health problems that the elderly experience cannot be cured. A system that focused more on the social dimensions of health and well-being, rather than simply on the absence of disease, would be more responsive to their needs.

| FICTION

High deductibles and co-payments result in the elderly usually paying thousands of dollars each year for their health care.

Our changing demographic structure, outlined in Chapter 14, has some potentially distressing repercussions for the Medicare program. Medicare is primarily funded through Social Security taxes—working people pay taxes today for programs used by the elderly today. In the future, as our population ages, there will be fewer working adults paying taxes relative to the number of elderly persons needing Medicare services. There were approximately 5 workers for each beneficiary in 1960, and 3 in 2000, but there will be only 1.9 by 2040 (De Lew, Greenbery, & Kinchen, 1992). Couple this with our rising health care costs, and we have the prescription for a major financing disaster. To deal with this problem, Congress will continue to increase the amount that elders pay out of their own pockets by raising deductibles and co-payments, and possibly covering fewer services. The goal is to keep Medicare solvent well into the future. We recognize that the health of our seniors is, at least in part, a social concern, not merely an individual problem. Compare this approach with our policies toward children.

Conclusion

What kind of family life do we want for the twenty-first century? Families are not socially isolated entities that can survive solely on their own accord. Families are woven into a network; they are part of a broader social system. Families will have the opportunity to flourish only when we provide the support that they need. Individual and community strengths are invaluable, but this support must also come in the form of broad social and economic policies designed to help us care for one another. Universal policies can bring families together and help us recognize our collective needs. Selective programs, designed to save money in the short run, have the potential to be divisive. They are premised on the view that families are responsible for their own plight and ignore the fact that families are likely to share certain needs—such as the need to help care for children and frail elders—and they mask the fact that we all benefit directly or indirectly from these types of services. The United States has much to learn about family policy from other countries. It is likely that no one country has a model that could, or even should, be superimposed on the United States. However, understanding the power of social structure, using a critical perspective, having respect for empirical data, and being able to link microlevel and macrolevel perspectives show us that other possibilities may indeed provide us with stronger, safer, and more resilient families.

Chapter Review

Why is social structure important?

Many of our personal experiences, choices, and beliefs are due to far more than individual inclinations. They are socially constructed and are shaped by historical and cultural forces, by our social positions, and by our social institutions.

What is a critical perspective?

It suggests that we should not blindly accept the commonsense explanations of why things are. A critical perspective does not consider the present organization of families as inviolable. It also examines the assumptions, values, and ideologies that are used to define and characterize families.

How does empirical research help us understand families?

Family scholars do not rely on common sense to help them understand and interpret family life. Instead, they rely on a scientific perspective, which draws on empirical data because data provide a far more objective window on the world.

What are microlevel and macrolevel perspectives?

A microlevel perspective focuses on individuals' interactions in specific settings. It stresses the importance of personal choices, and internal relationships among family members. A macrolevel perspective focuses on broader social factors in society. These two perspectives are interrelated.

What are the usual key components of family resiliency, and what is missing from the discussion?

Discussions of family resiliency usually focus on individual protective factors, family protective and recovery factors, and community institutions. Further consideration should be given to the importance of structural conditions in helping families flourish.

What are four themes of this book?

The text stresses (1) the importance of examining social structure for our everyday lives, (2) the usefulness of a critical perspective, (3) the importance of empirical research, and (4) the linkages between microlevel and macrolevel perspectives.

What is family resiliency?

Resiliency is a multifaceted phenomenon that produces the ability to thrive despite adversity. Family scholars generally point to individual attributes, family protective and recovery factors, and community features.

What is missing from the resiliency research?

A focus on structural factors, such as the role of family policy.

Does the United States have a strong family policy?

Compared to many other countries, the United States lags behind in a comprehensive family policy. Moreover, most of our programs are means-tested rather than universal.

What are some examples of general policies or programs needed to support families?

Examples include national health insurance, parental leaves, living wages, the Earned Income Tax Credit, and Temporary Assistance to Needy Families (TANF).

What are some examples of policies or programs to help children or the elderly?

Current policies include WIC, Head Start, child support policies, child-care policies, Social Security, and Medicaid.

Key Terms

agency: the ability to create viable lives even when constrained by structural forces *child support:* payment from the noncustodial parent to the custodial parent for the support of children

co-payment: the money that medical patients pay out of their own pockets to accompany insurance or government-supplied payments

community factors: community features that help promote resiliency, such as geographic space, social networks, and religious and faith-based fellowships

cumulative advantage and disadvantage: a syndrome in which early life chances influence one's status in later life

early childhood intervention: attempts to maintain or improve the quality of life of young children

earned income tax credit (EITC): refundable federal tax credit for low-income working families that reduces the amount of taxes owed

family protective factors (FPF): family characteristics or dynamics that shape the family's ability to endure in the face of risk factors

family recovery factors (FRF): factors that assist families in "bouncing back" from a crisis situation

flexplace: flexibility in the location of work

flextime: flexibility in the timing of work

individual-level protective factors: traits including a positive self-concept, sociability, intelligence and scholastic competence, autonomy, self-esteem, androgyny, communication and problem-solving skills, humor, and mental and physical health

living wage: a minimum wage that is deemed a "livable wage" in a particular community, usually from 150 percent to 225 percent of the federal minimum wage

means-tested programs: programs with income-based eligibility requirements

Medicare: a federal health insurance program for people aged sixty-five and older (and for some people with disabilities who are under age sixty-five)

national health insurance: a health care system for all citizens

parental leave: a guaranteed leave from work after the birth of a child (or some other serious family event, such as a child's illness or death)

progressive taxation: a form of taxation in which those who earn more pay a higher percentage of their income in taxes

resilience: a multifaceted phenomenon that produces the ability for individuals and families to thrive despite adversity

Temporary Assistance to Needy Families (TANF): the principal cash welfare program

universal programs: programs to help strengthen all families without any eligibility requirements

Resources on the Internet

These web sites have been selected for their relevance to the topics in this chapter. These sites are among the more stable, but please be aware that web site addresses change frequently.

Children's Defense Fund

http://www.childrensdefense.org

The mission of the Children's Defense Fund is to "Leave No Child Behind®" and to ensure every child a good start in life and successful passage to adulthood with the help of caring families and communities. CDF provides a strong, effective voice for *all* the children of the United States who cannot vote, lobby, or speak for themselves.

Head Start

http://www2.acf/dhhs.gov.programs/hsb

Head Start and Early Head Start are comprehensive child development programs that serve children from birth to age five, pregnant women, and their families. They are child-focused programs and have the overall goal of increasing the school readiness of young children in low-income families.

National Center for Policy Research (CPR) for Women and Families

http://www.cpr4womenandfamilies.org

The National Center for Policy Research (CPR) for Women and Families promotes the health and well-being of women and families by using objective, research-based information to encourage new, more effective programs and policies. The center achieves its mission by gathering and analyzing information and translating that information into clearly presented facts and policy implications that are made available to the public, the media, and policy makers.

United Nations

http://www.un.org

The United Nations is central to global efforts to solve the problems that challenge humanity, including work to promote respect for human rights, protect the environment, fight disease, foster development and reduce poverty, promote safe and efficient transport by air and sea, and fight drug trafficking and terrorism.

Companion Web Site for This Book

Virtual Society: The Wadsworth Sociology Resource Center

http://sociology.wadsworth.com

Begin by clicking the Student Resources section. Next, click Marriage and Family, and then click the cover image for this book. Se-lect from the pull-down menu the chapter you are presently studying. You will have easy access to chapter resources such as MicroCase Online exercises, additional Web links, flashcards, InfoTrac exercises, and practice tests (that can be scored). In addition, to enhance and help with your study of marriages and families, be sure to investigate the rest of the rich sociology resources at Virtual Society.

Visit InfoTrac College Edition

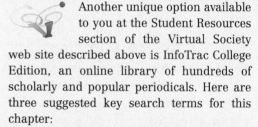 Another unique option available to you at the Student Resources section of the Virtual Society web site described above is InfoTrac College Edition, an online library of hundreds of scholarly and popular periodicals. Here are three suggested key search terms for this chapter:

* Search keywords: *policy + elderly*
* Search keywords: *minimum wage + United States*
* Search keywords: *welfare reform + children*

Search recent years to get the latest information on these issues.

Glossary

acquired immunodeficiency syndrome (AIDS): a deadly disease passed from one person to another through blood-to-blood transmission, sexual contact, and pregnancy, delivery, or breastfeeding.

activities of daily living (ADLs): general day-to-day activities such as cooking, cleaning, bathing, and home repair

adolescence: the period of life that occurs between childhood and adulthood. The term was not used until the twentieth century.

agency: the ability to create viable lives even when constrained by structural forces

agents of socialization: the primary groups responsible for gender socialization

agreement reality: a way of knowing about our world through information gathered from trusted others or through our culture

alcoholism: alcohol addiction—a chronic condition lasting a lifetime; therefore, it is often labeled a "disease"

alimony: payment by one partner to the other, designed to support the more dependent spouse for a period of time

Alzheimer's disease (AD): the most common form of dementia, or the loss of mental functions such as thinking, memory, and reasoning

androgynous love: a type of love that includes both traditional feminine traits and masculine traits

annihilated: exterminated

annual fertility rate: the number of births per 1,000 women in a given year

anti-gay prejudice: very strong negative feelings toward homosexuality. (This term is preferred over *homophobia.*)

anxious/ambivalent attachments: seen in infants who become nervous when their mother leaves the room and can show rejection when she returns

attachment theory: the theory that the way in which infants form attachment early in life will affect their relationships in later life

authoritarian parenting: parents using arbitrary or punitive means of controlling their children

authoritative parenting: includes communication that involves reasoning with children

avoidant attachments: seen in infants who show little attachment to their mother

baby boom: a cohort in which the average number of children born to women reaches a peak compared to cohorts prior to and subsequent to it—in the United States, the most significant baby boom took place between 1946 and 1964

baby boom generation: those persons born after World War II through the early 1960s

bilateral: descent traced through both male and female sides of the family

biochemical theories of love: biological theories that suggest humans are attracted to certain types of people. When the attraction occurs, the brain releases natural chemicals.

bisexual: an orientation in which a person is attracted to both males and females

bourgeoisie: the capitalist class, which owns the means of production

bundling: an arrangement in colonial America in which an unmarried couple would spend the night in a bed together, separated by a wooden board

calling: a dating practice of the eighteenth and nineteenth centuries in which a man would make a call on a woman in her home. It may have been more prevalent among the middle class.

career: an occupation with the opportunity for upward mobility and one that requires higher levels of education and training

Caucasian: part of a nineteenth-century biological definition of race comprising those individuals with relatively light skin

child support: payment from the noncustodial parent to the custodial parent for the support of children

child support order: a legal document delineating the amount and circumstances of the financial support of noncustodial children

childless versus childfree: terms referring to those who do not have children, either because they want to but cannot get pregnant or because they choose not to have children, respectively

children of alcoholics (COAs): children who still suffer the consequences of their parents' drinking. They often have little grasp of what is considered "normal" family behavior, suffer from low self-esteem, have trouble forming and maintaining close relationships, and experience other emotional difficulties.

class consciousness: people understanding their socioeconomic position in society and engaging in practices that help to maintain the system and their place in it

clitoridectomy: an operation in which the clitoris is cut out of the body

co-dependency: a relationship pattern in which people assume responsibility for meeting others' needs to the exclusion of acknowledging their own needs; they often lose their sense of their own identity.

cohabitation: the practice of unmarried couples who are sexual partners sharing a household

cohort effect: people born in a particular time period exhibiting similar behavior patterns compared to people born in a different time period

community factors: community features that help promote resiliency, such as geographic space, social networks, and religious and faith-based fellowships

companionate family: a marriage based on mutual affection, sexual attraction, compatibility, and personal happiness

companionate grandparenting: enjoying recreational activities, occasional overnight stays, and even babysitting, with an emphasis on fun and enjoyment

Conflict Tactics Scale (CTS): a commonly used scale based on how people deal with disagreements in relationships

conflict theory: a theoretical perspective that views social systems as always in flux. There is an uneven distribution of resources in society, and those with the most resources hold more power, or the ability to achieve their goals. Conflict theorists predict that those groups who have greater access to resources (education and income) will be more likely to have stable marriages.

conflicted bachelors: men who are ambivalent about their single status and the most likely to marry among long-term bachelors

conflict-habituated marriages: marriages that include frequent conflict. These may be enduring marriages, however.

control group: during experiments, the group members who do not receive the stimulus and are used for comparison

co-payment: the money that medical patients pay out of their own pockets to accompany insurance or government-supplied payments

courtly love: a term derived from the Middle Ages, when poets or troubadours would write songs of love and present them at the court of their aristocratic/royal masters. This type of love was initially considered to be unrequited.

crisis: a critical change of events that disrupts the functioning of a person's or a family's life

cross-dressing: wearing the clothing associated with the other sex

cross-sectional: a rate at only one point in time

cross-sectional data: data collected at one point in time

Cult of True Womanhood: the ideology of separate spheres for men and women

cumulative advantage and disadvantage: a syndrome in which early life chances influence one's status in later life

cunnilingus: oral stimulation of a woman's genitals by her partner

dating: used to describe the interactions that take place between romantically attached people away from the oversight of parents

deduction: the process beginning with a theory, developing a hypothesis, and then collecting data to test that hypothesis

deindustrialization: the process by which economies switch from being based on industry to ones based more on service sector production

delayed childbearing: putting off having children until someone is older, often related to the increased time spent in education and career development

delayed marriage: a trend for women and men to marry at a later age

dependent variable: the variable that we are interested in explaining. This variable changes as a result of changes in another (independent) variable.

descriptive research: the type of research designed to address basic quantitative questions such as "How many?" "How long?" "How much has changed?"

developmental perspective: a "stage" approach to analyzing family behavior. As relationships develop, they tend to go through somewhat predictable stages, just as the individual goes through developmental stages when growing up.

devitalized marriages: enduring marriages that exist without much passion

direct costs of raising children: expenditures for children, including housing, food, child care, and education

discrimination: behaviors, action, or practices that have harmful effects

division of domestic labor: the way in which domestic responsibilities are divided in a family

divorce mediation: a nonadversarial means of resolution whereby the divorcing couple, along with a third party such as a therapist or trained mediator, negotiate the terms of their financial, custody, and visitation settlement

domestic code: an ideology that emerged during the nineteenth century to help justify a system of gender difference

double standard: men being allowed far more permissiveness in sexual behavior

early childhood intervention: attempts to maintain or improve the quality of life of young children

earned income tax credit (EITC): refundable federal tax credit for low-income working families that reduces the amount of taxes owed

ecological perspective: a theoretical perspective identified with Urie Bronfenbrenner that studies human development and families by placing them in their environments. Environments range from the immediate day-to-day context (microsystem) to the broader cultural contexts (macrosystem).

economic hardship: low income, income loss, and unstable work

economic restructuring: transformations in the structure of employment

egalitarian: power and authority equally vested in both men and women

elder abuse: abuse of an elderly person that can include physical abuse, sexual abuse, psychological abuse, financial or material exploitation, and neglect

emotional abuse: verbal, mental, or psychological maltreatment that destroys self-esteem

empirical: that which is experienced through the senses. Empirical research is done by watching or listening to others to collect data.

enabling behaviors: doing things to cover for, support, or in many different ways enable the alcoholic or drug addict to continue without change

entrenched bachelors: single men who hold fast to their single status

epidemiologist: a "health detective" who works to piece together a picture of disease

equity theory: suggests that relationships work best when both people involved feel as though there is a fair exchange, or balance, in the relationship

ethnic group: people who share specific cultural features

ethnicity: shared cultural characteristics, such as language, place of origin, dress, food, and religion

evaluation research: the type of research designed to evaluate the effectiveness of structures or programs

experiential reality: understanding the world around us by using our own histories

experimental group: during experiments, the group members who receive the stimulus and are watched to note changes

experiments: a highly controlled research method for determining cause and effect. Used primarily by psychologists, it typically includes two groups of participants (experimental and control). One group receives a treatment; comparing the two groups over time can detect the effects of the given treatment.

explanatory research: the type of research designed to address questions of "why?"

exploratory research: the type of research designed to address questions about what it is like to experience a variety of situations

expressive roles: behaviors intended to manage the emotions and nurturing needs in families

extended families: families that include not only parents and children but also other family members, such as grandparents, uncles, aunts, and cousins

face-to-face surveys: a way of eliciting information in which the researcher and participant engage in conversation in the same place

family: a relationship by blood, marriage, or affection in which members may cooperate economically, may care for any children, and may consider their identity to be intimately connected to the larger group

family-based economy: a society in which households are the basic unit of economic production

family-consumer economy: a system in which family work focuses less on production and more on the organization of consumption and reproduction

family protective factors (FPF): family characteristics or dynamics that shape the family's ability to endure in the face of risk factors

family reconstitution: compiling all available information about significant family events and everyday life within a particular family

family recovery factors (FRF): factors that assist families in "bouncing back" from a crisis situation

family stress: tensions that test a family's emotional resources

family systems theory: a perspective incorporating the basic assumption of functionalism but having "interaction" (as opposed to the individual) as its primary focus. When there is a problem within the family, this perspective looks at how people interact or communicate, instead of looking at the characteristics of the people involved.

family-wage economy: a society in which the center of labor moves from the household to the factory

fecundity: women's biological capacity to reproduce

fellatio: oral stimulation of a man's genitals by his partner

feminist theoretical perspectives: theories that place women's and girls' experiences at the center instead of just applying knowledge based on samples of men to explain situations for women. Gender is always considered relevant because systems of power and inequality are found in all part of social life, including the family.

feminist theories of love: theories that see the organization of romantic relationships as mirroring the power of men over women in society

feminization of love: the process beginning in the nineteenth century whereby love became associated with the private work of women in the home—namely, nurturance and caring

fertility rate: the number of births to women

fetal alcohol syndrome (FAS): a series of mental and physical birth defects, including mental retardation, growth deficiencies, and abnormalities of the central nervous system and organs, caused by alcohol use by a pregnant woman

fictive kin: nonrelatives whose bonds are strong and intimate

field research: a method to study naturally occurring social phenomena as they occur

filter theory of love: sees relationships as developing over time and the traits that attract individuals to each other changing with that development

flexible bachelors: single men who are comfortable with their being long-term singles but are not opposed to marriage

flexplace: flexibility in the location of work

flextime: flexibility in the timing of work

focus group research: a method of eliciting information from people who are brought together in small groups for open discussion on a topic of research

formal care: care provided by social service agencies on a paid or volunteer basis

gender: culturally and socially constructed differences between males and females found in the meanings, beliefs, and practices associated with "femininity" and "masculinity"

gender ideology: belief systems about the similarities and differences between women and men

gender socialization: teaching the cultural norms associated with being male or female

gendered institution: gender organizing the way that people are organized, the way that they interact, their practices, and the distributions of power

gerontologists: persons who study the elderly

globalization: the process by which our economy is no longer bounded by national borders

hermaphrodites: those born with genitalia that do not clearly identify them as unambiguously male or female

heterogamous marriage: a marriage in which spouses do not share certain social characteristics, such as race, ethnicity, religion, education, age, and social class

heterosexual: attraction and preference for developing romantic and sexual relationships with persons of the other sex

hidden curriculum: gender socialization that is taught informally in school

his and her marriage: a term developed by Jessie Bernard to describe the different ways in which wives and husbands experience marriage

Home Observation of the Measurement of the Environment (HOME): interview and observation measure of parent–child interaction that examines maternal warmth and learning experiences provided to the child. It is associated with a variety of child outcomes.

homogamy: refers to the practice of dating or marrying someone who holds similar social characteristics

homophobia: an unrealistic fear of homosexuality. See *anti-gay prejudice*.

homosexual: attraction and preference for relationships with members of one's own sex

househusbands: husbands who focus their energies on unpaid domestic work

human agency: the ability of human beings to create viable lives even when they are constrained or limited by social forces

hypergamy: the practice of women marrying older men

hypothesis: a statement about the relationship between two or more variables (characteristics that can take on different values) that can be tested empirically (with observation)

ideology: a belief system that seeks to explain and justify certain conditions

immigration: moving to a country from another country

inaccurate observations: observations based on faulty perceptions

incidence: estimated number of new cases of a disease every year

income: wages or earnings from employment or investments

independent variable: the causal variable. When this variable changes, it causes another variable (the dependent variable) to change.

individual discrimination: one person exhibiting a negative behavior towards another individual

individual-level protective factors: traits including a positive self-concept, sociability, intelligence and scholastic competence, autonomy, self-esteem, androgyny, communication and problem-solving skills, humor, and mental and physical health

induction: the process of beginning with observations, noting patterns, and developing theoretical understandings from these patterns

industrialization: the transformation of an economy from a system based on small-family-based agriculture to one of large industrial capital

infant mortality rate: the number of deaths within the first year of life per 1,000 births in the population

infibulation: an operation in which the vaginal lips (and the clitoris) are cut or scraped away, and the outer portion of the vagina is stitched together

informal care: unpaid care by someone close to the care recipient

institutional discrimination: social institutions, such as the government, religion, and education, creating policies and practices that are systematically disadvantageous to certain groups

institutional review board: a committee that reviews research proposals at institutions, such as universities and institutes, to ensure the protection of human subjects in research. IRBs are required by law for those institutions that receive federal funding for research.

instrumental roles: behaviors intended to meet the tasks of financial support and leadership within families

intensive interviewing: collecting data through unstructured interviews in which questions are generally open-ended

intensive mothering: the view that a mother is the most appropriate parent and the one who should take on the primary responsibility for caring for children

intergenerational transmission of violence: the theory that sees violence as a cycle that is passed down to dependents

intergroup dating: the type of dating in which individuals hold different social characteristics (such as different religious beliefs or levels of education)

international adoption: children who are citizens of a foreign nation being adopted by U.S. individuals or families and brought to live in the United States

involved grandparenting: grandparents and grandchildren engaging in frequent interaction or possibly even living together

John Lee's styles of love: includes six types of love that describe the way in which couples are attracted to each other. For example, ludus is the love of passion while pragma is a down-to-earth type of love.

joint legal custody: a custody agreement allowing noncustodial parents (usually fathers) to retain their legal rights with respect to their children

joint physical custody: a custody agreement having children spend a substantial portion of time in the homes of both parents, perhaps alternating weeks or days within a week

kin-keeping: maintaining ties among family members

kin work: the conception, maintenance, and ritual celebration of cross-household kin ties

kissing: one of our earliest sensual experiences

labor force participation: the rate of involvement in paid labor

latent functions: the unintended, or unanticipated, reasons for the existence of some structure. While traditional family structures are assumed to be efficient, they also serve to reinforce gender inequality.

legal custody: given to the parent who has the legal authority to make important decisions concerning the children after a divorce, such as where they will go to school, in what community or state they will reside, or who will be notified in case of a health emergency or school problem

life-course perspective: a theory that sees age-related transitions as socially produced, socially recognized, and shared—a product of social structure, historical forces, and culture

life expectancy: how long a person can expect to live from birth

life-span perspective: a theory that sees development as a lifelong, multidirectional process that consists of both positive and negative changes involving gains and losses

life-stage perspective: a theory that sees development as proceeding through a fairly set pattern of sequential stages that most people experience

living wage: a minimum wage that is deemed a "livable wage" in a particular community, usually from 150 percent to 225 percent of the federal minimum wage

longitudinal data: data collected at more than one point in time

love: an enduring bond between two or more people who show affection and a sense of obligation toward one another

macrolevel: a focus on the interconnectedness of marriage, families, and intimate relationships with the rest of society and with other social institutions

mail surveys: respondents being asked to respond to questions by filling out a questionnaire. Mail surveys allow more privacy and time to answer, but may not produce detailed responses.

male privilege: the advantages, prerogatives, and benefits that feminists believe systematically accrue to men and are denied to women

manifest functions: the intended reasons for the existence of some structure. Bearing and rearing children is a manifest function of the family in society.

marital locus of control: the extent to which spouses believe they are in charge of their married lives

marital satisfaction: typically measured by asking spouses how happy they are with their marriage

marriage: a legally and socially recognized relationship between a woman and a man that includes sexual, economic, and social rights and responsibilities

marriage premium: people receiving more benefits (higher incomes, better health) when married as compared to being single

master status: the major defining status or statuses that a person occupies

masturbation: sexually stimulating one's own body

matriarchy: a form of social organization in which the norm or the expectation is that power and authority in society are vested in women

matrilineal: lineage traced exclusively or primarily through women's families

matrilocal residence: the expectation that the newly married couple will live with the family of the wife

means-tested programs: programs with income-based eligibility requirements

Medicaid: government-sponsored insurance program for low-income persons

medicalization of childbirth: a transition in the nineteenth century away from the use of midwives in childbirth, instead relying on physicians

Medicare: a federal health insurance program for people aged sixty-five and older (and for some people with disabilities who are under age sixty-five)

menarche: a woman's first menstrual period

microlevel: a focus on individuals' interactions in specific settings

mid-life crisis: a time of trauma during which people focus on what they have failed to achieve (e.g., in employment) or focus on the changes in their family (e.g., children leaving home)

midwives: women who are trained to help women give birth

minority group: a category of people who have less power than the dominant group and who are subject to unequal treatment

miscegenation laws: laws forbidding interracial marriage. These laws existed at the state level until 1967.

Mongoloid: part of a nineteenth-century biological definition of race, comprising individ-uals who have characteristics such yellow or brown skin and folds on their eyelids

monitoring: observation and/or management of children's schedules, activities, and friends

monogamy: marriage between one man and one woman

national health insurance: a health care system for all citizens

negative relationship: one variable increasing (such as education), resulting in another variable decreasing (such as the likelihood to divorce)

neglect: the failure to provide for basic needs

Negroid: part of a nineteenth-century biological definition of race, comprising people with darker skin and features such as coarse, curly hair

neolocal residence: the expectation that the newly married couple establishes its own residence and lives there independently

new home socioeconomics: a perspective on marriage that views roles as taking on a more symmetrical pattern

no-fault divorce: a style of divorce in which a divorcing couple can go before a judge without having to blame each other

nonmarital childbearing: having children outside of marriage

nonprobability sample: the type of sample in which there is no way of estimating the likelihood that the people selected represent the population from which they were drawn

nuclear families: families consisting of only parents and their children

official poverty line: a measure established by the Social Security Administration in 1964 as a way to determine the number of people living in poverty

opportunity costs of raising children: negative effect of childbearing and child rearing on women's employment in terms of experience and income

oral sex: oral stimulation of the genitals

overgeneralization: using what we know from a subset of a group to incorrectly conclude something for the entire group

parental control: behaviors exhibited by parents in their attempts to influence their children's lives

parental induction: a type of control in which parents actively communicate with their children using rational thought

parental involvement: parents spending more time with their children in a variety of interactions, from play and conversation to helping out with homework or attending children's events

parental leave: a guaranteed leave from work after the birth of a child (or some other serious family event, such as a child's illness or death)

parental support: supportive behaviors exhibited by parents to encourage social competence

participant observation: a type of field method in which the researcher makes observations of a particular population by joining in on their activities

passive–congenial marriages: enduring marriages that include little conflict but also little excitement

patriarchy: form of social organization in which the norm or the expectation is that men have a natural right to be in positions of authority over women

patrilineal: lineage traced exclusively (or at least primarily) through the man's family line

patrilocal residence: the expectation that the couple will live with the husband's family

peer marriages: marriages in which couples consider themselves to have equal status or standing in the relationship

period effect: patterns of behavior correlated because they occur during the same time period

permissive parenting: a style of parenting whereby parents are very nurturing and supportive, and do not exert very much control over their children

physical abuse: inflicting physical injury and harm

physical custody: the home where the children actually reside after a divorce

polyandry: wives allowed to have more than one husband

polygamy: allows for more than one spouse at a time

polygyny: husbands allowed to have more than one wife

positive relationship: one variable increasing (such as age), resulting in another variable also increasing (such as income)

post-traumatic stress disorder: a condition in which previous trauma manifests itself as (1) re-experiencing the trauma, (2) psychic numbing, (3) hypervigilance, and (4) survivor guilt

power: the ability to carry out goals, wishes, and desires, even in the face of opposition

prejudice: a negative attitude about members of selected racial and ethnic groups

prestige: the esteem or respect a person is afforded

prevalence: estimated number of people currently infected with a disease

private adoption: the placement of a child in a nonrelative home through the services of a nonprofit or for-profit agency that is licensed

by the state. Also called an *independent adoption.*

probability sample: a sample that is drawn in such a way that the researcher can estimate the extent to which it represents the target population. Random sampling is just one type of probability sample.

progressive taxation: a form of taxation in which those who earn more pay a higher percentage of their income in taxes

proletariate: those individuals who sell their labor to the owners

pronatalism: an attitude embedded in culture and social policy that supports and encourages childbearing

public adoption: an adoption in which a child who is in the public child welfare system is placed in a permanent home by either a government-operated agency or by a private agency that is contracted by a public agency to place such children

punitiveness: verbal or physical attempts at controlling children's behavior that do not have a rational explanation

putting-out system: in pre-industrial society, a practice in which parents would send their children to live with another family in order to learn a skill or trade

quintiles: the population as broken down into fifths of equal size

quota sampling: a nonprobability technique used to get a desired number of people (quota) in each category of people desired

race: a category composed of people who share real or alleged physical traits that members of a society deem as socially significant

racism: the belief that certain racial or ethnic categories are innately superior or inferior to others

random sample: a sample in which every person in the population has an equal chance of being selected for a study

ratio of divorces to marriages in a given year: a misleading way to calculate the divorce rate suggesting that if 100,000 marriages took place last year, and 50,000 divorces occurred, then 50 percent of marriages end in divorce

reciprocal socialization: a recognition that parents influence child development but that children also influence the development of parenting

refined divorce rate: the most appropriate way to measure divorce, based on the number of divorces per every 1,000 married women

Reiss's wheel theory of love: a developmental theory that shows relationships moving from the establishment of rapport, to self-revelation, to mutual dependence, and finally to need fulfillment

relative poverty: the condition of the poorest U.S. households relative to others in society

reliability: a measure producing consistent results over time

remarriage: a subsequent marriage. This area is gaining new interest because divorce rather than death has now become the leading precursor to remarriage.

remote grandparenting: emotionally or physically distant grandparent behaviors

repartnering: establishing a new relationship after divorce but not remarrying

replacement rate: the number of children who need to be born to each woman to maintain the current population

resilience: a multifaceted phenomenon that produces the ability for individuals and families to thrive despite adversity

rite of passage: one of the mechanisms used by society to denote movement from one phase of life to another

role overload: a situation that occurs when people take on too many roles that have conflicting demands

sandwich generation: family members who are in the middle, providing care to members of cohorts on both sides of them—parents and children

secondary research: research based on data collected by someone else

secure attachments: seen in infants who feel safe when their mothers are out of sight

selection bias: the results from a study being produced only because of the characteristics of the sample used. The results are non-generalizable.

selection effect: occurs when the factors that give rise to one family process are the same as those that give rise to another. For example, married people are generally healthier than single people, in part because healthier people are more likely to marry in the first place.

selective observation: seeing only those things that are in line with our preferences or beliefs

self-care: children in charge of taking care of themselves

self-disclosure: telling your spouse something about yourself (thoughts or feelings) in an honest fashion

serial monogamy: marriage to one person at a time, but may include many marriages over the lifetime because of divorce, widowhood, and remarriage

service sector: part of the economy that includes the provision of services (cleaning, child care, food preparation) as well as information processing (banking, computer operations, and clerical work)

sex: the biological differences between men and women, and the role of these differences in reproduction

sexology: a field made up of a multidisciplinary group of clinicians, researchers, and educators concerned with sexuality

sexual abuse: inappropriate sexual behavior with a child for sexual gratification

sexual intercourse: penetration, including vaginal and anal

sexual orientation: the sexual and romantic partner of choice

sexual scripts: the norms or rules regarding sexual behavior

sexual trafficking: a multi-billion-dollar industry in which children are coerced, kidnapped, sold, deceived, or otherwise trafficked into sexual encounters

shift work: a type of employment that runs by the clock and can occur at intervals around the clock

single mothers by choice: women who choose to have children without being married

singlehood: the state of being unmarried and noncohabiting

snowball sampling: a nonprobability technique that starts with a few people with the desired characteristics, then branches to people they know who also hold those desired characteristics

social capital: regarding children, this term refers to the value of children for integrating families into the broader community

social class: a hierarchy, based on income and wealth most apparently, but also on other resources, such as occupational prestige and educational level

social desirability bias: responses given by a participant in a study because of an anticipated judgment by others. Respondents say what they thing they should, or what is socially acceptable.

social exchange theory: a microlevel perspective that assumes that all interactions are based on rational self-interest. People will engage in an interaction if the benefits outweigh the costs.

social institution: major sphere of social life, with a set of beliefs and rules that is organized to meet basic human needs

social learning theory: learning ways of living by observing people as they engage in certain types of behavior

social mobility: upward movement from one social class to another

social norms: expectations that our society holds

social science: a set of systematic methods for investigating social relationship and social structure

Social Security: many programs under one umbrella, including Medicare, Medicaid, cash welfare assistance, and cash assistance for survivors and for seniors

social stratification: the hierarchical ranking of categories of people within society

social structure: a stable framework of social relationships that guides our interactions with others

socialization: the process of interaction whereby individuals acquire the knowledge, skills, norms, and values of their society

sociobiology: an evolutionary theory that argues that all humans have an instinctive impulse to pass on their genetic material

socioeconomic status (SES): a combination of education, occupation, and income

sociological imagination: the recognition that our personal experiences are, in large part, shaped by social forces within the larger society

specialization model of marriage: a type of marriage in which each spouse focuses his or her primary energy on a certain set of activities. For example, one spouse may be the breadwinner while the other spouse takes care of domestic responsibilities.

spillover: a situation in which the demands involved in one sphere of work can carry over into work in another sphere

spurious relationship: a relationship that exists only because of a third variable. Spurious relationships are correlational, not causal.

stable versus temporary singles: singlehood that is long-standing as opposed to short term or transitory

stalled revolution: the dramatic changes made by women in taking on both paid and unpaid work for the family while men made fewer changes in their level of domestic work

stations of divorce: the interrelated emotional, legal, economic, co-parental, community, and psychic dimensions of divorce, which together begin to describe the complexity of the divorce experience

status: the social positions that people occupy and the privileges and constraints that are attached to these positions

stepfamilies: families in which one or both of the adult partners has at least one child, either residing with them or elsewhere

stepfamilies as a normless norm: the idea that stepfamilies are common but that the expectations, obligations, and rules within these families are vague and confusing

stereotype: an oversimplified set of beliefs about a group of people

stimulus: during experiments, the independent variable that is tested

structural functionalism: a theoretical perspective aligned with Talcott Parsons and Robert Bales that sees the family as a structure meeting fundamental needs in society. Families produce and socialize new members to society.

surveys: the type of research that includes asking people to give information about themselves

symbolic interaction: a theoretical perspective aligned with the work of Herbert Blumer. The primary focus is on how relationships are formed through the use and exchange of symbols.

telephone surveys: the type of survey in which interviewers call people and ask them a series of questions

Temporary Assistance to Needy Families (TANF): the principal cash welfare program

theory: a set of statements that explains why certain relationships occur

total fertility rate: the total number of children ever born to women

transgendered: a condition in which a person feels as comfortable, if not more so, in expressing gendered traits that are associated with the other sex

transracial adoption: the placement of a child in a home with a family of a different race

transsexuals: individuals who undergo sex reassignment surgery and hormone treatments

triangular theory of love: sees love as having three elements: intimacy, passion, and commitment. Each relationship will vary depending on the type and level of these elements.

triple quandary of socialization: the additional socialization responsibilities of parents of color

unit of analysis: the individual, group, or subject of study

universal programs: programs to help strengthen all families without any eligibility requirements

validity: a measure producing an accurate picture of the concept or variable of interest

variable: a characteristic that can take on different values

vital (total) marriages: marriages in which couples give primacy to the marriage over other aspects of their lives

voluntary versus involuntary singles: those who want to be single as opposed to those who would rather be married but have not been successful in finding a partner

wealth: a person's or family's total economic package, including stocks, real estate, and other assets in addition to income

work: activity that creates something of value, either goods or services

References

Abbott, D. A., & Meredith, W. (1998). Characteristics of strong families: Perceptions of ethnic parents. *Home Economics Research Journal, 17,* 140–147.

Abrahamse, A. F., Morrison, P. A., & Waite, L. J. (1988). Teenagers willing to consider single parenthood: Who is at greatest risk? *Family Planning Perspectives, 20,* 13–18.

Abramovitz, M. (1996). *Regulating the lives of women: Social welfare policy from colonial times to the present.* Boston: South End.

Achenbaum, W. A. (1978). *Old age in the new land: The American experience since 1790.* Baltimore: Johns Hopkins University Press.

Adams, D., & Kocik, S. M. (1997). Perinatal social work with childbearing adolescents. *Social Work in Health Care, 24,* 85–97.

Adams, M. (1976). *Single blessedness: Observations on the single status in married society.* New York: Basic.

African Americans: Voices of triumph—perseverance (1993) (Vol. 1). Alexandria, VA: Time-Life Custom Publishers.

Ahlburg, D. A., & De Vita, C. J. (1992). New realities of the American family. *Population Bulletin,* Vol. 47. Washington, DC: Population Reference Bureau.

Ahrons, C. R. (1994). *The good divorce: Keeping your family together when your marriage comes apart.* New York: Harper-Collins.

Ahrons, C. R., & Rodgers, R. H. (1987). *Divorced families: A multidisciplinary development view.* New York: Norton.

Ainsworth, M. (1964). Patterns of attachment behavior shown by the infant in interaction with his mother. *Merrill-Palmer Quarterly, 10,* 51–58.

Ainsworth, M. D. S., Blehar, M., Waters, E., & Wall, S. (1978). *Patterns of attachment: A psychological study of the strange situation.* Hillsdale, NJ: Erlbaum.

Alan Guttmacher Institute (1998). *Facts in brief: Teen sex and pregnancy.* Retrieved from http://www.agi-usa.org/pubs/fb_teen_sex.html

Alan Guttmacher Institute (1999, April). Http://www.agi-usa.org/pubs/tenn_preg_stats.html. In *Teenage pregnancy: Overall trends and state-by-state information.*

Alan Guttmacher Institute (2000). *Why is teenage pregnancy declining? The roles of abstinence, sexual activity and contraceptive use.* Retrieved from http://www.agi-usa.org/pubs/or_teen_preg_decline.html

Albrecht, S. L., Bahr, H. M., & Goodman, K. L. (1983). *Divorce and remarriage: Problems, adaptations, and adjustments.* Westport, CT: Greenwood.

Aldous, J., Mulligan, G. M., & Bjarnason, T. (1998). Fathering over time: What makes the difference? *Journal of Marriage and the Family, 60,* 809–820.

Allen, E. S., Baucom, D. H., Charles K. Burnett, Epstein, N., & Rankin-Esquer, L. (2001). Decision-making power, autonomy, and communication in remarried spouses compared with first-married spouses. *Family Relations, 50,* 326–334.

Allen, K. R. (2000). A conscious and inclusive family studies. *Journal of Marriage and the Family, 62,* 4–17.

Allen, K. R., Blieszner, R., & Roberto, K. A. (2000). Families in the middle and later years: A review and critique of research in the 1990's. *Journal of Marriage and the Family, 62,* 911–926.

Allgeier, E. R., & Wiederman, M. W. (1991). Love and mate selection in the 1990s. *Free Inquiry, 11,* 25–27.

Altman, I., & Ginat, J. (1996). *Polygamous families in contemporary society.* Cambridge, England: Cambridge University Press.

Alwin, D. F. (1996). From childbearing to childrearing: The link between declines in fertility and changes in the socialization of children. *Population and Development Review, 22,* 176–196.

Amato, P. (1998). More than money? Men's contributions to their children's lives. In A. Booth & Crouter N. (Eds.), *Men in families: When do they get involved? What difference does it make?* (pp. 241–278). Mahweh, NJ: Erlbaum.

Amato, P., & Gilbreth, J. G. (1999). Nonresident fathers and children's well-being: A meta-analysis. *Journal of Marriage and the Family, 61,* 557–573.

Amato, P. R. (1994). The impact of divorce on men and women in India and the United States. *Journal of Comparative Family Studies, 25,* 207–221.

Amato, P. R. (1996). Explaining the intergenerational transmission of divorce. *Journal of Marriage and the Family, 58,* 628–640.

Amato, P. R., & Booth, A. (1991). The consequences of parental divorce and marital unhappiness for adult well-being. *Social Forces, 69,* 895–914.

Amato, P. R., & Booth, A. (1997). *A generation at risk: Growing up in an era of family upheaval.* Cambridge, MA: Harvard University Press.

Amato, P. R., & Keith, B. (1991). Parental divorce and adult well-being: A meta-analysis. *Journal of Marriage and the Family, 53,* 43–58.

Amato, P. R., & Rivera, F. (1999). Paternal involvement and children's behavior problems. *Journal of Marriage and the Family, 61,* 375–384.

Amato, P. R., & Rogers, S. J. (1997). A longitudinal study of marital problems and subsequent divorce. *Journal of Marriage and the Family, 59,* 612–624.

Ambert, A.-M. (1992). *The effects of children on parents.* Binghamton, NY: Haworth.

Ambert, A.-M. (2001). *Families in the new millennium.* Boston: Allyn & Bacon.

American Association of Retired Persons (AARP) & Administration on Aging (1997). *A profile of older Americans.* Washington, DC: AARP.

American Association of Retired Persons (AARP) & Travelers Foundation (1988). *A national study of caregivers: Final report.* Washington, DC: AARP.

American Association of University Women (AAUW) (1992). *How schools shortchange girls.* Washington, DC: AAUW Education Foundation.

American Council on Education and University of California (1998). *The American freshman: National norms for fall, 1998.* Los Angeles: Los Angeles Higher Education Research Institute.

American Psychological Association (1998). *Answers to your questions about sexual orientation and homosexuality.* Retrieved from http://www.apa.org/pubinfo/answers.html

American Values (2002). *Does divorce make people happy?* Retrieved from www.americanvalues.org

Amey, C., Seccombe, K., & Duncan, R. P. (1995). Health insurance coverage of Mexican-American families in the United States. *Journal of Family Issues, 16,* 488–510.

Amott, T. L., & Matthaei, J. A. (1996). *Race, gender, and work: A multicultural history of women in the United States* (Revised ed.). Boston: South End.

Andersen, M. L., & Taylor, H. F. (2002). *Sociology: Understanding a diverse society.* Belmont, CA: Wadsworth.

Anderson, M., & Collins, P. H. (1995). *Race, class and gender: An anthology.* Belmont, CA: Wadsworth.

Annie E. Casey Foundation (1998). *When teens have sex—issues and trends* (Kids Count special report). Baltimore: Author.

Apple, R. D. (1997). Constructing mothers: Scientific motherhood in the nineteenth and twentieth centuries. In R. D. Apple & J. Golden (Eds.), *Mothers and motherhood: Readings in American history* (pp. 90–110). Columbus: Ohio State University Press.

Aquilino, W. S. (1997). From adolescent to young adult: A prospective study of parent–child relations during the transition to adulthood. *Journal of Marriage and the Family, 59,* 670–686.

Aquilino, W. S., & Supple, A. J. (2001). Long-term effects of parenting practices during adolescence on well-being outcomes in young adulthood. *Journal of Family Issues, 22,* 289–308.

Aquilino, W. S., & Supple, K. (1991). Parent–child relations and parents' satisfaction with living arrangements when adult children leave home. *Journal of Marriage and the Family, 53,* 13–27.

Arditti, J. A. (1999). Rethinking relationships between divorced mothers and their children: Capitalizing on family strengths. *Family Relations, 48,* 109–119.

Arditti, J. A., & Madden-Derdich, D. A. (1997). No regrets: Custodial mothers' accounts of the difficulties and benefits of divorce. *Contemporary Family Therapy, 25,* 61–81.

Arendell, T. (1986). *Mothers and divorce: Legal, economic, and social dilemmas.* Berkeley: University of California Press.

Arendell, T. (1995). *Fathers and divorce.* New York: Sage.

Aries, P. (1962). *Centuries of childhood: A social history of family life.* New York: Vintage.

Ashe, A., & Rampersad, A. (1994). *Days of grace: A memoir.* New York: Ballantine.

Aswad, B. C. (1997). Arab American families. In M. K. DeGenova (Ed.), *Families in cultural context: Strengths and challenges in diversity* (pp. 213–237). Mountain View, CA: Mayfield.

Atoh, M. (1995). *The recent fertility decline in Japan: Changes in women's role and status and their policy implications* (Institute of Population Problems, Ministry of Health and Welfare, IPR Reprint Series No. 23). Tokyo.

Auerback, J. A., & Belous, R. S. (1998). *The inequality paradox: Growth of income.* Washington, DC: National Policy Association.

Axinn, W. G., & Barber, J. S. (1997). Living arrangements and family formation attitudes in early adulthood. *Journal of Marriage and the Family, 59,* 595–611.

Axinn, W. G., & Thornton, A. (1992). The relationship between cohabitation and divorce: Selectivity or causal influence? *Demography, 29,* 357–274.

Axinn, W. G., & Thornton, A. (2000). The transformation in the meaning of marriage. In L. J. Waite, C. Bachrach, M. J. Hindin, L. Thompson, & A. Thornton (Eds.), *The ties that bind: Perspectives on marriage and cohabitation* (pp. 147–165). New York: Aldine de Gruyter.

Babbie, E. (2001). *The practice of social research.* Belmont, CA: Wadsworth.

Baca Zinn, M., & Dill, B. T. (1994). Difference and domination. In M. Baca Zinn & B. T. Dill (Eds.), *Women of color in U.S. society* (pp. 3–12). Philadelphia: Temple University Press.

Baca Zinn, M., & Eitzen, D. S. (1996). *Diversity in families.* New York: HarperCollins.

Bachu, A. (1993). *Fertility of American women: June 1992* (U.S. Census Bureau, Current Population Reports No. P20–470). Washington, DC: U.S. Census Bureau.

Bachu, A. (1999). *Trends in remarital childbearing* (U.S. Census Bureau, Current Population Reports No. P23–197). Washington, DC: U.S. Census Bureau.

Bachu, A., & O'Connell, M. (2000). *Fertility of American women* (U.S. Census Bureau, Current Population Reports No. PS2–526). Washington, DC: U.S. Census Bureau.

Bachu, A., & O'Connell, M. (2001). *Fertility of American women* (U.S. Census Bureau, Current Population Reports No. P20–5543RV). Washington, DC: U.S. Census Bureau.

Badinter, E. (1981). *Mother love: Myth and reality.* New York: Macmillan.

Bahr, K. S. (1994). The strengths of Apache grandmothers: Observations on commitment, culture and caretaking. *Journal of Comparative Family Studies, 25,* 233–248.

Bailey, B. (1988). *From front porch to back seat: Courtship in twentieth century America.* Baltimore: Johns Hopkins University Press.

Bailey, J. M., Bobrow, D., Wolfe, M., & Mikach, S. (1995). Sexual orientation of adult sons of gay fathers. *Developmental Psychology, 31,* 124–129.

Bailey, J. M., & Pillard, R. C. (1991). A genetic study of male sexual orientation. *Archives of General Psychiatry, 48,* 1089–1096.

Bailey, J. M., Pillard, R. C., Neale, M. C., & Agyei, Y. (1993). Heritable factors influence sexual orientation in women. *Archives of General Psychiatry, 50,* 217–223.

Baker, S. (2000). Marriages, informal unions, and gender ideologies in revolutionary rural Nicaragua. In R. Miller & S. L. Browning (Eds.), *With this ring: Divorce, intimacy, and cohabitation from a multicultural perspective* (pp. 287–312). Stamford, CT: JAI.

Baldwin-Grossman, J. B., Walker, K. E., Kotloff, L. J., & Pepper, S. (2001). *Adult communication and teen sex: Changing a community.* Baltimore: Anne E. Casey Foundation and Public/Private Ventures.

Ball, F. L. J., Cowan, P., & Cowan, C. P. (1995). Who's got the power? Gender differences in partner's perceptions of influence during marital problem-solving discussions. *Family Process, 34,* 303–321.

Barber, B. (1992). Family, personality, and adolescent problem behaviors. *Journal of Marriage and the Family, 54,* 69–79.

Barber, B. K., Olsen, J. E., & Shagle, S. C. (1994). Associations between parental psychological and behavioral control and youth internalized and externalized behaviors. *Child Development, 65,* 1120–1136.

Barcas, F. E. (1983). *Images of life on children's television: Sex roles, minorities, and families.* New York: Praeger.

Bardwell, J. R., Cochran, S. W., & Walker, S. (1986). Relationship of parental education, race, and gender to sex-role stereotyping in five-year old kindergartners. *Sex Roles, 15,* 275–281.

Barich, R. R., & Bielby, D. D. (1996, March). Rethinking marriage: Change and stability in expectations, 1967–1994. *Journal of Family Issues, 17*(2), 139–169.

Barnett, R. C., & Baruch, G. K. (1987). Determinants of fathers' participation in family work. *Journal of Marriage and the Family, 49,* 29–40.

Barnett, R. C., & Shen, Y. (1997). Gender, high- and low-schedule-control housework tasks, and psychological distress: A study of dual-earner couples. *Journal of Family Issues, 18,* 403–428.

Bartholomew, K. (1990). Avoidance of intimacy: An attachment perspective. *Journal of Social and Personal Relationships, 7,* 147–178.

Bates, J. E. (1989). Temperament in infancy. In J. D. Osofsky (Ed.), *Handbook of infant development* (2nd ed., pp. 1101–1149). New York: Wiley.

Bauman, K. J. (1999). Shifting family definitions: The effect of cohabitation and other nonfamily household relationships on measures of poverty. *Demography, 36*(3), 315–325.

Baumrind, D. (1978). Parental disciplinary patterns and social competence in children. *Youth & Society, 9*(3), 239–276.

Baumrind, D. (1991). Effective parenting during the early adolescent transition. In P. A. Cowan & M. Hetherington (Eds.), *Family transitions* (pp. 111–163). Hillsdale, NJ: Erlbaum.

Ba-Yunus, I. (1991). Muslims in North America: Mate selection as an indicator of change. In E. Waugh, S. McIrvin Abu-Laban, & R. Qurashi (Eds.), *Muslim families in North America* (pp. 232–249). Alberta, Canada: University of Alberta Press.

Beatty, C. A. (1996). The stress of managerial and professional women: Is the price too high? *Journal of Organizational Behavior, 17,* 233–251.

Beck, U., & Beck-Gernsheim, E. (1995). *The normal chaos of love* (M. Ritter & J. Wiebel, Trans.). Cambridge, England: Polity.

Becker, G. S. (1981). *A treatise on the family.* Cambridge, MA: Harvard University Press.

Bedford, V. H. (1995). Sibling relationships in middle and old age. In R. Blieszner & V. H. Bedford (Eds.), *Handbook of aging and the family* (pp. 201–222). Westport, CT: Greenwood.

Beech, H. (2002, July 1). With women so scarce, what can men do? *Time,* p. 8.

Beer, W. R. (1992). *American stepfamilies.* New Brunswick, NY: Transaction.

Belcastro, P. (1985). Sexual behavior differences between black and white students. *Journal of Sex Research, 21,* 56–67.

Belmont Report, The (1979, April 18). Retrieved from http://ohrp.osophs.dhhs.gov/humansubjects/guidance/belmont.htm

Belsky, J., Weinraub, M., Owen, M., & Kelly, J. F. (2001). *Quantity of child care and problem behavior.* Presented at the Biennial meeting of the Society for Research on Child Development, Minneapolis, MN.

Bem, S. L. (1993). *The lenses of gender.* New Haven, CT: Yale University Press.

Bengston, V., Rosenthal, C., & Burton, L. (1990). *Families and aging: Diversity and heterogeneity* (R. H. Binstock & L. K. George, Eds.) (3rd ed., pp. 263–287). New York: Harcourt.

Benin, M. H., & Edwards, D. A. (1990). Adolescents' chores: The difference between dual- and single-earner families. *Journal of Marriage and the Family, 52,* 361–373.

Bennet, J. (1995, January 29). Soaring new car prices: Will they ever stop? *Denver Post,* p. 3G.

Bennett, N. G., Bloom, D. E., & Craig, P. H. (1989). The divergence of black and white marriage patterns. *American Journal of Sociology, 95,* 692–722.

Berardo, F. M. (1970). Survivorship and social isolation: The case of the aged widower. *Family Coordinator, 19,* 11–25.

Berardo, F. M., & Berardo, D. H. (2000). Widowhood. In *Encyclopedia of sociology* (E. F. Borgatta & R. J. Montgomery, Eds.) (2nd ed., pp. 3255–3261). New York: Macmillan.

Berger, R. (1998). *Stepfamilies: A multidimensional perspective.* New York: Haworth.

Bergmann, B. R. (1996). *Saving our children from poverty: What the United States can learn from France.* New York: Russell Sage Foundation.

Berk, M. L., & Wilensky, G. R. (1987). Health insurance coverage of the working poor. *Social Science and Medicine, 25,* 1183–1187.

Bernard, J. (1972). *The future of marriage.* New York: World.

Berne, L., & Huberman, B. (1999). *European approaches to adolescent sexual behavior and responsibility.* Washington, DC: Advocates for Youth.

Berns, N. (1999). "My problem and how I solved it": Domestic violence in women's magazines. *Sociological Quarterly, 40,* 85–108.

Berrick, J. D. (1995). *Faces of poverty.* New York: Oxford University Press.

Berscheid, E., Snyder, M., & Omoto, A. M. (1989). The relationship closeness of interpersonal relationships. *Journal of Personality and Social Psychology, 57,* 792–807.

Bianchi, S. (1990, June). America's children: Mixed prospects. *Population Bulletin, 45,* 3–41.

Bianchi, S. M., Milkie, M. A., Sayer, L. C., & Robinson, J. P. (2000). Is anyone doing the housework? Trends in the gender division of household labor. *Social Forces, 79*(1), 191–228.

Bianchi, S. M., & Robinson, J. (1997). What did you do today? Children's use of time, family composition, and the acquisition of social capital. *Journal of Marriage and the Family, 59,* 332–344.

Bianchi, S. M., & Spain, D. (1986). *American women in transition.* New York: Russell Sage Foundation.

Biblarz, T. J., & Gottainer, G. (2000). Family structure and children's success: A comparison of widowed and divorced single-mother families. *Journal of Marriage and the Family, 62,* 533–548.

Bielby, W. T., & Bielby, D. D. (1989). Family ties: Balancing commitments to work and family in dual career households. *American Sociological Review, 54,* 776–789.

Billingsley, A. (1992). *Climbing Jacob's ladder.* New York: Simon and Schuster.

Bird, C. E. (1999). Gender, household labor, and psychological distress: The impact of the amount and division of housework. *Journal of Health and Social Behavior, 40,* 32–45.

Bird, C. E., & Fremont, A. M. (1991). Gender, time use, and health. *Journal of Health and Social Behavior, 32,* 114–129.

Blackless, M., Charuvastra, A., Derryck, A., Fausto-Sterling, A., Lauzanne, K., & Lee, E. (2000). How sexually dimorphic are we? *American Journal of Human Biology, 12,* 151–166.

Blackwell, D. L., & Lichter, D. T. (2000). Mate selection among married and cohabiting couples. *Journal of Family Issues, 21*(3), 275–302.

Blair, S. L. (1993). Employment, family, and perceptions of marital quality among husbands and wives. *Journal of Family Issues, 14,* 189–212.

Blair, S. L., & Johnson, M. P. (1992). Wives' perceptions of the fairness of the division of household labor: The intersection of housework and ideology. *Journal of Marriage and the Family, 54,* 570–581.

Blaisure, K. R., & Allen, K. R. (1995). Feminists and the ideology and practice of marital equality. *Journal of Marriage and the Family, 57,* 5–19.

Blanc, A. K. (1987). The formation and dissolution of second unions: Marriage and cohabitation in Sweden and Norway. *Journal of Marriage and the Family, 49,* 391–400.

Blankenhorn, D. (1995). *Fatherless America: Confronting our most urgent social problem.* New York: Basic.

Blassingame, J. W. (1972). *The slave community: Plantation life in the antebellum South.* New York: Oxford University Press.

Blood, R. O., & Wolfe, D. M. (1960). *Husbands and wives: The dynamics of married living.* New York: Free Press.

Blumstein, P., & Schwartz, P. (1983). *American couples: Money, work, sex.* New York: Morrow.

Blyth, D. A., & Roelkepartian, E. C. (1993). *Healthy communities, healthy youth.* Minneapolis: Search Institute.

Bock, J. D. (2000). Doing the right thing? Single mothers by choice and the struggle for legitimacy. *Gender & Society, 14,* 62–86.

Bogenschneider, K. (1997). Parental involvement in adolescent schooling: A proximal process with transcontextual validity. *Journal of Marriage and the Family, 59,* 718–733.

Bogenschneider, K. (2000). Has family policy come of age? A decade review of the state of U.S. family policy in the 1990s. *Journal of Marriage and the Family, 62,* 1136–1159.

Bohannan, P. (1971). The six stations of divorce. In P. Bohannan (Ed.), *Divorce and after: An analysis of the emotional and social problems of divorce* (pp. 33–62). New York: Doubleday.

Booth, A., & Hess, B. (1974). Cross-sex friendship. *Journal of Marriage and the Family, 36,* 38–47.

Boston Medical and Surgical Journal (1915). Pp. 784–785.

Bowen, G. L., & Chapman, M. V. (1996). Poverty, neighborhood danger, social support, and the individual adaptation among at-risk youth. *Journal of Family Issues, 17,* 641–666.

Bowers, B. F., & Myers, B. J. (1999). Grandmothers providing care for grandchildren: Consequences of various levels of caregiving. *Family Relations, 48,* 303–311.

Bowlby, J. (1969). *Attachment and loss* (Vol. 1). New York: Basic.

Boykin, A. W., & Toms, F. (1985). Black child socialization: A conceptual framework. In H. McAdoo & J. McAdoo (Eds.), *Black children* (pp. 33–51). Beverly Hills, CA: Sage.

Bradbury, T., Fincham, F. D., & Beach, S. R. (2000). Research on the nature and determinants of marital satisfaction: A decade in review. *Journal of Marriage and the Family, 62,* 964–980.

Bramlett, M. D., & Mosher, W. D. (2001). First marriage dissolution, divorce, and remarriage: United States (Tech. Rep. No. 323). Hyattsville, MD: National Center for Health Statistics.

Bramlett, M. K., & Mosher, W. D. (2002). Cohabitation, remarriage, divorce, and remarriage in the United States [National Center for Health Statistics]. *Vital Health Statistics, 23*(22).

Braver, S. L., Whitley, M., & Ng, C. (1993). Who divorced whom? Methodological and theoretical issues. *Journal of Divorce and Remarriage, 20,* 1–19.

Bray, J. H. (1992). Family relationships and children's adjustment in clinical and nonclinical stepfather families. *Journal of Family Psychology, 6,* 60–68.

Brewster, K. L., & Padavic, I. (2000). Change in gender-ideology, 1977–1996. *Journal of Marriage and the Family, 62,* 477–487.

Brien, M. J., & Willis, R. J. (1997). The partners of welfare mothers: Potential earnings and child support. *The Future of Children, 7,* 65–73.

Briere, J. (1992). *Child abuse trauma: Theory and treatment of lasting effects.* Newbury Park, CA: Sage.

Brines, J. (1993). The exchange value of housework. *Rationality and Society, 5,* 302–340.

Brines, J., & Joyner, K. (1999). The ties that bind: Principles of cohesion in cohabitation and marriage. *American Sociological Review, 64,* 333–355.

Bronfenbrenner, U. (1979). *The ecology of human development.* Cambridge, MA: Harvard University Press.

Brooks-Gunn, J., & Chase-Lansdale, P. L. (1991). Children having children: Effects of the family system. *Pediatric Annals, 20,* 467–481.

Brooks-Gunn, J., Klebanov, P. K., Liaw, F. R., & Spiker, D. (1993). Enhancing the development of low-birth weight, premature infants: Changes in cognition and behavior over the first three years. *Child Development, 64,* 736–753.

Brown, J. K. (1975). Iroquois women: An ethnohistoric note. In R. R. Reiter (Ed.), *Toward an anthropology of women* (pp. 235–251). New York: Monthly Review Press.

Brown, S. L., & Booth, A. (1996). Cohabitation versus marriage: A comparison of relationship quality. *Journal of Marriage and the Family, 58,* 668–678.

Browne, J. (1997). *Dating for dummies.* Foster City, CA: IDG.

Browning, J. J., & Dutton, D. G. (1986). Assessment of wife assault with the Conflict Tactics Scale: Using couple data to quantify the differential reporting effect. *Journal of Marriage and the Family, 48,* 375–379.

Brubaker, T. H. (1990). Families in later life: A burgeoning research area. *Journal of Marriage and the Family, 52,* 959–982.

Brubaker, T. H., & Kinsel, B. I. (1985). Who is responsible for household tasks in long term marriages of "young-old" elderly? *Lifestyles: A Journal of Changing Patterns, 7,* 238–247.

Bryson, K., & Casper, L. M. (1999, May). *Coresident grandparents and grandchildren* (Current Population Reports: Special Studies, P23–198). Washington, DC: U.S. Census Bureau.

Buchanan, C. M., Maccoby, E. E., & Dornbusch, S. M. (1991). Caught between parents: Adolescents' experiences in divorced homes. *Child Development, 62,* 1008–1029.

Bulcroft, K. A., & Bulcroft, R. A. (1991). The nature and functions of dating in later life. *Research on Aging, 13,* 244–260.

Bulcroft, R. A., & Bulcroft, K. A. (1993). Race differences in attitudinal and motivational factors in the decision to marry. *Journal of Marriage and the Family, 55,* 338–355.

Bullough, V. (1976). *Sexual variance in society and history.* New York: Wiley.

Bumpas, M. F., Crouter, A. C., & McHale, S. M. (1999). Work demands of dual-earner couples: Implications for parents' knowledge about children's daily lives in middle school. *Journal of Marriage and the Family, 61,* 465–475.

Bumpass, L., & Lu, H.-H. (2000). Trends in cohabitation and implications for children's family contexts in the United States. *Population Studies, 54,* 29–41.

Bumpass, L., & McLanahan, S. (1989). Unmarried motherhood: Recent trends, composition, and black–white differences. *Demography, 26,* 279–286.

Bumpass, L., & Sweet, J. (1989). National estimates of cohabitation. *Demography, 26,* 615–625.

Bumpass, L. L., Raley, R. K., & Sweet, J. A. (1995). The changing character of stepfamilies: Implications of cohabitation and nonmarital childbearing. *Demography, 32,* 425–436.

Bureau of Labor Statistics. (2002, March 29). *Employment characteristics of families summary.* Retrieved from http://www.bls.gov/news.release/famee.nr0.htm

Burgess, E. W., & Locke, H. J. (1945). *The family: From institution to companionship.* New York: American Book Company.

Burgess, J. K. (1988). Widowers. In C. S. Chilman, E. W. Nunnally, & F. M. Cox (Eds.), *Variant family forms* (Vol. 5, pp. 150–164). Families in Trouble Series. Newbury Park, CA: Sage.

Burr, W. R., & Klein, S. R. (1994). *Reexamining family stress: New theory and research.* Newbury Park, CA: Sage.

Burstyn, L. (1995). Female circumcision comes to America. In *Atlantic Unbound.* Retrieved from http://www.theatlantic.com/unbound/flasbks/fgm.htm

Burt, M. A., & Aron, L. (2000, February). *America's homeless.* Retrieved from www.urban.org/housing/homeless/numbers/index.htm

Buss, D. M. (1989). Sex differences in human mate preferences: Evolutionary hypotheses tested in 37 cultures. *Behavioral and Brain Sciences, 12,* 1–49.

Buss, D. M. (1994). *The evolution of desire: Strategies of human mating.* New York: Basic.

Caetano, R., Nelson, S., & Cunradi, C. (2001). Intimate partner violence, dependence symptoms, and social consequences from drinking among white, black, and Hispanic couples in the United States. *American Journal on Addictions, 10,* 60–69.

Cain, M. (2001). *The childless revolution.* Cambridge, MA: Perseus.

Calasanti, T. M., & Bailey, C. A. (1991). Gender inequality and the division of household labor in the United States and Sweden: A socialist–feminist approach. *Social Problems, 38,* 34–53.

Caldwell, J. C. (1982). *Theory of fertility decline.* London: Academic Press.

Call, V., Sprecher, S., & Schwartz, P. (1995). The incidence and frequency of marital sex in a national sample. *Journal of Marriage and the Family, 57,* 639–650.

Campbell, D., & Stanley, J. (1963). *Experimental and quasi-experimental designs for research.* Chicago: Rand McNally.

Campbell, J. C., Rose, L., Kub, J. & Nedd, D. (1998). Voices of strength and resistance: A contextual and longitudinal analysis of women's responses to battering. *Journal of Interpersonal Violence, 13,* 743–762.

Cancian, F. M. (1987). *Love in America: Gender and self-development.* New York: Cambridge University Press.

Cancian, F. M. (1989). Love and the rise of capitalism. In B. J. Risman & P. Schwartz (Eds.), *Gender in intimate relations: A microstructural approach* (pp. 12–25). Belmont, CA: Wadsworth.

Cancian, M., & Meyer, D. R. (1998). Who gets custody? *Demography, 35,* 147–157.

Cargan, L., & Melko, M. (1982). *Singles: Myths and realities.* Beverly Hills, CA: Sage.

Carmichael, G. A. (1990). A cohort analysis of marriage and informal cohabitation among Australian men. *Australian and New Zealand Journal of Sociology, 27,* 53–72.

Carnoy, M. (1990). *Fathers of a certain age: The joys and problems of middle-aged fatherhood.* London: Faber & Faber.

Carrington, C. (1999). *No place like home: Relationships and family life among lesbians and gay men.* Chicago: University of Chicago Press.

Carter, M. (1998, August 2). Polygamy bedevils Utah governor. *Sunday Oregonian,* p. A9.

Casper, L. M., & Cohen, P. N. (2000). How does POSSLQ measure up? Historical estimates of cohabitation. *Demography, 37,* 237–245.

Cassidy, J. (2000). Adult romantic attachments: A developmental perspective on individual differences. *Review of General Psychology, 4,* 111–131.

Cassidy, M., & Lee, G. R. (1989). The study of polyandry: A critique and synthesis. *Journal of Comparative Family Studies, 20,* 1–11.

Castro, J. (1993, March 29). Disposable workers. *Time,* pp. 43–47.

Cates, W. (1999). Estimates of the incidence and prevalence of sexually transmitted diseases in the United States. *Sexually Transmitted Disease, 26* (Supplement), S2–S7.

Cawthon, L. (1996). *Planned homebirths: Outcomes among Medicaid women in Washington State* (Department of Social and Health Services, Office of Research and Data Analysis). Washington, DC.

Ceglian, C. P., & Gardner, S. (1999). Attachment style: A risk for multiple marriages. *Journal of Divorce and Remarriage, 31,* 125–139.

Center for Families, W., Well-Being (2001). *Response to extension of parental leaves.* Retrieved from http://www.worklife-

canada.ca/index.shtml

Center for the Study of Women and Society (2001). *Oregon families who left Temporary Assistance to Needy Families (TANF) or food stamps: A study of economic and family well-being from 1998–2000* (Vol. 1). Eugene, OR: Author.

Centers for Disease Control and Prevention (2001a). *HIV/AIDS update. A glance at the HIV epidemic.* Retrieved from http://www.cdc.nchstp/od/news/At-a-Glance.pdf

Centers for Disease Control and Prevention (2001b). *National vital statistics report* (Department of Health and Human Services). Hyattsville, MD: National Center for Health Statistics.

Centers for Disease Control (2001c). *Tracking the hidden epidemics: Trends in STDs in the United States, 2000.* Retrieved from http://www.cdc.gov/nchstp/dstd/stats_Trends/Trends2000.pdf

Centers for Disease Control and Prevention, Division of HIV/AIDS Prevention (2001). *HIV/AIDS among Hispanics in the United States.* Retrieved from http://www.cdc.gov/hiv/pubs/facts/hispanic.htm

Chadwick, B., & Heaton, T. (1999). *Statistical abstract on the American family.* Phoenix, AZ: Oryx.

Chambers-Schiller, L. (1984). *Liberty, a better husband: Single women in America.* New Haven, CT: Yale University Press.

Chang, W. (1993). Unequal terms. *Free China Review, 43*(11), 26–31.

Chao, R. (1994). Beyond parental control and authoritarian parenting style: Understanding Chinese parenting through the cultural notion of training. *Child Development, 65,* 1111–1119.

Chase-Lansdale, P. L., Cherlin, A. J., & Kiernan, K. E. (1995). The long-term effects of parental divorce on the mental health of young adults: A developmental perspective. *Child Development, 66,* 1614–1634.

Chase-Lansdale, P. L., & Hetherington, E. M. (1990). The impact of divorce on life-span development: Short and long term effects. In P. B. Baltes, D. L. Featherman, & R. Learner (Eds.), *Life-span development and behavior* (Vol. 10, pp. 105–150). Hillsdale, NJ: Erlbaum.

Cheal, D. J. (1989). Women together: Bridal showers and gender membership. In B. J. Risman & P. Schwartz (Eds.), *Gender in intimate relationships: A microstructural approach* (pp. 87–93). Belmont, CA: Wadsworth.

Cherlin, A. J. (1992). *Marriage, divorce, and remarriage: Social trends in the United States.* Cambridge, MA: Harvard University Press.

Cherlin, A. J. (1999). *Public and private families: An introduction* (2nd ed.). Boston: McGraw-Hill.

Cherlin, A. J. (2000). Toward a new home socioeconomics. In L. J. Waite, C. Bachrach, M. Hindlin, E. Thomson, & A. Thornton (Eds.), *The ties that bind: Perspectives on marriage and cohabitation* (pp. 126–144). New York: Aldine de Gruyter.

Cherlin, A. J., Chase-Lansdale, P. L., & McRae, C. (1998). Effects of parental divorce on mental health throughout the life course. *American Sociological Review, 63,* 239–249.

Cherlin, A. J., & Furstenberg, F. F. (1986). *The new American grandparent: A place in the family, a life apart.* New York: Basic.

Cherlin, A. J., & Furstenberg, F. F. (1994). Stepfamilies in the United States: A reconsideration. *Annual Review of Sociology, 20,* 359–381.

Chevalier, R., & Lynn, M. S. (1991). Questions asked by wives and mates of cross-dressers. In J. Dixon & D. Dixon (Eds.), *Wives, partners, and others: Living with cross-dressing.* Wayland, MA: Educational Resources.

Chevan, A. (1996). As cheaply as one: Cohabitation in the older population. *Journal of Marriage and the Family, 58,* 656–667.

Child Welfare League of America (2000). *About transracial adoption.* Retrieved from http://www.cwla.org/programs/adoption/transracialadopt.htm

Children's Defense Fund (1994). *Wasting America's future: The Children's Defense Fund report on the cost of child poverty.* Washington, DC: Author.

Children's Defense Fund (1997). *The state of America's children yearbook 1997.* Washington, DC: Author.

Children's Defense Fund (1998). *The state of America's children yearbook.* Washington, DC: Author.

Children's Defense Fund (2000). *The state of America's children yearbook 2000.* Washington, DC: Author.

Children's Defense Fund (2001). *The state of America's children yearbook 2001.* Washington, DC: Author.

Christoffersen, M. (2000). Growing up with unemployment: A study of parental unemployment and children's risk of abuse and neglect based on national longitudinal 1973 birth cohorts in Denmark. *Childhood, 7*(4), 421–438.

Christopher, F. S., & Sprecher, S. (2000). Sexuality in marriage, dating, and other relationships: A decade review. *Journal of Marriage and the Family, 62,* 999–1017.

Chudacoff, H. P. (1999). *The age of the bachelor: Creating an American subculture.* Princeton, NJ: Princeton University Press.

Chun, H., & Lee, I. (2001). Why do married men earn more? Productivity or marriage selection? *Economic Inquiry, 39,* 307–319.

Church, E. (1999). Who are the people in your family? Stepmothers' diverse notions of kinship. *Journal of Divorce and Remarriage, 31,* 83–105.

Cicirelli, V. G. (1983). Adult children and their elderly parents. In T. H. Brubaker (Ed.), *Family relationships in later life* (pp. 31–46). Beverly Hills, CA: Sage.

Clark-Ibáñez, M. (2000). *Gender, race and friendships: Structural and social factors leading to the likelihood of inter-ethnic dating.* Unpublished paper, Department of Sociology, University of California, Davis.

Clarkberg, M. E., Stolzenberg, R. M., & Waite, L. J. (1995). Attitudes, values, and entrance into cohabitational versus marital unions. *Social Forces, 74,* 609–634.

Clarke, S. C., & Wilson, B. F. (1994). The relative stability of remarriages: A cohort approach using vital statistics. *Family Relations, 43,* 305–310.

Clawson, M. A. (1980). Early modern fraternalism and the patriarchal family. *Feminist Studies, 6,* 368–391.

Clinton, W. J. (President). (1996, July 29). *Children's television conference* [Opening remarks]. Washington, DC: White House Office of the Press Secretary.

Cloud, J. (1998, July 20). Trans across America. *Time,* pp. 48–49.

Cockerham, W. C. (1997). *This aging society.* Upper Saddle River, NJ: Prentice Hall.

Cockerham, W. C. (2001). *Medical sociology* (8th ed.). Upper Saddle River, NJ: Prentice Hall.

Cohen, K. M., & Savin-Williams, R. C. (1996). Developmental perspectives on coming out to self and others. In R. C. Savin-Williams & K. M. Cohen (Eds.), *The lives of lesbians, gays, and bisexuals: Children to adults* (pp. 113–151). New York: Harcourt.

Cohen, P. N. (1999). *Racial–ethnic and gender differences in returns to cohabitation and marriage: Evidence from the Current Population Survey* (U.S. Census Bureau Population Division Working Paper No. 35). Washington, DC: U.S. Census Bureau.

Cohen, P. N., & Bianchi, S. M. (1999, December). Marriage, children, and women's employment: What do we know? *Monthly Labor Review,* pp. 22–31.

Coleman, J. S. (1990). *Foundations of social theory.* Cambridge, MA: Belknap Press of Harvard University Press.

Coleman, M., Ganong, L. H., & Fine, M. (2000). Reinvestigating remarriage: Another decade of progress. *Journal of Marriage and the Family, 62,* 1288–1307.

Coleman, M., Ganong, L., & Goodwin, C. (1994). The presentation of stepfamilies in marriage and family textbooks: A reexamination. *Family Relations, 43,* 289–297.

Coley, R. L., & Chase-Lansdale, P. L. (1998). Adolescent pregnancy and parenthood: Recent evidence and future directions. *American Psychologist, 53,* 152–166.

Collins, P. H. (1996). Shifting the center: Race, class, and feminist theorizing about motherhood. In D. Bassin, M. Honey, & M. M. Kaplan (Eds.), *Representations of motherhood* (pp. 56–74). New Haven, CT: Yale University Press.

Collins, R. (1986). *Sociology of marriage and the family: Gender, love, and property.* Chicago: Nelson-Hall.

Coltrane, S. (1998). *Gender and families.* Thousand Oaks, CA: Pine Forge.

Coltrane, S. (2000). Research on household labor: Modeling and measuring the social embeddedness of routine family work. *Journal of Marriage and the Family, 62,* 1208–1233.

Coltrane, S., & Ishii-Kuntz, M. (1992). Men's housework: A life course perspective. *Journal of Marriage and the Family, 54,* 43–57.

Coltrane, S., & Valdez, E. O. (1993). Reluctant compliance: Work–family role allocation in dual-earner Chicano families. In J. C. Hood (Ed.), *Men, work, and family* (pp. 151–175). Newbury Park, CA: Sage.

Commission on Family and Medical Leave (1996, April). *A workable balance: Report to Congress on family and medical leave policies.* Retrieved from http://www.dol.gov/dol/esa/fmla.htm

Committee on Ways and Means (1997). *Medicare and health care chartbook* (U.S. House of Representatives). Washington, DC: U.S. Government Printing Office.

Conger, R., Conger, K., & Elder, G. (1997). Family economic hardship and adolescent adjustment: Mediating and moderating processes. In G. J. Duncan & J. Brooks-Gunn (Eds.), *Consequences of growing up poor* (pp. 288–310). New York: Russell Sage Foundation.

Conger, R. D., Conger, K., Elder, G., Lorenz, F., Simons, R., & Whitbeck, L. (1992). A family process model of economic hardship and adjustment of early adolescent boys. *Child Development, 63,* 526–541.

Conger, R. D., Elder, G. H., Lorenz, F. O., Conger, K. J., Simons, R. L., Whitbeck, L. B., et al. (1990). Linking economic hardship to marital quality and instability. *Journal of Marriage and the Family, 52,* 643–656.

Conger, R. D., Ge, X.-J., & Lorenz, F. O. (1994). Economic stress and marital relations. In R. D. Conger & G. H. Elder Jr. (Eds.), *Families in troubled times: Adapting to change in rural America* (pp. 187–203). New York: Aldine de Gruyter.

Conger, R. D., Rueter, M. A., & Elder, Jr., G. H. (1999). Couple resilience to economic pressure. *Journal of Personality and Social Psychology, 76,* 54–71.

Connell, R. W. (1995). *Masculinities.* Berkeley: University of California Press.

Connidis, I. A., & McMullin, J. A. (1994). Social supports in older age: Assessing the impact of marital and parent status. *Canadian Journal on Aging, 13,* 510–527.

Connidis, I. A., & McMullin, J. A. (1999). Permanent childlessness: Perceived advantages and disadvantages among older persons. *Canadian Journal on Aging, 18,* 447–465.

Conway, F. D. L., Gilden, J., & Zvonkovic, A. (2002). Changing communication and roles: Innovations in Oregon's fishing families, communities, and management. *Fisheries, 27,* 20–29.

Coontz, S. (1988). *The social origins of private life: A history of American families, 1600–1900.* London: Verso.

Coontz, S. (1992). *The way we never were: American families and the nostalgia trap.* New York: Basic.

Coontz, S. (1997). *The way we really are: Coming to terms with America's changing families.* New York: Basic.

Coontz, S. (2000). *The way we never were: American families and the nostalgia trap* (2nd ed.). New York: Basic.

Cooper, P. F., & Shone, B. S. (1997, November/December). More offers, fewer takers for employment base health insurance: 1987 and 1996. *Health Affairs, 16,* 142–149.

Cornell Gerontology Research Institute (2000, Fall). His and her retirement? The role of gender and marriage in the retirement process [Issue Brief]. *The Edward R. Roybal Centers for Research on Applied Gerontology.*

Cornell, L. L. (1989). Gender differences in remarriage after divorce in Japan and the United States. *Journal of Marriage and the Family, 51,* 457–463.

Cornwell, C., & Rupert, P. (1997). Unobservable individual effects, marriage and the earnings of young men. *Economic Inquiry, 35,* 285–294.

Cost of food at home (1997). *Family Economics and Nutrition Review, 10,* 56.

Cott, N. F. (1977). *The bonds of womanhood.* New Haven, CT: Yale University Press.

Cott, N. F. (1978). Passionlessness: An interpretation of Victorian sexual ideology, 1790–1850. *Signs, 4,* 219–236.

Cott, N. F. (2000). *Public vows: A history of marriage and the nation.* Cambridge, MA: Harvard University Press.

Coughlin, C., & Vuchinich, S. (1996). Family experience in preadolescence and the development of male delinquency. *Journal of Marriage and the Family, 58,* 491–501.

Coulton, C. J., Korbin, J. E., Su, M., & Chow, J. (1995). Community level factors and child maltreatment rates. *Child Development, 66,* 1262–1276.

Coverman, S. (1983). Gender, domestic labor time, and wage inequality. *American Sociological Review, 48,* 623–637.

Covey, H. C., & Lockman, P. T. (1996). Narrative references of older African Americans living under slavery. *Social Science Journal, 3,* 23–37.

Cowan, R. S. (1983). *More work for Mother.* New York: Basic.

Cox, M. J., Paley, B., Burchinal, M., & Payne, C. C. (1999). Marital perceptions and interactions across the transition to parenthood. *Journal of Marriage and the Family, 61,* 611–625.

Crabb, P. B., & Bielawski, D. (1994). The social representation of material culture and gender in children's books. *Sex Roles, 30,* 69–79.

Croll, E. (2001). *Endangered daughters: Discrimination and development in Asia.* New York: Routledge.

Crosbie-Burnett, M. (1989). Application of family stress theory to remarriage: A model for assessing and helping stepfamilies. *Family Relations, 38,* 323–331.

Crosbie-Burnett, M., & Giles-Sims, J. (1991). Marital power in stepfather families: A test of normative-resource theory. *Journal of Family Psychology, 4,* 484–496.

Crosbie-Burnett, M., & Lewis, E. A. (1993). Use of African-American family structures and functioning to address the challenges of European-American postdivorce families. *Family Relations, 42,* 243–248.

Crossette, B. (1998, March 23). Mutilation seen as risk for the girls of immigrants. *New York Times,* p. A3.

Crouter, A., McHale, S. M., & Bartko, W. T. (1993). Gender as an organizing feature in parent–child relationships. *Journal of Social Issues, 49,* 161–174.

Crouter, A., Perry-Jenkins, M., Huston, T., & Crawford, D. (1989). The influence of work-induced psychological states on behavior at home. *Basic and Applied Social Psychology, 10,* 273–292.

Crouter, A. C., Bumpus, M. F., Head, M. R., & McHale, S. M. (2001). Implications of overwork and overload for the quality of men's family relationships. *Journal of Marriage and Family, 63,* 404–416.

Crouter, A. C., Bumpus, M. F., Maguire, M. C., & McHale, S. M. (1999). Linking parents' work pressure and adolescents' well-being: Insights into dynamics in dual-earner families. *Developmental Psychology, 35,* 1453–1461.

Crouter, A. C., Manke, B. A., & McHale, S. M. (1995). The family context of gender intensification in early adolescence. *Child Development, 66,* 317–329.

Crouter, A. C., & McHale, S. M. (1993). The long arms of the job: Influences of parental work on childrearing. In T. Luster & L. O. Okagi (Eds.), *Parenting: An ecological perspective* (pp. 179–202). Hillsdale, NJ: Erlbaum.

Cuber, J. F., & Harroff, P. B. (1966). *The significant Americans.* New York: Random.

Cunningham, J., Pearce, T., & Pearce, P. (1988). Childhood sexual abuse and medical complaints in adult women. *Journal of Interpersonal Violence, 3,* 131–144.

Cunningham, M. (2001). Parental influences on the gendered division of housework. *American Sociological Review, 66,* 184–203.

Cunningham-Burley, S. (2001). The experience of grandfatherhood. In A. J. Walker, M. Manoogian-O'Dell, L. A. McGraw, & D. L. White (Eds.), *Later life: Connections and transitions* (pp. 92–96). Thousand Oaks, CA: Pine Forge.

Curran, D. (1987). *Stress and the healthy family: How healthy families handle the 10 most common stresses.* New York: HarperCollins.

Currie, D. (1993). Here comes the bride: The making of a "modern traditional" wedding in Western culture. *Journal of Comparative Family Studies, 24,* 403–421.

Dalaker, J. (2001). *Current population report.* Washington, DC: U.S. Census Bureau.

Dalton, S. E., & Bielby, D. D. (2000). "That's our kind of constellation": Lesbian mothers negotiate institutionalized understandings of gender within the family. *Gender & Society, 14,* 36–61.

Davidson, B., Balswick, J., & Halverson, C. (1983). Affective self-disclosure and marital adjustment: A test of equity theory. *Journal of Marriage and the Family, 45,* 93–102.

Day, R. D., Peterson, G. W., & McCracken, C. (1998). Predicting spanking of younger and older children by mothers and fathers. *Journal of Marriage and the Family, 60,* 79–94.

De Lew, N., Greenbery, G., & Kinchen, K. (1992). A layman's guide to the U.S. health care system. *Health Care Financing Review, 14,* 151–165.

de Rougemont, D. (1956). *Love in the Western world.* New York: Pantheon.

Deaux, K. (1984). From individual differences to social categories: Analysis of a decade's research on gender. *American Psychologist, 39,* 105–116.

Degler, C. N. (1980). *At odds: Women and the family in America from the revolution to the present.* New York: Oxford University Press.

DeMaris, A., & MacDonald, W. (1993). Premarital cohabitation and marital instability: A test of the unconventionality hypothesis. *Journal of Marriage and the Family, 55,* 399–407.

D'Emilio, H., & Freedman, E. B. (1988). *Intimate matters: A history of sexuality in America.* New York: Harper & Row.

Demo, D., Allen, K., & Fine, M. A. (2000). *Handbook of family diversity.* New York: Oxford University Press.

Demo, D. H. (1992). Parent–child relations: Assessing recent changes. *Journal of Marriage and the Family, 54,* 104–117.

Demo, D. H., & Acock, A. C. (1993). Family diversity and the division of domestic labor: How much have things changed? *Family Relations, 42,* 323–331.

Demos, J. (1970). *A little commonwealth.* New York: Oxford University Press.

Demos, J. (1986). *Past, present and personal: The family and life course in American history.* New York: Oxford University Press.

Derlega, V. J., Metts, S., Petronio, S., & Margulis, S. T. (1993). *Self-disclosure.* Thousand Oaks, CA: Sage.

Deutsch, F. M., Lussier, J. B., & Servis, L. J. (1993). Husbands at home: Predictors of paternal participation in child care and housework. *Journal of Personality and Social Psychology, 65,* 1154–1166.

di Leonardo, M. (1987). The female world of cards and holidays: Women, families, and the work of kinship. *Signs, 12,* 440–453.

Dick-Read, G. (1972). *Childbirth without fear* (4th ed.). New York: Harper and Row.

Dillaway, H., & Broman, C. (2001). Race, class, and gender differences in marital satisfaction and divisions of household labor among dual-earner couples. *Journal of Family Issues, 22,* 309–327.

Dillman, D.A. (1978). *Mail and telephone surveys: The total design method.* New York: Wiley.

Dillman, D. A. (2001). *Mail and Internet surveys: The tailored design method.* New York: Wiley.

Dilworth-Anderson, P. (2001). Extended kin networks in black families. In A. J. Walker, M. Manoogian-O'Dell, L. A. McGraw, & D. L. White (Eds.), *Families in later life: Connections and transitions* (pp. 104–106). Thousand Oaks, CA: Pine Forge.

Dix, T., Ruble, D. N., & Zambarano, R. J. (1989). Mothers' implicit theories of discipline: Child effects, parent effects, and the attribution process. *Child Development, 60,* 1373–1391.

Dixon, J., & Dixon, D. (1991). *Wives, partners and others: Living with cross dressing.* Wayland, MA: Educational Resources.

Domhoff, G. W. (1998). *Who rules America: Power and politics in the year 2000* (3rd ed.). Mountain View, CA: Mayfield.

Donatelle, R. J., Davis, L. G., & Hoover, C. F. (1991). *Access to health* (2nd ed.). Englewood Cliffs, NJ: Prentice Hall.

Dornbusch, S. M., Ritter, P. L., Leiderman, P. H., Roberts, D. F., & Fraleigh, J. J. (1987). The relation of parenting style to adolescent school performance. *Child Development, 59,* 1244–1257.

Doumas, D. M., Margolin, G., & John, R. S. (2002). The relationship between daily marital interaction, work, and health promoting behavior in dual-earner couples: An extension of the work–family spillover model. *Journal of Family Issues, 24,* 3–20.

Downey, D. B. (1994). The school performance of children from single-mother and single-father families: Economics or interpersonal deprivation? *Journal of Family Issues, 15,* 129–147.

Downey, D. B. (1995). Understanding academic achievement among children in stephouseholds: The role of parental resources, sex of stepparent, and sex of child. *Social Forces, 73,* 875–894.

Drake, B., & Pandey, S. (1995). Understanding the relationship between neighborhood poverty and specific types of child maltreatment. *Child Abuse and Neglect, 20,* 1003–1018.

Dugger, C. W. (1996, December 12). Tug of taboos: African genital rite vs. U.S. law. *New York Times* (Late Edition), sec. 1, p. 1.

Dumka, L. E., Roosa, M. W., & Jackson, K. M. (1997). Risk, conflict, mother's parenting and children's adjustments in low-income Mexican immigrant and Mexican-American families. *Journal of Marriage and the Family, 59,* 309–323.

Duncan, G. J., Brooks-Gunn, J., & Klebanov, P. K. (1994). Economic deprivation and early childhood development. *Child Development, 65,* 296–318.

Duncan, G. J., Brooks-Gunn, J., Yeung, W.-J., & Smith, J. R. (1998). How much does childhood poverty affect the life chances of children? *American Sociological Review, 63,* 406–423.

Dunne, G. A. (2000). Opting into motherhood: Lesbians blurring the boundaries

and transforming the meaning of parenthood and kinship. *Gender & Society, 14,* 11–35.

Durbin, D. D., Darling, N., Steinberg, L., & Brown, B. B. (1993). Parenting style and peer group orientation among European-American adolescents. *Journal of Research on Adolescence, 3,* 87–100.

Duvall, E. (1977). *Marriage and family development.* Philadelphia: Lippincott.

Duvander, A.-Z. E. (1999). The transition from cohabitation to marriage: A longitudinal study of the propensity to marry in Sweden in the early 1990s. *Journal of Family Issues, 20,* 698–717.

Dwyer, J. W., & Seccombe, K. (1991). Elder care as family labor: The influence of gender and family position. *Journal of Family Issues, 12,* 229–247.

The Economist (1998, December 17). 6.3 brides for seven brothers. Retrieved from Economist.com/displayStory.cfm?story_ID=179826

Edin, K. (2000a, January 3). Few good men: Why poor mothers don't marry or remarry. *American Prospect,* pp. 26–31.

Edin, K. (2000b). What do low-income single mothers say about marriage? *Social Problems, 47,* 112–133.

Edin, K., & Lein, L. (1997). *Making ends meet.* New York: Russell Sage Foundation.

Edleson, J. L., & Brygger, M. P. (1986). Gender differences in reporting of battering incidences. *Family Relations, 35,* 377–382.

Edwards, J. N., & Booth, A. (1994). Sexuality, marriage, and well-being: The middle years. In A. S. Rossi (Ed.), *Sexuality across the life course* (pp. 233–259). Chicago: University of Chicago Press.

Edwards, M. E. (2001). Uncertainty and the rise of the work–family dilemma. *Journal of Marriage and Family, 63,* 183–196.

Egeland, B. (1993). A history of abuse is a major risk factor for abusing the next generation. In R. J. Gelles & D. R. Loseke (Eds.), *Current Controversies on Family Violence* (pp. 197–208). Newbury Park, CA: Sage.

Eggebeen, D. J., & Hogan, D. P. (1990). Giving between generations in American families. *Human Nature, 1,* 211–232.

Ehrenreich, B., & English, D. (1989). *For her own good: 150 years of experts' advice to women.* New York: Anchor/Doubleday.

Eisner, M. (1996). Ari's story. United States Embassy, Stockholm, Sweden. Retrieved from http://www.usemb.se/children/csec/press_contact.html

Elder, G., Liker, J., & Cross, C. (1984). Parent–child behavior in the Great Depression: Life course and intergenerational

influences. In P. Baltes & O. Brim (Eds.), *Life-span development and behavior* (pp. 109–158). Orlando, FL: Academic Press.

Elder, Jr., G. H. (1998). The life course and human development. In R. M. Lerner (Ed.), *Handbook of child psychology* (5th ed., Vol. 1, pp. 939–991). New York: Wiley.

Elder, G. H., Conger, R. D., Foster, E. M., & Ardelt, M. (1992). Families under economic pressure. *Journal of Family Issues, 13,* 5–37.

Elliott, L., Brantley, C., & Johnson, C. (1997). *Sex on campus: The naked truth about the real sex lives of college students.* New York: Random.

Ellwood, D. T. (1999). *The impact of the EITC on work and social policy reforms on work, marriage, and living arrangements.* Unpublished manuscript, Kennedy School of Government, Harvard University, Cambridge, MA.

Elrod, L. (1999). Epilogue: Of families, federalism, and a quest for policy. *Family Law Quarterly, 33,* 843–863.

Employment Policies Institute (2001, July). *The case for a targeted living wage subsidy.* Retrieved from http://www.epi-online.org/study_epi_living-wage_07–2001.html

Employee Benefit Research Institute (2000). *Domestic partner benefits: Facts and background.* Retrieved from http://www.ebri.org/facts/0600fact2.htm

Eng, T. R., & Butler, W. T. (Eds.) (1997). *The hidden epidemic: Confronting sexually transmitted diseases.* Washington, DC: National Academy Press.

Engel, J. W. (1982). *Changes in male–female relationships and family life in the People's Republic of China* (College of Tropical Agriculture and Human Resources, Hawaii Institute of Tropical Agriculture and Human Resources). Honolulu: University of Hawaii.

England, P. (2000). Marriage, the costs of children, and gender inequality. In L. J. Waite, C. Bachrach, M. J. Hindin, E. Thomson, & A. Thornton (Eds.), *The ties that bind: Perspectives on marriage and cohabitation* (pp. 320–342). New York: Aldine de Gruyter.

England, P., & Horowitz, R. (1998). *Birthing from within.* Albuquerque, NM: Partera.

Epstein, A. (1922). *Facing old age: A study of old age dependency in the United States and old age pensions.* New York: Knopf.

Faison, S. (1994, August 22). Divorce in modern China. *New York Times.* Cited in *Chinese cultural studies: Women in China: Past and the present.* Available: http://acc6.its.brooklyn.cuny.edu/~phalsall/texts/chinwomn.html

Farber, B. (1964). *Family: Organization and interaction*. San Francisco: Chandler.

Farber, N. (1990). The significance of race and class in marital decisions among unmarried adolescent mothers. *Social Problems, 37,* 51–63.

Farrell, B. G. (1999). *Family: The making of an idea, an institution, and a controversy in American culture*. Boulder, CO: Westview.

Farrington, K., & Chertok, E. (1993). Social conflict theories of the family. In P. G. Boss, W. J. Doherty, R. LaRossa, W. R. Schumm, & S. K. Steinmetz (Eds.), *Sourcebook of family theories and methods: A contextual approach* (pp. 357–381). New York: Plenum.

Feagin, J. R. (1975). *Subordinating the poor: Welfare and American beliefs*. Englewood Cliffs, NJ: Prentice Hall.

Feagin, J. R., & Feagin, C. B. (1994). *Social problems: A critical power–conflict perspective* (4th ed.). Englewood Cliffs, NJ: Prentice Hall.

Feagin, J. R., Vera, H., & Imani, N. (1996). *The agony of education*. New York: Routledge.

Federal Interagency Forum on Child and Family Statistics (2000). *America's children: Key national indicators of well-being*. Retrieved from http://www.childstats.gov

Federal Register (2002). Annual update of the HHS poverty guidelines. February 14, pp. 6931–6933.

Feeney, J., Noller, P., & Callan, V. J. (1994). Attachment style, communication, and satisfaction in the early years of marriage. In K. Bartholomew & D. Perlman (Eds.), *Attachment processes in adulthood* (pp. 269–308). London: Jessica Kingsley.

Felmlee, D. H. (1995). Fatal attractions: Affection and disaffection in intimate relationships. *Journal of Social and Personal Relationships, 12,* 295–311.

Felmlee, D. H. (2001). From appealing to appalling: Disenchantment with a romantic partner. *Sociological Perspectives, 44*(3), 263–280.

Ferber, M. A., & O'Farrell, B. (1991). *Work and family—policies for a changing workforce*. Washington, DC: National Academy Press.

Fergusson, D. M., & Woodward, L. J. (2000). Teenage pregnancy and female educational underachievement: A prospective study of a New Zealand birth cohort. *Journal of Marriage and the Family, 62,* 147–161.

Ferree, M. M. (1991). Feminism and fam-ily research. In A. Booth (Ed.), *Contemporary families* (pp. 103–121). Minneapolis, MN: National Council on Family Relations.

Fields, J. (2001). *Living arrangements of children: Fall 1996*. (Current Population Reports, P70–74.) Washington, DC: U.S. Census Bureau.

Fields, J., & Casper, L. M. (2001). *America's families and living arrangements: March 2000*. (Current Population Reports, P20–537.) Washington, DC: U.S. Census Bureau.

Fine, G. A. (1987). *With the boys: Little League baseball and preadolescent culture*. Chicago: University of Chicago Press.

Fine, M. (1997). *The role of the stepparent: How similar are the views of stepparents, parents, and stepchildren?* Retrieved from Stepfamily Association of America: http://www.tepfam.org/faqs/findings/6.htm

Firestone, S. (1970). *The dialectic of sex: The case for feminist revolution*. New York: Morrow.

Fischer, D. H. (1977). *Growing old in America*. New York: Oxford University Press.

Fisher, B., & Alberti, R. (2000). *Rebuilding when your relationship ends*. Atascadero, CA: Impact.

Fitch, C. A., & Ruggles, S. (2000). Historical trends in marriage formation: The United States 1950–1999. In L. J. Waite, C. Bachrach, M. J. Hindin, E. Thomson, & A. Thornton (Eds.), *The ties that bind: Perspectives on marriage and cohabitation* (pp. 59–88). New York: Aldine de Gruyter.

Fitzpatrick, M. A. (1988). *Between husbands and wives: Communication in marriage*. Beverly Hills, CA: Sage.

Fleming, D. T., McQuillan, G. M., Johnson, R. E., Nahmias, A. J., Aral, S. O., Lee, F. K., et al. (1997). Herpes simplex virus type 2 in the United States, 1976 to 1994. *New England Journal of Medicine, 337,* 1105–1111.

Flinn, M. (1992). Paternal care in a Caribbean village. In B. S. Hewlett (Ed.), *Father–child relations: Cultural and biosocial contexts* (pp. 57–84). New York: Aldine de Gruyter.

Flynn, C. P. (1999). Exploring the link between corporal punishment and children's cruelty to animals. *Journal of Marriage and the Family, 61,* 971–981.

Forste, R., & Tienda, M. (1996). What's behind racial and ethnic fertility differentials? *Population and Development Review, 22* (Supplement: Fertility in the United States: New Patterns, New Theories), 109–133.

Forsyth, C. J., & Johnson, E. L. (1995). A sociological view of the never married. *International Journal of Sociology of the Family, 25,* 91–104.

Foshee, V. A., Bauman, K. E., & Linder, G. F. (1999). Family violence and the perpetration of adolescent dating violence: Examining social learning and social control processes. *Journal of Marriage and the Family, 61,* 331–342.

Fracher, J., & Kimmel, M. S. (1992). Hard issues and soft spots: Counseling men about sexuality. In M. S. Kimmel & M. A. Messner (Eds.), *Men's lives* (2nd ed., pp. 438–450). New York: Macmillan.

Fraley, R. C., & Shaver, P. R. (2000). Adult romantic attachment: Theoretical developments, emerging controversies and unanswered questions. *Review of General Psychology, 4*(2), 132–154.

Francoeur, R. T., Koch, P., & Weis, D. L. (1998). *Sexuality in America: Understanding our sexual values and behavior*. New York: Continuum.

Franklin, C., Grant, D., Corcoran, J., Miller, P. O., & Bultman, L. (1997). Effectiveness of prevention programs for adolescent pregnancy: A meta-analysis. *Journal of Marriage and the Family, 59,* 551–567.

Franklin II, C. W. (1992). "Hey, home—yo, bro." Friendship among black men. In P. M. Nardi (Ed.), *Men's friendships* (pp. 201–214). Newbury Park, CA: Sage.

Friedan, B. (1963). *The feminine mystique*. New York: Dell.

Friedman, D., Hechter, M., & Kanazawa, S. (1994). A theory of the value of children. *Demography, 31,* 375–401.

Fry, R., & Lowell, B. L. (2002). *Work or study: Different fortunes of U.S. Latino generations*. Retrieved from Pew Charitable Trust: http://www.pewhispanic.org

Fujino, D. C. (1997). The rates, patterns and reasons for forming heterosexual interracial dating relationships among Asian Americans. *Journal of Social and Personal Relationships, 14*(6), 809–828.

Furstenberg, F. F., Jr. (1981). Remarriage and intergenerational relationships. In R. Fogel, E. Hatfield, S. Kiesler, & E. Shanas (Eds.), *Aging: Stability and change* (pp. 115–142). New York: Academic Press.

Furstenberg, F. F., Jr. (1987). The new extended family: The experience of parents and children after remarriage. In K. Pasley & M. Ihinger-Tallman (Eds.), *Remarriage and stepparenting: Current research and theory* (pp. 42–61). New York: Guilford.

Furstenberg, F. F., Jr., & Cherlin, A. J. (1991). *Divided families: What happens to children when parents part*. Cambridge, MA: Harvard University Press.

Gale Encyclopedia of Childhood & Adolescence (1998). *Head Start programs*. Retrieved from Gale Research: http://www.findarticles.com/cf_dls/g2602/2602000293/pl/articl.jhtml

Galinsky, E. (2001). Toward a new view of work and family life. In R. Hertz & N. L.

Marshall (Eds.), *Working families: The transformation of the American home* (pp. 168–186). Berkeley: University of California Press.

Galinsky, E., & Bond, J. T. (1998). *The 1998 business work–life study: A sourcebook.* New York: Families and Work Institute.

Gallagher, S. K. (1994). Doing their share: Comparing patterns of help given by older and younger adults. *Journal of Marriage and the Family, 56,* 567–578.

Gallagher, S. K. (2003). *Evangelical identity and gendered family life.* New Brunswick, NJ: Rutgers University Press.

Gallagher, S. K., & Gerstel, N. (2001). Connections and constraints: The effects of children on caregiving. *Journal of Marriage and Family, 63,* 265–275.

Gallup Organization (1997). *Global study of family values.* Retrieved from http://www.gallup.com/poll/specialreports/pollsummaries/family.asp

Gallup Poll (2001, May 1). *What's the best arrangement for today's families?* Retrieved from http://www.gallup.com/tuesdaybriefing.asp

Galtry, J. (1997). Suckling and silence in the USA: The costs and benefits of breast feeding. *Feminist Economics, 3*(3), 1–24. Retrieved from http://www.lawsocietyalberta.com/legalinfo/parental.htm

Ganong, L. H., & Coleman, M. (1989). Preparing for remarriage: Anticipating the issues, seeking solutions. *Family Relations, 38,* 28–33.

Ganong, L. H., & Coleman, M. (1994). *Remarried family relationships.* Newbury Park, CA: Sage.

Ganong, L. H., & Coleman, M. (1997). How society views stepfamilies. *Marriage and Family Review, 26,* 85–106.

Ganong, L. H., Coleman, M., Fine, M., & Martin, P. (1999). Stepparents' affinity-seeking and affinity-maintaining strategies with stepchildren. *Journal of Family Issues, 20,* 299–327.

Garasky, S., & Meyer, D. R. (1996). Reconsidering the increase in father-only families. *Demography, 33,* 385–394.

Gardecki, R. M. (2001). Racial differences in youth employment. *Monthly Labor Review, 124,* 51–67.

Garfinkel, I., McLanahan, S. S., & Robins, P. K. (1994). *Child support and child well-being.* Washington, DC: Urban Institute Press.

Garfinkel, I., Meyer, D. R., & McLanahan, S. S. (1998). A brief history of child support policies in the United States. In I. Garfinkel, S. S. McLanahan, D. R. Meyer, & J. A. Seltzer (Eds.), *Fathers under fire: The revolution in child support enforcement* (pp. 14–30). New York: Russell Sage Foundation.

Garmezy, N. (1991). Resilience and vulnerability to adverse developmental outcomes associated with poverty. *American Behavioral Scientist, 34,* 416–430.

Gattai, F. B., & Musatti, T. (1999). Grandmothers' involvement in grandchildren's care: Attitudes, feelings, and emotions. *Family Relations, 48,* 35–42.

Gay, P. (1984). *The bourgeois experience: Victoria to Freud.* New York: Oxford University Press.

Gelles, R. (1979). *Family violence.* Beverly Hills, CA: Sage.

Gelles, R. J. (1992). Poverty and violence toward children. *American Behavioral Scientist, 335,* 258–274.

Gelles, R. J., & Straus, M. A. (1988). *Intimate violence.* New York: Simon and Schuster.

Gender Test, The (1999). Retrieved from http://www.thespark.com/gendertest

Genovese, E. (1972). *Roll, Jordan, roll.* New York: Pantheon.

Gerard, J. M., & Buehler, C. (1999). Multiple risk factors in the family environment and youth problem behaviors. *Journal of Marriage and the Family, 61,* 343–361.

Germano, E., & Bernstein, J. (1997). Home births and short-stay delivery: Lessons in health care financing for providers of health care for women. *Journal of Nurse-Midwifery, 42,* 489–498.

Gerson, K. (1993). *No man's land: Men's changing commitments to family and work.* New York: Basic.

Gerstel, N. (1987). Divorce and stigma. *Social Problems, 34,* 172–186.

Gillespie, R. (2000). When no means no: Disbelief, disregard and deviance as discourses of voluntary childlessness. *Women's Studies International Forum, 23,* 223–234.

Gillis, J. R. (1996). *A world of their own making: Myth, ritual, and the quest for family values.* Cambridge, MA: Harvard University Press.

Glass, J. L., & Riley, L. (1998). Family responsive policies and employee retention following childbirth. *Social Forces, 76*(4), 1401–1435.

Glenn, E. N. (1983). Split household, small producer, and dual wage earner: An analysis of Chinese-American family strategies. *Journal of Marriage and the Family, 45,* 35–46.

Glenn, E. N. (1993). Chinese American families. In R. L. Taylor (Ed.), *Minority families in the United States: Comparative perspectives* (pp. 115–145). Englewood Cliffs, NJ: Prentice-Hall.

Glenn, N. (1996). Values, attitudes, and American marriage. In N. Glenn, D. Popenoe, J. B. Elshtain, & D. Blankenhorn (Eds.), *Promises to keep: Decline and renewal of marriage in America* (pp. 15–33). Lanham, MD: Rowman and Littlefield.

Glenn, N., & McLanahan, S. (1981). The effects of offspring on the psychological well-being of older adults. *Journal of Marriage and the Family, 43,* 409–421.

Glenn, N. D. (1982). Interreligious marriage in the United States: Patterns and recent trends. *Journal of Marriage and the Family, 44,* 555–566.

Glenn, N. D. (1997). Feedback: A reconsideration of the effect of no-fault divorce on divorce rates. *Journal of Marriage and the Family, 59,* 1023–1025.

Glenn, N. D. (1998). The course of marital success and failure in five American 10-year marriage cohorts. *Journal of Marriage and the Family, 60,* 569–576.

Glick, J. E., Bean, F. D., & Van Hook, J. (1997). Immigration and changing patterns of extended family household structure in the United States: 1970–1990. *Journal of Marriage and the Family, 59,* 177–191.

Glick, J. E., & Van Hook, J. (2002). Parent's coresidence with adult children: Can immigration explain race and ethnic variation? *Journal of Marriage and Family, 64,* 240–253.

Goldscheider, F. (1997). Recent changes in U.S. young adult living arrangements in comparative perspective. *Journal of Family Issues, 18,* 708–724.

Goldscheider, F., & Goldscheider, C. (1994). Leaving and returning home in 20th century America. *Population Bulletin, 48*(4), 1–35.

Goldscheider, F., & Lawton, L. (1998). Family experiences and the erosion of support for intergenerational coresidence. *Journal of Marriage and the Family, 60,* 623–632.

Goldscheider, F. K., & Waite, L. J. (1991). *New families, no families? The transformation of the American home.* Berkeley: University of California Press.

Goldstein, J. R., & Kenney, C. (2001). Marriage delayed or marriage forgone? New cohort forecasts of first marriage for U.S. women. *American Sociological Review, 66,* 506–519.

Gonzales, A. (2002). *The impact of the 2001/2002 economic recession on Hispanic workers: A cross-sectional comparison of three generations.* Retrieved from Pew Charitable Trust: http://www.pewhispanic.org

Goode, W. J. (1993). *World changes in divorce patterns.* New Haven, CT: Yale University Press.

Gordon, L. (1994). *Pitied but not entitled.* New York: Free Press.

Gordon, M. (1981). Was Waller ever right? The rating and dating complex reconsidered. *Journal of Marriage and the Family, 43,* 67–76.

Gottman, J. M. (1994). *Why marriages succeed or fail.* New York: Simon and Schuster.

Gottman, J. M. (1996). *What predicts divorce: The measures.* Hillsdale, NJ: Erlbaum.

Gottman, J. M., Coan, J., Carrere, S., & Swanson, C. (1998). Predicting marital happiness and stability from newlywed interactions. *Journal of Marriage and the Family, 60,* 5–22.

Graefe, D. R., & Lichter, D. T. (1999). Life course transitions of American children: Parental cohabitation, marriage and single motherhood. *Demography, 36,* 205–217.

Grant, B. F. (2000). Estimates of children exposed to alcohol abuse and dependence in the family. *American Journal of Holistic Health, 90,* 112–115.

Grant, J. (1998). *Raising baby by the book: The education of American mothers.* New Haven, CT: Yale University Press.

Green, R., Mandel, J. B., Hotvedt, M. W., Gray, J., & Smith, L. (1986). Lesbian mothers and their children: A comparison with solo parent heterosexual mothers and their children. *Archives of Sexual Behavior, 15,* 167–184.

Greenstein, T. N. (1990). Marital disruption and the employment of married women. *Journal of Marriage and the Family, 52,* 657–676.

Greenstein, T. N. (1996). Husband's participation in domestic labor: Interactive effects of wives' and husbands' gender ideologies. *Journal of Marriage and the Family, 58,* 585–595.

Greenwald, J. (1996, November 11). Barbie boots up. *Time,* pp. 48–50.

Greven, P. (1970). *Four generations: Population, land, and family in colonial Andover, Massachusetts.* Ithaca, NY: Cornell University Press.

Grief, G. L. (1995). Single fathers with custody following separation and divorce. *Marriage & Family Review, 20,* 213–231.

Griswold del Castillo, R. (1998). La familia: Family cohesion among Mexican American families in the urban Southwest. In S. J. Ferguson (Ed.), *Shifting the center: Understanding contemporary families* (pp. 78–92). Mountain View, CA: Mayfield.

Gupta, S. (1999). The effects of marital status transitions on men's housework performance. *Journal of Marriage and the Family, 61,* 700–711.

Gutman, H. (1976). *The black family in slavery and freedom, 1750–1925.* New York: Pantheon.

Guttman, J. (1993). *Divorce in psychosocial perspective.* Hillsdale, NJ: Erlbaum.

Haas, L. (1992). *Equal parenthood and social policy: A study of parental leave in Sweden.* Albany: State University of New York Press.

Haas, L. (1999). Families and work. In M. B. Sussman, S. K. Steinmetz, & G. W. Peterson (Eds.), *Handbook of marriage and families* (2nd ed., pp. 571–612). New York: Plenum.

Haas, L., & Hwang, P. (1995). Company culture and men's usage of family leave benefits in Sweden. *Family Relations, 44,* 28–36.

Haber, C. (1983). *Beyond sixty-five: The dilemma of old age in America's past.* Cambridge, England: Cambridge University Press.

Haddad, Y., & Lummis, A. (1987). *Islamic values in the United States.* New York: Oxford University Press.

Hagestad, G. O. (1985). Continuity and connectedness. In V. L. Bengston & J. L. Robertson (Eds.), *Grandparenthood* (pp. 31–48). Thousand Oaks, CA: Sage.

Hale-Benson, J. E. (1986). *Black children: Their roots, culture, and learning styles.* Provo, UT: Brigham Young University Press.

Hamby, S. L., & Sugarman, D. B. (1999). Acts of psychological aggression against a partner and their relation to physical assault and gender. *Journal of Marriage and the Family, 61,* 959–970.

Hamer, D., & Copeland, P. (1994). *The science of desire.* New York: Simon and Schuster.

Hamer, J., & Marchioro, K. (2002). Becoming custodial dads: Exploring parenting among low-income and working-class African American fathers. *Journal of Marriage and Family, 64,* 116–129.

Hamilton, V. L., Hoffman, W. S., Broman, W. S., & Rauma, D. (1993). Unemployment, distress, and coping: A panel study of autoworkers. *Journal of Personality and Social Psychology, 65*(2), 234–247.

Hammersmith, S. (1987). A sociological approach to counseling homosexual clients and their families. *Journal of Homosexuality, 14,* 173–190.

Hammonds, K. H. (1998). *Business Week* Harris poll: He said, she said. *Business Week.* Retrieved from www.businessweek.com/1998/31/b3589005.htm

Han, S.-K., & Moen, P. (1999). Work and family over time: A life course approach. *Annals of the American Academy of Political and Social Sciences, 562,* 98–110.

Han, W.-J., Waldfogel, J., & Brooks-Gunn, J. (2001). The effects of early maternal employment on later cognitive and behav-

ioral outcomes. *Journal of Marriage and Family, 63,* 336–354.

Hanson, K. V. (1992). "Our eyes behold each other": Masculinity and intimate friendship in antebellum New England. In P. M. Nardi (Ed.), *Men's friendships* (pp. 35–58). Newbury Park, CA: Sage.

Hanson, T. L., McLanahan, S. S., & Thomson, E. (1996). Double jeopardy: Parental conflict and stepfamily outcomes for children. *Journal of Marriage and the Family, 58,* 141–154.

Hantover, J. P. (1978). The Boy Scouts and the validation of masculinity. *Journal of Social Issues, 34,* 184–195.

Hao, L. (1996). Family structure, private transfers, and the economic well-being of families with children. *Social Forces, 75,* 269–292.

Hardesty, C., Wenk, K., & Morgan, C. S. (1995). Paternal involvement and the development of gender expectations in sons and daughters. *Youth & Society, 26,* 283–297.

Hardy, M. A., & Shuey, K. (2000). Retirement. In E. F. Borgatta & R. J. Montgomery (Eds.), *Encyclopedia of sociology* (2nd ed., pp. 2401–2410). New York: Macmillan.

Hareven, T. K. (1977). The historical study of the family in urban society. In T. K. Hareven (Ed.), *Family and kin in American urban communities, 1780–1940.* New York: Franklin and Watts.

Hareven, T. K. (2000). *Families, history, and social change: Life course cross-cultural perspectives.* Boulder, CO: Westview.

Harris, K., Furstenberg, F., & Marmer, J. (1998). Paternal involvement with adolescents in intact families: The influence of fathers over the life course. *Demography, 35,* 201–216.

Harris, K. M., & Morgan, S. P. (1991). Fathers, sons, and daughters: Differential paternal involvement in parenting. *Journal of Marriage and the Family, 53,* 531–544.

Hartog, H. (2000). *Man and wife in America: A history.* Cambridge, MA: Harvard University Press.

Harvey, E. (1999). Short-term and long-term effects of parental employment of children of the National Longitudinal Survey of Youth. *Developmental Psychology, 35,* 445–459.

Hashima, P. Y., & Amato, P. R. (1994). Poverty, social support, and parental behavior. *Child Development, 65,* 394–403.

Hatchett, S., & Jackson, J. S. (1993). African-American extended kin system: An assessment. In H. P. McAdoo (Ed.), *Family ethnicity: Strength in diversity* (pp. 90–108). Newbury Park, CA: Sage.

Hatfield, E., & Rapson, R. L. (1996). *Love and sex: Cross cultural perspectives.* Boston: Allyn & Bacon.

Hawkins, A. J., Nock, S. L., Wilson, J. C., Sanchez, L., & Wright, J. (2002). Attitudes about covenant marriage and divorce: Policy implications from a three-state comparison. *Family Relations, 51,* 166–175.

Hays, S. (1996). *The cultural contradictions of motherhood.* New Haven, CT: Yale University Press.

Hayslip, Jr., B., Shore, R. J., Henderson, C. E., & Lambert, P. L. (1998). Custodial grandparenting and the impact of grandchildren with problems on role satisfaction and role meaning. *Journal of Gerontology: Social Sciences, 53,* S164–S173.

Hazan, C., & Shaver, P. (1987). Romantic love conceptualized as an attachment process. *Journal of Personality and Social Psychology, 52,* 511–524.

Hazan, C., & Shaver, P. (1990). Love and work: An attachment theoretical perspective. *Journal of Personality and Social Psychology, 59,* 270–280.

Head Start (1999). *Early Head Start.* Retrieved from http://www2.acf.dhhs.gov/programs/hsb/about/programs/ehs.htm

Head Start (2002). *2002 Head Start fact sheet.* Retrieved from http://www2.acf.dhhs.gov/programs/hsb/about/fact2001.htm

Heath, D. T. (1995). Parents' socialization of children in global perspective. In B. B. Ingoldsby & S. Smith (Eds.), *Families in multicultural perspective* (pp. 161–186). New York: Guilford.

Heath, D. T., & Orthner, D. K. (1999). Stress and adaptation among male and female single parents. *Journal of Family Issues, 20*(4), 557–588.

Heaton, T. B., Jacobson, C. K., & Holland, K. (1999). Persistence and change in decisions to remain childless. *Journal of Marriage and the Family, 61,* 531–539.

Heckert, D. A., Nowak, T. C., & Snyder, K. A. (1998). The impact of husbands' and wives' relative earnings on marital disruption. *Journal of Marriage and the Family, 60,* 690–703.

Heidemann, B., Suhomlinova, O., & O'Rand, A. (1998). Economic independence economic status, and empty nest in midlife marital disruption. *Journal of Marriage and the Family, 60,* 219–231.

Helburn, S. (1995). *Cost, quality and child outcomes in child care centers.* Department of Economics, University of Colorado at Denver.

Hemstrom, O. (1996). Is marriage dissolution linked to difference in mortality risks for men and women? *Journal of Marriage and the Family, 58,* 366–378.

Hendrick, C., & Hendrick, S. (1996). Gender and the experience of heterosexual love. In J. T. Wood (Ed.), *Gendered relationships* (pp. 144–146). Mountain View, CA: Mayfield.

Hendrick, S. S., & Hendrick, C. (1992). *Romantic love.* Newbury Park, CA: Sage.

Henry, C. S., & Lovelace, S. G. (1995). Family resources and adolescent family life satisfaction in remarried family households. *Journal of Family Issues, 16,* 765–786.

Henshaw, S. K. (1999). *U.S. teenage pregnancy statistics, with comparable statistics for women aged 20–24.* New York: Alan Guttmacher Institute.

Herbert, B. (1997, October 31). China's missing girls. *New York Times,* p. A31.

Hesse-Biber, S., & Carter, G. L. (2000). *Working women in America: Split dreams.* New York: Oxford University Press.

Hetherington, E. M. (1993). An overview of the Virginia longitudinal study of divorce and remarriage with a focus on early adolescence. *Journal of Family Psychology, 7,* 39–56.

Hetherington, E. M., & Clingempeel, W. G. (1992). Coping with marital transitions: A family systems perspective [Serial No. 227]. *Monographs of the Society for Research in Child Development, 57,* 2–3.

Hetherington, E. M., Law, T. C., & O'Conner, T. G. (1993). Divorce: Challenges, changes, and new chances. In A. S. Skolnick & J. H. Skolnick (Eds.), *Family in transition* (10th ed., pp. 163–172). New York: Longman.

Hetzel, L., & Smith, A. (2001). *The 65 years and over population: 2000* (Census 2000 Brief No. C2KBR/01–10). Washington, DC: U.S. Census Bureau.

Hill, E. J., Hawkins, A. J., Ferris, M., & Weitzman, M. (2001). Finding an extra day a week: The positive influence of perceived job flexibility on work and family life balance. *Family Relations, 50,* 49–58.

Hill, R. B. (1999). *The strengths of African American families: Twenty-five years later.* Lanham, MD: University Press of America.

Hill, S. A. (1999). *African American children: Socialization and development in families.* Thousand Oaks, CA: Sage.

Hird, M. J., & Abshoff, K. (2000). Women without children: A contradiction in terms? *Journal of Comparative Family Studies, 31,* 347–366.

Hite, S. (1977). *The Hite report.* New York: Dell.

Hobart, C. (1991). Conflict in remarriages. *Journal of Divorce and Remarriage, 15,* 69–86.

Hochschild, A. (1989). *The second shift: Working parents and the revolution at home.* New York: Viking.

Hofferth, S., & Collins, N. (2000). Child care and employment turnover. *Population Research and Policy Review, 19,* 357–395.

Hoffman, L. W., & Manis, J. D. (1979). The value of children in the United States: A new approach to the study of fertility. *Journal of Marriage and the Family, 41,* 583–596.

Hoffman, S. D. (1998). Teenage childbearing is not so bad after all . . . or is it? A review of the new literature. *Family Planning Perspectives, 30,* 236–239, 243.

Hoffman, S. D., Foster, E. M., & Furstenberg, Jr., F. F. (1993). Reevaluating the costs of teenage childbearing. *Demography, 30,* 1–13.

Hoffmann, J. P., & Johnson, R. A. (1998). A national portrait of family structure and adolescent drug use. *Journal of Marriage and the Family, 60,* 633–645.

Hogan, D. P., & Astone, N. M. (1986). The transition to adulthood. *Annual Review of Sociology, 12,* 109–130.

Hogan, D. P., Eggebeen, D. J., & Clogg, C. C. (1993). The structure of intergenerational exchanges in American families. *American Journal of Sociology, 98,* 1428–1458.

Hojat, M., Shapurian, R., Foroughi, D., Nayerahmadi, H., Farzneh, M., Shafieyen, M., et al. (2000). Gender differences in traditional attitudes toward marriage and the family: An empirical study of Iranian immigrants in the United States. *Journal of Family Issues, 21,* 419–434.

Holloway, S. L., & Valentine, G. (2000). Children's geographies and the new social studies of childhood. In S. L. Holloway & G. Valentine (Eds.), *Children's geographies: Playing, living, learning* (pp. 1–26). London: Routledge.

Holroyd, R., & Sheppard, A. (1997). Parental separation: Effects on children; implications for service. *Child: Care, Health and Development, 23,* 369–378.

Holtzman, D., & Rubinson, R. (1995). Parent and peer communication effects on AIDS-related behavior among U.S. high school students. *Family Planning Perspectives, 27,* 235–268.

Hopper, J. (1993). The rhetoric of motives in divorce. *Journal of Marriage and the Family, 55,* 801–813.

Hotz, V. J., Mullin, C. H., & Scholz, J. K. (2001, May–June). The earned income tax credit and labor market participation of families on welfare [Newsletter]. *Poverty Research News* (Northwestern University/University of Chicago Joint Center for Poverty Research), 5.3, 13–15.

Houseknecht, S. K., & Sastry, J. (1996). Family "decline" and child well-being: A comparative assessment. *Journal of Marriage and the Family, 58,* 726–739.

Hughes, D., & Johnson, D. (2001). Correlates in children's experiences of parents' racial socialization behaviors. *Journal of Marriage and Family, 63,* 981–995.

Hull, J. D. (1995, January 30). The state of the union. *Time,* pp. 53–75.

Human Resources Development Canada (2002). *Overview of the Old Age Security Program.* Retrieved from http://www.hrdc-drhc.gc.ca/isp/oas/oasind_e.shtml

Human Rights Campaign Foundation (2002). *Frequently asked questions on domestic partner benefits.* Retrieved from http://www.hrc.org/worknet/dp/dp_facts.asp

Humphreys, L. (1975). *Tearoom trade: Impersonal sex in public places.* Chicago: Aldine.

Hunt, M. (1974). *Sexual behavior in the Seventies.* Chicago: Playboy Press.

Hunt, M. O. (1996). The individual, society, or both? A comparison of black, Latino, and white beliefs about the causes of poverty. *Social Forces, 75,* 293–322.

Hunter, A. G. (1997). Counting on grandmothers: Black mothers' and fathers' reliance on grandmothers for parenting support. *Journal of Family Issues, 18,* 251–269.

Hunter, A. G., & Ensminger, M. E. (1992). Diversity and fluidity in children's living arrangements: Family transitions in an urban Afro-American community. *Journal of Marriage and the Family, 54,* 418–426.

Huston, M., & Schwartz, P. (1996). Gendered dynamics in the romantic relationships of lesbians and gay men. In J. T. Wood (Ed.), *Gendered relationships* (pp. 163–176). Mountain View, CA: Mayfield.

Hutchinson, M. K., & Cooney, T. M. (1998). Patterns of parent–teen sexual risk communication: Implications for intervention. *Family Relations, 47,* 185–194.

Hyde, J., & Linn, M. (1988). Gender differences in verbal ability: A meta-analysis. *Psychological Bulletin, 104,* 53–69.

Hyman, B. (2000). The economic consequences of child sexual abuse for adult lesbian women. *Journal of Marriage and the Family, 62,* 199–211.

Hynie, M. J., Lydon, J. E., & Taradash, A. (1997). Commitment, intimacy, and women's perceptions of premarital sex and contraceptive readiness. *Psychology of Women Quarterly, 21,* 447–464.

Ihara, T. L., Hertz, F., & Warner, R. E. (2001). *Living together: A legal guide for unmarried couples.* Soquel, CA: Nolo.

Ihinger-Tallman, M., & Pasley, K. (1987). *Remarriage.* Newbury Park, CA: Sage.

Illouz, E. (1999). *Consuming the romantic utopia: Love and the cultural contradictions of capitalism.* Berkeley: University of California Press.

Ingoldsby, B., Smith, S., & Miller, J. E. (In press). *Exploring family theories.* Los Angeles: Roxbury.

Ingraham, C. (1999). *White weddings: Romancing heterosexuality in popular culture.* New York: Routledge.

Institute for Research on Poverty (2000). Child support enforcement policy and low-income families. *Focus, 21,* 1–86.

Institute of Medicine (1996). *Pathways of addiction: Opportunities in drug abuse research.* Washington, DC: National Academy Press.

Irazuzta, J. E., McJunkin, J. E., Danadian, K., Arnold, F., & Zhang, J. (1997). Outcome and cost of child abuse. *Child Abuse and Neglect, 21,* 751–757.

Ishii-Kuntz, M. (1994). Paternal involvement and perception toward fathers' roles: A comparison between Japan and the United States. *Journal of Family Issues, 15,* 30–48.

Ishii-Kuntz, M., & Coltrane, S. (1992). Remarriage, stepparenting, and household labor. *Journal of Family Issues, 14,* 215–233.

Ishii-Kuntz, M., & Seccombe, K. (1989). The impact of children upon social support networks throughout the life course. *Journal of Marriage and the Family, 51,* 777–790.

Jackson, S. A. (1993). Opportunity to learn: The health connection. *Journal of Negro Education, 62,* 377–393.

Jacob, H. (1992). The elusive shadow of the law. *Law and Society Review, 26,* 565–590.

Janssen, P. A., Holt, V., & Myers, S. J. (1994). Licensed midwife-attended, out-of-hospital births in Washington State: Are they safe? *Birth, 21,* 141–148.

Jekielek, S. M. (1998). Parental conflict, marital disruption, and children's emotional well-being. *Social Forces, 76,* 905–936.

Jendrek, M. P. (1994). Grandparents who parent their grandchildren: Circumstances and decisions. *The Gerontologist, 34,* 206–216.

Johnson, C. L. (2001). Divorced and reconstituted families: Effects on the older generation. In A. J. Walker, M. Manoogian-O'Dell, L. A. McGraw, & D. L. White (Eds.), *Families in later life: Connections and transitions* (pp. 253–257). Thousand Oaks, CA: Pine Forge.

Johnson, C. L., & Barer, B. M. (1997). *Life beyond 85 years: The aura of survivorship.* New York: Springer.

Johnson, M. P. (2001). Conflict and control: Images of symmetry and asymmetry in domestic violence. In A. Booth, A. C. Crouter, & M. Clements (Eds.), *Couples in conflict* (pp. 95–104). Mahweh, NJ: Erlbaum.

Johnson, M. P., Coughlin, J. P., & Huston, T. L. (1999). The tripartite nature of marital commitment: Personal, moral, and structural reasons to stay married. *Journal of Marriage and the Family, 61,* 160–177.

Johnson, M. P., & Ferraro, K. J. (2000). Research on domestic violence in the 1990's: Making distinctions. *Journal of Marriage and the Family, 62,* 948–963.

Jolivet, M. (1997). *Japan: Childless society?* New York: Routledge.

Jones, F. L. (1996). Convergence and divergence in ethnic divorce patterns: A research note. *Journal of Marriage and the Family, 58,* 213–218.

Jones, J. (1985). *Labor of love, labor of sorrow: Black women, work and the family from slavery to the present.* New York: Basic.

Jones, K. W. (1999). *Taming the troublesome child: American families, child guidance, and the limits of psychiatric authority.* Cambridge, MA: Harvard University Press.

Jordan, M., & Sulivan, K. (1999, May 9). Japan pushes dads to spend more than 17 minutes a day with kids. *Sunday Oregonian,* p. A16.

Joyner, K., & Udry, J. R. (2000). You don't bring me anything but down: Adolescent romance and depression. *Journal of Health and Social Behavior, 41,* 369–391.

Julian, T., McKenry, P. C., & McKelvey, M. W. (1994). Cultural variations in parenting: Perceptions of Causasian, African-American, Hispanic, and Asian-American parents. *Family Relations, 43,* 30–37.

Kageyama, Y. (1999, February 11). A tale of two drugs irks Japan's women. *The Oregonian,* p. A-6.

Kaiser Commission on Medicaid and the Uninsured (1998). *The uninsured and their access to health care.* Washington, DC: Henry J. Kaiser Family Foundation.

Kaiser Foundation & Health Research Educational Trust (1999). *Employer health benefits: 1999 annual survey.* Menlo Park, CA: Henry J. Kaiser Family Foundation and Chicago: Health Research Educational Trust.

Kalleberg, A. L., Reskin, B. F., & Hudson, K. (2000). Bad jobs in America: Standard and nonstandard employment relations and job quality in the United States. *American Sociological Review, 65,* 256–278.

Kalmijn, M. (1991). Status homogamy in the United States. *American Journal of Sociology, 97*, 496–523.

Kalmijn, M. (1998). Intermarriage and homogamy: Causes, patterns, trends. *Annual Review of Sociology, 24*, 395–421.

Kammerman, S. B., & Kahn, A. J. (1978). Families and the idea of family policy. In S. B. Kammerman & A. J. Kahn (Eds.), *Family policy: Government and families in fourteen countries* (pp. 1–16). New York: Columbia University Press.

Kamo, Y. (1990). Husbands and wives living in nuclear and stem family households in Japan. *Sociological Perspectives, 33*, 397–417.

Kamo, Y., & Zhou, M. (1994). Living arrangements of elderly Chinese and Japanese in the United States. *Journal of Marriage and the Family, 56*, 544–558.

Kaplan, L. (2001). A couplehood typology for spouses of institutionalized persons with Alzheimer's disease: Perceptions of "we"—"I." *Family Relations, 50*, 87–98.

Karney, B. R., & Bradbury, T. N. (1995). The longitudinal course of marital quality and stability: A review of theory, method, and research. *Psychological Bulletin, 118*, 3–34.

Karoly, L. A., Greenwood, P. W., Everingham, J. H., et al. (1998). *Investing in our children: What we know and don't know about the costs and benefits of early childhood interventions.* Santa Monica, CA: Rand.

Katzev, A. R., Warner, R. L., & Acock, A. C. (1994). Girls or boys? Relationship of child gender to marital stability. *Journal of Marriage and the Family, 56*, 89–100.

Kaufman, J., & Zigler, E. (1987). Do abused children become abusive parents? *Journal of Orthopsychiatry, 57*, 186–192.

Keefe, J., & Fancey, P. (2000). The care continues: Responsibility for elderly relatives before and after admission to a long term care facility. *Family Relations, 49*, 235–244.

Kemp, A. (1998). *Abuse in the family: An introduction.* Pacific Grove, CA: Brooks/Cole.

Kendall, D. (1999). *Sociology in our times* (2nd ed.). Belmont, CA: Wadsworth.

Kephart, W. M. (1967). Some correlates of romantic love. *Journal of Marriage and the Family, 29*, 470–474.

Kerchoff, A. C., & Davis, K. E. (1962). Value consensus and need complementarity in mate selection. *American Sociological Review, 27*, 295–303.

Kerr, M., & Stattin, H. (2001). *Parenting of adolescents: Action or reaction?* Paper presented at the Children's Influence on Family Dynamics Conference, Pennsylvania State University, December 6–7.

Kessler-Harris, A. (1981). *Women have always worked: A historical overview.* Old Westbury, New York: Feminist Press.

Kessler-Harris, A. (1982). *Out to work: A history of wage-earning women in the United States.* New York: Oxford University Press.

Kibria, N. (1997). The construction of "Asian American": Reflections on intermarriage and ethnic identity among second-generation Chinese and Korean Americans. *Ethnic and Racial Studies, 20*, 523–544.

Kimball, M. M. (1986). Television and sex-role attitudes. In T. M. Williams (Ed.), *Impact of television: A natural experiment in three communities* (pp. 265–301). Orlando, FL: Academic Press.

Kimmel, M. (2000). *The gendered society.* New York: Oxford University Press.

King, V., & Heard, H. E. (1999). Nonresident father visitation, parental conflict, and mother's satisfaction: What's best for child well-being? *Journal of Marriage and the Family, 61*, 385–396.

Kinsella, K., & Tauber, C. M. (1993). *An aging world II.* (U.S. Census Bureau International Population Reports P95/92–3.) Washington, DC: U.S. Government Printing Office.

Kinsey, A., Pomeroy, W. B., & Martin, C. E. (1953). *Sexual behavior in the human female.* Philadelphia: Saunders.

Kirby, D. (1997). *No easy answers: Research findings on programs to reduce teen pregnancy.* Washington, DC: National Campaign to Prevent Teen Pregnancy.

Kitchens, J. (1991). *Understanding and treating codependence.* Englewood Cliffs, NJ: Prentice Hall.

Kitson, G. (1992). *Portrait of divorce: Adjustment to marital breakdown.* New York: Guilford.

Kivett, V. R. (1993). Racial comparisons of the grandmother role: Implications for strengthening the family support system of older black women. *Family Relations, 42*, 165–172.

Klein, D., & White, J. (1996). *Family theories: An introduction.* Thousand Oaks, CA: Sage.

Knoester, C., & Booth, A. (2000). Barriers to divorce: When are they effective? When are they not? *Journal of Family Issues, 21*, 78–99.

Knox, D., & Zusman, M. E. (1998). Unpublished data on 620 students at East Carolina University. In D. Knox & C. Schacht (Eds.), *Choices in relationships: An introduction to marriage and the family* (6th ed., p. 372). Belmont, CA: Wadsworth.

Kohn, M. (1977). *Class and conformity: A study in values* (2nd ed.). Chicago: University of Chicago Press.

Kohn, M., & Schooler, C. (1983). *Work and personality: An inquiry into the impact of social stratification.* Norwood, NJ: Ablex.

Kolata, G. (1998, June 21). Women and sex: On this topic, science blushes. *New York Times,* Women's Health, p. 3.

Kolder, V. E. B., Gallagher, J., & Parsons, M. T. (1987). Court-ordered obstetrical interventions. *New England Journal of Medicine, 316*, 1192–1196.

Komarovsky, M. (1940). *The unemployed man and his family: The effect of unemployment upon the status of the man in fifty-nine families.* New York: Dryden.

Koss, M. P., Gidyzc, C. J., & Wisniewski, N. (1987). The scope of rape: Incidence and prevalence in a national sample of higher education students. *Journal of Consulting and Clinical Psychology, 55*, 162–170.

Kraditor, E. (1968). *Up from the pedestal: Selected writings in the history of American feminism.* Chicago: Quadrangle.

Kübler-Ross, E. (1969). *On death and dying.* New York: Macmillan.

Kulik, L. (2000). The impact of education and family attributes on attitudes and responses to unemployment among men and women. *Journal of Sociology and Social Welfare, 27*(2), 161–183.

Kurdek, L. (1999). The nature and predictions of the trajectory of change and marital quality for husbands and wives over the first 10 years of marriage. *Developmental Psychology, 35*, 1283–1296.

Kurdek, L. A. (1991). The dissolution of gay and lesbian couples. *Journal of Social and Personal Relationships, 8*, 265–278.

Kurdek, L. A. (1993a). The allocation of household labor in gay, lesbian, and heterosexual married couples. *Journal of Social Issues, 49*, 127–134.

Kurdek, L. A. (1993b). Predicting marital dissolution: A 5-year longitudinal study of newlywed couples. *Journal of Personality and Social Psychology, 64*, 221–242.

Kurdek, L. A. (1994). Areas of conflict for gay, lesbian, and heterosexual couples: What couples argue about influences relationship satisfaction. *Journal of Marriage and the Family, 56*, 923–934.

Kuriansky, J. (1996). *The complete idiot's guide to dating.* New York: Alpha.

Kurz, D. (2002). Caring for teenage children. *Journal of Family Issues, 23*, 748–767.

Ladner, J. A. (1971). *Tomorrow's tomorrow: The black woman.* New York: Doubleday.

Lamanna, M. A., & Riedmann, A. (1997). *Marriages and families: Making choices in a diverse society* (6th ed.). Belmont, CA: Wadsworth.

Lamaze, F. (1970). *Painless childbirth.* Chicago: Regnery.

Lampard, R., & Peggs, K. (1999). Repartnering: The relevance of parenthood and gender to cohabitation and remarriage among the formerly married. *British Journal of Sociology, 50,* 443–465.

Laner, M. R., & Ventrone, N. A. (1998). Egalitarian daters/traditionalist dates. *Journal of Family Issues, 19*(4), 468–477.

Laner, M. R., & Ventrone, N. A. (2000). Dating scripts revisited. *Journal of Family Issues, 21*(4), 488–500.

Lareau, A. (2002). Invisible inequality: Social class and childrearing in black families and white families. *American Sociological Review, 67,* 747–776.

Larson, R. W., Clore, G. L., & Wood, G. A. (1999). The emotions of romantic relationships: Do they wreak havoc on adolescents? In W. Furman, B. B. Brown, & C. Feiring (Eds.), *The development of romantic relationships in adolescents* (pp. 14–49). New York: Cambridge University Press.

Lasch, C. (1977). *Haven in a heartless world.* New York: Basic.

Laslett, P. (1971). *The world we have lost.* New York: Scribner.

Laumann, E., Paik, A., & Rosen, R. (1999). Sexual dysfunction in the United States: Prevalence and predictors. *Journal of the American Medical Association, 281,* 537–544.

Laumann, E. O., Gagnon, J. H., Michael, R. T., & Michaels, S. (1994). *The social organization of sexuality: Sexual practices in the United States.* Chicago: University of Chicago Press.

Lavee, Y., & Katz, R. (2002). Division of labor, perceived fairness, and marital quality: The effect of gender ideology. *Journal of Marriage and Family, 64,* 27–39.

Leaper, C. (2002). Parenting girls and boys. In M. H. Bornstein (Ed.), *Handbook of parenting* (Vol. 3, pp. 189–225). Mahweh, NJ: Erlbaum.

Lee, G. R., & Dwyer, J. W. (1996). Aging parent–adult child coresidence: Further evidence on the effects of parental characteristics. *Journal of Family Issues, 17,* 46–59.

Lee, G. R., Dwyer, J. W., & Coward, R. (1993). Gender differences in parent care: Demographic factors and same-gender preferences. *Journal of Gerontology: Social Sciences, 48,* S9–S16.

Lee, G. R., & Shehan, C. L. (1989). Retirement and marital satisfaction. *Journal of Gerontology: Social Sciences, 44,* S226–S230.

Lee, J. A. (1973). *The colors of love: An exploration of the ways of loving.* Don Mills, Ontario: New Press.

Lee, J. A. (1988). Love-styles. In R. J. Sternberg & M. L. Barnes (Eds.), *The psychology of love* (pp. 38–67). New Haven, CT: Yale University Press.

Lehne, G. K. (1998). Homophobia among men: Supporting and defining the male role. In M. S. Kimmel & M. A. Messner (Eds.), *Men's lives* (4th ed., pp. 237–249). Boston: Allyn & Bacon.

LeMasters, E. E. (1957). *Modern courtship and marriage.* New York: Macmillan.

Leridon, H. (1990). Cohabitation, marriage, separation: An analysis of life histories of French cohorts from 1965 to 1985. *Population Studies, 44,* 127–144.

Lesthaeghe, R. (1995). The second demographic transition: An interpretation. In K. O. Mason & A. M. Jensen (Eds.), *Gender and family change in industrialized countries* (pp. 17–62). Oxford, England: Clarendon.

Lesthaeghe, R. (1998). On theory development: Applications to the study of family formation. *Population and Development Review, 24*(1), 1–14.

Letherby, G., & Williams, C. (1999). Nonmotherhood: Ambivalent autobiographies. *Feminist Studies, 25,* 719–728.

LeVay, J. (1991). A difference in hypothalmic structure between heterosexual and homosexual men. *Science, 253,* 1034–1037.

Levenson, R. W., & Gottman, J. M. (1983). Marital interaction: Physiological linkage and affective exchange. *Journal of Personality and Social Psychology, 45,* 587–597.

Lever, J. (1994, August 23). Sexual revelations. *The Advocate,* pp. 17–24.

Levine, R. J. (1988). *Ethics and regulation of clinical research* (2nd ed.). New Haven, CT: Yale University Press.

Levy, K. N., Blatt, S. J., & Shaver, P. R. (1998). Attachment styles and parental representations. *Journal of Personality and Social Psychology, 74,* 407–419.

Lewis, O. (1966). The culture of poverty. *Scientific American, 215,* 19–25.

Lewit, E. M., & Kerrebrock, N. (1997). Childhood hunger. In *The future of children* (Vol. 7, pp. 128–137). Los Altos, CA: Center for the Future of Children.

Leyendecker, B., & Lamb, M. E. (1999). Latino families. In M. E. Lamb (Ed.), *Parenting and child development in "nontraditional" families* (pp. 247–262). Mahweh, NJ: Erlbaum.

Lichter, D. T., McLaughlin, D. K., Kephart, G., & Landry, G. (1992). Race and the retreat from marriage: A shortage of marriageable men? *American Sociological Review, 57,* 781–799.

Lillard, L., Brien, M. J., & Waite, L. J. (1995). Premarital cohabitation and subsequent marital dissolution: A matter of self-selection? *Demography, 32,* 437–457.

Lillard, L. A., & Panis, C. (1996). Marital status and mortality: The role of health. *Demography, 33,* 313–327.

Lillard, L. A., & Waite, L. J. (1993). A joint model of marital childbearing and marital disruption. *Demography, 30,* 653–682.

Lillard, L. A., & Waite, L. J. (1995). 'Til death do us part: Marital disruption and mortality. *American Journal of Sociology, 100,* 1131–1156.

Lindberg, L. D. (1996). Women's decisions about breastfeeding and maternal employment. *Journal of Marriage and the Family, 58,* 239–251.

Lino, M. (2001). *Expenditures on children by families, 2000 annual report* (U.S. Department of Agriculture Miscellaneous Publications No. 1528–2000). Washington, DC: USDA, Center for Nutrition Policy and Promotion.

Lips, H. (1993). *Sex and gender* (2nd ed.). Mountain View, CA: Mayfield.

Litoff, J. (1978). *American midwives: 1860 to the present.* Westport, CT: Greenwood.

Lloyd, S. (1991). The darkside of courtship: Violence and sexual exploitation. *Family Relations, 40,* 14–20.

London, R. A. (1996). The difference between divorced and never-married mothers' participation in the AFDC program. *Journal of Family Issues, 17,* 170–185.

Longman, P. J. (1998, March 30). What's the cost of having a child? [Electronic version]. *U.S. News & World Report,* cover story.

Lopata, H. Z. (1973). *Widowhood in an American city.* Cambridge, MA: Shenckman.

Lopata, H. Z. (1979). *Women as widows: Support systems.* New York: Elsevier.

Loprest, P. (1999). *Families leaving welfare: Who are they and how are they doing?* (Discussion Papers 99–02). Washington, DC: Urban Institute.

Lorber, J. (1994). *Paradoxes of gender.* New Haven, CT: Yale University Press.

Lorence, J. (1987). A test of "gender" and "job" models of sex differences in job involvement. *Social Forces, 66,* 121–142.

Lowe Family Foundation (2001). *Families and communities together.* Retrieved from http://www.lowefamily.org/communities/factsheet.html

Lukenbill, G. (1995). *Untold millions: Positioning your business for the gay and lesbian consumer revolution.* New York: Harper Business.

Luker, K. (1996). *Dubious conceptions: The politics of teenage pregnancy.* Cambridge, MA: Harvard University Press.

Luker, K. (1999). Is academic sociology politically obsolete? *Contemporary Sociology, 28,* 5–9.

Lundberg, S., & Rose, E. (1999, March). *The determinants of specialization within marriage.* Department of Economics, University of Washington (mimeo).

Lupton, D., & Barclay, L. (1997). *Constructing fatherhood: Discourses and experiences.* London: Sage.

Lynott, P. P., & Roberts, R. E. (1997). The developmental stake hypothesis and changing perceptions of intergenerational relations, 1971–1985. *The Gerontologist, 37,* 394–405.

Maccoby, E. E. (1998). *The two sexes: Growing up apart, coming together.* Cambridge, MA: Harvard University Press.

Maccoby, E. E., & Jacklin, C. N. (1974). *The psychology of sex differences.* Stanford, CA: Stanford University Press.

Maccoby, E. E., & Martin, J. A. (1983). Socialization in the context of the family: Parent–child interaction. In E. M. Heatherington (Ed.), *Handbook of child psychology: Socialization, personality, and social development* (Vol. 4, pp. 1–101). New York: Wiley.

MacDermid, S. M., & Williams, M. L. (1997). A within-industry comparison of employed mothers' experiences in small and large workplaces. *Journal of Family Issues, 18,* 545–566.

Macionis, J. J. (2001). *Sociology* (8th ed.). Upper Saddle River, NJ: Prentice Hall.

Mackey, R. A., & O'Brien, B. A. (1998). Marital conflict management: Gender and ethnic differences. *Social Work, 43,* 128–141.

Mackey, R. A., O'Brien, B. A., & Mackey, E. F. (1997). *Gay and lesbian couples: Voices from lasting relationships.* Westport, CT: Praeger.

Mackie, G. (1996). Ending footbinding and infibulation: A convention account. *American Sociological Review, 61,* 999–1017.

Mahoney, M. (1994). *Stepfamilies and the law.* Ann Arbor: University of Michigan Press.

Management and Coordination Agency (1991). *Rojin no seikatsu to ishiki: Dai sankai kokusai hikaku chosa kekka hokokusho [Life and perceptions of the elderly: Report of the results on the third international comparative survey].* Tokyo: Chuo Hoke Shuppan.

Manke, B., Seery, B. L., Crouter, A. C., & McHale, S. (1994). The three corners of domestic labor: Mothers,' fathers,' and children's weekday and weekend housework. *Journal of Marriage and the Family, 56,* 657–668.

Mann, J. (1994, April 29). From victims to agents of change. *Washington Post,* p. E3.

Manning, W. D. (1993). Marriage and cohabitation following premarital conception. *Journal of Marriage and the Family, 57,* 191–200.

Manning, W. D., & Landale, N. S. (1996). Racial and ethnic differences in the role of cohabitation in premarital childbearing. *Journal of Marriage and the Family, 58,* 63–77.

Manning, W. D., & Lichter, D. T. (1996). Parental cohabitation and children's economic well-being. *Journal of Marriage and the Family, 58,* 998–1010.

Manning, W. D., & Smock, P. J. (2002). First comes cohabitation and then comes marriage? A research note. *Journal of Marriage and Family, 64,* 1065–1087.

Mansnerus, L. (1995, February). The divorce backlash. *Working Woman,* pp. 38–47.

March, K. (1995). Perception of adoption as a social stigma: Motivation for search and reunion. *Journal of Marriage and the Family, 57,* 653–660.

Marini, M. M., & Shelton, B. A. (1993). Measuring household work: Recent experience in the United States. *Social Science Research, 22,* 361–382.

Marks, N. F., & Lambert, J. D. (1998). Marital status continuity and change among young and midlife adults: Longitudinal effects on psychological well-being. *Journal of Family Issues, 19,* 652–686.

Marks, S. R., Huston, T. L., Johnson, E. M., & MacDermid, S. M. (2001). Role balance among white married couples. *Journal of Marriage and Family, 63,* 1083–1098.

Marmor, J. (Ed.) (1980). *Homosexual behavior.* New York: Basic.

Marshall, N. L., Coll, C. G., Marx, F., McCartney, K., Keefe, N., & Ruh, J. (1997). After-school time and children's behavioral adjustment. *Merrill-Palmer Quarterly, 43,* 497–514.

Marshall, S. K., & Markstrom-Adams, C. (1995). Attitudes on interfaith dating among Jewish adolescents. *Journal of Family Issues, 16*(6), 787–811.

Marsiglio, W. (1992). Stepfathers with minor children living at home: Parenting perceptions and relationship quality. *Journal of Family Issues, 13,* 195–214.

Marsiglio, W., & Donnelly, D. (1991). Sexual relations in later life: A national study of married persons. *Journal of Gerontology: Social Sciences, 46,* S338–S344.

Marsiglio, W., Scanzoni, J. H., & Broad, K. L. (2000). Sexual behavior patterns. In E. F. Borgatta & R. J. Montgomery (Eds.), *Encyclopedia of sociology* (2nd ed., pp. 2549–2564). New York: Macmillan.

Martin, J. A., Park, M. M., & Sutton, P. D. (2002). Births: Preliminary data for 2001. *National Vital Statistics Reports, 50*(10).

Martin, P., & Luke, L. (1991). Divorce and the wheel theory of love. *Journal of Divorce and Remarriage, 15*(1–2), 3–21.

Martin, S. P. (2000). Diverging fertility among U.S. women who delay childbearing past age 30. *Demography, 37,* 523–533.

Martin, S. P. (2002). *Delayed marriage and childbearing: Implications and measurement of diverging trends in family timing.* Retrieved from http://www.russell-sage.org/special_interest/socialinequality/revmartin01.pdf

Martin, T. C., & Bumpass, L. L. (1989). Recent trends in marital disruption. *Demography, 26,* 37–51.

Masheter, C. (1997). Health and unhealthy friendship and hostility between ex-spouses. *Journal of Marriage and the Family, 59,* 463–475.

Mason, M. A. (1998). The modern American stepfamily: Problems and possibilities. In M. A. Mason, A. Slolnick, & S. D. Sugarman (Eds.), *All our families: New policies for a new century* (pp. 95–116). New York: Oxford.

Mason, M. A., & Simon, D. (1995). The ambiguous stepparent: Federal legislation in search of a model. *Family Law Quarterly, 29,* 446–448.

Massey, D. S., & Denton, N. A. (1993). *American apartheid: Segregation and the making of the underclass.* Cambridge, MA: Harvard University Press.

Masters, W. H., & Johnson, V. E. (1966). *Human sexual response.* Boston: Little, Brown.

Masters, W. H., & Johnson, V. E. (1970). *Human sexual inadequacy.* Boston: Little, Brown.

Masters, W. H., & Johnson, V. E. (1979). *Homosexuality in perspective.* Boston: Little, Brown.

Matthews, R. D., & Martin Matthews, A. (1986). Infertility and involuntary childlessness: The transition to nonparenthood. *Journal of Marriage and the Family, 48,* 641–649.

Maynard, R. A. (1997). *Kids having kids.* Washington, DC: Urban Institute Press.

Maza, P. L. (2002). *About single mother adoption.* Retrieved from http://www.clwl.org/programs/adoption/singlmother.htm

McBride, B. A., Schoppe, S. J., & Rane, T. R. (2002). Child characteristics, parenting stress, and parental involvement: Fathers versus mothers. *Journal of Marriage and Family, 64,* 998–1011.

McCabe, K. M. (1997). Sex differences in the long-term effects of divorce on children: Depression and heterosexual relationship difficulties in the young adult years. *Journal of Divorce and Remarriage, 27,* 123–135.

McCubbin, H. I., & McCubbin, M. A. (1988). Typologies of resilient families: Emerging roles of social class and ethnicity. *Family Relations, 37,* 247–254.

McCubbin, H. I., McCubbin, M. A., Thompson, A. I., Han, S.-Y., & Allen, C. T. (1997, June 22). Families under stress: What makes them resilient [Commemorative Lecture]. Washington, DC: AAFCS.

McElvaine, R. S. (1993). *The Great Depression: America, 1929–1941.* New York: Times Books.

McGaha, J. E., Stokes, J. L., & Nielson, J. (2000). *Children of alcoholism: Implications for juvenile justice.* Retrieved from Texas Youth Commission: www.tyc.state.tx.us/prevention/mcgaha.html

McGoldrick, M., Heiman, M., & Carter, B. (1993). The changing family life cycle: A perspective on normalcy. In F. Walsh (Ed.), *Normal family processes* (pp. 405–441). New York: Guilford.

McLanahan, S. (1983). Family structure and stress: A longitudinal comparison of two-parent and female-headed families. *Journal of Marriage and the Family, 45,* 347–357.

McLanahan, S., & Bumpass, L. (1988). Intergenerational consequences of family disruption. *American Journal of Sociology, 94,* 130–152.

McLanahan, S., & Sandefur, G. (1994). *Growing up with a single parent: What hurts, what helps.* Cambridge, MA: Harvard University Press.

McLoyd, V. C. (1990). The impact of economic hardship on black families and children: Psychological distress, parenting, and socioemotional development. *Child Development, 61,* 311–346.

McLoyd, V. C. (1993). Employment among African American mothers in dual earner families: Antecedents and consequences for family life and child development. In J. Frankel (Ed.), *The employed mother and the family context* (pp. 180–226). New York: Springer.

McLoyd, V. C., Cauce, A. M., Takeuchi, D., & Wilson, L. (2000). Marital processes and parental socialization in families of color: A decade review of research. *Journal of Marriage and the Family, 62,* 1070–1093.

McLoyd, V. C., Jayaratne, T. E., Ceballo, R., & Borques, J. (1994). Unemployment and work interruption among African American single mothers: Effects on parenting and adolescent socioemotional functioning. *Child Development, 65,* 562–589.

McMahon, M. (1995). *Engendering motherhood: Identity and self-transformation in women's lives.* New York: Guilford.

McQuillan, G. M. (2000, September 7–10). *Implications of a national survey for STDs: Results from the NHANES survey.* Presented at the Infectious Disease Society of America Conference, New Orleans.

Mead, M. (1935). *Sex and temperament in three primitive societies.* New York: Morrow.

Mehl, L., Peterson, G., Witt, M., & Hawes, W. E. (1977). Outcomes of elective home births: A series of 1,146 cases. *Journal of Reproductive Medicine, 19,* 281–290.

Menaghan, E. G. (1989). Role changes and psychological well-being: Variations in effects by gender and role repertoire. *Social Forces, 67,* 693–714.

Menaghan, E. G., Kowalski-Jones, L., & Mott, F. L. (1997). The intergenerational costs of parental social stressors: Academic and social difficulties in early adolescence for children of young mothers. *Journal of Health and Social Behavior, 38,* 72–86.

Menocal, M. R. (1987). *The Arabic role in medieval literary history: A forgotten heritage.* Philadelphia: University of Pennsylvania Press.

Michael, R. T., Gagnon, J., Laumann, E. O., & Kolata, G. (1994). *Sex in America: A definitive survey.* New York: Little, Brown.

Mikheyeva, A. (2000). Cohabitation, non-marital births, and traditionalism: Marriages in rural Siberia from a life cycle perspective. In R. Miller & S. L. Browning (Eds.), *With this ring: Divorce, intimacy, and cohabitation from a multicultural perspective* (pp. 313–328). Stamford, CT: JAI.

Milkman, R. (1976). Women's work and the economic crisis: Some lessons from the Great Depression. *Review of Radical Political Economics, 8,* 73–97.

Miller, J. E. (2000). Religion and families over the life course. In S. Price, S. McKenry, & M. Murphy (Eds.), *Families across time: A life course perspective* (pp. 173–186). Los Angeles: Roxbury.

Miller, N. B., Smerglia, V. L., Gaudet, D. S., & Kitson, G. C. (1998). Stressful life events, social support, and the distress of widowed and divorced women. *Journal of Family Issues, 19,* 181–203.

Miller, S. L., & Simpson, S. S. (1991). Courtship violence and social control: Does gender matter? *Law and Society Review, 25,* 335–365.

Mills, C. W. (1959). *The sociological imagination.* New York: Oxford University Press.

Mintz, S., & Kellogg, S. (1989). *Domestic revolution: A social history of family life.* New York: Free Press.

Mirowsky, J., & Ross, C. E. (1989). *Social causes of psychological distress.* New York: Aldine.

Mirowsky, J., & Ross, C. E. (1995). Sex differences in distress: Real or artifact? *American Sociological Review, 60,* 449–468.

Mitscherlich, A., & Mielke, F. (1992). Epilogue: Seven were hanged. In G. J. Annas & M. A. Grodin (Eds.), *The Nazi doctors and the Nuremberg Code: Human rights in human experimentation* (pp. 105–107). New York: Oxford University Press.

Mitterauer, M., & Sieder, R. (1982). *The European family: Patriarchy to partnership from the Middle Ages to present.* Chicago: University of Chicago Press.

Moen, P., Kim, J., & Hofmeister, H. (2001). Couples' work/retirement transitions, gender, and marital quality. *Social Psychology Quarterly, 64,* 55–71.

Monach, J. H. (1993). *Childless: No choice.* London and New York: Routledge.

Montgomery, M., Anderson, E., Herington, E., & Clingempeel, W. (1992). Patterns of courtship for remarriage: Implications for child adjustment and parent–child relationships. *Journal of Marriage and the Family, 54,* 686–698.

Montgomery, M. J., & Sorell, G. T. (1997). Differences in love attitudes across family life stages. *Family Relations, 46,* 55–61.

Montgomery, M. J., & Sorell, G. T. (1998). Love and dating experience in early and middle adolescence: Grade and gender comparisons. *Journal of Adolescence, 21,* 677–689.

Montgomery, P. (1996). The influence of social context on the caregiving experience. In Z. Khachaturian & T. Radenbaugh (Eds.), *Alzheimer's disease: Causes, diagnosis, treatment, and care* (pp. 313–321). New York: CRC.

Morales, E. S. (1990). Ethnic minority families and minority gays and lesbians. In F. W. Bozett & M. B. Sussman (Eds.), *Homosexuality and family relations* (pp. 217–239). New York: Harrington Park.

Morell, C. (2000). Saying no: Women's experiences with reproductive refusal. *Feminism & Psychology, 10,* 313–322.

Morgan, D. L. (1997). *Focus groups as qualitative research.* Thousand Oaks, CA: Sage.

Morgan, D. L., & Kruger, R. A. (1993). When to use focus groups and why. In D. L. Morgan (Ed.), *Successful focus groups: Advancing the state of the art* (pp. 3–19). Newbury Park, CA: Sage.

Morgan, L. (1988). Outcomes of marital separation: A longitudinal test of predictors. *Journal of Marriage and the Family, 50,* 493–498.

Morgan, L., & Kunkel, S. (1998). *Aging: The social context.* Thousand Oaks, CA: Pine Forge.

Morgan, S. P. (1991). Late nineteenth- and early twentieth-century childlessness.

American Journal of Sociology, 97, 779–807.

Morgan, S. P., Lye, D. N., & Condran, G. A. (1988). Sons, daughters, and the risk of marital disruption. *American Journal of Sociology, 94,* 110–129.

Morrison, D. R., & Ritualo, A. (2000). Routes to children's economic recovery after divorce: Are cohabitation and remarriage equivalent? *American Sociological Review, 65,* 560–580.

Moynihan, D. P. (1965). *The negro family: The case for national action.* Washington, DC: U.S. Department of Labor.

Muller, C. (1995). Maternal employment, parent involvement, and mathematics achievement among adolescents. *Journal of Marriage and the Family, 57,* 85–100.

Murray, C. (1984). *Losing ground: American social policy, 1950–1980.* New York: Basic.

Murray, C. (1988). *In pursuit of happiness and good government.* New York: Simon and Schuster.

Murray, C. A. (1984). *Losing ground: American social policy 1950–1980.* New York: Basic.

Murry, V. M. (2000). Challenges and experiences of black American families. In P. McKenry & S. J. Price (Eds.), *Families and change: Coping with stressful events* (2nd ed., pp. 333–358). Thousand Oaks, CA: Sage.

Murry, V. M., Brown, P. A., Brody, G. H., Cutrona, C. E., & Simons, R. L. (2001). Racial discrimination as a moderator of the links among stress, maternal functioning, and family relationships. *Journal of Marriage and Family, 63,* 915–926.

Murry, V. M., Smith, E. P., & Hill, N. E. (2001). Race, ethnicity, and culture in studies of families in context. *Journal of Marriage and Family, 63,* 911–914.

Myers, S. M., & Booth, A. (1996). Men's retirement and marital quality. *Journal of Family Issues, 17,* 336–357.

Myers, S. M., & Booth, A. (1999). Marital strains and marital quality: The role of high and low locus of control. *Journal of Marriage and the Family, 61,* 423–436.

Nakonezny, P. A., Shull, R. D., & Rodgers, J. L. (1995). The effect of no-fault divorce law on the divorce rate across the 50 states and its relation to income, education, and religiosity. *Journal of Marriage and the Family, 57,* 477–488.

Nardi, P. M. (1998). The politics of gay men's friendships. In M. S. Kimmel & M. A. Messner (Eds.), *Men's lives* (4th ed., pp. 250–253). Boston: Allyn & Bacon.

National Center for Health Statistics (2001). *Fastfacts: Life expectancy.* Retrieved from http://www.cdc.gov/nchs/fastats/lifexpec.htm

National Center on Elder Abuse (1999). *Types of elder abuse in domestic settings.* Washington, DC: Author.

National Clearinghouse for Alcohol and Drug Information (1995). *The fact is alcoholism tends to run in families.* Retrieved from http://www.health.org/govpubs/ph318

National Council on Family Relations (2001, November 16). *Journal of Marriage and Family* press release. Retrieved from http://www.ncfr.org/about_us/j_press_release.asp

National Family Caregivers Association (2002). *Ten tips for family caregivers.* Retrieved from http://www.nfcacares.org

National Institute of Justice and Centers for Disease Control and Prevention (1998, November). *Prevalence, incidence, and consequences of violence against women: Findings from the National Violence Against Women Survey* (Research in Brief). Retrieved from http:/www.ojp.usdoj.gov/hii/bubs-sum/172837.htm

National Institute on Alcohol Abuse and Alcoholism (1992, July). *Alcohol alert, the genetics of alcoholism* (No. 18 PH 357). Retrieved from http://www.niaaa.nih.gov/publications/aa18.htm

National Institute on Alcohol Abuse and Alcoholism (2000). The genetics of alcoholism. Retrieved from http://www.niaaa.nih.gov/publications/aa18.htm

National Institute on Alcohol Abuse and Alcoholism (2001). *Frequently asked questions.* Retrieved from http://www.niaaa.nih.gov/faq/q-a.htm

National Low Income Housing Coalition (2001). *Out of reach 2001: America's growing wage-rent disparity.* Retrieved from http://www.nlihc.org/oor2001/introduction.htm

National Opinion Research Center (NORC) (1994). *General Social Surveys, 1972–1994. Cumulative codebook.* University of Chicago: National Opinion Research Center.

National Organization on Fetal Alcohol Syndrome (2001). *No FAS.* Retrieved from http://www.nofas.org/main/what_is_FAS.htm

Needleman, H. L., Schell, A., Bellinger, D., Leviton, A., & Allred, E. L. (1990). The long-term effects of exposure to low doses of lead in childhood. *New England Journal of Medicine, 322,* 83–88.

Neft, N., & Levine, A. D. (1997). *Where women stand: An international report on the status of women in over 140 countries, 1997–1998.* New York: Random.

New York Times Week in Review (1998, November 8). The content of Jefferson's character is revealed at last, or is it?

New York Times. Retrieved from http://search.nytimes.com/search/daily/... te+site+60427+3+wAAA+Thomas%7EJefferson

NICHD Early Child Care Research Network (1997). The effects of infant child care on infant–mother attachment security: Results of the NICHD Study of Early Childhood Care. *Child Development, 68,* 860–879.

NICHD Early Child Care Research Network (1998). Early child care and self-control, compliance, and problem behavior at twenty-four and thirty-six months. *Child Development, 69,* 1145–1170.

Nitzy, A. (1998, August). A poppy in the rain. *Runner's World,* p. 22.

Nock, S. L. (1998). *Marriage in men's lives.* New York: Oxford University Press.

Noonan, M. C. 2001. The impact of domestic work on men's and women's wages. *Journal of Marriage and Family, 63,* 1134–1145.

Nye, R. (Ed.). (1999). *Sexuality.* New York: Oxford University Press.

O'Brien, E., & Feder, J. (1998). *How well does the employment-based health insurance system work for low income families?* (Kaiser Commission on Medicaid and the Uninsured). Washington, DC: Henry J. Kaiser Family Foundation.

Odent, M. (1984). *Birth reborn.* New York: Pantheon.

Office of Health Policy (1998). *Chartbook on children's insurance status.* Retrieved from Assistant Secretary for Planning and Evaluation: http://www.aspe.os.dhhs.gov/health/98Chartbk/98-chtbk.htm

Office of Research, Evaluation, and Statistics (1999). *Social security programs throughout the world 1999.* Washington, DC: U.S. Social Security Administration.

Officials may gain welfare insight. (1997, September 2). *Gainesville Sun,* pp. 1B, 2B.

Ogawa, N., & Retherford, R. D. (1993). Care of elderly in Japan: Changing norms and expectations. *Journal of Marriage and the Family, 55,* 585–597.

O'Hare, W. P. (1995). 3.9 million U.S. children in distressed neighborhoods. *Population Today, 22,* 4–5.

Okagaki, L., & Divecha, D. J. (1993). Development of parental beliefs. In T. Luster & L. Okagaki (Eds.), *Parenting: An ecological perspective* (pp. 35–67). Hillsdale, NJ: Erlbaum.

Olsen, C. (1996, Summer). African American adolescent women. Perceptions of gender, race, and class. *Marriage and Family Review, 24*(1–2), 107–115.

Omi, M., & Winant, H. (1986). *Racial formation in the United States: From the 1960s to the 1980s.* New York: Routledge & Kegan Paul.

Ono, H. (1998). Husbands' and wives' resources and marital dissolution. *Journal of Marriage and the Family, 60,* 674–689.

Ontario Coalition for Better Child Care (2000). *When Mom must work.* Retrieved from www.childcarecanada.org

Oppenheimer, V. K. (1982). *Work and the family: A study in social demography.* New York: Academic Press.

Oppenheimer, V. K. (2000). The continuing importance of men's economic position in marriage formation. In L. J. Waite, C. Bachrach, M. Hindlin, E. Thomson, & A. Thornton (Eds.), *The ties that bind: Perspectives on marriage and cohabitation* (pp. 283–301). New York: Aldine de Gruyter.

Oppenheimer, V. K., Kalmijn, M., & Lim, N. (1997). Men's career development and marriage timing during a period of rising inequality. *Demography, 34,* 311–330.

O'Rand, A. M. (1990). Stratification and the life course. In R. H. Binstock & L. K. George (Eds.), *Handbook of aging and the social sciences* (3rd ed., pp. 130–148). San Diego: Academic Press.

Orenstein, P. (1994). *School girls.* New York: Anchor.

Oropesa, R. S. (1996). Normative beliefs about marriage and cohabitation: A comparison of non-Latino whites, Mexican Americans, and Puerto Ricans. *Journal of Marriage and the Family, 58,* 49–62.

Oropesa, R. S., & Gorman, B. K. (2000). Ethnicity, immigration, and beliefs about marriage as a "tie that binds." In L. J. Waite, C. Bachrach, M. J. Hindin, E. Thomson, & A. Thornton (Eds.), *The ties that bind: Perspectives on marriage and cohabitation* (pp. 188–211). New York: Aldine de Gruyter.

Oropesa, R. S., Lichter, D. T., & Anderson, R. N. (1994). Marriage markets and the paradox of Mexican American nuptiality. *Journal of Marriage and the Family, 56,* 889–907.

Orshansky, M. (1965). Counting the poor: Another look at poverty. *Social Security Bulletin, 28,* 3–29.

Osmond, M. W., & Thorne, B. (1993). Feminist theories: The social construction of gender in families and society. In P. G. Boss, W. J. Doherty, R. LaRossa, W. R. Schumm, & S. K. Steinmetz (Eds.), *Sourcebook of family theories and methods: A contextual approach* (pp. 591–623). New York: Plenum.

Ostrander, S. A. (1980). Upper class women: The feminine side of privilege. *Qualitative Sociology, 3,* 23–44.

Oswald, R. F. (2000). A member of the wedding? Heterosexism and family ritual. *Journal of Social and Personal Relationships, 17*(3), 349–368.

Oswald, R. F. (2002). Resilience within the family networks of lesbian and gay men: Intentionality and redefinition. *Journal of Marriage and Family, 64,* 374–383.

Owen, D. D. R. (1975). *Noble lovers.* New York: New York University Press.

Ozretich, R., Vuchinich, S., Pratt, C., & Bowman, S. (2001). *Enriching foster family relationships through problem solving: Guidelines for foster parents* (Oregon State University Extension Service No. EC 1517). Corvallis: Oregon State University.

Pagani, L., Boulerice, B., Tremblay, R. E., & Vitaro, F. (1997). Behavioral development in children of divorce and remarriage. *Journal of Divorce and Remarriage, 38,* 769–781.

Parker, G. (1999, June 2). Japan approves birth control pill. Associated Press. Retrieved from http://www.yorkweekly.com/1999news/6_2_w2.htm

Parrillo, V. N. (1996). *Diversity in America.* Thousand Oaks, CA: Pine Forge.

Parsons, T., & Bales, R. F. (1955). *Family, socialization, and the interaction process.* New York: Free Press.

Patterson, C. J. (1998). Family lives of children with lesbian mothers. In C. J. Patterson & A. R. D'Augelli (Eds.), *Lesbian, gay and bisexual identities in families: Psychological perspectives* (pp. 154–176). New York: Oxford University Press.

Patterson, C. J. (2000). Family relationships of lesbians and gay men. *Journal of Marriage and the Family, 62,* 1052–1069.

Pavalko, E. K., & Elder, G. H., Jr. (1993). Women behind the men: Variations in wives' support of husbands' careers. *Gender & Society, 7,* 548–567.

Pearson, J., & Thoennes, N. (1998). Programs to increase fathers' access to their children. In I. Garfinkel, S. S. McLanahan, D. R. Meyer, & J. A. Selzer (Eds.), *Fathers under fire* (pp. 220–252). New York: Russell Sage Foundation.

Pederson, F. A. (1982). Mother, father, and infant as an interactive system. In J. Belsky (Ed.), *In the beginning* (pp. 216–226). New York: Columbia University Press.

Peiss, K. L. (1986). *Cheap amusements: Working women and leisure in turn-of-the-century New York.* Philadelphia: Temple University Press.

Peplau, L. A., & Cochran, S. D. (1990). A relationship perspective on homosexuality. In D. P. McWhirter, S. A. Sanders, & J. M. Reinisch (Eds.), *Homosexuality/heterosexuality: Concepts of sexual orientation* (pp. 321–349). New York: Oxford University Press.

Peplau, L. A., Veniegas, R. C., & Campbell, S. M. (1996). Gay and lesbian relationships. In R. C. Savin-Williams & K. M. Cohen (Eds.), *The lives of lesbians, gays, and bisexuals: Children to adults* (pp. 250–273). New York: Harcourt.

Perrucci, C. D., Perrucci, R., Targ, D. B., & Targ, H. R. (1988). *Plant closings: International context and social costs.* Hawthorne, NY: Aldine de Gruyter.

Peters, M. (1985). Racial socialization of young black children. In H. McAdoo & J. McAdoo (Eds.), *Black children* (pp. 159–173). Beverly Hills, CA: Sage.

Peterson, G. W., & Hann, D. (1999). Socializing children and parents in families. In M. B. Sussman, S. K. Steinmetz, & G. W. Peterson (Eds.), *Handbook of marriage and the family* (2nd ed., pp. 327–370). New York: Plenum.

Peterson, G. W., & Rollins, B. C. (1987). Parent–child socialization. In M. B. Sussman & S. K. Steinmetz (Eds.), *Handbook of marriage and the family* (pp. 471–507). New York: Plenum.

Peterson, R. R. (1996). A re-evaluation of the economic consequences of divorce. *American Sociological Review, 61,* 528–636.

Phillips, R. (1997). Stepfamilies from a historical perspective. In I. Levin & M. Sussman (Eds.), *Stepfamilies: History, research and policy* (pp. 5–18). New York: Haworth.

Phillips, R. (1991). *Untying the knot: A short history of divorce.* Cambridge, England: Cambridge University Press.

Phinney, J. S., & Chavira, V. (1995). Parental ethnic socialization and adolescent coping with problems related to ethnicity. *Journal of Research on Adolescence, 5,* 31–54.

Pimentel, E. E. (2000). Just how do I love thee? Marital relations in urban China. *Journal of Marriage and the Family, 62,* 32–47.

Pineo, P. (1961). Disenchantment in the later years of marriage. *Marriage and Family Living, 23,* 3–11.

Pines, A. M. (1997). Fatal attractions or wise unconscious choices: The relationship between causes for entering and breaking intimate relationships. *Personal Relationship Issues, 4,* 1–6.

Pirog-Good, M. A., & Amerson, L. (1997). The long arm of justice: The potential for seizing the assets of child support obligors. *Family Relations, 46,* 47–54.

The Plantation (2002). *Thomas Jefferson and Sally Hemings: A brief account.* Retrieved from http://www.monticello.org/plantation/hemings-jefferson_contro.html

Pleck, J. (1975). Man to man: Is brotherhood possible? In N. Glazer-Malbin (Ed.), *Old family/new family: Interpersonal relationships* (pp. 229–244). New York: Van Nostrand.

Pleck, J. H. (1977). The work–family role system. *Social Problems, 24,* 417–427.

Pleck, J. H. (1997). Paternal involvement: Levels, sources, and consequences. In M. E. Lamb (Ed.), *The role of the father in child development* (3rd ed., pp. 325–332). New York: Wiley.

Polatnick, M. R. (2002). Too old for child care? Too young for self-care? Negotiating after school arrangements for middle school. *Journal of Marriage and Family, 64,* 728–747.

Pong, S.-L. (1997). Family structure, school context, and eighth-grade math and reading achievement. *Journal of Marriage and the Family, 59,* 734–746.

Popenoe, D. (1987). Beyond the nuclear family: A statistical portrait of the changing family in Sweden. *Journal of Marriage and the Family, 49,* 173–183.

Popenoe, D. (1993). American family decline, 1960–1990: A review and appraisal. *Journal of Marriage and the Family, 55,* 527–555.

Popenoe, D., & Whitehead, B. D. (1999). *Should we live together? What young adults need to know about cohabitation before marriage* (The National Marriage Project). New Brunswick, NJ: National Marriage Project.

Popenoe, D., & Whitehead, B. D. (2002). *Should we live together? What young adults need to know about cohabitation before marriage: A comprehensive review of recent research* (2nd ed.). New Brunswick, NJ: National Marriage Project.

Posner, P. (2002). *One family's journey to healing.* Retrieved from Stepfamily Network: http://www.stepfamily.net

Presser, H. (2000). Nonstandard work schedules and marital instability. *Journal of Marriage and the Family, 62,* 93–110.

Presser, H. B. (1995). Job, family, and gender: Determinants on nonstandard work schedules among employed Americans in 1991. *Demography, 32,* 577–598.

Prevent Child Abuse America (2001). *Total estimated cost of child abuse and neglect in the United States: Statistical evidence.* Retrieved from http://www.preventchild-abuse.org

Price, J. (2002). Polygamy could help moms who work, says Utah NOW. Retrieved from http://www.polygamy.com

Purcell, P., & Stewart, L. (1990). Dick and Jane in 1989. *Sex Roles, 22,* 177–185.

Purdy, J. (2000). *Hale and hearty at 100.* Retrieved from www.geron.uga.edu/centarian_study.html

Pyke, K. (1994). Women's employment as a gift or a burden? Marital power across marriage, divorce, and remarriage. *Gender & Society, 8,* 73–91.

Pyke, K., & Coltrane, S. (1996). Entitlement, obligation, and gratitude in family work. *Journal of Family Issues, 17,* 60–82.

Quadagno, J. (1982). *Aging in early industrial society.* New York: Academic Press.

Quayle, D. (2001, May 28). Why I think I'm still right. *Newsweek,* p. 52.

Quick, H. E., & Moen, P. (1998). Gender, employment, and retirement quality: A life-course approach to the differential experiences of men and women. *Journal of Occupational Health Psychology, 3,* 44–64.

Quinn, J. B. (1993, January 25). Sauce for the goose. *Newsweek,* p. 64.

Raffaelli, M., Bogenschneider, K., & Flood, M. F. (1998). Parent–teen communication about sexual topics. *Journal of Family Issues, 19*(3), 315–333.

Rainwater, L., & Smeeding, T. A. (1995). *Doing poorly: The real income of American children in a comparative perspective.* (Maxwell School of Citizenship and Public Affairs, Syracuse University, Syracuse, NY, Working Paper No. 127, Luxembourg Income Study).

Raley, R. K. (2001). Increasing fertility in cohabiting unions: Evidence for the second demographic transition in the United States. *Demography, 38*(1), 59–66.

Ramafedi, G., Resnick, M., Blum, R., & Harris, L. (1992). Demography of sexual orientation in adolescents. *Pediatrics, 89,* 714–721.

Ramu, G. N., & Tavuchis, N. (1986). The valuation of children and parenthood among the voluntarily childless and parental couples in Canada. *Journal of Comparative Family Studies, 17,* 99–116.

Rank, M. R., & Davis, L. E. (1996). Perceived happiness outside of marriage among black and white spouses. *Family Relations, 45,* 435–441.

Rathus, S. A., Nevid, J. S., & Fichner-Rathus, L. (1993). *Human sexuality in a world of diversity.* Boston: Allyn & Bacon.

Raymo, J. M. (1998). Later marriages or fewer? Changes in the marital behavior of Japanese women. *Journal of Marriage and the Family, 60,* 1023–1034.

Reeder, H. (1996). The subjective experience of love through adult life. *International Journal of Aging and Human Development, 43*(4), 325–340.

Reilly, L. (1996). *Women living single: Thirty women share their stories of navigating through a married world.* Boston: Faber and Faber.

Reiss, I. L. (1960). Toward a sociology of the heterosexual love relationship. *Marriage and Family Living, 22,* 139–145.

Reiss, I. L. (1980). *Family systems in America* (3rd ed.). New York: Holt, Rinehart and Winston.

Reiss, I. L., & Lee, G. R. (1988). *Family systems in America* (4th ed.). New York: Holt, Rinehart & Winston.

Religious Action Center of Reform Judaism (2001). *Issues: Living wage campaigns.* Retrieved from http://www.rac.org/issues/issuemwcsa.html

Rempel, J. (1985). Childless elderly: What are they missing? *Journal of Marriage and the Family, 43,* 941–955.

Reskin, B., & Padavic, I. (1999). Sex, race, and ethnic inequality in United States workplaces. In J. Chafetz (Ed.), *Handbook of the sociology of gender* (pp. 343–374). New York: Plenum.

Rice, F. P. (1999). *Intimate relationships, marriages, and families* (4th ed.). Mountain View, CA: Mayfield.

Riessman, C. K., & Gerstel, N. (1985). Marital dissolution and health: Do males or females have greater risks? *Social Science and Medicine, 20,* 627–635.

Rindfuss, R. R., Morgan, S. P., & Swicegood, G. (1988). *First births in America: Changing patterns of parenthood.* Berkeley and Los Angeles: University of California Press.

Risman, B. J., & Johnson-Sumerford, D. (1998). Doing it fairly: A study of post-gender marriages. *Journal of Marriage and the Family, 60,* 23–40.

Roberts, N. A., & Levenson, R. W. (2001). The remains of the workday: Impact of job stress and exhaustion on marital interaction in police couples. *Journal of Marriage and Family, 63,* 1052–1067.

Robinson, B. A. (2002). *How interfaith and intra-faith couples handle religious differences.* Retrieved from http://www.religioustolerance.org/ifm_diff.htm

Robinson, J. P., & Godbey, G. (1997). *Time for life: The surprising ways Americans use their time.* University Park: Pennsylvania State University Press.

Rodgers, J. L., Nakonezny, P. A., & Shull, R. D. (1997). Feedback: The effect of no-fault divorce legislation on divorce rates: A response to a reconsideration. *Journal of Marriage and the Family, 59,* 1026–1030.

Rodgers, K. B. (1999). Parenting processes related to sexual risk-taking behaviors of adolescent males and females. *Journal of Marriage and the Family, 61,* 99–109.

Rodgers, R. H., & White, J. M. (1993). Family development theory. In P. G. Boss, W. J. Doherty, R. LaRossa, W. R. Schumm, & S.

K. Steinmetz (Eds.), *Sourcebook of family theories and methods: A contextual approach* (pp. 225–254). New York: Plenum.

Rodgers-Farmer, A. Y., & Jones, R. L. (1999). Grandmothers who are caregivers: An overlooked population. *Child and Adolescent Social Work Journal, 16,* 455–466.

Rogers, S. J., & Amato, P. R. (2000). Have changes in gender relations affected marital quality? *Social Forces, 79,* 731–753.

Rollins, B. C., & Feldman, H. (1970). Marital satisfaction over the marital life cycle. *Journal of Marriage and the Family, 32,* 20–28.

Romero, M. (1992). *Maid in the U.S.A.* Philadelphia: Temple University Press.

Ronfeldt, H. M., Kimerling, R., & Arias, I. (1998). Satisfaction with relationship power and the perpetration of dating violence. *Journal of Marriage and the Family, 60,* 70–78.

Rooks, J. (1997). *Midwifery and childbirth in America.* Philadelphia: Temple University Press.

Rose, S., & Frieze, I. H. (1989). Young singles' scripts for a first date. *Gender & Society, 3,* 258–268.

Rose, S., & Frieze, I. H. (1993). Young singles' contemporary dating scripts. *Sex Roles, 28,* 499–509.

Rosenfeld, M. J. (2002). Measures of assimilation in the marriage market: Mexican Americans 1970–1990. *Journal of Marriage and Family, 64,* 152–162.

Rosenthal, A. M. (1993, July 27). The torture continues. *New York Times,* p. A13.

Ross, C. E., & Mirowsky, J. (1988). Child care and emotional adjustment to wives' employment. *Journal of Health and Social Behavior, 29,* 127–138.

Ross, C. E., Mirowsky, J., & Goldsteen, K. (1990). The impact of the family on health: Decade in review. *Journal of Marriage and the Family, 52,* 1059–1078.

Ross, H. G., & Milgram, J. I. (1982). Important variables in adult sibling relationships: A qualitative analysis. In M. E. Lamb & B. Sutton-Smith (Eds.), *Sibling relationships: Their nature and significance across the lifespan* (pp. 225–266). Hillsdale, NJ: Erlbaum.

Ross, L. E. (1997). Mate selection preferences among African American college students. *Journal of Black Studies, 27,* 554–569.

Rossi, A. S., & Rossi, P. H. (1990). *Of human bonding: Parent–child relations across the life course.* New York: Aldine de Gruyter.

Rossi, P. H. (1999). Three encounters. *Contemporary Sociology, 28,* 1–4.

Rothman, B. K. (1991). *In labor: Women and power in the birthplace.* New York: Norton.

Rouse, K. G. (1998, Spring). Resilience from poverty and stress. *Human Development and Family Life Bulletin* (Ohio State University, College of Human Ecology), 4.

Roy, K. (1999). Low-income single fathers in an African American community and the requirements of welfare reform. *Journal of Family Issues, 20*(4), 432–457.

Rubin, J., Provenzano, F., & Luria, Z. (1974). The eye of the beholder: Parents' views on sex of newborns. *American Journal of Orthopsychiatry, 44,* 512–519.

Rubin, L. B. (1983). *Intimate strangers: Men and women together.* New York: Harper & Row.

Rubin, L. B. (1985). *Just friends: The role of friendship in our lives.* New York: Harper & Row.

Rubin, L. B. (1990). *Erotic wars: What happened to the sexual revolution?* New York: Farrar, Straus and Giroux.

Rubin, L. B. (1994). *Families on the fault line: America's working class speaks about the family, the economy, and ethnicity.* New York: HarperCollins.

Ruddick, S. (1989). *Maternal thinking: Toward a politics of peace.* Boston: Beacon.

Ruhm, C. J. (1998). *Parental leave and child health.* Working Paper 6554. Retrieved from National Bureau of Economic Research: http://papers.nber.org/papers/W6554.pdf

Russell, A., & Searcy, E. (1997). The contributions of affective reactions and relationship qualities to adolescents' reported responses to parents. *Journal of Social and Personal Relationships, 14,* 539–548.

Ryan, C., & Futterman, D. (1997). Lesbian and gay youth: Care and counseling. *Adolescent Medicine, State of the Art Reviews, 8,* 221.

Ryan, M. P. (1979). *Womanhood in America: From colonial times to the present* (2nd ed.). New York: New Viewpoints.

Sabatelli, R. M., & Shehan, C. L. (1993). Exchange and resource theories. In P. G. Boss, W. J. Doherty, R. LaRossa, W. R. Schumm, & S. K. Steinmetz (Eds.), *Sourcebook of family theories and methods: A contextual approach* (pp. 385–411). New York: Plenum.

Sachs, S. (2000, March 2). Egypt grants wives equality in divorce court. New York Times News Service.

Sadker, M., & Sadker, D. (1994). *Failing at fairness: How America's schools cheat girls.* New York: Scribner.

Saluter, A. F., & Lugaila, T. A. (1998). *Marital status and living arrangements: March 1996* (Current Population Reports, P20–496). Washington, DC: U.S. Census Bureau.

Sample, N. (1999). *What I felt like being adopted.* Retrieved from http://www.step-familynetwork.net/Adoption.htm

Sanday, P. R. (1981). The socio-cultural context of rape: A cross-cultural study. *Journal of Social Issues, 37,* 5–27.

Sandberg, J. F., & Hofferth, S. L. (2001). Changes in children's time with parents: United States, 1981–1997. *Demography, 38,* 423–436.

Sands, R. G., & Goldberg-Glen, R. S. (2000). Factors associated with stress among grandparents raising their grandchildren. *Family Relations, 49,* 97–105.

Savage, H. A., & Fronczek, P. J. (1993). Who can afford to buy a house in 1991? (*Current Housing Reports,* H121/93–3). Washington, DC: U.S. Department of Commerce, Economics and Statistics Administration, Bureau of the Census.

Savin-Williams, R. C. (2001). *Mom, Dad. I'm gay. How families negotiate coming out.* Washington, DC: American Psychological Association.

Scanzoni, J. (1988). Families in the 1980s. *Journal of Family Issues, 8,* 394–421.

Schacter, S. (1964). The interaction of cognitive and physiological determinants of emotional state. In L. Berkowitz (Ed.), *Advances in experimental social psychology* (Vol. 1, pp. 49–80). New York: Academic Press.

Schaefer, S. (2001). *What does the NICHD study really tell us about child care and aggression?* Retrieved from http://www.contemporaryfamilies.org/control.htm

Scharlach, A. E. (1991). *Elder care and the work force: Blue print for action.* Toronto: Lexington.

Scheuble, L., & Johnson, D. R. (1993). Marital name change: Plans and attitudes of college students. *Journal of Marriage and the Family, 55,* 747–754.

Schiller, B. R. (2001). *The economics of poverty and discrimination.* Englewood Cliffs, NJ: Prentice Hall.

Schneider, H. (2000, April 14). Women in Egypt gain broader divorce rights. *Washington Post Foreign Service,* p. A16.

Schneider Institute for Health Policy (2001). *Substance abuse: The nation's number one health problem* (Brandeis University, Prepared for the Robert Wood Johnson Foundation). Princeton, NJ: Author.

Schoen, R. (1992). First unions and the stability of first marriages. *Journal of Marriage and the Family, 54,* 281–284.

Schoen, R., Kim, Y. J., Nathanson, C. A., Fields, J., & Astone, N. M. (1997). Why do

Americans want children? *Population and Development Review, 23,* 333–358.

Schor, J. B. (1998). *The overspent American: Upscaling, downshifting, and the new consumer.* New York: Basic.

Schor, J. B. (1991). *The overworked American: The unexpected decline of leisure.* New York: Basic.

Schrock, J. J. (1989). Pseudoscience of animals and plants: A teacher's guide to non-scientific beliefs. *Kansas School Naturalist, 35,* 3–15.

Schulman, K. (2000). *The high cost of child care puts quality care out of reach for many families.* Washington, DC: Children's Defense Fund.

Schvaneveldt, J. D., Pickett, R. S., & Young, M. H. (1993). Historical methods in family research. In P. G. Boss, W. J. Doherty, R. LaRossa, W. R. Schum, & S. K. Steinmetz (Eds.), *Sourcebook of family theories and methods: A contextual approach* (pp. 591–623). New York: Plenum.

Schwartz, P. (1995). *Peer marriage.* New York: Free Press.

Schwartzberg, N., Berliner, K., & Jacob, D. (1995). *Single in a married world: A life cycle framework for working with the unmarried adult.* New York: Norton.

Seccombe, K. (1995). Health insurance and use of services among low income elders: Does residence influence the relationship? *Journal of Rural Health, 11,* 86–97.

Seccombe, K. (1999). *"So you think I drive a Cadillac?" Welfare recipients' perspectives on the system and its reform.* Needham Heights, MA: Allyn & Bacon.

Seccombe, K. (2000). Families in poverty in the 1990s: Trends, causes, consequences, and lessons learned. *Journal of Marriage and the Family, 62,* 1094–1113.

Sedlak, A. J., & Broadhurst, D. D. (1998, May 21). *Executive summary of the Third National Incidence Study of Child Abuse and Neglect.* Retrieved from www.casanet.org/library/abuse/stabuse.htm

Seigel, J. M. (1995). Looking for Mr. Right? Older single women who become mothers. *Journal of Family Issues, 16,* 194–211.

Seiter, E. (1993). *Sold separately: Children and parents in consumer culture.* New Brunswick, NJ: Rutgers University Press.

Seltzer, J. A. (1991). Relationships between fathers and children who live apart: The father's role after separation. *Journal of Marriage and the Family, 53,* 79–101.

Seltzer, J. A. (1998). Fathers by law: Effects of joint legal custody on nonresidential fathers' involvement with children. *Demography, 35,* 135–146.

Seltzer, J. A. (2000). Families formed outside of marriage. *Journal of Marriage and the Family, 62,* 1247–1268.

Settersten, R. A., & Hagestad, G. O. (1996). What's the latest? Cultural age deadlines for family transitions. *The Gerontologist, 36,* 602–613.

Shapiro, A., & Lambert, J. D. (1999). Longitudinal effects of divorce on the quality of father–child relationship and on fathers' psychological well-being. *Journal of Marriage and the Family, 61,* 397–408.

Shapiro, A. D. (1996). Explaining psychological distress in a sample of remarried and divorced persons: The influence of economic distress. *Journal of Family Issues, 17,* 186–203.

Shapiro, I., Greenstein, R., & Primus, W. (2001, May 31). *Pathbreaking CBO study shows dramatic increases in income disparities in 1980s and 1990s: An analysis of the CBO data.* Retrieved from http://www.cbpp.org/5-3-01tax.htm

Shapiro, J., Diamond, M. J., & Greenber, M. (1995). *Becoming a father: Contemporary, social, developmental, and clinical perspectives.* New York: Springer.

Sheets, V. L., & Braver, S. L. (1996). Gender differences in satisfaction with divorce settlements. *Family Relations, 45,* 336–342.

Shelton, B. A. (1992). *Women, men, and time: Gender differences in paid work, housework, and leisure.* Westport, CT: Greenwood.

Shelton, B. A., & John, D. (1993). Ethnicity, race, and difference: A comparison of white, black, and Hispanic men's household labor time. In J. C. Hood (Ed.), *Men, work, and family* (pp. 131–150). Newbury Park, CA: Sage.

Shelton, B. A., & John, D. (1996). The division of household labor. *Annual Review of Sociology, 22,* 299–322.

Shibazaki, K., & Brennan, K. A. (1998). When birds of different feathers flock together: A preliminary comparison of intra-ethnic and inter-ethnic dating relationships. *Journal of Social and Personal Relationships, 15*(2), 248–256.

Shilts, R. (2000). *And the band played on: Politics, people, and the AIDS epidemic.* New York: St. Martin's.

Shofield, J. (1982). *Black and white in school.* New York: Praeger.

Shore, R. (1998). *Ahead of the curve: Why America's leading employers are addressing the needs of new and expectant parents.* New York: Families and Work Institute.

Shorter, E. (1975). *The making of the modern family.* New York: Basic.

Sidel, R. (1996). *Keeping women and children last.* New York: Penguin.

Siegel, J. M., & Kuykendall, D. H. (1990). Loss, widowhood, and psychological distress among the elderly. *Journal of Consulting and Clinical Psychology, 58,* 519–524.

Silliman, B. (1994). *1994 resiliency research review: Conceptual & research foundations.* Retrieved from http://www.cyfernet.org/research/resilreview.html

Silliman, B. (1998, Spring). The resiliency paradigm: A critical tool for practitioners. *Human Development and Family Life Bulletin* (Ohio State University, College of Human Ecology), 4:1.

Silverstein, M., & Bengtson, V. L. (2001). Intergenerational solidarity and the structure of adult child–parent relationships in American families. *American Journal of Sociology, 103*(2), 429–460.

Simon, R. J., & Alstein, H. (2000). *Adoption across borders: Serving the children in transracial and intercountry adoptions.* Lanham, MD: Rowman & Littlefield.

Simpson, G. E., & Yinger, M. J. (1985). *Racial and cultural minorities: An analysis of prejudice and discrimination* (4th ed.). New York: Harper & Row.

Sinclair, U. 1906/1981. *The jungle.* New York: Bantam.

Singer, J. (1997). Husbands, wives, and human capital: Why the shoe won't fit. *Family Law Quarterly, 31,* 119–132.

Singh, D. (1993). Adaptive significance of female physical attractiveness: Role of waist-to-hip ratio. *Journal of Personality & Social Psychology, 65,* 293–307.

Singh, S., & Darroch, J. (2000). Adolescent pregnancy and childbearing: Levels and trends in developed countries. *Family Planning Perspectives, 32,* 14–23.

Sinson, F. S., Yi, H., Grant, B. F., Chou, P., Dawson, D. A., & Pickering, R. (1998). Drinking in the United States: Main findings from the 1992 National Longitudinal Alcohol Epidemiological Survey (NLAES). *U.S. alcohol data reference manual* (Vol. 6). Bethesda, MD: National Institute on Alcohol Abuse and Alcoholism.

Smith, D., & Wade, N. (1998, November 1). DNA tests offer evidence that Jefferson fathered a child with his slave. *New York Times.* Retrieved from http://search.nytimes.com/search/daily/...te+site+23051+wAAA+Thomas%7EJefferson

Smith, D. E. (1993). The standard North American family: SNAF as an ideological code. *Journal of Family Issues, 14,* 50–65.

Smith, D. S. (1973). Parental power and marriage patterns: An analysis of historical trends in Hingham, Massachusetts. *Journal of Marriage and the Family, 35,* 419–429.

Smith, J., Brooks-Gunn, J., & Klebanov, P. (1997). Consequences of growing up poor for young children. In G. J. Duncan & J. Brooks-Gunn (Eds.), *Consequences of growing up poor* (pp. 132–189). New York: Russell Sage Foundation.

Smith, K. (2000). *Who's minding the kids? Child care arrangements: Fall 1995* (Current Population Reports No. P70–70). Washington, DC: U.S. Census Bureau.

Smith-Rosenberg, C. (1975). The female world of love and ritual: Relations between women in nineteenth-century America. *Signs: A Journal of Women in Culture and Society, 1,* 1–29.

Smock, P. J. (2000). Cohabitation in the United States: An appraisal of research themes, findings, and implications. *Annual Review of Sociology, 26,* 1–20.

Snipp, M. (1989). *American Indians: The first of this land.* New York: Russell Sage Foundation.

Soldo, B. J., & Agree, E. M. (1988). America's elderly. *Population Bulletin, 43,* 3.

Somary, K., & Stricker, G. (1998). Becoming a grandparent: A longitudinal study of expectations and early experiences as a function of sex and lineage. *The Gerontologist, 38,* 53–61.

Sorensen, E. (1997). A national profile of nonresident fathers and their ability to pay child support. *Journal of Marriage and the Family, 59,* 785–797.

Sorensen, E., & Halpern, A. (1999). Child support enforcement is working better than we think. In *New federalism: Issues and options for states* (Tech. Rep. No. Series A31). Washington, DC: Urban Institute.

South, S. (1991). Sociodemographic differentials in mate selections preferences. *Journal of Marriage and the Family, 53,* 928–940.

South, S. J., & Spitze, G. (1994). Housework in marital and nonmarital households. *American Sociological Review, 59,* 327–347.

South, S. J., Trent, K., & Shen, Y. (2001). Changing partners: Toward a macrostructural–opportunity theory of marital dissolution. *Journal of Marriage and Family, 63,* 743–754.

Spain, D. (1992). The spatial foundations of men's friendships and men's power. In P. M. Nardi (Ed.), *Men's friendships* (pp. 59–73). Newbury Park, CA: Sage.

Spanier, G. B., & Thompson, L. (1987). *Parting: The aftermath of separation and divorce* (updated edition). Newbury Park, CA: Sage.

Spark.com (1999). The gender test. Retrieved from www.thespark.com/gendertest

Spenser, C. (1995). *Homosexuality in history.* New York: Harcourt.

Spicher, C. H., & Hudak, M. A. (1997, August 18). *Gender role portrayal on Saturday morning cartoons: An update.* Presented at the American Psychological Association, Chicago, IL.

Spitze, G., Logan, J., Deane, G., & Zerger, S. (1994). Adult children's divorce and intergenerational relationships. *Journal of Marriage and the Family, 56,* 279–293.

Sprecher, S. (1994). Two sides to the breakup of dating relationships. *Personal Relationships, 1,* 199–222.

Sprecher, S., & Felmlee, D. (1992). The influence of parents and friends on the quality and stability of romantic relationships: A 3-wave longitudinal investigation. *Journal of Marriage and the Family, 54,* 888–900.

Spruijt, E., & de Goede, M. (1997). Transitions in family structure and adolescent well-being. *Adolescence, 32,* 89–112.

Stacey, J. (1993). Good riddance to the family: A response to David Popenoe. *Journal of Marriage and the Family, 55,* 545–547.

Stacey, J., & Biblarz, T. J. (2001). (How) does the sexual orientation of parents matter? *American Sociological Review, 66,* 159–183.

Stack, S. (1992). The effect of divorce on suicide in Japan: A time series analysis, 1950–1980. *Journal of Marriage and the Family, 54,* 327–334.

Stack, S., & Eshleman, J. R. (1998). Marital status and happiness: A 17-nation study. *Journal of Marriage and the Family, 60,* 527–537.

Stafford, L., & Bayer, C. L. (1993). *Interaction between parents and children.* Newbury Park, CA: Sage.

Staples, R. (1973). *The black woman in America: Sex, marriage, and the family.* Chicago: Nelson Hall.

Staples, R. (1994). *The black family* (5th ed.). Belmont, CA: Wadsworth.

Starr, P. (1982). *The social transformation of American medicine.* New York: Basic.

Stattin, H., & Kerr, M. (2000). Parental monitoring: A reinterpretation. *Child Development, 71,* 1070–1083.

Steele, J., Waters, E., Crowell, J., & Treboux, D. (1998, June). *Self-report measures of attachment: Secure bonds to other attachment measures and attachment theory.* Presented at the Biennial meeting of the International Society for the Study of Personal Relationships, Saratoga Springs, New York.

Stein, P. (1976). *Single.* Englewood Cliffs, NJ: Prentice Hall.

Stein, P. (1981). Understanding single adulthood. In P. Stein (Ed.), *Single life: Unmarried adults in social contexts* (pp. 9–20). New York: St. Martin's.

Steinberg, L., Lamborn, S., Dombusch, S., & Darling, N. (1992). Impact of parenting practices on adolescent achievement: Authoritative parenting, school involvement, and encouragement to succeed. *Developmental Psychology, 63,* 1266–1281.

Stepfamily Association of America (2000). *Frequently asked questions.* Retrieved from http://www.stepfam.org/faqs/faqs.htm

Stephens, W. N. (1963). *The family in cross cultural perspective.* New York: Holt, Rinehart and Winston.

Sterk-Elifson, C. (1994). Sexuality among African American women. In A. Rossi (Ed.), *Sexuality across the life course* (pp. 99–127). Chicago: University of Chicago Press.

Stern, M., & Karraker, K. H. (1989). Sex stereotyping of infants: A review of gender labeling studies. *Sex Roles, 20,* 501–522.

Sternberg, R. J. (1986). A triangular theory of love. *Psychological Review, 93*(2), 119–135.

Sternberg, R. J. (1988). *The triangle of love.* New York: Basic.

Stinnett, N., & DeFrain, J. (1985). *Secrets of strong families.* Boston: Little, Brown.

Stinson, F. S., & Nephew, T. M. (1996). State trends in alcohol-related mortality, 1979–92. In *U.S. alcohol epidemiological data reference manual* (Vol. 5). Bethesda, MD: National Institute on Alcohol Abuse and Alcoholism.

Stockard, J. E. (2002). *Marriage in culture.* Orlando, FL: Harcourt.

Stone, R., Cafferata, G. L., & Sangle, J. (1987). Caregivers of the frail elderly: A national profile. *The Gerontologist, 27,* 616–626.

Strasser, S. (1982). *Never done.* New York: Henry Holt.

Straus, M. A. (1979). Measuring intrafamily conflict and violence: The Conflict Tactics (CT) Scale. *Journal of Marriage and the Family, 41,* 75–88.

Straus, M. A. (1994). *Beating the devil out of them: Corporal punishment in American families.* New York: Lexington.

Straus, M. A., Gelles, R. J., & Steinmetz, S. K. (1980). *Behind closed doors: Violence in the American family.* New York: Anchor.

Stroebe, M. S., & Stroebe, W. (1983). Who suffers more: Sex differences in health risks of the widowed. *Psychological Bulletin, 93,* 279–299.

Strong, B., DeVault, C., Sayad, B. W., & Yarber, W. L. (2002). *Human sexuality: Diversity in contemporary America* (4th ed.). Boston: McGraw-Hill.

Sudarkasa, N. (1997). African American families and family values. In H. P. McAdoo (Ed.), *Black families* (3rd ed., pp. 9–40). Thousand Oaks, CA: Sage.

Sudarkasa, N. (1999). Interpreting the African heritage in Afro-American family organization. In S. Coontz, M. Parson, & G. Raley (Eds.), *American families: A multicultural reader* (pp. 59–73). New York: Routledge.

Sugarman, D. B., & Hotaling, G. T. (1989). Dating violence: Prevalence, context, and risk markers. In M. A. Pirog-Good & J. E. Stets (Eds.), *Violence in dating relationships: Emerging social issues* (pp. 3–32). New York: Praeger.

Suitor, J. (1991). Marital quality and satisfaction with division of household labor. *Journal of Marriage and the Family, 53,* 221–230.

Sullivan, D. A., & Beeman, R. (1983). Four years experience with homebirth by licensed midwives in Arizona. *American Journal of Public Health, 73,* 641–645.

Sullivan, D. A., & Weitz, R. (1988). *Labor pains: Modern midwives and home birth.* New Haven, CT: Yale University Press.

Sun, Y., & Li, Y. (2002). Child well-being during parents' marital disruption process: A pooled time-series analysis. *Journal of Marriage and Family, 64,* 472–488.

Swain, S. (1989). Covert intimacy: Closeness in men's friendships. In B. J. Risman & P. Schwartz (Eds.), *Gender in intimate relationships: A microstructural approach* (pp. 71–86). Belmont, CA: Wadsworth.

Swain, S. O. (1992). Men's friendships with women: Intimacy, sexual boundaries, and the informant role. In P. M. Nardi (Ed.), *Men's friendships* (pp. 153–171). Newbury Park, CA: Sage.

Sweeney, M. M. (2002). Two decades of family change: The shifting economic foundations of marriage. *American Sociological Review, 67,* 132–147.

Swidler, A. (1980). Love and adulthood in America. In N. J. Smelser & E. H. Erikson (Eds.), *Themes of work and love in adulthood* (pp. 120–147). Boston: Harvard University Press.

Szinovacz, M. E. (1998). Grandparents today: A demographic profile. *The Gerontologist, 38,* 37–52.

Szinovacz, M. E. (2000). Changes in housework after retirement: A panel analysis. *Journal of Marriage and the Family, 62,* 78–92.

Szinovacz, M. E., & Harpster, P. (1993). Employment status, gender role attitudes, and marital dependence in later life.

Journal of Marriage and the Family, 49, 927–940.

Tannen, D. (1990). *You just don't understand: Women and men in conversation.* New York: Morrow.

Tasker, F. L., & Golombok, S. (1997). *Growing up in a lesbian family: Effects on child development.* New York: Guilford.

Tatara, T., & Kuzmeskus, L. (1997). *Summaries of statistical data on elder abuse in domestic settings for FY 95 and FY 96.* Washington, DC: National Center on Elder Abuse.

Taylor, R. J., Chatters, L. M., Tucker, M. B., & Lewis, E. (1990). Developments in research on black families: A decade review. *Journal of Marriage and the Family, 52,* 993–1014.

Taylor, S. E., Klein, L. C., Lewis, B. P., Gruenewald, T. L., Gurung, R. A. R., & Upedegraff, J. A. (2000). Biobehavioral responses to stress in females: Tend-and-befriend, not fight-or-flight. *Psychological Review, 107*(3), 411–429.

Teachman, J. D., Paasch, K., & Carver, K. (1996). Social capital and dropping out of school early. *Journal of Marriage and the Family, 58,* 773–783.

Teachman, J. D., Paasch, K. M., Day, R., & Carver, K. (1997). Poverty during adolescence and subsequent educational attainment. In G. J. Duncan & J. Brooks-Gunn (Eds.), *Consequences of growing up poor.* New York: Russell Sage Foundation.

Testa, M., Astone, N. M., Krogh, M., & Neckerman, K. M. (1989). Employment and marriage among inner-city fathers. *Annals of the American Academy of Political and Social Science, 501,* 79–91.

Thompson, L. (1991). Family work: Women's sense of fairness. *Journal of Family Issues, 12,* 181–196.

Thompson, L., & Walker, A. J. (1989). Gender in families: Women and men in marriage, work, and parenthood. *Journal of Marriage and the Family, 51,* 845–871.

Thorne, B., & Luria, Z. (1986). Sexuality and gender in children's daily worlds. *Social Problems, 33,* 176–190.

Thornton, A., Axinn, W. G., & Teachman, J. D. (1995). The influence of school enrollment and accumulation on cohabitation and marriage in early adulthood. *American Sociological Review, 60,* 762–774.

Thornton, A., & Young-DeMarcho, L. (2001). Four decades of trends in attitudes towards family issues in the United States: The 1960s through the 1990s. *Journal of Marriage and Family, 63,* 1009–1037.

Thornton, M. C. (1997). Strategies of racial socialization among black parents: Mainstream, minority, and cultural messages. In R. J. Taylor, J. S. Jackson, & L. M. Chatters (Eds.), *Family life in black*

America (pp. 201–215). Thousand Oaks, CA: Sage.

Tichenor, V. J. (1999). Status and income as gendered resources: The case of marital power. *Journal of Marriage and the Family, 61,* 638–650.

Tilly, L. A., & Scott, J. W. (1978). *Women, work, and family.* New York: Holt, Rinehart and Winston.

Tohidi, N. (1993). Iranian women and gender relations in Los Angeles. In R. Kelley, J. Friedlander, & A. Colby (Eds.), *Irangeles: Iranians in Los Angeles* (pp. 175–217). Berkeley: University of California Press.

Trattner, W. I. (1999). *From poor law to welfare state: A history of social welfare in America* (6th ed.). New York: Free Press.

Trent, K., & Crowder, K. (1997). Adolescent birth intentions, social disadvantage, and behavior outcomes. *Journal of Marriage and the Family, 59,* 523–535.

Trent, K., & South, S. J. (1989). Structural determinants of the divorce rate: A cross-societal analysis. *Journal of Marriage and the Family, 51,* 391–404.

Trent, K., & South, S. J. (1992). Sociodemographic status, parental background, childhood family structure, and attitudes toward family formation. *Journal of Marriage and the Family, 54,* 427–439.

Tucker, M. B. (2000). Marital values and expectations in context: Results from a 21-city survey. In L. J. Waite, C. Bachrach, M. J. Hindin, E. Thomson, & A. Thornton (Eds.), *The ties that bind: Perspectives on marriage and cohabitation* (pp. 166–187). New York: Aldine de Gruyter.

Tucker, M. B., & Mitchell-Kernan. (1995). Marital behavior and expectations: Ethnic comparisons of attitudinal and structural correlates. In M. B. Tucker & C. Mitchell-Kernan (Eds.), *The decline in marriage among African Americans: Causes, consequences and policy implications* (pp. 145–171). New York: Russell Sage Foundation.

Tucker, M. B., & Mitchell-Kernan, C. (1998). Psychological well-being and perceived marital opportunity among single African Americans, Latina and white women. *Journal of Comparative Family Studies, 28,* 57–72.

Tucker, R. K., Marvin, M. G., & Vivian, B. (1991). What constitutes a romantic act. *Psychology Reports, 89,* 651–654.

TV sex misses opportunities to educate audiences on safer sex. (1999). *Public Health Reports, 114*(3), 209.

Tweedie, J., Reichert, D., & O'Connor, M. (1999, July). *Tracking recipients after they leave welfare.* Presented at the National Conference of State Legislatures, Denver, CO.

Uhlenberg, P., & Kirby, J. B. (1998). Grand-parenthood over time: Historical and demographic trends. In M. E. Szinovacz (Ed.), *Handbook on grandparenthood* (pp. 23–39). Westport, CT: Greenwood.

Ulrich, M., & Weatherall, A. (2000). Motherhood and infertility: Viewing motherhood through the lens of infertility. *Feminism & Psychology, 10,* 323–336.

Umberson, D. (1992). Gender, marital status, and the social control of health behavior. *Social Science and Medicine, 34,* 907–917.

Umberson, D., Wortman, C. B., & Kessler, R. C. (1992). Widowhood and depression: Explaining long-term gender differences in vulnerability. *Journal of Health and Social Behavior, 33,* 10–24.

United Nations (1998). *Demographic yearbook, 1996.* New York: Author.

United Nations Statistics Division (2000). *Indicators on HIV/AIDS, maternity care and maternal mortality.* Retrieved from http://www.un.org/Depts/unsd/ww2000/table3b.htm

United Nations Statistics Division (2000). *Maternity leave benefits, as of 1998.* Retrieved from http://www.un.org/Depts/unsd/ww2000/table5c.htm

Urban Institute, The (1999). Child support enforcement: How well is it doing? Available: http://www.urban.org/uploaded-pdf/discussion99–11.pdf

U.S. Census Bureau (1975). *Historical statistics of the United States, colonial times to 1970.* Part 1, Series D11–25. Washington, DC: Author.

U.S. Census Bureau (1983). Child support and alimony: 1978. In *Current Population Reports* (Series P23–112). Washington, DC: U.S. Government Printing Office.

U.S. Census Bureau (1997a). Poverty in the United States, 1996. In *Current Population Report,* No. 198 (Series P60). Washington, DC: U.S. Government Printing Office.

U.S. Census Bureau (1997b). 1992 and 1997 Current Population Surveys as reported in *Marital status and living arrangements: March 1992,* Table H, and *Marital status and living arrangements: March 1997,* Table 4.

U.S. Census Bureau (2000). (Press Release). Retrieved from http://www.census.gov/Press-Release/www/1999/cb99–03.html

U.S. Census Bureau (2000a). The older population in the United States: Population characteristics, March 1999. In *Current Population Reports.* Retrieved from www.census.gov

U.S. Census Bureau (2000b). Health insurance coverage: 1999. In *Current Population Reports* (Series P60–211). Washington, DC: U.S. Government Printing Office.

U.S. Census Bureau (2000c). Child support for custodial mothers and fathers: 1997. In *Current Population Reports* (Series P60–212). Washington, DC: U.S. Government Printing Office.

U.S. Census Bureau (2000, October 24). Distribution of women by number of children ever born, by race, age, and marital status. Retrieved from http://www.census.gov/population/socdemo/fertility

U.S. Census Bureau (2001). *Statistical abstract of the United States.* Washington, DC: Author.

U.S. Census Bureau (2001, October 18). Retrieved from http://www.census.gov/population/socdemo/fertility/tabH4.pdf

U.S. Census Bureau (2002). Current population survey. *Annual demographics supplements.* Retrieved from http://www.census.gov/hhes/income/histinc/p36.html

U.S. Census Bureau (2002). Current population survey. *Poverty status of people by selected characteristics in 2001.* Retrieved from http://ferret.bls.census.gov/macro/032002/pov/new01_003.htm

U.S. Census Bureau (2002). *Statistical abstract of the United States.* Washington, DC: Author.

U.S. Census Bureau Public Information Office (2001, March 14). *Poverty rate lowest in 20 years, household income at record high, Census Bureau reports.* Retrieved from http://www.census.gov/Press-Release/www/2000/cb00–158.html

U.S. Census Bureau Public Information Office (2001, September 28). *More people have health insurance, Census Bureau reports.* Retrieved from http://www.census.gov/Press-Release/www.2001-cb01–162.html

U.S. Congress (1992). *Does health insurance make a difference?* (Office of Technology Assessment, Background Paper). Washington, DC: U.S. Government Printing Office.

U.S. Department of Health and Human Services (2002). *The 2002 HHS poverty guidelines.* Retrieved from http://aspe.os.dhhs.gov/poverty/02poverty.htm

U.S. Department of Health and Human Services, Administration on Aging (2001). *Elder abuse prevention.* Retrieved from wysiwyg://8/http://www.aoa.dhhs.gov/factsheets/abuse.html

U.S. Department of Health and Human Services, Administration on Aging (2001). *Grandparents raising grandchildren.* Retrieved from wysiwyg://2/http://www.aoa.dhhs.gov/factsheets.grandparents.html

U.S. Department of Health and Human Services, National Clearinghouse on Child Abuse and Neglect Information (2002). Retrieved from http://www.calib.com/nccanch/pubs/factsheets/canstats.cfm

U.S. Department of Justice, Bureau of Justice Statistics (1998). National Crime Victimization Survey. *Alcohol and crime, 1998.* Washington, DC: Author.

U.S. Department of Labor (2000). *Report on the youth labor force.* Retrieved from http://www.bls.gov/opub/rylf/rylfhome.htm

U.S. Department of Transportation (2000). *Traffic safety facts, 1999: Alcohol.* Washington, DC: National Highway Safety Administration.

U.S. House of Representatives, Committee on Ways and Means (1996). *1996 green book.* Washington, DC: U.S. Government Printing Office.

U.S. National Center for Health Statistics (1997). Fertility, family planning, and women's health: New data from the 1995 National Survey of Family Growth. *Vital and Health Statistics, 23,* 19.

U.S. National Center for Health Statistics (2000). Births: Final data for 1998. *National Vital Statistics Reports, 48,* 3.

U.S. News & World Report (1996, April 29, p. 54). Raise the minimum wage?

U.S. Social Security Administration (1999). *Social security programs throughout the world 1999.* Washington, DC: U.S. Government Printing Office.

Uttal, L. (1999). Using kin for child care: Embedment in the socioeconomic networks of extended families. *Journal of Marriage and the Family, 61,* 845–857.

van Gennep, A. (1960). *The rites of passage.* Chicago: University of Chicago Press.

Vanek, J. (1974). Time spent in housework. *Scientific American, 231,* 116–120.

VanLaningham, J., Johnson, D. R., & Amato, P. (2001). Marital happiness, marital duration, and the U-shaped curve: Evidence from a five-wave panel study. *Social Forces, 78,* 1313–1341.

Vannoy, P. (1991). Social differentiation, contemporary marriage, and human development. *Journal of Family Issues, 12,* 251–267.

Varnis, S. L. (2001). Regulating the global adoption of children. *Society, 38,* 39–46.

Vaughan, D. (1990). *Uncoupling: Turning points in intimate relationships.* New York: Vintage.

Ventura, S. J., & Bachrach, C. A. (2000). Nonmarital childbearing in the United States, 1940–1999. *National Vital Statistics Reports, 48*(16) (revised).

Ventura, S. J., Matthews, T., & Curin, S. C. (1999). Declines in teenage birth rates, 1991–1998: Update of national and state trends. In *National Vital Statistics Reports* (Vol. 47, No. 26). Hyattsville, MD: National Center for Health Statistics.

Vinokur, A. D., Price, R. H., & Caplan, R. D. (1996). Hard times and hurtful partners:

How financial strain affects depression and relationship satisfaction of unemployed persons and their spouses. *Journal of Personality and Social Psychology, 71,* 166–179.

Vinovskis, M. A. (2001). Historical perspectives on parent–child interactions. In S. J. Ferguson (Ed.), *Shifting the center: Understanding contemporary families* (pp. 215–230). Mountain View, CA: Mayfield.

Visher, E. B., & Visher, J. S. (1979). *Stepfamilies: A guide to working with stepparents and stepchildren.* New York: Brunner/Mazel.

Visher, E. B., & Visher, J. S. (1996). *Therapy with stepfamilies.* New York: Brunner/Mazel.

Vosler, N. R. (1994). Displaced manufacturing workers and their families: A research-based practice model. *Families in Society: The Journal of Contemporary Human Services, 75*(2), 105–115.

Vosler, N. R. (1996). *New approaches to family practice: Confronting economic stress.* Thousand Oaks, CA: Sage.

Voydanoff, P. (1987). *Work and family life.* Beverly Hills, CA: Sage.

Voydanoff, P. (2002). Linkages between the work–family interface and work, family, and individual outcomes: An integrative model. *Journal of Family Issues, 23,* 138–164.

Vreeland, R. S. (1972). Sex at Harvard. *Sexual Behavior.*

Waehler, C. A. (1996). *Bachelors: The psychology of men who haven't married.* Westport, CT: Praeger.

Waite, L. J. (2000). Trends in men's and women's well-being in marriage. In L. J. Waite, C. Bachrach, M. Hindin, E. Thomson, & A. Thornton (Eds.), *The ties that bind: Perspectives on marriage and cohabitation* (pp. 368–392). New York: Aldine de Gruyter.

Waite, L. J., & Gallagher, M. (2000). *The case for marriage.* New York: Doubleday.

Waite, L. J., & Lillard, L. A. (1991). Children and marital disruption. *American Journal of Sociology, 96,* 930–953.

Waite, L. J., & Nielsen, M. (2001). The rise of the dual-earner family, 1963–1997. In R. Hertz & N. L. Marshall (Eds.), *Working families: The transformation of the American home* (pp. 23–41). Berkeley: University of California Press.

Walker, A. J. (1999). Gender and family relationships. In M. B. Sussman, S. K. Steinmetz, & G. W. Peterson (Eds.), *Handbook of marriage and the family* (pp. 439–474). New York: Plenum.

Walker, A. J., & Allen, K. R. (1991). Relationships between caregiving daughters and their elderly mothers. *The Gerontologist, 31,* 389–396.

Walker, A. J., Manoogian-O'Dell, M., McGraw, L. A., & White, D. L. (2001). *Families in later life: Connections and transitions.* Thousand Oaks, CA: Pine Forge.

Walker, K. (1994). Men, women, and friendship: What they say, what they do. *Gender & Society, 8,* 246–265.

Walker, K. (2001). "I'm not friends the way she's friends": Ideological and behavioral constructions of masculinity in men's friendships. In M. S. Kimmel & M. A. Messner (Eds.), *Men's lives* (pp. 367–379). Boston: Allyn & Bacon.

Waller, W. (1937). The rating and dating complex. *American Sociological Review, 2,* 727–734.

Wallerstein, J. S. (1983). Children of divorce: The psychological tasks of the child. *American Journal of Orthopsychiatry, 53,* 230–243.

Wallerstein, J. S., & Blakeslee, S. (1989). *Second chances: Men, women and children a decade after divorce.* New York: Ticknor & Fields.

Walling, W. H. (Ed.) (1904). *Sexology, the family medical edition.* Philadelphia: Puritan.

Walsh, F. (1998). *Strengthening family resilience.* New York: Guilford.

Walsh, F. (2002). A family resilience framework: Innovative practice applications. *Family Relations, 51,* 130–137.

Walster, E., & Walster, G. W. (1978). *A new look at love.* Reading, MA: Addison-Wesley.

Walzer, S. (1998). *Thinking about the baby: Gender and transitions into parenthood.* Philadelphia: Temple University Press.

Ward, R., & Spitze, G. (1996). Will the children ever leave? Parent–child coresidence history and plans. *Journal of Family Issues, 17,* 514–539.

Ware, H. (1979). Polygyny: Women's views in a transitional society, Nigeria 1975. *Journal of Marriage and the Family, 41,* 185–195.

Warner, R. L. (1986). Alternative strategies for measuring household division of labor: A comparison. *Journal of Family Issues, 7,* 179–195.

Washington Post, The/Kaiser Family Foundation/Harvard University (2001, August). *Race and ethnicity in 2001: Attitudes, perceptions, and experiences.* Retrieved from http://www.kff.org/content/2001/3143/RacialBiracialToplines.pdf

Watkins, T. H. (1993). *The Great Depression: America in the 1930's.* New York: Little, Brown.

Weatherford, D. (1986). *Foreign and female: Immigrant women in America, 1840–1930.* New York: Schocken.

Wegar, K. (2000). Adoption, family ideology, and social stigma: Bias in community attitudes, adoption research, and practice. *Family Relations, 49,* 363–370.

Weigers, M. W., Weinick, R. M., & Cohen, J. W. (1998). Children's health insurance, access to care, and health status: New findings. *Health Affairs, 17,* 127–136.

Weinger, S. (1998). Poor children "know their place": Perceptions of poverty, class, and public messages. *Journal of Sociology and Social Welfare, 25,* 100–118.

Weiss, D. L. (1998). Basic sexological premises. In R. T. Francoeur, P. Barthalow, & D. L. Weis (Eds.), *Sexuality in America: Understanding our sexual values and behavior* (pp. 10–18). New York: Continuum.

Weissman, J. (1996). Uncompensated hospital care: Will it be there if we need it? *Journal of the American Medical Association, 276*(22), 823–828.

Weitz, R. (2001). *The sociology of health, illness, and health care: A critical approach* (2nd ed.). Belmont, CA: Wadsworth.

Weitzman, L. J. (1985). *The divorce revolution: The unexpected consequences for women and their children in America.* New York: Free Press.

Welch, C. E. III, & Glick, P. C. (1981). The incidence of polygamy in contemporary Africa: A research note. *Journal of Marriage and the Family, 43,* 191–193.

Wells, J. (1982, Fall). Alcohol: The number one drug of abuse in the United States. *Athletic Training.* p. 172.

Welter, B. (1966, Summer). The cult of true womanhood: 1820–1860. *American Quarterly,* pp. 151–174.

Werner, E. E. (1994). Overcoming the odds. *Developmental and Behavioral Pediatrics, 15,* 131–136.

Werner, E. E. (1995). Resilience in development. *American Psychological Society, 4,* 81–85.

Werner, E. E., & Smith, R. S. (1989). *Vulnerable but invincible: A longitudinal study of resilient children and youth.* New York: Adams, Bannister, Cox.

Werner, E. E., & Smith, R. S. (1992). *Overcoming the odds.* Ithaca, NY: Cornell University Press.

Wertheimer, D. M. (1988, January). Victims of violence: A rising tide of anti-gay sentiment. *USA Today Magazine,* pp. 52–54.

Wertz, R., & Wertz, D. (1989). *Lying-in.* New Haven, CT: Yale University Press.

West, C., & Zimmerman, D. (1987). Doing gender. *Gender & Society, 1,* 125–151.

Weston, K. (1991). *Families we choose: Lesbians, gays, kinship.* New York: Columbia University Press.

White, L. (1998). Who's counting? Quasi-facts and stepfamilies in reports of number of siblings. *Journal of Marriage and the Family, 60,* 725–733.

White, L., & Gilbreth, J. G. (2001). When children have two fathers: Effects of relationships with stepfathers and noncustodial fathers on adolescent outcomes. *Journal of Marriage and Family, 63,* 155–167.

White, L., & Rogers, S. J. (1997). Strong support but uneasy relationships: Coresidence and adult children's relationships with their parents. *Journal of Marriage and the Family, 59,* 62–76.

White, L., & Rogers, S. J. (2000). Families in social locations: Economic circumstances and family outcomes: A review of 1990s. *Journal of Marriage and Family, 62,* 1035–1051.

White, L. K., & Booth, A. (1985). Transition to parenthood and marital quality. *Journal of Marriage and the Family, 6,* 435–450.

White, L. R., & Riedmann, A. (1992). Ties among adult siblings. *Social Forces, 71,* 85–102.

Whitehead, B. D. (1993). Dan Quayle was right. *Atlantic Monthly, 271,* 47–50.

Whitehead, B. D., & Popenoe, D. (1999). *Why wed? Young adults talk about sex, love, and first unions.* New Brunswick, NJ: National Marriage Project.

Whitehead, B. D., & Popenoe, D. (2002). Why men won't commit. In *The state of our unions: The social health of marriage in America* (pp. 6–16). New Brunswick, NJ: National Marriage Project.

Wilcox, K., L., Wolchik, S. A., & Braver, S. L. (1998). Of maternal preference for joint or sole legal custody. *Family Relations, 47,* 93–101.

Wilkinson, D. Y. (1997). American families of African descent. In M. K. DeGenova (Ed.), *Families in cultural context: Strength and challenges in diversity* (pp. 35–59). Mountain View, CA: Mayfield.

Williams, L., & Sobieszczyk, T. (1997). Attitudes surrounding the continuation of female circumcision in the Sudan: Passing the tradition to the next generation. *Journal of Marriage and the Family, 59,* 966–981.

Williams, R. M., Jr. (1970). *American society: A sociological interpretation* (3rd ed.). New York: Knopf.

Wilmoth, J., & Koso, G. (2002). Does marital history matter? Marital status and wealth outcomes among preretirement adults. *Journal of Marriage and Family, 64,* 254–268.

Wilson, P. M. (1986). Black culture and sexuality. *Journal of Social Work and Human Sexuality, 4,* 29–46.

Wilson, W. J. (1987). *The truly disadvantaged: The inner city, the underclass, and public policy.* Chicago: University of Chicago Press.

Wilson, W. J. (1993). *The new urban poverty and the problem of race.* Ann Arbor: University of Michigan Press.

Wilson, W. J. (1996). *When work disappears: The world of the new urban poor.* New York: Knopf.

Wineberg, H. (1994). Marital reconciliation in the United States: Which couples are successful? *Journal of Marriage and the Family, 56,* 80–88.

Winfield, F. E. (1985). *Commuter marriage: Living together, apart.* New York: Columbia University Press.

Winton, C. (1995). *Frameworks for studying families.* Guilford, CT: Duskin.

Winton, C. A. (2003). *Children as caregivers: Parental and parentified children.* Boston: Allyn & Bacon.

Wisensale, S. K., & Heckart, K. E. (1998). Domestic partnerships: A concept paper and policy discussion. In S. J. Ferguson (Ed.), *Shifting the center: Understanding contemporary families* (pp. 654–667). Mountain View, CA: Mayfield.

Wohlmut, T. (2001). *Thanks to a stepfather on Father's Day.* Retrieved from Stepfamily Network: http://www.stepfamily.net

Wolf, A. (1998). Exposing the great equalizer: Demythologizing Internet equity. In B. Ebo (Ed.), *Cyberghetto or cybertopia? Race, class, and gender on the Internet* (pp. 15–32). Westport, CT: Praeger.

Wolin, S., & Wolin, S. (1993). *The resilient self.* New York: Villard.

Workman, J. E., & Freeburg, E. W. (1999). An examination of date rape, victim dress, and perceiver variables within the context of attribution theory. *Sex Roles, 41,* 261–277.

World Congress Against the Commercial Exploitation of Children (2001). *CSEC homepage.* Retrieved from www.usis.usemb.se/children/csec

World Values Survey (1994). *World Values Survey, 1990–1993.* Ann Arbor, MI: Inter-University Consortium for Political and Social Research.

Wright, C. (1889). *A report on marriage and divorce in the United States 1867–1886.* Washington, DC: U.S. Bureau of Labor.

Writing Group for the Women's Health Initiative Investigators (2002, July 10). Risks and benefits of estrogen plus progestin in healthy postmenopausal women. *Journal of the American Medical Association, 288*(3). Retrieved from http:www.jama.com

Wu, L. (1996). Effects of family instability, income, and income instability on the risk of premarital birth. *American Sociological Review, 61,* 386–406.

Wu, L. L., & Martinson, B. C. (1993). Family structure and the risk of premarital birth. *American Sociological Review, 58,* 210–232.

Wu, Z., & Pollard, M. S. (2000). Economic circumstances and the stability of nonmarital cohabitation. *Journal of Family Issues, 21*(3), 303–328.

Yardley, J. (2001, April 7). Well-off but still pressed, doctor could use tax cut. *New York Times.* Retrieved from http://www.nytimes.com/2001/04/07TEXA.html

YM (2000, February). New York: Gruner & Jahr, USA Publishing.

Yoon, Y-H., & Waite, L. J. (1994). Converging employment patterns of black, white, and Hispanic women: Return to work after first birth. *Journal of Marriage and the Family, 56,* 209–217.

Zarit, S. H., & Eggebeen, D. J. (1995). Parent–child relationships in adulthood and old age. In M. H. Bornstein (Ed.), *Handbook of parenting* (Vol. 1, pp. 119–140). Mahweh, NJ: Erlbaum.

Zeiss, A. M., Zeiss, R. A., & Johnson, S. M. (1980). Sex differences in initiation of and adjustment to divorce. *Journal of Divorce, 4,* 21–33.

Zelizer, V. A. (1985). *Pricing the priceless child: The changing social values of children.* New York: Basic.

Zhang, Z., Huang, L. X., & Brittingham, A. M. (1999). *Worker drug use and workplace policies and programs: Results from the 1994 and 1997 NHSDA.* Rockville, MD: U.S. Substance Abuse and Mental Health Services Administration, Office of Applied Studies.

Zill, N., Morrison, D. R., & Cioro, M. J. (1993). Long-term effects of parental divorce on parent–child relationships, adjustment, and achievement in young adulthood. *Journal of Family Psychology, 7,* 91–103.

Zinn, M. B. (1993). Feminist rethinking from racial–ethnic families. In M. B. Zinn & B. T. Dill (Eds.), *Women of color in U.S. society* (pp. 303–314). Philadelphia: Temple University Press.

Ziv, L. (1997, May). The horror of female genital mutilation. *Cosmopolitan,* pp. 242–246.

Zvonkovic, A. M., Manoogian, M. M., & McGraw, L. A. (2001). The ebb and flow of family life: How families experience being together and apart. In K. J. Daly (Ed.), *Minding the time in family experience: Emerging perspectives and issues* (pp. 135–160). New York: JAI.

Photo Credits

This page constitutes an extension of the copyright page. We have made every effort to trace the ownership of all copyrighted material and to secure permission from copyright holders. In the event of any question arising as to the use of any material, we will be pleased to make the necessary corrections in future printings. Thanks are due to the following authors, publishers, and agents for permission to use the material indicated.

Chapter 1. 1: © Tom Stewart/Corbis **3:** (top right) © Bob Krist/CORBIS **3:** (bottom right) © A. Ramey/Stock, Boston **8:** © Amy Etra/PhotoEdit **12:** © AFP/Corbis **17:** © Roger Ressmeyer/Corbis **19:** © Geoffrey Clements/Corbis **23:** © Bettmann/Corbis **26:** © Bettmann/Corbis **30:** The Kobal Collection **39:** © Mark Richards/PhotoEdit

Chapter 2. 46: © John Henley/Corbis **56:** © MIT Museum **57:** © Laima Druskis/Stock, Boston **60:** (top) © Michael Newman/PhotoEdit **60:** (bottom) © Chuck Savage/Corbis **75:** © Natalie Fobes/Corbis **81:** © Myrleen Ferguson Cate/PhotoEdit

Chapter 3. 92: © Gina Minielli/Corbis **96:** © Christopher Morris/VII **98:** © Peter Turnley/Corbis **99:** © 2002 AP/Wide World Photos **109:** © Mark Richards/PhotoEdit **111:** Photo by Aris Economopoulos © The Star-Ledger. All Rights Reserved **114:** © Tony Freeman/PhotoEdit **117:** © 2002 AP/Wide World Photos **119:** © Ariel Skelley/Corbis **125:** © John Coletti/Stock, Boston **127:** © Syracuse Newspaper/ Carl J. Single/ The Image Works

Chapter 4. 139: © Helen Norman/Corbis **142:** © Owen Franken/Stock, Boston **146:** © The Kobal Collection **151:** (top) © Ryan McVay/PhotoDisc/Getty Images **151:** (bottom) © Neil Rabinowitz/Corbis **164:** © Bettmann/Corbis **172:** © Davis Barber/PhotoEdit **174:** © Michael Newman/PhotoEdit **180:** © Steve Mason/PhotoDisc/Getty Images

Chapter 5. 186: © Yang Liu/Corbis **190:** (top left) © Spencer Grant/Stock, Boston **190:** (top right) © Robert Brenner/PhotoEdit **196:** © Amy Etra/PhotoEdit **198:** © Steve Liss/Corbis-Sygma **203:** The Granger Collection, New York **213:** Copyright © 2002 by Playboy **217:** © 2002 AP/Wide World Photos **219:** © A. Ramey/PhotoEdit **221:** © Sondra Dawes/The Image Works

Chapter 6. 230: © Claudia Kunin/Corbis **235:** © Bettmann/Corbis **237:** (left) The Granger Collection, New York **237:** (right) © Werner Bokelberg/The Image Bank-Getty Images **241:** © EyeWire Collection-Getty Images **251:** © John Henley/Corbis **255:** © Tom Stewart/Corbis **259:** © Jose Luis Pelaez, Inc/Corbis **263:** © Romilly Lockyer/The Image Bank-Getty Images **272:** © Bruce Davidson/Magnum Photos

Chapter 7. 277: © Larry Williams/Corbis **285:** Kautz Family YMCA Archives, University of Minnesota, Minnesota Collection **287:** © Stock Image/SuperStock **291:** © Robert Harding Picture Library **294:** © 2001 AP/Wide World Photos **299:** © Digital Vision/Getty Images **305:** © Thor Swift/The Image Works **310:** © Zigy Kaluzny/Stone-Getty Images **314:** © Abbas/Magnum Photos

Chapter 8. 320: © Ariel Skelley/Corbis **329:** © Monika Graff/The Image Works **333:** © Paul Barton/Corbis **335:** © John Henley/Corbis **338:** © Scott Markewitz/Taxi-Getty Images **343:** © Geoff Manasse/Aurora Photos **347:** © Tom Stewart/Corbis **349:** © 1999 AP/Wide World Photos **353:** © Steve Skjold/PhotoEdit **358:** (top left) © Harriet Gans/The Image Works **358:** (center left) © Suzanne Arms/Jeroboam

Chapter 9. 366: © Walter Hodges/Corbis **368:** © Michael Newman/PhotoEdit **370:** Photo by Lewis Wickes Hine © Corbis **375:** © Rhoda Sidney/The Image Works **378:** © Nubar Alexanian/Stock, Boston **389:** © Jose Carillo/PhotoEdit **391:** © Roy McMahon/Corbis **396:** © Najlah Feanny/Stock, Boston **398:** (top) © Michael Newman/PhotoEdit **398:** (bottom) © Bob Daemmrich/Stock, Boston

Chapter 10. 410: © Jim Craigmyle/Corbis **412:** © Bettmann/Corbis **414:** © The Mariner's Museum/Corbis **416:** © Corbis **425:** © Spencer Grant/PhotoEdit **432:** Photo by Philip Gendreau © Bettmann/Corbis

436: © Tony Freeman/PhotoEdit **437:** © RF/Corbis **444:** © Margaret Ross/Stock, Boston **451:** © Dorothy Littell Greco/The Image Works **453:** © Mark Richards/PhotoEdit

Chapter 11. 458: © DiMaggio/Kalish/Corbis **462:** © Tony Freeman/PhotoEdit **465:** © Dennis MacDonald/PhotoEdit **468:** © Skjold/Jeroboam, Inc. **469:** © Paul Fusco/Magnum Photos **473:** © Inc. Yuri Dojc/The Image Bank-Getty Images **477:** © Mary Kate Denny/PhotoEdit **483:** © Way Gary/Corbis Sygma **489:** © Jim Arbogast/PhotoDisc-Getty Images **491:** © David H. Wells/Corbis **496:** © Mary Kate Denny/PhotoEdit

Chapter 12. 502: © Bob Mitchell/Corbis **503:** © Larry Williams/Corbis **506:** © Peter Sanders/HAFA/The Image Works **509:** © Corbis **512:** © John Neubauer/PhotoEdit **515:** © ThinkStock/SuperStock **518:** © Yellow Dog Productions/The Image Bank-Getty Images **523:** © Zigy Kaluzny/Stone-Getty Images **526:** © Stephen Simpson/Taxi-Getty Images **529:** © Rob & Sas/Corbis **535:** © Andrea Pizzi/Corbis

Chapter 13. 540: © Philip Lee Harvey/Stone-Getty Images **542:** © V.C.L./Taxi-Getty Images **545:** © Elizabeth Young/ Stone-Getty Images **547:** © RF/Corbis **552:** © Michelle D. Bridwell/PhotoEdit **555:** © George DeSota/Newsmakers-Getty Images **564:** © Bob Daemmrich/The Images Works **565:** The Kobal Collection **571:** © Laura Dwight/PhotoEdit **572:** © Tony Freeman/PhotoEdit

Chapter 14. 579: © Jim Erickson/Corbis **584:** © Bettmann/Corbis **586:** Courtesy of Karen Seccombe **587:** © Darren Modricker/Corbis **592:** © Susan Van Etten/PhotoEdit **596:** © George Shelley/Corbis **601:** © Dwayne Newton/PhotoEdit **604:** © Michael Newman/PhotoEdit **608:** © Myrleen Ferguson Cate/PhotoEdit **609:** © Benelux Press/Index Stock/PictureQuest **612:** © Barros & Barros/The Image Bank-Getty Images

Chapter 15. 617: © Macduff Everton/Corbis **619:** © Myrleen Ferguson Cate/PhotoEdit **620:** © Annie Griffiths Belt/Corbis **624:** © Jeff Greenberg/PhotoEdit **628:** © Spencer Grant/PhotoEdit **631:** Courtesy of Karen Seccombe **633:** © Robert Brenner/PhotoEdit **636:** © Jeff Greenberg/PhotoEdit **640:** © Michael Newman/PhotoEdit **641:** © Tom Rosenthal/SuperStock **646:** © Jose Luis Pelaez Inc./Corbis

Name Index

Subject Index

patriarchy and, 96–97
polygamy and, 12
Remarriage, 548–559. *See also*
  Stepfamilies
    age for remarrying, 552–553
    Arab American families and,
      550–551
    children and, 555–556
    cohesiveness, development of,
      558
    in colonial America, 20
    commitment to, 558
    cross-cultural norms,
      549–551
    custodial mothers and,
      555–556
    division of domestic labor and,
      556–557
    double standard of aging,
      554–556
    equity issues in, 556–557
    gender differences, 553–556
    instability of, 558
    in Japan, 549–551
    maintenance issues, 558
    of older adults, 558–559
    power issues in, 556–557
    race and ethnicity and, 553
    re-divorce after, 557–558
    satisfaction in, 557–558
    social network, men and, 554
    stability of, 557–558
    timing of, 552–553
    widowhood and, 609
Remote grandparents, 596
Repartnering after divorce, 548
Replacement rate, 322
Representative sampling, 68
Research
    appreciation for, 620–621
    data analysis, 82–86
    descriptive research, 53
    on division of domestic labor,
      113
    ethics in, 77–82, 79
    evaluation research, 54
    experiments, 76–77
    explanatory research, 54
    exploratory research, 53
    field research, 72–76
    focus group research, 73, 76
    human research and ethics,
      80–82
    institutional review boards
      (IRBs), 80
    on marital satisfaction, 74–75
    misleading statistics, 84
    secondary research, 71–72
    on sexual behaviors, 203–206
    social theories and, 66–77
    surveys, 70–71
    techniques of, 68–70
Residence, patterns of, 14–15
Resiliency of families, 622–624
Retirement, 6, 603–605
Rites of passage, 238
Role overload, 439
Roller-coaster pattern, 460
Rolling Stone, 321
Russia, adoption from, 354

Sadie Hawkins dance, 554
Salaries. *See* Wages
Same-sex friendships. *See*
  Friendships
Same-sex marriage
    Canada, support in, 295
    debate over, 312–313
    views about, 309
Sampling, 50, 68–69
    surveys and, 72
Sandwich generation, 612
Sati, India, 549
Saving Our Children from Poverty
  (Bergmann), 636
Scapegoat, child as, 492

Schizophrenia, delayed child-
  bearing and, 335
School Girls (Orenstein), 214
Scientific manipulation, 50
Scientific modes of investigation,
  49
Seasonal workers, 425
Secondary orgasm dysfunction,
  212
Secondary research, 71–72
Secure attachments
    in adults, 144
    in infants, 143
Security in adult romantic rela-
    tionships, 144–145
Selection bias, 51
Selection effect, 301
Selective family policies, 625–
  627
Selective observation, 51
Self-care by children, 400–401
Self-disclosure
    in marriage, 262
    women and, 264
Self-esteem and resilience, 623
Self-revelation, love and, 159
Seneca Falls Convention, 237
*Separating Together: How Di-
    vorce Transforms Families*
    (Guttman), 542
Separation. *See* Divorce
Serial monogamy, 10, 172
Servants
    in colonial America, 20–21,
      21
    women working as, 413
Service sector, 423
Seventeen, 187
Sex, defining, 189
Sex education, 224
*Sex in America: A Definitive Sur-
    vey* (Michael et al.), 205
Sexology, 188
Sexology (Walling), 200–202
Sexual abuse. *See also* Rape
    cultural differences in, 487
    in dating, 473–474
    elder abuse as, 486
    poverty and, 471
Sexual attraction and love, 158
*Sexual Behavior in the Human
    Male/Sexual Behavior
    in the Human Female*
    (Kinsey), 204
Sexual behaviors. *See also*
    Double standard; Mastur-
    bation; Premarital sex
    of adolescents, 219–224
    in adult romantic relation-
      ships, 144
    aging and, 606–608
    contemporary research on,
      205–206
    in early America, 199–202
    expression of, 206–212
    Freud, Sigmund on, 203
    historical influences, 187–188
    industrialization and,
      202–203
    Kinsey, Alfred on, 203–204
    kissing, 208
    marital satisfaction and, 260
    Masters and Johnson, re-
      search by, 204–205
    in modern America, 202–203
    oral sex, 208–209
    research on, 203–206
    sociological imagination and,
      94
    women, sexual response of,
      206–207
Sexual child abuse, 482
Sexual harassment, 94
Sexual intercourse, 209–211
    dysfunctions in women, 212
    women and, 211–212

Sexual orientations, 191–192.
    See also Homosexuals
    causes of, 195–197
    classifications of, 191,
      194–195
    disclosure of, 310
Sexual response cycle, 204
Sexual risk-taking behaviors,
  378–379
Sexual scripts, 212–215
    gender and, 213
Shakespeare in Love, 147
Siblings. *See also* Stepfamilies
    aging and relationships with,
      603
    in colonial America, 20
    homosexuality and, 196
    parent-child relations and,
      392
Sick leave, 630
Side jobs, 638
SIDS (Sudden Infant Death Syn-
    drome), 489
Single fatherhood, 345–348, 429,
    544–547
Singlehood, 278, 279–293. *See
    also* Bachelors; Single
    fatherhood; Single
    motherhood; Single-parent
    households
    alternative scripts for,
      288–289
    changing rates of, 283–285
    consequences of, 290–293
    control issues, 287
    cultural factors and, 284–285
    demographics and, 283
    economics and, 283–284,
      292–293
    for homosexuals, 290
    involuntary singles, 285–286
    living arrangements, 279–283
    never married persons, 280
    in older adults, 280
    personal experience of, 289
    physical well-being and,
      290–292
    psychological well-being and,
      290–292
    race and ethnicity and, 292–
      293
    social class and, 284
    stages in life cycle for,
      287–290
    successful singlehood, 293
    tolerance to, 35
    twilight zone of, 288
    variations among singles,
      285–287
    voluntary singles, 285
Single motherhood. *See also*
    African Americans
    adoption by single mother,
      354
    as choice, 341–343
    compromise and, 343
    divorce and, 528–529
    in France, 636–637
    middle-class women and,
      341–342
    race and ethnicity and,
      342–343
    survival strategies, 638–639
    value of marriage and, 343
Single Mothers By Choice (SMC),
    341–342
Single-parent households, 4–5,
    321
    in Arab American families,
      551
    child abuse in, 483
    child care in, 400
    commitment to employment,
      447–448
    rise in rates of, 37–38
    single motherhood and, 342

success of children from, 534
    working families as, 451–452
Sisters and brothers. *See* Siblings
Situational discrimination, 118
Skepticism, 50
Slavery
    in colonial America, 23–25
    elderly slaves, treatment of,
      580
    extended families and, 120
    families and, 25
    gender and work, 413
    jobs in, 413
    rape, vulnerability to, 21
Sleeping Beauty myth, 140
Smoking, SIDS (Sudden Infant
    Death Syndrome) and,
    489
Snowball sampling, 69
Social capital
    children as, 333–334
    poverty and, 470
    in stepfamilies, 572
Social class, 122–133
    approaches to measuring,
      123–127
    cohabitation variations,
      296–297
    in colonial America child-
      rearing patterns, 22–23
    friendships and, 179–180
    gender socialization and, 112
    heterogamous marriages, 267,
      269–271
    industrialization and, 26–28
    influence of, 127, 130–133
    interaction of statuses,
      133–134
    parent-child relations and,
      386–387
    profiles of, 127, 131–133
    single motherhood and,
      341–342
    social status and, 10
    upper middle class, 126
    widowhood and, 610
Social clubs, singlehood and,
    284
Social constructionist perspec-
    tive, 59, 603–604
Social desirability bias, 70, 179
Social exchange theory, 55,
    61–62
    market relations analogy,
      61–62
Social history, 18–19
Social institution, family as, 9
Socialization, 106
    control of parents and, 379
    Khasi matriliny, 372–373
    media and, 111–112
    parenthood and, 106–107,
      394–395
    racial socialization, 389–390
    reciprocal socialization,
      384–386
    triple quandary of, 389–390
Social learning theory, 488
Social mobility, 132
Social network theory, 173–174
Social norms, 93
*The Social Organization of
    Sexuality: Sexual Practices
    in the United States*
    (Laumann et al.), 205
*The Social Organization of Sexu-
    ality* (Laumann et al.),
    607–608
Social problems, 460
Social science, 49. *See also*
    Research
    attitudes, 50
    types of research, 53–54
Social Security, 584, 644–645
    retirement age and, 603
Social stratification, 93–94